2012

alan rogers

the best campsites
in France.

over 940 independent reviews

D1495149

alan rogers  publishing

experts in camping for over 40 years

Compiled by: Alan Rogers Guides Ltd

Designed by: Vine Design Ltd

Additional photography: T Lambelin, www.lambelin.com
Maps created by Customised Mapping (01769 540044)
contain background data provided by GisDATA Ltd

Maps are © Alan Rogers Guides and GisDATA Ltd 2012

© Alan Rogers Guides Ltd 2012

Published by: Alan Rogers Guides Ltd,
Spelmonden Old Oast, Goudhurst, Kent TN17 1HE
www.alanrogers.com Tel: 01580 214000

British Library Cataloguing-in-Publication Data:
A catalogue record for this book is available
from the British Library.

ISBN 978-1-906215-78-1

Printed in Great Britain by Stephens & George Print Group

While every effort is taken to ensure the accuracy of the information
given in this book, no liability can be accepted by the authors or publishers
for any loss, damage or injury caused by errors in, or omissions from,
the information given.

All rights reserved. No part of this publication may be reproduced,
stored in a retrieval system or transmitted, in any form or by any means,
electronic, mechanical, photocopying, recording or otherwise, without
prior permission in writing from the publishers.

Contents

Alan Rogers - in search of 'the best'

Alan Rogers Guides were first published over 40 years ago. Since Alan Rogers published the first campsite guide that bore his name, the range has expanded and now covers 27 countries in six separate guides. No fewer than 20 of the campsites selected by Alan for the first guide are still featured in our 2012 editions.

There are over 11,000 campsites in France of varying quality: this guide contains impartially written reports on almost 1,000, including many of the very finest, each being individually inspected and selected. We aim to provide you with a selection of the best, rather than information on all – in short, a more selective, qualitative approach. New, improved maps and indexes are also included, designed to help you find the choice of campsite that's right for you.

We hope you enjoy some happy and safe travels – and some pleasurable 'armchair touring' in the meantime!

" ...the campsites included in this book have been chosen entirely on merit, and no payment of any sort is made by them for their inclusion."

Alan Rogers, 1968

How do we find the best?

The criteria we use when inspecting and selecting campsites are numerous, but the most important by far is the question of good quality. People want different things from their choice of site so we try to include a range of campsite 'styles' to cater for a wide variety of preferences: from those seeking a small peaceful campsite in the heart of the countryside, to visitors looking for an 'all singing, all dancing' site in a popular seaside resort. Those with more specific interests, such as sporting facilities, cultural events or historical attractions, are also catered for.

The size of the site, whether it's part of a chain or privately owned, makes no difference in terms of it being required to meet our exacting standards in respect of its quality and it being 'fit for purpose'. In other words, irrespective of the size of the site, or the number of facilities it offers, we consider and evaluate the welcome, the pitches, the sanitary facilities, the cleanliness, the general maintenance and even the location.

Expert opinions

We rely on our dedicated team of Site Assessors, all of whom are experienced campers, caravanners or motorcaravanners, to visit and recommend campsites. Each year they travel some 100,000 miles around Europe inspecting new campsites for the guide and re-inspecting the existing ones. Our thanks are due to them for their enthusiastic efforts, their diligence and integrity.

We also appreciate the feedback we receive from many of our readers and we always make a point of following up complaints, suggestions or recommendations for possible new campsites. Of course we get a few grumbles too – but it really is a few, and those we do receive usually relate to overcrowding or to poor maintenance during the peak school holiday period. Please bear in mind that, although we are interested to hear about any complaints, we have no contractual relationship with the campsites featured in our guides and are therefore not in a position to intervene in any dispute between a reader and a campsite.

Independent and honest

Whilst the content and scope of the Alan Rogers guides have expanded considerably since the early editions, our selection of campsites still employs exactly the same philosophy and criteria as defined by Alan Rogers in 1968.

'telling it how it is'

Firstly, and most importantly, our selection is based entirely on our own rigorous and independent inspection and selection process. Campsites cannot buy their way into our guides – indeed the extensive Site Report which is written by us, not by the site owner, is provided free of charge so we are free to say what we think and to provide an honest, 'warts and all' description. This is written in plain English and without the use of confusing icons or symbols.

Looking for the best

Highly respected by site owners and readers alike, there is no better guide when it comes to forming an independent view of a campsite's quality. When you need to be confident in your choice of campsite, you need the Alan Rogers Guide.

- Sites only included on merit

- Sites cannot pay to be included

- Independently inspected, rigorously assessed

- Impartial reviews

- Over 40 years of expertise

Written in plain English, our guides are exceptionally easy to use, but a few words of explanation regarding the layout and content may be helpful. Regular readers will see that our site reports are grouped into 23 official regions (plus the Vendée) and then by the various départements in each of these regions in numerical order.

Index town
Site name
Postal address (including département) T: telephone number. E: email address
alanrogers.com web address (including Alan Rogers reference number)

A description of the site in which we try to give an idea of its general features – its size, its situation, its strengths and its weaknesses. This section should provide a picture of the site itself with reference to the facilities that are provided and if they impact on its appearance or character. We include details on pitch numbers, electricity (with amperage), hardstandings etc. in this section as pitch design, planning and terracing affects the site's overall appearance. Similarly we include reference to pitches used for caravan holiday homes, chalets, and the like. Importantly at the end of this column we indicate if there are any restrictions, e.g. no tents, no children, naturist sites.

Facilities
Lists more specific information on the site's facilities and amenities and, where available, the dates when these facilities are open (if not for the whole season). Off site: here we give distances to various local amenities, for example, local shops, the nearest beach, plus our featured activities (bicycle hire, fishing, horse riding, boat launching). Where we have space we list suggestions for activities and local tourist attractions.

Open: Site opening dates.

Directions
Separated from the main text in order that they may be read and assimilated more easily by a navigator en-route. Bear in mind that road improvement schemes can result in road numbers being altered.

GPS: references are provided in decimal format. All latitudes are North. Longitudes are East unless preceeded by a minus sign e.g. 48.71695 is North, 0.31254 is East and -0.31254 is West.

Charges 2012 (or a general guide)

Maps, campsite listings and indexes

For this 2012 guide we have changed the way in which we list our featured campsites and also the way in which we help you locate the sites within each region.

We now include a map immediately after our Introduction to that region. These maps show the towns near which one or more of our featured campsites are located.

Within each regional section of the guide, we list these towns and the site(s) in that vicinity in alphabetical order.

You will certainly need more detailed maps for navigation, for example the Michelin atlas. We provide G.P.S. coordinates for each site to assist you. Our three indexes will also help you to find a site by its reference number and name, by region and site name, or by the town where the site is situated.

Understanding the entries

Regions and départements

For administrative purposes France is divided into 23 official regions covering the 95 départements (similar to our counties). The départements included in each region are stated in our introductions, together with their official number (eg. the département of Manche is number 50). We use these département numbers as the first two digits of our campsite reference numbers, so any campsite in the Manche département will start with the number 50, prefixed with FR.

Facilities

Toilet blocks

We assume that toilet blocks will be equipped with WCs, washbasins with hot and cold water and hot showers with dividers or curtains, and will have all necessary shelves, hooks, plugs and mirrors. We also assume that there will be an identified chemical toilet disposal point, and that the campsite will provide water and waste water drainage points and bin areas. If not the case, we comment. We do mention certain features that some readers find important: washbasins in cubicles, facilities for babies, facilities for those with disabilities and motorcaravan service points. Readers with disabilities are advised to contact the site of their choice to ensure that facilities are appropriate to their needs.

Shop

Basic or fully supplied, and opening dates.

Bars, restaurants, takeaway facilities and entertainment

We try hard to supply opening and closing dates (if other than the campsite opening dates) and to identify if there are discos or other entertainment.

Children's play areas

Fenced and with safety surface (e.g. sand, bark or pea-gravel).

Swimming pools

If particularly special, we cover in detail in our main campsite description but reference is always included under our Facilities listings. We will also indicate the existence of water slides, sunbathing areas and other features. Opening dates, charges and levels of supervision are provided where we have been notified. There is a regulation whereby Bermuda shorts may not be worn in swimming pools (for health and hygiene reasons). It is worth ensuring that you do take 'proper' swimming trunks with you.

Leisure facilities

For example, playing fields, bicycle hire, organised activities and entertainment.

Dogs

If dogs are not accepted or restrictions apply, we state it here. Check the quick reference list at the back of the guide.

Off site

This briefly covers leisure facilities, tourist attractions, restaurants etc. nearby.

Charges

These are the latest provided to us by the sites. In those cases where 2012 prices have not been provided to us by the sites, we try to give a general guide.

Reservations

Necessary for high season (roughly mid-July to mid-August) in popular holiday areas (i.e. beach resorts). You can reserve many sites via our own Alan Rogers Travel Service or through other tour operators. Or be wholly independent and contact the campsite(s) of your choice direct, using the phone or e-mail numbers shown in the site reports, but please bear in mind that many sites are closed all winter.

Telephone Numbers

All numbers assume that you are phoning from within France.

To phone France from outside that country, prefix the number shown with the relevant International Code (00 33) and drop the first 0, shown as (0) in the numbers indicated.

Opening dates

These are advised to us during the early autumn of the previous year – sites can, and sometimes do, alter these dates before the start of the following season, often for good reasons. If you intend to visit shortly after a published opening date, or shortly before the closing date, it is wise to check that it will actually be open at the time required. Similarly some sites operate a restricted service during the low season, only opening some of their facilities (e.g. swimming pools) during the main season; where we know about this, and have the relevant dates, we indicate it – again if you are at all doubtful it is wise to check.

Sometimes, campsite amenities may be dependent on there being enough customers on site to justify their opening and, for this reason, actual opening dates may vary from those indicated.

Some French site owners are very relaxed when it comes to opening and closing dates. They may not be fully ready by their stated opening dates – grass and hedges may not all be cut or perhaps only limited sanitary facilities open. At the end of the season they also tend to close down some facilities and generally wind down prior to the closing date. Bear this in mind if you are travelling early or late in the season – it is worth phoning ahead.

The Camping Cheque low season touring system goes some way to addressing this in that many participating campsites will have all key facilities open and running by the opening date and these will remain fully operational until the closing date.

You're on your way!

Whether you're an 'old hand' in terms of camping and caravanning or are contemplating your first trip, a regular reader of our Guides or a new 'convert', we wish you well in your travels and hope we have been able to help in some way.

We are, of course, also out and about ourselves, visiting sites, talking to owners and readers, and generally checking on standards and new developments.

Our Accommodation section

Over recent years, more and more campsites have added high quality mobile home and chalet accommodation. In response to feedback from many of our readers, and to reflect this evolution in campsites, we have now decided to include a separate section on mobile homes and chalets. If a site offers this accommodation, it is indicated above the site report with a page reference where full details are given. We have chosen a number of sites offering some of the best accommodation available and have included full details of one or two accommodation types at these sites.

Please note however that many other campsites listed in this guide may also have a selection of accommodation for rent.

We wish all our readers thoroughly enjoyable Camping and Caravanning in 2012 – favoured by good weather of course!

The Alan Rogers Team

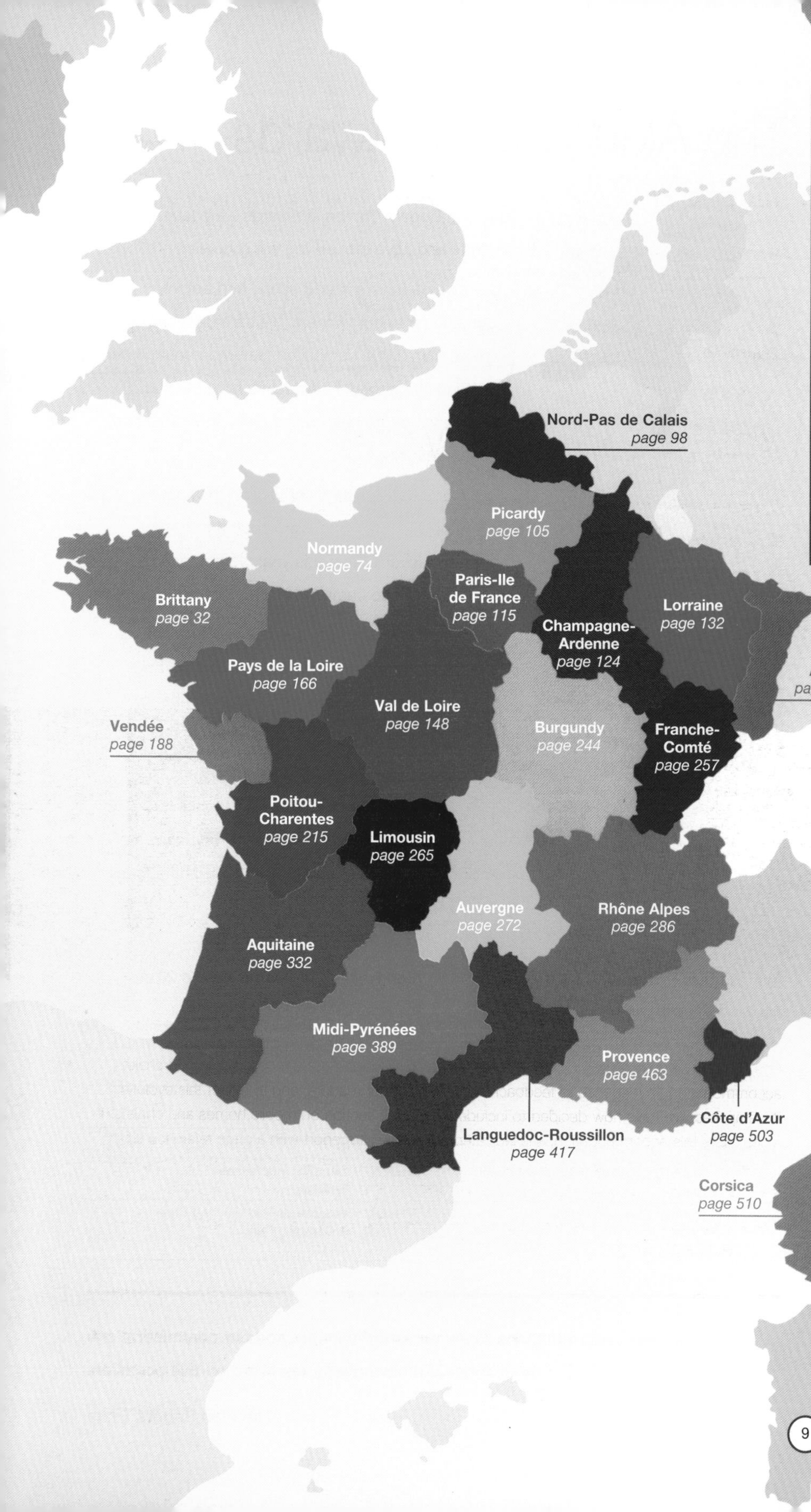

Nord-Pas de Calais
page 98

Picardy
page 105

Normandy
page 74

Brittany
page 32

Paris-Ile
de France
page 115

Lorraine
page 132

Champagne-
Ardenne
page 124

Alsace
page 141

Pays de la Loire
page 166

Val de Loire
page 148

Burgundy
page 244

Franche-
Comté
page 257

Vendée
page 188

Poitou-
Charentes
page 215

Limousin
page 265

Auvergne
page 272

Rhône Alpes
page 286

Aquitaine
page 332

Midi-Pyrénées
page 389

Provence
page 463

Côte d'Azur
page 503

Languedoc-Roussillon
page 417

Corsica
page 510

The Alan Rogers Awards

The Alan Rogers Campsite Awards were launched in 2004 and have proved a great success.

Our awards have a broad scope and before committing to our winners, we carefully consider more than 2,000 campsites featured in our guides, taking into account comments from our site assessors, our head office team and, of course, our readers.

Our award winners come from the four corners of Europe, from southern Portugal to Slovenia, and this year we are making awards to campsites in 10 different countries.

Needless to say, it's an extremely difficult task to choose our eventual winners, but we believe that we have identified a number of campsites with truly outstanding characteristics.

In each case, we have selected an outright winner, along with two highly commended runners-up. Listed below are full details of each of our award categories and our winners for 2011.

Alan Rogers Progress Award 2011

This award reflects the hard work and commitment undertaken by particular site owners to improve and upgrade their site.

Winner	
IT62290	Camping Lago di Levico
	Italy

Runners-up	
ES87430	Marjal Camping & Bungalows Resort
	Spain
CR6731	Naturist Camping Valalta
	Croatia

Alan Rogers Welcome Award 2011

This award takes account of sites offering a particularly friendly welcome and maintaining a friendly ambience throughout readers' holidays.

Winner	
ES80500	Camping Aquarius
	Spain

Runners-up	
DE3670	Camping Hopfensee
	Germany
IR9650	Woodlands Park Touring Caravan & Camping Park
	Ireland

Our warmest congratulations to all our award winners and our commiserations to all those not having won an award on this occasion.

The Alan Rogers Team

Alan Rogers Active Holiday Award 2011

This award reflects sites in outstanding locations which are ideally suited for active holidays, notably walking or cycling, but which could extend to include such activities as winter sports or watersports.

Winner

FR24060	Camping le Paradis *France*

Runners-up

ES86250	Kiko Park Rural *Spain*
IT62030	Caravan Park Sexten *Italy*

Alan Rogers Innovation Award 2011

Our new Innovation Award acknowledges campsites with creative and original concepts, possibly with features which are unique, and cannot therefore be found elsewhere. We have identified innovation both in campsite amenities and also in rentable accommodation.

Winner

AU0265	Park Grubhof *Austria*

Runners-up

IT60370	Camping Jesolo International *Italy*
SV4200	Camping Bled *Slovenia*

Alan Rogers Small Campsite Award 2011

This new award acknowledges excellent small campsites (less than 75 pitches) which offer a friendly welcome and top quality amenities throughout the season to their guests.

Winner

FR38040	Camping à la Rencontre du Soleil *France*

Runners-up

UK0065	Wayfarers Camping & Caravan Park *England*
DE3750	Camping Schloss Issigau *Germany*

Alan Rogers Seaside Award 2011

This award is made for sites which we feel are outstandingly suitable for a really excellent seaside holiday.

Winner

IT60200	Camping Union Lido Vacanze *Italy*

Runners-up

NL6948	Camping Strandpark De Zeeuwse Kust *Netherlands*
FR66560	Camping la Sirène *France*

Alan Rogers Country Award 2011

This award contrasts with our former award and acknowledges sites which are attractively located in delightful, rural locations.

Winner

FR37140	Huttopia Rillé *France*

Runners-up

UK3430	Kelling Heath Holiday Park *England*
FR19200	Les Hameaux de Miel *France*

Alan Rogers Family Site Award 2011

Many sites claim to be child friendly but this award acknowledges the sites we feel to be the very best in this respect.

Winner

NL5985	Vrijetijdspark Beerze Bulten *Netherlands*

Runners-up

IT60450	Camping Marina di Venezia *Italy*
FR40060	Club Camping International Eurosol *France*

Alan Rogers Readers' Award 2011

We believe our Readers' Award to be the most important. We simply invite our readers (by means of an on-line poll at www.alanrogers.com) to nominate the site they enjoyed most.

The outright winner for 2011 is:

Winner

FR17010	Camping Bois Soleil *France*

11

Book with us for the best holidays
on the best campsites

The Alan Rogers Travel Service was originally set up to provide a low cost booking service for readers. We pride ourselves on being able to put together a bespoke holiday, taking advantage of our experience, knowledge and contacts. We can even arrange low cost ferry crossings – ask us about our famous Ferry Deals!

FREE 2012 Brochure
call 01580 214000
Over 100 campsites in France, Italy and Spain hand picked for you

www.alanrogers.com/travel

The aims of the
Travel Service are simple

- **To provide convenience - a one-stop shop to make life easier.**

- **To provide peace of mind - when you need it most.**

- **To provide a friendly, knowledgeable, efficient service
  – when this can be hard to find.**

- **To provide a low cost means of organising your holiday
  – when prices can be so complicated.**

When you book with us, you will be allocated an experienced Personal Travel Consultant to provide you with personal advice and manage every stage of your booking. Our Personal Travel Consultants have first-hand experience of many of our campsites and access to a wealth of information. They can check availability, provide a competitive price and tailor your holiday arrangements to your specific needs.

- Discuss your holiday plans with a friendly person with first-hand experience

- Let us reassure you that your holiday arrangements really are taken care of

- Tell us about your special requests and allow us to pass these on

- Benefit from advice which will save you money – the latest ferry deals and more

- Remember, our offices are in Kent not overseas and we do NOT operate a queuing system!

Call us for advice or an instant quote

01580 214000 or visit
www.alanrogers.com/travel

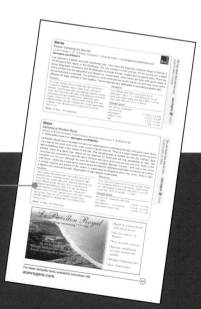

Look for a campsite entry like this to indicate
which campsites we can book for you.

The list is growing so please call for
up to the minute information.

alan rogers ⬭ travel

Value, Value, Value

Great Savings AND Complete Service

We work hard to offer quality and choice at remarkably low prices. And we pride ourselves on providing a friendly, personal service coupled with the in-depth knowledge of a specialist tour operator. We are not a large company and your holiday is important to us.

Our prices are based on the campsite's 'at-the-gate' prices. The campsite's own booking fees are not charged but are replaced by a standard Travel Service fee of just £45 per booking (up to 3 sites). Please bear in mind campsites typically charge a booking fee of around 30€ (perhaps £25) to customers booking direct - you will avoid this by booking with our Travel Service.

What's more, a campsite's own booking fee is charged at each campsite you visit. Our booking fee applies only **once**.

Our in-house travel team handles all aspects of your booking, for your peace of mind.

- Payment in sterling with **no risk** of exchange rate fluctuations

- **Secure bookings** – all campsite fees and deposits are paid in advance*
  with all ferry-inclusive holidays fully protected by our **ABTA bond**

- We have long-standing relationships with all campsites and **Special Requests**
  are passed on – details that can make a real difference

- Low cost ferries – **special fares** only available when booking a ferry-inclusive holiday

- A one-stop-shop for all your travel plans – campsite booking, overnight stops,
  low cost ferries and travel insurance – all in one place

excluding any nominal local tourist taxes, payable locally

Pitch only bookings

We're confident that our ferry inclusive booking service offers unbeatable value.

However, if you have already booked your ferry then we can still make a pitch-only reservation for you (minimum 5 nights). Since our prices are based on our ferry inclusive service, you need to be aware that a non-ferry booking may result in slightly higher prices than if you were to book direct with the site.

Want independent campsite reviews at your fingertips?

You'll find them here...

Over 3,000 in-depth campsite reviews at
www.alanrogers.com

Getting the most from
off peak touring

£13.95/night
single tariff
2 people

There are many reasons to avoid high season, if you can. Queues are shorter, there's less traffic, a calmer atmosphere and prices are cheaper. And it's usually still nice and sunny!

And when you use Camping Cheques you'll find great quality facilities that are actually open and a welcoming conviviality.

Did you know?
Camping Cheques can be used right into mid-July and from late August on many sites. Over 90 campsites in France alone accept Camping Cheques from 20th August.

Save up to 60% with Camping Cheques

Camping Cheque is a fixed price scheme allowing you to go as you please, staying on over 600 campsites across Europe, always paying the same rate and saving you up to 60% on regular pitch fees. One Cheque gives you one night for 2 people + unit on a standard pitch, with electricity. It's as simple as that.

Special offers mean you can stay extra nights free (eg 7 nights for 6 Cheques) or even a month free for a month paid! Especially popular in Spain during the winter, these longer-term offers can effectively halve the nightly rate. See Site Directory for details.

Check out our amazing Ferry Deals!

Why should I use Camping Cheques?

- It's a proven system, recognised by all 600+ participating campsites
  - so no nasty surprises.

- It's flexible, allowing you to travel between campsites, and also countries, on a whim - so no need to pre-book. (It's low season, so campsites are rarely full, though advance bookings can be made).

- Stay as long as you like, where you like - so you travel in complete freedom.

- Camping Cheques are valid 2 years - so no pressure to use them up.
  (If you have a couple left over after your trip, simply keep them for the following year, or use them up in the UK).

Tell me more... (but keep it brief!)

Camping Cheques was started in 1999 and has since grown in popularity each year (nearly 2 million were used last year). That should speak for itself. There are 'copycat' schemes, but none has the same range of quality campsites that save you up to 60%.

Ask for your **FREE** continental road map,
which explains how Camping Cheque works

01580 214002

FREE

downloadable Site Directory
alanrogers.com/directory

campingcheque.co.uk

NEW digital
iPad editions

Available on the
App Store

FREE Alan Rogers bookstore app
- digital editions of all 2012 guides

alanrogers.com/digital

GO THERE NOW!

What's In A Name?
Differentiating between the groups

At Alan Rogers we have been inspecting and reviewing campsites since 1968. There's no question things are very different today: facilities, standards, professionalism, technology have all evolved beyond all recognition. But we find there is still room for individuality, style and personality.

Campsites may still be small and uncommercial with modest facilities and the charm of a family-run establishment. Others may be larger and offer the impressive amenities of a modern resort. Some may favour highlighting their historic pedigree and ambience, others prefer to stress their rural location.

To achieve these various aims, many have joined forces with other like-minded campsites to raise their profile via glossy brochures and the like. Of course it's not black and white but over the following pages we try to clarify the distinctions between some of these groups of campsites, each of which claim to be unique in their own way.

Campéole

CAMPSITES AND RENTED ACCOMMODATION

Most Campéole campsites enjoy a great location close to water, first-class infrastructures and are designed where possible to sit harmoniously within their environments. They are popular with families with children of all ages, as well as couples and small groups.

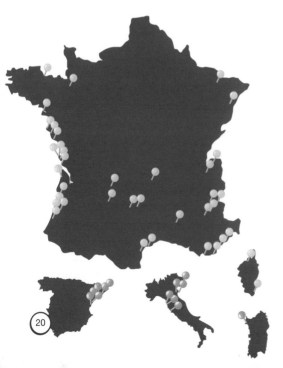

Campsites

Saint-Grégoire
Les Monts Colleux
Les Paludiers
La Grande Côte
Les Sirènes
Dornier
Le Platin
La Redoute
Les Amis de la Plage
Clairefontaine
Montalivet
Le Lac de Sanguinet
Le Vivier
Plage Sud
Navarrosse
Les Tourterelles
Le Val de Coise
Le Coiroux
Les Reflets du Quercy
La Boissière
Le Domaine de Combelles
La Côte des Roses
Les Mûriers
Île des Papes
Eurosurf
Les Arbousiers
La Croix du Sud
Le Dramont
Le Belgodère
L'Avena
Le Clos du Lac
Camping du Lac
Le Courounba
Les Vaudois
La Nublière
La Pinède
Le Giessen
Le Brabois
Castell Mar
Castell Montgri
Neptuno
Interpals
Montblanc park
Torre del Sol
Ca' Savio
Club del Sole Spina
Adriano
Il capannino
Free Time
Orbetello
Torre del Porticciolo

Campéole

In Their Own Words...

We will listen to you and advise you

Our helpful booking office is there to listen to you and to advise you accordingly. We can recommend a campsite suited to your needs and making a reservation is only a simple phone call away.

We will offer you a variety of holiday options

With over 50 destinations in France and elsewhere, around ten different types of accommodation, several possible lengths of stay and two arrival days per week, Campéole aims to provide maximum choice and flexibility.

We will ensure that our holidays are affordable for everyone

A range of services is available to make life easier for you during your holiday. We also guarantee the quality and comfort of our accommodation and therefore offer several solutions at different price levels.

We will all be committed to making a success of your holiday

The Campéole teams are professionals set on providing a holiday to remember. Each team member has your holiday at heart and will take it on themselves to make your stay as pleasant as possible.

We will cater for young children and teenagers

Campéole welcomes children and has created special amenities for them in its campsite villages: like Campitoo, popular with the little ones, or activity clubs for each age bracket and a dedicated Teen Space for teenagers.

We will create a friendly and festive atmosphere

On Campéole campsites you can take your pick from a range of sporting activities and join in the evening entertainments. Each site has a specific entertainment programme for all ages.

We will respect nature

Do your bit for the environment by opting for the unique Campéole holiday experience in unspoilt natural surroundings. Come and join us – we look forward to welcoming you!

www.campeole.co.uk

LES ★★★★ CASTELS
Hôtellerie de Plein Air

Les Castels is a well-established and highly regarded group of campsites set in the grounds of stunning châteaux, beautiful manors and charming country houses. This ensures unique natural settings for some of France's finest touring sites. You will be assured of a warm and courteous welcome, tranquil surroundings, great service and a taste of authentic French 'art de vivre'.

Campsites

Le Château de Galinée
Domaine de Keravel
Le Domaine des Ormes
La Grande Métairie
L'Orangerie de Lanniron
Le Ty Nadan
Château de la Grenouillère
Le Parc de Fierbois
L'Anse du Brick
Le Brévedent
Le Château de lez Eaux
Le Château de Martragny
Le Château de Chanteloup
Le Domaine des Forges
L'Étang de la Brèche
La Garangeoire
La Forge de Sainte Marie
Le Val de Bonnal
La Pergola
La Bien-Assise
Le Domaine de Drancourt
Le Moulin du Roch
Le Ruisseau des Pyrénées
Saint-Avit Loisirs
Le Château de Leychoisier
Le Château de Poinsouze
Le Caussanel
Le Domaine de la Paille Basse
Les Gorges du Chambon
Le Petit Trianon de Saint Ustre
Séquoia Parc
Le Château de Boisson
Les Criques de Porteils
Le Domaine de Massereau
Domaine du Verdon
Douce Quiétude
Le Château de Rochetaillée
Camping l'Ardéchois
Le Domaine de Sévenier

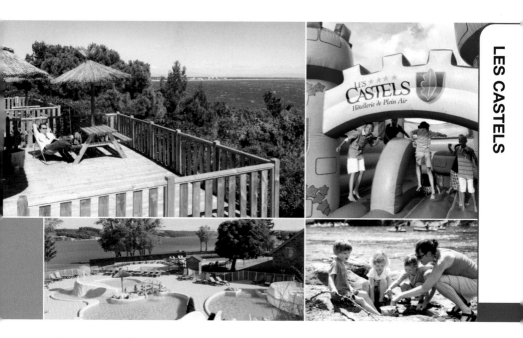

Les Castels

In Their Own Words...

Quality Assured

All campsites subscribe to the Les Castels Quality Charter and it was the first group to join the respected Camping Qualité label - a guarantee of excellence in facilities and services.

Whether you're on the move or just lazing...

Many Les Castels campsites offer supervised activities for children: organised games, fun workshops, outings and picnics, singing, dancing and real shows. You can go off and leave your children behind with your mind at rest because you know they'll have fun and make new friends. There is a wide range of activities for the whole family: football, tennis, mountain biking, aqua aerobics, tree climbing, pedal boats, canoeing, archery, boules and more.

Preserving our environmental heritage

Choosing to holiday on a Les Castels campsite means you already share our values. Each property contributes largely to the historical, environmental and architectural heritage of its region.

Benefit with our loyalty programme, the Castellissime Card

Enjoy Castellissime Card advantages, all year round. Earn points during your stay in any of Les Castels campsites, then redeem them for up to 15%* price reductions on your next stay.
*season-based, from 2% to 15% (see website for details)

Premium offer: the freedom of the outdoor life plus the very best in contemporary comfort

All our sites can now offer the Les Castels essential art-of-living package:

- Prestigious, secluded, large pitches in magnificent settings.
- Stylishly furnished and decorated spacious accommodation (bungalows, mobile homes or chalets) offering their own private terraces.
- All you need to enjoy a heavenly holiday: barbecue, garden furniture, lounge chairs and a sunshade.
- VIP services: bed linen and towels included, cleaning supply kit, television or hi-fi sound system, free internet access, etc.

www.camping-castels.co.uk

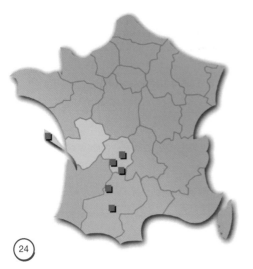

Chalets en France

Chalets en France offer a chance to holiday in beautiful French landscapes, enjoying natural surroundings and staying in comfortable chalets.
The friendly, knowledgeable staff have a good understanding of local areas, the history and culture and offer various activities to help visitors explore.

Corrèze

Les Hameaux de Miel,
Beynat

Les Hameaux du Perrier,
Lissac sur Couze

Les Cottages du Puy d'Agnoux,
Meyrignac l'Eglise

Tarn et Garonne

Les Hameaux des Lacs,
Monclar de Quercy

Lot

Les Hameaux de Pomette,
Cazals

Ile d'Oléron

Les Hameaux des Marines,
St Denis d'Oléron

Chalets en France

In Their Own Words...

The environment and heritage

We aim to give you a great holiday, while allowing you to experience and support the natural surroundings and local culture and commerce. We help you to discover the local region and each campsite offers a number of excursions, visits and activities that we hope you will find interesting.

A great welcome makes for a great holiday

We aim to provide a first-rate welcome and personal service from our bilingual staff. Throughout the season our staff are well presented and courteous and we hope you will get to know them and value their expert input to your holiday. Our high quality chalets ensure a good night's sleep, pleasant surroundings and comfort in which to enjoy your holiday.

A little bit extra....

We aim to ensure that the little touches make a big difference.

- Fresh bread and pastries can be delivered daily to your door.
- Free WiFi in reception and bar is welcome for many these days.
- Sensible and considerate rules to ensure the enjoyment of all holidaymakers.
- Free children's club, all season, for children aged 5 – 12 years.

www.chalets-en-france.com

Campsites on a human scale

The Flower philosophy is to avoid the style of so-called 'factory campsites'; to ignore anonymous standardisation but celebrate individuality and personality. Campsites in this group are all modestly sized: high quality facilities, for sure, but all on a very personable level and with a distinct personal touch.

Campsites

By the sea
Les Vertes Feuilles
Les Aubépines
Le Domaine du Rompval
La Chênaie
Utah Beach
Le Haut Dick
Les Chevaliers
Camping des Vallées
Camping de la Baie de Douarnenez
Aux 2 Chênes
Le Cabellou-Plage
Camping de l'Océan
Le Conleau
Le Kernest
Le Domaine de Pont Mahé
Les Brillas
La Bretonnière
Les Ilates
Les Maraises
Le Bel Air
Les Côtes de Saintonge
La Canadienne
Camping Harrobia
La Garenne
Le Mas de Mourgues
Le Marius

In the mountains
La Pène Blanche
L'Eden
Les Lanchettes

In the countryside
Le Domaine de Kervallon
Camping du Lac
L'Hermitage
Le Bois Fleuri
Le Val de Loire
L'Ile d'Offard
Le Val de Blois
Les Côteaux du Lac
Les Etangs
Le Martinet – Val de Loire
Les Portes de Sancerre
La Ferté Gaucher

Flower Campings

In Their Own Words...

Campsites on a human scale

On a Flower campsite you are not a number; you are not lost in the crowd. It's a sociable place, and camping is all about enjoying the company of others so the staff like to say hello and chat. We often remark on the warm and friendly 'micro climate' among residents on our campsites.

Quality campsites

On all our campsites, neither too big nor too small, quality is uppermost. We like small scale but we insist on high quality. We run campsites, we often live on campsites and we enjoy campsite life – we want you to enjoy it too. We have developed our ideal: camping on a human scale where you get to become part of the 'family', great facilities, wonderful locations. We hope this is your ideal too.

Discover the locality

The best advice we can give you is to get out of the campsite to explore our various regions. Each adds a real flavour to life: meet the local people, attend the local festivals and markets, and enjoy the local produce and the local traditions.

www.flowercampings.com

Countryside

Mediterranean

Your holiday "in nature's colours"
SUNELIA, WITH THE SUN!

Sunêlia
CAMPSITES - LEISURE RESORTS

Emerging in 2006, this is a group of
30 professionally run campsites sharing
a common view towards quality and
investment. With campsites located on
the coast, countryside and mountains,
there is 'something for everyone'.
What's more, campsites are rated as either
Sunêlia Club (livelier, plenty going on) or
Sunêlia Zen (calmer, relaxed).

Campsites

La Ribeyre
Aluna Vacances
Le Ranc Davaine
L'Hippocampe
Lac de Panthier
Le Soleil Fruité
Port'Land
L'Escale Saint-Gilles
L'Atlantique
Le Fief
Interlude
La Pointe du Médoc
Le Col Vert
Berrua
Le Col d'Ibardin
La Loubine
Framissima Nature
Les Pins
Les Tropiques
Le California
Domaine de la Dragonnière
Holiday Green
Perla di Mare
Résidence Lisa Maria
Villaggio dei Fiori
Rubina Resort
Le Clos du Rhône
Les Chalets du Logis d'Orres
Les Trois Vallées
Le Malazéou

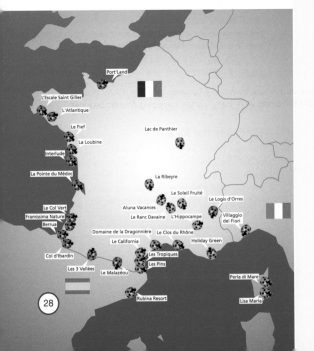

Sunêlia

In Their Own Words...

All Sunêlia campsites are 3- or 4-star rated and guarantee facilities of the highest standards.

On each campsite you will receive a warm, personal welcome from Sunêlia-trained staff keen to ensure your stay is pleasant and comfortable.

Rather like a village, each Sunêlia campsite offers a range of services: restaurant, grocery store, barbecue, etc.

On Sunêlia sites, everything is laid on for children so that you can make the most of your free time with full peace of mind.

What is your Sunêlia style?

At the seaside, in the countryside, in the mountains, by the ocean: Sunêlia offers holidays tailored to your every whim...

Mountains: at the heart of the Alps or the Pyrenees, you can make the most of the pure air and exceptional environment to let off steam or recharge your batteries, as a family or with friends!

Countryside: An Auvergne campsite, or perhaps an Ardèche or Provence one... whatever your favourite destination, beautiful surroundings are guaranteed.

Seaside: From the glorious beaches of the Med (choose from many between the Côte d'Azur and the Pyrenees) to the charming little bays and rockpools of Brittany, via the sweeping Atlantic beaches. The choice is yours.

Sunêlia quality

Sunêlia is committed to sustainable tourism standards and the Clef Verte accreditation and Camping Qualité standards testify to this (Camping Qualité alone conforms to over 500 quality criteria).

www.sunelia.com

Village Center is a group that has expanded from three sites in 2008 to its current network of over 30 sites, located in some of the most beautiful regions of France. There's quite a range of styles from simple (with limited amenities) to those which are rather more sophisticated. All sites in this group are owner-managed and most meet the standards of La Clef Verte. Village Center offers you holiday homes too.

Phare
Dune Blanche

Isles de Sola
Domaine de la Corniche

Baie du Karnic
Fontainebleau

Ile du Rhin
Parc de la Fecht

Bois de Pleuven
Lupins

Ker Goh Lenn

Bois d'Amour
Parc des Alais

Almadies
Côte Sauvage

Iles

Atlantic Club Montalivet
Catalpas
Domaine du Bosquet

Clos du Rocher

Forêt
Aqua Viva

Eurolac
Aurilandes
Tours
Rieumontagné
Demeures du Ventoux
Coteau de la Marine
Prés du Verdon

Vignes
Mas des Cigales
Côte Green
Domaine des Iscles

Domaine du Golf
Domaine de Manon

7 Fonts
Europe
Castellas

Fonserane
Saint-Clair

Domaine d'Ensérune
Ensoya
Neptune
Demeures Torrellanes

Demeures de la Massane
Domaine d'Anghione

30
• Campsite
• Holiday Home

Village Center

In Their Own Words...

With their 30 campsites, whatever kind of camping you fancy, Village Center can offer a great base for your holiday. Large pitches and modern accommodation in beautiful surroundings.

Mobile homes, chalets & equipped tents

There's always a friendly atmosphere and a great choice of accommodation for families or groups of friends. Choose between mobile homes, wooden chalets, bungalows and fully equipped tents: all the advantages of camping plus the comfort of custom-built accommodation.

Green credentials

We want you to enjoy your holiday and leave behind the routines and chores of daily life at home. That's why Village Center works together with La Clef Verte to guarantee the development of our sites (80% of our sites carry La Clef Verte accreditation). Moreover each year we invest in new accommodations.

Activities for the active

In high season you'll find a range of activities and entertainment designed to appeal to children and adults of all ages and preferences. Some of our campsites open their children's mini-clubs

during all French school holidays.

Stunning locations

Village Center offers diverse destinations amid stunning scenery in beautiful French regions: the legends of Brittany, the endless horizons of the Atlantic coast, the soft sunsets of the south of France or the fantastic landscapes of the Midi-Pyrénées.

www.village-center.com

Rolling sandy beaches, hidden coves, pretty villages and a picturesque coastline all combine to make Brittany a very popular holiday destination. Full of Celtic culture steeped in myths and legends, Brittany is one of the most distinctive regions of France.

DÉPARTEMENTS: 22 CÔTES D'ARMOR, 29 FINISTÈRE, 35 ILLE-ET-VILAINE, 56 MORBIHAN

MAJOR CITIES: RENNES AND BREST

Brittany's 800 miles of rocky coastline offer numerous bays, busy little fishing villages and broad sandy beaches dotted with charming seaside resorts. The coastline to the north of Brittany is rugged with a maze of rocky coves, while to the south, the shore is flatter with long sandy beaches. Inland you'll find wooded valleys, rolling fields, moors and giant granite boulders, but most impressive is the wealth of prehistoric sites, notably the Carnac standing stones.

Breton culture offers a rich history of menhirs, crosses, cathedrals and castles. Strong Celtic roots provide this region with its own distinctive traditions, evident in the local Breton costume and music, traditional religious festivals and the cuisine, featuring crêpes and cider. Many castles and manor houses, countless chapels and old towns and villages provide evidence of Brittany's eventful history and wealth of traditions. The abbey fortress of Mont St-Michel on the north coast (in Normandy) should not be missed and Concarneau in the south is a lovely walled town enclosed by granite rocks.

Places of interest

Cancale: small fishing port famous for oysters.

Carnac: 3,000 standing stones (menhirs).

Concarneau: fishing port, old walled town.

Dinan: historic walled town.

Perros-Guirec: leading resort of the 'Pink Granite Coast'.

Quiberon: boat service to three islands: Belle Ile (largest of the Breton islands), Houat, Hoedic.

Rennes: capital of Brittany, medieval streets, half-timbered houses; Brittany Museum.

St Malo: historic walled city, fishing port.

Cuisine of the region

Fish and shellfish are commonplace; traditional *crêperies* abound and welcome visitors with a cup of local cider.

Agneau de pré-salé: leg of lamb from animals pastured in the salt marshes and meadows.

Beurre blanc: sauce for fish dishes made with shallots, wine vinegar and butter.

Cotriade: fish soup with potatoes, onions, garlic and butter.

Crêpes Bretonnes: the thinnest of pancakes with a variety of sweet fillings.

Galette: can be a biscuit, cake or pancake; with sweet or savoury fillings.

Gâteau Breton: rich cake.

Poulet blanc Breton: free-range, quality, white Breton chicken.

www.brittanytourism.com
tourism-crtb@tourismebretagne.com
(0)2 99 28 44 30

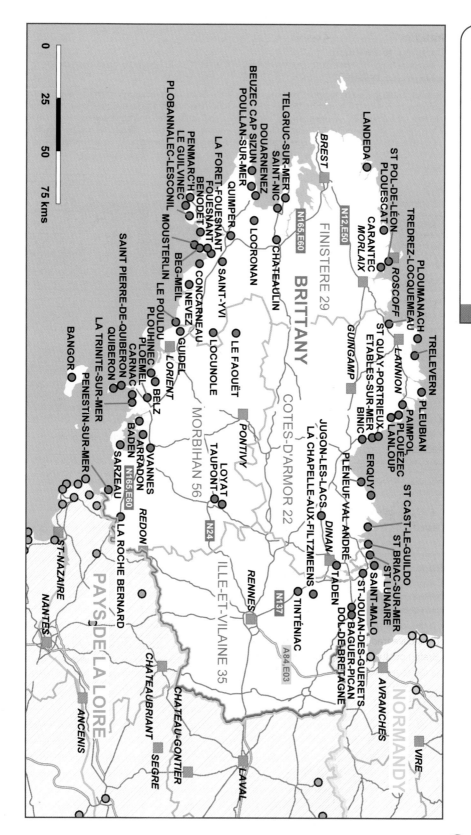

For latest campsite news, availability and prices visit
alanrogers.com

Call 01580 214000 We can book this site for you! alan rogers ◉ travel

Arradon
Camping de Penboch

9 chemin de Penboch, F-56610 Arradon (Morbihan) T: 02 97 44 71 29. E: camping.penboch@wanadoo.fr

alanrogers.com/FR56040

Penboch is 200 metres by footpath from the shores of the Golfe du Morbihan with its many islands, and plenty to do including watersports, fishing and boat trips. The site, in a peaceful, rural area, is divided into two – the main part, on open ground, with hedges and young trees, the other across a minor road in woodland with lots of shade. Penboch offers 175 pitches on flat grass, 105 are for touring and they are mostly divided into groups. Electricity (6/10A) is available on all pitches and most also have water and drainage. A Sites et Paysages member.

Facilities

Three toilet blocks, two on the main part (one heated) and one in the annex, include washbasins in cabins. New washing facilities include private family cabins (charged). Laundry facilities. Motorcaravan service point. Bar with snacks and takeaway. Shop (all 15/5-10/9). Heated pool with slide and paddling pool (15/5-15/9). Indoor pool (all season). Playground. Games room. American motorhomes accepted in low season. WiFi in bar. Off site: Beach, fishing 200 m. Sailing, windsurfing and bicycle hire 2 km.

Open: 7 April - 29 September.

Directions

From N165 at Auray or Vannes, take D101 along northern shores of Golfe du Morbihan; or leave N165 at D127 signed Ploeren and Arradon. Take turn to Arradon and site is signed. GPS: 47.62206, -2.8007

Charges guide

Per unit incl. 2 persons and electricity (10A)	€ 19.40 - € 39.30
extra person	€ 4.00 - € 6.20
child (2-7 yrs)	€ 3.00 - € 4.50

Arradon
Camping de l'Allée

L'Allée, F-56610 Arradon (Morbihan) T: 02 97 44 01 98. E: contact@camping-allee.com

alanrogers.com/FR56530

Camping de l'Allée is a pleasant family site close to the town of Arradon. There are 150 pitches extending across this six-acre site. The site has been developed in an orchard and pitches are of a good size, grassy and well shaded. A number of mobile homes and chalets are available for rent. Leisure amenities include a swimming pool (with separate paddling pool) and a good children's play area. Activities and evening entertainment are organised in peak season. The site is located close to the Morbihan gulf, with many opportunities for watersports and fishing.

Facilities

Shop, bar and restaurant (July/Aug). Swimming and paddling pools (heated 28/5-15/9). Play area. Tourist information. Activity and entertainment programme. Chalets and mobile homes for rent. Off site: Beach 600 m. Shops and restaurants in Arradon. Watersports. Fishing 3 km. Golf and riding 10 km. Vannes. .

Open: 2 April - 30 September.

Directions

Travelling on the N165 from Lorient to Vannes, take the D127 turn signed Ploeren. Then the D101 to Baden. After 2 km. site is well signed on the left. GPS: 47.621086, -2.840251

Charges guide

Per unit incl. 2 persons and electricity	€ 17.00 - € 23.15
extra person	€ 3.00 - € 4.85

Baden
Camping Mané Guernehué

52 rue Mané er Groez, F-56870 Baden (Morbihan) T: 02 97 57 02 06. E: info@camping-baden.com

alanrogers.com/FR56130

Located close to the Morbihan gulf, Mané Guernehué is a smart, modern site with excellent amenities and a variety of pitches. Some are terraced beneath pine trees, others in a former orchard with delightful views of the surrounding countryside. The 377 pitches are generally large, 210 being occupied by mobile homes and chalets. Most pitches have 10A electricity and a few also have water and drainage. Many are level but a few, particularly in the centre of the site, slope to varying degrees. An impressive new indoor pool complex has been added to the existing complex of outdoor pools and there is an equally impressive new spa and wellbeing facility.

Facilities

Three modern toilet blocks include washbasins in cabins. Facilities for disabled visitors. Washing machines and dryers. Small shop, bar and takeaway (9/4-20/9). Heated outdoor swimming pool (1/5-20/9). Heated indoor pool, waterslide, jacuzzi, gym and spa. Fishing. Minigolf. Pony trekking. Fitness room. Teenagers' room with games and TV. Play area. Tree top adventure area. Entertainment programme (high season). Mobile homes for rent. WiFi (charged). Off site: Beach and golf 3 km.

Open: 9 April - 1 November.

Directions

From Auray or Vannes use the D101 to Baden and watch for signs to site. GPS: 47.61419, -2.92596

Charges guide

Per unit incl. 2 persons and electricity	€ 19.90 - € 42.90
Camping Cheques accepted.	

For latest campsite news, availability and prices visit
alanrogers.com

Baguer-Pican
Camping le Vieux Chêne

Baguer-Pican, F-35120 Dol-de-Bretagne (Ille-et-Vilaine) T: 02 99 48 09 55. E: vieux.chene@wanadoo.fr
alanrogers.com/FR35000

This attractive, family owned site is situated between Saint-Malo and Mont Saint-Michel. Developed in the grounds of a country farmhouse dating from 1638, its young and enthusiastic owner has created a really pleasant, traditional atmosphere. In spacious, rural surroundings it offers 199 good sized pitches on gently sloping grass, most with 10A electricity, water tap and a light. They are separated by bushes and flowers, with mature trees for shade. A very attractive tenting area (without electricity) is in the orchard. The site is used by a Dutch tour operator (20 pitches). There are three lakes in the grounds and centrally located leisure facilities include a restaurant with a terrace overlooking an attractive pool complex. Some entertainment is provided in high season, which is free for children. A Sites et Paysages member.

Facilities

Three very good, unisex toilet blocks, which can be heated, include washbasins in cabins, a baby room and facilities for disabled visitors. Small laundry. Motorcaravan services. Shop, bar, takeaway and restaurant (1/6-4/9). Heated swimming pool, paddling pool, slides (17/5-11/9; lifeguard July/Aug). TV room (satellite). Games room. Tennis. Minigolf. Giant chess. Play area. Riding in July/Aug. Fishing. WiFi (charged). Off site: Supermarket in Dol 3 km. Riding 2 km. Bicycle hire 4 km. Golf 15 km.

Open: 17 May - 25 September.

Directions

Site is by the D576 Dol-de-Bretagne - Pontorson road, just east of Baguer-Pican. It can be reached from the new N176 taking exit for Dol-Est and Baguer-Pican. GPS: 48.54924, -1.684

Charges guide

Per unit incl. 2 persons	
and electricity	€ 19.00 - € 33.00
extra person	€ 4.50 - € 6.00
child (4-13 yrs)	€ 2.50 - € 3.90
dog	€ 3.00

BRITTANY
le vieux chêne
camping caravaning
★★★★
★ ★ ★ ★
• 200 pitches   • Aquatic Park   • Mini-golf   • Snack-bar
• Tennis   • Fishing ponds   • Mini-club   • Shop
Baguer Pican - 35120 Dol de Bretagne
Tél. 0033 2 99 48 09 55 - Email: vieux.chene@wanadoo.fr
Website: www.camping-vieuxchene.fr

Bangor
Flower Camping le Kernest

Bangor, F-56360 Belle Ile-en-Mer (Morbihan) T: 02 97 31 56 26. E: info@camping-kernest.com
alanrogers.com/FR56460

Belle Ile is a large island lying around 14 km. off the Quiberon peninsula. Access to the island can be made by ferry from either Quiberon, Vannes or Lorient (reservation is recommended in high season). Le Kernest is a family site and a member of the Flower group. It is located around 800 m. from a sandy beach with direct access via a footpath. There are 100 pitches here, some of which are occupied by wooden chalets. Touring pitches are grassy and well shaded, and all have electrical connections. Leisure facilities on site include a tennis court and multisports terrain, as well as a snack bar. Numerous cycle tracks cross the island, including one around the perimeter.

Facilities

Shop. Snack bar. Takeaway. Tennis. Multisports terrain. Play area. TV room. Activity and entertainment programme. Chalets for rent. Off site: Nearest beach 800 m. (direct path). Riding. Fishing. Cycle tracks.

Open: 1 June - 30 September.

Directions

Upon arrival at Le Palais, follow signs to Bangor on D90 and then to Kernest. Site is well signed from here. GPS: 47.31479, -3.18912

Charges guide

Per unit incl. 2 persons	
and electricity	€ 14.90 - € 22.50
extra person	€ 3.50 - € 4.50
child (2-7 yrs)	€ 2.20 - € 3.00
dog	€ 2.50 - € 3.00

We can book this site for you! alan rogers ⦿ travel
Call 01580 214000

For latest campsite news, availability and prices visit
alanrogers.com

Call 01580 214000 We can book this site for you! alan rogers ⊛ travel

Beg-Meil
Camping de la Piscine

(handwritten notes)

B.P. 12 Kerleya, Beg-Meil, F-29170 Fouesnant (Finistère) T: 02 98 56 56 06.
E: contact@campingdelapiscine.com alanrogers.com/FR29170

There are many campsites in this area but la Piscine is notable for the care and attention to detail that contribute to the well-being of its visitors. Created by the Caradec family from an orchard, the 199 level, grass pitches are of generous size and are separated by an interesting variety of hedges and trees. Water, drainage and electricity points are provided, normally one stand between two pitches. The small bar and takeaway with terrace overlooking the pool complex provides a relaxing focal point. A quiet site, set back from the sea, la Piscine will appeal to families looking for good quality without too many on-site activities. A new covered, heated pool with sauna and massage facilities was added in 2011.

Facilities
Two refurbished toilet units include washbasins in cabins and showers. Facilities for disabled visitors. Laundry facilities. Motorcaravan service point. Shop (25/5-16/9). Bar and takeaway (2/7-31/8). Pool complex with three slides, waterfall and jacuzzi. Covered, heated pool (all season). Sauna and turkish bath. Play area. BMX track. Bicycle hire. Half-court tennis. TV room. Entertainment organised in high season. WiFi (charged 1/7-31/8). Off site: Restaurants, bars, shops and supermarkets in Fouesnant 3 km. Beach 1 km. Fishing and riding 4 km.

Open: 11 May - 16 September.

Directions
Site is 5 km. south of Fouesnant. Turn off N165 expressway at Coat Conq signed Concarneau and Fouesnant. At Fouesnant join D45 signed Beg Meil and shortly turn right on D145 signed Mousterlin. In 1 km. turn left and follow signs to site. GPS: 47.86568, -4.01553

Charges guide
Per unit incl. 2 persons
and electricity   € 21.00 - € 32.10
extra person   € 4.20 - € 6.50
child (2-10 yrs)   € 2.10 - € 3.20

Belz
Camping le Moulin des Oies

21 rue de la Côte, F-56550 Belz (Morbihan) T: 02 97 55 53 26. E: moulindesoies@wanadoo.fr
alanrogers.com/FR56500

This delightful rural site is lovingly cared for by the owners M. and Mme. Tregret. The 68 generously sized pitches (with electricity 6A) are grassy, level and marked by trees and shrubs. Separated from the sea by the width of a small road, the campsite has its own saltwater inlet, controlled by a sluice, not being affected by the tide and with a small sandy beach, there is safe bathing at all times. To the side of this there is a shady, grassed picnic area.

Facilities
Sanitary block with showers. Facilities for disabled visitors. Washing machine, games room, TV. Multisports court. Bar, restaurant and takeaway (Jul/Aug). Saltwater swimming pool with beach. Kitchen with dining area for campers. Only certain breeds of dog accepted. WiFi (free). Off site: Boat launching 50 m. Bicycle hire 500 m. Belz town 1 km. for shops, restaurants and transport services. Golf and riding 6 km.

Open: 7 April - 29 September.

Directions
Leave the N165 at Auray. Take the D22 signed Lorient. At Belz the campsite is signed on the right after entering Belz. The campsite is 1 km. further. GPS: 47.680403, -3.175821

Charges guide
Per unit incl. 2 persons
and electricity   € 16.10 - € 18.10
No credit cards.

Beuzec Cap Sizun
Camping Pors Peron

F-29790 Beuzec Cap Sizun (Finistère) T: 02 98 70 40 24. E: info@campingporsperon.com
alanrogers.com/FR29540

This small site situated on the Cap Sizun peninsula is lovingly cared for by English owners Graham and Nikki Hatch. The site is hilly but the terrain has been terraced to provide 98 fairly level pitches. Many mature trees and shrubs provide some shade and areas of privacy. Long leads are required for the 60 electric hook-ups (10A). A 200 m. walk takes you to a delightful sandy bay and you can also access a coastal path. Although Pors Peron is set in a quiet and rural part of the Breton countryside, a short drive will take you to the busy port of Douarnenez.

Facilities
One central toilet block has open style washbasins and pre-set showers. Facilities for disabled visitors and babies (kept locked). Laundry facilities. No shop but bread delivered daily. Small, unfenced but safe play area with trampoline. Bicycle hire. Boules and board games. WiFi. Off site: Medieval town of Pont Croix 5 km. Douarnenez for shops, market and restaurants 12 km.

Open: 1 March - 31 October.

Directions
Travel west from Douarnenez on the D7 for 12 km. Site is signed on right towards Pors Peron. GPS: 48.08435, -4.48191

Charges guide
Per unit incl. 2 persons
and electricity   € 12.60 - € 13.40
extra person   € 3.30 - € 3.50

For latest campsite news, availability and prices visit
alanrogers.com

Bénodet
Camping du Letty

F-29950 Bénodet (Finistère) T: 02 98 57 04 69. E: reception@campingduletty.com

alanrogers.com/FR29030

The Guyader family have ensured that this excellent and attractive site has plenty to offer for all the family. With a charming ambience, the site on the outskirts of the popular resort of Bénodet spreads over 22 acres with 493 pitches, all for touring units. Groups of four to eight pitches are set in cul-de-sacs with mature hedging and trees to divide each group. All pitches have electricity, water and drainage. As well as direct access to a small sandy beach, with a floating pontoon (safe bathing depends on the tides), the site has recently built a grand aquatic parc, with heated open air and indoor pools including children's pools, jacuzzi, and slides. At the attractive floral entrance, former farm buildings provide a host of facilities including an extensively equipped fitness room and new wellness rooms for massage and jacuzzis. There is also a modern, purpose built nightclub and bar providing high quality live entertainment most evenings (situated well away from most pitches to avoid disturbance).

Facilities

Six well placed toilet blocks are of good quality and include mixed style WCs, washbasins in large cabins and controllable hot showers (charged). One block includes a separate laundry and dog washing enclosures. Baby rooms. Separate facility for disabled visitors. Launderette. Hairdressing room. Motorcaravan service points. Well stocked shop. Extensive snack bar and takeaway. Bar with games room and night club. Library/reading room with four computer stations. Entertainment room with satellite TV. New pool complex with indoor and outdoor pools, children's pool, jacuzzi and slide. Fitness centre (no charge). Saunas, jacuzzi and solarium (all charged). Tennis and squash (charged). Boules. Archery. Well equipped play area. Entertainment and activities (July/Aug). WiFi in reception. Off site: Sailing, fishing, riding and golf all nearby. Bénodet and Quimper.

Open: 11 June - 6 September.

Directions

From N165 take D70 Concarneau exit. At first roundabout take D44 to Fouesnant. Turn right at T-junction. After 2 km. turn left to Fouesnant (still D44). Continue through La Forêt Fouesnant and Fouesnant, picking up signs for Bénodet. Shortly before Bénodet at roundabout turn left (signed Le Letty). Turn right at next mini-roundabout and site is 500 m. on left. GPS: 47.86700, -4.08783

Charges guide

Per unit incl. 2 persons	
and electricity	€ 20.50 - € 36.00
extra person	€ 4.00 - € 7.50
child (1-6 yrs)	€ 2.00 - € 3.75
dog	€ 2.30

Direct access to the beach

Camping

Le Letty

Bénodet - South Brittany
Tel. + 33 (0)2 98 57 04 69

Waterpark

www.campingduletty.com

Campsite without any mobile home

For latest campsite news, availability and prices visit

alanrogers.com

We can book this site for you! alanrogers ◉ travel
Call 01580 214000

Binic
Camping le Panoramic

Rue Gasselin, F-22520 Binic (Côtes d'Armor) T: 02 96 73 60 43. E: camping.le.panoramic@wanadoo.fr
alanrogers.com/FR22310

You will receive a warm welcome from the owners of this newly renovated site on the Gäelo Coast. It is in a woodland setting, yet only 800 m. from the beaches and the popular resort of Binic. It is ideally situated for visiting the many charming little resorts along this coast. A feature of this campsite is the vast range of activities for all ages that are arranged during July and August. There are 200 attractive, terraced pitches with half for touring. They are separated by bushes and hedges giving some shade, some are slightly sloping and most have electricity (10A).

Facilities

Two new, well appointed toilet blocks with all necessary facilities, including those for campers with disabilities. Bar with basic shop (all season). Snack bar and takeaway (July/Aug). Bread to order (July/Aug). Indoor heated pool (all season). Fenced play area. Boules. Games/TV room. Extensive range of entertainment, morning, afternoon, evening (except Sat) July/Aug. WiFi. Off site: Casino. Zoo. Fishing, bicycle hire, boat ramp, sailing 800 m.

Open: 1 April - 30 September.

Directions

From the N12 St Brieuc bypass head north on D786 to Paimpol (par la Côte). On approaching Binic look for white campsite sign to the right. GPS: 48.591895, -2.824237

Charges guide

Per unit incl. 2 persons	€ 15.00 - € 18.50
extra person	€ 4.30 - € 5.30
electricity	€ 5.00

Carantec
Yelloh! Village les Mouettes

50 route de La Grande Grève, F-29660 Carantec (Finistère) T: 02 98 67 02 46.
E: camping@les-mouettes.com **alanrogers.com/FR29000**

Les Mouettes is a sheltered site on the edge of an attractive bay with access to the sea at the front of the site. In a wooded setting with many attractive trees and shrubs, the 434 pitches include just 90 for touring units, all with electricity, water and drainage. The remainder are taken by tour operators and by 207 mobile homes and rental chalets. At the centre of the 'village' are shops, a bar, a restaurant, a stage, sports facilities and an impressive heated pool complex with swimming, paddling and water slide pools, plus a 'tropical river', jacuzzi and sauna. The indoor swimming pool is a recent addition.

Facilities

Two clean sanitary blocks include controllable showers, washbasins in cabins and mainly British toilets. Facilities for disabled visitors. Laundry. Motorcaravan services. Shop (limited hours outside the main season). Takeaway. Bar with TV. Restaurant/pizzeria/grill. Pool complex. Beauty salon. Games rooms. Play area. Half-court tennis. Minigolf. Bicycle hire (July/Aug). Entertainment in main season. Large units should phone first. WiFi in central area (charged). Off site: Fishing 1 km. Beach, sailing and golf all 2 km. Riding 6 km. Bicycle hire 10 km.

Open: 6 April - 9 September.

Directions

Carantec is 15 km. northwest of Morlaix and 15 km. from Roscoff. From D58 Roscoff - Morlaix road, turn east to Carantec on D173. In 4 km. site is signed to the left at roundabout immediately after passing supermarket on right. GPS: 48.65807, -3.92833

Charges 2012

Per unit incl. 2 persons, electricity and water	€ 17.00 - € 46.00
extra person	€ 6.00 - € 9.00
child (0-7 yrs)	free - € 7.00

Carnac
Camping Moulin de Kermaux

F-56340 Carnac (Morbihan) T: 02 97 52 15 90. E: moulin-de-kermaux@wanadoo.fr
alanrogers.com/FR56090

Only 100 m. from the famous Carnac megaliths, le Moulin de Kermaux is an excellent base from which to see these ancient stones as they portray their ever changing mood, colour and profile. Family run, the site has 150 pitches, all with 6/10A electricity. There are 75 pitches for touring units and 75 mobile homes, mostly separated by hedges and with many mature trees offering welcome shade. The compact nature of the site offers a safe environment for parents and children. Ideal for children of all ages, there is an aquatic complex with a heated pool and a slide with an indoor pool planned. This is a well run, quiet and comfortable site.

Facilities

The fully equipped heated toilet block has washbasins in cabins. Facilities for disabled visitors. Baby bath. Laundry facilities. Motorcaravan service point. Shop (26/6-31/8). Bar with satellite TV. Takeaway (26/6-31/8). Swimming and paddling pools. Sauna and jacuzzi. Adventure playground. Minigolf. Organised activities (July/Aug). WiFi (charged). Off site: Bus service 100 m. Beaches 3 km.

Open: 29 April - 10 September.

Directions

From N165 take Quiberon/Carnac exit onto D768. After 5 km. turn south on D119 towards Carnac. After 4 km. at roundabout turn left (northeast) on D196 to site. GPS: 47.59675, -3.06162

Charges guide

Per unit incl. 2 persons and electricity	€ 21.70 - € 30.90

For latest campsite news, availability and prices visit
alanrogers.com

Carnac
Castel Camping la Grande Métairie

Route des Alignements de Kermario, B.P. 85, F-56342 Carnac (Morbihan) T: 02 97 52 24 01.
E: info@lagrandemetairie.com **alanrogers.com/FR56010**

La Grande Métairie is a good quality site situated a little back from the sea, close to the impressive rows of the famous Carnac menhirs (giant prehistoric standing stones). The site has 575 individual pitches (108 for touring units), surrounded by hedges and trees. All have electricity (some need long leads). The site is well known and popular and has many British visitors with 314 pitches taken by tour operators. It is ideal for families with children of all ages and is lively and busy over a long season. Musical evenings, barbecues and other organised events including occasional dances are held in an outdoor amphitheatre (pitches near these facilities may be noisy late at night – the bar closes at midnight). Paddocks with ponds are home for ducks, goats and ponies to watch and feed. There are also pony rides around the site. A super pool complex comprises heated indoor and outdoor pools, water slides and toboggans and a jacuzzi. A local market takes place at Carnac on Wednesdays and Sundays.

Facilities

Three large well maintained toilet blocks with washbasins in cabins. Facilities for babies and disabled visitors. Laundry facilities. Motorcaravan service points. Shops (from 19/5). Bar lounge and terrace, restaurant and takeaway (all from 19/5). TV and games rooms. Swimming pool complex with bar. Playgrounds and playing field. Tennis. Minigolf. BMX track. Bicycle hire. Fishing. Zip-wire. Paintball. Helicopter rides (July/Aug). Amphitheatre. Organised events and entertainment. American motorhomes accepted up to 27 ft. Off site: Riding 1 km. Nearest beach 3 km. Golf 12 km.

Open: 2 April - 10 September (all services from 19/5).

Directions

From N165 take Quiberon/Carnac exit onto D768. After 5 km. turn south onto D119 towards Carnac. At roundabout and after 4 km. turn left (northeast) onto D196 to the site. GPS: 47.5973, -3.0607

Charges guide

Per unit incl. 2 persons	
and electricity	€ 18.00 - € 43.80
extra person	€ 4.00 - € 7.90
child (4-7 yrs)	free - € 5.40
dog	€ 4.00

Less 20% 22/5-29/6 and after 1/9.

Route des Alignements de Kermario   **Tél. 33(0)2 97 52 24 01**
B.P. 85 - 56342 Carnac Cedex   **Fax 33(0)2 97 52 83 58**
www.lagrandemetairie.com

For latest campsite news, availability and prices visit
alanrogers.com

Call 01580 214000 We can book this site for you! alan rogers ◉ travel

Carnac
Kawan Village le Moustoir

Route du Moustoir, F-56340 Carnac (Morbihan) T: 02 97 52 16 18. E: info@lemoustoir.com

alanrogers.com/FR56110

Camping le Moustoir is a friendly, family run site situated about three kilometres inland from the many beaches of the area and close to the famous alignments of standing stones. Pitches are grassy and separated by shrubs and hedges, with several shaded by tall pine trees. There is a popular pool area with slides, swimming pool and a paddling pool with 'mushroom' fountain and a second covered pool complex. The bar and terrace become the social centre of the site in the evenings. A high season entertainment programme includes a daily 'Kids' Club' attracting children of several nationalities. Whilst younger children can enjoy pony rides around the campsite, the older ones can swoop through the treetops on the new aerial adventure complex. For those who like to experience local cuisine, nearby Carnac, Trinité-sur-Mer and Auray have restaurants and crêperies to suit all tastes. Carnac's Wednesday and Sunday markets are not to be missed.

Facilities

The substantial, traditional style toilet block is well maintained (outside peak season some sections may be closed). Motorcaravan service facilities. Shop, bar, restaurant and takeaway (all season). Heated swimming pool (21x8 m), water slides, and paddling pool (from 1/5). Heated indoor swimming pool (all season). Wellness area (added in 2011). Adventure playground. Tennis. Boules. Volleyball, football and basketball. Kids' Club. Barrier deposit € 20. WiFi. Off site: Watersports at Carnac Plage. Fishing, bicycle hire, riding 2 km. Beach 3 km. Golf 10 km.

Open: 1 April - 30 September.

Directions

From N165, take exit to D768 (Carnac and Quiberon). At second crossroads after 5 km. turn left (D119) towards Carnac. After 3 km. turn left (oblique turning) after a hotel. Site is 500 m. on left. GPS: 47.60825, -3.06587

Charges guide

Per unit incl. 2 persons and electricity	€ 20.60 - € 34.60
extra person	€ 5.20

Camping Cheques accepted.

Kawan Village Le Moustoir

Kawan Village Le Moustoir | 71 Route du Moustoir | F-56340 Carnac
Tel: 0033 297 52 16 18 | info@le-moustoir.com | www.lemoustoir.com

Carnac
Camping du Lac

F-56340 Carnac (Morbihan) T: 02 97 55 78 78. E: info@lelac-carnac.com

alanrogers.com/FR56390

Overlooking the lake and situated between the Morbihan Gulf and the Quiberon peninsula, this site is only 3 km. from the port of La Trinité-sur-Mer while the famous megaliths are even closer. The site is well maintained with flowering landscaped gardens and mature trees and shrubs, giving plenty of shade and some privacy. The 140 pitches are of various sizes and some are terraced towards the lake; there is good access for larger units. The free-form pool with sun loungers is fenced, but low glass panels give superb views across the lake and surrounding countryside.

Facilities

Two sanitary blocks, kept clean and well maintained, have British style WCs, baby bath and laundry units. Small shop (all season) with takeaway food (1/7-30/8). Swimming pool (15/5-30/9). Play areas with trampolines. Games room with electronic games, table football and TV. Fishing. Bicycle hire. Cycling and canoe activities arranged regularly. Kayaks, surfboards and cars for hire. WiFi (free). Off site: Riding 3 km. Sailing 4 km. Coastal beaches 5 km. Golf 8 km.

Open: 1 April - 30 October.

Directions

From the N165 Vannes - Lorient dual carriageway, south of Auray, take exit for Carnac/Ploemel. Head southwest on the D768 for 4 km. then turn south on the D186 La Trinité-sur-Mer road. Camping du Lac is well signed from here and at the end of a long access road. GPS: 47.61135, -3.0288

Charges guide

Per unit incl. 2 persons and electricity	€ 19.30 - € 26.30
extra person	€ 5.20

For latest campsite news, availability and prices visit
alanrogers.com

Carnac
Camping les Menhirs

Allée Saint-Michel, F-56340 Carnac (Morbihan) T: 02 97 52 94 67. E: contact@lesmenhirs.com
alanrogers.com/FR56270

Although located within the built-up area of the popular resort of Carnac, and only 300 m. from the beach, this campsite feels much more rural. Catering for all ages, this is a friendly site and lively in high season with plenty of activities including evening entertainment and a club for children. There are 350 pitches; 142 touring pitches and the remainder used for mobile homes and chalets, of which the majority are used by tour operators. The touring pitches are in groups and are large, level and hedged. 19 pitches are designated Luxe, being a little larger (110-120 sq. m) and six are Privilege (115-130 sq. m. including barbecue). All have 10A electricity, water and drainage. The central complex, containing the pools and games areas, overlooked by the bar and its terrace, makes a convivial focal point. The town and seafront can be explored on foot and the Brittany coast and the Gulf of Morbihan are within easy reach by car or bicycle. American style motorhomes should book ahead.

Facilities

Three spotless, modern, light toilet blocks with washbasins in cabins, facilities for children, babies and disabled visitors. A further en-suite unit for disabled campers is by the pool complex. Laundry. Shop. Bar with satellite TV and takeaway (26/5-16/9). Heated indoor and outdoor swimming pools (all season). Fitness complex with massage, multigym, jacuzzi, sauna and solarium. Multisports pitch. Tennis. Boules. Play areas. Children's club and evening entertainment (July/Aug). WiFi (charged). Off site: Beach 300 m. Bicycle hire 500 m. Town centre 1 km. Bars and restaurants within walking distance.

Open: 14 April - 22 September.

Directions

From Auray take D786 to Carnac and Quiberon. After 5 km. turn south on D119 towards Carnac at roundabout. 600 m. beyond next roundabout fork left, signed La Trinité-sur-Mer and Plages. Keep straight on at lights. Fork left at first roundabout. Turn left at next roundabout (T-junction) and site is signed at 250 m. on left. GPS: 47.57653, -3.06890

Charges guide

Per unit incl. 2 persons and electricity	€ 29.80 - € 40.50
extra person	€ 8.00
child (2-7 yrs)	€ 5.95

CAMPING LES MENHIRS

Situated 300 m from the sandy beach and close to the centre of Carnac Plage, the Camping des menhirs offers a variety of high standard facilities: heated outdoor swimming pool, heated indoor swimming pool, sauna, jacuzzi, etc...

Bp 167 - Allée St Michel - 56343 Carnac - France
Tel: 0033 (0)2 97 52 94 67 - Fax: 0033 (0)2 97 52 25 38
contact@lesmenhirs.com
www.lesmenhirs.com

Carnac
Camping le Dolmen

Chemin de Beaumer, F-56340 Carnac (Morbihan) T: 02 97 52 12 35. E: camping.ledolmen@gmail.com
alanrogers.com/FR56510

Le Dolmen is a family site located on the eastern edge of Carnac. The site has 130 pitches, of which around 70 are available to tourers. Other pitches are taken by mobile homes (around 12 are to rent). Pitches are of a good size and are mostly equipped with electricity. A number of pitches outside the main gate in a parking area have been specially equipped for motorcaravans (with services). On-site amenities include a small snack bar and a swimming pool. The nearest beach, le Men Dû, is around 600 m. away. This is a particularly attractive beach, shelving gently and with crystal waters.

Facilities

Two toilet blocks (one due for total refurbishment ahead of the 2012 season). Snack bar. Morning bread service. Heated swimming pool (1/6-31/8). Play area. Volleyball. Activity and entertainment programme. Motorcaravan services. WiFi in some areas (charged). Mobile homes for rent. Off site: Nearest beach 600 m. Fishing and bicycle hire 1 km. Sailing 1 km. Riding 3 km.

Open: 1 April - 11 September.

Directions

Approaching from the north (Auray) take D768 towards Quiberon and then D119 to Carnac. Upon arriving in Carnac, follow signs to Carnac-Plage and then to La Trinité-sur-Mer using D186 (Avenue des Druides). The site is clearly indicated to the left, on the edge of the town. GPS: 47.58076, -3.05751

Charges guide

Per unit incl. 2 persons	€ 21.50 - € 32.50
extra person	€ 4.30 - € 7.00

Carnac
Camping les Druides

55 chemin de Beaumer, B.P. 128, F-56343 Carnac (Morbihan) T: 02 97 52 08 18.
E: contact@camping-les-druides.com **alanrogers.com/FR56370**

Situated in a small village just two kilometres from the town of Carnac, this very pleasant site has 110 pitches on level grass, most having high mature hedges giving a good feel of privacy. All have good access to electricity (6-10A) and water. We had a very warm welcome from Mme. Simon and her daughter, who have built this site up over many years. The new reception building is impressive and registration is dealt with efficiently. This is a lovely base from which to explore the region; the famous megaliths are close by and the beaches are only 500 m. away.

Facilities

Two modern sanitary blocks, some basins in cubicles, pre-set showers and British style WCs. Baby changing room. Laundry room with washer/dryer and sinks (all kept very clean). Excellent facilities for disabled visitors. Bread and snacks available from reception. Superb fenced swimming pool (heated 16/6-3/9) with jacuzzi and tropical plants. Games room with TV, table football, pool, table tennis and electronic games. Play areas. Multisports court. Pétanque. WiFi (charged). Off site: Beaches 500 m. Fishing and bicycle hire 1 km. Sailing 3 km. Riding 4 km. Golf 15 km.

Open: 7 April - 8 September.

Directions

From the N165 Vannes - Lorient dual carriageway south of Auray, take the Carnac/Ploemel exit. Head southwest on the D768 for 7 km. Turn south on D119 signed Carnac. On entering Carnac centre, head east on the D781 towards St Philibert. Take a right turn and follow signs for the site. Les Druides is on the right just before you reach the Carnac Plage areas. GPS: 47.58033, -3.05685

Charges guide

Per unit incl. 2 persons and electricity	€ 23.00 - € 35.70
extra person	€ 3.80 - € 5.80
child (under 7 yrs)	€ 2.30 - € 4.00
dog	€ 1.70 - € 2.30

Opened from 7 April till 8 September 2012

3 star family campsite with 110 pitches. No animation. Well located at Carnac-Plage, close to facilities (supermarket, beaches, city centre). Sanitary bloc renewed in 2011!

Camping les Druides***   55, Chemin de Beaumer   56340 Carnac
E-mail : contact@camping-les-druides.com   Web : www.camping-les-druides.com

Châteaulin
Camping la Pointe

Route de Saint-Coulitz, F-29150 Châteaulin (Finistère) T: 02 98 86 51 53. E: lapointecamping@aol.com
alanrogers.com/FR29280

This small, rural campsite situated by the river Aulne on the outskirts of Châteaulin, was taken over by new English owners Julie and Marcus Gregory in 2008. They have developed the site to provide a friendly and relaxed atmosphere. The 60 pitches vary in size and quality, all have 10A electricity and a few provide hardstanding for heavier units. There is a small kitchen garden complete with chickens where campers can purchase free range eggs and other produce and are also welcome to just sit and relax. A family/games room can be found above the well maintained toilet block.

Facilities

The toilet and shower block also provides facilities for disabled visitors. Baby changing area. Laundry facilities. Motorcaravan service point. Family/games room. Small shop for basics and bread. Fresh eggs and produce available from the kitchen garden. WiFi (charged). Bicycle hire. Off site: Fishing in the Aulne 200 m (permit needed). Bicycle hire 2 km. Châteaulin 1.5 km. with shops, bars and restaurants. Medieval village of Locronan 15 km. Nearest beach 20 km with windsurfing and yachting.

Open: 15 March - 15 October.

Directions

From Quimper or Brest on N165, exit at 'Châteaulin Centre'. From Châteaulin follow signs for St Coulitz. After 1.5 km. turn left and continue 100 m. Site well signed. GPS: 48.18746, -4.0848

Charges guide

Per unit incl. 2 persons and electricity	€ 19.50
extra person	€ 4.00
child (under 10 yrs)	€ 2.50
dog	€ 1.00

No credit cards.
Camping Cheques accepted.

For latest campsite news, availability and prices visit
alanrogers.com

Châteaulin
Camping de Rodaven

Rocade de Prat Bihan, F-29150 Châteaulin (Finistère) T: 02 98 86 32 93. E: campingderodaven@orange.fr
alanrogers.com/FR29640

This former municipal campsite has been transformed by its enthusiastic owner M. Gerente into a most delightful place to stay. There are 94 generously sized, level, grassy pitches (40 with 10A electricity). They are divided by various flowering shrubs, small trees and, in the more open area of the site, by white lines on the grass. There is a small bar with a covered terrace. The site is alongside the Nantes-Brest canal, which offers good fishing (permit required). Canoes are also available for hire on the site. The riverside town of Châteaulin is only ten minutes walk away.

Facilities

Toilet and shower block with facilities for disabled campers. Washing machine and dryer. Bar. Play area. Bicycle and canoe hire. Archery, table tennis and boules. Fishing on canal (permit required). Off site: Swimming pool and tennis courts 200 m. Town centre 350 m. Nearest beach 15 km. Locronan and Quimper.

Open: 7 April - 30 September.

Directions

From the direction of Brest on N165 leave at first sign for Châteaulin and follow D770 to the town. Within the town follow signs for Piscine. Opposite Piscine you will see sign for the campsite. GPS: 48.189855, -4.090122

Charges guide

Per unit incl. 2 persons	
and electricity	€ 12.20 - € 13.70
extra person	€ 3.00
child (0-12 yrs)	€ 1.00 - € 2.00

Concarneau
Camping les Sables Blancs

Avenue Le Dorlett, F-29900 Concarneau (Finistère) T: 02 98 97 16 44.
E: contact@camping-lessablesblancs.com **alanrogers.com/FR29150**

This is an attractive terraced site overlooking the sea on the outskirts of Concarneau. Most of the 108 touring pitches are shaded by large mature trees and shrubs. All with 10A electricity, they are level and well shaded though access to some could prove a little difficult for large units. A traditionally styled bar, restaurant and conservatory opens out onto a terrace with swimming pool overlooking the Baie de la Forêt. Although the site is terraced with steep steps in places, the main touring pitches are on the top part of the site close to the main facilities.

Facilities

One new modern toilet block provides very good facilities including washbasins (both open and in cubicles) and showers. Facilities for babies and disabled visitors. New laundry facilities. Bar and restaurant (3/4-30/9). Heated outdoor swimming pool (23/4-15/9). Play area. Evening entertainment (July/Aug). Billiards room. WiFi in bar. Off site: Concarneau with shops, bars and restaurants. Beach 150 m. Riding 1 km. Bicycle hire 1.5 km.

Open: 2 April - 31 October.

Directions

Leave the N165 for Concarneau on D70. Site is situated on the northern edge of town on the coast road. Well signed. GPS: 47.88195, -3.92915

Charges guide

Per unit incl. 2 persons	
and electricity (10A)	€ 17.00 - € 27.00
extra person	€ 2.00 - € 7.00
child (under 7 yrs)	€ 1.00 - € 2.50
dog	€ 2.00

Concarneau
Camping les Prés Verts

B.P. 612, Kernous-Plage, F-29186 Concarneau (Finistère) T: 02 98 97 09 74. E: info@presverts.com
alanrogers.com/FR29190

What sets this family site apart from the many others in this region are its more unusual features – its stylish pool complex with Romanesque style columns and statue, and its plants and flower tubs. The 150 pitches are mostly arranged on long, open, grassy areas either side of main access roads. Specimen trees, shrubs and hedges divide the site into smaller areas. There is an area towards the rear of the site where the pitches have sea views. There is direct access to the sandy beach with no roads to cross (300 m). Concarneau is just 2.5 km. A Sites et Paysages member.

Facilities

Two toilet blocks provide unisex WCs, but separate washing facilities for ladies and men. Preset hot showers and washbasins in cabins for ladies, both closed 21.00-08.00 hrs. Some child-size toilets. Laundry facilities. Shop (1/7-25/8). Pizza service twice weekly. Heated swimming pool (1/6-31/8) and paddling pool. Playground (0-5 yrs). Minigolf (charged). Off site: Path to sandy/rocky beach 300 m. Coastal path. Riding 1 km. Bicycle hire 1.5 km. Supermarket 2 km. Golf 5 km.

Open: 1 May - 22 September.

Directions

Turn off C7 road, 2.5 km. north of Concarneau, where site is signed. Take third left after Hotel de l'Océan. GPS: 47.89616, -3.95433

Charges guide

Per unit incl. 2 persons	
and electricity (6A)	€ 24.75 - € 28.20
extra person	€ 5.95 - € 7.00
child (2-7 yrs)	€ 4.25 - € 5.00
dog	€ 1.70 - € 2.00

For latest campsite news, availability and prices visit

alanrogers.com

Concarneau
Flower Camping le Cabellou Plage

Avenue du Cabellou, F-29185 Concarneau (Finistère) T: 02 98 97 37 41. E: info@le-cabellou-plage.com

alanrogers.com/FR29520

Le Cabellou Plage is a very pleasant, well maintained site located close to Concarneau. The large, grassy pitches are divided by young hedges, all have 10A electricity and some also have water and drainage. Many have fine views to the nearby beach and the old walled town beyond. The enthusiastic owner has tastefully landscaped many areas of the site with a profusion of shrubs and flowers. A large swimming pool on site is overlooked by a terrace and bar and the beach is just 25 m. away. La Cabellou is ideally situated for those wishing to visit Concarneau with its twice weekly market, Pont Aven and the cathedral city of Quimper.

Facilities

One modern toilet block is bright and cheerful and provides mainly open style washbasins and preset showers. Baby room. Facilities for disabled visitors. Laundry room. Shop. Bar with television and Internet access. Outdoor heated swimming pool (all season). Scuba lessons and water gymnastics. Bicycle hire. Off site: Bus stop outside site. Supermarkets, shops and restaurants in Concarneau 4 km. Tennis 3 km. Riding 7 km. Golf 10 km.

Open: 7 April - 15 September.

Directions

Site is just south of Concarneau. Take the D783 towards Tregunc. Turn right onto Avenue Cabellou. Site is well signed from here. GPS: 47.85516, -3.90521

Charges guide

Per unit incl. 2 persons and electricity	€ 15.00 - € 29.00
extra person	€ 3.00 - € 5.50
child (2-7 yrs)	free - € 4.00
pet	€ 2.00

Camping
le Cabellou Plage
✳ ✳ Bretagne Sud

A peninsula facing
Concarneau

Camping Qualité

Tél : 00 (33) 2 98 97 37 41

QUALITÉ TOURISME

www.le-cabellou-plage.com

Dol-de-Bretagne
Castel Camping le Domaine des Ormes

[handwritten: OVER PRICED, TOO MANY BOATS & PACTS!]

Epiniac, F-35120 Dol-de-Bretagne (Ille-et-Vilaine) T: 02 99 73 53 00. E: info@lesormes.com

alanrogers.com/FR35020

This impressive site in the grounds of the Château des Ormes is in the north east part of Brittany, about 30 km. from the old town and ferry port of Saint Malo. In an estate of wooded parkland and lakes, it has a pleasant atmosphere, busy in high season but peaceful at other times, with an impressive range of facilities. Of the 800 pitches, only 160 are for tourers (120 with 6A electricity). They are of varying sizes and there is a choice of terrain – flat or gently sloping, wooded or open. The rest are occupied by tour operators (550) and by mobile homes (60 to rent).

Facilities

The toilet blocks are of fair standard, one recently refurbished but still rather cramped, including washbasins in cabins and ample facilities for disabled visitors. A new, more spacious, block has family cubicles. Motorcaravan services. Supermarket, bar, restaurant, pizzeria and takeaway. Games room, bar and disco. Indoor and outdoor pools, an impressive aqua park and new wave pool. Adventure play area. Golf. Bicycle hire. Fishing. Equestrian centre. Minigolf. Tennis. Sports ground. Paintball. Archery. Cricket club. Charcoal barbecues are permitted. WiFi in bar area (free). Off site: Beaches, sailing and boat launching 25 km. Historic Saint Malo and Dinan, and fashionable Dinard are all an easy drive away.

Open: 28 April - 23 September (with all services).

Directions

Site is off D795 8 km. south of Dol-de-Bretagne, 11 km. north of Combourg. GPS: 48.49030, -1.72787

Charges guide

Per person	€ 4.20 - € 7.50
child (under 13 yrs)	free - € 4.60
pitch incl. electricity (6A)	€ 18.60 - € 29.60
drainage	€ 1.70 - € 2.00
dog	€ 1.70 - € 2.00

For latest campsite news, availability and prices visit
alanrogers.com

Douarnenez
Camping Indigo Douarnenez

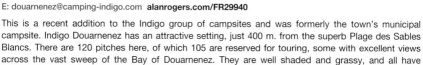

Avenue du Bois d'Isis, F-29100 Douarnenez (Finistère) T: 02 98 74 05 67.
E: douarnenez@camping-indigo.com **alanrogers.com/FR29940**

This is a recent addition to the Indigo group of campsites and was formerly the town's municipal campsite. Indigo Douarnenez has an attractive setting, just 400 m. from the superb Plage des Sables Blancs. There are 120 pitches here, of which 105 are reserved for touring, some with excellent views across the vast sweep of the Bay of Douarnenez. They are well shaded and grassy, and all have 13A electricity. There are also 15 fully equipped safari style tents for hire. An impressive range of new amenities will be added for 2012, including a swimming pool and bar/restaurant.

Facilities

Shop. Snack bar. Takeaway food. Swimming pool Children's playground. Activity programme. Bicycle hire. Tourist information. Fully equipped tents for rent. Off site: Beach 400 m. Fishing. Shops and restaurants in Douarnenez. Golf. Riding.

Open: 27 March - 30 September.

Directions

The site is west of the centre of Douarnenez. From Quimper go north on D765 to Douarnenez, then follow D207 passing to western side of Pouldavid. The site can be found on Avenue du Bois d'Isis and is well signed. GPS: 48.103056, -4.358889

Charges 2012

Per unit incl. 2 persons and electricity	€ 16.00 - € 23.60

Erquy
Camping le Vieux Moulin

14 rue des Moulins, F-22430 Erquy (Côtes d'Armor) T: 02 96 72 34 23. E: camp.vieux.moulin@wanadoo.fr
alanrogers.com/FR22050

Le Vieux Moulin is a family run site, just 2 km. from the little fishing port of Erquy on Brittany's Emerald Coast on the edge of a pine forest and nature reserve. It is about 900 m. from a beach of sand and shingle. Taking its name from the old mill opposite, the site has 173 pitches all with electricity (6/9A) and some with electricity, water and drainage. One section of 39 pitches is arranged around a pond. Most pitches are of a fair size, arranged in square boxes, with trees giving shade. Evening entertainment is organised and there is a friendly pizzeria.

Facilities

Two good quality toilet blocks have mostly British style toilets and plenty of individual washbasins, facilities for disabled visitors, and babies. A further small block provides toilets and dishwashing only. Washing machines and dryer. Motorcaravan service point. Shop. Pizzeria and takeaway. Bar and terrace. Heated, covered pool complex. Play areas. Tennis. Fitness gym. TV and games room. Bicycle hire. No electric barbecues. WiFi.

Open: 9 April - 17 September.

Directions

Site is 2 km. east of Erquy. Take minor road towards Les Hôpitaux and site is signed from junction of D786 and D34 roads. GPS: 48.63858, -2.44189

Charges guide

Per unit incl. 2 persons and electricity	€ 24.80 - € 39.00
extra person	€ 4.90 - € 6.80
child (under 7 yrs)	€ 3.80 - € 4.90

Erquy
Camping Bellevue

Route de la libération, F-22430 Erquy (Côtes d'Armor) T: 02 96 72 33 04. E: campingbellevue@yahoo.fr
alanrogers.com/FR22210

Situated a mile from the beaches between Erquy and Pléneuf Val-André, Camping Bellevue offers a quiet country retreat with easy access to the cliffs of Cap Fréhel, Sables d'Or and St Cast. There are 160 pitches of which 120 are available for touring units, most with electricity (6/10A) and 50 extra large ones with water and drainage. The site also has 20 mobile homes and tents to rent. Children are well catered for at this campsite – there are heated swimming and paddling pools, three play areas with minigolf, petanque and volleyball. A Sites et Paysages member.

Facilities

Two modern, unisex toilet blocks are of a high standard. Some washbasins in cubicles. Facilities for disabled visitors. Laundry facilities. Shop and bar (15/6-10/9). Restaurant and takeaway (12/6-30/9). Swimming and paddling pools (April-Sept). Play areas. Games room and library. Minigolf. Pétanque. Entertainment and organised activities in high season. There is also a multi-sport area with basketball, football etc. Max. 1 dog. WiFi. Off site: Beach and fishing 2 km. Golf 4 km. Bicycle hire and boat launching 5 km. Riding 6 km.

Open: 6 April - 20 September.

Directions

From St Brieuc road take D786 towards Erquy. Site is adjacent to the D786 at St Pabu and is well signed. GPS: 48.59426, -2.48475

Charges guide

Per unit incl. 2 persons and electricity (10A)	€ 20.80 - € 26.80
child (0-12 yrs)	free - € 4.50
extra person	€ 4.30 - € 5.30
dog	€ 1.30 - € 1.80

We can book this site for you! Call 01580 214000 alan rogers travel

For latest campsite news, availability and prices visit
alanrogers.com

Erquy

Yelloh! Village les Pins

Route du Guen, le Guen, F-22430 Erquy (Côtes d'Armor) T: 04 66 73 97 39.
E: info@yellohvillage-les-pins.com **alanrogers.com/FR22360**

Erquy is a pretty holiday resort nestling between two promontories. There are plenty of great sandy beaches around here, and one of the best is just 900 m. from this wooded site. Les Pins is a long-established site with many of the original facilities still in use. There are 235 touring pitches here and a further 148 pitches are occupied by mobile homes and chalets. The site boasts some impressive amenities including a top class swimming pool complex extending over 600 sq.m. with water slides, lazy river and various other water features.

Facilities

Four very old toilet blocks, all with mostly Turkish style toilets and other poor facilities. New facilities at the pools. Shop. Bar. Restaurant. Snack bar and takeaway (from 15/6). Large swimming pool complex with water slides and other features. Children's pool. Fitness centre. Sauna. Tennis. Play area. Activity and entertainment programme. Off site: Fishing and nearest beach 900 m. Sailing. Sand yachting. Sea kayaking. Golf, riding and bicycle hire 2.5 km. Casino. Diving school. Walking and cycle trails.
Open: 26 April - 13 September.

Directions

From St Brieuc, take the northbound D786 to Erquy. Continue through the town following signs to Cap d'Erquy and the site is well indicated. GPS: 48.63841, -2.45565

Charges guide

Per unit incl. 2 persons and electricity	€ 15.00 - € 36.00
extra person	€ 5.00 - € 6.00
child (0-7 yrs)	free - € 6.00
dog	free - € 4.00

Etables-sur-Mer

Camping l'Abri Côtier

Ville Es Rouxel, F-22680 Etables-sur-Mer (Côtes d'Armor) T: 02 96 70 61 57.
E: camping.abricotier@wanadoo.fr **alanrogers.com/FR22100**

L'Abri Côtier is a well cared for, family run site 500 m. from a sandy beach. Small and tranquil, it is arranged in two sections separated by a lane. The pitches are marked out on part level, part sloping grass, divided by mature trees and shrubs with some in a charming walled area. The second section has an orchard type setting. There are 125 touring pitches, all with electrical connections (long leads useful) and 60 are fully serviced. Tim and Pierrette Lee are busy with ideas for this very popular, friendly site.

Facilities

Good clean sanitary facilities include some washbasins in cabins and pushbutton showers. Facilities for disabled visitors. Baby bath/shower. Laundry room. Well stocked shop. Bar providing a simple takeaway service (plus set menu in high season). Covered terrace and games area. Sheltered, heated swimming pool with paddling pool and outdoor jacuzzi. Small play area. Some entertainment in peak season. WiFi in bar (charged). Off site: Beach and sailing 500 m. Restaurants and indoor pool in the village. Riding 1 km. Fishing and boat launching 2 km. Bicycle hire 4 km. Golf 10 km.
Open: 1 May - 13 September.

Directions

Etables-sur-Mer is 20 km. north of Saint Brieuc, roughly half-way between Roscoff and Saint Malo. From N12 (Saint Brieuc bypass) take D786 towards St Quay Portrieux. After 12 km. ignore signs to Etables, pass Aire de la Chapelle on the right and take second left back towards Etables-sur-Mer (site signed). Take second right at top of hill to site at crossroads in 100 m. GPS: 48.63559, -2.83546

Charges guide

Per unit incl. 2 persons and electricity (10A)	€ 19.60 - € 22.60
extra person	€ 4.40 - € 4.90

Fouesnant

Camping de PenHoat

Pointe de Mousterlin, 5 chemin de Kost ar Moor, F-29170 Fouesnant (Finistère) T: 02 98 56 51 89.
E: caradec2@wanadoo.fr **alanrogers.com/FR29630**

This small rural campsite is set in two acres of trees, shrubs and well-tended flowerbeds. The 87 touring pitches are level, grassy, generous in size and separated by hedges and/or small trees. The 58 pitches with electricity (5A and 10A) may need long leads. The 32 mobile homes are mostly separated from the touring pitches. There are also six traditional gîtes for hire. The pleasant wooden chalet-style bar and takeaway has a covered terrace. Kayaks can be hired at the campsite. The long sandy beach is 300 m. away. And for lovers of wildlife, the protected Mousterlin nature reserve is next to the campsite.

Facilities

Two toilet and shower blocks with facilities for campers with disabilities. Laundry. Nursery. Bar, takeaway and restaurant. Games room. Playground. Trampoline. Bicycle and kayak hire. Gîtes for hire. Off site: Beach 300 m. Riding 1 km. Shops in Fouesnant 6 km. Golf 6 km.
Open: 3 April - 30 September.

Directions

Site is 5 km. south of Fouesnant. Turn off N165 at Coat Cong signed Concarneau and Fouesnant. Join D45 signed Beg Meil and shortly turn right on D145 signed Mousterlin. Site signed in approx. 5 km. GPS: 47.851024, -4.035341

Charges guide

Per unit incl. 2 persons and electricity	€ 16.40 - € 20.10

For latest campsite news, availability and prices visit

alanrogers.com

Guidel

Camping les Jardins de Kergal

Route de Guidel Plages, F-56520 Guidel (Morbihan) T: 02 97 05 98 18. E: jardins.kergal@wanadoo.fr
alanrogers.com/FR56220

This is a long established campsite that offers a variety of well cared for pitches. Most are shaded by mature trees and unusually many are triangular in shape. Access could be tricky for larger units. The toilet facilities have been refurbished to a very high standard, complete with soft music and potted plants. A comfortable lounge contains a small library, board games and a television. The site's pool complex is impressive with a heated, covered pool, an open pool with slides and a paddling pool. Many sporting facilities are provided, and in high season there is entertainment and activities for children.

Facilities	Directions
The good toilet block includes facilities for disabled visitors and babies. Washing machine and dryer. Shop. Bar (July-Aug). Pizza and rotisserie vans visit (high season). Covered swimming pool (all season). Outdoor pool and slides (15/5-15/9). Multisports court. Bicycle hire. Minigolf. WiFi (charged). Off site: Beaches 1.5 km. Guidel town for shops and restaurants. Fishing 3 km. Golf 10 km.	From the RN165 west of Lorient take exit for Guidel, then the D306 from Guidel towards the beach (plage). Site is well signed on the left. GPS: 47.77466, -3.50616

Open: 1 April - 30 September.

Charges guide

Per unit incl. 2 persons	
and electricity (10A)	€ 8.50 - € 15.90
extra person	€ 4.50 - € 6.90
child (2-10 yrs)	€ 2.90 - € 4.90
dog	€ 3.00 - € 5.00

Jugon-les-Lacs

Camping Au Bocage du Lac

Rue du Bocage, F-22270 Jugon-les-Lacs (Côtes d'Armor) T: 02 96 31 60 16.
E: contact@campinglacbretagne.com alanrogers.com/FR22200

This well kept former municipal site has been updated over the past few years by the current owners, M. and Mme. Rivière. It is on the edge of the village beside a lake, 25 km. from the sea. It offers 183 good sized pitches, all with electrical connections, set on gently sloping grass and divided by shrubs and bushes, with mature trees providing shade. Some 45 wooden chalets and mobile homes are intermingled with the touring pitches. On-site facilities include a good pool with children's section and sunbathing patio. There is also a small animal park.

Facilities	Directions
Two main sanitary blocks include facilities for disabled visitors. British and Turkish style WCs and some washbasins in cabins. Washing machine. Small shop. Bar. Swimming pool (1/5-19/9). Tennis. Football. Play area. Activity programmes July/Aug. Fishing. Bicycle hire. Off site: Supermarket in village 1 km. River 1 km. Beach 20 km.	From N176 (E401) Lamballe - Dinan road, about 15 km. from Lamballe take turning for Jugon-les-Lacs. Site is signed shortly after. GPS: 48.40120, -2.31736

Open: 6 April - 6 October.

Charges 2012

Per unit incl. 2 persons	
and electricity (10A)	€ 17.35 - € 27.20
extra person	€ 3.90 - € 5.90
child (under 7 yrs)	€ 2.70 - € 4.50
dog	€ 2.50 - € 3.00

On the lakeside, in the pretty and historical town of Jugon Les Lacs, for both relaxation and leisure, you will find a wide range of activities : heated pool, water slide, paddling pool, childrens' mini camp, tennis, minigolf, sailing, fishing, walking. New sanitary block includes private cabins, facilities for babies. Rental of Chalets, Mobile Homes with view over the lake.
WELCOME TO BRITTANY!!
22270 Jugon les Lacs / Tél : 02.96.31.60.16
contact@campinglacbretagne.com / www.camping-location-bretagne.com

For latest campsite news, availability and prices visit
alanrogers.com

La Chapelle-aux-Filtzmeens

Domaine du Logis

Le Logis, F-35190 La Chapelle-aux-Filtzmeens (Ille-et-Vilaine) T: 02 99 45 25 45.
E: domainedulogis@wanadoo.fr **alanrogers.com/FR35080**

This is an attractive rural site under new, young and enthusiastic ownership, set in the grounds of an old château. The site's upgraded modern facilities are housed in traditional converted barns and farm buildings, which are well maintained and equipped. There are a total of 188 pitches, 70 of which are for touring. The grass pitches are level, of a generous size and divided by mature hedges and trees. All have 10A electricity connections. This site would appeal to most age groups with plenty to offer the active including a new fitness room with a good range of modern equipment and a sauna for those who prefer to relax, perhaps a quiet days fishing beside the lake. Although set in a quiet, rural part of the Brittany countryside, the nearby village of La Chapelle-aux-Filtzmeens has a bar, restaurant and shops. A 20 minute car ride will get you into the large town of Rennes, or perhaps travel north for 30 minutes to Mont Saint-Michel, Dinan, Dinard and the old fishing port of Saint Malo to sample the famous seafood.

Facilities

One comfortable toilet block with washbasins and showers. Toilet and shower for disabled visitors. Laundry facilities. Bar with Sky TV (1/4-7/11). Restaurant and takeaway (1/7-29/8). Outdoor swimming pool (from 1/5). Fitness and games rooms. Sauna. BMX circuit. Bicycle hire. Unfenced play areas. Children's club (high season). Free WiFi-Internet access. Lake fishing. Off site: Boating on the canal. Riding 10 km. Golf 15 km.

Open: 1 April - 7 November.

Directions

Turn south off N176 onto D795 signed Dol-de-Bretagne. Continue to Combourg and then take D13 to La Chapelle-aux-Filtsmeens. Continue for 2 km. to site on right. GPS: 48.37716, -1.83705

Charges guide

Per unit incl. 2 persons and electricity	€ 20.60 - € 27.60
extra person	€ 4.00 - € 4.50
child (2-12 yrs)	€ 2.50

Camping Cheques accepted.

Camping Le Domaine du Logis****

35190 LA CHAPELLE AUX FILTZMEENS (Ille et Vilaine)
Tél.: 02 99 45 25 45 - Fax: 02 99 45 30 40 - E-mail: domainedulogis@wanadoo.fr - www.domainedulogis.com

La Forêt-Fouesnant

Domaine du Saint-Laurent

Kerleven, F-29940 La Forêt-Fouesnant (Finistère) T: 02 98 56 97 65. E: info@camping-du-saint-laurent.fr
alanrogers.com/FR29020

Saint-Laurent is a well established site, situated on a sheltered wooded slope bordering one of the many attractive little inlets that typify the Brittany coastline. The site is on the coastal footpath that leads from Kerleven to Concarneau. The 260 pitches are on level terraces, under tall trees. All are of average size (100 sq.m) and divided by hedges and partly shaded, all with electricity connections. Around 60% of the pitches are occupied by site owned mobile homes. Touring pitches with the best sea views tend to be adjacent to the cliff edge and may not be suitable for families with young children.

Facilities

Two sanitary blocks provide combined shower and washbasin cubicles, separate washbasin cubicles, baby changing and facilities for disabled visitors. Washing machines, dryers and ironing. Small shop at reception (all season). Bar, snack bar and takeaway (1/7-31/8). Swimming pools. Gym and sauna. Canoe and boat hire. Two tennis courts (free). Play area. Entertainment in July/Aug. for adults and children (in English and French) with discos in the bar each evening. Bicycle hire. Internet access.

Open: 5 April - 29 September.

Directions

From N165 take D70 Concarneau exit. At first roundabout take first exit D44 (Fouesnant). After 2.5 km. turn right at T-junction, follow for 2.5 km, then turn left (Port La Forêt). Continue to roundabout, straight ahead (Port La Forêt) and after 1 km. turn left (site signed here). In 400 m. left turn to site. GPS: 47.8961, -3.9551

Charges guide

| Per unit incl. 2 persons and electricity | € 15.00 - € 33.00 |
| extra person | € 4.70 - € 7.00 |

For latest campsite news, availability and prices visit

alanrogers.com

La Forêt-Fouesnant
Camping du Manoir de Pen-ar-Ster

2 chemin de Penn Ar Ster, F-29940 La Forêt-Fouesnant (Finistère) T: 02 98 56 97 75.
E: info@camping-pennarster.com **alanrogers.com/FR29100**

In the grounds of an old Breton house and arranged on terraces up the steep sides of a valley, this site has a picturesque, garden-like quality. There are 105 pitches, of which about half are for touring units (the remainder used for mobile homes). Pitches vary in size (80-100 sq.m) and some are accessed by steep slopes, but all are on flat, grassy terraces, with low hedging and all have electricity (6/10A), water and drainage. The campsite is open for a long season and its location in the village of La Forêt-Fouesnant makes it popular with those camping by bicycle, motorbike or in a motorcaravan.

Facilities

Two sanitary blocks include mixed British and Turkish style toilets, cabins with washbasins and showers, baby areas and children's toilets. One block is heated in low season and contains facilities for disabled campers. At the rear of the old house is a laundry room with washing machines and dryers. Play area. Tennis. Bicycle hire. Barrier with card. Off site: Baker 50 m. Village with all amenities 150 m. Golf 800 m. Riding 2 km.

Open: 2 April - 31 October.

Directions

From N165 take D70 Concarneau exit. At first roundabout take D44 (Forêt-Fouesnant). Follow to T-junction and turn right on D783. After 2 km. turn left back onto D44 to Forêt-Fouesnant. In village take first exit right at roundabout to site 150 m. on left. GPS: 47.911316, -3.979679

Charges guide

Per unit incl. 2 persons	€ 21.00 - € 27.00
extra person	€ 5.00 - € 7.00
No credit cards.	

La Forêt-Fouesnant
Camping de Kéranterec

Route de Port la Forêt, F-29940 La Forêt-Fouesnant (Finistère) T: 02 98 56 98 11.
E: info@camping-keranterec.com **alanrogers.com/FR29240**

A well established family run site with a very French ambience, Keranterec has 265 grassy pitches in two areas. The upper part of the site is open and has little shade, and is also largely taken up by private mobile homes. The lower, more mature area is predominantly for tourers, with terraced pitches set in a former orchard. Spacious and divided by mature hedging, all pitches have electrical connections (25 m. cable advised) and most also offer water and drainage. Some pitches have shade from the many trees on the lower part of the site, and some also overlook the little cove at the rear of the site.

Facilities

Two modern, fully equipped toilet blocks kept very clean include washbasins in cubicles, baby baths and facilities for disabled visitors. Laundry facilities. Small shop and bar (15/6-10/9) and takeaway (1/7-31/8). TV room with satellite. Heated outdoor swimming pool (1/6-10/9) with paddling pool, jacuzzi and three slides and a covered, heated pool. Tennis. Boules. Play area. In July/Aug organised events and activities for all the family, and a free children's club. Free WiFi. Off site: Attractive sandy beach of Kerleven 10 minutes walk. Golf 0.8 km. Riding 2 km.

Open: 5 April - 21 September.

Directions

From N165 take D70 Concarneau exit. At first roundabout take D44 signed Fouesnant. After 2.5 km. turn right at T-junction, and follow for 2.5 km. and turn left (Port La Forêt). Continue to roundabout and take second exit (straight ahead), signed Port La Forêt. After 1 km. turn left (site signed). GPS: 47.8991, -3.95198

Charges guide

per unit incl. 2 persons and electricity	€ 15.00 - € 34.00
extra person	€ 7.00 - € 8.50

La Roche Bernard
Camping Municipal le Pâtis

3 chemin du Pâtis, F-56130 La Roche Bernard (Morbihan) T: 02 99 90 60 13. E: camping.lrb@gmail.com
alanrogers.com/FR56080

This is another of those excellent municipal sites one comes across in France. Situated beside the River Vilaine, a five minute walk from the centre of the very attractive old town of La Roche Bernard and beside the port and marina, it provides 69 level grass, part-hedged pitches in bays of four, with 7A electricity and water. Eighteen special pitches for motorcaravans have been created at the entrance, along with two wooden chalets to hire. Next door is a sailing school, boats to hire, fishing, tennis, archery, etc. A restaurant and bar are on the quayside, with others uphill in the town.

Facilities

There are two fully equipped sanitary blocks, one new and very modern, the other fully refurbished. Laundry room behind reception with washing machine and dryer. Small play area. Bicycle hire. WiFi. Off site: Fishing 500 m. Riding 5 km. Golf 15 km.

Open: April - 30 September (or mid October).

Directions

Go into town centre and follow signs for the port around a one-way system and then a sharp turn down hill. GPS: 47.51817, -2.30317

Charges guide

Per unit incl. 2 persons and electricity	€ 13.50 - € 19.00
extra person	€ 3.50 - € 4.00

For latest campsite news, availability and prices visit
alanrogers.com

La Trinité-sur-Mer

Camping de la Baie

Plage de Kervillen, F-56470 La Trinité-sur-Mer (Morbihan) T: 02 97 55 73 42.

E: contact@campingdelabaie.com **alanrogers.com/FR56030**

This site is one of two owned by members of the same family. It is situated on the coast overlooking the safe, sandy beach of Kervillen Plage, with its little rocky outcrops providing a naturally enclosed swimming area. This is a very friendly site, which is ideal for quiet or family holidays in an area with lots of local interest. There are 170 pitches, of which around 50 are used by tour operators. The 92 touring pitches are all of good size, hedged and all have electricity (6/10A) water and drainage. Some shade is provided by mature and maturing trees. In the bar and restaurant complex, just outside the entrance, one can sit and watch the sun set over the bay. The restaurant has an extensive menu, from seafood to snacks, and much is also available from the takeaway. American motorhomes should book ahead.

Facilities

Two very clean toilet blocks include well equipped baby rooms and full en-suite facilities for disabled visitors. Laundry facilities. Bar, restaurant and takeaway (open to the public all season). Well stocked shop (all season). Small (12 m.) swimming pool with slide. Play areas. Multi-sport pitches. TV room. Indoor games room. Bicycle hire. Off site: Beach, fishing and boat ramp 50 m. Tennis and minigolf 200 m. (shared with Camping de la Plage). Sailing school 1.5 km. Riding and golf 5 km.

Open: 12 May - 16 September.

Directions

From the N165 at Auray take D28 signed La Trinité-sur-Mer. Keep on through the town following signs to Carnac Plage on D186. Site is well signed off this road to the south. Be careful to take the road signed to Kervillen Plage where it forks.
GPS: 47.57364, -3.02758

Charges guide

Per unit incl. 2 persons	
and electricity (10A)	€ 17.20 - € 47.90
extra person	€ 2.90 - € 8.00
dog	free - € 1.30

www.campingdelabaie.com

Mobile-homes for rent

On a privileged location between two fine sand beaches. you will enjoy all the comfort of a 4-star campsite

Activities:
• Swimming pool
• Toboggan
• Tennis
• Mini golf
• Animations
• Kids club

Camping de LA BAIE • Plage de Kervillen • 56470 La Trinite sur Mer
Tél. 0033 (0)2 97 55 73 42 • contact@campingdelabaie.com

La Trinité-sur-Mer

Camping de la Plage

Plage de Kervillen, F-56470 La Trinité-sur-Mer (Morbihan) T: 02 97 55 73 28.

E: camping@camping-plage.com **alanrogers.com/FR56020**

The Carnac and La Trinité area of Brittany is popular with British holidaymakers. Camping de la Plage is one of two sites, close to each other and owned by members of the same family, with direct access to the safe, sandy beach of Kervillen Plage. There are 195 grass pitches of which 122 are for touring (34 are used by tour operators). All are hedged and have electricity (6/10A), water and drainage. The site has a slight slope and a few pitches reflect this. With narrow roads and sharp bends, it is not suitable for large units.

Facilities

Toilet blocks (one heated) have free hot water, washbasins in cubicles, baby baths and facilities for children and disabled visitors. Laundry facilities. Small swimming pool with water slides. Play areas including ball pool. Tennis. TV. Entertainment programme in high season for all ages. Bicycle hire. Beach. Guided tours. Internet access and WiFi (charged). Communal barbecue areas (gas or electric only on pitches). Off site: Fishing 50 m. Shop with bakery. Bar, restaurant, crêperie, takeaway all 200 m. Sailing 1.5 km. Riding 3.5 km. Golf 13 km.

Open: 5 May - 16 September.

Directions

From N165 at Auray take D28 (La Trinité-sur-Mer). On through town following signs to Carnac-Plage on D186. Site signed off this road to the south. Take care to take road signed to Kervillen Plage where it forks. At seafront turn right. Site is 300 m. on right. Site is well signed. GPS: 47.57563, -3.02890

Charges guide

Per unit incl. 2 persons	
and electricity (10A)	€ 20.80 - € 40.80
extra person	€ 5.20
child (2-17 yrs)	€ 2.00 - € 4.20

For latest campsite news, availability and prices visit

alanrogers.com

La Trinité-sur-Mer
Camping de Kervilor

Kervilor, F-56470 La Trinité-sur-Mer (Morbihan) T: 02 97 55 76 75. E: camping.kervilor@wanadoo.fr
alanrogers.com/FR56050

Kervilor may be a good alternative for those who find the beachside sites in La Trinité too busy and lively. In a village on the outskirts of the town, it has 250 pitches on flat grass and is attractively landscaped with trees (silver birch) and flowers giving a sense of spaciousness. The pitches are in groups divided by hedges, separated by shrubs and trees and all have electricity (6/10A). Around 116 are used for touring units. Used by tour operators (10 pitches). The site has a central pool complex with covered swimming and paddling pools, slides and fountains. Activities and entertainment are organised in high season. The pleasant port is only 1.5 km. with sandy beaches within 2 km.

Facilities

Two modern toilet blocks of a good standard with further facilities in an older block. They include many washbasins in cabins, facilities for disabled visitors and babies. Small laundry. Small shop and takeaway. Bar with terrace. Pool complex with covered pool. Play area. Minigolf, pétanque, tennis and volleyball. Bicycle hire. Only charcoal barbecues are permitted. WiFi in bar area (free). Off site: Town facilities 1.5 km. Sandy beach, fishing and riding 2 km. Golf 12 km.

Open: 1 April - 23 September.

Directions

Site is north of La Trinité-sur-Mer and is signed in the town centre. From Auray take D186 Quiberon road; turn left at site sign at Kergroix on D186 to La Trinité-sur-Mer, and left again at outskirts of town. GPS: 47.60213, -3.03672

Charges guide

Per unit incl. 2 persons	
and electricity (10A)	€ 22.00 - € 33.10
extra person	€ 3.95 - € 5.45
child (under 7 yrs)	€ 2.60 - € 3.60

Camping Caravaning Kervilor
56470 La Trinité sur Mer, France
Tel: +33 297 55 76 75
Fax: +33 297 55 87 26
ebideau@camping-kervilor.com
www.camping-kervilor.com

Landéda
Camping des Abers

Dunes de Sainte Marguerite, F-29870 Landéda (Finistère) T: 02 98 04 93 35.
E: camping-des-abers@wanadoo.fr **alanrogers.com/FR29130**

This delightful 12-acre site is in a beautiful location almost at the tip of the Presqu'île Sainte Marguerite on the northwestern shores of Brittany. The peninsula lies between the mouths (abers) of two rivers, Aber Wrac'h and Aber Benoît. Camping des Abers is set just back from a wonderful sandy beach with rocky outcrops and islands you can walk to at low tide. There are 180 pitches, landscaped and terraced, some with amazing views, others sheltered by mature hedges, trees and flowering shrubs. Hubert le Cuff and his team make you very welcome and speak excellent English.

Facilities

Three toilet blocks, recently refurbished are kept clean and provide washbasins in cubicles and roomy showers (token € 0.65-0.85). Good facilities for disabled visitors and babies. Laundry. Motorcaravan service point. Shop stocks essentials (25/5-22/9, limited hours low season). Simple takeaway dishes (1/7-31/8). Good play area. Games room. Hairdresser. Breton music and dancing, cooking classes and guided walks arranged. Splendid beach with good bathing. Long leads needed in places. Torch useful. Free Internet and WiFi. Off site: Pizzeria next door. Tennis nearby. Sailing club 3 km. Riding 7 km. Golf 30 km. The nearby town of L'Aber Wrac'h has many restaurants.

Open: 28 April - 30 September.

Directions

Landéda is 55 km. west of Roscoff via the D10 to Plougerneau then D13 crossing river bridge (Aber Wrac'h) and turning west to Lannilis. From N12 Morlaix-Brest road turn north on D59 to Lannilis. Continue through town taking road to Landéda and from there follow signs for Dunes de Ste Marguerite, 'camping' and des Abers. GPS: 48.59306, -4.60305

Charges guide

Per unit incl. 2 persons	
and electricity	€ 16.20 - € 18.00
extra person	€ 3.24 - € 3.60
child (under 7 yrs)	€ 1.90 - € 2.10
dog	€ 1.80 - € 2.00

For latest campsite news, availability and prices visit
alanrogers.com

We can book this site for you! Call 01580 214000 alanrogers ◯ travel

Lanloup
Camping le Neptune

Ker Guistin, F-22580 Lanloup (Côtes d'Armor) T: 02 96 22 33 35. E: contact@leneptune.com

alanrogers.com/FR22160

Situated on the Côte de Goëlo at Lanloup, le Neptune offers a peaceful, rural retreat for families. The friendly owners, François and Marie Jo Camard, keep the site neat and tidy and there is a regular programme of renovation. There are 84 level, grass pitches (65 for touring units) separated by trimmed hedges providing privacy and all with electricity (10A). There are also 21 mobile homes to rent. Within walking distance is the local village, with a restaurant and shop, and sandy beaches are only a short drive away. The area is good for cycling and walking.

Facilities

The modern, heated, toilet block is of a good standard, clean and well maintained and provides washbasins in cubicles and pushbutton showers. Facilities for disabled visitors. Laundry. Motorcaravan services. No restaurant but good takeaway (all season). Small shop well stocked for basic needs. Bar with indoor and outdoor seating. Heated swimming pool with retractable roof (Easter-end Oct). Pétanque. Play area. Entertainment and children's activities in high season. WiFi. Off site: Tennis 300 m. Fishing and beach 2 km. Golf 4 km. Riding 8 km. Restaurant and shop within walking distance.

Open: 1 April - 17 October.

Directions

Lanloup is 30 km. northwest of Saint Brieuc and 100 km. from both Roscoff and Saint Malo. From N12 Saint Brieuc bypass take D786 Paimpol (par la côte). After 28 km. on approaching Lanloup, site is well signed, turning right at crossroads by café. GPS: 48.71372, -2.96704

Charges guide

Per unit incl. 2 persons	
and electricity	€ 19.00 - € 25.00
extra person	€ 4.00 - € 5.50

Camping Cheques accepted.

Le Faouët
Camping Municipal Beg Er Roch

Route de Lorient, F-56320 Le Faouët (Morbihan) T: 02 97 23 15 11. E: camping.lefaouet@wanadoo.fr

alanrogers.com/FR56310

Like many of today's municipal campsites, this one is immaculate and offers excellent value. There are 57 well kept grassy pitches with electricity (10A) available. There are also eight mobile homes for rent. Unusually for a municipal site, there is a large games room and provision for other sporting activities. For those campers that are anglers a river at the bottom of the site (fenced) provides salmon and trout fishing at a supplement. For the more energetic, the manager can provide details and maps of local walks. For shops and other amenities the town of Le Faouët is only 2 km. away.

Facilities

A single toilet block provides toilets, washbasins and showers. Facilities for campers with disabilities. Washing machine and dryer. Play area. Minigolf. Boules. Fishing. Games room with TV and bar billiards. Off site: le Faouët with museums, the chapel of St Barbe and a market housed in a 16th-century building.

Open: 15 March - 30 September.

Directions

Take the D769 north from Lorient to Le Faouët. Site is well signed from this road. GPS: 48.01823, -3.47009

Charges guide

Per unit incl. 2 persons	
and electricity	€ 12.35 - € 16.90
extra person	€ 2.90 - € 4.00

Le Guilvinec
Yelloh! Village la Plage

F-29730 Le Guilvinec (Finistère) T: 02 98 58 61 90. E: info@yellohvillage-la-plage.com

alanrogers.com/FR29110

La Plage is a spacious site with direct access to a long sandy beach between the fishing town of Le Guilvinec and the watersports beaches of Penmarc'h on the southwest tip of Brittany. It is surrounded by tall trees which provide shelter and is made up of several flat, sandy meadows. The 410 pitches (200 for touring units) are arranged on either side of sandy access roads, mostly not separated but all numbered. There is less shade in the newer areas. Electricity is available on most pitches. Like all beach-side sites, the facilities receive heavy use.

Facilities

Four sanitary blocks provide modern, bright facilities including washbasins in cabins, good facilities for children and disabled visitors. Laundry facilities. Motorcaravan service point. Shop with gas supplies. Bar, restaurant and takeaway. Covered heated swimming pool with paddling pool and slide. Sauna and fitness complex. Play area. TV room. Tennis. Minigolf. Pétanque. Giant chess. Bicycle hire. Beach. Multisports fields. Entertainment. WiFi (free). Off site: Fishing and watersports nearby. Riding 5 km.

Open: 1 April - 15 September.

Directions

Site is west of Le Guilvinec. From Pont l'Abbé, take the D785 road towards Penmarc'h. In Plomeur, turn left on D57 signed Le Guilvinec. On entering Le Guilvinec fork right signed Port and camping. Follow road along coast to site on left. GPS: 47.8025, -4.3072

Charges guide

Per unit incl. 2 persons	
and electricity	€ 17.00 - € 43.00
extra person	€ 6.00 - € 8.00

We can book this site for you! Call 01580 214000

alanrogers travel

Le Pouldu
Camping les Embruns

533

2 rue du Philosophe Alain, Le Pouldu Plages, F-29360 Clohars-Carnoët (Finistère) T: 02 98 39 91 07.
E: camping-les-embruns@orange.fr **alanrogers.com/FR29180**

This site is unusual in that it is located in the heart of a village, yet is only 250 metres from a sandy cove. The entrance with its code operated barrier and wonderful floral displays, is the first indication that this is a well tended and well organised site, and the owners have won numerous regional and national awards for its superb presentation. The 180 pitches (100 occupied by mobile homes) are separated by trees, shrubs and bushes, and most have electricity (16A Europlug), water and drainage. There is a covered, heated swimming pool, a circular paddling pool and a water play pool and slide. It is only a short walk to the village centre with all its attractions and services. It is also close to beautiful countryside and the Carnoët Forest which are good for walking and cycling.

Facilities

Two modern sanitary blocks, recently completely renewed and heated in winter, include mainly British style toilets, some washbasins in cubicles, baby baths and good facilities for disabled visitors. Family bathrooms. Laundry facilities. Motorcaravan service point (€ 4 charge). Shop (all season). Restaurant by entrance, bar and terrace, takeaway (6/4-15/9). Covered, heated swimming and paddling pools. Large games hall. Play area. Football field. Minigolf. Communal barbecue area. Daily activities for children and adults organised in July/Aug. Bicycle hire. Internet access and WiFi in reception area (charged). Off site: Nearby sea and river fishing and watersports. Beach 250 m. Riding 2 km.

Open: 6 April - 22 September.

Directions

From N165 take either 'Kervidanou, Quimperlé Ouest' exit or 'Kergostiou, Quimperlé Centre, Clohars Carnoët' exit and follow D16 to Clohars Carnoët. Then take D24 for Le Pouldu and follow site signs in village. GPS: 47.76867, -3.54508

Charges 2012

Per unit incl. 2 persons and electricity	€ 10.50 - € 31.50
extra person	€ 3.95 - € 5.90
child (under 7 yrs)	€ 2.80 - € 3.80
dog	€ 2.70
Low season reductions	

250 m from one of Brittany's sandy beaches Gwénaëlle & Gisèle welcome you in their particularly well maintained campsite where you are assured of a good holiday.

- First class facilities and amenities in a green and floral environment
- Mobile homes to rent
- Motorcaravan service point
- Covered swimming pool is heated from the opening date
- NEW! Heated sanitary blocks
- Discover the delights of our 2 waterslides

LE POULDU - F-29360 CLOHARS-CARNOET
tel: 0033 298 39 91 07 - fax: 0033 298 39 97 87

www.camping-les-embruns.com
E-mail: camping-les-embruns@orange.fr

HÔTELLERIE DE PLEIN AIR - CAMPING CARAVANING

Les Embruns ★★★★

Locronan
Camping Locronan

Rue de la Troménie, F-29180 Locronan (Finistère) T: 02 98 91 87 76. E: contact@camping-locronan.fr
alanrogers.com/FR29650

Camping Locronan is a well cared for, friendly site on the edge of the village of Locronan (400 m). The site has a heated covered pool and a children's play area. The 100 pitches are level, grassy and divided by low hedges. These are arranged on four different levels as the site is on the side of a steep hill. Vehicle access between the levels is steep and pedestrian access is by wooden steps which would not be suitable for the disabled visitor. Many of the pitches offer panoramic views across the countryside to the distant bay of Douarnenez.

Facilities

Two modern toilet blocks have facilities for campers with disabilities. Laundry facilities. Covered swimming pool. Children's play area, shop. WiFi. Mobile homes and equipped tents for hire. Off site: Shops and restaurants in Locronan 300 m. Riding, tennis 300 m. Nearest beach 5 km. Walking and cycling tracks. Quimper 13 km.

Open: 9 April - 3 November.

Directions

Locronan lies to the northwest of Quimper. From there, head north on D39 and D63 (towards Douarnenez) until you reach the village. The site is clearly signed in the village.
GPS: 48.095824, -4.199181

Charges guide

Per unit incl. 2 persons and electricity (10A)	€ 17.90 - € 19.80
extra person	€ 4.00 - € 4.60

For latest campsite news, availability and prices visit
alanrogers.com

We can book this site for you! alan rogers travel
Call 01580 214000

Locunolé
Castel Camping le Ty-Nadan

Route d'Arzano, F-29310 Locunolé (Finistère) T: 02 98 71 75 47. E: infos@camping-ty-nadan.fr
alanrogers.com/FR29010

Camping le Ty-Nadan is a well organised site set amongst wooded countryside along the bank of the River Elle. There are 183 grassy pitches for touring units, many with shade and 99 fully serviced. The pool complex with slides and paddling pool is very popular as are the large indoor pool complex and indoor games area with a climbing wall. There is also an adventure play park and a minikids park for 5-8 year olds, not to mention tennis courts, table tennis, pool tables, archery and trampolines. This is a wonderful site for families with children. Several tour operators use the site. An exciting and varied programme of activities is offered throughout the season – canoeing and sea kayaking expeditions, rock climbing, mountain biking, aquagym, paintball, riding and walking – all supervised by qualified staff. A full programme of entertainment for all ages is provided in high season including concerts, Breton evenings with pig roasts, dancing, etc. (be warned, you will be actively encouraged to join in!).

Facilities

Two older, split-level toilet blocks are of fair quality and include washbasins in cabins and baby rooms. A newer block provides easier access for disabled campers. Washing machines and dryers. Restaurant, takeaway, bar and well stocked shop. Heated outdoor pool (17x8 m). Indoor pool. Small river beach (unfenced). Indoor badminton and rock climbing facility. Activity and entertainment programmes (all season). Horse riding centre. Bicycle hire. Boat hire. Canoe trips. Fishing. Internet access and WiFi (charged). Off site: Beaches 20 minutes by car. Golf 12 km.

Open: 27 March - 2 September.

Directions

Make for Arzano which is northeast of Quimperlé on the Pontivy road and turn off D22 just west of village at site sign. Site is about 3 km.
GPS: 47.90468, -3.47477

Charges guide

Per unit incl. 2 persons	
and electricity	€ 20.10 - € 46.00
extra person	€ 4.30 - € 8.80
child (2-6 yrs)	€ 2.00 - € 5.40
dog	€ 2.10 - € 5.80

Camping Cheques accepted.

Camping "Le Ty Nadan" ★★★★
NADAN
For unforgettable holidays!
CAMPING PLUS BRETAGNE
LES CASTELS ★★★★ Hôtellerie de Plein Air
www.tynadan-vacances.fr

Loyat
Camping Merlin l'Enchanteur

La Vallée de l'Yvel, 8 rue du Pont, F-56800 Loyat (Morbihan) T: 02 97 93 05 52. E: qualitypark1@wanadoo.fr

alanrogers.com/FR56210

This fairly basic ex-municipal site is located a few hundred metres from the village of Loyat and 5 km. from the large town of Ploërmel. The 65 grass touring pitches are level and each pitch is separated by well established trees. Long leads may be required for the 10A electricity hook-ups, and the water points may be some distance from certain pitches. This simple site is open all year and is ideally suited for anglers as there is a fishing lake and river adjacent. A short walk takes you into the village where most basic requirements can be bought. The long distance cycle route, 'voie verte', is nearby.

Facilities

One small sanitary block has open style washbasins and preset showers. There is a second newer Portacabin style block. No facilities for disabled visitors. Laundry facilities. Covered swimming pool (April-Sept). Play area. Fishing. Bicycle hire. Internet access. Torches useful. A mobile home specially adapted for disabled visitors is available to rent. WiFi (charged). Off site: Loyat Village. Riding 3 km. Plo'rmel 5 km. Golf 5 km.

Open: All year.

Directions

Site is in a northern direction from Ploërmel on the D766. Take D13 signed Loyat. Site is on left after 1 km. before entering Loyat Village. GPS: 47.98425, -2.38191

Charges guide

Per unit incl. 2 persons	
and electricity	€ 15.50 - € 18.00
extra person	€ 3.50
child (7-13 yrs)	€ 2.00

Camping Cheques accepted.

Mousterlin
Sunêlia l'Atlantique

Kerbader, B.P. 11, F-29170 Fouesnant (Finistère) T: 02 98 56 14 44. E: sunelia@latlantique.fr

alanrogers.com/FR29350

L'Atlantique is quietly situated just outside Beg-Meil. The 432 pitches are predominantly used by tour operators with about 90 for independent visitors. Pitches are level and grassy, all with electricity, and separated by low shrubs. Apple orchards used for cider production are also on the site. All the facilities are grouped together in the centre including an innovative play area and pool complex with both indoor and outdoor pools, water slides and a paddling pool. The sandy beach faces the Glénan Islands and is a pleasant 400 m. walk away through a nature reserve. Coastal paths await exploration and Concarneau, Pont-Aven and La Pointe du Raz are all nearby. An innovation for 2010 are ready erected and furnished tents and yurts. Pamper breaks are also available. These include massage, body treatments and accommodation. L'Atlantique is attempting to stay 'ahead of the game' and is succeeding. A lively family would find it difficult to become bored here, as there is something for all ages.

Facilities

Fully equipped toilet blocks (cleaned three times a day) include facilities for disabled visitors. Shop, bar, snack bar with takeaway meals and pizza (all 1/5-12/9). Heated outdoor and indoor pools, water complex with slides (all 1/5-12/9). Tennis. TV room. Billiards. Minigolf. Sports ground. Play area. Children's club (4-12 yrs) and evening entertainment in July/Aug. Bicycle hire. WiFi in bar (charged). Off site: Fishing 300 m. Windsurf hire 1 km. Boat hire 3 and 5 km. Riding 3 km. Golf 8 km.

Open: 23 April - 11 September.

Directions

From Fouesnant follow directions for Mousterlin for 2 km., then follow Chapelle de Kerbader. Site is signed. GPS: 47.856564, -4.020658

Charges guide

Per unit incl. 2 persons	
and electricity (6A)	€ 22.00 - € 41.00
extra person	€ 3.00 - € 7.00
child (0-10 yrs)	€ 2.00 - € 4.00

Camping Cheques accepted.

Village CAMPING L'Atlantique
www.lAtlantique.fr
sunelia@lAtlantique.fr

with a great pool complex, indoor, outdoor, a wellness center, and a direct access to a fine sandy beach. Accomodations: tents, mobile homes, offer all the comforts of home.

Tel: 0033298561444
Fax: 0033298561867
Sunelia Atlantique
Mousterlin BP11 - 29170 Fouesnant

4 * Campingsite in South Brittany

We can book this site for you! Call 01580 214000 alan rogers travel

For latest campsite news, availability and prices visit
alanrogers.com

Call 01580 214000 We can book this site for you! alan rogers ◗ travel

Névez
Camping le Raguénès-Plage

19 rue des Iles, F-29920 Névez (Finistère) T: 02 98 06 80 69. E: info@camping-le-raguenes-plage.com
alanrogers.com/FR29090

Mme. Guyader and her family will ensure you receive a warm welcome on arrival at this well kept and pleasant site. Le Raguénès-Plage is an attractive and well laid out campsite with many shrubs and trees. The 287 pitches are a good size, flat and grassy, separated by trees and hedges. All have electricity, water and drainage. The site is used by two tour operators (15 pitches), and has 61 mobile homes of its own. A pool complex complete with new heated indoor pool and water toboggan is a key feature and is close to the friendly bar, restaurant, shop and takeaway. From the far end of the campsite a delightful five minute walk along a path and through a cornfield takes you down to a pleasant, sandy beach looking out towards the Ile Verte and the Presqu'île de Raguénès.

Facilities
Two clean, well maintained sanitary blocks include mixed style toilets, washbasins in cabins, baby baths and facilities for disabled visitors. Laundry room. Motorcaravan service point. Small shop (from 15/5). Bar and restaurant (from 1/6) with outside terrace and takeaway. Reading and TV room, Internet access point. Heated indoor and outdoor pools with sun terrace and paddling pool. Sauna (charged). Play areas. Games room. Various activities are organised in July/Aug. WiFi (charged). Off site: Beach, fishing and watersports 300 m. Supermarket 3 km. Riding 4 km.

Open: 1 April - 30 September.

Directions
From N165 take D24 Kerampaou exit. After 3 km. turn right towards Nizon and bear right at church in village following signs to Névez (D77). Continue through Névez, following signs to Raguénès. Continue for 3 km. to site entrance on left (entrance is quite small and easy to miss). GPS: 47.79337, -3.80049

Charges 2012
Per unit incl. 2 persons	
and electricity	€ 20.30 - € 39.70
extra person	€ 4.40 - € 6.00
child (under 7 yrs)	free - € 3.90

Névez
Camping les Deux Fontaines

Feunteun Vilian, Raguenèz, F-29920 Névez (Finistère) T: 02 98 06 81 91. E: info@les2fontaines.fr
alanrogers.com/FR29470

Les Deux Fontaines is a large site with 288 pitches. Of these 115 are for touring, 118 are used by tour operators, and the remainder for mobile homes. The well cared for pitches are on grass, level and attractively laid out amongst mature trees and shrubs. All have 6/10A electricity connections (Europlug). Trees have been carefully planted creating one area with silver birch, one with apple trees and another with palms and tropical plants. The pool complex is an excellent feature complete with chutes, flumes and waterfalls, and new in 2010, a covered pool with adjacent gym and massage room. There are numerous daytime activities for all the family to enjoy and a variety of entertainment in the evening.

Facilities
Two modern toilet blocks are of good quality and provide washbasins in cabins and preset showers. Separate facilities for disabled visitors. Laundry facilities. Well stocked shop, bar, takeaway (all season). Basic motorcaravan services. Large indoor and outdoor swimming pool complex (all season). Fitness and pamper room. Play area. Skateboard park. 6-hole golf course. Driving range. Rollerblade hire. Archery. WiFi in bar (free). Bicycle hire Off site: Fishing 1 km. Riding 5 km.

Open: 5 May - 2 September.

Directions
Travel south from Névez on the D1. The site is on the left after 3 km. and is well signed. GPS: 47.79337, -3.79017

Charges 2012
Per unit incl. 2 persons	
and electricity	€ 20.90 - € 38.70
extra person	€ 3.70 - € 6.60
child (2-7 yrs)	€ 1.50 - € 4.20
No credit cards.	

For latest campsite news, availability and prices visit
alanrogers.com

Paimpol

Camping Municipal de Cruckin

Rue de Cruckin, Kérity, F-22500 Paimpol (Côtes d'Armor) T: 02 96 20 78 47.
E: contact@camping-paimpol.com **alanrogers.com/FR22250**

A neat and well managed municipal site situated close to the historical fishing port of Cité des Islandais and within easy reach of the Ile de Bréhat. This is an ideal location for many interesting walks. The site has 130 well maintained, mostly level pitches set in both wooded and open areas and all have electricity connections (5-12A). A very large area has been provided for sports, a play area and picnic tables. Although the site does not have its own swimming pool, the beach is just a short walk away.

Facilities

One modern and heated toilet block. Washbasins in cabins and showers. Facilities for babies and disabled visitors. Laundry facilities. Bread and milk (high season). Snack bar/takeaway (July/Aug). Motorcaravan service point. Large field for football. Pétanque. Fenced play area. Internet access on request. Bicycle hire. Fishing. Off site: Beach. Kérity village with shops, restaurants and cafés. Riding 2 km. Golf 10 km.

Open: 1 April - 10 October.

Directions

From N12 St Brieuc bypass, take D786 north towards Paimpol. Village of Kérity is 3 km. south of Paimpol. Site is signed. GPS: 48.76966, -3.02209

Charges guide

Per unit incl. 2 persons and electricity	€ 15.40 - € 17.50
child (under 7 yrs)	€ 1.70 - € 2.20
dog	€ 1.30 - € 1.60

Pénestin-sur-Mer

Camping le Cénic

F-56760 Pénestin-sur-Mer (Morbihan) T: 02 99 90 33 14. E: info@lecenic.com
alanrogers.com/FR56180

Le Cénic is attractively set amidst trees and flowers, providing activities for all tastes. An attractive, covered aquatic complex has water slides, bridges, rivers and a jacuzzi, whilst the outdoor pool comes complete with water slide, 'mushroom' fountain and sunbathing areas. You may fish in the lake or use inflatables, watched by the peacock, the geese and turkeys. There is a hall for table tennis and a range of indoor games. There are 310 pitches, 160 of which are for touring. Of these, 90 have 6A electricity, but long leads will be required. The area has much to offer from the beaches of La Mine d'Or, the harbour at Trébiguier-Pénestin, the Golfe du Morbihan with its numerous islands, La Baule with its magnificent beach and the medieval city of Guérande to the unique Brière nature reserve.

Facilities

Good new toilet block includes washbasins in cabins, facilities for disabled visitors, baby room and laundry and dishwashing sinks. Separate laundry. Bar and shop (1/7-31/8). TV and games rooms (1/7-31/8). Indoor (15/4-15/9) and outdoor (1/7-31/8) swimming pools. Play area. Fishing. Off site: Riding 500 m. Bicycle hire 1 km. Sailing 2 km. Pénestin town 2 km. Sandy beaches 2.5 km. Golf 30 km.

Open: 1 May - 30 September.

Directions

From D34 (La Roche-Bernard), at roundabout just after entering Pénestin take D201 south (Assérac). After 100 m. take first turning on left. After 800 m. turn left and campsite is 300 m. on right down a narrow winding lane. GPS: 47.47910, -2.45643

Charges guide

Per unit incl. 2 persons and electricity	€ 18.00 - € 31.00
extra person	€ 4.50 - € 6.00
child (under 7 yrs)	€ 2.00 - € 3.00

We can book this site for you! Call 01580 214000 alanrogers travel

Covered Aquatic Centre (heated swimming pool, balneotherapy area, children's pool), outdoor pool, water chute, games room, bar, fishing in the lake.
Le Cénic offers a range of accommodation: static caravans, chalets to rent.

www.lecenic.com
56760 Pénestin-sur-Mer
Tél: +33 (0)2 99 90 33 14

info@lecenic.com
Fax: +33 (0)2 99 90 45 05

For latest campsite news, availability and prices visit
alanrogers.com

Pénestin-sur-Mer

Yelloh! Village Domaine d'Inly

Route de Couarne, B.P. 24, F-56760 Pénestin-sur-Mer (Morbihan) T: 02 99 90 35 09. E: inly-info@wanadoo.fr

alanrogers.com/FR56240

This very large site is mainly taken up with mobile homes and cottages, some belonging to the site owner, some private and some belonging to tour operators. Most of these pitches are arranged in groups of 10 to 14 around a central stone circle with a water point in the middle. Of the 500 pitches, 100 are for touring units and all are large (150-200 sq.m) with a 10A electrical connection (Europlug). Most are level and are situated by the attractive lake at the bottom of the site where one can fish or canoe. Pony rides are possible around the lake. The heated swimming pool, with its slides, and the bar and restaurant area, form two sides of an attractive courtyard. You will enjoy the indoor swimming pool which opens every day of the season, as well as a beauty area and many sporting and leisure activities.

Facilities

One toilet block (an additional block is planned) with facilities for disabled visitors, and a baby room. Laundry. Shop. Small, comfortable bar with large screen satellite TV, attractive restaurant and takeaway (all season). Heated swimming pool complex with slide (outdoor 15/5-15/9, indoor all season). Games room. Play areas. Football pitch (weekly games organised in July/Aug). Wellness (all season). Lake for fishing/canoeing. Pony rides. Bicycle hire. Sports and activities. WiFi. Off site: Supermarket 1 km. Pénestin town centre 2 km. Beach 2 km. Sailing and boat launching 2.5 km. Riding 15 km. Golf 25 km.

Open: 6 April - 22 September.

Directions

From D34 from La Roche-Bernard, at roundabout just after entering Pénestin take D201 south, signed Assérac. After 100 m. take first turning on left (site signed) opposite Carrefour supermarket. After 650 m. turn right, again signed, and campsite is 400 m. on left. GPS: 47.471483, -2.467267

Charges 2012

Per unit incl. 2 persons	
and electricity	€ 17.00 - € 42.00
extra person	€ 6.00 - € 7.00
child (3-7 yrs)	free - € 6.00
dog	€ 4.00

In SOUTH BRITTANY, France, relaxation, activities and entertainment in woodland estate, 2km from the beaches. Pond for fishing, indoor and outside pools, slide and numerous facilities available from April to September.

Domaine d'Inly

www.camping-inly.com • Tél. 0033 (0)2 99 90 35 09 • inly-info@wanadoo.fr

Pénestin-sur-Mer

Camping des Iles

La Pointe du Bile, B.P. 4, F-56760 Pénestin-sur-Mer (Morbihan) T: 02 99 90 30 24.
E: contact@camping-des-iles.fr **alanrogers.com/FR56120**

You will receive a warm, friendly welcome at this family run campsite. The owner, Madame Communal, encourages everyone to make the most of this beautiful region. Of the 184 pitches, 103 are for touring. Most are flat, hedged and of a reasonable size (larger caravans and American motorhomes are advised to book) and all have electricity. Some pitches have sea views and overlook the beach. There is direct access to cliff-top walks and local beaches (you can even walk to small off-shore islands at low tide).

Facilities

The new large central toilet block is spotlessly clean with washbasins in cabins and showers. Laundry facilities. Facilities for disabled campers, and baby room. Motorcaravan service point. Shop. Bar and restaurant with takeaway (15/5-15/9). Pool complex (15/5-30/9). Bicycle hire. Riding. Activities and entertainment in July/Aug. Across the road in Parc des Iles (mobile home section of site): TV room, multisports pitch, tennis court. No electric barbecues. Internet access in bar (charged). Off site: Windsurfing 500 m. Sailing 3 km. Golf 20 km.

Open: 2 April - 17 October.

Directions

From D34 (La Roche-Bernard), at roundabout just after entering Pénestin take D201 south (Assérac). Take right fork to Pointe-du-Bile after 2 km. Turn right at crossroads just before beach. Site is on left. GPS: 47.44543, -2.48396

Charges guide

Per unit incl. 2 persons	
and electricity	€ 20.50 - € 39.50
extra person (over 7 yrs)	€ 2.30 - € 5.80
child (0-7 yrs)	free - € 3.20
Camping Cheques accepted.	

For latest campsite news, availability and prices visit

alanrogers.com

Penmarc'h
Camping les Genêts

Rue de Gouesnac'h Nevez, F-29760 Penmarc'h (Finistère) T: 02 98 58 66 93. E: nohartp@wanadoo.fr
alanrogers.com/FR29260

Les Genêts' owners, Bridgette and Pascal Rohart, bought this rural campsite a few years ago and have enthusiastically transformed it beyond recognition. The modern reception is in front of a modestly sized swimming pool that has a section for small children. A covered pool should now be open. There are two new heated toilet blocks. The 100 pitches are divided by trees and hedges and vary in both size and quality. The clever design of the flower beds and shrubs around the site is particularly attractive. There are 52 pitches for mobile homes which are placed to one side of the campsite.

Facilities	Directions
Two new heated toilet blocks with showers and wash cubicles. Laundry room. Bar and snack bar (July/Aug). Bread available (July/Aug). Outdoor swimming pool. Play area and trampoline. Free WiFi by pool and office. Off site: Shops and restaurants 1.5 km. Riding, beach, fishing and boat launching 1.5 km. Golf 3 km.	From Pont l'Abbé, take the D785 southwest towards Penmarc'h. Before the town turn left eastwards on the D53 (Loc Tudy) and site is on left in about 2 km. GPS: 47.81838, -4.309452

Open: 1 April - 30 September.

Charges guide

Per unit incl. 2 persons	€ 12.00 - € 17.00
extra person	€ 3.20 - € 4.50
child (0-7 yrs)	€ 1.80 - € 2.70
electricity (10A)	€ 3.00 - € 3.40

Pléneuf Val André

Campé●le

Campéole les Monts Colleux

26 rue Jean Lebrun, F-22370 Pléneuf Val André (Côtes d'Armor) T: 02 96 72 95 10.
E: monts-colleux@campeole.com **alanrogers.com/FR22380**

Les Monts Colleux is a member of the Campéole group with an unusual town centre location in Le Val André. The site, however, has a hilltop setting and some pitches have fine views of the sea. This was formerly a municipal site and is well managed with well kept hedges and pitches. The reception area and shop have been added recently, although the wash blocks are older. Pitches are generally flat, although, given its hillside location, there are a number of sloping pitches. The 115 pitches all have electrical connections (10A). Although there is no swimming pool on site, there is a large covered municipal pool adjacent with limited free access for campers. Around 71 pitches are occupied by mobile homes, chalets and fully equipped bungalow tents (available for rent). The nearest beach is close – just 300 m, and boats can be launched nearby. An attractive golf course is 1 km. distant. Val André is an attractive resort and the town centre is just 300 m. from the site. There are many activities here during the high season, including weekly free jazz concerts.

Facilities	Directions
Play area. Bouncy castle. Shop. Snack bar. Takeaway meals. Games/TV room. Activity and entertainment programme. Tourist information. Mobile homes and chalets for rent. Off site: Municipal covered swimming pool adjacent. Val André centre and beach 300 m. Golf 1 km. Fishing.	Approaching from the east (St Malo and Dinard) on the D786, bypass Erquy and continue to Pléneuf-Val-André and then to Le Val-André. Follow signs to 'Piscine Municipale' – the site is adjacent. GPS: 48.5894, -2.5508

Open: 1 April - 30 September.

Charges guide

Per unit incl. 2 persons and electricity	€ 15.10 - € 22.00

Campé●le
CAMPSITES AND RENTALS

Les Monts Colleux ★★★

Beautiful site in Brittany at 300 meters of the village Val André and a fine sandy beach. Pitches and accommodations of high quality.

BRITTANY

22370 Pleneuf Val André - Tel.: +33-296-7295-10 - www.campeole.co.uk / monts-colleux@campeole.com

For latest campsite news, availability and prices visit
alanrogers.com

Pleubian
Camping de Port la Chaine

F-22610 Pleubian (Côtes d'Armor) T: 02 96 22 92 38. E: info@portlachaine.com

alanrogers.com/FR22140

Michelle and Thierry Suquet offer a warm welcome to this comfortable, quiet, family site. In a beautiful location on the Presqu'île Sauvage between Paimpol and Perros-Guirec, attractive trees and shrubs provide a balance of sun and shade for the 200 pitches. Of these, 140 are for touring, all with electricity (long leads may be needed in places) and some also have water and drainage. Pitches are on grassy terraces on the gradual descent towards the bay and the sea (a sandy bay with rocks). Most terraces have a slight slope, so those with motorcaravans will need to choose their pitch carefully.

Facilities

Two fully renovated toilet blocks are comfortable and fully equipped with washbasins in cabins, British and Turkish style toilets. Cabins for families and disabled visitors. Washing machines and dryer. Bar/snacks with terrace and takeaway (30/6-24/8). Bread and croissants (all season). Heated swimming pool (21/5-3/9). Play area. Games room. Pétanque. Children's entertainer in July/Aug. Beach, fishing and sailing. WiFi (free) in reception area. Off site: Bus 1 km. Boat launching 1 km. Good fishing and diving. Village 2 km. for tennis, bicycle hire, market, shops and restaurants. Riding 6 km. Golf 18 km.

Open: 4 April - 22 September.

Directions

Pleubian is 37 km. north of Guingamp and 87 km. by road east of Roscoff. From D786 Lannion - Paimpol road, east of Tréguier turn north on D20 to Pleubian and on for 2 km. towards l'Armor Pleubian. Site signed to left. GPS: 48.8555, -3.1327

Charges 2012

Per unit incl. 2 persons	
and electricity	€ 18.00 - € 26.60
extra person	€ 4.10 - € 6.40
child (2-7 yrs)	€ 3.50 - € 4.20
dog	€ 2.90

Plobannalec-Lesconil
Yelloh! Village l'Océan Breton

Lieu dit le Manoir de Kerlut, F-29740 Plobannalec-Lesconil (Finistère) T: 02 98 82 23 89.
E: info@yellohvillage-loceanbreton.com **alanrogers.com/FR29120**

L'Océan Breton is a comfortable site in the grounds of a manor house on a river estuary near Pont l'Abbé. The campsite itself has neat, modern buildings and is laid out on flat grass providing 240 pitches (90 for touring units). All have electricity connections, some also have water and drainage and around ten pitches have hardstanding. One area is rather open with separating hedges planted, the other part being amongst more mature bushes and some trees which provide shade. Site amenities are of good quality. A Yelloh! Village member.

Facilities

New sanitary facilities including washbasins all in cabins, and facilities for babies and disabled visitors. Laundry. Small shop. Restaurant. Takeaway. Large modern bar with TV (satellite) and entertainment all season. New aquatic area with large children's pool, swimming pool and water slide. Sauna, solarium and small gym. Fitness centre. Play area. Tennis. Pétanque. Games room. Bicycle hire. Off site: Beach 2 km. Riding 5 km. Golf 15 km.

Open: 29 May - 9 September (with all services).

Directions

From Pont l'Abbé, on D785, take D102 road towards Lesconil. Site is signed on the left, shortly after the village of Plobannalec. GPS: 47.81234, -4.22105

Charges 2012

Per unit incl. 2 persons	
and electricity	€ 17.00 - € 42.00
extra person	€ 6.00 - € 8.00

Ploemel
Camping Saint-Laurent

Kergonvo, F-56400 Ploemel (Morbihan) T: 02 97 56 85 90. E: camping.saint-laurent@wanadoo.fr

alanrogers.com/FR56330

This is an attractive, peaceful and rural site ten minutes from the beaches and 10 km. from Carnac. There are 70 touring pitches out of a total of 90 which are set among pine trees and wiry hedges giving some shade. Long leads are required. There is a more casual camping area further away amongst some trees. A well fenced small paddling pool and heated swimming pool with sun loungers are pleasantly sheltered by a well manicured hedge. The welcoming bar and patio area also has a communal barbecue. Basic provisions are available from reception where good English is spoken. This pleasant site is open all year.

Facilities

One bright modern sanitary block provides adequate facilities with excellent en suite facilities for disabled visitors and is centrally located. Heated swimming pool and paddling pool. Volleyball. Basketball. Small children's play area. Bicycle hire. Off site: Golf 1 km. Riding 5 km. Fishing and beaches 10 km.

Open: All year.

Directions

From the N165 Vannes - Lorient dual carriageway, take the exit signed D768 Ploemel/Carnac. After about 4 km. turn right heading northwest towards Ploemel. Once in the village centre follow signs to St Laurent Camping. GPS: 47.66406, -3.09985

Charges guide

Per unit incl. 2 persons	
and electricity	€ 15.10 - € 17.30

We can book this site for you! alan rogers ✺ travel
Call 01580 214000

For latest campsite news, availability and prices visit

alanrogers.com

Plouescat
Village Center Baie du Kernic

Rue de Pen An Theven, F-29430 Plouescat (Finistère) T: 04 99 57 21 21. E: contact@village-center.com

alanrogers.com/FR29440

This is a large site close to the beach near Plouescat and only 15 minutes from the popular beach resort of Roscoff. At present the site is still in the process of renovation, although the indoor heated pool is now open. The new owners, the Village Center Group, have plans for a new bar, reception area and a pool complex and upgrades to the rest of the site, and when completed this will be a good, lively site in an interesting location. There are 256 rough grass pitches separated by hedges with 143 for touring, only 45 with electricity.

Facilities	Directions
Three adequate but tired toilet blocks. Motorcaravan services. Shop. Bar, snack bar, restaurant (July/Aug). Outdoor swimming and paddling pools, covered pool (all season). Games/TV room. Organised activities (July/Aug). Bicycle hire. Internet. Off site: Fishing, beach, sailing 100 m. Bicycle hire 3 km. Golf 30 km. Tennis. Watersports. Thalassotherapy. Casino.	Site is on the D788 between Brignogan Plage and Roscoff, well signed from Plouescat centre. GPS: 48.65868, -4.21744

Open: 27 May - 18 September.

Charges guide

Per unit incl. 2 persons	
and electricity	€ 14.00 - € 22.00
extra person	€ 3.00 - € 5.00
dog	€ 3.00

No credit cards.

Plouézec
Camping le Cap Horn

Port Lazo, F-22470 Plouézec (Côtes d'Armor) T: 02 96 20 64 28. E: lecaphorn@hotmail.com

alanrogers.com/FR22320

Le Cap Horn is in a magnificent setting with exceptional views of the Bay of Paimpol and the Ile de Bréhat. The enthusiastic owners are keen to make visitors welcome at their site which is well positioned for exploring the Goëlo Coast, Paimpol and the Pink Granite Coast. The campsite is in two sections and slopes down to the beach. The upper section is mostly devoted to mobile homes and is reached by a road or a series of steep steps, the lower section is for tourers. There are 149 pitches with 115 good sized grass pitches for touring (90 with 6A electricity).

Facilities	Directions
Two toilet blocks including facilities for campers with disabilities but site not ideal for those with walking difficulties. Small shop. Bar, restaurant with takeaway and terrace with views over the bay (July/Aug). Heated swimming pool, paddling pool (1/6-15/9). Play area. Boules. Fishing. Watersports. Sports area. Bicycle hire, Organised activities (July/Aug). Internet access. Off site: Beach 100 m. Boat ramp 300 m. Riding 6 km. Golf 12 km. Shops, bars and restaurants at Plouézec and Paimpol.	From Saint Brieuc take D786 north to Paimpol (par la Côte). Site is at Plouézec, south of Paimpol, well signed from D786. GPS: 48.759792, -2.962795

Open: 7 April - 30 September.

Charges guide

Per unit incl. 2 persons	
and electricity (6A)	€ 15.00 - € 26.50
extra person	€ 3.50 - € 5.50
child (under 7 yrs)	€ 2.50 - € 4.90
dog (max. 1)	€ 1.00 - € 4.00

NEW digital iPad editions

alan rogers

NEW 2012

Available on the App Store

FREE Alan Rogers bookstore app - digital editions of all 2012 guides

alanrogers.com/digital

For latest campsite news, availability and prices visit

alanrogers.com

Plouhinec
Camping Moténo
Route du Magouër, F-56680 Plouhinec (Morbihan) T: 02 97 36 76 63. E: camping-moteno@wanadoo.fr

alanrogers.com/FR56440

This site is situated on the east side of the river d'Etel, just before it enters the sea. The grass pitches are of average size, hedged and shaded by large trees. Of the 256 pitches, 181 are occupied by mobile homes, mostly for rent. The new aqua park complex with covered and open areas is superb and includes slides, flumes and various pools. The beach is easily accessible, just 800 m. away, as is the little port facing Etel which can be reached by a regular ferry service. Plouhinec, the nearest town, is 5 km. by road where you will find shops and restaurants. A little further is the large town of Lorient.

Facilities
New modern toilet block for 2012 season. Washing machines and dryer. Shop and bar (July/Aug). New aqua complex. Multisports court. Gym. Bicycle hire. Play area. Entertainment (July/Aug). WiFi. Off site: Beach 800 m. Ferry to Etel for bars and shopping. Riding 3 km. Golf 15 km. Nearby towns of Lorient, Auray and the Quiberon peninsular.

Open: 5 April - 13 September.

Directions
From Plouhinec, southeast of Lorient, take the D781 in the direction of Carnac. Site is signed on right in 4 km. Follow signs for Plage. GPS: 47.66457, -3.22098

Charges guide
Per unit incl. 2 persons and electricity	€ 18.20 - € 33.50
extra person (over 7 yrs)	€ 3.60 - € 6.50

Ploumanach
Yelloh! Village le Ranolien
Ploumanach, F-22700 Perros-Guirec (Côtes d'Armor) T: 02 96 91 65 65. E: info@yellohvillage-ranolien.com

alanrogers.com/FR22080

Le Ranolien has been attractively developed around a former Breton farm – everything here is either made from, or placed on or around the often massive pink rocks. Of the 520 pitches 110 are for touring, mostly large and flat, but some quite small, all with electricity (10A) and some with water and drainage. The rest of the site is taken up with mobile homes and chalets for hire and several tour operators. The site is on the coast, with beaches and coves within walking distance and there are spectacular views from some pitches. Member of Leading Campings group.

Facilities
The main toilet block is heated in cool weather and has washbasins in cabins, mostly British style WCs and good showers. Facilities for disabled visitors. Laundry. Motorcaravan service point. Supermarket and gift shop. Restaurant, crêperie and bar. Indoor and outdoor (from end May) swimming pool complex. Wellness centre. Disco in high season. Minigolf. Games room. Play area. Cinema. Gym and steam room. Internet and WiFi (on payment). Off site: Beach, boat launching and sailing 1.5 km. Riding and bicycle hire 3 km. Golf 10 km.

Open: 6 April - 23 September.

Directions
From Lannion take D788 to Perros-Guirec. Follow signs to 'Centre Ville' past harbour area, then turn right along coast road ('Centre Ville par la Corniche and Trégastel'). Continue through north of town and on to la Clarté. After a sharp left hand bend site is immediately on the right. GPS: 48.82798, -3.47623

Charges 2012
Per unit incl. 2 persons and electricity	€ 17.00 - € 43.00
extra person	€ 6.00 - € 9.00

Poullan-sur-Mer
Flower Camping Caravaning le Pil-Koad
Route de Douarnenez, F-29100 Poullan-sur-Mer (Finistère) T: 02 98 74 26 39. E: info@pil-koad.com

alanrogers.com/FR29060

Pil-Koad is an attractive, family run site just back from the sea near Douarnenez in Finistère. It has 190 pitches on fairly flat ground, marked out by separating hedges and of quite good quality, though varying in size and shape. With 88 pitches used for touring units, the site also has a number of mobile homes and chalets. All pitches have electrical connections and the original trees provide shade in some areas. A large room, the Woodpecker Bar, is used for entertainment with discos and cabaret in July/Aug. Weekly outings and clubs for children are organised (30/6-30/8).

Facilities
Two main toilet blocks in modern style include washbasins mostly in cabins and facilities for disabled visitors. Laundry facilities. Motorcaravan service point. Gas supplies. Small shop for basics (1/4-30/9). Bar, new restaurant and takeaway (all 1/6-31/8). Heated swimming and paddling pools (1/4-30/9, no Bermuda-style shorts). Tennis. Minigolf. Fishing. Bicycle hire. Playground. Off site: Restaurants in village 500 m. Riding 4 km.

Open: 4 April - 27 September.

Directions
From Douarnenez take circular bypass route towards Audierne; if you see road for Poullan sign at roundabout, take it, otherwise there is a camping sign at turning to Poullan from the D765 road. GPS: 48.0824, -4.40805

Charges guide
Per unit incl. 2 persons and electricity	€ 16.80 - € 30.90
extra person	€ 3.60 - € 5.10

For latest campsite news, availability and prices visit
alanrogers.com

Quiberon

Camping Do Mi Si La Mi

31 rue de la Vierge, Saint Julien-Plage, F-56170 Quiberon (Morbihan) T: 02 97 50 22 52.
E: camping@domisilami.com **alanrogers.com/FR56360**

Occupying a five-hectare site on the Quiberon Peninsula just 100 metres from the sandy beaches, this campsite has plenty to offer and is particularly quiet and laid back in low season. Of the 350 pitches, 194 are for touring and are set amongst high mature hedges giving plenty of shade and privacy; some have sea views. Long leads are required on a few pitches as hook-ups can be shared between three or four pitches. The excellent facilities for children are in a well fenced area and include climbing frames, bouncy castles and multisports courts. Treasure hunts and other activities are organised daily in high season. Well managed reception on the opposite side of the road to the campsite. This site is ideally situated for exploring this fascinating area.

Facilities

Seven sanitary blocks, with good hot showers. Separate laundry. Shop. Bar. TV room. Bouncy castles. Multisports courts. Children's club. Off site: Bar, restaurant, supermarket 50 m. Beaches and bicycle hire 100 m. Town centre 2 km. Golf and riding 3 km.

Open: 1 April - 11 November.

Directions

From the N165 Vannes - Lorient dual carriageway south of Auray, take the exit for Carnac/Ploemel. Continue southwest on D768 through the town of Plouharmel following signs for Quiberon. About 25 km. from the N165 but before reaching the town of Quiberon, the site is signed to the left at St Julien Plage. GPS: 47.49974, -3.12026

Charges guide

Per unit incl. 2 persons and electricity	€ 16.80 - € 25.90
extra person	€ 3.10 - € 4.50
child (under 7 yrs)	€ 1.90 - € 2.70
dog	€ 1.50 - € 2.40

Quiberon

Camping Bois d'Amour

87 rue Saint Clement, F-56170 Quiberon (Morbihan) T: 02 97 50 13 52. E: boisdamour@hotmail.com
alanrogers.com/FR56520

Le Bois d'Amour faces toward Belle Ile and lies just 150 m. from the attractive, sandy Goviro beach at the southern end of the Quiberon peninsula. There are 290 pitches here, of which around 110 are for touring units, most with electricity. Other pitches are occupied by mobile homes and chalets (available for rent). On-site amenities include a large outdoor pool and a separate children's pool. Quiberon is explored by bicycle and these are available to rent on site. In high season, a regular programme of activities and entertainment is organised, including activities for children.

Facilities

Three good toilet blocks include facilities for children and disabled visitors. Laundry facilities. Bar/snack bar. Shop. Takeaway. Swimming and paddling pools (heated all season). Gym. Bicycle hire. Games room. Playground. Activity and entertainment programme. Mobile homes and chalets for rent. Off site: Golf 100 m. Nearest beach 150 m. Fishing. Riding 200 m. Tennis. Quiberon. Carnac. Excursions to Belle Ile.

Open: 2 April - 2 October.

Directions

From Auray (RN 165) take the southbound D768 to Plouharmel and on to Quiberon. Upon arrival in Quiberon, follow signs to 'Thalassotherapie' and then the site. GPS: 47.47634, -3.110364

Charges guide

Per unit incl. 2 persons and electricity	€ 15.00 - € 40.00
extra person	€ 3.00 - € 7.00
child (3-6 yrs)	€ 2.50 - € 5.00
dog	€ 2.00

For latest campsite news, availability and prices visit

alanrogers.com

Call 01580 214000 We can book this site for you! alan rogers ● travel

Quimper
Castel Camping l'Orangerie de Lanniron

Château de Lanniron, F-29336 Quimper (Finistère) T: 02 98 90 62 02. E: camping@lanniron.com

alanrogers.com/FR29050

L'Orangerie is a beautiful and peaceful family site set in ten acres of a 17th-century, 38-hectare country estate on the banks of the Odet river, formerly the home of the Bishops of Quimper. The site has 199 grassy pitches (156 for touring units) of three types varying in size and services. They are on flat ground, laid out in rows alongside access roads with shrubs and bushes providing pleasant pitches. All have electricity and 88 have three services. The original outbuildings have been attractively converted around a walled courtyard. Used by tour operators (30 pitches). There are lovely walks within the grounds and in spring the rhododendrons and azaleas are magnificent – the gardens and the restaurant are both open to the public. The site is just to the south of Quimper and about 15 km. from the sea and beaches at Bénodet. The restoration of the park, including the original canal, fountains, ornamental 'bassin de Neptune', the boathouse and gardens, is now complete. In addition to the golf course (9 holes) and driving range, a training bunker and pitching area have been created along with a second putting green. The Aqua-park has a new waterfall and exotic plants; it provides in excess of 600 sq.m. of heated water and includes balneotherapy, spa, jacuzzi, fountains, slides and games.

Facilities

Excellent heated block in the courtyard and second modern block serving the top areas of the site. Facilities for disabled visitors and babies. Washing machines and dryers. Motorcaravan services. Shop (15/5-9/9). Gas supplies. Bar, snacks and takeaway. New restaurant (open daily). Swimming and paddling pools. Aqua-park with waterfall, balnéo, spa, jacuzzi, fountains, water slides and games. Small play area. Tennis. Minigolf. Golf course, driving range, two putting greens, training bunker and pitching area (weekly green fee package available). Fishing. Archery. Bicycle hire. Reading, games and billiards rooms. TV/video room. Karaoke. Outdoor activities. Pony rides and tree climbing (high season). WiFi throughout (charged). Off site: Two hypermarkets 1 km. Quimper under 3 km. Beach 15 km.

Open: 15 May - 15 September.

Directions

From Quimper follow Quimper Sud signs, then 'Toutes Directions' and general camping signs, finally signs for Lanniron. GPS: 47.97685, -4.11102

Charges 2012

Per unit incl. 2 persons	
and electricity	€ 23.20 - € 41.00
extra person	€ 4.50 - € 7.90
child (2-9 yrs)	€ 3.00 - € 5.10
dog	€ 3.20 - € 4.70

Less 15% outside July/Aug.

94 acres of park, gardens and nature reserve.
Gites, cottages, mobile homes and studios for rent. Aqua park with paddling pool, spa, balnéo and 4 waterslides. 9-holes golf, golf practice, restaurant, bar, tennis, kayak, fishing, ponies, children's farm.

Castel L'Orangerie de Lanniron★★★★ - **Château de Lanniron**
Chemin de Lanniron - F-29000 Quimper - Finistère Sud Bretagne
Tel.: +33(0)2 98 90 62 02 - Fax: +33(0)2 98 52 15 56
camping@lanniron.com - GPS: 47°58,57 N 4°6,64 W
www.lanniron.com

L'Orangerie de Lanniron ★★★★

For latest campsite news, availability and prices visit
alanrogers.com

Saint Briac-sur-Mer
Camping Emeraude

7 chemin de la Souris, F-35800 Saint Briac-sur-Mer (Ille-et-Vilaine) T: 02 99 88 34 55.
E: camping.emeraude@wanadoo.fr **alanrogers.com/FR35100**

M. et Mme. Giroux have, over the past ten years, created a pleasant site with a French feel and some surprising features for such a compact site. Notably these include an attractive heated leisure pool with water slides, whirlpool and a paddling pool, safely separated from the main pool and with its own little slide. There are 71 level pitches for touring, separated by hedges or shrubs and all with electricity connection adjacent (6A). Beyond these are 121 mobile homes and chalets (65 for rent). Although in an urban setting, the sandy beaches of the attractive Côte Eméraude are only a short drive away. Saint Briac has a choice of shops, bars and restaurants and the resort of Dinard is only seven kilometres to the east. A bus service will take you there and you could then hop on the sea bus across to Saint Malo.

Facilities

Large toilet block with washbasins in cubicles and controllable showers. Facilities for disabled visitors. Baby room. Washing machine and dryer. Motorcaravan service points. Swimming pool (8/5-10/9). Shop and takeaway (all season). Bar (July/Aug). Games room. Excellent play area. Minigolf. Bicycle hire. Children's activities and evening entertainment for families (July/Aug). Gas barbecues only (available to hire). No twin-axle caravans or motorhomes. Off site: Beach, fishing, sailing and boat launching 900 m. Golf 3 km. Shops, bars and restaurants nearby.

Open: 3 April - 19 September.

Directions

Saint Briac is 7 km. west of Dinard and 14 km. from Saint Malo by road. From ferry terminal follow signs for Dinard. Turn west onto D168. Keep west onto D603 and follow signs for 'Camping Eméraude par la côte' (avoids town centre); site is well signed from there. From other directions take D976/N176 and follow signs for Dinard. GPS: 48.62776, -2.130865

Charges guide

Per unit incl. 2 persons	
and electricity	€ 22.80 - € 32.00
extra person	€ 5.50 - € 6.50
child (under 7 yrs)	€ 3.00 - € 4.50

CAMPING
Emeraude★★★ **Camping Emeraude**✹✹✹
Saint-Briac sur mer / Bretagne

7, Chemin de la Souris - 35800 Saint Briac sur Mer - France
Tel. 0033 299 88 34 55 - camping.emeraude@wanadoo.fr - www.campingemeraude.com

Saint Cast-le-Guildo
Castel Camping le Château de Galinée

La Galinée, F-22380 Saint Cast-le-Guildo (Côtes d'Armor) T: 02 96 41 10 56. E: chateaugalinee@wanadoo.fr
alanrogers.com/FR22090

Situated a few kilometres back from Saint Cast and owned and managed by the Vervel family, Galinée is in a parkland setting on level grass with numerous and varied mature trees. It has 273 pitches, all with electricity, water and drainage and separated by many mature shrubs and bushes. The top section is mostly for mobile homes. An attractive outdoor pool complex has swimming and paddling pools and two pools with a water slide and a 'magic stream'. A new indoor complex has now also been added and includes a swimming pool, bar, restaurant and large entertainment hall.

Facilities

The large modern sanitary block includes washbasins in private cabins, facilities for babies and a good unit for disabled visitors. Laundry room. Shop for basics, bar and excellent takeaway menu (all 25/5-4/9). Attractive heated pool complex (indoor 16/4 and outdoor 14/5-10/9) with swimming and paddling pools. New covered complex with heated swimming pool, bar, restaurant, entertainment hall and Internet access. Outside terrace with large play area. Tennis. Fishing. Field for ball games. Off site: Beach and golf 3.5 km. Riding 6 km.

Open: 14 May - 10 September.

Directions

From D168 Ploubalay - Plancoet road turn onto D786 towards Matignon and Saint Cast. Site is very well signed 1 km. after leaving Notre Dame de Guildo. GPS: 48.58475, -2.25656

Charges guide

Per unit incl. 2 persons	
and electricity	€ 21.70 - € 41.30
extra person	€ 4.00 - € 6.80
child (under 7 yrs)	€ 2.50 - € 4.80
dog	€ 4.00

Camping Cheques accepted.

We can book this site for you! Call 01580 214000 alanrogers ◉ travel

For latest campsite news, availability and prices visit
alanrogers.com

Call 01580 214000 We can book this site for you! alan rogers ◉ travel

Saint Cast-le-Guildo

Camping le Châtelet

Rue des Nouettes, F-22380 Saint Cast-le-Guildo (Côtes d'Armor) T: 02 96 41 96 33. E: chateletcp@aol.com

alanrogers.com/FR22040

Carefully developed over the years from a former quarry, le Châtelet is pleasantly and quietly situated with lovely views over the estuary from many pitches. It is well laid out, mainly in terraces with fairly narrow access roads. There are 216 good-sized pitches separated by hedges, all with electricity and 112 with water and drainage. Some pitches are around a little lake (unfenced) which can be used for fishing. Used by three different tour operators (73 pitches). A 'green' walking area is a nice feature around the lower edge of the site and a path leads from the site directly down to a beach (about 200 m. but including steps). Saint Cast, 1 km. away to the centre, has a very long beach with many opportunities for sail-boarding and other watersports. The nearby towns of Dinan, Dinard and the old walled town of Saint Malo are all within a comfortable distance for a day's excursion. The campsite has added a few well equipped Safari style tents for hire.

Facilities

Four toilet blocks with access at different levels include washbasins in cabins and facilities for children. Three small toilet blocks on the lower terraces. Some facilities are closed outside July/Aug. Motorcaravan services. Heated swimming and paddling pools. Shop for basics, takeaway, bar lounge and general room with satellite TV and pool table. 'Zen' room for rest, meditation and massage sessions (high season). Games room. Play area. Organised games and activities in season. Dancing (June, July and Aug). Off site: Beach 200 m. Bicycle hire 1.5 km.

Open: 23 April - 14 September.

Directions

Best approach is to turn off D786 road at Matignon towards St Cast; just inside St Cast limits turn left at sign for 'campings' and follow camp signs on C90. GPS: 48.63723, -2.26934

Charges guide

Per unit incl. 2 persons	
and electricity	€ 22.00 - € 42.00
extra person	€ 4.00 - € 7.00
child (2-7 yrs)	€ 3.00 - € 5.00
dog	€ 4.00

CAMPING LE CHATELET★★★★

Campsite is situated on terraces, overlooking the sea. Direct access to hiking paths and to two beaches.
Covered and heated swimming pool (telescopic roof). Fishing lake. Childrens playground, Wifi.

Openingdates : from the 23th of April until the 14th of September 2012

CAMPING LE CHATELET ★★★★ • Rue des Nouettes • 22380 Saint Cast le Guido

Tél : +33 (0)2.96.41.96.33 • Mail : info@lechatelet.com • Web : www.lechatelet.com

Saint Jouan-des-Guerets

Camping le P'tit Bois

Saint Malo, F-35430 Saint Jouan-des-Guerets (Ille-et-Vilaine) T: 02 99 21 14 30.

E: camping.ptitbois@wanadoo.fr alanrogers.com/FR35040

On the outskirts of Saint Malo, this neat, family oriented site is very popular with British visitors, being ideal for one night stops or for longer stays in this interesting area. Le P'tit Bois provides 274 large level pitches with 114 for touring units. In two main areas, either side of the entrance lane, these are divided into groups by mature hedges and trees, separated by shrubs and flowers and with access from tarmac roads. Nearly all have electrical hook-ups and over half have water taps. There are site-owned mobile homes and chalets, meaning that the facilities are open over a long season (if only for limited hours).

Facilities

Two fully equipped toilet blocks, include washbasins in cabins. Baby baths. Laundry facilities. Simple facilities for disabled campers. Motorcaravan service point. Small shop, bar (with entertainment in July/Aug), snack bar with takeaway (all open all season). TV room. Games rooms. Heated swimming pool, paddling pool and two water slides (from 15/5). Heated indoor pool with Turkish baths and jacuzzi (all season). Playground. Multisports court. Tennis. Minigolf. Charcoal barbecues not permitted. WiFi (free). Off site: Beach and fishing 2 km. Buses 2 km.

Open: 2 April - 11 September.

Directions

St Jouan is west off the Saint Malo-Rennes road (N137) just outside Saint Malo. Site is signed from the N137 (take second exit for St Jouan on the D4). GPS: 48.60993, -1.98665

Charges guide

Per unit incl. 2 persons	
and electricity	€ 23.00 - € 41.00
extra person	€ 5.00 - € 8.00
child (1-6 yrs)	€ 3.00 - € 6.00
dog	€ 4.00 - € 6.00

For latest campsite news, availability and prices visit

alanrogers.com

Saint Lunaire
Camping la Touesse

171 rue Ville Gehan, F-35800 Saint Lunaire (Ille-et-Vilaine) T: 02 99 46 61 13.
E: camping.la.touesse@wanadoo.fr **alanrogers.com/FR35060**

This family campsite was purpose built and has been developed since 1987 by Alain Clément who is keen to welcome more British visitors. Set just back from the coast road, 300 metres from a sandy beach, it is in a semi-residential area. It is, nevertheless, a pleasant, sheltered site with a range of trees and shrubs. Of the 141 level, grass pitches in bays, 90 are for touring units, all with electricity. The plus factor of this site, besides its proximity to Dinard, is the fine sandy beach which is sheltered – so useful in early season – and safe for children. The owners speak English.

Facilities

The central toilet block is well maintained, heated in low season with all modern facilities. Part of it may not be open outside July/Aug. Baby bath. Toilet for disabled visitors. Laundry facilities. Motorcaravan service point. Shop for basics (1/4-20/9). Pleasant bar/restaurant with TV. Video games for children. Sauna. Internet access in reception and WiFi (free) at reception. Bouncy castle. Off site: Buses 100 m. Sandy beach, fishing 300 m. Sailing 400 m. Riding 500 m. Bicycle hire 1.5 km. Golf 3 km. Shops, bars and restaurants nearby.

Open: 1 April - 30 September.

Directions

From ferry terminal follow signs for Dinard. From other directions take D976/N176 and follow signs for Dinard. Turn west onto D168, then northwest onto D64 towards St Lunaire. Follow signs to campsite at La Fourberie east of town. GPS: 48.63084, -2.08418

Charges guide

Per unit incl. 2 persons and electricity (10A)	€ 19.20 - € 25.50
extra person	€ 3.90 - € 5.40
child (under 7 yrs)	€ 2.70 - € 3.00
dog	€ 1.50

No credit cards.

Saint Malo
Domaine de la Ville Huchet

Route de la Passagère, Quelmer, F-35400 Saint Malo (Ille-et-Vilaine) T: 02 99 81 11 83.
E: info@villehuchet.com **alanrogers.com/FR35050**

Domaine de la Ville Huchet was taken over a few years ago by the owners of Camping Les Ormes (FR35020). It has been transformed into a superb site with modern facilities and lots of character. The pitches are well laid out and of generous size, most with 6A electricity and some with shade. They are set around an old manor house (disused) at the centre of the site. A splendid pool complex with its slides and pirate theme is particularly exciting for children, and alongside is a large, new, covered pool. A range of entertainment for young and old takes place in the spacious bar area and a new crêperie provides a range of food. This is a useful site, positioned on the edge of St Malo with easy access to the ferry terminal, old town and beaches. A bus service to take you into the town is 400 m. away.

Facilities

The sanitary blocks are modern and clean. Facilities for disabled visitors. Shop. Bar, crêperie and snack bar. Aqua park with water slides (June-Aug). Covered pool (all season). Bicycle hire. Play area. Entertainment programme in peak season (including live bands). WiFi. Off site: Aquarium 700 m. Fishing 1.5 km. Riding 6 km. Golf 12 km. Saint Malo (beaches, ferry terminal and old town) 4 km.

Open: 10 April - 12 September.

Directions

From St Malo take D137 towards Rennes. Take exit for St Jouan (D4) heading south. The site is well signed (2 km). GPS: 48.61507, -1.98782

Charges guide

Per unit incl. 2 persons and electricity	€ 21.45 - € 33.50
extra person	€ 3.90 - € 6.40
child (2-13 yrs)	€ 2.55 - € 3.85
dog	€ 3.20

Domaine de la Ville Huchet ★★★★

Holiday resort in St-Malo
On a 6-hectare estate,
4 km from the beaches.

• Campsite ★★★★
• Aquatic Park
• Indoor swimming pool
• Mobile homes, Wooden cottages, Cottages, Apartments for rent

WiFi

Tel. 33(0)2 99 81 11 83 • Fax 33(0)2 99 81 51 89
info@lavillehuchet.com
www.lavillehuchet.com

For latest campsite news, availability and prices visit
alanrogers.com

Saint Nic

Camping Domaine de Ker Ys

Pentrez-Plage, F-29550 Saint Nic (Finistère) T: 02 98 26 53 95. E: camping-kerys@wanadoo.fr

alanrogers.com/FR29410

Camping Domeaine de Ker Ys and Les Tamaris are adjacent sites that have been joined to form a camping village. Miles of wide sandy beach are just 20 m. away. The site has no bar or restaurant, but there is a bar next door and a snack stall in front of the site. The pool complex is very good with its slides, fountains and paddling pools. Entertainment such as karaoke and dance evenings are organised in high season. The 71 touring pitches vary in size and are divided by hedges. The site is concentrating now on the provision of mobile home holidays, and touring visitors may feel overwhelmed by these.

Facilities	Directions
Three unisex toilet blocks have British style toilets, showers and washbasins in cabins. Facilities for disabled visitors. Washing machines and dryers. Small shop. Swimming pool complex with slides, fountains and paddling pools. Play area. Mini-tennis. TV and games rooms. Beach 20 m. WiFi (charged). Off site: Shops, bars and restaurants nearby (but not many). Riding 15 km. Beach 20 m.	From the N165 (Quimper - Brest) take exit west at Châteaulin on D887 towards Crozon. Turn left to Saint Nic, then follow signs for Pentrez Plage and site. At the promenade turn left and site is 300 m. on the left. GPS: 48.192161, -4.301303

Open: 4 April - 19 September.

Charges guide

Per unit incl. 1 or 2 persons	€ 15.00 - € 27.50
extra person	€ 2.50 - € 5.00
child (3-6 yrs)	€ 1.50 - € 4.00
dog	€ 2.00

Saint Pierre-de-Quiberon

Flower Camping l'Océan

16 avenue de Groix, B.P. 18 Kerhostin, F-56510 Saint Pierre-de-Quiberon (Morbihan) T: 02 97 30 91 29.
E: info@relaisdelocean.com **alanrogers.com/FR56470**

L'Océan is a member of the Flower group and can be found just 100 m. from the nearest beach, halfway down the Quiberon peninsula. The site is a part of a holiday complex that was established in 1925 and which also includes a large hostel. There are 275 pitches which are generally well shaded, although some sunnier pitches are also available. A selection of mobile homes and fully equipped tents are for rent. In peak season, a varied entertainment programme is on offer, including traditional Celtic folk evenings and magic shows, as well as discos and concerts. The site's bar/restaurant, Ty Mouss, is the focal point, specialising in pizzas and crêpes, and other light meals. In low season, these facilities are unavailable. The nearest beach is sandy and various activities take place there, including volleyball and children's games. Bicycle hire is available on site and there are miles of marked cycle tracks around the peninsula, and further afield, for example, to the prehistoric standing stones at Carnac.

Facilities	Directions
Sanitary facilities provide hot showers, but are a little dated. Facilities for disabled visitors. Laundry facilities. Motorcaravan services. Shop, bar/restaurant and takeaway (July/Aug). Multisports terrain. Fishing. Bicycle hire. Tennis. Bicycle hire. Canoe hire. Play area. TV/games room. Activity and entertainment programme. Mobile homes and equipped tents for rent. WiFi (charged). Off site: Nearest beach 100 m. Riding 3 km. Golf 15 km. Cycle tracks. Prehistoric stones at Carnac.	Leave the N165 at the Quiberon exit and head south on the D768. Continue towards St Pierre-de-Quiberon, passing through Plouharnel. Site is located at Kerhostin and is signed to the right, before St Pierre. GPS: 47.534327, -3.139558

Open: April - November.

Charges guide

Per unit incl. 2 persons and electricity	€ 15.50 - € 24.50
extra person	€ 3.50 - € 5.00
child (2-7 yrs)	€ 2.20 - € 3.50
dog	€ 3.00 - € 4.00

Camping de l'Océan

16 Avenue de Groix Kerhostin
BP18 - 56510 St. Pierre Quiberon

Situated on the Presqu'Ile de Quiberon (South Brittany), 30 meters from the sea on open terrain with many trees. Flower Camping de l'Océan is a perfect destination for your family holiday.

Flower Camping de l'Océan welcomes you from April till October for a relaxing holiday in the heart of the Morbihan (South Brittany)

Campsite is part of Camping Qualité

Information: 0033 297 30 91 29 / Reservations: www.relaisdelocean.com

Saint Pol-de-Léon

Camping Ar Kleguer

Plage Sainte Anne, F-29250 Saint Pol-de-Léon (Finistère) T: 02 98 69 18 81. E: info@camping-ar-kleguer.com
alanrogers.com/FR29040

Ar Kleguer is less than 20 minutes from the Roscoff ferry terminal in the heart of the Pays du Léon in north Finistère. One section of the site (used in high season) has a 'country' feel and incorporates a small domestic animal park. The main section is divided into several areas, some on terraces at the edge of the sea with spectacular views overlooking the Bay of Morlaix. There are 173 large and well kept pitches, 125 for touring units, all with 10A electricity connections. Of these, 125 are for touring units. This neat site is decorated with attractive flowers, shrubs and trees.

Facilities	Directions
Three modern, tiled toilet blocks are well maintained and kept clean. Facilities for babies, children and disabled visitors. Laundry room. Shop, bar and takeaway (July/Aug). Good heated pool complex with paddling pools and slide (20/6-5/9). Pool table. Tennis. Bicycle hire. Animal park. Play area. Activities for children and some entertainment in high season. Beach adjacent with fishing and sailing. Free WiFi. Off site: Restaurant at site entrance. Sailing and boat launching 1 km. Riding 4 km. Golf 7 km.	Saint Pol is 18 km. northwest of Morlaix just off the D58 Morlaix-Roscoff road. Site is best approached from south, leaving D58 on the D769 signed Saint Pol Littoral. Turn right at cemetery following signs for 'Plages et Port' and campsites. Turn left along seafront to site at end. GPS: 48.69151, -3.96717

Open: Easter - 30 September.

Charges guide

Per unit incl. 2 persons and electricity	€ 20.20 - € 26.00
extra person	€ 4.20 - € 5.60
child (2-7 yrs)	€ 2.50 - € 3.80
dog	€ 2.20 - € 2.90

Saint Quay-Portrieux

Camping Bellevue

68 boulevard du Littoral, F-22410 Saint Quay-Portrieux (Côtes d'Armor) T: 02 96 70 41 84.
E: campingbellevue22@orange.fr **alanrogers.com/FR22230**

With magnificent coastal views, this attractive and well cared for site lives up to its name. Family owned for many years, it is situated on the outskirts of the popular seaside resort of St Quay-Portrieux and you will be made to feel most welcome by the owners. The 173 numbered touring pitches vary in size and 140 have 6A electricity. Some are separated by hedges, whilst others are in groups of four. Entertainment on site is limited but there is plenty to do and see around the area and a great opportunity for exploring the Goelo coast. Lazy hours could be spent gazing at the superb views of this spectacular part of the Brittany coast which can be seen from many of the Bellevue pitches. Further afield a days excursion could take you to Dinan, Dinard or the old walled town of St Malo. Some of the finest seafood can be found in this area of France.

Facilities	Directions
Two clean sanitary blocks provide both open and cubicled washbasins and controllable showers. Facilities for disabled visitors and babies. Laundry facilities. Motorcaravan service point. Shop for basics. Simple snack bar (1/7-31/8). Outdoor pool (1/6-18/9; no Bermuda shorts). Paddling pool. Volleyball. Boules. Play area. WiFi (free). Off site: Within walking distance of St Quay-Portrieux with shops, bars, restaurants and casino. Bicycle hire 1 km. Riding 8 km. Golf 10 km.	From N12 Saint Brieuc by-pass, take D786 north towards Paimpol. Site is well signed northwest of Saint Quay-Portrieux, 13 km. from the bypass. GPS: 48.66277, -2.84443

Open: 28 April - 16 September.

Charges 2012

Per unit incl. 2 persons and electricity	€ 17.00 - € 22.10
extra person	€ 4.00 - € 5.40
child (under 7 yrs)	€ 3.00 - € 3.40
dog	free

Camping Bellevue***

Exceptional view on the bay, lovely situated at the seaside. Direct access to a small creek. Situated 800m from the village and the beaches through a nice hiking path (GR34)

Opening dates:
23 April till 17 September 2011

68 Boulevard du Littoral - 22410 Saint Quay Portrieux - tel: +33 296 704 184 fax: +33 296 705 546 - campingbellevue22@orange.fr - www.campingbellevue.net

For latest campsite news, availability and prices visit
alanrogers.com

Saint Yvi

Village Center du Bois de Pleuven

Bois de Pleuven, route de Saint Yvi, F-29140 Saint Yvi (Finistère) T: 04 99 57 21 21.
E: contact@village-center.com **alanrogers.com/FR29200**

Camping du Bois de Pleuven is a member of the Village Center group and can be found within the 17-hectare Pleuven wood, between Quimper and Concarneau. The nearest beaches are a ten minute drive away. Given its wooded location, pitches are large and quite private. The majority are reserved for mobile homes to rent. This is a lively site in peak season with many activities, including a daily children's miniclub and Breton folk dancing classes. On-site amenities include two swimming pools, one of which is covered, as well as a children's paddling pool and a water slide. Concarneau is within easy access and is undeniably worth a visit. The town has two distinct identities: the modern town which is one of France's foremost fishing port, and the medieval Ville Close, a picturesque walled town on an island in the harbour. The Ville Close is connected to the main town by a drawbridge.

Facilities

Sanitary facilities include those for disabled visitors. Washing machine. Shop. Bar. Snack bar. Swimming pool with water slide. Covered pool. Paddling pool. Games room. Tennis courts. Sports field. Play area. Tourist information. Activity and entertainment programme. Mobile homes for rent. Off site: Nearest beach 10 km. Fishing. Cycle and walking tracks. Concarneau 12 km. Golf.

Open: 4 April - 20 September.

Directions

Approaching from the south, leave the N165 at the first Quimper exit and head east on D765 (towards Rosporden). Before reaching St Yvi turn right following signs to the site and Bois de Pleuven. The site is clearly signed from here.
GPS: 47.95055, -3.9675

Charges guide

Per unit incl. 2 persons	€ 14.00 - € 22.00
extra person	€ 3.00 - € 6.00

Camping Cheques accepted.

Sarzeau

Camping la Ferme de Lann-Hoëdic

Rue Jean de la Fontaine, F-56370 Sarzeau (Morbihan) T: 02 97 48 01 73. E: contact@camping-lannhoedic.fr
alanrogers.com/FR56200

Camping la Ferme de Lanne-Hoëdic is an attractively landscaped site with many flowering shrubs and trees. The 108 touring pitches, all with electricity (10A) are large and mostly level, with maturing trees which offer some shade. The 20 pitches with mobile homes are in a separate area. The working farm produces cereal crops and the summer months are an interesting time for children to see the harvest in progress. Mireille and Tim, the owners, go out of their way to make this a welcoming and happy place to stay. Located in the countryside on the Rhuys Peninsula, Golfe du Morbihan, it is an ideal base for cycling, walking and water-based activities.

Facilities

Two high quality toilet blocks with facilities for disabled visitors and babies. Washing machines and dryers. Bread delivery. Ice creams and soft drinks available at reception. Takeaway meals and traditional Breton 'soirées' (high season). Bicycle hire. Playground with modern well designed equipment. Pétanque. Internet access and free WiFi. Off site: Beach, fishing and boating 800 m. Sarzeau 2 km. Riding 2 km. Golf 6 km.

Open: 1 April - 31 October.

Directions

East of Vannes on the N165, join the D780 in the direction of Sarzeau. Exit D780 at the 'Super U'; roundabout south of Sarzeau, following signs for Le Roaliguen. Campsite is signed.
GPS: 47.50745, -2.76092

Charges 2012

Per unit incl. 2 persons and electricity	€ 16.10 - € 21.00
extra person	€ 3.60 - € 4.80

No credit cards.
Camping Cheques accepted.

★ ★ ★

The comfort of a 3-star campsite, the charm of a country setting.

Rue Jean de la Fontaine - 56370 Sarzeau   Tél : +33 297 48 01 73   www.camping-lannhoedic.fr

For latest campsite news, availability and prices visit

alanrogers.com

Taden

Camping International la Hallerais

4 rue de la Robardais, F-22100 Taden (Côtes d'Armor) T: 02 96 39 15 93. E: camping.la.hallerais@wanadoo.fr
alanrogers.com/FR22060

La Hallerais has a lot more to offer than most municipal sites. It is ideally located for exploring this fascinating area and is a short run from Saint Malo and from the resorts of the Côte d'Armor. It is just outside the attractive old medieval town of Dinan, beyond and above the little harbour on the Rance estuary. There is a pleasant riverside walk to the port and up into the town. Of the 226 pitches, 107 are for touring, all with electricity (6A), water and drainage, and are mainly on level, shallow terraces, with trees and hedges giving a park-like atmosphere.

Facilities

Two toilet blocks have pushbutton showers and washbasins in cubicles, and also some spacious cabins with shower and washbasin. Unit for disabled visitors. Launderette. Shop. Bar/restaurant with outside terrace and takeaway (all season). Swimming and paddling pools (15/5-30/9). Tennis. Minigolf. Games/TV room. Play area. Fishing. Mobile homes for rent. Free Internet and WiFi. Off site: Riding 2 km. Restaurants and bars at port 3 km.

Open: 12 March - 13 November.

Directions

Dinan is due south of Saint Malo (32 km. by road). From N176 (Avranches/Saint Brieuc) take Taden exit north of Dinan, turn towards Taden and follow blue signs to site. GPS: 48.47148, -2.02284

Charges 2012

Per unit incl. 2 persons	
and electricity	€ 13.70 - € 20.05
extra person	€ 3.30 - € 3.90

Taupont

Camping la Vallée du Ninian

Le Rocher, F-56800 Taupont (Morbihan) T: 02 97 93 53 01. E: infos@camping-ninian.fr
alanrogers.com/FR56160

Murielle and Stéphane Veaux have recently acquired this peaceful family run site in central Brittany from a former farm and they continue to make improvements to ensure that their visitors have an enjoyable holiday. The level site falls into three areas – the orchard with 100 large, hedged pitches with electricity, the wood with about 13 pitches more suited to tents, and the meadow by the river providing a further 35 pitches delineated by small trees and shrubs, with electricity. The bar has as its centrepiece a working cider press with which Stéphane makes his own 'potion magique'.

Facilities

A central building houses unisex toilet facilities including washbasins in cubicles, large cubicle with facilities for disabled visitors and laundry area. Shop (1/6-31/8) selling bread. Bar and takeaway (1/7-31/8). Small (7x12 m) heated swimming pool and children's pool with slide and fountain (15/6-31/8). Swings, slides and large trampoline. Trout fishing (permits from office). WiFi (free). Off site: Riding 2 km. Bicycle hire and golf 7 km.

Open: 7 April - 30 September.

Directions

From Ploërmel follow signs to Taupont north on N8. Continue through Taupont and turn left (east) signed Vallée du Ninian. Follow road for 3 km. to site on left. From Josselin follow signs for Hellean. Through village, sharp right after river Ninian bridge. Site is 400 m. on right. GPS: 47.96931, -2.47014

Charges guide

Per unit incl. 2 persons	
and electricity	€ 14.10 - € 19.70

Credit cards accepted in July/Aug. only.

Tinténiac

Camping Les Peupliers

Domaine de la Besnelais, F-35190 Tinténiac (Ille-et-Vilaine) T: 02 99 45 49 75.
E: camping.les.peupliers@wanadoo.fr alanrogers.com/FR35110

In the grounds of la Domaine de Besnelais, this little site has a very French feel. It is in a quiet area with wonderful opportunities for walking and cycling, with a flight of eleven locks on the attractive canal nearby. Of the 100 level, grassy pitches separated by hedges and bushes, 40 are for touring, all with electricity (10A). There are a couple of small fishing lakes. The site is close to the D137 Saint Malo - Rennes expressway and could be used as a peaceful base from which to visit Dinan and Dinard, Mont Saint-Michel and the bustling city of Rennes.

Facilities

The traditional, clean toilet block has mainly British style toilets, controllable showers and some washbasins in cubicles. Laundry room. Swimming and paddling pools (15/5-30/9). Bar with terrace. Weekly themed evening and some children's activities (high season). Takeaway food). Friterie (July/Aug). Basic supplies in reception. Tennis. Minigolf. Pitch and putt. Boules. Fishing. Bicycle hire. Free WiFi. Mobile homes to rent (1/3-31/10). Off site: Bars and restaurants nearby. Riding 200 m. Boat launching 2 km.

Open: 1 April - 30 September.

Directions

Tinténiac is 43 km. south of Saint Malo and 30 km. north of Rennes. Site is 2.5 km. south of village and is signed. From D137, leave at exit for Hédé and turn east then north towards Tinténiac. Site is 1.5 km. GPS: 48.310016, -1.821075

Charges guide

Per unit incl. 2 persons	
and electricity	€ 19.40 - € 21.10
extra person	€ 4.90 - € 5.50
child (under 12 yrs)	€ 3.80 - € 4.00

For latest campsite news, availability and prices visit

alanrogers.com

We can book this site for you! Call 01580 214000

alan rogers ● travel

Telgruc-sur-Mer

Camping le Panoramic

Route de la Plage-Penker, F-29560 Telgruc-sur-Mer (Finistère) T: 02 98 27 78 41.
E: info@camping-panoramic.com **alanrogers.com/FR29080**

This medium sized, traditional site is situated on quite a steep, ten-acre hillside with fine views. It is personally run by M. Jacq and his family who all speak good English. The 200 pitches are arranged on flat, shady terraces, in small groups with hedges and flowering shrubs, and 20 pitches have services for motorcaravans. Divided into two parts, the main upper site is where most of the facilities are located, with the swimming pool, its terrace and a playground located with the lower pitches across the road. Some up-and-down walking is therefore necessary, but this is a small price to pay for such pleasant and comfortable surroundings. This area provides lovely coastal footpaths. The sandy beach and a sailing school at Trez-Bellec-Plage are a 700 m. walk. A Sites et Paysages member.

Facilities

The main site has two well kept toilet blocks with another very good block opened for main season across the road. All three include British and Turkish style WCs, washbasins in cubicles, facilities for disabled visitors, baby baths, plus laundry facilities. Motorcaravan services. Small shop (1/7-31/8). Refurbished bar/restaurant with takeaway (1/7-31/8). Barbecue area. Heated pool, paddling pool and jacuzzi (1/6-15/9). Playground. Games and TV rooms. Tennis. Bicycle hire. WiFi. Off site: Beach and fishing 700 m. Riding 6 km. Golf 14 km. Sailing school nearby.

Open: 1 May - 15 September.

Directions

Site is just south of Telgruc-sur-Mer. On D887 pass through Ste Marie du Ménez Horn. Turn left on D208 signed Telgruc-sur-Mer. Continue straight on through town and site is on right within 1 km.
GPS: 48.22409, -4.37186

Charges guide

Per unit incl. 2 persons and electricity (10A)	€ 26.50
extra person	€ 5.00
child (under 7 yrs)	€ 3.00
dog	€ 2.00
Less 20% outside July/Aug.	

Camping **LE PANORAMIC** ★★★★ BRITTANY

Family run campsite bordering the sea on the Crozon Peninsula in the Armorique Regional Park. Large sunny or partly shaded private pitches with panoramic view on the beach and the bay of Douarnenez. Outdoor heated pool 26°C, paddling pool 26°C, jacuzzi 28°C, tennis, sailing school, water sports, cultural activities, museums, folklore evenings... *Family Jacq*

29560 Telgruc-sur-Mer - France
Tel. 0033 298 27 78 41 - Fax: 0033 298 27 36 10
Email : info@camping-panoramic.com / www.camping-panoramic.com

CAMPINGS SITES PAYSAGES

Tredrez-Locquémeau

Camping les Capucines

Kervourdon, F-22300 Tredrez-Locquémeau (Côtes d'Armor) T: 02 96 35 72 28. E: les.capucines@wanadoo.fr
alanrogers.com/FR22010

A warm welcome awaits at les Capucines, which is quietly situated about a kilometre from the village of Saint Michel with its good, sandy beach and also very near Locquémeau, a pretty fishing village. This attractive, family run site has 100 pitches on flat or slightly sloping ground. All are well marked out by hedges, with mature trees and with more recently planted. There are 70 pitches with electricity, water and drainage, including ten for larger units. A good value restaurant/crêperie can be found at Trédrez; others at Saint Michel. A Sites et Paysages member.

Facilities

Two modern toilet blocks, clean and very well kept, include washbasins mainly in cabins, facilities for babies and disabled visitors. Laundry with washing machines and dryer. Small shop for essentials (bread to order). Takeaway, bar with TV and games room. New covered and heated swimming pool (all season). Paddling pool. Playground. Tennis. Minigolf. New multisports area. Charcoal barbecues are not permitted. Chalets and mobile homes to rent. WiFi. Off site: Beach and fishing 1 km. Riding 2 km. Golf 15 km.

Open: 2 April - 23 September.

Directions

Turn off main D786 road northeast of St Michel where site is signed, and 1 km. to site.
GPS: 48.69274, -3.55663

Charges 2012

Per unit incl. 2 persons	
and electricity	€ 18.00 - € 27.00
extra person	€ 4.00 - € 5.50
child (under 7 yrs)	€ 2.90 - € 3.60
dog	€ 2.00

For latest campsite news, availability and prices visit
alanrogers.com

Trélévern

RCN Camping de Port l'Epine

Venelle de Pors Garo, F-22660 Trélévern (Côtes d'Armor) T: 02 96 23 71 94. E: info@rcn-portlepine.fr

alanrogers.com/FR22130

Port l'Epine is a pretty little site in a unique situation on a promontory with direct access to the sea, and views across the attractive bay to Perros Guirec. There are 160 grass pitches, 101 for touring, all with electricity (16A) and some fully serviced. They are separated by attractive hedging and trees. The rest are used for mobile homes. This site is ideal for families with young children, though not for teenagers looking for lots to do! On the north side is a little port facing an archipelago of seven small islands.

Facilities

The original toilet block is well equipped and a second block has been refurbished in a modern style with thermostatically controllable showers and washbasin in cubicles. Baby room. Facilities for disabled visitors. Modern launderette. Shop and bar (all season) restaurant with takeaway (1/7-31/8). Small heated swimming pool and paddling pool (May-Sept). Fenced play area near the bar/restaurant. Video games. Bicycle hire. Fishing and boat launching. Internet and WiFi in bar. Off site: Riding 2 km. Sailing 5 km. Golf 15 km. Useful small supermarket up hill from site. Many coastal paths to enjoy.

Open: Mid May - 11 September.

Directions

Trélévern is 14 km. northeast of Lannion and 70 km. by road east of Roscoff. From roundabout south of Perros Guirec take D6 towards Tréguier. After passing through Louannec, turn left at crossroads for Trélévern. Go through village following camping signs. Port l'Epine is then clearly marked as distinct from the municipal site. GPS: 48.81311, -3.38598

Charges guide

Per unit incl. 2 persons	
and electricity	€ 14.50 - € 30.00
with services	€ 17.00 - € 33.00
extra person	€ 5.00 - € 7.00

Vannes

Camping du Haras

Aérodrome Vannes-Meucon, Kersimon, F-56250 Vannes-Meucon-Monterblanc (Morbihan)
T: 02 97 44 66 06. E: contact@campingvannes.com **alanrogers.com/FR56150**

Close to Vannes and the Golfe du Morbihan in southern Brittany, le Haras is a small, family run, rural site that is open all year. There are 140 pitches, in a variety of settings, both open and wooded, the pitches are well kept and of a good size, all with electricity (4/10A) and most with water and drainage. Whilst M. Danard intends keeping the site quiet and in keeping with its rural setting, he provides plenty of activities for lively youngsters, including some organised games and evening parties.

Facilities

The two modern toilet blocks (heated in winter) provide a few washbasins in cabins and controllable showers. Facilities for babies and disabled visitors. Laundry facilities. No shop but basics are kept in the bar. Bar with snacks (May-Oct). Takeaway (July/Aug). Swimming pool with waves and slide (1/5-31/10). Play area. Animal park. Trampoline. Minigolf. Bicycle hire. Organised activities (high season). Off site: Riding 400 m. Fishing 3 km. Beach 15 km. Golf 25 km.

Open: All year.

Directions

From Vannes on N165 take exit signed Pontivy and airport on the D767. Follow signs for airport and Meucon. Turn right on the D778, follow airport and yellow campsite signs. GPS: 47.730477, -2.72801

Charges guide

Per unit incl. 2 persons	
and electricity (10A)	€ 20.00 - € 31.00
extra person	€ 4.00 - € 5.00
child (0-7 yrs)	€ 2.00 - € 3.00
dog	€ 3.00 - € 4.00

Vannes

Flower Camping de Conleau

188 avenue Maréchal Juin, F-56000 Vannes (Morbihan) T: 02 97 63 13 88. E: camping@mairie-vannes.fr

alanrogers.com/FR56410

This well maintained site is in a great location on the edge of the Gulf of Morbihan. Many of the 226 slightly sloping pitches have sea views. One area is for caravans and another for tents whilst mobile homes occupy the front part of the site. There are no numbered pitches, you choose where you want to go and get given a number to display on your unit. A bar and restaurant and organised activities are available in high season. Historic Vannes is only a five minute drive away and has all the amenities you would expect from a large town.

Facilities

Three well positioned sanitary blocks provide very good modern facilities and are kept very clean. Separate laundry room. Bar/restaurant (July/Aug). TV/games room with pool tables and electronic games. Bicycle hire. Activities on offer included free pony rides when we were on site. Off site: Small seawater swimming pool and beach 500 m. Boat trips 500 m. Town centre 3 km.

Open: 1 April - 30 September.

Directions

From the N165 Vannes - Lorient dual carriageway, take any of the four exits south towards Vannes town centre. Site is well signed from any of these points, as is the Port of Conleau which is where the site is located. GPS: 47.63365, -2.78008

Charges guide

Per person	€ 4.20
pitch	€ 6.10
electricity (6A)	€ 4.50

(73)

A striking area whose beauty lies not only in the landscape. Famed for its seafood and Celtic tradition, certain areas of Normandy remain untouched and wonderfully old fashioned.

DÉPARTEMENTS: 14 CALVADOS, 27 EURE, 50 MANCHE, 61 ORNE, 76 SEINE MARITIME

MAJOR CITIES: CAEN AND ROUEN

Normandy has a rich landscape full of variety. From the wild, craggy granite coastline of the northern Cotentin to the long sandy beaches and chalk cliffs of the south. It also boasts a superb coastline including the Cotentin Peninsula, cliffs of the Côte d'Albâtre and the fine beaches and fashionable resorts of the Côte Fleurie. Plus a wealth of quiet villages and unspoilt countryside for leisurely exploration.

The history of Normandy is closely linked with our own. The famous Bayeux Tapestry chronicles the exploits of the Battle of Hastings and there are many museums, exhibitions, sites and monuments, including the Caen Memorial Museum, which commemorate operations that took place during the D-Day Landings of 1944.

Known as the dairy of France you'll also find plenty of fresh fish, rich cream, butter, and fine cheeses such as Camembert and Pont l'Evêque. The many apple orchards are used in producing cider and the well known Calvados, Normandy's apple brandy.

Places of interest

Bayeux: home to the famous tapestry; 15th-18th-century houses, cathedral, museums.

Caen: feudal castle, Museum of Normandy, Museum for Peace.

Omaha Beach: D-Day beaches, Landing site monuments, American Cemetery.

Deauville: seaside resort, horse racing centre.

Giverny: home of impressionist painter Claude Monet, Monet Museum.

Honfleur: picturesque port city with old town.

Lisieux: pilgrimage site, shrine of Ste Thérèse.

Mont St-Michel: world famous abbey on island.

Rouen: Joan of Arc Museum; Gothic churches, cathedrals, abbey, clock tower.

Cuisine of the region

Andouillette de Vire: small chitterling (tripe) sausage.

Barbue au cidre: brill cooked in cider and Calvados.

Douillons de pommes à la Normande: baked apples in pastry.

Escalope (Vallée d'Auge): veal sautéed and flamed in Calvados with cream and apples.

Ficelle Normande: pancake with ham, mushrooms and cheese.

Tripes à la Mode de Caen: stewed beef tripe with onions, carrots, leeks, garlic, cider and Calvados.

www.normandy-tourism.travel
info@normandie-tourisme.org
(0)2 32 33 79 00

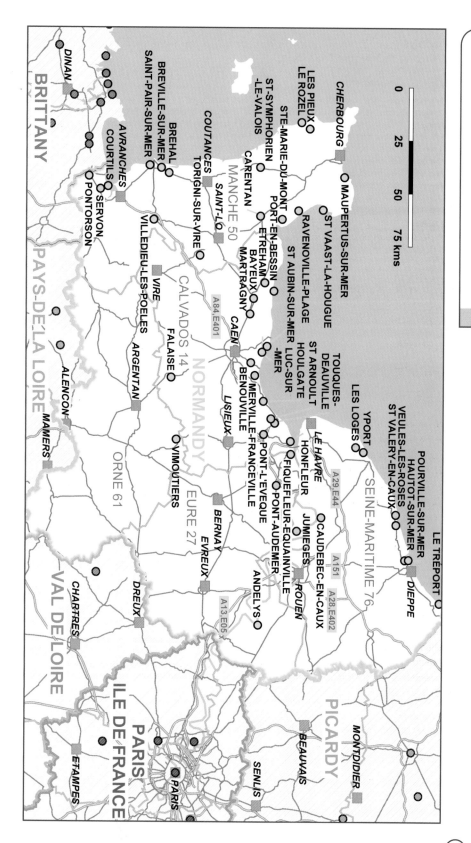

For latest campsite news, availability and prices visit
alanrogers.com

Andelys
Camping de l'Ile des Trois Rois

1 rue Gilles Nicolle, F-27700 Andelys (Eure) T: 02 32 54 23 79. E: campingtroisrois@aol.com

alanrogers.com/FR27070

One hour from Paris, on the banks of the Seine and overlooked by the impressive remains of Château Gaillard (Richard Coeur de Lion), this attractive and very spacious ten-hectare site will appeal to everyone. There is easy access to the 108 touring pitches on level grass, in a well landscaped setting and all with electricity (6A), although some long leads may be required. Many of these back onto the River Seine where you can watch the barges, and most have views of the château. Of the 80 mobile homes on site, there are five to let, leaving lots of space to enjoy the surroundings, including the large lake full of perch and bream for those eager fishermen. A nearby station will whisk you to Paris for the day, or a short drive will bring the delights of Monet's house and garden. A Medieval Festival is held in Les Andelys in the last weekend of June. Walk along the banks of the Seine and watch the huge passenger boats cruising there, or stroll into the main town for shopping and restaurants.

Facilities

Four small, unheated toilet blocks have British style toilets (no seats), showers and washbasins, all in cubicles; dishwashing and laundry sinks. One has facilities for disabled visitors, another has a laundry facility. Motorcaravan service point. Heated swimming and paddling pools (15/5-30/9). Bar and restaurant (1/4-30/9). Fenced play area. Evening entertainment (4/7-30/8). Bicycles and barbecues for hire. Satellite TV. Internet access and WiFi (charged). Adult open-air exercise area. Off site: Riding 5 km. Golf 9 km. Giverny 20 km.

Open: 15 March - 15 November.

Directions

Les Andelys is 40 km. southeast of Rouen. From the town centre, continue on D125 and follow signs until roundabout by bridge where second exit leads directly into site. GPS: 49.23564, 1.40005

Charges guide

Per unit incl. 2 persons and electricity	€ 21.00
extra person	€ 5.50
child (under 3 yrs)	free
dog	€ 2.00

L'Ile des Trois Rois

The park Ile des Trois Rois is situated in the most beautiful bend of the Seine nearby Castle Gaillard in Normandy and is a haven of peace. Paris is situated of less than than an hour and Rouen is half an hour driving from the camp site. Facilities: two heated swimming pools, ping pong, camper service, bar and restaurant (high season) and play area

1, Rue Gilles Nicole - F-27700 Les Andelys - France - Tel. 0033 (0) 2 32 54 23 79
Fax 0033 (0) 2 32 51 14 54 - Email campingtroisrois@aol.com - www.camping-troisrois.com

Bayeux
Camping des Bords de l'Aure

Boulevard Eindhoven, F-14400 Bayeux (Calvados) T: 02 31 92 08 43. E: campingmunicipal@mairie-bayeux.fr

alanrogers.com/FR14020

Only a few kilometres from the coast and the landing beaches, this excellent site makes a very useful night stop on the way to or from Cherbourg, whether or not you want to see the tapestry at Bayeux. The 140 pitches are in two areas (many on hardstanding), well marked and generally of good size with electricity. The site is busy over a long season – early arrival is advised as reservations are not taken. Reception is open 08.00 to 12.30 and 14.00 to 19.00 (all day in July/August). There is no parking outside for tourers. There may be some road noise on one side of the site.

Facilities

The two good quality toilet blocks have British style WCs, washbasins in cabins in main block, and units for disabled visitors. Baby changing. Motorcaravan service point. Laundry room. Van calls with takeaway food (Mon-Fri eves). Bread to order. Two playgrounds. Reading room with TV. Games room. Five mobile homes to rent. Off site: Free public indoor swimming pool adjacent to site. Supermarket. Bayeux Tapestry, town centre and bicycle hire 1 km. Riding 5 km. D-Day beaches 8 km.

Open: 16 April - 29 October.

Directions

On the northernmost point of the inner ring road (D613), just west of the junction to Arromanches (D516), the site is well signed in this area. GPS: 49.2839, -0.6976

Charges guide

Per unit incl. 2 persons and electricity	€ 16.20
extra person	€ 4.10
child (under 7 yrs)	€ 2.40
dog	free

For latest campsite news, availability and prices visit

alanrogers.com

Bénouville
Camping les Hautes Coutures

Ave de la Côte de Nacre, F-14970 Bénouville (Calvados) T: 02 31 44 73 08.
E: info@campinghautescoutures.com **alanrogers.com/FR14060**

Les Hautes Coutures is a pleasant site beside the Caen ship canal and a short walk from Pegasus Bridge. Being ten minutes from the ferry, it is very good for overnight stops although there is a minimum stay of two nights in the peak season. However, with the D-Day Beaches of Sword, Juno, Gold, Omaha and Utah on your doostep, one day is not enough. This well laid out site has 277 pitches, 99 for touring and the remainder for mobile homes, both private and rental. Of the touring pitches, some are among those homes in the upper part of the site and are of variable sizes, separated by mature hedging. Those alongside the canal are larger and trees mark their boundaries. All are on grass and have electricity (6-10A). The up-to-date, open-air heated pool complex includes, slides and whirlpools, and part is under a sliding roof. After the activities of the day, relax in the chic cocktail bar alongside the restaurant.

Facilities

Two main sanitary blocks include showers, washbasins in cabins (warm water). Facilities can be under pressure at peak times despite the addition of a third block. Facilities for disabled visitors. Laundry. Motorcaravan service point. Small shop and bar. Restaurant and takeaway (July/Aug). Outdoor heated pool complex. Small lounge with TV area and games room. Children's play area and outdoor fitness equipment. Multisports court. Children's club (July/Aug). Fishing. Minigolf. Boules. WiFi.
Off site: Pegasus Bridge and Memorial Museum. Beach, sailing, boat launching, water-skiing and riding all 2-3 km.

Open: 1 April - 30 October.

Directions

From Ouistreham ferry, follow D84 towards Caen for 4.5 km. and take first exit signed Z.A. Bénouville. At T-junction turn right and after 400 m. turn left and site is on right in 300 m, immediately before re-joining dual-carriageway. From Caen, follow the D515 (Ouistreham), after sign for Pegasus Bridge continue for 1 km. take next exit and site is at end of the slip road. GPS: 49.24948, -0.27217

Charges guide

Per unit incl. 2 persons	
and electricity	€ 23.00 - € 27.00
extra person	€ 5.50 - € 9.40

Bréhal
Camping La Vanlée

Rue des Gabions, F-50290 Bréhal (Manche) T: 02 33 61 63 80. E: contact@camping-vanlee.com
alanrogers.com/FR50220

A typical French beach holiday is on offer when you stay at la Vanlée. The resident manager, who enthusiastically runs this municipal site on the outskirts of Saint Martin de Bréhal, is passionate about the area and the type of holiday offered by the site. There are 470 pitches which are open, marked and numbered. All are on sandy grass and in some areas the ground is undulating. The roads around the site are tarmac but it is necessary to drive over grass to access most of the pitches. The swimming and paddling pools are a little dated without slide or flume, but there is direct access to the beach.

Facilities

There are five toilet blocks, although only two were open at the time of our visit. Heating in two blocks (recently upgraded). Washbasins in cabins (no doors). Pushbutton showers. Good facilities for disabled visitors. Washing and drying facilities. Shop, bar and takeaway (July/Aug). TV room, multisports pitch, boules, games room (July/Aug). Activities for all ages. Internet access. Torches useful.
Off site: Golf and horse riding 500 m. Supermarket and shops at Bréhal 4 km. Boat trips from Granville 10 km.

Open: 1 May - 30 September.

Directions

From North or South on D971 enter Bréhal. Leave on D592, signed Camping La Vanlée. Entering Saint Martin de Bréhal follow signs for 'camping-golf'. Continue alongside golf course directly to site. GPS: 48.908405, -1.564897

Charges guide

Per unit incl. 2 persons	
and electricity (6A)	€ 15.40 - € 18.70
extra person	€ 3.80 - € 4.70

For latest campsite news, availability and prices visit
alanrogers.com

Breville-sur-Mer

Kawan Village la Route Blanche

F-50290 Breville-sur-Mer (Manche) T: 02 33 50 23 31. E: larouteblanche@camping-breville.com

alanrogers.com/FR50150

La Route Blanche has a bright and cheerful atmosphere and Philippe and Corinne, the owners, are working continually to make an excellent site even better. The 140 pitches for touring are average in size, numbered, on well-cut grass and divided by young conifers. There are many shrubs and flowers and mature trees give shade to some areas. Sixty seven pitches have 6/10A electricity and long leads may be necessary for some. Although the site does not have its own restaurant, there are five to choose from within a short distance. Three hundred and twenty square metres of swimming pool complex with exceptional facilities for campers with disabilities will be enjoyed by all. If golf is your game, then you will not be disappointed. There is an 18-hole course and a nine-hole course only 400 m. away. The area has the highest tides in Europe and each visitor to the site is given a current tide timetable. The sandy beach is only 800 m. away and there are several walking routes waymarked through the dunes. Corinne cooks moules and frites a couple of times in the high season for site visitors and on-site entertainment is arranged during July and August. After 21.00 hours late arrivals are not accepted. WiFi is available all round the site.

Facilities

Well maintained sanitary facilities with British style toilets, washbasins in cabins and showers. Good provision for disabled visitors. Laundry and dishwashing facilities. Bread available all season. Bar and takeaway (July/Aug). Large swimming pool complex. Play area. Multisports court. Entertainment in high season. WiFi (charged). Off site: Golf (opposite). Fishing 500 m. Riding 1 km. Shops, restaurants and supermarket at Donville-les-Bains 3 km. Boat trips to the Channel Islands and the Isles de Chausey from Granville. Mont-Saint Michel. Cruises on board old tall ships.

Open: 1 April - 17 October.

Directions

Take D971 that runs between Granville and Coutance. Then one of the roads west to Breville-sur-Mer. Site is well signed. GPS: 48.869658, -1.563873

Charges guide

Per unit incl. 2 persons	
and electricity	€ 23.00 - € 34.00
extra person	€ 5.00 - € 7.00
child (2-7 yrs)	free - € 4.80
dog	€ 2.50 - € 3.00

Camping Cheques accepted.

Situated in the Mont Saint Michel Bay, in front of Chausey and Chanel Islands (Jersey, Guernesey and Sark), our campsite La Route Blanche*** is located at sea shore and in the country, at 5 km from Granville.

CAMPING CARAVANING La Route Blanche*(*)**
6 La Route Blanche • F-50290 Bréville sur Mer • France
Tel: 0033 233 50 23 31 • larouteblanche@camping-breville.com
www.camping-breville.com

(*) Pending classification

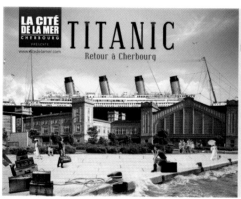

TITANIC
Retour à Cherbourg

New in 2012 !

Relive the unique and tragic voyage of the "Titanic", 100 years on.

In a new area of 2,500m² at the Museum of the Sea in Cherbourg :

Follow the journey of emigrants to Americas.

Discover the exhibition dedicated to the cruise ship the "Titanic".

Carentan
Flower Camping Le Haut Dick

30 chemin du Grand Bas Pays, F-50500 Carentan (Manche) T: 02 33 42 16 89.
E: contact@camping-lehautdick.com **alanrogers.com/FR50240**

Le Haut Dick is located at the heart of the south Cotentin peninsula. On the banks of the Haut Dick canal, this is a simple campsite but offers all comforts required. It comprises 120 good-sized pitches which are flat, grassy and well divided by hedges. The village of Carentan is a 10 minute walk away and features a brand new pool complex. Le Haut Dick is an ideal departure point for visiting the Landing Beaches, such as Omaha Beach, and Arromanches. The famous Mont Saint-Michel is also a short drive.

Facilities

Sanitary buildings include showers, baby rooms and facilities for disabled visitors. Washing machine. Snack bar. Table tennis. Minigolf. Play area. Bicycle hire. Boules courts. Accommodation to rent.

Open: 1 April - 15 October.

Directions

Leave the A13 and follow the RN13 and then the E46 to Carentan. GPS: 49.309859, -1.238869

Charges guide

Per unit incl. 2 persons and electricity	€ 18.00 - € 25.00
extra person	€ 3.50 - € 4.50
child (under 7 yrs)	€ 3.00 - € 4.00
dog	€ 1.50

Caudebec-en-Caux
Camping Barre Y Va

Route de Villequier, F-76490 Vilequier (Seine-Maritime) T: 02 35 96 26 38. E: campingbarreyva@orange.fr
alanrogers.com/FR76280

Camping Barre Y Va is a gem of a site, close to the riverside town of Caudebec-en-Caux with its attractive promenade and landing stage for the passing cruise ships. Across the road from the site, the River Seine is full of interest with all manner of shipping. The 70 pitches along the length of the site are on level grass and the 52 for touring, divided by small trees and bushes, all have 10A electricity. There is a special gravel area for motorcaravans, enabling use to the end of October. The friendly owners take great care of their customers and enjoy a chat in the bar in the evenings.

Facilities

Two older style unheated unisex toilet blocks with washbasins in cabins, preset showers and British style toilets (no seats). Facilities for disabled visitors. Washing machines, dryers and ironing board. Motorcaravan services. Bar and snack bar (all season). Bicycle hire. Play area. Volleyball. Minigolf. Tourist information. Mobile homes for rent. WiFi. Off site: Shops, bars and restaurants in Caudebec-en-Caux. Swimming pool and tennis adjacent (high season). Riding, sailing and boat launching 3 km. Walking and cycle trails. Rouen 38 km.

Open: 6 April - 26 October.

Directions

Site is midway between the village of Villequier and the town of Caudebec-en-Caux on the D81, alongside the River Seine. The entrance is narrow and larger units may have difficulty. Late arrivals have a dedicated fenced area 50 m. west of main entry. GPS: 49.521761, 0.702153

Charges guide

Per unit incl. 2 persons and electricity	€ 18.55 - € 22.80
extra person	€ 3.70 - € 4.50
child (2-7 yrs)	€ 2.45 - € 3.05
dog	€ 2.25 - € 2.65

For latest campsite news, availability and prices visit
alanrogers.com

We can book this site for you! alan rogers ◎ travel   Call 01580 214000

Courtils

Camping Saint-Michel

35 route du Mont Saint-Michel, F-50220 Courtils (Manche) T: 02 33 70 96 90.

E: infos@campingsaintmichel.com alanrogers.com/FR50110

This delightful site is located in a peaceful, rural setting, yet is only 8 km. from the busy tourist attraction of Mont Saint-Michel. The site has 100 pitches which include 43 for touring units and 30 for mobile homes to rent. Electricity connections (6A) are available to all pitches and many trees and shrubs provide a good amount of shade. From the restaurant and its terrace overlooking the pool, the site slopes gently down to a small enclosure of farm animals kept to entertain children and adults alike. Meet Nestor and Napoléon, the donkeys and Linotte the mare, as well as miniature goats, sheep, chickens and ducks. It is the intention of M. and Mme. Duschesne to maintain a quiet and peaceful site, hence there are no discos or organised clubs.

Facilities

Two small, well maintained toilet blocks have washbasins in cubicles and pushbutton showers. Separate laundry. Baby room. En-suite facilities for disabled visitors. Motorcaravan service point. Shop. Bar (15/3-15/10). Restaurant and takeaway (15/6-10/9). Heated swimming pool (1/5-20/9). Animal farm. Play area. Games room. Bicycle hire. Internet access and WiFi (free) in reception area. Off site: Fishing (sea) 2 km, (river) 6 km. Beach 2 km. and (for swimming) 30 km. Riding 9 km.

Open: 10 February - 11 November.

Directions

Courtils is 8 km. east of Mont Saint-Michel. From south on A84 and from north on A84/N175 leave at junction 33/34 and follow signs for Mont Saint-Michel (N175/D43) and Courtils. From Saint Malo take D137 south and join N176 east to Pontorson where it becomes N175. In 12 km. turn northwest on D43 signed Courtils. Site is through village on the left. GPS: 48.627616, -1.416

Charges 2012

Per unit incl. 2 persons	€ 19.00 - € 25.00
extra person	€ 5.00 - € 7.00

CAMPING SAINT MICHEL *

35 Route du Mont Saint Michel - 50220 Courtils
Tél: 0033 (0)2 33 70 96 90
infos@campingsaintmichel.com - www.campingsaintmichel.com

Etreham

Camping la Reine Mathilde

Route de Sainte Honorine, F-14400 Etreham/Bayeux (Calvados) T: 02 31 21 76 55.

E: campingreinemathilde@gmail.com alanrogers.com/FR14300

Camping la Reine Mathilde can be found at Etreham, close to the fine city of Bayeux, the D-Day beaches and the interesting fishing port of Port-en-Bessin. The site is in the grounds of a large stone farmhouse. The 76 touring pitches are grassy and of variable sizes. Most are equipped with electrical connections (6A). Fifty pitches are occupied by mobile homes, chalets and fully equipped bungalow-style tents, with 14 available for rent. The excellent Omaha Beach Golf Course (36 holes) is close at hand and Port-en-Bessin is an important centre for watersports. The cider and Calvados tastings are a must.

Facilities

All main facilities are housed in a converted stone outbuilding fronted by a piazza with tables and chairs. Baby changing and facilities for disabled visitors. Laundry room. Motorcaravan services. Shop. Bar, snack bar and takeaway. Heated swimming pool (1/6-15/9). Play area. Entertainment and activities (high season). Mobile homes and tents for rent. WiFi. Off site: Port-en-Bessin 4 km. Riding 3 km. Golf 4 km. Beaches 6 km.

Open: 1 April - 30 September.

Directions

Etreham can be found northwest of Bayeux. From there take the westbound N13 and leave shortly after Tour en Bessin, following signs to Etreham (D206). The site is well signed in the village. Continue through village to boundary sign, take first right and follow signs to site. GPS: 49.331316, -0.802447

Charges guide

Per unit incl. 2 persons	€ 21.70 - € 23.80
extra person	€ 5.80 - € 6.50

For latest campsite news, availability and prices visit

alanrogers.com

THE MERVILLE BATTERY

The Merville Battery, a German army strongpoint in the Atlantic Wall, was situated at the eastern flank of the allied invasion of 6 June 1944.
Bombed ineffectively many times, it was neutralised by the British 9th Parachute Battalion after an incredible attack.
On this totally preserved historic site, an educational trail winds between the different bunkers and invites you to learn the story of the Merville Battery.
Every 20 minutes, you can experience "total immersion". Sound, light smoke and odours will convey you for a few short minutes into the hell that was the bombardment and the attack on the Battery.

The 9th Battalion
The Parachute Regiment

MUSÉE DE LA BATTERIE DE MERVILLE
Place du 9è Bataillon
14810 MERVILLE-FRANCEVILLE
Tél : 02 31 91 47 53
E-mail : museebatterie@wanadoo.fr
Web : www.batterie-merville.com

Falaise
Camping Municipal du Château

3 rue du Val d'Ante, F-14700 Falaise (Calvados) T: 02 31 90 16 55. E: camping@falaise.fr

alanrogers.com/FR14100

The location of this site is really quite spectacular, lying in the shadow of the Château of William the Conqueror, within walking distance of the historic town of Falaise in the 'coeur de Normandie'. The site itself is small, with only 66 pitches (most with electricity) either beside the little river, on a terrace above or on gently sloping ground. With trees and hedges providing some shade as well as open grassed areas, this site has a rather intimate 'up-market' feel about it, different from the average municipal site.

Facilities

Although the sanitary facilities are dated, they are of good quality and kept clean. Free hot water to showers, washbasins in cubicles for the ladies and laundry and dishwashing sinks (all closed overnight). Unit for disabled visitors (shower room and separate WC). Motorcaravan service point. Excellent play area for younger children. Tennis courts and boules pitch. TV room. Fishing. Free WiFi access. Off site: Bicycle hire 300 m. Riding 500 m. Tree-top adventure park 17 km. Kayak club with canoe hire and river descent 19 km.

Open: 1 May - 30 September.

Directions

Falaise is 35 km. southeast of Caen on the route to Alençon and Le Mans. Site on western side of town, well signed from ring road. From N158 heading south take first roundabout into Falaise and follow site signs through suburb to site. Roads become one way and 0.6 km. from turn into the suburb, there is a 180º left-hand turn downwards; should you overshoot, continue until signage indicates the route back. GPS: 48.89556, -0.20468

Charges guide

Per unit incl. 2 persons and electricity	€ 16.60
extra person	€ 2.70 - € 3.80

Fiquefleur-Equainville
Camping du Domaine Catinière

Route de Honfleur, F-27210 Fiquefleur-Equainville (Eure) T: 02 32 57 63 51. E: info@camping-catiniere.com

alanrogers.com/FR27020

A peaceful, friendly site, close to the Normandy coast, in the countryside yet in the middle of a very long village, this site is steadily achieving a modern look, whilst retaining its original French flavour. In addition to 20 rental and 23 privately owned mobile homes, there are 87 pitches for touring units, plus a large open field for tents and units not needing electricity. Caravan pitches are separated, some with shade, others are more open and all have electricity hook-ups. The site is divided by well fenced streams, popular with young anglers. The site is a good base for visiting this part of Normandy. A Sites et Paysages member.

Facilities

Toilet facilities include mostly British style WCs, some washbasins in cubicles, and facilities for disabled visitors and babies. Washing machine and dryer. Reception with shop. Small bar/restaurant with regional dishes and snacks. Heated swimming pool with slides and flume (1/6-15/9). Two playgrounds. Trampoline. Children's farm. Boules. Barrier (card deposit). WiFi throughout (charged). Off site: Large supermarket close to southern end of the bridge. Smaller supermarket in Beuzeville 7 km. Beach 7 km. Golf 15 km.

Open: 6 April - 18 September.

Directions

From the Pont de Normandie (toll bridge). Take first exit on leaving bridge (exit 3, A29) signed Honfleur. At roundabout turn left under motorway in direction of Le Mans and Alencon on D180. Take second exit on right after about 2.5 km, onto D22 towards Beuzeville. Site is on right after about 1 km. GPS: 49.40090, 0.30608

Charges guide

Per unit incl. 2 persons and electricity	€ 20.00 - € 28.50
extra person	€ 4.00 - € 6.00
Credit cards accepted (minimum € 70).	

For latest campsite news, availability and prices visit

alanrogers.com

Hautot-sur-Mer

Camping la Source

Petit Appeville, F-76550 Hautot-sur-Mer (Seine-Maritime) T: 02 35 84 27 04. E: info@camping-la-source.fr
alanrogers.com/FR76040

This friendly, attractive site with a new heated pool is just four kilometres from Dieppe and is useful for those using the Newhaven-Dieppe ferry crossing, either as a one-night stopover or for a few days' break before heading on. The 120 pitches (54 with electricity 10A) are flat and there is some shade. There are good hardstandings for motorcaravans. The site is quietly located in a valley with the only disturbance from the occasional passing train. A fast-flowing small river runs along one border (not protected for young children). There are opportunities for fishing, rowing and canoeing.

Facilities

A good, clean single toilet block includes washbasins in cubicles and mainly British style WCs. Unit for disabled visitors but the unmade gravel roads may cause problems. Laundry. Motorcaravan service point. Small bar and terrace. Swimming pool. Playing field. TV and games rooms. Fishing. Bicycle hire. Mobile homes (3) for rent. WiFi throughout (charged). Off site: Baker in the village. Riding 2 km. Beach 3 km. Golf 4 km.

Open: 15 March - 15 October.

Directions

From Dieppe follow D925 west to Fécamp. At foot of descent at traffic lights in Petit Appeville turn left. From west, turn right (signed D153 Saint Aubin). Just after railway, turn left under bridge and ahead on narrow road (limited passing places). Site is shortly on left. GPS: 49.89846, 1.05694

Charges guide

Per unit incl. 2 persons	€ 20.70 - € 23.70

Camping Cheques accepted.

Honfleur

Camping la Briquerie

Equemauville, F-14600 Honfleur (Calvados) T: 02 31 89 28 32. E: info@campinglabriquerie.com
alanrogers.com/FR14180

La Briquerie is a large, neat municipal site on the outskirts of the attractive and popular harbour town of Honfleur. Very well cared for and efficiently run by a family team, the site has 420 pitches, many of which are let on a seasonal basis. There are also 130 medium to large, hedged touring pitches. All have electricity (5/10A), water and drainage. Among the main attractions here are the swimming complex with indoor and outdoor pools, and the close proximity to Honfleur where one can watch the fishing boats from the quay or browse the work of the artists who display their paintings in the galleries.

Facilities

The sanitary facilities were completely renovated in 2011. Good facilities for disabled visitors. Laundry room. Large restaurant (July/Aug). Takeaway (1/6-15/9). Bar (1/6-30/9). Small shop (July/Aug). Large pool complex with two flumes (7/4-30/9). Sauna. Jacuzzi. Fitness room. Boules. Minigolf. Astroturf multisports pitch. TV. Internet access and WiFi throughout. Off site: Supermarket 100 m. Bus stop 100 m. Town centre 2 km. Beach 2.5 km. Fishing 5 km.

Open: 31 March - 30 September.

Directions

Site is well signed from Honfleur on the D579, beside the Intermarché on the D62. GPS: 49.39735, 0.20849

Charges guide

Per unit incl. 2 persons, electricity, water and drainage	€ 21.00 - € 31.00
extra person	€ 5.00 - € 8.00

No credit cards.

Houlgate

Camping de la Vallée

88 rue de la Vallée, F-14510 Houlgate (Calvados) T: 02 31 24 40 69. E: camping.lavallee@wanadoo.fr
alanrogers.com/FR14070

Camping de la Vallée is an attractive site with good, well maintained facilities, situated on the rolling hillside above the seaside resort of Houlgate. The original farmhouse building has been converted to house a bar/brasserie and a comfortable TV lounge and billiards room overlooking the pool. The site has 373 pitches with 98 for touring units. Large, open and separated by hedges, all the pitches have 4 or 6A electricity and some also have water and drainage. Part of the site is sloping, the rest level, with gravel or tarmac roads. Shade is provided by a variety of well kept trees and shrubs.

Facilities

Three good toilet blocks include washbasins in cabins, mainly British style toilets, facilities for disabled visitors and baby bathrooms. Laundry facilities (no washing lines allowed). Motorcaravan services. Shop (from 1/5). Bar. Snack bar with takeaway in season (from 1/5). Heated swimming pool (1/4-31/10; no Bermuda shorts). Games room. Playground. Bicycle hire. Volleyball, football, tennis, pétanque. Entertainment in Jul/Aug. WiFi (charged). Only one dog per pitch. Off site: Riding 500 m. Town 1 km.

Open: 1 April - 30 September.

Directions

From A13 take exit for Cabourg and follow D400 to Dives-sur-Mer, then D513 (Hougate/Deauville) until you reach the seafront. After 1 km. at lights turn right and follow site signs to campsite on right in about 1 km. (No arrivals 12.00-14.00 in low season). GPS: 49.2940, -0.0683

Charges guide

Per unit incl. 2 persons	€ 21.00 - € 32.00
extra person	€ 5.00 - € 7.00

Camping Cheques accepted.

For latest campsite news, availability and prices visit
alanrogers.com

Jumièges
Camping de la Forêt

Rue Mainberthe, F-76480 Jumièges (Seine-Maritime) T: 02 35 37 93 43. E: info@campinglaforet.com

alanrogers.com/FR76130

This is a pretty family site with a friendly, relaxed atmosphere. It is located just 10 km. from the A13 Paris - Caen autoroute. Cars and smaller motorcaravans can approach by ferry across the River Seine (not caravans). Formerly a municipal site, it has recently been taken over by the Hoste family. The 111 grassy pitches (84 for tourers) are attractively located in woodland. Many pitches have some shade and all have 10A electrical connections. There is a separate area for tents. The site organises some activities in high season and these include treasure hunts and guided walks. Jumièges is just 600 m. away. The great abbey at Jumièges was founded in 654 by Saint Philibert, rebuilt by the Normans and consecrated in the presence of William the Conqueror – well worth a visit!

Facilities

Two toilet blocks, both of modern construction and maintained to a good standard with British toilets, some basins in cubicles and preset showers. Baby room. Facilities for disabled visitors. Laundry facilities. Motorcaravan service point. Shop. Baker calls daily. Pizzas on Friday and Saturday evenings 18.30 hrs. Small swimming pool and paddling pool (heated 1/6-15/9). Playground. Boules. Games room with TV. Bicycle hire. Chalets and mobile homes to let. Off site: Bar/restaurant 600 m. Rouen 20 km. Riding and golf 8 km.

Open: 11 April - 25 October.

Directions

From A29, junction 8, follow Yvetot - Pont de Brotonne. Before bridge, turn left and follow Le Trait and Jumièges. Site clearly signed.
GPS: 49.43487, 0.82897

Charges guide

Per unit incl. 2 persons	
and electricity	€ 21.00 - € 23.50
extra person	€ 4.50
child (under 7 yrs)	€ 2.00 - € 2.50
dog	free

Camping Cheques accepted.

Le Rozel
Camping le Ranch

La Mielle, F-50340 Le Rozel (Manche) T: 02 33 10 07 10. E: contact@camping-leranch.com

alanrogers.com/FR50230

Le Ranch is a pleasantly situated, family run site with direct access to a long and wide sandy beach that extends to some 3 km. The reception area is well presented and has a small shop that stocks all the basic provisions. An outdoor pool complex has a large heated pool, paddling pool and a small separate pool with water slides. The whole area is surrounded by clear screening and incorporates ample space with sun loungers for soaking up the sunshine. Access to site is controlled by a magnetic key, which is also used to activate the showers in the splendid sanitary block. Touring pitches are large and well defined by small hedges; some are on raised terraces but are easily accessed.

Facilities

One modern heated toilet block was spotlessly clean and had piped music. Sinks in closed cabins and showers operated by barrier entry key. Baby changing area. Facilities for disabled visitors. Excellent laundry and dishwashing area. Shop. Bar with TV, pizzeria (eat in or take away). Covered games area. Outdoor pool complex with heated pool, paddling pool and small pool with slides. Play area. Exercise machines. Boules. TV in bar. Barbecue areas. WiFi (charged). Off site: Restaurant by site entrance. Riding and bicycle hire 4 km. Two supermarkets at Les Pieux 7 km.

Open: 1 April - 30 September.

Directions

Heading to or from Cherbourg on D650, 3 km. South of Les Pieux take D62 signed Le Rozel. D62 leads directly to the site which is well signed.
GPS: 49.480199, -1.842055

Charges guide

Per unit incl. 2 persons	
and electricity	€ 21.60 - € 33.70
extra person	€ 4.50 - € 7.00
child (3-11 yrs)	€ 3.00 - € 5.00
dog	€ 2.10 - € 2.30

For latest campsite news, availability and prices visit
alanrogers.com

Les Loges
Camping l'Aiguille Creuse

F-76790 Les Loges (Seine-Maritime) T: 02 35 29 52 10. E: camping@aiguillecreuse.com

alanrogers.com/FR76160

L'Aiguille Creuse, not far from Le Havre and Dieppe, is named after a rock, alleged to be hollow, near Etretat. The site is set back from the Côte d'Albâtre in the village of Les Loges, only 10 km. from Fécamp. There are 89 good sized grassy pitches, slightly sloping in parts, of which 80 are for touring, all with 10A electricity. They are divided by neat hedges and some trees while the remaining nine are chalets for rent. The site, being three hectares, is left with lots of space for playing or just quiet enjoyment. The local shops and bar are within easy walking distance. The fishing port of Fécamp has many festivities connected with the sea as well as the Bénédictine distillery. The picturesque villages of Etretat and Yport were an attraction for the Impressionist painters of the late 19th century and have largely remained intact.

Facilities

Modern toilet block (2012) with unisex toilets (no seats), showers, washbasins in cubicles, baby changing and facilities for disabled visitors. Laundry. Motorcaravan services. Bar and snack bar (all season). Takeaway (July/Aug). Heated covered pool (15/4-15/9). WiFi (charged). Card-operated barrier. Off site: Local shops and bicycle hire 1 km. Beach, golf, riding, sailing, Etretat 5 km. Supermarket 7 km. Fécamp with banks, bars, restaurants and shops 10 km.

Open: 1 April - 30 September.

Directions

From Fécamp, take the D940 towards Etretat. Passing through Les Loges, site is well signed to the left. GPS: 49.698782, 0.275602

Charges guide

Per unit incl. 2 persons	
and electricity	€ 19.30 - € 23.30
extra person	€ 4.00 - € 5.50
child (2-6 yrs)	€ 2.30 - € 3.20
dog	€ 2.50 - € 3.00

Camping Cheques accepted.

Camping Airotel L'Aiguille Creuse***

On a preserved natural site, ideally situated at 5 km of the famous Etretat cliffs, we propose you to discover the Albatre coast in a very quiet family campsite.

Camping Airotel L'Aiguille Creuse*** - 24, résidence de l'Aiguille Creuse F - 76790 LES LOGES
Tel: 0033(0)2.35.29.52.10 - E-mail: camping@aiguillecreuse.com - **www.campingaiguillecreuse.com**

Been to any good campsites lately? **We have**

alan rogers

the BIG selection 2012

NEW 2012

The UK's market leading independent guides to the best campsites
Also available on iPad alanrogers.com/digital

Le Tréport
Camping Municipal les Boucaniers

Rue Pierre Mendès France, F-76470 Le Tréport (Seine-Maritime) T: 02 35 86 35 47.
E: camping@ville-le-treport.fr **alanrogers.com/FR76110**

This is a large, good quality, modern municipal site. It has an attractive floral entrance, tarmac roads and easy access to pitches. The 193 touring pitches (176 with electricity 6A: some long leads necessary) are on level grass, some with dividing hedges, with trees to provide a little shade. There are 50 good quality wooden chalets for rent, and some privately owned mobile homes. A small unit acts as shop, bar and takeaway all season, the baker calls daily in high season, and every day except Wednesday in low season. The town centre is within walking distance with a choice of many good seafood restaurants.

Facilities

Three well equipped sanitary blocks (the larger one can be heated) provide mainly British style WCs, washbasins in cubicles, preset hot showers, with facilities for small children and disabled visitors in one block. Multisports court. Minigolf. Boules. Max. 2 dogs. Motorcaravan parking and services adjacent (€ 5.00) Off site: Tennis, football and gym nearby. Fishing, golf and beach 2 km.

Open: 1 April - 30 September.

Directions

From D925 Abbeville - Dieppe road take D1915 towards Le Tréport centre. At new roundabout take first exit to right. Site is 150 m. on the right in rue Pierre Mendès-France. GPS: 50.05772, 1.38870

Charges guide

Per unit incl. 2 persons	
and electricity	€ 20.80 - € 22.20
extra person	€ 4.20 - € 4.80

Les Pieux
Camping le Grand Large

F-50340 Les Pieux (Manche) T: 02 33 52 40 75. E: info@legrandlarge.com
alanrogers.com/FR50060

Le Grand Large is a well established, quality family site with direct access to a long sandy beach and within a 20 km. drive of Cherbourg. It is a neat and tidy site with 132 touring pitches divided and separated by hedging giving an orderly, well laid out and attractive appearance. A separate area has 40 mobile homes for rent. The reception area is at the entrance (with a security barrier) and the forecourt is decorated with flower beds. To the rear of the site and laid out in the sandhills is an excellent play area with swings, slides and climbing frame. Not surprisingly the sandy beach is the big attraction. The length of units is restricted to eight metres to prevent any problems accessing pitches. Roads around the site are tarmac and many of the delightful plants and shrubs that you see bordering these carry name tags in four languages. The pleasant views from the site stretch across the bay to the tip of the Cherbourg peninsula. Every effort is made at le Grand Large to attract and cater for families with young children, so noisy entertainment is not an option. Most of the pitches have electricity (10A), water and drainage.

Facilities

Two well maintained toilet blocks (new showers in all cubicles planned). The main one includes washbasins in cubicles and some family rooms. WCs are mostly to the outside of the building. Provision for disabled visitors. Baby bathroom. Laundry area. Motorcaravan services. Shop for basics. Bar. Restaurant and takeaway (30/6-31/8). WiFi throughout (charged). Swimming and paddling pools (21/4-23/9). Play area. Tennis. Boules. Fishing. TV room. Some entertainment (July/Aug). Off site: Bicycle hire and riding 5 km. Golf 15 km. Supermarkets in Les Pieux.

Open: 7 April - 23 September.

Directions

From Cherbourg port take N13 south for about 2 km. Branch right on D650 (previously D904) signed Carteret. Continue for 18 km. to Les Pieux. Take the D4 in town, turn left just after supermarket. Follow site signs via D117/517. GPS: 49.49452, -1.84246

Charges guide

Per unit incl. 2 persons	
and electricity	€ 21.00 - € 36.00
extra person	€ 4.50 - € 7.50
Camping Cheques accepted.	

We can book this site for you! alanrogers ◑ travel
Call 01580 214000

F - 50340 LES PIEUX
CAMPING
Tél : 02 33 52 40 75 - Fax : 02 33 52 58 20 - Site Internet : Legrandlarge.com

For latest campsite news, availability and prices visit
alanrogers.com

We can book this site for you! Call 01580 214000 alan rogers ◉ travel

Luc-sur-Mer

Camping la Capricieuse

2 rue Brummel, F-14530 Luc-sur-Mer (Calvados) T: 02 31 97 34 43. E: info@campinglacapricieuse.com
alanrogers.com/FR14170

La Capricieuse is situated on the edge of the delightful, small, seaside town of Luc-sur-Mer. It is an ideal location for visiting the D-Day landing beaches, which are just a few minutes drive from the Ouistreham car ferry. This immaculate site has 204 touring pitches of varying sizes, most are on level grass with hedges and a variety of trees giving some shade. One hundred and five have electricity and 52 also have water and drainage. Although the site does not have its own shop, bar or restaurant, these can be found within walking distance in Luc-sur-Mer.

Facilities	Directions
Three modern toilet blocks with washbasins in cubicles and showers are kept very clean. Facilities for disabled visitors. Laundry facilities. Motorcaravan service point. Large TV room. Games room with WiFi. Adventure playground (unfenced). Tennis. Boules. Off site: Public transport outside gate. Fishing and bicycle hire nearby. Beach and watersports 200 m. Riding 3 km. Golf 30 km.	Take the D514 from Ouistreham car ferry and head west to Luc-sur-Mer. Campsite is well signed from the western end of St Luc. GPS: 49.31797, -0.35780

Open: 1 April - 30 September.

Charges guide

Per unit incl. 2 persons and electricity	€ 21.25

Martragny

Castel Camping le Château de Martragny

F-14740 Martragny (Calvados) T: 02 31 80 21 40. E: chateau.martragny@wanadoo.fr
alanrogers.com/FR14030

Martragny is an attractive site in the parkland of a château. Close to D-Day beaches and Bayeux, it is convenient for the ports of Caen and Cherbourg, and has the facilities and charm to encourage both long stays and stopovers. The pleasant lawns surrounding and approaching the château take 160 units, with electricity connections (10A). Most pitches are divided by either a small hedge or a few trees. Bed and breakfast accommodation is available in the château (reservation essential). The de Chassey family ensure you can enjoy the peace and calm of their home with a glass of wine in the lovely courtyard.

Facilities	Directions
Three modernised sanitary blocks include washbasins in cabins, showers, sinks for dishwashing and laundry, and two baby baths. Disabled visitors are well catered for. Good laundry. Shop (all season). Bar, brasserie and takeaway (24/5-10/9). Swimming pool (20x6 m) and paddling pool heated in poor weather. Play areas. Tennis. Minigolf. Games and TV room. Fishing pond. WiFi. Off site: Riding 1 km. Bayeux Tapestry 8 km. Fishing 12 km. D-Day Beaches 15 km. Golf 20 km.	From Caen on N13 take exit for Martragny, ignore turning to village. Continue for 100 m, site signed on right. From Bayeux (8 km) on N13, follow exit signs for Martragny, at D82B turn left (ignore village sign), on for 100 m. as above. GPS: 49.24941, -0.60237

Open: 1 May - 12 September.

Charges guide

Per unit incl. 2 persons	€ 29.50 - € 33.50
extra person	€ 6.50 - € 7.50
Camping Cheques accepted.	

Maupertus-sur-Mer

Castel Camping Caravaning l'Anse du Brick

Route du Val de Saire, F-50330 Maupertus-sur-Mer (Manche) T: 02 33 54 33 57.
E: welcome@anse-du-brick.com **alanrogers.com/FR50070**

A friendly, family site, l'Anse du Brick overlooks a picturesque bay on the northern tip of the Cotentin peninsula, eight kilometres east of Cherbourg port. This quality site with its pleasing location offers direct access to a small sandy beach and a woodland walk. This is a mature, terraced site with magnificent views from certain pitches. Tarmac roads lead to the 117 touring pitches (all with 10A electricity) which are level, separated and mostly well shaded by many trees, bushes and shrubs.

Facilities	Directions
New sanitary facilities are kept spotlessly clean and are well maintained. British style toilets, washbasins mainly in cubicles and push button showers. Provision for disabled visitors. Laundry area. Motorcaravan service point. Shop (1/4-30/9). Restaurant and bar/pizzeria (1/5-10/9). Heated swimming pool (all season). Tennis. Play area. Organised entertainment in season. Miniclub (6-12 yrs). Bicycle and kayak hire. WiFi throughout (charged). Off site: Fishing 100 m. Riding 4 km. Golf 10 km.	From Cherbourg port follow signs for Caen and Rennes. After third roundabout, take slip road to right, under road towards Bretteville-en-Saire (D116). From southeast on N13 at first (Auchan) roundabout, take slip road to right towards Tourlaville (N13 car ferry), ahead at next roundabout, right at third lights on D116 to Bretteville. Continue for 7 km. Site signed to north. GPS: 49.66715, -1.48704

Open: 1 April - 30 September.

Charges 2012

Per unit incl. 2 persons	€ 21.90 - € 39.60
extra person	€ 4.50 - € 8.00

For latest campsite news, availability and prices visit
alanrogers.com

Merville-Franceville
Camping les Peupliers

Allée des Pins, F-14810 Merville-Franceville (Calvados) T: 02 31 24 05 07. E: asl-mondeville@wanadoo.fr
alanrogers.com/FR14190

Les Peupliers is run by friendly, family managers who keep this site attractive and tidy. It is just 300 metres from a long, wide, sandy beach. The touring pitches, of which there are 85, are on level open ground, all with 10A electricity. Those in the newest part are hedged but, with just a few trees on the edge of the site, there is little shade. The campsite amenities are near the entrance, housed in modern buildings. An animation programme for children and various activities are organised in high season. This site is ideally located for visiting Caen, Bayeux and the seaside towns of Deauville and Trouville.

Facilities

Two excellent heated toilet blocks with washbasins in cabins and showers. Good facilities for disabled visitors and for babies. Laundry room. Small shop, bar with terrace and takeaway (all July/Aug). Heated outdoor swimming pool and paddling pool (May-Sept). Play area. Games room. Entertainment in high season. WiFi. Off site: Public transport 400 m. Fishing, riding and golf all within 1 km. Bicycle hire 2 km.

Open: 1 April - 31 October.

Directions

From Ouistreham take the D514 to Merville-Franceville. Site is well signed off Allée des Pins. From Rouen on A13 (exit 29B), take D400 to Cabourg then the D514 to Merville-Franceville. GPS: 49.28326, -0.17053

Charges guide

Per unit incl. 2 persons and electricity	€ 20.10 - € 26.80
extra person	€ 5.55 - € 6.90

Merville-Franceville
Camping le Point du Jour

Route de Cabourg, F-14810 Merville-Franceville-Plage (Calvados) T: 02 31 24 23 34.
E: camp.lepointdujour@wanadoo.fr **alanrogers.com/FR14210**

Camping le Point du Jour has a very French flavour and is an ideal location for family holidays as it has direct access to a fine sandy beach. There are 142 pitches bordered by shrubs and hedging, including 20 occupied by mobile homes and chalets (10 for hire). Although there are quite a few seasonal units, most have to be removed for high season. All touring pitches have 10A electricity, including those on the sea-dyke looking down onto the beach. Facilities are simple, but there is a smart new heated pool with retractable roof. Fishing is possible from the beach and small boats may be launched.

Facilities

Two toilet blocks (one heated) provide washbasins in cubicles, pushbutton showers, and fairly basic facilities for babies and for disabled visitors. Laundry facilities. Motorcaravan service points. All-purpose room has small bar (serving basic drinks and snacks except in very low season), projector for films and football matches, pool table and exercise machines. Play area. Bicycle hire. Bread delivery. Entertainment and activities in high season. Internet and WiFi in reception area. Off site: Fishing 0.5 km. Shops, bars and restaurants all within 2 km.

Open: 1 March - 15 November.

Directions

Merville-Franceville is 17 km. northeast of Caen. From A13 motorway at junction 29 take D400 towards Dives-sur-Mer and bear left on D400a to Cabourg. Follow signs for Merville-Franceville along D514. Site is on right in 2 km. From Ouistreham Car Ferry (16 km) follow signs for Caen and turn east on D514 over Pegasus Bridge and through Merville to site on left. GPS: 49.28319, -0.19098

Charges guide

Per unit incl. 2 persons	€ 20.00 - € 29.40
extra person	€ 4.80 - € 7.80

Pont-Audemer
Camping Caravaning des Etangs Risle-Seine

19 route des Etangs, Toutainville, F-27500 Pont-Audemer (Eure) T: 02 32 42 46 65.
E: camping@ville-pont-audemer.fr **alanrogers.com/FR27010**

This attractive and well maintained site is owned by the Pont-Audemer local authority and run by an enthusiastic manager. It is well laid out with 61 hedged pitches on level grass and electricity for 28 of them. Fishing and watersports are possible as the site is positioned next to some large lakes, but swimming is not allowed. In high season a shuttle bus goes to Pont-Audemer where you will find shops, restaurants and a good swimming complex.

Facilities

Two well equipped and maintained toilet blocks with facilities for disabled visitors. They include washbasins in cabins and pre-set showers. Laundry facilities. Bar area with terrace (soft drinks only as there is no alcohol licence, visitors may bring their own). Bread and milk available. Playing field. TV. Bicycle hire. Fishing. Takeaway and courtesy bus (high season). Accommodation available. Off site: Pont-Audemer swimming complex.

Open: 15 March - 15 November.

Directions

Approaching from north or south on D810, at the bridge over the River Risle, turn to the west on south side of river and travel 1.5 km. on rue des Etangs. Site is well signed. GPS: 49.3666, 0.48739

Charges guide

Per unit incl. 2 persons and electricity (10A)	€ 16.70 - € 18.10
extra person	€ 3.15

For latest campsite news, availability and prices visit
alanrogers.com

We can book this site for you! alan rogers ◑ travel   Call 01580 214000

Pontorson
Kawan Village Haliotis

Chemin des Soupirs, F-50170 Pontorson (Manche) T: 02 33 68 11 59. E: camping.haliotis@wanadoo.fr
alanrogers.com/FR50080

The whole staff at this beautiful campsite offer a warm welcome to visitors. Situated on the edge of the little town of Pontorson, the site has 152 pitches, including 118 for touring units. Most have electricity (16A) and 34 really large ones also have water and drainage. Excellent private sanitary facilities are available on 12 'luxury' pitches. The comfortable reception area incorporates a pleasant bar, opening onto the swimming pool terrace. The site is attractively laid out and includes a Japanese garden. Haliotis (which takes its name from a large shell) is next to the river Couesnon and it is possible to walk, cycle and canoe along the river to Mont Saint-Michel, 9 km. away. An auberge at half-distance could provide a welcome break! A good bus service is available to all major towns in the area.

Facilities

Well equipped heated toilet block with controllable showers and washbasins in cubicles. Good facilities for disabled visitors incorporating baby room. Laundry facilities. Bar where breakfast is served. Bread to order. Outdoor heated swimming pool (1/5-30/9) with jacuzzi and separate paddling pool. Sauna and solarium. Fenced play areas. Trampoline. Pétanque. Archery. Games room. Tennis. Golf practice range. Multisports court. Outdoor fitness equipment. Bicycle hire. River fishing. Japanese garden and animal park. Club for children. Internet access in bar and WiFi throughout. Off site: Large supermarket, bars, restaurants and takeaways within easy walking distance. Riding 3 km. Golf 20 km. Beach 30 km.

Open: 16 March - 11 November.

Directions

Pontorson is 22 km. southwest of Avranches and is bypassed by the N176 which links with D137 from Saint Malo to the west and (via N175) with A84 (Caen - Rennes) to the east. Site is 300 m. north of the town centre and is well signed. NB. Entrance is on rue du Général Patton. Satnav users should follow signs! GPS: 48.55836, -1.51429

Charges 2012

Per unit incl. 2 persons	
and electricity	€ 19.50 - € 25.50
with individual sanitary facility	€ 25.00 - € 31.00
extra person	€ 5.00 - € 6.00

Camping Cheques accepted.

Camping - Caravaning - Cottages ★★★

At 9 km of Mont Saint Michel, cycle track starting at the camp-site, heated pool, jacuzzi, sauna, mini farm..

Camping Qualité   La Clef Verte

www.camping-haliotis-mont-saint-michel.com

CAMPING ★★★ **HALIOTIS** Chemin des Soupirs 50170 PONTORSON
Tel : (33) 02 33 68 11 59 Fax : (33) 02 33 58 95 36 E-mail : camping.haliotis@wanadoo.fr

Pont-l'Evêque
Castel Camping du Brévedent

Le Brévedent, F-14130 Pont-l'Evêque (Calvados) T: 02 31 64 72 88. E: contact@campinglebrevedent.com
alanrogers.com/FR14090

Le Brévedent is a well established, traditional site with 144 pitches (109 for tourists, 31 used by tour operators) set in the grounds of an elegant 18th-century hunting pavilion. Pitches are either around the fishing lake, in the lower gardens (level), or in the old orchard (gently sloping). Most have electricity. It is an excellent holiday destination within easy reach of the Channel ports and its peaceful, friendly environment makes it ideal for mature campers or families with younger children (note: lake is unfenced).

Facilities

Three toilet blocks include washbasins in cubicles and facilities for disabled visitors. One has been refurbished with en-suite cubicles. Laundry facilities. Motorcaravan service point. Shop. Bar (evenings). Restaurant (15/5-19/9). Takeaway (1/5-25/9). Clubroom. TV and library. Heated swimming and paddling pools (1/5-25/9, unsupervised). Playground. Minigolf. Boules. Fishing. Rowing. Bicycle and buggy hire. Organised excursions. Entertainment and children's club (high season). WiFi. No dogs accepted. Off site: Riding 1 km. Beach 25 km.

Open: 28 April - 23 September.

Directions

Pont-l'Evêque is due south of Le Havre. Le Brévedent is 13 km. southeast from Pont-l'Evêque: take D579 toward Lisieux for 4 km. then D51 towards Moyaux. At Blangy le Château continue ahead on D51 to Le Brévedent. GPS: 49.22525, 0.30438

Charges guide

Per unit incl. 2 persons	
and electricity	€ 21.00 - € 31.10
extra person	€ 5.00 - € 8.00

For latest campsite news, availability and prices visit
alanrogers.com

Port-en-Bessin

Sunêlia Port'land

Chemin du Castel, F-14520 Port-en-Bessin (Calvados) T: 02 31 51 07 06. E: campingportland@wanadoo.fr

alanrogers.com/FR14150

We can book this site for you! Call 01580 214000   alan rogers ◉ travel

The Gerardin family will make you most welcome at Port'land, now a mature site lying 700 m. to the east of the little resort of Port-en-Bessin, one of Normandy's busiest fishing ports. The 300 pitches are large and grassy with 202 available for touring units, including 128 with 15A electricity. There is a separate area for tents without electricity. The camping area has been imaginatively divided into zones, some overlooking small fishing ponds and another radiating out from a central barbecue area. An attractive modern building houses reception and the good amenities which include a shop and a bar/restaurant with fine views over the Normandy coastline. In peak season a range of entertainment is organised including disco and karaoke evenings, and a range of children's activities. A coastal path leads to the little town, and the nearest beach (the sandy Omaha Beach) is 4 km. There are ten site-owned mobile homes for rent. A member of the Sunelia Group.

Facilities	Directions
The two sanitary blocks are modern and well maintained. Special disabled facilities. Heated swimming pool (covered in low season) and paddling pool. Bar, restaurant, takeaway (all open all season). Large TV and games room. Multisports pitch. Fishing. Play area. WiFi. Off site: 27-hole Omaha Beach International Golf Course adjacent. Fishing 600 m. Nearest beach 4 km. Bicycle hire and riding 10 km. D-Day beaches. Colleville American war Cemetery. Bayeux.	Site is clearly signed off the D514, 4 km. west of Port-en-Bessin. GPS: 49.3463, -0.7732

Open: 1 April - 3 November.

Directions

Site is clearly signed off the D514, 4 km. west of Port-en-Bessin. GPS: 49.3463, -0.7732

Charges guide

Per unit incl. 2 persons	
and electricity	€ 20.50 - € 32.00
extra person	€ 5.00 - € 8.00
child (2-10 yrs)	€ 3.00 - € 5.00
dog	€ 3.00

Reductions for stays over 7 nights.

Port'land is situated at the heart of the Normandy beaches.

Ideal for visiting the D.Day sites and only 10km from the world famous UNESCO site «The Bayeux Tapestry»

Chemin du Castel - 14520 Port-en-Bessin - Tel : 0033 (0)2.31.51.07.06 - Fax : 0033 (0)2.31.51.76.49
Email : campingportland@wanadoo.fr - Site : www.camping-portland.com

Pourville-sur-Mer

Camping le Marqueval

1210 rue de la Mer, F-76550 Pourville-sur-Mer (Seine-Maritime) T: 02 35 82 66 46.
E: contact@campinglemarqueval.com **alanrogers.com/FR76010**

Le Marqueval is a well established, family site of 290 pitches, located close to the seaside town of Hautot-sur-Mer, just west of Dieppe. The site has been developed around three small lakes (one unfenced, suitable for fishing). There are 60 grass pitches for touring units, all of a good size, separated by hedges and 40 with electrical connections (6A). The majority of the pitches here are used for privately owned mobile homes. Leisure amenities include a swimming pool and smaller children's pools. The site's bar also functions as a snack bar and during the high season evening entertainment is occasionally organised here.

Facilities	Directions
The single toilet block is at the entrance to the site. Motorcaravan service point (charged). Snack bar. Swimming pool. Fishing (charged). Playground. Entertainment and activity programme. Mobile homes for rent. Off site: Nearest beach 1.2 km. Riding 1.5 km. Tennis. Cycle and walking tracks. Dieppe 5 km. St Valery-en-Caux (fishing port). Supermarket in Dieppe.	Head west from Dieppe on the D925 as far as Hautot-sur-Mer. Then turn right onto the D153 towards Pourville. Site is well signed from here. GPS: 49.9088, 1.0406

Open: 17 March - 15 October.

Charges guide

Per unit incl. 2 persons	
and electricity	€ 16.50 - € 23.50
extra person	€ 4.00 - € 7.00
child (under 7 yrs)	€ 3.00 - € 4.00

For latest campsite news, availability and prices visit
alanrogers.com

Call 01580 214000 We can book this site for you! alan rogers ◖ travel

Ravenoville-Plage
Kawan Village le Cormoran

2 le Cormoran, F-50480 Ravenoville Plage (Manche) T: 02 33 41 33 94. E: lecormoran@wanadoo.fr
alanrogers.com/FR50050

This welcoming, environmentally friendly, family run site, close to Cherbourg and Caen, is situated just across the road from a long sandy beach. It is also close to Utah beach and is ideally located for those wishing to visit the many museums, landing beaches and remembrance gardens of WW2. On flat, quite open ground, the site has 110 good size pitches on level grass, all with 6/10A electricity (Europlug). Some extra large pitches are available. The well kept pitches are separated by mature hedges and the site is decorated with flowering shrubs. A covered pool, a sauna and a gym are among recent improvements. This modern, clean and fresh looking campsite caters for both families and couples and would be ideal for a holiday in this interesting area of France. The country roads provide opportunities for exploring on foot or by bike. There are many small towns in the area and in early June, you may find historical groups re-enacting battles and the events of 1944-1945. There is a large enclosure of pygmy goats where children are encouraged to mingle. A dedicated entrance is provided for large American units and a hard stand area for motorcaravans. Car hire is now available on site.

Facilities

Four toilet blocks, three heated, are of varying styles and ages but all are maintained to a good standard. Laundry facilities. Shop. Bar and terrace. Snacks and takeaway. Outdoor pool (1/6-15/9, unsupervised). New covered pool, sauna and gym (all season). Play areas. Tennis. Boules. Entertainment, TV and games room. Billiard golf. Playing field, archery (July/Aug). Hairdresser. Masseuse. Bicycle and shrimp net hire. Riding (July/Aug). Communal barbecues. BMX park. WiFi (charged). Off site: Beach 20 m. Sand yachting. Golf 3 km. Ste-Mère-Eglise 9 km.

Open: 7 April - 29 September.

Directions

From N13 take Ste. Mère-Eglise exit and in centre of town take road to Ravenoville (6 km), then Ravenoville-Plage (3 km). Just before beach turn right and site is 500 m. GPS: 49.46643, -1.23533

Charges 2012

Per unit incl. 2 persons and electricity	€ 21.00 - € 33.00
extra person	€ 4.00 - € 7.90
child (5-10 yrs)	€ 2.00 - € 3.00

Camping Cheques accepted.

Camping Le Cormoran****

2, Rue du Cormoran - 50480 Ravenoville-Plage - France
Tel: 0033 233 41 33 94 - fax: 0033 233 95 16 08
E-mail: lecormoran@wanadoo.fr - www.lecormoran.com

covered heated pool

Saint Arnoult
Camping la Vallée de Deauville

Avenue de la Vallée, F-14800 Saint Arnoult (Calvados) T: 02 31 88 58 17. E: contact@camping-deauville.com
alanrogers.com/FR14200

Close to the traditional seaside resorts of Deauville and Trouville, this large, modern site is owned and run by a delightful Belgian couple. With a total of 450 pitches, there are many mobile homes, both for rent and privately owned, and 150 used for touring units. These pitches are level, of a reasonable size and mostly hedged, and 60 have 10A electricity connections. A new pool complex complete with flumes, lazy river, jacuzzi and fun pool makes an attractive focal point near the entrance and there is a large fishing lake. The bar and restaurant are large and comfortable and there is a very good shop on the site.

Facilities

Two heated toilet blocks with showers and washbasins in cubicles. Good facilities for babies and disabled visitors. Laundry facilities. Small shop, bar and restaurant (high season). Takeaway (all season). New swimming pool complex. Good play area and play room. Entertainment in high season. WiFi (charged). Off site: Golf and riding 2 km.

Open: 1 April - 31 October.

Directions

From the north, take the A29, then the A13 at Pont l'Eveque. Join the N177 (Deauville/Trouville) and after 9 km. take the D27 signed St Arnoult. Site is well signed on edge of village. GPS: 49.32864, 0.086

Charges guide

| Per unit incl. 2 persons | € 20.40 - € 34.00 |
| extra person | € 5.40 - € 9.00 |

For latest campsite news, availability and prices visit
alanrogers.com

Saint Aubin-sur-Mer
Yelloh! Village la Côte de Nacre

Rue du Général Moulton, F-14750 Saint Aubin-sur-Mer (Calvados) T: 02 31 97 14 45.
E: info@yellohvillage-cote-de-nacre.com **alanrogers.com/FR14010**

La Côte de Nacre is a large, popular, commercial site with many facilities, all of a high standard. It is an ideal holiday location for families. Two thirds is given over to mobile homes and there are four tour operators on the site. The 149 touring pitches are reasonable, both in size and condition, all having 10A electricity. With pleasant, well cared for flowerbeds, there is some hedging and a few trees. A state- of-the-art heated pool complex includes both open and covered (sliding roof) areas, slides, whirlpools and water jets, and on a hot day becomes the focal point of the campsite. The small seaside town of Saint Aubin-sur-Mer with its delightful promenade is only a few minutes away.

Facilities

The toilet block, with modern black and grey décor, provides toilets and showers, washbasins in cubicles, and a large room for toddlers and babies. Facilities for disabled visitors. Dishwashing and laundry room. Motorcaravan services. Grocery with fresh bread baked on site. Bar, restaurant and takeaway. Pool complex. Hammam, sauna, dry and humid heat, body treatments. Play area for young children with bouncy castle and climbing frames. Multisports pitch. Synthetic skating rink. Games room. Bicycle hire. Children's clubs and mini-discos. Entertainment. WiFi. Mobile homes for rent. Off site: Town 1 km. Pegasus Bridge 16 km. Bayeux 25 km.

Open: 30 March - 23 September.

Directions

Travel west from Ouistreham on D514 to Saint Aubin-sur-Mer. Site is well signed, to the left, just off the main road in a residential area. Take care as signage is small and you are in an urban area with no turning back. GPS: 49.322333, -0.387333

Charges guide

Per unit incl. 2 persons	
and electricity	€ 23.00 - € 44.00
extra person	€ 5.00 - € 8.00
child (3-7 yrs)	free - € 5.00
dog	€ 4.00

Saint Pair-sur-Mer
Castel Camping le Château de lez Eaux

Saint Aubin des Préaux, F-50380 Saint Pair-sur-Mer (Manche) T: 02 33 51 66 09. E: bonjour@lez-eaux.com
alanrogers.com/FR50030

Set in the spacious grounds of a château, lez Eaux lies in a rural situation just off the main route south, under two hours from Cherbourg. There are 229 pitches of which 113 are for touring, all with electricity (10A Europlug) and 84 fully serviced. Most of the pitches are of a very good size, partly separated by trees and shrubs on either flat or very slightly sloping, grassy ground overlooking Normandy farmland or beside a small lake (with carp and other fish). There is a considerable tour operator presence, but these units by no means dominate, being generally tucked away in their own areas. This is a very pleasant location from which to explore this corner of the Cotentin peninsula.

Facilities

Three modern clean toilet blocks include hot showers and washbasins in cabins, facilities for children and babies, and for disabled visitors. Shop, small bar, snacks and takeaway (all from 1/5). Small heated swimming pool and indoor tropical-style fun pool (from 1/5, no T-shirts or Bermuda-style shorts). Play area. Tennis. Games and TV rooms. Bicycle hire. Lake fishing. Cash machine at reception. Torches useful. Internet access and WiFi (charged). Only one dog per pitch. Off site: Beach 4 km. Riding 5 km. Golf 7 km.

Open: 30 March - 18 September.

Directions

Lez Eaux is just to the west of the D973 about 17 km. northwest of Avranches and 7 km. southeast of Granville. Site is between the two turnings east to St Aubin des Préaux and well signed. GPS: 48.79778, -1.52498

Charges guide

Per unit incl. 2 persons	
and electricity	€ 20.00 - € 49.00
extra person	€ 8.00
child (under 7 yrs)	€ 6.00
dog	free

For latest campsite news, availability and prices visit
alanrogers.com

Saint Symphorien-le-Valois

Camping l'Etang des Haizes

43 rue Cauticotte, F-50250 Saint Symphorien-le-Valois (Manche) T: 02 33 46 01 16.

E: info@campingetangdeshaizes.com **alanrogers.com/FR50000**

This is an attractive and very friendly site with a swimming pool complex that has a four-lane slide, jacuzzi and a paddling pool. L'Etang des Haizes has 160 good sized pitches, of which 100 are for touring units, on fairly level ground and all with electricity (10A). They are set in a mixture of conifers, orchard and shrubbery, with some very attractive, slightly smaller pitches overlooking the lake and 60 mobile homes inconspicuously sited. The fenced lake has a small beach (swimming is permitted), with ducks and pedaloes, and offers good coarse fishing for huge carp (we are told!). There are good toilet and shower facilities where children and campers with disabilities are well catered for. Monsieur Laurent, the friendly owner of the site, who speaks excellent English, has recently had an outdoor fitness park installed consisting of eight different pieces of equipment all designed to exercise different parts of the body in the fresh air. This is a good area for walking and cycling and an eight kilometre round trip to experience the views from Le Mont de Doville is a must. Just one kilometre away is La Haye-du-Puits with two supermarkets, restaurants and a market on Wednesdays. A good sandy beach is within 10 km. at Bretville sur Ay and in July and August you can try your hand at archery or water polo.

Facilities

Two well kept and modern unisex toilet blocks have British style toilets, washbasins in cabins, units for disabled visitors, and two family cabins. Small laundry. Motorcaravan services. Milk, bread and takeaway snacks available (no gas). Snack bar/bar with TV and terrace. Swimming pool complex (all amenities 26/5-2/9). Play areas. Bicycle hire. Pétanque. Organised activities including treasure hunts, archery, water polo and food tasting (5/7-25/8). Well stocked tourist information cabin. WiFi (charged). Off site: Riding 1 km. Beach, kayaking and Forest Adventure 10 km. Walking (routes are well signposted). Cycling. Normandy landing beaches 30 km.

Open: 1 April - 15 October.

Directions

Site is just north of La Haye-du-Puits on the primary route from Cherbourg to Mont St-Michel, St Malo and Rennes. It is 24 km. south of N13 at Valognes and 29 km. north of Coutances: leave D900 at roundabout at northern end of bypass (towards town). Site signed on right.
GPS: 49.300413, -1.544775

Charges guide

Per unit incl. 2 persons and electricity	€ 16.00 - € 37.00
extra person (over 4 yrs)	€ 5.00 - € 7.00
dog	€ 1.00 - € 2.00

Camping Cheques accepted.

Camping Caravaning

★★★★

L'étang des Haizes

Club Airotel

A very relaxing atmosphere with a fantastic swimming pool the lake is a wonderful attraction and excellent facilities

In between Nature Park and a Lovely Coast with sandy beaches

Camping L'étang des Haizes

Tél. : 0033 233 460 116
Fax : 0033 233 472 380
St-Symphorien-le-Valois
F 50250 LA HAYE DU PUITS
in NORMANDY

Http:/www.campingetangdeshaizes.com
Email: info@campingetangdeshaizes.com

Création 3D © 02 97 41 69 42

For latest campsite news, availability and prices visit
alanrogers.com

Saint Vaast-la-Hougue
Camping la Gallouette

10 bis rue de la Gallouette, F-50550 Saint Vaast-la-Hougue (Manche) T: 02 33 54 20 57.
E: contact@camping-lagallouette.fr **alanrogers.com/FR50010**

Claudine and Jean Luc Boblin will give you a warm welcome at their seaside campsite which is ideally placed for visiting Barfleur, Ste. Mère-Eglise and the Normandy landing beaches. There are 176 level pitches in total, 111 of which are for touring and all have 6/10A electricity. Some are separated by hedges and there are many colourful flower beds, shrubs and trees but little shade. A light and airy bar faces onto a terrace and swimming pool and there is also a state-of-the-art multisports court. The site is close to the cross-channel ferry terminal at Cherbourg. Saint Vaast-la-Hougue is a busy fishing port with freshly caught fish on sale and a good choice of fish restaurants. Just a couple of hundred yards from the site on a Saturday morning finds you in the midst of a bustling, traditional French market. A regular bus service from near the site entrance will take you to most of the surrounding areas including Barfleur and Cherbourg. For those wanting to take a leisurely stroll there is a pleasant walk along the raised sea wall to Fort de la Hougue which can be seen from the site. Whilst motorcaravans are welcome on grass pitches, there is a dedicated area within the site for approximately 16 to overnight on hardstanding with access to all facilities at a reduced rate.

Facilities

Three modern sanitary blocks, one open and two enclosed, have British style toilets, showers and washbasins (some in cabins). Area for disabled visitors and for babies. Laundry facilities. Small shop. Snack bar. Bar with terrace. Swimming pool. Multisports court. Play area. Pétanque. WiFi throughout (charged). Entertainment in high season. Off site: Beach 300 m. Shops and restaurant in St Vaast. Riding 5 km. Golf 12 km. Fishing. Sailing. Boat trips to Ile de Tatihou.

Open: 1 April - 30 September.

Directions

The D902 runs between Barfleur and Valognes on the eastern side of the Cherbourg peninsula. About half way along at Quettehou take the D1 to St Vaast. Site signed on right on entering town. GPS: 49.58400, -1.26783

Charges guide

Per unit incl. 2 persons and electricity (6A)	€ 19.40 - € 26.70
extra person	€ 4.60 - € 6.20

Camping La Gallouette ★★★★

10 bis rue de la Gallouette 50550
Saint Vaast la Hougue
Tel 02.33.54.20.57
Fax 02.33.54.16.71
contact@camping-lagallouette.fr

La Gallouette is a family campsite, situated at 400 m of the fishing and trading port, in between the two towers of Vauban, which are listed as UN world heritage.

Cotentin,
ce pays comme une île...

www.lagallouette.com

Saint Valery-en-Caux
Camping Municipal d'Etennemare

Hameau d'Etennemare, F-76460 Saint Valery-en-Caux (Seine-Maritime) T: 02 35 97 15 79
alanrogers.com/FR76090

This comfortable, neat site is two kilometres from the picturesque harbour and town, 30 km. west of Dieppe. Quietly located, it has 116 pitches of which 49 are available for touring units. The grassy pitches are all on a slight slope, with electricity (6/10A), but there is very little shade. Reception is open all day in July and August, but in low season is closed 12.00-15.00 daily and all day Wednesday: there is a card-operated security barrier. Not far from Fécamp, with its Benedictine Distillery – indeed, the chalky cliffs along this coast were made famous by the many artists and sculptors who visited here in the late 1800s.

Facilities

Two modern, clean and well maintained sanitary buildings are side by side, one containing showers and the other toilets, with open and cubicle washbasins and facilities for disabled visitors. Both blocks are heated in winter. Dishwashing and laundry sinks. Washing machines. Small shop (July/Aug). Playground. Off site: Hypermarket 1.5 km. Harbour and pebble beach 2 km.

Open: All year.

Directions

From Dieppe keep to D925 Fécamp road (not through town). At third roundabout turn right on D925E towards hypermarket. From Fécamp turn left on D925E as before. Take first right (site signed) to site on left in 1 km. GPS: 49.8585, 0.7046

Charges guide

Per unit incl. 2 persons and electricity	€ 14.90
extra person	€ 3.05

For latest campsite news, availability and prices visit
alanrogers.com

Sainte Marie-du-Mont
Flower Camping Utah Beach

F-50480 Sainte Marie-du-Mont (Manche) T: 02 33 71 53 69. E: utah.beach@wanadoo.fr
alanrogers.com/FR50140

This family-run campsite has a very French atmosphere. It is very well cared for with landscaped areas, flowerbeds and shrubs. Pitches (32 for touring) are quite generous in size and separated by hedges on mainly level ground. All have electricity connections (6A). Situated in an area full of history, the site's main attraction is probably its very close proximity to Utah beach (just 50 m). On site a very good sports facility is provided including a BMX field. You will also be able to enjoy a delightful, well stocked aviary and just 500 m. away you'll find a museum.

Facilities

One well equipped and clean sanitary block provides British style toilets, washbasins in cabins and showers. Baby bath. Laundry facilities. Shop. Bar, restaurant and takeaway. Motorcaravan service point. Swimming pool (15/5-30/9). Multisports court. Play area (unfenced). Volleyball. Tennis. Games room. Aviary. Entertainment in high season. WiFi. Off site: Bicycle hire and golf 15 km.

Open: 1 April - 20 September.

Directions

From the N13 south of Sainte Mère-Église take D70 west to Sainte Marie-du-Mont, then D913 to the coast. Turn left on D421 coast road and site is 500 m. on left. GPS: 49.41931, -1.18058

Charges guide

Per unit incl. 2 persons and electricity	€ 21.00 - € 25.50

Servon
Campéole Saint Grégoire

Campé·le

47 rue Saint Grégoire, F-50170 Servon (Manche) T: 02 33 60 26 03.
E: saint-gregoire@campeole.com **alanrogers.com/FR50190**

This small rural site is simple and well cared for. Modestly sized pitches are in groups of three or four with very little indication of pitch boundaries. Shrubs and well trimmed hedges are planted throughout. Twenty nine of the 72 pitches are occupied by chalets and mobile homes. One building houses all of the facilities which are modern, bright and of a high standard. The site is now managed by a young couple who work hard to ensure the comfort of their visitors. It would particularly suit families with very young children. Le Mont Saint-Michel is a 20 minute drive and well worth a visit. Do remember that this is one of the tourist Meccas of France and a visit outside of July/August is recommended. A little further away, the old port of Saint Malo is splended, with many restaurants where you can enjoy the local seafood. Dinan and Dinard are also popular destinations.

Facilities

One modern sanitary block has washbasins in cabins and controllable showers. Baby room. Very good facilities for disabled visitors. Washing machine. Takeaway (July/Aug). Small swimming pool (7/4-15/9). Boules. Play area (3-8 yrs). WiFi. Torches required. Off site: Several beaches can be reached by car. Le Mont Saint-Michel. Saint Malo. Avranches.

Open: 1 April - 22 September.

Directions

On the RN175 from Avranches towards Saint Malo, take exit for Servon on the right. Site is on the right in 200 m. GPS: 48.59703, -1.41316

Charges guide

Per unit incl. 2 persons and electricity	€ 15.10 - € 20.40
extra person	€ 4.00 - € 6.90
child (2-6 yrs)	free - € 3.90

Campé·le

CAMPSITES AND RENTALS

Saint Grégoire ★★★
At 8 kilometers of the Mont Saint-Michel.
Pitches and accommodations
of high quality, with swimming pool.

NORMANDIE

50170 Servon - Tel.: +33-233-6026-03 - www.campeole.co.uk / saint-gregoire@campeole.com

Torigni-sur-Vire

Camping le Lac des Charmilles

Route de Vire, F-50160 Torigni-sur-Vire (Manche) T: 02 33 56 91 74.
E: contact@camping-lacdescharmilles.com **alanrogers.com/FR50170**

The very friendly new owners have recently acquired this former municipal site and have already made some outstanding changes. Situated next to a lake on the outskirts of Torigni-sur-Vire and surrounded by farmers' fields, the 39 touring pitches are divided by mature hedges giving plenty of privacy. Additions have included an exceptional new bar and restaurant with an attractive wooden terrace, a new sanitary block providing the most modern facilities and a multisports court along with trampolines and bouncy castle. Although lacking some facilities, this small rural site makes this a great choice if visiting this area. This is a delightful campsite set in the heart of the Normandy countryside, it is only 1 km. from the nearby village of Torigni-sur-Vire, which makes it ideal for those who do not wish to drive all the time. A nearby lake offers canoeing, kayaks and a vélorail. Avranches, Le Mont Saint-Michel and Saint Malo are all within driving distance for a day's excursion.

Facilities

Two sanitary blocks including one new central block with excellent facilities including those for disabled visitors. Bar/restaurant with full menu and takeaway. Outdoor swimming pool (heated 15/6-15/9). TV, table tennis, go-karts, pétanque, multisports court, trampoline, bouncy castle. Motorcaravan service point. Large units accepted. WiFi (1st hour free). Off site: Fishing 200 m. Village with shops, bars, banks etc. 1 km. Canoes 5 km. Riding 13 km. Golf 30 km. Beaches of Normandy 45 mins.

Open: 1 April - 15 October.

Directions

Exit the A84 Caen - Rennes motorway at junction 40 and head north on the N174 towards Saint Lô. The site is on your right just before you enter the town of Torigni-sur-Vire. GPS: 49.02851, -0.97190

Charges guide

Per unit incl. 2 persons	
and electricity	€ 18.00 - € 24.90
extra person	€ 3.50 - € 4.50
child (0-6 yrs)	€ 2.90 - € 4.00
dog	€ 1.50

Camping Cheques accepted.

Camping le Lac des Charmilles*
Route de Vire - 50160 Torigni sur Vire
Tel: 0033 (0) 233 569 174 - contact@camping-lacdescharmilles.com
www.camping-lacdescharmilles.com

Camping des Chevaliers*
2 Impasse Pré de la Rose - 50800 Villedieu-les-Poêles
Tel: 0033 (0) 233 610 244 - contact@camping-deschevaliers.com
www.camping-deschevaliers.com

Veules-les-Roses

Camping les Mouettes

Avenue Jean Moulin, F-76980 Veules-les-Roses (Seine-Maritime) T: 02 35 97 61 98.
E: contact@camping-lesmouettes-normandie.com **alanrogers.com/FR76060**

Les Mouettes is set back from the cliffs, with the pretty seaside resort of Veules-les-Roses below. It is a busy site, attracting many visitors en route from Dieppe. There are 152 pitches in total but many are occupied by mobile homes and seasonal caravans, leaving only 82 for touring, all with 6A electricity, and 21 for tents without electricity. They are level, grassy and divided by hedges, but have no shade. The narrow roads may cause difficulty for larger units. A special area for 16 motorcaravans is by the entrance. The site is open for a longer season and may be useful for those travelling south for winter.

Facilities

Toilet facilities are in a central group of buildings and provide separate male and female facilities, and those for disabled visitors. Washbasins in cubicles, showers, toilets (no seats) and baby changing. Motorcaravan services. Covered heated swimming pool (15/4-15/10). Play area. Games room. Bicycle hire. Tourist information. WiFi (charged). Off site: Village and beach 300 m. Tennis. Walking and cycle trails. Cinema, shops and restaurants.

Open: 1 April - 4 November.

Directions

Veules-les-Roses is west of Dieppe. From there, head west on the D925 towards St Valery-en-Caux. On arrival at town sign for Veules-les-Roses, site is immediately on left. GPS: 49.876239, 0.802935

Charges guide

Per unit incl. 2 persons	
and electricity	€ 18.80 - € 25.50
extra person	€ 3.70 - € 5.40
child (5-10 yrs)	€ 2.60 - € 3.60

Touques-Deauville
Camping des Haras

Chemin du Calvaire, F-14800 Touques-Deauville (Calvados) T: 02 31 88 44 84.
E: campingdesharas@orange.fr alanrogers.com/FR14270

Les Haras is located in Touques, just outside the stylish resort of Deauville. This is a mature site with grassy and well shaded pitches. A number of mobile homes are available for rent. Leisure amenities include a heated pool (July and August) with a separate children's pool and spa bath. There is a bar and snack bar, with many other restaurants in nearby Deauville. The sandy beaches of Deauville and its neighbour, Trouville, are deservedly renowned and are likely to be the main appeal here. The site is open for a long season and may appeal as a short break destination. The Duke of Morny, half brother of Napoleon III, founded Deauville in 1861 and inaugurated the Deauville - La Touques race course in 1864, even before the church was built! The resort quickly grew around the race course and is still one of the most important in France. Indeed, les Haras translates as a stud farm. Golf is also popular here and the Barrière club has a fine location, overlooking the town.

Facilities	Directions
Bar and snack bar. Swimming pool and children's pool. Playground. Games room. Mobile homes for rent. Off site: Shops and restaurants in Deauville and Trouville. Golf. Riding.	Site is south of Trouville. Approaching from A132 motorway, continue on D677 towards Trouville and Deauville. On reaching Touques, take eastbound D62 (Route d'Honfleur) and the site is well signed. GPS: 49.349567, 0.111711
Open: 1 March - 30 October.	

Charges guide

Per unit incl. 2 persons and electricity	€ 20.00 - € 35.00
extra person	€ 5.50 - € 9.00

Near Deauville, 2 km from the beaches, visit us to enjoy the panoramic view of the country of Auge with their horses in the green meadows. You will appreciate the peace and the serinity of a raised and spacious campsite where the family can enjoy the life in fresh-air, with good activities, facilities and various possibilities the regio offers you.

Chemin du Calvaire · F-14800 Touques · Deauville · France
Tél: +33 231 88 44 84 · contact@camping-des-haras.com
www.camping-des-haras.com

Villedieu-les-Poêles
Flower Camping les Chevaliers

2 impasse Pré de la Rose, F-50800 Villedieu-les-Poêles (Manche) T: 02 33 61 02 44.
E: contact@camping-deschevaliers.com alanrogers.com/FR50180

This pleasant site is situated less than a five minute walk from the attractive and interesting town of Villedieu-les-Poêles with its history of metalwork shops and foundries. There are five museums to visit, three of which are close by. This former municipal site has undergone extensive modernisation. So far the sanitary facilities have been renovated, a heated (15/6-15/9) outdoor swimming pool added, and a new bar/restaurant with terrace. The 80 touring pitches are separated by low hedges and there are many mature trees giving plenty of shade. There are plenty of electrical connections (8A). A small river runs alongside the site which is safely fenced with gate access.

Facilities	Directions
Two sanitary blocks provide adequate facilities. One main block situated behind reception has all modern facilities, the other centrally located with toilets and sinks only. Shop. Bar and restaurant with terrace. Takeaway snacks and pizzas. Heated swimming pool (15/6-15/9). Multisports court. Purpose-built skateboard park. Playground with trampoline and bouncy castle. Go-karts and bicycle hire. WiFi (charged). Off site: Shops, bars, restaurants in town 500 m.	From the A84 Rennes - Caen motorway, take exit 37 and head east on the D524 to Villedieu-les-Poêles. Follow signs for the Office de Tourisme and continue on, keeping the Office and Post Office on the left. The campsite is 200 m. on the left. GPS: 48.83665, -1.21697
Open: 1 April - 15 October.	

Charges guide

Per unit incl. 2 persons and electricity	€ 18.00 - € 24.90
extra person	€ 3.50 - € 4.50
child (0-6 yrs)	€ 2.90 - € 4.00

For latest campsite news, availability and prices visit
alanrogers.com

Vimoutiers
Camping Municipal la Campière

Boulevard du Docteur Dentu, F-61120 Vimoutiers (Orne) T: 02 33 39 18 86. E: mairie.vimoutiers@wanadoo.fr

alanrogers.com/FR61010

This small, well kept site is situated in a valley on the northern side of the town, which is on both the Normandy cheese and cider routes. Indeed the town is famous for its cheese and has a Camembert Museum, five minutes walk away. Fifteen minutes by car, at Mont-Ormel, the events of the Falaise Gap are brought vividly to life. The 36 pitches here are flat and grassy, separated by laurel hedging and laid out amongst attractive and well maintained flower and shrub beds. There is some shade around the perimeter and all pitches have electricity. Also, there are four mobile homes to rent.

Facilities

The single central sanitary block is clean and heated, providing open washbasins, good sized, well designed showers, children's toilets and a bathroom for disabled visitors. Dishwashing and laundry facilities under cover. Off site: Tennis courts and a park adjacent. Large supermarket 300 m. Restaurant and shops in town. Watersports facilities and riding 2 km.

Open: 1 April - 30 October.

Directions

Site is on northern edge of town, signed from main Lisieux - Argentan road next to large sports complex. GPS: 48.93245, 0.19609

Charges guide

Per unit incl. 2 persons and electricity	€ 13.80
extra person	€ 3.30
child (0-10)	€ 2.00
dog	€ 1.50

Reductions for 7th and subsequent days.

Yport
Flower Camping la Chênaie

Rue Henry Simon, F-76111 Yport (Seine-Maritime) T: 02 35 27 33 56. E: camping.yport@flowercampings.com

alanrogers.com/FR76170

La Chênaie, part of the Flower Camping group, is set in a wooded valley, just 1 km. from the traditional fishing village of Yport, renowned for its fishermen's houses and beautiful 19th-century villas. Of the 114 pitches, 50 are for touring and the rest are wooden chalets and FreeFlower tents, all for rent. The touring pitches are on open level grass with no shade, so may not offer the privacy some may require. All have 6A electricity. The nearby village of Etretat, with its famous chalk cliffs, inspired the paintings of Claude Monet and Gustave Courbet. Only 6 km. east is the much larger fishing town of Fécamp with many festive activities connected with the sea, a haven for thousands of small vessels, plus all the usual commercial facilities. The Benedictine Distillery needs no further introduction.

Facilities

Modern toilet block with toilets, washbasins in cubicles and showers. Facilities for babies and disabled visitors. Laundry. Dishwashing. Heated covered pool (all season). Games room and play area. Communal barbecue. WiFi (charged). Off site: Local shops, bars, restaurants in village. Fishing 1 km. Riding 4 km. Bicycle hire, sailing and boat launching 5 km. Golf 10 km.

Open: 1 April - 15 October.

Directions

Yport is located between Etretat and Fécamp. From Fécamp (42 km. NE of Le Havre), take the D940 southwest for 5 km, turn right on the D104 towards Yport. Site is on left in 1 km. GPS: 49.732805, 0.320682

Charges guide

Per unit incl. 2 persons and electricity	€ 13.90 - € 23.90
extra person	€ 3.00 - € 5.00
child (2-7 yrs)	€ 2.00 - € 3.00
dog	€ 2.00

Want independent campsite reviews at your fingertips?

NOW ON ANDROID TOO

alan rogers

Available on the App Store

Download for Android

An exciting **FREE** app for both iPhone and Android

alanrogers.com/apps

Nord-Pas de Calais

Nord-Pas de Calais, with its lush countryside and market towns, is much more than just a stopover en-route to or from the ports. The peaceful, rural, unspoilt charms of the region provide a real breath of fresh air.

DÉPARTEMENTS: 59 NORD, 62 PAS DE CALAIS

MAJOR CITIES: LILLE AND ARRAS

Nord-Pas de Calais is jam-packed with history, culture, seaside resorts and bustling towns and cities. A region known for its hospitality, it most recently found fame among the French as the setting for the box office hit comedy 'Bienvenue chez les Ch'tis', mocking northern and southern stereotypes while portraying the region as the friendly and welcoming place that it is.

Nord-Pas de Calais offers a large range of sporting activities, a variety of landscapes and historic sites and museums that will captivate all visitors. Stay for a day or for a week, within a few hours you could be a million miles from home. This is a region where good living is an everyday event.

It is certainly a region that will surprise and delight: traditional fairs and festivals where you too can join in the fun; long, sandy expanses of coast where you can try your hand at sand-yachting, the undulating countryside with its lush, green meadows and vivid blue and yellow fields of flax and rapeseed, bustling towns with their colourful markets and festive night life, and of course a warm welcome everywhere.

Tourism in
Nord-Pas de Calais

www.**northernfrance-tourism.com**

Places of interest

Lille
For shopping and culture.

The Opal Coast
Cap Blanc Nez and Cap Gris Nez and
seaside resorts.

Arras
Its squares and Flemish architecture.

Boulogne-sur-Mer
Nausicaa: unique sea centre offers insights
into the world's seas and oceans.

Roubaix
Museum La Piscine, fashion design and
outlet centres.

Avesnois
Le Quesnoy and the Regional Natural Park.

Saint-Omer
Audomarois Marshland.

Le Cateau-Cambrésis
Matisse Museum.

Lewarde
Coalmine museum.

Cassel
French Flanders hills, new Flanders Museum.

Cuisine of the region

In the Nord-Pas de Calais region, you
can enjoy good French gastronomy as
well as regional dishes that must be tasted
in typical regional restaurants, called
'estaminets'. Cheese, beers, sweets…
the region has plenty to offer gourmets.

Hochepot: A thick Flemish soup with virtually
everything in it but the kitchen sink.

Carbonade flamande: Beef in a beer and
gingerbread sauce served with French fries.

Waterzooï: A cross between soup and stew,
usually of fish or chicken.

Langue de Lucullus: Foie gras with thin slices
of ox tongue.

Maroilles and Vieux Lille: cheeses.

Waffles

Images © Xavier Alphand, Eric Desaunois

Boiry-Notre-Dame
Camping la Paille Haute

145 rue de Sailly, F-62156 Boiry-Notre-Dame (Pas-de-Calais) T: 03 21 48 15 40.
E: la-paillehaute@wanadoo.fr alanrogers.com/FR62080

Quietly situated in a small village overlooking beautiful countryside, yet easily accessed from the A1, A2 and A26 autoroutes, this is an ideal overnight stop on your holiday route whilst also a great base for exploring the Flemish city of Arras with its underground tunnels, begun in the 10th century and used in both world wars; the battlefields of the Somme and the Thiépval Memorial. Of the 149 pitches, 60 are for touring on level grass and all with 6/10A electricity. The friendly owner has worked hard over the years expanding and developing this site to what it is today. Northern France is often overlooked by holidaymakers but is full of folklore and traditions.

Facilities

One modern, basic unisex toilet block. Extra toilets by pool. One toilet/shower room for disabled visitors. Washing machine and dryer under canopy. Motorcaravan service point. Swimming pool (1/6-15/9). Poolside bar, snacks and pizza oven (15/6-15/9). TV in bar. Fishing pond. Playground. Boules. WiFi. Entertainment (in season). Off site: Supermarket 500 m. Riding 10 km. Golf 15 km. WW1 Canadian memorial at Vimy Ridge.

Open: 1 April - 31 October.

Directions

From A1 take exit 15 and D939 southeast. After 3 km. turn left for Boiry-Notre-Dame and follow camping signs to site. GPS: 50.273533, 2.948667

Charges guide

Per unit incl. 2 persons	
and electricity (6A)	€ 20.00 - € 23.50
extra person	€ 2.50 - € 3.50
child (under 7 yrs)	€ 2.00 - € 2.50

For latest campsite news, availability and prices visit

alanrogers.com

Buysscheure
Camping Caravaning la Chaumière

529 Langhemast Straete, F-59285 Buysscheure (Nord) T: 03 28 43 03 57.
E: camping.LaChaumiere@wanadoo.fr **alanrogers.com/FR59010**

This is a very friendly, pleasant site, in the département du Nord with a strong Flanders influence. There is a real welcome here. Set just behind the village of Buysscheure, the site has 29 touring pitches separated by trees and bushes. Each pair shares a light, electricity connections, water points and rubbish container. Access from narrow site roads can be difficult, although once on site there are several pitches available for extra large units. A small, fenced fishing lake contains some large carp. A bonus is that Bernadette works for the local vet and can arrange all the documentation for British visitors' pets.

Facilities

Modern unisex toilet facilities are simple and small in number, with two WCs, one shower and one washbasin cabin. Facilities for disabled visitors may also be used (a toilet and separate washbasin/shower room). Laundry facilities. Motorcaravan services. Basic chemical disposal. Bar (daily) and restaurant (weekends only, all day, in season). Dog exercise area. Heated outdoor pools (July/Aug). Play area. Minigolf. Archery. Fishing. WiFi (free). Off site: Local market (Monday) at Bergues. St Omer. Beach 30 km. Lille 60 km.

Open: 1 April - 30 September.

Directions

From Dunkirk ferry take D300 south (St Omer). From Calais take N43 (St Omer) for 25 km. Just beyond Nordausques take D221 left (Watten). In Watten turn left for centre, then right on D26 (Cassel). Soon after Lederzeele site signed to right. On reaching Buysscheure turn left, then right, site signed. Single track road with bend. GPS: 50.80152, 2.33924

Charges guide

Per unit incl. 2 persons	€ 19.00 - € 20.00
extra person	€ 8.00
No credit cards.	

Camiers
Village Center la Dune Blanche

Route d'Etaples, F-62176 Camiers (Pas-de-Calais) T: 03 21 09 78 48. E: contact@village-center.com
alanrogers.com/FR62210

Camping la Dune Blanche is a member of the Village Center group and can be found between Le Touquet and Hardelot. This is a spacious site extending over 20 hectares, encompassing a lake (suitable for fishing) and well shaded by pine trees. There are 353 pitches here, most with electrical connections. There are also a small number of mobile homes to rent. This is a quiet site in low season, but livelier in July and August, with an activity and entertainment programme for all ages. The nearest beach is 3 km. distant and a shuttle service is available in peak season.

Facilities

Bar/snack bar. Takeaway. Swimming pool. Play area. Entertainment and activity programme. Archery. Tennis. Fishing. Canoeing. Tourist information. Mobile homes for rent. Off site: Nearest beach 3 km. Shops and restaurants in Le Touquet. Golf. Riding. Boulogne-sur-Mer (aquarium).

Open: 2 February - 30 November.

Directions

Approaching from the north (Boulogne), leave A16 motorway at the Le Touquet/Etaples exit and head north on D940. The site is well signed before you reach St Gabriel Plage. GPS: 50.55844, 1.618295

Charges 2012

Contact the site for details.

Condette
Caravaning du Château d'Hardelot

21 rue Nouvelle, F-62360 Condette (Pas-de-Calais) T: 03 21 87 59 59. E: campingduchateau@libertysurf.fr
alanrogers.com/FR62040

Within about 15 minutes drive of Boulogne and only five minutes by car from the long sandy beach at Hardelot, this modern site has 70 pitches with around 50 for touring units, the rest occupied by long stay or units to rent. Pitches are of varying size on level grass, all with access to electricity (10A). Hedging plants between the pitches are maturing well and there is shade from mature trees around the site. With friendly and accommodating owners, this site provides a useful overnight stop, but is also an excellent base for longer stays. British visitors enjoy the welcome they receive here and return year after year.

Facilities

Modern sanitary facilities in two small units (one heated) include large hot showers and baby bath (all spotless). Laundry facilities (washing machine and dryer). Motorcaravan services. Excellent playground and entertainment for children in season. Small fitness room. WiFi (charged). Off site: English-run pub/restaurant within walking distance. Fishing 800 m. Riding 1 km. Bicycle hire, golf and boat launching 3 km.

Open: 1 April - 31 October.

Directions

South of Boulogne, take N1 Amiens (Paris) road, then on the outskirts take right fork for Le Touquet-Paris Plage (D940). Continue for about 5 km. passing a garage and signs for Condette, then right at new roundabout. Continue to next roundabout and turn right again. Site entrance (narrow) is on the right after a short distance. GPS: 50.6466, 1.6256

Charges guide

Per unit incl. 2 persons	€ 20.20 - € 26.00
extra person	€ 5.00 - € 6.00
No credit cards.	

For latest campsite news, availability and prices visit
alanrogers.com

Call 01580 214000 We can book this site for you!

alan rogers ⊚ travel

Eperlecques

Kawan Village Château du Gandspette

133 rue de Gandspette, F-62910 Eperlecques (Pas-de-Calais) T: 03 21 93 43 93.
E: contact@chateau-gandspette.com **alanrogers.com/FR62030**

This spacious family run site, in the grounds of a 19th-century château, conveniently situated for the Channel ports and tunnel, provides overnight accommodation together with a range of facilities for longer stays. There are 110 touring pitches, all with electric hook-ups, intermingled with 20 privately owned mobile homes and caravans, with a further 18 for hire. Pitches are delineated by trees and hedging. Mature trees form the perimeter of the site, through which there is access to woodland walks. The WW2 'Blockhaus' nearby is worthy of a visit, as is La Coupole at Saint Omer, which also dates from WW2 and is equally fascinating. There is a market at Watten on Fridays and at Saint Omer on Saturdays.

Facilities

Two sanitary blocks with a mixture of open and cubicled washbasins. Good facilities for disabled visitors and babies. Laundry facilities. Motorcaravan service point. Bar, grill restaurant and takeaway (all 1/5-15/9). Swimming pools (15/5-15/9). Playground. Multisports court. Tennis. Pétanque. Children's room. Entertainment in season. WiFi in bar area (charged). Off site: Supermarket 1 km. Fishing 3 km. Riding and golf 5 km. Beach 30 km.

Open: 1 April - 30 September.

Directions

From Calais follow D943 (St Omer) for 25 km. Southeast of Nordausques take D221 (east). Follow site signs for 5-6 km. From St Omer follow D943 to roundabout at junction with D300. Turn right on D300 (Dunkirk). After 5 km. turn left on D221. Site is 1.5 km. on right. From Dunkirk ferry follow signs for St Omer D300. At Watten roundabout exit right (Gandspette) following site signs.
GPS: 50.81924, 2.17753

Charges guide

Per unit incl. 2 persons and electricity (6A)	€ 18.00 - € 28.00
extra person	€ 5.00 - € 6.00
child (3-6 yrs)	€ 3.00 - € 4.00

Camping Cheques accepted.

Escalles

Camping les Erables

17 rue du Château d'Eau, F-62179 Escalles (Pas-de-Calais) T: 03 21 85 25 36.
E: boutroy-les.erables@wanadoo.fr **alanrogers.com/FR62200**

This small site on the Cote d'Opale is very convenient for the Calais ferries and Eurotunnel as well as being just a few minutes from the A16. The 41 pitches are terraced and set on open ground separated by low privet hedging. There is some shade around the perimeter and all pitches have electricity (6A Europlug). Just two kilometres from the beach, the pitches have spectacular views over the coast towards the Channel, Cap Blanc-Nez and the English coastline. Some pitches have a hardstanding area for motorcaravans. With few facilities or activities for children, this site is perhaps better suited to those who appreciate peace and quiet. The gate is closed 22.00-08.00 and no vehicle can enter the site during lunch break 12.00-14.00.

Facilities

One small toilet block, heated in low season, has British style toilets, washbasins and pushbutton showers in cubicles. Facilities for disabled visitors. Washing machine and dryer. Motorcaravan service point. No shop, but bread available to order. Caravan storage. Ice packs frozen. Off site: Shops, bar and restaurant in village. Beach 1.5 km. Golf 3 km. Boat launching and sailing 4 km. Fishing and bicycle hire 5 km. Riding 8 km. Coastal Walks. Cité de l'Europe 15 km.

Open: 1 April - 11 November.

Directions

Leave A16/E402 at Junction 40. Join D243 west bound. After passing the village sign, take the second turning on the left. Watch out for small site sign at road junction. The site entrance is approx. 300 yds. on the left. N.B. Turn left when leaving the site. GPS: 50.91229, 1.72047

Charges guide

Per unit incl. 2 persons and electricity	€ 16.00
extra person	€ 3.50
child (5-12 yrs)	€ 2.50

Credit Cards not accepted.

For latest campsite news, availability and prices visit

alanrogers.com

Guînes

Castel Camping Caravaning la Bien-Assise

D231, F-62340 Guînes (Pas-de-Calais) T: 03 21 35 20 77. E: castels@bien-assise.com

alanrogers.com/FR62010

A mature and well developed site, the history of la Bien-Assise goes back to the 1500s. There are 198 grass pitches mainly set among mature trees with others on a newer field. Connected by gravel roads and of a good size (up to 300 sq.m), shrubs and bushes divide most of the pitches. Being close to Calais, the Channel Tunnel exit and Boulogne, makes it a good stopping point en-route, but it is well worth a longer stay. The site can have heavy usage at times (when maintenance can be variable). Used by tour operators (40 pitches).The château, farm and mill form the focal point for this popular campsite.

Facilities

Three well equipped toilet blocks provide many washbasins in cabins, mostly British style WCs and provision for babies, laundry and dishwashing. The main block is in four sections, two unisex. Motorcaravan service point. Shop. Restaurant. Bar/grill and takeaway (evenings from 1/5). TV room. Pool complex (1/5-20/9) with toboggan, covered paddling pool and outdoor pool. Play areas. Minigolf. Tennis. Bicycle hire. Only gas and charcoal barbecues are allowed. WiFi (charged). Off site: Riding 3 km. Fishing 8 km. Beach 12 km.

Open: 30 March - 26 September.

Directions

From ferry or tunnel follow signs for A16 Boulogne. Take exit 11 (Frethun, Gare TGV) and RD215 (Frethun). At first roundabout take third exit (Guines). Pass under the TGV. In Frethun take RD246 (Guines and St Tricat) and at roundabout take exit for Guines. Pass through St Tricat and Hames Boucres, and in Guines follow site signs. GPS: 50.86632, 1.85698

Charges guide

Per unit incl. 2 persons and electricity	€ 23.00 - € 32.50
extra person	€ 4.50 - € 6.50

Le Portel

Village Center le Phare

2 rue de la Mer, F-62480 Le Portel (Pas-de-Calais) T: 03 21 31 69 20. E: contact@village-center.com

alanrogers.com/FR62220

Camping le Phare is a member of the Village Center group and is located to the south of Boulogne-sur-Mer, with easy access to an excellent sandy beach. There are 88 touring pitches on this eight-hectare site, most of which have electrical connections. There are also around 14 mobile homes to rent. Le Phare comes to life in the high season with an activity and entertainment programme for all ages. On-site amenities include a shop and bar (all season). A wide range of restaurants, cafés and shops are available in nearby Boulogne, is a lively town with a number of notable monuments.

Facilities

Shop. Bar/snack bar. Takeaway food. Children's play area. Entertainment and activity programme. Tourist information. Mobile homes for rent. Off site: Swimming pool. Beach. Shops and restaurants in Boulogne. Golf. Riding.

Open: 1 April - 30 September.

Directions

Approaching from the north (Boulogne), leave the A16 motorway at the Boulogne exit and head south on N1 and then D236 following signs to Outreau and Le Portel. The site is well signposted from Le Portel. GPS: 50.704055, 1.566303

Charges 2012

Contact the site for details.
Camping Cheques accepted.

Licques

Camping les Pommiers des 3 Pays

273 rue du Breuil, F-62850 Licques (Pas-de-Calais) T: 03 21 35 02 02. E: contact@pommiers-3pays.com

alanrogers.com/FR62190

This delightful site, close to Channel ports and A26 and A16 autoroutes, on the outskirts of Licques, is in the beautiful Boulonnais countryside. Of the 58 level, grassy pitches, 20 are for touring, all with 16A electricity and some fully serviced. Motorcaravans are especially welcome. The pretty brasserie caters for dining and takeaway in pleasant surroundings near the pool. There is a small, fenced play area for children. A longer stay enables visits to the beaches of the Opal Coast, and many sites of both World Wars, Dunkirk and Ypres for example.

Facilities

One toilet block with British style toilets, showers, washbasins, baby changing and a separate facility for disabled visitors. A second block with toilets only. Laundry facilities. Bar/restaurant/snack bar (1/4-15/10). Small heated swimming pool (25/4-15/9). Children's play area. Children's activities (July/Aug). TV/games room. Chalets and mobile homes to rent. WiFi. Off site: Supermarket 1 km. Larger shops and vet at Ardres 10 km. Golf 22 km.

Open: 15 March - 15 November.

Directions

From Calais to Ardres on D943, turn left at traffic lights then, after 200 m, right on D224 and follow to Licques. Take D191 and site is on left in 1 km. GPS: 50.779825, 1.947707

Charges guide

Per unit incl. 2 persons and electricity	€ 19.30 - € 23.30
extra person	€ 4.20 - € 5.50
child (2-10 yrs)	€ 3.20 - € 3.50

For latest campsite news, availability and prices visit

alanrogers.com

Wimereux

Camping l'Eté Indien

Hameau Honvault, F-62930 Wimereux (Pas-de-Calais) T: 03 21 30 23 50. E: ete.indien@wanadoo.fr

alanrogers.com/FR62120

L'Eté Indien is a new site located near the resort of Wimereux, a little to the north of Boulogne. It offers a quiet and tranquil environment in which to enjoy your holiday – apart from some train noise (every 30 minutes, daytime only). Pitches for touring and camping are furthest from the entrance and vary in size. All have electrical connections (10A). In keeping with its Wild West theme, there is a small village of four Indian 'teepees' for rent, as well as more conventional mobile homes and chalets. The swimming pool and children's pool are a fair distance from the touring pitches. Other amenities include a fishing pond and a snack bar, Le Jardin de l'Eté Indien. The site lies at the heart of the Côte d'Opale, which boasts over 130 km. of coastline. Wimereux is an old-fashioned resort with plenty of shops and restaurants, and is renowned as a centre for kite surfing and speed sailing. This is an ideal stopover for Calais, Dunkerque or Boulogne.

Facilities

Two toilet blocks include facilities for babies and disabled visitors. Laundry. Small shop. Bar. Snack bar and takeaway. Motorcaravan services. Swimming pool. Children's pool. Play area with trampoline. Boules. Games room. Internet access and WiFi. Fishing pond. Off site: Wimereux, Le Touquet, Boulogne and the Nausicaa museum. Cité de l'Europe shopping complex at Calais. Beach 1 km. Riding adjacent. Golf 1.5 km.

Open: All year.

Directions

From the A16 take exit 32 (Wimereux) and follow signs to Wimereux (D96 and D940). After 1.5 km. turn right. Site is well signed from here and is located on the left, close to a riding centre. Approach is rather narrow, with speed ramps and is poorly surfaced. GPS: 50.75142, 1.60728

Charges guide

Per unit incl. 2 persons	
and electricity	€ 16.00 - € 23.00
extra person	€ 4.00 - € 6.00
child (2-7 yrs)	€ 3.00 - € 5.00
dog	€ 2.00 - € 3.00

For latest campsite news, availability and prices visit

alanrogers.com

The birthplace of Gothic architecture in France with no less than six cathedrals, the region is still predominately rural with deep river valleys, forests of mature beech and oak, peaceful lakes and sandy beaches, providing plenty of contrast.

DÉPARTEMENTS: 02 AISNE, 60 OISE, 80 SOMME

MAJOR CITY: AMIENS

France itself was born in this northern province located between the Marne and the Somme rivers, for it was here that the Franks – ancestors of the French – first settled. Picardy tends to be a region that most people travel through and this was the invaders route. Evidence of this is visible in the 17th-century defensive citadels designed by Vauban at the end of a long period of conquests by English kings and Burgundian dukes. From a more recent age, acres of immaculately tended war graves are a sobering reminder of two Great Wars. At Vimy Ridge near Arras, World War One trenches have been preserved intact, a most poignant sight. Elsewhere, almost every village between Arras and Amiens has its memorial.

Picardy's coastline is the least urbanised in all France with miles upon miles of beautiful sandy beaches and dunes – great for windsurfing, land yachting, sailing, swimming and building castles. Do not miss the magnificent 'Baie de Somme' or the largest bird park in Europe, the Marquenterre.

Places of interest

Abbeville: church of St Vulfran, Bagatelle Château, Baie de Somme nature reserve.

Amiens: Notre Dame cathedral, impressive for its size and richly sculpted façade and the stone carvings of the choir; monument to the 1918 Battle of the Somme; remarkable 'hortillonnages' (water gardens) and interlocking canals.

Aisne: surrounded by 60 fortified churches.

Chantilly: Château of Chantilly with a 17th-century stable with a 'live' Horse Museum.

Compiègne: Seven miles east of the town is Clairière de l'Armistice. The railway coach here is a replica of the one in which the 1918 Armistice was signed and in which Hitler received the French surrender in 1942.

Laon: 12th-century cathedral, WW1 trenches, Vauclair Abbey.

Marquenterre: one of Europe's most important bird sanctuaries.

Cuisine of the region

Fresh fish and seafood is popular, as is chicory flavoured coffee.

Carbonnade de Boeuf à la Flamande: braised beef with beer, onions and bacon.

Caudière (Chaudière, Caudrée): versions of fish and potato soup.

Ficelles Picardes: ham pancakes with mushroom sauce.

Flamiche aux poireaux: puff pastry tart with cream and leeks.

Soupe courquignoise: soup with white wine, fish, moules, leeks and Gruyère cheese.

www.picardietourisme.com/en
documentation@picardietourisme.com
(0)3 22 22 33 63

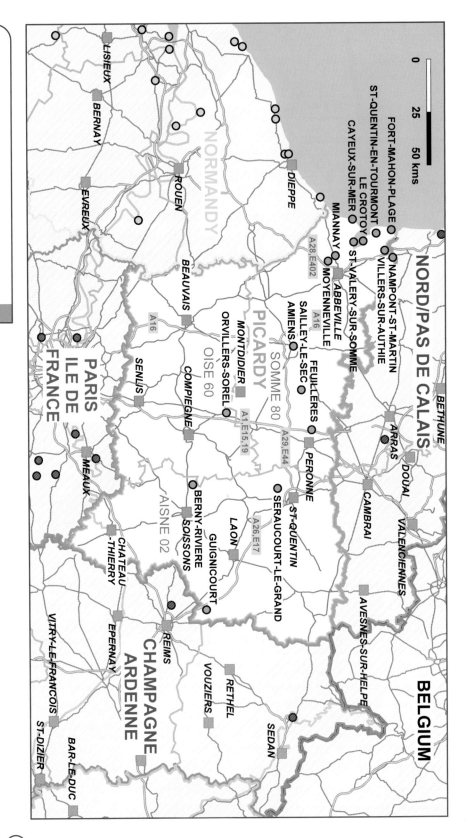

NORD/PAS DE CALAIS

BELGIUM

PICARDY

NORMANDY

PARIS
ILE DE
FRANCE

CHAMPAGNE
ARDENNE

0   25   50 kms

LISIEUX
BERNAY
EVREUX
ROUEN
DIEPPE
BEAUVAIS
SENLIS
COMPIEGNE
MEAUX
BETHUNE
ARRAS
DOUAI
VALENCIENNES
CAMBRAI
AVESNES-SUR-HELPE
SEDAN
VOUZIERS
RETHEL
REIMS
EPERNAY
CHATEAU
-THIERRY
VITRY-LE-FRANCOIS
BAR-LE-DUC
ST-DIZIER
SOISSONS
LAON
ST-QUENTIN
PERONNE
AMIENS
ABBEVILLE
MOYENNEVILLE
MIANNAY
ST-VALERY-SUR-SOMME
CAYEUX-SUR-MER
LE CROTOY
ST-QUENTIN-EN-TOURMONT
FORT-MAHON-PLAGE
NAMPONT-ST-MARTIN
VILLERS-SUR-AUTHIE
FEUILLERES
SAILLEY-LE-SEC
MONTDIDIER
ORVILLERS-SOREL
BERNY-RIVIERE
GUIGNICOURT
SERAUCOURT-LE-GRAND

SOMME 80
OISE 60
AISNE 02

A28.E402
A16
A16
A1.E15.19
A29.E44
A26.E17

For latest campsite news, availability and prices visit
alanrogers.com

Amiens
Camping Parc des Cygnes

111 avenue des Cygnes, F-80080 Amiens (Somme) T: 03 22 43 29 28. E: camping.amiens@wanadoo.fr
alanrogers.com/FR80100

This 3.2 hectare site has been completely levelled and attractively landscaped. Bushes and shrubs divide the site into areas and trees around the perimeter provide some shade. The 145 pitches are for touring, with five mobile homes for rent. All pitches are grassed with plenty of space on the tarmac roads in front of them for motorcaravans to park in wet conditions. There are 81 pitches with electricity (10A), of which 37 also have water and drainage and further water points can be accessed throughout the rest of the site. The site is just a few minutes from the N1, the A16 Paris - Calais motorway and the A29/A26 route to Rouen and the south, so it is useful as a stop-over being about 50 km. from the ports. Amiens itself is an attractive cathedral city where you can eat out on the waterfront of the 'Venice of the North' or take a boat trip around the 'floating gardens' of 'Les Hortillonnages'. Information is available and reduced prices are offered for visits to these historical locations as the site is a 'Somme Battlefields Partner'. A Sites et Paysages member.

Facilities

Two toilet blocks (both open when site is busy) with separate toilet facilities but unisex shower and washbasin area. Baby bath. Facilities for disabled visitors. Reception building also has toilets, showers and washbasins (heated when necessary). Laundry facilities. Shop (open on request all season), bar and takeaway (7/5-12/9; weekends only in low season). Games and TV room. Bicycle hire. Fishing. Off site: Golf and riding 12 km. Beaches 70 km.

Open: 1 April - 14 October.

Directions

From A16, leave at exit 20. Take the Rocade Nord (northern bypass) to exit 40, follow signs for Amiens Longpré. At roundabout take second exit to Parc de Loisirs, then right to site (signed). For sat nav use Rue du Grand Marais. GPS: 49.920916, 2.258833

Charges guide

Per unit incl. 2 persons and electricity	€ 19.10 - € 24.80
extra person	€ 6.00

Parc des Cygnes★★★★
Camping & Caravaning, Cottages

For quality holidays!

111 Avenue des Cygnes - 80080 AMIENS
Tél.: +33 (0)3 22 43 29 28
Fax: +33 (0)3 22 43 59 42
E-mail: alban@parcdescygnes.com
Web: www.parcdescygnes.com
GPS: 49.920916 / 2.258833

Berny-Rivière
Caravaning la Croix du Vieux Pont

F-02290 Berny-Rivière (Aisne) T: 03 23 55 50 02. E: info@la-croix-du-vieux-pont.com
alanrogers.com/FR02030

Located on the banks of the River Aisne, la Croix du Vieux Pont is a very smart, modern 34 hectare site offering a high standard of facilities. Many pitches are occupied by mobile homes and tour operator tents, but there are 100 large and pleasant touring pitches, some on the banks of the Aisne. Maintained to a high standard, the excellent amenities include three heated swimming pools, two indoors with a waterslide and jacuzzi. At the heart of the site are two well stocked fishing lakes which are also used for pedaloes and canoes. There are two tennis courts, an amusement arcade and multisports court.

Facilities

The nine toilet blocks are modern and kept very clean, with washbasins in cabins and free hot showers. Laundry facilities. Facilities for disabled visitors and babies. Motorcaravn service point. Supermarket. Bar, takeaway and good value restaurant (most amenities 1/4-30/9). Swimming pool complex (covered pool 1/4-30/10, outdoor 1/4-30/9). Play area. Fishing. Bicycle hire. Trampoline. Minigolf. Archery. Climbing tower. Multisports area. Apartments, chalets and mobile homes to let. WiFi (charged). Off site: Pony club adjacent. Golf 30 km.

Open: 2 weeks before Easter - 31 October.

Directions

From Compiègne take N31 towards Soissons. At site sign, turn left onto D13. At Vic-sur-Aisne turn right, towards Berny-Riviere and follow site signs. GPS: 49.40487, 3.12840

Charges guide

Per unit incl. 2 persons and electricity	€ 25.50 - € 30.50
incl. 4 persons	€ 36.00 - € 41.00
Camping Cheques accepted.	

For latest campsite news, availability and prices visit
alanrogers.com

Cayeux-sur-Mer

Camping les Galets de la Mollière

Rue Faidherbe, la Mollière, F-80410 Cayeux-sur-Mer (Somme) T: 03 22 26 61 85.
E: info@campinglesgaletsdelamolliere.com **alanrogers.com/FR80190**

Cayeux-sur-Mer is an attractive, traditional seaside resort close to the Somme estuary and les Galets de la Mollière is located just to the north of the town. Formerly a municipal site, it has undergone a recent renovation programme. The site extends over six hectares and has 195 pitches, of which 96 are reserved for touring units, all with 10A electrical connections (French style). An attractive swimming pool complex, bar, shop and a games room were added in 2008. A fine sandy beach is adjacent to the site, a short walk across the sand dunes. Cayeux is just 3 km. away and has a good range of shops and restaurants.

Facilities

Toilet blocks housed in small wooden huts include facilities for babies and disabled visitors. Laundry. Small shop. Bar, snack bar and takeaway (all 1/7-31/8). Games room. Play area. A heated outdoor swimming pool (1/5-15/9). Boules. Motorcaravan services (across the road from the site entrance). WiFi (charge). Off site: Nearest beach 300 m. Riding and fishing 1 km. Cayeux-sur-Mer 3 km. Tennis 3 km. Bicycle hire 7 km. Golf 15 km.

Open: 1 April - 1 November.

Directions

From the A16 take exit 24 (Le Crotoy) and join the D32 to Rue, and then the D940 to St Valery. Bypass St Valery on the D940 and then join the D3 signed Cayeux-sur-Mer. After a further 4 km. you will arrive at La Mollière (site signed). GPS: 50.2026, 1.5251

Charges guide

Per unit incl. 3 persons and electricity	€ 17.50 - € 29.00
extra person (over 1 yr)	€ 7.00

Feuillères

Camping du Chateau et de l'Oseraie

12 rue du Château, F-80200 Feuillères (Somme) T: 03 22 83 17 59. E: jsg-bred@wanadoo.fr
alanrogers.com/FR80180

Situated very close to the A1 autoroute, this site would make a lovely stopover for a few days to break a journey, but would be equally ideal for a longer stay. Despite the closeness to the autoroute and the railway, the site is very quiet and peaceful. Immaculately kept, there are just 18 grass pitches for touring, each with 6A electricity. They are of a good size and most are hedged. There are five modern chalets for hire, and the rest of the site is occupied by privately owned mobile homes. It is an easy, pleasant stroll into the peaceful village of Feuillères, with its fishing ponds, and the River Somme nearby.

Facilities

Excellent toilet facilities, modern and spotlessly clean. Showers on payment. Separate shower room for disabled visitors, access by key. Laundry facilities. Motorcaravan service point. Small shop in reception, baker calls in high season. Bar with TV. Snacks. Games for children in high season. Multisports court. Tennis. Playground. Internet. Off site: Peronne with its WWI Museum and good shopping. Fishing 500 m. Boating on River Somme.

Open: 1 April - 31 October.

Directions

Leave A1 at exit 13.1 and take D938 westwards towards Albert. After crossing the autoroute take D146 south to Feuillères. Site well signed in village. GPS: 49.94813, 2.84364

Charges guide

Per unit incl. 2 persons and electricity	€ 17.10 - € 17.70

Guignicourt

Camping Municipal Guignicourt

14 bis rue des Godins, F-02190 Guignicourt (Aisne) T: 03 23 79 74 58. E: mairie-guignicourt@wanadoo.fr
alanrogers.com/FR02060

This very pleasant, little municipal site has 100 pitches, 20 for long stay units and 80 for touring units. These two sections are separated by the main facilities on a higher terrace. Pitches are generally large and level, although you might need an extra long electricity lead for some, but there are few dividing hedges. Pitches along the river bank have most shade, with a few specimen trees providing a little shade to some of the more open pitches. On a quiet evening you are likely to hear the site's nightingales. The town is quite attractive and is worthy of an evening stroll.

Facilities

The modern sanitary unit has British and Turkish style toilets, washbasins (cold only except for the one in a cubicle), pushbutton hot showers, dishwashing and laundry sinks. Playground. Boules. Fishing. Off site: The town has all services including a supermarket and bank. Golf 3 km. Beach 15 km. Good train service into Reims with its spectacular cathedral.

Open: 1 April - 30 September.

Directions

Guignicourt is about 20 km. north of Reims, just east of the A26, junction 14. The site is well signed from D925 in the village. GPS: 49.4320, 3.9704

Charges guide

Per person	€ 2.20
child (under 12 yrs)	€ 1.50
pitch incl. electricity	€ 11.10 - € 13.20

For latest campsite news, availability and prices visit

alanrogers.com

Fort-Mahon-Plage
Camping le Royon

1271 route de Quend, F-80120 Fort-Mahon-Plage (Somme) T: 03 22 23 40 30. E: info@campingleroyon.com
alanrogers.com/FR80040

This busy site, some two kilometres from the sea, has 397 pitches of which 116 are used for touring units. Most are near the entrance, some are set amongst the mobile homes. They are of either 95 or 120 sq.m, marked, numbered and divided by hedges and are arranged either side of access roads. Electricity (6A) and water points are available to all. The remaining 281 pitches are used for mobile homes. The site is well lit, fenced and guarded at night (€ 30 deposit for barrier card). Entertainment is organised for adults and children in July/Aug when it will be very full. Nearby there are opportunities for windsurfing, sailing, sand yachting, canoeing, swimming, climbing and shooting. The site is close to the Baie de l'Authie which is an area noted for migrating birds.

Facilities

Four toilet blocks provide unisex facilities with British and Turkish style WCs and washbasins in cubicles. Units for disabled people. Baby baths. Laundry facilities. Shop (15/3-1/11). Gas supplies. Mobile takeaway calls evenings in July/Aug. Clubroom and bar (15/3-1/11). Heated, open air and covered pools. Open air children's pool and sun terrace. Play area. Games room with TV. Multisports court. Tennis. Boules. Bicycle hire. Internet access and WiFi. Off site: Fishing, riding, golf and watersports centre within 1 km. Public transport nearby (July/Aug). Train station 15 km.

Open: 15 March - 1 November.

Directions

From A16 exit 24, take D32 around Rue (road becomes D940 for a while then continues as the D32 Fort-Mahon-Plage). Site is on right after 19 km. GPS: 50.33229, 1.5796

Charges guide

Per unit incl. up to 3 persons and electricity	€ 18.00 - € 31.00
extra person (over 1 yr)	€ 7.00
dog	€ 3.00

Open from 9th of March until the 1st of November 2012.

Campsite at 2.5 km of the beach.
Mobil Homes for rent per night or per week.

Covered and heated swimmingpool (Easter until September). Animations, Kidsclub, Sportsterrain, Fitnessarea, playground.

Camping le Royon**
1271 route de quend - 80120 fort mahon plage
téléphone 03.22.23.40.30
info@campingleroyon.com - www.campingleroyon.com

Le Crotoy
Kawan Village le Ridin

Lieu-dit Mayocq, F-80550 Le Crotoy (Somme) T: 03 22 27 03 22. E: contact@campingleridin.com
alanrogers.com/FR80110

Le Ridin is a popular family site in the countryside just 2 km. from Le Crotoy with its beaches and marina, and 6 km. from the famous bird reserve of Le Marquenterre. The site has 162 pitches, including 40 for touring, the remainder occupied by mobile homes and chalets (for rent). There is some shade. The pitches and roads are unsuitable for large units. The site amenities are housed in beautifully converted barns across the road and these include a heated pool, fitness centre, bar/restaurant and bicycles for hire. Reception staff are helpful and will advise on local excursions.

Facilities

Toilet blocks are heated in cool weather and provide good showers and special facilities for children. Laundry facilities. Motorcaravan service point. Restaurant/bar. Small shop. Swimming and paddling pools. Fitness centre. Games room. Play area. TV room. Bicycle hire. Entertainment and activity programme in high season. WiFi (free). Off site: Golf 2 km. Fishing and riding 3 km. Birdwatching 6 km.

Open: 1 April - 7 November.

Directions

From A16 (Calais - Abbeville) take exit 24 and follow signs to Le Crotoy. At roundabout on arrival at Le Crotoy turn towards St Férmin, then second road on right. GPS: 50.23905, 1.63182

Charges guide

Per unit incl. 2 persons and electricity	€ 19.50 - € 30.00
extra person	€ 5.30 - € 5.80
child (2-7 yrs)	€ 4.30 - € 4.80
Camping Cheques accepted.	

For latest campsite news, availability and prices visit
alanrogers.com

Moyenneville

Camping le Val de Trie

Rue des Sources, Bouillancourt-sous-Miannay, F-80870 Moyenneville (Somme) T: 03 22 31 48 88.
E: raphael@camping-levaldetrie.fr **alanrogers.com/FR80060**

Le Val de Trie is a natural countryside site in woodland, near a small village. The 80 numbered, grassy touring pitches are of a good size, divided by hedges and shrubs with mature trees providing good shade in most areas, and all have electricity (6A) and water. It can be very quiet in April, June, September and October. If there is no-one on site, just choose a pitch or call at the farm to book in. This is maturing into a well managed site with modern facilities and a friendly, relaxed atmosphere. It is well situated for the coast and also the cities of Amiens and Abbeville. There are five new wooden chalets (including one for campers with disabilities). There are good walks around the area and a notice board keeps campers up to date with local market, shopping and activity news. English is spoken. The owners of le Val de Trie have recently opened a new campsite nearby, le Clos Cacheleux (FR80210), where larger units can be accommodated.

Facilities

Two clean, recently renovated sanitary buildings include washbasins in cubicles, units for disabled visitors, babies and children. Laundry facilities. Microwave. Shop (all season), bread to order and butcher visits in season. Bar with TV (23/4-4/9), snack bar with takeaway (27/4-2/9). Room above bar for children. Covered heated swimming pool with jacuzzi (14/4-30/9). Outdoor pool for children (26/4-10/9). WiFi in bar area (free). Electric barbecues not permitted. Off site: Riding 4 km. Golf 10 km. Beach 12 km.

Open: 1 April - 15 October.

Directions

From A28 take exit 2 near Abbeville and D925 to Miannay. Turn left on D86 to Bouillancourt-sous-Miannay: site is signed in village.
GPS: 50.08539, 1.71499

Charges 2012

Per unit incl. 2 persons	
and electricity	€ 18.90 - € 25.90
extra person	€ 3.10 - € 5.30
child (under 7 yrs)	€ 2.00 - € 3.40
dog	€ 1.80 - € 2.00
Camping Cheques accepted.	

Sites & Paysages DE FRANCE

Le Clos Cacheleux ***
Nature and Culture
1h from Calais (A 16)
Fishing pound
10 km from the Bay of Somme
Ideal spot for first or last night or longer stay

+ 33 (0) 3 22 19 17 47 route de Bouillancourt
80132 MIANNAY
raphael@camping-lecloscacheleux.fr

www.camping-lecloscacheleux.fr

Le Val de Trie ***
* Indoor Swimming pool
* Children club (season)
* Farm and animals
* Cottages to rent
* Near sandy beach and cliffs

raphael@camping-levaldetrie.fr
www.camping-levaldetrie.fr
+ 33 (0) 3 22 31 48 88 Bouillancourt sous Miannay 80870 MOYENNEVILLE

Camping Qualité   La Clef Verte

New Indoor Pool

Camping Cheque

We can book this site for you! Call 01580 214000   alan rogers ● travel

For latest campsite news, availability and prices visit
alanrogers.com

Miannay
Camping le Clos Cacheleux

Route de Bouillancourt, F-80132 Miannay (Somme) T: 03 22 19 17 47.
E: raphael@camping-lecloscacheleux.fr **alanrogers.com/FR80210**

Le Clos Cacheleux is a well situated campsite of eight hectares bordering woodland in the park of the Château Bouillancourt which dates from the 18th century. The site was first opened in July 2008. It is 11 km. from the Bay of the Somme, regarded as being amongst the most beautiful bays in France. There are 100 very large, grassy pitches (200 sq.m) and all have electricity (10A Europlug). The aim of the owners is to provide high quality services and activities. Visitors have access to the swimming pool, bar and children's club of the sister site – le Val de Trie (20 m). A Sites et Paysages member.

Facilities	Directions
The single sanitary block is clean and well maintained. Facilities for disabled visitors. Baby room. Laundry room. Motorcaravan service point. At the sister site: shop, bar with terrace (22/4-10/9), library and TV room, restaurant and takeaway (27/4-2/9). Play area. Boules. Picnic tables. Barbecue hire. Bicycle hire. Fishing pond. Caravan storage. Covered pool (15/4-30/9) on the sister site and a second sanitary block. WiFi. Off site: Village 1 km. Hypermarket in Abbeville. Riding 4 km. Golf 9 km. **Open:** 15 March - 15 October.	From the A28 at Abbeville take the D925 towards Eu and Le Tréport; do not go towards Moyenville. Turn left in Miannay village on the D86 towards Toeufles. The road to Bouillancourt-sous-Miannay is on the left after 2 km. and site is signed in the village. GPS: 50.08352, 1.71343

Charges guide

Per unit incl. 2 persons and electricity	€ 18.50 - € 25.80
extra person	€ 3.10 - € 5.30

Orvillers-Sorel
Aestiva Camping de Sorel

Rue Saint-Claude, F-60490 Orvillers-Sorel (Oise) T: 03 44 85 02 74. E: contact@aestiva.fr
alanrogers.com/FR60020

Aestiva Camping de Sorel is located north of Compiègne, close to the A1 motorway and is ideal as an overnight stop. The site has 80 large grassy pitches, of which 50 are available for touring, all with electrical connections (three with water and waste water). The original farm buildings have been carefully converted to house the site's amenities including a bar, TV room and the toilet facilities. The site is open for a long season but most amenities are only open from April to September. The site is, however, close to the village of Sorel with its shops and restaurants. There are four mobile homes for rent.

Facilities	Directions
Toilet block with facilities for children and disabled visitors. Motorcaravan service point. Small shop. Bar, snack bar and takeaway (15/5-15/10). TV room. Play area. Boules. Hairdressing service. Bicycle hire. WiFi. Off site: Tennis. Riding 5 km. Fishing 2 km. Golf 7 km. Compiègne 15 km. **Open:** 1 February - 14 December.	Take exit 11 from the A1 motorway (Lille - Paris) and join the northbound N17. Site is signed to the right on reaching village of Sorel after around 8 km. GPS: 49.56688, 2.70841

Charges guide

Per unit incl. 2 persons	€ 16.50 - € 18.00
extra person	€ 6.00
Camping Cheques accepted.	

Sailly-le-Sec
Camping les Puits Tournants

6 rue du Marais, F-80800 Sailly-le-Sec (Somme) T: 03 22 76 65 56. E: camping.puitstournants@wanadoo.fr
alanrogers.com/FR80160

Les Puits Tournants is a simple, rural site, situated in lovely countryside in the battlefield area of the Somme, a short stroll from the River Somme along a quiet country lane. The owners, the Lebon family, speak very little English, but are extremely warm and friendly. The site has 80 pitches, 30 of which are for touring, and all have 4/6A electricity, water and a drain. A few pitches are individual with surrounding hedges, but most are placed informally in unmarked areas around the fishing lake. A lot of development is taking place, and parts of the site are overgrown and untidy, particularly around the mobile home area.

Facilities	Directions
One modern, heated toilet block, unisex, very clean. There will be more toilets once the pool complex is finished. Laundry facilities. Motorcaravan service point. Small shop in reception. One pitch on site is specifically for disabled visitors, and has a small, wooden building on it containing toilet/shower facilities. Swimming and paddling pools (15/4-15/10). Small playground. Fishing. Off site: An ideal location for visiting the WWI Museums in Peronne 22 km. and Albert I4 km. and the cathedral in Amiens. **Open:** 1 April - 31 October.	From A16 take A29 easterly to exit 52. Turn north to Villers Bretonneux, then take N29 towards Lamotte Warfusée. From there take D42 north to Sailly-Laurette and continue on D333 to Sailly-Le-Sec. Site is 100 m. from the church. GPS: 49.91925, 2.57824

Charges guide

Per unit incl. 2 persons and electricity	€ 19.10
extra person	€ 4.50
Camping Cheques accepted.	

For latest campsite news, availability and prices visit
alanrogers.com

We can book this site for you! Call 01580 214000 alanrogers travel

We can book this site for you! alan rogers ◉ travel
Call 01580 214000

Nampont-Saint Martin
Kawan Village la Ferme des Aulnes

535

1 rue du Marais, Fresne-sur-Authie, F-80120 Nampont-Saint Martin (Somme) T: 03 22 29 22 69.
E: contact@fermedesaulnes.com **alanrogers.com/FR80070**

This peaceful site, with 120 pitches, has been developed on the meadows of a small, 17th-century farm on the edge of Fresne and is lovingly cared for by its new enthusiastic owners, Marie and Denis Lefort and their hard working team. Restored outbuildings house reception and the facilities, around a central courtyard that boasts a fine heated swimming pool. A new development includes a bar and entertainment room. Outside, facing the main gate, are 20 large level grass pitches for touring. There is also an area for tents. The remaining 22 touring pitches are in the main complex, hedged and fairly level. Activities are organised for children and there are indoor facilities for poor weather. From here you can visit Crécy, Agincourt, St Valery and Montreuil (where Victor Hugo wrote Les Misérables). The nearby Bay of the Somme has wonderful sandy beaches and many watersports.

Facilities

Both sanitary areas are heated and include washbasins in cubicles with a large cubicle for disabled visitors. Dishwashing and laundry sinks. Shop. Piano bar and restaurant. Motorcaravan service point. TV room. Swimming pool (16x9 m; heated and with cover for cooler weather). Jacuzzi and sauna. Fitness room. Aquagym and balnéotherapy. Playground. Boules. Archery. Rooms with PlayStations and videos. Internet café. WiFi (free). Shuttle service to stations and airports. Off site: Private lake fishing (free) 2 minutes away. River fishing 100 m. Golf 1 km. Riding 8 km.

Open: 1 April - 1 November.

Directions

From Calais, take A16 to exit 25 and turn for Arras for 2 km. and then towards Abbeville on N1. At Nampont-St Martin turn west on D485 and site will be found in 2 km. GPS: 50.33645, 1.71285

Charges guide

Per unit incl. 2 persons	
and electricity	€ 27.00 - € 33.00
extra person	€ 7.00
child (under 7 yrs)	€ 4.00
dog	€ 4.00
Camping Cheques accepted.	

For latest campsite news, availability and prices visit
alanrogers.com

Saint Quentin-en-Tourmont
Camping Caravaning le Champ Neuf

Rue du Champ Neuf, F-80120 Saint Quentin-en-Tourmont (Somme) T: 03 22 25 07 94.
E: contact@camping-lechampneuf.com **alanrogers.com/FR80020**

Le Champ Neuf is located in Saint Quentin in Tourmont, on the Bay of the Somme. It is a quiet site, 900 m. from the ornithological reserve of Marquenterre, the favourite stop for thousands of migratory birds; birdwatchers will appreciate the dawn chorus and varied species. This eight-hectare site has 157 pitches with 34 for touring, on level grass with 6/10A electricity. The site is only 75 minutes from Calais, 18 km. from the motorway. An excellent covered pool complex has been added, including a flume, jacuzzi and pool for toddlers, and a fitness room and sauna.

Facilities	Directions
Four unisex toilet blocks have showers, washbasins in cubicles, family cubicles and facilities for disabled visitors. Laundry facilities. Motorcaravan service point. Bar, entertainment area and snack bar. Play area. TV. Games room. Covered, heated pool complex including slides, jacuzzi and children's pool. Fitness room. Sauna. Multisports court. WiFi in bar area (free). Off site: Shops, restaurants and bars in Rue 7 km.	From A16 exit 24, take D32 towards and around Rue. At second roundabout take second exit on D940, then left on D4 for 1.5 km. before turning right on D204 to Le Bout des Crocs. Site is signed to the left. GPS: 50.26895, 1.60263

Open: 1 April - 1 November.

Charges guide

Per unit incl. 2 persons and electricity	€ 20.00 - € 30.00
extra person	€ 5.00 - € 6.50

Saint Valery-sur-Somme
Camping Airotel Le Walric

536

Route d'Eu, F-80230 Saint Valery-sur-Somme (Somme) T: 03 22 26 81 97. E: info@campinglewalric.com
alanrogers.com/FR80150

A clean, well-kept and managed site, Le Walric is about 75 minutes from Calais. A former municipal site, it has been completely updated with a new bar and snack bar, a pool complex, two play areas and entertainment in high season. There are 263 well laid out, large and level grass pitches. Of these, 47 with electricity connections are for touring, with the remainder used for a mix of new mobile homes and semi-residential caravans. The site's situation on the outskirts of the town make it an ideal holiday location.

Facilities	Directions
Two heated toilet blocks include British style WCs, washbasins in cubicles and showers. Facilities for disabled visitors. Laundry room with baby changing. Motorcaravan services. Shop. Bar with snacks and TV (1/4-1/11). Heated outdoor pool (1/5-15/9). Play areas. Tennis. Volleyball. Boules. Internet access (charged). Children's club and entertainment (July/Aug). Off site: Shops, restaurants, bars in St Valery. Bicycle hire and beach 2 km.	From A16 exit 24, follow D32 across N1. At roundabout take D235 to Morlay; turn left on D940 and continue around Saint Valery until second roundabout where take first exit on D3 to site on right. GPS: 50.1838, 1.61791

Open: 1 April - 1 November.

Charges guide

Per unit incl. 3 persons and electricity	€ 18.00 - € 31.00
extra person	€ 7.00

Saint Valery-sur-Somme
Castel Camping le Château de Drancourt

B.P. 80022, F-80230 Saint Valery-sur-Somme (Somme) T: 03 22 26 93 45. E: chateau.drancourt@wanadoo.fr
alanrogers.com/FR80010

This is a popular, busy and lively site within easy distance of the Channel ports, between Boulogne and Dieppe. There are 356 pitches in total, of which 130 are occupied by several tour operators; 30 units for rent, and 26 privately owned. The 170 touring pitches are on level grass, of good size, some in shade and others in the open, all with electricity (10A). The site is well landscaped and, in spite of the numbers in high season, does not feel overcrowded. It can be dusty around the reception buildings and the château in dry weather. English is spoken and the site is run by the energetic owner and his staff.

Facilities	Directions
Three toilet blocks include washbasins in cubicles, family bathrooms and facilities for disabled visitors. Laundry facilities. Drainage difficulties can cause occasional problems. Shop, restaurant and takeaway, several bars (all Easter-mid Sept). TV rooms. Games room. Heated pools, one indoor, one outside (1/6-15/9) and paddling pool. Tennis. Golf practise range. Minigolf. Bicycle hire. Fishing. Field for ball games and kite flying. WiFi in bar area (charged). Off site: Beach 14 km. Riding 15 km. Golf 30 km. Many traffic-free cycle paths.	Site is 2.5 km. south of Saint Valery and signed from the D940 Berck - Le Tréport road. Turn south on D48 Estreboeuf road. Turn immediately left to Drancourt and site. GPS: 50.15281, 1.63614

Open: Easter - 1 November.

Charges guide

Per unit incl. 2 persons and electricity	€ 17.00 - € 35.00
extra person	€ 4.50 - € 7.50
child (under 5 yrs)	€ 3.50 - € 5.20

For latest campsite news, availability and prices visit
alanrogers.com

Call 01580 214000 We can book this site for you! alan rogers ◉ travel

Seraucourt-le-Grand

Camping du Vivier aux Carpes

10 rue Charles Voyeux, F-02790 Seraucourt-le-Grand (Aisne) T: 03 23 60 50 10.
E: contact@camping-picardie.com **alanrogers.com/FR02000**

Vivier aux Carpes is a small quiet site, close to the A26, two hours from Calais, so is an ideal overnight stop but is also worthy of a longer stay. The 59 well spaced pitches, are at least 100 sq.m. on flat grass with dividing hedges. The 40 for touring units all have electricity (6A), some also with water points, and there are special pitches for motorcaravans. This is a neat, purpose designed site imaginatively set out with a comfortable feel. The enthusiastic owners and manager speak excellent English and are keen to welcome British visitors. The layout takes full benefit of large ponds which are well stocked for fishing.

Facilities

The spacious, clean toilet block has separate, heated facilities for disabled visitors. Laundry facilities. Motorcaravan service point. Bar, snack bar and takeaway (July-August). Large TV/games room. Play area. Bicycle hire. Pétanque. Fishing (about € 5.50 p/day). Gates open 07.00-22.00. Rallies welcome. WiFi (free). Cycling and walking tours from site. Off site: Village has a little shop, brasserie, café, nurse. Supermarket 8 km. Special rates for campers at local golf course, tennis and horse riding.

Open: 1 March - 31 October.

Directions

Leave A26 (Calais - Reims) at exit 11. Take D1 left towards Soissons for 4 km. Take D8, on entering Essigny-le-Grand (4 km) turn sharp right on the D72 signed Seraucourt-le-Grand (5 km). Site signed. GPS: 49.78217, 3.21403

Charges 2012

Per unit incl. 2 persons and electricity	€ 20.50
extra person	€ 4.00
child (under 10 yrs)	€ 3.00

No credit cards.

Villers-sur-Authie

Kawan Village Caravaning le Val d'Authie

20 route de Vercourt, F-80120 Villers-sur-Authie (Somme) T: 03 22 29 92 47. E: camping@valdauthie.fr
alanrogers.com/FR80090

In a village location, this well organised site is fairly close to several beaches, but also has its own excellent pool complex, small restaurant and bar. The owner has carefully controlled the size of the site, leaving space for a leisure area with an indoor pool complex. There are 170 pitches in total, but with many holiday homes and chalets, there are only 60 for touring units. These are on grass, some are divided by small hedges, with 6/10A electric hook-ups, and ten have full services. The site has a fitness trail and running track, mountain bike circuit, and plenty of good paths for evening strolls. Ideas for excursions include the 15/16th century chapel and hospice and the Aviation Museum at Rue, Valloire Abbey and gardens, and the steam railway which runs from Le Crotoy to Cayeux-sur-Mer around the Baie de Somme. Another family day out would be to cycle the traffic-free route around the bay.

Facilities

Good toilet facilities, some unisex, include shower and washbasin units, washbasins in cubicles, and limited facilities for disabled visitors and babies. Shop (not October). Bar/restaurant (5/4-12/10; hours vary). Swimming and paddling pools (lifeguards in July/Aug). Playground, club room with TV. Weekend entertainment in season. Multisports court, beach volleyball, football, boules and tennis court. Trampoline. Internet room. Fitness room including sauna (charged). WiFi throughout (charged). Off site: Shops, banks and restaurants in Rue 6 km.

Open: 1 April - 10 October.

Directions

Villers-sur-Authie is about 25 km. NNW of Abbeville. From A16 exit 24 take N1 to Vron, then left on D175 to Villers-sur-Authie. Or use D85 from Rue, or D485 from Nampont St Martin. Site is at southern end of village at road junction. GPS: 50.31357, 1.69488

Charges guide

Per unit incl. 2 persons and electricity	€ 24.00 - € 33.00
extra person	€ 6.00
child (2-6 yrs)	€ 3.00

Camping Cheques accepted.

LE VAL D'AUTHIE
★★★★★

20 route de Vercourt
80120 - Villers sur Authie

Tel : 0033 (0)3 22 29 92 47
Fax : 0033 (0)3 22 29 93 30

www.valdauthie.fr

For latest campsite news, availability and prices visit

alanrogers.com

With its tree lined boulevards, museums, art galleries, the Arc de Triomphe and of course the famous Eiffel Tower, this cosmopolitan city has plenty to offer. Less than 30 miles from the heart of the capital, a fun-packed trip to Disneyland Paris is also within reach.

DÉPARTEMENTS: 75 PARIS, 77 SEINE-ET-MARNE, 78 YVELINES, 91 ESSONE, 92 HAUTS-DE-SEINE, 93 SEINE-ST-DENIS, 94 VAL DE MARNE, 95 VAL D'OISE

MAJOR CITIES: PARIS, VERSAILLES, IVRY, MELUN, NANTERRE, BOBIGNY, CRETEIL AND PONTOISE

One of the most chic and culturally rewarding cities in the world, Paris has something for everyone. The list of things to do is virtually endless and could easily fill many holidays - window shopping, the Eiffel Tower, Notre Dame, Montmartre, trips on the Seine, pavement cafés and the Moulin Rouge; the list goes on.

As a peaceful retreat, you can relax and enjoy the lush scenery of surrounding hills and secret woodlands of the Ile de France. Square bell towers in gentle valleys, white silos on endless plains of wheat; soft and harmonious landscapes painted and praised by La Fontaine, Corot and all the landscape painters. Paris is surrounded by forests, Fontainebleau, Compiègne, Saint-Germain-en-Laye and majestic châteaux such as Fontainbleau and Vaux-le-Vicomte.

Disneyland Resort Paris provides a great day out for all the family with two fantastic theme parks with over 70 attractions and shows to choose from. On the outskirts of Paris is Parc Astérix, with one of Europe's most impressive roller-coasters.

Places of interest

Fontainebleau: château and national museum, history of Napoléon from 1804-1815.

Malmaison: château and national museum.

Meaux: agricultural centre, Gothic cathedral, chapter house and palace.

Paris: obviously! The list of places is too extensive to include here.

St Germain-en-Laye: château, Gallo-roman and Merovingian archaeological museum.

Sèvres: ceramics museum.

Thoiry: château and Parc Zoologique, 450-hectare park with gardens and African reserve containing 800 animals.

Versailles: Royal Castle, Royal Apartments, Hall of Mirrors, Royal Opera and French History Museum.

Cuisine of the region

Although without a specific cuisine of its own, Paris and Ile de France offer a wide selection of dishes from all the regions of France. Paris also has a wide choice of foreign restaurants, such as Vietnamese and North African.

www.new-paris-idf.com
info@nouveau-paris-idf.com
(0)1 44 50 19 98

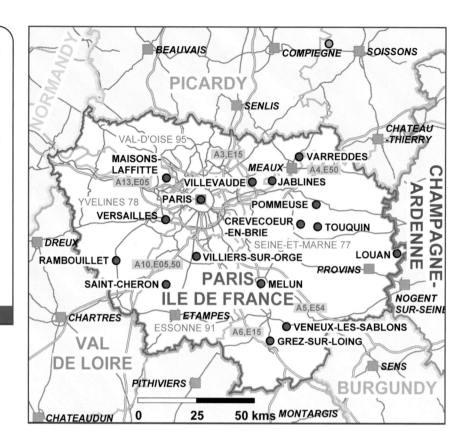

Crèvecoeur-en-Brie

Caravaning des 4 Vents

Rue de Beauregard, F-77610 Crèvecoeur-en-Brie (Seine-et-Marne) T: 01 64 07 41 11. E: f.george@free.fr

alanrogers.com/FR77040

This peaceful, pleasant site has been owned and run by the same family for over 35 years. There are around 200 pitches, with many permanent and seasonal units, however, there are 140 spacious grassy pitches for tourists, well separated by good hedges, all with 6A electricity and a water tap shared between two pitches. The whole site is well landscaped with flowers and trees everywhere. This is a great family site with pool and games facilities located at the top end of the site so that campers are not disturbed.

Facilities

Three modern sanitary units (heated in cooler weather) provide British style WCs, washbasins (mainly in cubicles) and pushbutton showers. Facilities for disabled visitors. Laundry facilities. Motorcaravan service point. In high season (July/Aug) a mobile snack bar and pizzeria (open 16.00-23.00), and a baker (07.30-11.00). Well fenced, circular swimming pool (16 m. diameter; May to Sept). Playground, games room, volleyball and boules court. Riding (high season). Free WiFi. Off site: La Houssaye 1 km. Fontenay Tresigny 5 km.

Open: 15 March - 1 November.

Directions

Crèvecoeur is just off the D231 between A4 exit 13 and Provins. From north, pass obelisk and turn right onto the C3 in 3 km. From south 19 km. after junction with N4, turn left at signs to village. Follow site signs. GPS: 48.75060, 2.89714

Charges guide

Per unit incl. 2 persons and electricity	€ 27.00
extra person (over 5 yrs)	€ 6.00
dog	€ 3.00

For latest campsite news, availability and prices visit

alanrogers.com

Grez-sur-Loing
Camping Municipal les Prés

Chemin des Prés, F-77880 Grez-sur-Loing (Seine-et-Marne) T: 01 64 45 72 75. E: camping-grez@wanadoo.fr
alanrogers.com/FR77080

A typical municipal site, although now leased to a French/English couple who live on site. Les Prés has 136 grassy pitches and a fair number of long stay units. However, there are usually around 35 pitches available for tourists, all with 5A electricity hook-ups. The town of Grez-sur-Loing dates back to medieval times and is well worth investigating. The site makes an ideal base for fishing, cycling (the warden can provide a booklet with five suggested routes – in French, of course), walking and rock climbing in Fontainebleau.

Facilities

A two-storey building has separate, unheated, male and female facilities on the upper level and unisex facilities at ground level. British and Turkish style toilets, dishwashing and laundry facilities. Excellent suite for disabled visitors in a separate building. Children's cubicle. Very small shop. Takeaway (pizza and pannini, 15/3-11/11, Sat, Sun and B.Hs). Sauna. Play area. Fishing lake. WiFi (charged). Off site: Bicycle hire 200 m. Supermarket, bank and ATM 1 km. Riding 5 km. Golf 10 km.

Open: 15 March - 11 November.

Directions

Grez-sur-Loing is just off the D607 north of Nemours and south of Fontainebleau. From both directions turn east at roundabout north of the town towards Montcourt, cross river bridge and almost immediately turn right (signed). Note: this site access road is one-way. Do not follow campsite signs south of village due to narrow roads. GPS: 48.317301, 2.69658

Charges guide

Per unit incl. 2 persons and electricity	€ 13.90
extra person	€ 2.90

Jablines
International de Jablines

Base de Loisirs, F-77450 Jablines (Seine-et-Marne) T: 01 60 26 09 37. E: welcome@camping-jablines.com
alanrogers.com/FR77030

Jablines is a modern site which, with the leisure facilities of the adjacent Espace Loisirs, offers an interesting, if a little impersonal, alternative to other sites in the region. Man-made lakes provide opportunities for many water-based activities. The Grand Lac is said to have the largest beach on the Ile-de-France. The site itself has 150 pitches, of which 141 are for touring units. Most are of a good size, often slightly sloping, with gravel hardstanding and grass, accessed by tarmac roads and marked by young trees. All have 10A electrical connections, 60 with water and waste connections also. The whole complex close to the Marne has been developed around old gravel workings. Whilst staying on the campsite admission to the Base de Loisirs is free. Water activities include catamaran sailing, windsurfing, water boarding, canoeing, fishing and supervised bathing, plus a large equestrian centre, an orienteering course, a multisports court and mountain-bike trails.

Facilities

Two toilet blocks, heated in cool weather, include pushbutton showers, some washbasins in cubicles. Dishwashing and laundry facilities. Motorcaravan service point (charged). Shop (all season). Play area. Internet point in reception. Ticket sales for Disneyland and Parc Astérix. Mobile homes for rent. Off site: Bar/restaurant adjacent (500 m) at Base de Loisirs with watersports, riding, tennis and minigolf. Fishing, horse riding, bicycle hire, beach, boat launching all 500 m. Golf 15 km.

Open: 31 March - 29 September.

Directions

From A4 Paris - Rouen turn north on A104. Take exit 8 on D404 Meaux/Base de Loisirs Jablines. From A1 going south, follow signs for Marne-la-Vallée using A104. Take exit 6A Clay-Souilly on N3 (Meaux). After 6 km. turn south on D404 and follow signs. At park entry keep left. GPS: 48.91378, 2.73451

Charges 2012

Per unit incl. 2 persons and electricity	€ 25.00 - € 28.00
extra person	€ 6.50 - € 7.50
Camping Cheques accepted.	

L'international de Jablines - www.camping-jablines.com - Tel: 0160260937

Base de loisirs de Jablines-Annet (77450)

For latest campsite news, availability and prices visit
alanrogers.com

We can book this site for you! Call 01580 214000 alan rogers ○ travel

Louan

Yelloh! Village Paris/Ile-de-France

Route de Montaiguillon, F-77560 Louan (Seine-et-Marne) T: 04 66 73 97 39.
E: info@yellohvillage-paris-iledefrance.com alanrogers.com/FR77140

Formerly known as La Cerclière, this Yelloh! Village site 80 km. east of Paris lies at the heart of the Montaiguillon forest. This 11 hectare site contains 220 pitches, of which 40 are for touring units; the rest are occupied by chalets including 40, which are privately owned. The touring pitches occupy a small corner of the site, they are on sandy soil, are generally small and access to some is difficult; most are well shaded. The site boasts some impressive amenities including a swimming pool with water slides.

Facilities

The toilet block nearest the touring area was being refurbished to provide family rooms with shower and washbasin. Facilities for disabled visitors, motorcaravans and chemical disposal appear to be in older, distant blocks and are limited. Shop. Bar. Restaurant. Takeaway. Swimming pool complex with slides. Covered balnéo pool. Multisports pitch. Bicycle hire (chalets only). Tennis. Fishing. Overhead cable runway (over 8 yrs; charged). Pony rides (charged). Activity programme. Play area. WiFi (charged). Off site: Riding 2 km. Disneyland Paris 50 km.

Open: All year.

Directions

Louan is 17 km. northeast of Provins. From the N4 Paris - Nancy road at Montceaux (west of Esterhay) turn south on D403 to Villiers St Georges, then east on D60 to Louan Villegruis Fontaine. The site is signed to the left. GPS: 48.63095, 3.49193

Charges guide

Per unit incl. 2 persons and electricity	€ 15.00 - € 36.00
extra person	€ 5.00 - € 7.00
child (under 7 yrs)	free - € 7.00

Maisons-Laffitte

Camping Caravaning International

1 rue Johnson, F-78600 Maisons-Laffitte (Yvelines) T: 01 39 12 21 91. E: ci.mlaffitte@wanadoo.fr
alanrogers.com/FR78010

This site, on the banks of the Seine, is consistently busy, has multilingual, friendly reception staff and occupies a grassy, tree covered area bordering the river. There are 317 pitches, 107 occupied by mobile homes and tour operators, plus two areas dedicated to tents. Most pitches are separated by hedges, are of a good size with some overlooking the Seine (unfenced access), and all 210 touring pitches have electricity hook-ups (6A). The roads leading to the site are a little narrow so large vehicles need to take care. Train noise can be expected.

Facilities

Three sanitary blocks, two insulated for winter use and one more open (used July/Aug). Facilities are clean with constant supervision due to volume of visitors. Provision for disabled visitors. Laundry and dishwashing areas. Motorcaravan service point. Self-service shop. Restaurant/bar. Takeaway food and pizzeria (all open all season). TV in restaurant, table tennis, football area. Fishing (with licence). WiFi (charged). Off site: Sports complex adjoining. Riding 500 m. Bicycle hire 5 km.

Open: 1 week before Easter - 31 October.

Directions

From A15 exit 7 take D184 towards Saint Germain, after 11 km. turn left on D308 (Maisons-Laffitte). Follow site signs. From A1 take A86, then at exit 2 (Bezons) take D308 (Maisons-Laffitte). Follow signs to site. GPS: 48.9399, 2.14589

Charges guide

| Per unit incl. 2 persons and electricity | € 26.70 - € 32.20 |
| extra person | € 5.70 - € 6.40 |

We can book this site for you! Call 01580 214000 alan rogers ○ travel

Melun

Kawan Village la Belle Etoile

Quai Joffre, la Rochette, F-77000 Melun (Seine-et-Marne) T: 01 64 39 48 12.
E: info@campinglabelleetoile.com alanrogers.com/FR77070

Alongside the River Seine, this site has an overall mature and neat appearance, although the approach road is somewhat off-putting with several industrial plants. However, you will discover that la Belle Etoile enjoys a pleasant position with pitches to the fore of the site within view of the barges which continually pass up and down. The 170 touring pitches, 130 with 6A electricity connections, are on grass and laid out between the many shrubs and trees. There are ten units for hire. A friendly, family run site with pleasant and helpful English speaking owners, it is ideal for visiting Fontainebleau and Paris.

Facilities

The toilet blocks are not new but they are kept very clean and the water is very hot. Laundry room. Baby bath. Facilities for disabled visitors. Motorcaravan service point. Small bar, snacks, shop and takeaway (all 1/7-29/8). Heated outdoor swimming pool (1/5-15/9). Play area. Bicycle hire. WiFi (charged). Only gas and charcoal barbecues allowed. Tickets for Disney and Vaux le Vicomte are sold. Off site: Fishing 100 m. Golf 15 km.

Open: 31 March - 14 October.

Directions

Travelling north on RD606 Fontainebleau - Melun road, on entering La Rochette, pass petrol station on left. Turn immediately right into Ave de la Seine. At end of road turn left at river, site on left in 500 m. GPS: 48.52502, 2.66940

Charges 2012

| Per unit incl. 2 persons and electricity | € 21.00 - € 25.00 |

Camping Cheques accepted.

For latest campsite news, availability and prices visit

alanrogers.com

Paris
Camping du Bois de Boulogne

2 allée du Bord de l'eau, F-75016 Paris (Paris) T: 01 45 24 30 00. E: paris@campingparis.fr
alanrogers.com/FR75020

A busy site and the nearest to the city, set in a wooded area between the Seine and the Bois de Boulogne. The site is quite extensive but nevertheless becomes very full with many international visitors, with noise well into the night, despite the rules. There are 510 pitches of varying size (including mobile homes) of which 280 are marked, with electricity (10A), water, drainage and TV aerial connections. The site is under new management and as a result an improvement and development programme is in progress including the refurbishment of some toilet blocks. Reservations are made for pitches – if not booked, arrive early in season (mornings).

Facilities	Directions
Most toilet blocks have British style WCs, washbasins in cubicles and showers with divider (warm water). All suffer from heavy use in season. Laundry room. Two motorcaravan service points. Shop. Bar and restaurant (1/4-15/10). Bar open 07.00-24.00 most times and until 02.00 in peak season. Pizza bar and takeaway. Small playground. Bicycle hire. Information service. Off site: Fishing 1 km.	Site is on east side of Seine between the river and the Bois de Boulogne, just north of the Pont de Suresnes. Easiest approach is from Port Maillot. Traffic lights at site entrance. Follow signs closely and use a good map. GPS: 48.86829, 2.23545

Open: All year.

Charges guide

Per unit incl. 2 persons and electricity	€ 27.55 - € 37.25

Pommeuse
Camping le Chêne Gris

24 place de la Gare de Faremoutiers, F-77515 Pommeuse (Seine-et-Marne) T: 01 64 04 21 80.
E: info@lechenegris.com **alanrogers.com/FR77020**

This site is being progressively developed by a Dutch holiday company. A principal building houses reception on the ground floor and also an airy restaurant/bar plus a takeaway. Of the 350 pitches, 53 are for touring, many of which are on aggregate stone, the rest (higher up the hill on which the site is built) being occupied by over 217 mobile homes and 80 tents belonging to a Dutch tour operator. The pitches are not suitable for larger units (over 7 m). Terraces look out onto the heated leisure pool complex and an outdoor adventure-type play area for over-fives, whilst the indoor soft play area is in a large tent at the side of the bar.

Facilities	Directions
One toilet block with pushbutton showers, washbasins in cubicles and a dishwashing/laundry area. At busy times these may be under pressure. Facilities for disabled visitors and children. Bar, restaurant, takeaway and swimming pool complex (from Easter weekend). Indoor and outdoor play areas. WiFi (charged). Off site: Shops, bars and restaurants within walking distance. Fishing and riding 2 km.	Pommeuse is 55 km. east of Paris. From A4 at exit 16 take N34 towards Coulommiers. In 10 km. turn south for 2 km. on D25 to Pommeuse; site on right after level-crossing. Also signed from south on D402 Guignes - Coulommiers road, taking D25 to Faremoutiers. GPS: 48.808213, 2.993935

Open: 20 April - 8 November.

Charges guide

Per unit incl. 2 persons	€ 25.00 - € 44.00
Camping Cheques accepted.	

Saint Chéron
Village Parisien le Parc des Roches

La Petite Beauce, F-91530 Saint Chéron (Essonne) T: 01 64 56 65 50. E: info@camping-parcdesroches.com
alanrogers.com/FR91020

Parc des Roches is a 23-hectare holiday park in an attractive setting surrounded by woodland, and is ideal for visiting Paris. There are 320 average sized, marked pitches with only 100 for touring, all with 6A electricity and laid out amongst the trees. The other pitches are used for mobile homes, tents and chalets, some of which are privately owned. Paris is only 50 minutes from the RER Saint Chéron Station, 2 km. from the site. Fontainebleau is also a major attraction and the town certainly merits a visit. The château was once the home of the Kings of France.

Facilities	Directions
The two main sanitary blocks are spacious, and include some washbasins in cubicles, and facilities for babies and disabled visitors. Laundry and dishwashing facilities. Motorcaravan services. Restaurant, bar and snack bar/takeaway (1/4-31/10). Small shop. Games room. Heated outdoor swimming and paddling pools (15/6-15/9). Fitness facility. Football pitch. Tennis. Boules. Play area. Volleyball. WiFi (charged). Off site: Golf 20 km.	Leave A10 autoroute southwest of Paris, exit 10. Take D149 south to bypass Dourdan, road number changes to D116. Continue east on D116 to Chéron. Site is signed 3 km. from village. GPS: 48.543448, 2.138077

Open: 1st March - 15th December.

Charges guide

Per unit incl. 2 persons and electricity	€ 18.00 - € 30.00

For latest campsite news, availability and prices visit
alanrogers.com

Call 01580 214000 We can book this site for you! alan rogers ● travel

Rambouillet

Huttopia Rambouillet

Rue du Château d'Eau, F-78120 Rambouillet (Yvelines) T: 01 30 41 07 34.
E: rambouillet@huttopia.com alanrogers.com/FR78040

HUTTOPIA

This pleasant site is now part of the Huttopia group whose philosophy is to 'rediscover the camping spirit'. It is in a peaceful forest location beside a lake, with good tarmac access roads and site lighting. The 141 touring pitches, 100 with electrical connections (10A), are set among the trees and in clearings. As a result, shade is plentiful and grass sparse. The main area is kept traffic-free but there is a section for motorcaravans and those who need or prefer to have their car with them. The result is a safe, child-friendly site. There is an 'espace nature' with 40 huge pitches for campers. As part of their efforts to be environmentally friendly, Huttopia have built a 'natural swimming pool'. The water is filtered by reeds and it was used for the first time in 2008 and passed the stringent tests of France's Ministry of Health. The opening date each year depends on how quickly the reeds do their work, but it will certainly be open from June to September. From your pitch, you can stroll out into the forest and there are many good cycle routes and footpaths in the area. Rambouillet itself is an interesting town and Chartres and Versailles are within easy reach. It is possible to visit Paris by rail (a 30 minute journey) and the Mobilis 'transport package' ticket is available from the railway station.

Facilities

The brand new sanitary block has controllable showers, some washbasins in cubicles and a number of more spacious 'family' cubicles. Facilities for disabled visitors. Laundry facilities. Three outlying 'rondavels' each with two family rooms. Motorcaravan service point. Small shop (all season) selling basics plus bar/restaurant with terrace (weekends in low season and daily in July and August). Games room with TV. Play area. 'Natural' swimming pool (June-Sept, earlier if possible). Bicycle hire. Fishing. Children's and family activities with a 'natural' theme (July-Aug). Off site: Riding 5 km. Golf and lake with beach 15 km. Sailing 20 km. Shops, bars and restaurants in town plus large supermarket nearby.

Open: 30 March - 7 November.

Directions

Rambouillet is 52 km. southwest of Paris. Site is southeast of town: from N10 southbound take Rambouillet/Les Eveuses exit, northbound take Rambouillet centre exit, loop round (site signed) and rejoin N10 southbound, taking next exit. Pass under N10, following signs to site in 1.7 km.
GPS: 48.62638, 1.84375

Charges guide

Per unit incl. 2 persons and electricity	€ 23.00 - € 32.20
extra person	€ 5.50 - € 7.10
child (2-7 yrs)	€ 3.10 - € 4.50
dog	€ 4.00

HUTTOPIA

In the heart of the famous forest of Rambouillet
by the «Etang d'Or» pond...

Rambouillet ***

Wood & Canvas Tents, Gipsy caravans, Chalets, Cahuttes to rent

Natural swimming pool, Bar, Restaurant, Play area...

www.huttopia.com
Route du Château d'Eau - 78120 Rambouillet - Tel : +33 (0) 1 30 41 07 34

Touquin

Camping les Etangs Fleuris

Route Couture, F-77131 Touquin (Seine-et-Marne) T: 01 64 04 16 36. E: contact@etangs-fleuris.com

alanrogers.com/FR77090

This is a pleasant, peaceful site which has a very French feel. The 90 touring pitches are grouped on the level ground around the three attractive lakes, all with electricity (10A) and water, separated by hedges and with shade from mature trees. The life of the site centres round a smart bar/function room which doubles as reception and a shop, as well as the lakes and an attractive, irregularly shaped pool. The lakes are home to some sizeable carp as well as being restocked daily with trout (fishing € 5 for half a day). This is an ideal base to visit Paris (50 km) and Disneyland (23 km) and to provide a practical alternative to the busier sites nearer the centre.

Facilities

A fairly simple, heated toilet block has pushbutton showers and open washbasins (with dividers and hooks) for men but mainly in cubicles for ladies. No facilities for disabled visitors. Another heated block is only opened when site is very busy. Laundry facilities. Motorcaravan service area. Shop for basics in bar (1/4-15/9). Heated pool with paddling section (15/4-15/9). Takeaway meals and snacks (weekends and B.Hs in low season, every night high season). Internet access and WiFi (free). Multisports pitch. Minigolf. Trampoline. Off site: Riding and zoo 5 km. Golf 15 km.

Open: 4 April - 15 September.

Directions

Touquin is off the D231, 21 km. from exit 13 of the A4 motorway and 30 km. northeast of Provins. From D231 follow signs for Touquin, then Etangs Fleuris. Site is 2.5 km. west of village. Well signed from D231. GPS: 48.733054, 3.046978

Charges guide

Per unit incl. 2 persons and electricity	€ 19.00
extra person	€ 9.50
child (3-11 yrs)	€ 4.00
dog	€ 1.50

CAMPING Les Etangs Fleuris★★★

Only 25 minutes from Disneyland Resort Paris!

CAMPING Les Etangs Fleuris★★★ • Route de la Couture • 77131 Touquin
Tél.: +33 164 04 16 36 • Fax: +33 164 04 12 28
E-mail: contact@etangs-fleuris.com • www.etangs-fleuris.com

GPS location:
48.733054 / 3.046978

Want independent campsite reviews at your fingertips?

alan rogers

NOW ON ANDROID TOO

Available on the App Store
Download for Android

An exciting **FREE** app for both iPhone and Android

alanrogers.com/apps

For latest campsite news, availability and prices visit

alanrogers.com

Varreddes

Le Village Parisien

Route de Congis (D121), F-77910 Varreddes (Seine-et-Marne) T: 01 64 34 80 80.
E: contact@villageparisien.com **alanrogers.com/FR77050**

If you are intending to visit Disneyland, this site is ideally situated 12 km. away. Tickets can be purchased at the site and taxi travel can be arranged. The site has 224 pitches and is reasonably well cared for with mature hedges dividing the pitches. There are 50 used for touring units and these vary both in size and quality. Access on some could be difficult for larger units. Le Village Parisien is unfortunately rather dominated by the large number of seasonal pitches (80%). The three toilet blocks are old and only just adequate. There is a reasonably large swimming pool (unheated).

Facilities

Three toilet blocks (old and in need of refurbishment, one closed in low season). Facilities for disabled visitors. Motorcaravan service point. Dishwashing and laundry facilities. Small shop and takeaway, bar with entertainment and TV (1/5-15/9). Swimming and paddling pools (1/5-15/9, unheated). Tennis. Play area. Fishing. Minigolf. Tickets and taxis for Disneyland. WiFi (charged).

Open: 15 March - 1 November.

Directions

Heading south on the A1 towards Paris, turn southeast on N330 at Senlis. Head towards Meaux, then turn left on D405 for Varreddes. Site is well signed from here (about 2 km). GPS: 49.002938, 2.941412

Charges guide

Per unit incl. 2 persons
and electricity   € 19.00 - € 27.00

Veneux-les-Sablons

Camping les Courtilles du Lido

Les Courtilles du Lido, chemin du Passeur, F-77250 Veneux-les-Sablons (Seine-et-Marne)
T: 01 60 70 46 05. E: lescourtilles-dulido@wanadoo.fr **alanrogers.com/FR77130**

Les Courtilles du Lido is a well established, family-run site located just outside the 14th-century village of Moret-sur-Loing on the edge of the Forêt de Fontainebleau. There are 180 well shaded grassy pitches with 10A electricity, dispersed throughout the five-hectare terrain, although access to some may be difficult due to low branches on overhanging trees. A good range of amenities includes a pool and an 18-hole minigolf course, as well as a pizzeria and bar. There are 19 mobile homes for rent. Paris lies 55 km. to the north and can be accessed by either the A5 or A6 motorways or by rail from the local station (within walking distance). Some train noise can be heard from the site.

Facilities

A single toilet block provides adequate facilities including those for children. Shop. Pizzeria, bar and takeaway (all season). Outdoor swimming pool (15/5-22/9). Play area. Games room. Motorcaravan services. Minigolf. Short tennis, Boules. Internet access and free WiFi. Off site: Fishing 500 m. Canoeing. Moret-sur-Loing 2 km.

Open: 1 April - 30 September.

Directions

From Fontainebleau take southbound D606 (towards Sens). At Veneux-les-Sablons follow signs for Moret-sur-Loing, then St Mammès. Final approach is via a tunnel. Site is well signed. GPS: 48.38321, 2.80303

Charges guide

Per unit incl. 2 persons and electricity   € 19.50
extra person   € 4.00

Versailles

Huttopia Versailles

31 rue Berthelot, F-78000 Versailles (Yvelines) T: 01 39 51 23 61.
E: versailles@huttopia.com **alanrogers.com/FR78060**

This Huttopia site is rather different. When the French owners visited Canada and experienced 'back to nature' camping, they were so impressed that they decided to introduce the idea to France. This is probably a little like camping as it used to be, but with some big differences. Gone are the formal pitches with neatly trimmed hedges, and instead there are 141 of ample size arranged informally amongst the trees, 93 with electricity (10A) and 14 with water and drainage as well. The terrain is as nature intended with very little grass and much of it steep and rugged. Long electricity leads are required and be prepared to use blocks and corner steadies on many pitches.

Facilities

Three well designed toilet blocks provide basic facilities, including for children and disabled visitors. Laundry. Motorcaravan service point. Special bivouacs for cooking and washing up. Restaurant with takeaway (July/Aug and weekends). Bar. Games room. Simple swimming and paddling pools (13/4-23/9). Playground. Bicycle hire. Children's club (high season). Boules. No charcoal barbecues. Off site: Versailles and its château (tickets can be purchased at the site). Supermarket. Hiking. Cycling trails. Fishing 1 km. Golf 3 km. Riding 5 km.

Open: 23 March - 7 November.

Directions

From the front of the château of Versailles take the Avenue de Paris and the site is signed after 2 km. GPS: 48.79396, 2.16075

Charges guide

Per unit incl. 2 persons
and electricity   € 29.10 - € 39.10
extra person   € 6.40 - € 8.90
child (2-7 yrs)   € 3.10 - € 4.70
dog   € 4.00

We can book this site for you! Call 01580 214000 alan rogers travel

Villevaudé

Camping Club le Parc de Paris

Rue Adèle Claret, Montjay la Tour, F-77410 Villevaudé (Seine-et-Marne) T: 01 60 26 20 79.
E: info@campingleparc.fr **alanrogers.com/FR77110**

This rural, sloping site (open all year) is conveniently situated as an overnight stop or for a visit to Disneyland or to Paris. The 200 largely level, grassy touring pitches all have access to 6A electricity, though some areas have yet to be fully prepared for use. There are 100 mobile homes for rent. The new owners have ongoing plans for improving the site. A ten minute drive takes you to a station on a Metro (RER) line to Paris and there is free parking. Disneyland and Parc Astérix are easily reached via the motorways. The Base de Loisirs, with its man-made lakes, at nearby Jablines (7 km) provides great opportunities for many types of water-based and other leisure activities and it has the largest beach in the Ile-de-France region. There is a small shop in the nearby village of Villaudé and a bar/restaurant in the next hamlet.

Facilities

The three toilet blocks have some washbasins in cabins, mainly British-style toilets and pushbutton showers. Facilities for young children and disabled visitors. Laundry. Motorcaravan service point. Bar, snack bar and takeaway. Play area. Games area. TV room. Internet access in reception and WiFi throughout (charged). Off site: Fishing, riding and golf 6 km. Paris 20 km. Disneyland 20 km. Astérix Park 40 km.

Open: All year.

Directions

From the north: A1 Paris, join A104 Marne la Vallée and leave at exit 6B onto N3. After Claye-Souilly turn right on D404 towards Villevaudé and follow signs to site on left. From the south: A4 Reims, Metz, Nancy, join A104 Lille and take exit 8 to join D404 towards Claye-Souilly and Villevaudé then follow signs to site on right after village. GPS: 48.91282, 2.67465

Charges guide

Per unit incl. 2 persons	
and electricity	€ 21.00 - € 30.00
extra person	€ 4.00 - € 8.00
child (3-11 yrs)	€ 3.00 - € 5.00

Open all the year

www.campingleparc.fr

CAMPING CLUB LE PARC DE PARIS
Rue Adèle Claret MONTJAY LA TOUR 77410 VILLEVAUDE
TEL : +33 1 60 26 20 79
info@campingleparc.fr
G.P.S. North 48°54,720—East 2°40,330

Villiers-sur-Orge

Camping le Beau Village de Paris

1 voie des Prés, F-91700 Villiers-sur-Orge (Essonne) T: 01 60 16 17 86. E: le-beau-village@wanadoo.fr
alanrogers.com/FR91010

This is a pleasant, typically French campsite just 25 km. south of Paris and conveniently located at the centre of a triangle formed by the A6 motorway, the N20/A10 to Orleans and the N104 east/west link road, 'la Francilienne'. Half of its 124 pitches are occupied on a seasonal basis by Parisians or by mobile homes to rent; the remainder are touring pitches, all hedged and with 10A electricity. Trees provide some shade. Reception, in a traditionally-styled building, also has a pleasant little bar, a games room and an attractive terrace with wooden tables, benches, thatched canopies and a stone-built barbecue.

Facilities

Three toilet blocks have controllable showers and some washbasins in cabins. The refurbished main block has a baby changing room and laundry facilities. A second block has adequate facilities for disabled visitors. Small bar (high season and on demand). Games room. WiFi in reception (free sessions). Adventure play area. Free loan of canoes. Boules. Off site: Station with trains to Paris (20 mins) 700 m. Shops and restaurants nearby. Golf, riding 2 km. River beach and sailing 3 km.

Open: All year.

Directions

Villiers-sur-Orge is 25 km. south of Paris. From A6 leave at exit 6 (Savigny-sur-Orge). Turn southwest, follow signs for Quartier Latin on D25 then right at roundabout on D35 to Villiers-sur-Orge. Turn left immediately after river on Voie des Prés along river bank to site on left. GPS: 48.65527, 2.30409

Charges guide

Per unit incl. 2 persons	
and electricity	€ 18.00 - € 20.00
extra person	€ 4.50 - € 5.00

For latest campsite news, availability and prices visit
alanrogers.com

The varied landscapes of Champagne-Ardenne include dense forests, vineyards and winding rivers. The whole area is dotted with fascinating ancient churches and castles, towns and villages.

DÉPARTEMENTS: 08 ARDENNES, 10 AUBE, 51 MARNE, 52 HAUTE-MARNE

MAJOR CITY: REIMS, TROYES

Situated on the flatlands of Champagne are the most northerly vineyards in France where special processing turns the light, dry wine into 'le Champagne'. Nowhere else in the world are you allowed to make sparkling wine and call it Champagne. Reims and Epernay are the centres for the wine trade. It is not the names of the vineyards that have become famous but those of the shippers, such as Moët & Chandon and Veuve Clicquot.

Champagne-Ardenne is a very rich cultural land which offers, from the Belgian border to the gates of Burgundy, a rich heritage and diverse sites which shouldn't be missed: the cathedral of Reims, a listed UNESCO World Heritage Site, the largest fortified castle in Europe in Sedan, the picturesque medieval alleys of Troyes, the loft of Renoir in Essoyes or the all new Memorial of General de Gaulle in Colombey-les-Deux-Eglises. Nature is all around: meanders of the Meuse River deeply embanked in the Ardennes Massif, the great lakes of Champagne between Saint-Dizier and Troyes, hiking trails leading into deep forests. A wonderful preserved environment ideal for getting in touch with nature.

CHAMPAGNE ARDENNE

TOURISME

www.**tourisme-champagne-ardenne.com**

Champagne

Perching Bar in Verzy

Perched over 18 feet high in a tree, the Perching Bar enjoys an exceptional view over the plains of Champagne. The bar offers a large choice of great brands and wine growers' champagnes.

www.**perchingbar.eu**

Cellier Saint-Pierre

In the heart of Troyes, opposite the cathedral, discover a unique place and taste different wines and fine liquors.

www.**celliersaintpierre.fr**

Cycling

La Voie Verte Trans-Ardennes

Running along the spectacular Meuse River valley, the Trans-Ardennes cycle path offers an easy 85 km. ride between Charleville-Mézières and Givet, near the Belgian border. The route passes through the beautiful landscape of the Ardenne massif from north to south.

www.**ardennes.com**

Les Voies Vertes du Lac du Der

Several 'green tracks' run through the Pays du Der: the loop around the lake (38 km) mainly uses the dykes and offers panoramic views of the 4,800 ha. lake. The loop can be extended to reach Saint-Dizier (12 km), Montier-en-Der (12 km) and Vitry-le-François (20 km).

www.**lacduder.com**

Heritage

Reims Cathedral

The Cathedral of Notre Dame de Reims, built in the 13th century is a masterpiece of Gothic art and one of the most important buildings of the European Middle Ages.

www.**reims-tourisme.com**

Mémorial du Général De Gaulle

The new Général De Gaulle Memorial is equipped with the most modern techniques to celebrate the history of Charles de Gaulle and of France in the 20th century.

www.**memorial-charlesdegaulle.fr**

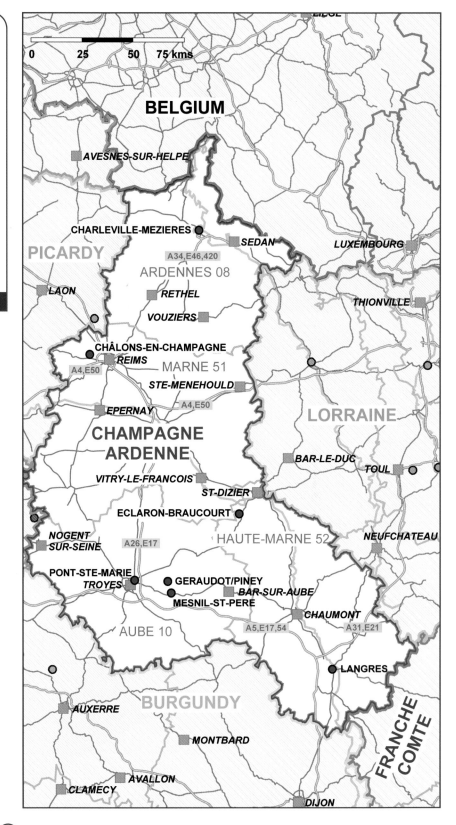

For latest campsite news, availability and prices visit
alanrogers.com

Champagne and land
AUTHENTIC FLAVOURS

- Let your imagination enjoy this unique vineyard.
- Follow the slopes for unexpected walks.
- Visit the oldest cellars.
- Discover the secret of the most mythical of wines.
- Enjoy its exuberant effervescence !

A region full of history where our love of good things is second nature which amateurs and professionals love to share throughout the year. There is a 350 miles Champagne Route to discover. Behind every slope and each vintage, legends and secrets are transmitted from generation to generation. Come and shed light on the mystery of its bubbles.

Don't wait anymore, find all the information on
www.champagne-ardenne-tourism.co.uk
To organise your next tasting

Châlons-en-Champagne

Camping de Châlons-en-Champagne

Rue de Plaisance, F-51000 Châlons-en-Champagne (Marne) T: 03 26 68 38 00.
E: camping.chalons@orange.fr **alanrogers.com/FR51020**

The location of Châlons, south of Reims and near the A4 and A26 autoroutes, about 300 km. from Calais and Boulogne, makes this an ideal stopover. This site on the southern edge of town bears all the hallmarks of the good municipal site it was formerly: the wide entrance with its neatly mown grass and flowerbeds leads to tidy rows of large pitches separated by hedges, many with taps and drains adjacent. Of the 148 pitches, 89 are on gravel, the rest on grass; 96 have electricity (10A). Some overlook a lake.

Facilities	Directions
Two fairly basic toilet blocks (one open only in high season, the other can be heated) include washbasins in cabins, baby room and hairdressing station. Good en-suite unit for disabled visitors. Laundry and dishwashing facilities. Bread to order. Open-air bar, snack bar and takeaway (1/5-30/9). Games (pool and babyfoot) and TV rooms. Fishing lake. Playground. Minigolf, tennis, volleyball, boules, mini-football. Motorcaravan service point. WiFi. Mobile homes to rent. Off site: Bus stop 800 m. Fishing. Horse riding 1 km. Bicycle hire 3 km. Golf 15 km.	Châlons-en-Champagne is 50 km. southeast of Rheims and the site is 3 km. south of the town on the D20. From north on A4, take La Veuve exit (27) onto N44 Rheims - Vitry road which bypasses town. Leave at most southerly exit (St Memmie) and follow camping signs. GPS: 48.9359, 4.3832

Open: 15 March - 15 November.

Charges guide

Per unit incl. 2 persons and electricity	€ 27.50
extra person	€ 5.15
child (under 16 yrs)	€ 2.50 - € 5.15

Camping Cheques accepted.

Charleville-Mezieres

Camping Municipal du Mont Olympe

Rue des Paquis, F-08000 Charleville-Mezieres (Ardennes) T: 03 24 33 23 60.
E: camping-charlevillemezieres@wanadoo.fr **alanrogers.com/FR08010**

Attractively situated alongside the Meuse River, within easy walking distance across a footbridge to the centre of the pleasant large town, this site was completely rebuilt in 2002. It now offers excellent facilities, with 121 grass pitches, 112 with electricity (10A), water and waste water connections. There are 66 from 108 to 219 sq.m. in size, 49 up to 106 sq.m. and seven hardstandings for motorcaravans. Many pitches are shaded by mature trees and all are separated by well kept hedges.

Facilities	Directions
Two heated buildings provide first class showers, private cabins, baby rooms and facilities for disabled visitors. Well equipped laundry room. Motorcaravan service point. Shop (July/Aug). Play area. TV and games room. Barbecues allowed at communal area only. WiFi. Off site: Municipal pool next door. Boat trips on the river. Attractive town centre close by. Bicycle hire 1 km. Golf 20 km.	Site north of Charleville on island of Montcy St Pierre. From north D988/D1 follow river, over bridge, then immediately left. From southeast (A203/N51/N43) take 'centre' exit, head for 'Gare' then follow Avenue Forest north and sharp left after bridge. Site is 150 m. on from old site. GPS: 49.7790, 4.7207

Open: 1 April - 1 October.

Charges guide

Per unit incl. 2 persons and electricity	€ 16.25
extra person	€ 3.50
child (2-10 yrs)	€ 1.75

Eclaron-Braucourt

Flower Camping la Presqu'île de Champaubert

F-52290 Eclaron-Braucourt (Haute-Marne) T: 03 25 04 13 20. E: ilechampaubert@free.fr
alanrogers.com/FR52010

This site is situated beside what is said to be the largest man-made inland lake in Europe (4,800 ha), the Lac du Der Chantecoq. This provides superb facilities for windsurfing, sailing, etc. and even for swimming from a 100 m. beach alongside the site (lifeguard in main season). The site itself is situated on the shores of the lake, with 195 fairly level grassy pitches of a good size, 70 for tourers, all with electrical connections (7A) and many with hardstanding. They are separated by hedges and trees that also provide a fair amount of shade. The views across the lake are very attractive.

Facilities	Directions
The toilet block, although old, is fully equipped and clean. There are plans to replace it. Laundry facilities. Motorcaravan service point. Small shop for essentials. Bar/restaurant. New heated swimming pool is planned. Playground. Bicycle hire. Fishing. Mobile homes for rent. Off site: Beach for swimming. Miles of walking and cycle tracks. Birdwatching. Sailing and windsurfing on Lac de Der. Shops and restaurants in Montier-en-Der 10 km.	From St Dizier, take D384 past Eclaron to Braucourt and follow signs to the site (3 km). GPS: 48.55425, 4.79235

Open: 3 April - 11 September.

Charges guide

Per unit incl. 2 persons and electricity	€ 15.00 - € 31.00
extra person	€ 4.00 - € 5.00
child (3-7 yrs)	free - € 5.00

For latest campsite news, availability and prices visit
alanrogers.com

Eclaron-Braucourt
Yelloh! Village en Champagne

F-52290 Eclaron-Braucourt (Haute-Marne) T: 04 66 73 97 39. E: info@yellohvillage-en-champagne.com
alanrogers.com/FR52050

Formerly known as Les Sources du Lac, this Yelloh! Village site is located close to the village of Eclaron and has direct access to the Lac du Der. This is a very large lake with 77 km. of shoreline and is home to over 270 species of birds. Part of the lake is an ornithological reserve but a wide range of water based activities are on offer in other areas. These include fishing, windsurfing and sailing, and a separate area is reserved for motor boats. There are just 30 touring pitches here and around 120 mobile homes and chalets for rent.

Facilities	Directions
Two toilet blocks include facilities for babies. The facilities may be under pressure at busy times. Shop (July/Aug). Bar. Restaurant. Takeaway. Swimming pool. Paddling pool. Direct access to the lake and beach. Play area. Bicycle hire. Fishing. Ornithological activities. Activity and entertainment programme. Off site: Riding 10 km. Walking and cycle trails. Fishing. The 'Champagne route'. Grange aux Abeilles (bee barn) at Giffaumont Champaubert.	Take the southbound N44 from Chalons-en-Champagne as far as Vitry-le François and then join the eastbound N4 as far as St Dizier. From the St Dizier ring road take the D384 towards Montier-en-Der and upon reaching Eclaron-Braucourt follow signs to the site. GPS: 48.57213, 4.84891

Open: 1 May - 30 September.

Charges guide

Per unit incl. 2 persons	
and electricity	€ 15.00 - € 30.00
extra person (over 3 yrs)	€ 4.00 - € 6.00
child (3-7 yrs)	free - € 5.00
dog	€ 4.00

Géraudot/Piney
Camping les Rives du Lac

Rue du Fort Saint Georges, F-10220 Géraudot/Piney (Aube) T: 03 25 41 24 36.
E: camping.lepinauxmoines@orange.fr **alanrogers.com/FR10060**

This is a friendly, relaxed site in the heart of the Parc Naturel de la Forêt d'Orient and a very short stroll from the Lac d'Orient with swimming and fishing, and opportunities for sailing and boating (with your own equipment). There are 181 pitches on level or gently sloping ground separated by hedges or bushes and with a choice of sunny or shady spots. All have 6A electricity and water nearby; just two are occupied by caravans for rent. There are excellent walking and mountain biking routes in the nearby forest or you could just stroll to the nearby bar and restaurant!

Facilities	Directions
Two toilet blocks, one heated when necessary, the other open only in high season. Hot showers, some washbasins in cabins. Dishwashing and laundry under cover. Facilities for disabled visitors. Filling point for motorcaravans. Bread etc. can be ordered. Small shop planned for 2012. Children's play area (2-6 yrs). Tourist information. Off site: Water-based activities. Fishing. Walking and cycling trails. Golf 3 km. Riding 7 km. Sailing school 11 km. Troyes 25 km.	Géraudot is due east of Troyes, From Rheims on the A26 leave at exit 23 (Thennellières) and follow the D619 for 7 km. Turn north on D1F to Géraudot from where site is well signposted to the east on the D43. From A5 Paris - Nancy join A26 Rheims then as above. GPS: 48.302756, 4.337473

Open: All year.

Charges guide

Per unit incl. 2 persons	
and electricity	€ 15.00 - € 22.00
extra person	€ 3.00 - € 4.50
child (3-7 yrs)	free - € 2.50
dog	€ 2.00

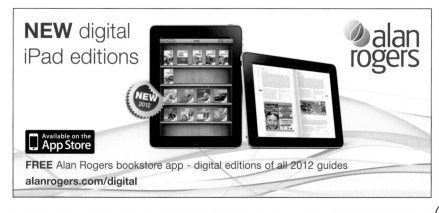

NEW digital iPad editions

alan rogers

NEW 2012

Available on the App Store

FREE Alan Rogers bookstore app - digital editions of all 2012 guides
alanrogers.com/digital

For latest campsite news, availability and prices visit
alanrogers.com

Call 01580 214000 We can book this site for you! alan rogers ◐ travel

Langres

Kawan Village Lac de la Liez

Peigney, F-52200 Langres (Haute-Marne) T: 03 25 90 27 79. E: campingliez@free.fr

alanrogers.com/FR52030

Managed by the enthusiastic Baude family, this excellent lakeside site is near the city of Langres. Only ten minutes from the A5, Camping Lac de la Liez provides an ideal spot for an overnight stop en route to the south of France. There is also a lot on offer for a longer stay. The site provides 131 fully serviced pitches, some with panoramic views of the 250 hectare lake with its sandy beach and small harbour where boats and pedalos may be hired. Ideal for swimming and watersports, access to the lake is down steps and across quite a fast road (in total 150 m). Amenities on the site include indoor and outdoor swimming pools, a restaurant and bar and a shop. As well as all the activities on the lake, sporting activities on site include a tennis court, archery and bicycle hire. The city of Langres with its old ramparts and ancient city centre is within easy reach – it was elected one of the 50 most historic cities in France – and it is well worth a visit.

Facilities

Two toilet blocks have all facilities in cabins (only one is open in low season). Facilities for disabled visitors and babies. Laundry facilities. Motorcaravan services. Shop, bar and restaurant (with takeaway food). Indoor pool complex with spa and sauna. Heated outdoor pool (15/6-15/9). Games room. Playground. Extensive games area. Tennis (free in low season). WiFi. Off site: Lake with beach. Boat and bicycle hire and cycle tracks around lake. Fishing 100 m. Riding 5 km. Golf 40 km.

Open: 1 April - 15 October.

Directions

From Langres take the N19 towards Vesoul. After 3 km. turn right, straight after the large river bridge, then follow site signs. GPS: 47.87022, 5.37627

Charges guide

Per unit incl. 2 persons and electricity	€ 22.00 - € 31.00
extra person	€ 6.00 - € 8.00
child (2-12 yrs)	€ 3.00 - € 4.50

Camping Cheques accepted.

KAWAN CAMPING DE LA LIEZ★★★★

kawan

The team of Camping la la Liez welcomes you on their campsite!

NEW in 2012:
- Toboggan
- Pitches with private sanitary block
- 'Stop&Go' pitches
- Poney Club

Kawan Camping de la Liez★★★★ - Rue des Voiliers - 52200 Peigney
Tel : 0033 (0)3.25.90.27.79 - Fax : 0033 (0)3.25.90.66.79
email: campingliez@free.fr - web: www.campingliez.com

Mesnil Saint Père

Kawan Resort Lac d'Orient

Rue du Lac, F-10140 Mesnil Saint Père (Aube) T: 03 25 40 61 85. E: info@camping-lacdorient.com

alanrogers.com/FR10020

Le Lac d'Orient opened in 2009 and is one of the first Kawan Resorts, a new group of campsites in attractive rural locations and equipped with a good range of leisure amenities. The site can be found at the centre of the large Forêt d'Orient natural park and is just 100 m. from the Lac d'Orient which is ideal for all manner of watersports. Previously, a small municipal site, Kawan Resort Lac d'Orient has been rebuilt and offers a new restaurant, bar and takeaway, as well as a heated indoor pool and outdoor swimming pools with slides, all in one complex with the reception and the shop. The pitches here are large and are semi-shaded with mature trees.

Facilities

One new, purpose built toilet block and one refurbished, both of a high standard. Facilities for disabled visitors. Laundry facilities. Motorcaravan services (outside site). Restaurant, bar and takeaway (31/3-16/9). Shop (as site). Heated indoor pool (as site) and outdoor pools with slides (28/4-16/9). Spa bath. TV room. Play area. Multisports court. Only one dog per pitch accepted. WiFi (free). Off site: Lac de l'Orient 100 m. Windsurfing and sailing. Canoe and pedalo hire. Fishing. Troyes 20 km.

Open: 31 March - 30 September.

Directions

Mesnil Saint-Père is close to the intersection of the A5 and A26 motorways, 20 km. east of Troyes. From the north, leave the A26 at exit 23 and join the eastbound D619, signed Lac d'Orient. Turn left on D43 following signs to Mesnil Saint-Père and then site. GPS: 48.254856, 4.341359

Charges guide

Per unit incl. 2 persons and electricity	€ 25.00 - € 34.00

Camping Cheques accepted.

Langres
Camping Navarre

9 boulevard Maréchal de Lattre de Tassigny, F-52200 Langres (Haute-Marne) T: 03 25 87 37 92.
E: campingnavarre@free.fr **alanrogers.com/FR52060**

Camping Navarre is a small municipal site of 60 pitches, with the advantage of being located in a unique position within the town of Langres. The pitches here are grassy, well shaded and of a good size (80-120 sq.m.), all with electrical connections (10A). The site's toilet block has all the usual facilities and is a new building of architectural merit. Although there are few amenities on site, the town centre is just a short walk away with a wide selection of shops, cafés and restaurants. Langres, with its 3.5 km. of ancient ramparts and imposing towers, is classified as one of the 50 most beautiful towns in France and makes a popular overnight stop. For those choosing to spend longer in the Haute-Marne, the surrounding countryside, Lac de la Liez (resulting from the construction of the Marne - Saône canal) and the Marne valley are well worth exploration. The Liez sailing school offers opportunities for windsurfing, sailing, and canoe and pedalo hire.

Facilities	Directions
Modern, heated toilet block with facilities for disabled visitors. Play area. WiFi (free, near reception). Off site: Langres centre. Fishing (river) 3 km. Lac de la Liez 5 km. Cycle and walking tracks.	Langres is close to the intersection of the A5 and A31 motorways. Leave either motorway and head for the town centre. Site is well signed. GPS: 47.86085, 5.33029

Open: 15 March - 31 October.

Charges guide

Per unit incl. 2 persons	
and electricity	€ 13.10 - € 15.30
extra person	€ 2.60 - € 3.30
child (2-13 yrs)	€ 1.30 - € 1.50

For a one-night stop or a longer stay in the historical city of Langres the campsite Navarre is ready to welcome you with a brand new toilet block

Camping Navarre • 9, Boulevard Marechal de Lattre de Tassigny • 52200 Langres
Tél./fax: 0033 (0)325 87 37 92 • E-mail: campingnavarre@free.fr • www.campingnavarre.fr

Pont-Sainte-Marie
Camping Municipal de Troyes

7 rue Roger Salengro, F-10150 Pont-Sainte-Marie (Aube) T: 03 25 81 02 64. E: info@troyescamping.net
alanrogers.com/FR10010

This municipal campsite, within the Troyes city boundary and about 2 km. from the centre, has been developed by two young enthusiastic managers who are turning it into an attractive place to stay. There are 140 level, grassy pitches (six with hardstanding), all for tourers, about equally shaded and open and with electricity (10A Europlug). Being on one of the main routes from Luxembourg to the southwest of France, and on the main route from Calais to the Mediterranean, Troyes makes a good night stop or a base for discovering the lively city.

Facilities	Directions
Two modern toilet blocks contain British style WCs, washbasins and preset showers. Facilities for disabled visitors. Motorcaravan services. Washing machines and dryer. Shop for basics. Gas supplies. Restaurant, snack bar and takeaway (15/5-15/9), bar (20/6-10/9). Heated outdoor swimming pool (15/5-15/9). WiFi throughout (free). TV room. Games room. Playground. Minigolf. Boules. Bicycle hire. Off site: Bus to Troyes centre 100 m. Supermarket 100 m. Other shops, restaurants, bars, ATM 300 m. Riding 8 km.	From all routes follow signs for Troyes and Pont-Sainte-Marie (just north of the old city centre), then signs for Camping Municipal. Site is on the Chalons road no. 77. GPS: 48.31124, 4.09683

Open: 1 April - 15 October.

Charges 2012

Per unit incl. 2 persons	
and electricity	€ 20.50 - € 24.80
extra person	€ 5.20 - € 6.20
child (2-11 yrs)	€ 3.35 - € 4.40
dog	€ 1.00

For latest campsite news, availability and prices visit
alanrogers.com

For centuries, Lorraine has been a major European crossroads, resulting in a rich mixture of cultural influences. Today, it is an idyllic setting for holidays with a diverse historical and cultural heritage, plus endless forests, lakes, rivers and mountains to explore.

DÉPARTEMENTS: 54 MEURTHE-ET-MOSELLE, 55 MEUSE, 57 MOSELLE, 88 VOSGES

MAJOR CITIES: NANCY, METZ

Along with Alsace, Lorraine has suffered as a tract of Europe over which nations have incessantly waged war. Lorraine became part of France in the late 18th century, after which there was a further period of German rule from 1872-1918, followed by a temporary re-annexation under Hitler. In the north and the east of the region, architecture, cuisine and language show Germanic influence, yet the people consider themselves thoroughly French.

From Nancy, north to the border, is a region of outstanding beauty with dense woodlands, the haunt of deer and boar. South of Nancy are spa towns and villages such as Vittel, Bains-les-Bains and Plombières, and the birthplace of St Joan of Arc at Domrémy. The Vosges crests formed part of the battle front in World War One and military requirements led to the building of the road now known as the Route des Cretes which runs near to the highest peaks. It goes past more WWI sites than vineyards, and more 'ballons' (the highest peaks are so-called because they are round and bald) than villages but the view from the top is utterly breathtaking.

Places of interest

Epinal: picturesque town and capital of the Vosges.

Fermont: underground fort at Longuyon, 50 km. north of Verdun.

Metz: a Gallo-Roman city, situated in a strategic defensive position and as a crossroads of trade routes. Some medieval walls and arches, but pride of place goes to the 13th-century cathedral of St Etienne.

Nancy: at the confluence of the Meurthe and Moselle rivers, owes many of its architectural attractions to Duke Stanislas, an exiled king of Poland. Influenced by Louis XV (his son-in-law), he modelled the town on the mode favoured by the court at that time – elaborate façades, imaginative gardens and fountains and vanities such as the Arc de Triomphe of Place Stanislas.

Verdun: hill forts such as Fort de Vaux and Fort de Douaumont, large military cemetery at Douaumont.

Cuisine of the region

The cooking is peppery and hearty and quite unlike any other region.

Bar-le-Duc ('Lorraine caviar'): redcurrant jam de-seeded with a goose quill.

Quiche Lorraine: made only in the classical manner with cream, eggs and bacon.

Vittel and Contrexéville: famous as the sources of mineral waters.

Eaux-de-vie: a strong, white alcohol liqueur distilled from fermented fruit juices, including mirabelles (small yellow plums), cherries and pears.

www.tourism-lorraine.com
contact@tourisme-lorraine.fr
(0)3 83 80 01 80

BELGIUM LUXEMBOURG

0   25   50 kms

LUXEMBOURG

GERMANY

THIONVILLE
A30

SAARBRUCKEN

BURTONCOURT

A4,E25,50

VERDUN   A4,E50   METZ

SARREGUEMINES

FRANCALTROFF

MEUSE 55   A31,E21,E23   MOSELLE 57

LORRAINE

SARREBOURG

BAR-LE-DUC

NANCY
TOUL   VILLERS-LES-NANCY
VILLEY-LE-SEC   LUNEVILLE

ALSACE

MEURTHE-ET-MOSELLE 54

A31,E21
NEUFCHATEAU

HERPELMONT   CORCIEUX
SANCHEY   GRANGES-
REHAUPAL   SUR-VOLOGNE
VOSGES 88   LE THOLY
LA BRESSE
CHAUMONT   SAULXURES-SUR-MOSELOTTE
CHAMPAGNE   BUSSANG
ARDENNE   ST-MAURICE-SUR-MOSELLE   THANN

FRANCHE
COMTE   LURE
VESOUL

For latest campsite news, availability and prices visit
alanrogers.com

Burtoncourt

Camping la Croix du Bois Sacker

F-57220 Burtoncourt (Moselle) T: 03 87 35 74 08. E: camping.croixsacker@wanadoo.fr

alanrogers.com/FR57080

This very attractive site is quiet and child friendly and has been run for the last few years by a young and enthusiastic couple who have made many improvements to this former municipal site. For example, the terrace has been enlarged, a small shop added and the facilities for disabled visitors improved. There are 60 small to medium, uneven and open pitches, some with shade and all with electricity and water taps. The site is not far from Metz and is well suited for travellers going south to Germany, Switzerland or Italy. Forming part of the site, a lake is good for fishing (carp).

Facilities	Directions
The seasonal and touring parts of the site have separate facilities. Showers are on payment (token). Turkish style toilets outnumber British style. Washbasins, some in cabins. Facilities may become stretched at peak times. Shop. Bar. Sports field and tennis court. Play area. Lake swimming (July/Aug). Fishing. WiFi. Off site: Woodland walks.	From the A4 take exit 37 (Argancy) and follow signs for Malroy, Chieulles and Vany on RD3 towards Bouzonville. Then take D53 to Burtoncourt and site. GPS: 49.22499, 6.39943

Open: 1 April - 20 October.

Charges guide

Per unit incl. 2 persons and electricity	€ 16.00
extra person	€ 4.00
child (2-12 yrs)	€ 2.50

Bussang

Kawan Village Domaine de Champé

14 rue des Champs-Navés, F-88540 Bussang (Vosges) T: 03 29 61 61 51. E: info@domaine-de-champe.com

alanrogers.com/FR88050

Bordered by the Moselle river, surrounded by the mountains of the Vosges and located just off the town square, this site is open all year making it a good base from which to explore in summer, and ideal for skiing in winter, when you might be tempted to rent one of the 12 chalets. Domaine de Champé is a level site with 110 touring pitches, all with electricity (4-12A), spread over a fairly large area on both sides of a tributary stream, so some are quite a distance from the facilities. There are two heated pools, one large outside and a smaller one inside. The village boasts a Theatre of the People, founded in 1895, giving shows in July and August. The Casino is open all year and is very popular.

Facilities	Directions
Two sanitary units, one behind reception, a smaller one in a more central position, are adequate rather than luxurious and include two family rooms. Facilities for disabled campers. Motorcaravan services. Bar and restaurant (all year), takeaway (high season). Swimming pools (outdoor 1/5-30/9, indoor all year). Wellness centre (charged) including sauna, hammam and relaxation room. Tennis. Two large play areas. WiFi (charged). Off site: Skiing 3 km. Lake fishing 3.5 km. Riding 4 km. Shops and all other services at Le Thillot 10 km.	Bussang is about midway between Remiremont and Mulhouse on N66, almost due north of Belfort. Site is signed from town. GPS: 47.888617, 6.85715

Open: All year.

Charges guide

Per unit incl. 2 persons and electricity	€ 22.00 - € 34.00
extra person	€ 5.00 - € 8.00
child (4-10 yrs)	€ 3.00 - € 6.00
Camping Cheques accepted.	

Corcieux

Camping Au Clos de la Chaume

21 rue d'Alsace, F-88430 Corcieux (Vosges) T: 03 29 50 76 76. E: info@camping-closdelachaume.com

alanrogers.com/FR88120

This pleasant site is within walking distance of the town, on level ground with a small stream adjacent. The friendly family owners, who are British and French, live on site and do their best to ensure campers have an enjoyable relaxing stay. There are 100 level grassy pitches of varying sizes and with varying amounts of sun and shade. All pitches have electricity hook-ups (6/10A) and some are divided by shrubs and trees. There are some chalets and caravan holiday homes on the site. The site has an attractive, well fenced, new swimming pool and a small adventure style playground. A Sites et Paysages member.

Facilities	Directions
Two units (one newly refurbished) provide well maintained facilities including a dual-purpose room for families and disabled visitors. Laundry with washing machines and dryers. Motorcaravan service point. Reception keeps basic supplies (July/Aug). New swimming pool (July-Sept). Play area. Games room. Boules. Volleyball. WiFi (charged). Off site: Bicycle hire 800 m. Riding 2 km. Fishing 3 and 10 km. Golf 30 km. Corcieux market (Mon).	Corcieux is 17 km. southwest of St Dié-des-Vosges. Site is on the D60, east of town centre, by the town boundary sign. GPS: 48.16826, 6.89025

Open: 28 April - 18 September.

Charges guide

Per unit incl. 2 persons and electricity	€ 16.00 - € 20.80
extra person	€ 4.80
child (2-7 yrs)	€ 3.00

For latest campsite news, availability and prices visit

alanrogers.com

Francaltroff
Parc Résidentiel de la Tensch

536

F-57670 Francaltroff (Moselle) T: 03 87 01 79 04. E: tensch@tensch.com
alanrogers.com/FR57090

La Tensch is a large leisure park located south of Saint Avold in the Moselle départment. The park has been developed around three lakes and fishing is understandably very popular here, although many watersports are also possible, including windsurfing, canoeing and jet skiing. Although there are 100 touring pitches, this is primarily a 'parc résidentiel' with a few mobile homes and chalets for rent, as well as residential units. Many footpaths lead around the lakes passing picnic areas and well designed playgrounds. There are two swimming pools, one especially for children with a water slide.

Facilities

Shop. Bar/restaurant. Takeaway. Swimming pool. Children's pool. Pedaloes. Canoe hire. Bicycle hire. Tennis. Trampolines. Play area. Games room. Activity and entertainment programme. Mobile homes and chalets for rent. Off site: Riding. Fishing. Cycle and walking tracks. St Avold.

Open: 20 March - 19 December.

Directions

Leave the A4 autoroute at exit 39 for Saint Avold and head south on D633 to Saint Avold. Continue south on D22 to Francaltroff and the site is clearly signed. GPS: 48.96083, 6.77444

Charges guide

Per unit incl. 2 persons and electricity	€ 17.50
extra person	€ 3.80

Granges-sur-Vologne
Camping Gadémont Plage

2 Gadémont, F-88640 Granges sur Vologne (Vosges) T: 03 29 51 44 60. E: deleeuw697@aol.com
alanrogers.com/FR88400

Camping Gadémont Plage is open all year and can be found within the Parc Naturel Régional des Ballons des Vosges, close to the town of Granges-sur-Vologne. Pitches here are terraced and are generally well shaded. A number of pitches can be found on the banks of the little river which runs through the site. There is also direct access to a small lake (canoeing is possible – courses are available) with fishing (free to campers). This is a good base for exploring the Vosges, which is, of course, a very popular region for adventure sports. Various activities are organised on site in peak season including occasional discos and sports competitions.

Facilities

Two modern, clean toilet blocks, one by reception is heated. Showers by token in July/Aug. Facilities for disabled visitors in one block. Restaurant/snack bar. Takeaway. Activity and entertainment programme. Canoeing. Fishing. Play area. Tourist information. Fully equipped chalets and mobile homes for rent. WiFi. English and Dutch spoken. Off site: Shops, restaurants and cafés in Granges-sur-Vologne 2 km. Bicycle hire 3 km. Riding 4 km. Boat launching, sailing and skiing 10 km. Gérardmer 10 km. Cycle and walking tracks.

Open: All year.

Directions

Approaching from Gérardmer, head north on D423 to Granges-sur-Vologne. You will see the site signed to the left around 100 m. before reaching the village. GPS: 48.123783, 6.818449

Charges guide

Per unit incl. 2 persons and electricity	€ 10.20 - € 17.00
dog	€ 1.50

Granges-sur-Vologne
Camping la Sténiole

1 le Haut Rain, F-88640 Granges-sur-Vologne (Vosges) T: 03 29 51 43 75. E: steniole@wanadoo.fr
alanrogers.com/FR88110

Set in a lovely rural area in the heart of the Vosges massif, this attractive site is run by a dedicated young couple who are constantly improving the site and its facilities. There are 70 pitches, either separated by hedges or beside the water. A small river has been used to form a small lake for fishing and swimming and a series of separate ponds (water quality is checked regularly). An atmosphere of relaxation is encouraged and the whole family can have a good time here. At an altitude of 720 m. there is easy access to 160 km. of paths and tracks for walking and cycling.

Facilities

A new toilet block now supplements the original, together with further facilities in the main building provide all necessities including 4 private cabins. Washing machines and dryers. Bar. Restaurant (July/Aug). Takeaway (1/6-30/8). Internet access on the terrace. Lake swimming. Fishing. Games room with TV and library. Play area. Tennis. Apartments and mobile homes to rent. Off site: Woods and hills for walking and cycling. Riding 5 km. Bicycle hire 4.5 km. Golf 30 km.

Open: 1 May - 30 September.

Directions

Take the N420 from Epinal to Gérardmer then the D423 to Granges. There are two sites not far away from each other. GPS: 48.1217, 6.8284

Charges guide

Per unit incl. 2 persons and electricity	€ 17.00
extra person	€ 3.50
child (under 8 yrs)	€ 2.50
dog	€ 1.00

For latest campsite news, availability and prices visit
alanrogers.com

Herpelmont

Camping Caravaning Domaine des Messires

1 rue des Messires, F-88600 Herpelmont (Vosges) T: 03 29 58 56 29. E: mail@domainedesmessires.com

alanrogers.com/FR88070

Nestling in woods beside a lake, des Messires is a haven of peace and is perfect for nature lovers – not just birds and flowers but beavers, too. The Vosges is famous for its mountains and you can easily cross the Col de Schlucht to the Moselle vineyards and the medieval villages like Riquewihr with their old walls and storks on chimneys. The 110 good sized and fully serviced pitches are on grass over stone, with some directly by the lakeside, excellent for fishing. When the day is over, enjoy a leisurely meal at the restaurant overlooking the lake or just relax over a glass of wine. There are 22 mobile homes for rent.

Facilities	Directions
The fully equipped, modern, airy toilet block includes all washbasins in cabins, provision for disabled visitors (key from reception), baby room and laundry. Bar and restaurant overlooking the lake (both 1/5-1/10). Takeaway (1/5-1/10). Two small play areas. Games and TV room. Canoeing and lake swimming. Programme of activities for children and adults in high season. WiFi (charged). Off site: Weekly markets in Bruyères, Corcieux and St Dié.	From Épinal, exit N57 on N420 for St Dié and follow signs until you pick up signs for Bruyères. Lac du Messires is signed as you leave Bruyères on D423, at Laveline go south to Herpelmont and site. GPS: 48.1787, 6.74309
Open: 23 April - 18 September.	

Charges guide

Per unit incl. 2 persons and electricity	€ 18.00 - € 26.00
extra person	€ 4.00 - € 6.50

La Bresse

Domaine du Haut des Bluches

5 route des Planches, F-88250 La Bresse (Vosges) T: 03 29 25 64 80. E: hautdesbluches@labresse.fr

alanrogers.com/FR88210

Le Haut des Bluches is attractively located in the rolling hills of the Vosges and is close to the ski resorts of Gérardmer and La Bresse. The site is open most of the year with skiing possible in winter and it is a good base for nature lovers in summer. There are 140 slightly uneven and sloping grass/gravel pitches informally laid out in groups on terraces. These include 105 for touring, all with electricity (4/8/13A Europlug), long leads and rock pegs advised. Special areas of hardstanding for motorcaravans include some electricity hook-ups. Although there is little organised on the site, La Bresse (4 km) has a wide range of activities on offer.

Facilities	Directions
Two well appointed, modern, heated toilet blocks include cabins with WC, basin and shower. Facilities for babies and disabled visitors. Motorcaravan services. Small shop (bread to order) and bar. Restaurant and takeaway (high season; weekends in low season). Games/TV room. Play area. Multisports court. Boules. Internet. Off site: ski resorts, 5-8 km. La Bresse with all amenities 4 km.	La Bresse is 25 km. south of Gérardmer on the D486. At the eastern end of the town turn south on Route des Planches. Site is signed, entrance in 350 m. GPS: 47.998986, 6.918324
Open: All year excluding November to mid December.	

Charges guide

Per unit incl. 2 persons and electricity	€ 13.90 - € 23.20
extra person	€ 3.10

Le Tholy

Camping de Noirrupt

15 chemin de l'Etang, F-88530 Le Tholy (Vosges) T: 03 29 61 81 27. E: info@jpvacances.com

alanrogers.com/FR88030

An attractive, modern, family-run site, Camping de Noirrupt has a commanding mountainside position with some magnificent views, especially from the upper terraces. This is a very comfortable and high quality site and one that is sure to please. The tarmac site road winds up through the site with pitches being terraced and cars parked in separate small car parks close by. The 70 lawn-like tourist pitches are generally spacious, and the whole site is beautifully landscaped and divided up with many attractive shrubs, flower beds, decking and trees. Paved paths and steps take more direct routes between levels.

Facilities	Directions
Two modern buildings at different levels, plus a small unit behind reception, all immaculate with modern fittings. Washbasins in cubicles, facilities for babies, children and disabled campers. Washing machines and dryer. Shop. Bar, snack bar and takeaway (6/7-22/8). Swimming pool (15x10 m. 1/6-15/9). TV room (1/6-15/9). Tennis. Organised activities in high season. WiFi (charged). Heated chalets for rent. Gas and charcoal barbecues only. No double-axle caravans or American RVs. Off site: Riding 300 m. Fishing 2 km. Supermarket at Le Tholy 2 km.	From Gérardmer take D417 west towards Remiremont. In Le Tholy turn right on D11, continue up hill for 2 km., and site is signed to your left. GPS: 48.0889, 6.728483
Open: 1 May - 15 October.	

Charges guide

Per unit incl. 2 persons and electricity	€ 19.10 - € 28.00
extra person	€ 4.13 - € 5.90
child (under 7 yrs)	€ 2.45 - € 3.50
dog	€ 1.40 - € 2.00

Metz

Camping Municipal de Metz-Plage

Allée de Metz-Plage, F-57000 Metz (Moselle) T: 03 87 68 26 48. E: campingmetz@mairie-metz.fr

alanrogers.com/FR57050

As this site is just a short way from the autoroute exit and within easy walking distance for the city centre, it could make a useful night stop if travelling from Luxembourg to Nancy or for a longer stay if exploring the area. By the Moselle river, the 151 pitches are on fairly level grass and most are under shade from tall trees. Sixty five pitches are fully serviced and 84 have electricity (10A). Tent pitches have a separate place beside the river.

Facilities

The two sanitary blocks, one newer than the other, are acceptable if not luxurious. Facilities for disabled visitors. Baby room. Laundry and dishwashing facilities. Motorcaravan service point. Shop. Bar, restaurant and takeaway. Hardstanding pitches for overnight stops for motorcaravans without electricity. WiFi (free). Bicycle hire. Fishing (permits for sale). Off site: Indoor pool adjacent (free entry). Riding 5 km. Golf 8 km.

Open: 24 April - 5 October.

Directions

From autoroute take the Metz-Nord-Pontiffray exit 33 and follow site signs. GPS: 49.12402, 6.16917

Charges guide

Per unit incl. 2 persons and electricity	€ 18.00
extra person	€ 3.00
child (4-10 yrs)	€ 1.50
dog	€ 0.50

Rehaupal

Camping du Barba

45 le village, F-88640 Rehaupal (Vosges) T: 03 29 66 35 57. E: barba@campingdubarba.com

alanrogers.com/FR88100

Located in the refreshing and beautiful Haute-Vosges region, this small, very pleasant campsite is owned and run by a dedicated couple. There is room for 50 units on well tended, unmarked grass where you pitch where you like. This creates a very relaxed, natural environment with hedges and mature trees providing shelter and shade (overhanging trees could cause problems for large units). The site is in the heart of the village with an auberge next door for fine wines and good food, including local specialities. The surrounding hills offer 150 km. of marked walking and bike trails. Gérardmer and the Valley of the Lakes are just 15 minutes away.

Facilities

The single toilet block, built in chalet style, is of an acceptable standard and should be sufficient. Washing machine and dryer. Bread delivered. Auberge next door for meals and takeaway (to order) and small shop. Off site: Supermarket 5 km. Walking, cycling, skiing and fishing. Riding 6 km.

Open: 1 May - 1 October.

Directions

From Gérardmer follow signs to Rehaupal. Site is very well signed. GPS: 48.11892, 6.73130

Charges guide

Per unit incl. 2 persons and electricity	€ 14.90 - € 19.50
extra person	€ 3.60 - € 4.20
child (under 7 yrs)	€ 2.00

Saint Maurice-sur-Moselle

Camping les Deux Ballons

17 rue du Stade, F-88560 Saint Maurice-sur-Moselle (Vosges) T: 03 29 25 17 14. E: stan0268@orange.fr

alanrogers.com/FR88010

Les Deux Ballons is in a narrow valley near the source of the River Moselle in the Vosges. The 168 pitches (150 fully serviced, 4-15A electricity) are on stoney ground or grass, some under trees and others in the open by a stream that runs through the site. Wild birds are abundant, including kingfishers. Try an exhilarating walk to the top of the nearby Ballon d'Alsace, 1250 m. (or drive and walk the last half a mile). Theatre lovers should visit Bussang (6 km) and see the large wooden People's Theatre, built in 1895 and still performing in July and August every year; you will marvel at the raked stage and the enormous backstage areas which may be visited at any time.

Facilities

Two new up-to-date toilet blocks (open all season) and two older ones (high season only). Facilities for disabled campers and babies. Laundry. Motorcaravan service point. Gas supplies. Bar and takeaway (July/Aug). Large heated swimming pool with slide and children's pool (15/6-31/8). Walks, fishing, boules, TV. Internet point and WiFi (charged). Tennis. Bicycle hire. Off site: Shops and restaurant nearby. Riding 3 km. Paragliding 6 km. Mulhouse and car museum 30 mins.

Open: 10 April - 15 September.

Directions

Site is on main N66 Le Thillot - Bussang road on western edge of St Maurice behind Avia filling station (entrance partly obscured - keep a look out). GPS: 47.85517, 6.81108

Charges guide

Per unit incl. 2 persons and electricity	€ 20.80 - € 34.00
extra person	€ 5.50 - € 5.80
child (2-7 yrs)	€ 4.10 - € 4.20
dog	€ 3.00 - € 3.50

No credit cards (except for on-line bookings).

For latest campsite news, availability and prices visit

alanrogers.com

Sanchey
Kawan Village Lac de Bouzey

19 rue du Lac, F-88390 Sanchey (Vosges) T: 03 29 82 49 41. E: lacdebouzey@orange.fr

alanrogers.com/FR88040

Open all year, Camping Lac de Bouzey is 8 km. west of Épinal, at the start of the Vosges Massif. The 147 reasonably level grass pitches are separated by very tall trees and some hedging giving varying amounts of shade. There are 107 for touring, all with electricity (6/10A) and 100 fully serviced. They are on a gently sloping hillside above the lake and there are views over the lake and its sandy beaches. In high season there is entertainment for all ages, especially teenagers, and the site will be very lively. English is spoken.

Facilities	Directions
The refurbished toilet block includes a baby room and one for disabled visitors (some gradients). Small, heated section in main building with toilet, washbasin and shower is used in winter. Laundry facilities. Motorcaravan service point. Shop and bar (all year), restaurant and takeaway (1/3-1/11). Heated pool (1/5-30/9). Fishing. Riding. Games room. Archery. Bicycle hire. Internet access. Soundproofed room for cinema and discos (high season). Lake beach, bathing and boating. WiFi. Off site: Golf 8 km.	Site is 8 km. west of Épinal on the D460. From Épinal follow signs for Lac de Bouzey and Sanchey. At western end of Sanchey turn south, site signed. GPS: 48.16692, 6.35990

Charges guide

Per unit incl. 2 persons and electricity	€ 23.00 - € 34.00
extra person	€ 6.00 - € 10.00

Camping Cheques accepted.

Open: All year.

Saulxures-sur-Moselotte
Base de Loisirs du Lac de la Moselotte

Les Amias B.P. 34, F-88290 Saulxures-sur-Moselotte (Vosges) T: 03 29 24 56 56. E: contact@lac-moselotte.fr

alanrogers.com/FR88090

This neat, well run, spacious lakeside site, part of a leisure village complex, has 105 grassy pitches with 63 for touring. All have electricity (10A) and 30 of these also have water and a drain. They are individually hedged and a variety of young trees give only a little shade. The site is fully fenced with a security barrier with a key used for the gates to the lakeside. The adjacent 'Base de Loisirs' has a wide variety of activities on offer and the area is very good for walking and cycling. This is a good base for both summer and winter.

Facilities	Directions
The heated toilet block has key entry, controllable hot showers, some washbasins in cubicles and good facilities for babies and disabled campers. Laundry facilities. Shop (July/Aug). Bread to order. Bar/snack bar and terrace. Bicycle hire. Play area. Outdoor skittle alley. Entertainment programme (July/Aug). Base de Loisirs adjacent with lake (swimming supervised July/Aug), sandy beach, play area, climbing wall, fishing, archery and hire of pedaloes, canoes and kayaks. 30 chalets for rent. Off site: Saulxures-sur-Moselotte 1.5 km. with shops, bars and restaurants.	Saulxures-sur-Moselotte is 20 km. east of Remiremont. From Remiremont take D417 east (St Amé), then right (southeast) on D43 towards La Bresse for 10.5 km. Turn left into Saulxures (site signed), entrance on right by lake after 700 m. GPS: 47.95273, 6.75212

Charges guide

Per unit incl. 2 persons and electricity	€ 18.00 - € 21.00
extra person	€ 4.00 - € 5.00

Open: All year.

Verdun
Camping les Breuils

Allée des Breuils, F-55100 Verdun (Meuse) T: 03 29 86 15 31. E: contact@camping-lesbreuils.com

alanrogers.com/FR55010

Thousands of soldiers of many nations are buried in the cemeteries around this famous town and the city is justly proud of its determined First World War resistance. Les Breuils is a neat, attractive site beside a small fishing lake and close to the town and Citadel. It provides 162 flat pitches of varying sizes on two levels (144 for touring units), many with shade. Separated by trees or hedges, they are beside the lake and 120 offer electricity connection (6A) – long leads will be necessary for some. The 'Citadelle Souterraine' is well worth a visit and is within walking distance of the site.

Facilities	Directions
Two sanitary blocks are a mixture of old and new, including washbasins in cabins for ladies. Laundry. Facilities for disabled visitors and babies. Cleaning variable. Motorcaravan services. Shop (1/5-30/9). Guide books on sale at reception (1/5-31/8). Restaurant (1/6-20/8), bar (evenings 1/5-30/9). Swimming pool (200 sq.m) and children's pool (15/5-31/8). Fenced gravel play area. Multisports complex. Bicycle hire. WiFi.	The RN3 forms a sort of ring road round the north of the town. Site is signed from this on the west side of the town (500 m. to site). GPS: 49.15404, 5.36573

Charges guide

Per unit incl. 2 persons and electricity	€ 17.10 - € 20.80
extra person	€ 4.20 - € 5.80

Credit cards accepted (minimum € 15).

Open: 1 April - 30 September.

For latest campsite news, availability and prices visit

alanrogers.com

Villers-les-Nancy

Campéole le Brabois

Campé●le

Avenue Paul Muller, F-54600 Villers-les-Nancy (Meurthe-et-Moselle) T: 03 83 27 18 28.
E: brabois@campeole.com alanrogers.com/FR54000

This former municipal site is within the Nancy city boundary and 5 km. from the centre. Situated within a forest area, there is shade in most parts and, although the site is on a slight slope, the 185 good-sized, numbered and separated pitches are level. Of these, 160 pitches have electrical connections (5/15A) and 30 also have water and drainage. Being on one of the main routes from Luxembourg to the south of France, Le Brabois makes a good night stop. However, Nancy is a delightful city in the heart of Lorraine and well worth a longer stay. There are many attractions in the area including the interesting 18th-century Place Stanislas (pedestrianised) and 11th-century city centre. The British manager has a wide range of tourist literature, publishes a monthly English newsletter and is pleased to help plan visits and day trips. Horse racing takes place every two weeks at the Nancy race track next to the campsite, and good wine is produced nearby.

Facilities

Four sanitary blocks have been completely updated. Facilities for babies and disabled visitors. Laundry facilities. Motorcaravan service point. Shop (incl. eggs and other produce grown on site). Bread to order. Restaurant with bar, takeaway and small shop (15/6-15/9). Library. Two playgrounds. WiFi (free from 2nd night). Off site: Restaurants, shops 1 km. Walking and cycling. Regular buses to Nancy.

Open: 1 April - 15 October.

Directions

From autoroute A33 take exit 2b for Brabois and continue for 500 m. to 'Quick' restaurant on left. Turn left, pass racetrack to T-junction, turn right and after 400 m. turn right on to site entrance road. GPS: 48.66440, 6.14330

Charges guide

Per unit incl. 2 persons	
and electricity	€ 13.60 - € 18.70
extra person	€ 4.00 - € 5.60
child (2-6 yrs)	free - € 3.60
Credit cards minimum € 15.	

Campé●le
CAMPSITES AND RENTALS
LORRAINE

Le Brabois★★★
Peaceful, ideal to visit Nancy (Stanilas square).
Amenities, pitches and accommodations of high quality.

54600 Villers Les Nancy · Tel.: +33-383-2718-28 · www.campeole.co.uk / brabois@campeole.com

Villey-le-Sec

Camping de Villey-le-Sec

34 rue de la Gare, F-54840 Villey-le-Sec (Meurthe-et-Moselle) T: 03 83 63 64 28.
E: info@campingvilleylesec.com alanrogers.com/FR54010

This neat campsite is a popular overnight stop, but the area is worth a longer stay. Villey-le-Sec has its own fortifications, part of the defensive system built along France's frontiers after the 1870 war, and a long cycle track passes near the site. On a bank of the Moselle river, there are 96 level grassy marked touring pitches, with electricity (6/10A) and plenty of water taps. There are also individual water taps and waste water drainage for eight of these pitches. Another area without electricity accommodates 11 tents. Just outside the site is an overnight stopping place for motorcaravans.

Facilities

Two modern toilet blocks (one heated) contain British style WCs, washbasins in cabins and controllable showers. Facilities for disabled visitors and babies. Motorcaravan services. Washing machine and dryer. Bar/restaurant. Snack bar and takeaway (all 15/4-20/9). Shop. Playground. Playing field. Table tennis. Boules. Fishing. Off site: Riding 2 km. Rock climbing 4 km. Golf 15 km.

Open: 1 April - 30 September.

Directions

Villey-le-Sec is 7 km. east of Toul. Leave A31 west of Nancy at exit 15 and after 1 km. at roundabout (Leclerc supermarket) take D909 to Villey-le-Sec. In village follow signs 'Camping' to the right. At bottom of hill turn left to site in 300 m. GPS: 48.65281, 5.99151

Charges guide

Per unit incl. 2 persons	
and electricity (6A)	€ 17.50 - € 20.30
extra person	€ 3.50

(139)

Sites & Paysages DE FRANCE

Discover our selection
of 58 campsites, 3, 4 and 5 stars,
very comfortable, very natural
and in the middle of the most beautiful
sites of France!

58 destinations
for your future holidays,
so don't hesitate any longer!

16€

Special offer:
A special price of 16 € for
a Confort pitch for 2 persons,
caravan or tent or camper van,
electricity included, except July and August
at the presentation of this Guide!
Children younger than 2 years can stay
free of charge and one pet is included!

So we'll see you very soon at our place..
where you can make yourself at home!!!

Make your reservation on our website 24/7:
www.sites-et-paysages.com
or contact us at 0033 475.352.236.

Sites & Paysages de France
89, rue du Petit Bois - 07120 RUOMS (FRANCE)
Tél. 04 75 35 22 36 - Fax 04 75 93 95 50
contact@sites-et-paysages.com
www.sites-et-paysages.com

Lying between the Rhine and the Vosges mountains, to the north and east, Alsace shares a border with Germany, to the south with German-speaking Switzerland and to the west with Lorraine and Franche Comté.

DÉPARTMENTS: 67 BAS-RHIN, 68 HAUT-RHIN

MAJOR CITY: STRASBOURG

Historically speaking, Alsace was part of the German-speaking area of central Europe and to this day a large proportion of the population, of all generations, speak or understand Alsatian, a dialectal form of German closely resembling the German spoken in Switzerland. In the last two centuries, Alsace has passed back and forth between Germany and France and back and back again; consequently, it is a region that was not part of France at the time of the makings of the modern-day nation, and has held on to a number of institutional differences, particularly concerning religious affairs. For example, Good Friday is a public holiday in Alsace, but not in the rest of France.

In architectural terms, Alsace is definitely Germanic. Descend from the Vosges mountains into the Alsace vineyards and the fairytale wine villages and towns which fringe the broad Rhine Valley with the Grand Canal d'Alsace running parallel. Follow the well signed tourist route, the 'Route des Vins' and look in on the most picturesque towns – Obernai, Riquewihr and Ribeauville. Strasbourg is the capital, a busy city with a wide industrial girdle and an exquisite medieval centre, now the home of the European Parliament.

Places of interest

Colmar: interesting for its 16th-century timber houses. Musée d'Unterlinden.

Kayserberg: small town, birthplace of Albert Schweitzer. Special Christmas market.

Le Linge: a football pitch-sized hilltop where in 1915, 17,000 French and German soldiers lost their lives. The opposing trenches including rusty barbed wire have been left as they were as a reminder of the pain and futility of war.

Mulhouse: famous for the Musée National de l'Automobile and the Musée Français de Chemin de Fer.

Riquewihr: almost untouched since the 18th century (whilst almost every other village was decimated by war) with 13/14th-century fortifications and medieval houses.

Cuisine of the region

Beckenoffe (Baeckeoffe): a hotpot of potatoes, lamb, beef, pork and onions, cooked in local wine.

Choucroute: sauerkraut with peppercorns, boiled ham, pork, Strasbourg sausages and boiled potatoes.

Chou farci: stuffed cabbage.

Foie gras: goose liver.

Tarte a l'oignon Alsacienne: onion and cream tart.

www.tourisme-alsace.com
crt@tourisme-alsace.com
(0)3 89 24 73 50

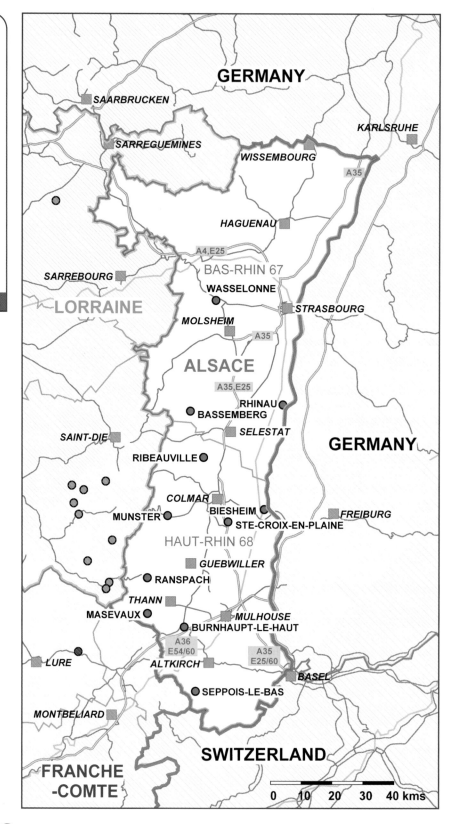

GERMANY

SAARBRUCKEN

KARLSRUHE

SARREGUEMINES

WISSEMBOURG

A35

HAGUENAU

A4,E25

SARREBOURG

BAS-RHIN 67

WASSELONNE

LORRAINE

MOLSHEIM

STRASBOURG

A35

ALSACE

A35,E25

RHINAU

BASSEMBERG

SELESTAT

SAINT-DIE

GERMANY

RIBEAUVILLE

COLMAR

BIESHEIM

FREIBURG

MUNSTER

STE-CROIX-EN-PLAINE

HAUT-RHIN 68

GUEBWILLER

RANSPACH

THANN

MASEVAUX

MULHOUSE

BURNHAUPT-LE-HAUT

A36
E54/60

A35
E25/60

LURE

ALTKIRCH

BASEL

SEPPOIS-LE-BAS

MONTBELIARD

SWITZERLAND

FRANCHE
-COMTE

0   10   20   30   40 kms

Bassemberg

Campéole le Giessen

Campé●le

Route de Villé, F-67220 Bassemberg (Bas-Rhin) T: 03 88 58 98 14. E: giessen@campeole.com

alanrogers.com/FR67070

Le Giessen is a member of the Campéole group and can be found at the foot of the Vosges mountains, with easy access to many of the best loved sights in Alsace. Although there is no pool on site, a large complex, comprising indoor and outdoor pools with a water slide, can be found adjacent to the site, with free admission for all campers. The 80 touring pitches here are grassy and of a good size, mostly with 6A electrical connections and some shaded by mature trees. A number of mobile homes and fully equipped tents are available for rent. Various activities are organised in high season including a children's club and disco evenings. Nearby places of interest include the magnificent fortified castle of Haut-Koenigsbourg, as well as the great cities of Strasbourg and Colmar. This is a good base for exploring the Vosges and the Route du Vin (bicycle hire in the village). The site's friendly managers will be pleased to recommend possible itineraries.

Facilities

Three toilet blocks with all facilities including controllable hot showers and facilities for disabled visitors. Laundry and dishwashing. Bar. Snack bar/takeaway (July/Aug). Play area. Multisports court. Activities and entertainment. Bicycle hire. Tourist information. Mobile homes and equipped tents for rent. WiFi (charged).
Off site: Swimming pool complex adjacent. Tennis. Rollerblading rink. Hiking and mountain biking. Fishing 1.5 km. Riding 5 km. Strasbourg 50 km.

Open: 1 April - 18 September.

Directions

Leave the A35 autoroute at exit 17 (Villé) and follow the D697 to Villé. Continue south on D39 to Bassemberg from where the site is well indicated. GPS: 48.33722, 7.28862

Charges guide

Per unit incl. 2 persons and electricity	€ 15.10 - € 24.50
extra person	€ 4.00 - € 6.10
child (2-6 yrs)	free - € 4.00
dog	€ 2.00 - € 2.60

ALSACE

Campé●le

CAMPSITES AND RENTALS

Le Giessen ★★★

At the foot of the Vosges mountains and many beautiful villages of Alsace. Amenities, pitches and accommodations of high quality. Free entrance to aquatic center.

67220 Bassemberg - Tel.: +33-388-5898-14 - www.campeole.co.uk / giessen@campeole.com

Biesheim

Village Center l'Ile du Rhin

Zone Touristique, Ile du Rhin, F-68600 Biesheim (Haut-Rhin) T: 03 89 72 57 95.
E: contact@village-center.com **alanrogers.com/FR68010**

In a pleasant island situation between the Rhine and the Canal d'Alsace, this site has views across the river to Breisach in Germany. It is well situated to explore the Vosges and the Black Forest. There are 251 hedged pitches, many occupied by seasonal static caravans, but including 65 touring pitches. Some vary in size but all have electrical connections and are on flat grass with good shade.

Facilities

Three well kept sanitary blocks (one heated) include washbasins in cabins. Laundry and dishwashing sinks. Washing machine and dryer. Shop. Bar, small restaurant with covered terrace, and takeaway (all 15/6-15/9, weekends only until 30/9). Playground. Table tennis and boules. Bicycle hire. Caravan storage. Off site: Fishing 100 m. Restaurant, heated pool (free entry for campers), sports ground and marina 200 m. Riding 1.5 km.

Open: All year excl. Christmas and New Year.

Directions

Site is reached from the bridge into Germany using the N415 Colmar - Freiburg road, signed beside the frontier post. Proceed under bridge northwards and site is to left past the restaurant. GPS: 48.02739, 7.57283

Charges guide

Per unit incl. 2 persons	€ 13.11
extra person	€ 3.75
child (under 7 yrs)	€ 1.90
electricity (4-10A)	€ 3.00 - € 5.75

No credit cards.
Camping Cheques accepted.

For latest campsite news, availability and prices visit

alanrogers.com

Burnhaupt le Haut

Camping les Castors

4 route de Guewenheim, F-68520 Burnhaupt le Haut (Haut-Rhin) T: 03 89 48 78 58.
E: camping.les.castors@wanadoo.fr **alanrogers.com/FR68300**

Camping les Castors provides a convenient starting point from which to explore the Alsace region. It is close to the Vosges mountains which are dominated by the Ballon d'Alsace (1427 m). This well cared for site with its stream and small lake offers 135 pitches with electricity 5/10A. Most are of a reasonable size and some have some shade. Fishing is possible in the lake and the site is on the banks of the river. Bicycle hire is available and there are walks in the adjacent forest and the surrounding countryside. The small village of Burnhaupt-le-Haut is within 1.5 km and has a supermarket, ATM and pharmacy.

Facilities	Directions
A new sanitary block offers modern facilities with showers and wash cubicles. Facilities for babies and disabled visitors. Laundry facilities. Attractive restaurant and bar with terrace serving traditional local food. Takeaway. Bread can be ordered from reception. Small play area. Fishing. Bicycle hire. WiFi on the terrace (charged). Off site: Excursions. Hiking. Supermarket 1.5 km.	Exit the D38 signed to Masevaux and Burnhapt-le-Haut. Take the D466 towards Masevaux. The site is signed to the right after 1 km. GPS: 47.746877, 7.124494

Open: 1 April - 31 October.

Charges guide

Per unit incl. 2 persons and electricity	€ 16.00 - € 16.80
extra person	€ 4.00
child (under 10 yrs)	€ 2.00
dog	€ 1.20

Masevaux

Camping de Masevaux

3 rue du Stade, F-68290 Masevaux (Haut-Rhin) T: 03 89 82 42 29. E: camping-masevaux@tv-com.net
alanrogers.com/FR68030

Masevaux is a pleasant little town in the Haut-Rhin département of Alsace, just north of the A36 Belfort - Mulhouse motorway. The neatly mown 110 pitches for tourers are on level grass, of reasonable size, marked by trees and hedges, and all have electricity (3/6A). Most are well shaded with good views of the surrounding hills. The pleasant and helpful Scottish managers, who take pride in the site, would like to welcome more British visitors. A good choice for one night or a longer stay to explore this interesting region, and an ideal destination for serious walkers.

Facilities	Directions
A modern, well designed and well equipped sanitary block has most washbasins in private cabins. Baby room. Laundry. Café/bar serving snacks. Baker calls in high season. Ice creams and soft drinks from reception. TV room, small library. Boules. Play area. Tennis (extra charge). Fishing. WiFi. Off site: Supermarket, restaurants and indoor pool. Wed. market in Masevaux. Bicycle hire 300 m. Golf 7 km. Riding 10 km. Beach 15 km.	From D466 in Masevaux follow signs for Belfort and then 'Camping Complexe Sportif'. GPS: 47.7782, 6.9909

Open: 10 January - 10 December.

Charges guide

Per unit incl. 2 persons and electricity	€ 17.30
extra person	€ 4.40
child (2-16 yrs)	€ 2.00 - € 3.20
dog	free

Munster

Village Center le Parc de la Fecht

Route de Gunsbach, F-68140 Munster (Haut-Rhin) T: 04 99 57 21 21. E: contact@village-center.com
alanrogers.com/FR68100

Part of the Village Center Group, this site has 228 pitches, some of which are occupied by mobile homes and chalets. The 139 touring pitches are on two levels in woodland and heavily shaded. Electricity (6A) is available to all but long leads may be necessary. A fast flowing river borders the length of the site on one side. This part of the Vosges is beautiful and great for walking and mountain-biking. The site is not far from the famous wine routes of Alsace and is close to historic Colmar and the medieval villages with storks nesting on chimneys.

Facilities	Directions
Two toilet blocks. Small play area for children. Mobile homes for rent. Off site: Supermarket, shops and restaurants in Munster. Riding 10 km. Swimming pool with water slides. Extensive walking and cycle (mountain bike) opportunities. Many picturesque Alsatian villages.	Site is 1 km east of the town centre on D10 and is well signed. GPS: 48.04325, 7.15118

Open: 15 December - 13 March, 15 June - 11 September.

Charges guide

Per unit incl. 2 persons and electricity	€ 14.00 - € 16.00
extra person	€ 3.00 - € 4.00
Camping Cheques accepted.	

For latest campsite news, availability and prices visit

alanrogers.com

Ranspach
Flower Camping les Bouleaux

8 rue des Bouleaux, F-68470 Ranspach (Haut-Rhin) T: 03 89 82 64 70. E: contact@alsace-camping.com

alanrogers.com/FR68140

Les Bouleaux is a well maintained site with 100 touring pitches of a rather small size (80 sq.m), although they are flat and grassy. The site is open all year round, although the outdoor swimming pools and the shop are only opened during the high season. The site is ideally situated if you are coming by motorbike or are planning to go paragliding or skiing. Les Bouleaux is set in the heart of the Thur valley, at the foot of the Vosges mountains. It offers many possibilities for outdoor activities such as climbing, playing golf, hiking and fishing, to name just a few. Also recommended is a visit to the Wesserling park and its beautiful gardens, which were established in 1699!

Facilities

Two traditional, clean sanitary blocks with showers. Good baby room. Facilities for disabled visitors. Laundry and dishwashing. Shop (July/Aug). Bar, restaurant, snack bar/takeaway (all year except Nov). Outdoor swimming and paddling pools (hats compulsory, no Bermuda shorts). Boules. Volleyball. Minigolf. Children's play area. WiFi (charged). Accommodation to rent. Off site: Fishing 1 km. Bicycle hire, beach and sailing 3 km.

Open: All year.

Directions

Leave the A31 and follow signs for Epinal on the E23. Approaching Epinal follow the E512 towards Mulhouse. Continue on the E512 until Ranspach. Drive on 700 m. on the 'route national', then turn right on rue des Bouleaux to the site. GPS: 47.880743, 7.010334

Charges guide

Per unit incl. 2 persons	
and electricity	€ 15.50 - € 21.50
extra person	€ 3.50 - € 4.50
child (under 8 yrs)	€ 2.80 - € 3.50
dog	€ 2.50 - € 3.00

château du
Haut-Kœnigsbourg

Bien plus qu'un monument

This fairy tale castle looks down majestically across the Alsace plain for more than 850 years. The château is open every day, all year round, except January 1st, May 1st and December 25th. Admission is free for under-18s visiting the castle with their family.

www.haut-koenigsbourg.fr/en

château du Haut-Kœnigsbourg

CONSEIL GÉNÉRAL
Bas-Rhin

For latest campsite news, availability and prices visit
alanrogers.com

Rhinau

Camping la Ferme des Tuileries

1 rue des Tuileries, F-67860 Rhinau (Bas-Rhin) T: 03 88 74 60 45. E: camping.fermetuileries@neuf.fr

alanrogers.com/FR67040

Close to the German border, this ten-hectare, family run site has 150 large open pitches, hardstanding for 15 motorcaravans and room for 50 seasonal caravans. The site buildings have a traditional external appearance but all have modern interiors. Welcoming reception staff will provide information about the site and the local area. A small lake with two water slides is used for swimming, fishing and boating (divided into two areas) and there is also a small unsupervised swimming pool (hats compulsory). A newly built restaurant and bar are at the lakeside. A ferry crosses the Rhine river into Germany from 1 km. away.

Facilities

Three modern, bright and cheerful blocks with the usual facilities. Two washing machines and two dryers. Controllable showers. Family bathroom at no extra charge. Fully equipped facilities for disabled visitors (no key, no coins). Motorcaravan services. Bar, restaurant and takeaway (July/Aug). Small lake for swimming, fishing, boating, two water slides. Swimming pool (unguarded) open July/Aug. Tennis. Pétanque. Minigolf. Bicycle hire. Dogs are not accepted. Off site: Supermarket 500 m.

Open: 1 April - 30 September.

Directions

Coming from Colmar (A35) take exit 14 (Kogenheim-Benfeld-Erstein) then the N83 to exit for Benfeld-Rhinau, following site signs. From Strasbourg on A35 take exit 7 (Erstein-Fegersheim) then the N83. GPS: 48.321, 7.698

Charges guide

Per unit incl. 2 persons and electricity	€ 14.60
extra person	€ 3.80
child (under 7 yrs)	€ 1.80

No credit cards or cheques.

Ribeauvillé

Camping Municipal Pierre de Coubertin

23 rue de Landau, F-68150 Ribeauvillé (Haut-Rhin) T: 03 89 73 66 71. E: camping.ribeauville@wanadoo.fr

alanrogers.com/FR68050

The fascinating medieval town of Ribeauvillé on the Alsace Wine Route is within walking distance of this attractive, quietly located site. Popular and well run, it has 226 touring pitches, all with 16A electricity and some separated by shrubs or railings. There are tarmac and gravel access roads. This is a site solely for touring units – there are no mobile homes or seasonal units here. The small shop is open daily for most of the season (hours vary) providing bread, basic supplies and some wines. Only breathable groundsheets are permitted.

Facilities

Large, heated block provides modern facilities with washbasins in cubicles. Baby facilities. Large laundry and dishwashing rooms. A smaller unit at the far end of the site is opened for July/Aug. Very good facilities for disabled campers at both units. Shop (Easter-Oct). Excellent adventure style play area with rubber base. Tennis. Boules. TV room. WiFi throughout. Off site: Outdoor pool (June-Aug). Bicycle hire 200 m.

Open: 15 March - 15 November.

Directions

Ribeauvillé is 13 km. southwest of Sélestat and site is well signed. Turn north off the D106 at traffic lights by large car park, east of the town centre. GPS: 48.19482, 7.33654

Charges guide

Per unit incl. 2 persons and electricity	€ 15.50 - € 16.50
extra person	€ 4.00

Saint Croix-en-Plaine

Camping Clair Vacances

Route de Herrlisheim, F-68127 Saint Croix-en-Plaine (Haut-Rhin) T: 03 89 49 27 28. E: clairvacances@orange.fr **alanrogers.com/FR68080**

Clair Vacances is a very neat, tidy and pretty site with 135 level pitches of generous size which are numbered and most are separated by trees and shrubs. All have electricity connections (16A) and 12 are fully serviced with water and drainage. The site has been imaginatively laid out with the pitches reached from hard access roads. This is a quiet family site. The friendly couple who own and run it will be pleased to advise on the attractions of the area. The site is 1 km. from the A35 exit, not far from Colmar in the region of Alsace, a popular and picturesque area.

Facilities

Two excellent, modern toilet blocks include washbasins in cabins, well equipped baby rooms and good facilities for disabled visitors. Laundry facilities. Swimming and paddling pools (heated) with large sunbathing area (1/5-15/9). Playground. Community room. Archery in high season. Camping Gaz. Dogs are not accepted. No barbecues or football. American motorhomes and twin axle caravans are not accepted. WiFi. Off site: Colmar.

Open: Week before Easter - 15 October.

Directions

Site is signed from exit 27 of the A35 on D1, halfway between St Croix-en-Plaine and Herrlisheim. GPS: 48.01606, 7.35016

Charges guide

Per unit incl. 2 persons and electricity	€ 16.50 - € 25.00
extra person	€ 4.50 - € 7.50
child (2-12 yrs)	€ 1.50 - € 5.00

For latest campsite news, availability and prices visit

alanrogers.com

Seppois-le-Bas

Village Center les Lupins

1 rue de la Gare, F-68580 Seppois-le-Bas (Haut-Rhin) T: 04 99 57 21 21. E: contact@village-center.com
alanrogers.com/FR68120

Only ten kilometres from the Swiss border and within walking distance of a small village (800 m), this is a very attractive site. It has 142 grass touring pitches, which are not separated and 25 chalets to rent. Attractive trees have been planted throughout the site. The main site building houses reception, a small shop, two pool tables and a television, and used to be the old local railway station (1910-1970). A very pleasant, small, fenced swimming pool is guarded in July and August, as is a playground for small children. The site is a member of the Village Center group.

Facilities	Directions
One good toilet block provides plenty of facilities in a traditional style. A second block is older but with similar facilities. Cabins for disabled visitors. Free hot water. Small shop. Bar and terrace. Swimming pool. Play area. Internet access. Off site: Village 800 m. Restaurant across the road. Forest walks.	Leave Belfort - Basel (CH) autoroute at Grandvillars. From Colmar/Strasbourg to Altkirch-Férette and Seppois-le-Bas. Leave A36 at Burnhaupt (exit 14) and take D103 towards Dannemarie, then the D7b to Seppois. From there follow signs to site. GPS: 47.53913, 7.17998

Open: 24 June - 4 September.

Charges guide

Per unit incl. 2 persons and electricity	€ 14.00 - € 16.00

Wasselonne

Camping Municipal Wasselonne

Route de Romanswiller, F-67310 Wasselonne (Bas-Rhin) T: 03 88 87 00 08.
E: camping-wasselonne@wanadoo.fr **alanrogers.com/FR67050**

A good quality municipal site with a resident warden. Facilities include a well stocked small shop, a crêperie in season and the added bonus of free admission to the superb indoor heated swimming pool adjacent to the site. There are 80 tourist pitches and around 20 seasonal units, on grass with a slight slope, all with electricity hook-ups (16A). Six new rental chalets are in a separate fenced area and there are six new private chalets. This could be an excellent base from which to visit Strasbourg.

Facilities	Directions
The single, large and well maintained sanitary unit has unisex facilities with ample sized showers and washbasins in cubicles. Laundry facilities and covered dishwashing sinks. No specific facilities for disabled visitors but the rooms are spacious and should be accessible to many. Excellent drive-over motorcaravan service point. Off site: Heated pool, hotel with restaurant, tennis courts and athletics stadium, all adjacent. Supermarket 500 m. Fishing and fitness trail 1 km. Riding 1.5 km.	Wasselonne is 25 km. west of Strasbourg. Site lies southwest of town centre on D224 towards Romanswiller, and is well signed. GPS: 48.6377, 7.4318

Open: 15 April - 15 October.

Charges guide

Per unit incl. 2 persons and electricity	€ 14.20 - € 14.80
extra person	€ 3.60 - € 3.80
child (0-10 yrs)	€ 2.00 - € 2.10
dog	€ 0.50 - € 0.60

Been to any good campsites lately?
We have

alan rogers

101 great campsites, ideal for your specific hobby, pastime or passion
Also available on iPad **alanrogers.com/digital**

For latest campsite news, availability and prices visit
alanrogers.com

With over one hundred of France's finest châteaux, this is a region to inspire the imagination. Stunning châteaux, peaceful gardens, fine food and wine, the Loire Valley has it all.

DÉPARTEMENTS: 18 CHER, 28 EURE-ET-LOIR, 36 INDRE, 37 INDRE-ET-LOIRE, 41 LOIR-ET-CHER, 45 LOIRET

MAJOR CITIES: ORLÉANS, BLOIS AND TOURS

In 2000, UNESCO gave official recognition to the Loire Valley for its architectural heritage combined with its exceptional unspoilt nature. The region is remarkable for its monumental architecture and the quality of its urban sites. Nowhere else in Europe do you find such a density of Renaissance castles or such quality of urban facades built on the riverbanks: Chambord, Amboise, Villandry, Chenonceau, all dotted along the Loire River and its tributaries. The Loire à Vélo long-distance cycle trail offers a delightful way to get back to nature and enjoy the unspoilt river banks, beautiful villages and historic cities.

Known as the Garden of France, the Loire's mild climate and fertile landscape of soft green valleys, lush vineyards and fields of flowers makes it a favourite with visitors. Renowned for its wines, with hundreds to choose from, all are produced from vineyards stretching along the main course of the River Loire. Cities such as Blois and Tours are elegant with fine architecture and museums, and Paris is only one hour by TGV.

Région Centre

Loire Valley

Architectural & Cultural Heritage

Amboise
Château, Leonardo da Vinci museum.

Beauregard
Château with Delft tiled floors.

Blois
Château with architecture from Middle Ages to Neo-Classical periods.

Chambord
Renaissance château.

Chaumont-sur-Loire
A world renowned International Garden Festival.

Chartres
Cathedral with stained glass windows.

Chinon
Old town, fine wines, Joan of Arc museum.

Orléans
Holy Cross cathedral, house of Joan of Arc.

Sancerre
Its vineyard and the Maison des Sancerre.

Sully-sur-Loire
A medieval fortress home to a number of tapestries, paintings, sculptures and pieces of furniture.

Tours
Renaissance and Neo-Classical mansions, cathedral of St Gatien.

Villandry
Famous Renaissance gardens.

Outdoor activities

Balloon Flights
France Montgolfières.

Cycling
www.**cycling-loire.com**

Cuisine of the region

Wild duck, pheasant, hare, deer and quail are classics, and freshwater fish such as zander, perch and eel are favourites.

Specialities
Rillettes, Rillons de Tours, Pâté de Chartres, mushrooms, green lentils of Berry and five different designations of origin (AOC) of goat's cheese are found in the region.

The home-made pears, 'Poires tapées à l'ancienne', the result of long and meticulous drying, served with salted dishes, pastries or ice cream.

Tarte Tatin: a succulent upside-down tart of caramelised apples and pastry.

Almond Pithiviers: puff pastry pie.

IImages © (left to right, top to bottom): Léonard de Serres; J. Damase – CRT Centre Val de Loire; S Le Donne; CL; C Mouton.

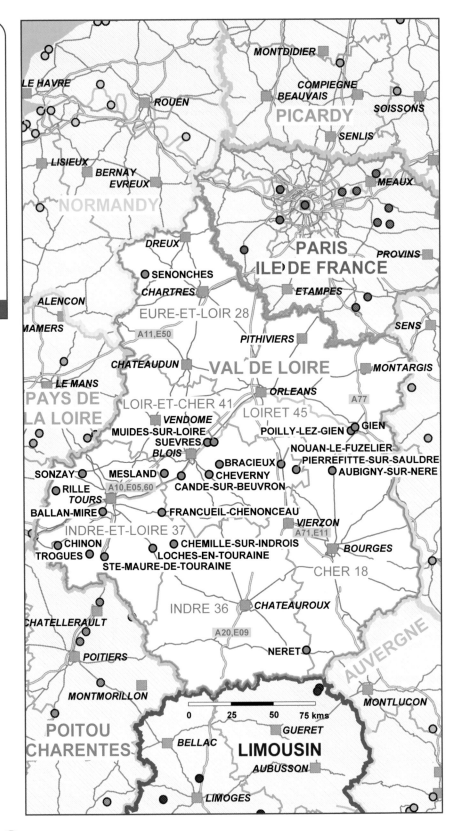

For latest campsite news, availability and prices visit

alanrogers.com

Aubigny-sur-Nère
Flower Camping les Etangs

Route de Sancerre, F-18700 Aubigny-sur-Nère (Cher) T: 02 48 58 02 37. E: camping.aubigny@orange.fr

alanrogers.com/FR18010

Les Etangs is a site of 100 pitches, close to the Sancerre vineyards and the lakes of the Sologne. A member of the Flower group, this site extends over two hectares and borders a small lake (suitable for fishing). Pitches are large and grassy (most have electrical connections). There are chalets available for rent. The town of Aubigny-sur-Nère is very close (1 km) and has a close attachment with Scotland, thanks to the 'Auld Alliance'. The town is the only one in France to celebrate French – Scottish friendship on Bastille Day. Bring your bicycle as there are many tracks running through the surrounding forests. A covered municipal swimming pool is 50 m. from the site (a charge is made). Various activities are organised on site during the high season, including special events for children.

Facilities

Two heated toilet blocks are a good provision and are well located. Bar (high season). Play area. Fishing (permit required). Activity and entertainment programme. WiFi (free). Chalets and tents for rent. Off site: Swimming pool 50 m. (with aqua-gym). Aubigny-sur-Nère 1 km. Riding 20 km. Sancerre vineyards. Walking and cycle tracks.

Open: 1 April - 30 September.

Directions

Aubigny is southeast of Orléans. Approaching from the north (Orléans) on the A71 autoroute take exit 4 for Salbris and head east on the D724 and D924 until Aubigny. Take the D923 towards Sancerre and site is 1 km. GPS: 47.48435, 2.45703

Charges guide

Per unit incl. 2 persons	€ 11.50 - € 18.90
extra person	€ 3.00 - € 4.00
child (2-7 yrs)	€ 2.00 - € 2.50
dog	free

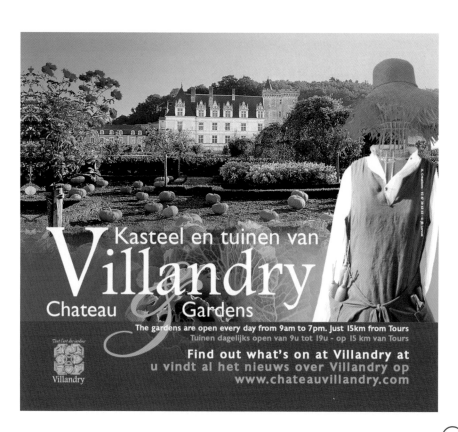

Kasteel en tuinen van **Villandry**

Chateau & Gardens

The gardens are open every day from 9am to 7pm. Just 15km from Tours
Tuinen dagelijks open van 9u tot 19u - op 15 km van Tours

Find out what's on at Villandry at
u vindt al het nieuws over Villandry op
www.chateauvillandry.com

Villandry

For latest campsite news, availability and prices visit

alanrogers.com

We can book this site for you! alan rogers ◐ travel

Call 01580 214000

Bracieux

Camping Indigo les Châteaux

11 rue Roger Brun, F-41250 Bracieux (Loir-et-Cher) T: 02 54 46 41 84.
E: chateaux@camping-indigo.com **alanrogers.com/FR41120**

Camping des Châteaux has recently joined the Indigo group and there are major plans for development and modernisation. This is a well-located site on the outskirts of Bracieux, convenient for many of the best known châteaux of the Loire valley. There are 350 flat, grassy pitches here, most of which are reserved for touring. Some pitches are grouped in blocks of four between hedges with electricity, water and drainage provided for each group. The majority, however, are more open with scattered water points and electrical connection boxes. Mature trees provide shade to most pitches. Rental accommodation is available in mobile homes or safari style tents. There is a good municipal swimming pool next door. The church is immediately opposite the site, and the bustling village centre is an easy 300 m. walk away. A new central building is planned for 2012, and will include a café/restaurant, tourist information and reception area. Bicycle hire is on offer and the site managers will be pleased to recommend possible routes. Of the many châteaux close at hand, Chambord (8 km) and Cheverny (9 km) are amongst the most celebrated.

Facilities

Four toilet blocks, well spaced among the pitches, have modern, clean facilities including those for disabled visitors. Motorcaravan service point. Small shop. Bar/snack bar/pizzeria. Bicycle hire. Children's play area. Games/TV room and library. Activity and entertainment programme. Internet access. Mobile homes and tents for rent. Off site: Municipal swimming pool 50 m. Shops, restaurants and bars 300 m. Château de Chambord 8 km. Cheverny 9 km. Golf 12 km. Riding 18 km.

Open: 27 March - 29 November.

Directions

From Blois take D765 south towards Cheverny. At roundabout (junction with D956) turn east on D923, signed Bracieux. Turn south on D112 at roundabout and the site is 300 m. on right, just over the river. GPS: 47.550883, 1.537867

Charges guide

Per unit incl. 2 persons and electricity	€ 17.80 - € 18.95
extra person	€ 4.55 - € 5.05
child (2-13 yrs)	€ 2.02 - € 2.25
dog	€ 2.80

LES Châteaux ★★★
Pays de Chambord - Bracieux

Surrounded by the castles of The Loire, in between Chambord and Cheverny

Wood and Canvas Tents, mobile homes and chalets for rent

Spacious pitches, café-restaurant, swimming pool, children's playground, nature and culture activities in summer, 150 m from the village ...

www.camping-indigo.com

11 rue Roger Brun - 41 250 Bracieux - Pays de Chambord - Tel : +33 (0)2 54 46 41 84

Ballan-Miré

Camping de la Mignardière

22 avenue des Aubépines, F-37510 Ballan-Miré (Indre-et-Loire) T: 02 47 73 31 00. E: info@mignardiere.com
alanrogers.com/FR37010

Southwest of the city of Tours, this site is within easy reach of several of the Loire châteaux, notably Azay-le-Rideau. There are also many varied sports amenities on the site or very close by. The site has 177 numbered pitches of which 139 are for touring units, all with electricity (6/10A) and 37 with drainage and water. Pitches are of a good size on rather uneven grass with limestone gravel paths (which are rather 'sticky' when wet). The barrier gates (coded access) are closed 22.30-07.30 hrs. Reservation is essential for most of July/August.

Facilities

Three toilet blocks include washbasins in private cabins, a unit for disabled visitors, baby bath and laundry facilities. Motorcaravan service point. Shop. Takeaway. Two large, heated swimming pools (one covered). Paddling pool. Tennis. Bicycle hire. Off site: Attractive lake 300 m. Family fitness run. Fishing 500 m. Riding 1 km. Golf 3 km. Tours centre 8 km.

Open: 1 April - 25 September.

Directions

From A10 autoroute take exit 24 and D751 towards Chinon. Turn right after 5 km. at Campanile Hotel following signs to site. From Tours take the D751 towards Chinon. GPS: 47.35509, 0.63408

Charges guide

Per unit incl. 2 persons incl. electricity,	€ 16.00 - € 24.00
water and drainage	€ 21.00 - € 34.00
extra person	€ 4.20 - € 5.80

Chemillé-sur-Indrois

Flower Camping les Coteaux du Lac

Base de Loisirs, F-37460 Chemillé-sur-Indrois (Indre-et-Loire) T: 02 47 92 77 83.
E: lescoteauxdulac@wanadoo.fr alanrogers.com/FR37150

This former municipal site has been completely refurbished to a high standard and is being operated efficiently by a private company owned by the present enthusiastic manager, Emmanuel duGas. There are 47 touring pitches, all with electricity (10A) and individual water tap; four have hard standing for motorcaravans. At present there is little shade apart from that offered by a few mature trees, but new trees and bushes have been planted and flower beds are to be added. In a few years this promises to be a delightful site; meanwhile it is smart and very well tended. The site is in pleasant countryside above a lake and next to a rapidly developing Base de Loisirs with watersports provision and a bar/restaurant. There is a good, well-equipped little swimming pool with paddling area securely separated from the main pool (open and heated 1/6-30/9). The site is near the town of Loches which has an attractive château, and is an easy drive from Tours and from the many châteaux along the Loire and the Indre, including Chenonceaux.

Facilities

Excellent sanitary block with controllable showers, some washbasins in cabins and en-suite facilities for disabled visitors. Laundry facilities. Reception sells a few basic supplies and bread can be ordered. Swimming and paddling pools. Playing field. Play equipment for different ages. Fishing. Bicycle hire. Chalets to rent (15) are grouped at far end of site. Off site: Fishing 100 m. Lakeside beach, sailing and other water sports 200 m. Riding 4 km. Golf 15 km.

Open: 1 May - 30 September.

Directions

Chemillé-sur-Indrois is 55 km. southeast of Tours and 14 km. east of Loches, just off the D760 from Loches to Montrésor. Site is to the north of this road and is signed just west of Montrésor. GPS: 47.15786, 1.15986

Charges guide

Per unit incl. 2 persons	€ 13.90 - € 19.00
extra person	€ 3.90 - € 5.70
child (2-9 yrs)	€ 2.30 - € 3.60
electricity	€ 3.90

Les Coteaux du Lac
CAMPING - VILLAGE DE CHALETS ****

Situated between the Loire châteaux and the mediaeval city of Loches, Les Coteaux du Lac welcomes you in a superb natural setting situated at a 35 acre lake. You will enjoy a great stay in a friendly atmosphere and profit from the ideal location to discover the region of Touraine Côté Sud.

Our campsite offers you a heated swimming pool, a shop, animation and take-away from the campsite restaurant, attractively located at the lakeside. The campsite or the outdoor park offers you various activities like ATB, canoeing and pedalo.

Base de loisirs - F-37460 Chemillé-sur-Indrois
Tél. +33 247 92 77 83 - lescoteauxdulac@wanadoo.fr
www.lescoteauxdulac.com

For latest campsite news, availability and prices visit
alanrogers.com

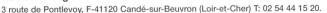
Call 01580 214000 We can book this site for you! alan rogers ◉ travel

Candé-sur-Beuvron

Kawan Village la Grande Tortue

3 route de Pontlevoy, F-41120 Candé-sur-Beuvron (Loir-et-Cher) T: 02 54 44 15 20.
E: grandetortue@wanadoo.fr **alanrogers.com/FR41070**

F 536

In the region that the Kings of France chose to build their most beautiful residences, this pleasant, shady site has been developed in the surroundings of an old 800-hectare forest, just 1 km. from the banks of the Loire river. For those seeking a relaxing holiday, it provides 169 touring pitches (the majority of more than 100 sq.m), all with 10A electricity and includes 58 fully serviced pitches. The friendly family owners continue to develop the site with a new multisport court and an attractive swimming pool complex. During July and August, they organise a programme of trips including canoeing and horse riding excursions, as well as twice weekly concerts and shows. La Grande Tortue is very well placed for visiting the châteaux of the Loire or the cities of Orléans and Tours. It is located on the long distance 'Loire á Vélo' cycle track and this leads from the site to Chaumont, Blois and Chambord, with over 300 km. of marked cycle tracks in the surrounding area. There are some good restaurants close at hand, although the site restaurant is also recommended with a range of good-value meals.

Facilities

Three sanitary blocks offer British style WCs, washbasins in cabins and pushbutton showers. Facilities for disabled visitors in one block. Laundry facilities. Motorcaravan service point. Shop, terraced bar and restaurant with reasonably priced food and drink plus a takeaway service (all 2/4-15/9). Covered, heated swimming pool (2/4-15/9) and two shallower pools for children (15/5-30/9). Trampolines, a ball crawl with slide and climbing wall, two bouncy inflatables. Club for children (July/Aug). Multisport court. Bicycle hire. Off site: Walking and cycling. Fishing 500 m. Golf 10 km. Châteaux at Blois 10 km. Riding 12 km. Chambord 20 km. Chenonceau 20 km.

Open: 2 April - 25 September.

Directions

Site is just outside Candé-sur-Beuvron on D751, between Amboise and Blois. From Amboise, turn right just before Candé, then left into site.
GPS: 47.4900069, 1.2583208

Charges guide

Per unit incl. 2 persons and electricity	€ 22.00 - € 32.50
extra person	€ 6.75 - € 9.00
child (3-9 yrs)	€ 3.75 - € 5.75
dog	€ 3.70

Camping Cheques accepted.

Camping Caravaning International ★★★★

La Grande Tortue

3, route de Pontlevoy
41120 CANDÉ-sur-BEUVRON
Tel: 0033 254 44 15 20 - Fax: 0033 254 44 19 45
Website: www.la-grande-tortue.com

Cheverny
Camping les Saules

Route de Contres (D102), F-41700 Cheverny (Loir-et-Cher) T: 02 54 79 90 01.
E: contact@camping-cheverny.com **alanrogers.com/FR41100**

Set in the heart of the château region, les Saules has developed into a popular, friendly campsite run by a local family. The well renovated, traditional reception buildings in their lakeside setting give a very pleasant welcome. There are 164 good size, level pitches with 146 available for touring units. All have shade from the many trees on the site, and electrical connections (a few will require leads longer than 25 m), and there are ample water taps. A large, grassy field provides room for youngsters to play safely. There are many designated cycle paths and walking circuits in the area, often linking châteaux through attractive, sleepy countryside. Cheverny, just a five-minute cycle ride away, is considered to have the best interior and furnishings of all the châteaux in the Loire region, and many others are within easy reach (Chambord, Chenonceaux, Chaumont and more). A Sites et Paysages member.

Facilities	Directions
Two sanitary blocks with toilets, showers, washbasins in cubicles and facilities for disabled visitors. Laundry facilities. Motorcaravan service point. Gas supplies. Shop. Restaurant (July/Aug). Bar. Snack bar and takeaway. Swimming and paddling pools. TV/social room with toys, board games, books. Two play areas. Large grass area for ball games. Minigolf (free). Fishing. Bicycle hire. Internet and WiFi. Off site: Golf and riding 3 km.	From Cheverny take D102 south towards Contres. Site is on the right after about 2 km. GPS: 47.478003, 1.450842

Open: 1 April - 23 September.

Charges guide

Per unit incl. 2 persons and electricity	€ 19.50 - € 30.00
extra person	€ 4.50
child (4-10 yrs)	€ 2.00
dog	€ 2.00

We can book this site for you! Call 01580 214000 alan rogers travel

CHEVERNY CAMPING LES SAULES ★★★★

In the heart of the Kings Valley, next to the Château of Cheverny and its 18-hole golf course, just near the forest, welcome to the quiet atmosphere of the Camping Les Saules and its green and shady setting of 8 hectares.

Excellent starting point for walking and cycling.

Rental of chalets.

CAMPING LES SAULES F. 41700 CHEVERNY
Tel. : 33 (0) 254 799 001
Fax : 33 (0) 254 792 834
www.camping-cheverny.com - contact@camping-cheverny.com

Chinon
Camping de l'Ile Auger

Quai Danton, F-37500 Chinon (Indre-et-Loire) T: 02 47 93 08 35. E: camping-ile-auger@hotmail.fr
alanrogers.com/FR37070

This traditional, good value site is well placed for exploring the old medieval town of Chinon. It lies alongside the River Vienne with views of the impressive château, which has a museum to Joan of Arc and was once the home of England's Henry II. A five minute walk over the bridge takes you to the château and town centre. The 277 level pitches are numbered but not separated and trees provide some shade. All have 8/12A electricity (long leads may be needed). Nearby are châteaux at Ussé, Azay-le-Rideau and Villandry, and the abbey at Fontevraud.

Facilities	Directions
The main toilet block by the entrance, with all the usual facilities, is undergoing refurbishment. Three small blocks around the rest of the site, have WCs and basins with cold water. Motorcaravan service point. Laundry facilities. Playground. Boules court. Fishing. Canoes. Barrier locked 22.00-07.00. A warden lives on site. WiFi (charged). Off site: Indoor and outdoor swimming pools nearby. Bicycle hire and boat launching 100 m. Town with shops, bars, restaurants, bus service and railway station 400 m. Tennis. River beach (no swimming) 1 km. Boat trips. Riding 10 km.	Chinon is 45 km. southwest of Tours. West of Chinon, at roundabout, leave Chinon bypass (D751) and take D8 east to town centre (3 km). Turn south, cross river and immediately turn west to site in 300 m. GPS: 47.16433, 0.23327

Open: 1 April - 31 October.

Charges guide

Per unit incl. 2 persons and electricity (12A)	€ 13.10
extra person	€ 2.20
child (under 7 yrs)	€ 1.50

For latest campsite news, availability and prices visit
alanrogers.com

We can book this site for you! Call 01580 214000 alan rogers ● travel

Francueil-Chenonceau

Camping le Moulin Fort

F-37150 Francueil-Chenonceau (Indre-et-Loire) T: 02 47 23 86 22. E: lemoulinfort@wanadoo.fr

alanrogers.com/FR37030

Camping le Moulin Fort is a tranquil, riverside site with British owners, John and Sarah Scarratt. The 130 pitches are enhanced by trees and shrubs offering plenty of shade and 110 pitches have electricity (6A). From the snack bar terrace adjacent to the restored mill building, a timber walkway over the mill race leads to the unheated swimming pool and paddling pools. The site is ideal for couples and families with young children, although the river is unfenced. There is occasional noise from trains passing on the opposite bank of the river. All over the campsite, visitors will find little information boards about local nature (birds, fish, trees and shrubs), about the history of the mill and fascinating facts about recycling. The owners are keen to encourage recycling on the site. The picturesque Château of Chenonceau is little more than 1 km. along the Cher riverbank and many of the Loire châteaux are within easy reach, particularly Amboise and its famous Leonardo de Vinci museum.

Facilities

Two toilet blocks with all the usual amenities of a good standard, include washbasins in cubicles, baby baths and facilities for disabled visitors. Motorcaravan service point. Shop, bar (limited hours), restaurant and takeaway (all 25/5-16/9). Swimming pool (25/5-16/9). Excellent play area. Minigolf. Petanque. Games room and TV. Library. Fishing. Bicycle and canoe hire. In high season regular family entertainment including wine tasting, quiz evenings, activities for children, lighthearted games tournaments and live music events. WiFi (charged). Off site: Trains to Tours 1.5 km. Boat launching 2 km. River beach 4 km. Riding 12 km. Golf 20 km.

Open: 1 April - 30 September.

Directions

Site is 35 km. east of Tours off the D976 Vierzon road. From A85 at exit 11 take D31 towards Bléré and turn east on D976 (Vierzon) for 7 km. then turn north on D80 (Chenonceau) to site. From north bank of Cher (D140/D40) turn south on D80 to cross river between Chenonceau and Chisseaux. Site on left just after bridge. GPS: 47.32735, 1.08936

Charges 2012

Per unit incl. 2 persons and electricity	€ 19.00 - € 27.00
extra person	€ 4.00 - € 5.00
child (4-12 yrs)	€ 3.00 - € 4.00
dog	€ 2.00 - € 3.00

CAMPING LE MOULIN FORT***

www.lemoulinfort.com

Camping Le Moulin Fort is ideally situated, a calm and peaceful site on the banks of the river Cher, a short walk from Chenonceau château, one of France's most popular tourist attractions. The pitches are flat and well-maintained, the wash blocks are clean and well-equipped, facilities on site offer you all you need and more, without going over the top! With no mobile homes or tour operators, the campsite is for camping as it used to be!

Break your journey by stopping for a few nights, or make the Loire valley the centre of your holiday this year. Whatever your schedule, we look forward to welcoming you on our site.

Camping Le Moulin Fort* • John & Sarah Scarratt
37150 Francueil-Chenonceaux • France
Tel. +33 (0)2 47 23 86 22 • lemoulinfort@wanadoo.fr

For latest campsite news, availability and prices visit

alanrogers.com

Gien

Kawan Village les Bois du Bardelet

Route de Bourges, Le Petit Bardelet, F-45500 Gien (Loiret) T: 02 38 67 47 39. E: contact@bardelet.com
alanrogers.com/FR45010

This attractive, high quality and lively site, ideal for families with young children, is in a rural setting and well situated for exploring the less well known eastern part of the Loire Valley. Two lakes (one for boating, one for fishing) and a pool complex have been attractively landscaped in 12 hectares of former farmland, blending old and new with natural wooded areas and more open field areas with rural views. There are 260 large, level grass pitches with 130 for touring units. All have 8A or 16A electricity, 20 have water and waste water and some have hardstanding.

Facilities

Two toilet blocks include facilities for disabled visitors and babies. Laundry facilities. Minimart (3/4-16/9). Bar and takeaway (3/4-16/9). Restaurant (high season and weekends). Heated outdoor pool (1/5-31/8). Heated indoor pool and children's pool. Aquagym, fitness and jacuzzi room. Games area. Archery. Canoeing and fishing. Tennis. Minigolf. Boules. Volleyball. Pétanque. Children's playground. Sports tournaments (July/Aug). Bicycle hire. WiFi in bar area (charged). Off site: Supermarket 5 km.

Open: 1 April - 30 September.

Directions

Leave the A77 autoroute (exit 19 Gien). Take the D940 (signed Bourges) to Gien, cross river Loire, continue D940 for 5 km. At junction with D53 turn right and right again to cross D940 (no left turn). Follow signs for 1.5 km. to site. GPS: 47.64152, 2.61528

Charges 2012

Per unit incl. 2 persons and electricity	€ 19.80 - € 33.00

Camping Cheques accepted.

Loches-en-Touraine

Camping la Citadelle

Avenue Aristide Briand, F-37600 Loches-en-Touraine (Indre-et-Loire) T: 02 47 59 05 91.
E: camping@lacitadelle.com **alanrogers.com/FR37050**

A pleasant, well maintained site, one of la Citadelle's best features is that it is within walking distance of Loches, noted for its perfect architecture and its glorious history, yet at the same time the site has a rural atmosphere. The 86 standard touring pitches are all level, of a good size and with 10A electricity. Numerous trees offer varying degrees of shade. The 30 larger, serviced pitches have 16A electricity but little shade. Mobile homes occupy the other 48 pitches (28 for hire).

Facilities

Three sanitary blocks (one could be under pressure in high season) provide mainly British style WCs, washbasins (mostly in cabins) and controllable showers. Laundry facilities. Motorcaravan service point. Two baby units and provision for disabled visitors (both in need of attention). Heated pool (May-Sept). Paddling pool and play area (adult supervision strongly recommended). Bar and snack bar (15/6-15/9). Boules, volleyball and games room. Internet access and TV. Off site: Bicycle hire 50 m. Supermarket within 1 km. Riding 5 km. River beach 10 km.

Open: 19 March - 10 October.

Directions

Loches is 45 km. southeast of Tours. Site is well signed from most directions. Do not enter town centre. Approach from roundabout by supermarket at southern end of bypass (D943). Site signed towards town centre and is on right in 800 m. GPS: 47.12303, 1.00223

Charges guide

Per unit incl. 2 persons and electricity	€ 19.50 - € 29.00

Mesland

Yelloh! Village Parc du Val de Loire

155 route de Fleuray, F-41150 Mesland (Loir-et-Cher) T: 02 54 70 27 18. E: parcduvaldeloire@wanadoo.fr
alanrogers.com/FR41010

Between Blois and Amboise, quietly situated among vineyards away from the main roads and towns, this site is nevertheless centrally placed for visits to the châteaux; Chaumont, Amboise and Blois (21 km) are the nearest in that order. There are 150 touring pitches of reasonable size (80-120 sq.m), either in light woodland marked by trees or on open meadow with separators. All the pitches have electricity (10A) and 50 of them also have water and drainage. Sports and competitions are organised.

Facilities

Three original toilet blocks of varying ages are barely acceptable. One is very old and only open in July/Aug. Units for disabled visitors and babies. Laundry facilities. Motorcaravan services. Shop with bakery, bar, restaurant, snack service, pizzeria and takeaway. TV and recreation rooms. Three swimming pools, one heated and covered (outdoor 25/4-11/9). Balnéo. Tennis. Three playgrounds. Bicycle hire. Minigolf. Barbecue area. WiFi. Off site: Golf 5 km. Fishing 7 km. Riding and boat launching 10 km.

Open: 6 April - 23 September.

Directions

From A10 exit 18 (Château-Renault, Amboise) take D31 south to Autrèche (2 km). Turn left on D55 for 3.5 km. In Darne-Marie Les Bois turn left, then right onto D43 to Mesland. Follow site signs. From south, site signed from Onzain. GPS: 47.51002, 1.10481

Charges 2012

Per unit incl. 2 persons	€ 17.00 - € 35.00
large pitch with services	€ 19.00 - € 41.00
extra person	€ 6.00 - € 8.00

We can book this site for you! Call 01580 214000 alan rogers travel

For latest campsite news, availability and prices visit

alanrogers.com

Park & Château de BEAUREGARD

Gallery of 327 portraits
40 ha park & gardens
5600 Delft tiles
Expo: 100 atypical portraits

www.beauregard-loire.com

expo 2012

Muides-sur-Loire

Camping Château des Marais

27 rue de Chambord, F-41500 Muides-sur-Loire (Loir-et-Cher) T: 02 54 87 05 42.
E: chateau.des.marais@wanadoo.fr **alanrogers.com/FR41040**

The Château des Marais campsite is well situated to visit the château at Chambord (its park is impressive) and the other châteaux in the Vallée des Rois. The site, providing 134 large touring pitches, all with electricity (6/10A), water and drainage and with ample shade, is situated in the oak and hornbeam woods of its own small château. An excellent swimming complex offers pools with two slides, two flumes and a lazy river. A new wellness centre is a recent addition. The reception from the enthusiastic owners and the staff is very welcoming.

Facilities

Four modern sanitary blocks have good facilities including some large showers and washbasins en-suite which would also be suitable for visitors with disabilities. Washing machines and dryers. Motorcaravan service point. Shop and takeaway. Bar/restaurant with large terrace. Swimming complex with heated and unheated pools, slide and cover for cooler weather. New wellness spa centre. Bicycle and go-kart hire. Games room. Children's club (high season). Fishing pond. Entertainment programme and canoe trips in high season. Free WiFi throughout. Off site: Riding 5 km. Golf 12 km. Muides-sur-Loire (five minutes walk).

Open: 5 May - 15 September.

Directions

From A10 autoroute take exit 16 to Mer. Turn left off the N152 to cross the Loire. Turn right to join the D951. Opposite car park in centre of Muides-sur-Loire, turn left onto D103. Site is signed off the D103 to the southwest of the village, 600 m. from junction with D112. GPS: 47.66580, 1.52877

Charges 2012

Per unit incl. 2 persons and electricity	€ 31.00 - € 45.00
extra person	€ 8.00
child	free - € 7.00

Credit cards accepted for amounts over € 80.

Néret

Camping le Bonhomme

Mulles, F-36400 Néret (Indre) T: 02 54 31 46 11. E: info@camping-lebonhomme.com
alanrogers.com/FR36120

You are assured of a warm welcome by the friendly Dutch owners at this small, neat and tidy site. Le Bonhomme is in the verdant countryside of the Indre, between Châteauroux and Montluçon. There are just 25 large and grassy, slightly sloping pitches laid out around the edge of a small meadow. There is some shade from a variety of fruit trees and all the pitches have electricity (6A). This is excellent walking and cycling country and the owners will be pleased to recommend routes. Le Bonhomme is a very restful site but may also be a good choice for an en-route stop.

Facilities

The toilet blocks are situated in one side of the farmhouse, a long walk from some pitches, with open washbasins and controllable showers. Disabled toilet. Washing machine in farmhouse. Weekly pizza van. Restaurant (Tue, Fri, Sun) and pizzas. Small, raised fun pool (June-Aug). Boules. Happy hour (5-6pm). Accompanied walking and cycle trips. Tourist information. Cottage for rent. Off site: Châteaumeillant with shops, bar and restaurants 6 km. Fishing 6 km. Riding 8 km. Golf 20 km. Ainay-le-Vieil and its château.

Open: 15 April - 1 October.

Directions

Leave A71 autoroute at exit 8 (St Amand-Montrond) through town, then southwest on D951 then D997 to Culan. Take D943 west and bypass Châteaumeillant, then D68 northwest to Néret. Site is 3 km. north of Néret on D71, well signed 'Aire Naturelle'. GPS: 46.588826, 2.13329

Charges guide

| Per unit incl. 2 persons and electricity | € 16.90 |
| extra person | € 3.00 |

For latest campsite news, availability and prices visit

alanrogers.com

Nouan-le-Fuzelier

Camping la Grande Sologne

Rue des Peupliers, F-41600 Nouan-le-Fuzelier (Loir-et-Cher) T: 02 54 88 70 22.
E: info@campinggrandesologne.com **alanrogers.com/FR41180**

The enthusiastic new managers, who speak many languages, are working hard to raise this site to a high standard. It is in a parkland setting on the southern edge of Nouan-le-Fuzelier close to the A71 Autoroute, making this an ideal spot to spend some time relaxing whilst en route north or south. It has 165 spacious, level, grass pitches with a variety of mature trees giving some shade, with 150 for touring. All have 10A electricity, but long leads may be necessary. They are marked but not delineated; but some hedges will be planted for 2012. Access is easy for large outfits. The site is entered through a very attractive park which has some interesting sculptures and holds the excellent municipal swimming pool and tennis courts, which are free to campers.

Facilities	Directions
Three modern toilet blocks with all necessary facilities including those for campers with disabilities. Washing machine, dryer. Snack bar (July/Aug). Small shop (all season). Games/TV room. Motorcaravan services. Fishing. Bicycle hire. Children's play area. WiFi. Off site: Municipal swimming pool, tennis courts, adjacent (free). Many interesting old market towns and villages within easy reach. Famous equestrian centre 7 km. Chambord and other famous châteaux. Lakes for fishing.	Nouan-le-Fuzelier is between exits 3 and 4 on the A71 autoroute, south of Orléans. Take D2020 to site at southern edge of Nouan-le-Fuzelier, opposite railway station. Well signed. GPS: 47.533863, 2.037674

Open: 1 April - 15 October.

Charges guide

Per unit incl. 2 persons	
and electricity	€ 18.00 - € 22.00
extra person	€ 4.50 - € 5.50
child (2-12 yrs)	€ 3.40
dog	€ 1.00

Château Royal de Blois

6 Place du Château
41000 Blois

The Royal Château of Blois, residence of 7 kings and 9 queens of France is a true synthesis of the art and history of the Loire Valley châteaux and makes it an ideal introduction for their visit.

Tel: 0033 (0)2 54 90 33 32 | contact@chateaudeblois.fr | www.chateaudeblois.fr

Parc d'attractions et Camping ★★★★

DE LA RÉCRÉ DES 3 CURÉS

La Récré DES TROIS CURÉS

29290 MILIZAC - www.larecredes3cures.fr
Tel: (+33) 02 98 07 95 59

By renting a mobile home on Campsite La Récré des 3 Curés for 1 week, you'll have access to attraction parc La Récré des 3 Curés during the entire week.

For latest campsite news, availability and prices visit
alanrogers.com

Pierrefitte-sur-Sauldre

Leading Camping les Alicourts

Domaine des Alicourts, F-41300 Pierrefitte-sur-Sauldre (Loir-et-Cher) T: 02 54 88 63 34.
E: info@lesalicourts.com **alanrogers.com/FR41030**

A secluded holiday village set in the heart of the forest, with many sporting facilities and a super spa centre, Camping les Alicourts is midway between Orléans and Bourges, to the east of the A71. There are 490 pitches, 150 for touring and the remainder occupied by mobile homes and chalets. All pitches have electricity connections (6A) and good provision for water, and most are 150 sq.m. (min. 100 sq.m). Locations vary, from wooded to more open areas, thus giving a choice of amount of shade. All facilities are open all season and the leisure amenities are exceptional. The Senseo Balnéo centre offers indoor pools, hydrotherapy, massage and spa treatments for over 18s only (some special family sessions are provided). An inviting outdoor water complex (all season) includes two swimming pools, a pool with wave machine and a beach area, not forgetting three water slides. Competitions and activities are organised for adults and children including a high season club for children with an entertainer twice a day, a disco once a week and a dance for adults. A member of Leading Campings group.

Facilities

Three modern sanitary blocks include some washbasins in cabins and baby bathrooms. Laundry facilities. Facilities for disabled visitors. Motorcaravan services. Shop. Restaurant. Takeaway in bar with terrace. Pool complex. Spa centre. 7-hectare lake (fishing, bathing, canoes, pedaloes). 9-hole golf course. Adventure play area. Tennis. Minigolf. Boules. Roller skating/skateboarding (bring own equipment). Bicycle hire. Internet access and WiFi (charged).

Open: 29 April - 9 September.

Directions

From A71, take Lamotte Beuvron exit (no. 3) or from N20 Orléans to Vierzon turn left on to D923 towards Aubigny. After 14 km. turn right at camping sign on to D24E. Site signed in 4 km.
GPS: 47.54398, 2.19193

Charges guide

Per unit incl. 2 persons	
and electricity	€ 20.00 - € 44.00
extra person	€ 7.00 - € 10.00
child (5-17 yrs)	€ 6.00 - € 8.00
child (1-4 yrs)	free - € 6.00
dog	€ 5.00 - € 7.00

Reductions for low season longer stays.

Been to any good campsites lately? **We have**

alan rogers

The UK's market leading independent guides to the best campsites
Also available on iPad alanrogers.com/digital

For latest campsite news, availability and prices visit
alanrogers.com

Poilly-lez-Gien
Camping Touristique de Gien

Rue des Iris, F-45500 Poilly-lez-Gien (Loiret) T: 02 38 67 12 50. E: camping-gien@wanadoo.fr

alanrogers.com/FR45030

This open, attractive, well cared for site lies on a bank of the Loire with views of the town of Gien and its château. It has a long river frontage, which includes a good expanse of sandy beach. There are 200 well-sized, level, grassy pitches with 150 for touring. All have 4/10A electricity, 18 have water and drainage (between two). Some are shaded by mature trees and many have good views over the river. The bar and restaurant, with a large outdoor area, are open to the public. Soirées with different themes are held at least weekly in July and August. No twin-axle caravans. The town of Gien, with its shops, bars, restaurants and château, is within a kilometre just across the bridge. A long distance cycle path passes the entrance. This is an excellent base for exploring the eastern end of the Loire valley, and Gien has a festival celebrating the heritage of this part of the Loire at Ascensiontide, well worth a visit. The tourist office organises a wide range of activities both sporting and cultural. There is a regular bus service to Orléans, an ancient city well known for its association with Joan of Arc.

Facilities

Three toilet blocks, one heated, and one new with an en-suite unit for disabled visitors. Laundry. Bar and restaurant (1/4-30/9), both open to the public. Shop 20 m. outside gates (all year). Swimming pool and paddling pools (15/6-15/9). Play area and grassed games area. Minigolf. Bicycle and pedal cart hire. Canoe hire. Fishing. Large sandy beach. Some organised activities (July/Aug). Off site: Children's club on beach. Town centre less than 1 km. Hypermarket 1 km. Riding 2 km. Golf 25 km. Many sporting activities, excursions and visits can be arranged from the site or the tourist office.

Open: 1 March - 7 November.

Directions

Leave A77 autoroute at exit 19 (Gien). Take D940 (signed Bourges) to Gien, follow signs to Centre Ville and cross the river Loire. Immediately, at traffic lights, turn west (D951) signed Poilly-lez-Gien. Fork right to site in 300 m. on right. GPS: 47.68229, 2.62315

Charges guide

Per unit incl. 2 persons and electricity	€ 21.50 - € 24.00
extra person	€ 6.00
child (under 12 yrs)	€ 4.00
dog	€ 2.00

CAMPING TOURISTIQUE DE GIEN ***
Rue des iris - 45500 Poilly lez Gien (GIEN)
Tél : 02 38 67 12 50 - Fax : 02 38 67 12 18
Email : camping-gien@wanadoo.fr - www.camping-gien.com

Plenty of touristic and cultural sites
Trips, canoes and montainbikes (for rent), fishing
Covered swimming pool, crazy golf, maxi trampoline
Entertainment and themed evenings

Mobile homes and roulottes for rent
Restaurant, bar, ice cream
Supermarket, Laundry

Poilly-lez-Gien
Les Roulottes des Bords de Loire

537

Rue des Iris, F-45500 Poilly-lez-Gien (Loiret) T: 02 38 67 12 50. E: info@roulottes-bords-de-loire.com

alanrogers.com/FR45050

Les Roulottes des Bords de Loire is a small parc résidentiel, close to the attractive town of Gien in the eastern Loire Valley. Although it is attached to a site with touring pitches, please note that there are none here. Instead, accommodation is in attractive Romany style caravans, albeit equipped with all home comforts. Each caravan can accommodate up to five people and has its own fully equipped kitchen and en-suite bathroom. The site, although small, is well equipped with a swimming pool (covered in low season), minigolf and direct access to the River Loire.

Facilities

Swimming pool. Direct access to River Loire. Beach volleyball. Bicycle hire. Minigolf. Fishing. Play area. Canoe trips. Tourist information. Activity and entertainment programme. Romany style mobile homes for rent. Off site: Gien centre 2 km. Golf 35 km. Loire valley and vineyards. Cycle and walking tracks. Orléans.

Open: 1 March - 6 November.

Directions

Site is at Poilly-lez-Gien on the south side of the Loire. From the A77 take the Gien exit and bypass the town on the D940 following signs to Bourges. Arrive in Poilly-lez-Gien shortly after crossing the Loire and site is well signed from here. GPS: 47.68229, 2.62315

Charges 2012

Contact the site for details.

For latest campsite news, availability and prices visit
alanrogers.com

Call 01580 214000 We can book this site for you! alan rogers ● travel

Rillé

Huttopia Rillé

Lac de Rillé, F-37340 Rillé (Indre-et-Loire) T: 02 47 24 62 97.
E: rille@huttopia.com **alanrogers.com/FR37140**

Huttopia Rillé is a rural site ideal for tent campers seeking a more natural, environmentally friendly, peaceful campsite close to a lake. Cars are parked outside the barrier but allowed on site to unload and load. The 146 slightly uneven and sloping pitches, 80 for touring, are scattered between the pine trees. All have 10A electricity (very long leads needed) and 24 are fully serviced. They vary in size and are numbered but not marked. This site is designed for those with tents, though small caravans and motorcaravans (special area) are accepted. It is not ideal for those with walking difficulties. Communal barbecues only. The site is situated in an area ideal for exploring and there are numerous marked footpaths and cycle tracks close by. The area north of the lake, in easy reach of the site, is designated a nature reserve offering excellent opportunities for birdwatching. After a long day exploring the region, you can unwind with a refreshing drink or a light meal on the terrace overlooking the lake and small swimming pool. In July and August there is a wide range of interesting family activities, both on site and nearby. These include nature trails, a goat farm, jam making and star gazing.

Facilities

Modern central toilet block with family rooms and facilities for disabled visitors (no ramps and difficult access for wheelchairs). A smaller block has separate showers, washbasins and facilities for disabled visitors. Motorcaravan service point. Small heated swimming pool with paddling area (21/4-30/9). Play area. Fishing. Canoes on lake. Communal barbecue areas (no charcoal barbecues). Max. 1 dog. Off site: Small steam train passes site. Châteaux to visit. Marked walks and cycle tracks. Nature reserve at lake. Riding 6 km. Golf 15 km.

Open: 21 April - 7 November.

Directions

Rillé is 40 km. west of Tours. Leave D766 Angers - Blois road at Château la Vallière take D749 southwest. In Rillé turn west on D49. Site is on right in 2 km. GPS: 47.45811, 0.2192

Charges guide

Per unit incl. 2 persons	
and electricity	€ 20.20 - € 31.90
extra person	€ 5.30 - € 7.10
child (2-7 yrs)	€ 3.20 - € 4.75
dog	€ 4.00

Near the Châteaux of the Loire Valley
in the heart of the forest, around a lake

Rillé ***

Wood & Canvas Tents, Gipsy caravans, Chalets, Cahuttes to rent

Heated swimming pool, Bar restaurant, Tennis courts, Beach, Play area...

www.huttopia.com
Lac de Rillé - 37340 Rillé - Tel : +33 (0)2 47 24 62 97

Senonches
Huttopia Senonches

Etang de Badouleau, avenue de Badouleau, F-28250 Senonches (Eure-et-Loir) T: 02 37 37 81 40.
E: senonches@huttopia.com alanrogers.com/FR28140

Huttopia Senonches is hidden away in the huge Forêt Dominiale de Senonches and in keeping with other Huttopia sites, combines a high standard of comfort with a real sense of backwoods camping. There are 91 touring pitches here, some with electricity (10A). The pitches are very large ranging from 100 sq.m. to no less than 300 sq.m. There are also 30 Canadian style log cabins and tents available for rent. A good range of on-site amenities includes a shop and a bar/restaurant. The chlorine free natural pool, with terrace, overlooks a lake and is open from early July until September. The forest can be explored on foot or by cycle (rental available on site) and beyond the forest, the great city of Chartres is easily visited, with its stunning Gothic cathedral, widely considered to be the finest in France.

Facilities

The toilet blocks are modern and heated in low season, with special facilities for disabled visitors. Shop (all season). Bar, snack bar and takeaway (limited in low season). Swimming pool. Fishing. Play area. Bicycle hire and horse riding. Entertainment and activity programme. Tents, Cahuttes and chalets for rent. Gas barbecues only. Max. 1 dog. Off site: Riding 4 km. Senonches (good selection of shops, bars and restaurants). Cycle and walking tracks. Chartres.

Open: 6 April - 7 November.

Directions

Approaching from Chartres, use the ringroad (N154) and then take the D24 in a northwesterly direction. Drive through Digny and continue to Senonches, from where the site is well signed.
GPS: 48.5533, 1.04146

Charges guide

Per unit incl. 2 persons and electricity	€ 19.70 - € 28.60
extra person	€ 4.30 - € 6.00
child (2-7 yrs)	€ 2.70 - € 4.20
dog	€ 4.00

We can book this site for you! Call 01580 214000 alan rogers travel

HUTTOPIA

Close to Chartres
In the middle of the forest, at the shore of a pond...

SENONCHES

Wood & Canvas Tents, Chalets, Cahuttes to rent
Natural swimming pool, Bar, Restaurant, Play area...

www.huttopia.com
Etang de Badouleau - 28250 SENONCHES - Tel : +33 (0)2 37 37 81 40

Sainte Maure-de-Touraine
Castel Camping Parc de Fierbois

F-37800 Sainte Catherine de Fierbois (Indre-et-Loire) T: 02 47 65 43 35.
E: contact@fierbois.com **alanrogers.com/FR37120**

Parc de Fierbois has an impressive entrance and a tree lined driveway and is set among 250 acres of lakes and forest in the heart of the Loire Valley. In all, there are 420 pitches including 125 for touring units, the remainder being used by tour operators and for chalets and mobile homes. Of the 125 touring pitches, mostly level and separated by low hedging or small trees, all have 10A electricity. The other pitches are small or medium in size, many unmarked and some sloping and in the shade.

Facilities

Three toilet blocks provide British style WCs, hot showers and washbasins in cubicles. Baby room. Laundry facilities. Motorcaravan service point. Shop. Bar. Restaurant. Takeaway. Water park complex (pools, slides, paddling pool). Indoor heated pool. Entertainment and games bar. Tennis. Pétanque. Minigolf. Bicycle hire. Go-karts and electric cars. TV/video room. Gym. Fishing. Pedaloes, canoeing and entertainment programme (July/Aug). WiFi throughout (charged). Off site: Riding 10 km. Golf 30 km.

Open: 16 April - 7 September.

Directions

Travelling south on N10 from Tours, go through Montbazon and on towards Saint Maure and Chatellerault. Site signed 16 km. outside Montbazon near Sainte Catherine. Turn off main road. Follow site signs. From A10 autoroute use Saint Maure exit and turn north up N10. GPS: 47.1487, 0.6548

Charges 2012

Per unit incl. 2 persons	€ 16.00 - € 44.00
extra person	€ 7.00 - € 9.00
electricity	€ 5.00

Sonzay
Camping l'Arada Parc

537

Rue de la Baratière, F-37360 Sonzay (Indre-et-Loire) T: 02 47 24 72 69. E: info@laradaparc.com
alanrogers.com/FR37060

A good, well maintained site in a quiet location, easy to find from the motorway and popular as an overnight stop. Camping l'Arada Parc is an attractive family site nestling in the heart of the Touranelle countryside between the Loire and Loir valleys. The 73 grass touring pitches all have electricity and 19 have water and drainage. The clearly marked pitches, some slightly sloping, are separated by trees and shrubs, some of which are now providing a degree of shade. An attractive, heated pool is on a pleasant terrace beside the restaurant. Entertainment is organised in July/August.

Facilities

Two modern toilet blocks provide unisex toilets, showers and washbasins in cubicles. Baby room. Facilities for disabled visitors (wheelchair users may find the gravel access difficult). Laundry facilities. Shop, bar, restaurant and takeaway (all season). Motorcaravan service point. Outdoor swimming pool (no Bermuda-style shorts; 1/5-15/9). Heated, covered pool (all season). Fitness room. Play area. Games area. Boules. TV room. Bicycle hire. Internet access. WiFi throughout. Footpath to village. Off site: Tennis 200 m. Fishing 500 m. Golf 12 km.

Open: 26 March - 1 November.

Directions

Sonzay is northwest of Tours. From the new A28 north of Tours take the exit to Neuillé-Pont-Pierre which is on the N138 Le Mans - Tours road. Then take D766 towards Château la Vallière and turn southwest to Sonzay. Follow campsite signs. GPS: 47.625963, 0.452843

Charges guide

Per unit incl. 2 persons and electricity (10A)	€ 19.00 - € 25.10
extra person	€ 4.00 - € 5.30
Camping Cheques accepted.	

We can book this site for you! Call 01580 214000   alan rogers ◖ travel

Suèvres
Castel Camping Château de la Grenouillère

RN152, F-41500 Suèvres (Loir-et-Cher) T: 02 54 87 80 37. E: la.grenouillere@wanadoo.fr
alanrogers.com/FR41020

Château de la Grenouillère is an attractive site set in a 28-acre park midway between Orléans and Tours, well situated for visiting many of the Loire châteaux. The 280 pitches, with 130 for touring, are in three distinct areas. The majority are in a wooded area, with about 60 in the old orchard and the remainder in open meadows. There are varying amounts of shade from the trees. There is one water point for every four pitches and all have electric hook-up (10A). Additionally, there are 14 fully serviced pitches with a separate sanitary block in the outbuildings of the château.

Facilities

Three excellent sanitary blocks are well appointed. Laundry facilities. Shop. Bar. Pizzeria and pizza takeaway. Restaurant and grill takeaway. Swimming complex of four pools (one covered) and slide. Spa with whirlpool, jacuzzi, sauna, massage. Tennis. Games room. Bicycle and canoe hire (July/Aug). Fishing. WiFi (charged). Off site: Suèvres 3 km. Riding and watersports 5 km. Golf 10 km.

Open: 17 April - 11 September.

Directions

Site is on the D2155 between Suèvres and Mer, 3 km. from Mer and is well signed. GPS: 47.68557, 1.48686

Charges guide

Per unit incl. 2 persons and electricity	€ 26.00 - € 39.00
incl. full services	€ 30.00 - € 45.00
extra person	€ 5.00 - € 8.00

For latest campsite news, availability and prices visit
alanrogers.com

Trogues

Camping du Château de la Rolandière

F-37220 Trogues (Indre-et-Loire) T: 02 47 58 53 71. E: contact@larolandiere.com

alanrogers.com/FR37090

This is a charming site set in the grounds of a château and you are assured of a very warm welcome here. There are 50 medium sized, level or gently sloping pitches, separated by hedges with a variety of trees giving some shade. Most have 6A electricity (long leads advised) with water taps nearby. There is a large chalet and mobile homes for hire and bed and breakfast is also available. The site has a pleasant swimming pool, paddling pool, fitness room and games/TV room. The bar and restaurant have a sunny terrace overlooking the château. Minigolf, swings, slides and an area for ball games are adjacent. The site is a peaceful spot from which to visit the châteaux at Chinon, Loches, Villandry or Azay-le-Rideau and the villages of Richelieu and Crissay-sur-Manse. There are many excursions to beautiful gardens and grottos and you should find time to enjoy the local gastronomy and wines. In July and August, a programme of activities is aimed at families with younger children. A Sites et Paysages member.

Facilities

The older style toilet block has been refurbished to provide good facilities with modern showers, washbasin and laundry areas. Provision for disabled visitors. Small shop for basics. Bar with terrace. Snacks and takeaway (July/Aug). Swimming pool (15/5-30/9). Minigolf. Play area. Fitness room. TV lounge. WiFi. Off site: Fishing 1 km. on River Vienne. River beach and boat launching 4 km. Restaurant 4 km. Bicycle hire and shops 6 km. St Maure 7 km. Golf 15 km.

Open: 23 April - 24 September.

Directions

Trogues is 40 km. southwest of Tours on the D760 Loches - Chinon road. Site is on D760, midway between Trogues and A10 (exit 25). Entrance is signed and marked by a model of the château. GPS: 47.10767, 0.51052

Charges guide

Per unit incl. 2 persons and electricity	€ 20.90 - € 28.90
extra person	€ 4.50 - € 6.00

No credit cards.

Château de La Rolandière ★★★

Tel/Fax: (0033) 247 585 371   37220 TROGUES

CAMPING / BED & BREAKFAST

**CALM
CONFORT
CONVIVIALITY**

*In the heart
of the Loire Valley*

Swimming-pool
snack-bar

WiFi

**A10 EXIT 25
6km direction Chinon**

**GPS Position:
N 47° 06' 25,4" E 0° 30' 36,6"**

www.larolandiere.com   contact@larolandiere.com

Trogues

Village Center le Parc des Allais

Les Allais, F-37220 Trogues (Indre-et-Loire) T: 04 99 57 21 21. E: contact@village-center.com

alanrogers.com/FR37130

Village Center le Parc des Allais is a mainly residential site situated in the heart of the Loire Valley. It is convenient for exploring the surrounding countryside and the region's world class châteaux. The site lies within a 16-hectare park and borders a small lake. It has a large indoor and outdoor pool next to the bar/restaurant, with a large terrace overlooking the Vienne River. Of the 241 pitches there are only about 10 small pitches for touring (10A electricity), all in a group by the entrance. They are separated by hedges and a variety of trees give good shade.

Facilities

Toilet block includes facilities for disabled visitors. Shop, bar, takeaway, restaurant (July/Aug and some weekends). Indoor pool (all season), outdoor pool, slides, paddling pool (June-Aug). Miniclub. Entertainment (July/Aug). Themed evenings. Minigolf. Tennis. Boules. Fishing. Bicycle hire. Boat and go-kart rental (July/Aug). Play area. Fitness facilities. Games room. Internet. Motorcaravan services outside entrance. WiFi (charged). Off site: Riding and beach 3 km. Futuroscope (45 minutes). Tours (less than an hour). Golf 30 km. Caves. Wine Route.

Open: 8 April - 2 October.

Directions

Site is between Pouzay and Trogues. South of Tours leave A10 autoroute at exit 25 signed Ste Maure de Touraine. Take D760 west for about 3 km. At roundabout turn south, D58 to Pouzay. At traffic lights, turn west, D109 to site in 3 km. GPS: 47.099233, 0.504183

Charges guide

Per unit incl. 2 persons and electricity	€ 16.00 - € 26.00
extra person	€ 3.00 - € 6.00

Camping Cheques accepted.

For latest campsite news, availability and prices visit

alanrogers.com

The Pays de la Loire covers the area of Western France to the south of Brittany and Normandy. It lies along the lower stretches of the River Loire, the longest river in France, downstream from the châteaux of the Val de Loire region.

DÉPARTEMENTS: 44 LOIRE-ATLANTIQUE, 49 MAINE-ET-LOIRE, 53 MAYENNE, 72 SARTHE

Strictly speaking, the department of 85 Vendée is also part of this region. Because of its importance as a holiday destination for British people, we have featured it separately in this guide.

MAJOR CITIES: ANGERS, NANTES

Pays de la Loire is one of the regions created in the late 20th century to serve as an administrative zone of influence for its capital, Nantes. Whilst the great Loire châteaux lie in the Val de Loire region, the Pays de la Loire is home to many great monuments, such as the castles of Angers, Laval and Mayenne and the Château des Ducs de Bretagne at Nantes, the Royal Fontevraud Abbey and the old city of Le Mans. It also contains many natural parks including the Brière and the Poitou marshes.

The region has become very popular with British visitors involving no more than a day's drive from the Channel ports. It includes 300 km. of Atlantic coastline that offers long, sandy beaches and islands such as the Ile de Noirmoutier and the Ile d'Yeu, contrasting with the lush green countryside through which flows the River Loire.

At the region's heart lies Angers, the capital of the historic province of Anjou, home to the feudal warlords and the Plantagenet kings of England. To the southeast, the Vendée, is a peaceful holiday area very popular with summer visitors.

Places of interest

Angers: art town, medieval castle and tapestries, cathedral.

Brissac: 15th-century castle.

Le Croisic: small fishing port, Naval Museum.

Fontevraud: 11th-century Royal abbey.

Laval: castle, 'Douanier Rousseau' art gallery, boat trips on the Mayenne.

La Baule: holiday resort with lovely sandy bay.

Le Mans: the annual 24-hour car race attracting visitors from all over the world; car museum, old town, cathedral.

Le Puy de Fou: 15-16th-century castle, sound and light show involving over 700 participants.

Les Sables d'Olonne: fishing port and seaside resort.

Noirmoutier: linked to the mainland by a three mile bridge.

Saumer: 13th-century castle, Cadre Noir National School of Horse Riding, wine cellars and Mushroom Museum.

Cuisine of the region

Beurre blanc: a buttery sauce that goes well with fish.

Rillauds d'Anjou: muscadet sausages.

Curé Nantais and Port-Salut: local cheeses.

Pâté aux prunes: A speciality of the Angers region and found in all good local bakers in July and August, this sugary pastry is filled with plums.

www.paysdelaloire.co.uk
infotourisme@sem-paysdelaloire.fr
(0)2 40 48 24 20

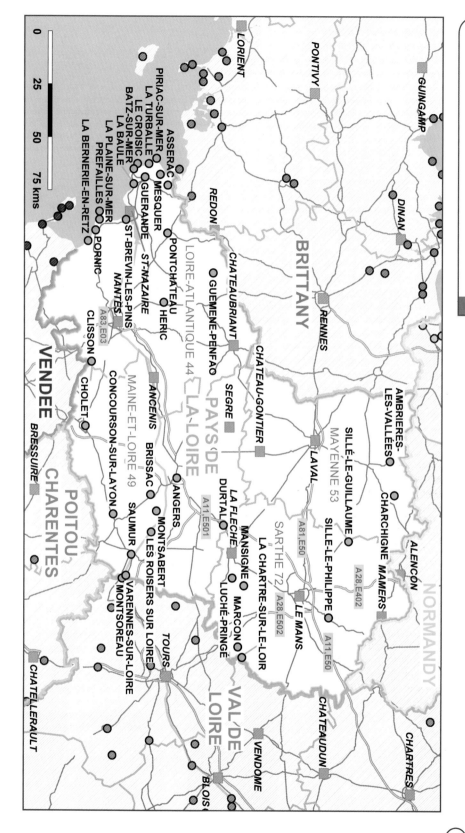

For latest campsite news, availability and prices visit
alanrogers.com

Call 01580 214000 We can book this site for you! alan rogers ◉ travel

Ambrières-les-Vallées
Camping Parc de Vaux

35 rue des Colverts, F-53300 Ambrières-les-Vallées (Mayenne) T: 02 43 04 90 25.
E: parcdevaux@camp-in-ouest.com **alanrogers.com/FR53010**

Parc de Vaux is an ex-municipal site which was acquired in 2010 by the owners of FR72080. This 3.5 hectare site has 90 pitches, 18 occupied by mobile homes, chalets and bungalow tents, available to rent. The 59 touring pitches are generally grassy and well sized (mostly with 10A electricity and water). The site is located close to the pretty village of Ambrières-les-Vallées, and there is direct access to the village from the site by a footbridge over the river. The village is around 12 km. north of Mayenne, and may prove a convenient en-route stop. There is a swimming pool adjacent (with water slide) and the site also has access to a lake and a good range of amenities.

Facilities

Three small toilet blocks, one with facilities for disabled visitors. No children's facilities. Laundry. Motorcaravan service point. Bar and snack bar/takeaway in high season. Heated outdoor swimming pool. Sports field. Fishing. Football. Basketball. Minigolf. Boules. Canoes. Pedaloes. Bicycle hire. Archery and tennis adjacent. Games room with TV and library. Play area. Tourist information. Mobile homes/chalets/bungalow tents for rent. Off site: Ambrières-les-Vallées (shops and restaurants). Boating on the River Mayenne. Walking and cycle tracks.

Open: 1 April - 1 November.

Directions

From Mayenne head north on D23 to Ambrières-les-Vallées. The site is clearly signed on your right-hand side from from here. GPS: 48.391908, -0.61709

Charges guide

Per unit incl. 2 persons	€ 10.40 - € 12.90
extra person	€ 3.20 - € 4.20
child (under 13 yrs)	€ 1.70 - € 2.30
electricity	€ 3.10
dog	€ 1.30 - € 1.80

Angers
Camping du Lac de Maine

Avenue du Lac de Maine, F-49000 Angers (Maine-et-Loire) T: 02 41 73 05 03. E: camping@lacdemaine.fr
alanrogers.com/FR49000

The Lac de Maine campsite is situated in the heart of the Anjou region. Most of the 143 level touring pitches are part grass and part gravel hardstanding, with the remainder all gravel. All have water, drainage and electricity (10A). Some pitches are not suitable for awnings. The main entrance has a height restriction of 3.2 m, although there is an alternative gate for higher vehicles. This is a useful site, open for a long season and only five minutes from the centre of Angers. With wide access roads, it is also suitable for American RVs. This site has the advantage of being at the southern end of the Parc de Loisirs du Lac de Maine. The adjacent 220 acre lake has a sandy beach for swimmers, windsurfing, sailing and pedaloes available, while the parkland provides tennis courts and a nature reserve.

Facilities

Two sanitary blocks, one which can be heated and includes some washbasins in cubicles. British style WCs. Facilities for babies and disabled visitors. Laundry facilities. Motorcaravan service point. Restaurant/bar (both 15/6-5/9). Heated L-shaped swimming pool (1/6-15/9). Spa. Pétanque. Bicycle hire. Play area. Internet point and WiFi (free). Barrier card deposit (€ 20). Off site: Supermarket within walking distance. Lake beach 500 m. Fishing 1 km. Riding 3 km. Golf 5 km.

Open: 25 March - 10 October.

Directions

Site is just west of Angers near the N23 (Angers - Nantes road). Turn south at signs for Quartier de Maine and Lac de Maine. Follow signs for Pruniers and Bouchemaine. Site on D111 and signed. GPS: 47.45434, -0.59619

Charges guide

Per unit incl. 2 persons and electricity	€ 16.50 - € 22.20
extra person	€ 3.20
Camping Cheques accepted.	

Camping du Lac de Maine
★★★★

Discover this pretty campsite nestling in the heart of the Anjou wine region, close to the historic town of Angers and a beautiful vast 100 ha lake.

Openingdates:
25/03 to 10/10/2011

Mobile homes and bungalows for rent

Heated Swimming Pool, Paddling pool, SPA, Restaurant, Bar, Takeaway, Bike hire, Internet Facilities (WiFi)...

Avenue du Lac de Maine - F-49000 Angers - Tel: 0033 (0)2.41.73.05.03
Fax: 0033 (0)2.41.73.02.20 - camping@lacdemaine.fr - www.camping-angers.fr

Asserac
Flower Camping Domaine du Pont Mahé

Pont Mahé, F-44410 Asserac (Loire-Atlantique) T: 02 40 01 74 98. E: contact@pont-mahe.com
alanrogers.com/FR44400

La Grande Brière is a vast area of marshland to the north of the Loire estuary. This is an area rich in flora and fauna, arguably best explored using the traditional punts (chalands). Domaine du Pont Mahé is a seaside site to the north of the Brière. Of the 81 pitches, 36 are for touring and the remainder are occupied by mobile homes (27 for rent). Pitches are generally well shaded and of a good size. The site's covered swimming pool is a focal point and is attractively surrounded by a terrace with straw parasols. Bicycle hire is on offer and a number of cycle tracks run close to the site.

Facilities

Sanitary facilities include hot showers and washbasins in cabins. Facilities for disabled visitors. Laundry facilities. Shop. Bar. Takeaway. Covered swimming pool. Children's pool. Play area. Games room. Bicycle and canoe hire. Activity and entertainment programme. Mobile homes and equipped tents for rent. Off site: Nearest beach 250 m. Grande Brière natural park. Fishing. Cycle tracks. La Baule 18 km.

Open: 1 April - 31 October.

Directions

Leave the N165 at Arzal exit and head south on the D139 (which becomes the D83) as far as Assérac. Head west here on D82 to Pont Mahé and site is well signed. GPS: 47.44737, -2.45043

Charges guide

Per unit incl. 2 persons	
and electricity	€ 14.50 - € 27.90
extra person	€ 3.00 - € 5.00
child (2-7 yrs)	€ 2.00 - € 4.00

Batz-sur-Mer

Campé●le

Campéole les Paludiers

Rue Nicolas Appert, F-44740 Batz-sur-Mer (Loire-Atlantique) T: 02 40 23 85 84.
E: paludiers@campeole.com **alanrogers.com/FR44360**

Les Paludiers, part of the Campéole group, is pleasantly situated at Batz-sur-Mer, a typical Breton village between La Baule and the fortified town of Guérande. The site has 300 pitches, with 99 used for touring units on sandy ground, marked and divided by shrubs. There are 70 with 10A electricity. The remainder of the pitches are occupied by mobile homes and canvas bungalows. At the rear of the modern reception building there is a bar and games room. Outside, a patio area overlooks a small heated pool and a play area for children. Entertainment is provided for both children and adults in the high season. This site is ideal for families with young children, with a good pool and a safe environment for play. The added bonus here is the close proximity of a lovely sandy beach – just five minutes walk. The drive along the Côte Sauvage to Le Croisic is quite spectacular.

Facilities

Three modern toilet blocks each with good facilities for disabled visitors and a baby room. Laundry facilities. Shop with limited but essential stocks. Bar and snacks (1/7-31/8). Swimming and paddling pools (15/5-15/9). Play area. Games room. Barbecues are only permitted in a dedicated area. Off site: Beach 100 m. Fishing 500 m. Town centre 800 m. Golf, bicycle hire and riding 1 km. Salt marshes and coastal walking paths.

Open: 1 April - 30 September.

Directions

From Nantes take the N171 to Saint Nazaire and then the D213 towards Guérande. At the D774 follow signs to Batz-sur-Mer, continue through village and take exit from the roundabout into rue Nicolas Appert. Site entrance is on the left. GPS: 47.2788, -2.4913

Charges guide

Per unit incl. 2 persons	
and electricity	€ 17.10 - € 26.60
extra person	€ 4.50 - € 7.10
child (under 6 yrs)	free - € 4.40
dog	€ 2.50 - € 3.20

Campé●le
CAMPSITES AND RENTALS
Les Paludiers***
At 100 meters of the beach and 800 meters of the centre, with swimming pool. Pitches and accommodations of high quality.
PAYS DE LA LOIRE
44740 Batz Sur Mer - Tel.: +33-240-2385-84 - www.campeole.co.uk / paludiers@campeole.com

For latest campsite news, availability and prices visit
alanrogers.com

Call 01580 214000

We can book this site for you!

alan rogers ● travel

Brissac
Camping de l'Etang
Route de Saint-Mathurin, F-49320 Brissac (Maine-et-Loire) T: 02 41 91 70 61. E: info@campingetang.com

alanrogers.com/FR49040

At Camping de l'Etang many of the 124 level touring pitches have pleasant views across the countryside. Separated and numbered, some have a little shade and all have electricity (10A) with water and drainage nearby; 21 are fully serviced. A small bridge crosses the river Aubance which runs through the site (well fenced) and there are two lakes where fisherman can enjoy free fishing. The site has its own vineyard and the wine produced can be purchased on the campsite. The adjacent Parc de Loisirs is a paradise for young children with many activities (free for campers). A Sites et Paysages member.

Facilities

Three well maintained toilet blocks. Laundry facilities. Baby room. Disabled visitors are well catered for. Motorcaravan service point. The farmhouse houses reception, small shop and takeaway snacks (July/Aug) when bar is closed. Bar/restaurant (evenings July/Aug). Swimming pool (heated and covered) and paddling pool. Fishing. Play area. Bicycle hire. Evening entertainment in high season. WiFi. Off site: Golf and riding 10 km.

Open: 1 May - 15 September.

Directions

Brissac-Quincé is 17 km. southeast of Angers on D748 towards Poitiers. Do not enter the town but turn north on D55 (site signed) in direction of St Mathurin. GPS: 47.3611, -0.4353

Charges guide

Per unit incl. 2 persons and electricity	€ 18.00 - € 30.00
extra person	€ 4.00 - € 5.00

Charchigne
Camping le Malidor
F-53250 Charchigne (Mayenne) T: 02 43 00 11 12. E: lemalidor@gmail.com

alanrogers.com/FR53020

This attractive, small, rural site is surrounded by farmland and it provides a real taste of the French countryside. The three private lakes provide great fishing and only a short walk away the path leads to the village where you will find the local bakery and restaurant. There are 27 pitches, 17 for touring, all with 10A electricity. They are terraced and divided by mature hedges. Fly pitches are allowed by prior arrangement with the manager, to within three metres of the main lake for the keen fisherman.

Facilities

One sanitary block provides good facilities including a disabled access shower. Bar and restaurant (all year). Play area. Boules. Darts and pool table plus a hall for groups up to 90. Minigolf. Fishing on all three lakes. Fishing platform for wheelchair users. Off site: Village with bar/restaurant and shop 500 m. Riding 3.5 km. Beaches 20 km. Golf 25 km.

Open: Said to be all year, but check before visiting.

Directions

From A81 (Rennes - Le Mans) take exit 3 for Laval. Head northeast on N162 to Mayenne. Then take N12 in the same direction towards Alençon for 20 km. Just before Javron turn left on D33 to Charchigne. Then follow signs to site just before Charchigne. GPS: 48.41857, -0.40141

Charges guide

Per unit incl. 2 persons and electricity	€ 15.00
extra person	€ 2.00

Cholet
Centre Touristique Lac de Ribou
Allée Léon Mandin, F-49300 Cholet (Maine-et-Loire) T: 02 41 49 74 30. E: info@lacderibou.com

alanrogers.com/FR49120

Situated just 58 km. southeast of Nantes and a similar distance from the River Loire at Angers and Saumur, this could be a useful place to break a journey or to spend a few days relaxing. Camping Lac de Ribou, with the adjacent 'Village Vacances', forms a holiday complex in pleasant parkland next to an extensive lake on the outskirts of the busy market town of Cholet. One hundred and sixty two touring pitches are on undulating land (some are sloping), divided by hedges and with mature trees providing shade on many; most have electricity (10A) and 115 also have individual water tap and drainage.

Facilities

One sanitary block with preset showers and washbasins in cabins. Facilities for disabled visitors. Motorcaravan service points. Small shop (July/Aug). Bar and snack bar with takeaway (July/Aug). Heated swimming pool plus smaller pool with slide and a paddling pool (1/6-30/9). Play area. Multisport pitch. Volleyball. Boules. Activities for all ages (July/Aug) including archery, art workshop for children, sub-aqua, aquagym. Professional cabaret evenings. Night club (high season). WiFi (with deposit). Off site: Fishing and small beach (no swimming) 500 m.

Open: 1 April - 30 September.

Directions

From Cholet ring road east of town, turn east on D20 towards Maulévrier and Mauléon. At roundabout by Leclerc supermarket, take first exit signed to site which is signed 'Parc de Loisirs de Ribou' all around the town. GPS: 47.036367, -0.843733

Charges guide

Per unit incl. 1 or 2 persons and electricity	€ 10.20 - € 23.00
extra person	€ 3.05 - € 5.10
dog	€ 1.55 - € 3.10

No credit cards.

For latest campsite news, availability and prices visit
alanrogers.com

Clisson

Camping Municipal du Moulin

Route de Nantes, F-44190 Clisson (Loire-Atlantique) T: 02 40 54 44 48

alanrogers.com/FR44020

This good value, small site is conveniently located on one of the main north – south routes on the edge of the interesting old town of Clisson and in the middle of the wine-growing region. A typical municipal site, it is useful for short stays. There are 45 good sized, marked and level pitches with electricity and divided by hedges and trees giving a good degree of privacy and some shade. There is also an unmarked, wooded area for small tents. A barbecue and campfire area is to the rear of the site above the river where one can fish or canoe (via a steep path). The town is within walking distance.

Facilities

The fully equipped toilet block, cleaned each afternoon, includes some washbasins in cabins and others in a separate large room, with hot and cold water. Unit for disabled visitors. Laundry facilities. Bread delivered daily. Small playground. Fishing. No double axle or commercial vehicles accepted. Off site: Supermarket with fuel just across the road. Bicycle hire, riding 5 km. Sailing 15 km. Golf 30 km.

Open: Mid April - mid October.

Directions

From N249 Nantes-Cholet road, take exit for Vallet/Clisson and D763 south for 7 km. then fork right towards Clisson town centre. At roundabout after passing Leclerc supermarket on your right take second exit (into site). GPS: 47.09594, -1.28271

Charges guide

Per unit incl. 1 person and electricity	€ 12.91 - € 13.62
extra person	€ 2.57 - € 2.71

No credit cards.

Concourson-sur-Layon

Camping Caravaning la Vallée des Vignes

La Croix Patron, F-49700 Concourson-sur-Layon (Maine-et-Loire) T: 02 41 59 86 35.

E: info@campingvdv.com **alanrogers.com/FR49070**

The enthusiasm of the English owners here comes across instantly in the warm welcome received by their guests. Bordering the Layon river, the 79 good sized touring pitches are reasonably level and fully serviced (10A electricity, water tap and drain). Five pitches have a hardstanding for cars. Attractions include an enclosed bar and restaurant, a generously sized sun terrace surrounding the pool and high season activities for children and adults. These include wine tasting, competitions and treasure hunts. An ideal base for visiting the châteaux of the Loire and the many caves and vineyards.

Facilities

The toilet block includes washbasins in cabins, and dishwashing facilities at either end. Baby room. Facilities for disabled visitors. Laundry facilities. Bar (from 15/5 or on request) serving meals, snacks and takeaway (from 15/5). Swimming and paddling pools (from 15/5). Playground, games area and football pitch. Minigolf, volleyball, basketball, table tennis. Internet access. Fishing. Caravan storage. Pets corner. Off site: Zoo at Doué-la-Fontaine. Grand Parc Puy du Fou.

Open: 15 April - 30 September.

Directions

Site signed off D960 Doué - Vihiers road, just west of Concourson-sur-Layon. GPS: 47.17431, -0.34730

Charges guide

Per unit incl. 2 persons and electricity	€ 20.50 - € 28.00
extra person	€ 4.00 - € 6.00
child (2-12 yrs)	€ 2.00 - € 4.00
dog	€ 2.50 - € 3.50

Special offers available.

Durtal

Camping les Portes de l'Anjou

9 rue du Camping, F-49340 Durtal (Maine-et-Loire) T: 02 41 76 31 80.

E: lesportesdelanjou@camp-in-ouest.com **alanrogers.com/FR49160**

Les Portes de L'Anjou is an ex-municipal site which has recently been acquired by the owners of FR72080. The site can be found at Durtal, an attractive town around 30 km. north of Angers. There are 122 pitches here, all of which are surrounded by hedges and are of a good size (with 6A electricity). A number of mobile homes are available for rent. The town centre is around 500m away and a good range of shops and restaurants can be found there. The site enjoys direct access to the Loir and fishing is said to be good here. Various activities are organised on site in the peak season.

Facilities

Three modern sanitary blocks have British style toilets, basins in cubicles, preset showers and separate facilities for disabled visitors. Bar/snack bar. Swimming pool. Fishing. Games room. Canoe hire. Play area. Tourist information. Entertainment and activity programme. Direct river access. Mobile homes for rent. Off site: Durtal (shops, restaurants and château). Walking and cycling. Aerial adventure park in the forest of Ecouflant.

Open: 21 March - 28 September.

Directions

Durtal is located close to exit 11 of the A11. From there head for the town centre and then follow signs to the site. GPS: 47.671269, -0.235991

Charges guide

Per unit incl. 2 persons and electricity	€ 12.40 - € 14.70

For latest campsite news, availability and prices visit

alanrogers.com

Guemene-Penfao
Flower Camping l'Hermitage

36 ave. du Paradis, F-44290 Guemene-Penfao (Loire-Atlantique) T: 02 40 79 23 48.
E: camping.heritage@wanadoo.fr **alanrogers.com/FR44130**

L'Hermitage is a pretty wooded site set in the Vallée du Don and would be useful for en-route stops or for longer stays. The enthusiastic staff, even though their English is a little limited, provide a warm welcome and maintain this reasonably priced site to a good standard. There are 110 pitches of which 80 are a good size for touring and camping. Some are formally arranged on open, level grass pitches, whereas others are informal amongst light woodland. Electricity (6A) is available to all (a long lead may be useful). A further 18 pitches are taken by mobile homes, most of which are for rent.

Facilities

A clean and well serviced toilet block includes some washbasins in cabins with warm water. Laundry and dishwashing sinks under cover (cold water but a hot tap is provided). Smallish pool, paddling pool and slide. Small play area. Pétanque. Bicycle hire. Games room with video games. WiFi (free). Off site: Leisure complex with indoor pool opposite. Fishing 500 m. Village 1 km. for all facilities. Riding 2 km. Many walking trails.

Open: 1 April - 31 October.

Directions

Exit N137 at Derval (signed Châteaubriant) but take D775 for Redon. Guémené-Penfao is about 13 km. Watch for site signs before village centre. Site is on the outskirts in a semi-residential area to the northeast. GPS: 47.62595, -1.8181

Charges guide

Per unit incl. 2 persons and electricity	€ 16.00 - € 21.50
extra person	€ 3.50 - € 5.00

Guérande
Le Domaine de Léveno

537

Route de Sandun, F-44350 Guérande (Loire-Atlantique) T: 02 40 24 79 30.
E: domaine.leveno@wanadoo.fr **alanrogers.com/FR44220**

There have been many changes to this extensive site over the past years and considerable investment has been made to provide some excellent new facilities. The number of mobile homes and chalets has increased considerably, leaving just 38 touring pitches. However, these are mainly grouped at the far end of the site and are rather worn with little grass. Pitches are divided by hedges and trees which offer a good deal of shade and all have electricity (10A). Access is tricky to some and the site is not recommended for larger units. Twin-axle caravans and American motorhomes are not accepted.

Facilities

Main refurbished toilet block offers preset showers, washbasins in cubicles and facilities for disabled visitors. Laundry facilities. Small shop selling basics and takeaway snacks. Restaurant, bar with TV and games (April-Sept). Indoor pool. Heated outdoor pool complex with water slides and a flume, paddling pool (15/5-30/9). Fitness room. Play area. Multisport court. Crazy golf. Programme of activities and events (high season). Electric barbecues are not permitted. WiFi in bar. Off site: Hypermarket 1 km. Fishing 2 km. Beach, golf and riding all 5 km.

Open: 4 April - 30 September.

Directions

Site is less than 3 km. from the centre of Guérande. From D774 and from D99/N171 take D99E Guérande bypass. Turn east following signs for Villejames and Leclerc hypermarket and continue on D247 to site on right. GPS: 47.33352, -2.3906

Charges guide

Per unit incl. 2 persons, electricity and water	€ 22.00 - € 42.00
extra person	€ 5.00 - € 9.00
child (under 7 yrs)	€ 3.00 - € 7.00

Heric
Camping la Pindière

F-44810 Heric (Loire-Atlantique) T: 02 40 57 65 41. E: camping.pindiere@free.fr
alanrogers.com/FR44430

Camping la Pindière can be found between Nantes and Rennes, close to the Nantes – Brest canal. The site is open all year and may appeal as an en-route stop, although there is much to see in the area. Pitches here are of a good size and generally well shaded. Most have electrical connections. A number of mobile homes and roulottes are available for rent. The adjacent Auberge des Pyrénées is a pleasant restaurant, open throughout the year. Cycling is popular in the area, with a number of excellent cycle tracks, including routes alongside the canal. The great city of Nantes is within easy reach.

Facilities

New toilet block. Small shop. Restaurant and takeaway. Children's pool (July/Aug). Play area. Volleyball. Tourist information. Mobile homes for rent. WiFi. Off site: Shops, bars and restaurants in Heric. Cycle trails along the banks of the Nantes – Brest canal. Nantes.

Open: All year.

Directions

Heric is north of Nantes. If approaching from the north, use the N137 Rennes – Nantes road and leave at Fay-de-Bretagne exit. The site is well signed from here. GPS: 47.41329, -1.6705

Charges guide

Per unit incl. 2 persons and electricity	€ 16.50 - € 18.80
extra person	€ 3.50 - € 4.00

For latest campsite news, availability and prices visit
alanrogers.com

La Baule
Camping les Ajoncs d'Or

Chemin du Rocher, F-44500 La Baule (Loire-Atlantique) T: 02 40 60 33 29. E: contact@ajoncs.com
alanrogers.com/FR44170

This site is situated in pine woods, 1.5 km. on the inland side of La Baule and its beautiful bay. A well maintained, natural woodland setting provides a wide variety of pitch types (just over 200), some level and bordered with hedges and tall trees to provide shade and many others that maintain the natural characteristics of the woodland. Most pitches have electricity and water nearby and are usually of a larger size. A central building provides a shop and an open friendly bar that serves snacks and takeaways. The new, English-speaking owner has extensive plans for this campsite. Large areas of woodland have been retained for quiet and recreational purposes and are safe for children to roam. It can be difficult to find an informal campsite close to an exciting seaside resort that retains its touring and camping identity, but les Ajoncs d'Or does this. Enjoy the gentle breezes off the sea that constantly rustle the trees. The family are justifiably proud of their site.

Facilities

Two good quality sanitary blocks are clean and well maintained providing plenty of facilities including a baby room. Washing machines and dryers. Shop and bar (July/Aug). Snack bar (July/Aug). Good size swimming pool and paddling pool (1/6-5/9). Sports and playground areas. Bicycle hire. Reception with security barrier (closed 22.30-07.30). Off site: Everything for an enjoyable holiday can be found in nearby La Baule. Beach, fishing and riding 1.5 km. Golf 3 km.

Open: 1 April - 30 October.

Directions

From N171 take exit for La Baule les Pins. Follow signs for 'La Baule Centre', then left at roundabout in front of Carrefour supermarket and follow site signs. GPS: 47.28950, -2.37367

Charges guide

Per unit incl. 2 persons	
and electricity	€ 18.00 - € 30.00
extra person	€ 4.20 - € 7.00
child (2-7 yrs)	€ 2.10 - € 3.50
dog	€ 1.20 - € 2.00

CAMPING ✫ ✫ ✫
Les Ajoncs d'Or

• 800m from store
• 1km from center of LA BAULE
• 2km from the sea
• Les Ajoncs d'Or a naturel parc of 6ha

www.ajoncs.com – contact@ajoncs.com
Tel: (+33)2 40 60 33 29
Chemin du Rocher – 44 500 – La Baule

La Baule
Village Center le Bois d'Amour

Allée de Diane, F-44500 La Baule (Loire-Atlantique) T: 08 25 00 20 30. E: contact@village-center.com
alanrogers.com/FR44470

Camping le Bois d'Amour is a member of the Village Center group and can be found on the edge of the Escoublac forest, close to La Baule and its celebrated beach. There are 200 pitches, some of which are very large (150 sq.m). The camping area is well shaded and most pitches have electrical connections. Several mobile homes and fully equipped 'Ecolodge' tents are available for rent. This is a quiet site in low season, but livelier in July and August, with an activity and entertainment programme for all ages. La Baule is one of France's great traditional resorts, but only became popular in the late 19th century with the arrival of the railway from Saint Nazaire. Many of the town's great buildings, such as the very grand Hermitage Hotel and the stylish casino date from this period.

Facilities

Motorcaravan service point. Small shop. Snack bar. Takeaway. Swimming pool. Volleyball. Play area. Children's activity programme. Bicycle hire. Mobile homes and tents for rent. Off site: Nearest beach 1.5 km. Shops and restaurants at La Baule. Golf. Riding. Château de Careil 7 km. Le Croisic (aquarium) 13 km.

Open: 2 April - 1 October.

Directions

Approaching from the east (St Nazaire), leave the N171 at the La Baule - Escoublac exit and the site is well signed before you reach the town centre (Allée de Diane). GPS: 47.288721, -2.372312

Charges guide

Per unit incl. 2 persons	
and electricity	€ 17.00 - € 24.00
dog	€ 3.00

La Bernerie-en-Retz

Camping les Ecureuils

24 avenue Gilbert Burlot, F-44760 La Bernerie-en-Retz (Loire-Atlantique) T: 02 40 82 76 95.
E: camping.les-ecureuils@wanadoo.fr **alanrogers.com/FR44050**

Just 350 metres from both the sea and the centre of the little town of La Bernerie, les Ecureuils is a family run site. The sandy beach here is great for children; swimming is restricted to high tide, since the sea goes out a long way, although at low tide a shallow lagoon remains which is perfect for young children. The site has 163 touring pitches, all with electricity (10A) close by and 19 with their own water tap and drain. There are also 86 mobile homes and chalets for rent and a further 62 privately owned.

Facilities

Two toilet blocks are in traditional French style; some have controllable showers and washbasins in cubicles. Facilities for disabled visitors are not all easily accessible. Baby room. Bar with terrace, also selling bread (1/7-31/8). Snack bar and takeaway (July/Aug). Swimming pools (15/5-15/9). Playground. Only gas barbecues are permitted. WiFi in bar area. Off site: Shops, restaurants and bars 350 m. Also beach, fishing, sailing and boat launching. Golf, riding and bicycle hire 6 km.

Open: 1 May - 16 September.

Directions

La Bernerie-en-Retz is 5 km. south of Pornic and 26 km. south of the Saint Nazaire bridge. From the D213/D13 (Saint Nazaire - Noirmoutier) turn west on D66 to La Bernerie. Site is signed to right by railway station before reaching town.
GPS: 47.0845, -2.036667

Charges 2012

Per unit incl. 2 persons	
and electricity	€ 21.00 - € 36.00
extra person	€ 4.00 - € 7.00
child (0-10 yrs)	free - € 5.50

La Plaine-sur-Mer

Camping la Tabardière

F-44770 La Plaine-sur-Mer (Loire-Atlantique) T: 02 40 21 58 83. E: info@camping-la-tabardiere.com
alanrogers.com/FR44150

Owned and managed by the Barré family, this campsite is pleasant, peaceful and immaculate. It will suit those who want to enjoy the local coast and towns but return to an 'oasis' for relaxation. However, it still provides activities and fun for those with energy remaining. The pitches are mostly terraced and care needs to be taken in manoeuvring caravans into position – although the effort is well worth it. The pitches have access to electricity and water taps are conveniently situated nearby. The site is probably not suitable for people using wheelchairs. Whilst this is a rural site, its amenities are excellent with a covered swimming pool, paddling pool and water slides, volleyball, tennis, boules and a very challenging 18-hole minigolf to keep you occupied, plus a friendly bar. The beautiful beaches are 3 km. away with the fishing harbour town, Pornic, some 5 km, ideal for cafés, restaurants and evening strolls. A Sites et Paysages member.

Facilities

Two good, clean toilet blocks are well equipped and include laundry facilities. Motorcaravan service point. Shop, bar, snacks and takeaway (high season). Good sized covered swimming pool, paddling pool and slides (supervised). Playground. Minigolf. Volleyball and basketball. Half size tennis courts. Boules. Fitness programme. Bicycle hire (July/Aug). Overnight area for motorcaravans (€14 per night). Off site: Beach and sea fishing 3 km. Golf, riding and bicycle hire all 5 km.

Open: 16 April - 25 September.

Directions

Site is well signed, situated inland off the D13 Pornic - La Plaine-sur-Mer road. GPS: 47.140767, -2.15052

Charges guide

Per unit incl. 2 persons	
extra person	€ 15.50 - € 28.60
child (2-9 yrs)	€ 3.00 - € 6.90
dog	€ 3.00 - € 4.75
electricity (3/10A)	€ 3.40
	€ 3.50 - € 6.00
Camping Cheques accepted.	

Call 01580 214000
We can book this site for you! alan rogers ◉ travel

CAMPING LA TABARDIÈRE ★★★★ *Camping Caravaning*

South Loire - North Vendée

Situated in a green environment, with covered heated swimming pool.

3 km from the sea, 4 km from the shops, 6 km from a 18 holes golf terrain in Pornic, 8 km from a tha-lasso centre.

Open from 16 April till 25 September

44770 la Plaine sur Mer - Tél.: 0033 240 215 883
info@camping-la-tabardiere.com - www.camping-la-tabardiere.com

La Chartre-sur-le-Loir

Camping du Vieux Moulin

Chemin des Bergivaux, F-72340 La Chartre-sur-le-Loir (Sarthe) T: 02 43 44 41 18. E: camping@lachartre.com
alanrogers.com/FR72070

Le Vieux Moulin is a pleasant family site, located on the banks of the Loir, close to the pretty town of La Chartre-sur-le-Loir, to the south east of Le Mans. Pitches here are grassy and of a good size. There are also a number of mobile homes and fully equipped tents available for rent. On-site amenities include a heated swimming pool, a paddling pool and a sports field. Canoeing is popular here and canoes can be rented on site. The site becomes livelier in peak season with limited entertainment and activities.

Facilities

Traditional sanitary block provides pushbutton showers and some washbasins in cubicles. Facilities for disabled visitors. Washing machine and dryer. Motorcaravan service point. Small shop selling basics, restaurant and takeaway with licence (weekends and July/Aug). Swimming and paddling pools (1/6-20/9). Fishing. Canoeing. Bicycle hire. Large sports field. Play area. Tourist information. Mobile homes and equipped tents for rent. Internet access and free WiFi. Off site: Village with shops, bars and restaurants 1 km. Lake with swimming, sailing and watersports 4 km. Cycle and walking tracks.

Open: 1 May - 20 September.

Directions

La Chartre-sur-le-Loir is 47 km. southeast of Le Mans and 44 km. north of Tours. From A28 exit 26, head east to Château du Loir, turn south on the D938/D338 (Caen - Tours road) and cross the Loir. Then head northeast on the D305 to La Chartre-sur-Le Loir. After one-way system follow signs to the site, turning left immediately after crossing river. GPS: 47.7324, 0.57095

Charges guide

Per unit incl. 2 persons	
and electricity	€ 13.10 - € 18.20
extra person	€ 2.70 - € 3.60

La Plaine-sur-Mer

Camping le Ranch

Les Hautes Raillères, F-44770 La Plaine-sur-Mer (Loire-Atlantique) T: 02 40 21 52 62.
E: info@camping-le-ranch.com **alanrogers.com/FR44240**

This is a pleasant, family run campsite with a friendly atmosphere, close to the beaches of the Jade Coast between Pornic and Saint Brévin-les-Pins, yet not right on the seashore. The 88 touring pitches all have access to 10A electricity although on some a long cable may be required; these occupy the central part of the site, with the fringe areas taken up by mobile homes and chalets, 28 for rent and 74 privately owned (although 30 of these are also available for rent in high season). The rows of pitches are separated by well kept hedges, and small trees mark the corners of most plots. In high season there is a very lively atmosphere, and at less busy times it is almost certainly a very peaceful site. A bar and terrace overlook the pool complex with swimming and paddling pools, together with water slides and a flume. Linked to the bar is a large barn with a stage and a dance floor, which at other times is a games room and volleyball court. The central area, complete with boules, gives the site a very French ambience.

Facilities

The central sanitary block has preset showers and washbasins in cubicles. Facilities for disabled visitors. Baby room. Further small toilet block. Heated swimming pool complex with slides and flume (1/5-15/9). Bar has small shop selling bread, basics and camping gaz. Good takeaway (July/Aug). Activities for children and entertainment and sports events for families in high season. Electric barbecues not permitted. WiFi. Off site: Beach and fishing 800 m. Bicycle hire 1.5 km. Boat launching and sailing 3 km. Riding 4 km. Golf 6 km.

Open: 1 April - 30 September.

Directions

La Plaine-sur-Mer is 16 km. south of the St Nazaire bridge. Site is on D96 5 km. northeast of the town. From D213 (Route Bleue) just south of St Michel-Chef-Chef turn southwest on D96 towards La Plaine. Site on left in about 2 km. GPS: 47.155216, -2.1649

Charges guide

Per unit incl. 2 persons	
and electricity	€ 17.20 - € 29.70
extra person	€ 3.20 - € 5.70
child (under 8 yrs)	€ 2.20 - € 3.50

Friendly summer holiday, near the sea in the south of Brittany

Camping ★★★ Le Ranch

Camping Qualité

www.camping-le-ranch.com

Chemin des Hautes Raillères - 44770 LA PLAINE SUR MER - Tél. 02 40 21 52 62 - info@camping-le-ranch.com

For latest campsite news, availability and prices visit
alanrogers.com

La Turballe
Camping la Falaise

1 boulevard de Belmont, F-44420 La Turballe (Loire-Atlantique) T: 02 40 23 32 53.
E: info@camping-de-la-falaise.com **alanrogers.com/FR44340**

La Falaise is a simple site enjoying direct access to a wide sandy beach. There are 150 pitches of which 67 are available to tourers with water and electricity. Other pitches are occupied by mobile homes and chalets (some to rent). The pitches are of a reasonable size and marked by low hedges, but are unshaded. This is a quiet site in low season becoming much livelier in July and August. There are relatively few amenities on site but nearby La Turballe has a good selection of shops and restaurants. In high season, a takeaway food service is available. There is one main building housing reception and rather dated washing and toilet facilities. La Turballe is a bustling fishing port and nearby Guérande, on the edge of the Grande Brière natural park, merits a visit with its excellent market.

Facilities

Central toilet block (over half the toilets are Turkish style). Bar, snack bar and takeaway (1/6-15/9). Play area (unfenced). Mobile homes and chalets for rent. Direct access to the beach. Off site: Shops 300 m. Fishing. Boat launching 500 m. Shops and restaurants in La Turballe 2 km. Golf 2 km. Riding 10 km. Walking and cycle trails.

Open: 1 April - 31 October.

Directions

Take the D99 from Guèrande to La Turballe and then continue towards Piriac sur Mer. Bypass La Turballe and the site is on this road after a further kilometre. GPS: 47.353833, -2.517333

Charges guide

Per unit incl. 2 persons and electricity	€ 21.00 - € 32.00
extra person (over 4 yrs)	€ 4.45 - € 5.10
dog	€ 2.35 - € 3.00

Camping La Falaise

2 entrance to the beach, on 400 m distance from the fisher harbour and marina. The center is at 600 meters distance, you will find a supermarket at 400 meter distance. La Falaise is near various places of interest. The mediaeval city of Guérande, ferries to the islands, the Parc Naturel Régional de Brière and the Côte Sauvage.

1 Boulevard de Belmont - 44420 La Turballe - Tel: 0033 240 23 32 53 - Fax: 0033 240 62 87 07
E-mail: info@camping-de-la-falaise.com - www.camping-la-falaise.co.uk

La Turballe
Camping le Parc Sainte-Brigitte

Domaine de Bréhet, chemin des Routes, F-44420 La Turballe (Loire-Atlantique) T: 02 40 24 88 91.
E: saintebrigitte@wanadoo.fr **alanrogers.com/FR44040**

Le Parc Sainte-Brigitte is a well established site in the attractive grounds of a manor house, three kilometres from the beaches. It is a spacious site with 150 good pitches, 110 with electricity, water and drainage. Some are arranged in a circular, park-like setting near the entrance, others are in wooded areas under tall trees and the remainder are on more open grass in an unmarked area near the pool. This is a quiet place to stay outside the main season, whilst in high season, it can become very busy. One can walk around many of the areas of the estate that are not used for camping; there are farm animals to see and a carp fishing lake will be popular with anglers.

Facilities

The main toilet block, supplemented by a second block, is of good quality. They include washbasins in cabins and two bathrooms. Laundry facilities and lines provided. Motorcaravan services. Small shop. Pleasant restaurant/bar with takeaway (both 15/5-15/9). Heated swimming pool with retractable roof and paddling pool. Playground. Bicycle hire. Boules. TV room and traditional 'salle de réunion'. Fishing. WiFi (free). Off site: Riding 2 km. Nearest beach 2.5 km. Golf 15 km.

Open: 1 April - 1 October.

Directions

Entrance is off the busy La Turballe-Guérande D99 road, 3 km. east of La Turballe. A one-way system operates – in one lane, out via another. GPS: 47.34253, -2.47168

Charges guide

Per unit incl. 2 persons, water, waste water and electricity	€ 29.80
extra person	€ 6.30
child (under 7 yrs)	€ 5.00
No credit cards.	

For latest campsite news, availability and prices visit

alanrogers.com

Le Croisic
Camping de l'Océan

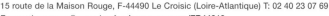

538

15 route de la Maison Rouge, F-44490 Le Croisic (Loire-Atlantique) T: 02 40 23 07 69
E: camping-ocean@wanadoo.fr **alanrogers.com/FR44210**

Camping de l'Océan is situated on the Le Croisic peninsula, an attractive part of the Brittany coastline. Out of a total of 400 pitches, 60 are available for tourers with the remainder being taken by mobile homes either privately owned or for rent. The pitches are level and 80-100 sq.m. in size (they were rather worn when we visited). The leisure facilities, which include a restaurant, bar and pool complex, are of an excellent standard. This site, probably more suitable for families with young teenagers, can be very lively in high season with a wealth of activities and entertainment for all ages. Sports are well catered for and there are tournaments in high season. After an excellent meal in the restaurant you can enjoy different entertainment on most evenings in July and August. The site is within walking distance of the Atlantic Ocean and white sandy beaches are just 150 m. away.

Facilities

Three adequate toilet blocks, however there are no facilities for disabled visitors. Washing machines and dryers. Good restaurant and bar. Takeaway. Shop. Motorcaravan service point. Swimming pool complex comprising an indoor pool, outdoor pool and paddling pool, hammam, sauna and balnéo. Volleyball. Football. Basketball. Tennis. Bicycle hire. Charcoal barbecues are permitted. WiFi throughout (charged; free in bar area). Off site: Market (most days). Le Croisic for shops, bars and restaurants. Sailing, riding and golf.

Open: 6 April - 30 September.

Directions

From Le Pouliguen, travel west on N171 to Le Croisic. Site is well signed from here and found in about 1.5 km. GPS: 47.29752, -2.53593

Charges 2012

Per unit incl. 2 persons and electricity	€ 25.00 - € 52.00
extra person	€ 6.00 - € 9.00
child (2-7 yrs)	€ 4.00 - € 7.00
dog	€ 5.00 - € 7.00

3 campings-villages for a successful holiday!
Visit our website: www.campsite-atlantic-coast.co.uk

LE DOMAINE DE LÉVENO

At 7 km from La Baule beach!
Lieu dit Léveno
44350 GUÉRANDE - France
tel. : 0033 2 40 24 79 30
or 0033 2 40 24 79 50
fax : 0033 2 40 62 01 23
www.camping-leveno.com

NEW : wave pool and waterslide to sensations

L'OCÉAN

At 150 m from the beach!
15, route Maison Rouge
B.P. 15
44490 LE CROISIC - France
tel. : 0033 2 40 23 07 69
fax : 0033 2 40 15 70 63
www.camping-ocean.com

LA BOUTINARDIÈRE Kid's Club

At 200 m from the beach!
23, rue de la plage
de la Boutinardière
44210 PORNIC - France
tel. : 0033 2 40 82 05 68
fax : 0033 2 40 82 49 01
www.camping-boutinardiere.com

For latest campsite news, availability and prices visit
alanrogers.com

Le Croisic
Camping la Pierre Longue

B.P 13, rue Henri Dunant, F-44490 Le Croisic (Loire-Atlantique) T: 02 40 23 13 44
E: lapierrelongue@orange.fr **alanrogers.com/FR44320**

Le Croisic can be found on a peninsula which stretches over 5 km. into the ocean. The friendly owners have a great sense of humour at this delightful site. There are a total of 60 grass touring pitches of ample size which are well tended and divided by small trees and young shrubs. There is a little, but not much shade. A comfortable bar and restaurant with a comprehensive menu serving speciality seafood dishes, both open out onto a terrace and small swimming pool. This site is open for a long season.

Facilities

The main modern toilet block is heated with washbasins both open and in cubicles. Large shower area. Facilities for disabled visitors. Laundry facilities. Small shop (June-Sept). Bar, restaurant and takeaway (May-Sept). Outdoor heated swimming pool and paddling pool (May-Sept). WiFi. Off site: Riding, golf, boat launching within 1.5 km. Town of Guérande. Beaches of La Baule.

Open: 1 March - 30 November.

Directions

Take D774 from Guérande south to Pouliguen. Follow northwest to Le Croisic. Site is well signed and on left after 1.5 km. GPS: 47.29244, -2.52923

Charges guide

Per unit incl. 2 persons and electricity	€ 18.90 - € 23.70
extra person	€ 4.60 - € 6.60

Les Roisers-sur-Loire
Flower Camping Val de Loire

6 rue Sainte-Baudruehe, F-49350 Les Roisers-sur-Loire (Maine-et-Loire) T: 02 41 51 94 33.
E: contact@camping-valdeloire.com **alanrogers.com/FR49180**

This former municipal site on the outskirts of a village on the River Loire between Saumur and Angers has 84 touring pitches, all with electricity (5/10A), individual water taps and waste water drainage. A further 28 pitches are used for mobile homes, mostly for hire. Recent additions include a pleasant little bar with a terrace and an adjacent marquee used for games and entertainment. There are two new heated swimming pools, one covered, the other surrounded by sunbathing terraces and with a large (linked) paddling pool. In July and August there is a busy programme of activities.

Facilities

The main sanitary block is modern if rather drab, with controllable showers and washbasins in cubicles. Two older blocks and a new 'portacabin' unit provide additional facilities. Facilities for disabled visitors. Laundry room. Bar with TV serves snacks and fresh bread to order (July/Aug). Covered pool (1/5-15/9). Outdoor pool (1/5-15/9). Children's activities, events and entertainment in season. Play area. Games room. Minigolf. Tennis. Bicycle hire. Off site: Shops, bar and restaurant in village 800 m. Fishing 800 m. Boat launching 1 km. Riding 2 km.

Open: 1 April - 30 September.

Directions

Les Rosiers is 17 km. northwest of Saumur. From A85 motorway at exit 1 take southbound D144 to Beaufort-en-Vallée, then continue south on D59. Site is signed to right on approach to village. From D952 Saumur-Angers road turn north in village to site on left in 800 m. GPS: 47.35877, -0.22604

Charges guide

Per unit incl. 2 persons and electricity	€ 20.40 - € 26.00
extra person	€ 4.00 - € 5.50

Luché-Pringé
Camping La Chabotière

Place des Tilleuils, F-72800 Luché-Pringé (Sarthe) T: 02 43 45 10 00. E: contact@lachabotiere.com
alanrogers.com/FR72100

This is a delightful little municipal site on the River Loir, just a few steps from the main square of an interesting village classed as a Petite Cité de Caractère. There are 85 pitches, 65 for touring and all with access to electricity and the remainder used for wooden chalets and canvas 'bungalows' for rent. The main part of the site down by the river is kept vehicle free in July and August. A child-proof gate leads out onto the river bank and footpath. There are many opportunities for walking, cycling and sightseeing.

Facilities

The traditional toilet block is well maintained with pushbutton showers and some washbasins in cubicles. Baby room and washbasins for children. Facilities for disabled visitors. Laundry facilities. Motorcaravan service point. Quiet room. Internet access (adults only). Adventure play area. Sports field. Bicycle hire. Fishing. Activities for children. WiFi over site. Chalets for rent. Off site: Espace de Loisirs (July/Aug) at entrance with free access from site: swimming and paddling pools (unheated), minigolf, tennis, bar with games, and hire of boats, canoes and pedaloes. Shops, bar and restaurants in village.

Open: 1 April - 15 October.

Directions

Luché-Pringé is 40 km. south of Le Mans. From A11 between Le Mans and Angers, leave at exits 10 or 11 and head eastwards to La Flêche, then north on D323 towards Le Mans. At Clermont-Créans turn east on D13 to Luché-Pringé. In main square (ignore earlier campsite sign) turn sharp right then left, signed 'Minigolf' then site. GPS: 47.70252, 0.07364

Charges 2012

Per unit incl. 2 persons and electricity	€ 11.90 - € 14.50
extra person	€ 2.50 - € 3.80

For latest campsite news, availability and prices visit
alanrogers.com

Mansigné
Camping de la Plage

Rue du Plessis, F-72510 Mansigné (Sarthe) T: 02 43 46 14 17. E: camping-mansigne@wanadoo.fr
alanrogers.com/FR72050

Situated just a couple of hundred metres from the village of Mansigné (Village in Bloom), this municipal site offers 176 flat and numbered pitches separated by a variety of low hedges with young and mature trees giving a feeling of spaciousness. Long leads are required for many of the pitches. The main attraction to this site is the adjacent 60 acre lake which offers all kinds of watersports. There are ten bungalows for rent, with a further 20 mobile homes available away from the main site close to the lake. The modern reception building is full of information for exploring this delightful region of the Loire Valley.

Facilities

Three sanitary blocks, one more modern central block with some washbasins in cabins. Laundry. Three children's play areas. Bar and snack bar (June-Sept). Swimming pools. Minigolf, tennis and table tennis. Pétanque. Volleyball, football and basketball. Mountain bike track (bikes available from reception). Athletics track. Lake with sailing, pedaloes, canoes and fishing. Off site: Riding 1.5 km.

Open: 15 April - 15 October.

Directions

Mansigné is signed off the N23 between Le Mans and Angers. Follow D13 for 21 km. Reaching Mansigné, follow signs for the 'Base de Loisirs'. The campsite is on the right just before the lake. GPS: 47.751055, 0.132533

Charges guide

Per person	€ 2.45 - € 7.40
child (under 7 yrs)	€ 1.25 - € 3.70
pitch	€ 2.80 - € 5.60
electricity (10A)	€ 2.30 - € 4.60

Heavy supplements for twin-axle caravans (including pitch, occupants and electricity).

Marçon
Camping Lac des Varennes

Saint Lezin, route de Port-Gauthier, F-72340 Marçon (Sarthe) T: 02 43 44 13 72.
E: lacdesvarennes@camp-in-ouest.com **alanrogers.com/FR72080**

This extensive site is located near the massive forest of Bercé in the Vallée du Loir and is on the shore of the lake from which it takes its name. There are 250 pitches here, with 175 for tourers, all grassy and with electrical connections (10A). Many also have lake views. The site has its own sandy beach (with a beach volleyball court) and canoes are available for rent. In high season, various activities are organised including a club for children and riding. Mobile homes are available for rent. A gate gives free access to the Base de Loisirs which offers a variety of water and land-based activities.

Facilities

Three traditional sanitary blocks are kept clean and provide pushbutton showers, some washbasins in cubicles and a mix of British and Turkish-style toilets. Washing machines and dryer. Basic facilities for disabled visitors. Motorcaravan service point. Shop, snack bar and takeaway (July/Aug). Simple bar with games and TV. Play area. Motorcaravan services. Organised entertainment (July/Aug). Direct access to lake with fishing and swimming. Off site: Base de Loisirs with sailing, boat launching, water slide, carp fishing, tennis, multisport court plus (weekends and July/Aug) minigolf, pedaloes and archery. Riding 5 km. Walking and cycling in the forest 8 km. Golf 38 km.

Open: 27 March - 12 November.

Directions

Marçon is 50 km. southeast of Le Mans and 47 km. northwest of Tours. From A28 exit 26, head east to Château du Loir, turn south on the D938/D338 (Caen-Tours road) and cross the Loir. Then head northeast on the D305 to Marçon, and turn west in village centre to Base de Loisirs and site on right in 1 km. GPS: 47.7125, 0.4993

Charges guide

Per unit incl. 2 persons and electricity	€ 13.60 - € 17.10
extra person	€ 3.50 - € 4.70
child (under 13 yrs)	€ 1.70 - € 2.30
dog	€ 1.30 - € 1.80

For latest campsite news, availability and prices visit
alanrogers.com

Call 01580 214000   We can book this site for you!   alan rogers ● travel

Mesquer

Camping le Château du Petit Bois

1820 route de kerlagadec, F-44420 Mesquer (Loire-Atlantique) T: 02 40 42 68 77.
E: info@campingdupetitbois.com **alanrogers.com/FR44270**

This pleasant campsite is located in the wooded grounds of a small château. The 125 good-sized touring pitches, all with electricity (3/ 6A) have varying degrees of shade and a few are in the open for those who like a sunny plot. Reception is housed in a wooden chalet and is welcoming and informative. The Marin family and their staff are friendly and helpful and the site is very well run. On site there is an attractive swimming pool complex: a heated main pool and paddling pool, and a separate pool with two good water slides which is only open when the pool is supervised. The sea is just over a kilometre away, as is the village of Mesquer and nearby are the salt marshes which produce the famous Sel de Guérande.

Facilities	Directions
The main sanitary block has preset showers and open style washbasins together with some cubicles with controllable shower and a washbasin. Dishwashing and laundry facilities. Facilities for disabled visitors. Combined bar, snack bar and takeaway. Small shop selling bread and basics (July/Aug). Pool complex with heated main pool, paddling pool and pool with water slides (only open when supervised). Programme of activities (all July/Aug). WiFi in bar (free). Off site: Fishing, bicycle hire, riding and sailing all nearby. Golf 12 km.	From N165 Nantes - Vannes road, leave at exit 15 towards La Roche Bernard, turn left to join the D774 towards La Baule. 8 km. after Herbignac, turn right on D52 to St Molt and Mesquer. Site is on the D52 just west of village. GPS: 47.399016, -2.471316

Open: 1 April - 30 October.

Charges guide

Per unit incl. 2 persons	
and electricity	€ 13.00 - € 27.60
extra person	€ 4.90 - € 6.40
child (3-7 yrs)	€ 3.40 - € 4.40

Camping & Rental accommodations

The Celtic spirit in Southern Brittany !

LE CHATEAU
DU PETIT BOIS
★★★

1820, route de Kerlagadec
44420 MESQUER - France
tél. : (+33) (0)2 40 42 68 77
fax : (+33) (0)2 40 42 65 58
www.campingdupetitbois.com

Montsabert

Yelloh! Village Parc de Montsabert

Montsabert, F-49320 Coutures (Maine-et-Loire) T: 02 41 57 91 63.
E: info@yellohvillage-parcdemontsabert.com **alanrogers.com/FR49060**

This extensive site has recently been taken over by a friendly French couple who already have plans for improvements. It has a rural atmosphere in the shadow of Montsabert château, from where visiting peacocks happily roam in the spacious surroundings. The main features are the heated swimming pool (with cover) and the adjoining refurbished, rustic style restaurant. There are 111 large, well marked touring pitches, divided by hedges and all with water tap, drain and electricity (10A). Picnic tables are provided. The site is used by several small tour operators (12 pitches). Partially wooded by a variety of trees, this site offers the peace of the countryside.

Facilities	Directions
The main toilet block can be heated and has washbasins and bidets in cabins and a baby room. Laundry facilities. A second block serves the pool and another provides more WCs. Shop, bar and takeaway. Restaurant. Heated pool (no Bermuda style shorts) and paddling pool. Sports hall. Minigolf. Tennis. Play area. Bicycle hire. Entertainment (high season). Archery. Riding. Off site: Canoeing nearby. Fishing 5 km. Golf 8 km.	Coutures is 25 km. southeast of Angers on the D751 to Saumur. From A11 take exit 14 and follow signs for Cholet/Poitiers, then Poitiers on D748. At Brissac-Quincé turn northeast on D55 and in 5 km. turn right to Coutures. Montsabert is north of village. GPS: 47.3744, -0.3469

Open: 10 April - 12 September.

Charges guide

Per unit incl. 2 persons	
and electricity	€ 15.00 - € 29.00
extra person	€ 4.00 - € 5.00
child (3-7 yrs)	free - € 5.00
dog (max. 2)	€ 4.00

Montsoreau
Kawan Village l'Isle Verte

Avenue de la Loire, F-49730 Montsoreau (Maine-et-Loire) T: 02 41 51 76 60. E: isleverte@cvtloisirs.fr

alanrogers.com/FR49090

This friendly, natural site, with pitches overlooking the Loire, is just 200 m. from the nearest shop, bar and restaurant in Montsoreau, and is an ideal base from which to explore the western Loire area. Most of the 90 shaded, level and good-sized tourist pitches are separated by low hedges but grass tends to be rather sparse during dry spells. All have electricity (16A). Excellent English is spoken in the reception and bar/restaurant. Attractions within walking distance include the château, troglodyte caves (used for traditional mushroom production) and restaurant, wine tasting in the cellars nearby, and a Sunday market in the town. Fishermen are particularly well catered for at Isle verte, with an area to store equipment and live bait (permits are available in Saumur). Cyclists and walkers could also well be in their element here. For the less energetic, there is a bus service into Saumur with its château and other historic buildings, and all its shops, bars and restaurants. Trains or buses are available in Saumur to take you on to other towns along the Vallée de la Loire. Just 5 km. south of Montsoreau is the fascinating 12th-century Abbaye Royale de Fontévraud.

Facilities

A single building provides separate male and female toilets. Washbasins, some in cabins, and showers are unisex. Separate facilities for disabled campers. Baby room. Laundry facilities. Motorcaravan service point. Bar and restaurant(1/5-30/9). Swimming and paddling pools (25/5-30/9). Small play area. Table tennis, volleyball and boules. Fishing. Boat launching. WiFi (charged). Off site: Beach on river 300 m. Bicycle hire and sailing 1 km. Golf and riding both 7 km.

Open: 1 April - 30 September.

Directions

Montsoreau is 12 km. southeast of Saumur on the D947 towards Chinon. Site is clearly signed on left along the road into town. GPS: 47.21820, 0.05265

Charges guide

Per unit incl. 2 persons and electricity	€ 18.50 - € 22.50
extra person	€ 3.00 - € 4.00
child (5-10 yrs)	€ 2.00 - € 2.50
dog	€ 1.50

Camping Cheques accepted.

Located on the banks of the Loire river, KAWAN VILLAGE ISLE VERTE**** is ideal for relaxing holidays, in one of the "Plus Beaux Villages de France", and discover the Loire valley castles and vineyards...

KAWAN VILLAGE L'ISLE VERTE** • Avenue de la Loire • 49730 Montsoreau**
Tel: 00.33.(0) 241.51.76.60 • Fax: 00.33.(0) 241.51.08.83
E-mail: isleverte@cvtloisirs.fr • Web: www.campingisleverte.com

For latest campsite news, availability and prices visit
alanrogers.com

We can book this site for you! alan rogers ◉ travel

Call 01580 214000

Piriac-sur-Mer

Camping Parc du Guibel

Route de Kerdrien, F-44420 Piriac-sur-Mer (Loire-Atlantique) T: 02 40 23 52 67.

E: camping@parcduguibel.com alanrogers.com/FR44070

This is a very large site situated in extensive woodland and just back from the coast. A keen birdwatcher once told the owner that he had seen 50 different species of birds. There are 450 pitches of which 300 are for touring, mainly shaded but some in small clearings. One section at the top of the site across a minor road is always quiet and peaceful. One hundred and sixty pitches have electricity (10A), of which 60 also have a water tap and drainage. There are also 134 mobile homes and chalets for rent.

Facilities

Five sanitary blocks: the newest is smart and well equipped, with controllable showers and washbasins. Two others have been partially refurbished to the same standards. The others are rather old-fashioned, with preset showers and washbasins in cubicles. Facilities for disabled visitors. Baby room. Laundry facilities. Motorcaravan service point. Swimming pool complex and paddling pool (1/4-30/9). Bar, snack bar, takeaway and restaurant (July-Aug only). WiFi. Off site: Riding 400 m. Fishing 1 km. Beach 1.2 km. Sailing 3.5 km.

Open: 1 April - 30 September.

Directions

On N165 from Vannes, leave at exit 15 towards La Roche Bernard, turn left to join D774 towards La Baule. 8 km. after Herbignac, turn right on D52 to St Molt and Mesquer towards Piriac. Do not take the coast road but turn left on D52. Site signed on right in 3 km. GPS: 47.38616, -2.51029

Charges guide

Per unit incl. 2 persons and electricity (10A)	€ 13.80 - € 22.20
extra person	€ 3.10 - € 5.90

Pontchâteau

538

Kawan Village du Deffay

B.P. 18 Le Deffay, Sainte Reine-de-Bretagne, F-44160 Pontchâteau (Loire-Atlantique) T: 02 40 88 00 57.

E: campingdudeffay@wanadoo.fr alanrogers.com/FR44090

A family managed site, Château du Deffay is a refreshing departure from the usual formula in that it is not over organised or supervised and has no tour operator units. The 170 good sized, fairly level pitches have pleasant views and are either on open grass, on shallow terraces divided by hedges, or informally arranged in a central, slightly sloping wooded area. Most have electricity (6/10A). The bar, restaurant and covered pool are located within the old courtyard area of the smaller château that dates from before 1400. A significant attraction of the site is the large, unfenced lake which is well stocked for fishermen and even has free pedaloes for children. The landscape is wonderfully natural and the site blends well with the rural environment of the estate, lake and farmland which surround it. Alpine type chalets overlook the lake and fit in well with the environment and the larger château (built 1880 and which now offers B&B) stands slightly away from the camping area but provides a wonderful backdrop for an evening stroll. The site is close to the Brière Regional Park, the Guérande Peninsula, and La Baule and is just 20 minutes drive from the nearest beach.

Facilities

The main toilet block is well maintained, if a little dated, and includes washbasins in cabins, provision for disabled visitors, and a baby bathroom. Laundry facilities. Shop. Bar and small restaurant with takeaway (1/5-15/9). Covered and heated swimming pool and paddling pool. Play area. TV. Entertainment in season including miniclub. Lake fishing. Pedalos. Torches useful. WiFi (charged). Off site: Golf 7 km. Riding 10 km. Beach 25 km.

Open: 1 May - 30 September.

Directions

Site is signed from D33 Pontchâteau - Herbignac road near Ste Reine. Also signed from the D773 and N165-E60 (exit 13). GPS: 47.44106, -2.15981

Charges guide

Per unit incl. 2 persons and electricity	€ 18.30 - € 28.20
extra person	€ 3.35 - € 5.60
Camping Cheques accepted.	

Le Deffay Camping Caravaning

Family campsite in the natural surroundings of the Grande Brière only 20 minutes from the beach. Quiet and relaxing camping. All services are open from beginning of May till mid-September.

Covered heated swimming pool, tennis, fishing, pedaloes, walks around the property, table-tennis, playgrounds are free of charge.

BP 18 - 44160 Pontchateau
Tel: 0033 240 88 00 57 - (winter) 0033 685 21 15 79
Fax: 0033 240 01 66 55

Camping Cheque

www.camping-le-deffay.com - email : campingdudeffay@wanadoo.fr

For latest campsite news, availability and prices visit

alanrogers.com

Pornic
Yelloh! Village La Chênaie

36 rue du Patisseau, F-44210 Pornic (Loire-Atlantique) T: 02 40 82 07 31. E: accueil@campinglachenaie.com
alanrogers.com/FR44080

La Chênaie is a pleasant, family run campsite in countryside close to the fishing port of Pornic and less than three kilometres from the nearest beach. There are 94 touring pitches in two areas on gently sloping ground, with the pool and other leisure facilities in the dip between. All the pitches are well tended with electricity available (10A; longer leads may be needed in places) and there is some shade in places from maturing trees and bushes. Some of the 50 mobile homes (35 for rent) are scattered among the touring pitches, others are at the top of the site. There is a sense of spaciousness everywhere on this friendly site which has joined the Yelloh! Village group for the first time in 2012. Even in high season the site seems quiet and peaceful, except perhaps if you are near the bar area on the weekly disco evening or when an occasional daytime train passes on the line which runs behind the site.

Facilities

Two good sanitary blocks, one central to each area. Some washbasins in cubicles. Baby room. Facilities for disabled visitors. Large washing machines and dryer. Motorcaravan service point. Heated indoor swimming pool and paddling pool (6/4-16/9). Outdoor pool (1/7-31/8). Bar and shop selling bread and a few basics. Restaurant and snack bar with takeaway. Play area. Some activities for children and adults. Off site: Fishing 300 m. Sailing and boat launching 3 km. Golf 4 km. Riding 5 km.

Open: 6 April - 16 September.

Directions

Pornic is 19 km. south of St Nazaire bridge. Road to site is at junction of D751 (Nantes - Pornic) with the D213 (St Nazaire - Noirmoutier) 'Route Bleue'. From north take exit D751 Nantes. From south follow D751 Clion-sur-Mer. At roundabout on D751 north of D213 take exit for Le Chenaic and follow site signs. Avoid Pornic town centre. GPS: 47.118483, -2.070817

Charges guide

Per unit incl. 2 persons	
and electricity	€ 19.00 - € 35.00
extra person	€ 5.00 - € 8.00

La Chênaie★★★★
Camping - Pornic

36 rue du Patisseau
44210 PORNIC - FRANCE
accueil@campinglachenaie.com
Tél.: 02 33 240 820 731
www.campinglachenaie.com

● Camping - Caravanning - Rental
● Situated near the beaches and the old harbour
● Spacious pitches - green surroudings

yelloh!

Pornic
Camping le Patisseau

29 rue du Patisseau, F-44210 Pornic (Loire-Atlantique) T: 02 40 82 10 39. E: contact@lepatisseau.com
alanrogers.com/FR44100

Le Patisseau is situated in the countryside just a short drive from the fishing village of Pornic. It is a relaxed site with a large number of mobile homes and chalets, and is popular with young families and teenagers. The 102 touring pitches, all with electrical connections (6A), are divided between the attractive 'forest' area with plenty of shade from mature trees and the more open 'prairie' area. Some are on a slight slope and access to others might be tricky for larger units. A railway runs along the bottom half of the site with trains several times a day, (but none overnight) and the noise is minimal.

Facilities

The modern heated toilet block is very spacious and well fitted; most washbasins are open style, but the controllable showers are all in large cubicles which have washbasins. Also good facilities for disabled visitors and babies. Laundry rooms. Shop (1/7-30/8). Bar, restaurant and takeaway (all season). Indoor heated pool with sauna, jacuzzi and spa (all season). Small heated outdoor pools and water slides (1/6-30/9). Play area. Multisport court. Bicycle hire. WiFi in bar area. Off site: Fishing and beach 2.5 km. Riding, golf, sailing and boat launching all 5 km.

Open: 3 April - 11 November.

Directions

Pornic is 19 km. south of St Nazaire bridge. Access to site is at junction of D751 Nantes - Pornic road with the D213 St Nazaire - Noirmoutier Route Bleue. From north take exit D751 Nantes. From south follow D751 Clion-sur-Mer. At roundabout north of D213 take exit for le Patisseau and follow site signs. Avoid Pornic town centre. GPS: 47.118833, -2.072833

Charges guide

Per unit incl. 2 persons	
and electricity (6A)	€ 25.00 - € 41.00
extra person	€ 4.00 - € 8.00

For latest campsite news, availability and prices visit
alanrogers.com

Pornic

Camping de la Boutinardière

538

Rue de la Plage de la Boutinardière 23, F-44210 Pornic (Loire-Atlantique) T: 02 40 82 05 68.
E: info@laboutinardiere.com **alanrogers.com/FR44180**

This is truly a holiday site to suit all the family, whatever their ages, just 200 m. from the beach. It has 250 individual good sized pitches, 100-120 sq.m. in size, many bordered by three metre high, well maintained hedges for shade and privacy. All pitches have electricity available. It is a family owned site and English is spoken by the helpful, obliging reception staff. Beside reception is the excellent site shop and across the road is a complex of indoor and outdoor pools, paddling pool and a twin toboggan water slide. On site there are sports and entertainment areas.

Facilities

Toilet facilities are in three good blocks. Washbasins are in cabins. Laundry facilities. Shop. New complex of bar, restaurant, terraces. Three heated swimming pools, one indoor (April-Sept), a paddling pool and water slides (15/5-22/9). Games room. Sports and activity area. Playground. Minigolf. Fitness equipment and sauna. Off site: Sandy cove 200 m. Golf, riding, sea fishing, restaurants, cafés, boat trips and sailing all within 5 km.

Open: 3 April - 28 September.

Directions

From north or south on D213, take Nantes D751 exit. At roundabout (with McDonalds) take D13 signed Bernarie-en-Retz. After 4 km. site is signed to right. Note: do NOT exit from D213 at Pornic Ouest or Centre. GPS: 47.09150, -2.05133

Charges guide

Per unit incl. 2 persons	
and electricity	€ 22.00 - € 48.20
extra person	€ 4.00 - € 8.00

Préfailles   *CRAMPTED SITE - GOOD CONDITION FOR WALKS*

Camping EléoVic   *BETTER IN LOW SEASON. COVERED POOL OK.*

Route de la Pointe St-Gildas, F-44770 Préfailles (Loire-Atlantique) T: 02 40 21 61 60.
E: contact@camping-eleovic.com **alanrogers.com/FR44230**

This is a well situated site overlooking the sea on the attractive Jade Coast west of Pornic. There are 70 touring pitches which are rather worn, some with wonderful views of the sea, and a similar number of mobile homes, many of which are available for rent. All pitches have access to electricity (10A), though on some you may need a long cable. Much of the ground is sloping, so a really level pitch may not be available and access for larger units to some pitches may be tricky. The site has so much to offer, however, that any extra effort that may be needed to get installed is likely soon to be forgotten. There is an excellent covered, heated pool (with paddling pool) which has a canopy that can be opened up in good weather. A path from the site leads directly to a small rocky cove where you can gather oysters and mussels freely at low tide. Other wider sandy beaches are a short distance away.

Facilities

Central sanitary block has spacious pre-set showers and washbasins in cabins. Facilities for disabled visitors. Room for dishwashing and laundry. Further facilities are in the pool building and another smaller block. Good restaurant (July-Aug; not Wednesdays) with small bar and terrace. Fitness room. Playground. Boules. Children's activities and entertainment and sporting events for families (high season). Bicycle hire. WiFi. Off site: Beach, sailing and boat launching 800 m. Riding 3 km. Golf 7 km.

Open: 3 April - 26 October.

Directions

Préfailles is 20 km. south of the St Nazaire bridge and 9 km. west of Pornic. From north on D213 (Route Bleue) turn southwest just south of St Michel-Chef-Chef on D96 to La Plaine-sur-Mer and follow signs for Préfailles. From Pornic take D13 to La Plaine but do not enter town. Follow signs for Préfailles. Continue on D313 past village towards La Pointe Saint-Gildas and at 50 km. sign turn left, then left again to site on right. GPS: 47.132616, -2.2315

Charges guide

Per unit incl. 2 persons	
and electricity	€ 18.20 - € 33.50
extra person	€ 3.60 - € 6.50

★★★★ **Eléovic**
c a m p i n g - c a r a v a n i n g

Route de la pointe St Gildas - 44770 Préfailles
Loire Atlantique - Bretagne sud
Tel: 0033 240 21 61 60 - E-mail: contact@camping-eleovic.com
www.camping-eleovic.com

The campsite Eleovic with its direct access to the beach, overhang the bay of Bourgneuf and made in front of the island of Noirmoutier.
Relaxation and user-friendliness are gathered to spend pleasant holidays!

For latest campsite news, availability and prices visit

alanrogers.com

Saint Brévin-les-Pins

Camping le Fief

57 chemin du Fief, F-44250 Saint Brévin-les-Pins (Loire-Atlantique) T: 02 40 27 23 86.

E: camping@lefief.com **alanrogers.com/FR44190**

If you are a family with young children or lively teenagers, this could be the campsite for you. Le Fief is a well established site only 800 m. from sandy beaches on the southern Brittany coast. It has a magnificent aquapark with outdoor and covered swimming pools, paddling pools, slides, river rapids, fountains, jets and more. The site has 174 pitches for touring units (out of 405). Whilst these all have 5A electricity, they vary in size and many are worn and may be untidy. There are also 183 mobile homes and chalets to rent and 48 privately-owned units. This is a lively site in high season with a variety of entertainment and organised activity for all ages. This ranges from a miniclub for 5-12 year olds, to Tonic Days in a state-of-the-art wellness centre with aquagym, jogging and sports competitions, and to evening events which include karaoke, themed dinners and cabaret. There are plenty of sporting facilities for active youngsters.

Facilities

One excellent new toilet block and three others of a lower standard. Laundry facilities. Shop (1/6-31/8). Bar, restaurant and takeaway (3/4-26/9) with terrace overlooking the pool complex. Outdoor pools, etc. (1/5-15/9). Covered pool (all season). Wellness centre. Play area. Tennis. Pétanque. Archery. Games room. Internet access. Organised entertainment and activities (weekends April/June, daily July/Aug). Bicycle hire. Off site: Beach 800 m. Bus stop 1 km. Riding 1 km. Golf 15 km. Planète Sauvage safari park.

Open: 3 April - 3 October.

Directions

From the St Nazaire bridge take the fourth exit from the D213 signed St Brévin-l'Océan. Continue over first roundabout and bear right at the second to join Chemin du Fief. The site is on the right, well signed. GPS: 47.23486, -2.16757

Charges guide

Per unit incl. 2 persons	
and electricity	€ 22.00 - € 45.00
extra person	€ 5.00 - € 10.00
child (0-7 yrs)	€ 2.50 - € 5.00
dog	€ 3.00 - € 8.00

No credit cards.

We can book this site for you! Call 01580 214000 alan rogers travel

Sunêlia
le fief
Sunêlia © 2010
www.koramarketing.com

Camping Qualité

camping le fief

57, chemin du Fief 44250 SAINT BRÉVIN LES PINS
tel. : 0033 2 40 27 23 86
fax : 0033 2 40 64 46 19   www.lefief.com

SAINT BRÉVIN LES PINS — CÔTE DE JADE — SUD BRETAGNE — FRANCE

CAMPING, HIRE & SPA

GROCERY
BAR - RESTAURANT
TAKE AWAY
CHILDREN'S PLAYGROUND
TENNIS
MULTISPORTS GROUNDS
INDOORS,
HEATED SWIMMING POOL
9 ENTERTAINERS IN SEASON

WELLNESS
Sauna, Turkish bath, Gymnasium, Spa, Power Plate®, LPG®

FULL AND HALF PENSION

For latest campsite news, availability and prices visit
alanrogers.com

Call 01580 214000   We can book this site for you! alan rogers ⬤ travel

Saumur

Camping de Chantepie

Saint Hilaire-Saint Florent, F-49400 Saumur (Maine-et-Loire) T: 02 41 67 95 34.
E: info@campingchantepie.com **alanrogers.com/FR49020**

On arriving at Camping de Chantepie with its colourful, floral entrance, a friendly greeting awaits at reception, set beside a restored farmhouse. The site is owned by a charitable organisation which provides employment for local people with disabilities. Linked by gravel roads (which can be dusty), the 150 grass touring pitches are level and spacious, with some new larger ones (200 sq.m. at extra cost – state preference when booking). All pitches have electricity (6/10A) and are separated by low hedges of flowers and trees which offer some shade. This is a good site for families. The panoramic views over the Loire from the pitches on the terraced perimeter of the meadow are stunning and from here a footpath leads to the river valley. Leisure activities for all ages are catered for in July/August by the Chantepie Club, including wine tastings, excursions and canoeing. A Sites et Paysages member.

Facilities

The toilet block is clean and facilities are good with washbasins in cubicles, new showers (men and women separately) and facilities for disabled visitors. Baby area. Laundry facilities. Shop, bar, terraced café and takeaway (all 15/6-31/8). Covered and heated pool, outdoor pool and paddling pool. Play area with apparatus. Terraced minigolf. TV. Video games. Pony rides. Bicycle hire. WiFi (charged). Off site: Fishing 500 m. Golf, riding 2 km. Sailing 7 km.

Open: 15 May - 15 September.

Directions

St Hilaire-St Florent is 2 km. west of Saumur. Take D751 (Gennes). Right at roundabout in St Hilaire-St Florent and on until Le Poitrineau and campsite sign, then turn left. Continue for 3 km. then turn right into site road. GPS: 47.29381, -0.14264

Charges guide

| Per unit incl. 2 persons and electricity | € 18.50 - € 30.60 |
| extra person | € 4.00 - € 6.00 |

Camping Cheques accepted.

Panoramic view of the *Loire*.
Quiet Holidays with family.

Camping Chantepie

Camping Qualité

Route de Chantepie - Saint Hilaire Saint Florent - 49400 SAUMUR (FR.)
Tél. +33(0)2 41 67 95 34 - Fax. +33(0)2 41 67 95 85
info@campingchantepie.com - www.campingchantepie.com

Saumur

Flower Camping de Ile d'Offard

Bvd. de Verden, Ile d'Offard, F-49400 Saumur (Maine-et-Loire) T: 02 41 40 30 00. E: iledoffard@cvtloisirs.fr
alanrogers.com/FR49080

This site occupies a prime position on an island in the River Loire within walking distance of the centre of the historic town of Saumur. The 207 touring pitches are mainly on grass with plenty of shade provided by mature trees. Twelve hardstandings nearer the entrance can be rather dusty in dry weather. One hundred and fifty pitches have access to electricity (10A) and some also have water and drainage. Ile d'Offard is useful as an overnight stop on the journey south (or north) but it is also an excellent base from which to visit the numerous châteaux in the region.

Facilities

Three unisex sanitary blocks, one heated in winter, include provision for disabled visitors. Laundry facilities. The other blocks are only open in high season. These facilities are generally kept reasonably clean, but are fairly basic and lack finesse. Motorcaravan services. Restaurant and bar (1/5-30/9) with takeaway. Heated swimming, paddling and spa pools (15/4-30/9). Internet access and WiFi (charged). Play area. Some activities and a children's club, wine tastings, etc. in high season. Off site: Thursday market 500 m. Saturday morning market 2 km. Beach on river, sailing and bicycle hire all 1 km. Golf and riding 10 km.

Open: 1 March - 15 November.

Directions

From north and A85 exit 3, take D347 south (Saumur). After 2.5 km. go left at roundabout signed 'Saumur touristique'. Follow old road towards river and town. Cross bridge onto island and immediately go left at roundabout. Site is ahead in 1 km. GPS: 47.25762, -0.06100

Charges guide

Per unit incl. 2 persons and electricity	€ 20.00 - € 33.00
extra person	€ 5.00 - € 6.00
child (5-10 yrs)	€ 2.50

Sillé-le-Guillaume
Camping Indigo les Molières

Sillé Plage, F-72140 Sillé-le-Guillaume (Sarthe) T: 02 43 20 16 12.
E: molieres@camping-indigo.com **alanrogers.com/FR72040**

Les Molières is an attractive recent addition to the Indigo group. It can be found close to Sillé-le-Guillaume, around 30 km. north of Le Mans. There are 120 large shady pitches here. Most are equipped with electrical connections (10A). A large lake of 32 hectares is ideal for sailing and windsurfing, and the forested surrounds of the Parc Naturel Régional provide an excellent environment for cycling or walking. Swimming is also popular from the large sandy beach. The Maison du Lac et de la Forêt is an interesting centre with a wealth of information about the area.

Facilities

Direct access to lake. Sailing. Fishing. Bicycle hire. Play area. Tourist information. Max. 1 dog. Off site: Walking and cycling tracks. Le Mans 30 km.

Open: 30 April - 26 September.

Directions

From Le Mans head north on D338, then D304 to Sillé-le-Guillaume. Follow signs to the Parc Naturel Régional and site. GPS: 48.203383, -0.127667

Charges guide

Per unit incl. 2 persons and electricity	€ 18.20 - € 26.70
extra person	€ 3.10 - € 4.50

Sillé-le-Philippe
Castel Camping le Château de Chanteloup

Chanteloup, F-72460 Sillé-le-Philippe (Sarthe) T: 02 43 27 51 07. E: chanteloup.souffront@wanadoo.fr
alanrogers.com/FR72030

An attractive and peaceful site close to Le Mans, Chanteloup is situated in the park of a 19th-century château in the heart of the Sarthe countryside. There are 100 pitches all with 6A electricity although long leads will be required in some places. Some are in the woods, many are around the edges of the lawns and completely open, and a few overlook the lake, so there are differing degrees of shade throughout the site. This lack of regimentation enhances the atmosphere and feeling of spaciousness in the grounds surrounding the old château. Tours of the grounds and the village by pony and cart can be arranged.

Facilities

All sanitary facilities are in the château outbuildings and are well maintained and kept very clean. Washbasins are in cabins. Dishwashing and laundry facilities. Small shop, takeaway and restaurant with covered outdoor seating (all 5/7-24/8). Bar (all season). Swimming pool (all season). Play area (parental supervision essential). Games room, volleyball, table tennis. Organised activities (high season). WiFi. Off site: Riding 7 km. Golf 10 km. Tennis club in Le Mans.

Open: 28 May - 31 August.

Directions

Sillé-le-Philippe is 18 km. northeast of Le Mans on the D301 to Bonnétable. From autoroute take exit 23, follow signs for Le Mans and Tours, then Le Mans and Savigné l'Evèque. Site is to the east just off main road and signed on southern edge of Sillé. GPS: 48.10586, 0.34108

Charges guide

Per unit incl. 2 persons and electricity	€ 26.90 - € 43.40
extra person	€ 6.30 - € 11.50

Charges are higher during Le Mans 24 hr race week.

Varennes-sur-Loire
Castel Camping l'Etang de la Brèche

5 impasse de la Breche (RN152), F-49730 Varennes-sur-Loire (Maine-et-Loire) T: 02 41 51 22 92.
E: mail@etang-breche.com **alanrogers.com/FR49010**

The Saint Cast family have developed l'Etang de la Brèche with care and attention. The site provides 135 large, level touring pitches with shade from trees and bushes. Less shaded areas are used for recreation. There are 16A (Europlug) electrical connections to all pitches (some long cables may be required), with water and drainage on 80 of them. The restaurant, bar and terrace, also open to the public, provides a social base and is popular with British visitors. The pool complex includes one with a removable cover, one outdoor, and one for toddlers.

Facilities

Three toilet blocks, modernised to good standards, include facilities for babies and disabled visitors. Laundry facilities. Shop and epicerie. Restaurant, pizzeria and takeaway. Heated swimming pools. Tennis. Multisport pitch. Go-karts. Minigolf. Bicycle hire. General room, games and TV rooms. Internet point. Varied sporting and entertainment programme (10/7-25/8). Pony riding. Torch useful. WiFi throughout. Off site: Golf 7 km.

Open: 28 April - 15 September.

Directions

Site is 100 m. north off the main D952, about 5 km. northeast of Saumur on the north bank of the Loire. GPS: 47.24731, -0.00048

Charges 2012

Per unit incl. 2 persons and electricity	€ 17.50 - € 38.00
with water and drainage	€ 19.00 - € 40.50
extra person	€ 6.50 - € 8.50

For latest campsite news, availability and prices visit
alanrogers.com

It's not only the fine beaches that make this holiday region so appealing – sleepy fishing harbours, historic ports and charming towns all create a great holiday atmosphere.

DÉPARTEMENT: VENDÉE

MAJOR CITY: LA ROCHE-SUR-YON

Because of its importance as a holiday destination for British visitors to France we have decided in this guide to list the Vendée départment as a region in its own right. Administratively the department lies in the region of Pays de la Loire.

With a sunshine record to rival the south of France, the Vendée is among the most popular areas in France. Visitors flock to the region to enjoy the exceptionally mild climate and 160 km. stretch of gently shelving, mostly sandy beaches. Popular resorts in the Vendée include Les Sables-d'Olonne, La Tranche-sur-Mer, and St Jean-de-Monts. Explore the coasts for traditional fishing villages or head inland for fields of sunflowers and unspoilt rural villages.

The Vendée was the centre of the counter-revolutionary movement between 1793 and 1799 and a 'son et lumière' held at Le Puy-du-Fou tells the whole story. Les Sables-d'Olonne is its main resort renowned for its excellent sandy beach. The area between the Vendée and Charente, the Marais Poitevin, is one of the most unusual in France – a vast tract of marshland with a thousand or more tree-lined canals and slow moving streams.

Places of interest

L'Aiguillon-sur-Mer: The Vendéan mussel-growing capital, famous for its shellfish, marsh, and sea.

Apremont: picturesque village which seems to cling to the rocky sides of the valley of Vie; Renaissance castle and a lake (largest lake in the Vendée) with a sandy beach.

Île-d'Yeu: an hour by boat off the coast where time is believed to have stood still. Colourful shops and bars line the main town. Bicycles and cars for hire.

Jard-sur-Mer: Abbey of Lieu-Dieu (financed by Richard the Lionheart), seaside with attractive, colourful houses.

Le Puy-du-Fou: 15/16th-century castle, sound and light show involving over 700 participants.

Les Sables-d'Olonne: the start and finish line of the grand Vendée Globe; arts and crafts shops.

Cuisine of the region

Locally-produced meat and poultry include Charolais beef, salt-marsh lamb, duck from Challans and foie gras. Seafood includes sole sablaise, cooked with lemon, barbecued sardines from Saint Gilles Croix-de-Vie, baked white tuna and mussels from the Baie de l'Aiguillon cooked in white wine.

Samphire: a herb that grows on the edges of the salt marshes.

Bonnottes: potatoes with the taste of hazelnuts, served for a few days each year in France's best restaurants.

www.vendee-tourisme.com/en
info@vendee-tourisme.com
(0)2 51 47 88 20

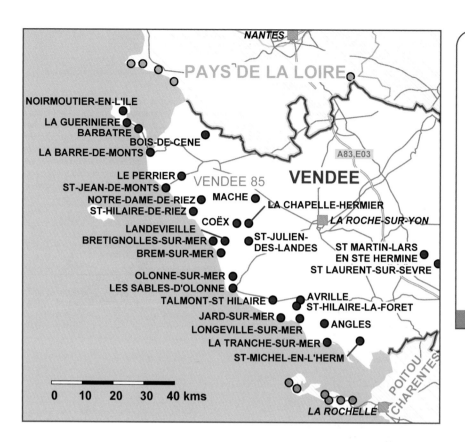

Angles
Camping le Clos Cottet

Route de la Tranche-sur-Mer, F-85750 Angles (Vendée) T: 02 51 28 90 72.
E: contact@camping-clos-cottet.com **alanrogers.com/FR85950**

Le Clos Cottet is an attractive family site, based around an old Vendéan farm. This is a lively site in high season with activities for children and the whole family, including regular discos and karaoke evenings, as well as many sports tournaments. There are 196 pitches here, all of which have reasonable shade. Many of them are occupied by mobile homes and chalets, but 70 are available for touring, all with electricity (10A). In high season (July and August) a free shuttle bus service runs to the nearest beach (6 km). On site, a fine swimming pool complex provides a large outdoor pool with water slides and a heated indoor pool, plus a sauna and Turkish bath.

Facilities

Two traditional toilet blocks provide preset showers and washbasins in cubicles. Baby room. En-suite unit for disabled visitors. Hot water to dishwashing and laundry sinks. Washing machine and dryer. Motorcaravan service point. Shop, plus bar with snack bar and takeaway (July/Aug). Pool complex (all season). Sauna. Fitness room. Play area. Multisports court. Sports field. Minigolf. Fishing lake. Activity and entertainment programme (July/Aug plus holiday weekends). Free WiFi in bar area. Mobile homes and chalets for rent. Off site: Cycle and walking tracks. Angles village centre 1.5 km. Riding 5 km. Nearest beach, sailing 6 km. Golf 30km. Les Sables d'Olonne 37 km. Marais Poitevin 70km. Puy du Fou 75 km.

Open: 5 April - 20 September.

Directions

Angles is 34 km south of La Roche-sur-Yon. From A87 Cholet/La Roche-sur-Yon leave at exit 32 for La Tranche-sur-Mer and follow D747 towards La Tranche. Site is south of Angles and is well signed to the right. GPS: 46.39239, -1.40365

Charges guide

Per unit incl. 2 persons	
and electricity	€ 18.00 - € 29.00
extra person	€ 4.00 - € 6.00
child (under 4 yrs)	€ 2.50 - € 4.00
dog	€ 3.00

For latest campsite news, availability and prices visit
alanrogers.com

Call 01580 214000   We can book this site for you!   alan rogers ⬤ travel

Avrillé

Castel Camping Domaine des Forges

Rue des Forges, F-85440 Avrillé (Vendée) T: 02 51 22 38 85. E: contact@campingdomainedesforges.com

alanrogers.com/FR85930

Le Domaine des Forges was acquired by Cathy and Thierry Pacteau a few years ago, and since then they have undertaken a vast improvement programme with huge investments made to improve the site's infrastructure. Arranged in the beautiful grounds of a 16th-century manor house, the 295 touring pitches are very generous in size (170-300 sq.m) and fully serviced, including 32A electricity, internet access and cable TV. The owners' aim is to develop a prestige campsite with the highest quality of services and they have made a very good start. An extension to the site was opened for the first time in 2011 with two new toilet blocks and it will take a little time for trees and shrubs to mature here. A new heated indoor pool was also opened in 2011, as was an area of hardstanding pitches for motorcaravans and a TV room.

Facilities

Four brand new toilet blocks including facilities for disabled visitors and babies. Laundry facilities. Shop (15/6-31/8). Restaurant (15/6-31/8). Bar and takeaway (15/6-15/9). Heated outdoor pool (15/5-15/9). Heated indoor pool (15/3-31/10). Tennis. Minigolf. Fishing lake. Internet access (charged). One dog per pitch.
Off site: Village 400 m. Vendée beaches 7 km. Golf de la Domangère and Golf Port Bourgenay (with discount) 10 km. Riding 10 km. Les Sables d'Olonne 25 km.

Open: All year.

Directions

Travel south from La Roche-sur-Yon on the D747 for about 21 km. At the D19, turn right for Avrille (about 6 km). At junction with the D949 turn right and first right again into rue des Forges. Site at the end of the road. GPS: 46.47609, -1.49454

Charges guide

Per unit incl. 2 persons,	
electricity, water and drainage	€ 16.00 - € 38.40
extra person	€ 2.00 - € 6.00
child (2-6 yrs)	free - € 4.00
dog	€ 3.00 - € 4.00

Camping Domaine des Forges ★★★★

LES ★★★★★
CASTELS
Hôtellerie de Plein Air

**Open February till November
Very comfortable pitches of 220 m²
5 star Member of 'Les Castels'**

• Rue des Forges • F-85440 Avrillé • Tél: 0033 2 51 22 38 85 •
contact@campingdomainedesforges.com • www.campingdomainedesforges.com

For latest campsite news, availability and prices visit

alanrogers.com

Barbâtre

Camping du Midi

Rue du camping, F-85630 Barbâtre (Vendée) T: 02 51 39 63 74. E: contact@campingdumidi.com
alanrogers.com/FR85014

This family site is a member of the Original Camping Group and is located close to the village of Barbâtre, on the west coast of the island of Noirmoutier. The site has direct access to a fine sandy beach. There are 539 pitches, of which around 335 are available for touring units (the rest are occupied by an imaginative range of chalets, mobile homes and fully equipped tents, including teepees, many of which are for rent). Touring pitches are mostly equipped with 6/10A electricity. On-site amenities include two swimming pools and a paddling pool. These are surrounded by a wide sunbathing area. A children's beach club is organised in peak season and evening entertainment is also on offer.

Facilities	Directions
Shop (July/Aug). Swimming pool complex (1/6-15/9). Sailing school. Games room. Play area. Tourist information. Activity and entertainment programme. Mobile homes, tents and chalets for rent. Direct beach access. Off site: Shops and restaurants in Barbâtre 5 minutes walk. Tennis. Riding. Watersports. Fishing. Riding 10 km. Golf 15 km.	Noirmoutier can be accessed either by the Gois causeway (at low tide only) or by the bridge from Fromentine, to the south of the island. From the bridge head north to Barbâtre on D944 and the site is well signed. GPS: 46.94508, -2.1853

Open: 1 April - 30 September.

Charges guide

Per unit incl. 2 persons	€ 17.00 - € 32.90

Bois-de-Céné

Camping le Bois Joli

2 rue de Châteauneuf, F-85710 Bois-de-Céné (Vendée) T: 02 51 68 20 05.
E: contact@camping-leboisjoli.com **alanrogers.com/FR85510**

A warm welcome is given by the English-speaking owners, Martine and Eric Malard, who make every effort to ensure that your stay is enjoyable. On site is a small, attractive lake with fishing and a large sports field. Next to the small swimming pool and paddling pool are a pleasant bar with terrace and a dancing area. There are 152 pitches of which 91 are for touring units, all with electricity; water taps may be less close. The site has 24 mobile homes for rent, including one equipped for disabled visitors, and there are 37 which are privately owned.

Facilities	Directions
Three toilet blocks provide washbasins in cubicles, some controllable showers, two family shower cubicles, washing machines and dryer, dishwashing and laundry sinks. Facilities for disabled visitors. Motorcaravan service point. Bar serving simple meals (all season). Takeaway food (July/Aug and busy weekends). Play area. Tennis court. Volleyball. Pétanque. Bicycle hire. WiFi (charged). Activities and entertainment (July/Aug). Off site: Shops in village (two minutes walk). Riding 5 km. Beach and sailing 18 km.	Bois de Céné is 47 km. southwest of Nantes and 10 km. north of Challans. Site is south of the village where the D58 from Challans meets the D21 and D28 and is signed. GPS: 46.93382, -1.88791

Open: 1 April - 15 October.

Charges guide

Per unit incl. 2 persons and electricity	€ 15.80 - € 20.80

Brem-sur-Mer

Camping l'Océan

Rue des Gabelous, F-85470 Brem-sur-Mer (Vendée) T: 02 51 90 59 16. E: contact@campingdelocean.fr
alanrogers.com/FR85110

Set amongst grapevines and fir trees, Camping l'Océan is only 600 metres from a beautiful sandy beach while the village centre is also within walking distance. A warm welcome awaits you at the modern reception area which is well stocked with local information. The 90 touring pitches, all with electric connections reasonably close, are of a good size, separated by bushes (and in some cases vines) and with some mature trees providing shade. They are centrally located close to the entrance and you are largely unaware of the 260 mobile homes (120 available to rent) on either side.

Facilities	Directions
Two toilet blocks have free preset showers, British style WCs, and washbasins in cubicles. Separate facilities for disabled visitors. Dishwashing and laundry sinks. Washing machines and dryers. Shop (July/Aug). Bar, snack bar and takeaway service (July/Aug and busy weekends). Heated swimming pool (15/6-15/9). Heated indoor pool (all season). Fitness room. Bicycle hire. Two playgrounds. WiFi (charged). Organised activities and entertainment (July/Aug). Off site: Beach 600 m. Brem-sur-Mer 900 m.	From A87 at La Roche-sur-Yon, continue on the D160 towards Les Sables-d'Olonne. Take exit for La Mothe-Achard and Brétignolles-sur-Mer. Follow the D54 to Brem-sur-Mer. Site is to north of village on D38 to Brétignolles. GPS: 46.601654, -1.84404

Open: 1 April - 31 October.

Charges guide

Per unit incl. 2 persons and electricity	€ 17.00 - € 27.00
extra person	€ 4.00 - € 6.00

We can book this site for you! alan rogers travel
Call 01580 214000

For latest campsite news, availability and prices visit
alanrogers.com

We can book this site for you! Call 01580 214000 alanrogers ◉ travel

Brétignolles-sur-Mer

Chadotel Camping la Trévillière

1 rue de Bellevue, F-85470 Brétignolles-sur-Mer (Vendée) T: 02 51 90 09 65. E: info@chadotel.com

alanrogers.com/FR85310

In a pleasant rural setting, la Trévillière is on the edge of the little resort town of Brétignolles. There are 200 pitches, 110 for tourers, all with access to water and electricity (long leads required in places). Some are level, some sloping; all are separated by hedges or low bushes either with shade or more open. Although just 2 km. from the nearest beach and less than 5 km. from the Plage des Dunes (one of southern Vendée's best beaches), la Trévillière has a more 'laid back' feel than many other sites in the area, particularly in low season. There is a heated swimming pool with water slide, a small paddling pool and a large sunbathing terrace with plenty of loungers, one part has a retractable cover. Overlooking the pool is the building housing the bar and reception. In early season the site is very quiet, becoming much livelier in July and August when there is a good range of activities for all.

Facilities

Three traditional toilet blocks, a little tired in parts, include washbasins in cubicles, pushbutton showers, a unit for disabled visitors and a baby room with bath, shower and toilet. Warm water for dishwashing and laundry sinks. Washing machines and dryers. Bar (1/5-30/9). Small shop (15/6-10/9). Snack bar with takeaway (1/6-10/9). Heated pool with slide and paddling pool. Play area. Minigolf. Max. 1 dog. Off site: Shops, restaurants and bars 1 km. Beach 2 km. Fishing, sailing, riding all 3 km. Golf 10 km.

Open: 3 April - 1 November.

Directions

Brétignolles is 40 km. west of La Roche-sur-Yon and is on the D38 coast road. From north, after St Gilles go through Brétignolles-La Sauzaie (left fork) and before reaching Brétignolles turn left on sharp right hand bend, heading for water tower. Site on right in 800 m. GPS: 46.63632, -1.85844

Charges guide

Per unit incl. 2 persons	€ 14.60 - € 29.60
extra person	€ 5.80

Brem-sur-Mer

Camping Caravaning le Chaponnet

Rue du Chaponnet (N16), F-85470 Brem-sur-Mer (Vendée) T: 02 51 90 55 56.
E: campingchaponnet@wanadoo.fr **alanrogers.com/FR85480**

This well established, family run site is within five minutes' walk of Brem village and 1.5 km. from a sandy beach. The 81 touring pitches are level with varying amounts of grass, some with shade from mature trees. Pitches are separated by tall hedges and serviced by tarmac or gravel roads and have frequent water and electricity points (long leads may be required). Tour operators have mobile homes and tents on 100 pitches and there are 146 other mobile homes and chalets, over half available for rent. The swimming pool complex features heated indoor and outdoor pools with a jacuzzi, slides and a children's pool, together with a sauna and fitness centre. It is overlooked by the spacious bar and restaurant/snack bar. Entertainment and activities for all ages are organised in high season.

Facilities

The five sanitary blocks are well maintained with washbasins in cubicles, and some showers and basins with controllable water temperature. Facilities for babies and disabled visitors. Laundry facilities. Bar, restaurant, snack bar and pizzeria (early June-late Aug). Indoor and outdoor heated pools. Waterslide, jacuzzi and sauna. Play area. Tennis. Bicycle hire. Indoor games room. WiFi (charged). Children's club (4-14 yrs) and entertainment for families (July/Aug). Off site: Shops and bus stops 200 m.

Open: 2 April - 30 September.

Directions

Brem is 35 km. west of La Roche-sur-Yon. From A87 at La Roche continue on D160 towards Les Sables-d'Olonne. Take exit for La Mothe-Achard and Brétignolles-sur-Mer. Follow D54 to Brem-sur-Mer. Site is clearly signed, just off the one-way system in centre of village. GPS: 46.60433, -1.83244

Charges guide

Per unit incl. 2 persons and electricity	€ 21.60 - € 30.80

CAMPING LE CHAPONNET ★★★★

Le Chaponnet ★★★★

Please visit our special **iPhone** website: www.lechaponnet.mobi

CAMPING LE CHAPONNET ★★★★ • 16 Rue du Chaponnet • BP 20 • F-85470 Brem sur Mer • France
T: [33] 2 51 90 55 56 • F: [33] 2 51 90 91 67 • campingchaponnet@wanadoo.fr
www.le-chaponnet.com

For latest campsite news, availability and prices visit

alanrogers.com

Camping Holidays
chadOtel

7 campsites in VENDEE
Atlantic Coast

Pitches for tents, caravans & motorhomes
Quality mobile homes & chalets

Entertainment for adults
and children (July & August)

Cycle path
Swimming pool and waterslide

Le Bahamas Beach - St Gilles Croix de Vie
Le Domaine de Beaulieu - St Gilles Croix de Vie
La Trévillière - Brétignolles sur Mer
La Dune des Sables - Les Sables d'Olonne
Les Roses - Les Sables d'Olonne

L'Océano d'Or - Jard sur Mer
La Bolée d'Air - St Vincent sur Jard

CHADOTEL
BP 12 - 85520 Jard sur Mer
Tél. +33 (0)2 51 33 05 05 - Fax. +33 (0) 2 51 33 94 04
info@chadotel.com - www.chadotel.com

We can book this site for you! Call 01580 214000

alan rogers travel

Coëx

RCN Camping la Ferme du Latois

Le Latoi, F-85220 Coëx (Vendée) T: 02 51 54 67 30. E: ferme@rcn.fr

alanrogers.com/FR85770

Originally a simple 'camping à la ferme', this site has been developed by a Dutch organisation into an extensive, very well equipped and well maintained campsite. Located round two attractive fishing lakes, the 215 pitches, most available for touring, are spacious and attractively laid out with plenty of grass, hedges and trees, some young, some mature. All have electricity and a few are very large. There are 30 mobile homes for rent. An old barn has been converted into a large restaurant offering an extensive French menu, including a 'menu du jour'. Also here are a small bar and a shop selling basic provisions.

Facilities

Two sanitary blocks have excellent toilets, showers and washbasins in cubicles. Good facilities for disabled visitors, babies and children. Two smaller blocks provide additional facilities. Laundry room. Small shop. Bar counter with terrace. Restaurant. All facilities available all season. Heated outdoor swimming pool with slides. Play area. Bicycle hire. Fishing lakes. WiFi over site (charged). Accommodation for rent. Off site: Shops in Coëx 2 km.

Open: 14 April - 29 September.

Directions

Coëx is 29 km. west of La Roche-sur-Yon via the D938 to Aizenay, then the D6 St Gilles Croix-de-Vie road. Site is south of village just off the D40 to La Chaize-Giraud. GPS: 46.677033, -1.76885

Charges 2012

Per unit incl. 2 persons	
and electricity	€ 17.50 - € 42.15
extra person	€ 2.20 - € 5.10
dog (max. 1)	€ 7.00

Jard-sur-Mer

Camping les Ecureuils

Route des Goffineaux, F-85520 Jard-sur-Mer (Vendée) T: 02 51 33 42 74. E: ecureuils@franceloc.fr

alanrogers.com/FR85210

Les Ecureuils is a wooded site in a quieter part of the southern Vendée. It is undoubtedly one of the prettiest sites on this stretch of coast, with an elegant reception area, attractive vegetation and large pitches separated by low hedges with plenty of shade. Of the 278 pitches, some 128 are for touring units, each with water and drainage, as well as easy access to 10A electricity. This site is popular with tour operators (54 pitches). Jard is rated among the most pleasant and least hectic of Vendée towns. The harbour is home to some fishing boats and rather more pleasure craft.

Facilities

Two toilet blocks include baby baths, and laundry rooms. Small shop (bread baked on site). Snack bar and takeaway (1/6-30/8). Bar with snacks. Swimming pool and separate paddling pool (30/5-15/9). New large flume into separate pool. Indoor pool and fitness centre (all season). New play area (3-10 yrs). Minigolf. Boules. Multisports pitch. Bouncy castle. Club for children (5-10 yrs, July/Aug). Games room. Bicycle hire. WiFi (free). Only gas barbecues are allowed. Dogs are not accepted. Off site: Beach and fishing 400 m.

Open: 9 April - 25 September.

Directions

From Les Sables-d'Olonne take the N949 towards Talmont-Saint Hilaire. Keep right in the centre (D21 towards Jard). From La Roche-sur-Yon follow the D474 and the D49 towards Jard-sur-Mer. Do not use sat nav for final approach. From the village follow the signs 'Autres campings' or Camping les Ecureuils. Site is on the left. GPS: 46.4113, -1.5896

Charges guide

Per unit incl. 2 persons,	
and electricity	€ 16.00 - € 32.00

Jard-sur-Mer

Chadotel Camping l'Océano d'Or

Rue Georges Clémenceau, B.P. 12, F-85520 Jard-sur-Mer (Vendée) T: 02 51 33 05 05. E: info@chadotel.com

alanrogers.com/FR85270

This eight-hectare site should appeal to families with children of all ages. It is very lively in high season but appears to be well managed, with a full programme of activities (it can therefore be noisy, sometimes late at night). The site is only 1 km. from the excellent beach. There are 430 flat, grass and sand pitches of which 40% are occupied by tour operators and mobile homes. The 260 for touring units, all with 10A electricity (French sockets, long leads may be required), are quite large (about 100 sq.m). Some are separated by high hedges, others are more open with low bushes between them.

Facilities

Four refurbished toilet blocks include washbasins in cabins. Facilities for disabled visitors. Dishwashing and laundry facilities. Shop (1/6-10/9). Bar, snack bar and takeaway (1/6-10/9). Swimming pool (heated 20/5-20/9) with children's pool. Fitness suite. Play area. Tennis. Bicycle hire. Pétanque. Minigolf. Multisports pitch. Electric barbecues are not allowed. Max. 1 dog. WiFi (charged). Off site: Excellent beach within walking distance.

Open: 8 April - 25 September.

Directions

Site is on the D21 Talmont-Saint Hilaire - Longeville-sur-Mer, just east of the turning to the town centre. GPS: 46.42075, -1.5694

Charges guide

Per unit incl. 2 persons	
and electricity	€ 19.60 - € 32.00
extra person	€ 5.80

For latest campsite news, availability and prices visit

alanrogers.com

La Barre-de-Monts

Campéole

Campéole la Grande Côte

Route de la Grande Côte, F-85550 La Barre-de-Monts (Vendée) T: 02 51 68 51 89.
E: grande-cote@campeole.com alanrogers.com/FR85840

A site that lives up to its name, this one is very large, with 727 pitches. However, 245 are occupied by Bengali tents to rent, 60 by private caravans and 29 by tour operators. There are still 394 numbered touring pitches in rows, all with 10A electricity and spread over undulating sand dunes with sparse grass under pine trees. The site is served by eight fairly modern and fairly well maintained toilet blocks around the site. Some of the terraced pitches at the rear of the site have views of the impressive bridge onto the Ile de Noirmoutier, and there is direct access to a sandy beach via a gate. Also on site is an outdoor heated swimming pool. In July and August, the site offers clubs for children of all ages whilst adults can enjoy themed tapas, karaoke, cabaret, and aquagym. Whilst in high season this site is very busy, in low season it is rather quiet with only the pool and the playground open.

Facilities

Eight toilet blocks include some washbasins in cubicles, seatless toilets, baby bath, and a good unit for disabled campers. One laundry room. Outdoor heated swimming pool (15/5-19/9). Shop for bread and basics. Bar and takeaway (1/7-31/8). Playgrounds, trampoline and bouncy castle. Entertainment and clubs for children (1/7-31/8). Multisports court. Boules. Bicycle hire. No charcoal barbecues. Supplement for twin-axle caravans. WiFi (charged). Off site: Fishing, sailing 50 m. Riding 2 km. Golf 15 km. Boat launching 25 km. Nearby is Ecomuseum du Daviaud.

Open: 1 April - 19 September.

Directions

Site is on the mainland at the approach to the Ile de Noirmoutier. From the north via Bourgneuf-en-Retz take D758 to Beauvoir-sur-Mer, then D22 to La Barre-de-Monts. Continue through town. At town boundary turn right on D38b, signed Ile de Noirmoutier. In 500 m, straight on at roundabout for about 1 km. then right signed Grand Côte and Fromentine. Take next left for 1 km. to site (entrance on right). GPS: 46.8858, -2.1477

Charges guide

Per unit incl. 2 persons and electricity	€ 17.10 - € 26.60
extra person	€ 7.20 - € 12.30

Campéole

CAMPSITES AND RENTALS

PAYS DE LA LOIRE

La Grande Côte***

Close to Ile de Noirmoutier, swimming pool, direct access to the beach and the village. Amenities, pitches and accommodations of high quality.

85550 La Barre de Monts - Tel.: +33 251-6851-89 - www.campeole.co.uk / grande-cote@campeole.com

La Chapelle-Hermier

Camping le Pin Parasol

Lac du Jaunay, F-85220 La Chapelle-Hermier (Vendée) T: 02 51 34 64 72. E: contact@campingpinparasol.fr
alanrogers.com/FR85680

Tucked away in the Vendée countryside, yet just 15 minutes' drive from the beach, this attractive friendly campsite enjoys a pleasant setting above the Lac du Jaunay, well away from the bustle of the coast. There are 229 good sized touring pitches, all with electricity (10A) and 32 with water tap and drainage. Some have shade, others are in the open with maturing hedges and trees. The enthusiastic family owners are very hands-on and the facilities are of a high standard, most notably the elegant entrance and reception building, and the pool area with its indoor pool, jacuzzi, steam room and fitness suite.

Facilities

Four fully equipped toilet blocks (one heated) include hot showers, washbasins in cabins and facilities for babies and disabled visitors. Washing machines and dryers. Shop and bar with terrace (15/5-25/9). Takeaway (July/Aug). Heated outdoor pool with paddling pool (15/6-15/9). Indoor pool (all season). Play areas. Multisports pitch. Boules. Bicycle hire. Entertainment in high season. Fishing. Tennis. WiFi (charged). Off site: Golf 5 km. Riding 10 km. Beaches and sailing 12 km.

Open: 23 April - 25 September.

Directions

La Chapelle-Hermier is 26 km. west of La Roche-sur-Yon. Site is to the south of the D42 La Chapelle-Hermier - l'Aiguillon-sur-Vie road, 2 km. east of the junction with the D40 Coëx-La Chaize - Giraud road and is well signed. GPS: 46.66622, -1.75528

Charges guide

Per unit incl. 2 persons and electricity	€ 16.50 - € 33.50
extra person	€ 4.50 - € 6.50

We can book this site for you! Call 01580 214000 alan rogers ◉ travel

For latest campsite news, availability and prices visit

alanrogers.com

La Guérinière
Camping le Caravan'ile

1 rue de la Tresson B.P. 4, La Guérinière, F-85680 Ile de Noirmoutier (Vendée) T: 02 51 39 50 29.
E: contact@caravanile.com **alanrogers.com/FR85620**

This well appointed, family run site on the island of Noirmoutier has direct access across a dune and an extensive sandy beach, although swimming is only possible at high tide. It has a good pool and leisure complex, and a variety of entertainment is arranged in high season. Most of the 103 reasonably level touring pitches are on sand beneath the dunes. All have electricity (5A) and are separated by bushes and the occasional maturing tree; there is little shade. The site has a very French ambience, with many privately owned mobile homes, plus 90 for rent.

Facilities

Three sanitary blocks with preset showers, warm water to washbasins, in cabins. Facilities for babies and disabled visitors. Washing machines and dryers. Supermarket at entrance (15/4-15/9). Bar, snack bar and takeaway (15/4-15/9; limited opening until mid-June). Heated indoor pool and paddling pool. Outdoor pool (15/5-15/9; heated July/Aug). Small play area and bouncy castle. Multisports court. Games room with digital TV. WiFi (charged) in bar area. Off site: Restaurant, shop and bicycle hire nearby.
Open: 15 March - 15 November.

Directions

The Ile de Noirmoutier is 70 km. southwest of Nantes. At La Barre-de-Monts, take D38 across bridge to island and continue to fifth roundabout. Take exit for La Guérinière and immediately turn left to site. GPS: 46.96631, -2.216073

Charges guide

Per unit incl. 2 persons and electricity (5A)	€ 17.00 - € 28.00
extra person	€ 3.60 - € 6.50

La Guérinière
Domaine les Moulins

54 rue des Moulins, F-85680 La Guérinière (Vendée) T: 02 51 39 51 38. E: contact@camping-les-moulins.com
alanrogers.com/FR85625

New owners have completely transformed this site on the Ile de Noirmoutier, making it an ideal choice for a seaside holiday. It is on the edge of a forest with direct access across dunes to a pleasant sandy beach. One area has 113 touring pitches on generally level ground and separated by hedges; most have electricity and a few also have water and drainage. Two other areas have an impressive range of innovative tented accommodation, fully in keeping with the forest setting. The heated pool has two paddling pools and a jacuzzi, whilst the bar also serves a full range of meals and snacks. Other facilities are of an equally high standard, with attention to detail in evidence everywhere.

Facilities

Two modern sanitary blocks provide unisex, preset showers and washbasins, segregated WCs, baby bath and changing station, and good facilities for disabled visitors. Washing machines and dryers. Motorcaravan service point. Bar/restaurant and takeaway (Jul/Aug; weekends May-Sept). Heated pool complex (15/4-15/9). Wellness suite. Small gym. WiFi (charged). Small theatre. Multisports court. Pétanque. Cycle hire.
Open: 1 April - 30 September.

Directions

The Ile de Noirmoutier is 70 km. southwest of Nantes. At la Barre-de-Monts take D38 across bridge to island and continue to fifth roundabout. Take exit for La Guérinière and immediately turn left to site. GPS: 46.966233, -2.217173

Charges guide

Per unit incl. 2 persons and electricity	€ 22.00 - € 42.00

We can book this site for you! Call 01580 214000 alan rogers ⊕ travel

La Tranche-sur-Mer
Camping du Jard

123 boulevard Maréchal de Lattre de Tassigny, F-85360 La Tranche-sur-Mer (Vendée) T: 02 51 27 43 79.
E: info@campingdujard.fr **alanrogers.com/FR85020**

Camping du Jard is a well maintained site between La Rochelle and Les Sables-d'Olonne. First impressions are good, with a friendly welcome from M. Marton or his staff. The 160 touring pitches, all with electricity and 60 also with water and drainage, are level and grassy; many are hedged by bushes and a large variety of trees provide shade in places. An impressive pool complex has a heated outdoor pool with toboggan and paddling pool, plus an indoor pool with jacuzzi. The site is 700 m. from a sandy beach with many shops and restaurants nearby.

Facilities

Three toilet blocks provide basic facilities for babies and disabled visitors. Controllable showers in one block; some washbasins in cabins. Washing machines and dryers. Motorcaravan service point. Shop (1/6-10/9), restaurant and bar (25/5-10/9). Heated outdoor pool (from 25/5); heated indoor pool (all season). Tennis. Minigolf. Bicycle hire. Play area, TV/games rooms. Free WiFi around bar. American motorhomes not accepted. No pets.
Open: 26 April - 15 September.

Directions

From A87 Cholet/La Roche-sur-Yon leave at exit 32 for La Tranche-sur-Mer and take D747 to La Tranche. Turn east following signs for La Faute-sur-Mer along bypass. Take exit for La Grière and then turn east to site. GPS: 46.34836, -1.38738

Charges guide

Per unit incl. 2 persons and electricity	€ 23.50 - € 32.00

For latest campsite news, availability and prices visit
alanrogers.com

La Tranche-sur-Mer
Camping Baie d'Aunis

10 rue du Pertuis Breton, F-85360 La Tranche-sur-Mer (Vendée) T: 02 51 27 47 36.
E: info@camping-baiedaunis.com **alanrogers.com/FR85870**

This very popular 2.5-hectare site has direct access to a sandy beach through a pedestrian gate (with key code) and across a car park. The town centre is also only 500 m. away. Shady and level, there are 153 individual pitches, all with electricity (10A). A good number of pitches are on a gravel base and a few are suitable only for smaller units. There are chalets and mobile homes (19) to rent. On-site amenities include a heated swimming pool and a good restaurant and bar. This is a popular seaside resort with 13 km. of good quality sandy beaches. All have first aid posts, lifeguards in season and dogs are forbidden on the sands. From the pier by the Centre Nautique, just 50 m. from the site's rear pedestrian gate, you can catch ferries to the islands of Aix and Ré and to the larger resort of La Rochelle.

Facilities

The main centrally located sanitary unit is large, good quality and very well appointed. A smaller simpler unit is at the far end of the site. British style WCs, washbasins in cubicles, provision for babies and disabled campers. Laundry room at each block. Motorcaravan service point. Bar/restaurant and takeaway (20/5-13/9, Thu. & Sun. only in low season). Outdoor swimming pool (10x20 m; heated May-Sept). Playground. Games Room. TV room. Volleyball. Dogs and other animals not accepted July/Aug. WiFi over site (free). Off site: La Tranche is a major sailboarding/kite surfing centre, with teaching facilities in a special lagoon, plus a surf school. Bicycle hire adjacent. Beach and sea fishing within 50 m. Town centre 500 m. Riding 12 km.

Open: 30 April - 19 September.

Directions

La Tranche-sur-Mer is 35 km. south of La Roche-sur-Yon. From La Roche-sur-Yon take the D747 to La Tranche. At roundabout (D747 and D1046) carry straight on to next roundabout and turn right towards town centre. At next (new) roundabout continue straight on to site on left (well signed). GPS: 46.34638, -1.43184

Charges guide

Per unit incl. 2 persons and electricity	€ 25.10 - € 33.40
extra person	€ 5.80 - € 7.00
child (under 5 yrs)	€ 3.60 - € 3.80
dog (not 1/7-31/8)	€ 2.30

CAMPING BAiE D'AUNiS••••

Camping Baie d'Aunis | 10, Rue du Pertuis Breton | 85360 La Tranche sur Mer
Tel: 0033 (0) 251 27 47 36 | Fax: 0033 (0) 251 27 44 54
info@camping-baiedaunis.com | www.camping-baiedaunis.com

La Tranche-sur-Mer
Village Center les Almadies

Route de la Roche sur Yon, F-85360 La Tranche-sur-Mer (Vendée) T: 08 25 00 20 30.
E: contact@village-center.com **alanrogers.com/FR85585**

Les Almadies has recently been acquired by the Village Center Group who have built an impressive covered pool complex (open all year) and increased the number of mobile homes available for rent. Of the 520 pitches, all on level ground, 132 are available for touring, most in blocks, numbered but otherwise unmarked; all but two have electricity. A shop, restaurant and takeaway and the outdoor pool are open in high season only. The sophisticated resort of Les Sables d'Olonne is 40 km. to the northwest and offers up-market shopping and dining, a zoo and a fine sandy beach.

Facilities

Six traditional toilet blocks with preset showers and washbasins in cabins. Hot water to dishwashing sinks. Washing machines and dryers. Baby bath in one block. Facilities for disabled visitors in three blocks. Bar (all season). Shop, restaurant and takeaway (July/Aug). Heated indoor pool. Outdoor pool (July/Aug). Play area. Cycle hire. WiFi in bar area (charged). Off site: Beaches sailing and sea fishing 3 km. Supermarket 3 km. Shops and bars 5 km.

Open: Easter - 26 September.

Directions

Site is on the D747 north of La Tranche-sur-Mer and 36 km. south of La Roche-sur-Yon. From A87 Cholet - La Roche-sur-Yon leave at exit 32 for La Tranche-sur-Mer and follow D747 towards La Tranche. Site is on right, 4/5 km. after passing Angles. GPS: 46.372221, -1.414002

Charges guide

Per unit incl. 2 persons	€ 14.00 - € 25.00
extra person	€ 3.00 - € 5.00
Camping Cheques accepted.	

For latest campsite news, availability and prices visit
alanrogers.com

Call 01580 214000 We can book this site for you! alanrogers ◖travel

Landevieille

Camping Pong

Rue du Stade, F-85220 Landevieille (Vendée) T: 02 51 22 92 63. E: info@lepong.com

alanrogers.com/FR85130

A comfortable family run site, in a rural situation close to St Gilles Croix-de-Vie, and just 5 km. from the coast at Brétignolles, Camping Pong has 237 pitches of which 177 are for tourers. All are of a good size and have electricity; most also have a water tap and drainage. The bar, snack bar, function room, games room, gym and shop are in a neat group of buildings next to the reception. The original area around the small, lightly-fenced fishing lake has mature trees, whilst in the newer section, trees and shrubs are developing well.

Facilities

A modern, well equipped sanitary block has controllable showers, washbasins in cabins, facilities for disabled visitors, baby room, dishwashing and laundry room. Shop (July/Aug), Bar plus snack bar and takeaway (15/6-15/9). Heated pool with paddling pool (from 15/5). Small gym, TV/games room. Bicycle hire. Fishing. Fenced play area. Children's club and family entertainment (July/Aug). WiFi in bar area (charged). Off site: Small supermarket, restaurant and bakery close by. Tennis 200 m. Lac du Jaunay 2.5 km. Beach, sailing, golf, and riding all 5 km.

Open: 1 April - 15 September.

Directions

Landevieille is 32 km. west of La Roche-sur-Yon via the A87/D160 Les Sables road; take exit for La Motte Achard and follow D12 for St Gilles Croix-de-Vie. Site is on the edge of Landevieille and is signed from the D12 and from the D32 (Challans - Les Sables-d'Olonne). GPS: 46.64231, -1.79935

Charges guide

Per unit incl. 2 persons and electricity	€ 15.00 - € 24.00
extra person	€ 3.20 - € 4.90

Le Perrier

Domaine le Jardin du Marais

208 route de Saint-Gilles, F-85300 Le Perrier (Vendée) T: 02 51 68 09 17. E: info@lejardindumarais.eu

alanrogers.com/FR85635

A delightful, family campsite situated, as its name suggests, in a country setting on the edge of the marshes. It is beautifully kept and has excellent facilities including a well stocked shop, a pleasant bar/restaurant and a good pool complex. The enthusiastic and hard-working owners are keen to welcome more British visitors who will be sure of a warm reception. Of the 120 pitches, 52 are available for touring. The established pitches offer some shade and have electricity and water nearby; a new area offers large pitches with electricity, water and drainage, but bushes and trees have yet to mature. The beaches are just seven kilometres away. For shops, bars and restaurants you can use the nearby village of Le Perrier or head for the resorts of Saint Jean-de-Monts or Saint Hilaire-de-Riez where there are also large supermarkets and frequent markets.

Facilities

Two bright, modern sanitary blocks provide hot showers and washbasins in cubicles. Baby bath and changing. En-suite facility for disabled visitors. Washing machine and dryer. Motorcaravan services arranged. Shop, bar/restaurant and takeaway (all season, on demand). Outdoor pool with paddling pool (15/6-15/9). Indoor heated pool (15/4-15/9). Solarium. Fitness room. Play area. Free fishing on small lake (fenced and gated). Children's club, activities and evening entertainment (July/Aug). Games area. Bicycle hire. WiFi (charged) in bar area. Off site: Riding 4 km. Beach and sailing 7 km.

Open: 1 April - 2 October.

Directions

Le Perrier is 51 km. northwest of La Roche-sur-Yon and 11 km. southwest of Challans. Site is 2 km. to the south on the D59 to Le Pissot and St Gilles; from the new route of the D753 Challans - St Jean-de-Monts road turn south on D59 and site is on right in 300m. GPS: 46.80133, -1.980656

Charges guide

Per unit incl. 2 persons and electricity	€ 18.00 - € 31.00
extra person	€ 5.00 - € 7.50
child (2-11 yrs)	€ 3.00 - € 6.00

DOMAINE ✦✦✦✦✦ FAMILY CAMPSITE
Le Jardin du Marais
Sites & Paysages DE FRANCE
Phone : 0033 02 51 68 09 17
Web : http://www.lejardindumarais.eu
Family campsite with a beautiful swimming pool and a strech of water to go fishing.
Seats, bar, restaurant and snack bar. Only a few kilometers away from the Atlantic Ocean.
Sites et Paysages Le Jardin du Marais - 208 Route de Saint Gilles - F85300 LE PERRIER - Vendée des Iles

Les Sables-d'Olonne
Chadotel Camping les Roses

Rue des Roses, F-85100 Les Sables-d'Olonne (Vendée) T: 02 51 33 05 05. E: info@chadotel.com

alanrogers.com/FR85450

Les Roses has an urban location, with the fashionable town centre and lovely beach of Les Sables just a short walk away. It has an informal air with 210 pitches arranged interestingly on a knoll. Mature trees give good shade to some areas. There are 90 touring pitches of varying sizes, all with access to water and electricity (long cables may be needed). The site has 120 mobile homes and chalets, some for rent and some owned by a tour operator. Roads around the site can get crowded in high season.

Facilities

Three fairly basic toilet blocks have pushbutton showers, washbasins in cubicles, a unit for disabled visitors, a baby room, washing machines and dryers. Simple bar and takeaway and small shop (10/6-15/9). Small outdoor pool with water slide and paddling pool (15/5-15/9). Play area. Volleyball, basketball and pétanque. Bicycle hire. Gas barbecues only (for hire). WiFi in bar area (charged). Max. 1 dog. Off site: Beach 500 m. Golf, riding, karting, watersports, zoo, sea and river fishing all within 5 km.

Open: 3 April - 7 November.

Directions

Les Sables-d'Olonne is 40 km. southwest of La Roche-sur-Yon. From end of A87 Cholet/La Roche at exit 33, continue on D160 to Les Sables ring road. At eastern end of ring road in Château d'Olonne ('Géant Casino' roundabout), turn west along Ave d'Aquitaine towards town centre. Site signed at small roundabout. GPS: 46.49167, -1.76517

Charges guide

Per unit incl. 2 persons and electricity	€ 19.60 - € 32.00

Longeville-sur-Mer
Camping le Petit Rocher

1250 avenue de Docteur Mathevet, F-85560 Longeville-sur-Mer (Vendée) T: 02 51 33 17 00.
E: info@campinglepetitrocher.com **alanrogers.com/FR85000**

A former municipal site, le Petit Rocher is now under the same management (M. Guignard) as another local campsite, les Brunelles. With its seaside location set in a pine forest, there is an air of peace and tranquillity. Although the area is undulating, the 150 good sized touring pitches are flat and arranged in terraces throughout the wooded area. Electricity hook-ups are available (Euro style plugs) and there are adequate water points. A grassy play area for children is thoughtfully situated in a hollow, but has limited equipment. A fun pool was added in 2008.

Facilities

Three new, spacious sanitary blocks are clean and well maintained with showers, British style WCs. Facilities for visitors with disabilities. Washing machine and dryer. Bar, restaurant and takeaway (July/Aug). Tennis court. New heated outdoor pool (28/5-17/9). Max. 1 dog. Off site: Beach 200 m. Bars, restaurant, and small shops nearby. Riding and bicycle hire 2 km. Boat launching 11 km. Fishing 15 km. Golf 20 km.

Open: 28 May - 17 September.

Directions

From Longeville-sur-Mer follow signs for le Rocher towards La Tranche-sur-Mer. Turn right at first roundabout, following campsite signs to site on right. GPS: 46.403767, -1.507183

Charges guide

Per unit incl. 2 persons and electricity	€ 16.00 - € 25.00
extra person	€ 3.00 - € 5.00

Longeville-sur-Mer
Camping le Zagarella

Route de La Tranche, F-85560 Longeville-sur-Mer (Vendée) T: 02 51 33 30 60. E: zagarella@franceloc.com

alanrogers.com/FR85010

This pleasant campsite is set in a wooded, six hectare area, a 1,300 metre walk from the beach (or 1.5 km. by road). Scattered among the 130 mobile homes (110 to rent) are 70 touring pitches, which are of a reasonable size, though the site is probably unsuitable for larger units. On well drained grass and shaded, the pitches are hedged and all have water and electricity. An impressive landscaped pool complex with indoor and outdoor pools, includes water slides paddling pool and a pirate-themed adventure area. Nearby is a large adventure playground with a huge bouncy castle.

Facilities

Three well maintained toilet blocks of traditional design include washbasins in cubicles and free preset showers. Separate baby room and facilities for disabled visitors. Washing machines and dryers. Shop (from 25/5). Bar (from 20/5). Restaurant and takeaway (all season). Outdoor heated pool (from 1/6) and indoor pool (all season). Adventure playground. Multisports court. Tennis. Bicycle hire. Free WiFi in bar area. Gas barbecues only. Off site: Riding 1 km. Beach 1.3 km. Sailing 1.5 km. Shops, bars and restaurants in Longeville 3 km.

Open: 1 May - 30 September.

Directions

Longeville-sur-Mer is 32 km south of La Roche-sur-Yon. Site is 3 km south of the town on D105 to La Tranche-sur-Mer. From A87 Cholet/La Roche leave at exit 32 for La Tranche and take D747 to La Tranche. Turn northwest on D105 for 8.5 km. to site on right. GPS: 46.40390, -1.48810

Charges guide

Per unit incl. 2 persons	€ 16.00 - € 33.00
extra person	€ 4.70 - € 8.00
child (0-7 yrs)	€ 2.60 - € 5.00

We can book this site for you! Call 01580 214000 alanrogers travel

For latest campsite news, availability and prices visit
alanrogers.com

Call 01580 214000   We can book this site for you!   alanrogers ◉ travel

Longeville-sur-Mer
Camping les Brunelles

Le Bouil, F-85560 Longeville-sur-Mer (Vendée) T: 02 51 33 17 00. E: camping@les-brunelles.com
alanrogers.com/FR85440

This is a well managed site with a wide range of facilities and a varied programme of high season entertainment for all the family. A busy site in high season, there are plenty of activities to keep children happy and occupied. In 2007, les Brunelles was combined with an adjacent campsite to provide 600 pitches of which 200 are for touring units; all have electricity (10A) and 20 of the new touring pitches also have water and a drain. All are in excess of 100 sq.m. to allow easier access for larger units. On the original les Brunelles site, the touring pitches are all level on sandy grass and separated by hedges, away from most of the mobile homes. A large aquapark provides a swimming pool of 1,000 sq.m. with indoor and outdoor pools, slides, a sauna, steam room, jacuzzi, and a fitness centre. A good, supervised, sandy beach is 900 m. away.

Facilities

Four well maintained and modernised toilet blocks have British and Turkish style toilets and washbasins, both open style and in cabins. Laundry facilities. Shop, takeaway and large modern, airy bar (all season). Covered pool with jacuzzi (all season). Outdoor pool with slides and paddling pools (21/5-24/9). Tennis. Bicycle hire. Max. 1 dog. Off site: Riding 3 km. Good, supervised, sandy beach 900 m. St Vincent-sur-Jard 2 km. Golf 20 km.

Open: 2 April - 24 September.

Directions

From D21 (Talmont-Longeville), between St Vincent and Longeville, site signed south from main road towards coast. Turn left in Le Bouil (site is signed). Site is 800 m. on left. GPS: 46.41330, -1.52313

Charges guide

Per unit incl. 2 persons	
and electricity	€ 21.00 - € 35.00
incl. water and waste water	€ 25.00 - € 40.00
extra person	€ 5.00 - € 9.00
child (under 5 yrs)	free - € 6.00
dog	€ 5.00

Camping Cheques accepted.

Noirmoutier-en-l'Ile
Camping Indigo Noirmoutier

23 allée des Sableaux, Bois de la Chaize, F-85330 Noirmoutier-en-l'Ile (Vendée) T: 02 51 39 06 24.
E: noirmoutier@camping-indigo.com   **alanrogers.com/FR85720**

Located in woodland and on dunes along a two kilometre stretch of sandy beach. just east of the attractive little town of Noirmoutier on the island of the same name, this could be paradise for those who enjoy a simple campsite in a natural setting. On land belonging to France's forestry commission, this site is operated by Huttopia whose aim is to adapt to the environment rather than take it over. The 398 touring pitches, all with electricity (10A), are situated among the pine trees and accessed along tracks. Those on the sand dunes have fantastic views across the Baie de Bourgneuf. They cost a few euros extra – if you are lucky enough to get one. Cars are only allowed in these areas on arrival and departure. There are no mobile homes, but Indigo have installed 80 large and well equipped canvas tents on wooden bases for rent. Nearby are salt marshes, an aquarium and a water theme park and there are opportunities to walk, cycle, sail and windsurf.

Facilities

Five sanitary blocks currently provide basic facilities including preset showers and some washbasins (with warm water) in cubicles. The central one is larger and more modern, and another has been refurbished with controllable showers and hot and cold water to washbasins, although these are open-style; there are two cubicles with shower and washbasin. Facilities for babies and disabled visitors. Hot water to dishwashing and laundry sinks. Washing machines and dryers. Basic motorcaravan services point. Play area. Bicycle hire. Free internet point in reception. Only electric barbecues allowed. Off site: Shops, bars and restaurants in Noirmoutier-en-l'Ile 2 km. Riding 4 km. Sailing 5 km. Golf 25 km.

Open: 30 March - 7 October.

Directions

The Ile de Noirmoutier is 70 km. southwest of Nantes. At La Barre-de-Monts, take D38 across bridge to island and continue 20 km. to Noirmoutier-en-l'Ile. Go through town past three sets of traffic lights and at roundabout turn right following blue signs to 'Campings'. Site is ahead at roundabout in about 2 km. GPS: 46.9969, -2.2201

Charges guide

Per unit incl. 2 persons	
and electricity	€ 18.80 - € 25.80
extra person	€ 3.40 - € 5.00
child (2-7 yrs)	€ 1.90 - € 2.90
dog	€ 4.00

Camping Cheques accepted.

Des campings à 2 pas de la plage...

VENDÉE

Its magnificent landscapes will enchant you by offering a guaranteed, mindblowing change of scene: its large beaches of fine sand, the islands, le Marais Poitevin...Come and discover the Vendée and its authenticity.

Campsite les Brunelles

Come and enjoy your holidays at campsite les Brunelles, a 5 star campsite located at only 800m from the beach, with a unique aquatic area.

Le Bouil - 85560 Longeville sur Mer

Campsite le Petit Rocher

Campsite le Petit Rocher*** is ideal for nature lovers and guarantees you serenity at only 150m from the beach and 50m from different shops.

1250 Avenue du Dr. Mathevet
85560 Longeville sur Mer

CAMP'ATLANTIQUE

Les Plantes de la Brunelle - 85560 LONGEVILLE sur MER
Tél: 0033 (0)2 51 33 17 00 - contact@camp-atlantique.com
www.camp-atlantique.com

Maché

Camping Caravaning Val de Vie

Rue du Stade, F-85190 Maché (Vendée) T: 02 51 60 21 02. E: campingvaldevie@orange.fr

alanrogers.com/FR85320

Opened in 1999, Val de Vie is a small, good quality site run with enthusiasm and dedication by its owners, on the outskirts of a rural village set back from the coast. There are 64 pitches for touring units with electricity (6/10A), that vary in size from 100-130 sq.m. on mostly level grass with hedging. There are nine extra large super pitches (which must be pre-booked for high season). The ground can become very hard, so steel pegs are advised. The pitches are arranged in circular fashion around the toilet block which, with reception, is built in local style with attractive, red tiled roofs. If you are looking for a beach, the Vendée coast is 20 km. away.

Facilities

The two toilet blocks provide excellent, modern facilities including some washbasins in cabins, baby bath, facilities for disabled visitors, dishwashing and laundry facilities. Reception also offers wine, beer, soft drinks and ice cream. Small play area. Heated swimming pool (from mid May). Bicycle hire. Off site: Tennis courts, shops, bar, tabac within walking distance. Lake d'Apremont 300 m. Apremont itself with Renaissance château 4 km. Vendée coast 20 km.

Open: 1 May - 30 September.

Directions

From La Roche-sur-Yon take D948 northwest. At end of Aizenay bypass continue for 2 km; cross River Vie and take next right, following the signs for Maché into the village centre. GPS: 46.75268, -1.68633

Charges guide

Per unit incl. 2 persons and electricity	€ 15.80 - € 23.50
extra person	€ 3.50 - € 4.80
child (under 10 yrs)	€ 2.00 - € 3.80
dog	€ 1.50 - € 2.50

Val de Vie CAMPING CARAVANING ★ ★ ★

The new owners give you a warm welcome at their 3* campsite in the middle of nature, close to the Apremont lake.

Facilities: heated pool, children's playground, bouncy castle, skelters, boules, etc.

Camping Val de Vie* - 05, rue du Stade - F- 85190 MACHE**
Tel : 0033 (0)2.51.60.21.02 - E-mail: campingvaldevie@bbox.fr - www.campingvaldevie.fr

Notre-Dame-de-Riez

Camping Domaine des Renardières

13 chemin du Chêne Vert, F-85270 Notre-Dame-de-Riez (Vendée) T: 02 51 55 14 17. E: caroline.raffin@free.fr

alanrogers.com/FR85520

Just 7 km. from the busy coastal strip, Domaine des Renardières is an oasis of calm in the traditional French manner. Converted from the family farm in 1970, the site consists of three fields with varying amounts of shade and two further open fields in full sun. The 74 touring pitches, all with electricity (10A), are well grassed and level. Solar lighting. Torches and long cables are advisable. Mme. Raffin's benevolent authority is to be seen everywhere and the welfare of her clients is of paramount importance to her. Recycling of waste is encouraged – there are collection points for batteries and green waste and the site has a La Clef Verte (green key) status. There is an entertainment programme in high season.

Facilities

The new unisex toilet block has private cubicles, baby changing room and a bathroom for disabled visitors. Showers are closed at night except for one cold shower. Laundry facilities. Motorcaravan service point. Shop. Air-conditioned bar with TV and takeaway (1/7-27/8). Small heated pool (all season). Play area. Boules. Gas and electric barbecues only. WiFi (charged). Off site: Fishing 1 km. VeloRail 5 km. Bicycle hire and Atlantic Toboggan 7 km. St Hilaire-de-Riez 7 km. with good sandy beach. Riding 9 km. Golf 11 km. Puy du Fou 80 km.

Open: 1 April - 2 September.

Directions

Site is northeast of the village of Notre-Dame-de-Riez. Turn in centre of village and cross railway. Fork right and site is on left. Well signed. GPS: 46.75523, -1.89814

Charges guide

Per unit incl. 2 persons and electricity	€ 16.50 - € 22.00
extra person	€ 3.37 - € 4.50
child (under 5 yrs)	€ 2.00 - € 2.50
dog	€ 2.00 - € 3.00
No credit cards.	

For latest campsite news, availability and prices visit

alanrogers.com

Olonne-sur-Mer
Camping la Loubine

1 route de la Mer, F-85340 Olonne-sur-Mer (Vendée) T: 02 51 33 12 92. E: camping.la.loubine@wanadoo.fr

alanrogers.com/FR85030

On the edge of a forest and just 1.8 kilometres from a sandy beach, La Loubine is a busy campsite close to Les Sables-d'Olonne. Under new ownership from 2011, the site has 60 grass touring pitches which are mostly shaded, all with electricity and with water points nearby. Mobile homes and chalets, many for rent, and tour operator tents occupy the remaining 300 pitches. The focal point is an excellent restaurant with an attractive covered terrace and bar with an entertainment area for karaoke and discos, plus a patio overlooking the splendid pool complex with its water slides and heated indoor pool. The camping areas have many mature trees and hedges, some quite high, providing plenty of shade. A shuttle bus to the beach operates in high season, the area has a network of cycle tracks and there are occasional buses to Les Sables and Saint Gilles from close by. Olonne-sur-Mer has shops, bars, restaurants and a hypermarket, whilst ten minutes away is fashionable Les Sables with its sandy beach.

Facilities

Four toilet blocks have British style WCs, washbasins in cubicles and controllable showers. Facilities for disabled visitors. Hot water to dishwashing and laundry sinks. Washing machines and dryers. Shop, bar, restaurant and takeaway (15/5-15/9). Outdoor pools and heated indoor pool (all season). Tennis. Fitness room. Minigolf. Play area. Bicycle hire. Free WiFi in bar area. Internet (charged). Shuttle bus to beach (July/Aug). Dogs are not allowed in high season. Off site: Restaurant and occasional buses nearby. Riding 200 m. Canoeing 1 km. Beach 1.8 km.

Open: 2 April - 25 September.

Directions

Site is off D80 coast road between Olonne-sur-Mer and Brem-sur-Mer, signed at small roundabout. From La Roche-sur-Yon via A87/D160, turn west on the D949 Les Sables ring road then west on D32 to Olonne-sur-Mer. Site is signed to left in town centre. GPS: 46.54626, -1.80556

Charges guide

Per unit incl. 2 persons and electricity	€ 19.80 - € 31.80
extra person	€ 3.30 - € 5.20

Camping La Loubine

Traditional-style facilities set in the grounds of an old farm only 1800 m from the beach; La Loubine is a lively site with one of the best pool complexes in the area. (1 heated indoor pool with 3 waterslides, whirlpool bath and sauna).

Bar - Restaurant - Take Away - Shop - Tennis Court - Crazy Golf - Playground - Fitness Room - Multi Sport Pitch - Bicycle Hire - Entertainment in high season.

1, Route de la Mer - 85340 Olonne Sur mer - France
Tel.: 0033 (0)2 51 33 12 92 - Fax: 0033 (0)2 51 33 12 71
camping.la.loubine@wanadoo.fr
www.la-loubine.fr

Olonne-sur-Mer
Domaine de l'Orée

13 route des Amis de la Nature, F-85340 Olonne-sur-Mer (Vendée) T: 02 51 33 10 59. E: loree@free.fr

alanrogers.com/FR85180

On the edge of a national forest, close to marshes and a bird sanctuary, and just 1,800 m. from a fine sandy beach, Domaine de l'Orée will provide ample opportunities for an active holiday whether in the impressive pool complex, using the many sports facilities, venturing out onto the network of footpaths and cycle tracks or just going to the beach. The 53 touring pitches are level and separated by bushes; all have electricity (16A) and 40 also have a water tap and drainage. The remaining 243 pitches are occupied by chalets and mobile homes, many available for rent.

Facilities

Two blocks provide British style WCs, good, hot showers (preset) and washbasins in cabins. Basic facilities for disabled visitors. Washing machines, dryers and ironing facilities. Small, well-stocked shop, bar with TV, snack bar and takeaway (all from 1/5). Heated outdoor swimming pool and fun pool (from 1/5) plus heated indoor pool with jacuzzi (all season). Play areas. Trampolines. Tennis (free). Bicycle hire. Free WiFi in bar and pool area. Off site: Restaurant nearby. Riding 50 m. Canoeing 500 m. Beach 1.8 km. Shops in Olonne-sur-Mer 5 km.

Open: 11 April - 13 September.

Directions

From La Roche-sur-Yon via A87/D160, turn west on D949 Les Sables ring road then north on D32 to Olonne-sur-Mer. Site is signed to left in town centre. GPS: 46.54979, -1.80159

Charges guide

Per unit incl. 2 persons and electricity	€ 18.30 - € 33.50
extra person	€ 3.00 - € 6.00
child (2-6 yrs)	€ 2.00 - € 4.00
dog	free - € 3.50

For latest campsite news, availability and prices visit
alanrogers.com

Saint Hilaire-de-Riez
Camping les Ecureuils

100 avenue de la Pège, F-85270 Saint Hilaire-de-Riez (Vendée) T: 02 51 54 33 71.
E: info@camping-aux-ecureuils.com **alanrogers.com/FR85230**

Of the seaside sites on the Vendée, Les Ecureuils has to be one of the best, run by a friendly and most helpful family. Just 300 m. from a superb beach, the site is ideally situated for exploring from Les Sables-d'Olonne to Noirmoutier. Developed on what was originally a farm, there are 215 pitches (42 for touring units). On sandy grass, all have electricity (6A, Euro adaptors available free of charge), water and drainage. Well kept hedges and mature trees give shade and privacy, although some more open pitches are also available for sun lovers. The site is popular with British tour operators (60%).

Facilities

The two main sanitary blocks include some washbasins in cubicles, and facilities for babies and disabled visitors. Laundry and dishwashing facilities. Motorcaravn service point. Small shop (1/5-4/9). Restaurant. Bar with screened terrace. Pool complex. Lazy river. Indoor pool, paddling pool and jacuzzi. Gym. Tennis court. Games room. Play area. Off site: Bicycle hire 200 m. Beach 300 m. Fishing 4 km. Riding 5 km.

Open: 28 April - 9 September.

Directions

Driving south D38 (St Jean-de-Monts - St Gilles), turn right at L'Oasis hotel in Orouet (6 km. outside St Jean-de-Monts), signed Les Mouettes. After 1.5 km. at roundabout turn left (St Hilaire-de-Riez). Site is 500 m. on left. GPS: 46.74473, -2.00869

Charges guide

Per unit incl. 2 persons and electricity	€ 27.15 - € 36.70

Saint Hilaire-de-Riez
Camping Caravaning la Ningle

Chemin des Roselières 66, F-85270 Saint Hilaire-de-Riez (Vendée) T: 02 51 54 07 11.
E: campingdelaningle@wanadoo.fr **alanrogers.com/FR85350**

At Camping la Ningle you are guaranteed to receive a warm welcome from M. et Mme. Guibert, who have established a very pleasant campsite with a friendly, family atmosphere. There are 153 pitches, 54 available for touring units. All are fully serviced (electricity 6/10A, water and drainage). Pitches are spacious with dividing hedges and all have some shade. The nearest beach is a 500 m. walk through a pine forest, but there are also three small heated swimming pools on site.

Facilities

Two clean toilet blocks include some washbasins in cubicles. Toilet/shower room for disabled visitors, and large family shower room. Laundry facilities. Bread (July/Aug). Takeaway three evenings per week. Bar (July/Aug). Main swimming pool, larger children's pool, paddling pool and slide (20/5-10/9). Fitness suite. Tennis court. Games room. Games room. Fishing lake. Children's activities (July/Aug), and regular pétanque competitions. WiFi in bar area. Off site: Small supermarket and takeaway 200 m.

Open: 20 May - 10 September.

Directions

Driving south on D38 (St Jean-de-Monts - St Gilles), turn right at L'Oasis hotel in Orouet, signed Les Mouettes. After 1.5 km. at roundabout, turn left (St Hilaire-de-Riez). Pass two campsites, then next left, signed La Ningle. GPS: 46.7447, -2.0044

Charges guide

Per unit incl. 2 persons and electricity	€ 18.00 - € 32.90
extra person	€ 3.10 - € 4.80

We can book this site for you! Call 01580 214000 alan rogers travel

Saint Hilaire-la-Forêt
Camping la Grand Métairie

8 rue de la Vineuse en Plaine, F-85440 Saint Hilaire-la-Forêt (Vendée) T: 02 51 33 32 38.
E: info@camping-grandmetairie.com **alanrogers.com/FR85300**

Just five kilometres from the super sandy beach at Jard-sur-Mer, La Grand Métairie offers many of the amenities of its seaside counterparts, but with the important advantage of being on the edge of a delightful, sleepy village otherwise untouched by tourism. It is a busy well run site with a programme of lively entertainment in high season. The site has 172 pitches (39 touring pitches), all with electricity (10A). The pitches have good shade, are all separated by mature trees and hedges and are reasonable in size, although access to some may prove difficult for larger units.

Facilities

Two modern toilet blocks include washbasins mainly in cabins. Units for disabled visitors. Washing machines and dryers. Fridge hire. Shop (all season). Smart bar/restaurant and takeaway (all 2/7-27/8). Attractive, heated outdoor pool and paddling pool (20/5-10/9). Indoor pool (all season). Large inflatable slide. Sauna, jacuzzi. Gym. Tennis, minigolf (both free in low season). Games room. Play area. Visiting hairdressing salon. WiFi (charged). Children's club in high season. Off site: Village shop 100 m. Riding and fishing 5 km. Golf 15 km.

Open: 2 April - 24 September.

Directions

From Les Sables-d'Olonne take D949 (La Rochelle) towards Talmont-St Hilaire and Luçon; 7 km. after Talmont turn right on D70 to St Hilaire-la-Forêt. Site is on left before village centre. GPS: 46.44862, -1.52626

Charges guide

Per unit incl. 2 persons and electricity	€ 17.00 - € 28.00
extra person	€ 5.00 - € 8.00
child (under 7 yrs)	€ 3.00 - € 4.00

For latest campsite news, availability and prices visit

alanrogers.com

Saint Hilaire-la-Forêt

Camping des Batardières

2, rue des Batardières, F-85440 Saint Hilaire-la-Forêt (Vendée) T: 02 51 33 33 85.

alanrogers.com/FR85390

Camping des Batardières is a haven of tranquillity on the edge of an unspoilt village, yet just 5 km. from the sea. It is an attractive, unsophisticated little site, lovingly maintained by its owners for more than 25 years. Many visitors return year after year. There are 75 good-sized pitches (a few up to 130 sq.m) and all are available for touring units (there are no mobile homes and no tour operators). All have easy access to water and electricity (6A). Otherwise there are few facilities on site.

Facilities

The sanitary block is kept very clean and visitors are encouraged to keep it that way (no shoes in the shower cubicles, for instance). Some washbasin and shower combination cubicles. Laundry facilities. Tennis court. Play area and field for games, kite-flying etc. Not suitable for American motorhomes or twin-axle caravans. Off site: Village shop and bar 200 m. Jard-sur-Mer 5 km. Bicycle hire 3 km. Fishing 5 km. Golf 16 km.

Open: 1 July - 1 September.

Directions

From Les Sables-d'Olonne take D949 (la Rochelle) towards Talmont-St Hilaire and Luçon. 7 km. after Talmont turn right on D70 to St Hilaire-la-Forêt. Site signed to the right approaching village. GPS: 46.4486, -1.5286

Charges 2012

Per unit incl. 2 persons and electricity	€ 23.50
extra person	€ 4.00

No credit cards.

Saint Jean-de-Monts

Camping l'Abri des Pins

Route de Notre-Dame-de-Monts, F-85160 Saint Jean-de-Monts (Vendée) T: 02 51 58 83 86.

E: contact@abridespins.com alanrogers.com/FR85090

L'Abri des Pins is situated on the outskirts of St Jean-de-Monts and is separated from the sea and a long sandy beach by a strip of pine forest. The site has 218 pitches, 30 of which are for touring units, most with electricity and water; they are separated by hedges and most have shade. Seventy pitches have mobile homes and chalets for rent, the rest being occupied by privately-owned mobiles. It has an impressive entrance, good leisure facilities which include a recently added indoor pool and the sanitary blocks are modern and clean. From the site, it is a pleasant 15 minute walk to the beach.

Facilities

The two sanitary blocks have washbasins in cabins, preset showers, basic facilities for babies and disabled visitors. Laundry and dishwashing facilities. Bar/restaurant (July/Aug) with takeaway. Heated indoor and outdoor pools, small pool for children. Sauna and steam room. Gym equipment. Daily children's club (July/Aug). Play area. Games rooms. Tennis court. Pétanque. Bicycle hire arranged. WiFi in bar area (charged). Off site: Bar, restaurant and supermarket 500 m. Beach 700 m.

Open: 15 June - 16 September.

Directions

Site is 4 km. north of St Jean-de-Monts town centre on western side of D38 Notre Dame-de-Monts road, almost opposite Les Places Dorées. GPS: 46.8093, -2.109

Charges guide

Per unit incl. 3 persons and electricity	€ 24.20 - € 36.20
extra person	€ 3.90 - € 6.70

Saint Jean-de-Monts

Siblu Camping le Bois Dormant

168 rue des Sables, F-85160 Saint Jean-de-Monts (Vendée) T: 02 51 58 01 30. E: boisdormant@siblu.fr

alanrogers.com/FR85100

Le Bois Dormant is on the outskirts of the pleasant, modern resort of Saint Jean-de-Monts with its shops, bars, restaurants and market, just 3 km. from the beach. The site is well managed, with a full programme of activities (so it can be noisy, sometimes late at night). Parents of young children should be aware that there is a small lake on the site. The site has 500 pitches, most occupied by privately owned mobile homes. Well kept hedges and mature trees give shade and privacy, although some more open pitches are also available for sun lovers. This site can be expected to be very busy for most of the season, with many organised activities for children of all ages.

Facilities

Four sanitary blocks offer washbasins in cabins, baby baths and toilets. Facilities for disabled visitors. Washing machines and dryers. Small shop. Bar/restaurant, also serves takeaway snacks. Large swimming pool, paddling pool, flume and water slides (no Bermuda style shorts). Games room. Play areas. Boules. Multisports pitch and tennis courts. Gas barbecues only. WiFi (charged). Off site: All the facilities of the site's larger, busier sister site, Le Bois Masson. Beach 3 km. Golf 5 km.

Open: 7 April - 16 September.

Directions

Site is well signed from roundabout at southeast end of the St Jean-de-Monts bypass (CD38). Follow signs off the roundabout to 'centre ville' and site is about 500 m. on the left. GPS: 46.78549, -2.03075

Charges guide

Per unit incl. up to 6 persons and electricity	€ 13.00 - € 34.00

For latest campsite news, availability and prices visit

alanrogers.com

Saint Jean-de-Monts

Camping Acapulco

Avenue des Epines, F-85160 Saint Jean-de-Monts (Vendée) T: 02 51 54 33 87. E: info@sunmarina.com

alanrogers.com/FR85220

Ideal for family beach holidays, this large, friendly site is just 600 m. from the beach. Most of the 450 pitches here are taken by mobile homes; at present there are 40 available for touring, although some of these are destined for more mobiles. The few existing touring pitches, which have electricity and water nearby, are of average size on grass and divided by hedges. There is an excellent pool complex with waterslides, a children's pool, an imaginative new balnéo area and a sunbathing terrace. Adjacent to this is a spacious bar/restaurant. Acapulco is midway between the popular resort of St Jean-de-Monts and the more laid-back Saint Hilaire-de-Riez; as a result the opportunities for shopping and eating out are numerous. The busy fishing port of Saint Gilles Croix-de-Vie, a little further south, has quayside bars and restaurants, pedestrianised streets and a thriving marina. Fashionable Les Sables d'Olonne, famous for its superb sandy beach and its great range of shops, bars and restaurants, is an easy drive away. The more adventurous might choose a day out to visit le Puy du Fou, an amazing historical theme park, or to take out a punt or canoe on the waterways of La Venise Verte.

Facilities

Three sanitary blocks are clean and include washbasins in cabins and preset showers. Facilities for disabled visitors. Washing machines and dryers. Shop, takeaway and bar/restaurant. Heated, open-air pool complex. Play area. Tennis. Cycle hire. WiFi over site (charged). Children's club, activities and entertainment plus excursions (July/Aug). Off site: Shopping centre 400 m. Sandy beach 600 m. Riding 2 km. Fishing, sailing and golf 6 km. St Jean-de-Monts 6 km. St Hilaire-de-Riez 8 km.

Open: 1 May - 11 September.

Directions

Saint Jean-de-Monts is 55 km. northwest of La Roche-sur-Yon. The site is off the D38 St Jean-de-Monts - Saint Gilles road at Orouët. At mini-roundabout by l'Oasis hotel/restaurant turn southwest signed les Mouettes and campsite. Site is on left in 2 km. GPS: 46.7637, -2.009

Charges guide

Per unit incl. 3 persons and electricity	€ 25.00 - € 35.00
extra person	€ 9.00

WWW.SUNMARINA.COM

SUN MARINA: 3 FIVE STAR CAMPSITES IN THE VENDÉE.

For you family holidays, discover our campsites at the Atlantic coast with a waterpark, toboggan, spa, bar, animations, 100% wifi.

Groupe **SUN MARINA** - 3 campings***** en Vendée • 201 Avenue de le Forêt 85270 SAINT HILAIRE DE RIEZ • Tél : 0033 (0)2 51 54 33 87 • info@sunmarina.com

We can book this site for you Call 01580 214000 alanrogers travel

Saint Jean-de-Monts

Camping les Places Dorées

Route de Notre-Dame-de-Monts, F-85160 Saint Jean-de-Monts (Vendée) T: 02 51 59 02 93.
E: contact@placesdorees.com **alanrogers.com/FR85280**

Les Places Dorées is, in high season, a busy, popular site with a lively programme of activities and entertainment. At other times it is quieter, but still has plenty to offer. There are 288 grassy pitches, of which just 60 are available for touring units, the quietest being towards the back of the site. Those nearer the leisure complex can be noisy in high season with the bar and disco closing late. Pitches are separated by hedges and there is some shade. A 20 minute walk will take you to a long sandy beach.

Facilities

Three traditional toilet blocks offer preset showers and washbasins in cubicles. Facilities for disabled visitors. Laundry facilities. Bread to order. Bar/restaurant, snack bar and takeaway. Outdoor pool complex. Covered, heated pool, spa facilities, gym. Multisports pitch. Entertainment and children's club (July/Aug). Bicycle hire arranged. WiFi in bar area (charged). Facilities at L'Abri des Pins (opposite) may be used. Max. 1 small dog. Off site: Beach 800 m. on foot, 2 km. by road.

Open: 11 June - 11 September.

Directions

Site is 4 km. north of St Jean-de-Monts on the D38 St Jean-de-Monts - Notre Dames-de-Monts road on the eastern side, almost opposite L'Abri des Pins. GPS: 46.80993, -2.10992

Charges guide

Per unit incl. 3 persons and electricity	€ 24.20 - € 36.20
No credit cards.	

For latest campsite news, availability and prices visit

alanrogers.com

Saint Jean-de-Monts

Camping la Yole

Chemin des Bosses, Orouet, F-85160 Saint Jean-de-Monts (Vendée) T: 02 51 58 67 17.

E: contact@la-yole.com **alanrogers.com/FR85150**

La Yole is an attractive and well run site, two kilometres from a sandy beach. It offers 369 pitches, some of which are occupied by tour operators and mobile homes to rent. There are 180 touring pitches, most with shade and separated by bushes and trees. A newer area at the rear of the site is a little more open. All the pitches are of at least 100 sq.m. and have electricity (10A), water and drainage. The pool complex includes an attractive outdoor pool, a paddling pool, slide and an indoor heated pool with jacuzzi. There are also new gym facilities. Entertainment is organised in high season. This is a clean and tidy site, ideal for families with children and you will receive a helpful and friendly welcome.

Facilities

Two toilet blocks include washbasins in cabins and facilities for disabled visitors and babies. A third block has a baby room. Laundry facilities. Shop (15/5-5/9). Bar, restaurant and takeaway (1/5-15/9). Outdoor pool and paddling pool. Indoor heated pool with jacuzzi (all season, no shorts). Gym centre. Play area. Club room. Tennis. Games room. Entertainment in high season. WiFi (charged). Gas barbecues only. Off site: Beach, bus service, bicycle hire 2 km. Riding 3 km. Fishing, golf and watersports 6 km.

Open: 2 April - 21 September.

Directions

Site is signed off the D38, 6 km. south of St Jean-de-Monts in the village of Orouet. Coming from St Jean-de-Monts turn right at l'Oasis restaurant towards Mouette and follow signs to site. GPS: 46.75659, -2.00792

Charges guide

Per unit incl. 2 persons and electricity	€ 16.00 - € 31.00
extra person	€ 3.70 - € 6.80
child (under 9 yrs)	free - € 5.50
dog (max. 1)	€ 4.00 - € 5.00

Camping Cheques accepted.

We can book this site for you! Call 01580 214000 alan rogers ◗ travel

Hot Spot WiFi

Camping La Yole ★★★★

Camping Cheque

Wake up to the sound of birdsong in a wooded park of 17 acres with four star comfort. Space, security, informal atmosphere: la yole, tucked away between fields and pine trees, only 2 km from the beach.

– Chemin des Bosses - Orouet - F 85160 Saint Jean de Monts –
– Tel: 0033 251 58 67 17 - Fax: 0033 251 59 05 35 –
– contact@la-yole.com / www.la-yole.com –

For latest campsite news, availability and prices visit
alanrogers.com

Saint Jean-de-Monts
Camping Caravaning le Bois Joly

46 route de Notre-Dame-de-Monts, B.P. 507, F-85165 Saint Jean-de-Monts (Vendée) T: 02 51 59 11 63.
E: campingboisjoly@wanadoo.fr alanrogers.com/FR85780

This is an attractive, family run holiday site with indoor and outdoor pool complexes and 385 pitches, most of which are fully serviced. Of these 202 are taken by mobile homes and chalets, leaving 183 good sized, hedged pitches with 10A electric hook-ups for tourists. Grassy and level, these are served by tarmac roads and four fresh, clean, modern, toilet blocks. A good family holiday location, there are lots of activities and entertainment in July and August. The indoor pool is open all season, the L-shaped outdoor pool complex has a 'menhirs' theme and attractive flower beds. There are four toboggans, a paddling pool and a raised solarium deck. On site there are several small playgrounds for younger children, plus a very large and comprehensive adventure playground. The river behind the site offers opportunities for fishing and canoeing.

Facilities

Four modern toilet blocks with controllable showers, washbasins in cubicles. Facilities for babies and disabled visitors. Laundry facilities. Motorcaravan service point. Bar and snack bar, takeaway (15/6-15/9). Indoor pool (all season). Outdoor pools (15/6-15/9). Sauna, solarium and gym (July/Aug, charged). Playgrounds. Multisports court. Pétanque. TV room. Games room. Entertainment and canoeing on site in July/Aug. River fishing. No charcoal barbecues allowed. No double-axle caravans accepted. Off site: Riding and tennis 500 m. Bicycle hire, beach and boat launching 1.5 km. Shops within 2 km. Golf 2 km.

Open: 7 April - 30 September.

Directions

Site is at the northern end of St Jean-de-Monts, on the eastern side of the D38, about 300 m. north of junction (roundabout) with the D51.
GPS: 46.79915, -2.0744

Charges guide

Per unit incl. 2 persons	
and electricity	€ 18.00 - € 32.00
extra person	€ 2.00 - € 5.00
child (1-7 yrs)	€ 1.00 - € 2.50
dog	€ 1.50 - € 3.00

Camping Qualité · ancv

LE BOIS JOLY
46 Rte de Notre-Dame - BP 507
85165 ST-JEAN DE MONTS Cedex
Tél. 00 33 (0)2 51 59 11 63
Fax 00 33 (0)2 51 59 11 06
www.camping-leboisjoly.com
e-mail : campingboisjoly@wanadoo.fr

OPEN FROM APRIL TO SEPTEMBER
· Aquatic complex   · Bar
· SPA   · Sauna
· Fitness   · Sports ground
· Entertainment   · Restaurant
RENTAL OF MOBILE-HOMES
and CHALETS
(per week, weekends and 10 nights)
LOW SEASON DISCOUNT

WiFi

Saint Jean-de-Monts
Camping la Forêt

190 chemin de la Rive, F-85160 Saint Jean-de-Monts (Vendée) T: 02 51 58 84 63.
E: camping-la-foret@wanadoo.fr alanrogers.com/FR85360

Camping la Forêt is an attractive, well run site with a friendly family atmosphere, thanks to the hard working owners, M. and Mme. Jolivet. It provides just 61 pitches with 46 for touring units. They are of a reasonable size and surrounded by mature hedges; all have water and electricity, and some also have drainage. A variety of trees provides shade to every pitch. There are 15 mobile homes for rent and one tour operator on site (11 pitches), but their presence is not intrusive and the site has a quiet and relaxed atmosphere.

Facilities

The central toilet block provides hot showers and washbasins in cubicles. Laundry and dishwashing facilities. Baby bath. Facilities for disabled visitors. Motorcaravan waste tanks emptied on request. Basics sold in reception, including fresh bread. Takeaway (15/5-15/9). Small heated swimming pool (15/5-15/9). Small TV/games room. WiFi over site (charged). Play area. Bicycle hire. Only gas and electric barbecues allowed, communal barbecue in centre of site. Not suitable for American motorhomes. Off site: Beach 400 m.

Open: 1 May - 28 September.

Directions

The site is 6 km. north of St Jean just off the D38 towards Notre Dame-de-Monts. At southern end of Notre Dame, turn west at sign for site and Plage de Pont d'Yeu. Bear left and site is on left in about 200 m. GPS: 46.80807, -2.11384

Charges guide

Per unit incl. 2 persons	
and electricity	€ 17.00 - € 31.90
extra person	€ 3.50 - € 5.00

For latest campsite news, availability and prices visit
alanrogers.com

Saint Jean-de-Monts
Campéole Dornier

Route de la Tonnelle, F-85161 Saint Jean-de-Monts (Vendée) T: 02 51 58 81 16. E: dornier@campeole.com
alanrogers.com/FR85960

Le Dornier is an extensive site, located on land belonging to the French forestry commission and close to the popular resort of St Jean-de-Monts. The site has direct access to a superb sandy beach and also has a good sized heated swimming pool. The 232 touring pitches, all with electricity (6A) available, are mostly sandy and of a reasonable size. A range of chalets, fully equipped bungalow tents and mobile homes are available for rent including some models specially adapted for campers with disabilities. The site has a small bar and snack bar (July/Aug) just along the road. There is also a small supermarket and a large bar and restaurant close by. The site can become quite lively in high season with a daily children's club and a wide range of daytime activities and evening entertainment, including concerts and discos. However, touring pitches are well scattered on this vast site, so it should be possible to ask to be located well away from these events if desired.

Facilities
Three sanitary blocks have been refurbished to a very high standard with modern preset showers, washbasins in cubicles, and excellent facilities for children and disabled visitors. Hot water for dishwashing and laundry sinks. Washing machines and dryers. Motorcaravan service point. Direct beach access. Heated swimming pool and paddling pool (8/5-11/09, supervised July/Aug). Bicycle hire. Archery (July/Aug). Multisports court. Bouncy castle. Snack bar adjacent (July/Aug). Play area. Activities and entertainment programme (July/Aug). Tourist information. WiFi around reception (charged). Mobile homes, chalets and equipped tents for rent. Gas or electric barbecues only. Off site: Beach, golf and riding 3 km.

Open: 1 April - 11 September.

Directions
The site is 6 km. north of St Jean-de-Monts on the D38 towards Notre Dame-de-Monts. Turn west at the roundabout at Les Tonnelles where site is signed and is on right in 300 m. GPS: 46.8094, -2.1208

Charges guide

Per unit incl. 2 persons	
and electricity	€ 17.10 - € 26.60
extra person	€ 4.50 - € 7.10
child (2-6 yrs)	free - € 4.40

Campéole
CAMPSITES AND RENTALS

PAYS DE LA LOIRE

Dornier ★★★★

Close to Saint-Jean-de-Monts, swimming pool, direct access to fine sandy beach. Amenities, pitches and accommodations of high quality.

85160 St Jean de Monts · Tel.: +33-251-5881-16 · www.campeole.co.uk / dornier@campeole.com

Saint Jean-de-Monts
Camping Plein Sud

246 route de Notre-Dame-de-Monts, F-85160 Saint Jean-de-Monts (Vendée) T: 02 51 59 10 40.
E: info@campingpleinsud.com **alanrogers.com/FR85590**

Plein Sud is a small, friendly site, immaculately kept and with a very French ambience. Of the 110 grassy pitches separated by hedges, 40 are available for touring. They are of a reasonable size and all have electricity and water; most also have drainage. Twenty pitches have site-owned mobile homes, cabins or tents for rent, the rest have privately-owned mobiles. The touring pitches at the far end of this long, narrow site are particularly peaceful. Only 800 m. away, via another campsite across the road and through a strip of forest, is a long stretch of safe, sandy beach.

Facilities
Two well maintained sanitary blocks provide pushbutton showers and washbasins in cabins. Good facilities for disabled visitors. Baby room. Dishwashing and laundry facilities. Small bar with TV and terrace (July/Aug). Bread and milk to order daily (high season). Takeaway (Tue-Sun). Heated pool with paddling pool (15/5-15/9). Play areas. Bicycle hire. Children's club (July/Aug).

Open: 1 May - 15 September.

Directions
Site is about 4 km. north of Saint Jean-de-Monts on the D38 towards Notre Dame-de-Monts, on the right almost opposite Camping L'Abri des Pins. GPS: 46.809805, -2.109557

Charges guide

Per unit incl. 2 persons	
and electricity	€ 14.00 - € 29.00

For latest campsite news, availability and prices visit
alanrogers.com

Saint Jean-de-Monts

Campéole

Campéole les Sirènes

Avenue des Demoiselles, F-85164 Saint Jean-de-Monts (Vendée) T: 02 51 58 01 31.
E: sirenes@campeole.com **alanrogers.com/FR85970**

Les Sirènes is a large campsite located in the forest behind the popular resort of St Jean-de-Monts. The nearest beach, just 700 m. away, is long and sandy, shelving very gradually into the sea. Pitches here vary considerably; some, ideal for tents, are among the tall pine trees, whilst others are on flat ground but still with shade provided by a variety of younger trees. Most have electrical connections and water taps nearby. A number of equipped tents and mobile homes (including specially adapted models for disabled visitors) are available for rent. On-site amenities include a swimming pool and separate children's pool, a multi-sport pitch and archery. This is a lively site in high season with plenty going on, including a daily children's club and regular sporting competitions. Evenings, however, are generally quiet, with just a weekly 'soirée dansante'. Les Sirènes has a good location with easy pedestrian access to the beach, and to lively Saint Jean-de-Monts with shops, bars and restaurants plus a daily market.

Facilities

Several small sanitary blocks are fairly basic, but a programme of refurbishment has begun. Some modern preset showers and mainly open-style washbasins (a few in cabins) with only cold water. Washing machines and dryers. Shop, takeaway (July/Aug). Heated swimming pools with paddling pool (1/06-11/09, supervised July/Aug). Multisports pitch. Bicycle hire. Bouncy castle. Archery. Play area. Children's club and activities (July/Aug). Tourist information. WiFi (charged) around reception. Mobile homes and equipped tents for rent. Off site: Restaurant at site entrance. Beach 700 m.

Open: 1 April - 11 September.

Directions

From southern end of D38/D38bis St Jean bypass turn north on D38 Route des Sables towards town. At next roundabout go left on D123 Ave. Valentin, signed La Plage. Bear right at second roundabout, then after 1.2 km. turn right at roundabout along Ave des Mimosas into Ave des Demoiselles. The site is on right in 400 m. GPS: 46.780083, -2.055881

Charges guide

Per unit incl. 2 persons and electricity	€ 17.10 - € 26.60
extra person	€ 4.50 - € 7.10
child (2-6 yrs)	free - € 4.40

Campéole

CAMPSITES AND RENTALS

VENDÉE

Les Sirènes ***

Beautiful site, new amenities, swimming pool, beach and shops at walking distance. Pitches and accommodations of high quality.

85164 St Jean de Monts - Tel.: +33-251-5801-31 - www.campeole.co.uk / sirenes@campeole.com

We can book this site for you! alanrogers ◉ travel
Call 01580 214000

Saint Julien-des-Landes

Castel Camping Caravaning la Garangeoire

F-85150 Saint Julien-des-Landes (Vendée) T: 02 51 46 65 39. E: info@garangeoire.com
alanrogers.com/FR85040

La Garangeoire is a stunning campsite, situated some 15 km. inland near the village of St Julien-des-Landes. Set in 200 hectares of parkland surrounding the small château of la Garangeoire, of which there is an outstanding view as you approach through the gates. With a spacious, relaxed atmosphere, the main camping areas are on either side of the old road which is edged with mature trees. The 356 pitches, all named rather than numbered, are individually hedged, some with shade. They are well spaced and are especially large (most 150-200 sq.m), all with electricity (16A) and some with water and drainage.

Facilities

First class sanitary facilities have washbasins in cabins, facilities for babies and disabled campers. Laundry facilities. Motorcaravan service point. Shop, restaurant and takeaway (10/5-22/9) with bars and terrace. Pool complex with a new covered pool and a children's pool. Play equipment. Games room. Tennis courts. Multisports court. Bicycle hire. Minigolf. Archery. Riding (July/Aug). WiFi (charged). Off site: Lac de Jaunay 2 km. Golf 8 km.

Open: 7 April - 24 September.

Directions

Site is signed from St Julien; entrance is to the east off the D21 road, 2.5 km. north of St Julien-des-Landes. GPS: 46.663648, -1.713395

Charges 2012

Per unit incl. 2 persons and electricity	€ 17.50 - € 37.00
extra person	€ 4.50 - € 7.90
Camping Cheques accepted.	

For latest campsite news, availability and prices visit
alanrogers.com

Saint Julien-des-Landes

Village de la Guyonnière

La Guyonnière, F-85150 Saint Julien-des-Landes (Vendée) T: 02 51 46 62 59. E: info@laguyonniere.com

alanrogers.com/FR85260

La Guyonnière is a spacious, rural site. It is Dutch owned but English is spoken and all visitors are made very welcome. The pitches are arranged on eight different fields, each being reasonably level and seven having a toilet block. There are 270 mostly large pitches (225 sq.m) with a mix of sun and shade. Some are open, others are separated by a tree and a few bushes. All have access to electricity connections and 86 are occupied by mobile homes and chalets. A new pool complex includes an outdoor pool with a 'wild water river' and a heated indoor pool with a waterfall. Bar and restaurant facilities are housed in original farm buildings, attractively converted. Entertainment is provided in the bar on high season evenings. This is a perfect place for families, with large play areas on sand and grass, and a paddling pond with shower. Visitors with disabilities are made especially welcome with a range of facilities (for example, a lift in the pool and special scooters to rent). Being in the country, it is ideal for cyclists and walkers with many signed routes from the site. A pleasant 500 m. walk takes you to the Jaunay Lake where fishing is possible (permits from the village), canoeing (life jackets from reception) and pedaloes to hire. There are no tour operators and, needless to say, no road noise. This site is popular for many reasons, the main one being the relaxed atmosphere.

Facilities

Modern toilet blocks. Most cubicles are quite small. Washbasins are in cubicles. Provision for disabled visitors (including lift in the pool, scooters to rent). Laundry facilities. Shop. Bar with TV and pool table (both 1/5-15/9). Restaurant (15/6-15/9). Pizzeria with takeaway (1/5-29/9). New pool complex with outdoor pool and 'wild water river' and covered pool (1/5-20/9) with waterfall. Paddling pool. Play areas, sand pit. Tennis. Bicycle hire. Car wash. WiFi. Off site: Riding 3 km. Golf 8 km. Beaches 10 km.

Open: 25 April - 25 September.

Directions

Site is signed off the D12 road (La Mothe Achard - St Gilles Croix-de-Vie), about 4 km. west of St Julien-des-Landes. The site is about 1 km. from the main road. GPS: 46.65273, -1.74987

Charges guide

Per unit incl. 2 persons	
and electricity	€ 18.00 - € 36.90
extra person	€ 4.90 - € 6.00
child (3-9 yrs)	€ 3.30 - € 3.90
dog	€ 3.50

Less 10-20% outside high season.

We can book this site for you! Call 01580 214000 alan rogers travel

Camping Vendée ★ ★ ★ ★ ★

VILLAGE de la GUYONNIÈRE

A beautiful, rural campsite with a tranquil atmosphere within 15 minutes' drive of large sandy beaches and 400 m from a large lake. The campsite has many quality amenities and the green spacious pitches, which are up to 225 m², are unique! Children love to see the many animals around the site.

NEW: outdoor pool with contra flow river!

The Vendée is a sunny destination - only a half day's drive from the ferry ports - as it has as many hours of sunshine as the French Rivièra!

Camping Qualité

85150 St Julien des Landes
Tel. 0033 251 46 62 59 Fax 0033 251 46 62 89
Internet: www.laguyonniere.com
E-mail: info@laguyonniere.com

For latest campsite news, availability and prices visit

alanrogers.com

Saint Julien-des-Landes
Flower Camping la Bretonnière

F-85150 Saint Julien-des-Landes (Vendée) T: 02 51 46 62 44. E: camp.la-bretonniere@wanadoo.fr

alanrogers.com/FR85850

An attractive, modern site on a family farm surrounded by beautiful peaceful countryside, this site is sure to please. With 150 pitches in an area of six hectares, there is plenty of space for everyone. There are 101 touring pitches, 28 tour operator tents and 17 Alpine style chalets, spread around several fields, some quite open, others with some shade from perimeter hedges. The grassy pitches are all of a really generous size with electricity (12A). Two swimming pools, one covered, the other outdoor, are surrounded by a pleasant terrace, with the bar and reception close by. Also on site is a lovely large fishing lake (unfenced) with a pleasant walk all around. The bar and takeaway operate in July/August, ices and basic tinned food items are available from reception and there is a motorcaravan service point. A kids' club runs in July and August. The village of Saint Julien-des-Landes is 2.5 km. and the larger town of La Mothe-Achard is 7 km.

Facilities

Three modern, clean and well appointed toilet blocks are spread around the site, with baby rooms and facilities for disabled visitors at two blocks (may be closed April/May). Motorcaravan service point. Bar, snack bar and takeaway (July/Aug). Covered swimming pool, outdoor pool and wellness centre (June-Sept). Free WiFi around bar and reception. Playgrounds. Games/TV room. Tennis. Boules. Basketball. Volleyball. Indoor and outdoor football pitches. Fishing lake. Caravan storage. Off site: Paintball and tree-climbing adventure trail 2 km. Village 2.5 km. Riding 3 km.

Open: 1 April - 15 October.

Directions

Saint Julien-des-Landes is 18 km. northeast of Les Sables-d'Olonne and 5 km. northwest of La Mothe-Achard. From La Mothe-Achard take D12 west towards Bretignolles-sur-Mer, pass through St Julien and after 2 km. take first turn right (site signed). Site is 500 m. GPS: 46.64463, -1.73328

Charges guide

Per unit incl. 2 persons and electricity	€ 14.00 - € 26.90
extra person	€ 3.50 - € 4.50

www.la-bretonniere.com

Saint Julien-des-Landes
Yelloh! Village Château La Forêt

Route de Martinet, F-85150 Saint Julien-des-Landes (Vendée) T: 02 51 46 62 11.
E: camping@domainelaforet.com **alanrogers.com/FR85820**

Set in the tranquil and beautiful natural parkland surrounding an 18th-century château, this lovely site has 200 large pitches, of which 167 are for touring units. There are five units for rent and 28 pitches are occupied by tour operators. All are on grass and fully serviced including 6A electricity; some are in shady woodland and others, for sun worshippers, are more open. The camping area is only a small part of the 50-hectare estate, with a mix of woodland, open meadows and fishing lakes, all accessible to campers. The outbuildings have been converted and include a bar and restaurant in the old stables.

Facilities

Two large, good quality sanitary blocks offer washbasins in cubicles, with good provision for babies and disabled campers. Laundry. Bar/restaurant with TV. Two heated outdoor swimming pools. Evening entertainment, children's clubs and disco (July/Aug). Adventure playground. Tennis. Boules. Fishing lakes. 6-hole swing golf course. Canoeing. WiFi. Only gas barbecues permitted. No double-axle caravans. Off site: Equestrian centre, bicycle hire 200 m. ATM at La Mothe-Achard 5 km.

Open: 15 May - 15 September.

Directions

St Julien-des-Landes is about 25 km. west of La Roche-sur-Yon, northwest of La Mothe-Achard. From La Mothe-Achard take D12 to St Julien, turn northeast on D55 at crossroads towards Martinet. Site is on left almost immediately (signed). GPS: 46.6432, -1.71198

Charges guide

Per unit incl. 2 persons and electricity	€ 17.70 - € 33.20
extra person	€ 3.10 - € 6.30

For latest campsite news, availability and prices visit

alanrogers.com

Saint Laurent-sur-Sèvre
Camping le Rouge Gorge

Route de la verrie, F-85290 Saint Laurent-sur-Sèvre (Vendée) T: 02 51 67 86 39.
E: campinglerougegorge@wanadoo.fr **alanrogers.com/FR85890**

A family run site, le Rouge Gorge has 72 touring pitches, plus some units for rent and privately-owned caravans and chalets. The site does accept a small number of workers' units. Slightly sloping and undulating pitches are on grass in a garden-like setting and a small wildlife pond (fenced) is in the centre of the site. It would make a suitable base from which to visit the spectacles of Puy de Fou and the steam railway which runs from Mortagne-sur-Sèvre to Les Herbiers. This is also an excellent stopover for those heading to and from southern France and Spain, or the ski-resorts. The largest Japanese garden in Europe, at Maulevrier, is worth a visit.

Facilities

Two toilet blocks with washbasins in cubicles. Facilities for disabled campers and babies. Washing machine and dryer. Bar. Shop (1/7-31/8). Snack bar/takeaway (15/6-15/9). Heated swimming pool (5/5-30/9). Children's club and occasional evening entertainment (July-Aug). Boules. Bouncy castle. Trampoline. Playground. No charcoal barbecues. WiFi. Off site: Fishing 200 m. Riding 2 km.

Open: 1 March - 30 December.

Directions

St Laurent-sur-Sèvre is about 10 km. due south of Cholet, just south of the N149. Site is on D111 west of town towards la Verrie, entrance at top of hill on right. GPS: 46.95781, -0.90309

Charges guide

Per unit incl. 2 persons	€ 17.50 - € 22.70
extra person	€ 3.90

Saint Michel-en-l'Herm
Camping la Dive

12 route de la Mer, F-85580 Saint Michel-en-l'Herm (Vendée) T: 02 51 30 26 94.
E: camping-la-dive@wanadoo.fr **alanrogers.com/FR85013**

Camping la Dive can be found south of the popular resort of La Tranche-sur-Mer, close to the broad, sweeping bay of l'Aiguillon-sur-Mer. The eight-hectare site is located on the edge of the pleasant village of St Michel-en-l'Herm. The beach can be accessed in around five minutes by car. The 130 touring pitches here are of average size, grassy, part shaded and have 6A electricity. A wide range of mobile homes and chalets are available for rent in a new area of the site. On-site amenities include an outdoor swimming pool with slides and a flume (1/4-30/9), a minigolf course and pony rides. There is a good range of shops in the village (500 m).

Facilities

Three toilet blocks with facilities for children and disabled visitors. Laundry. Bar, restaurant and takeaway (1/6-30/8). Swimming pool. Paddling pool. Jacuzzi and sauna. Gym. Games room. Bouncy castle. Multisports pitch. Boules. Bicycle hire. Pony rides. Minigolf. Children's zoo. Play area. Tourist information. Entertainment and activity programme (July/Aug). Mobile homes, roulottes and chalets for rent. Off site: Shops in village 500 m.

Open: 1 April - 30 September.

Directions

St Michel-en-l'Herm is around 8 km. east of l'Aiguillon-sur-Mer. From there, head east on D746. The site is 500 m. from the village centre and is well signed. Beware of tight turn into entrance. GPS: 46.34912, -1.24786

Charges guide

Per unit incl. 2 persons and electricity	€ 17.20 - € 23.40
extra person	€ 4.20

Talmont-Saint-Hilaire
Yelloh! Village le Littoral

Le Porteau, F-85440 Talmont-Saint-Hilaire (Vendée) T: 02 51 22 04 64. E: info@campinglelittoral.com
alanrogers.com/FR85250

One hundred metres from the sea, five minutes from Les Sables-d'Olonne, le Littoral is situated on the south Vendée coast. It has been fully modernised over recent years by the Boursin family. The site's 484 pitches are mainly used for mobile homes and chalets, but there are 85 touring pitches, hedged, of a good size and all with water, electricity and drainage. The site has a heated outdoor pool complex with outdoor and indoor pools. The minimarket, bar and restaurant are open all season with frequent themed evenings and lots of entertainment and activities in high season.

Facilities

Three sanitary blocks have British and Turkish style WCs, showers and washbasins in cubicles. Baby rooms. Facilities for disabled visitors. Laundry facilities. Fridge hire. Shop, bar, restaurant and takeaway, pizzeria and crêperie. Indoor pool. Outdoor pool complex (14/5-9/9). Bicycle hire. Multisports court. Tennis. Play areas. Games room with TV. Children's club (all season). Activities and excursions. WiFi (charged). Mobile homes and chalets for hire. Off site: Sea fishing 200 m. Riding 500 m. Beach 3 km.

Open: 6 April - 9 September.

Directions

From La Roche-sur-Yon on A87/D160 turn east on ring road and continue on D949 towards Talmont. Soon after end of dual carriageway, site is signed to the south opposite a market garden; in 3.5 km. turn right to site in 300 m. GPS: 46.451633, -1.702017

Charges guide

Per unit incl. 2 persons and electricity	€ 15.00 - € 41.00
extra person	€ 5.00 - € 6.00

We can book this site for you! **alanrogers** ◉ travel
Call 01580 214000

For latest campsite news, availability and prices visit
alanrogers.com

Discover wonderful outdoor holidays in France!

With Vacances Krusoë, discover a new way of enjoying your holidays in comfort, and come stay in a fantastic place with family or friends.

- 27 campsites in France
- The same quality standards in each location
- Our fully equipped mobile homes are all less than 5 years old, with decks and sleeping accommodations for 2 to 6 people
- A wide choice of free activities and entertainment at select campgrounds
- 3 environments to choose from: garden, active or village

Book online at **www.alanrogers.com/travel**
or call us on **01580 214000**
Find all our promotions on **www.vacances-krusoe.com**

PROJET ATLANTIQUE - N11305 - ATOUT France : IM085100026 - Groupe BENETEAU - S.A.S. au capital de 100 000 € Siret 449 625 920 000 11 - R.C.S. La Roche sur Yon - TVA intracommunautaire FR 40449625920.

vacances
Krusoë
L'art de vivre au grand air

On the Atlantic coast, between the châteaux of the Loire Valley and the Bordeaux vineyards, lies Poitou-Charentes, one of the sunniest parts of the French western coast. Its mild climate – 2,250 hours of sunshine per year – makes it popular with visitors from early spring to late autumn.

DÉPARTEMENTS: 16 CHARENTE, 17 CHARENTE-MARITIME, 79 DEUX SÈVRES, 86 VIENNE

MAJOR CITIES: POITIERS, LA ROCHELLE, COGNAC

Three hundred miles of coastline with fine sandy beaches backed by fragrant pine forests, lively resorts such as La Rochelle and Royan, and the islands of Oléron, Aix and Ré attract many holiday makers, particularly the French themselves. The scenery inland is in marked contrast: vast horizons and wooded valleys, the vineyards of Cognac, the Poitou fens and Marais Poitevin, the soothing tranquillity of canals, the valley of Vienne and the foothills of Charente.

Farming is important to the economy; wheat, corn and cattle are raised. Industries produce machinery, chemicals and dairy products. The region is renowned as the home of Cognac – such famous names as Martell, Hennessy and Rémy Martin line the river Charente around the towns of Cognac and Jarnac where the spirit is distilled.

The capital of the region and capital of the Vienne département, is the city of Poitier. Situated on high ground at the confluence of the Clain and Boivre rivers, the city commands the so-called gate of Poitou, a gap 44 miles (71 km) wide between the mountains south of the Loire River and the Massif Central that serves as the connecting link between northern and southern France.

Places of interest

Angoulême: hilltop town surrounded by ramparts, cathedral, Renaissance château.

Cognac: the most celebrated 'eau de vie' in the world, cellars, Valois castle.

Marais Poitevin: marshes also known as the 'Green Venice'.

Poitiers: Palais de Justice, Notre Dame la Grande Romanesque church, old city.

La Rochelle: port, Porte de la Grosse Horloge (clock gate), Museum of the New World.

Saint Savin: 17th-century abbey, mural painting.

Cuisine of the region

Fish predominates, both fresh water (eel, trout, pike) and sea water (shrimps, mussels, oysters).

Bouilliture (bouilleture): eel stew with shallots and prunes in Sauvignon white wine.

Boulaigou: thick sweet or savoury pancake.

Bréjaude: cabbage, leek and bacon soup.

Cagouilles: snails from Charente.

Casserons en matelote: squid in red wine sauce with garlic and shallots.

Farcidure: a dumpling (poached or sautéed).

Farci Poitevin: paté of cabbage, spinach and sorrel, encased in cabbage leaves.

Mouclade: mussels cooked in wine, egg yolks and cream, served with Pineau des Charentes.

www.visit-poitou-charentes.com
crt@poitou-charentes-vacances.com
(0)5 49 50 10 50

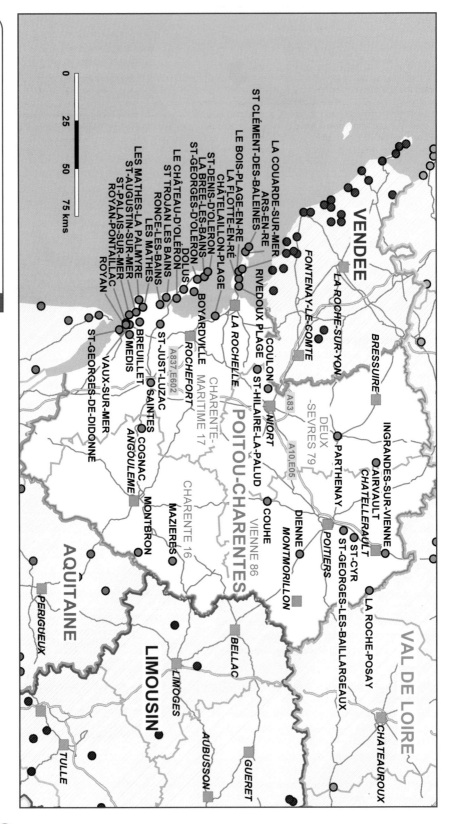

For latest campsite news, availability and prices visit
alanrogers.com

Ars-en-Ré
Camping le Cormoran

Route de Radia, Ars-en-Ré, F-17590 Ile de Ré (Charente-Maritime) T: 05 46 29 46 04. E: info@cormoran.com
alanrogers.com/FR17260

On the outskirts of Ars-en-Ré, le Cormoran offers a quiet rural holiday. Touring pitches vary in size and are a mixture of sand and grass. Large units may be advised to call ahead. There are 33 pitches for touring units (all with 10A electricity) and the clean sanitary facilities are a mix of modern and traditional. A small comfortable bar and restaurant are located next to the pleasant pool. Being close to the local oyster beds and with numerous cycle paths which include routes through a nature reserve, this campsite is popular with families of all ages. Although rural, the campsite is only 500 m. from the sea. During July and August children's clubs and evening entertainment are organised. The village of Ars-en-Ré is only 800 m. away and a local market is held regularly during the season.

Facilities

One traditional toilet block and one modern unit provide good facilities. Washbasins are mainly in cabins. Provision for disabled visitors. Laundry. Motorcaravan services. Bar, restaurant and takeaway meals (4/4-15/9). Swimming pool (unheated). Fitness centre. Tennis. Games room. Play area. Entertainment programme in high season. Bicycle hire. WiFi. Off site: Nearest beach and fishing 500 m. Ars-en-Ré 800 m. Boat launching 1 km. Riding 3 km. Golf 10 km.

Open: 4 April - 26 September.

Directions

Cross the toll bridge from La Rochelle onto the Ile de Ré and continue on D735 to Ars-en-Ré from where site is well signed. GPS: 46.21121, -1.5298

Charges guide

Per unit incl. 2 persons	
and electricity	€ 23.60 - € 32.75
extra person	€ 5.60 - € 13.00
child (1-9 yrs)	€ 3.60 - € 13.00
dog	€ 2.80 - € 5.80

For latest campsite news, availability and prices visit
alanrogers.com

Boyardville

Camping Signol

121 Avenue des Albatros, F-17190 Boyardville (Charente-Maritime) T: 02 51 33 17 00.
E: contact@signol.com **alanrogers.com/FR17600**

Occupying an eight-hectare site, just 800 metres from the sandy beaches, this campsite has plenty to offer. Of the 300 pitches, 107 are for touring and are set amongst high pine trees and one metre high hedges give plenty of shade and privacy; some have sea views. The pitches are generous (80-120 sq.m) although access to some is tight and may not be suitable for larger units. Levelling blocks are required on some. Electricity (6A) is available to all, although long leads are required occasionally as hook-ups can be shared between three or four pitches. There may be a short walk to the water supply. The facilities for children are in a fenced area and include climbing frames, bouncy castle and multisports court. The heated and supervised swimming pools are overlooked by the bar/snack bar. A club for children is organised in high season and treasure hunts and other activities are organised daily. Entertainment for adults is also arranged in high season.

Facilities

Three modern, fully equipped toilet blocks provide washbasins and showers in cubicles. They also include facilities for campers with disabilities, and for children. Laundry. Motorcaravan services. No shop. Bar/snack bar, terrace, takeaway, breakfast service. Two swimming pools (21/5-24/9). Enclosed play area with seats for parents. Children's club (from 1/7). Boules. Evening entertainment (from 1/7). WiFi (free). Dogs are not accepted in July/Aug. Barbecues are not allowed (communal area). Mobile homes and chalets available to hire. Off site: Nearest beach 800 m. Sailing and windsurfing. Fishing. Riding. Cycle and walking trails. St Pierre-d'Oléron (good choice of shops and restaurants and supermarket).

Open: 1 May - 12 September.

Directions

Cross the viaduct and continue on the D26 to Dolus and turn right on D126 signed Boyardville. Continue on this road for 6 km. until the canal bridge at the edge of the town. Cross bridge and turn immediately sharp right along the quayside. Site signed from here. GPS: 45.96807, -1.24456

Charges guide

Per unit incl. 2 persons and electricity	€ 21.00 - € 35.00
extra person	€ 5.00 - € 9.00
child (under 5 yrs)	free - € 6.00
dog (excl. July/Aug)	€ 5.00

Credit cards accepted.
Camping Cheques accepted.

Airvault

Camping de Courte Vallée

8 rue de Courte Vallée, F-79600 Airvault (Deux-Sèvres) T: 05 49 64 70 65.
E: camping@caravanningfrance.com **alanrogers.com/FR79020**

This small and beautifully landscaped site is family run. Set in ten acres of parkland close to the Thouet river, it is within walking distance of Airvault (the birthplace of Voltaire). In the heart of rural France and off the main tourist tracks, the site offers tranquillity and a warm and friendly atmosphere in surroundings maintained to the highest standards. There are 64 grass pitches, many with electricity, water and drainage which makes the site ideal for a long stay to explore the area. Nearby are Puy du Fou, Fontevraud Abbey, Doué la Fontaine zoo and the châteaux of Saumur and Oiron. Caravan storage facilities ensure that many regular campers arrive to find their 'home' washed and sited.

Facilities

A modern unisex block has spacious cubicles for showers and washbasins, and shower and WC cubicles for disabled visitors, all kept to a very high standard of cleanliness. Dishwashing area under cover. Washing machine and dryers. Reception sells 'frites', snacks, a selection of beers and wine and ice cream. Internet access. Swimming pool. Boules. Play area. Caravan storage. Wine tasting events and barbecues. Coffee bar. Off site: Airvault (birthplace of Voltaire) is a 10-15 minute walk. Fishing 300 m. Riding 8 km.

Open: 15 March - 31 October.

Directions

From D938 (Parthenay-Thouars) take D725 Airvault. On approaching village turn left over bridge. At T-junction turn sharp left, second exit at roundabout, left at junction to site on left. Note: caravans are not allowed in village. GPS: 46.833056, -0.148333

Charges guide

Per unit incl. 2 persons and electricity	€ 29.00 - € 33.00
extra person	€ 7.00 - € 8.00
child (under 11 yrs)	€ 3.00 - € 5.00
dog	€ 1.50

No credit cards.

For latest campsite news, availability and prices visit
alanrogers.com

Camp' Atlantique

Des campings à 2 pas de la plage...

CHARENTE-MARITIME

Ile de Ré:
Be charmed by the assets of a peaceful and protected island

Campsite les Peupliers***

Campsite les Peupliers guarantees you a pleasant stay at 800m from the beach and the city centre of Flotte-en-Ré.

RD 735 - 17630 La Flotte-en-Ré

Ile d'Oléron:
The wild delight of an island to be discovered by bike or on foot

Campsite Signol****

You will be charmed by the nature surrounding Campsite Signol, situated at 800m from the beach and Port de Boyardville.

Boyardville - 17190 Saint Georges d'Oléron

CAMP'ATLANTIQUE

Les Plantes de la Brunelle - 85560 LONGEVILLE sur MER
Tél: 0033 (0)2 51 33 17 00 - contact@camp-atlantique.com
www.camp-atlantique.com

Breuillet

Camping Transhumance

Route de Royan, F-17920 Breuillet (Charente-Maritime) T: 05 46 22 72 15. E: transhumance@wanadoo.fr

alanrogers.com/FR17550

The approach to Camping Transhumance looks out over pretty countryside and leads to a peaceful site with a pleasant, sociable atmosphere. There are 260 pitches here, made up of 100 touring pitches and 160 mobile homes. They are arranged in avenues with about 20 units in each and divided by hedges. Mainly on grass, the pitches are level and have 10A electricity. Some areas are shaded. Although quite a peaceful site, some entertainment is provided in high season, and there is a pleasant pool area. A recent addition is a very attractive heated indoor pool which is treated with ozone.

Facilities

Two toilet blocks, are unheated but clean and bright. Baby room. Good facilities for disabled visitors (key access). Excellent laundry. Small shop. Bar. Takeaway. Outdoor swimming pool. Heated indoor pool. Tennis. Boules. WiFi throughout (charged). Large units should contact site first. Off site: Village of Breuillet 2 km. with shops and bank. La Palmyre Zoo. Riding 2 km. Fishing 3 km. Golf, bicycle hire and beach 5 km.

Open: 28 May - 11 September.

Directions

From Saujon take the D14 northwest (La Tremblade). After about 8 km. turn left on D140 (Breuillet). Pass through village (with speed bumps) and site is 2 km. on the left, well signed. GPS: 45.67839, -1.05166

Charges guide

Per unit incl. 2 persons and electricity	€ 19.00 - € 33.00
extra person	€ 5.00
electricity (10A)	€ 4.00

Châtelaillon-Plage

Camping Au Port-Punay

Allée Bernard Moreau, les Boucholeurs, F-17340 Châtelaillon-Plage (Charente-Maritime) T: 05 46 56 01 53. E: contact@camping-port-punay.com **alanrogers.com/FR17340**

Au Port-Punay is a friendly, well run site just 200 metres from the beach and 3 km. from the centre of the resort of Châtelaillon-Plage. There are 115 touring pitches laid out on well trimmed grass, with many mature poplars and low shrubs. The site has a well stocked shop, open all season, and a small bar and restaurant open mid June - mid September. A heated swimming pool has a separate gated area for paddling. A good range of activities are available and in high season some entertainment is arranged. This is a family run site (Famille Moreau) and the son of the family speaks excellent English, as does his Dutch wife. Rochefort to the south and La Rochelle to the north are well worth a visit (buses from outside the site), as is the nearby town of Châtelaillon-Plage, which has an all-year covered market and, in summer, a street market every day.

Facilities

One large toilet block with good facilities including washbasins in cubicles and large shower cubicles. Facilities for disabled visitors and babies. Washing machines. Motorcaravan services. Shop. Bar, restaurant and takeaway (11/6-15/9). Swimming pool (heated May-Sept). New indoor pool and wellness facility planned for 2012 season. Games area. Play area. Bicycle hire. Internet access. WiFi (charged). Off site: Buses to Rochefort and La Rochelle from outside site. Beach 200 m. Châtelaillon-Plage 1.5 km. along the seafront on foot or bike, 3 km. by road. Riding 2 km. Golf 10 km.

Open: 7 April - 23 September.

Directions

From N137 (La Rochelle - Rochefort) take exit for Châtelaillon-Plage. At first roundabout follow sign for town centre. At second roundabout turn left (Les Boucholeurs). Follow signs to site at the seaside hamlet of Les Boucholeurs. Here drive to sea wall then turn left through village to site. Take care, as the road has many traffic calming measures and can be narrow in places. GPS: 46.05480, -1.08340

Charges guide

Per unit incl. 2 persons and electricity	€ 21.50 - € 34.00
extra person	€ 4.90 - € 5.90
child (0-3 yrs)	€ 3.30 - € 4.30

Camping Au Port-Punay

Cosy campsite, partly under large trees at 200m from the sea. Luxurious sanitary block maintained to a high standard. An ideal choice for families with small children. Charming fisherman's village, good starting point to visit the islands of Ré and Aix and located in between the historical and tourist cities of La Rochelle and Rochefort. Châtelaillon and its surroundings can be easily discovered by bicycle. Wireless internet available. French, English, Dutch and German spoken.

Camping Au Port-Punay • Les Boucholeurs • 17340 CHATELAILLON-PLAGE FRANCE • Tel. +33 (0)5 46 56 01 53 • Fax +33 (0)5 46 56 86 44 www.camping-port-punay.com • Email contact@camping-port-punay.com

We can book this site for you! **alan**rogers ◑ travel
Call 01580 214000

Couhé

Camping Caravaning les Peupliers

F-86700 Couhé (Vienne) T: 05 49 59 21 16. E: info@lespeupliers.fr

alanrogers.com/FR86080

Les Peupliers is situated in a valley just 25 km. south of Poitiers and close to the N10 motorway. The site has been family owned and run since 1968, and continually updated to provide good facilities. The camping area is divided in the middle by a small river (unfenced) with crossing points at various intervals. There are 180 pitches, 38 of which are for mobile homes available to rent. The 132 level touring pitches are on grass and separated by trees and shrubs. All have 10A electricity and 50 are fully serviced. The site enjoys a rural position and tends to benefit from long hours of sunshine.

Facilities

Three sanitary blocks also provide facilities for babies and disabled visitors. Laundry facilities. Motorcaravan service point. TV and fridge rental. Shop. Restaurant, bar and snack bar (July/Aug). Pool complex. Playgrounds. Fishing lake. Minigolf. Multisports court. Entertainment in high season. WiFi. Off site: Tennis 800 m. Bicycle hire 1 km. Riding 5 km. Golf 30 km.

Open: 2 May - 30 September.

Directions

Couhé is 30 km. south of Poitiers on N10. From north, follow signs (Couhé town centre) and campsite (a short distance from slip road on right). From south, take 2nd Couhé exit from N10. Entrance is opposite end of slip road. GPS: 46.31177, 0.17783

Charges guide

Per unit incl. 2 persons	
and electricity	€ 23.20 - € 31.00
extra person	€ 5.25 - € 7.00

Camping Cheques accepted.

Cognac

Camping de Cognac

Boulevard de Châtenay, route de Sainte-Sévère, F-16100 Cognac (Charente) T: 05 45 32 13 32.

E: info@campingdecognac.com **alanrogers.com/FR16050**

Situated close to the historic town of Cognac, this municipal site is set in parkland beside the river Charente. It has 168 pitches, 160 for touring, all have 6A electricity (long leads required), ten have hardstanding and a water tap but no drainage. The pitches are separated by shrubs and some hedging, with a variety of trees giving varying amounts of shade. Access for large units is good, though twin-axle caravans are not accepted. There is some noise from the adjacent road. Public transport is available to the town centre (daily July/Aug; Saturdays at other times).

Facilities

Two well equipped, fairly modern toilet blocks (access by steps) include children's toilets and washing machines. Separate ground level facilities for disabled visitors. Motorcaravan services. Small swimming pool (June-Sept, municipal pool nearby). Shop, snack bar and takeaway (mid June-mid Sept). Fishing. Play area on grass. Minigolf. WiFi by reception. Off site: Bicycle hire 1 km. Riverside walks. Restaurants, bars and shops in the town (2.3 km).

Open: 29 April - 25 September.

Directions

Site is 2.4 km. north west of the town on the D24 to St Sévère just after crossing the river. GPS: 45.70916, -0.31289

Charges guide

Per unit incl. 2 persons	
and electricity	€ 13.00 - € 20.00
extra person	€ 4.50 - € 5.50
child (2-13 yrs)	€ 3.50 - € 4.00
dog	€ 2.00

Coulon

Camping de la Venise Verte

178 route des Bords de Sèvre, F-79510 Coulon (Deux-Sèvres) T: 05 49 35 90 36.

E: accueil@camping-laveniseverte.fr **alanrogers.com/FR79040**

This family run site on the edge of the Sevre Nortaise and the Marais Poitevin is ideal for short or long stays. With canoe and bicycle hire on site you have no excuse for not exploring the local area. In the Deux-Sèvres, the 'department of discovery', so named because it has two rivers named Sevre, the Noirtaise and Nantaise, the Venise Verte provides an excellent site. There are 120 flat pitches here with 88 used for touring units, the remainder occupied by mobile homes. The pitches are of a good size, all with 10A electricity, water and drainage and with some shade. A Sites et Paysages member.

Facilities

Modern toilet facilities are of a high standard with free showers. Washing machine and dryer. Motorcaravan services. Bar (July/Aug). Restaurant. Takeaway on request. Swimming pool (1/6-31/8). Play area. Bicycle and canoe hire. Boules area. Fishing. WiFi throughout (free). Electric barbecues not permitted. Off site: Fishing 200 m. Coulon 1 km. Boat trips in the Marais. Ideal for walking, fishing, cycling or canoeing. Golf and riding 15 km.

Open: 1 April - 30 October.

Directions

From Niort take N11 towards La Rochelle. Turn on the D3 (Sansais), then north on D1 (Coulon). At traffic lights head towards 'centre ville' (Coulon) at mini-roundabout turn slightly right. Follow Sevre Noirtaise for 1.5 km. to site on right. GPS: 46.31492, -0.60835

Charges guide

Per unit incl. 2 persons	
and electricity	€ 18.50 - € 30.00
extra person	€ 4.00 - € 6.00

For latest campsite news, availability and prices visit

alanrogers.com

Dolus-d'Oléron

Camping Indigo les Chênes Verts

20 Passe de l'Ecuissiere, F-17550 Dolus-d'Oléron (Charente-Maritime) T: 05 46 75 32 88
alanrogers.com/FR17985

This former municipal site is a recent addition to the Indigo group of campsites and is located just 100 m. from the beach at Dolus-d'Oléron, on the eastern side of the Ile d'Oléron. Pitches here are of a good size and most have electrical connections. Several are occupied by mobile homes or fully equipped safari-style tents. Renovation work is planned during the winter and the site will have a small shop and snack bar for the 2012 season. During peak season, various activities are organised, including opportunities to discover more about the island and its inhabitants. Dolus is one of the larger towns on the Ile d'Oléron and is still reliant on fishing and oyster cultivation, as well as tourism. It is best known now for its broad sandy beach, and is also home to a cluster of excellent seafood restaurants. Cycling is popular across the island, with miles of dedicated cycle tracks. Back on the mainland, a popular excursion is the large zoo at La Palmyre, by some distance the most popular in France.

Facilities

Shop. Snack bar. Playground. Tourist information. Fully equipped tents and mobile homes for rent.
Off site: Nearest beach 100 m. Shops and restaurants in Dolus-d'Oléron. Fishing. Boat trips. Cycle tracks across the island.

Open: 21 June - 15 September.

Directions

Dolus-d'Oléron can be found north of Le Château d'Oléron. Approaching from the mainland, cross the (toll-free) bridge at Marennes and head north on D26 to Dolus-d'Oléron. The site is well signposted from here. GPS: 45.886995, -1.275433

Charges guide

Per unit incl. 2 persons and electricity € 20.00

For latest campsite news, availability and prices visit
alanrogers.com

Dienné

Camping Domaine de Dienné

F-86410 Dienné (Vienne) T: 05 49 45 87 63. E: info@domaine-de-dienne.fr

alanrogers.com/FR86120

This is without doubt a wonderful site and unique in what it offers. It concentrates on your well being and provides all the facilities you could wish for in achieving that aim. The site extends over 47 hectares but there are just 30 pitches for touring units and these are on large generous plots of 250 sq.m. All have their own water supply, drainage and 10A electricity and access for even the largest of units will not cause a problem. The accommodation to rent includes gypsy style caravans, tree houses, yurts, a gîte and cottages, which are all of superb quality and again on large plots. Domaine de Dienné cannot fail to impress from the moment you arrive.

Facilities

Restaurant. Heated swimming pools. Health and fitness centre. Hairdressing salon. Horse riding centre. Mountain biking. Adventure park. Climbing tower. Children's games. Walking trails. Fishing. Cooking lessons. WiFi. Off site: Poitiers airport 25 km. Futuroscope. Crocodile Planet. Monkey Park. Historical sites and castles.

Open: All year.

Directions

From Poitiers take N147 towards Limoges. After the village of Fleure the site is well signed. GPS: 46.445028, 0.559294

Charges guide

Per unit incl. 2 persons and electricity	€ 21.00 - € 39.00
extra person	€ 4.00 - € 7.50

La Brée-les-Bains

Camping Antioche d'Oléron

Route de Proires, F-17840 La Brée-les-Bains (Charente-Maritime) T: 05 46 47 92 00. E: info@camping-antiochedoleron.com **alanrogers.com/FR17570**

Situated to the northeast of the island, Camping Antioche is quietly located within a five minute walk of the beach. There are 130 pitches, of which 73 are occupied by mobile homes and 57 are for touring units. The pitches are set amongst attractive shrubs and palm trees and all have electricity (10A), water and a drain. A new pool area which comprises two swimming pools (heated), two jacuzzis, two paddling pools and a raised sunbathing deck, is beautifully landscaped with palms and flowers. A small bar, restaurant and takeaway offer reasonably priced food and drinks. The site is livelier in season with regular evening entertainment and activities for all the family. With specially prepared trails for cycling, and oyster farms and salt flats to visit, the Ile d'Oléron offers something for everyone. Bresnais market, selling local produce and products, is within easy access on foot and is held daily in high season.

Facilities

The single sanitary block is of a good standard and is kept clean and fresh. Facilities for disabled visitors. Laundry. Motorcaravan services. Bar, restaurant and snack bar (weekends only May and June, daily July/Aug). Swimming and paddling pools. Games room. Play area. WiFi. Bicycle hire (July/Aug). Off site: Beach and fishing 150 m. Riding 1.5 km. Golf 7 km.

Open: 1 April - 30 September.

Directions

Cross the bridge on the D26 and join the D734. After St Georges turn right onto the D273E1 towards La Brée-les-Baines. At T-junction turn left from where the campsite is signed. GPS: 46.02007, -1.35764

Charges guide

Per unit incl. 2 persons and electricity	€ 22.30 - € 37.30
extra person	€ 7.50 - € 8.70
child (1-14 yrs)	€ 4.20 - € 5.40
dog	€ 4.20

la Brée-les-Bains   Île d'Oléron - France

Camping 150 m from the sea

www.koronmarketing.com © 2011

Antioche d'Oléron
camping & locations ★★★

camping Antioche d'Oléron
Route de Proires
17840 La Brée-les-Bains - France
tel. : 0033 5 46 47 92 00

www.camping-antiochedoleron.com

For latest campsite news, availability and prices visit

alanrogers.com

Call 01580 214000 We can book this site for you! alan rogers ◉ travel

Ingrandes-sur-Vienne

Castel Camping le Petit Trianon

Saint-Ustre, 1 rue du Moulin de Saint-Ustre, F-86220 Ingrandes-sur-Vienne (Vienne) T: 05 49 02 61 47.
E: chateau@petit-trianon.fr **alanrogers.com/FR86010**

A family-owned site for many years, le Petit Trianon is situated halfway between Tours and Poitiers. It enjoys a countryside position within the lovely grounds of an 18th-century château. Visitors to the site often return several times after their first visit for the calm and tranquil atmosphere here. There are 99 pitches all with electricity (10A), set in seven hectares, which gives a real sense of spaciousness. Plants are well tended and shade is provided in parts by the many attractive trees. Access around the site is good and large units are accepted by prior arrangement.

Facilities	Directions
The sanitary facilities include washbasins in cabins, some washbasin and shower units, baby baths, washing machines and dryer. Facilities for disabled visitors. Motorcaravan service point. Shop. Snack bar. Takeaway. Heated swimming pool and paddling pool. Playground. Minigolf. Badminton, croquet, volleyball and boules. Satellite TV. Reading room. Bicycle hire. Bread making. Internet access. WiFi. Caravan storage. Off site: Restaurant 50 m. Tennis 2 km. Fishing 3 km. Riding 15 km. Local markets. Futuroscope.	Take the N10 to Ingrandes-sur-Vienne and take the D75 in the direction of Oyre. Follow D121 to St Ustre (1.5 km) and site is then well signed. GPS: 46.885533, 0.586133

Open: 20 May - 20 September.

Charges guide

Per unit incl. 2 persons	
and electricity	€ 23.10 - € 35.30
extra person	€ 6.00 - € 8.00
child (under 13 yrs)	€ 2.00 - € 3.50
dog	€ 2.10 - € 2.50

La Flotte-en-Ré

Camping la Grainetière

Route de Saint-Martin, F-17630 La Flotte-en-Ré (Charente-Maritime) T: 05 46 09 68 86.
E: la-grainetiere@orange.fr **alanrogers.com/FR17280**

A truly friendly welcome awaits you from the owners, Isabelle and Eric, at La Grainetière. It is a peaceful campsite set in almost three hectares of pine trees which provide some shade for the 88 touring pitches of various shapes and sizes. There are also 50 well spaced chalets for rent. Some pitches are suitable for units up to seven metres (these should be booked in advance). There are no hedges for privacy and the pitches are sandy with some grass. Ample new water points and electricity (10A) hook-ups (Euro plugs) serve the camping area. The site is well lit. At the site entrance there is a very attractive swimming pool surrounded by tropical plants and with plenty of space to sunbathe. There are no toboggans here and the atmosphere is convivial and relaxed. The site is situated just two kilometers from the beach and La Flotte-en-Ré with its harbour-side restaurants is even closer.

Facilities	Directions
The unisex sanitary block is first class, with washbasins in cubicles, showers, British style WCs, facilities for children and visitors with disabilities. Shop. Takeaway. Swimming pool (heated all season) and jacuzzi. Bicycle hire. Fridge hire. TV room. Charcoal barbecues are not permitted. WiFi (charged). Off site: Beach, fishing, boat launching and sailing 2 km. Bar and restaurant 2 km. Riding 3 km. Golf 10 km.	Follow camping signs from La Flotte, 1 km. from the village. GPS: 46.18755, -1.344933

Open: 1 April - 30 September.

Charges guide

Per unit incl. 2 persons	
and electricity	€ 19.50 - € 34.50
extra person	€ 5.00 - € 8.00
child (0-7 yrs)	€ 3.00 - € 4.00
dog	€ 2.50 - € 4.00

CAMPING LA GRAINETIERE

Isabelle, Eric and Fanny welcome you in a wooden site between St Martin & La Flotte.
Friendly and family atmosphere, all kinds of shops at proximity.

Route de St Martin - 17630 La Flotte - Ile de Ré - France
Tél : (0033)5.46.09.68.86   Fax : (0033)5.46.09.53.13
la-grainetiere@orange.fr   www.la-grainetiere.com

For latest campsite news, availability and prices visit
alanrogers.com

La Couarde-sur-Mer

Camping la Tour des Prises

Route d'Ars, F-17670 La Couarde-sur-Mer (Charente-Maritime) T: 05 46 29 84 82.
E: camping@lesprises.com **alanrogers.com/FR17630**

La Tour des Prises is a friendly, family site close to the village of La Couarde-sur-Mer on the southern side of the Ile de Ré. There are 140 pitches here, around 50 of which are occupied by fully equipped mobile homes and chalets (available for rent). The 88 touring pitches are of a good size and are mostly equipped with electricity (16A). The site is just 600 m. from a fine sandy beach, the plage des Prises. Cycling is particularly popular on the island, thanks to the quality and extent of its cycle tracks, one of which passes adjacent to the site. English is spoken at reception.

Facilities

Two unisex toilet blocks provide good facilities and are kept clean, with washbasins in cubicles and seatless WCs. Baby room and facilities for visitors with disabilities. Laundry. Basic motorcaravan service point. No bar, restaurant or takeaway. Pizza van (Tues. Thurs. and Sun). Small shop (1/6-15/9). Heated, covered swimming pool. Children's pool. Adult entertainment and children's club in high season. WiFi. Games room. Play area. Bicycle hire. Tourist information. Mobile homes and chalets to rent. No barbecues or washing lines. Off site: Nearest beach 600 m. Fishing 600 m. Sailing 1 km. Ecomuseum. Riding.

Open: 1 April - 30 September.

Directions

From La Rochelle, cross the toll bridge to the Ile de Ré (D735) and follow signs to St Martin and then La Couarde-sur-Mer. Do not tow/drive through village. Stay on D375 towards Ars-en-Ré. After 2 miles follow site signs on your right. GPS: 46.204451, -1.446301

Charges guide

Per unit incl. 2 persons	
and electricity	€ 22.20 - € 40.20
extra person	€ 3.70 - € 8.20
child (0-7 yrs)	€ 2.60 - € 4.70

La Roche-Posay

Airotel la Roche Posay Vacances

Route de Lesigny, F-86270 La Roche-Posay (Vienne) T: 05 49 86 21 23. E: info@larocheposay-vacances.com
alanrogers.com/FR86050

Camping la Roche Posay is set in eight hectares and has direct access to the Creuse river on which fishing and canoes are popular. There are 200 pitches, of which 30 are used for mobile homes to rent. The touring pitches include 19 with hardstanding, ideal for motorcaravans and with services nearby. Access around the site is good for larger units. The pitches are all large and 16A electricity is available. This is a good, well run site in very natural surroundings. There is a sense of spaciousness where you can relax in a convivial atmosphere. Many different types of trees offer a mix of shade and the site is pleasantly landscaped. A programme of entertainment is arranged for both adults and children and in high season there is a children's club. There are many places to visit and things to do within a 20 km. radius of the site. This campsite is good for a long stay in both low and high seasons and represents good value for money.

Facilities

Two fully equipped, heated toilet blocks, one in each section. Excellent facilities for disabled visitors and children. Bar and snack bar. Swimming and paddling pools. Play area. Games room. Fishing. Canoes. Boules. Riding. Barbecues are not permitted. Entertainment in high season. Off site: Shops, restaurants etc. 1 km. Golf 3 km.

Open: 14 April - 22 September.

Directions

Site is signed from the D725 town bypass, turning north at roundabout onto D5 towards Lesigny. Site is 50 m. on right. GPS: 46.799646, 0.80945

Charges 2012

Per unit incl. 2 persons	
and electricity	€ 16.00 - € 28.00
extra person	€ 6.00 - € 8.00
child	€ 4.00 - € 6.00
No credit cards.	

La Roche Posay Vacances Touraine - Loire

New for 2012:
- heated and covered pool
- waterpark with slides
- children's pool with water games
- snack/bar/take-away area
- children play area / sports field
- access to river/fishing/canoe
- cottage 2 or 3 bedroom to rent

www.larocheposay-vacances.com
+33 (0)549862123
info@larocheposay-vacances.com

For latest campsite news, availability and prices visit
alanrogers.com

La Flotte-en-Ré

Camping les Peupliers

RD735, F-17630 La Flotte-en-Ré (Charente-Maritime) T: 02 51 33 17 00. E: camping@les-peupliers.com

alanrogers.com/FR17290

On the Ile de Ré, you are never far from the sea and the location of this campsite is no exception. It is just 800 metres from the sea with sea views from some of the pitches. The staff here go out of their way to make your stay enjoyable. The 20 level touring pitches are in a separate area from 143 chalets for rent, in an area of light woodland. There are few water points. Trees provide some shade, but the very low hedges provide little privacy as the width and length of the pitches varies.

Facilities

Two new sanitary blocks are clean and well maintained. Both have unisex facilities including showers and vanity type units in cabins. Separate facilities for disabled visitors. Laundry facilities. Shop, restaurant, takeaway and bar with TV (all 2/4-24/9). Heated outdoor swimming pool (21/5-24/9). Play area. Children's club and entertainment (high season). Fridge hire. Bicycle hire. Max. 1 dog. WiFi throughout (charged). Off site: Riding 500 m. Beach, fishing, boat launching and sailing 800 m. Golf 20 km.

Open: 2 April - 24 September.

Directions

Over the toll bridge and turn left at second roundabout. Site is well signed. GPS: 46.18461, -1.3080

Charges guide

Per unit incl. 2 persons and electricity	€ 21.00 - € 35.00
extra person	€ 5.00 - € 9.00
child (under 5 yrs)	free - € 6.00

Camping Cheques accepted.

Le Bois-Plage-en-Ré

Campéole les Amis de la Plage

68, avenue du Pas des Boeufs, F-17580 Le Bois Plage en Ré (Charente-Maritime) T: 05 46 09 24 01.
E: les-amis-de-la-plage@campeole.com **alanrogers.com/FR17610**

Les Amis de la Plage, a former municipal site, is now a member of the Campéole group and located on the southern side of the Ile de Ré, at Le Bois-Plage-en-Ré. The site has direct access to a superb sandy beach (across sand dunes). This is a large site with 219 pitches, some of which are occupied by mobile homes, chalets and fully equipped tents. The 136 touring pitches are sandy with varying degrees of shade (some are rather small). Most have electrical connections (10A). The island's largest market is held daily, just 500 m. from the site. The Ile de Ré is well known for its cycle tracks and a number of these pass close to the site. It has to be the best way to explore the island (rental service close to site). We also recommend the Maison du Platin, an interesting ecomuseum, dedicated to the Ile de Ré's heritage and traditions. Back on the mainland, a visit to La Rochelle is a must, with its unique maritime heritage and stunning architecture. A small electric bus provides a free daily service to Amis de la Plage.

Facilities

Three toilet blocks (one closed low season) provide some washbasins in cubicles and facilities for disable visitors and children. Laundry. Motorcaravan service point. No shop, but bread to order daily (July/Aug). Play area with bouncy castle. Boules. Table tennis. Activities and entertainment (high season). Tourist information. Direct access to beach. Communal barbeque area. No charcoal barbecues on pitch. Mobile homes, chalets and tents for rent. WiFi (charged). Off site: Swimming pool and bar/restaurant near site entrance (charged). Bicycle hire 1 km. Riding 3km. Cycle and walking tracks. Tennis.

Open: 6 April - 30 September.

Directions

From La Rochelle, cross the toll bridge and take D201 along the southern coast of the island until you reach Le Bois-Plage-en-Ré, and then follow signs to the campsite. GPS: 46.177401, -1.386514

Charges guide

Per unit incl. 2 persons and electricity	€ 18.10 - € 24.00
extra person	€ 4.10 - € 6.30
child (2-6 yrs)	free - € 4.00
dog	€ 2.50 - € 2.60

Campéole

CAMPSITES AND RENTALS

POITOU-CHARENTES

Les Amis de la Plage ★★★

Magnificent site in the heart of the Ile de Ré, jewel in the Atlantic. Quality mobile homes, bungalows and touring pitches. Direct access to the fine sandy beach.

17580 Le bois plage en ré - Tel: +33-546-0924-01 - www.campeole.co.uk / les-amis-de-la-plage@campeole.com

Le Château-d'Oléron
Airotel Oléron

Domaine de Montravail, F-17480 Le Château-d'Oléron (Charente-Maritime) T: 05 46 47 61 82.
E: info@camping-airotel-oleron.com **alanrogers.com/FR17060**

This family run site on the outskirts of Le Château-d'Oléron has very good facilities, including a superb equestrian centre, a full range of sporting activites and an attractive heated pool complex. This is a mature site with 272 pitches of a good size, with varying degrees of shade provided by trees and attractive shrubs. It is well laid out and most of the 133 touring pitches have electricity (10A), 4 with individual water and drainage. The remaining pitches are used for mobile homes of which 30 are for rent. A full entertainment programme is provided in high season. Visitors can enjoy exploring the island with its fine sandy beaches on the Atlantic coast. There are miles of flat tracks on the island for walking, cycling or horse riding, and the equestrian centre offers courses up to a week in length.

Facilities

Two modern toilet blocks with facilities for disabled visitors and babies. Washing machine and dryer. Motorcaravan service point. Shop. Bar, restaurant and takeaway (15/6-15/9). Heated swimming and paddling pools. Equestrian centre. Playground. Multisports court. Tennis. Minigolf. Fishing. Canoe hire. Bicycle hire. TV and games room. Internet access. WiFi (charged). Off site: Supermarket. Local markets. Zoo. Aquarium.

Open: Easter - 30 September.

Directions

Cross the bridge onto the island and continue on D26. At second roundabout turn right, marked Dolus and Le Château. Proceed 500 m. and take first right, marked Campings. Site is 1 km. on the right. GPS: 45.88207, -1.20648

Charges guide

Per unit incl. 2 persons and electricity	€ 17.90 - € 26.90
extra person	€ 4.00 - € 6.90

web : www.camping-airotel-oleron.com   phone : 00335 46 47 61 82 - fax : 00335 46 47 79 67

Les Mathes
Camping l'Orée du Bois

225 route de la Bouverie, la Fouasse, F-17570 Les Mathes (Charente-Maritime) T: 05 46 22 42 43.
E: info@camping-oree-du-bois.fr **alanrogers.com/FR17050**

L'Orée du Bois has 341 pitches of about 100 sq.m. in a very spacious, pinewood setting. There are 88 for touring units, mainly scattered amongst the permanent chalets and tents. They include 40 large pitches with hardstanding and individual sanitary facilities (in blocks of four with shower, toilet, washbasin and dishwashing sink). Pitches are on flat, fairly sandy ground, separated by trees, shrubs and hedges and all have electrical connections (6A). The forest pines offer some shade. This is a family site with a good aqua park amongst the amenities as well as a splendid new children's playground.

Facilities

Four main toilet blocks include some washbasins in cabins. Three have a laundry and facilities for disabled visitors. Shop. Excellent bar, restaurant, crêperie and takeaway service (1/5-13/9). Heated swimming pools (1/5-13/9), water slide and paddling pool (trunks, not shorts). Play areas. Tennis court, boules, football and basketball. Games room and TV lounge. Adventure park. Bicycle hire. Discos. Entertainment in July/Aug. WiFi (charged). Off site: Riding 300 m. Fishing 4 km. Golf 5 km.

Open: 1 May - 13 September.

Directions

From north follow D14 La Tremblade. At roundabout before Arvert turn on D268 (Les Mathes, La Palmyre). Site is on the right in Fouasse. GPS: 45.7326, -1.1785

Charges guide

Per unit incl. 2 persons and electricity	€ 18.00 - € 41.50
incl. private sanitary facility	€ 27.00 - € 51.50

Camping Cheques accepted.

We can book this site for you! Call 01580 214000 alan rogers travel

For latest campsite news, availability and prices visit
alanrogers.com

Le Château-d'Oléron
Camping la Brande

Route des Huitres, F-17480 Le Château-d'Oléron (Charente-Maritime) T: 05 46 47 62 37.
E: info@camping-labrande.com **alanrogers.com/FR17220**

An environmentally-friendly site, run and maintained to a high standard, la Brande offers an ideal holiday environment on the delightful Ile d'Oléron, it is situated on the oyster route and close to a sandy beach. Pitches here are generous and mostly separated by hedges and trees, the greater number for touring outfits. All are on level grassy terrain and have electricity hook-ups, some are fully serviced. Some of the most attractive pitches are in a newer section towards the back of the site. The many activities during the high season, plus the natural surroundings, make this an ideal choice for families. A feature of this site is the heated indoor pool (28ºC) open all season. The Barcat family ensures that their visitors not only enjoy quality facilities, but Gerard Barcat offers guided bicycle tours and canoe trips. This way you discover the nature, oyster farming, vineyards and history of Oléron, which is joined to the mainland by a 3 km. bridge.

Facilities

Three clean sanitary blocks have spacious, well equipped showers and washbasins. Baby facilities. Excellent facilities for disabled visitors. Private facilities to rent. Laundry. Motorcaravan service point. Restaurant/takeaway and bar (July/Aug). Shop (July/Aug). Heated indoor swimming pool (all season). Jacuzzi. Sauna. Well equipped playground. Games room. Football field, tennis, minigolf, fishing and archery. Bicycle hire. Canoe hire. Free WiFi. New building for children. Off site: Beach 300 m.

Open: 20 March - 14 November.

Directions

After crossing bridge to the Ile d'Oléron turn right towards Château-d'Oléron. Continue through village and follow sign for Route des Huitres. Site is on left after 2.5 km. GPS: 45.90415, -1.21525

Charges guide

Per unit incl. 2 persons and electricity	€ 20.00 - € 43.00
extra person	€ 5.00 - € 8.00

Camping Cheques accepted.

Les Mathes
Camping Atlantique Parc

26 avenue des Mathes, F-17570 Les Mathes (Charente-Maritime) T: 05 46 02 17 17.
E: info@camping-atlantique-parc.com **alanrogers.com/FR17975**

Camping Atlantique Parc is a large, well-equipped holiday complex that has something to offer for campers of all ages, but particularly for families with children. It is ideally situated on the edge of Forêt de St Augustin-les-Mathes, only a short drive from the beautiful beaches of the holiday resort of La Palmyre. The site has almost 400 large pitches, the majority used for chalets and mobile homes for rent. There are 50 touring pitches with electricity, water and drainage, many with good shade from attractive mature trees. An attractive outdoor pool complex is heated. Entertainment is organised in high seaon, including a club for children and evening entertainment for adults three times weekly.

Facilities

Well maintained toilet blocks include facilities for disabled visitors and babies. Shop, bar and restaurant (all 1/6-10/9). Swimming pool (15/5-15/9). Play areas with inflatable slide. Pet corner. Bicycle hire. Boules. Video games room and TV. Minigolf. Football, volleyball and basketball. Entertainment and children's club (high season). WiFi in some areas (free). Off site: La Palmyre zoo within walking distance. Riding 200 m. Fishing 1 km. Beach 1.2 km.

Open: 25 June - 4 September
(holiday homes 15 May - 15 September).

Directions

From Royan take D25 towards La Palmyre. Pass the zoo on the right and at large roundabout take D141 towards Les Mathes. Site is on right after 500 m. GPS: 45.701348, -1.167686

Charges guide

Per unit incl. 2 persons and electricity	€ 27.00 - € 37.00
extra person	€ 6.60

Administration charge € 22 per stay.

For latest campsite news, availability and prices visit

alanrogers.com

Les Mathes-La Palmyre
Camping Caravaning Monplaisir

26 avenue de la Palmyre, F-17570 Les Mathes-La Palmyre (Charente-Maritime) T: 05 46 22 50 31.
E: camping-monplaisir@orange.fr **alanrogers.com/FR17110**

Monplaisir provides a small, quiet haven in an area with some very hectic campsites. It is ideal for couples or families with young children. Quite close to the town and set back from the road, the entrance leads through an avenue of trees, past the owner's home to a well kept, garden-like site with many trees and shrubs. There are 114 level, marked pitches and all but a few have 6A electrical connections. On 14 there are caravans for hire and a modern building provides flats and studios for rent. There is no shop, bar or restaurant but it is a happy, friendly site. Visitors return year after year.

Facilities	Directions
The toilet block has some washbasins in cabins and facilities for disabled visitors. Laundry and dishwashing facilities. Ice pack service in reception. Bread delivered daily. TV, games room and library. Heated swimming and paddling pools (early May-30/9). Small play area. Winter caravan storage. Off site: Bicycle hire opposite. Supermarket short walk. Minigolf adjacent (owned by site).	From north on D14 (La Tremblade) turn onto D268 (Les Mathes and La Palmyre) at roundabout just before Arvert. Keep straight on to Les Mathes, road becomes D141. Turn left (north) at roundabout. Site is 600 m. on left. GPS: 45.71530, -1.15533

Open: Easter - 1 October.

Charges guide

Per unit incl. 2 persons and electricity	€ 19.00 - € 22.50

Les Mathes-La Palmyre
Camping la Clé des Champs

1188 route de la Fouasse, F-17570 Les Mathes-La Palmyre (Charente-Maritime) T: 05 46 22 40 53.
E: contact@cledeschamps.com **alanrogers.com/FR17540**

Situated on the edge of the large Forêt de la Coubre and around 1.5 km. from the village of Les Mathes, la Clé des Champs is a large site (7.6 hectares) and has 129 grass touring pitches (90 sq.m). Set amongst avenues of small trees, 80 have electricity (6/10A). This quiet campsite is flat, with 170 mobile homes (51 available to rent, the others privately owned) well positioned at the top end of the site. A new toilet block has been added which can be heated in cool weather. The swimming pool can be covered by a polythene structure in low season and a bar and shop are open from mid June to September. Various cycle tracks lead through the forest to the beaches of the Côte Sauvage (bicycle hire is available on site). These stretch for 70 km. and sandy beaches alternate with rocky coves. The nearby zoo at La Palmyre, with over 1,600 animals, is France's second largest. La Palmyre is a stylish resort with many cafés and restaurants, as well as a fine sandy beach.

Facilities	Directions
New toilet block, heated in cool weather. Washing machine. Shop. Bar. Snack bar and takeaway (mid-June-Sept). Swimming pool. Paddling pool. Games room. Play area. Bicycle hire. Activity and entertainment programme (July/Aug). WiFi (charged). New wellness (jacuzzi, sauna) and fitness rooms. Mobile homes for rent. Charcoal barbecues are not permitted. Off site: Riding centre nearby. Minigolf 800 m. Les Mathes village 1.5 km. (good range of shops and restaurants). Nearest beach 4 km.	From Saujon take D14 northwest towards La Tremblade. At Arvert head south on D141 to Les Mathes. Beyond village, head right on Route de la Fouasse and the site is on the right after a further 500 m. GPS: 45.72098, -1.17149

Open: 31 March - 15 November.

Charges guide

Per unit incl. 2 persons and electricity	€ 16.10 - € 28.90
extra person	€ 3.50 - € 4.90
child (2-7 yrs)	€ 2.80 - € 3.90
dog	€ 2.80 - € 3.00

La Clé des Champs
Hôtellerie de plein air ★★★

Tel. 05 46 22 40 53
www.la-cledeschamps.com

Covered and heated swimming pool
Spa • Sauna • Animation • Gym
Mobil home rental
Multisport • Minigolf

1188, RTE DE LA FOUASSE • 17 570 LES MATHES-LA PALMYRE • FAX 05 46 22 56 96 • CONTACT@LA-CLEDESCHAMPS.COM

For latest campsite news, availability and prices visit
alanrogers.com

We can book this site for you! Call 01580 214000

alan rogers ⬤ travel

Les Mathes-La Palmyre

Camping Atlantique Fôret

Route de la Fouasse, F-17570 Les Mathes-La Palmyre (Charente-Maritime) T: 05 46 22 40 46.
E: atlantique-foret@orange.fr alanrogers.com/FR17970

This is a good value, family-run campsite which is almost completely dedicated to touring caravans and campers. The owners live on-site so there is a 24 hour presence. Access is excellent and should present no problems. There are 170 large pitches, on grass, spread out among the trees. All basic requirements are provided for and facilities are modern and well maintained. For the active, there is a boules area and a volleyball court, and for children, a fenced play area. The site is attractively situated in the countryside on the edge of a large forest, within easy reach of the beaches at la Palmyre and the unspoilt coastline of the Forêt de la Coubre.

Facilities

Three toilet blocks provide good facilities including those for children. Two toilets for disabled campers. Shop (July/Aug). Play area. Boules. Volleyball. WiFi in some areas (charged). Off site: Supermarket nearby. Luna Park and La Palmyre Zoo. Riding and bicycle hire 2 km. Beach 5 km. Golf 6 km. Fishing 8 km.

Open: 15 June - 15 September.

Directions

From Royan take D25 towards La Palmyre. At large roundabout on outskirts take D141 towards Les Mathes. At next roundabout take D268 towards La Tremblade. Site is 1 km. after the large Luna Park complex on the right. GPS: 45.734734, -1.176846

Charges guide

Per unit incl. 2 persons and electricity	€ 25.50
extra person	€ 3.80

Médis

Camping le Clos Fleuri

8 impasse du Clos Fleuri, F-17600 Médis (Charente-Maritime) T: 05 46 05 62 17.
E: clos-fleuri@wanadoo.fr alanrogers.com/FR17160

Camping le Clos Fleuri really does live up to its name. The profusion of different trees and the lawns and flower beds give this small site a very rural atmosphere. There is always a warm welcome from the Devais family who created this pretty site in 1974. The 123 touring pitches are mostly of generous size (a little uneven in places). They vary from being in full sun to well shaded and 100 have electrical connections. The bar/restaurant is a converted barn providing a cool haven on hot days and a very convivial venue for evening gatherings and entertainment. The season here is short and services are only fully open in the height of the summer. The surrounding countryside is very pleasant with crops of sunflowers, wheat and maize, while beaches of all sorts are within easy reach. All in all, le Clos Fleuri combines a great deal of charm, beauty and friendliness with a location from which the attractions of the Charente-Maritime may be discovered. There is occasional noise from light aircraft but this does not detract from the peaceful ambience on site.

Facilities

Toilet facilities are kept clean. One block is segregated male and female, the other is unisex with each unit in its own cubicle. Facility for disabled visitors. Baby baths. Laundry facilities. Small pool and paddling pool. Sauna. Shop (9/7-15/9). Restaurant (11/7-31/8) and bar (9/7-15/9). In high season there are twice weekly 'soirées' and boules and archery competitions. Minigolf. WiFi. Large units should call in high season to check there is space. Off site: Médis 2 km.

Open: 1 June - 18 September.

Directions

Médis is on the N150 from Saintes, halfway between Saujon and Royan. Drive into village. Site signed to south at various points in Médis and is about 2 km. outside village. GPS: 45.63011, -0.9458

Charges guide

Per unit incl. 2 persons and electricity	€ 22.90 - € 35.50
extra person	€ 6.50 - € 9.00
child	€ 5.00 - € 7.00
dog	€ 2.50 - € 3.50

In the land of Sun, Pineau, Cognac, Oysters, Mussels and Melons.

nr.ROYAN

Le Clos Fleuri

www.le-clos-fleuri.com

☆ ☆ ☆ ☆

Trees, bushes, flowers and birds.....
Smart & large grassy pitches. Chalets
& mobile homes with individual BBQ.
Bar & restaurant set in
a old stone built barn

country camping

Family barbecues are...recommended !

Mazières

Camping le Paradis

Mareuil, F-16270 Mazières (Charente) T: 05 45 84 92 06. E: info@le-paradis-camping.com

alanrogers.com/FR16130

Camping le Paradis is a small, immaculate, family run site open all year. You are assured of a very warm welcome here. There are 29 large, well spaced pitches with 24 for touring, separated by hedging and a variety of maturing trees give some shade. Nine are on grass and 15 have hardstanding. All have 10/16A electricity and many have a water tap. Five very large pitches are fully serviced with satellite TV point and drainage; ideal for very large units. The excellent facilities include large, spotlessly clean bathrooms with shower, washbasin and toilet.

Facilities

Superb toilet facilities with rooms having toilet, washbasin and shower, part heated in winter. Washing machine and dryer. Motorcaravan service point. Small shop for basics, bread to order (July/Aug). Internet point near reception. Caravan storage. Off site: Bakers and fishing 3 km, Riding, beach and bicycle hire 5 km. Supermarket 7 km. Golf 10 km. Many châteaux, chocolate factory, old towns and villages with links to the Resistance.

Open: All year (min. stay 3 nights 1 Nov - 1 March).

Directions

Midway between Angoulême and Limoges leave N141 at La Péruse. Take D16 south, continue through Mazières. Approx. 1 km. after Mazières turn right to site (signed). GPS: 45.832836, 0.558114

Charges guide

Per unit incl. 2 persons and electricity	€ 18.75 - € 21.75
extra person	€ 3.75

Credit cards not accepted.

Parthenay

Flower Camping du Bois Vert

14 rue Boisseau, le Tallud, F-79200 Parthenay (Deux-Sèvres) T: 05 49 64 78 43.
E: campingboisvert@orange.fr **alanrogers.com/FR79050**

Bois Vert is a former municipal site, now operated by a campsite group although so far it has changed little. There are 88 pitches of which 74 are for touring, all with electricity (10A) and 30 also with water and drainage. There are 15 mobile homes to rent. Pitches are separated by hedges and there are mature trees providing some shade. The site is on the River Thouet and although there is a secure fence, there is a steep drop to the river bank. Pleasant walkways along both sides and a footbridge close by enable you to walk into the old walled town. The medieval city of Parthenay is a place of art and history. It is the capital of the Gatine region, an agricultural area renowned for its sheep, farming, dairy products, apple orchards and cattle breeding. This is an ideal destination close to the Marais Poitevan and Venise Verte. In medieval times the city was also one of the important stops on the pilgrims' route to Santiago de Compostela.

Facilities

Two toilet blocks, one with unisex toilets, showers and washbasins in cubicles, and scheduled for refurbishment. The second was closed when we visited. Dishwashing and laundry sinks. Facilities for disabled visitors, including new mobile homes. Bar with snack bar and takeaway (1/5-30/9). Small shop. Bread can be ordered. Breakfast available at the bar. Heated swimming pool. TV. Boules. Badminton. Bicycle hire. Small play area. Security barrier. Tickets available for Futuroscope and Puy du Fou. Off site: Motorcaravan service point adjacent. Fishing 100 m. Base de Loisirs nearby. Riding and golf 15 km.

Open: 1 April - 31 October.

Directions

Parthenay is 50 km. west of Poitiers (and the A10) via the N149 to Bressuire and Nantes. Site is southwest of the town at Le Tallud on the D949 La Roche-sur-Yon road. Take ring road and site is on right as you join D949. GPS: 46.6414, -0.2672

Charges guide

Per unit incl. 2 persons	€ 15.50 - € 21.00
incl. electricity	€ 19.00 - € 24.50
extra person	€ 5.00 - € 6.00
child (5-10 yrs)	€ 2.50

Camping Cheques accepted.

CAMPING DU BOIS VERT ****

Camping du Bois Vert in Parthenay at the shores of the river Thouet is a perfect location to enjoy your family holiday in peace and quiet. We offer you calm a green environment in a true paradise. Perfectly situated for a cycle tour in the Vallée du Thouet or visit the characteristic medieval cities and the Châteaux de Gatines. Ideally located on only one hour distance from touristic features like: Park Futuroscope, Puy du Fou, Les Marais Poitevin, La Rochelle, the Loire Châteaux...

NEW SANITARY

kawan

Camping du Bois Vert** - 14 rue Boisseau Le Tallud - 79200 Parthenay - Tel: 0033 549 647 843
www.camping-boisvert.com - campingboisvert@orange.fr**

For latest campsite news, availability and prices visit
alanrogers.com

Montbron
Castel Camping les Gorges du Chambon

Eymouthiers, F-16220 Montbron (Charente) T: 05 45 70 71 70. E: info@gorgesduchambon.fr
alanrogers.com/FR16020

This is a wonderful Castel site with 28 hectares of protected natural environment to be enjoyed in the rolling Perigord Vert countryside. The 90 pitches are extremely generous in size (150 sq.m), slightly sloping and enjoy a mixture of sunshine and shade. There are 85 with water and 10A electricity, the remaining five are fully serviced. The spaciousness is immense, with fine walks through the woodlands and around the grounds. Flora and fauna are as nature intended. Here you can feel at peace and enjoy precious moments of quiet. There has been much work done with the ecology association.

Facilities

Traditional blocks include facilities for disabled visitors. Washing machine, dryer. Basic shop. Bar, restaurant. Takeaway. Swimming pool (all season), children's pool (high season). Large play area. Games/TV room. Tennis. Archery. Minigolf. Bicycle hire. Beach and canoe hire. Organised activities (July/Aug). Children's club. Teenagers' corner and disco. WiFi (charged). Dogs are not accepted. Off site: Private fishing (free) 6 km, with licence 200 m.

Open: 23 April - 17 September.

Directions

Leave N141 Angoulême - Limoges road at Rochefoucauld and take D6 to Montbron (14 km). Continue on D6 for 4 km., turn north on D163, site is signed. After 2 km. turn right and follow lane up to site. GPS: 45.6598, 0.557667

Charges guide

Per unit incl. 2 persons and electricity	€ 18.40 - € 31.90
extra person	€ 4.30 - € 8.75

Rivedoux Plage
Campéole le Platin

Campé●le

125 avenue Gustave Perreau, F-17940 Rivedoux Plage (Charente-Maritime) T: 05 46 09 84 10.
E: platin@campeole.com alanrogers.com/FR17560

Located at the gateway to the Ile de Ré, le Platin is just a short walk from the pleasant village of Rivedoux Plage where there are several good restaurants and shops. In high season a small market is held every morning in the village square. A long, narrow site, the beach is on one side and the main road on the other. It is divided into small avenues with around 20 pitches in each. All have 8/10A electricity and most are shaded, although the pitches nearest the beach have little shade (but the best views). Of the 200 pitches, 50 are used for canvas bungalows for hire, the rest are seasonal and for touring. Popular with motorcaravanners, le Platin has a short stay area outside the barrier, and a bus stop 100 m. away makes it easy to explore the island and also to visit La Rochelle on the mainland. A cycle track runs alongside the site. Direct access onto the beach makes it an ideal spot for families, and sea fishing is a popular activity here. The beach is a hive of activity at low tide when the oyster beds are exposed.

Facilities

The toilet facilities here are a little below standard, although one block has good showers and an en-suite bathroom for disabled visitors. This is only the second year Campéole have been here, and there are plans for improvements. A swimming pool complex is due for completion in June. Small bar. Entertainment in high season. WiFi. Off site: Bicycle hire 200 m.

Open: 6 April - 20 September.

Directions

After crossing the toll bridge from La Rochelle, continue on the D735 into Rivedoux Plage. Site is well signed on the right. GPS: 46.1588, -1.2708

Charges guide

Per unit incl. 2 persons and electricity	€ 19.50 - € 24.40

POITOU-CHARENTES

Campé●le

CAMPSITES AND RENTALS

Le Platin**

Two stars site facing the Ocean with direct access to the beach; quality facilities, touring pitches, and accommodations.

17940 Rivedoux-Plage - Tél.: +33-546-0984-10 - www.campeole.co.uk / platin@campeole.com

For latest campsite news, availability and prices visit
alanrogers.com

Ronce-les-Bains

Camping la Clairière

Rue des Roseaux, F-17390 Ronce-les-Bains (Charente-Maritime) T: 05 46 36 36 63.
E: info@camping-la-clairiere.com **alanrogers.com/FR17480**

This site is attractively laid out with flowers, shrubs and trees. It is set away from the other campsites in the area and only 2.5 km. from the sea. Tranquil and peaceful, there is a feeling of spaciousness due to its setting within 12 hectares. The 147 pitches are level, shady and have easy access for large units. There are 32 mobile homes and chalets for rent. On-site facilities are impressive and include a covered pool, as well as a large outdoor aquapark with water slides. The gym here is well equipped with a good range of muscular training equipment for the energetically minded. Massages are also on offer.

Facilities

Two modern sanitary blocks. Baby room. No facilities for disabled visitors. Washing machines. Shop, bar, restaurant and takeaway (from June). Indoor and outdoor heated swimming pools, children's pool and 55 metre toboggan. Games room. Gym. Massage. Tennis. Pétanque. Minigolf. Basketball. Children's club. Entertainment in July/Aug. No charcoal barbecues. WiFi in some areas (charged). Dog shower. Off site: Riding 100 m. Fishing 2 km. Beach 2.5 km. Bicycle hire 3 km. Golf 9 km. Cycle and walking tracks through the Forêt de la Coubre. Ile d'Oléron.

Open: 2 April - 24 September.

Directions

From roundabout at Les Mathes, take D25 to La Palmyre. Take first right and follow the signs for the site. GPS: 45.772933, -1.166734

Charges guide

Per unit incl. 2 persons	
and electricity	€ 20.00 - € 31.50
extra person	€ 5.00 - € 8.00
child (2-10 yrs)	free - € 5.00
dog	€ 3.50

Royan-Pontaillac

Campéole Clairefontaine

Campéole

6 rue du Colonel Lachaud, F-17200 Royan-Pontaillac (Charente-Maritime) T: 05 46 39 08 11.
E: clairefontaine@campeole.com **alanrogers.com/FR17100**

Camping Clairefontaine is situated on the outskirts of Royan, 300 m. from a golden sandy beach and a casino. This busy site has benefited from much recent investment, and many of the facilities, especially the sanitary facilities, are of a high standard. There are 300 pitches, of which 115 are available for touring units. Electricity is available to all pitches, but some may require long leads. The site is mostly shaded and level with easy access to pitches. American motorhomes are accepted but care is needed on the entrance road to the site as it is not wide enough for two vehicles to pass. The reception area is large and welcoming and English is spoken. A programme of entertainment is provided in July and August and includes karaoke, singers and folk groups. There are many places of interest to visit, notably the nature reserves, the lighthouse at Cordouan, forests and the oyster beds of Marennes and Oléron.

Facilities

Two very modern sanitary blocks with good facilities for disabled visitors. Washing machines. Ironing room. Motorcaravan services. Bar and restaurant with takeaway (June-mid Sept). Large swimming and paddling pools (from June). Four play areas. Games room with TV. Tennis. Basketball. Entertainment in high season. Internet access. WiFi in some areas (charged). Off site: Fishing 200 m. Beach and sailing 300 m. Bicycle hire 350 m. Riding and golf 10 km.

Open: 7 April - 30 September.

Directions

Exit Royan on Avenue de Pontaillac towards La Palmyre. Turn right at the casino on the front, up Avenue Louise. Site is on left after 200 m. and is signed. GPS: 45.631388, -1.050122

Charges guide

Per unit incl. 2 persons	
and electricity	€ 20.00 - € 31.70
extra person	€ 4.60 - € 9.60
child (2-10 yrs)	free - € 5.60
dog	€ 2.50 - € 3.50

Campéole
CAMPSITES AND RENTALS

Clairefontaine****

Luxurous four stars site in Royan
at 300 meters of the beach;
swimming pool, new accommodations,
large touring pitches.

17200 Royan-Pontaillac Tel.: +33-546-3908-11 · www.campeole.co.uk / clairefontaine@campeole.com

For latest campsite news, availability and prices visit
alanrogers.com

Royan

Camping Chant des Oiseaux

19, rue des Sansonnets, F-17200 Royan (Charente-Maritime) T: 05 46 39 39 47.
E: contact@chantdesoiseaux.fr **alanrogers.com/FR17680**

Le Chant des Oiseaux is located in the attractive, wooded Maine-Geoffroy district of the popular seaside resort of Royan. This is a good value, family site, open for a long season. There are 150 large grassy pitches, most of which have electrical connections. They are mostly shaded although a few sunnier ones are also available. There are also a number of fully equipped mobile homes for rent. The main appeal here is sure to be one of Royan's fine sandy beaches, but the site also boasts a large swimming pool (with separate children's pool). Other on-site amenities include a small shop and snack bar.

Facilities

Two sanitary blocks within easy reach of all pitches. Facilities for disabled visitors. Two baby baths. Laundry room. Shop (July/Aug). Bar and snack bar (July/Aug). Swimming and paddling pools (1/5-30/9). Sports area. Play area. Games room. Bicycle hire. Entertainment and activity programme (high season). Mobile homes for rent. Off site: Royan centre. Tennis. Shops and restaurants. Watersports. Zoo at La Palmyre. Roman city of Saintes.

Open: 1 May - 31 October.

Directions

Approaching from the north (A10 motorway). Take exit 35 (Saintes) and follow signs to Royan. On reaching the town, take Avenue de Rochefort (D733), then the first left (rue des Cendrilles) and follow signs to site. The entrance is 500 m. further on rue des Sansonnets. GPS: 45.646598, -1.028724

Charges guide

Per unit incl. 2 persons	€ 21.50 - € 32.00
extra person	€ 3.70 - € 5.50

Saint Augustin-sur-Mer

Le Logis du Breuil

F-17570 Saint Augustin-sur-Mer (Charente-Maritime) T: 05 46 23 23 45. E: info@logis-du-breuil.com
alanrogers.com/FR17190

The first impression on arrival at this impressive campsite is one of space. The site covers a 30-hectare expanse of farm pasture where (on different areas) cattle graze and children play. The 9 hectare camping areas are set among rows of mature and shady trees giving a dappled effect to the 320 grassy pitches. There are 250 with 3/10A electricity and all are very large with direct access to wide, unpaved alleys which lead on to the few tarmac roads around the site. The amenities are centred around the reception area and pool complex. The area around the site is very pleasant agricultural land and the beaches of the Atlantic coast are nearby. Also near are the oyster and mussel beds of Marennes and La Tremblade. The Gagnard family started the campsite over 25 years ago and obviously take great pride in what it has now become a peaceful, friendly and pleasant campsite from which to explore a delightful holiday area.

Facilities

Four well maintained toilet blocks are spaced around the camping area. Laundry facilities. Excellent shop, bar, restaurant and takeaway. Swimming pools (20/5-15/9). No evening entertainment. Play area. Indoor games area. Bicycle hire. Tennis. Excursions organised. WiFi. Gîtes, mobile homes and chalets to rent. Off site: Beach 10 mins drive to St Palais-sur-Mer and La Grande-Côte. Sailing 5 km.

Open: 1 May - 30 September.

Directions

From A10 exit 35, take the N150 to Saujon and continue on the N150 to Royan. Take the D25 towards La Palmyre (Zoo), then turn right onto the D145 towards Saint Augustin. Site is signed and is 2 km. on the left. GPS: 45.67555, -1.094817

Charges 2012

Per unit incl. 2 persons and electricity	€ 19.35 - € 28.10
extra person	€ 4.15 - € 7.20
child (under 7 yrs)	€ 3.60 - € 5.25
dog	€ 2.05 - € 3.10

Quiet - Rest - Space

Le Logis du Breuil ★★★

between land and sea

**Camping & Caravaning
Chalet & Mobilhomes
to rent**

Tel : (+33) 05 46 23 23 45
17570 Saint-Augustin-sur-mer

www.logis-du-breuil.com   info@logis-du-breuil.com

For latest campsite news, availability and prices visit
alanrogers.com

Saint Clément-des-Baleines
Camping la Plage
408 rue du Chaume, F-17590 Saint Clément-des-Baleines (Charente-Maritime) T: 05 46 29 42 62.
E: info@la-plage.com **alanrogers.com/FR17590**

This campsite, a member of the Airotel group, can be found at the western end of the Ile de Ré, very close to the imposing Phare des Baleines and just 100 m. from a sandy beach. Pitches are of average size and most are equipped with 10A electricity. Good selections of mobile homes are available for rent. Leisure facilities here include an attractive pool with a wide sunbathing terrace, and a multisports terrain. The bar/restaurant is the focal point for the site and a range of activities and entertainment take place there throughout the high season, including a daily children's club.

Facilities

One unisex toilet block provides good facilities and is kept clean and fresh. Washbasins in cubicles. Baby room and facilities for disabled visitors. Laundry. Basic motorcaravan service point. Bar. Restaurant. Takeaway food. Small shop.(July/Aug). Heated swimming pool and children's pool. Jacuzzi. Sauna and fitness suite. Games room. Multisports terrain. Play area. Entertainment and activities. Bicycle hire. WiFi (charged). Mobile homes to rent. Gas and electric barbecues only. Off site: Sandy beach 100 m. Phare des Baleines. Ars-en-Ré. Riding. Cycling. Walking.

Open: 4 April - 26 September.

Directions

From La Rochelle cross the toll bridge to the Ile de Ré. Continue on D735 to Ars-en-Ré, then to St Clement-des-Baleines and Phare des Baleines. Site is well signed from here. Large units take care when turning into site. GPS: 46.241186, -1.55345

Charges guide

Per unit incl. 3 persons and electricity	€ 42.75 - € 51.05
1 or 2 persons (excl. high season)	€ 17.85 - € 27.00
child (0-10 yrs)	€ 3.60 - € 13.00

Saint Clément-des-Baleines
Village Center la Côte Sauvage
336 rue de la Forêt, F-17590 Saint Clément-des-Baleines (Charente-Maritime) T: 08 25 00 20 30.
E: contact@village-center.com **alanrogers.com/FR17965**

Camping La Côte Sauvage is a member of the Village Center group, located on the Ile de Ré, close to the pretty village of Saint Clement-des-Baleines. There are 274 pitches here (80-100 sq.m), as well as a number of fully equipped tents which are available for rent. Unusually, the site also offers ten traditional yurts which have been attractively prepared in traditional style. Activities here are designed to take advantage of the site's natural setting and include ornithology and twilight nature trails. In high season, there is a snack bar which also serves ice creams.

Facilities

Snack bar. Children's play area. Children's activity programme. Volleyball. Bicycle hire. Tourist information. Fully equipped tents for rent. Off site: Shops and restaurants at St Clement-des-Baleines. Cycle tracks. Riding. Ornithology and nature trails.

Open: 2 April - 1 October.

Directions

Approaching from the toll bridge, follow D735 past La Couarde-sur-Mer and Ars-en-Ré as far as St Clement-des-Baleines. The site is well signed from here. GPS: 46.225423, -1.54462

Charges guide

| Per unit incl. 2 persons and electricity | € 18.00 - € 29.00 |

Saint Cyr
Flower Camping du Lac de Saint-Cyr
F-86130 Saint Cyr (Vienne) T: 05 49 62 57 22. E: contact@campinglacdesaintcyr.com
alanrogers.com/FR86090

This well organised, five-hectare campsite is part of a 300-hectare leisure park, based around a large lake with sailing and associated sports, and an area for swimming (supervised July/Aug). Land-based activities include tennis, two half courts, table tennis, fishing, badminton, pétanque, beach volleyball, TV room, and a well equipped fitness suite, all of which are free of charge. The campsite has around 185 touring pitches, ten mobile homes and three 'yurts' (canvas and wooden tents) for rent. The marked and generally separated pitches are all fully serviced with electricity (10A), water and drainage. Spacious and very natural, this is a tranquil setting.

Facilities

The main toilet block is modern and supplemented in peak season by a second unit, although they do attract some use by day trippers to the leisure facilities. Laundry facilities, and facilities for babies and disabled visitors. Shop, restaurant and takeaway (April-Sept). Playground on beach. Bicycle hire. Free WiFi. New heated swimming pool (2011). Off site: Riding 200 m. Golf 800 m. Watersports and activities around the lake.

Open: 1 April - 30 September.

Directions

Saint Cyr is about midway between Châtellerault and Poitiers. Site signed to east of N10 at Beaumont along D82 towards Bonneuil-Matours, and is part of the Parc de Loisirs de Saint Cyr. GPS: 46.71972, 0.46018

Charges guide

| Per unit incl. 2 persons and electricity | € 15.00 - € 27.00 |
| extra person | € 3.00 - € 5.00 |

For latest campsite news, availability and prices visit
alanrogers.com

Saint Denis d'Oléron
Les Hameaux des Marines

Rue des Seulières, F-17650 Saint Denis d'Oléron (Charente-Maritime) T: 05 55 84 34 48.
E: info@chalets-en-france.com **alanrogers.com/FR17660**

Les Hameaux des Marines is a member of the Chalets en France group. This group comprises four chalet parks in southern France. Please note, however, that there are no touring pitches here. This is the group's only coastal site and is attractively situated 300 m. from a fine sandy beach at the northern tip of the Ile d'Oleron. The nearest beach, the Plage des Huttes has been awarded the European Blue Flag accreditation for its cleanliness. The site is open all year and a new heated and covered swimming pool was recently added. The Ile d'Oleron has miles of excellent cycle tracks and a number of these run very close to the site. The 48 wooden chalets here are attractively dispersed around the site and are all available for rent.

Facilities

No bar, restaurant or snack bar, but bread can be ordered. Ice-creams for sale. Swimming pool (9x5 m). Play area. Games room. Boules. Communal barbecue - electric barbecues to hire. Tourist information. Chalets for rent. Security barrier. Off site: Nearest beach 300 m. Sailing and windsurfing. Fishing. Riding. Cycle and walking trails. Supermarket 6 km. St Denis d'Oléron with good shops and restaurants.

Open: All year.

Directions

Take exit 35 from the A10 motorway (Saintes) and then head west on the D728 to Marennes. Cross the bridge to the Ile d'Oléron and then follow the D26 and D734 to St Denis d'Oleron at the north of the island. Turn sharp left at 'Croustille Snack Bar' into rue St Denis signed Bétaudière. Follow this road for approx. 2 km. and at T junction, turn left and the site is on your left. GPS: 46.01355, -1.39182

Charges 2012

Contact the site for details.

Saint Georges-d'Oléron
Chadotel le Domaine d'Oléron

La Jousselinière, F-17190 Saint Georges-d'Oléron (Charente-Maritime) T: 05 46 76 54 97.
E: contact@chadotel.com **alanrogers.com/FR17470**

This is a neat, well presented and well managed site where you will receive a warm and friendly welcome from Anneke and Freddy who speak excellent English. The site is set in a peaceful rural location between St Pierre and St Georges and is part of the Chadotel group. At present there are 172 pitches of which 60 are for touring units. The pitches are generously sized (100-150 sq.m) and are mostly sunny, level and easily accessible, all with 10A electricity. The site is close to the Forest of Saumonards and is just 3 km. from the beach. The local port, shops and restaurants are also nearby. Boat trips are available around the island to see Fort Boyard, Chassiron lighthouse and the Château d'Oléron.

Facilities

Two modern sanitary blocks include facilities for disabled visitors and babies. Washing machines and dryers. Ironing room. Restaurant, snack bar and takeaway. Bar with TV. Bread delivered daily. Swimming pool with slides (1/5-14/9). Adventure style play area. Six pétanque lanes. Bicycle hire. Organised entertainment two or three times a week in July/Aug. Gas barbecues only on pitches, communal areas for charcoal. WiFi in some areas (charged). Off site: Fishing and riding 2 km. Golf 8 km. Royan Zoo. Cycle trails.

Open: 3 April - 25 September.

Directions

Take D734 to St Pierre. Turn right in St Pierre after Leclerc supermarket. At next roundabout turn left towards Le Bois Fleury. After passing airfield, turn right and left and site is on the left. GPS: 45.9674685, -1.3192605

Charges guide

Per unit incl. 2 persons	
and electricity	€ 15.00 - € 30.50
extra person	€ 5.80
child (2-13 yrs)	€ 3.80
dog (max. 1)	€ 3.20

Camping Holidays

Charente Maritime (17)

chad⊙tel

Domaine d'Oléron****

Chadotel
Camping Domaine d'Oléron
F- 17190 Saint Georges d'Oléron
Tél. +33 (0)2 51 33 05 05 - info@chadotel.com **www.chadotel.com**

Pitches for tents, caravans & motorhomes
Quality mobile homes
Swimming pool and waterslide
Entertainment for adults & children
Cycle path

For latest campsite news, availability and prices visit
alanrogers.com

Saint Georges-d'Oléron

Camping les Gros Joncs

850 route de Ponthezieres, les Sables Vignier B.P. 17, F-17190 Saint Georges-d'Oléron (Charente-Maritime)
T: 05 46 76 52 29. E: info@les-gros-joncs.fr **alanrogers.com/FR17070**

Situated on the west coast of the island of Ile d'Oléron, les Gros Joncs is owned and run by the Cavel family who work hard to keep the site up to date and of high quality. There are 50 or so touring pitches of a good size (some extra large) with tall pine trees providing a choice between full sun and varying degrees of shade. All have water and 12A electricity to hand. The main building not only houses a light and airy reception, but also a modern, beautifully presented bar and restaurant, a fully stocked and competitively priced shop, an attractive indoor swimming pool and a magnificent spa. The indoor pool, with water jets and jacuzzi, has glass sides which in good weather are opened out onto an outdoor pool area where there are also water slides, a paddling area and plenty of sunbathing terraces. Both pools are heated. The spa offers hydrotherapy and beauty treatments, sauna, and a comprehensive fitness room. Much attention has been given to the needs of disabled visitors here, including chalets where space and equipment are specially adapted. All the amenities are of a standard unusual on a campsite.

Facilities

Traditional style toilet facilities are kept to a high standard. Laundry facilities. Motorcaravan services. Well stocked shop with bakery and restaurant (all year). Indoor pool with first class spa and wellness centre (all year, with professional staff). Outdoor pool (heated, 1/4-15/9). Bicycle hire. Children's clubs (1/7-15/9). Internet access and WiFi (charged). ATM. No charcoal barbecues. Off site: Beach 200 and 400 m. via a sandy path. Bus service from Chéray. Fishing 2 km. Riding 6 km. Golf 8 km.

Open: All year.

Directions

Cross the viaduct onto the Ile d'Oléron. Take the D734 (St Georges-d'Oléron). At traffic lights in Chéray turn left. Follow signs for camping and Sable Vignier. Soon signs indicate directions to les Gros Joncs. GPS: 45.95356, -1.37979

Charges guide

Per unit incl. 2 persons and electricity	€ 18.70 - € 46.10
extra person	€ 6.12 - € 12.00
child (0-7 yrs)	€ 2.80 - € 7.40
dog	€ 3.00

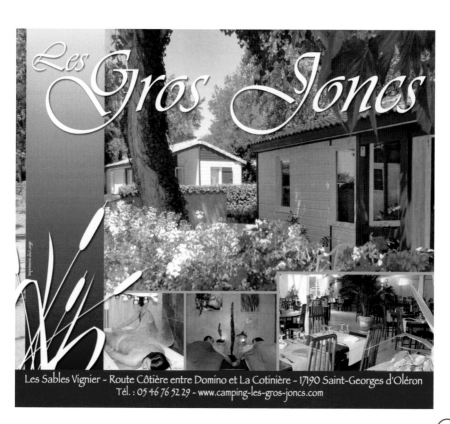

Les Sables Vignier - Route Côtière entre Domino et La Cotinière - 17190 Saint-Georges d'Oléron
Tél. : 05 46 76 52 29 - www.camping-les-gros-joncs.com

For latest campsite news, availability and prices visit
alanrogers.com

Saint Georges-de-Didonne
Camping Bois Soleil

2 avenue de Suzac, F-17110 Saint Georges-de-Didonne (Charente-Maritime)

T: 05 46 05 05 94. E: camping.bois.soleil@wanadoo.fr **alanrogers.com/FR17010**

Close to the sea, Bois Soleil is a large site in three parts, with 165 serviced pitches for touring units and a few for tents. All the touring pitches are hedged and have electricity, with water and drainage between two. The main part, Les Pins, is attractive with trees and shrubs providing shade. Opposite is La Mer with direct access to the beach, some areas with less shade and an area for tents. The third part, La Forêt, is for caravan holiday homes. It is best to book your preferred area as it can be full mid June to late August. Excellent private sanitary facilities are available to rent, either on your pitch or at a block (subject to availability). There are a few pitches with lockable gates. The areas are all well tended and are cleared and raked between visitors. This lively site offers something for everyone, whether it be a beach-side spot or a traditional pitch, plenty of activities or the quiet life. Recent additions include a new toilet block and some accommodation to rent with sea views. The wide sandy beach is popular with children and provides a pleasant walk to the pretty town of Saint Georges-de-Didonne.

Facilities

Each area has one large and one small sanitary block. Heated block near reception. Cleaned twice daily, they include facilities for disabled visitors and babies. Launderette. Supermarket, bakery, beach shop (all 15/4-15/9). Restaurant, bar and takeaway (all 15/4-15/9). Swimming pool (heated 15/6-15/9). Steam room. Tennis. Bicycle hire. Play area. TV room and library. Internet terminal and WiFi. Charcoal barbecues not permitted. Dogs are not accepted 26/6-5/9. Off site: Fishing, riding 500 m. Golf 20 km.

Open: 2 April - 9 October.

Directions

From Royan centre take coast road (D25) along the seafront of Saint Georges-de-Didonne towards Meschers. Site is signed at roundabout at end of the main beach. GPS: 45.583583, -0.986533

Charges guide

Per unit incl. 3 persons	
and electricity	€ 26.00 - € 50.00
extra person	€ 3.00 - € 8.50
child (3-7 yrs)	free - € 6.50
dog	€ 3.00 - € 4.00

Less 20% outside July/Aug.
Camping Cheques accepted.

Saint Georges-d'Oléron
Camping l'Anse des Pins

Chemin du Râteau-Domino, F-17190 Saint Georges-d'Oléron (Charente-Maritime) T: 05 46 76 55 97.

E: camping-apv@wanadoo.fr **alanrogers.com/FR17270**

Rock pools, sand dunes and spectacular sunsets, with sea views from many of the pitches, help to make this site attractive to those seeking an away from it all holiday in a quiet part of the island of the Ile d'Oléron. The campsite is arranged in three areas, some areas with good shade, others in full sun. There are 350 pitches including 137 for touring units, the remainder used for mobile homes. All pitches have electricity (3-10A) and 22 also have water and drainage. Across the road are the leisure facilities which include a complex of outdoor pools (unheated) with a toboggan and flume, and an indoor pool with a sauna. There is a bar and snack bar with takeaway and a small shop. Activities are organised for all (games, competitions) with some evening entertainment in high season. The nearest village (Domino) is about 500 m. away and has a daily market.

Facilities

Two main toilet blocks (plus two small blocks for high season use) with mainly British style toilets. Showers and washbasins in cabins. Laundry facilities. Gas supplies. Bar. Shop with limited takeaway and snack bar. Indoor pool (all season) and outdoor swimming and paddling pools (April-Sept). Play area. Activities in high season (1/7-31/8). Tennis. Boules. Bicycle hire. WiFi. Barbecues only permitted in a communal area. Off site: Beach 50 m. Bicycle hire 1 km. Riding 10 km. St Georges 5 km.

Open: April - October.

Directions

Cross the bridge onto Ile d'Oléron and follow the D734 (St Dennis). In Chéray, turn left at traffic lights (signed Camping). Stay on this road to Domino (avoid side roads). Follow green signs to Rex and l'Anse des Pins Camping. Narrow roads. GPS: 45.97059, -1.3864

Charges guide

Per unit incl. 2 persons	
and electricity	€ 22.50 - € 37.30
extra person	€ 7.80 - € 8.30
child (0-4 yrs)	€ 3.80 - € 4.50
dog	€ 2.60

Bois Soleil

Camping ★★★★
Charente-Maritime

Surrounded by pine trees and a sandy beach on the Atlantic Coast, with one direct access to the beach, Bois Soleil proposes to you many attractions like tennis, tabletennis, children playgrounds and entertainment. Shops, take-away and snack-bar with big TV screen.

Spring and Summer

2, avenue de Suzac - 17110 ST GEORGES DE DIDONNE
Tel: 0033 546 05 05 94 - Fax: 0033 546 06 27 43
www.bois-soleil.com / e-mail: camping.bois.soleil@wanadoo.fr

Saint Georges-les-Baillargeaux

Kawan Village le Futuriste

F-86130 Saint Georges-les-Baillargeaux (Vienne) T: 05 49 52 47 52. E: camping-le-futuriste@wanadoo.fr

alanrogers.com/FR86040

Le Futuriste is a neat, modern site, open all year and close to Futuroscope. It is very convenient for the A10 and N10 motorway network. There are 112 individual, level, grassy pitches of a generous size and divided by flowering hedges. Eighty-two have electricity (6A) and 30 also have water and waste water connections. Pitches are mostly open although some do have the benefit of shade from trees. All are accessed via tarmac roads. There are lovely panoramic views from this site and the popular attraction of Futuroscope can be clearly seen. Large units are accepted by prior arrangement. There is a pleasant restaurant on site offering good food at reasonable prices. Entertainment takes place in the daytime rather than in the evenings. This site is ideal for a short stay to visit Futuroscope which is only 2 km. away but it is equally good for longer stays to see the region.

Facilities

Excellent, clean sanitary facilities in two heated blocks. Good facilities for disabled visitors and babies. Laundry facilities. Shop (1/5-30/9, bread to order). Bar/restaurant snack bar and takeaway (1/7-31/8). Heated outdoor pool with slide and paddling pool (1/7-31/8). Covered pool. Games room. TV. Boules. Multisports area. Lake fishing. Daily activities in season. Youth groups not accepted. Only gas and electric barbecues allowed. Off site: Bicycle hire 500 m. Hypermarket 600 m. Futuroscope 2 km. Golf 5 km. Riding 10 km.

Open: All year.

Directions

From either A10 autoroute or N10, take Futuroscope exit. Site is east of both roads, off D20 (St Georges-les-Baillargeaux). Follow signs to St Georges. Site on hill; turn by water tower and site is on left. GPS: 46.3952, 0.2341

Charges 2012

Per unit incl. 3 persons	
and electricity	€ 20.60 - € 27.80
extra person	€ 2.30 - € 3.20
dog	€ 2.20

Camping Cheques accepted.

Open all year. Panoramic view over the Futuroscope situated at 2 kms.
Heated swimming pool, pond, snack, bar, restaurant.
Chalets for hire.

86130 St-Georges les Baillargeaux
Tel.: 0033 549 52 47 52
Fax: 0033 549 37 23 33
www.camping-le-futuriste.fr

For latest campsite news, availability and prices visit

alanrogers.com

Saint Georges-de-Didonne
Village Center les Catalpas

45 chemin d'Enlias, F-17110 Saint Georges-de-Didonne (Charente-Maritime) T: 04 99 57 21 21.
E: contact@village-center.com **alanrogers.com/FR17350**

Camping les Catalpas is a member of the Village Center group and is located close to the Gironde estuary at St Georges-de-Didonne. Pitches are grassy and there is a choice between sunny and more shady options. A number of chalets are available for rent. On-site amenities include a swimming pool, children's paddling pool, a small shop and a snack bar. A large supermarket is just 3 minutes' walk from the site. There are also some excellent beaches within a few minutes' walk of the site, and St Georges has all the amenities one would expect of a well established holiday resort.

Facilities

Two modern sanitary blocks with good facilities for disabled visitors and babies. Washing machines and dryers. Snack bar, pizzeria and bar (all season). Shop. Heated swimming pool with paddling pool. Games room. Pétanque. TV room. Entertainment July/Aug. Gas barbecues only on pitches. Chalets for rent. Internet access. Off site: Nearest beach 10 mins walk.

Open: 24 June - 4 September.

Directions

From Royan take the southbound coast road (D25) to St Georges-de-Didonne. The site is located in parkland close to the Avenue d'Aquitaine and is well indicated. GPS: 45.61529, -0.99477

Charges guide

Per unit incl. 2 persons	€ 16.00 - € 23.00
extra person (over 5 yrs)	€ 2.00 - € 5.00

Saint Just-Luzac
Castel Camping Séquoia Parc

La Josephtrie, F-17320 Saint Just-Luzac (Charente-Maritime) T: 05 46 85 55 55. E: info@sequoiaparc.com
alanrogers.com/FR17140

This is definitely a site not to be missed. Approached by an avenue of flowers, shrubs and trees, Séquoia Parc is a Castel site set in the grounds of La Josephtrie, a striking château with beautifully restored outbuildings and courtyard area with a bar and restaurant. Most of the 426 pitches are 140 sq.m. with 6/10A electricity connections and separated by mature shrubs providing plenty of privacy. The site has 300 mobile homes and chalets, with 126 used by tour operators. This is a popular site with a children's club and entertainment throughout the season and reservation is necessary in high season. The site itself is designed to a high specification with reception in a large, light and airy room retaining its original beams and leading to the courtyard area where you find the bar and restaurant. The pool complex with water slides, large paddling pool and sunbathing area is impressive. A new terraced area adjacent to the snack bar has been created so that you can buy a snack and then sit in a very pleasant garden setting with sunshades, to eat your meal. Member of Leading Campings group.

Facilities

Three spotlessly clean luxurious toilet blocks, include units with washbasin and shower and facilities for disabled visitors and children. Dishwashing sinks. Large laundry. Motorcaravan service point. Gas supplies. Large supermarket. Boutique. Restaurant/bar and takeaway. Impressive swimming pool complex with water slides and large paddling pool. Massage (July/Aug). Tennis. Games and TV rooms. Bicycle hire. Pony trekking. Organised entertainment/excursions all season. Children's farm. WiFi in reception area (charged). Electric barbecues not permitted. Off site: Supermarket 5 km. Fishing 5 km.

Open: 12 May - 9 September (with all services).

Directions

From Rochefort take D733 south for 12 km. Turn west on D123 to Ile d'Oléron. Continue for 12 km. Turn southeast on D728 (Saintes). Site signed, in 1 km. on left. From A10 at Saintes take D728 and leave this road by turning right shortly after St Just. Site is signed. GPS: 45.81095, -1.06109

Charges 2012

Per unit incl. 2 persons and electricity	€ 21.00 - € 48.00
extra person	€ 7.00 - € 9.00
child (3-11 yrs)	€ 3.00 - € 5.00

Near Oléron island and its beaches

Aquapark of 2000 m²!

Kids club during whole season

Animations and horseriding

Bar restaurant Le Carrousel

Large pitches

Luxurious cottages, mobilehomes

Online bookings: **www.sequoiaparc.com**
17320 Saint Just-Luzac, France, tel.: +33 5 46 85 55 55

Open from 12/05 to
05/09/2012

Séquoia Parc
Les Castels Camping Village
CHARENTE MARITIME - FRANCE

For latest campsite news, availability and prices visit
alanrogers.com

Saint-Hilaire-la-Palud

Camping le Lidon

F-79210 Saint-Hilaire-la-Palud (Deux-Sèvres) T: 05 49 35 33 64. E: info@le-lidon.com

alanrogers.com/FR79060

Le Lidon is located within the Marais Poitevin, an enchanting region of over 400 km. of rivers, canals and fens lying to the west of Niort. This site has 132 grassy pitches scattered across three hectares, 116 for touring. The site's selection of rented accommodation includes fully equipped, Canadian-style tents and chalets. The Marais Poitevin is undeniably best explored by canoe or punt and it is possible to rent these on site. During high season, an activity and entertainment programme is organised including a children's club and various family activities.

Facilities

Two toilet blocks with facilities for disabled visitors and children. Laundry. Motorcaravan service point. Shop, bar, snack bar. Bread available to order. Heated swimming pool (15/6-31/8). Bar/restaurant. Takeaway food. Games room. Play area. Direct access to river. Fishing. Bicycle and canoe hire. Entertainment programme (July/Aug). Tents and chalets for rent. Off site: St-Hilaire-la-Palud with shops and cafés, and an open-air cinema. Fishing (river). Riding 2 km. Tennis 3 km. Golf 25 km.

Open: 9 April - 17 September.

Directions

Approaching from the north (Niort) leave A10 autoroute at exit 33 and head west on the N248 as far as Epannes. Head north here on the D1 to Sansais and then west on the D3 to St-Hilaire-la-Palud. Site is well signed to the right just after the village. Long access road. GPS: 46.2838, -0.74345

Charges guide

Per unit incl. 2 persons
and electricity   € 20.10 - € 26.00
Camping Cheques accepted.

Saint-Palais-sur-Mer

Camping le Logis

22 rue des Palombes, F-17420 Saint-Palais-sur-Mer (Charente-Maritime) T: 05 46 23 20 23.
E: reservations@yukadivillages.com **alanrogers.com/FR17530**

Le Logis is a member of the Yukadi Villages group and is a popular site close to the attractive resort of St-Palais-sur-Mer on the edge of the forest of St Augustin. The site was established back in 1936 and there are now 750 pitches here. The majority of these are occupied by mobile homes and chalets (many for rent) but there are 216 touring pitches also available. These are grassy and of a reasonable size, and all have 5A electrical connections. This is a lively site in high season with a varied programme of entertainment and activities, including concerts and discovery excursions into the forest.

Facilities

Four heated sanitary blocks. Facilities for disabled visitors. Laundry. Shop, bar and snack bar. Waterpark with heated pools, children's pool and water slides. Games room. Tennis. Play area. TV room. Multisports area. Bicycle hire. Activity and entertainment programme. Mobile homes and chalets for rent. WiFi in some areas (free). Off site: Fishing and golf 600 m. Beach and riding 800 m. Royan 8 km. Cycle and walking tracks in the forest of St Augustin.

Open: 13 May - 4 September.

Directions

From Royan, head west on D25 towards La Palmyre. Pass the golf course (on the right), and then turn left immediately towards St-Palais-sur-Mer. Turn left at the next crossroads and site is 200 m. further on the right. GPS: 45.65208, -1.1159

Charges guide

Per unit incl. 2 persons
and electricity   € 21.00 - € 40.80

Saint-Trojan-les-Bains

Camping Indigo Oléron

11 avenue des Bris, F-17370 Saint-Trojan-les-Bains (Charente-Maritime) T: 05 46 76 02 39.
E: oleron@camping-indigo.com **alanrogers.com/FR17580**

This attractive four-hectare site is a member of the Indigo group. It is close to the popular seaside resort of St-Trojan-les-Bains on the south side of the island. There are 200 pitches, which vary in size, most of which have electrical connections (10A French type). Indigo Oléron is situated in a lightly wooded setting on undulating, sandy terrain, just 1 km. from the nearest sandy beach. Building materials must be sympathetic with the natural environment, for example, the use of wooden decking around the pool and you won't find mobile homes for rent here, only specially designed wood and canvas safari-style tents.

Facilities

Two modern toilet blocks provide washbasins in cabins, showers and British style toilets. Facilities for disabled visitors. Laundry. Motorcaravan service point. Heated swimming pool (June-Sept). Small bar. Very small shop (mainly bread). Bicycle hire. Sandy play area. Activities and entertainment. Gas or electric barbecues only. Tourist information. Max. 1 dog. Off site: Beach and fishing 0.5 km. Supermarket 3 km.

Open: Easter - 3 October.

Directions

From Marennes, cross bridge to Ile d'Oléron (D26) then follow signs to St-Trojan on D126. Drive through shopping area to second roundabout. Turn right and continue ahead. Follow the railway track and where the road bends left, follow the road and the site is then on your left. GPS: 45.83152, -1.213882

Charges guide

Per unit incl. 2 persons
and electricity   € 18.80 - € 30.00

We can book this site for you! Call 01580 214000   alan rogers ◑ travel

For latest campsite news, availability and prices visit
alanrogers.com

Saintes

Camping Municipal Au Fil de l'Eau

6 rue de Courbiac, F-17100 Saintes (Charente-Maritime) T: 05 46 93 08 00. E: campingaufildeleau@sfr.fr

alanrogers.com/FR17200

Saintes is a 2,000-year-old Gallo-Roman city, well worth a couple of days to visit the cathedral, the abbey, the Arch of Germanicus, the Amphitheatre and several museums, all within walking distance of the site (reception can provide a city map). Do take a stroll through the well tended, very pretty public gardens by the riverside. This large, pleasant site is run as a franchise from the local municipality and has 214 mostly shady and generally grassy level pitches, with 132 electric hook-ups, and six mobile homes for rent.

Facilities

The main toilet block is a large building, with two smaller older units opened at peak times. Washbasins in cubicles. Facilities for disabled visitors. Laundry building. Motorcaravan service point. Shop. Bar. Restaurant and takeaway (July/Aug). TV room. Boules. Badminton. Minigolf. Playground. Fishing. WiFi in some areas (charged). Barrier system and guardian lives on site. Twin-axle caravans not accepted. Off site: Adjacent open-air Olympic size pool complex, free for campers. Bicycle hire 2 km. Riding 3 km. Golf 6 km.

Open: 1 May - 30 September.

Directions

From east and northeast follow signs for town and site, turning right after river. Avoiding centre and from all other directions, use bypass following signs for N137 La Rochelle to large roundabout at northern end. Turn right for town centre and Camping Municipal (at this roundabout coming from La Rochelle N137, go straight on). Left at next roundabout, ahead at two more, right at next. Left at mini-roundabout. Site is 200 m. on right. GPS: 45.755283, -0.628133

Charges guide

Per unit incl. 2 persons and electricity	€ 17.00
extra person	€ 4.50

Vaux-sur-Mer

Camping le Val Vert

108 avenue Frederic Garnier, F-17640 Vaux-sur-Mer (Charente-Maritime) T: 05 46 38 25 51.
E: camping-val-vert@wanadoo.fr **alanrogers.com/FR17310**

Situated in seven acres of lush countryside (hence its name 'green valley'), this is a charming campsite, just 200 metres from the village of Vaux-sur-Mer, and 900 metres from the sandy beach at Nouzon. There are 95 touring pitches, all with either 6A or 10A electricity (French connections – adaptors available). Extra long cables are required for some pitches, which are of average size (100 sq.m) with good access, even for larger units. Some are terraced. Although entertainment is organised in high season, facilities on the site are minimal as the accent here is on peace and tranquillity.

Facilities

There are ample toilet and shower facilities. Separate facilities for visitors with disabilities. Laundry facilities. Shop, bar, restaurant and takeaway (all 10/6-10/9). Swimming and paddling pools (29/4-10/9; supervised in high season). Play area. Pétanque. Off site: Village facilities including bar, supermarket and bank with ATM 200 m. Beach 900 m. Fishing 1 km. Boat launching 5 km. Golf and riding 10 km.

Open: 8 April - 30 September.

Directions

Follow camping signs from the village of Vaux-sur-Mer. GPS: 45.64400, -1.0632

Charges guide

Per unit incl. 1-3 persons	€ 17.00 - € 25.50
extra person	€ 4.00 - € 5.40
child (1-7 yrs)	€ 3.40 - € 4.40
electricity (6/10A)	€ 4.10 - € 4.70

NEW digital iPad editions

alan rogers

Available on the App Store

FREE Alan Rogers bookstore app - digital editions of all 2012 guides

alanrogers.com/digital

For latest campsite news, availability and prices visit

alanrogers.com

Burgundy is a wonderfully evocative region offering breathtaking châteaux and cathedrals, rolling hills and heady mountain views, vineyards and superlative cuisine, not to mention of course, a wide variety of world-renowned wines.

DÉPARTEMENTS: 21 CÔTE D'OR, 58 NIÈVRE, 71 SAÔNE-ET-LOIRE, 89 YONNE

MAJOR CITY: DIJON

In the rich heartland of France, Burgundy was once a powerful independent state and important religious centre. Its golden age is reflected in the area's magnificent art and architecture: the grand palaces and art collections of Dijon, the great pilgrimage church of Vézelay, the Cistercian Abbaye de Fontenay and the evocative abbey remains at Cluny, once the most powerful monastery in Europe.

However, Burgundy is best known for its wine, including some of the world's finest, notably from the great vineyards of the Côte d'Or and Chablis, and also for its sublime cuisine. You'll also notice how driving through the country villages is like reading a wine merchant's list with plenty of opportunities for tasting and choosing your wine.

The area is criss-crossed by navigable waterways and includes the Parc Régional du Morvan; good walking country amidst lush, rolling wooded landscape.

Places of interest

Autun: 12th-century St Lazare cathedral.

Beaune: medieval town; Museum of Burgundy Wine.

Cluny: Europe's largest Benedictine abbey.

Dijon: Palace of the Dukes, Fine Arts Museum, Burgundian Folklore Museum.

Fontenay: Fontenay Abbey and Cloister.

Joigny: medieval town.

Mâcon: Maison des Vins (wine centre).

Paray-le-Monial: Romanesque basilica, pilgrimage centre.

Sens: historic buildings, museum with fine Gallo-Roman collections.

Vézelay: fortified medieval hillside.

Cuisine of the region

Many dishes are wine based, including *Poulet au Meursault* and *Coq au Chambertin*. Dijon is known for its *pain d'épice* (spiced honey cake) and spicy mustard.

Boeuf Bourguignon: braised beef simmered in a red wine-based sauce.

Garbure: heavy soup, a mixture of pork, cabbage, beans and sausages.

Gougère: cheese pastry based on Gruyère.

Jambon persillé: parsley-flavoured ham, served cold in jelly.

Matelote: freshwater fish soup, usually based on a red wine sauce.

Meurette: red wine-based sauce with small onions, used with fish or poached egg dishes.

www.burgundy-tourism.com
documentation@crt-bourgogne.fr
(0)3 80 28 02 80

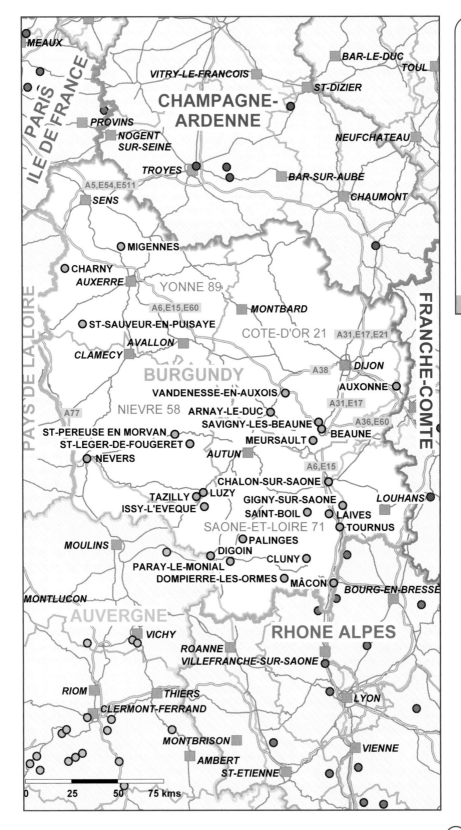

For latest campsite news, availability and prices visit
alanrogers.com

Arnay le Duc

Camping de l'Etang de Fouché

Rue du 8 mai 1945, F-21230 Arnay le Duc (Côte d'Or) T: 03 80 90 02 23. E: info@campingfouche.com
alanrogers.com/FR21040

Useful as a stop en route to or from the Mediterranean or indeed for longer stays, this quite large but peaceful, lakeside site with its new bar/restaurant and swimming pool complex, can be very busy during the school holidays, and is probably better visited outside the main season. There are over 200 good sized pitches, on fairly level grass and all with 10A electricity (some with water). Many are hedged and offer a choice of shade or more open aspect. In July/August there are regular activities for children and adults. A 2 km. stroll around the lake is very pleasant.

Facilities

Two new toilet blocks and third (totally refurbished) provide all the necessary modern facilities (male and female are separate). Facilities for disabled visitors. Baby room. Washing machines and dishwashing under cover. Shop, bar, restaurant, takeaway (all 15/5-15/9). New small heated outdoor swimming pool (15/5-10/9). Boules. TV/games room. Playground. Fishing. Bicycle hire. WiFi. Off site: Town centre 800 m. Lakeside beach with playground, water slides, pedaloes, canoes. Riding 2 km.

Open: 15 April - 15 October.

Directions

From A6 (exit 24) take D981, 16 km. to the town. Turn left on D906 for about 400 m. and site is signed to left. GPS: 47.13411, 4.49840

Charges guide

Per unit incl. 2 persons and electricity	€ 19.90 - € 25.90
extra person	€ 4.70 - € 6.50
child (2-10 yrs)	€ 2.40 - € 3.60
dog	€ 2.00

Auxonne

Camping de l'Arquebuse

Route d'Athée, F-21130 Auxonne (Côte d'Or) T: 03 80 31 06 89. E: camping.arquebuse@wanadoo.fr
alanrogers.com/FR21090

This is an all-year-round site located in the Northern Jura with a riverside setting on the Saône. L'Arquebuse has 100 level, unmarked pitches on grass, of which ten are occupied by mobile homes and chalets. All have 10A electricity and a variety of trees give shade to some pitches. Auxonne is close to both the A36 and A39 motorways and this site may prove a useful overnight stop. The site has bar/restaurant, Le Pinocchio, and the adjacent 'base nautique' offers a good range of leisure activities, including canoeing, windsurfing, mountain biking as well as a large swimming pool. Auxonne is an attractive town, fortified by Vauban, and is renowned as the capital of the Saône valley. The town's most famous former occupant is Napoleon and he spent two years at the Auxonne military academy. Not surprisingly there are several monuments celebrating his time here!

Facilities

Basic toilet block, heated in winter, provides mostly Turkish style toilets and open washbasins (cleaning can be variable). Washing machine. Small shop (1/5-31/10). Restaurant/bar (1/1-15/12). Pizzeria. Takeaway meals. Play area. WiFi. Chalets for rent. Off site: Swimming pool, windsurfing, canoeing, boat trips and fishing. Motorcaravan services. Fortified town of Auxonne with shops, bars and restaurants 1 km. Dijon 34 km.

Open: All year.

Directions

From the A39 autoroute take exit 5 and the N5 for about 6 km. to Auxonne. Site is signed to the left just before crossing the bridge over the Saône. Site is a few hundred metres. GPS: 47.19941, 5.38365

Charges guide

Per unit incl. 2 persons and electricity	€ 17.00 - € 18.80
extra person	€ 3.70
child (under 7 yrs)	€ 2.20
dog	€ 2.00

Camping l'Arquebuse ✱✱✱

- 3 star campsite
- Open all year
- Wifi
- Washing machines and dryers
- Restaurant with terrace
- At the bank of the Saône
- Pool 10 metres from the campsite
- Shop
- Bungalow tents and mobile homes for rent
- Play area for children

Camping l'Arquebuse - Route d'Athée - 21130 Auxonne - Tel: 0033 (0)380 31 06 89 - Fax: 0033 (0)380 31 12 62
E-mail: camping.arquebuse@wanadoo.fr - www.campingarquebuse.com - GPS: 47.198955, 5.382580

Beaune
Camping Municipal les Cent Vignes

10 rue Auguste Dubois, F-21200 Beaune (Côte d'Or) T: 03 80 22 03 91.
E: campinglescentvignes@mairie-beaune.fr **alanrogers.com/FR21020**

Les Cent Vignes is a very well kept site offering 116 individual pitches of good size, separated by neat beech hedges high enough to maintain a fair amount of privacy. Over half of the pitches are on grass, ostensibly for tents, the remainder on hardstandings with electricity for caravans. A popular site, within walking distance of the town centre, les Cent Vignes becomes full mid June to early September but with many short-stay campers there are departures each day and reservations can be made. The Côte de Beaune, situated southeast of the Côte d'Or, produces some of the very best French wines.

Facilities

Two modern and fully equipped sanitary blocks, one of which can be heated, should be large enough. Nearly all washbasins are in cabins. Laundry facilities. Shop, bar, restaurant with takeaway (all 1/4-15/10). Playground. Sports area with tennis, basketball, volleyball and boules. TV room. Barbecue area. WiFi. Off site: Centre of Beaune 1 km. Bicycle hire 1 km. Riding 2 km. Fishing and windsurfing 3 km. Golf 4 km.

Open: 15 March - 31 October.

Directions

From autoroute exit 24 follow signs for Beaune centre on D2 road, camping signs to site in about 1 km. Well signed from other routes.
GPS: 47.03304, 4.83911

Charges guide

Per unit incl. 2 persons and electricity	€ 14.90 - € 16.30
extra person	€ 3.40 - € 3.90
child (under 7 yrs)	€ 1.70 - € 1.90

Châlon-sur-Saône
Camping du Pont de Bourgogne

Rue Julien Leneveu, Saint-Marcel, F-71380 Châlon-sur-Saône (Saône-et-Loire) T: 03 85 48 26 86.
E: campingchalon71@wanadoo.fr **alanrogers.com/FR71140**

This is a well presented and cared for site, useful for an overnight stop or for a longer stay to explore the local area. It is close to the A6 Autoroute, and the interesting market town of Châlon-sur-Saône is only 2 km. There are 100 slightly sloping pitches (90 sq.m) all with 10A electricity, most on grass, but 30 have a gravel surface. They are separated by beach hedging, and a variety of mature trees gives varying amounts of shade. Many pitches overlook the river, a good spot to watch the passing boats. Access is easy for large outfits.

Facilities

Three toilet blocks, two traditional in style and fittings. The third is a superb modern building, including a children's bathroom, disabled bathroom and family shower. Motorcaravan services. Dishwashing facilities, laundry. No shop but essentials kept in the bar (bread to order). Modern bar/restaurant (July/Aug). Simple play area. Bicycle hire arranged. WiFi. Off site: Fishing and boat ramp 200 m. Municipal swimming pool 300 m. Golf, sailing 1 km. Riding 10 km. Châlon-sur-Saône with many shops, bars, banks etc.

Open: 1 April - 30 September.

Directions

From A6 exit 26 (Châlon-Sud), take N80 (signed Dôle) to second roundabout. Take fourth exit (signed Roseraie) and fork right (Les Chavannes). At traffic lights turn right (signed Roseraie) under bridge to site entrance 500 m. GPS: 46.78448, 4.87295

Charges guide

Per unit incl. 2 persons and electricity	€ 19.40 - € 26.10
extra person	€ 4.70 - € 6.30
child (under 7 yrs)	€ 3.30 - € 4.80
Camping Cheques accepted.	

Charny
Flower Camping des Platanes

41 route de la Mothe, F-89120 Charny (Yonne) T: 03 86 91 83 60. E: campingdesplatanes@wanadoo.fr
alanrogers.com/FR89070

Peacefully situated in the village of Charny, this is a tranquil, quiet site, yet within easy reach of the A6 autoroute and only 1.5 hours from Paris. The important archaeological site of Guédelon castle is nearby, the Chablis wines of the Yonne are ready for discovery and there are delightful walks around two local lakes. There are currently 82 level, grass pitches, all with 16A electricity. With 27 used for touring units (some now with water and waste water), the remainder are used for rented holiday homes and seasonal units.

Facilities

A modern, purpose-built, heated toilet block provides separate areas for men and women. Washbasins in cabins. Facilities for disabled visitors. Laundry. Motorcaravan service point. Takeaway (June-Sept). Heated swimming pool (15/5-30/9). Bicycle and barbecue hire. Play area for under fives. WiFi. Off site: Fishing 500 m. Riding 7 km. Walking.

Open: 15 March - 30 October.

Directions

Leave A6 at exit 18 and follow D943 towards Montargis for 14 km. Turn left on D950 and site is on right at start of village. GPS: 47.891, 3.092

Charges guide

Per unit incl. 2 persons and electricity	€ 15.50 - € 19.50
extra person	€ 3.00 - € 4.50
child (2-7 yrs)	€ 2.00 - € 3.00

(247)

We can book this site for you! Call 01580 214000 · alan rogers travel

Gigny-sur-Saône

Kawan Village Château de l'Epervière

 539

Rue du Château, F-71240 Gigny-sur-Saône (Saône-et-Loire) T: 03 85 94 16 90.
E: domaine-de-leperviere@wanadoo.fr **alanrogers.com/FR71070**

This popular and high quality site is peacefully situated in the wooded grounds of a 16th-century château, close to the A6 and near the village of Gigny-sur-Saône. It is within walking distance of the river where you can watch the cruise boats on their way to and from Châlon-sur-Saône. There are 160 pitches in two separate areas, of which 100 are used for touring, all with 6A electricity. Some are on hardstanding and 30 are fully serviced. Some pitches, close to the château and fishing lake, are hedged and have shade from mature trees; another area has a more open aspect. Red squirrels, ducks and the occasional heron can be found on the campsite and the pitches around the periphery are good for birdwatchers. The château's main restaurant serves regional dishes and there is a good range of takeaway meals. Gert-Jan, François and their team enthusiastically organise many activities, mainly for children, but including wine tasting in the cellars of the château. Don't forget, here you are in the Maconnais and Châlonnaise wine regions, so arrange some visits to the local caves.

Facilities

Two well equipped, very clean toilet blocks with all necessary facilities including those for babies and campers with disabilities. Washing machine/dryer. Basic shop (1/5-30/9). Restaurant with good menu and takeaway (1/4-30/9). Cellar with wine tasting. Converted barn with bar, large TV. Unheated outdoor swimming pool (1/5-30/9) partly enclosed by old stone walls. Smaller indoor heated pool, jacuzzi, sauna (1/4-30/9). Play areas with paddling pool. Fishing. Bicycle hire. Motorcaravan services. WiFi (free) in bar area. Off site: Boat launching 500 m. Riding 15 km. Golf 20 km. Historic towns of Châlon and Tournus, both 20 km. The Monday market of Louhans, to see the famous Bresse chickens 26 km.

Open: 30 March - 30 September.

Directions

From A6 heading south, take exit 26 Châlon-Sud, or from A6 heading north take exit 27 Tournus. Then N6 to Sennecey-le-Grand, turn east D18, signed Gigny. Follow site signs to site (6.5 km). GPS: 46.65485, 4.94463

Charges 2012

Per unit incl. 2 persons	
and electricity	€ 24.30 - € 35.10
extra person	€ 5.90 - € 8.50
child (under 7 yrs)	€ 3.60 - € 5.80
dog	€ 2.40 - € 3.00

Camping Cheques accepted.

Cluny

Camping Municipal Saint-Vital

Rue des Griottons, F-71250 Cluny (Saône-et-Loire) T: 03 85 59 08 34. E: cluny-camping@wanadoo.fr
alanrogers.com/FR71030

Close to this attractive small town (300 m. walk) with its magnificent abbey (the largest in Christendom) and next to the municipal swimming pool (free for campers), this site has 174 pitches. On gently sloping grass, with some small hedges and shade in parts, 6A electricity is available (long leads may be needed). Some rail noise is noticeable during the day but we are assured that trains do not run 23.30-07.00. On Monday and Thursday evenings during high season, there is a presentation of local produce in the 'salle de réunion'. The town also has the largest number of Roman houses in France, the National Stud farm, and don't miss the Cheese Tower for the best views of Cluny.

Facilities

Two sanitary buildings provide British and Turkish style WCs, some washbasins in cubicles and controllable showers. Facilities for disabled visitors. Dishwashing and laundry sinks. Washing machine, dryer and ironing board. Chemical disposal. Shop (July/Aug). Outdoor swimming pool (June-Sept). Children's play area. WiFi (charged). Off site: Fishing and bicycle hire 100 m. Riding 1 km. Wine routes, châteaux, churches. Traffic-free cycle path from Cluny to Givry.

Open: 26 April - 30 September.

Directions

Site is east of town, by the D15 road towards Azé and Blanot. GPS: 46.43196, 4.66755

Charges guide

Per unit incl. 2 persons and electricity	€ 16.85
extra person	€ 3.80
child (under 7 yrs)	€ 2.30

For latest campsite news, availability and prices visit
alanrogers.com

3 campsites in the heart of southern burgundy

www.campings-bourgogne.com

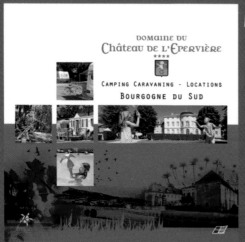

Holiday
in château park

www.domaine-eperviere.com

Discover Tournus

www.camping-tournus.com

City campsite

Bourgondië

www.camping-chalon.com

Digoin
Flower Camping la Chevrette

Rue de la Chevrette, F-71160 Digoin (Saône-et-Loire) T: 03 85 53 11 49. E: info@lachevrette.com

alanrogers.com/FR71180

This pretty town site has been leased from the municipality for the last few years by an enthusiastic couple. There are 100 neat and tidy pitches which are separated by hedges (even the pitches for tents) and flowers decorate the site. The level pitches include 75 with electricity (10A) for touring units, 23 for tents and two for caravan holiday homes for rent. At the far end of the site there is direct access to the Loire river and it is this aspect that attracts campers with canoes. The adjacent town swimming pool complex is free for campers. It incorporates a second pool for the sport of water jousting.

Facilities

Four small toilet blocks, one with cold water only, each provide separate facilities for men and women and some washbasins in cabins. Facilities for disabled visitors. Laundry facilities. Small restaurant/snack bar and takeaway (all 1/7-31/8). Club room with TV. Fishing and boat launching. WiFi. Off site: Swimming pool (adjacent 15/6-7/9). Supermarkets, restaurants and bars in the town. Cycle paths. Riding 3 km. Bicycle hire 15 km.

Open: 15 March - 15 October.

Directions

Digoin lies off the N79 and site is well signed from all directions. GPS: 46.47973, 3.96755

Charges guide

Per unit incl. 2 persons and electricity	€ 15.90 - € 17.80
extra person	€ 3.20 - € 4.00
child (under 13 yrs)	€ 1.90 - € 2.20

Twin-axle units are charged much more.

Dompierre-les-Ormes
Camping le Village des Meuniers

344 rue du Stade, F-71520 Dompierre-les-Ormes (Saône-et-Loire) T: 03 85 50 36 60.
E: contact@villagedesmeuniers.com **alanrogers.com/FR71020**

In a tranquil setting with panoramic views, the neat appearance of the reception building sets the tone for the rest of this attractive site. It is an excellent example of current trends in French tourism development. This is a super site, on the gentle slopes of a hill top, that is tastefully landscaped, with a high standard of cleanliness in all areas. The main part has 108 terraced, grassy pitches, some with hardstanding, are all fairly level, 86 with electricity and ample water points. Of these, 75 also have waste water outlets. A second section, used only in high season contains 16 standard pitches.

Facilities

Sanitary facilities are mainly in a purpose designed hexagonal block and are of a high standard. Excellent facilities for disabled visitors. Smaller unit in the lower area of the site, plus further toilets in the main reception building. Motorcaravan service point in car park. Shop. Bar, café and takeaway (all 15/3-1/11). Swimming pool complex with three heated pools and toboggan run (1/5-31/9). Activities for children (high season). Minigolf. WiFi. Off site: Village 500 m. (banks and some shops, closed Sun/Mon). Fishing 1.5 km. Riding 10 km.

Open: 15 March - 1 November.

Directions

Town is 35 km. west of Mâcon. Leave the A6 at exit 29 and follow N79/E62 (Charolles, Paray, Digoin) road and turn south onto D41 to Dompierre-les-Ormes (3 km). Site is clearly signed through village. GPS: 46.36369, 4.47460

Charges guide

Per unit incl. 2 persons and electricity	€ 21.00 - € 27.50
extra person	€ 5.00 - € 6.50
child (2-12 yrs)	€ 3.50 - € 4.00

Issy-l'Évêque
Camping de l'Etang Neuf

L'Etang Neuf, F-71760 Issy-l'Évêque (Saône-et-Loire) T: 03 85 24 96 05. E: info@issy-camping.com

alanrogers.com/FR71080

This well tended, tranquil campsite overlooking a lake, with views of a forest and the 19th-century Château de Montrifaut, is a real countryside haven for relaxation. The birdsong includes nightingales and golden orioles. The 61 marked, grass pitches have 6A electricity, a small hardstanding area for a car and are separated by a variety of maturing trees giving some shade. There is a separate area nearer the lake for tents. There is no organised entertainment but a play area and a fenced area of the lake, with beach for swimming and paddling plus plenty of space, will keep children happily amused.

Facilities

Two very clean sanitary blocks include washbasins in cabins. Separate shower and toilet rooms for disabled visitors are in the lower block. Laundry facilities. Motorcaravan services. Bar (1/7-31/8). Bread and croissants to order. Boules. TV/games room. Internet access (WiFi). Off site: Minigolf just outside the site entrance. Riding and tennis 500 m. Nearest shops 1.2 km. in Issy-l'Évêque. 120 km. of marked footpaths in the area.

Open: 13 May - 15 September.

Directions

From N81 (Autun - Bourbon-Lancy) turn left onto D27/D25 just west of Luzy and continue for about 11 km. Turn right, D42 in centre of Issy-l'Évêque, signed to campsite. The road narrows slightly, entrance on the right. GPS: 46.70773, 3.96018

Charges guide

Per unit incl. 2 persons and electricity	€ 17.00 - € 19.40
extra person	€ 3.00 - € 5.00

For latest campsite news, availability and prices visit

alanrogers.com

Laives
Camping la Heronnière
Lac de Laives, F-71240 Laives (Saône-et-Loire) T: 03 85 44 98 85. E: contact@camping-laheronniere.com
alanrogers.com/FR71120

Camping la Heronnière is a quiet relaxing site on the edge of a leisure lake in pleasant rolling woodland countryside. The 80 touring pitches are good sized, grassy and level. About half have shade, with electrical connections for 88 and there are plenty of water points. The site is within easy reach of Chalon-sur-Saône, Tournus and the Chalonnais vineyards and wine route. Cluny and the former industrial towns of Le Creusot and Montceau-les-Mines are each about 40 km. away.

Facilities

Well equipped modern sanitary block includes facilities for campers with disabilities. Snack bar (June-Aug). Covered area outside reception, with bread, drinks, ice cream, basic provisions and French breakfast. Heated outdoor pool. Boules. Bicycle hire. Fishing. Marquee with TV, board games. Playground. Off site: Lake swimming, beach, bar and restaurant 300 m. Exercise circuit, canoeing, windsurfing, pedalos. Riding 10 km. Golf 15 km. La Voie Verte, a 117 km. track for cycling or walking near the site.

Open: 6 April - 30 September.

Directions

Leave N6 (Chalon-sur-Saône - Mâcon) at Sennecy-le-Grand (about 18 km. south of the centre of Chalon), taking D18 west to Laives (4 km). In centre of village, take right fork and continue along D18, 4 km. to the northwest. GPS: 46.67198, 4.8333

Charges guide

Per unit incl. 2 persons and electricity	€ 20.40 - € 24.80
extra person	€ 5.20
child (under 7 yrs)	€ 3.60

Mâcon
Camping Municipal Mâcon
RN6, F-71000 Mâcon (Saône-et-Loire) T: 03 85 38 16 22. E: camping@ville-macon.fr
alanrogers.com/FR71010

A well cared for site worth considering as a stopover or for longer stays, as it is close to the main route south. The 266 good sized, level, grassy pitches, 190 with 5/10A electricity and 60 with fresh and waste water points, are easily accessed by tarmac roads. This is a pleasant site, remarkably quiet considering its location, and with a generally bright and cheerful ambience. Extra charge for outfits over 3.5 tonnes or with twin axles. Only gas and electric barbecues. Reservations are not accepted so, in July and August, arrive by late afternoon to avoid disappointment. Some road and rail noise.

Facilities

Four well maintained toilet blocks, one new, others being refurbished. Facilities for disabled visitors. Laundry facilities. Motorcaravan service point (with Fiamma sewage couplings). Shop/tabac, bar, takeaway and restaurant (le Tipi) open midday and evenings. Heated swimming and paddling pools (campers only, 15/5-15/9). TV lounge. Playground. Free WiFi. Off site: Sports centre on banks of river close by. Supermarket 400 m. Fishing 500 m. Golf, riding 10 km. Centre of Mâcon 3 km.

Open: 15 March - 31 October.

Directions

Site is on northern outskirts of Mâcon on main N6, 3 km. from the town centre, well signed (just south of A40 autoroute junction). GPS: 46.3021, 4.8325

Charges guide

Per unit incl. 2 persons	€ 15.30 - € 16.90
with electricity (10A)	€ 19.20 - € 21.40
extra person	€ 4.10 - € 4.60
child (under 7 yrs)	€ 2.30 - € 2.40
dog	€ 1.20 - € 1.40

Meursault
Camping la Grappe d'Or
2 route de Volnay, F-21190 Meursault (Côte d'Or) T: 03 80 21 22 48. E: info@camping-meursault.com
alanrogers.com/FR21050

Meursault, the capital of the great white wines of Burgundy, is southwest of Beaune and Camping la Grappe d'Or offers terraced pitches overlooking acres of vineyards. Most of the 130 touring pitches are flat, of varying sizes, and some have shade from mature trees. Almost all have electrical connections (15A). There is an outdoor pool and flume and, during July and August, aqua gym and other water activities are organised. There is a fenced play area for youngsters and, just across the road from the entrance, there are two tennis courts for campers.

Facilities

Sanitary facilities are in three blocks with some washbasins in cabins. Child/baby room. Facilities for visitors with disabilities. Laundry facilities. Shop. Bar, restaurant, takeaway (1/5-30/9). Swimming pool (15/6-15/9). Play area. Tennis. Bicycle hire. Off site: Golf and riding 7 km. Indoor pool 7 km. Fishing 8 km. Beaune 9 km.

Open: 1 April - 15 October.

Directions

Site is north of Meursault. Take N74 from Beaune and follow the sign for Meursault. Site is signed from town but not very clearly (tents with three arrows). GPS: 46.98574, 4.76858

Charges guide

Per unit incl. 2 persons and electricity	€ 18.00 - € 22.00
extra person	€ 3.00 - € 3.80

Camping Cheques accepted.

For latest campsite news, availability and prices visit
alanrogers.com

Migennes
Camping les Confluents

Allée Leo Lagrange, F-89400 Migennes (Yonne) T: 03 86 80 94 55. E: planethome2003@yahoo.fr

alanrogers.com/FR89090

Camping les Confluents can be found north of Auxerre, in the green countryside of the Yonne. There are 65 touring pitches here. These are very large (150 sq. m) and all have electrical connections. A number of smaller tent pitches are also available, as well as several mobile homes for rent. On-site amenities include a swimming pool with aqua gym and water polo, and a tennis court. The Canal de Bourgogne and River Yonne run close to the site and are popular with anglers. Excursions on pleasure boats start from here too. The nearest town is Migennes, accessible within 15 minutes on foot. It has a good selection of shops and a supermarket, and hosts a popular market on Thursday mornings. It is best known as the northern entry point of the Canal de Bourgogne from the Yonne and is popular with boaters. This is pleasant walking country and the site's friendly managers will be pleased to recommend routes.

Facilities

Shop. Bar/snack bar. Takeaway food. Swimming pool. Children's pool. Children's play area. Tennis. Archery. Entertainment and activity programme. Tourist information. Mobile homes for rent. Off site: River Yonne. Canal de Bourgogne. Shops and restaurants in Migennes. Golf. Riding.

Open: 1 April - 1 November.

Directions

From the north (Paris), leave the A6 motorway at the Joigny exit and head east on D943 to Joigny and continue on the same road to Migennes. The site is well signed here. GPS: 47.956809, 3.510218

Charges guide

Per unit incl. 2 persons	
and electricity	€ 12.60 - € 17.20
extra person	€ 3.40 - € 3.70
child (4-10 yrs)	€ 1.80 - € 2.00

CAMPING LES CONFLUENTS***

- Family atmosphere
- Animations
- Children's playground
- Swimming pool and paddling pool
- Fishing
- TV
- WIFI
- At 300m of the rivers
- At 800m of shops and the Canal de Bourgogne
- Mobile homes 4/6/8 pers.

Openings dates : from the 1st of April until the 1st of November

Allée Léo Lagrange - 89400 Migennes - Tel: 0033 (0)3.86.80.94.55
Email: planethome2003@yahoo.fr - Web: http://www.les-confluents.com/

Nevers
Camping de Nevers

Rue de la Jonction, F-58000 Nevers (Nièvre) T: 06 84 98 69 79. E: info@campingnevers.com

alanrogers.com/FR58100

On the banks of the Loire in Nevers, facing the cathedral and the Palais des Ducs across the river, this site has just 73 pitches. The area nearest the river is for tents and the terraces above for touring pitches, mainly grass but five hardstandings; there are 60 pitches with electricity (6/10A). The pitches are quite tight but larger units can be accommodated and the site is ideal for those who enjoy being able to wander into town or as a base to explore the region with its famous Burgundy wines of Sancerre and Pouilly Fumé. The shops, bars and restaurants of Nevers are within easy reach.

Facilities

One modern unisex toilet block with washbasins in cabins and controllable showers. Bright and clean, they may be under pressure in high season. Baby area. En-suite unit for disabled visitors. Laundry with washing machine, dryer and ironing facilities. Motorcaravan service point. Simple bar with basic snacks (all season). Bicycle hire. Children's play area (3-12 yrs). Pétanque. Internet (charged). Two mobile homes for rent. Off site: All the amenities of Nevers, including shops, restaurants, bars, large stores and supermarkets within easy reach. Bus stop at entrance. Boat launching 500 m. Golf and riding 15 km.

Open: 13 April - 14 October.

Directions

Nevers is 150 km. north of Clermont-Ferrand. Do not approach through the town. From the A77/N7 (Paris-Lyon) take exit 37 onto D976 (Bourges). Turn north at first roundabout towards 'Centre Ville'. Site is signed to the right immediately before bridge across the Loire. Avoid arriving between 12.00-15.00 (site is closed) as there is no waiting place outside. GPS: 46.98209, 3.16098

Charges guide

Per unit incl. 2 persons	€ 17.70 - € 21.45
extra person	€ 2.10 - € 3.10

Camping Cheques accepted.

For latest campsite news, availability and prices visit
alanrogers.com

Palinges
Camping du Lac

Le Fourneau, F-71430 Palinges (Saône-et-Loire) T: 03 85 88 14 49. E: camping.palinges@hotmail.fr
alanrogers.com/FR71110

Camping du Lac is a very special campsite and it is all due to M. Labille, the owner, who thinks of the campsite as his home and every visitor as his guest. The campsite has 40 pitches in total, 16 of which have 10A electricity and 16 are fully serviced. There are seven chalets to rent. The site is adjacent to a lake with a beach and safe bathing. Set in the countryside yet within easy reach of many tourist attractions, especially Cluny, the local Château Digoin and Mont St Vincent with distant views of Mont Blanc on a clear day. If you want to visit a specific place, then Monsieur knows exactly where you should go – he never recommends anything that he hasn't personally tried out. Monsieur Labille provides tables and chairs for tent campers and he freezes bottles of water for cyclists to take away (free of charge).

Facilities

The central sanitary block provides all necessary facilities including those for campers with disabilities. This site is particularly well adapted for disabled visitors. Motorcaravan services. Washing machine and fridge. Bread and croissants to order. Boules. Play area. TV room. Sports field, lake beach and swimming adjacent. WiFi. Off site: Bar/snack bar outside entrance (1/7-31/8). Palinges is within walking distance, cycle and walking routes, museums, cruises on canals, châteaux, 'museographical' complex. Riding 8 km.

Open: 1 April - 30 October.

Directions

Palinges is midway between Montceau les Mines and Paray le Monial. From Montceau take N70, then turn left onto D92 to Palinges. Follow campsite signs. Site is also well signed from D985 Toulon-sur-Arroux to Charolles road. GPS: 46.56095, 4.22492

Charges guide

Per unit incl. 2 persons and electricity	€ 20.00
extra person	€ 3.50

No credit cards.

CAMPING DU LAC ★★★
Open 1st April to 30th October
33(0)3 85 88 14 49
Silence, nature, peace
40 pitches 7 chalets
Palinges
South Burgundy

Paray-le-Monial
Camping de Mambré

Route du Gué Léger, F-71600 Paray-le-Monial (Saône-et-Loire) T: 03 85 88 89 20.
E: bureau-reservations@orange.fr **alanrogers.com/FR71240**

Paray-le-Monial is one of Burgundy's well established pilgrimage destinations and is well located for exploring southern Burgundy. Le Mambré is a well equipped family site and can be found close to the west of the town centre. There are 82 pitches reserved for caravans and motorcaravans, and a further 63 smaller pitches, reserved for tents. Please note that twin-axle caravans and large motorhomes are not accepted. Pitches are grassy and well shaded. A number of mobile homes and chalets are available for rent. On-site amenities include a swimming pool and paddling pool, and a small snack bar.

Facilities

Sanitary blocks with hot showers and facilities for disabled visitors. Laundry facilities. Café/snack bar. Shop (July/Aug). Swimming pool. Paddling pool. Playground. Picnic areas. Games room. Bicycle hire. Tourist information. Mobile homes and chalets for rent. Off site: Paray-le-Monial with a good selection of shops, cafés and restaurants. Walking and cycling trails. Fishing 2 km. Riding 3 km.

Open: 2 May - 30 September.

Directions

Approaching from the east (N79), follow signs to the centre of Paray-le-Monial (D979) and the site is well signed to the west of the town centre. GPS: 46.457379, 4.104858

Charges guide

Per unit incl. 2 persons and electricity	€ 15.60 - € 18.40
extra person	€ 3.20 - € 4.00
child (3-14 yrs)	€ 1.90 - € 2.50
dog	€ 2.00

For latest campsite news, availability and prices visit
alanrogers.com

We can book this site for you! Call 01580 214000 alan rogers ⦾ travel

Saint Boil

Camping le Moulin de Collonge

Moulin de Collonge, F-71390 Saint Boil (Saône-et-Loire) T: 03 85 44 00 32. E: millofcollonge@wanadoo.fr

alanrogers.com/FR71050

This small campsite is situated on the wine route between Beaune and Cluny and close to the long cycle route through the Burgundy vineyards. This well run, family site offers an 'away from it all' situation and it will appeal to those seeking a quiet, relaxing environment in a garden-like setting. There are 61 small to average-sized, level, grassy pitches, with 50 for touring (6A electricity) although long leads may be required. Most pitches are well shaded by a wide variety of mature trees making access for tall outfits quite difficult. No twin-axle caravans or large outfits accepted.

Facilities

Well kept toilet facilities housed in a converted barn. Laundry facilities. Freezer for campers' use. Bread each morning. Basic shop (1/5-30/9). Restaurant/pizzeria, snack bar. Swimming pool covered – some walls can be opened in good weather (all season). Playgrounds. Bouncy castle. Bicycle hire. Table tennis. Fishing. Pony trekking. WiFi. Off site: La Voie Verte, a 117 km. track for cycling or walking near the site. Riding 4 km.

Open: 1 April - 30 September.

Directions

From Chalon-sur-Saône, take N80 west 9 km. Turn south on D981 through Buxy (6 km). Continue south to Saint Boil 7 km. and site is signed at south end of the village. GPS: 46.64621, 4.69479

Charges guide

Per unit incl. 2 persons and electricity	€ 19.00 - € 23.60
extra person	€ 4.75 - € 5.80

Saint Léger-de-Fougeret

Camping l'Etang de la Fougeraie

Hameau de Champs, F-58120 Saint Léger-de-Fougeret (Nièvre) T: 03 86 85 11 85.
E: campingfougeraie@orange.fr **alanrogers.com/FR58040**

This is a quiet and peaceful, spacious campsite laid out on a hillside deep in the Parc Naturel Régional du Morvan, with views over the lake, meadows and surrounding hills. The spring water lake is ideal for fishing and swimming. There is a small bar and restaurant serving good quality regional meals and a well stocked shop with local produce. There are 60 terraced pitches, with 57 for touring, 36 with electricity (10/16A). The site is not suitable for double-axle or large outfits or people with walking difficulties, as the site roads are steep and narrow. Large RVs are not accepted.

Facilities

Traditional and modern buildings with all necessary facilities and a heated family/disabled room lie at the top of the site, a fair distance uphill from some pitches. Washing machine and dryer. Shop. Bar and restaurant (1/5-30/9). WiFi. Lake swimming. Fishing. Playgrounds. Caravan storage. American RVs not accepted, site not really suitable for large units. Off site: Riding 2 km. Shops, bank with ATM and services 7 km.

Open: 1 April - 30 September.

Directions

St Léger-de-Fougeret is about 10 km. south of Château-Chinon. From Château-Chinon take D27 south for 3 km, then fork right on D157 for 5.5 km. to St Léger. Continue through village, follow signs to site 1 km. GPS: 47.00587, 3.90548

Charges guide

Per unit incl. 2 persons and electricity	€ 16.20 - € 17.20
extra person	€ 5.00

Saint Sauveur-en-Puisaye

Camping Parc des Joumiers

F-89520 Saint Sauveur-en-Puisaye (Yonne) T: 03 86 45 66 28. E: camping-motel-joumiers@wanadoo.fr

alanrogers.com/FR89040

This is an attractive, spacious, family run site in the north of Burgundy and east of the Loire. It is set beside a lake and a forest which offers many opportunities for walks and bike rides. There are 200 large, slightly sloping, grass pitches separated by hedges with a variety of trees giving varying amounts of shade. All 174 for touring have 16A electricity, water, drainage and TV point. There are no organised on-site activities but within 10 km. are many interesting old towns, a medieval style castle being built using traditional methods and Château de Saint Fargeau with its pageants and 'son-et-lumière'.

Facilities

Two well appointed toilet blocks with all necessary facilities, including those for children and campers with disabilities. Washing machine. Motorcaravan services. Small swimming and paddling pools (June-mid Sept). Play area with bouncy castle. Bar, restaurant and takeaway (all season) overlooking lake (fishing only). WiFi near bar. Fishing. Off site: Village of St Sauveur with small shops, bar, restaurant 1 km. Riding 5 km. Bicycle hire 8 km. Children's pedal cars. Château de Saint Fargeau. Cyclorail (cycling along railway tracks).

Open: 28 March - 5 November.

Directions

Leave A77 at exit 21 and take D965 east for 17 km. to St Fargeau. Turn right on D85 southeast to St Sauveur-en-Puisaye in 11 km. In village turn hard left on D7. In 800 m. turn right (site well signed) to site in 800 m. GPS: 47.63083, 3.19405

Charges guide

Per unit incl. 2 persons and electricity	€ 17.80 - € 20.10
extra person	€ 3.80
child (under 7 yrs)	€ 1.80

For latest campsite news, availability and prices visit

alanrogers.com

We can book this site for you! Call 01580 214000

alan rogers travel

Saint Pereuse-en-Morvan
Camping le Manoir de Bezolle

F-58110 Saint Pereuse-en-Morvan (Nièvre) T: 03 86 84 42 55. E: info@camping-bezolle.com
alanrogers.com/FR58030

Manoir de Bezolle is in the heart of Burgundy, well situated to explore the Morvan Nature Park and the Nivernais area and is open all year round. It has been attractively landscaped to provide a number of different areas, some giving pleasant views over the surrounding countryside. There are 100 spacious pitches with 84 for touring, most with 10A electricity (long leads advised). One area is set out on terraces and some pitches are slightly sloping. Many have good shade from a variety of magnificent trees. There is a good children's play area and three well stocked, small lakes for anglers. There is a good bar, restaurant and takeaway with an attractive terrace overlooking the large, heated swimming pools. The lower, level area is more suitable for those with walking difficulties. There are many small towns and villages to visit in an area renowned for its gastronomy and history.

Facilities

Two main toilet blocks provide washbasins in cabins, mostly British style WCs, baths, provision for disabled visitors and a baby bath. A small unit contains two tiny family WC/basin/shower suites for rent. Facilities by the pools can be heated in winter. Laundry. Motorcaravan services. Shop. Bar and restaurant. Pizza and takeaway (all year). Internet point and WiFi (charged). Two heated pools (1/5-15/9). Large play area. Minigolf. Boules. Fishing. Off site: Châtillon-en-Bazois 14 km. Old towns and villages with their châteaux, museums and markets. Walking and cycling in the Morvan Regional Park.

Open: All year.

Directions

Site is between Nevers and Autun. Leave D978, 13 km. east of Châtillon-en-Bazois (site signed) onto D11. Site is a few hundred metres on the right. GPS: 47.05877, 3.81716

Charges guide

Per unit incl. 2 persons and electricity	€ 20.00 - € 31.00
extra person	€ 5.00 - € 5.50
child (0-6 yrs)	€ 4.00 - € 4.50
dog	€ 2.00

Camping Cheques accepted.

Camping Le Manoir de Bezolle ★★★★

4-star Les Castels campsite with 2 pools, restaurant, bar, take-away and shop.

Fresh baked bread every morning!

Camping Le Manoir de Bezolle★★★★ • 58110 Saint-Péreuse-en-Morvan • France
Tel 0033 (0)3 86 84 42 55 • Fax 0033 (0)3 86 84 43 77
info@camping-bezolle.com • www.camping-bezolle.com

Savigny-les-Beaune
Camping les Premier Pres

Route de Bouilland, F-21420 Savigny-les-Beaune (Côte d'Or) T: 03 80 26 15 06.
E: contact.camping@x-treme-bar.fr **alanrogers.com/FR21030**

This popular site is ideally located for visiting the Burgundy vineyards, for use as a transit site or for spending time in the town of Beaune. During the high season it is full every evening, so it is best to arrive by 4 pm. The 90 level pitches are marked and numbered, with 6A electric hook-ups and room for an awning. A former municipal site, now privately owned. Whilst the famed wine region alone attracts many visitors, Beaune, its capital, is unrivalled in its richness of art from times gone by. Narrow streets and squares are garlanded with flowers, pavement cafés are crammed with tourists and overlooking the scene is the glistening Hôtel Dieu.

Facilities

Well kept sanitary facilities are housed in a modern building behind reception. Additional WCs and water points are conveniently placed towards the middle of the site. Motorcaravan service point. Ice available to purchase. Torch useful. Fishing. Bicycle hire. WiFi. Off site: Village with Sunday market 1 km. Beaune 7 km.

Open: 15 March - 15 October.

Directions

From A6 autoroute take exit 24 signed Beaune and Savigny-les-Beaune onto D2. Turn right towards Savigny-les-Beaune (3 km) and follow signs to site. GPS: 47.069, 4.803

Charges guide

Per unit incl. 2 persons and electricity	€ 11.40 - € 12.70
extra person	€ 2.50 - € 2.90

No credit cards.

For latest campsite news, availability and prices visit
alanrogers.com

Tazilly

Airotel Château de Chigy

Chigy, F-58170 Tazilly (Nièvre) T: 03 86 30 10 80. E: reception@chateaudechigy.com.fr

alanrogers.com/FR58050

This very spacious site (20 ha. for pitches and another 50 ha. of fields, lakes and woods) lies at the southern tip of the Morvan Nature Park. The château houses the reception and apartments. Most of the facilities are nearby, and behind are 54 good sized, shaded and slightly sloping pitches, many uneven, all with electricity (6A). There is a large woodland area with paths, beyond which are 100 or so less shaded pitches, some of up to 150 sq.m. Most are slightly sloping and some are on low terraces, nearly all with electricity. Most have very good views.

Facilities

Two toilet blocks provide British style WCs, washbasins in cubicles, and showers but are a good distance from many pitches. Portacabin with 4 cubicles (for private hire in July/Aug). Facilities for disabled visitors and babies. Laundry facilities. Shop. Bar, restaurant and takeaway (July/Aug). Two outdoor pools, paddling pool (15/5-30/9). Swimming in lake. Covered pool. Games and TV rooms. Playground. Minigolf. Boules. All weather sports terrain. Playing field. Off site: Luzy 4 km. Riding 9 km.

Open: 26 April - 30 September.

Directions

Leave Autun on N81 southwest (signed Bourbon-Lancy) through Luzy (D973, signed Bourbon-Lancy). Site is signed to the left after approx. 4 km.
GPS: 46.75746, 3.94478

Charges guide

Per unit incl. 2 persons	
and electricity	€ 21.00 - € 28.00
extra person	€ 5.00 - € 7.00
child (6-17 yrs)	€ 4.00 - € 6.00

Tournus

Camping de Tournus

14 Rue des Canes, F-71700 Tournus (Saône-et-Loire) T: 03 85 51 16 58. E: info@camping-tournus.com

alanrogers.com/FR71190

This very well maintained, pleasant site is just a few minutes from the A6 autoroute, 200 metres from the River Saône and close to the interesting old market town of Tournus. It is ideal for a night halt but deserving of a longer stay. The new owners have made some hardstanding pitches to complement the fairly level grassy pitches. All 90 pitches are for touring and 70 have 6A electricity. A few trees give some pitches varying amounts of shade. A municipal outdoor swimming pool is adjacent to the site.

Facilities

Two clean toilet blocks near the entrance provide all necessary facilities, including those for disabled visitors. Motorcaravan services. Small bar and shop in the reception area where bread can be ordered daily and light snacks purchased. Small play area. Internet terminal. Bicycle hire. WiFi. Off site: Municipal pool next door. Fishing 100 m. Tournus, Saturday market, shops, bars, cafés, banks etc. short walk/cycle ride along river.

Open: 1 April - 30 September.

Directions

From the A6 take exit 12 for Tournus and the N6 south for just over 1 km. In Tournus (opposite railway station), turn left signed camping and follow signs to site, about 1 km. GPS: 46.57372, 4.909349

Charges guide

Per unit incl. 2 persons	
and electricity	€ 19.10 - € 24.50
extra person	€ 4.20 - € 5.60
Camping Cheques accepted.	

Vandenesse-en-Auxois

Sunêlia Lac de Panthier

RD977b, F-21320 Vandenesse-en-Auxois (Côte d'Or) T: 03 80 49 21 94. E: info@lac-de-panthier.com

alanrogers.com/FR21000

Camping Lac de Panthier is an attractively situated lakeside site in the Burgundy countryside. It is divided into two distinct areas, the smaller section houses the reception, shop, restaurant, indoor pool and sauna. The second, larger area is 200 m. along the lakeside road and is where the other site activities take place and the outdoor pools can be found. The 207 pitches (153 for touring) all have electricity (6A) and are mostly on gently sloping grass, although in parts there are shallow terraces. The restaurant and some of the pitches have panoramic views over the lake which offers many watersports.

Facilities

Each area has two adequate unisex toilet blocks including provision for babies and disabled visitors. Shop, bar and restaurant. Games and TV rooms. Swimming pool, children's pool and slide (15/5-15/9). Indoor pool, sauna and gym. Fishing. Riding. Bicycle hire. Canoe hire. Watersports. Entertainment and activities in high season and clubs for children and teenagers. Internet access on payment (WiFi charged). Trampoline. No electric barbecues. Off site: Boat excursions from Pouilly-en-Auxois (8 km). Riding and golf 10 km.

Open: 7 April - 7 October.

Directions

From the A6 join the A38 and exit immediately at junction 24. Take N81 south towards Arnay Le Duc, over A6, shortly turn left on D977 for 5 km. Fork left for Vandenesse-en-Auxois. Through village on D977 for 2.5 km, turn left and site is on left.
GPS: 47.23661, 4.62810

Charges 2012

Per unit incl. 2 persons	
and electricity	€ 19.00 - € 28.00
extra person	€ 5.00 - € 7.00
Camping Cheques accepted.	

For latest campsite news, availability and prices visit

alanrogers.com

Located to the south of Alsace, the historic province of Franche-Comté boasts a varied landscape ranging from flat plains to dense woodlands, rugged dramatic mountains and limestone valleys.

DÉPARTEMENTS: 25 DOUBS, 39 JURA, 70 HAUTE-SAÔNE, 90 TRE. DE BELFORT

MAJOR CITY: BESANÇON

Franche-Comté is really made up of two regions. The high valley of the Saône is wide, gently rolling farmland with a certain rustic simplicity, while the Jura mountains are more rugged with dense forests, sheer cliffs, craggy limestone escarpments and torrents of clear, sparkling water gushing through deep gorges. It is for this thrilling scenery that Franche-Comté is best known. Nature lovers can climb, bike and hike in the mountains or explore the hills honeycombed with over 4,000 caves. The streams and lakes provide world-class fishing. The spa towns of Salins les Bains and Besançon offer relaxation and a chance to 'take the waters'.

The region has a rich architectural heritage dating from many different periods, including medieval abbeys and châteaux and a poignant chapel in memory of the war. Roman remains, fortresses perched on cliff tops and elegant spa towns can all be explored at leisure. The region's position, bordering Switzerland and close to Germany, is reflected in its culture and also the great diversity of architectural style in the many fine buildings.

Places of interest

Arbois: Pasteur Family Home and Museum, Museum of Wine and Wine Growing.

Belfort: sandstone lion sculpted by Bartholdi; Memorial and Museum of the French Resistance.

Besançon: citadel with good views over the city.

Champlitte: Museum of Folk Art.

Dole: lovely old town, Louis Pasteur's birthplace.

Gray: Baron Martin Museum.

Luxeuil-les-Bains: Tour des Echevins Museum.

Ornans: Gustave Courbet birthplace, museum.

Ronchamp: Chapel of Notre-Dame du Haut de Ronchamp designed by Le Corbusier.

Salins-les-Bains: Salt mines and tunnels.

Sochaux: Peugeot Museum.

Cuisine of the region

Freshwater fish such as trout, grayling, pike and perch are local specialities. The region has a rare wine known as *vin de paille* as well as *vin jaune* (deep yellow and very dry) and *vin du jura*, Jura wine.

Brési: water-thin slices of dried beef; many local hams.

Gougère: hot cheese pastry based on the local *Comté* cheese.

Jésus de Morteau: fat pork sausage smoked over pine and juniper.

Poulet au vin jaune: chicken, cream and *morilles* cooked in *vin jaune*.

www.franche-comte.org
info@franche-comte.org
00800 2006 2010 (free from the UK)

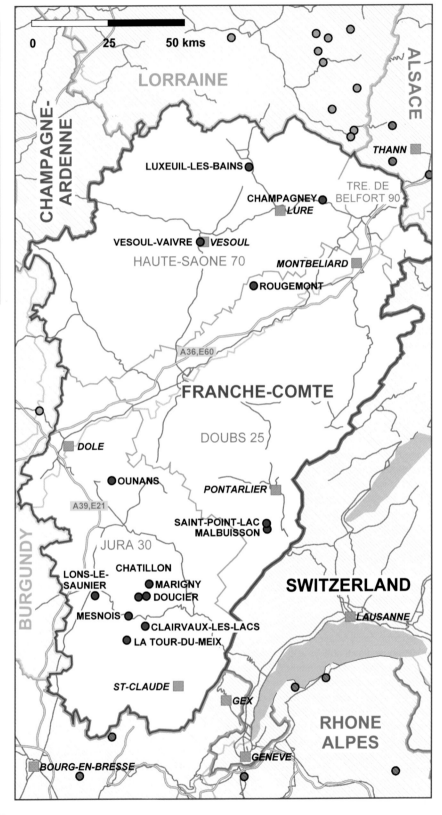

ALSACE

CHAMPAGNE-ARDENNE

LORRAINE

0   25   50 kms

THANN

LUXEUIL-LES-BAINS

CHAMPAGNEY
LURE

TRE. DE
BELFORT 90

VESOUL-VAIVRE   VESOUL

HAUTE-SAONE 70

MONTBELIARD

ROUGEMONT

A36,E60

FRANCHE-COMTE

DOUBS 25

DOLE

OUNANS

PONTARLIER

A39,E21

SAINT-POINT-LAC
MALBUISSON

JURA 30

CHATILLON

LONS-LE-
SAUNIER

MARIGNY

DOUCIER

SWITZERLAND

MESNOIS

CLAIRVAUX-LES-LACS

LA TOUR-DU-MEIX

LAUSANNE

ST-CLAUDE

GEX

RHONE
ALPES

BURGUNDY

GENEVE

BOURG-EN-BRESSE

For latest campsite news, availability and prices visit

alanrogers.com

Champagney

Camping Domaine les Ballastières

F-70290 Champagney (Haute-Saône) T: 03 84 23 11 22. E: contact@campinglesballastieres.com
alanrogers.com/FR70030

Within easy reach of the historic town of Belfort, les Ballastières opened in 2008. The landscaping is becoming established and the 100 touring pitches are very large, level and easily accessible. Reception building also houses the bar and snack bar, while outside a patio with tables and chairs overlooks the pool and adjacent lake. The site has been designed with disabled campers in mind, although there is a sloping path down to the pool; a hoist has been installed, and one of the ten mobile homes is ramped for easy access.

Facilities

Two toilet blocks each with good facilities including those for disabled visitors, but may become stretched in high season. Washbasins in cabins. Laundry. Swimming and paddling pools (July/Aug). Shop (Jul/Aug), bar with TV and snackbar (all season). Climbing for children (3-11) with supervisor. Kayaks and canoes. Play area. Motorcaravan services. Off site: Chapelle de Notre Dame du Haut, supermarket, restaurants, and bar in Ronchamp 4 km.

Open: 1 April - 31 October.

Directions

Site is 20 km. northwest of Belfort; from the roundabout on east side of Ronchamp on D19, take D4 eastwards for 2 km. Site is signed on left. GPS: 47.706841, 6.671437

Charges guide

Per unit incl. 2 persons and electricity	€ 18.00 - € 20.60
extra person	€ 3.70

Camping Cheques accepted.

Chatillon

Kawan Village Domaine de l'Epinette

15 rue de l'Epinette, F-39130 Chatillon (Jura) T: 03 84 25 71 44. E: info@domaine-epinette.com
alanrogers.com/FR39080

This site is set in charming wooded countryside on land sloping down to the river Ain, which is shallow and slow moving. There are 150 grassy pitches, 110 are available for touring units, some slightly sloping. These are arranged on terraces and separated by hedges, bushes and trees, about half being shaded. Nearly all have electricity hook-ups, although some long leads are needed. Ten pitches have hardstanding. There is an attractive swimming pool (heated 1/7-31/8) with a paddling pool. Guided canoe trips on the river start and finish at the campsite.

Facilities

Two modern toilet blocks. Unit for disabled visitors. Baby bath. Dishwashing and laundry sinks. Washing machine and dryer. Small shop for basics. Snack bar and takeaway (evenings). New reception, bar, TV room and shop. Swimming pool with toboggan. Playground. Boules. Direct access to river for swimming and canoeing. WiFi (free). Gas and charcoal barbecues permitted. Off site: Riding 6 km. Shops, etc. in Doucier 6 km. Golf 25 km.

Open: 9 June - 15 September.

Directions

From Lons-le-Saunier take D471 eastwards towards Pontarlier-Genève. After about 8 km. fork right onto D39 towards Vevy. After 11 km. at Chatillon turn right onto D151 south towards Blye. Site is less than 2 km. on the left. GPS: 46.65887, 5.72978

Charges guide

Per unit incl. 2 persons and electricity	€ 17.00 - € 27.00
extra person	€ 3.50 - € 4.50

Camping Cheques accepted.

Clairvaux-les-Lacs

Yelloh! Village Fayolan

B.P. 52, F-39130 Clairvaux-les-Lacs (Jura) T: 03 84 25 88 52. E: lefayolan@oclesia.eu
alanrogers.com/FR39050

This large, spacious site is modern and well equipped. Backed by wooded hills, it is situated on the shores of Le Petit Lac amid the lakes and forests of the Jure, about a mile from the town of Clairvaux-les-Lacs. It is in two parts, with 516 pitches either on terraces overlooking the lake or on the flatter area near the shore. With 456 for touring units, all have electricity (10A) and 200 are fully serviced. The pitches are separated by hedges and mature trees giving most some shade. Many activities are organised on site, some in low season. Used by tour operators (130 pitches).

Facilities

Four modern well equipped toilet units. Baby room. Laundry facilities. Shop. Restaurant. Bar. Snack bar/pizzeria and takeaway. Swimming pool complex with indoor pool (all season), outdoor pool (7/5-14/9; heated 5/6-31/8). Fitness centre, sauna, steam bath, massage (16/5-2/9). Entertainment area. Playground. Organised activities, children's club. Internet access. Fishing. Beach sports area and lake swimming. Boules. Organised walks. Off site: Bicycle hire 800 m. Riding 15 km.

Open: 28 April - 9 September.

Directions

Clairvaux-les-Lacs is on the D678 about 23 km. southeast of Lons-le-Saunier. In Clairvaux follow signs for 'Lacs Campings' and Fayolan (1.5 km. southeast of town). GPS: 46.56438, 5.75621

Charges 2012

Per unit incl. 2 persons and electricity	€ 17.00 - € 45.00
extra person	€ 6.00 - € 8.00
child (3-7 yrs)	free - € 6.00

For latest campsite news, availability and prices visit

alanrogers.com

Doucier

Camping Domaine de Chalain

F-39130 Doucier (Jura) T: 03 84 25 78 78. E: chalain@chalain.com

alanrogers.com/FR39030

Doucier lies 25 km. east of Lons-le-Saunier among the wooded hills of the Jura and rather away from the main routes. This large, spacious site is in a parkland setting beside Lac de Chalain and is surrounded by woods and cliffs. Large areas are left for sports and recreation. The lake shelves gently but then becomes deep quite suddenly. The site also has an attractive, well equipped pool complex. There are 800 good-sized, level pitches with 462 for touring units, Most have electricity (7A) and there are varying amounts of shade. Booking is obligatory for caravans and motorcaravans over 7 m.

Facilities

Nine well equipped sanitary blocks with facilities for babies and disabled visitors. Shops. Restaurant, takeaway and bar. Swimming pool complex with heated indoor pool (all season), outdoor pools (1/6-15/9) with slide, sauna and spa (one entrance per day). Play areas. Fishing. Pedalo and bicycle hire. Sports activities including rock climbing, archery, aquagym. TV room. Disco, entertainment, organised activities. Dogs not permitted on lake beach. Off site: Signed walk from site. Riding 2 km. Golf 25 km.

Open: 27 April - 18 September.

Directions

Doucier is 25 km. east of Lons-le-Saunier. In village turn left off D39, site signed, entrance in 3 km. GPS: 46.66435, 5.81315

Charges guide

Per unit incl. 3 persons	
and electricity	€ 21.00 - € 37.00
extra person	€ 4.00 - € 6.00
child (4-15 yrs)	€ 3.00 - € 5.00
dog	€ 2.00

Doucier

Camping les Mérilles

Rue des 3 Lacs, F-39130 Doucier (Jura) T: 03 84 25 73 06. E: camping.lesmerilles@wanadoo.fr

alanrogers.com/FR39170

Camping les Mérilles is a small, good quality, family run campsite 500 m. from the small town of Doucier and only 2 km. from the beautiful Lac de Chalain. It has 96 good sized, level, grass pitches separated by hedging. A variety of trees give some shade. There are 73 pitches for touring with 16 having a private bathroom. All have electricity (6/10A). This site is a quieter alternative to the much busier sites near the lake. The surrounding area is well worth exploring and is well known for its lakes, waterfalls and caves. Owners of large outfits should phone ahead to reserve the larger pitches.

Facilities

One modern, well appointed and heated toilet block, one older and very small block plus 16 private cabins to rent with certain pitches. Motorcaravan services. Basic shop and bar with TV (1/6-30/9). Takeaway (1/7-30/9). Outdoor heated pool and paddling pool (1/5-30/9). Playground. Bicycle hire. WiFi (charged). Organised family activities (July/Aug). Off site: Riding 50m. Fishing 100m. Doucier with small shops, bar and restaurant 500 m. Lac de Chalain, indoor pool, beach and watersports 2 km.

Open: 1 April - 30 September.

Directions

Doucier is 25 km. east of Lons-le-Saunier. The site is 500 m. east of Doucier on the D39 with the entrance on the right. GPS: 46.65178, 5.77491

Charges guide

Per unit incl. 2 persons	
and electricity	€ 15.50 - € 18.90
incl. private bathroom	€ 19.10 - € 25.95
extra person	€ 3.80 - € 4.00

La Tour-du-Meix

Camping de Surchauffant

Le Pont de la Pyle, F-39270 La Tour-du-Meix (Jura) T: 03 84 25 41 08. E: info@camping-surchauffant.fr

alanrogers.com/FR39020

With only 200 pitches, this site may appeal to those who prefer a more informal atmosphere, however it can be lively in high season. It is pleasantly situated above the beaches bordering the Lac de Vouglans, which can be reached quickly on foot directly from the site. The 157 touring pitches are of a reasonable size and are informally arranged, some are fully serviced and most have electricity (10A). They are divided by hedges and there is some shade. The lake offers a variety of watersports activities, boat trips, etc. and is used for fishing and swimming (guarded in high season as it shelves steeply).

Facilities

The sanitary facilities are older in style and adequate rather than luxurious, but reasonably well maintained and clean when we visited. They include some washbasins in private cabins. Laundry. Heated swimming pool (200 sq.m), paddling pool and surround (15/6-15/9). Three playgrounds. Entertainment (July/Aug). Safety deposit boxes. Off site: Bicycle hire and riding 5 km. Restaurant, takeaway and shops adjacent.

Open: 20 April - 17 September.

Directions

From A39 take exit 7 and N1082 to Lons-le-Saunier. Continue south on D52 for about 20 km. to Orgelet. Site is by the D470, at La Tour-du-Meix, about 4 km. east of Orgelet. GPS: 46.5231, 5.67401

Charges guide

Per unit incl. 2 persons	
and electricity	€ 15.00 - € 23.50
extra person (over 4 yrs)	€ 2.50 - € 4.70

For latest campsite news, availability and prices visit

alanrogers.com

Lons-le-Saunier
Camping la Marjorie

640 boulevard de l'Europe, F-39000 Lons-le-Saunier (Jura) T: 03 84 24 26 94. E: info@camping-marjorie.com
alanrogers.com/FR39060

La Marjorie is a spacious site set on the outskirts of the spa town of Lons-le-Saunier with a long season. Bordering one area of the site are open fields and woodlands. It has 200 level pitches, 180 for touring units and 127 with electricity (6/10A). Some are on hardstanding and 37 are fully serviced. They are separated by well trimmed hedges interspersed with tall trees which gives privacy plus some shade. There is a cycle path from the site into town (2.5 km) and a mountain bike track behind the site. This is a good site for a long or short stay. In July and August activities are organised for all the family.

Facilities

Three well maintained toilet blocks, two modern and heated. Baby baths. Facilities for disabled visitors. Shop (15/6-31/8). Small bar with takeaway meals (all 15/6-31/8). TV room. Play area. Boules. Football field. Archery, riding and canoeing. Motorcaravan service point (charged). Bicycle hire. WiFi throughout. Off site: Swimming pool 200 m. Bus stop 400 m. Restaurants 500 m. Fishing 3 km. Riding 5 km. Golf 6 km. Caves and waterfalls 17 km.

Open: 1 April - 15 October.

Directions

Site is off the N1083 Lons-le-Saunier - Besançon road, just north of Lons. Follow signs for 'camping' and 'piscine'. GPS: 46.68437, 5.56843

Charges 2012

Per unit incl. 2 persons	
and electricity	€ 15.95 - € 21.90
extra person	€ 3.50 - € 5.15
child (under 10 yrs)	€ 2.30 - € 3.40

Luxeuil-les-Bains
Domaine du Chatigny

14 rue du Gramont, F-70300 Luxeuil-les-Bains (Haute-Saône) T: 03 84 93 97 97.
E: camping.ot-luxeuil@wanadoo.fr **alanrogers.com/FR70010**

An excellent example of a well cared for municipal site, Domaine du Chatigny is located on a hillside backing onto woods, yet is only a five minute walk from the centre of the interesting old spa town of Luxeuil-les-Bains. As the site has only recently been opened, all facilities are of a high quality and were very clean when we visited. There are 98 good sized, level or slightly sloping, grass pitches separated by young shrubs and trees with not much shade. Of the 78 touring pitches 52 have electricity (16A) and 26 are fully serviced. Some activities are organised on site, but a programme of events is offered nearby.

Facilities

One modern, heated toilet block is excellent and provides all necessary facilities. Motorcaravan services. Snack bar, swimming and paddling pool (open weekends June, Sept and every day July/Aug). Games/TV room. Tennis. Internet, WiFi. Off site: Spa town of Luxeuil-les-Bains with good range of shops, bars, restaurants, Casino, Saturday market and many organised events, 5 minutes walk. Fishing and riding 2 km. Golf 10 km.

Open: 1 April - 31 October.

Directions

The site is 45 km. south of Epinal. No access for vehicles from the centre of Luxeuil-les-Bains. Bypass Luxeuil-les-Bains on the N57 and at supermarket (site signed) turn west into rue Ste Anne. Bear right three times to site (900 m). GPS: 47.8236, 6.381667

Charges guide

Per unit incl. 2 persons	
and electricity	€ 16.00 - € 20.00
extra person	€ 2.00 - € 4.00

Marigny
Castel Camping la Pergola

1 rue des Vernois, F-39130 Marigny (Jura) T: 03 84 25 70 03. E: contact@lapergola.com
alanrogers.com/FR39040

Close to the Swiss border and overlooking the sparkling waters of Lac de Chalain, la Pergola is a good quality terraced site set amongst the rolling hills of the Jura. Neat and tidy, it is very well appointed, with 350 pitches, 100 for touring, mainly on grass and gravel and separated by small hedges. All have electricity (6A), water and drainage and some have shade from a variety of mature trees. The well appointed bar/restaurant and terrace are next to the three swimming pools and the entertainment area, with good views over the lake. This is a good holiday base in high season for families. English is spoken.

Facilities

Three good quality and well appointed toilet blocks include facilities for disabled visitors and provision for children. Motorcaravan services. Shop (1/6-15/9). Bar. Restaurant. Pizzeria/takeaway (15/5-15/9). Pool complex, two pools heated. Play areas. Children's club. Archery. Boules. Lake swimming. Fishing. Pedalos, canoes and small boats for hire. Events (high season). Evening entertainment. Disco twice weekly. Internet access. WiFi. Off site: Hang-gliding 2 km. Riding 3 km. Golf 25 km.

Open: 15 May - 15 September.

Directions

Doucier is 25 km. east of Lons-le-Saunier. On the outskirts of Doucier turn north onto D27, site signed. Site in 3 km. beside Lac de Chalain. GPS: 46.6771, 5.78094

Charges guide

Per unit incl. 2 persons	
and electricity	€ 19.00 - € 38.00
extra person	€ 5.50 - € 7.00

Camping Cheques accepted.

We can book this site for you! Call 01580 214000 alanrogers travel

For latest campsite news, availability and prices visit
alanrogers.com

Malbuisson
Camping les Fuvettes

24 route de la Plage et des Perrières, F-25160 Malbuisson (Doubs) T: 03 81 69 31 50.
E: les-fuvettes@wanadoo.fr **alanrogers.com/FR25080**

High in the Jura and close to the Swiss border, les Fuvettes is a well established family site beside Lac Saint Point. The 320 reasonably sized grass pitches are separated by hedges and small trees with varying degrees of shade and many are slightly sloping. There are 250 for touring with 200 having electricity (6A). Only a few have views over the lake. The swimming pool complex is impressive with water slides and a separate children's pool. The site's bar/snack bar is housed in an attractive, steep roofed building and offers panoramic views across the lake. The lake is large – over 1,000 hectares and a wide range of watersports is possible from the site including sailing, windsurfing and pedaloes. Most equipment can be hired on site. Walking and mountain biking are popular pursuits and many trails are available in the surrounding countryside. The Château de Joux is a popular excursion and the nearby Mont d'Or offers fine views towards the Alps. In the high season, the site runs an entertainment and excursion programme, including a children's club.

Facilities

Three toilet blocks include facilities for babies and disabled visitors. Shop. Bar and snack bar. Swimming pool with water slides, jacuzzi and paddling pool (from June). Play area. Minigolf. Archery. Bicycle hire. Sports pitch. Fishing (permit needed). Boat and pedalo hire. Games room. TV room. Children's club in peak season. Entertainment and excursion programme (July/Aug). Mobile homes and chalets for rent. Gas and charcoal barbecues allowed. WiFi (charged). Off site: Lakeside beach. Sailing school. Tennis. Riding 1 km. Bicycle hire 3 km. Many cycling and walking trails. Many restaurants, cafes and shops in nearby Malbuisson (walking distance).

Open: 1 April - 30 September.

Directions

From Besançon, head south on the N57 to just beyond Pontarlier. Take the D437 signed Lac St Point and Mouthe. The road skirts the lake and through Malbuisson. Site is on right at the end of the village. GPS: 46.79197, 6.29334

Charges guide

Per unit incl. 2 persons	
and electricity	€ 18.90 - € 24.90
extra person	€ 3.80 - € 5.00
child (2-7 yrs)	€ 1.80 - € 3.00
dog	free - € 1.50

Camping***
Les Fuvettes
Malbuisson

Situated in the heart of the Jura and at the border of lake St. Point, this campsite is the perfect starting-place for many ramblings through the wild and preserved nature.

Camping Les Fuvettes* • 24, rte de la plage des perrières • 25160 Malbuisson
Tel : 03.81.69.31.50 • email: les-fuvettes@wandoo.fr
www.camping-fuvettes.com

Mesnois

Camping Beauregard

2 Grande Rue, F-39130 Mesnois (Jura) T: 03 84 48 32 51. E: reception@juracampingbeauregard.com
alanrogers.com/FR39120

A hillside site on the edge of a small village with views of the rolling countryside, Beauregard has 192 pitches. A fenced area encloses indoor and outdoor pools and sun terrace. The indoor area includes a jacuzzi, sauna and hot tub. Mobile homes and tents for rent leave around 155 for touring units, all with 6A electricity (long leads may be necessary). The tarmac roads are narrow in places, and many pitches are compact and could be more level. Larger outfits may have difficulty fitting everything on the pitch and with levelling, although the newer pitches on the lower level could be more suitable (but no shade).

Facilities

Three very clean toilet blocks fairly evenly distributed around the site make a good provision, although the newest one on the lower section is only opened in peak season. Baby room and facilities for disabled visitors. Indoor and outdoor pools (15/6-31/8) with toilet and shower facilities. Play areas. WiFi (charged). Off site: Restaurant, bar and takeway (1/4-30/9) adjacent to site. Fishing 500 m. Boat launching 2 km. Other shops, bank and ATM and services in Pont de Poitte 2 km. Riding 5 km.

Open: 1 April - 30 September.

Directions

From Lons-le-Saunier (easily accessed from the A39) take N78 southeast towards Clairvaux-les-Lacs. After about 17 km. in Thuron (before Pont-de-Poitte) turn left on D151 to Mesnois. Site is 1 km. on left by road junction. GPS: 46.59976, 5.68824

Charges guide

Per unit incl. 2 persons and electricity	€ 22.80 - € 27.50
extra person	€ 3.80 - € 4.80
child (2-10 yrs)	€ 2.80 - € 3.50
Less 20% in low season.	

Ounans

Camping la Plage Blanche

3 rue de la Plage, F-39380 Ounans (Jura) T: 03 84 37 69 63. E: reservation@la-plage-blanche.com
alanrogers.com/FR39010

In the Jura, by the rippling waters of the River Loue, this spacious eight-hectare site has 220 pitches (193 for touring, 70 on the riverbank). All are large, grassy and level with 10A electricity (Europlugs). In low season, this is a perfect site for couples; in high season it is ideal for family holidays with its children's club (5-11 yrs), two evening events per week in the bar/restaurant (DJ or live music), swimming pool, kayaking, canoeing, fishing, fly fishing and woodland walks in the site's own wood. La Plage Blanche is an excellent base for exploring Dole, Arbois and its vineyards and the famous Comté cheesemakers. At low water levels the river provides an ideal setting for children to swim and play safely in the gently flowing, shallow water.

Facilities

Modern, well kept sanitary facilities (heated in low season) in three blocks, one renovated for 2011, include showers, washbasins in cabins and facilities for babies and campers with disabilities. Launderette. Motorcaravan service area. Shop with basics, bar/restaurant with terrace, takeaway (all open all season). Swimming and paddling pools (1/5-30/9). Jacuzzi and sauna planned. Play area. Entertainment, activities and children's club (1/7-30/8). TV room. Library. Volleyball. Boules. River fishing and fishing lake. Woodland walks. Canoeing. WiFi (free). Off site: Activities centre at site entrance. Bicycle hire 200 m. Shop 1.5 km. Supermarket 6 km. Riding 10 km. Golf 13 km. Paragliding and hang-gliding.

Open: 1 April - 30 September.

Directions

Ounans is 20 km. southeast of Dole. From autoroute A39 exit 6 (Dole Choisey) follow signs for Pontarlier. In Ounans turn left just before the pizzeria (campsite signposted). GPS: 47.00284, 5.663

Charges 2012

Per unit incl. 2 persons and electricity	€ 26.00
extra person	€ 5.50
child (1-6 yrs)	€ 4.00
dog	€ 2.00

For latest campsite news, availability and prices visit
alanrogers.com

Rougemont
Castel Camping le Val de Bonnal

Bonnal, F-25680 Rougemont (Doubs) T: 03 81 86 90 87. E: val-de-bonnal@wanadoo.fr

alanrogers.com/FR25000

This is an impressive, generally peaceful, well managed site in a large country estate, designed to blend harmoniously with the surrounding countryside, well away from main roads and other intrusions. The site itself is very busy, with a wide range of activities and amenities. The 280 good sized, landscaped pitches (190 for touring) with electricity (6-10A) are separated by a mixture of trees and bushes. The main attraction must be the variety of watersports on the three large lakes and nearby river. The range of activities available in high season is almost inexhaustible, not to say exhausting!

Facilities

Four toilet blocks include washbasins in cabins, suites for disabled visitors and facilities for children and babies. Laundry facilities. Riverside restaurant, snack bar/takeaway, bar and terrace, shop (all 6/5-6/9). Swimming pool complex with water slides. Well equipped play areas. Sport and fitness facilities. Boules. Bicycle hire. Watersports. Fishing on the river and lake. Fitness suite. WiFi (charged). Off site: Rougemont 3.5 km. Golf 6 km. Riding 7 km. Day trips to Switzerland.

Open: 8 May - 9 September.

Directions

From Vesoul take D9 towards Villersexel. After about 20 km. turn right in Esprels signed Val-de-Bonnal. Continue for 3.5 km. to site on left. From autoroute A36, exit Baume-les-Dames; go north on D50, then D486 to Rougemont and follow site signs. GPS: 47.50698, 6.35487

Charges guide

Per unit incl. 2 persons and electricity	€ 25.50 - € 45.00
extra person	€ 6.95 - € 12.50

Saint Point-Lac
Camping Municipal de Saint-Point-Lac

8 rue du Port, F-25160 Saint-Point-Lac (Doubs) T: 03 81 69 61 64. E: camping-saintpointlac@wanadoo.fr

alanrogers.com/FR25050

A good example of a municipal campsite in which the village takes a pride, this site is on the banks of a small lake with views to the distant hills. The 84 level, numbered pitches are on grass and 60 have electricity (16A). It is worth making a detour from the Pontarlier - Vallorbe road or for a longer stay. The village shop and restaurant are an easy 200 m. walk from the site entrance. Units over 7 metres are not accepted.

Facilities

Well maintained, older style central sanitary block (partly refurbished) has British style WCs and free hot water. Suite for disabled visitors. Laundry facilities. Hot snacks and takeaway in high season (July/Aug). Fishing. Off site: Lakeside walk. Motorcaravan services opposite. Beach and swimming area. Pedalo hire. Bicycle hire 5 km.

Open: 1 May - 30 September.

Directions

From north, take D437 south of Pontarlier and keep on west side of the lake to the second village (Saint Point-Lac); from south exit N57 at Les Hopitaux-Neufs and turn west to lake. GPS: 46.8118, 6.3031

Charges guide

Per unit incl. 2 persons and electricity	€ 14.50 - € 16.00
extra person	€ 2.50 - € 3.00
child (4-10 yrs)	€ 1.50 - € 1.75

Vesoul-Vaivre
Camping International du Lac

Avenue des Rives du Lac, F-70000 Vesoul-Vaivre (Haute-Saône) T: 03 84 76 22 86. E: camping_dulac@yahoo.fr **alanrogers.com/FR70020**

This is one of the better examples of a town site and is part of a leisure park around a large lake. The campsite does not have direct access to the lake as it is separated by a security fence, but access is possible at the site entrance. There are 160 good sized, level, grass pitches, all with 10A electricity. Access is from hard roads and pitches are separated by shrubs and bushes. There is a large area in the centre of the site with a play area. A 5 km. path around the lake is used for jogging, walking and cycling.

Facilities

Three good quality toilet blocks, one heated, are well spaced around the site and provide a mix of British and Turkish style WCs, washbasins and showers. Baby room. Two superb suites for disabled visitors. Washing machines and dryers. Motorcaravan service point. Baker calls daily (July/Aug); bread ordered from reception at other times. Entertainment (July/Aug). Bicycle hire. TV and games room. Boules. Internet access. Fishing. Off site: Bar and restaurant adjacent. Lake beach 100 m. Sailing 2 km. Riding 4 km.

Open: 1 March - 31 October.

Directions

On road D457 to west of Vesoul on route to Besançon, well signed around the town. GPS: 47.63054, 6.12946

Charges guide

Per unit incl. 2 persons and electricity	€ 24.40
extra person	€ 3.80
child (under 7 yrs)	€ 1.80
dog	€ 2.00

For latest campsite news, availability and prices visit
alanrogers.com

This quiet and deeply rural province is right in the centre of France to the south of the tourist region of the Loire Valley. Unspoilt and thinly populated, it is unknown to many but by others is considered close to paradise.

DÉPARTEMENTS: 19 CORRÈZE, 23 CREUSE, 87 HAUTE-VIENNE

MAJOR CITIES: LIMOGES, BRIVE-LA-GAILLARDE

On the western side of the Massif Central, this stunningly beautiful region of still lakes, fast flowing streams, gentle rolling valleys and forested mountains has been one of the best kept secrets in France. Lush green meadows are grazed by the Limousin breed of cattle, numerous ancient villages and churches dot the landscape, as well as more imposing abbey churches and fortresses. The region's moorland has made it popular with horse breeders and the Anglo-Arab horse originated from the famous studs of Pompadour.

The city of Limoges, synonymous with porcelain production, produced the finest painted enamelware of Europe in the 16th and 17th centuries and today remains the porcelain capital of France. Aubusson is renowned for its beautiful and intricate tapestries.

But Limousin's appeal is more than anything the freedom of the countryside and it has not yet been discovered except by the discerning traveller. It is said that in Limousin a discovery awaits you at the end of every path and we consider this to be a fairly accurate description.

Places of interest

Aubusson: long tradition of tapestry making, Hotel de Ville tapestry collections.

Grimel-les-Cascades: a pretty hamlet set in a deep gorge.

Gueret: built around a monastery founded in the 8th century, the municipal museum houses a fine collection of porcelain.

Limoges: porcelain, enamel and faience work, château, church of St Michel-de-Lions, cathedral of St Etienne.

Noilac: abbey.

Segur-le-Château: picturesque village dominated by its fortified château. Henry IV's house.

Treignac: Rocher des Folles with a view of the Vézères gorges.

Tulle: 12th-century cathedral and cloister, City museum, Maison de Loyac.

Cuisine of the region

Traditional dishes include a variety of stews such as pote, cassoulet, beans and pork and sauced dishes accompanied by chestnuts of rye pancakes. Limousin beef is tender and full of flavour.

Bréjaude: a soup eaten with rye bread and so thick with cabbage and other vegetables that a spoon will stand up in it.

Clafoutis: a pancake batter poured, for example, over fruit.

Galette Corrzienne: almond cake.

Gargouillau and Milliard: clafoutis of pears and cherries, respectively.

www.tourismelimousin.com or
www.massifcentral-tourisme.com
documentation@crt-limousin.fr
(0)5 55 11 05 90

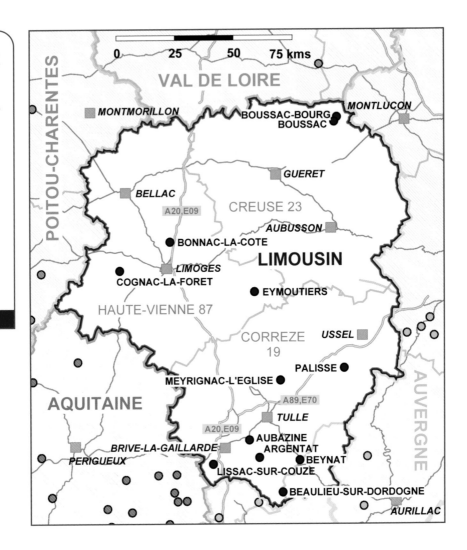

Argentat
Camping Château de Gibanel

Saint Martial Entraygues, F-19400 Argentat (Corrèze) T: 05 55 28 10 11. E: contact@camping-gibanel.com

alanrogers.com/FR19070

This slightly terraced campsite is located in a beautiful estate, dominated by the 16th-century château, on the banks of a very clean lake in this lesser known part of the Dordogne valley. The very friendly family ensures that everything is of a very high standard. Nearly all of the 250 grassy pitches are used for touring units. All have electricity (10A) and are separated by a variety of mature trees giving varying amounts of shade. Many of the trees have low branches making access to most pitches rather difficult for large motorcaravans. Some pitches have an ideal position alongside the lake.

Facilities

Four modern, spacious and clean toilet blocks include many large cubicles with a shower and washbasin. Good provision for disabled visitors. Laundry facilities. Shop for basics. Bar, snack and takeaway (July/Aug). Swimming and paddling pools. Family activities in July/Aug.Bicycle hire (July/Aug). TV room. Boules. Communal barbecue areas. WiFi. Off site: Argentat 5 km (canoe hire available). The river Dordogne is good for fishing and watersports.

Open: 1 June - 4 September.

Directions

Site is 5 km. northeast of Argentat. Take D18, signed Egletons, and after 4 km, alongside the lake, fork right at site sign. Follow lane down to site. GPS: 45.11083, 1.95893

Charges guide

Per unit incl. 2 persons and electricity	€ 18.50 - € 25.90
extra person	€ 4.20 - € 5.30

For latest campsite news, availability and prices visit
alanrogers.com

Argentat
Camping le Vaurette

Monceaux-sur-Dordogne, F-19400 Argentat (Corrèze) T: 05 55 28 09 67. E: info@vaurette.com
alanrogers.com/FR19090

You are assured of a warm welcome at this immaculate site, beautifully situated beside the shallow river Dordogne and just a few kilometres from Argentat. There are 120 large, gently sloping grass pitches, 118 for touring. Separated by a large variety of beautiful trees and shrubs offering varying amounts of shade, all have 6A electricity and many have good views over the river Dordogne as the pitches nearest the river are slightly terraced. The owners run an active campsite for all the family whilst maintaining an air of tranquillity (no radios). Excellent English and Dutch are spoken.

Facilities

Two very clean toilet blocks include facilities for disabled visitors. Further facilities are near the bar and heated pool. Motorcaravan service point. Shop and takeaway (July/Aug). Football. Gym. Boules. Tennis. Fishing. River bathing. Accompanied canoe trips, walks and mountain bike rides. Organised activities in (July/Aug) but no late discos etc. WiFi. Off site: Argentat 9 km. Riding 15 km.

Open: 1 May - 21 September.

Directions

From the A20 or A89 take the exit for Tulle then the N120 to Argentat, onto the D12 towards Beaulieu. The site is on the left. GPS: 45.0464, 1.8821

Charges guide

Per unit incl. 2 persons and electricity	€ 18.50 - € 28.50
extra person (over 2 yrs)	€ 3.50 - € 5.50

Argentat
Sunêlia Au Soleil d'Oc

Monceaux-sur-Dordogne, F-19400 Argentat (Corrèze) T: 05 55 28 84 84. E: info@dordogne-soleil.com
alanrogers.com/FR19100

You will be assured of a very warm welcome, throughout the long season, at this attractive family run site set amongst a variety of tall trees on the banks of the river Dordogne. The 120 large, level, grass pitches, 80 for tourists, all with 6A electricity, are mostly separated by neatly trimmed shrubs and hedges. They are set out on two levels; the lower level nearer the river, with fewer static pitches, being some distance from the toilet facilities and sports area. This site should appeal to lovers of watersports and other activities, particularly in July and August when there is plenty to do for all the family. The access roads on site are narrow with sharp corners and therefore not recommended for larger units.

Facilities

Two unisex toilet blocks offer all the facilities one would expect. Baby facilities. Shop (1/7-31/8). Bar (1/5-31/10). Restaurant and takeaway (1/6-30/9). Outdoor pool (1/5-15/10). New indoor pool planned. Motorcaravan service point. River bathing. Canoe hire and organised trips. Volleyball, football, pool table and electronic games. Archery. Minigolf. Fishing. Bicycle hire. Guided walks and bike rides. Entertainment (July/Aug). WiFi. Torches useful. Off site: River Dordogne. Argentat 4 km. Riding 15 km.

Open: 4 April - 15 November.

Directions

Leave Argentat on D12 heading southwest (Beaulieu). In 3.5 km. (village of Laygue) turn left across a single track bridge spanning the river Dordogne. Immediately turn left and site is a few hundred metres on left. GPS: 45.0753, 1.91699

Charges guide

Per unit incl. 2 persons and electricity (6A)	€ 17.90 - € 27.90

Camping Cheques accepted.

Beaulieu-sur-Dordogne
Flower Camping des Iles

Boulevard Rodolphe de Turenne, F-19120 Beaulieu-sur-Dordogne (Corrèze) T: 05 55 91 02 65.
E: info@campingdesiles.fr **alanrogers.com/FR19130**

This is a very pleasant and well equipped site in a beautiful location on a small island in the river Dordogne. Camping les Iles is a very attractive family run site only five minutes walk away from the centre of the medieval town of Beaulieu-sur-Dordogne with its ancient streets, old churches, many shops and restaurants. This 5 hectare site has 120 shady, grass pitches, 80 of which are available for touring all with 10A electricity. The added bonus of its close proximity to the centre of the village makes this an ideal site for tourers.

Facilities

Three modern, clean toilet blocks. Baby room. Facilities for campers with disabilities. Laundry room. Motorcaravan service point. Heated pool (June-Sept), poolside bar, snacks. Boules. Canoe hire. Fishing. Children's entertainment (3-12 yrs) 4 days per week. Evening soirees 2 evenings per week. No shop or bread on site because of its close proximity to the town. WiFi. Off site: Pizzeria and takeaway 200 m. Tennis 600 m. Bicycle hire 8 km. Golf or riding 18 km. Gouffre de Padirac.

Open: 23 April - 24 September.

Directions

Site is in the centre of the Beaulieu-sur-Dordogne on the D940. From Tulle turn right or from Montal turn left. Approach site with care through the narrow streets. Enter site through narrow archway (3 m. high). GPS: 44.979705, 1.840146

Charges guide

Per unit incl. 2 persons and electricity	€ 13.90 - € 26.90
extra person	€ 3.90 - € 6.90
child (2-7 yrs)	free - € 3.30

For latest campsite news, availability and prices visit
alanrogers.com

Aubazine

Campé**o**le

Campéole le Coiroux

Centre Touristique du Coiroux, F-19190 Aubazine (Corrèze) T: 05 55 27 21 96.

E: coiroux@campeole.com **alanrogers.com/FR19140**

Le Coiroux, part of the Campéole group, is set in a picturesque location in the heart of a forest on the edge of a large leisure park and lake. There are 174 large pitches, 62 for touring all with 10A electricity. They are flat and grassy with small dividing hedges and trees giving shade. The large number of mobile homes and chalets on site are separate from the camping area and not intrusive. There is everything one needs for a family holiday at this site which caters for adults and children of all ages.

Facilities

One large modern very well equipped sanitary block with all necessary facilities including those for campers with disabilities and baby room. Washing machines and tumble dryers. Second smaller sanitary block. Motorcaravan service point. Large heated swimming pool (1/5-30/9). Poolside bar, snack bar and large shop selling groceries, fruit and vegetables (1/7-31/8). Boules. Tennis. Organised activities for children, teenagers and adults throughout the day (July/Aug). Accommodation for hire. Free WiFi. Off site: Leisure park (reduced fees charged). Lake fishing 300 m. Excellent 27-hole golf complex 800 m. Tree walking adventure course. Paintball. Rocamadour and many other tourist destinations are within 1 hour's drive.

Open: 1 April - 30 September.

Directions

Leave A20 exit 50 Brive centre, take N28 towards Tulle. At the village of Gare d'Aubazine turn right to Aubazine. Continue for 6 km. through village, take road to Chastang and follow signs to Parc Touristique du Coiroux about 4 km. GPS: 45.18633, 1.70775

Charges guide

Per unit incl. 2 persons	
and electricity	€ 15.10 - € 24.50
extra person	€ 4.00 - € 5.90
child (2-6 yrs)	free - € 3.90
dog	€ 2.00 - € 2.60

Campé**o**le

CAMPSITES AND RENTALS

Le Coiroux***

Magnificent three stars site in the middle of a nature park. Swimming pool, golf, tree top adventure, touring pitches and quality accommodations.

19190 Aubazine · Tel.: +33-555-2721-96 · www.campeole.co.uk / coiroux@campeole.com

Beynat

alan rogers
Runner up 2011 Awards

Les Hameaux de Miel

F-19190 Beynat (Corrèze) T: 05 55 84 34 48.

E: info@chalets-en-france.com **alanrogers.com/FR19200**

Les Hameaux de Miel is a member of the Chalets en France group, which comprises six chalet parks in southern France. Please note, however, that there are no touring pitches here. The site is open all year and has a hilltop location with fine views of the surrounding valleys and forests of the Limousin. The Etang de Miel is three minutes walk away and has received the European Blue Flag accreditation for its cleanliness. The lake is ideal for sailing and windsurfing, as well as fishing, and also has special facilities for disabled visitors. A children's club operates during the peak season and various other activities are organised, including archery, rock climbing and riding. Chalets here are attractively dispersed around the site and are all available for rent. Bread and pastries can be delivered to your door each morning. The site makes a good base to explore the surrounding Corrèze area. The Dordogne and Lot rivers provide many opportunities for fishing, canoeing, walking and sightseeing. Foie gras, ceps, strawberries and walnuts are all here waiting to be tasted at the local market stalls.

Facilities

Two swimming pools (one covered in low season). Play area. Multisports pitch. Volleyball. Games room. Entertainment and activity programme. Children's club. Chalets for rent. Tourist information. Off site: Etang de Miel 300 m. Fishing 500 m. Golf, boat launching and sailing 5 km. Cycling and walking trails.

Open: 23 April - 24 September.

Directions

Take exit 50 from the A20 motorway (Brive) and then head east on the N89 to Malemort-sur-Corrèze. Shortly beyond this town, join the southbound D921 to Beynat. The site is beyond the town and is well signed. GPS: 45.12932, 1.76141

Charges 2012

Contact the site for details.

For latest campsite news, availability and prices visit

alanrogers.com

Boussac-Bourg

Castel Camping le Château de Poinsouze

Route de la Châtre, B.P. 12, F-23600 Boussac-Bourg (Creuse) T: 05 55 65 02 21.
E: info.camping-de.poinsouze@orange.fr **alanrogers.com/FR23010**

Le Château de Poinsouze is a well established site arranged on an open, gently sloping, grassy park with views over a small lake and Château. It is an attractive, well maintained, high quality site situated in the unspoilt Limousin region. The 118 touring pitches, some with lake frontage, all have electricity (6-20A Europlug), water and drainage and 68 have sewerage connections. The site has a friendly family atmosphere with many organised activities in main season including dances, children's games and crafts. There are marked walks around the park and woods. All facilities are open all season. This great site should ensure a stress-free, enjoyable holiday for all the family. Exceptionally well restored outbuildings on the opposite side of the drive house a shop, bar and a new restaurant serving excellent cuisine. The pool complex has a new superb water play area for children with many fun fountains. The château is not open to the public.

Facilities

High quality, sanitary unit, washing machines, dryer, ironing, suites for disabled visitors. Motorcaravan services. Well stocked shop. Takeaway. Bar, Internet and WiFi, two satellite TVs, library. Restaurant with new mini-bar for low season. Heated swimming pool, slide, children's pool and new water play area with fountains. Fenced playground. Pétanque. Bicycle hire. Free fishing in the lake, boats and lifejackets can be hired. Sports facilities. No dogs in high season (14/7-18/8). Off site: Boussac (2.5 km) has a market every Thursday morning. The massive 12th-/15th-century fortress, Château de Boussac, is open daily all year.

Open: 1 June - 1 September.

Directions

Boussac lies 35 km. west of Montluçon, between the A20 and A71 autoroutes. Site is 2.5 km. north of Boussac on D917 (towards La Châtre). GPS: 46.37243, 2.20268

Charges guide

Per unit incl. 2 persons and full services	€ 19.00 - € 35.00
extra person	€ 3.00 - € 6.00
child (2-7 yrs)	€ 2.00 - € 5.00
dog	€ 3.00

Centre of France

LES CASTELS
Hôtellerie de Plein Air

Château de Poinsouze

★★★★

Wi Fi

Camping Qualité

Ecolabel — EU Ecolabel FR/026/024

La Clef Verte

Family Campsite. Calm & Nature. Exceptional fully enclosed sanitary facilities.
Heated swimming pool. Animation 4-12 years. Chalets, gîtes & mobile homes for hire.

Route de la Châtre, 23600 Boussac-Bourg | Tel: 0033 555 65 02 21 | Fax: 0033 555 65 86 49
info.camping-de.poinsouze@orange.fr | www.camping-de-poinsouze.com

For latest campsite news, availability and prices visit
alanrogers.com

Bonnac-la-Côte

Castel Camping le Château de Leychoisier

Domaine de Leychoisier, 1 route de Leychoisier, F-87270 Bonnac-la-Côte (Haute-Vienne) T: 05 55 39 93 43.
E: contact@leychoisier.com **alanrogers.com/FR87020**

You will receive a warm welcome at this beautiful, family run 15th-century château site. It offers peace and quiet in superb surroundings. It is ideally situated for short or long stays being only 2 km. from the A20/N20 and 10 km. north of Limoges. The large, slightly sloping and grassy pitches are in a parkland setting with many magnificent mature trees offering a fair amount of shade. The 80 touring pitches have 10A electricity (reversed polarity) and many have a tap, although long leads and hoses may be necessary. Explore the grounds and walk down to the four hectare lake. The lake provides free fishing, boating, canoeing and a marked off area for swimming.

Facilities

The toilet block is very clean, but perhaps cramped at busy times. Some washbasins in cabins with good provision for disabled visitors. Washing machine and dryer. Basic food provisions (bread can be ordered). Restaurant (from 10/5). Bar, TV room and snack bar. Small swimming pool with sunbathing area (no Bermuda shorts). Lake. Play area. Tennis and boules courts (in need of repair when we visited). Torch useful. WiFi (charged). Off site: Shop 2 km. Supermarket 5 km. Riding 7 km. Golf 20 km.

Open: 15 April - 20 September.

Directions

From A20, north of Limoges, take exit 27 (west) signed Bonnac-La-Côte. In village turn left and follow signs to site. GPS: 45.93299, 1.29006

Charges guide

Per unit incl. 2 persons	
and electricity	€ 23.00 - € 30.00
extra person	€ 5.00 - € 8.00
child (under 7 yrs)	€ 4.00 - € 5.00
dog	€ 2.00 - € 3.00

No credit cards.

Château de Leychoisier
Camping & caravaning ★★★★

1 Route de Leychoisier
F-87270 Bonnac-la-Côte
Tél./fax: +33 (0)55 53 99 343
E-mail: contact@leychoisier.com
www.leychoisier.com

Europe Qualité

LES CASTELS ★★★★

Cognac-la-Forêt

Camping des Alouettes

Les Alouettes, F-87310 Cognac-la-Forêt (Haute-Vienne) T: 05 55 03 26 93.
E: info@camping-des-alouettes.com **alanrogers.com/FR87100**

Camping des Alouettes is run by a young Dutch couple who will do all they can to ensure your stay is enjoyable. The site has 68 large flat pitches all with 10A electricity. Almost all pitches enjoy panoramic views of the area. There is a mixture of mature and young trees providing some shade and pitches are separated by new shrubs or hedging. On arrival you are given a guided tour of the campsite and an explanation of what is available both on and off site, supplemented by extensive tourist information at reception. There are various walking and cycle routes direct from the site and the many tourist attractions include a porcelain museum and Parc Bellevue for children.

Facilities

Well kept traditional sanitary block includes facilities for disabled visitors. Washing machine (€ 4). Bread can be ordered daily and delivered to your pitch. Bar (open all season). Restaurant (Monday and Friday with limited menu). Takeaway spit roast chicken (Wednesday). Swimming pool planned. Small library. Football, volleyball, badminton, pétanque and table tennis. Small play area and trampoline. No charcoal barbecues. Internet access at bar. Off site: Village 250 m. with shops, café and bank. Walking and cycle routes direct from site. Oradour-sur-Glane 18 km. Limoges 25 km.

Open: 1 April - 30 September.

Directions

From the north take exit 28 from the A20 onto the D2000/N520. Continue towards Perigueux until Cognac-la-Forêt is signed to the right at the roundabout. Continue through the village on the D10. The site is on the left after 250 m. GPS: 45.8247, 0.99657

Charges guide

Per unit incl. 2 persons	
and electricity	€ 13.60 - € 17.00
extra person	€ 3.00 - € 3.60
child (under 10 yrs)	€ 2.00 - € 2.50
dog	€ 1.00

For latest campsite news, availability and prices visit
alanrogers.com

Lissac-sur-Couze

Les Hameaux du Perrier

F-19600 Lissac-sur-Couze (Corrèze) T: 05 55 84 34 48. E: info@chalets-en-france.com

alanrogers.com/FR19190

Les Hameaux du Perrier is a member of the Chalets en France group. This group comprises four chalet parks in southern France. Please note, however, that there are no touring pitches here. The site is open all year and can be found ten minutes south west of Brive-la-Gaillarde on the border between the Corrèze and Dordogne départements. The site enjoys fine views of the large Lac du Couze, popular for sailing and windsurfing. On-site amenities include two swimming pools and a bar/restaurant. During the peak season, there is a children's club and various other activities. Accommodation on offer here is an attractive range of 94 wooden chalets, thoughtfully dispersed around the site.

Facilities

Bar. Restaurant. Takeaway. Two swimming pools. Play area. Multisports pitch. Games room. Tourist information. Entertainment and activity programme. Children's club. Chalets for rent. Off site: Lac de Couze 500 m. Sailing and windsurfing. Fishing. Cycle and walking trails. Riding. Brive (large town with many shops and restaurants).

Open: All year.

Directions

Take exit 51 from the A20 motorway (Brive south) and then head west on the D59 to Lissac-sur-Couze. The site is well signed upon arrival at the village. GPS: 45.10029, 1.43848

Charges 2012

Contact the site for details.

Meyrignac l'Eglise

Les Cottages du Puy d'Agnoux

F-19800 Meyrignac l'Eglise (Corrèze) T: 05 55 84 34 48.
E: info@chalets-en-france.com **alanrogers.com/FR19240**

This attractive site offers high quality cottage accommodation for up to six persons in the lesser known, but beautiful, Corrèze region to the south west of the Auvergne. The cottages are in a wooded area close to a small lake. The hills and valleys surrounding the site offer a wealth of marked footpaths and cycle routes and will be greatly appreciated by nature lovers. There are many ancient villages, with their old houses, Romanesque churches and markets, which are well worth visiting. The chalet accommodation, available throughout the year, is spacious and very well equipped. There are three chalets specially equipped for visitors with disabilities.

Facilities

Laundry room. Bar, restaurant and snack bar. Heated indoor and outdoor swimming pools. Jacuzzi and sauna. Games and TV room. Tennis. Pool table. Playground. Family activities in high season, including a children's miniclub. WiFi. Off site: Minigolf and paintball 2 km. Picturesque old towns and villages. A small range of shops in St. Augustine 2 km. Corrèze with Sunday market 3 km. Riding 8 km. Fishing.

Open: All year.

Directions

Leave A89 autoroute, exit 21 northeast of Tulle. Take N89 northeast then D26 north to Corrèze. Continue through village to site in 2.5 km. GPS: 45.40162, 1.85967

Charges 2012

Contact the site for details.

Palisse

Camping le Vianon

F-19160 Palisse (Corrèze) T: 05 55 95 87 22. E: info@levianon.com

alanrogers.com/FR19080

You will receive a very warm welcome from the Dutch owners of this spacious and peaceful site and they speak excellent English. The site is tucked away in the lesser known, very beautiful Corrèze region yet it is only a few kilometres from the river Dordogne. This region is reputed to have the purest air in France. The grassy, slightly sloping pitches are of a good size in a natural woodland setting with tall trees offering shade and all have 16A electricity. The bar, restaurant and terrace overlook the swimming pool and sunbathing area and are open all season.

Facilities

Modern toilet blocks with all the necessary facilities. Unit for disabled visitors. Bar. Restaurant, takeaway. Shop. Boules. Spacious play area. Bicycle hire. Lake fishing. Off site: Small town Neuvic with shops, restaurants 9 km. Large lake with water sports, swimming. Canoeing in the Dordogne (30 minutes). Riding and golf course at Neuvic. Marked walks and cycle rides.

Open: All year (telephone first October-April).

Directions

Leave A89 southwest of Ussel and take N89 towards Egletons. In about 7 km. just before Combressol, turn left on D47 signed Palisse and Camping le Vianon. Site entrance is on the left in 7 km. GPS: 45.42678, 2.20583

Charges guide

Per unit incl. 2 persons and electricity	€ 20.30 - € 29.65
extra person (over 2 yrs)	€ 4.00 - € 5.50

For latest campsite news, availability and prices visit

alanrogers.com

Set in the heart of the Massif-Central, the Auvergne was formed by a series of volcanic eruptions and is a dramatic region of awe-inspiring, non-active volcanoes, lakes, sparkling rivers, green valleys and forests.

DÉPARTEMENTS: 03 ALLIER, 15 CANTAL, 43 HAUTE-LOIRE, 63 PUY-DE-DÔME

MAJOR CITY: CLERMONT-FERRAND

The Auvergne is one of the largest protected areas in Europe and includes two regional nature parks and the vast oak forest of Tronçais. The opportunities for outdoor activities are endless: hiking along one of the 11 long-distance trails, hang gliding above the volcano and rafting in the gorge of the Allier; cycling along the 'voies vertes' or, if you dare, on a volcano; enjoying the flora and fauna, swimming and fishing in one of the 50 lakes.

You can take a cultural tour and admire the beautiful Romanesque churches and some of the 50 castles open to the public, or the national museums (Theatrical Costumes, Michelin); and then there are many international festivals and local events.

Gastronomy is a key interest in the region, with 11 restaurants with Michelin stars, including one with three, and 30 so-called 'bibs gourmands' (good and inexpensive restaurants) where you must try one of the regional specialities based on cheese and potatoes.

AUVERGNE
YOUR NEW WORLD

www.**auvergne-tourism.com**
www.**auvergne-bike.com**

Places of interest

Le Panoramique des Dômes

Take this spectacular train to the top of the Puy-de-Dôme all year round. Besides an exceptional view of the mountains and volcanoes, you will find a restaurant, a shop and a Mercury Temple.

Vulcania

A beautiful park that celebrates the natural phenomenon of volcanoes around the world. In 2012 the park celebrates its 10th year: children up to 10 years old receive free admission.

UNESCO World Heritage

The cathedral of Puy-en-Velay and the Romanesque basilica of Notre Dame du Port at Clermont-Ferrand are designated as World Heritage Sites.

Historical towns and buildings

Eleven of the offically recognised 'most beautiful French villages', 250 Romanesque churches, a historic castle route and a route through ancient spa towns.

Great festivals

Short films in Clermont-Ferrand, street theatre in Aurillac, religious music in La Chaise Dieu, contemporary music in Clermont-Ferrand, world culture in Gannat.

Cuisine of the region

La truffade: Potatoes with fresh Tomme cheese from the Cantal.

La chou farci: Stuffed cabbage.

La lentille verte: green lentils.

Ham and sausages from Auvergne.

Five first-class cheeses: Cantal, St.-Nectaire, Bleu d'Auvergne, Salers, Fourme d'Ambert.

Red wine and rosé: Boudes, Côtes d'Auvergne, Saint Pourçain.

Mineral water: Volvic, Vichy Célestins.

La tarte aux myrtilles: blueberry pie.

Les pâtes de fruits: fruit pastes.

Liqueurs: Verveine du Velay, Eaux de vie.

Crafts

Enamelled lava, knives from Thiers, lace from Puy-en-Velay, umbrellas from Aurillac.

Images © : Comité Régional de Développement Touristique d'Auvergne; (left to right, top to bottom): FROBERT-David, SOISSONS-Pierre, DAMASE-Joël, DAMASE-Joël, DAMASE-Joël, FAYET-Gérard.

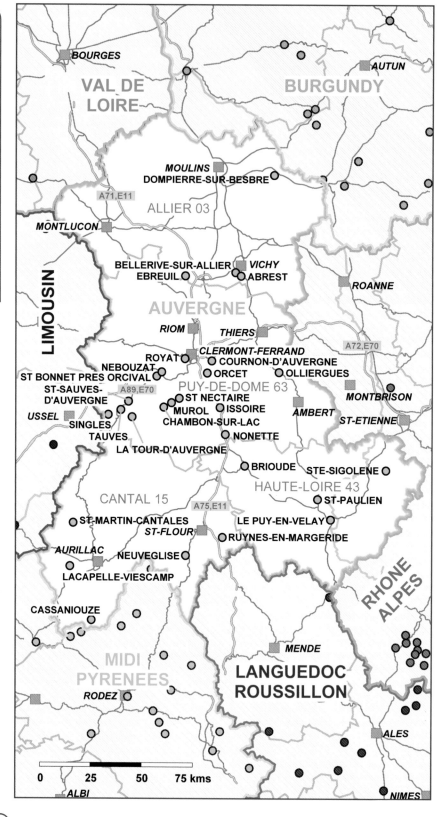

For latest campsite news, availability and prices visit

alanrogers.com

Abrest
Camping de la Croix Saint Martin

Allée du Camping, 99 avenue des Graviers, F-03200 Abrest (Allier) T: 04 70 32 67 74.
E: camping-vichy@orange.fr **alanrogers.com/FR03110**

La Croix Saint Martin is in Abrest on the edge of the attractive spa town of Vichy and close to the Bourbonnais mountains. The site is on the right bank of the Allier and extends over three hectares of wooded parkland. There are 89 level grassy pitches with 72 for touring and 65 with 10A electricity. They are separated by some hedging and a variety of mature trees give varying amounts of shade. Vichy's elegant parks are less than 30 minutes on foot and the town centre is only another ten minutes. No twin-axle caravans.

Facilities

Adequate toilet block with all necessary facilities. Swimming pool (1/5–30/9). Fishing. Play area. Volleyball. Table tennis, tennis, boules. Children's miniclub (July/Aug). Bouncy cushion. Tourist information. Motorcaravan services. Free WiFi. Off site: Vichy centre 40 minutes walk. Bus to Vichy. Canoeing, windsurfing, river bathing 3 km. Golf 5 km. Walking, cycling and riding in the Auvergne.

Open: 2 April - 15 October.

Directions

Abrest lies just south of Vichy. From town centre, head south D906 (Avenue de Thiers) to Abrest. Follow signs to site. GPS: 46.1073, 3.43747

Charges guide

Per unit incl. 2 persons and electricity	€ 14.60 - € 18.90
extra person	€ 3.70 - € 4.90
child (under 7 yrs)	€ 2.50 - € 3.50

Bellerive-sur-Allier
Camping Beau Rivage

Rue Claude Decloître, les Berges de l'Allier, F-03700 Bellerive-sur-Allier (Allier) T: 04 70 32 26 85.
E: camping-beaurivage@wanadoo.fr **alanrogers.com/FR03030**

This well maintained, compact, urban site is beside the River Allier and just over the water from the famous spa town of Vichy. It has recently been completely refurbished by the enthusiastic new owners (good English and Dutch spoken). There are 80 medium sized, reasonably level grass pitches with 47 for touring. Some have delightful views across the river to the beautiful Parc Napoléon beyond. They are separated by flowering shrubs and some tall hedging, and mature trees offer some shade. All pitches have 10A electricity and 12 are fully serviced. On-site access is not easy for large outfits. No twin-axle caravans. There is a high season overspill site adjacent.

Facilities

Very clean, modern airy sanitary facilities in individual cubicles in pleasantly decorated buildings. Fully equipped, including a baby room and facilities for campers with disabilities. Laundry facilities. Motorcaravan service point. Small bar with snacks (March-Oct). River fishing. Play area. Bicycles and pedaloes. Minigolf. Archery. Internet. WiFi (first hour free). Off site: Riding, canoeing and tennis nearby. Very close to the site are several bars and restaurants. Hypermarket within 1 km. Vichy 2 km.

Open: 1 April - 15 October.

Directions

From A71 exit 12 (Vichy), head east, A719 then D2209 to Bellerive-sur-Allier. Turn right at roundabout with fountains, follow signs to Berges des Allier, Campings and then Beau Rivage. Site is in 3 km. GPS: 46.11567, 3.43012

Charges guide

Per unit incl. 2 persons and electricity (6A)	€ 16.00 - € 20.30
extra person	€ 4.10 - € 5.30
Camping Cheques accepted.	

Cassaniouze
Camping de Coursavy

D141, F-15340 Cassaniouze (Cantal) T: 04 71 49 97 70. E: camping.coursavy@wanadoo.fr
alanrogers.com/FR15110

This is a tranquil, rural site located on the banks of the Lot river. There are just 50 pitches, of which four are used for chalets. All the pitches have electricity, although some require long leads. Many have shade and some are separated by hedges. Very large units may have difficulties reaching a few pitches. Fishing from the river bank on the site is possible, as is swimming. The site also has a small, unheated swimming pool. Many interesting walks are possible in the surrounding hills. A well-equipped basic site for a taste of the real countryside.

Facilities

One central, very clean toilet block includes facilities for disabled visitors and family and baby rooms. Washing machine, mangle and washing line. Fresh bread daily, fresh vegetables twice weekly. Small swimming pool. Sports field. Fishing. Chalets for rent. WiFi (free) throughout. Torches required. Off site: Walking and mountain biking. Riding. Golf. River sports.

Open: 20 April - 20 September.

Directions

Site is northwest of Rodez. From Entraygues-sur-Truyère take the D107 west for 8.5 km. where road number changes to D141. Continue 10 km. to site on the left. Go beyond the site for 500 m. to turn and enter site. GPS: 44.642551, 2.366282

Charges guide

Per unit incl. 2 persons	€ 23,20
extra person	€ 4.00

For latest campsite news, availability and prices visit
alanrogers.com

Chambon-sur-Lac
Camping les Bombes

Chemin de Pétary, F-63790 Chambon-sur-Lac (Puy-de-Dôme) T: 04 73 88 64 03.
E: les-bombes.camping@orange.fr **alanrogers.com/FR63250**

Les Bombes is a former municipal campsite, and has been refurbished over the past few years. Recently added amenities include a heated swimming pool, a snack bar and a number of chalets for rent (single night bookings accepted in low season). The site extends over 12.5 hectares and has 150 pitches. These are large (minimum 100 sq. m), flat, grassy and generally well shaded. The site is well located for walking and mountain biking with a number of routes leading direct from the site. The site owners will be delighted to recommend possible routes.

Facilities

Three toilet blocks are a mix of traditional and modern and can be a long way from some pitches. They have washbasins in cabins and preset showers. Baby changing. Facilities for disabled visitors. Laundry facilities. Shop. Bar/snack bar (15/6-30/8). Swimming pool. Paddling pool. Games room. Play area. Giant chess. Fishing. Bicycle hire. Weekly entertainment (high season). WiFi. Chalets for rent. Off site: Lac de Chambon 10 mins. on foot. Murol 3 km. St. Nectaire 10 km. Vulcania 48 km.

Open: 1 May - 15 September.

Directions

The site can be found to the west of the Lac de Chambon. From Murol, head west on D996 skirting the lake to Chambon-sur-Lac and follow signs to the site. GPS: 45.56979, 2.90185

Charges guide

Per unit incl. 2 persons and electricity	€ 18.10 - € 22.45
extra person	€ 4.20 - € 4.90
child (1-7 yrs)	€ 3.00 - € 3.90

Cournon-d'Auvergne
Camping le Pré des Laveuses

Rue des Laveuses, F-63800 Cournon-d'Auvergne (Puy-de-Dôme) T: 04 73 84 81 30.
E: camping@cournon-auvergne.fr **alanrogers.com/FR63230**

A well equipped municipal site, le Pré des Laveuses is adjacent to a boating and fishing lake and its beach, alongside the River Allier, close to Cournon-d'Auvergne and the A75 autoroute. This site will be busy in the high season due to its public bar/restaurant, new heated swimming pool complex, nearby activities and its proximity to Clermont-Ferrand. There are 150 large, grassy, mostly level pitches with 120 for touring (all with 10A electricity, long leads advised). They are in small groups separated from other groups by neat low hedges. Mature trees give some shade to some pitches.

Facilities

Two modern toilet blocks include facilities for disabled visitors, possibly stretched when site busy. Laundry facilities. Public bar/restaurant with TV (June/Sept). Swimming pool complex. Children's room (TV). Play area. Boules. Motorcaravan services outside gate. High season activities, children's club. WiFi (charged). Off site: Lake, bathing, boating and free fishing (adjacent). Canoeing (high season) and free fishing in River Allier. Minigolf. Tennis. Adjacent park. Cournon 2 km. Bicycle hire 2.5 km.

Open: 1 April - 31 October.

Directions

Site is 12 km. southeast of Clermont-Ferrand. Leave autoroute A75 at exit 1, taking D212 to Cournon d'Auvergne. Site is well signed to east of town, beside River Allier. Follow Zone de Loisirs. GPS: 45.74019, 3.22266

Charges guide

Per unit incl. 2 persons and electricity (10A)	€ 18.60 - € 22.50
extra person	€ 4.70 - € 5.20

Dompierre-sur-Besbre
Camping les bords de Besbre

F-03290 Dompierre-sur-Besbre (Allier) T: 04 70 34 55 57. E: camping.dompierre@free.fr
alanrogers.com/FR03170

This immaculate, attractive and excellent value-for-money site has 67 level, partly shaded, individually hedged, grassy pitches, all with easy access. There are a few long stay units, leaving about 65 for tourists, all with electricity (10A) and most being fully serviced. It is located next to the municipal sports fields and is ideal for motorcaravans being within easy walking distance of the town centre and supermarket (700 m). The warden is very proud of his efficiently run site and its award-winning floral displays. Twin-axle caravans are not accepted.

Facilities

Modernised, heated toilet blocks are very clean and include provision for disabled visitors. Some washbasins in curtained cubicles for ladies. Washing machine. Motorcaravan services. No charcoal barbecues. Heated indoor swimming pool (all season). Off site: The small town has shops, restaurants and a Saturday market. Vallée de la Besbre has several rivers and small lakes nearby for fishing. Cycle tracks and footpaths.

Open: 15 May - 15 September.

Directions

Dompierre is 35 km. east of Moulins. Leave N79 at eastern end of Dompierre bypass, turn southwest on N2079 towards town. Entrance to sports complex and campsite is on left beyond D55 before the river bridge and town centre. GPS: 46.51564, 3.68434

Charges guide

Per unit incl. 2 persons and electricity	€ 9.40
extra person	€ 2.40

For latest campsite news, availability and prices visit
alanrogers.com

Ebreuil
Camping de la Filature

Route de Chouvigny, F-03450 Ebreuil (Allier) T: 04 70 90 72 01. E: camping.filature@gmail.com

alanrogers.com/FR03010

Beside a fine fly fishing river, not far from the spa town of Vichy, this spacious family campsite makes a good base for exploring the Auvergne, the nearby river gorges, châteaux, mountains and lakes. There are 80 spacious, grassy pitches, 74 for touring, in a parkland setting. Most have 6A electricity and some shade from mature trees. Many are directly by the river, which is clean, shallow and pleasant to play in. There is a deeper area for swimming 500 m. away. You will receive a warm welcome from the English owners, who also provide good value and very popular takeaway food. In May and June, the fields abound with wild flowers, some quite rare. Bird songs are many and varied. Listen for the songs of the nightingale and golden oriole, often heard but seldom seen. The quiet country roads are ideal for walking and cycling, especially mountain biking and for touring by car. The interesting village of Ébreuil with its Thursday market, is just a 15 minute level stroll. Just west of the site are the gorges of the river Sioule, and the extinct volcanoes of the Puy-de-Dôme with the Vulcania Exhibition are well worth a visit.

Facilities

Clean, fully equipped sanitary facilities, bathroom and facilities for campers with disabilities. Laundry facilities. Small shop for essentials (1/5-30/9). Baker calls. Bar (15/5-30/9). Excellent takeaway (1/6-15/9). Barbecues and pizza nights organised in high season. River bathing and fishing. Play areas. Minigolf. WiFi. Electric barbecues only. Off site: Riding, canoeing, tennis, bicycle hire, motorcaravan services 500 m. Ébreuil with shops, bar, restaurants 1 km. Spa town of Vichy with large range of shops, bars, restaurants and sporting activities 30 km.

Open: 31 March - 1 October.

Directions

Site is well signed from exit 12 of A71 autoroute to Clermont-Ferrand in the direction of Ebreuil. It is about 6 km. from the A71 and 1 km. west of Ebreuil beside the river on the D915 towards the Chouvigny gorges. GPS: 46.10877, 3.07338

Charges 2012

Per unit incl. 2 persons and electricity	€ 21.50
extra person	€ 6.00
child (under 16 yrs)	€ 3.50
dog	free

Don't wait to die to go to heaven, visit the:

★★★★
CAMPING DE LA FILATURE DE LA SIOULE
03450 EBREUIL, FRANCE - 0033 (0)4 70 90 72 01
camping.filature@gmail.com

- Clean, quiet, comfortable site, open 31 March to 1 October;
- Large, shady pitches;
- 5 min from A71 (Paris - Millau);
- 6 Luxury mobile homes;
- Free WiFi, Low low-season prices;
- Perfect for canoeing, riding, cycling, swimming and walking;
- Bar and quality take-away, June - September.
- 30 days for 2 persons € 360,- except 14 July to 15 August.

www.campingfilature.com

Issoire
Château Camping la Grange Fort

Les Pradeaux, F-63500 Issoire (Puy-de-Dôme) T: 04 73 71 02 43. E: chateau@lagrangefort.com

alanrogers.com/FR63040

This tranquil campsite of seven hectares is within the 25 hectare estate of the picturesque 15th-century Chateau of Grange Fort. There are 120 pitches (90 for touring units) some with panoramic views over the river Allier, others with views of the historic château. There is a mix of well drained grass and hardstanding pitches with varying degrees of shade. A short steep path leads down to the river. Guided tours of the château are available and high quality evening meals are provided in its vaulted restaurant. The campsite is just ten minutes from the A75.

Facilities

Three good sanitary blocks have facilities for disabled visitors and a 'hydra shower'. Laundry room. Bread. Restaurant and takeaway (1/5-15/9). Bar (15/6-15/9). Indoor pool, sauna, massage table (15/4-15/10). Outdoor pools (15/6-1/10). Outdoor swimming pool with jacuzzi. Play area, games room. Internet. WiFi (charged). Tennis, minigolf, football, boules. Activities in season. Torches useful. Off site: Fishing 250 m. Riding 8 km. The Parc des Volcans and the Vulcania exhibition are nearby.

Open: 10 April - 15 October.

Directions

From A75 autoroute take exit 13 onto D996 east towards Parentignat. At first roundabout take first exit on D999 new road (St Remy, La Vernet). At next roundabout take first exit (D34) and follow campsite signs. GPS: 45.50875, 3.28488

Charges guide

Per unit incl. 2 persons and electricity	€ 19.50 - € 30.25
extra person	€ 3.50 - € 6.00

For latest campsite news, availability and prices visit
alanrogers.com

La Tour-d'Auvergne

Camping la Chauderie

Route de Besse, F-63680 La Tour-d'Auvergne (Puy-de-Dôme) T: 06 33 78 53 45. E: info@la-chauderie.com
alanrogers.com/FR63350

La Chauderie has recently been taken over by an enthusiastic young Dutch couple. It boasts its own beautiful and totally natural waterfall on the small La Burande river. There are 75 terraced pitches arranged in small groups radiating from the winding central site road. All have 6A electricity and some are separated by hedging. There are two well specified sanitary blocks, one with facilities for disabled campers and a baby room. A new bar serving light meals adds to the relaxed, family atmosphere at this happy, well run site. Views from the site include the Mont de Sancy and village of La Tour-d'Auvergne.

Facilities

Two very clean sanitary blocks with good separate facilities for ladies and men include provision for disabled visitors. Laundry facilities in lower block. New bar and snack bar. Takeaway meals (June-Aug). TV room. Games room. Playground for small children has recently been renewed. Minigolf course. Boules. WiFi. Off site: Shops, bars, restaurants and bank in town. Lake for swimming and fishing 900 m.

Open: 28 April - 30 September.

Directions

Leave A89 at exit 25 (St Julien Puy Laveze) and head south on D98. Join D922 Westbound for 8 km. then take D203 south to site 9 km. on left.
GPS: 45.527824, 2.700008

Charges guide

Per unit incl. 2 persons and electricity	€ 14.50 - € 16.50
extra person	€ 3.50

Lacapelle-Viescamp

Camping la Presqu'île du Puech des Ouilhes

F-15150 Lacapelle-Viescamp (Cantal) T: 04 71 46 42 38. E: contact@cantal-camping.fr
alanrogers.com/FR15080

La Presqu'île du Puech des Ouilhes is a small, family site located on a peninsula within the large St Etienne Cantales lake. There are 76 pitches set amongst mature trees, of which 68 have electrical connections. There are 21 chalets/simple camping huts (without bathrooms) available for rent. On-site amenities include a heated swimming pool (with attractive sun terrace) and adjacent paddling pool. A number of activities are focused on the lake, including canoeing, windsurfing and fishing. A number of other activities are on offer, including archery, themed meals and a children's club.

Facilities

Shop (July/Aug). Take away food. Swimming pool. Paddling pool. Fishing (boat available). Watersports. Children's play area. Tourist information. Chalets and mobile homes for rent. WiFi. Torches useful. Off site: Walking and mountain biking in the Cantal mountains. Adventure sports.

Open: 15 May - 15 September.

Directions

The site can be found to the west of Aurillac. From there, head west on D120 and follow signs to Puech des Ouilhes. Continue through Lacapelle-Viescamp and follow signs to Base de Loisirs.
GPS: 44.913058, 2.248887

Charges guide

Per unit incl. 2 persons	€ 17.00 - € 21.00
extra person	€ 4.50
Camping Cheques accepted.	

Le Puy-en-Velay

Camping de Bouthezard

Avenue d'Aiguilhe, Aiguilhe, F-43000 Le Puy-en-Velay (Haute-Loire) T: 04 71 09 55 09.
E: adamluc@wanadoo.fr alanrogers.com/FR43020

This city site is located at the foot of a towering needle of volcanic rock with a church on top, which is spectacularly lit at night. This is one of three major attractions in Puy-en-Velay, a World Heritage site. The excellent location, in a wooded area, within walking distance of the medieval city, is protected by a good security barrier and the manager, who speaks good English, lives on site. Tarmac roads lead to 80 marked, grassy pitches with 6A electricity, including some with water and drainage. Access is good and as the site may be popular in high season, early arrival is advised.

Facilities

Refurbished toilet block, facilities for disabled campers. Older and more basic unit at rear of site is used in peak season. The facilities may be stretched in high season. Motorcaravan services. Boules, volleyball and badminton. Restaurant (1/4-31/10). WiFi (free). Twin-axle caravans not accepted. Off site: Indoor pool and tennis adjacent. Fishing. Baker and small supermarket 5 minutes walk. Several other shops, bar and restaurants close by. Golf 4 km. Riding 5 km.

Open: 15 March - 31 October.

Directions

Site is northwest of town, close to where N102 crosses River Borne, and Rocher St Michel d'Aiguilhe (a church on a rocky pinnacle). Site is well signed from around town. GPS: 45.05042, 3.88094

Charges guide

Per unit incl. 2 persons and electricity	€ 13.60
extra person	€ 3.05
No credit cards.	

For latest campsite news, availability and prices visit

alanrogers.com

Murol

Camping du Pré Bas

Lac Chambon, F-63790 Chambon-sur-Lac (Puy-de-Dôme) T: 04 73 88 63 04.
E: prebas@campingauvergne.com **alanrogers.com/FR63070**

Le Pré Bas is suitable for families and those seeking the watersports opportunities that the lake provides. Level, grassy pitches are divided up by mature hedging and trees, with 108 mobile homes for rent, including one for visitors with mobility problems, and around 72 pitches available for tourers, all with electricity (6A). A gate leads to the lakeside, where in high season there is windsurfing, pedaloes, canoes and fishing, and 50 m. away is a beach with supervised bathing and a snack bar. There is a pool complex with heated swimming pools (one covered), a large slide and a paddling pool, plus a new wellness centre and supervised club for children. The site is in the heart of the Parc des Volcans d'Auvergne, beside the beautiful Lac de Chambon with its clear, clean water. The cable car ride up to the Puy-de-Sancy, the highest peak in the area, provides superb views. Superb scenery abounds; wooded mountains rising to over 6,000 feet, flower filled valleys and deep blue lakes. A large indoor adventure type play zone is adjacent to the wellness centre with its steam room, sauna and jacuzzi. Massage is available from trained staff. A reasonably priced restaurant is open daily in high season.

Facilities

Refurbished toilet building with facilities for disabled guests, plus four smaller units. Laundry facilities. Baby room. Motorcaravan services. Snack bar (10/6-10/9 and some weekends in low season). Three pools (20/5-10/9, lifeguard in July/Aug). Watersports, fishing in lake. Games room, TV, library. Adventure style playground. Football. Basketball. Bicycle hire. Activities. WiFi. Max. 1 dog. Off site: Lakeside bars, restaurants, shops. Murol 3 km. St Nectaire. Puy-de-Dôme, Vulcania Exhibition.

Open: 1 May - 20 September.

Directions

Leave A75 autoroute at exit 6 and take D978 signed St Nectaire and Murol, then D996. Site is located on left, 3 km, west of Murol towards Mont Dore, at far end of Lac de Chambon. GPS: 45.57516, 2.91428

Charges guide

Per unit incl. 2 persons and electricity	€ 17.30 - € 28.90
extra person	€ 3.90 - € 6.40
child (under 5 yrs)	€ 2.60 - € 4.20

New : Hélios 32M² Bungalow for persons in reduced mobility

Discover the family Center : this area of more than 300sqm, called "Family Center", is entirely covered. It includes spa, hammam, sauna, rest area and massage (on demand) – for the adults and a play area for children. This one is made of 4 levels (pool with balls, slides, trampoline and a mini-football pitches) for the greatest joy of children from 3 to 12. Mobile homes for rent. Situated at the Lac Chambon.

Lac Chambon – 63790 Murol – www.leprebas.com – prebas@campingauvergne.com

Murol

Sunêlia la Ribeyre

Jassat, F-63790 Murol (Puy-de-Dôme) T: 04 73 88 64 29. E: info@laribeyre.com
alanrogers.com/FR63050

The friendly Pommier family have put much personal care into the construction of this site. There are 400 level, grassy pitches, of which 310 are for tourers and 200 of these have electricity (6/10A). Electricity, water and drainage is available for 71 pitches. A superb large indoor/outdoor water park includes slides, toboggan and lazy river. A small man-made lake at one end of the campsite provides facilities for water sports. It is a great base for touring being only 1 km. from Murol, 6 km. from Saint Nectaire and about 20 km. from le Mont Dore and Puy-de-Sancy, the highest peak in the area.

Facilities

Six excellent, very clean modern toilet blocks with facilities for disabled visitors. Washing machines, dryers. Snack bar in peak season (15/6-31/8). Large indoor/outdoor water park (heated July/Aug). TV. Games room. Tennis. Fishing. Lake swimming and canoeing. Many organised activities in high season. WiFi (charged). Off site: Riding 300 m. Bicycle hire 1 km. Shops and restaurants in Murol 1.5 km. Fishing and watersports at Lac Chambon 3 km.

Open: 1 May - 15 September.

Directions

From A75 Autoroute, exit 6 signed St Nectaire. Continue to Murol, D978 then D996, several sites signed in town. Turn left up hill, D5, shortly turn right opposite car park, D618, site signed. Site is second on left. GPS: 45.56251, 2.93852

Charges guide

Per unit incl. 2 persons and electricity	€ 25.05 - € 33.55
extra person	€ 5.75 - € 7.40

For latest campsite news, availability and prices visit
alanrogers.com

Murol

Camping le Repos du Baladin

Groire, F-63790 Murol (Puy-de-Dôme) T: 04 73 88 61 93. E: reposbaladin@free.fr
alanrogers.com/FR63130

A lovely, small and friendly campsite that offers an alternative to the larger sites in this area. The owners are aiming for a quiet, relaxing site, attracting nature lovers who want to spend time walking, cycling or touring in this beautiful region. Attractively and well laid out, there are 91 good sized pitches, some with superb views of the château, 70 for touring (all with 5A electricity, 19 with water, waste water and 10A electricity), and many with good privacy. They are separated by neat conifer hedges with mature trees offering varying amounts of shade. Murol and its ancient château are half an hour's walk away.

Facilities

One excellent, very clean and central, heated toilet block provides all the necessary facilities including those for babies and disabled visitors. Small shop, bar with TV, restaurant with snacks and takeaway (all 15/6-30/8). Heated swimming pool and sunbathing area (1/5-10/9). Large play area. Boules. WiFi. Off site: Murol 1.5 km. Fishing, bicycle hire and boat launching at Lac Chambon 2 km.

Open: 28 April - 8 September.

Directions

Site is 40 km. southwest of Clermont-Ferrand. Leave A75 at exit 6 (St Nectaire) and take D978 beyond St Nectaire to Murol (34 km). At far end of the village turn left up hill on D5. In 800 m. turn right on D146, signed Groire and site. Entrance on right in 900 m. GPS: 45.57373, 2.95708

Charges guide

Per unit incl. 2 persons	€ 17.90 - € 22.70
extra person	€ 3.90 - € 4.80

Nébouzat

Camping les Domes

Les Quatre Routes de Nébouzat, F-63210 Nébouzat (Puy-de-Dôme) T: 04 73 87 14 06.
E: camping.les-domes@orange.fr **alanrogers.com/FR63090**

A popular site, it is ideally situated for exploring the beautiful region around the Puy-de-Dôme. The site has 65 small to medium sized pitches, most for touring, 50 with 10A electricity, separated by trees and hedges. Rock pegs are advised. The attractive reception area comprising the office, a small shop for essentials (high season only) and a meeting room has lots of local information and interesting artefacts. A small heated, covered swimming pool, which can be opened in good weather, is provided. There is some low-key entertainment in high season.

Facilities

Clean toilet block with limited facilities for disabled visitors. Basic shop (baker calls). Breakfast, snacks. Boules, pool table, table football, table tennis, giant chess, drafts. Play area. TV and games room. WiFi. Off site: Fishing 100 m. Restaurant 200 m. Nebouzat 1.3 km. (shops etc). Riding 6 km. Hang gliding and parascending Puy de Dôme 8 km. New Vulcania exhibition 15 minutes drive. Watersports 9 km. Golf 10 km. Clermond-Ferrand with its old town and hypermarkets 18 km. Marked walks and cycle routes.

Open: 1 May - 15 September.

Directions

Site is 18 km. southwest of Clermont-Ferrand and is well signed from the roundabout at the junction of the D2089 and the D941A. It is a few hundred metres from the roundabout along the D216 towards Orcival. GPS: 45.72562, 2.89005

Charges guide

Per unit incl. 2 persons and electricity (10A)	€ 17.70 - € 22.20
extra person	€ 5.50 - € 6.90
No credit cards.	

Neuvéglise

Camping le Belvédère du Pont de Lanau

F-15260 Neuvéglise (Cantal) T: 04 71 23 50 50. E: belvedere.Cantal@wanadoo.fr
alanrogers.com/FR15010

This is a very steeply terraced, family run site in the picturesque southern Auvergne. Of the 120 pitches around 80 are for touring. The highest pitches, with views, have no electricity and are only suitable for tents. The lower pitches have 6A electricity and some have a sink, draining board and barbecue. The pitches are of a good size and separated by tall conifers and pines, offering good shade and privacy. The site roads are very steep and have sharp bends, so access may be difficult for large units. Many pitches are some distance from the toilet blocks and access may involve climbing a large number of steep steps.

Facilities

Two basic toilet blocks include some basins in cabins. Baby room. Facilities for disabled visitors. Sauna. Laundry facilities. Motorcaravan service point. Small shop (mid June-mid Oct). Spacious bar/restaurant and TV room provides meals and takeaways (July/Aug). Exercise room. Activities (July/Aug). WiFi (charged). Off site: Fishing and boat launching 500 m. Bicycle hire 5 km. Chaudes-Aigues with the hottest thermal springs in Europe 5 km.

Open: 20 April - 15 October.

Directions

Site is 5 km. north of Chaudes-Aigues on D921 St Flour - Rodez road. Turn west at site sign, entrance is just beyond the Belvédère Centre de Vacances. GPS: 44.89518, 3.00130

Charges guide

Per unit incl. 2 persons and electricity	€ 18.00 - € 25.00
extra person	€ 3.00 - € 6.00

For latest campsite news, availability and prices visit

alanrogers.com

Nonette
Camping les Loges

F-63340 Nonette (Puy-de-Dôme) T: 04 73 71 65 82. E: les.loges.nonette@wanadoo.fr

alanrogers.com/FR63140

A pleasant, spacious, rural site bordering the River Allier and close to the A75 autoroute. There are 126 good sized, level, grassy pitches offering plenty of shade, 100 for touring and all with 6A electricity. This site would suit those seeking a quieter holiday without too many organised activities. The river is good for bathing and canoeing and there are walks and bike rides in the area. It is also well placed to explore the Auvergne countryside, the extinct volcanoes and the many attractive old towns and villages.

Facilities

Modern toilet blocks contain all the usual facilities. Small shop (July/Aug). Bar, restaurant, takeaway (mid June-mid Sept). TV room. Heated swimming pool with toboggan, paddling pool (June-Sept). Sauna, spa room (July/Aug). Volleyball. Play areas. Play room. River fishing, bathing. Sunday evening dances in high season. Canoe trips. Off site: Walking and cycling routes. Nonette 3 km. Riding 5 km. Saint Germain 5 km. Issoire 13 km. Parc des Volcans, Vulcania exhibition.

Open: 1 April - 13 October.

Directions

From A75 exit 17 (south of Issoire), turn left (D214) signed Le Breuil. Bypass Le Breuil, turn left (D123) signed Nonette. Cross river, turn left then immediately very sharp left just after roundabout - take care (site signed). Entrance is 1 km. GPS: 45.47310, 3.27223

Charges guide

Per unit incl. 2 persons	€ 13.10 - € 16.80
extra person	€ 3.90 - € 4.70
electricity (6A)	€ 3.70

Olliergues
Camping les Chelles

F-63880 Olliergues (Puy-de-Dôme) T: 04 73 95 54 34. E: info@camping-les-chelles.com

alanrogers.com/FR63220

A very rural, rustic site, les Chelles is run by enthusiastic Dutch owners. It is situated in the Parc Naturel Livradois, 25 km. south of Thiers, and is ideal for nature lovers and those seeking a quiet retreat. There are many marked walks and challenging cycle routes close by. There are 65 pitches with 55 slightly sloping, grassy pitches for touring, some with views over the surrounding wooded hills (15A electricity, long leads advised). The pitches are naturally laid out on woodland terraces but not ideal for those with walking difficulties or for large or underpowered units due to the hilly terrain.

Facilities

Centrally placed basic toilet block. Laundry facilities. Motorcaravan service point (charge). Bar/restaurant (all season) with TV. Bread to order. Small swimming and paddling pools near small play area. Tennis. Boules. Bicycle hire (high season). Small fishing lake. Some activities for younger children, bike rides (high season). WiFi near bar. Off site: Olliergues, bank, shops, restaurants, bars 5 km. Thiers, larger range of shops, cutlery museum 25 km. Many cycle rides and walks.

Open: 1 April - 30 October.

Directions

Olliergues is on D906 25 km. south of Thiers. On entering Olliergues bear left up hill, D37. Shortly turn sharp left on D87. In 1.5 km. at church turn right and shortly left to site. Well signed from Olliergues. GPS: 45.68987, 3.63336

Charges guide

Per unit incl. 2 persons and electricity	€ 15.80 - € 16.30
extra person	€ 3.00
child (under 13 yrs)	€ 1.80

Orcet
Camping le Clos Auroy

Rue de la Narse, F-63670 Orcet (Puy-de-Dôme) T: 04 73 84 26 97. E: info@campingclub.info

alanrogers.com/FR63060

Le Clos Auroy is a very well maintained and popular site, 300 metres from Orcet, a typical Auvergne village just south of Clermont-Ferrand. Being close (3 km) to the A75, and open all year, it makes an excellent stopping off point on the journey north and south, but you may be tempted to stay longer. The 85 good sized pitches are on level grass, separated by very high, neatly trimmed conifer hedges, offering lots of privacy but not much shade. All have electricity (10A) and 8 are fully serviced. In winter only 20 pitches are available. Access is possible for a limited number of large units.

Facilities

Three very clean high quality toilet blocks. Laundry facilities. Motorcaravan services. Small shop (1/7-31/8), bar and takeaway (1/6-31/8), small swimming pool (15/5-15/9), terrace near bar (1/6-31/8). Playground. Coffee evenings. Children's activities. Off site: Playground and tennis court nearby and riverside walk just outside gate. Village with shops and three wine 'caves' 300 m. Fishing and canoeing 500 m. Parc des Volcans. Walking and cycling.

Open: 4 January - 1 November.

Directions

From A75 take exit 4 or 5 towards Orcet and follow campsite signs. It is just before the village. GPS: 45.70018, 3.16902

Charges guide

Per unit incl. 2 persons and electricity	€ 28.80
extra person	€ 5.90
child (4-14 yrs)	€ 3.30 - € 5.90
dog	€ 2.00

Less for longer stays in low season.

For latest campsite news, availability and prices visit
alanrogers.com

We can book this site for you! Call 01580 214000 — alan rogers travel

Royat

Camping Indigo Royat

Route de Gravenoire, F-63130 Royat (Puy-de-Dôme) T: 04 73 35 97 05.
E: royat@camping-indigo.com **alanrogers.com/FR63120**

This is a spacious and attractive site sitting high on a hillside on the outskirts of Clermont-Ferrand, but close to the beautiful Auvergne countryside. It has 197 terraced pitches on part hardstanding. There are 138 available for touring units, all with 10A electricity (long leads may be needed) and in addition five pitches offer water and drainage. The pitches are informally arranged in groups, with each group widely separated by attractive trees and shrubs. The bar and terrace overlooks the irregularly shaped swimming pool. Although very peaceful off season, the site could be busy and lively in July and August.

Facilities

Five well appointed toilet blocks, some heated. They have all the usual amenities but it could be a long walk from some pitches. Small shop (all season). Bar, restaurant and takeaway (July/Aug). Attractive heated swimming and paddling pools (27/5-18/9), sunbathing area. Tennis. Boules. Two grassy play areas. Organised entertainment in high season. Internet. Torches advised. Max. 1 dog. Off site: Royat 20 minutes walk. Fishing 2 km. Golf 3 km. Riding 10 km. Clermont-Ferrand, Puy-de-Dôme, Parc des Volcans, Vulcania exhibition.

Open: 1 April - 29 October.

Directions

From A75 exit 2 (Clermont-Ferrand) follow signs for Bordeaux (D799). At third roundabout exit left (Bordeaux). Shortly take exit right then turn right (Ceyrat). Leaving Ceyrat, at traffic lights take D941C (Royat and Puy-de-Dôme). At top of hill turn left (D5) site signed. GPS: 45.7587, 3.05509

Charges guide

Per unit incl. 2 persons and electricity	€ 19.70 - € 27.70

Camping Cheques accepted.

Ruynes-en-Margeride

Camping Le Petit Bois

F-15320 Ruynes-en-Margeride (Cantal) T: 04 71 23 42 26. E: lepetitbois0639@orange.fr
alanrogers.com/FR15190

With spectacular views of the Auvergne countryside, this pleasant site on the edge of an interesting village could be no more than a convenient overnight stop when using the A75 Clermont-Ferrand/Béziers motorway. Yet it has a great deal more to offer, and we met some British visitors who came for a night and stayed a week. There are 90 touring pitches, all with 10A electricity; 16 also have water and drainage. Some are level with views across to the village, some on the hilltop among trees and others on sloping, grassy land with panoramic views of the Monts du Cantal and the distant volcanic mountains.

Facilities

The main central toilet block has preset showers, washbasins in cabins, children's WCs and en-suite units for disabled visitors (building is on a hill, so access may not be easy). Laundry facilities. Motorcaravan service point. Play areas. Children's club. Family entertainment evenings (July/Aug). TV room. Pétanque. Mobile homes and wooden 'huttes' for rent. WiFi (charged). Off site: Municipal swimming pool adjacent (July/Aug). Village 500 m. Riding 1 km. Fishing, river beach 7 km.

Open: 30 April - 17 September.

Directions

Ruynes-en-Margeride is 110 km. due south of Clermont-Ferrand and 6 km. east from exit 30 of the A75 motorway. Follow signs for village and campsite. Site is 500 m. southwest of village and is clearly signed. GPS: 44.99904, 3.21908

Charges guide

Per unit incl. 2 persons and electricity	€ 16.50 - € 20.00

Camping Cheques accepted.

Saint Bonnet près Orcival

Camping de la Haute Sioule

Route du Camping, F-63210 Saint Bonnet près Orcival (Puy-de-Dôme) T: 04 73 65 83 32.
E: info@chalets-auvergne.info **alanrogers.com/FR63210**

This simple, small site is family run in a quiet, rural location in the heart of the beautiful Parc des Volcans. With good views over the surrounding hills, it is close to the Puy-de-Dôme and several winter and summer resorts. Developed from a farm with sheep and geese roaming freely until mid June, the site has 70 sloping, slightly uneven, grassy pitches with about 45 for touring (4-13A electricity, long leads needed). Access is not easy for motorcaravans and large outfits. It would be a good base for touring the region but may be noisy in the high season due to the seasonal caravans.

Facilities

Central basic toilet block with mainly Turkish toilets. New heated sanitary block with baby changing and facilities for visitors with disabilities. Laundry facilities. Shop. Bar with TV. Restaurant (July/Aug). Play area for younger children. Minigolf. Boules. Fishing. WiFi. Off site: St Bonnet 200 m. with some small shops, a restaurant and a bar. Orcival 4 km. Puy-de-Dôme. Vulcania exhibition. Riding 7 km.

Open: All year.

Directions

From the A75 just south of Clermont-Ferrand at exit 2 (Bordeaux and La Bourboule). Continue on D2089 until Les Quatre Routes. Left at roundabout, D216. Bear left to site (500 m). GPS: 45.7084, 2.86087

Charges guide

Per unit incl. 2 persons and electricity (4-13A)	€ 18.70 - € 23.90

For latest campsite news, availability and prices visit
alanrogers.com

Saint Martin-Cantalès
Camping Pont du Rouffet

Pont du Rouffet, F-15140 Saint Martin-Cantalès (Cantal) T: 04 71 69 42 76. E: pontdurouffet@live.nl

alanrogers.com/FR15060

A very tranquil and rural site located on the banks of the Lac d'Enchanet. There are just 34 pitches, four of which have mobile homes for hire. All pitches have electricity (4/6/10A) and some require long leads. Many have shade and some are separated by young hedges. Fishing from the banks by the site is possible, as is swimming. Large units are advised to telephone in advance for suitable pitches. The showers and washing areas have recently been refurbished. This is a well equipped but basic site aimed at those wishing to get away from the fast pace of city life.

Facilities	Directions
Refurbished shower block. Laundry facilities. Fishing. Table tennis. Indoor games. Tourist information. Mobile homes for rent. Torches required WiFi. Off site: Nearest supermarket 9 km. Walking on marked routes and along disused railway viaducts and through tunnels. Fishing. Mountain trails for bikes. Bicycle hire 12 km. Riding 18 km. Golf 38 km. Lake sports. **Open:** 27 April - 8 September.	The site is 80 km. south-east of Clermont-Ferrand. From Mauriac take the D681 south for 9 km, bear right onto D680 (1 km) then left onto D37 (7 km). Turn right onto D27 then immediately left onto D6 (8.5 km) then right onto D42 (4.6 km) Site on right. GPS: 45.072187, 2.258865

Charges guide

Per unit incl. 2 persons and electricity	€ 14.75 - € 16.25

Saint Nectaire
Camping la Clé des Champs

Route des Granges, F-63710 Saint Nectaire (Puy-de-Dôme) T: 04 73 88 52 33.
E: campingcledeschamps@free.fr **alanrogers.com/FR63270**

Camping la Clé des Champs is a family run campsite in traditional French style. It is bisected by a small river, and close to the popular spa town of Saint Nectaire, at the heart of the Auvergne. Pitches are of a good size, most have some shade, and many have 2-6A electrical connections. A number of fully equipped mobile homes and chalets are available for rent. On-site amenities here include a swimming pool, a playground and a snack bar. The large Lac de Chambon is close at hand and is a popular centre for a variety of watersports. Saint Nectaire is a town of great interest with many small restaurants.

Facilities	Directions
Swimming pool. Bar/snack bar. Takeaway. Shop. Games room. Play area. Tourist information. Entertainment and activity programme. Mobile homes and chalets for rent. Free WiFi. Torches useful. Off site: Saint Nectaire. Watersports at Lac de Chambon. Walking and mountain biking.. **Open:** 15 April - 15 September.	Approaching from the east (Champeix and Issoire) use D996 to Saint Nectaire. The site is well signed at the entrance to the town. GPS: 45.575498, 3.001741

Charges guide

Per unit incl. 2 persons	€ 13,00 - € 21,50
extra person	€ 3.00 - € 5.00
child (under 5 yrs)	free - € 3.00
dog	free - € 2,00

Sainte Sigolène
Kawan Village Camping de Vaubarlet

Vaubarlet, F-43600 Sainte Sigolène (Haute-Loire) T: 04 71 66 64 95. E: camping@vaubarlet.com

alanrogers.com/FR43030

Expect a warm welcome at this peacefully and beautifully located, spacious riverside family site. It has 131 marked, level, grassy, open pitches, with those around the perimeter having shade. The family has made great efforts to offer equal opportunity to all guests throughout its rental and touring facilities. There are 102 pitches all with 6A electricity for touring units. The remaining places are occupied by site owned tents and mobile homes including two fully equipped for disabled guests. Excellent facilities for guests with disabilities including smooth paths, electric buggy and a hoist to assist entry into the pool.

Facilities	Directions
Very good, clean toilet blocks include a baby room. Two family bathrooms are also suitable for disabled visitors. Washing machine, dryer. Small shop, bread. Takeaway. bar. Swimming pool. Children's pool. Separate solarium. Boules. Extensive riverside grass games area. Playground. Activities in season include camp fire, music evenings, children's canoe lessons. Trout fishing. Bird watching. WiFi (free). Off site: Shops and supermarkets in Ste Sigolène 6 km. Riding 15 km. Walks and cycle tracks. Golf 30 km. **Open:** 1 May - 30 September.	Site is 6 km. southwest of Ste Sigolène on the D43 signed Grazac. Keep left by river bridge, site signed. Site is shortly on right. GPS: 45.2163, 4.2124

Charges guide

Per unit incl. 2 persons and electricity	€ 15.00 - € 24.00
extra person	€ 3.00 - € 4.00
child (2-7 yrs)	€ 2.25 - € 3.00
Camping Cheques accepted.	

For latest campsite news, availability and prices visit
alanrogers.com

Saint Paulien

Camping de la Rochelambert

Route de Lanthenas, F-43350 Saint Paulien (Haute-Loire) T: 04 71 00 54 02.
E: infos@camping-rochelambert.com **alanrogers.com/FR43060**

Rochelambert can be found at the beautiful heart of Auvergne, north of Le Puy-en-Velay. The site extends over four hectares and is located at the foot of the Château de la Rochelambert. It is bordered by a river and a wooded nature trail. There are 80 large pitches here (120 sq.m), mostly well shaded and equipped with 10A electricity. Some riverside pitches for 'back to nature' camping have no electricity. A number of good quality timber chalets are for rent. The emphasis here is on peace and tranquillity in an idyllic natural setting, and for this reason the site is run along very environmentally friendly lines. Several imaginative activities are organised in high season and these include children's workshops, treasure hunts, themed meals and outdoor cinema. The nearby village of Saint Paulien has a good range of shops and other amenities. There are many mountain bike and walking trails in the area and the site's friendly owners will be pleased to make recommendations. This campsite is well run and tidily maintained and prides itself on offering a place in the countryside with easy access to nature.

Facilities

Two well positioned toilet blocks (one heated) are well maintained and clean. Baby room. Excellent room for disabled visitors. Motorcaravan services. Small shop for basics. Snack bar serving pizza and regional specialities. Pleasant bar and terrace. Swimming and paddling pools. Fishing. Bicycle hire. Tennis. Archery. Boules. Play area. Entertainment and activity programme. Wooden chalets to rent and two caravans. WiFi (free). Off site: St Paulien 2.5 km. Walking and cycling. Riding 10 km. Golf 15 km.

Open: 1 April - 30 September.

Directions

Site is north of Le Puy-en-Velay. From there, head north on N102 and turn north to Saint Paulien from where the château and the site are well signed. GPS: 45.120173, 3.793674

Charges guide

Per unit incl. 2 persons and electricity	€ 15.20 - € 19.70
extra person	€ 1.70 - € 4.60
child (3-7 yrs)	€ 2.75 - € 3.70

CAMPING
de la Rochelambert***

At the heart of the Auvergne, this friendly family site is located at the foot of the Rochelambert castle, bordered by a wild river and greenery.

Chalets to hire, heated pools, animations, bar/snack, playground, fishing, hiking.

43350 Saint Paulien
Tel : 0033 (0)4.71.00.54.02
Email: infos@camping-rochelambert.com
Web: www.camping-rochelambert.com

Saint Sauves-d'Auvergne

Camping du Pont de la Dordogne

F-63950 Saint Sauves-d'Auvergne (Puy-de-Dôme) T: 04 73 81 01 92. E: promobat2@wanadoo.fr
alanrogers.com/FR63240

Camping du Pont de la Dordogne is attractively situated at the heart of the Auvergne, 4 km. from the important resort of La Bourboule. Given its proximity to the A89 autoroute (5 km), this site may also appeal as a stopover. There are 57 pitches here (on a 3.5 hectare site), some of which have fine views towards the chain of extinct volcanoes of the Auvergne. The site borders the River Dordogne, and therefore may appeal to anglers. There is also a small fishing lake. On-site amenities include a snack bar (with takeaway food), archery and a fitness trail.

Facilities

Direct access to river. Fishing. Shop. Bar/snack bar. Takeaway food. Children's play area. TV room. Fitness trail. Spa. Sauna. WiFi. Tourist information. Chalets and Romany caravans for rent. Off site: Shops and restaurants in Saint Sauves d'Auvergne. Walking and mountain biking. Rock climbing. Canoeing. Rafting. La Bourboule and Le Mont Dore.

Open: 15 May - 15 October.

Directions

Leave A89 autoroute at exit 25 (Saint Julien Puy Laveze) and head south on D98 to Le Trador. Then join the westbound D922 to Saint-Sauves d'Auvergne. The site is well signed in the town. GPS: 45.60249, 2.689861

Charges guide

| Per unit incl. 2 persons and electricity | € 19.00 - € 23.50 |
| extra person | € 6.00 |

Camping Cheques accepted.

For latest campsite news, availability and prices visit
alanrogers.com

Singles

Camping le Moulin de Serre

Vallée de la Burande (D73), F-63690 Singles (Puy-de-Dôme) T: 04 73 21 16 06. E: moulindeserre@orange.fr
alanrogers.com/FR63080

Off the beaten track, this spacious and well maintained site is set in a wooded valley beside a lively river where one can join the locals panning for gold. It offers a good base for those seeking quiet relaxation in this lesser known area of the Auvergne. The 90 large pitches (54 for touring) are separated by a variety of trees and hedges giving good shade. Some pitches have hardstanding and all have electricity (5/10A), long leads may be necessary. This tranquil site is an ideal base for walkers and cyclists.

Facilities	Directions
Two clean and well equipped central toilet blocks, one heated, have excellent facilities for disabled visitors and babies. Washing machine, dryer. Motorcaravan services. Takeaway (July/Aug), bar/snack bar. Restaurant (July/Aug). Bread to order. Heated swimming pool, terrace (28/5-11/9). Play area. Tennis. Canoe hire in high season. Organised activities (July/Aug). New communal barbecue. WiFi. Off site: Lake for fishing 2 km. Château de Val 20 km. Spa town of La Bourboule 25 km. Watersports.	Site is about 25 km. southwest of La Bourboule. Turn west off the D922 just south of Tauves at site sign. Follow site signs along the D29 and then the D73 for about 10 km. GPS: 45.54317, 2.54275

Open: 9 April - 18 September.

Charges guide

Per unit incl. 2 persons	
and electricity	€ 13.95 - € 23.00
extra person	€ 2.40 - € 4.35
child (under 10 yrs)	€ 1.60 - € 2.95

Tauves

Camping les Aurandeix

F-63690 Tauves (Puy-de-Dôme) T: 04 73 21 14 06. E: contact@camping-les-aurandeix.fr
alanrogers.com/FR63200

This municipal site is under a long term management contract by a friendly family with plans for refurbishment. It is only a few minutes walk from the centre of the village which is in the beautiful Parc des Volcans with its many extinct volcanoes and is ideal for touring on foot, bike or in the car. There are 80 small sized, grass pitches on terraces. There are 55 for touring, separated by hedges and trees offering good shade and some privacy (6/10A electricity).

Facilities	Directions
Two adequate toilet blocks with facilities for visitors with disabilities. Motorcaravan services. Shop (July/Aug). Bread to order. Heated swimming and paddling pools (mid June-end Sept). Play area. Volleyball, basketball, football. Communal barbecue (charcoal barbecues are not permitted). WiFi Internet. Off site: Small shops, bank, restaurant/takeaway in village 500 m. Fishing, riding and bicycle hire 1 km. Lakeside beach 8 km. Chain of extinct volcanoes.	Site is well signed in Tauves, 9 km. southwest of La Bourboule, just off the D922. GPS: 45.56089, 2.62446

Open: 4 April - 30 September.

Charges guide

Per unit incl. 2 persons	
and electricity	€ 15.55 - € 20.20
extra person	€ 3.45 - € 4.40
child (2-10 yrs)	free - € 3.85
dog	€ 1.75

Vieille Brioude

Camping la Bageasse

Avenue Bageasse, F-43100 Brioude (Haute-Loire) T: 04 71 50 07 70. E: aquadis1@wanadoo.fr
alanrogers.com/FR43040

La Bageasse is a member of the Aquadis Loisirs group. Popular with anglers, it is located on the banks of the River Allier, barraged to form a large lake with canoeing and bathing possible. It is near the stunning Gorges de l'Allier and the town of Brioude, home to the largest Romanesque church of the Auvergne, the St Julien basilica. The pitches here are large and grassy, most are equipped with electrical connections. There are 17 fully equipped chalets for rent. During peak season, several activities are organized, including a children's club (6-12 yrs).

Facilities	Directions
Two sanitary blocks are in traditional style and have been recently renovated. En-suite unit for disabled visitors. Laundry facilities. Small shop. Bar and snack bar with games (1/6-30/9). Swimming and paddling pools (1/6-15/9). Fishing. Play area. Activity and entertainment programme. Chalets for rent. Off site: Shops and restaurants in Brioude, 5 km. Tennis. Riding. Watersports. Walking and mountain biking. Allier gorges.	Brioude lies midway between Clermont-Ferrand and Le Puy-en-Velay. Head south from Clermont-Ferrand on A75 as far as exit 20 and then follow the southbound N102 to Brioude. The site is well signed from the town. GPS: 45.28127, 3.40548

Open: 1 April - 17 October.

Charges guide

Per unit incl. 2 persons	
and electricity	€ 15.30 - € 16.30
extra person	€ 4.10

Camping Cheques accepted.

For latest campsite news, availability and prices visit
alanrogers.com

With a rich and varied landscape, the Rhône Alpes offers a spectacular region that includes the craggy gorges and scented hills of the Rhône Valley, the deep valleys and mountain slopes of the Savoy Alps and the forbidding Dauphiné Alps, all offering spectacular scenery.

DÉPARTEMENTS: 01 AIN, 07 ARDÈCHE, 26 DRÔME, 38 ISÈRE, 42 LOIRE, 69 RHÔNE, 73 SAVOIE, 74 HAUTE-SAVOIE

MAJOR CITIES; LYON, GRENOBLE

The Rhône valley holds areas of great interest and natural beauty. From the sun-baked Drôme, with its ever-changing landscapes and the isolated mountains of the Vercors, to the deep gorges and high plateaux of the Ardèche, studded with prehistoric caves and lush valleys filled with orchards; and encompassing the vineyards of the Beaujolais and the Rhône Valley. For the energetic there are cycling, horse riding and even white-water rafting opportunities, while for the more leisurely inclined, the remote areas are a haven for bird watching and walking.

Lying between the Rhône Valley and the Alpine borders with Switzerland and Italy are the old provinces of Savoie and Dauphiné. This is an area of enormous granite outcrops, deeply riven by spectacular glacier hewn valleys. One of the world's leading winter playgrounds, there is also a range of outdoor activities in the summer. Despite development, great care has been taken to blend the old with the new and many traditional villages still retain their charm and historical interest. For many, it is an opportunity to escape the crowds and enjoy some clean air, unusual wildlife, stunning views and hidden lakes.

Places of interest

Aix-les-Bains: spa resort on the Lac du Bourget, boat excursions to the Royal Abbey of Hautecombe.

Annecy: canal-filled lakeside town, 12th-century château, old quarter.

Beaujolais: vineyards and golden stone villages.

Bourg-Saint-Maurice: centre of Savoie café society.

Chambéry: old quarter, Dukes of Savoie château, Savoie museum.

Chamonix: site of first Winter Olympics in 1924, world capital of mountain climbing.

Grenoble: University city, Fort de la Bastille.

Lyon: Gallo-Roman artifacts, Renaissance quarter, historical Fabric Museum, silk museum.

Vallon-Pont d'Arc: base from which to visit Gorges de l'Ardèche.

Cuisine of the region

Bresse (Poulet, Poularde, Volaille de): the best French poultry, fed on corn and when killed bathed in milk.

Farcement (Farçon Savoyard): potatoes baked with cream, eggs, bacon, dried pears and prunes.

Gratin Dauphinois: potato dish with cream, cheese and garlic.

Gratin Savoyard: another potato dish with cheese and butter.

Tartiflette: potato, bacon, onions and Reblochon cheese.

www.rhonealpes-tourism.co.uk
info@rhonealpes-tourisme.com
(0)4 72 59 21 59

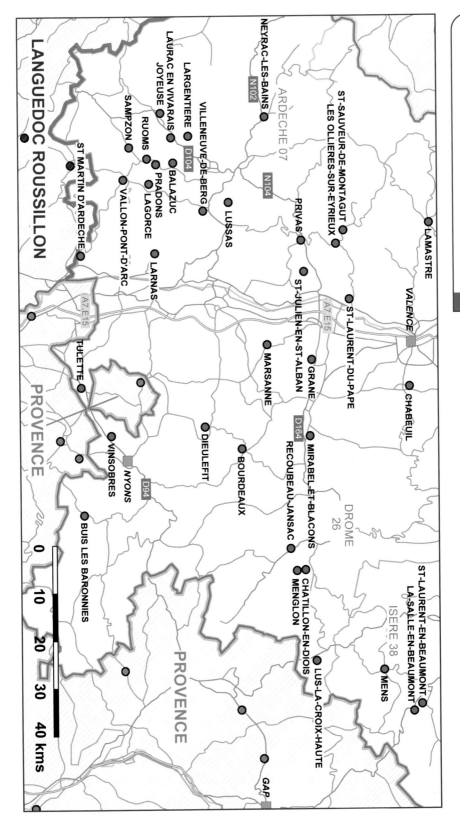

LANGUEDOC ROUSSILLON

PROVENCE

PROVENCE

ARDÈCHE 07

DRÔME 26

ISÈRE 38

NEYRAC-LES-BAINS

LAURAC EN VIVARAIS
JOYEUSE
LARGENTIERE
VILLENEUVE-DE-BERG
SAMPZON
RUOMS
BALAZUC
PRADONS
LAGORCE
LARNAS
ST MARTIN D'ARDECHE
VALLON-PONT-D'ARC
LUSSAS

ST-SAUVEUR-DE-MONTAGUT
LES OLLIERES-SUR-EYRIEUX
PRIVAS
ST-JULIEN-EN-ST-ALBAN
GRANE
ST-LAURENT-DU-PAPE
LAMASTRE
VALENCE
CHABEUIL

MARSANNE

MIRABEL-ET-BLACONS
RECOUBEAU-JANSAC
CHATILLON-EN-DIOIS
MENGLON
LUS-LA-CROIX-HAUTE
MENS

ST-LAURENT-EN-BEAUMONT
LA SALLE-EN-BEAUMONT

TULETTE
VINSOBRES
NYONS
DIEULEFIT
BOURDEAUX
BUIS LES BARONNIES

GAP

N102
N104
D104
A7-E15
A7-E15
D164
D94

0 10 20 30 40 kms

For latest campsite news, availability and prices visit

alanrogers.com

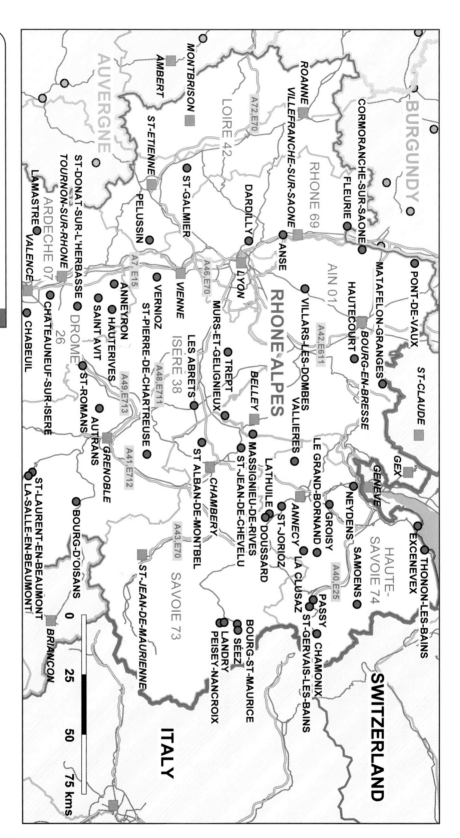

For latest campsite news, availability and prices visit

alanrogers.com

Anneyron
Flower Camping la Châtaigneraie

Route de Mantaille, F-26140 Anneyron (Drôme) T: 04 75 31 43 33. E: contact@chataigneraie.com

alanrogers.com/FR26140

La Châtaigneraie is a small, neat, terraced site run by a very friendly family (English spoken). It is tucked away in the countryside high above the village of Anneyron with magnificent far-reaching views over the valley of the Rhone. There are 71 medium sized, slightly sloping, grassy pitches, 30 for touring away from the static units. They are separated by a variety of hedges and young trees provide varying degrees of shade and all have 6/10A electricity. Twin-axle caravans and large outfits are not admitted and only gas and electric barbecues are allowed on site.

Facilities

A very clean toilet block has all necessary facilities including those for campers with disabilities. Bar and small shop. Good restaurant/takeaway. Swimming and paddling pools (15/5-15/9). Short tennis. Two small play areas, TV/games room. Bicycle hire. Farmers' market twice a week. Entertainment for children and adults (July/Aug). WiFi near bar. Off site: Fishing, riding and golf 3 km. Anneyron, with a few shops, bars, restaurants etc. 3 km.

Open: 1 April - 30 September.

Directions

Leave A7 Autoroute, exit 12, then N7 south for 7 km. Turn east, D1, to Anneyron (7 km). In the village turn right D161, signed Mantaille. In 3 km. turn right D301, signed Albon, to site immediately on right (well signed). GPS: 45.2547, 4.9039

Charges guide

Per unit incl. 2 persons	
and electricity	€ 15.50 - € 27.00
extra person	€ 4.00 - € 5.50

Autrans
Kawan Village Au Joyeux Réveil

Le Château, F-38880 Autrans (Isère) T: 04 76 95 33 44. E: camping-au-joyeux-reveil@wanadoo.fr

alanrogers.com/FR38080

This superb site is run by a very friendly family (English is spoken). It is on the outskirts of Autrans, high on a plateau (1,050 m) in the Vercors region close to a ski jump and short lift. There are 101 pitches with 70 for touring, with electricity (6A). They are mainly on gently sloping grass, in a sunny location with fantastic views over the surrounding wooded mountains with small trees giving just a little shade. There is a new swimming pool area with two pools, one covered, a river and slide plus a separate paddling pool. Here the days can be very hot and sunny and the nights quite chilly. This site is ideally situated for many of the activities that this wonderful area has to offer with magnificent scenery. The D531 and the D106 look a little daunting on the map and do involve a stiff climb but they are good roads and have no really difficult bends.

Facilities

The spotless toilet block is well appointed, with underfloor heating and all the expected facilities. Another chalet-style building houses a bar with terrace, snack bar/takeaway (July/Aug). Two pools, one covered, toboggan for children, sunbathing area and a separate paddling pool. Small play area. TV room. Internet point and WiFi (free). Family entertainment (July/Aug). Off site: Fishing 200 m. Riding 300 m. Autrans with a few shops 500 m. Bicycle hire 500 m. Villard de Lans, supermarket, shops, restaurants, bars, ice rink and many other activities 16 km. Bus to Villard de Lans and Grenoble. Golf 20 km.

Open: 1 May - 30 September.

Directions

Leave A48, northwest of Grenoble, exit 13 (going south) or 3A (north). Follow N532 to Sassenage, turn west at roundabout, D531 to Lans-en-Vercors. At roundabout turn right, D106 Autrans. At roundabout in Autrans turn right (site signed) and very shortly right again. Site is on the left. This is the only route recommended for caravans and motorcaravans. GPS: 45.17517, 5.54762

Charges 2012

Per unit incl. 2 persons	
and electricity	€ 24.00 - € 39.00
extra person	€ 5.00
Camping Cheques accepted.	

CAMPING AU JOYEUX REVEIL

We take pride in providing our guests with the very best service, including sharing our love of the Vercors, one of France's most beautiful regions. Our campsite is open in both summer and winter and offers a quiet, friendly environment perfect as a base for discovering all that nature has to offer in the Vercors.

The campsite has a very nice heated pool complex, including a covered pool, modern sanitary facilities with under-floor heating in winter and the pitches with clear views of the mountains.

Located right at the heart of the Vercors natural park (history, tradition and nature) in a beautiful, restful setting, our site is located just across from the Olympic ski jump from the 1968 Games and is just 300m from the town of Autrans (1050m) which offers a full range of shops and activities.

Christine and Franck Blanc

Camping Au Joyeux Réveil • 38880 Autrans • Tel: 0033.4.76.95.33.44 • www.camping-au-joyeux-reveil.fr

For latest campsite news, availability and prices visit
alanrogers.com

Anse

Camping les Portes du Beaujolais

Avenue Jean Vacher, F-69480 Anse (Rhône) T: 04 74 67 12 87. E: campingbeaujolais@wanadoo.fr

alanrogers.com/FR69030

Situated just off the A6 motorway at Anse, this campsite would make a good overnight stop. The good public transport from Anse also means that it could be used as a base for visiting Lyon. Despite some noise from the motorway and the main line railway, this well run site has much to offer. It has good facilities with modern buildings of traditional design and materials. There are 150 formal pitches which are shady, level, numbered and marked, with neatly trimmed grass and hedges, and 10A electrical connections. Around 40% of the pitches are fully serviced. Some space is available for those who prefer to pitch in more simple and open surroundings.

Facilities	Directions
Modern toilet blocks include facilities for disabled visitors, and baby rooms. Motorcaravan services. Washing machines. Shop (all season). Gas supplies. Bar, restaurant, takeaway (1/6-15/9). Swimming and paddling pools (1/5-30/9). Playground. Playing field. Tennis. Minigolf. Boules. Games room. WiFi. Free loan of barbecues. Chalets, mobile homes and 3 tepees to rent (sleeps 5). Off site: Fishing 200 m. Anse 1 km.	Leave the A6 at exit 32 and join the N6 to Anse. Site is signed from northern and southern ends of village. There are height limits on all approaches (3 or 3.2 m). GPS: 45.9405, 4.7268

Open: 1 March - 31 October.

Charges guide

Per unit incl. 2 persons and electricity	€ 21.90 - € 27.50

Camping Cheques accepted.

Balazuc

Camping le Chamadou

Mas de Chaussy, F-07120 Balazuc (Ardèche) T: 08 20 36 61 97. E: infos@camping-le-chamadou.com

alanrogers.com/FR07620

La Chamadou is a delightful, well maintained and calm site run by an enthusiastic and friendly family. It is situated in the southern Ardèche, close to the medieval, perched village of Balazuc, not far from the river Ardèche. There are 86 slightly sloping grassy/stony pitches with 69 for touring (electricity 10A). They are separated by hedges and flowering shrubs with a variety of trees giving some shade. A cosy restaurant and terrace have panoramic views. The narrow approach road makes access difficult for large outfits. In April, May and June the campsite offers access to an extensive trial biking area. It is some distance from the campsite and is well managed to minimise disturbance to campers.

Facilities	Directions
Several small, well appointed and very clean toilet blocks have all the necessary facilities including those for disabled visitors. Bar/TV. Small shop for basics, restaurant and takeaway (July/Aug). Swimming pool, paddling pool, toboggan. Good play area. Games room. Private trout fishing. Minigolf. Basketball. Canoe trips and bike hire organised. Electric and gas barbecues only. Winery. Free WiFi. Off site: Small shop 2 km. River bathing 2 km. Small village of Vogüé 3 km. Riding and bicycle hire 4 km.	Site is in southern Ardèche, south of Aubenas. Leave Aubenas on the D104, signed Alès. Shortly turn left on D579 signed Vallon-Pont-d'Arc. Bypass Vogüé, cross river and keep right. In 4.5 km. turn left at site sign along narrow lane to site in 2 km. GPS: 44.50778, 4.40347

Open: 1 April - 31 October.

Charges guide

Per unit incl. 2 persons and electricity	€ 21.00 - € 29.20
extra person	€ 4.50 - € 6.00

Bourg-d'Oisans

Camping la Cascade

Route de l'Alpe d'Huez, F-38520 Bourg-d'Oisans (Isère) T: 04 76 80 02 42. E: lacascade@wanadoo.fr

alanrogers.com/FR38030

La Cascade has a long season as it is at the heart of a popular skiing and cycling area. It is within sight and sound of the waterfall from which it takes its name. It is only 2 km. from Bourg-d'Oisans which lies in the Romanche valley 725 m. above sea level surrounded by high mountains. The area is a sun trap and gets very hot in summer. The site has 133 individual grassy pitches, 106 for touring units, all with 16A electricity, on mainly flat ground and of varying size. Although most are quite adequate, larger units are best near the entrance as the pitches and roads do become narrow.

Facilities	Directions
Two heated sanitary blocks with mainly British style toilets, washbasins in cabins and showers. Laundry facilities. Bar and snack bar (25/6-30/8). Fresh bread daily (July/Aug). Heated swimming pool and paddling pool (1/6-30/9). TV in bar. WiFi. Chalets for hire (all year). Off site: Fishing 100 m. Riding and supermarket 500 m. Bicycle hire 1 km.	From Grenoble take D1091 (previously N91) to Bourg d'Oisans, cross river bridge, after 730 m. turn left on to D211, signed Alpe d'Huez. Site is on right in 600 m. GPS: 45.06408, 6.03903

Open: 20 December - 30 September.

Charges guide

Per unit incl. 2 persons and electricity	€ 24.50 - € 31.00

For latest campsite news, availability and prices visit

alanrogers.com

Bourdeaux
Camping les Bois du Chatelas

540

Route de Dieulefit, F-26460 Bourdeaux (Drôme) T: 04 75 00 60 80. E: contact@chatelas.com

alanrogers.com/FR26210

Located at the heart of the Drôme Provençale, les Bois du Chatelas is a quality, family run site just 1.5 km. from the delightful village of Bourdeaux which offers some shops, cafés, etc. There are 138 level, good sized, terraced pitches, 70 for touring. They all have electricity, water and drainage. There is a superb swinmming pool complex with indoor and outdoor pools, toboggan, paddling pool, fitness room, jacuzzi and sauna. Overlooking the pool area is a restaurant with superb views over the valley and hills beyond. Les Bois du Chatelas is a good choice for those seeking an active holiday. The long distance GR9 footpath passes through the site and there are very many walking and cycle routes close at hand. A popular aquagym is organised in the large outdoor pool in peak season. In the high season, there is a lively entertainment programme as well as a number of cycling and walking excursions. A member of Sites et Paysages.

Facilities

Two excellent toilet blocks (one heated) with facilities for babies and disabled visitors (though not ideal). Shop. Bar. Restaurant/takeaway/pizzeria. Indoor and outdoor pools. Outdoor pool with water slide, waterfall, sauna, aquagym and jacuzzi. Sports pitch. Archery. Play area. Bicycle hire. Entertainment and excursion programme (July/Aug). WiFi everywhere. Off site: Fishing 1 km. Bourdeaux with some shops 1.5 km. Riding 5 km. Dieulefit with a wider range of shops, Friday market etc. 12 km. Rafting and canoe trips. Extensive walking and cycle (mountain bike) opportunities. Vercors mountain range. Many stunning medieval villages.

Open: 6 April - 16 September.

Directions

Leave A7 Autoroute, exit 16 Loriol. Take D104 east to Crest. Leave Crest bypass at traffic lights, take D538 south to Bourdeaux and continue towards Dieulefit for 1.5 km. Site is on the left (well signed). GPS: 44.57825, 5.12795

Charges 2012

Per unit incl. 2 persons	
and electricity	€ 21.70 - € 38.50
extra person	€ 4.90 - € 8.30
child (2-7 yrs)	€ 3.90 - € 5.20
dog	€ 2.20 - € 5.20

Route de Dieulefit - F-26460 Bourdeaux - Tél.: (33) 4 75 00 60 80 - Fax (33) 4 75 00 60 81
E-mail: contact@chatelas.com - www.chatelas.com

Bourg-d'Oisans
Camping à la Rencontre du Soleil

Route de l'Alpe d'Huez, F-38520 Bourg-d'Oisans (Isère) T: 04 76 79 12 22.

E: rencontre.soleil@wanadoo.fr **alanrogers.com/FR38040**

The Isère is an attractive and popular region with exceptional scenery. Bourg-d'Oisans lies in the Romanche valley 725 m. above sea level surrounded by high mountains. This compact site, pleasant, friendly and family run, nestles between two impressive mountain ranges, at the base of France's largest national park, Le Parc des Ecrins. It is only 2 km. from the busy town of Bourg-d'Oisans. It has 77 level, hedged pitches of small to average size with mature trees offering good shade (52 for touring with 10A electricity). Rock pegs are advised. A Sites et Paysages member.

Facilities

Heated toilet block provides all the usual amenities, but none for disabled visitors. Washing machine and dryer. Motorcaravan services. Bread to order. Restaurant and takeaway. Room with TV, children's play room. Small, sheltered swimming pool (all season). Play area. Children's club. Activities in high season include walking, mountain biking. WiFi over site (charged). Off site: Supermarket 1 km. Bicycle hire and riding 2 km. Fishing 5 km.

Open: 1 May - 30 September.

Directions

From Grenoble bypass Bourg-d'Oisans on N1091 towards Briançon. At end of bypass turn left at roundabout on D211 signed Alpe-d'Huez. Site is on left beyond Camping la Piscine and just before a sharp left-hand bend - take care. GPS: 45.06547, 6.0394

Charges 2012

Per unit incl. 2 persons	
and electricity	€ 25.00 - € 36.00

alan rogers

Winner 2011 Awards

We can book this site for you! Call 01580 214000 alan rogers travel

For latest campsite news, availability and prices visit
alanrogers.com

Bourg-d'Oisans

Camping le Colporteur

Le Mas du Plan, F-38520 Bourg-d'Oisans (Isère) T: 04 76 79 11 44. E: info@camping-colporteur.com

alanrogers.com/FR38140

The site is within a few minutes level walk of an attractive market town and ski resort, making this an ideal spot for motorcaravanners. There are 150 level grassy pitches, 120 for touring, including ten hardstandings for motorcaravans. All pitches have 15A electricity and rock pegs are advised. They are mostly separated by hedging and a variety of mature trees that offer some shade. There is no pool on site but campers have free entry to the adjacent municipal pool. In July and August the attractive bar/restaurant is the focal point for evening activities. Bourg-d'Oisans is in the largest national park in France. It is at an altitude of 700 m. and is surrounded by high mountains making it a real suntrap. The days can be very hot, especially in summer. The area is revered by serious cyclists as several mountain roads close by are regularly used by the Tour de France. This is an ideal base for exploring this scenic region with its abundance of wild flowers, old villages and rushing waterfalls; by car, on foot or by bike.

Facilities

Two large, clean toilet blocks are well equipped, modern and airy with all the necessary facilities including washbasins in cabins, baby room and en-suite room for disabled campers. Restaurant, bar and takeaway (mid June-end Aug). Games room. Boules. Play area. Organised family activities (July/Aug). Off site: Shops, bars, restaurants in town. Supermarket 500 m. Alpe-d'Huez 13 km. and Les Deux Alpes 19 km. Cycling, mountain biking, hiking, rafting, canoeing, climbing, riding, hang-gliding. Parc des Ecrins, cable cars (July/August).

Open: 17 May - 20 September.

Directions

Site is in Bourg-d'Oisans. From Grenoble follow the N91 into town and shortly after the road bears left in the town centre and then right (site signed). Follow signs to site, a few hundred metres. GPS: 45.0526, 6.0355

Charges guide

Per unit incl. 2 persons and electricity	€ 22.30 - € 26.00
extra person	€ 5.00 - € 7.00
child (5-10 yrs)	€ 2.70 - € 5.00

5 minutes walk from the town. Grassy touring pitches. Complete tranquility. Views of Alpe d'Huez. 36 Chalets & 2 Gipsy Wagons for rent info@camping-colporteur.com - www.camping-colporteur.com

Bourg-d'Oisans

RCN Camping Belledonne

Rochetaillée, F-38520 Bourg-d'Oisans (Isère) T: 04 76 80 07 18. E: info@rcn-belledonne.fr

alanrogers.com/FR38100

This spacious site is now owned by the RCN group and many improvements are planned. It has 180 well drained, level, generous, grassy pitches, most for touring, all with electricity (6A). Beech hedges and abundant mature trees provide ample privacy and shade. A bar/restaurant with terrace (open all season) is next to an attractive pool complex, comprising two swimming pools (one covered and heated), a paddling pool and large sunbathing space surrounded by gardens and grassy areas. In July and August the site becomes quite lively with many organised activities. No twin-axle caravans are accepted and large outfits should phone ahead.

Facilities

Four well appointed sanitary blocks include baby rooms and facilities for disabled visitors. Shop. Bar/restaurant and takeaway (all season). TV/games room. Swimming and paddling pools (one covered and heated). Sauna. Tennis. Good play area. Large meadow with fitness course. Football field. Bicycle hire (July/Aug). WiFi. Max. 1 dog. Off site: Riding 500 m. Allemont with shops 2 km. Fishing 4 km. Bourg-d'Oisans, shops, bars, restaurants and Saturday market 8 km. Cable car (high season).

Open: 23 April - 24 September.

Directions

Site is 8 km. west of Bourg-d'Oisans. From Grenoble take N85 to Vizille and then N91/D1091 towards Bourg-d'Oisans. In Rochetaillée branch left (site signed) onto D526, signed Allemont. Site is 250 m. on right. GPS: 45.11423, 6.00765

Charges guide

Per unit incl. 2 persons and electricity	€ 18.90 - € 39.90

Camping Cheques accepted.

For latest campsite news, availability and prices visit

alanrogers.com

Bourg-d'Oisans
Castel Camping le Château de Rochetaillée

Chemin de Bouthean, Rochetaillée, F-38520 Bourg-d'Oisans (Isère) T: 04 76 11 04 40.
E: jcp@camping-le-chateau.com **alanrogers.com/FR38180**

Set in the grounds of a small château with spectacular views, this site's ratings have recently been upgraded and it provides high quality amenities. The grounds are shared with chalets and tents to rent, with these in a separate area. There are 97 touring pitches, all with 6/10A electricity hook-ups on level areas (some large) separated by hedges and trees. The site has an excellent heated swimming pool, a fitness room, sauna, bar/restaurant and takeaway food together with a small shop selling bread and basic groceries. The site is in the centre of an area ideal for walkers, cyclists and climbers.

Facilities

Three good toilet blocks (two very large) are colourful and clean. Shower room with facilities for babies. Excellent, spacious facilities for disabled visitors. Small launderette. Freezer space. Shop. Bar, snacks, takeaway and separate restaurant (1/6-11/9). Heated swimming pool (1/6-11/9). Sauna, fitness room and jacuzzi (13/5-11/9). Climbing wall. Daily activities for children (July/Aug). Guided mountain walks. Fishing. Barbecue area. WiFi (charged).

Open: 13 May - 11 September.

Directions

South of Grenoble take exit 8 from A480 signed Stations de L'Oisans. Follow D1091 to Briançon. Site is signed just north of Rochetaillée at junction with D526. Turn here and site is immediately on the left. GPS: 45.11530, 6.00548

Charges guide

Per unit incl. 2 persons and electricity	€ 22.40 - € 36.50

Bourg-Saint-Maurice
Camping Caravaneige le Versoyen

Route des Arcs, F-73700 Bourg-Saint-Maurice (Savoie) T: 04 79 07 03 45. E: leversoyen@wanadoo.fr
alanrogers.com/FR73020

Bourg-St-Maurice is on a small, level plain at an altitude of 830 m. on the River Isère, surrounded by mountains. Le Versoyen attracts visitors all year round (except for a short time when they close). The site's 205 unseparated, flat pitches (180 for touring) are marked by numbers on the tarmac roads and all have electrical connections (4/6/10A). Most are on grass but some are on tarmac hardstanding making them ideal for use by motorcaravans or in winter. Trees give shade in some parts, although most pitches have almost none. Duckboards are provided for snow and wet weather.

Facilities

Two acceptable toilet blocks can be heated (but may be hard pressed in high season). British and Turkish style WCs. Laundry. Motorcaravan service facilities. Outdoor and covered pools (July/Aug). Heated rest room with TV. Small bar with takeaway in summer. Free shuttle in high season to funicular railway. Off site: Cross-country ski track behind the site. Fishing and bicycle hire 200 m. Tennis and swimming pool 500 m. Riding 1 km. Golf 15 km.

Open: All year excl. 7/11-14/12 and 2/5-25/5.

Directions

Site is 1.5 km. east of Bourg-Saint-Maurice on the CD119 Les Arcs road. GPS: 45.62248, 6.78475

Charges guide

Per unit incl. 2 persons and electricity	€ 17.40 - € 20.40
extra person	€ 4.30 - € 5.10

Buis-les-Baronnies
Camping Domaine de l'Ecluse

Bénivay, F-26170 Buis-les-Baronnies (Drôme) T: 04 75 28 07 32. E: camp.ecluse@wanadoo.fr
alanrogers.com/FR26200

Tucked away in the beautiful Drôme Provençale region, this quiet, rural site is situated high in the hills northeast of the Roman city of Vaison-la-Romaine and surrounded by vineyards. There are 75 level, stony pitches of average size, with 53 for touring (6A electricity, long leads necessary). They are separated by hedges and mature poplar trees giving varying amounts of shade. Some 15 of these are on an upper level, larger and more open, and separate from the rest of the site, with views of the hills. Rock pegs are advised. The attractive L-shaped swimming pool has a toboggan and sunbathing area.

Facilities

Two toilet blocks with all the necessary modern facilities include rooms for babies and campers with disabilities. Small shop. Bar/restaurant and takeaway (all July/Aug). Swimming pool (April-Sept). Games field. Simple programme of events and some excursions (July/Aug). Gas barbecues only. Internet link via a cable. Max. 1 dog. Off site: Restaurant nearby. Bicycle hire, fishing, lake bathing and riding 8 km. Historic villages of Buis-les-Baronnies 8 km. Mollans 8 km. Vaison la Romaine 14 km.

Open: 5 April - 15 November.

Directions

Site is northeast of Vaison la Romaine. Recommended access is via Buis-les-Baronnies. Just south of the village turn northwest on the D147 for 7 km. over the pass to Propiac. Turn right on D347 and climb to site in 2 km. At entry pull over into turning area provided to take sharp left-hand bend down to site. GPS: 44.28995, 5.1917

Charges guide

Per unit incl. 2 persons and electricity	€ 19.50 - € 25.50

We can book this site for you! Call 01580 214000 alan rogers travel

For latest campsite news, availability and prices visit
alanrogers.com

Chabeuil

Le Grand Lierne

B.P. 8, F-26120 Chabeuil (Drôme) T: 04 75 59 83 14. E: grand-lierne@franceloc.fr
alanrogers.com/FR26030

Le Grand Lierne is part of the FrancLoc group, and is fairly convenient for the A7 autoroute. It has 203 marked, stony pitches, 45 for touring units (6/10A electricity), separated by hedges and oak trees which offer varying amounts of shade. The site is clearly aimed at families with young children and has an attractive pool complex with several pools including a children's fun pool and a covered, heated pool for bathing in poor weather. The latest addition (2011) is a Disney style activity climb, close to the entrance, which children clearly adore.

Facilities

Two sanitary blocks with modern facilities including those for disabled visitors. Washing machines and dryers. Motorcaravan services. Shop/restaurant (22/4-18/9). Bar/takeaway. Fridge rental. Four pools, one covered and heated. Paddling pool, water slide, toboggans and lazy river. Playgrounds. Entertainment programme in high season. Minigolf. Archery. Only gas and electric barbecues are permitted. Dogs are not accepted in high season. WiFi. Off site: Golf 3 km. Bicycle hire 4.5 km. Fishing 5 km.

Open: 22 April - 18 September (with all services).

Directions

Site signed from Chabeuil about 11 km. east of Valence. Best approached from south side of Valence via Valence ring road. D68 to Chabeuil. Site is off D125 to Charpey, 5 km. from Chabeuil, well signed. GPS: 44.91572, 5.065

Charges guide

Per unit incl. 2 persons	
and electricity	€ 24.00 - € 39.00
extra person	€ 4.70 - € 7.00

Chamonix

Camping de la Mer de Glace

200 chemin de la Bagna, les Praz, F-74400 Chamonix (Haute-Savoie) T: 04 50 53 44 03.
E: info@chamonix-camping.com **alanrogers.com/FR74150**

This attractive site is convenient for Chamonix but is in a tranquil setting away from its hustle and bustle. The buildings are of typical regional timber construction, decorated with traditional painted flower designs. The English-speaking owners (since 2004) make every effort to keep it as natural as possible, therefore it is without a pool, restaurant, bar or disco and is well suited to those looking for quiet and relaxation. There are 150 pitches of varying sizes, most with shade and 75 have electricity connections (10A). Visitors are provided with a free bus in order to visit Chamonix town, as well as the surrounding area, during their stay.

Facilities

Three sanitary blocks with facilities for disabled visitors. Washing machine, dryer. Motorcaravan services. Bread. Pizza van twice weekly in July/Aug. Meeting room, snack preparation and meeting room. Small playground for young children. Free Internet and WiFi access. Free charging point for mobile phones etc. Off site: Fishing and golf 500 m. Shops etc. in Les Praz 700 m. Bicycle hire 1 km. Shops and swimming pools in Chamonix 1.5 km.

Open: 27 April - 30 September.

Directions

From Chamonix take D1506 (previously N506) northeast towards Les Praz. After 1 km. site signed to right. NOTE: the first two signs direct you under a 2.4 m. high bridge. Continue to a small roundabout at entrance to Les Praz, turn right and follow signs. GPS: 45.93805, 6.89267

Charges guide

Per unit incl. 2 persons	
and electricity	€ 21.60 - € 25.60

Chamonix

Camping l'Ile des Barrats

185 chemin de l'Ile des Barrats, F-74400 Chamonix (Haute-Savoie) T: 04 50 53 51 44.
E: campingiledesbarrats74@orange.fr **alanrogers.com/FR74160**

l'Ile des Barrats is a delightful neat, tidy, small and tranquil site. It is within easy walking distance of the beautiful town of Chamonix, although there are bus and train services close by if needed. There are 48 slightly sloping, grassy pitches, all for touring, mostly separated by small hedges and a variety of trees that offer some shade. All have electricity (10A) and 32 have water and drainage. This is an ideal site for those wishing to roam the mountain trails and for those seeking a peaceful and relaxing holiday in a most superb setting. There are four quality chalets available to rent. No twin-axle caravans.

Facilities

A modern, clean toilet block offers all necessary facilities, including those for disabled visitors. Covered picnic area with table and benches, ideal for those with small tents. Motorcaravan services. Store room for mountaineers. Mobile shop in July/Aug. No organised activities. WiFi (charged). Off site: Baker 500 m. Chamonix 800 m. level walk (summer and winter resort with colourful Sat. market).

Open: 15 May - 1 October.

Directions

On entering Chamonix from Geneva, turn left at first roundabout after turn off for the Mont Blanc Tunnel (follow hospital signs). A next roundabout, turn left, site is opposite hospital. GPS: 45.9143, 6.8615

Charges guide

Per unit incl. 2 persons	
and electricity	€ 24.20 - € 28.20
No credit cards.	

For latest campsite news, availability and prices visit
alanrogers.com

Châteauneuf-sur-Isère

Camping le Soleil Fruité

Les Peches, F-26300 Châteauneuf-sur-Isère (Drôme) T: 04 75 84 19 70. E: contact@lesoleilfruite.com

alanrogers.com/FR26220

Le Soleil Fruité is a new site conveniently located a little to the north of Valence, only 6 km. from the autoroute. The site lies amidst a large fruit farm with peaches, apricots and olives with views over the Ardèche mountains. Campers are invited to pick fruit and there is a twice weekly market featuring the farm's produce. There are 137 large, level, grassy pitches with 100 for touring (electricity 6A). They are separated by small shrubs and young trees giving little shade. Twin-axle caravans are not allowed on site. Only gas and electric barbecues. No dogs in July and August.

Facilities

Excellent, clean toilet block with facilities for babies and disabled visitors. Motorcaravan services. Bar, snack bar with TV, small shop. Twice weekly market (July/Aug). Swimming pool with jacuzzi. Paddling pool. Play area. Bicycle hire. WiFi (free). Trampolines. Entertainment and excursion programme (July/Aug). Off site: Canoeing on the River Drôme. Minigolf. Covered pool. Health club.

Open: 28 April - 15 September.

Directions

Leave A7 autoroute at exit 14 (Valence Nord) take the N7 north for 2 km. Turn right, D877, site signed. After 2km. turn left, then left at roundabout then left again to site. GPS: 45.002716, 4.895514

Charges guide

| Per unit incl. 2 persons and electricity | € 20.10 - € 27.90 |
| extra person | € 5.10 - € 6.80 |

Châtillon-en-Diois

Flower Camping Lac Bleu

Quarter la Touche, F-26410 Châtillon-en-Diois (Drôme) T: 04 75 21 85 30. E: info@lacbleu-diois.com

alanrogers.com/FR26150

This spacious and peaceful site is run by a very friendly family who have made many improvements to the site with many more in the pipeline. It lies in a beautiful valley surrounded by mountains, south of the Vercors National Park. The 199 pitches (76 for touring) are level with rough grass, slightly uneven and separated by a variety of trees offering some shade (rock pegs advised). All have electricity (10A). At the centre of the site is a lake of 2.5 hectares with warm clean water fed by springs, making it ideal for swimming and fishing. A good bar, restaurant and terrace overlook the lake and there is plenty of space for children to play. No dogs. Only gas and electric barbecues. An evening stroll around the lake is recommended. The site is near the very small Bez river and not far from the interesting and ancient small town of Die, the home of the famous Clairette de Die – a sparkling wine mentioned in dispatches by the Romans around 40AD. This is a very good site for exploring this picturesque part of France, and to completely unwind and enjoy the views, the beautiful sunset over the mountains and the very clean air.

Facilities

Two clean toilet blocks, one new, the other refurbished, with all the necessary facilities. Baby room. Facilities for disabled campers. Bar/restaurant, takeaway. TV/games room (all season). Covered heated swimming pool and paddling pool (all season). Motorcaravan service point. Play area by the lake, which has footpaths around it, bathing and fishing. Pedaloes. Large sports/play area. Bicycle hire. WiFi in bar/terrace area (charged). Only gas and electric barbecues allowed. Off site: Medieval villages (Châtillon 2 km). Riding 7 km. Canoeing, canyoning, grottos.

Open: 1 April - 30 September.

Directions

Take D93 southeast from Die, signed Gap. After about 5 km. turn left on D539 signed Châtillon-en-Diois. After 4.5 km. bear right onto D140, site signed. Site shortly on left. GPS: 44.6824, 5.44795

Charges guide

Per unit incl. 2 persons and electricity	€ 15.30 - € 25.20
extra person	€ 3.60 - € 5.80
child (2-7 yrs)	€ 2.50 - € 4.10
dog	€ 1.30 - € 2.50

Le Lac Bleu
★★★
Châtillon en Diois
Drôme - Rhône Alpes

At the foot of the Vercors, at the gate to the Provence
Bar, restaurant.
Tents, mobile homes and chalets to rent.
This campsite offers you all for both a family holiday as more active holiday.
All services available from 01/04 till 30/09.

Quartier la Touche
26410 Châtillon-en-Diois
Tél. 00 33 (0)4 75 21 85 30
www.lacbleu-diois.com

For latest campsite news, availability and prices visit
alanrogers.com

Cormoranche-sur-Saône

Camping du Lac

Base de Loisirs, les Luizants, F-01290 Cormoranche-sur-Saône (Ain) T: 03 85 23 97 10.
E: contact@lac-cormoranche.com **alanrogers.com/FR01090**

Situated in a region famous for its wines, gastronomy and picturesque old villages, this site is part of the 42-hectare, landscaped recreation park that surrounds a tree lined lake. The 117 generous pitches are level, grassed and enclosed by hedges, all with electricity and drainage. A small dam divides the lake into two areas, one for swimming, the other, larger part for fishing (also permitted at night) and boating. To the far side of the park is a TGV railway track. During the day the trains are fairly frequent, but there are no night services and the daytime noise is a moderate rumble. The reception office has a good selection of tourist information on a region lined with the wine routes of Beaujolais, Macon and Bourgogne. In addition, this is the region of Bresse chickens and fresh water fish and in the surrounding picturesque towns and villages there are many good restaurants, the most famous being that of Georges Blanc in Vonnas.

Facilities

Modern sanitary building provides free preset showers and washbasins in cabins (a little small). Facilities for disabled visitors. Laundry room with washing machine. Motorcaravan service point. Small shop (order bread for following morning). Bar and restaurant with takeaway, overlooking lake. Lake swimming with a separate area for small children. Off site: Macon, Bourg-en-Bresse and the village of Perouges.

Open: 1 April - 30 September.

Directions

Site is 5 km. south-southwest of Macon on the eastern site of the Saône. It is well signed from all directions 'Base de Loisirs'. If approaching from the west via Creches, there is a 2.6 m. height restriction. GPS: 46.25167, 4.8261

Charges guide

Per unit incl. 2 persons and electricity	€ 14.40 - € 19.00
extra person	€ 4.20 - € 5.10

BASE DE LOISIRS DU LAC
CAMPING ****
To rent - Chalets - Mobile Homes - Tipis
SNACK - BAR - ANIMATION
01290 Cormoranche-sur-Saône
00 33-(0)3-85-23-97-10
www.lac-cormoranche.com

COMMUNAUTE DE COMMUNES
CANTON DE PONT-DE-VEYLE

CORMORANCHE

PARIS
MÂCON
LYON
C'est ici

We can book this site for you! Call 01580 214000 alan rogers ○ travel

Dardilly

Camping Indigo Lyon

Porte de Lyon, Avenue du Camping International, F-69570 Dardilly (Rhône) T: 04 78 35 64 55.
E: lyon@camping-indigo.com **alanrogers.com/FR69010**

This is a modern overnight site just off the A6 autoroute. Kept busy with overnight trade, reception and the café (main season) open until quite late. There are 175 separate numbered plots all with 6/10A electricity and 140 of these also provide water and waste water drainage. Those for caravans are mostly on hardstandings on a slight slope, with another small grassy part, while those for tents are on a flatter area of grass. A very large commercial centre has been developed just outside the site, with eight hotels, restaurants, a supermarket, petrol station, etc. There is some road noise.

Facilities

Three sanitary blocks, one heated, have free hot water (solar heated) and washbasins in cabins. Baby changing facilities and washing machines. Bar open at weekends in low season and daily in July and August. Takeaway provision on Friday and Saturdays. Motorcaravan service point. Swimming and paddling pools (27/4-16/9, supervised and free). Playground. TV room. Games room. Reading room (books and local information). Boules. Picnic and barbecue area. Only electric barbecues allowed. Off site: Riding 2 km. Golf 12 km.

Open: All year.

Directions

Travelling south, do not take A46 motorway around Lyon, continue on A6, take exit Limonest, Dardilly, Porte de Lyon. About 8 km. north of Lyon tunnel; turn left for Porte de Lyon (well signed). GPS: 45.82035, 4.7604

Charges guide

Per unit incl. 2 persons and electricity	€ 20.90 - € 23.40
extra person	€ 4.20 - € 4.50
child (2-7 yrs)	€ 2.50 - € 3.10
Camping Cheques accepted.	

For latest campsite news, availability and prices visit
alanrogers.com

Dieulefit
Huttopia Dieulefit

Quartier d'Espeluche, F-26220 Dieulefit (Drôme) T: 04 37 64 22 35.
E: dieulefit@huttopia.com **alanrogers.com/FR26580**

The site is located just north of the town of Dieulefit. The name originates from Dieu l'a fait, meaning God made it, so it is not surprising to find this latest addition to the Huttopia group set in a managed forest, by a small lake, with stunning views over the town and across the valley. It follows the Huttopia philosophy of high standards combined with a sense of real camping, therefore no cars are generally allowed on pitches. Of 165 pitches, 50 are rental accommodation in the form of Cahuttes, Cabanes or Canadiennes, all varying types of wood and canvas structures. The remaining pitches are for camping amongst the trees, although there are some closer to the central lodge which are more open. 'Bivouac' outdoor cooking and eating areas are dotted around the site as no barbecues are allowed in the forest. There are two pools and a good range of on-site amenities including a shop, bar and restaurant.

Facilities

Modern well equipped heated sanitary facilities in the central lodge, plus strategically placed outlying 'rondavels' containing family rooms and toilets and water points. Bar/restaurant. Pizzeria. Small shop. Large central lodge with wood burning fire and communal area. Conference Centre. Bicycle hire. Off site: Dieulefit town 2 km. Acro Pole Adventure (tree walk and other activites) 2 km. Walking, cycling, hiking. Montelimar 10 km. Historic town of Grignon 10 km.

Open: 2 July - 1 October.

Directions

From A7 take junction 18 onto N7 to Montelimar. Go right on ring road and follow D540 towards La Batise Rolland. Continue on D540 to Dieulefit. On entering town go left at roundabout onto D538 (north). Continue through and once you pass the Pompiers on the right you will begin to see signs for campsite on left. GPS: 44.53505, 5.059274

Charges guide

Per unit incl. 2 persons and electricity	€ 23.20 - € 40.20
extra person	€ 4.50 - € 6.50
child (2-7 yrs)	€ 2.70 - € 4.00
dog	€ 4.00

In the Drôme Provençale,
in the very heart of the lavender country...

DIEULEFIT

Wood & Canvas Tents,
Chalets, Cahuttes to rent

Swimming pool, Bar,
Restaurant, Play area...

www.huttopia.com
Quartier d'Espeluche - 26220 Dieulefit - Tel : +33 (0)4 75 54 63 94

For latest campsite news, availability and prices visit
alanrogers.com

Doussard
Camping International le Lac Bleu

Route de la Plage, F-74210 Doussard (Haute-Savoie) T: 04 50 44 30 18. E: contact@camping-lac-bleu.com
alanrogers.com/FR74180

This lakeside site has its own beach and jetty and a short walk brings you to the lake ferry. The site has breathtaking views, a swimming pool (a 'fun pool' was added in 2010) and 220 pitches divided by privet and beech hedges. This site is perfect for walking, cycling or sailing and in low season provides a tranquil base for those just wishing to relax. In high season it will be busy and popular. The proximity of the public lakeside area, which is often used as a festival venue, could be either a source of noise or an exciting place to be, depending on your point of view. When we visited the music stopped at 23.00. A nearby cycle track on a disused railway to Annecy gives a level 16 km. ride with mountains on the left and the lake to the right. In high season there is a children's club for the under eights. The bar has a thriving takeaway (roast whole chickens and pizza) and an 'al fresco' eating area.

Facilities	Directions
Three toilet blocks are of a high standard with free showers. Good provision for babies and disabled visitors. Bar (15/5-15/9) and integral small shop. Takeaway. Swimming pool (15/5-15/9). Bicycle hire. Boat launching (sailing lessons and boat hire nearby). Multisports pitch. Private beach. Off site: Small supermarket 100 m. Village nearby with bars and restaurants. Fishing 100 m. Hypermarket 4 km. Riding and golf 7 km.	Site is 16 km. south of Annecy on Route d'Albertville, well signed. GPS: 46.317367, 6.362967

Open: 1 April - 25 September.

Charges guide

Per unit incl. 2 persons and electricity	€ 20.70 - € 37.00
extra person (over 3 yrs)	€ 4.00 - € 6.30
dog	€ 2.90 - € 4.50

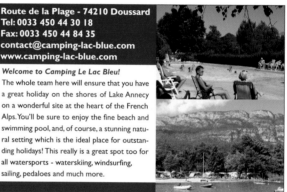

Route de la Plage - 74210 Doussard
Tel: 0033 450 44 30 18
Fax: 0033 450 44 84 35
contact@camping-lac-blue.com
www.camping-lac-blue.com

Welcome to Camping Le Lac Bleu!
The whole team here will ensure that you have a great holiday on the shores of Lake Annecy on a wonderful site at the heart of the French Alps. You'll be sure to enjoy the fine beach and swimming pool, and, of course, a stunning natural setting which is the ideal place for outstanding holidays! This really is a great spot too for all watersports - waterskiing, windsurfing, sailing, pedaloes and much more.

Doussard
Camp de la Ravoire

Bout-du-Lac, route de la Ravoire, F-74210 Doussard (Haute-Savoie) T: 04 50 44 37 80.
E: info@camping-la-ravoire.fr **alanrogers.com/FR74040**

La Ravoire is a high quality site, 800 m. from Lake Annecy. It is noted for its neat and tidy appearance and the quietness of its location in this popular tourist region. The 112 level pitches are on well mown grass with some shade, and separated by small shrubs and some hedging. The 90 pitches for touring (21 with water and drainage) have electricity (5-15A). Those looking for a campsite in this attractive region, without the 'animation' programmes that many French sites consider necessary, will find this a peaceful base.

Facilities	Directions
Very good toilet block with facilities for disabled visitors. Laundry room has washing machines, dryers and irons. Shop. Bar, snack bar and takeaway. Outdoor pool, water slide and paddling pool (all open all season). Good play area. Sports areas. Off site: Lake with restaurants 800 m. Cycle track (30 km) almost to Annecy passes close by. Fishing, boat launching, bicycle hire 1 km. Riding 6 km. Golf 8 km. Shops in Doussard and Annecy (18 km). Canyoning and hang-gliding. Boat trips.	Site signed from D1508 (previously N508) Annecy - Albertville road. About 13 km. south of Annecy, at traffic lights in Brédannaz, turn right (site signed) and then immediately left. Site on left in about 1 km. Large outfits should use alternative access at the next right turn after the traffic lights. GPS: 45.80256, 6.20977

Open: 15 May - 7 September.

Charges guide

Per unit incl. 2 persons and electricity	€ 24.50 - € 35.20
extra person	€ 5.00 - € 6.50
child (2-15 yrs)	€ 2.50 - € 4.50

Camping Cheques accepted.

For latest campsite news, availability and prices visit
alanrogers.com

Doussard

Campéole la Nublière

30 allée de la Nublière, F-74210 Doussard (Haute-Savoie) T: 04 50 44 33 44.
E: nubliere@wanadoo.fr **alanrogers.com/FR74190**

Campé●le

If you are looking for large pitches, shady trees, mountain views and direct access to a lakeside beach, this site is for you. There are 271 touring pitches, of which 243 have electrical hook-ups (6A). This area is very popular and the site is very likely to be busy in high season. There may be some noise from the road and the public beach. La Nublière is 16 km. from old Annecy and you are spoilt for choice in how to get there. Take a ferry trip, hire a sailing boat or pedalo, or walk or cycle along the traffic free track towards the town. The local beach and sailing club are close and there is a good restaurant on the site perimeter. Across the road from the site are courts for tennis and boules. The site is perfect for walking, cycling or sailing and in low season provides a tranquil base for those just wishing to relax in natural surroundings on the edge of a nature reserve.

Facilities

Large clean sanitary blocks include free hot showers and good facilities for disabled visitors. Laundry. Shop (1/5-15/9). Restaurant on site perimeter (closed Mon). Children's club (3/7-26/8) for 4-8 yrs. Safe deposit. WiFi (charged). Off site: Small supermarket adjacent to site. Good watersports area within 70 m. Access to town beach from site. Fishing 100 m. Golf and riding 4 km. Bicycle hire 7 km.

Open: 28 April - 18 September.

Directions

Site is 16 km. south of Annecy on Route d'Albertville, well signed. GPS: 45.7908, 6.2197

Charges guide

Per unit incl. 2 persons and electricity	€ 17.50 - € 26.60
extra person	€ 4.50 - € 6.80
child (2-6 yrs)	free - € 4.30

Campé●le
CAMPSITES AND RENTALS
RHÔNE-ALPES

La Nublière***

At the shore of Lac d'Annecy, direct acces to the beach and nautic base, with mountains all around. Pitches and accommodations of high quality.

74210 Doussard - Tel.: +33-450-4433-44 - www.campeole.co.uk / nubliere@campeole.com

Fleurie

Camping Municipal la Grappe Fleurie

La Lie, F-69820 Fleurie (Rhône) T: 04 74 69 80 07. E: camping@fleurie.org
alanrogers.com/FR69020

With easy access from both the A6 autoroute and the N6, this site is ideally situated for night stops or indeed for longer stays to explore the vineyards and historic attractions of the Beaujolais region. Virtually surrounded by vineyards, but within walking distance (less than 1 km) of the pretty village of Fleurie, this is an immaculate small site, with 85 separated touring pitches. All are generous, grassy and fairly level with the benefit of individual access to water, drainage and electrical connections (10A). A baker calls 07.30-08.30. Wine tasting is arranged twice weekly in high season. Restaurant and shopping facilities are available in the village.

Facilities

Sanitary facilities in two blocks have British and Turkish style toilets and very satisfactory shower and washing facilities (showers closed 22.00-07.00). Facilities for disabled visitors. Two cold showers are provided. Washing machine and dryer. Outdoor swimming pool (15x7 m). Small playground. Only gas or electric barbecues are allowed. WiFi (code). Off site: Fleurie 600 m. Bicycle hire 5 km. Fishing 10 km.

Open: Late March - end October.

Directions

From N6 at Le Maison Blanche/Romanech-Thorins, take D32 to village of Fleurie from where site is signed. GPS: 46.1879, 4.69916

Charges guide

Per unit incl. 2 persons and electricity	€ 18.50 - € 20.00
tent pitch incl. 2 persons and electricity	€ 16.50 - € 18.00
extra person	€ 6.00 - € 7.00
child (3-10 yrs)	€ 4.50 - € 5.00

For latest campsite news, availability and prices visit
alanrogers.com

Excenevex

Campéole la Pinède

Campé●le

F-74140 Excenevex Plage (Haute-Savoie) T: 04 50 72 85 05. E: pinede@campeole.com

alanrogers.com/FR74280

La Pinède is a member of the Campéole group and has direct access to Excenevex beach, the only naturally sandy beach on Lake Geneva. The site has a pleasant woodland setting and pitches are of a good size, all with electricity (10A). Mobile homes, chalets and fully equipped tents are available for rent (including specially adapted units for wheelchair users). There is a supervised bathing area on the beach, which shelves gradually, and a small harbour (suitable only for boats with a shallow draught). Other amenities include a shop and takeaway food service, as well as an entertainment marquee and children's play area. There is plenty of activity here in high season with a children's club and regular discos and karaoke evenings. Geneva is just 25 km. distant and other possible excursions include Thonon-les-Bains with its weekly market and, of course, boat trips on Lake Geneva. Dramatic mountain scenery is close at hand, notably the spectacular Dent d'Oche and the Gorges du Pont du Diable.

Facilities

Lake beach. Takeaway food. Play area. Bouncy castle. Activities and entertainment programme. Tourist information. Mobile homes, chalets and equipped tents for rent. Off site: Hiking and cycle tracks. Riding. Golf. Thonon-les-Bains 15 km. Geneva 25 km.

Open: 11 April - 11 September.

Directions

From Geneva head along the south side of the lake on the D1005 as far as Massongy and shortly beyond here take the northbound D324 to Escenevex. The site is well indicated from here. GPS: 46.34492, 6.35808

Charges guide

Per unit incl. 2 persons
and electricity   € 17.10 - € 26.60

Campé●le

CAMPSITES AND RENTALS

RHÔNE-ALPES

La Pinède***

Opposite Switzerland, direct access to the beach of Lake Geneva. Pitches and accommodations of high quality.

74140 Excenevex - Tel.: +33-450-7285-05 - www.campeole.co.uk / pinede@campeole.com

Groisy

Camping Moulin Dollay

206 rue du Moulin Dollay, F-74570 Groisy (Haute-Savoie) T: 04 50 68 00 31. E: moulin.dollay@orange.fr

alanrogers.com/FR74170

Nestling between Annecy (15 km) and Geneva (35 km), this spacious site is a gem with only 45 pitches, 30 for touring. The friendly and enthusiastic owner has worked hard to develop this site to a high quality. The large to very large, level, grass pitches are partially separated by hedging and a variety of trees provide some shade. All pitches have 6A electricity and rock pegs are recommended. As there are only a few activities organised for youngsters on site it is perhaps better suited to those who would appreciate a peaceful site in a parkland setting alongside a rushing stream.

Facilities

Spacious, well appointed, heated toilet block, including facilities for disabled visitors and a baby room. Washing machine, dryer. Motorcaravan services. Bar, TV corner. Large open play and sports area. Fishing and bathing in shallow river. Off site: Some shops, restaurants, bank and supermarkets at Groisy 1 km. Riding 4 km. Interesting little town of Thorens-Glières with its 11th-century château 5 km. Golf 6 km. Annecy with wide range of facilities 12 km. Lake Annecy and watersports 15 km.

Open: 1 May - 30 September.

Directions

Site is north of Annecy. Heading north on N1203 Annecy - Bonneville road, turn right on D2 signed Thorens-Glières and site, then immediately right again. Site is 300 m. GPS: 46.00238, 6.19079

Charges guide

Per unit incl. 2 persons and electricity	€ 18.00 - € 22.00
extra person	€ 5.00
child (under 7 yrs)	€ 2.00
dog	€ 1.00

No credit cards.

For latest campsite news, availability and prices visit

alanrogers.com

Grâne
Kawan Village les Quatre Saisons

Route de Roche-sur-Grâne, F-26400 Grâne (Drôme) T: 04 75 62 64 17. E: contact@camping-4-saisons.com

alanrogers.com/FR26110

This small, terraced site, open all year, nestles in the hillsides of the lower Drôme valley close to the Vercors Mountains. With its 80 pitches (69 for tourers), it provides mainly overnight accommodation but it is worth a longer stay. The pitches are level and stony, of variable size, cut out of the hillside and reached by a one-way system on tarmac roads. All pitches have electricity (6A), some with water and drainage. The modern main building houses reception on the upper level as you enter the site, with the pool, bar and other facilities to the side and below. The clever terracing provides commanding views across the valley towards Crest and the Vercors. This is a tranquil site in a rural setting yet close to Grane and the Drome river. The nearby, more bustling town of Crest, is well worth a visit with its historic keep high on the hill, and the narrow streets of the old town.

Facilities

Good sanitary facilities include baby room, en-suite facilities for disabled visitors (site is very sloping, so unsuitable for wheelchairs). Washing machine. Bar (1/5-30/9). TV/games room. Small swimming pool (1/5-15/9). Play area. Trampoline and bouncy castle. Children's club (high season). Only electric and gas barbecues are allowed on the pitch. Chalets available to rent. Off site: Village nearby with shops catering for most needs. Fishing 1 km. Bicycle hire 2/3 km. Riding 3 km. Canoeing in Crest 3 km.

Open: 1 April - 30 September.

Directions

From A7 exit 17, or the N7 at Loriol, take the D104 towards Crest. After 8 km. in Grâne take D113 south. Site is on left about 600 m. beyond the village. GPS: 44.7277, 4.9265

Charges guide

Per unit incl. 2 persons	
and electricity	€ 18.00 - € 29.00
extra person	€ 5.00
child (under 6 yrs)	€ 3.50
dog	free

Camping Cheques accepted.

Les 4 Saisons Camping et Caravanning★★★★

Only 10 minutes from exit 16 of the A7 highway. Ideal for a stop-over or a longer stay in a quiet and relaxing environment with lovely well situated pitches with a nice view on the Vercors. The campsite is perfectly located for cyclists and walkers. Lovers of antiquity will love the magnificent high situated villages.

Route de Roche sur Grâne - 26400 Grane
Tél. 0031 (0)4 75 62 64 17 - Fax 0031 (0)4 75 62 69 06
E-mail contact@camping-4-saisons.com

www.camping-4-saisons.com

Hautecourt
Camping de l'Ile Chambod

3232, route du Port, F-01250 Hautecourt (Ain) T: 04 74 37 25 41. E: camping.chambod@sholnet.fr

alanrogers.com/FR01020

This small, attractive rural site is situated in a valley close to the Gorges de l'Ain. Many improvements have been made by its current owners; it has two modern toilet blocks, a swimming pool and small café. The 110 medium-sized, slightly sloping, grassy pitches (many with views of the surrounding wooded hills) are separated by low hedges and most have some shade. All have access to water points and electricity (5/10A) although some may need extremely long leads. Some pitches are close to the pool and bar area, which may be noisy in July and August.

Facilities

Two modern toilet blocks include some washbasins in cabins, dishwashing, laundry and vegetable preparation sinks. Washing machines and dryer. Both blocks have facilities for disabled visitors and one has a baby room. Bread available to order. Small shop (June-Aug). Bar/restaurant and takeaway (May-Aug). Swimming pool (May-Aug). Small play area. Activities organised in high season for all the family. Off site: Fishing 100 m. Riding 5 km. Golf 20 km. Close to the spectacular gorges of the River Ain.

Open: 29 April - 1 October.

Directions

Site is 23 km. southeast of Bourg-en-Bresse via the D979. It is well signed from the crossroads in Hautecourt, and is a further 4 km. southeast down a long lane. GPS: 46.12777, 5.42818

Charges guide

Per unit incl. 2 persons	
and electricity	€ 18.00 - € 19.00
extra person	€ 4.70
child (2-12 yrs)	€ 3.20
dog	€ 1.10

For latest campsite news, availability and prices visit
alanrogers.com

Hauterives
Flower Camping le Château

5, route de Romans, F-26390 Hauterives (Drôme) T: 04 75 68 80 19. E: camping-hauterives@orange.fr
alanrogers.com/FR26360

Le Château is a former municipal campsite which is now run by the friendly and very helpful Valérie and Franck. It is a family oriented site set an hour south from Lyon near the motorway. In high season activities are organised for the whole family. This site comprises 137 neat, good sized touring pitches with 13 used for rental accommodation, well spread over an area of 4 ha. There is also a dedicated area for tent campers near the entrance of the site. The old château buildings are used for entertainment, bar and snacks, with the pools adjacent. The village of Hauterives is a short walk from the site.

Facilities

Sanitary buildings include controllable showers. Facilities for disabled visitors. Dishwashing sinks. Bar/snack bar (June-Aug). Heated outdoor pools (salt water) and children's pool (June-Aug). Table tennis. TV room. Playground. Library. Boules. Bicycle hire. Accommodation to rent. WiFi (charged). Off site: Supermarket by entrance. Shops, restaurants and weekly market in village. Fishing 1 km. Riding 5 km. Golf 15 km.

Open: 1 April - 30 September.

Directions

Leave the A7 at exit 12 (Chanas) and take the third exit from roundabout (D519 for Grenoble-Beaurepaire). At Beaurepaire take the D538 and go through Lens Lestang, then Hauterives. At roundabout by the church, turn left for Romans. Site is 200 m. on the left. GPS: 45.252796, 5.026717

Charges guide

Per unit incl. 2 persons and electricity	€ 14.50 - € 25.50

Joyeuse
Camping Caravaning les Cruses

Ribes, F-07260 Joyeuse (Ardèche) T: 04 75 39 54 69. E: les-cruses@wanadoo.fr
alanrogers.com/FR07260

High in the quiet hills of the southern Ardèche, among the sweet chestnut trees, this small site is carefully terraced. A warm welcome awaits you on arrival. M. and Mme. Rouvier are very keen to promote a quiet family atmosphere, personal contact with their guests is important and weekly entertainment is tailored to guests' needs. For instance he will lead walks, arrange boules competitions against other campsites, canyoning and canoe trips on the river. There are 45 pitches and 22 mobile homes and chalets for hire. Pitches are of varying sizes, some on grass and some gravel, and some are only accessible for tents.

Facilities

The toilet block is clean with preset showers and a few en-suite shower, toilet and basin cabins. Baby room. Facilities for disabled visitors. Laundry. Bar, restaurant and pizzeria serving good food (weekends only in low season). Swimming pool (1/5-20/9). Fishing. Play area. Covered area for pétanque. Games room. Activities arranged. Chalets, mobile homes and Romany caravans for rent. Gas barbecues only. WiFi (charged). Off site: Fishing and river beach 1 km. Riding 3 km. Bicycle hire 5 km.

Open: 4 April - 26 September.

Directions

From Joyeuse take the D203 towards Ribes. Turn left at D450 signed Ribes and continue for 1 km. The site is signed on the left some 1 km. before the village. GPS: 44.492417, 4.207267

Charges guide

Per unit incl. 2 persons and electricity	€ 15.50 - € 27.10
extra person	€ 4.20 - € 6.35

Joyeuse
Camping la Nouzarède

F-07260 Joyeuse (Ardèche) T: 04 75 39 92 01. E: campingnouzarede@wanadoo.fr
alanrogers.com/FR07270

On the outskirts of Joyeuse, this site will appeal to people, including children, who enjoy riding, for it has its own equestrian centre opposite the entrance. The site is open from 1 April until 30 September and, unusually, so are all the facilities, including the heated pool, restaurant, shop and bar. There are 63 pitches for touring units, including 25 which are fully serviced with water, drainage and electricity (10A). The site is flat with some shade provided by maturing trees. The small, busy town of Joyeuse has an extensive and notable market on a Wednesday morning – not the best time to arrive!

Facilities

Sanitary facilities are modern, clean and spacious, with a bathroom for young children and facilities for disabled visitors. Laundry room. Shop. Bar and restaurant with pizza oven. Swimming pool and children's pool with water features. Sports area. Play area. Evening entertainment and daytime activities for children. Horse and pony riding with lessons. Direct river access for fishing and bathing. Free WiFi. Off site: Town with bicycle hire and good supermarket nearby. Tennis.

Open: 1 April - 30 September.

Directions

Joyeuse is on the Rosières - Aubenas road. Site is signed from roundabout to town centre. Bear right at Renault garage (on right) and down 'Rampe de Cluchet'. At junction turn left and continue for 500 m. through market square and on over small bridge, site is on right. GPS: 44.48335, 4.235333

Charges guide

Per unit incl. 2 persons and electricity	€ 17.10 - € 28.60

For latest campsite news, availability and prices visit
alanrogers.com

La Clusaz
Camping le Plan du Fernuy
Route des Confins, F-74220 La Clusaz (Haute-Savoie) T: 04 50 02 44 75. E: info@plandufernuy.com
alanrogers.com/FR74090

This neat and open site has separate summer and winter seasons. It has 80 average sized, stony, grassy, pitches, 58 for tourists with electricity and 22 fully serviced. There are good mountain views but little shade, rock pegs essential. The site's crowning glory is an excellent indoor heated pool with large windows looking out on to the mountains. This is a good site for skiing in winter (with access to a ski-tow from the campsite and a free bus to other centres). In summer it is a good base for walking and cycling with other sporting opportunities nearby. The pleasant owners speak good English.

Facilities

Very good heated sanitary provision. Baby room. Facilities for disabled visitors. Washing machine and dryer. Drying room for ski clothing and boots. Motorcaravan services. Small shop and bar, snacks, takeaway. Games, TV room. Heated indoor pool and paddling pool. Skiing from site and ski excursions organised. Off site: Shops and restaurants in village 2 km. Riding 800 m. Golf, bicycle hire and fishing 1.5 km.

Open: 4 June - 4 September, 18 December - 24 April.

Directions

From Annecy take D909 to La Clusaz and at roundabout turn towards Les Confins. Site is on right after 2 km. (well signed). It is best to avoid using D909 from Flumat particularly with caravans or motorcaravans. GPS: 45.90922, 6.45203

Charges guide

Per unit incl. 2 persons	€ 20.00 - € 24.00
incl. electricity (4-13A)	€ 23.50 - € 32.00
extra person	€ 5.50 - € 6.50

Winter prices are higher.

La Salle-en-Beaumont
Camping le Champ Long
Le Champ Long, F-38350 La Salle-en-Beaumont (Isère) T: 04 76 30 41 81. E: champlong38@orange.fr
alanrogers.com/FR38190

Set at the entrance to the Ecrins national park and overlooked by the great Obiou massif, this site has been carved from a hilly forest. It provides 67 touring pitches (8/10A electricity) arranged in glades between mature trees. The setting is such that it is hard to see the other units around you, yet the mountain views through the trees are wonderful. The site is terraced and hilly and the winding access tracks need adequate power in reserve for towing, so it is not really suitable for large outfits. There are some steep paths to the sanitary blocks.

Facilities

Two sanitary blocks, one at reception, the other high on the steep terraces provide British and Turkish style WCs, washbasins in cabins and unexceptional showers. Facilities for children and babies. Laundry facilities. Motorcaravan service point. Milk, bread and a few essentials kept (May-Sept). Bar, good restaurant and takeaway (all April-Oct). Heated outdoor swimming pool (1/5-31/8). Play area and games room. Barbecues to rent. Chalets and mobile homes to rent. WiFi (charged).

Open: 1 April - 15 October.

Directions

From the D1085 turn off at sign for La Roche which is close to La Salle en Beaumont. Site is signed through long country roads.
GPS: 44.85554, 5.84503

Charges guide

Per unit incl. 2 persons and electricity	€ 17.50 - € 19.50
extra person	€ 3.50 - € 3.80
child (0-7 yrs)	€ 2.50 - € 2.80

Lagorce

Castel Domaine de Sévenier
F-07150 Lagorce (Ardèche) T: 04 75 88 29 44. E: domainedesevenier@orange.fr
alanrogers.com/FR07660

Le Domaine de Sévenier is a modern, high quality chalet complex enjoying a hilltop location with fine panoramic views over the surrounding garrigue, a unique mix of oak trees, juniper, rosemary and thyme. Located 4 km. from Vallon-Pont-d'Arc and 800 m. from the pretty village of Lagorce, the domaine is an old winery which has been sensitively converted and offers accommodation in well appointed wooden chalets, serving the needs of different sized families. Rest and relaxation is the theme here and the restaurant has a good reputation. On-site amenities include a swimming pool and a separate children's pool. The site has links to Nature Parc Camping de l'Ardèche and guests are welcome to use the camping site's evening entertainment but there are no touring pitches at Sévenier.

Facilities

Restaurant. Bar. Shop. Swimming pool. Children's pool. Activity programme. Play area. Minigolf. Tourist information. Fully equipped chalets for rent. No touring pitches. Off site: Lagorce 800 m. (shops and cafés). Cycle and walking tracks. Riding. Vallon Pont d'Arc 5 km.

Open: 13 March - 15 November.

Directions

Head north from Vallon-Pont-d'Arc (at western end of the Ardèche gorges) on D1 and upon reaching Lagorce, follow signs to the site.
GPS: 44.434151, 4.410989

Charges guide

Contact the site for details.

For latest campsite news, availability and prices visit
alanrogers.com

Lamastre
Camping de Retourtour

1 rue de Retourtour, F-07270 Lamastre (Ardèche) T: 04 75 06 40 71. E: campingderetourtour@wanadoo.fr

alanrogers.com/FR07460

This family run site is situated in the lesser-known, but beautiful, northern Ardèche and, you can be sure of a good welcome here. Delightfully situated near a tiny village below the ruins of a chateau, there are 130 good sized, level, grass pitches with 70 for touring (all with 4-13A electricity). They are separated by hedges and mature trees which offer varying amounts of shade. There are some with views over the wooded valley. Entertainment for all the family is organised in July and August making this a good site for those seeking a more relaxing holiday. The site is situated in the valley of the Doux river, and a beautiful natural river swimming area is within 150 m.

Facilities

Three clean, refurbished toilet blocks with all necessary facilities including those for babies and disabled visitors. Small shop. Bar. Restaurant/takeaway (July/Aug otherwise weekends). Good play area. Multisports area. Fitness room. Boules. Minigolf. Climbing. Fishing. WiFi (charged). Only gas and electric barbecues are allowed. Mobile homes to rent. Off site: Fishing and small riverside beach 150 m. Restaurant nearby. Amenities in Lamastre 1.5 km.

Open: Easter - 30 September.

Directions

Leave A7 autoroute at exit 13 (Tournon) or 15 (Valence). Go west to Lamastre following signs to Le Puy (about 35 km). Continue through Lamastre (site well signed). After 1.5 km. turn right (site signed) down lane to site. GPS: 44.99165, 4.56477

Charges guide

Per unit incl. 2 persons and electricity	€ 16.16 - € 20.66

No credit cards.

Landry
Flower Camping l'Eden

F-73210 Landry (Savoie) T: 04 79 07 61 81. E: info@camping-eden.net

alanrogers.com/FR73060

L'Eden is open to tourers in summer and winter. It is beside the Isere river and set in beautiful woodland glades, and is perfect for winter skiing and walking and cycling in summer. The site is set in a valley with the Alpine peaks as a backdrop. The 133 good, spacious pitches all have 10A electrical hook-ups and individual water supplies (available when no frost is likely). The clean, modern sanitary blocks are heated in colder weather and include a large drying room. There is a pool for summer lounging, a bar and a welcoming communal area with bar, TV and Internet access.

Facilities

Two heated toilet blocks have good facilities for babies and disabled visitors, and drying room. Small launderette. Communal area with bar, TV and Internet. Snack bar and takeaway (July/Aug). Swimming pool (June-Sept). Games room. Play area. Fishing. Ski passes for sale on-site. Off site: Rafting and canoeing opposite entrance. Shops and restaurants in village. Riding 10 km. Golf 15 km.

Open: 25 May - 15 September and 15 December - 5 May.

Directions

From the RN90 take D87 towards Landry. Site is on left after 250 m. and is well signed from the RN90. GPS: 45.57652, 6.73457

Charges guide

Per unit incl. 2 persons and electricity	€ 27.40
extra person	€ 5.30
child (under 12 yrs)	€ 2.80 - € 4.00

Largentière
Kawan Village les Ranchisses

Route de Rocher, F-07110 Largentière (Ardèche) T: 04 75 88 31 97. E: reception@lesranchisses.fr

alanrogers.com/FR07070

This is a very well equipped, modern campsite in a lesser known area of the Ardèche. There are 93 good-sized, level, grassy pitches, 38 for touring with electricity (10A) including 55 which are fully serviced, both shaded and part shaded. Good quality mobile homes and chalets are available to rent. A small river pool provides opportunities for bathing, fishing or canoeing (free life jackets), with one part of the area quite safe for youngsters. A high quality pool area, close to a wellness centre provides good free exercise and relaxation. Well run and with the emphasis on personal attention, this is a highly recommended site.

Facilities

Comprehensive toilet buildings include facilities for babies and disabled visitors. Laundry facilities. Motorcaravan services. Shop. Bar. Restaurant, takeaway/pizzeria. Two large pools, paddling pool (heated). Separate water slides. Wellness centre with sauna, gym, jacuzzi and hammam. Adventure style playground. Organised amusements for adults and children (from 1/7). Miniclub and mini theatre. Skate park. Tennis. Minigolf. Boules. Canoeing. WiFi over site (charged). Only one dog per pitch. Off site: Canoe, kayaking arranged (mid June-end Aug). Largentière 1.5 km.

Open: 16 April - 25 September.

Directions

Largentière is southwest of Aubenas and best approached using D104. Just beyond Uzer, 16 km. from Aubenas, turn northwest on D5. After 5 km. at far end of Largentière, fork left downhill signed Rocher and Valgorge. Site on left in 1.8 km. just beyond rocky gorge. The approach from Valgorge is not recommended. GPS: 44.56071, 4.28463

Charges guide

Per unit incl. 2 persons	€ 19.00 - € 43.00

Camping Cheques accepted.

For latest campsite news, availability and prices visit
alanrogers.com

Larnas
La Domaine d'Imbours

F-07220 Larnas (Ardèche) T: 04 75 54 39 50. E: imbours@franceloc.fr
alanrogers.com/FR07290

This large site is part of a holiday complex with many mobile homes (99), chalets (41), an hotel and 200 camping pitches. These are on scrub grass with some shade from mature trees and 6A electricity (long leads may be helpful). For those looking for organised activities in high season this complex is ideal, but fewer are arranged in low season. Many of the activities are found by the hotel which is about 1 km. from the camping area along a descending site road. Here is a large, exciting and well designed pool complex and in high season there are evening shows and dancing. There is a free shuttle service around the campsite in high season.

Facilities

Two fully equipped sanitary units. Facilities for children and disabled visitors. Laundry. Well stocked supermarket (site is remote). ATM. Bars and restaurants. Takeaway (1/6-3/9). Two pool complexes with excellent water chutes (outdoor pools heated 9/4-25/9, indoor pool all season). Adventure play area. Tennis. Bicycle hire. Quad bikes (school holidays). Riding. Aerial walkways and zipwires. Activity clubs and entertainment (high season). WiFi (free). Off site: Caves and the Ardèche Gorge within 25 km.

Open: 9 April - 25 September.

Directions

From N86 Bagnols-Aubanas road, exit onto D4 at Bourg St Andeo to Remeze (good road). Turn right at entrance to village on D362 towards Larnas and site is on right in Imbours. Do not attempt other routes with a caravan. GPS: 44.43681, 4.57754

Charges guide

Per unit incl. 2 persons	
and electricity	€ 20.00 - € 34.00
extra person	€ 4.70 - € 7.00

Lathuile
Camping l'Idéal

715 route de Chaparon, F-74210 Lathuile (Haute-Savoie) T: 04 50 44 32 97. E: camping-ideal@wanadoo.fr
alanrogers.com/FR74200

For panoramic views of mountains and the lake, this family run site is excellent. Trim and neat, the site is well cared for and the welcome is warm. The 300 pitches are generally large and well drained, some with small hedges but mostly open and with 6A electricity. These pitches share the site with chalets which are located at the top of the site well away from the tourers. L'Idéal is far enough from the lake to avoid the noise and crowds but close enough to take advantage of the facilities there. From the site you can cycle downhill to the Annecy cycle route.

Facilities

Three very well designed toilet blocks include excellent facilities for babies and disabled visitors. A further new block is planned. Laundry facilities. Shop (June-Sept). Bar. Restaurant, snack bar and takeaway (June-mid Aug). Two swimming pools. Tennis. Paragliding lessons. Bicycle hire. Play area. Children's club. Activities and excursions in high season. WiFi (charged). Off site: Lake 900 m. Golf 5 km.

Open: 8 May - 5 September.

Directions

Lathuile is 18 km. southeast of Annecy and site is well signed in the village. GPS: 45.79514, 6.20564

Charges guide

Per unit incl. 2 persons	
and electricity	€ 21.30 - € 29.30
extra person	€ 4.00 - € 7.00
child (2-6 yrs)	€ 3.00 - € 6.00

Laurac-en-Vivarais
Flower Camping Saint-Amand

Route des Défilés de Ruoms, quartier Saint Amand, F-07110 Laurac-en-Vivarais (Ardèche)
T: 04 75 36 84 45. E: st-amand@wanadoo.fr **alanrogers.com/FR07640**

Saint-Amand is a member of the Flower group and can be found around 15 km. west of Vallon Pont d'Arc, close to the appropriately named village of Bellevue. There are 68 touring pitches, most with electrical connections (6A) and good shade. A further 42 pitches are occupied by mobile homes and fully equipped tents available for rent. From the site's pool, there are some fine views across the surrounding scrubland and vineyards. Other amenities include a small restaurant, specialising in homemade pizzas and a new playing area for children. The closest shops are in the village of Laurac (2.5 km).

Facilities

Sanitary building with family shower and laundry facilities. Facilities for disabled visitors. Small shop. Pizzeria and snack bar. Takeaway. Swimming pool. Children's pool. Play area. Activity and entertainment programme. Mobile homes for rent. Free WiFi. Off site: Laurac 2.5 km. Vallon-Pont-d'Arc 15 km. Cycle and walking tracks.

Open: 2 April - 17 September.

Directions

From the north (Privas), head southwest using D104 towards Aubenas, continuing via Uzer and on for 3 km. to Bellevue. Turn left and site is signed from here to a right turn down a track which may be difficult for larger units. GPS: 44.49964, 4.30619

Charges guide

Per unit incl. 2 persons	
and electricity	€ 15.50 - € 23.90
extra person	€ 3.00 - € 4.50

For latest campsite news, availability and prices visit
alanrogers.com

Le Grand-Bornand
Camping Caravaning l'Escale

Route de la Patinoire, F-74450 Le Grand-Bornand (Haute-Savoie) T: 04 50 02 20 69.
E: contact@campinglescale.com **alanrogers.com/FR74070**

You are assured a good welcome in English from the Baur family at this beautifully maintained and picturesque site, situated at the foot of the Aravis mountain range. There are 149 pitches with 122 for touring. Of average size, part grass, part gravel, they are separated by trees and shrubs that give a little shade. All pitches have electricity and 86 are fully serviced. Rock pegs are essential. A 200-year-old building houses a bar/restaurant decorated in traditional style and offering regional dishes in a delightful, warm ambience. The village is 200 m. away and has all the facilities of a resort with activities for both summer and winter holidays. In summer, a variety of well signed footpaths and cycle tracks provide forest and mountain excursions. In winter the area provides superb facilities for downhill and cross-country skiing. This very popular campsite, set beside the picture postcard ski resort of Le Grand-Bornand, has wonderful views and is surrounded by fields of flowers in summer.

Facilities

Good toilet blocks (heated in winter) have all the necessary facilities. Drying room for skis, clothing and boots. Superb pool complex with interconnected indoor (all season) and outdoor pools and paddling pools (15/6-29/8), jacuzzi and water jets. Cosy bar/restaurant and takeaway (all season). Play area. Tennis. WiFi. Activities for adults and children. Video games. Discounts on organised walks and visits to Chamonix-Mont Blanc. Off site: Village (5 minutes walk), shops, bars, restaurants, archery, paragliding, golf, minigolf. Signed walks. Ice skating, snow shoes in winter. Free bus to cable car (500 m). Bicycle hire 200 m. Riding and golf 3 km.

Open: 15 December - 25 April, 1 June - 25 September.

Directions

From Annecy follow the D16 and D909 towards La Clusaz. At Saint Jean-de-Sixt, turn left at the roundabout D4 signed Grand-Bornand. Just before village fork right signed Vallée de Bouchet and camping. Site entrance is on right at roundabout in 1.2 km. GPS: 45.94036, 6.42842

Charges guide

Per unit incl. 2 persons and electricity	€ 20.30 - € 34.40
extra person (over 2 yrs)	€ 5.00 - € 5.90
dog	€ 2.30

Camping Caravaneige L'Escale

74450 Le Grand Bornand - France - Tel: +33 (0)4 50 02 20 69 - Fax: +33 (0)4 50 02 36 04
Email: contact@campinglescale.com - www.rentlescale.com

Les Abrets
Kawan Village le Coin Tranquille

6 chemin des Vignes, F-38490 Les Abrets (Isère) T: 04 76 32 13 48. E: contact@coin-tranquille.com
alanrogers.com/FR38010

Les Abrets is well placed for visits to the Savoie regions and the Alps. It is an attractive, well maintained site of 192 grass pitches (178 for tourers), all with 6A electricity. They are separated by neat hedges of hydrangea, flowering shrubs and a range of trees to make a lovely environment doubly enhanced by the rural aspect and marvellous views across to the mountains. This is a popular, family run site with friendly staff, making it a wonderful base for exploring the area. Set in the Dauphiny countryside north of Grenoble, le Coin Tranquille is truly a 'quiet corner', especially outside school holiday times.

Facilities

The central well appointed sanitary block is well kept, heated in low season. Facilities for children and disabled visitors. Two smaller blocks provide facilities in high season. Busy shop. Excellent restaurant. Heated swimming pool (1/5-30/9; no Bermuda style shorts) . Play area. Weekly entertainment (July/Aug) including live music (not discos). Bicycle hire (limited). WiFi. Off site: Les Abrets 2 km. Riding 6 km. Fishing 8 km. Golf 25 km.

Open: 1 April - 31 October.

Directions

From roundabout in Les Abrets take N6 towards Chambéry, turning left in 2 km. (signed Camping). Follow signs along country lane for just over 1 km. and entrance is on right. GPS: 45.54115, 5.60778

Charges guide

Per unit incl. 2 persons	€ 18.00 - € 32.00

Camping Cheques accepted.

For latest campsite news, availability and prices visit
alanrogers.com

Les Ollières-sur-Eyrieux
Camping le Domaine des Plantas

F-07360 Les Ollières-sur-Eyrieux (Ardèche) T: 04 75 66 21 53. E: plantas.ardeche@wanadoo.fr

alanrogers.com/FR07090

This is a good quality site in the beautiful, steep sided Eyrieux valley. There is a sandy beach beside the fairly fast-flowing river but the attractive swimming pool complex tempts you back for either sedate bathing or exciting slides. There are 76 steeply terraced and shaded touring pitches with 10A electricity. The walk up from some pitches to the original old farm buildings housing the reception, restaurant and bar is rewarded by a terrace with a spectacular viewpoint. Sporting and play areas near the river and an unusual themed adventure play area, children's clubs and evening entertainment should appeal to all.

Facilities

Two well equipped toilet blocks (one heated) including facilities to please the very young. Washing machines. Motorcaravan services. Small shop, bar, restaurant, disco. Heated, covered and outdoor swimming pools, paddling pool and toboggans. Themed adventure play area. Games area. Pétanque. High season children's activities, discos for 14-18 year olds (strictly no alcohol). Activities and excursions. WiFi (free). Chalets and mobile homes to rent. Only gas and electric barbecues. Off site: Riding 15 km.

Open: 21 April - 19 September.

Directions

Leave A7 exit 15 (Valence Sud). Follow signs to Montélimar via N7 for 7 km. At Beauchastel, take D120 to Ollières-sur-Eyrieux. Cross river, turn left and campsite signs give reassurance along the (3 km) narrow road with wider passing places (possible problem for larger outfits). GPS: 44.80917, 4.63581

Charges guide

Per unit incl. 2 persons	€ 24.00 - € 40.00
extra person	€ 4.70 - € 7.00

Les Ollières-sur-Eyrieux
Flower Camping le Chambourlas

F-07360 Les Ollières-sur-Eyrieux (Ardèche) T: 04 75 66 24 31. E: info@chambourlas.com

alanrogers.com/FR07190

Tucked away in a beautiful setting, in the hills above Privas, this is a small, neat and tidy, family owned site. The 78 large, grassy, some slightly sloping pitches (72 for touring, electricity 10A) are set on low terraces, separated by an interesting variety of trees with excellent views over the wooded hills. The attractive reception, restaurant and shop are in one building close to all the facilities. There is a private lake with a beach making it a tranquil place for fishing or canoeing. The site is not ideal for very large units due to the steep and narrow local roads.

Facilities

One modern, very clean toilet block with all necessary facilities including for disabled visitors. Bar (1/7-31/8). Restaurant and takeaway (15/5-28/8). Small shop (mid May-Oct). Swimming pool, paddling pool and sunbathing area (1/5-30/9). Play area. Boules. Good range of activities, some in low season, no discos. River fishing. Only gas or electric barbecues. WiFi (free). Wooden chalets and tents for rent. Off site: Many walks and bike rides. Bicycle hire 6 km. Les Ollières-sur-Eyrieux 6 km.

Open: 1 May - 1 October.

Directions

At traffic lights in Privas take D2 north, signed Les Ollieres/Le Cheylard. Follow road over two river bridges climbing gradually through the hills before descending to the site entrance on the right after 14 km. Site access road appears steeper and narrower than it actually is. GPS: 44.78155, 4.61806

Charges guide

Per unit incl. 2 persons	€ 17.50 - € 31.50
extra person	€ 6.00 - € 6.50

Les Ollières-sur-Eyrieux
Kawan Village Mas de Champel

Quartier Champel, F-07360 Les Ollières-sur-Eyrieux (Ardèche) T: 04 75 66 23 23.

E: masdechampel@wanadoo.fr **alanrogers.com/FR07440**

At Mas de Champel you will be invited to relax in a region of natural beauty. Once a farm with orchards located at the heart of the valley of the Eyrieux, rounded river worn boulders are featured in the buildings that house the site's very good restaurant, bar, wellness centre and reception. With 51 generously sized touring pitches with 6A electricity and varying degrees of shade and 44 chalets and mobile homes to rent, the campsite is able to provide a programme of entertainment for all family members. There are pools and a riverside beach offers fishing, bathing and canoeing.

Facilities

Two clean toilet blocks with all the necessary facilities, with a third opened in high season. Motorcaravan services. Bar, good restaurant with terrace and takeaway. Swimming pool, heated paddling pool, fun pool, jacuzzi and sunbathing area. Wellness centre. Games/TV room. Play area. Pétanque. Bicycle hire. Fishing. Canoe hire. Organised family activities (July/Aug). Only gas barbecues permitted. WiFi (free). Off site: Aquarock Centre canoeing and aerial adventure park 1 km. Riding 7 km.

Open: 14 April - 23 September.

Directions

Leave N86 south of Valence at Beauchastel. Turn west, D120, to Ollières-sur-Eyrieux (about 20 km). Site is on right at entrance to village and is signed. GPS: 44.80721, 4.61489

Charges guide

Per unit incl. 2 persons and electricity	€ 19.00 - € 28.30
extra person	€ 4.40 - € 6.90

For latest campsite news, availability and prices visit
alanrogers.com

Lus-la-Croix-Haute

Camping Champ la Chèvre

F-26220 Lus-la-Croix-Haute (Drôme) T: 04 92 58 50 14. E: info@campingchamplachevre.com

alanrogers.com/FR26270

This is a pleasant, unpretentious site with some really magnificent views across towards the western Alps. Formerly a farm (hence its name!) and now under new management, Champ la Chèvre is undergoing a steady process of refurbishment and is attractively located just 200 m. from the village and 500 m. from the D1075. There are 100 pitches, for the most part sunny and quite spacious, and many with fine mountain views. Some pitches are sloping and most pitches have 6A electrical connections. A new heated and covered pool and a further heated shower block will be completed for 2012. This is a good base for exploring the mountains and the owners have many ideas for excursions in the area, including downhill mountain biking, swimming in local rivers and hundreds of kilometres of walking trails. The village of Lus-La-Croix-Haute is pretty and has a good range of shops and a small railway station.

Facilities

Centrally located toilet block with facilities for disabled visitors, and a second block by the entrance. Motorcaravan services. Bar, restaurant and takeaway (all season). Heated swimming pool (15/6-31/8). Play area. Children's club (July/Aug). Minigolf. Mobile homes and chalets for rent. WiFi. Off site: Riding 100 m. Village of Lus-La-Croix-Haute 200 m. Railway station 300 m. Bicycle hire 500 m. Fishing 3 km. Tennis. Many walking and cycle trails.

Open: 23 April - 17 September.

Directions

From the north, head south from Grenoble initially on the A480 and then the A51 towards Sisteron. Then join the southbound N75 for around 35 km. to Lus-La-Croix-Haute. Drive through the village and site is well signed. GPS: 44.66440, 5.70742

Charges guide

Per unit incl. 2 persons
and electricity   € 19.00 - € 23.30
extra person   € 4.30 - € 5.50

Camping** Champ la Chèvre

Mobile Homes, chalets and cabins for rent. Bar, restaurant, take-away and pizza during high season, covered and heated pool. New sanitary facilities, table tennis, soccer, volleyball, jeu de boules and evening entertainment

Please make reservations for high season

D505 - 26620 Lus La Croix Haute - Tel.: 0033 (0)4 92 58 50 14
E-mail: info@campingchamplachevre.com - www.campingchamplachevre.com

Summerseason from 26/4 to 28/9
Winterseason from 28/9 to 26/4

Marsanne

Camping les Bastets

Quartier les Bastets, F-26740 Marsanne (Drôme) T: 04 75 90 35 03. E: contact@campinglesbastets.com

alanrogers.com/FR26190

You will find a warm welcome from Thierry and Marie Jose at this small, family run site. It has been carved out of the rocky hillside and has wonderful views over the beautiful Drôme Provençale and the mountains beyond. The whole site is dotted with lavender plants growing between the shrubs and mature trees. There are 62 pitches with 54 for touring, all with 10A electricity and most with their own water supply and drainage. The upper pitches are only suitable for tents, and access to the irregularly shaped touring pitches can be difficult – Thierry will provide tractor assistance when necessary. An area for motorcaravans near the entrance has easy access. This site is ideal for discovering the historic towns and villages of the Drôme Provençale by car, bike (those strong of limb) and on foot.

Facilities

One toilet block at the bottom of the site and another higher up provide good modern facilities. Motorcaravan service point. Shop (July/Aug). Restaurant and takeaway (full service July/Aug; to order off season). Excellent swimming pool next to bar (all season). TV/games room. Play area. Organised family activities and excursions (high season). Central barbecue area. Electric barbecues only. Off site: Marsanne 2 km. Montélimar (home of Nougat) 10 km. Fishing, riding and golf 10 km.

Open: 1 April - 15 October.

Directions

Leave A7 at exit 17 (Montélimar Nord) and head south on the N7 for just over 3 km. Turn left on D74 and in 1.5 km. turn left on D107. In a further 5.5 km. turn left on the D105 signed Marsanne. Pass through village and in 2 km. turn right (site signed). Site is 300 m. on the left. GPS: 44.657733, 4.89075

Charges guide

Per unit incl. 2 persons
and electricity   € 20.00 - € 30.00
Camping Cheques accepted.

For latest campsite news, availability and prices visit

alanrogers.com

Lussas
Ludocamping

Route de Lavilledieu, F-07170 Lussas (Ardèche) T: 04 75 94 21 22. E: info@ludocamping.com

alanrogers.com/FR07170

Ludocamping is set amongst the magnificent scenery of the Auzon valley. This is a quiet family campsite run by a very friendly French family with access to a wide range of activities. The 160 grassy pitches, all for touring, with 5/10A electricity, are in two areas. The upper terrace has large pitches with wonderful views but little shade. The lower area, closer to the small river, has pitches set naturally amongst the trees and they have good shade. There is a large swimming pool (heated all season) and a good sized paddling pool, both with attractively terraced sunbathing areas with views of the forested slopes. The site's restaurant area offers both a traditional fixed price menu with a children's option and snacks. The valley is a delight for nature lovers, particularly in early season when the many wild flowers and cherry trees are at their best. There are numerous birds including eagles and the elusive golden oriole, heard but seldom seen. A ride through Darbres and Mirabel has breathtaking views.

Facilities

Clean, good quality toilet blocks offer all necessary facilities. Bar, restaurant and takeaway (15/5-15/9) with terrace. Play area. Recreational area next to river. Fishing. Bicycle hire. Club for over 6/7 yr olds offering a very wide range of activities. Off season club for older children. Seniors excursions in campsite coach. Only gas and electric barbecues. Free WiFi around the bar. Chalets, mobile homes and tents for rent. Off site: Lussas 600 m. Riding 6 km. Gliding, hang-gliding, canoeing.

Open: 15 April - 15 October.

Directions

From Montélimar take N102 west towards Aubenas, pass around Villeneuve, at traffic lights in Lavilledieu turn right onto D224 towards Lussas. Site entrance is on right just before village (about 4 km. from N102). GPS: 44.60495, 4.4712

Charges guide

Per unit incl. 2 persons and electricity	€ 18.00 - € 31.00
extra person	€ 3.00 - € 6.50

Mobile homes for rent

L'Ardèche du sud

Heated pool 220M² and paddling pool . 6ha of spacious, comfortable and shady pitches on the side of the river. Bar, snack bar, shop, children's animation in July and August. Sports activities.

**LUDO CAMPING
07170 LUSSAS - FRANCE**
Tél. (+33) (0)4 75 94 21 22
info@ludocamping.com

www.ludocamping.com

Massignieu-de-Rives
Kawan Village Lac du Lit du Roi

La Tuillière, F-01300 Massignieu-de-Rives (Ain) T: 04 79 42 12 03. E: info@camping-savoie.com

alanrogers.com/FR01040

This attractive and well cared for, family run site is ideal for those seeking an active holiday in a peaceful setting. This superb, picturesque area offers wonderful opportunities for exploration by foot, bicycle, car and boat. Take time to sample the wines and other local produce on offer. Of the 120 pitches (electricity 10A), 90 are available for touring, all being close to the lake and many having wonderful views over the lake and the wooded hills beyond. The slightly sloping, grassy pitches are set on low terraces and are partly separated by hedging and a variety of trees give some shade.

Facilities

Two modern toilet blocks offer all necessary facilities with provision for disabled visitors. Washing machines. Motorcaravan services. Small shop, bar, restaurant and terrace. Bread. Swimming pool, children's play area with water features. Tennis. Play area by lake. Grassy beach, pedaloes, canoes, surf bikes for hire. Bicycle hire. Lake fishing. Winter caravan storage. Free WiFi. Fridge and barbecue rental. Off site: Shops at Belley 8 km. Lac du Bourget (watersports, boat hire). Golf 8 km. Riding 15 km.

Open: 11 April - 4 October.

Directions

Site is about 8 km. east of Belley. Travelling south on N504 towards Aix-les-Bains bypass Belley and at roundabout (Champion supermarket) turn east D992, signed Culoz and Seyssel. After 4 km. turn right over bridge, D37 signed Massignieu. Follow signs to site (2 km). GPS: 45.76883, 5.76942

Charges guide

Per unit incl. 2 persons and electricity	€ 17.50 - € 28.00

Camping Cheques accepted.

For latest campsite news, availability and prices visit
alanrogers.com

Matafelon-Granges
Camping des Gorges de l'Oignin

Rue du Lac, F-01580 Matafelon-Granges (Ain) T: 04 74 76 80 97. E: camping.lesgorgesdeloignin@wanadoo.fr
alanrogers.com/FR01050

This family run, terraced site (English spoken) offers lovely views across the lake to the hills beyond. There are 132 good sized pitches, 102 for touring, separated by young trees and flowering shrubs and with a choice of grass or hardstanding. About half have their own water point and all have 10A electricity. Twin-axle caravans are not accepted. The reception, bar/restaurant and the pool complex are at the top of the site with a steep road down to the terraces and the rest of the campsite. At the bottom of the site is a large grassy area next to the lake for sunbathing and activities.

Facilities

Two modern, well equipped and clean toilet blocks with all the usual facilities except facilities for disabled visitors. Bar/restaurant, takeaway and TV room (July/Aug). Swimming pool, paddling pool and 'lazy river' (1/6-30/9). Playground and sports area. Swimming, fishing and boating on the lake (no motorboats). Off site: Matafelon 800 m. Golf and riding 2 km. Thoirette 6 km. Oyonnax with range of shops, market, bar/restaurants 10 km.

Open: 1 April - 30 September.

Directions

Matafelon is 40 km. east of Bourg-en-Bresse. Leave autoroute A404 at Oyonnax, exit 11 and head west on D13 to Matafelon (10 km). On entering village and opposite the Mairie turn left, signed camping, and descend to site (800 m). GPS: 46.25535, 5.55717

Charges guide

Per unit incl. 2 persons and electricity	€ 17.00 - € 26.20
extra person	€ 3.60 - € 5.80

Menglon
Kawan Village l'Hirondelle

Bois Saint Ferreol, F-26410 Menglon (Drôme) T: 04 75 21 82 08. E: contact@campinghirondelle.com
alanrogers.com/FR26130

This is a natural, spacious and popular, family run site; you are assured of a good welcome. It lies in a beautiful valley, south of the Vercors mountains and the Vercors National Park, beside the River Bez. The 170 large to very large pitches, 112 for touring, are stony and slightly uneven (rock pegs advised). They lie in natural openings in woodland and some have views over the fields and hills beyond. For 2012 there are 53 new huge pitches, some with good views and 16 have a private bathroom. All have electricity (3/6/10A) and long leads are advised.

Facilities

Six large toilet blocks offer all the necessary facilities (16 private bathrooms). Good bar/restaurant/takeaway. Small shop sells bread. Excellent pool complex with toboggans, paddling pool, water games and beach area (1/5-13/9). Ample play room. River bathing. Club/TV room. Fishing. Football, boules, volleyball, archery. Multisports court. Bicycle hire. Organised events (high season). WiFi (charged). Off site: Riding 3 km. Canoeing, kayaking, climbing, rambling, mountain biking and cycling.

Open: 28 April - 15 September.

Directions

From Die follow D93 southwards and after 6 km. at Pont de Quart, turn left on D539 signed Châtillon. After about 4 km. turn right on D140, signed Menglon. Site entrance is shortly on right just after crossing a small river. GPS: 44.68142, 5.44743

Charges 2012

Per unit incl. 2 persons	€ 20.90 - € 38.20
extra person	€ 5.20 - € 9.30

Camping Cheques accepted.

Mens
Camping le Pré Rolland

Rue de la Piscine, F-38710 Mens (Isère) T: 04 76 34 65 80. E: contact@camping-prerolland.fr
alanrogers.com/FR38230

Le Pré Rolland is a small, well maintained family run site on the outskirts of the little town of Mens. It is surrounded by beautiful mountain scenery making it an ideal base for nature lovers touring this little known region of the Trièves. There are 98 mainly level, good sized grass pitches, 90 for touring and all having electricity (10A). Some are delineated by flowering shrubs and mature trees and are quite shady, others are more open and sunny. The snack bar and bar, with terrace overlooking the pool is a peaceful place to unwind after a day exploring the region. There is no on-site entertainment.

Facilities

Two well maintained and clean toilet blocks with all the necessary facilities, including those for babies and campers with disabilities. Covered area with tables, small kitchen and bunk room. Bar/snack bar (all season). Adjacent municipal swimming pool, free (1/6-31/8). Day room/TV. Playground. WiFi (free). Off site: Small town of Mens with small shops, bar and restaurant 500 m. Fishing 1.5 km. Riding 2 km. Marked walks and cycle rides. Rock climbing, bungee jumping. Many small towns and villages.

Open: 1 May - 30 September.

Directions

From the A51 going south from Grenoble take the N75 towards Sisteron. After about 50 km, at Clelles, turn east D521 to Mens. On entering town turn right, signed site and 'piscine'. GPS: 44.814807, 5.7485

Charges guide

Per unit incl. 2 persons and electricity	€ 18.00 - € 20.50
extra person	€ 6.00 - € 7.50

For latest campsite news, availability and prices visit
alanrogers.com

Mirabel-et-Blacons

Gervanne Camping

Bellevue, F-26400 Mirabel-et-Blacons (Drôme) T: 04 75 40 00 20. E: info@gervanne-camping.com

alanrogers.com/FR26120

This spacious, riverside site, run by a friendly family, has 174 pitches, with 154 for touring (with 6A electricity). It is in two sections either side of a road, connected by an underpass. The upper section is adjacent to the bar, restaurant and good swimming pool with mountain views. The pitches are of average size with some shade and are separated by a few small shrubs and trees. The lower section, closer to the river, is less formally laid out with mature trees offering plenty of shade. Access to and on site is easy here.

Facilities

Four very clean toilet blocks including good facilities for babies and disabled visitors. Laundry. Motorcaravan service point. Bar/restaurant (15/5-15/9) with simple menu, takeaway service and free WiFi. Heated swimming pool (28/4-30/9). Small play area. Football pitch. Boules. Bicycle hire. Electric and gas barbecues only. WiFi. Off site: Supermarket next door. Canoeing and bathing in adjacent River Drôme. Old village of Mirabelle 1.5 km. Riding 5 km. Golf 13 km. Crest with ancient Château.

Open: 2 April - 30 September.

Directions

Leave A7 autoroute, exit 16 Loriol. Take D104, then D164 bypassing Crest. After 6 km, at roundabout, turn left D164A. Cross river into Mirabel-et-Blacons, left at roundabout, site is in 200m. GPS: 44.71110, 5.09015

Charges 2012

| Per unit incl. 2 persons and electricity | € 18.00 - € 27.00 |
| extra person | € 4.00 - € 6.70 |

Murs-et-Gèlignieux

Camping Ile de la Comtesse

Route des Abrets, F-01300 Murs-et-Gélignieux (Ain) T: 04 79 87 23 33. E: camping.comtesse@wanadoo.fr

alanrogers.com/FR01060

A very pleasant, family run, lakeside site, there are 100 medium to large, level grassy pitches here. With 58 for touring, many are separated by low hedges and tall poplar trees offer some shade. All have 6A electricity (but very long leads may be necessary) and most have views over the lake and craggy hills beyond. High season activities are aimed mainly at younger children and the family. Fishing, sailing, canoeing and bathing are possible on the lake that borders the site. There is plenty of space around the lake for leisure activities, including marked walks and cycle trails.

Facilities

Traditionally styled, modern and well appointed toilet block with all the necessary facilities. Facilities for disabled visitors. Motorcaravan service point. Small bar/restaurant with takeaway and small shop. Large marquee for TV and organised activities. Heated outdoor swimming and paddling pools. Daily programme of activities for young children and the family in high season. Bicycle hire. WiFi. Off site: Restaurant adjacent. Beach 300 m. Shops in Aost 5 km. Walaibi Theme Park 10 km. Riding 10 km.

Open: 3 April - 30 September.

Directions

From the A43 (Lyon - Chambery) autoroute, take exit 10 and go north on D592 for about 10 km. After crossing the lake turn right on the D992 and site is shortly on the right. GPS: 45.63995, 5.64900

Charges guide

| Per unit incl. 2 persons and electricity | € 15.00 - € 29.80 |
| extra person | € 4.90 - € 7.50 |

Neydens

Camping la Colombière

Saint Julien-en-Genevois, F-74160 Neydens (Haute-Savoie) T: 04 50 35 13 14. E: la.colombiere@wanadoo.fr

alanrogers.com/FR74060

La Colombière, a family owned site, is on the edge of the small village of Neydens, a few minutes from the A40 autoroute and only a short drive from Geneva. It is an attractive site with 115 pitches (93 for touring with electricity 5-15A), all reasonably level and separated by fruit trees, flowering shrubs and hedges. Neydens makes a good base for visiting Geneva and the region around the lake. It is a very pleasant, friendly site where you may drop in for a night stop – and stay for several days! The site is open all year for motorcaravans and suitable caravans. English is spoken. A Sites et Paysages member.

Facilities

Good sanitary blocks (one heated) include facilities for disabled visitors. Motorcaravan services. Fridge hire. Gas supplies. Good bar/restaurant with terrace (1/5-15/9). New heated, indoor pool, spa pool and jacuzzi (21/3-11/11). Organised activities. Bicycle hire. Archery. Boules. Playground. WiFi. Max.1 dog. Off site: Fishing and riding 1 km. Switzerland 3 km. St Julien-en-Genevois 5 km.

Open: 20 March - 11 November
(all year for motorcaravans and suitable caravans).

Directions

From A40 south of Geneva take exit 13 and then N201 towards Annecy. After 2 km. turn left into village of Neydens and follow campsite signs to site in just over 1 km. GPS: 46.1201, 6.10552

Charges guide

Per unit incl. 2 persons and electricity	€ 21.00 - € 32.00
extra person	€ 4.00 - € 6.00
child (2-12 yrs)	€ 3.50 - € 4.50

For latest campsite news, availability and prices visit

alanrogers.com

Neyrac-les-Bains

Domaine de la Plage

Neyrac-les-Bains, F-07380 Aubenas (Ardèche) T: 04 75 36 40 59. E: contact@lecampingdelaplage.com

alanrogers.com/FR07570

A great deal of care and attention to detail has gone into developing this compact site and its superb facilities. Of its 45 pitches, only 12 are available for camping and advance booking is essential. The site is beautifully landscaped and the facilities are sympathetically incorporated into a former textile factory. It has a very attractive solar heated pool and sunbathing terrace, with bar and snack service, on-site shop, games room and library. The river is directly accessed from the site with a bridge walkway crossing a waterfall and leading to a sports and picnic area. A Sites et Paysages member.

Facilities

Modern sanitary facilities include facilities for disabled visitors (access around the site is quite steep). Laundry room. Fridge hire. Microwave and oven facilities. Gas. Bar. Snack service. Shop. Solar heated swimming pool and poolside bar. Games room. Library/TV room. Pétanque. Play area. Multisports area. Entertainment programmes. Fishing. Canoeing excursions. WiFi (free). Off site: Thermal baths 700 m. Bicycle hire 2 km. Tennis 3 km. Golf 8 km.

Open: 29 March - 23 October.

Directions

From A7 exit 17 take N7 (Montélimar) for 20 km. Turn west on N102 to Aubenas. Continue on N102 for 30 km. towards Neyrac-les-Bains. Cross river at Pont-de-Labeaume and site is 2 km, on left just before entering village. GPS: 44.6733, 4.2594

Charges guide

Per unit incl. 2 persons and electricity	€ 19.00 - € 31.00
extra person	€ 4.00 - € 5.00

Passy

Village Center les Iles

245 route des Lacs, F-74190 Passy (Haute-Savoie) T: 04 99 57 21 21. E: contact@village-center.com

alanrogers.com/FR74210

This Alpine site is approached by a lakeside road with mountains to the left and with stunning views of Mont Blanc straight ahead. Set in an area with oak trees giving shade, there are 253 pitches (196 for tourers, most with 10A electricity), which are divided by 1.2 m. high beech hedges. A small, high season takeaway is located close to the play area allowing relaxed child supervision. An electric railway next to the site and a distant motorway may cause some noise. This is a good base for walking and cycling, and the municipal watersports area in which the site is set offers a range of water-based activities as well as an adventure course set amongst the trees around the lake.

Facilities

Three older but acceptable toilet blocks include hot showers and a WC/shower for disabled visitors. Laundry facilities. A new bar/restaurant for the 2012 season. Chalets to rent. WiFi (charged). Off site: Adjacent activity area centred around the lake. Buses nearby. Fishing 500 m. Shops, restaurants and bars in Passy 2 km. Riding 10 km. Golf 20 km. Excellent centre for walking and cycling.

Open: 5 December - 13 March, 14 May - 10 December.

Directions

Site is west of Passy. From the A40 take exit 21 (Chamonix) and drive through Passy and take the D199, first right over level crossing. Site is at end of road behind municipal car park (signed). GPS: 45.9239, 6.6504

Charges guide

Per unit incl. 2 persons and electricity	€ 14.00 - € 18.00

Peisey-Nancroix

Flower Camping les Lanchettes

Route de Boverêche (D87), Nancroix, F-73210 Peisey-Nancroix (Savoie) T: 04 79 07 93 07. E: lanchettes@free.fr **alanrogers.com/FR73030**

This site is close to the beautiful Vanoise National Park and at 1,470 m. is one of the highest campsites in this guide. There is a climb to the site but the spectacular scenery is well worth the effort. It is a natural, terraced site with 90 good size, reasonably level and well drained, grassy pitches, with 70 used for touring units, all having electricity (3-10A). Outside taps are only available in summer because of the altitude and cold winters. For those who love walking and mountain biking, wonderful scenery, flora and fauna, this is the site for you.

Facilities

Well appointed heated toilet block. Motorcaravan services. Restaurant, takeaway (July/Aug. and winter). Playground. Club/TV room. Large tent/marquee used in bad weather. In winter a small bus (free) runs to the ski lifts every 30 minutes. Free WiFi. Off site: Riding next to site. Peisey-Nancroix, restaurants, bars and shops 3 km. Les Arcs winter sports centre, outdoor swimming pool and bicycle hire 6 km. Golf and indoor pool 8 km. Lakeside beach 10 km. Walks in National Park.

Open: 15 December - 30 April, 1 June - 15 October.

Directions

From Albertville take N90 towards Bourg-St-Maurice, through Aime. In 9 km. turn right on D87, signed Peisey-Nancroix. Follow a winding hilly road (with hairpin bends) for 10 km. Pass through Peisey-Nancroix; site on right about 1 km. beyond Nancroix. GPS: 45.53137, 6.77560

Charges guide

Per unit incl. 2 persons and electricity	€ 12.50 - € 14.10
extra person	€ 4.20 - € 4.70

For latest campsite news, availability and prices visit

alanrogers.com

Pélussin
Camping Bel'Epoque du Pilat

Route de Malleval, F-42410 Pélussin (Loire) T: 04 74 87 66 60. E: camping-belepoque@orange.fr
alanrogers.com/FR42030

This is a peaceful, family run site located within the relatively little known Pilat Regional Park overlooking the attractive town of Pélussin. There are 70 good sized, slightly uneven and sloping, grassy pitches, of which 50 are for touring (electricity 6A). They are separated by trees and some hedging with most having some shade and some having good views over the valley below. The site is well maintained with an attractive pool and small bar and snack bar with takeaways (only July and August). Large outfits accepted but care needed on narrow winding roads, please use recommended route.

Facilities

Well appointed toilet block with facilities for disabled visitors. Bar (1/5-30/8), snack bar, takeaway (1/7-31/8). Swimming pool (May-Sept). Tennis. Play area. WiFi. Bicycle hire. Entertainment for young children (high season). Off site: Fishing, riding 500 m. Water sports 7 km. Golf 25 km. Vienne (Roman town). Safari park at Peaugres. Excursions to Côtes du Rhone vineyards (côtes rôties, Condrieu). Lyon (50 km. to the north).

Open: 1 April - 30 September.

Directions

Leave A7 autoroute, exit 10 Vienne 34 km. south of Lyon, take N86 south to Chavanay. Turn west D7, climb to Pélussin. On entering the village bear left, site signed. Site on right in 1.5 km. Only recommended route. GPS: 45.4139, 4.69139

Charges guide

Per unit incl. 2 persons and electricity (6A)	€ 19.50 - € 23.50
extra person	€ 5.00

Pont-de-Vaux
Camping les Ripettes

Chavannes-sur-Reyssouze, F-01190 Pont-de-Vaux (Ain) T: 03 85 30 66 58. E: info@camping-les-ripettes.com
alanrogers.com/FR01030

A friendly welcome is assured from the owners of this spacious site situated in quiet, flat countryside near the pleasant small town of Pont-de-Vaux. The 2.5-hectare site has 54 large (100 sq.m. to 400 sq.m) level grassy pitches, 51 of which are available to tourists. Nearly all are separated by hedges and about half are shaded by the many trees on the site. All but two have electrical connections (10A), and there are ample water points. The site is a useful stop on the way to or from the south of France, and also serves as a centre to explore the interesting surrounding area.

Facilities

Two well appointed, small sanitary blocks contain a suite for disabled visitors. Washing machine and dryer. Limited range of food stocked and wine, ice cream, meat for barbecues at reception. Two swimming pools. Areas for ball games. Board games, books. WiFi. Communal Sunday barbecues are popular. Off site: Restaurant 1 km. Riding 2 km. Shops in Pont-de-Vaux 4 km. Fishing 4 km.

Open: 1 April - 30 September.

Directions

Site is 18 km. northeast of Macon. Leave N6 at Fleurville (14 km. south of Tournus). Go east on D933A to Pont-de-Vaux (5 km) where site is signed. GPS: 46.44455, 4.98067

Charges guide

Per unit incl. 2 persons and electricity	€ 16.50 - € 20.00
extra person	€ 3.60 - € 4.00

Pont-de-Vaux
Camping Aux Rives du Soleil

Le Port, F-01190 Pont-de-Vaux (Ain) T: 03 85 30 33 65. E: info@rivesdusoleil.com
alanrogers.com/FR01070

Aux Rives du Soleil is a spacious and relaxed, family run campsite beside the unfenced, wide and sometimes powerful river Saône, which forms the border between Burgundy and Rhône-Alpes. There are 160 grass pitches with 140 used for touring units. Some are separated by beech hedges with shade, sometimes heavy, while others are on open grassland. Many have pleasant river or country views. All have electricity (6A) but extremely long leads are sometimes needed. There is some occasional noise from the river, the distant motorway and the TGV. At certain times, access for heavy outfits may be difficult due to soft pitches. Twin-axle caravans are not accepted.

Facilities

Two toilet blocks with acceptable facilities, one accessed by steep stairs. Some pitches far from these blocks. Very small shop in reception. Bar/restaurant with TV room. Takeaway (mid June-end Aug). Unheated swimming pool (15/5-15/9). Unheated paddling pool and play area by entrance. Entertainment for children under 12 (July/Aug). Small children's club and some family activities (high season). Bicycle hire. River bathing and fishing. Boat launching and canoeing. WiFi. Off site: Shops, bars, restaurants and weekly market in Pont-de-Vaux 3 km.

Open: 22 April - 17 October.

Directions

Leave A6 at Tournus and head south on the D906. At Fleurville take the D933a across the Saône. The entrance is immediately on the right after crossing the river. Well signed. GPS: 46.446967, 4.898867

Charges guide

Per unit incl. 2 persons and electricity	€ 22.00 - € 25.00
extra person	€ 5.00 - € 6.00
child (under 3 yrs)	free
dog	€ 3.50

For latest campsite news, availability and prices visit
alanrogers.com

Pradons

Camping les Coudoulets

Pradons, F-07120 Ruoms (Ardèche) T: 04 75 93 94 95. E: camping@coudoulets.com

alanrogers.com/FR07130

Situated beside the river Ardèche between Ruoms and the pretty village of Balazuc, Camping les Coudoulets is well cared for and would suit those who prefer a more intimate and peaceful campsite. It is run by a very friendly family who also own a small vineyard and their highly recommended wine is on sale in the bar. There are 125 good sized, grassy and well shaded pitches, separated by trees and shrubs. There are 109 for touring, all with 10-16A electricity. There is an area for bathing in the river and it is an ideal spot for canoeists. Organised family activities take place in July/August.

Facilities

Very good, clean and modern sanitary block with all the necessary facilities including excellent facilities for disabled visitors. Motorcaravan services. Bar, TV, terrace (May-Sept). Bread and newspapers to order, ices, drinks. Snacks and takeaway (July/Aug). Small heated swimming pool, paddling pool. Superb new aquatic play area and pool for children (May-Sept). Play areas. Bouncy castles. Fishing. WiFi (charged). Organised activities in high season. Tourist information. Off site: Shop 300 m.

Open: 15 April - 15 September.

Directions

Leave Montélimar westwards on N102 towards Aubenas. After passing Villeneuve-de-Berg turn left on D103 towards Vogüé for 5 km. Turn left on D579 towards Ruoms, site on right on entering Pradons (10 km). GPS: 44.47663, 4.35857

Charges guide

Per unit incl. 2 persons	
and electricity	€ 17.00 - € 31.00
extra person	€ 4.00 - € 7.00

Privas

Kawan Village Ardèche

Boulevard de Paste, F-07000 Privas (Ardèche) T: 04 75 64 05 80. E: jcray@wanadoo.fr

alanrogers.com/FR07180

This spacious, family run site is on the southern outskirts of Privas and aims to provide a warm friendly atmosphere. There are 166 large, grass, mostly level pitches, of which 131 are for tourers with 10A electricity and trees offering varying degrees of shade. It is a good base for exploring the lesser known parts of the Ardèche, with bus and coach trips available. On site there is something for young and old with bar, restaurant, heated swimming pool complex, and multisports area with outdoor gym equipment. There is also a play area and a miniclub with an emphasis on children aged 6-12 yrs. Music and dancing are organised near the bar and a welcome drink is offered when details of local attractions are given.

Facilities

Two toilet blocks, only one open in low season. Facilities for disabled visitords. Motorcaravan service point. Bar and restaurant (1/5-30/9). Swimming pool planned. Boules. Play area. Trampoline. Multisports area. Miniclub (1/5-11/9). Entertainment (high season). WiFi at the bar (free). Only gas barbecues are permitted. Chalets, mobile homes and tents for rent. Off site: Supermarket 100 m. Bicycle hire 2 km. Riding 5 km.

Open: 15 April - 30 September.

Directions

From the A7 motorway (Loriol) take exit 16 towards Privas. At Le Pouzin use heavy goods route, D86, D22 then D2. In Privas at roundabout (near Intermarché) look for signs Espace Ouvéze exit left and take second left, signed campsite and Espace Ouvéze. GPS: 44.72611, 4.59845

Charges guide

Per unit incl. 2 persons	
and electricity	€ 19.50 - € 26.80

Camping Cheques accepted.

Recoubeau-Jansac

Camping le Couriou

F-26310 Recoubeau-Jansac (Drôme) T: 04 75 21 33 23. E: camping.lecouriou@wanadoo.fr

alanrogers.com/FR26340

Le Couriou is a family run site in the beautiful Drôme countryside just south of Die. There are 131 stony/grassy, level pitches of varying sizes with 102 for touring (6A electricity). They are laid out on high terraces with views over the surrounding wooded hills; not ideal for those with walking difficulties. The pitches are separated by some shrubs and a variety of trees giving some shade. Though the site roads are quite steep, access is not difficult for large outfits. It has a large swimming pool complex, bar and restaurant, all open to the public. Only electric barbecues allowed on site.

Facilities

Three adequate toilet blocks with facilities for babies and campers with disabilities. Washing machines/dryer. Shop, bar, restaurant/takeaway (1/6-30/8). Four heated swimming pools, toboggans, paddling pool, sauna, massage (open to public). Multisports area, table tennis, boules. Off site: Fishing 500m. Recoubeau 1 km. Luc-en-Diois 5 km. Riding 5 km. Bike hire 10 km.

Open: 1 May - 30 August

Directions

From Die take D93 south for 14 km. Just before Recoubeau turn right, site signed, to site. GPS: 44.658534, 5.407172

Charges guide

Per unit incl. 2 persons	
and electricity	€ 16.60 - € 28.90
extra person	€ 4.00 - € 7.30

For latest campsite news, availability and prices visit

alanrogers.com

Ruoms
Yelloh! Village la Plaine
F-07120 Ruoms (Ardèche) T: 04 75 39 65 83. E: info@yellohvillage-la-plaine.com
alanrogers.com/FR07250

This is a high quality campsite with full provision for families of all ages with a beautiful riverside location. La Plaine is quiet in low season, but in high season with all-day and evening activities for both teenagers and adults, and a miniclub each day, there should be something for everyone! There are 212 pitches of moderate size, of which 160 have electricity. They are protected from the sun and marked by many trees. A varied programme of entertainment is provided most evenings in high season. This is a young family site for people with lots of energy, perhaps not for a quiet holiday in high season! There are 77 pitches used for their own air-conditioned mobile homes.

Facilities

Three clean, modern sanitary blocks with all facilities for young children and disabled visitors. Laundry room. Fridge hire. Shop, restaurant, bar and takeaway. Heated pool complex. Gym. Games area and TV. Boules. Football field. Play area. Fitness room. Activity programme. Miniclub. Fishing. River beach. Multisports area. Bicycle hire. WiFi over site (charged). Off site: Riding 2 km. Shops 3 km.

Open: 16 April - 17 September.

Directions

Exit Ruoms south on the D579 and at junction 2 km, south, take D111 signed St Ambroix. Site is on the left. GPS: 44.427067, 4.335617

Charges guide

Per unit incl. 2 persons and electricity (6A)	€ 15.00 - € 42.00
extra person	€ 5.00 - € 8.00

Ruoms
Camping la Digue
Chauzon, F-07120 Ruoms (Ardèche) T: 04 75 39 63 57. E: info@camping-la-digue.fr
alanrogers.com/FR07330

The circuitous route to la Digue is worth the effort as you will be greeted with a warm welcome from its resident owners, who provide their visitors with a great, yet calm, family atmosphere. There are plenty of outdoor activities available, both on and off the site. M. Elne and his busy small team organise many activities, including canoeing and fishing on the River Ardèche which flows past the site, mountain biking, hill walking and caving. It is less than 200 metres to the river and a wide beach that can be a mixture of sand and rounded pebbles. The 74 touring pitches are on grass and of a good size, with 6-10A electricity available to all. La Digue is open for an unusually long season.

Facilities

The first rate sanitary unit is kept in excellent condition. Attractive cubicles for young children and babies and good facilities for disabled visitors. Laundry room. Well stocked shop. Restaurant, bar and takeaway (1/4-21/10). Swimming pool (heated) in season. Play area. Pony ride. Bicycle hire. Canoe hire. Tennis. Fishing. Free WiFi near bar and reception. Mobile homes to rent. Winter caravan storage. Off site: River beach 200 m. Riding 5 km.

Open: 15 March - 3 November.

Directions

From the D579 Vallon-Pont-d'Arc - Ruoms road, turn left on entering Pradon, signed Chauzon. Site is signed here. Immediately after crossing river bridge, bear right about 400 m. taking ring road on left around the village following Campings signs. GPS: 44.48485, 4.372983

Charges guide

Per unit incl. 2 persons	€ 17.90 - € 31.30
extra person	€ 4.20 - € 6.20

Ruoms
Camping le Petit Bois
87 rue du Petit Bois, F-07120 Ruoms (Ardèche) T: 04 75 39 60 72. E: vacances@campinglepetitbois.fr
alanrogers.com/FR07360

Situated only 800 metres from the ancient town centre of Ruoms, and yet within an area of trees and rocky outcrops, this site offers a centre for those wishing to explore this part of the Ardèche valley. The 110 pitches are of irregular shape and size and a mix of stone and grass, with 76 spaces for touring units. There is some shade and access to the river for swimming and fishing. The site is now thirty years old and is needing some restoration, which is now underway. Some standpipes have coils of tubing attached. Perhaps these should not be used for domestic water purposes. A Sites et Paysages member.

Facilities

Refurbished toilet block, older second block (high season). Motorcaravan service point. Bar. Restaurant, pizzeria and takeaway (1/7-31/8). Heated swimming pool (1/4-30/6) and solarium. Slides and child splash pool. Pétanque. Playground. Games and TV rooms in season. Fishing. Entertainment organised in high season. Mobile homes and tents for rent. WiFi in the bar (free). Off site: Town with shops, etc. 800 m. Riding 1 km.

Open: 1 April - 30 September.

Directions

Approaching Ruoms on the D579 from Vallon-Pont-d'Arc go straight on at first (Super U) and second roundabouts. At third roundabout turn left (southwest) signed Largentier (site is signed). GPS: 44.46063, 4.3373

Charges guide

Per unit incl. 2 persons and electricity	€ 21.00 - € 33.00
extra person	€ 5.90 - € 6.90

For latest campsite news, availability and prices visit
alanrogers.com

Ruoms

Aluna Vacances

Route de Lagorce, F-07120 Ruoms (Ardèche) T: 04 75 93 93 15. E: alunavacances@wanadoo.fr

alanrogers.com/FR07630

Aluna is a high quality, large holiday park close to the market town of Ruoms in the southern Ardèche, famous for its gorges and the large range of watersports and other tourist activities. This will be a very lively site in July and August with a wide range of activities organised for all age groups, all day and into the night. There are 200 pitches mainly occupied by mobile homes and tour operators with 61 slightly uneven and sloping pitches for touring (electricity 6A, rock pegs advised). All the main activities take place in a single area, including a magnificent aqua park.

Facilities	Directions
Well appointed and very clean modern toilet blocks with all necessary facilities including those for campers with disabilities. Motorcaravan services. Shop, bar, restaurant, takeaway (15/4-18/9). Superb aqua park complex (all season). Fitness room. Large play area. Miniclubs (over 5 years). Tennis. Multisports court. Boules. Mini football stadium with artificial surface. Underground disco (until 02.00), outdoor stage (both July/Aug). Extensive activity programme (July/Aug). Gas and electric barbecues only. Max. 1 dog. WiFi throughout. Off site: Bicycle hire and river bathing 2 km. Riding 5 km.	Site is in southern Ardèche south of Aubenas. Leave Aubenas on D104 signed Alès. Turn left on D579 signed Vallon-Pont-d'Arc. Bypass Vogüé, cross river and keep right. At Ruoms turn left at roundabout on D559 signed Lagorce. In about 1 km. turn right to site on right. GPS: 44.44407, 4.36704

Open: 1 April - 18 September.

Charges guide

Per unit incl. 2 persons and electricity	€ 20.00 - € 43.00
extra person	€ 6.50 - € 10.30
child (2-12 yrs)	€ 3.80 - € 9.20

Saint-Alban-de-Montbel

Camping le Sougey

Lac Rive Ouest, F-73610 Saint-Alban-de-Montbel (Savoie) T: 04 79 36 01 44. E: info@camping-sougey.com

alanrogers.com/FR73120

In scenic surroundings, this site is only 200 m. from Lake Aiguebelette, the third largest natural lake in France. The 165 pitches (140 for touring units) all have 6/10A electricity and are set amongst many mature trees and well-manicured hedges, giving a tropical feel and plenty of shade and privacy. Most pitches are flat, but some are on a steep hillside and therefore sloping. There are adequate water points around the site and there are 30 serviced pitches available. This is a very peaceful, quality site with good views of the surrounding countryside and mountains. The owner, Philippe Kremer, is very friendly and speaks excellent English. The restaurant and shop are in a converted barn just outside the main entrance and the patio has terrific views across the lake. A traditional wood oven is used for pancakes and pizzas or there is a good choice of speciality Savoyard dishes. The beach is free for campsite users, and lifeguards are present in July and August (dogs are not permitted).

Facilities	Directions
Two identical sanitary blocks provide excellent facilities, washbasins in cabins, controllable showers, baby bath, 2 shower units with en-suite washbasin. Good facilities for disabled visitors. Separate laundry. Freezer. Shop (1/7-21/8). Bar and restaurant (open to public, just outside main gate). Well maintained play area. Miniclub. TV room. Chalets to rent. Off site: Fishing, boating etc. at lake 200 m. Bicycle hire 3 km. Walks with llamas and paragliding.	From A43 Chambéry - Lyon motorway, take exit 12 and D921 south towards Lac d'Aiguebelette. Follow signs to Plage du Sougey. Site is on the left just before the beach. GPS: 45.55582, 5.79081

Open: 1 May - 16 September.

Charges guide

Per unit incl. 2 persons and electricity	€ 16.90 - € 21.90
with full services	€ 18.30 - € 25.80
extra person (over 5 yrs)	€ 3.90

CAMPING LE SOUGEY****

Campsite du Sougey is nestled in the heart of a site naturally rich in exceptional panoramas, located at a height of 380 meters at the foot of the 'Massif de l'Epine'. You are looking for quality services and service, for a complete and diversified atmosphere of tourism then do not hesitate: **you found your place for holidays!**

Lac Rive Ouest - 73610 Saint Alban de Montbel
Tel : 0033 479 36 01 44 - Fax : 0033 479 44 19 01
E-mail : info@camping-sougey.com - Internet : www.camping-sougey.com

Saint Avit

Domaine la Garenne

156 chemin de Chablezin, F-26330 Saint Avit (Drôme) T: 04 75 68 62 26. E: garenne.drome@wanadoo.fr
alanrogers.com/FR26160

This very spacious, and cleverly terraced rural site lies in pleasant countryside, quite hidden from the roads by its own wood, and situated to the east of the Rhône valley. Most of the very large pitches are spread out and appear to form natural clearings under pine trees. A grassy lower area is more open and young trees give little shade. Although all the pitches have electricity (3/6A) very long leads are necessary. Of the 74 touring pitches, 25 are taken up by long stay units. The facilities are old but very clean and could entail a long walk. A new pool complex has been added (in 2011) with two pools, a children's fun pool and a sunbathing area adjacent to the covered bar and terrace. Torches and rock pegs essential. Good English is spoken by the friendly owners.

Facilities

Four basic toilet blocks with washbasins in cabins. Some facilities for disabled visitors, but site is generally unsuitable due to steep paths and terracing. Washing machine. Motorcaravan services. Baker calls July/Aug. Small bar plus takeaway food (July/Aug). Kitchen area. Swimming pool, shallow pool and fun pool. Large sports area. Play area. Communal barbecue (not allowed on the pitches). Some family activities (July/Aug). WiFi at reception.

Open: 16 April - 15 September.

Directions

Leave the N7 16 km. north of Tournon. Turn east on D51, signed Châteauneuf. After about 15 km. at Mureils, turn right on D363, signed St Avit. After 2 km. turn left on D53 (site signed) and site entrance is shortly on the right. GPS: 45.20205, 4.95719

Charges guide

Per unit incl. 2 persons and electricity	€ 19.50 - € 25.00

Saint Galmier

Campéole

Campéole Val de Coise

Route de la Thiéry, F-42330 Saint Galmier (Loire) T: 04 77 54 14 82.
E: val-de-coise@campeole.com **alanrogers.com/FR42040**

Val de Coise is a member of the Campéole group and is situated in the undulating landscape of the Massif Central, north of St Etienne. It is an attractive site located between the River Coise and a dense forest. The 92 pitches are grassy and of a good size with most of the 52 for touring units with 16A electricity. Mobile homes, chalets and fully equipped tents are available for rent. There is plenty of activity here in high season with a children's club and regular discos and karaoke evenings. This is rugged, dramatic country – ideal for walking and mountain biking. The nearby spa town of St Galmier is home to the Badoit water plant, a casino, restaurants and a number of art galleries. The Badoit plant has guided tours available and locals refill their water bottles from the source of this naturally sparkling spa water. In St Galmier guided walks are organised by the local tourist office, both a town trail and in the surrounding forests, and the Monts du Forez and Monts du Lyonnais are within easy reach.

Facilities

The single toilet block is central. It is kept clean and is neatly tiled and painted. Small baby room. Facilities for disabled visitors. Good motorcaravan services. Small shop in reception. No bar or snacks. Swimming pool (July/Aug). Multisports area. TV room. Play area. Minigolf. Boules. Bouncy castle. Activities and entertainment programme. Fishing. WiFi (first hour free). Mobile homes, chalets and equipped tents for rent. Off site: St Galmier and tennis 2 km. Fishing (in River Coise). St Etienne 22 km.

Open: 15 April - 15 October.

Directions

From St Etienne, head north on the A72 and leave at the Andrezieux Bouthéon St Galmier exit. Take the D100, then the D12 to St Galmier. Site is well signed from here. GPS: 45.59272, 4.33542

Charges guide

Per unit incl. 2 persons and electricity	€ 15.10 - € 19.10
extra person	€ 4.00 - € 5.40
child (2-6 yrs)	€ 3.00 - € 3.50

Campéole
CAMPSITES AND RENTALS
Val de Coise ***
Pitches and accommodations of high quality, with swimming pool.

RHÔNE-ALPES

42330 St Galmier- Tel.: +33-477-5414-82 - www.campeole.co.uk / val-de-coise@campeole.com

For latest campsite news, availability and prices visit
alanrogers.com

Saint Donat-sur-Herbasse

Domaine des Ulèzes

Route de Romans, F-26260 Saint Donat-sur-Herbasse (Drôme) T: 04 75 47 83 20.
E: contact@domaine-des-ulezes.com **alanrogers.com/FR26330**

A neat and tidy family run site with a long season only five minutes' walk from St Donat and only 16 km. from the A7 and A49 Autoroutes. There are 85 level, grassy pitches with 77 for touring; all are fully serviced with 10A electricity and close to one of the nine toilet blocks. Those in the older section are separated by hedging and a variety of mature trees giving good shade to most pitches. The hedges and trees in the newer section offer little shade at the moment. No twin-axle caravans and only gas and electric barbecues.

Facilities

Nine small toilet blocks with all the necessary facilities, some new, others awaiting refurbishment. Facilities for children and disabled visitors. Washing machines. Basic shop, bar and restaurant with takeaway. Small swimming pool (8/5-15/9). Children's play area, mini-golf, boules. Games/TV room. Off site: St Donat with a few shops, bars, restaurants five minutes on foot, 1 km. by car. River bathing close by. Riding 3 km. Fishing 10 km. Golf 15 km.

Open: 1 April - 31 October.

Directions

Leave A7 autoroute at exit 13, take D532 east for 5 km. to Curson. Take D67 north 10 km. through St Donat. At a roundabout turn south, D53 and follow signs to site (1 km). GPS: 45.1192, 4.9927

Charges guide

Per unit incl. 2 persons and electricity	€ 18.50 - € 22.50
extra person	€ 4.00

Saint Jean-de-Chevelu

Camping Lacs de Chevelu

F-73170 Saint Jean-de-Chevelu (Savoie) T: 04 79 36 72 21. E: camping-des-lacs@wanadoo.fr
alanrogers.com/FR73080

This is a small, beautifully kept, family orientated campsite, which is run by a friendly family and surrounded by delightful scenery, not far from Lac du Bourget. Beside the site is a small lake which is fed by springs and has a small sandy beach ideal for swimming and playing around in small boats. The site has 120 average to large sized, grass pitches with 110 for touring. There are 50 with 10A electricity (long leads advised). They are numbered and marked by very small trees with a few having some shade. This site is ideal for families who are happy to make their own entertainment.

Facilities

Excellent newly refurbished toilet block with all necessary facilities including those for babies and disabled visitors. Motorcaravan services. Shop. Bar (1/6-30/8). Takeaway snacks (1/6-30/8). Fishing. Lake bathing. Organised walks and cycle rides. Covered games area. Boules. TV room. Play area. Some family entertainment in high season. WiFi. Off site: Riding, bicycle hire, canoeing, hang-gliding 5 km. Shops, bars and restaurants in Yenne 5 km.

Open: 1 May - 11 September.

Directions

Leave A43 at exit 13 (Chambéry) and take the D1504 (previously N504) north towards Belley. After the 'Tunnel du Chat', continue into St Jean-de-Chevelu, turn right at roundabout (site signed). Site is just over 1 km. GPS: 45.69378, 5.82491

Charges guide

Per unit incl. 2 persons and electricity	€ 17.90 - € 28.50
extra person	€ 3.70 - € 5.50

Saint Jorioz

Village Camping Europa

1444 route Albertville, F-74410 Saint Jorioz (Haute-Savoie) T: 04 50 68 51 01. E: info@camping-europa.com
alanrogers.com/FR74100

You will receive a friendly welcome at this quality, family run site. The flowers, shrubs and trees are lovely and everything is kept neat and tidy. There are 210 medium to large sized pitches (110 for touring) on level stony grass. Rock pegs are advised. All pitches have electricity (6A) nearby and 18 have 10A electricity, water and drainage. The static units are to one side of the site giving the impression that you are on a small site. Expect some noise from the adjacent main road. This is a good base from which to tour the Lake Annecy area and there is direct access to a 30 km. cycle path, which travels the length of the lake.

Facilities

Two very good toilet blocks, modernised to a high standard, have all the necessary facilities including some large cubicles with both showers and washbasins. Good bar and restaurant (26/5-10/9). Boulangerie (1/6-15/9). Swimming pool complex (entry bracelet € 2 each 1/5-17/9). Bicycle hire. WiFi (charged). Miniclub. Some musical evenings. Off site: Fishing 300 m. Boat launching 500 m. Lakeside beach 2 km. Riding 3 km. Golf 8 km. Lakeside bike ride (40 km). St Jorioz. Boat trips around lake.

Open: 30 April - 17 September.

Directions

From Annecy take D1508 (previously N508) signed Albertville. Site is well signed on the right on leaving Saint Jorioz. GPS: 45.8246, 6.1758

Charges guide

Per unit incl. 2 persons and electricity	€ 19.00 - € 35.50
serviced pitch	€ 23.50 - € 40.00
extra person	€ 4.20 - € 6.80
dog	€ 4.00

For latest campsite news, availability and prices visit
alanrogers.com

Saint Gervais-les-Bains

Camping les Dômes de Miage

197 route des Contamines, F-74170 Saint Gervais-les-Bains (Haute-Savoie) T: 04 50 93 45 96.
E: info@camping-mont-blanc.com **alanrogers.com/FR74140**

Saint Gervais is a pretty spa town in the picturesque Val-Monjoie valley and this site is 2 km. from its centre. It is 22 km. west of Chamonix and centrally located for discovering this marvellous mountain region. Nestled among the mountains, this sheltered, well equipped site provides 150 flat, grassy pitches. Of a good size, about half have shade and there are 100 with electricity points (3/10A). The remainder on terraced ground are used for tents. Third generation hosts, Stéphane and Sophie, will welcome you to the site and their passion for this area at the foot of Mont Blanc is infectious. A number of Savoyard style chalets to let are planned for the future. This is a good site for large motorcaravans. There is no on-site entertainment programme, but a wealth of information about the area and activities available nearby is provided at reception where they will help you plan your itinerary. The region is good for walking and there is a bus service into Saint Gervais, from where there is a frequent shuttle bus to its spa and a tramway to the Mont Blanc range. There is also public transport from town to Chamonix.

Facilities

Two sanitary blocks, one heated, with a suite for disabled visitors and baby room. Washing machines, dryer. Motorcaravan services. Small basic shop. Bar/restaurant. TV room, library, ironing board. Excellent playground. Playing field. WiFi (free). Off site: Fishing 100 m. Bicycle hire 1 km. Riding 7 km. Shops, etc. and outdoor swimming pool in St Gervais.

Open: 1 May - 12 September.

Directions

From St Gervais take D902 towards Les Contamines and site is on left after 2 km.
GPS: 45.87389, 6.7199

Charges guide

Per unit incl. 2 persons	
and electricity	€ 20.10 - € 26.10
extra person	€ 3.00 - € 4.10
child (2-9 yrs)	€ 2.50 - € 3.50
dog	free - € 2.00

A NEW WAY TO DISCOVER THE MOUNTAINS...

A campsite in the middle of untouched nature, in a quiet location at the foot of Mont-Blanc, in the center of many hiking paths. A wide choice of activities and services, sports centre with swiming pool, tennis, etc... 800 yards away. Aiguille du Midi, Mer de glace & Chamonix 15 miles, St-Gervais 1,2 miles , Megève 7 miles.

CAMPING
Les Dômes de Miage
★ ★ ★

197, route des Contamines - F-74170 Saint-Gervais-les-bains
Tél. + 33 (0)4 50 93 45 96
e-mail : info@camping-mont-blanc.com
WWW.CAMPING-MONT-BLANC.COM

La Clef Verte

Camping Qualité

For latest campsite news, availability and prices visit
alanrogers.com

Saint Julien-en-Saint Alban

Camping l'Albanou

Quartier Pampelonne, F-07000 Saint Julien-en-Saint Alban (Ardèche) T: 04 75 66 00 97.
E: camping.albanou@wanadoo.fr **alanrogers.com/FR07210**

Guests are warmly welcomed at this small, very clean and neat site. It is situated in the beautiful northern Ardèche region with its many old villages, markets and museums – well worth exploring. The site's 87 large, level and easily accessible pitches (84 for touring) are in groups separated by tall hedges, all with electricity (6A). An attractive modern building houses the reception and a small bar with a terrace. Snacks and bread are available to order. In high season a few games are organised for younger children but the emphasis here is on a quiet and peaceful site.

Facilities

Refurbished toilet block has all the necessary facilities including those for disabled visitors. Motorcaravan services. Small shop. Bar, snacks, takeaway. Good, heated swimming pool, paddling pool and small slide (1/5-22/9). Spa/jacuzzi. Spacious play area. Area for ball games. Information and maps for walking and driving. WiFi throughout (charged). Only gas or electric barbecues. Off site: Fishing 300 m. St Julien 2 km. Le Pouzin 4 km.

Open: 28 April - 22 September.

Directions

From A7 autoroute take exit 16 for Loriol, head west across the Rhône to Le Pouzin. At roundabout take N104, signed Aubenas, follow road up hill. Turn left in 4 km. just before St Julien. Site is signed. GPS: 44.75716, 4.71286

Charges guide

Per unit incl. 2 persons and electricity	€ 20.00 - € 24.00
extra person	€ 4.00 - € 5.00

Saint Laurent-du-Pape

Camping la Garenne

Montée de la Garenne, F-07800 Saint Laurent-du-Pape (Ardèche) T: 04 75 62 24 62. E: info@lagarenne.org
alanrogers.com/FR07100

This spacious, split level site has a long season and is within easy reach of the A7/N7 south of Valence. The 120 pitches on open flat land or on terraced sloping land, all have 6A electricity and varying degrees of shade. Some pitches are separated by hedges, and some need longer leads or rock pegs. It is only a short walk from the village which has a few shops. Guests are predominantly Dutch but all are made welcome and English is widely spoken. Visitors' pursuits have been carefully considered resulting in a varied programme of activities from mid May to mid September.

Facilities

Excellent and very clean, modern toilet blocks provide all necessary facilities including those for children and disabled visitors. Small shop for basics. Bar, restaurant and takeaway (all 15/5-15/9). Swimming pool and sunbathing terrace (20/5-30/9). Paddling pool. Boules. Games room. Barbecues are not permitted. WiFi (charged). Two mobile homes and four tents for rent. Off site: Village. Fishing 1 km. Riding 2 km.

Open: 1 March - 1 November.

Directions

Leave the N86 at Beauchastel, 20 km. south of Valence and follow the D21 to Saint Laurent-du-Pape. In the village, turn right just before the post office and the site is at the end of this road, beyond the tennis court. GPS: 44.82616, 4.76184

Charges guide

Per unit incl. 2 persons and electricity	€ 18.50 - € 31.50
extra person	€ 5.50

Saint Laurent-en-Beaumont

Camping Belvédère de l'Obiou

Les Egats, F-38350 Saint Laurent-en-Beaumont (Isère) T: 04 76 30 40 80. E: info@camping-obiou.com
alanrogers.com/FR38130

This extremely good and well maintained small Alpine site with just 45 pitches is in the centre of the Ecrins National Park. It is therefore ideal for walkers and cyclists looking to take advantage of the well marked trails. It has most things a good site should have, with its restaurant, heated pool and sitting room with TV and library. The welcoming owners will even supply you with breakfast. The views from the 45 terraced pitches are spectacular and there is a wealth of activities in the area ranging from bungee jumping and high walkways across the lake to a more sedate trip by boat to take in the stunning views. Mobile homes are available to rent as well as two comfortable rooms (B&B).

Facilities

Two modern toilet blocks, one part of the main building, the other Portacabin style, are immaculate and can be heated. High standard facilities for disabled visitors. Excellent laundry. Motorcaravan services. Small shop for ice cream and soft drinks. Restaurant (May-Sept) with local speciality menu, high quality takeaway and breakfast. Heated swimming pool (May-Sept). Bicycle hire. Good play area. WiFi. Off site: Fishing 5 km.

Open: 15 April - 15 October.

Directions

From Grenoble take exit 8 onto the D1085. After 9 km. left onto D529 towards La Motte d'Aveillans and back onto the D1085 at La Mure. 7 km. south of La Mure site is clearly signed on the left. GPS: 44.87593, 5.83741

Charges guide

Per unit incl. 2 persons and electricity	€ 16.50 - € 24.00
Camping Cheques accepted.	

For latest campsite news, availability and prices visit
alanrogers.com

Saint Pierre-de-Chartreuse
Camping de Martinière

Route du Col de Porte, F-38380 Saint Pierre-de-Chartreuse (Isère) T: 04 76 88 60 36.
E: camping-de-martiniere@orange.fr **alanrogers.com/FR38160**

Chamechaude, the 2,082 m. Eiger-like peak, presides benevolently over the 90 touring pitches at this beautiful, high alpine site open from May to September for the summer season. The large touring pitches, all with electricity (2-10A), have some shade and are slightly sloping. The site has a heated outdoor pool so that none of the view is missed. This well run, family owned enterprise, set around a traditional Savoyard farmhouse, is a peaceful centre for walking, climbing, cycling or just soaking up the air and ambience. It is in the centre of the Chartreuse National Forest. A Sites et Paysages member.

Facilities

Two heated toilet blocks provide excellent, clean facilities. Facilities for babies and disabled visitors. Laundry. Shop (1/6-11/9). Bar (10/6-5/9) with snacks (1/7-31/8). Swimming and paddling pools (1/6-5/9; heated July/Aug). Play area. Indoor sitting area for poor weather. Extensive paperback library (NL, IT, Fr, UK). Off site: Restaurant 50 m. from site entrance. Fishing 500 m. Bicycle hire 3 km. Skiing 6 km. Walking, cycling and mountain activities.

Open: 30 April - 11 September.

Directions

From St Laurent-du-Pont (north from Voiron or south from Chambery), take D512 signed St Pierre-de-Chartreuse. Site is well signed in the village (the road south from St Pierre-d'Entremont is not recommended for towing). GPS: 45.3258, 5.7972

Charges guide

Per unit incl. 2 persons	
and electricity	€ 17.00 - € 26.20
extra person	€ 4.90 - € 5.60

Saint Romans
Flower Camping Lac du Marandan

F-38160 Saint Romans (Isère) T: 04 76 64 41 77. E: contact@camping-lac-marandan.com
alanrogers.com/FR38250

Lac du Marandan is ideally situated at the foot of the regional park of the Vercors. It has direct access to an inviting lake which has a temperature of 28 degrees at its shallowest point and is surrounded by a fine sandy beach. Christelle and Yannick will make sure you enjoy your stay. The site has 100 pitches (88 for touring, all with 6A electricity) from 100-200 sq.m. in size and located in a wooded area where old oaks will provide shade. Many activities are possible around the lake and the area itself also offers a rich variety of sporting activities and sightseeing.

Facilities

Sanitary buildings with showers. Facilities for disabled visitors. Washing machine. Shop. Bar/restaurant (weekends only in low season). Tennis courts. Boules court. Playground. Canoe hire. Fishing. Accommodation to rent. WiFi. Off site: Lakeside restaurant. St Roman 2 km. Mountain bike hire and riding 5 km. Hiking. Gorges.

Open: 7 April - 30 September.

Directions

South of Grenoble, leave the A49 at exit 9 and follow the D518 towards Saint Romans. Then take the D1532, to Base de Loisirs du Marandan (signed). GPS: 45.103198, 5.292631

Charges guide

Per unit incl. 2 persons	
and electricity	€ 15.00 - € 24.00

Saint Sauveur-de-Montagut
Camping Caravaning l'Ardéchois

Le Chambon, Gluiras, F-07190 Saint Sauveur-de-Montagut (Ardèche) T: 04 75 66 61 87.
E: ardechois.camping@wanadoo.fr **alanrogers.com/FR07020**

This attractive site is quite a way off the beaten track but it is worth the effort to find it in this spectacular and peaceful setting. This site has 106 spacious pitches (83 for touring with 10A electricity) laid out on steep terraces and many separated by trees and plants. Some are alongside the Glueyre river that tumbles between pools, while the rest are on higher, terraced ground nearer the restaurant, bar and pool. The main site access roads are quite steep but are made of good tarmac. A convivial family atmosphere is encouraged by the owners and entertainment is tailored to the guests' needs. There is weekly live music and a comprehensive entertainment package for children centred around a room near a fenced play area.

Facilities

Two very good sanitary blocks include facilities for families and disabled campers. Laundry facilities. Motorcaravan services. Shop. Cosy restaurant. Swimming and paddling pools (heated), adjacent bar, snack bar, terrace. TV. Bicycle hire, archery, fishing. Large sports field with football. Courts for volleyball/badminton and a second adventure play area. Entertainment programme. Only gas/electric barbecues. WiFi (charged). Off site: Aquarock Adventure Park. Canoeing trips organised.

Open: 11 May - 20 September.

Directions

From Valence take N86 south for 12 km. At La Voulte-sur-Rhône turn right onto D120 to St Sauveur-de-Montagut (site well signed), in centre turn left onto D102 towards Mézilhac for 8 km. to site. The road narrows in places but has wider stretches. GPS: 44.82842, 4.52332

Charges guide

Per unit incl. 2 persons	
and electricity	€ 19.00 - € 28.75

Camping Cheques accepted.

For latest campsite news, availability and prices visit
alanrogers.com

We can book this site for you! Call 01580 214000 alan rogers ◉ travel

Saint Martin-d'Ardèche

Camping Indigo le Moulin

F-07700 Saint Martin-d'Ardèche (Ardèche) T: 04 75 04 66 20. E: moulin@camping-indigo.com

alanrogers.com/FR07650

Le Moulin is a member of the Indigo group and is situated just 300 m. from the centre of St Martin-d'Ardèche. The site has its own river beach and is very well placed for canoe trips on the Ardèche. There are 141 touring pitches here, extending over the site's seven hectares. The pitches are well shaded and most have 10A electrical connections. Rental accommodation includes innovative wood and canvas tents (40) and Romany-style caravans (16). Amenities include a pleasant snack bar and a café. A children's club (recré-enfants) operates in peak season, focusing on craft activities and games.

Facilities

Three modern well-appointed sanitary units placed over the site. Snack bar/café. Pizza. Bread to order and local produce at reception. Play area with climbing frame. Children's activity programme. Heated outdoor swimming pool (all season). Direct river access. Canoeing. Football. Internet access. Tents and caravans for rent. Max. 1 dog per pitch. Off site: Bicycle hire 100 m. St Martin 300 m. (shops, cafés and restaurants). Cycle and walking tracks. Aiguèze (pretty craft village). Riding 3 km.

Open: 6 April - 7 October.

Directions

From Pont St Esprit, take northbound D6086, becoming D86 after crossing the river, and then D290 to St Martin-d'Ardèche. The site is clearly signed. GPS: 44.300272, 4.571171

Charges guide

Per unit incl. 2 persons and electricity	€ 19.90 - € 28.90
extra person	€ 3.90 - € 6.00

Camping Cheques accepted.

Samoëns

Camping Caravaneige le Giffre

La Glière, F-74340 Samoëns (Haute-Savoie) T: 04 50 34 41 92. E: camping.samoens@wanadoo.fr

alanrogers.com/FR74230

Surrounded by magnificent mountains in this lesser known Alpine area, yet accessible to major ski resorts, le Giffre could be the perfect spot for those seeking an active, yet relaxing holiday. There are 300 firm, level pitches on stony grass (rock pegs advised) with 288 for touring units. Most have electricity (6/10A) but long leads may be needed. They are spaced out amongst mature trees which give varying amounts of shade and some overlook the attractive lake and leisure park. The small winter/summer resort of Samoëns is only a 15 minute, level stroll away. Mr Dominach loves gardening and the site is bedecked with flowers. Make sure you do not miss the small vegetable and herb garden at the entrance. There is little in the way of on-site entertainment but there are many activities available in Samoëns and the surrounding area.

Facilities

Three adequate toilet blocks, heated in winter with facilities for campers with disabilities. Games room. Play area. Boules. Fishing. Accommodation for hire. Off site: Leisure park next to site with pool (entry free summer), ice skating (entry free winter), tennis (summer), archery, adventure park. Paragliding. Rafting, many walks and bike rides (summer) and ski runs (winter). Snack bar and baker (high season) 100 m. Samoëns with a good range of shops, bars, restaurants 1 km. Grand Massif Express cable car 150 m. Bicycle hire 200 m. Riding 2 km.

Open: All year.

Directions

Leave A40 autoroute at Cluses (exit 18 or 19). Go north on D902 towards Taninges. Just before Taninges turn east on D4 to Samoëns. After crossing river, at roundabout, turn left and site is immediately on the left. Park outside the entrance. GPS: 46.07731, 6.71851

Charges guide

Per unit incl. 2 persons and electricity	€ 16.20 - € 27.15
extra person	€ 3.95
child (4-12 yrs)	€ 2.70
dog	€ 2.10

Camping Caravaneige Le Giffre★★★

Open all year, located on the edge of the Giffre and the 'Lacs aux Dames', 700m from the town and its shops and at the heart of the leisure park, our campsite has 312 level grass pitches on a well shaded site of 6.9h.

In winter, departures for cross-country skiing from the campsite and ski lifts 150m away. Access within 8 min to 265 km of downhill slopes.

Camping Caravaneige Le Giffre • La Glière • F-74340 Samoens
www.camping-samoens.com

For latest campsite news, availability and prices visit
alanrogers.com

Sampzon
Yelloh! Village Soleil Vivarais
F-07120 Sampzon (Ardèche) T: 04 75 39 67 56. E: info@yellohvillage-soleil-vivarais.com
alanrogers.com/FR07030

A large, lively, high quality site bordering the River Ardèche, complete with beach, Soleil Vivarais offers much to visitors, particularly families with children. Of the 350 pitches, 104 generously sized, shady and level pitches are for tourers, all with 10A electricity. During the day the proximity of the swimming pools to the terraces of the bar and restaurant make it a pleasantly social area. In the evening the purpose built stage, with professional lighting and sound system, provides regular family entertainment programmes, six evenings a week. An additional attractive pool complex can be used by guests located in a separate mobile home section beyond the beach.

Facilities

Modern, clean, well equipped toilet blocks. Attractive facilities for babies and children. Facilities for visitors with disabilities. Washing machines, dryers. Motorcaravan services. Small supermarket. Bar/restaurant, takeaways and pizzas. Heated pool complexes and paddling pool. Water polo. Aquarobics. Fishing. Boules. Archery. Bicycle and canoe hire. River bathing. Entertainment programme (June-Aug). Massage and beauty parlour. Free WiFi near bars. Off site: Riding 800 m. Canoeing, rafting, climbing etc.

Open: 1 April - 12 September.

Directions

On D579, 2 km. south of Ruoms, turn left at roundabout, (Vallon-Pont-d'Arc). Turn right over river bridge, site is on right. GPS: 44.42917, 4.35531

Charges guide

Per unit incl. 2 persons and electricity	€ 15.00 - € 44.00
extra person	€ 5.00 - € 8.00
child (3-7 yrs)	free - € 7.00

Sampzon
RCN la Bastide en Ardèche
Route d'Alès (D111), Sampzon, F-07120 Ruoms (Ardèche) T: 04 75 39 64 72. E: bastide@rcn.fr
alanrogers.com/FR07080

You are assured of a good welcome at this site and much attention has been paid to the layout of the park with floral areas around the buildings and the separation of rented accommodation and touring pitches. There are 300 good sized, level, grassy pitches marked out by trees giving plenty of shade. There are 260 for touring units, all with 6A electricity, and 86 with full services. Canoe trips are arranged down the Gorge d'Ardèche and annually a large section of the river bank next to the site is cleared of boulders and sand put down. Security patrols ensure quiet nights. There is an emphasis on families and whilst there is lots of activity available on site, there are a number of other providers within easy reach.

Facilities

Two well equipped toilet blocks with baby room and facilities for disabled visitors. Shop, restaurant, pizzeria and bar (1/4-1/10). Heated swimming pool (1/4-1/10). Play area. Tennis. Fishing. Organised activities. Recreation room. Bicycle hire. WiFi (charged). Very useful information leaflet given on arrival. Only gas barbecues permitted. Max. 1 dog. Off site: Riding 3 km. Ruoms 3 km.

Open: 19 March - 8 October.

Directions

Going south from Ruoms on the D579, after 2.5 km. at roundabout, turn right on D111 signed Alès. After 1 km. cross river bridge and site is 200 m. on the left. GPS: 44.42292, 4.32162

Charges guide

Per unit incl. 2 persons, electricity and water	€ 19.90 - € 43.90
extra person	€ 2.50 - € 4.90

Sampzon
Flower Camping le Riviera
F-07120 Sampzon (Ardèche) T: 04 75 39 67 57. E: leriviera@wanadoo.fr
alanrogers.com/FR07400

This well organised, family run and orientated site is situated beside the River Ardèche, not far from Vallon-Pont-d'Arc. There are 180 pitches with 114 of varying size for touring units, although access to some may prove difficult for larger units. Separated by hedges and trees, pitches have varying degrees of shade and 10A electricity connections. The site's facilities are of a high standard and disabled visitors are well provided for. In July and August, daily and evening activities are organised for all the family. The site maintains a sandy beach by the river with good opportunities for fishing and canoeing.

Facilities

Two modern toilet blocks provide cubicles with washbasins, showers, baby room and excellent facilities for disabled visitors. Washing machines and dryer. Bar. Restaurant with terrace (July/Aug). Shop (July/Aug). Swimming and paddling pools (heated). New play and multisports areas. Bicycle and canoe hire (July/Aug). Fishing. River beach. Activities and entertainment. Free WiFi near bar/reception. Off site: Shop close to entrance.

Open: 1 April - 30 September.

Directions

On D579 2 km. south of Ruoms, turn left at roundabout signed Vallon-Pont-d'Arc. Shortly turn right over river bridge. Site on left. GPS: 44.42838, 4.35527

Charges guide

Per unit incl. 2 persons and electricity (10A)	€ 19.50 - € 47.00
extra person	€ 5.50 - € 8.40

For latest campsite news, availability and prices visit
alanrogers.com

Séez

Camping le Reclus

F-73700 Séez (Savoie) T: 04 79 41 01 05. E: contact@campinglereclus.com

alanrogers.com/FR73100

Bordering a fast flowing but well-fenced stream, this small mountain campsite, set in the hills above Bourg-St-Maurice in the Vanoise National Park, is enthusiastically run by Mélanie Bonato. The 90 sunny pitches, most with electricity (4-10A), are on terraces. The village of Séez is a few minutes' walk away. Winter sports enthusiasts are well catered for here, with a drying room and ski-shoe heating, plus discounts on ski passes and other activities. There is a free shuttle to Les Arcs and La Rosière and it is centrally situated for the Tarentaise ski lifts. This site is not recommended for larger units.

Facilities

Two sanitary blocks have been renovated, the central one more modern, have small shower cubicles with preset hot water; and open style basins. Laundry room with washer/dryer and indoor drying area. Restaurant and takeaway (1/7-5/9). Small play area. Bread, drinks and ice cream for sale. Bicycle hire. TV room. Off site: Shops and bars in the village of Séez. Riding 1 km. Access to the ski resort of Les Arcs via the funicular railway in Bourg-St-Maurice 2 km. Swimming pools 2 km. Golf 15 km.

Open: All year.

Directions

From A43 Lyon - Chambéry - Grenoble motorway take A430 to Albertville and RN90 to Moutiers and Bourg-St-Maurice. Drive through town, at third roundabout follow signs for Tignes and Val d'Isère. Site is 2 km. up the hill on the right on entering village of Séez. GPS: 45.625844, 6.792794

Charges guide

Per unit incl. 2 persons and electricity	€ 16.50 - € 18.80
extra person	€ 4.20 - € 4.70
child (4-13 yrs)	€ 2.50 - € 4.20

Thonon-les-Bains

Camping Saint Disdille

117 avenue de Saint Disdille, F-74200 Thonon-les-Bains (Haute-Savoie) T: 04 50 71 14 11. E: camping@disdille.com **alanrogers.com/FR74220**

Saint-Disdille is situated close to the beautiful Lake Geneva and the famous spa towns of Thonon-les-Bains, which can be reached on a bus that passes the site and Evian-les-Bains. There are 300 large, level pitches on stone and rough grass (rock pegs are essential). Large trees give some shade. The 200 pitches reserved for touring have 10A electricity and are scattered amongst mobile homes and permanent weekender caravans and can be some distance from the facilities. The site is ideally situated for the large range of watersports in the area and Switzerland is easily accessible by car, bus, train or boat. This site will be lively in the high season due to the large number of long stay units and the on-site and adjacent discos finish after midnight. A new bypass around Thonon makes access easier.

Facilities

Five adequate toilet blocks, 4 recently refurbished inside. Shop. Bar with TV, restaurant with takeaways. Diving and rafting clubs. Play area with bouncy castle. Multisports court. Boules. Games room with pool table. WiFi (free) and Internet point (charged). Bicycle hire. Tennis court. Off site: Small lakeside public beach and disco 300 m. Fishing 500 m. Large open-air pool 1 km. Boat ramp, windsurfing, bicycle hire 2 km. Many other watersports in the area. Thonon-les-Bains 2 km. Golf 5 km.

Open: 1 April - 30 September.

Directions

From Annemasse take N5 to Thonon-les-Bains. In Thonon follow signs for Evian to Intermarché supermarket. At next roundabout follow signs to campsite and Parc de la Chataigneraie. GPS: 46.39765, 6.50335

Charges 2012

Per unit incl. 2 persons and electricity	€ 18.40 - € 27.40
extra person	€ 4.20 - € 5.20
child (3-10 yrs)	€ 3.20 - € 4.20
dog	€ 2.00

★★★ St Disdille
Camping Locations
Haute-Savoie
Thonon-les-Bains
www.disdille.com
Camping Qualité
camping@disdille.com
Tel: 0033 (0)4.50.71.14.11

For latest campsite news, availability and prices visit

alanrogers.com

Trept
Domaine les Trois Lacs du Soleil

⌐ 540

La Plaine, F-38460 Trept (Isère) T: 04 74 92 92 06. E: les3lacsdusoleil@hotmail.fr
alanrogers.com/FR38060

Les Trois Lacs is situated on the edge of three lakes in flat, open country in the north of Dauphine. The camping area is on one side of the largest lake with tall trees on one edge and views of distant mountains. The 200 good sized pitches, with 150 for tourists, are well spaced and separated by trees and hedges. All have 6A electricity. There is plenty of activity on offer for the whole family including fishing in one lake, swimming in the other two and, for the more energetic, roller blading. There is plenty of space around the lake for children to play. The land around the lakes has been well landscaped with grassy banks and a variety of shrubs and trees. This is a good base from which to enjoy either the countryside, the historic places of the region or the programme of leisure activities provided by the site.

Facilities

Two modern fully equipped toilet blocks are in the centre of the camping area. Toilets for children. Baby room. Laundry facilities. Small shop (May-Aug). Bar/snack bar and restaurant (June-Aug). New outdoor pool and paddling pool. (May-Aug). Lakeside beach and water slide. Discos and entertainment in high season. TV and sports hall. Roller blade hire. Fitness. Walking. Fishing. Gas barbecues only. WiFi. Off site: Riding 500 m. Trept 2 km. Mountain bike hire 10 km.

Open: 1 May - 17 September.

Directions

From A43 take exit 7 on to D522 north. Turn left after 7 km. on to D65 then after 5 km. turn right on the D517. Site is 2 km. east of Trept with signs in village. GPS: 45.68699, 5.35191

Charges guide

Per unit incl. 2 persons	
and electricity	€ 19.00 - € 32.50
extra person	€ 3.50 - € 7.00
child (0-10 yrs)	free - € 3.50
dog	€ 2.50

CAMPING VILLAGE
DOMAINE
LES 3 LACS DU SOLEIL
Cat.1 ★ ★ ★ ★

A holiday park of 26 acres with 3 lakes, a 'nature' swimming pool of 5000 m², swimming pool, paddling pool, shady pitches of 100 m², tennis, mini golf, sporting facilities, fishing. Cottages, chalets and bungalow tents for rent, free WiFi

Opening dates: 30/04/2011 - 10/09/2011

Camping Village les 3 Lacs du Soleil★★★★
38460 Trept | Tél.: 0033 4 74 92 92 06
www.camping-les3lacsdusoleil.com

Tulette
Camping les Rives de l'Aygues

Route de Cairanne, F-26790 Tulette (Drôme) T: 04 75 98 37 50. E: camping.aygues@wanadoo.fr
alanrogers.com/FR26240

As the name implies, this spacious, family run site is situated by the bank of the river. Set in beautiful countryside and surrounded by vineyards for the famous Côtes du Rhône wines, this is a delightful site to unwind and explore this picturesque region. There are 100 very large, stony pitches with some grass laid out in the natural landscape and separated by attractive shrubs and trees giving good shade and privacy. There are 92 for touring units (electricity 6A, long leads advised). A number of pitches back onto the bank separating the site from the river, which is accessible for sunbathing and paddling. The area around the site is fairly flat and ideal for exploring by bike. For the more serious cyclist, Mont Ventoux is not far away.

Facilities

A single, large building provides adequate facilities including some washbasins in cabins. It is quite a walk from some pitches. Bread to order. Bar, restaurant and takeaway (July/Aug). Games/TV room. Swimming and paddling pools (May-Sept). Play areas. Boules. Playing field. Only gas barbecues are permitted. WiFi (charged). Off site: Fishing 200 m. Bicycle hire 2 km. Riding 3 km. Shops and restaurants in Tulette 3 km. and Sainte Cecile-les-Vignes 3.5 km. Golf 15 km. Vaison la Romaine 16 km.

Open: 1 May - 25 September.

Directions

Leave A7 at exit 19 (Bollène) and take D94 towards Nyons. On entering Tulette (about 16 km) turn hard right onto D193 (site signed) and follow signs to site (2 km). GPS: 44.26518, 4.93149

Charges guide

Per unit incl. 2 persons	
and electricity	€ 20.20 - € 24.20
extra person	€ 5.10
child (under 7 yrs)	€ 3.50

No credit cards.

For latest campsite news, availability and prices visit
alanrogers.com

Vallon-Pont-d'Arc

Castel Camping Nature Parc l'Ardéchois

Route touristique des Gorges, F-07150 Vallon-Pont-d'Arc (Ardèche) T: 04 75 88 06 63.
E: ardecamp@bigfoot.com alanrogers.com/FR07120

This very high quality, family run site is within walking distance of Vallon-Pont-d'Arc. It borders the River Ardèche and canoe trips are run, professionally, direct from the site. This campsite is ideal for families with younger children seeking an active holiday. The facilities are comprehensive and the central toilet unit is of an extremely high standard. Of the 244 pitches, there are 225 for tourers, separated by trees and individual shrubs. All have electrical connections (6/10A) and 125 have full services. Forming a focal point are the bar and restaurant (good menus), with a terrace and stage overlooking the attractive heated pool. There is also a large paddling pool and sunbathing terrace. For children, there is a well thought out play area plus plenty of other space for youngsters to play, both on the site and along the river. Activities are organised throughout the season; these are family based – no discos. Patrols at night ensure a good night's sleep. Access is easy, so site is suitable for large outfits. Member of Leading Campings Group.

Facilities

Two well equipped toilet blocks, one superb with everything working automatically. Facilities are of the highest standard, very clean and provide for babies and disabled visitors. Dishwashing and laundry. Private bathrooms to hire. Washing machines. Well stocked shop. Swimming pool and paddling pool (no Bermuda shorts). Tennis. Play area. Internet access. Organised activities, canoe trips. Communal barbecue area. WiFi (charged). Off site: Vallon-Pont-d'Arc 800 m).

Open: 15 April - 30 September.

Directions

From Vallon-Pont-d'Arc (western end of Ardèche Gorge) at a roundabout go east on the D290. Site entrance is shortly on the right.
GPS: 44.39804, 4.39878

Charges guide

Per unit incl. 2 persons and electricity	€ 30.00 - € 55.00
extra person	€ 5.90 - € 9.80

Vallières

Camping les Charmilles

D14, 625 route du val de fier, F-74150 Vallières (Haute-Savoie) T: 04 50 62 10 60.
E: les.charmilles.camping@wanadoo.fr alanrogers.com/FR74290

Les Charmilles is a friendly site in the village of Vallières, to the west of Annecy. There are 67 pitches, most with electricity (6/8A). A number of pitches are occupied by chalets and caravans (for rent). The site restaurant, Le Marilyn, is open to the general public and specialises in Savoyard cuisine. Takeaway meals are also possible. On-site leisure amenities include a new, large swimming pool, paddling pool and volleyball. During peak season, various activities are organised including theme evenings, as well as a children's club specialising in craft activities and games. The village centre is around 500 m. distant and has a number of shops including a post office and a specialist cheese shop. Rumilly, a larger village around 5 km. to the south, has two supermarkets and a wider selection of shops, cafés and restaurants.

Facilities

Facilities for disabled visitors. Washing machine. Motorcaravan service point. Bar, restaurant, takeaway service. Swimming pool (all 1/4-31/10). Paddling pool. Play area. Tourist information. Entertainment and activity programme. Chalets and caravans for rent. WiFi (free). Off site: Village centre 500 m. Rumilly 5 km. Vineyards. Mountain biking. Fishing and riding 5 km. Bicycle hire 6 km.

Open: 1 April - 31 October.

Directions

Approaching from the north, leave A40 autoroute at exit 11 and head south on D1508 and D1504 to Frangy. Then continue south on D910 to Vallières and then follow signs to the site.
GPS: 45.90194, 5.92766

Charges guide

Per unit incl. 2 persons	€ 15.50
extra person	€ 3.50 - € 19.00

Camping les Charmilles*
Tél 0033 450 62 10 60
www.campinglescharmilles.com
les.charmilles.camping@wanadoo.fr

This quiet 3-star family campsite is set on the countryside at the foot of the mountains, centrally situated between 3 lakes (Annecy, Genève and Aix-les-Bains). 2 swimming pools and 2 trampolines, restaurant with terrace. Good pizzas and Savoy specialties, good wine card!

IN SOUTH ARDECHE,
1 FAMILY, 2 CASTELS,
10 STARS!

The *Ardèche* riverfront,
at Vallon Pont d'Arc

In the charming little
village of *Lagorce*,
the peaceful

Camping Nature Parc
L'Ardechois
★★★★★

PRL
Domaine
de Sévenier
★★★★★

LES
CASTELS
Hôtellerie de Plein Air

Wooden house rentals

Route des Gorges de l'Ardèche
07150 VALLON PONT D'ARC
ardecamp@bigfoot.fr

Tel: 33(0)4 75 88 06 63
www.ardechois-camping.com
GPS: N44,398 E4,399

LeadingCampings

Quartier Sévenier
07150 LAGORCE
domainedesevenier@orange.fr

Tel: 33(0)4 75 88 29 44
www.sevenier.net
GPS: N44, 434 E4,411

La Clef
Verte

Vallon-Pont-d'Arc

Camping la Roubine

Route de Ruoms, F-07150 Vallon-Pont-d'Arc (Ardèche) T: 04 75 88 04 56. E: roubine.ardeche@wanadoo.fr

alanrogers.com/FR07310

This site on the bank of the Ardèche has been in the same family ownership for some 30 years. During this time there has been constant upgrading and it must now be considered one of the best sites in the area. There are 114 touring pitches, all with electricity (10A) and quite spacious. Well tended grass, trimmed hedging and mature trees and smart tarmac roads create a calm and well kept atmosphere. The proprietors, M. Moulin and Mme. Van Eck like to welcome their guests and are available to help during the day – they are rightly proud of their well run campsite. Much attention is given to cleanliness – the toilet blocks are cleaned three times a day. A variety of sporting facilities are available on the site. The pool complex is heated when necessary throughout the season. There is a bar and restaurant of most modern design which, together with a mini-market, are open throughout the season. The campsite also caters for their young visitors with a children's club in high season complete with an adventure playground and even an amphitheatre. There is an Internet room for visitors.

Facilities

Several small sanitary blocks include washbasins in cubicles. The main toilet block has showers, washbasins in vanity units, a baby bathroom and facilities for disabled visitors. Laundry. Swimming pools, paddling pool and separate children's pool. Tennis. Boules. Fishing. Barbecues only permitted on communal sites. River beach. Off site: Footpath to town 700 m. Supermarket in town. Bicycle hire and riding 1 km.

Open: 26 April - 18 September.

Directions

From Vallon take the D579 towards Ruoms. The site is well signed on left 400 m. from town. From west (Ruoms) site signed on right near Vallon town sign. If missed proceed to roundabout at entrance to Vallon, go around and return some 400 m. (as above). GPS: 44.40547, 4.37916

Charges guide

Per unit incl. 2 persons and electricity	€ 22.50 - € 45.00
extra person	€ 3.40 - € 9.20

NATURE, REST AND SPACE...
On the banks of the Ardèche river at only 800 m from Vallon-Pont-d'Arc

CAMPING ★★★★★

Comfortable pitches separated by natural hedges - Mobile homes with air conditioning and private terrace - Heated swimming pool and water play ground - Multi sports platform, midget golf, beach volley, half-court tennis - Excellent restaurant, open throughout the whole season - Free Wifi - English spoken

Route de Ruoms 07150 Vallon Pont d'Arc - Ardèche
Tél. (00 33) 04 75 88 04 56
www.camping-roubine.com
roubine.ardeche@wanadoo.fr
GPS : N 44°24'20» E 4°22'45»

Vernioz

Kawan Village le Bontemps

5 impasse du Bontemps, F-38150 Vernioz (Isère) T: 04 74 57 83 52. E: info@campinglebontemps.com

alanrogers.com/FR38120

This spacious, attractive and extremely well cared for site between Lyon and Valence in the Rhone Alpes is enhanced by a variety of trees planted by the original owner nearly 30 years ago. The 175 large, level and grassy pitches are arranged in groups, partly separated by neat hedges, all with water and 6A electricity. Fifteen pitches are used for mobile homes and chalets and a group at the back is used by weekenders. This is an excellent site for both short and long stays and the Dutch director and his wife, who speak English, have have spared no efforts in making this a most attractive and comfortable site.

Facilities

Two toilet blocks, one recently refurbished to a high standard. Motorcaravan service point. Shop (15/5-15/9). Bar, restaurant and takeaway (all 1/4-15/9). Heated swimming pool, children's fun pool and slide pool (all season). Several play areas. Minigolf. Tennis. Badminton. Electronic games. Fitness equipment. Bicycle hire. Extensive list of activities for all the family (high season). Small fishing lake. WiFi (charged). Off site: Small river for fishing. Vernioz 2 km. Pilat Regional Park 15 km. Golf.

Open: 26 March - 1 October.

Directions

Exit A7 south of Lyons at junction 9. Continue south for about 7 km. on N7. Just north of Auberives turn left on D37. Follow campsite signs for 7 km. Entrance is on right 4 km. beyond Vernioz. GPS: 45.4283, 4.928233

Charges guide

Per unit incl. 2 persons and electricity	€ 22.00 - € 30.00
extra person	€ 6.00 - € 7.00
child (under 7 yrs)	€ 3.00 - € 4.00

For latest campsite news, availability and prices visit
alanrogers.com

Vallon-Pont-d'Arc
Mondial Camping

Route des Gorges de l'Ardèche, F-07150 Vallon-Pont-d'Arc (Ardèche) T: 04 75 88 00 44.
E: reserv-info@mondial-camping.com **alanrogers.com/FR07370**

Located at the head of the spectacular Ardèche Gorges, Mondial Camping is one of many campsites along the banks of the river and offers the experience of canoe trips downstream with minibuses provided for the return. There are 217 pitches with 6/10A electricity and 32 of these also provide water and drainage. The grass pitches are an acceptable size, with good shade and separated by some topiary styled hedges. There are 23 mobile homes available for rent. The site has a good sports provision and a pool complex with one pool for swimming, one for children and another with water slides. Mondial is located at the head of the Gorge de l'Ardèche close to Vallon-Pont-d'Arc. It is some nine hours by river down to the end of the canoe trip. A number of canoe hire agencies exist but Mondial has one on site. Shorter trips are available and the trip can be made with an overnight stop. The Gorges de l'Ardèche has a route for those who prefer tarmac. A good wide road, the D290, takes you along the sides of the valley with numerous stunning viewpoints conveniently sited on your side of the road.

Facilities

Three modern sanitary units are tiled, very clean and heated in low season. Good facilities for disabled visitors. A fourth smaller block services the campsite and heated pools and has facilities for babies. Motorcaravan service point. Restaurant and takeaway. Bar. Good mini-supermarket. Games room. Play area, organised entertainment for children and sports in high season. Archery. Canoe hire and launching. Fishing (licence required). Internet access. WiFi (free). Off site: Bicycle hire 500 m. Riding 100 m. Town facilities 1 km.

Open: 28 March - 30 September.

Directions

From Vallon Pont-d'Arc take the Route Gorges de l'Ardèche.(D290). Site is 1 km. on the right and well signed. GPS: 44.397313, 4.40107

Charges guide

Per unit incl. 2 persons	
and electricity	€ 22.50 - € 42.00
extra person	€ 5.50 - € 9.20
child (1-13 yrs)	€ 4.00 - € 6.50
dog	€ 3.00 - € 4.50

On the banks of the Ardèche
Heated swimming pool

In a beautiful green environment
Open 30.03 - 30.09.2012

Off-season heated sanitation • Illuminated tennis courts • Comfortable sanitation Rental of canoes • Rental of mobil-homes • Camper service station • Bar with air conditioning • Ice cubes for sale • Accessible places for cars with water and drainage • Restaurant • Small supermarket • Activity program • Archery • Discounts outside the season • We speak english

Route des Gorges - 07150 Vallon-Pont-d'Arc
Tél. : 33 4 75 88 00 44 • Fax : 33 4 75 37 13 73
www.mondial-camping.com
reserv-info@mondial-camping.com

Duo + 60 years
- 15%
off season on stay
camping site

Free wifi

Villeneuve-de-Berg
Domaine le Pommier

RN102, F-07170 Villeneuve-de-Berg (Ardèche) T: 04 75 94 82 81. E: info@campinglepommier.com
alanrogers.com/FR07110

Domaine le Pommier is an extremely spacious, Dutch owned site of 10 hectares in 32 hectares of wooded grounds centred around a spectacular pirate themed water park. The site is steeply terraced and has wonderful views over the Ardèche mountains and beyond. There are 611 pitches, with 275 for touring units, the rest used for mobile homes and chalets for rent. They are on sandy grass, of a good size and well spaced. Separated by trees and hedges, some have less shade. All have access to electricity and water is close by. The site is not recommended for very large units. Extensive amenities feature a mini-farm, including llamas, goats and ponies. The site has first class facilities.

Facilities

Four excellent toilet blocks, one with underfloor heating, provide all the necessary facilities. Shop. Bar/restaurant. Swimming pool complex. Boules. Minigolf. Large multisports area. Bridge and watercolour classes. Tennis. Soundproofed disco. Extensive programme of events on and off site. Entertainment programme exclusively in Dutch. WiFi (charged). Off site: Villeneuve-de-Berg 1.5 km.

Open: 21 April - 15 September.

Directions

Site is west of Montélimar on the N102. The entrance is adjacent to the roundabout at the eastern end of the Villeneuve-de-Berg bypass. GPS: 44.57250, 4.51115

Charges guide

Per unit incl. 2 persons	
and electricity	€ 23.50 - € 43.50
extra person	€ 5.50 - € 9.50

For latest campsite news, availability and prices visit
alanrogers.com

Call 01580 214000 We can book this site for you! alanrogers ◊ travel

Villars-les-Dombes
Camping Indigo Parc des Oiseaux

Avenue des Nations, F-01330 Villars-les-Dombes (Ain) T: 04 74 98 00 21.
E: parc-des-oiseaux@camping-indigo.com **alanrogers.com/FR01110**

The Parc des Oiseaux is one of Europe's largest and most popular ornithological parks and can be found at Villars-les-Dombes, northeast of Lyon. This campsite is a new member of the Indigo group, reopening in 2011 (it was formerly a municipal site). The 199 pitches here are large and grassy, and are mostly supplied with electricity. A range of wooden chalets and specially made tents are available for rent. On-site amenities include a swimming pool and a small bar/restaurant. The River Chalaronne runs alongside the site and fishing is popular. A children's activity programme is run in high season, focusing on nature and the countryside. A great diversity of birds from around the world are on display at the nearby parc, and the emphasis there is very firmly on replicating birds' natural habitat and conservation. The park has won several major awards for this reason. Villars-les-Dombes lies at the heart of the Dombes, a region notable for its hundreds of lakes which are suited for fish rearing and water fowl.

Facilities

Bar/restaurant. Shop. Takeaway food. Swimming pool. Fishing. Playground. Children's activity programme. Tourist information. Chalets and tents for rent. Off site: Parc des Oiseaux. Cycle tracks and footpaths. Golf 1 km. Riding 10 km. Villars-les-Dombes. Lyon 33 km.

Open: 8 April - 28 October.

Directions

From A46, northeast of Lyons take exit 3 signed Bourg-en-Bresse. Take N83 northeast to Villars-les-Dombes, about 20 km. On entering town turn right to site (D904) which is well signed. GPS: 45.99723, 5.03047

Charges 2012

Contact the site for details.
Camping Cheques accepted.

In a peaceful green sanctuary, at the gateway of the Parc des Oiseaux

Parc des Oiseaux ★★★★
«Wood & canvas» tents for rent

Completely renovated Indigo campsite for outdoor holidays, spacious pitches, swimming pool, close to the village and next to the famous bird park «Parc des Oiseaux»
Indigo Parc des Oiseaux - 01330 Villars-les-Dombes
In between Lyon and Genève in the Ain
Tel : +33 (0)4 74 98 00 21

www.camping-indigo.com

Vinsobres
Camping le Sagittaire

Pont de Mirabel, F-26110 Vinsobres (Drôme) T: 04 75 27 00 00. E: camping.sagittaire@wanadoo.fr
alanrogers.com/FR26100

Le Sagittaire is a FranceLoc site, situated in this picturesque region with its Côtes du Rhône vineyards, lavender fields and medieval hilltop villages. It is only 2.5 km. from Vinsobres and 6 km. from Nyons, well known for its olives and its Provençal market. There are 297 level, grassy pitches with 100 for touring, all with 10A electricity. Most are separated by hedges and there are mature trees offering some shade. The hub of the site is a water park with indoor and outdoor pools, slides and toboggans, a restaurant, bar and small supermarket.

Facilities

Three excellent modern toilet blocks. Facilities for disabled campers and families. Motorcaravan services. Shop. Bar with TVs. Restaurant. Takeaway. Outdoor swimming pool, toboggan, slides, lazy river, cascades (1/5-30/8). Heated covered pool, paddling pool, jacuzzi (1/4-30/9). Games room (1/4-30/9). Cinema room. Small lake with sandy beach, picnic area. Excellent range of sporting facilities. Play areas. Fitness room. Extensive programme of family activities (July/Aug). Fishing. Bicycle hire. Minigolf. WiFi. Charcoal barbecues not allowed. Cycling is forbidden. Off site: Riding nearby. Nyons, Vaison la Romaine, Chateaux at Grignan and Suze la Rousse.

Open: All year.

Directions

Leave A7 at exit 19 (Bollène) and follow signs for Nyons (D94). Site is well signed on right just beyond Vinsobres (about 30 km) just before junction with D4. GPS: 44.32773, 5.07905

Charges guide

Per unit incl. 2 persons	
and electricity	€ 23.00 - € 40.00
extra person	€ 4.70 - € 8.00
child (under 7 yrs)	€ 3.50 - € 5.00

Long stay off season discounts.

Insurance Service

High quality, low cost insurance you can trust

Price Beater **GUARANTEE***

Caravan Insurance **SAVE** UP TO 60%

We've been entrusted with readers' campsite-based holidays since 1968, and they have asked us for good value, good quality insurance.

We have teamed up with Shield Total Insurance – one of the leading names in outdoor leisure insurances – to bring you peace of mind and huge savings. Call or visit our website for a no obligation quote – there's no reason not to – and trust us to cover your valued possessions for you.

*Price Beater **GUARANTEE**
  Motorhomes and Static Caravans
  We guarantee to beat any genuine 'like for like' insurance renewal quote by at least £25. Subject to terms & conditions.

• Caravans - **Discounts up to 60%**

• Park Homes - **Fantastic low rates**

• Tents - **Prices from only £30**

Instant quote

Call **0844 824 6314**

alanrogers.com/insurance

Alan Rogers Insurance Services is a trading name of Mark Hammerton Travel Limited which is an Appointed Representative of ITC Compliance Ltd and is authorised and regulated by the Financial Services Authority. Insurance products featured in this advertisement are provided by Shield Total Insurance which is a trading name of Vantage Insurance Services Limited (VISL). VISL is a subsidiary of Vantage Holdings Ltd and is authorised and regulated by the Financial Services Authority. VISL is registered in England No. 3441136. Registered Office: 41 Eastcheap, London EC3M 1DT.

From the endless shimmering beaches and dunes, and the fragrant pine forests of the Atlantic coast to the historical and beautiful Dordogne with its gastronomic delights, it's easy to see the attraction of this popular holiday region.

DÉPARTEMENTS: 24 DORDOGNE, 33 GIRONDE, 40 LANDES, 47 LOT-ET-GARONNE, 64 PYRÉNÉES-ATLANTIQUES

MAJOR CITY: BORDEAUX

The history of Aquitaine goes back many thousands of years to when man lived in the caves of the Périgord and left cave paintings at sites such as Les Eyzies and Lascaux. The ancient dukedom of Aquitaine was ruled by the English for 300 years following the marriage of Eleanor of Aquitaine to Henry Plantagenet, the future king, in 1154. The fortified villages and castles of the area bear evidence of the resulting conflict between the French and the English for control of Aquitaine, and today add character to the countryside.

This is a diverse region of mountains and vineyards, vast beaches, fertile river valleys, rolling grasslands and dense forests. Within its boundaries are the beautiful valleys of the Dordogne and Vézère, the forests of the Landes, and the beaches of the Atlantic which stretch from the Gironde estuary to the Basque Country, and the rocky Pyrenees mountains on the Spanish border.

Some of the world's most famous vineyards are around Bordeaux, the capital of the region. These are especially famous for their Médoc, Sauternes and St Emilion wines and most châteaux allow visits to their cellars and wine tastings.

Places of interest

Agen: a rich agricultural area, famous for its prunes.

Bordeaux: 14,000-piece Bohemian glass chandelier in foyer of the Grand Theatre, 29-acre Esplanade des Quinconces.

Rocamadour: cliffside medieval pilgrimage site.

Saint Cirq-La Popie: medieval village perched on a cliff.

St Emilion: visit the castle ramparts or drink 'premier cru' St Emilion at pavement cafés.

St Jean-de-Luz: seaside resort and fishing village.

St Jean-Pied-de-Port: ancient city with citadel, bright Basque houses in steep streets.

Cuisine of the region

Local specialities include fish dishes: carp stuffed with foie gras, mullet in red wine and besugo (sea bream), plus cagouilles (snails from Charentes).

Cassoulet: a hearty stew of duck, sausages and beans.

Cèpes: fine, delicate mushrooms; sometimes dried.

Chorizos: spicy sausages.

Chou farci: stuffed cabbage, sometimes aux marrons (with chestnuts).

Foie Gras: specially prepared livers of geese and ducks, stuffed with truffles.

Magret de canard: duck breast fillets.

Lamproie: eel-like fish with leeks, onions and red Bordeaux wine.

www.tourisme-aquitaine.fr/en
tourisme@tourisme-aquitaine.fr
(0)5 56 01 70 00

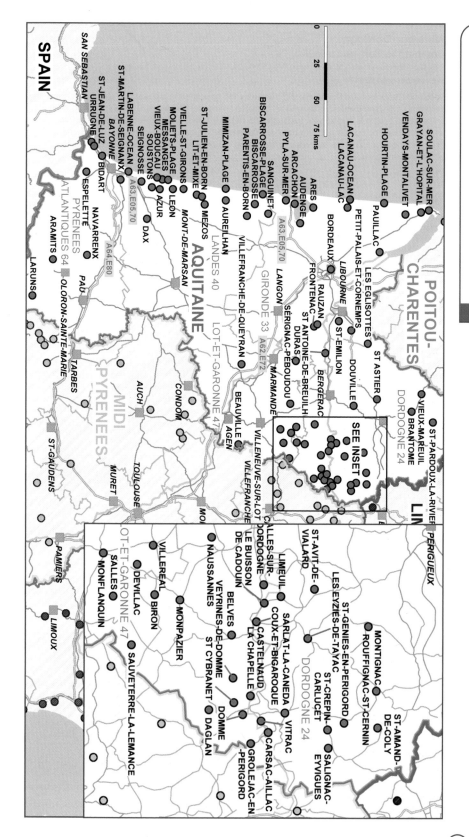

For latest campsite news, availability and prices visit

alanrogers.com

Allés-sur-Dordogne

Camping le Port de Limeuil

F-24480 Allés-sur-Dordogne (Dordogne) T: 05 53 63 29 76. E: didierbonvallet@aol.com

alanrogers.com/FR24170

At the confluence of the Dordogne and Vézère rivers, opposite the picturesque village of Limeuil, this delightful family site exudes a peaceful and relaxed ambience. There are 75 marked touring pitches on grass, some spacious and all with electricity (5/10A). The buildings are in traditional Périgourdine style and surrounded by flowers and shrubs. A sports area on a large, open, grassy space between the river bank and the main camping area adds to the feeling of space and provides an additional recreation and picnic area (there are additional unmarked pitches for tents and camper vans along the bank here).

Facilities

Two clean, modern toilet blocks provide excellent facilities. Bar/restaurant with snacks and takeaway (all 20/5-5/9). Small shop. Swimming pool with jacuzzi, paddling pool and children's slide (1/5-30/9). Badminton. Tennis. Volleyball. Football. Boules. Trampoline. Mountain bike hire. Canoe hire, launched from the site's own pebble beach. WiFi in bar area (free). Off site: The pretty medieval village of Limeuil 200 m. Riding 1 km. Golf 10 km.

Open: 1 May - 30 September.

Directions

Site is 7 km. south of Le Bugue. From D51/D31E Le Buisson to Le Bugue road turn west towards Limeuil. Just before bridge into Limeuil, turn left (site signed), across another bridge. Site shortly on the right. GPS: 44.87977, 0.88587

Charges guide

Per unit incl. 2 persons and electricity	€ 16.50 - € 30.00
extra person	€ 4.50 - € 6.50

Aramits

Camping Barétous-Pyrénées

Quartier Ripaude, F-64570 Aramits (Pyrénées-Atlantiques) T: 05 59 34 12 21. E: atso64@hotmail.com

alanrogers.com/FR64020

Located on the edge of the Pyrenees, this quiet site is well away from the tourist bustle, particularly in early or late season. It is now owned by the Drapeaus, a hard working and welcoming French couple. Set in a rural location, yet close to the town, its excellent position is ideal for exploring the region and offers a peaceful haven for those wishing to stay in quiet surroundings. The 61 shady, grass pitches are attractive and of a good size with hedges. They offer both water and electricity (10A). The welcoming reception (English spoken) sells local produce and organic food. The heated swimming and paddling pool area is overlooked by a small sun terrace with a café/bar.

Facilities

Two sanitary blocks, one old, one modern, offer clean facilities with unisex toilets and showers. Facilities for disabled visitors. Laundry facilities. Small shop selling organic food. Café/bar. Swimming and paddling pools (heated July/Aug). Sauna and spa pool. Communal room with TV, games, library and drinks. Boules. Play area with sandpit. WiFi (charged). Off site: Fishing 50 m. Town with supermarket and ATM 250 m. Riding 3 km.

Open: 1 March - 20 October.

Directions

From Oloron-Sainte-Marie, head southwest on D919 to Aramits. Through village bear right on D918. Cross river and immediately turn right at campsite sign. GPS: 43.1214, -0.732317

Charges guide

Per unit incl. 2 persons and electricity	€ 19.60 - € 26.20

Camping Cheques accepted.

Arès

Camping la Cigale

53 rue du Général de Gaulle, F-33740 Arès (Gironde) T: 05 56 60 22 59. E: contact.lacigale@gmail.com

alanrogers.com/FR33120

La Cigale is an attractive little site with charm and ambience where the owners extend a very warm welcome. Small and beautifully maintained, it is set amid a variety of trees that give some dappled shade. M. Pallet's floral displays add colour to the 41 neatly hedged, grassy touring pitches (100 sq.m. and most with 6A electricity, ten also with water and a drain). There is a small unheated swimming pool and a paddling pool. The bar has a terrace where drinks, meals and snacks are served under the shade of large plane trees. Six delightful chalets for rent are spacious, modern and very well presented.

Facilities

Well equipped toilet block includes a family room with two showers and facilities for disabled visitors. Washing machine and dryer. Motorcaravan services. Simple shop. Bar, terrace, meals, snacks. Pizza takeaway (all 17/6-10/9). Swimming and paddling pools (25/5-12/9). Small play area. Entertainers for children and adults in July/Aug. Free donkey cart rides every Sunday in season. Off site: Site is convenient for a wide choice of beaches. Village centre 800 m. Fishing and riding 1 km.

Open: 23 April - 26 September.

Directions

Leave Bordeaux ring road at exit 10 (D213) or exit 11 (D106) and continue direct to Arès. Turn into Arès following road to church square. Turn right following signs for Lège - Cap Ferret. Site is 800 m. on left. GPS: 44.77287, -1.14147

Charges guide

Per unit incl. 2 persons and electricity	€ 25.50 - € 35.50
extra person	€ 6.00

For latest campsite news, availability and prices visit

alanrogers.com

Arcachon

Camping Club Arcachon

5 allée Galaxie, B.P. 46, F-33312 Arcachon Cedex (Gironde) T: 05 56 83 24 15.
E: info@camping-arcachon.com **alanrogers.com/FR33030**

This campsite enjoys a position well back from the hustle and bustle, where nights are quiet and facilities are of a high standard. The 176 touring pitches are divided into areas for caravans, motorcaravans and tents and are on neatly formed terraces beneath tall pine trees. Most have electricity (6/10A). The site is quite hilly and the narrow roads that wind around it could possibly make it difficult for larger motorcaravans to manoeuvre and find suitable pitches. At night, wardens ensure that security and noise levels are controlled. A 1 km. walk takes you to the town of Arcachon where there are plenty of shops, bars and restaurants. However, the campsite bar, restaurant and takeaway are open at weekends from April to September (daily July/Aug) if you prefer to stay on site. Watersports, paragliding, sailing, tennis tournaments, climbing the biggest sand dune in Europe, and not forgetting such gastronomic delights as oysters and mussels, are readily available.

Facilities

Three sanitary blocks with the usual facilities. Washing machine, dryers. Fridge hire. Motorcaravan services. Shop (15/6-15/9). Bar, restaurant, snack bar, takeaway (April-Sept). Swimming pool (1/5-30/9). Bicycle hire. Play area. Games room. Children's club and entertainment for all age groups (1/7-31/8). Barbecues are only permitted in communal areas. Internet access and WiFi.
Off site: Beach 1 km. on foot. Riding 1 km. Golf 2 km. Arcachon 2-3 km.

Open: All year (excl. 12 November - 12 December).

Directions

Approaching Arcachon from Bordeaux on the N250 take exit for 'Hôpital Jean Hameau' (D217). Cross over bypass following signs for hospital, then signs for Abatilles. At next roundabout follow signs for 'Camping'. Take care as the route travels through suburban housing. Follow campsite signs, not sat nav. GPS: 44.6513, -1.174083

Charges guide

Per unit incl. 2 persons and electricity	€ 17.00 - € 36.00
extra person	€ 4.00 - € 8.50
child (4-10 yrs)	€ 1.00
dog	€ 2.00 - € 4.00

Camping Cheques accepted.

We can book this site for you! Call 01580 214000 alan rogers travel

Camping Club Arcachon ★★★★

Atlantic Ocean

Bassin d'Arcachon

Discover nature

Water Slides

Special offer April, May, June and September :
1 week 7days/7nights
for the price of 4 days in mobil-home
4 persons 220 €* or
1 week-end 2days/2nights in mobil-home
4 persons 80 €*
*Prices without tourist tax
limited offer (subject to availability)

Online booking

5, ALLÉE DE LA GALAXIE
LES ABATILLES - BP 46
33312 ARCACHON CEDEX
Tel. +33 (0)5 56 83 24 15
Fax. +33 (0)5 57 52 28 51
Internet :
www.camping-arcachon.com
Email :
info@camping-arcachon.com

Audenge

Camping le Braou

Route de Bordeaux, F-33980 Audenge (Gironde) T: 05 56 26 90 03. E: info@camping-audenge.com
alanrogers.com/FR33260

The present owners, M. and Mme. Gharbi, were the wardens of this simple, former municipal site and now lease it from the town. They have funded several developments since they took over in 2003 including a swimming pool, a snack bar, play area and new electrical hook-ups. The site is flat with easy access, and the large pitches are in avenues, separated by newly-planted small shrubs. There is little natural shade. The new electric hook-ups (on 116 of the 148 pitches) are 6A. Outside high season this is a pleasant, reasonably priced place to stay while exploring the Bassin d'Arcachon with its bird reserve, oyster beds, waymarked walks and cycle tracks.

Facilities

The two toilet blocks have been recently refurbished and are very adequate. Washbasins are in cubicles, showers are controllable for temperature, pushbutton operated. Bar and snack bar (July/Aug). Swimming pool (1/4-31/8). Play area. Internet access. Motorcaravan service point and overnight pitches outside site. Mobile homes to rent. Off site: Town facilities 800 m. Riding 2 km. Golf 5 km.

Open: 1 April - 30 September.

Directions

From A63 take exit 22 onto A660 towards Arcachon. From A660 take exit 2 towards Facture, then D3 through Biganos to Audenge. Site is signed 'Camping Municipal' at lights in town. GPS: 44.6841, -1.00433

Charges guide

Per unit incl. 2 persons and electricity	€ 22.00 - € 33.50

Aureilhan

Village Center Eurolac

236 promenade de l'Etang, F-40200 Aureilhan (Landes) T: 05 58 09 02 87. E: contact@village-center.com
alanrogers.com/FR40270

This well shaded and wooded site is located on the banks of Lac de l'Aureilhan (with a road in between), just 8 km. from the Atlantic beaches. The natural surroundings of the lake shore provide many bicycle and walking tracks, together with a sandy beach. This is a mobile home park (most privately owned). They do not accept touring units, but the sister site just a few yards further along the same road does.

Facilities

Four traditional toilet blocks provide washbasins in cabins, showers and British style toilets. Ramped facilities for disabled visitors. (key provided). Laundry. Heated swimming pool (May-Sept). Games room. Multisports area. Minigolf. Bicycle Hire. Fishing (licence from Mimizan). Sandy play area with good equipment for young children. Miniclub (4-12 yrs) and evening entertainment (July/Aug). Barbecues not permitted (communal area provided). Off site: Fishing 20 m. (permit). Boat launching. Riding 1 km. Golf 5 km. Sea and beach 8 km.

Open: 4 April - 13 September.

Directions

Approaching from north take A63 motorway (Bayonne). Leave at exit 16 (Labouheyre). Follow signs to Mimizan. After St Paul-en-Born, turn right signed Aureilhan and site. Continue to stop sign and turn left. Go through the village to the lake and turn right down the promenade to site on the right. GPS: 44.22245, -1.20345

Charges guide

Per unit incl. 1 person	€ 8.50 - € 22.00

Camping Cheques accepted.

Aureilhan

Village Center Aurilandes

1001 promenade de l'Etang, F-40200 Aureilhan (Landes) T: 04 99 57 21 21. E: contact@village-center.com
alanrogers.com/FR40300

Ten minutes from the beach, this well-shaded and wooded eight-hectare site is located on the banks of Lac de l'Aureilhan (with a road in between), just eight kilometres from the Atlantic beaches. It has 300 average sized pitches, most with 6-10A electricity. There are also mobile homes and bungalow tents to hire. The natural surroundings of the lake shore provide many bicycle and walking tracks, together with a sandy beach. Facilities for sport and activities are excellent, with a 580 sq.m. swimming pool, sauna, spa, and fitness room. There are many walks and cycle paths nearby, as well as boat launching facilities. Sports tournaments and water polo are arranged in high season.

Facilities

Traditional toilet blocks provide washbasins in cabins, showers and British style toilets. Facilities for disabled visitors. Laundry. Heated swimming pool with jacuzzi (July-Sept). Shop. Bar, restaurant, snack bar and takeaway (1/7-30/9). Games room. Boules. Multisports area. Bicycle hire. Fishing. Miniclub (4-12 yrs). Teenage club (13-17 yrs) and evening entertainment (July/Aug). Barbecues not permitted (communal area provided). Off site: Fishing (permit). Boat launching, riding 1 km.

Open: 25 May - 13 September.

Directions

Heading east from the centre of Mimizan, take the D626. After 2 km. take next left signed Aureilhan. Continue to stop sign and turn left. Go through village to lake and turn right down the promenade to site on right. GPS: 44.22296, -1.19445

Charges guide

Per unit incl. 2 persons and electricity	€ 16.00 - € 24.00

Camping Cheques accepted.

For latest campsite news, availability and prices visit
alanrogers.com

Azur
Camping Village la Paillotte

66 route des Campings, F-40140 Azur (Landes) T: 05 58 48 12 12. E: info@paillotte.com

alanrogers.com/FR40040

La Paillotte, in the Landes area of southwest France, is a site with a character of its own. It lies beside the Soustons Lake only 1.5 km. from Azur village, with its own sandy beach. This is suitable for young children because the lake is shallow and slopes gradually. All 310 pitches at La Paillotte are mostly shady with shrubs and trees. The 75 pitches for touring vary in price according to size, position and whether they are serviced. La Paillotte is an unusual site with its own atmosphere which appeals to many regular clients. The campsite buildings (reception, shop, restaurant, sanitary blocks) are Tahitian in style.

Facilities

Well equipped toilet blocks. Washing machines, dryers. Shop (1/6-1/9). Good restaurant with terrace overlooking lake, bar, takeaway (all 22/4-24/9). Swimming pool complex (22/4-24/9). Sports, games and organised activities. Miniclub. TV room, library. Fishing. Bicycle hire. Sailing, rowing boats and pedaloes for hire. Torches useful. Free WiFi. Dogs are not accepted. Off site: Riding 5 km. Golf and Atlantic beaches 10 km.

Open: 30 May - 20 September.

Directions

Coming from the north along N10, turn west on D150 at Magescq. From south go via Soustons. In Azur turn left before church (site signed). GPS: 43.78696, -1.3093

Charges guide

Per unit incl. 2 persons and 10A electricity	€ 15.50 - € 38.00
incl. water	€ 17.50 - € 40.00

Beauville
Camping Les 2 Lacs

F-47470 Beauville (Lot-et-Garonne) T: 05 53 95 45 41. E: camping-les-2-lacs@wanadoo.fr

alanrogers.com/FR47170

Les 2 Lacs is a spacious family campsite, attractively situated at the heart of a 22-hectare estate, with two lakes suitable for swimming and fishing. Pitches are large (minimum 100 sq. m) and surrounded by hedges. It is a good site for anglers and the fishing lake is stocked with bream, carp, perch and pike, amongst others. It is possible to hire rowing boats, pedaloes and canoes. The site's bar/restaurant is located between the two lakes. There is plenty of activity in peak season with campfires, evening walks and musical evenings, but these activities do not disturb the site's tranquillity. A walk around the site may offer the opportunity to see badgers, deer or even wild boar, with large birds of prey overhead.

Facilities

One traditional toilet block has good clean facilities including controllable hot showers, washbasins in cabins, a baby bath and facilities for disabled visitors. Washing machine and dryer. Restaurant (April-Oct) and snack bar (July/Aug). Swimming and fishing lakes (no lifeguard). Boat, pedalo and canoe hire. Country walks. Volleyball. Tennis. Children's play area. Entertainment and activities in peak season. Tourist information. Mobile homes and equipped tents for rent. WiFi. Off site: Beauville 800 m.

Open: 1 April - 31 October.

Directions

From Cahors head west on the D656 to Tournon d'Agenais and then to St Amans-du-Pech. Here, head south on the D80 and then the D215 to Beauville. The site is well signposted from this point. GPS: 44.27217, 0.88821

Charges guide

Per unit incl. 2 persons and electricity	€ 13.95 - € 17.70
extra person	€ 3.10 - € 4.30

Belvès
RCN le Moulin de la Pique

F-24170 Belvès (Dordogne) T: 05 53 29 01 15. E: moulin@rcn.fr

alanrogers.com/FR24350

This high quality campsite set in the heart of the Dordogne has fine views looking up to the fortified town of Belvès. It is a splendid rural estate where there is plenty of space and a good mixture of trees and shrubs. Set in the grounds of a former mill, the superb traditional buildings date back to the 18th century. There are 200 level pitches with 154 for touring units, all with 6A electricity, a water point and drainage. The remainder are used for mobile homes to rent. The site is ideally suited for families with young and teenage children as there is so much to do, both on site and in the surrounding area.

Facilities

Three modern sanitary blocks include facilities for disabled visitors. Launderette. Shop, bar, restaurant, snack bar and takeaway (all open all season). Swimming pools (two heated). Recreational lake. Playgrounds. Library. Fossil field. Sports field. Tennis. Minigolf. Boules. Satellite TV. Games room. Bicycle hire. WiFi (charged). Off site: Bars, restaurants and shops in Belvès 2 km. Canoeing 2 km. Riding 5 km. Golf 7 km.

Open: 9 April - 1 October.

Directions

Site is 35 km. southwest of Sarlat on the D710, about 7 km. south of Siorac-en-Périgord. GPS: 44.76228, 1.01412

Charges guide

Per unit incl. 2 persons, electricity and water	€ 19.90 - € 43.90
extra person (over 3 yrs)	€ 2.50 - € 4.90
Camping Cheques accepted.	

For latest campsite news, availability and prices visit
alanrogers.com

Belvès

Flower Camping les Nauves

Le Bos Rouge, F-24170 Belvès (Dordogne) T: 05 53 29 12 64. E: campinglesnauves@hotmail.com
alanrogers.com/FR24470

Les Nauves is a pretty and well maintained site, 4 km. from the beautiful medieval village of Belvès in the Périgord Noir region of the Dordogne. The site consists of 100 pitches, 60 for touring (on a slight slope, long leads necessary) and 40 dedicated to mobile homes, chalets and bungalow tents. There are some pitches that are separated and shaded by mature trees, while others are open with good views of the surrounding countryside. The ground on most of the pitches is soft, sandy soil and may cause some difficulty for large vehicles in wet weather. The owners are very dedicated to providing a quality site.

Facilities

The single sanitary block is clean and well maintained. Facilities for disabled visitors. Baby room. Laundry area with washing machine. Good shop. Bar/restaurant with patio, and takeaway on request. Swimming pool and paddling pool. Good play area. Boules. Library (FR, NL). Games room. Riding. WiFi. Off site: Fishing 2 km. Small supermarket in Belvès 4 km. Bicycle and mountain bike hire 4 km. Golf 10 km.

Open: 23 April - 24 September.

Directions

From Belvès take D53 southwest towards Monpazier. Site is 4 km. from Belvès on the left hand side. Follow signs and site is 800 m. off the main road. GPS: 44.75275, 0.98445

Charges guide

Per unit incl. 2 persons and electricity	€ 13.95 - € 24.50
extra person	€ 2.50 - € 4.90

Bidart

Camping le Pavillon Royal

Avenue du Prince de Galles, F-64210 Bidart (Pyrénées-Atlantiques) T: 05 59 23 00 54. E: info@pavillon-royal.com alanrogers.com/FR64060

Le Pavillon Royal has an excellent situation on raised ground overlooking the sea, with good views along the coast to the south and to the north coast of Spain beyond. There is a large heated swimming pool and sunbathing area in the centre of the site. The camping area is divided up into 303 marked, level pitches, many of a good size. About 50 are reserved for tents and are only accessible on foot. The remainder are connected by asphalt roads. All have electricity and most are fully serviced. Much of the campsite is in full sun, although the area for tents is shaded.

Facilities

Good quality toilet blocks with baby baths and two units for disabled visitors. Washing facilities (only two open at night). Washing machines, dryers. Motorcaravan services. Shop (including gas). Restaurant and takeaway (from 1/6). Bar (all season). Heated swimming and paddling pools. Playground. General room, TV room, games room, films. Fishing. Surf school. Wellness facilities (1/6-25/9). Dogs are not accepted. WiFi (charged). Off site: Golf 500 m. Bicycle hire 2 km. Riding 3 km.

Open: 14 May - 30 September.

Directions

From A63 exit 4, take the N10 south towards Bidart. At roundabout after the Intermarché supermarket turn right (signed for Biarritz). After 600 m. turn left at site sign. GPS: 43.45458, -1.57649

Charges guide

Per unit incl. 2 persons, electricity and water	€ 30.00 - € 51.00
tent pitch	€ 24.00 - € 41.00
extra person	€ 8.00 - € 11.00

Bidart

Castel Camping le Ruisseau des Pyrénées

Route d'Arbonne, F-64210 Bidart (Pyrénées-Atlantiques) T: 05 59 41 94 50. E: francoise.dumont3@wanadoo.fr alanrogers.com/FR64070

This busy site, with a large play area filled with equipment, is ideal for young families. It is about 2 km. from Bidart and 2.5 km. from a sandy beach. There are two swimming pools with slides on the main site and, across the road, there is an indoor heated pool and new spa complex (charged in July/August) with outdoor fitness equipment. Pitches on the main campsite are individual, marked and of a good size, either on flat terraces or around the lake. The terrain is wooded so the great majority of them have some shade. Electrical connections are available throughout. The site has a number of steep slopes.

Facilities

Two main blocks and some extra smaller units. Washing machines. Motorcaravan service point. Shop, large self-service restaurant with takeaway and bar with terraces, and TV (all 22/5-4/9). Outdoor swimming pools, indoor heated pool and spa complex (all season). Sauna. Large play area. Two tennis courts (free outside July/Aug). Fitness track. TV and games rooms. Minigolf. Bicycle hire. Fishing. Small animal sanctuary. WiFi throughout (charged). Off site: Riding and golf 3 km.

Open: 7 April - 18 September.

Directions

Site is east of Bidart on a minor road towards Arbonne. From A63 autoroute take Biarritz exit (4), turn towards St Jean-de-Luz and Bidart on N10. After Intermarché turn left at roundabout and follow signs to site. GPS: 43.4367, -1.5677

Charges guide

Per unit incl. 2 persons and electricity	€ 19.00 - € 44.00
extra person	€ 5.00 - € 7.00

We can book this site for you! Call 01580 214000 alanrogers travel

For latest campsite news, availability and prices visit
alanrogers.com

Bidart
Sunêlia Berrua
Rue Berrua, F-64210 Bidart (Pyrénées-Atlantiques) T: 05 59 54 96 66. E: contact@berrua.com
alanrogers.com/FR64140

Berrua is in a useful situation on the Basque coast, 10 km. from the Pyrenees, 20 km. from Spain and a five minute drive from Biarritz. Just 1 km. from the sea, it is an ideal location for visiting the beaches in southwest France. A neat and tidy site, it has 270 level pitches (140 for touring units) set amongst trees. Most have electricity (6A) and some are fully serviced. The focal point of the site is an excellent swimming pool complex with several pools, slides and paddling pools which is surrounded by sunbeds for sunbathing. Organised activities and entertainment for both adults and children in high season, guided walks, dances, sporting competitions, bingo and karaoke. A member of the Sunêlia group.

Facilities

Toilet facilities are good (unisex) consisting of two blocks with washbasins in cabins, baby rooms, facilities for disabled visitors, washing machines and dishwashing sinks (cold water only). Motorcaravan services. Shop, bar/restaurant and takeaway. New pool complex. Games room. Play area (3-10 yrs only). Archery. Boules. WiFi throughout (charged). Off site: Fishing and beach 1 km.

Open: 1 April - 30 September.

Directions

From A63 exit 4, take N10 south towards Bidart. At roundabout after the Intermarché supermarket, turn left. Bear right then take next right (site signed). GPS: 43.43822, -1.58237

Charges guide

Per unit incl. 2 persons
and electricity € 19.00 - € 41.00
Camping Cheques accepted.

Bidart
Yelloh! Village Ilbarritz
Avenue de Biarritz, F-64210 Bidart (Pyrénées-Atlantiques) T: 04 66 73 97 39.
E: info@yellohvillage-ilbarritz.com **alanrogers.com/FR64150**

This is a very pleasant member of the Yelloh! Village group (formerly called Résidence des Pins), which will appeal greatly to couples and young families. Set on a fairly gentle hillside, the top level has reception and a bar. Slightly lower are the impressive new paddling and swimming pools in a sunny location with sunbeds. Next comes the well stocked shop, tennis courts and the rest of the pitches. Some pitches are behind reception and others, lower down, some slightly sloping, are under trees and separated by hydrangea hedges. Some have electricity (10A, long leads required). There is a varied entertainment programme in July and August. The site is not suitable for American motorhomes.

Facilities

The two toilet blocks have some washbasins and showers together. Washing machines, dryers, ironing boards and facilities for disabled visitors. Motorcaravan services. Shop and bar open all season, restaurant (1/6-10/9) and takeaway (1/7-31/8). 2 swimming pools (one open all season). Games room. Table tennis. Tennis (charged in July/Aug). Play area (3-8 yrs). Bicycle hire. Off site: Lake beach with lifeguard and fishing (no licence needed) 600 m.

Open: 31 March - 10 November.

Directions

Heading south on the A63 towards Spain, take exit J4 onto the N10 towards Bidart. At the roundabout straight after Intermarche turn right towards Biarritz. The site is on the right after 1 km. GPS: 43.4531, -1.5737

Charges guide

Per unit incl. 2 persons
and electricity € 20.00 - € 46.00
extra person € 6.00

Bidart
Camping Ur-Onea
Rue de la Chapelle, F-64210 Bidart (Pyrénées-Atlantiques) T: 05 59 26 53 61. E: uronea@wanadoo.fr
alanrogers.com/FR64280

Situated on the outskirts of Bidart and 600 m. from a fine sandy beach, this large, attractively terraced site has 280 grass pitches with little shade, 142 are for touring with electricity (10A) and 10 have water and drainage. There are some hardstandings for motorcaravans. A separate area is reserved for washing surf boards, barbecues and there is even a shower for washing dogs. With local transport available all year (600 m) this campsite is ideal for exploring the surrounding areas. During the summer months, aquarobics, dancing and discos are arranged, with organised sports events and children's clubs.

Facilities

Three well maintained and clean sanitary blocks are of good size with large showers (all also have washbasins) and wall mounted hairdryers. Facilities for babies and disabled visitors. Laundry. Shop. Bar, restaurant and takeaway (12/6-10/9). New heated swimming pool (1/5-18/9). Two excellent play areas for younger children. Organised activities in high season. Internet. Off site: Beach, bars, restaurants and shops 600 m.

Open: 3 April - 18 September.

Directions

Take N10 north from St Jean-de-Luz. Continue through Guethary and site sign is on the right. Turn right and site is on the left in 800 m. GPS: 43.43397, -1.59074

Charges guide

Per unit incl. 2 persons
and electricity € 18.50 - € 32.50
extra person € 3.50 - € 6.50

(339)

Call 01580 214000 We can book this site for you! alan rogers ◉ travel

Biscarrosse
Camping du Domaine de la Rive

541

Route de Bordeaux, F-40600 Biscarrosse (Landes) T: 05 58 78 12 33. E: info@larive.fr
alanrogers.com/FR40100

Surrounded by pine woods, la Rive has a superb beach-side location on Lac de Sanguinet. It provides 250 mostly level, numbered and clearly defined touring pitches of 100 sq. m. all with electricity connections (10A). The swimming pool complex is wonderful with pools linked by water channels and bridges. There is also a jacuzzi, paddling pool and two large swimming pools all surrounded by sunbathing areas and decorated with palm trees. An indoor pool is heated and open all season. This is a friendly site with a good mix of nationalities. The latest additions are a super children's aquapark with various games, and a top quality bar/restaurant complex where regular entertainment is organised. The beach is excellent, shelving gently to provide safe bathing for all ages. There are windsurfers and small craft can be launched from the site's slipway.

Facilities

Five good clean toilet blocks have washbasins in cabins and mainly British style toilets. Facilities for disabled visitors. Baby baths. Motorcaravan service point. Shop with gas. New bar/restaurant complex with entertainment. Swimming pool complex (supervised July/Aug). Games room. Play area. Tennis. Bicycle hire. Boules. Archery. Fishing. Waterskiing. Watersports equipment hire. Tournaments (June-Aug). Skateboard park. Trampolines. Miniclub. No charcoal barbecues on pitches. WiFi (charged). Off site: Riding 2 km. Golf 8 km. Beach 17 km.

Open: 6 April - 9 September.

Directions

Take D652 from Sanguinet to Biscarrosse and site is signed on right in about 6 km. Turn right and follow tarmac road for 2 km. GPS: 44.46052, -1.13065

Charges guide

Per unit incl. 2 persons and electricity	€ 24.50 - € 47.00
extra person	€ 3.80 - € 8.50
child (3-7 yrs)	€ 2.50 - € 7.00
dog	€ 5.00 - € 7.00

Camping Cheques accepted.

Biron
Camping le Moulinal

F-24540 Biron (Dordogne) T: 05 53 40 84 60. E: lemoulinal@franceloc.fr
alanrogers.com/FR24100

A rural, lakeside site in woodland, now owned and run by the FranceLoc company, le Moulinal offers activities for campers of all ages. Of the 300 grassy pitches, only around 72 are available for touring units and these are spread amongst the site's own mobile homes, chalets and a small number of Dutch tour operator tents. All pitches are flat, grassy and have 6A electricity, but vary considerably in size (75-100 sq.m). The five acre lake has a sandy beach and is suitable for boating (canoe hire available), swimming and fishing. Ambitious, well organised animation is run throughout the season including craft activities and a children's club.

Facilities

Toilet facilities, built to harmonise with the surroundings, include facilities for disabled campers and babies. Washing machines, dryers. Motorcaravan services. Excellent restaurant. Bar. Snack bar/takeaway. Large, heated swimming pool with jacuzzi and paddling pool. Rustic play area. Children's club. Multisports court. Boules. Tennis. Archery. Roller skating. Mountain bike hire. Canoeing. Fishing and swimming in lake. WiFi. Evening entertainment (July/Aug). All facilities are open all season. Max. 1 dog. Off site: Riding and climbing 5 km. Potholing 10 km. Shops and supermarket in Villeréal 12 km. Bastide towns of Monpazier and Monflanquin 15 km. Castles (Biron, Bonaguil, Gavaudun).

Open: 1 April - 16 September.

Directions

Site is 53 km. southeast of Bergerac. From D104 Villeréal - Monpazier road take the D53/D150 south. Just before Lacapelle Biron turn right onto D255 towards Dévillac, (site signed). Site is 1.5 km. on the left. GPS: 44.5998, 0.8708

Charges guide

Per unit incl. 2 persons and electricity	€ 19.00 - € 37.00
extra person	€ 5.00 - € 7.00

For latest campsite news, availability and prices visit
alanrogers.com

CAMPING RESORT
★★★★★

La Rive

Leisure pool - Slides - Jacuzzi - Rapid river - Massage jet. Aquatic area more than 3000 m² included 1000 m² covered and heated aquatic park. Bar - restaurant - Theatre - Kids club - Animation. Chalets and mobile homes to rent - Attractively situated at the lakeside in the heart of the Les Landes forest.

www.larive.fr

Biscarrosse

Club Airotel

Route de Bordeaux 40600 Biscarrosse
Tél : + 33 5 58 78 12 33   Fax : + 33 5 58 78 12 92
info@larive.fr   www.campingaquitaine.com

Biscarrosse

Campéole Navarrosse

712 chemin de Navarrosse, F-40600 Biscarrosse (Landes) T: 05 58 09 84 32. E: navarrosse@campeole.com

alanrogers.com/FR40230

Navarosse is a member of the Campéole group and is located on the very large Lac de Sanguinet, just 7 km. from the Atlantic beaches. The location of this traditional campsite is attractive, with a long sandy beach and a small harbour (ideal for mooring small boats) on one side, and to the other, a small canal. Pitches are of a good size, mostly on fairly level, sandy soil with good shade. Most have 10A electricity. Many water-based activities take place on the lake, including sailing jet skiing and windsurfing. For cyclists there are many tracks to various places. Mobile homes, chalets and fully equipped tents are available for rent. Some units are specially adapted for disabled visitors. The lake, which is one of the largest in western Europe and the Dune de Pyla, Europe's highest sand dune is close by, as well as the Arcachon basin, the great city of Bordeaux and the world renowned Médoc vineyards.

Facilities

Two sanitary units are made up of separate blocks of toilets and showers. One modern block has all facilities under one roof including for disabled people. Laundry facilities. Motorcaravan services. Bar, snack bar and takeaway (1/7-31/8). Tennis. Multisports pitch. Archery. Bicycle hire. Play area. Bouncy castle. Activity and entertainment programme (1/7-31/8). Tourist information. WiFi (charged). Charcoal barbecues are not permitted. Mobile homes, equipped tents and chalets for rent. Off site: Riding. Sailing 300 m. Biscarrosse 3 km. Golf and fishing 5 km. Nearest beach 8 km.

Open: 27 April - 16 September.

Directions

From the north on the D652 turn right onto the D305. After about 1.5 km. turn right at campsite sign and towards lake. GPS: 44.43192, -1.16885

Charges guide

Per unit incl. 2 persons	
and electricity	€ 17.90 - € 31.60
extra person	€ 4.60 - € 9.40
child (2-6 yrs)	€ 4.80 - € 5.70
dog	€ 2.50 - € 3.50

AQUITAINE

Campéole
CAMPSITES AND RENTALS

Navarrosse***
On the side of Lake Biscarrosse with sandy beach. Pitches, quality accommodations, possibility to moor boat.

40600 Biscarrosse - Tel: +33-558-0984-32 - www.campeole.co.uk / navarrosse@campeole.com

Want independent campsite reviews at your fingertips?

NOW ON ANDROID TOO

alan rogers

Available on the App Store
Download for Android

An exciting **FREE** app for both iPhone and Android
alanrogers.com/apps

Biscarrosse
Camping Mayotte Vacances

368 chemin des Roseaux, F-40600 Biscarrosse (Landes) T: 05 58 78 00 00.
E: camping@mayottevacances.com **alanrogers.com/FR40240**

This appealing site is set amongst pine trees on the edge of Lac de Biscarrosse. Drive down a tree- and flower-lined avenue and proceed toward the lake to shady, good sized pitches which blend well with the many tidy mobile homes that share the area. Divided by hedges, all 208 touring pitches have electricity (16A) and water taps. There may be some aircraft noise at times from a nearby army base. The pool complex is impressive, with various pools, slides, chutes, jacuzzi and sauna, all surrounded by paved sunbathing areas. The excellent lakeside beach provides safe bathing for all ages with plenty of watersports available. A comfortable restaurant and bar overlook the pool. A new, fully equipped gym is available free of charge. Children of all ages are catered for with organised clubs, play and sports areas and a games room. This well managed, clean and friendly site with helpful multi-lingual staff in reception should appeal to all and the facilities are open all season.

Facilities

Four good quality, clean toilet blocks (one open early season). Good facilities for visitors with disabilities. Unusual baby/toddler bathroom. Motorcaravan services. Laundry. Supermarket. Boutique. Comprehensive rental shop (July/Aug). Restaurant. Swimming pools (one heated; supervised July/Aug. and weekends). Play area. Further children's area (extra cost) with trampolines, inflatables and a small train. Bicycle hire. Fishing. Watersports. Organised activities and entertainment (July/Aug). Clubs for toddlers and teenagers (July/Aug). Charcoal barbecues not permitted. Hairdressers (seasonal). ATM. Internet access. Off site: Riding 100 m. Golf 4 km. Town 2 km. with restaurants, shops and bars. Beach 8 km.

Open: 1 April - 1 October.

Directions

From the north on D652 turn right on D333 (Chemin de Goubern). Pass through Goubern and Mayotte village. Take next right (signed to site) into Chemin des Roseaux. GPS: 44.43495, -1.15505

Charges guide

Per unit incl. 2 persons	€ 18.00 - € 45.00
extra person	€ 4.00 - € 7.00
child (3-7 yrs)	free - € 4.00
dog	€ 3.00 - € 5.00

★★★★☆
CAMPING VILLAGE

Mayotte Vacances
BISCARROSSE - FRANCE

Like an island's breeze

Welcome to the shores of Lake Biscarosse where beauty and tranquillity are unrivalled. Quality accommodations are awaiting you in combination with many sporting activities, exclusive concerts and performances for children and adults. The new additions of 2012: a modern spa of 250 m² and a refurbished pool area of 650m² (250 m² balnéo pool - 400 m² beach).

368, chemin des Roseaux - 40600 Biscarrosse
Tél : 00 33(0)5 58 78 00 00 - Fax 00 33(0)5 58 78 83 91 · camping@mayottevacances.com · www.mayottevacances.com

For latest campsite news, availability and prices visit
alanrogers.com

Biscarrosse

Camping Bimbo

176 chemin du Bimbo, Navarrosse, F-40600 Biscarrosse (Landes) T: 05 58 09 82 33.
E: camping.bimbo@free.fr **alanrogers.com/FR40460**

Camping Bimbo is a well-maintained site in the popular resort of Biscarrosse. An excellent new aquapark was opened in 2010. This features a spa pool and an excellent children's pool with many water games. The complex is surrounded by a large 700 sq. m. sun terrace. The 70 touring pitches are of a good size and are well shaded. Most have 6/8A electrical connections. A good range of mobile homes and chalets are available for rent. Bimbo is a lively site in peak season with a varied activity and entertainment programme, including special activities for children. The site is located on the south side of the massive Etang de Cazaux, where a wide range of water sports are possible. Alternatively, the magnificent Atlantic beach is a short drive away, at Biscarrosse-Plage. Biscarrosse itself is a pleasant resort, and home to an interesting seaplane museum. The surrounding forest is ideal cycling and walking country (cycle hire available on site).

Facilities

Toilet blocks have hot showers, washbasins in cabins and facilities for disabled visitors. Shop. Restaurant, bar/snack bar and takeaway (15/6-15/9, weekends in low season). Swimming pool complex. Sports area. Children's play area. Games room. Fitness room. Sauna and spa. Entertainment and activity programme (high season). Bicycle hire. Tourist information. Mobile homes and chalets for rent. WiFi (charged). Off site: Sailing and boat launching 600 m. Shops and restaurants in Biscarrosse centre. Riding and golf 2 km. Biscarrosse-Plage 9 km.

Open: 1 May - 30 September.

Directions

Approaching Biscarrosse on D652 from Sanguinet, follow signs to Navarrosse. Pass through the hamlet of En Belliard, and the site is soon signposted, and can be found on the right.
GPS: 44.426828, -1.161091

Charges guide

Per unit incl. 2 persons and electricity	€ 20.00 - € 39.50
extra person	€ 4.00 - € 8.50
child (2-7 yrs)	free - € 5.50

Camping BIMBO
176, chemin de Bimbo
NAVARROSSE
40600 BISCARROSSE
tél : 05 58 09 82 33
fax : 05 58 09 80 14
www.campingbimbo.fr

Bimbo is a friendly 4-star campsite, between the sea and a lake. Fantastic facilities: waterpark with toboggan, sportsterrain, spa, animationprogrammes for adults and children, beautiful beaches. Accomodations for all budgets. Biscarrosse Landes Côte Atlantique

Biscarrosse-Plage

Campé•le

Campéole Plage Sud

230 rue des Bécasses, F-40600 Biscarrosse-Plage (Landes) T: 05 58 78 21 24. E: plage-sud@campeole.com
alanrogers.com/FR40420

Biscarrosse-Plage is a lively holiday resort with a fabulous beach. La Plage Sud is a member of the Campéole group and is located around 800 m. from the beach. This is a massive site with 905 touring pitches and a further 479 pitches occupied by mobile homes, chalets and fully equipped tents (available for rent). The site is lively in peak season with a varied programme of activities and entertainment (N.B. numbers are limited for some activities). On-site amenities include a swimming pool and paddling pool. Pitches are sandy and generally well shaded. Most are equipped with electricity.

Facilities

Five modern toilet blocks were clean, with some washbasins in cabins, warm water and preset showers. Facilities for children and babies. Motorcaravan service point. Bar/snack bar. Shop. Swimming pool (4/6-18/9). Paddling pool. Multisports terrain. Play area. Activity and entertainment programme. Tourist information. Mobile homes, chalets and tents for rent. WiFi (charged). Charcoal barbecues not allowed. Off site: Nearest beach 800 m. Surfing. Cycle and walking tracks. Dune de Pyla. Minigolf. Canoeing in the Leyre river. Wine tasting.

Open: 29 April - 18 September.

Directions

From A63 motorway, take A66 towards Bassin d'Arcachon, Dune du Pyla and Biscarrosse. Take the Biscarrosse exit, then D216 towards Sanguinet and Biscarrosse. In Biscarrosse, take right turning off the second roundabout, towards la Plage. The campsite can be found before reaching Biscarrosse Plage. Entrance to site is tight - large units may ask to access via side gate. GPS: 44.4419, -1.2455

Charges guide

Per unit incl. 2 persons	€ 17.90 - € 31.70

For latest campsite news, availability and prices visit
alanrogers.com

Biscarrosse-Plage

Campéole

Campéole le Vivier

681 rue du Tit, F-40600 Biscarrosse-Plage (Landes) T: 05 58 78 25 76. E: vivier@campeole.com
alanrogers.com/FR40430

Le Vivier is a member of the Campéole group and can be found 2 km. from the seaside resort of Biscarrosse-Plage. The nearest beach is 800 m. away and the crashing Atlantic breakers can be heard on site. Pitches are located amongst the towering pine trees and mostly have electrical connections. Mobile homes and chalets are available for rent (including specially adapted units for wheelchair users). Although close to the beach, there is a large swimming pool on site, and other sports amenities include volleyball, basketball and tennis. This large, lively site in high season with plenty going on, including discos and karaoke evenings, as well as sports tournaments. The Arcachon Basin is easily accessible to the north, as well as the Dune de Pyla, Europe's highest sand dune and the Aqualand water theme park. Another popular day trip could be the great city of Bordeaux, accessible within an hour's drive. Closer to the site, there are miles of cycle trails through the forest and bikes can be hired on site. Riding is also popular – there are stables close to Biscarrosse.

Facilities

Bar/snack bar and takeaway food (25/6-31/8). Swimming pool (12/6-18/9). Tennis. Bicycle hire. Bouncy castle. Children's play area. Activities and entertainment programme. Tourist information. Mobile homes, chalets and equipped tents for rent. Only communal barbecues are permitted. WiFi (charged). Off site: Nearest beach 800 m. Treetop adventure park 2 km. Lake beach 5 km. Hiking and cycle tracks. Riding 8 km. Golf 10 km.

Open: 26 April - 21 September.

Directions

Head south from Arcachon on D218 passing the Dune de Pyla and continue to Biscarrosse Plage. The site is well signed from here. GPS: 44.45804, -1.23968

Charges guide

Per unit incl. 2 persons	
and electricity	€ 17.90 - € 31.70
extra person	€ 4.60 - € 9.50
child (2-6 yrs)	free - € 5.60
dog	€ 2.50 - € 3.50

AQUITAINE

Campéole
CAMPSITES AND RENTALS

Le Vivier ★★★

Three stars site with swimming pool at 800 meters of a sandy beach. Quality facilities, touring pitches and accomodations for rent.

40600 Biscarrosse-Plage - Tel.: +33-558-7825-76 - www.campeole.co.uk / vivier@campeole.com

Bordeaux

Camping Bordeaux Lac

Boulevard Jacques Chaban Delmas, F-33000 Bordeaux Lac (Gironde) T: 05 57 87 70 60.
E: contact@village-du-lac.com alanrogers.com/FR33410

Bordeaux is undeniably one of France's 'must see' cities and now it has a superior campsite. Adjacent to the exhibition centre and beside Bordeaux Lac, the site opened in 2009 and is open all year. The facilities and accommodation are of top quality. There are 119 touring pitches, some on well kept grass, others, primarily for motorcaravans, have hardstanding. All have electricity, 40 have water and drainage and 70 also have sewerage disposal. Within the 14 hectare campsite there are also 93 well equipped chalets and mobile homes (three specifically for disabled visitors) for rent. The site is arranged around five attractive, man-made lakes and set amongst tall trees.

Facilities

Modern, heated sanitary block. Laundry. Restaurant, bar and supermarket. Swimming pool. Play area. Table tennis, handball and basketball court. Mobile homes and chalets for rent. WiFi (charged). Off site: Golf and fishing (Bordeaux Lac complex). Large shopping centre. Cycle and walking tracks. Bordeaux centre 5 km. with public transport daily from site.

Open: All year.

Directions

At Bordeaux, take the A630 ring road and exit 4A. Follow signs for Parc des Expositions and signs for campsite. At roundabout take second exit (right) and site is 700 m. on the right. GPS: 44.89805, -0.58194

Charges guide

Per unit incl. 2 persons	
and electricity	€ 16.00 - € 31.00
extra person	€ 4.00 - € 9.00

For latest campsite news, availability and prices visit
alanrogers.com

Brantôme

Camping Brantôme Peyrelevade

Avenue André Maurois, F-24310 Brantôme (Dordogne) T: 05 53 05 75 24. E: info@camping-dordogne.net

alanrogers.com/FR24540

Le Peyrelevade is a quiet and peaceful site in the Périgord Vert region. Of a very good standard, it comprises 170 spacious and well kept touring pitches and 17 mobile homes for rent. Most pitches have 6A electricity and 12 are fully serviced. The site is set in an area that is part open, part wooded and most pitches have partial shade from well sited trees and hedges. The beautiful village of Brantôme on an island surrounded by a river, is close by and there you will find small bars, restaurants and other amenities. There is a 3.5 tonne weight restriction on the main road through the village.

Facilities

Two heated sanitary blocks are well maintained, clean and adequate for the number of pitches. One is new and includes good facilities for disabled visitors. Baby area with bath. Laundry with washing machine. Shop (1/6-15/9). Bar. Takeaway (1/7-31/8). Games room with TV. Open air swimming pool. Play area. River beach suitable for paddling. Fishing. WiFi (charge). Max. 2 dogs accepted. Off site: Boat trips. Riding 3 km. Golf 25 km.

Open: 1 May - 30 September.

Directions

Take D939 south from Angoulême, or north from Périgueux. Brantôme is around 20 km. north of Périgueux. Drive through town and look for sign for site which is about 1.5 km. north outside Brantôme. There is a 3.5 tonne weight restriction on the main road through the village. GPS: 45.361, 0.661

Charges guide

Per unit incl. 2 persons	
and electricity	€ 14.50 - € 22.50

Carsac-Aillac

Village Center Aqua Viva

Route Sarlat-Souillac, Carsac-Aillac, F-24200 Sarlat-la-Canéda (Dordogne) T: 08 25 00 20 30.
E: contact@village-center.com **alanrogers.com/FR24110**

This shaded woodland site is ideally situated for visits to Rocamadour and Padirac, as well as exploring the Dordogne region, including the medieval town of Sarlat, only 7 km. away. The site is divided into two sections, separated by a small access road. The 179 pitches are flat, mainly on grass, divided by shrubs and they vary in size (80-150 sq.m). Many have shade from the numerous trees and all have electricity (6/10A). A wide range of organised activities, children's clubs and entertainments run throughout the season, making this site popular with families, especially those with pre-teens and young teenagers.

Facilities

Each part of the site has a modern toilet block, with facilities for disabled visitors and babies. Bar, restaurant and takeaway with terrace. Good shop. Heated swimming pool (open all season, heated 1/6-13/9) plus a children's pool. Small fishing lake. Minigolf. Half tennis. Good play park for under 7s. Floodlit boules pitch and multisports court. Bicycle hire. Off site: Aerial woodland assault course 500 m. Riding and golf 5 km.

Open: 3 April - 12 September.

Directions

Site is 6 km. from Sarlat south of the D704A road from Sarlat to Souillac. From Souillac, the access road to the site is just around a left-hand bend, not easy to see. GPS: 44.8677581, 1.2794936

Charges guide

Per unit incl. 2 persons	
and electricity	€ 16.00 - € 29.00
extra person	€ 3.00 - € 5.00

Castelnaud-la-Chapelle

Camping Maisonneuve

Vallée du Céou, F-24250 Castelnaud-la-Chapelle (Dordogne) T: 05 53 29 51 29.
E: contact@campingmaisonneuve.com **alanrogers.com/FR24450**

This family run site is beautifully situated in the Céou Valley, in the Périgord. There are 130 spacious touring pitches, all with 6/10A electricity. Some are well separated, whilst others are on two open, grassy areas. Most pitches have some shade. The site's facilities are grouped around the old farmhouse. Swimming, diving, fishing and canoeing are all possible in the Céou river which borders the site and can be accessed directly. There are also swimming and paddling pools on site and in high season entertainment is organised several evenings each week. This is an excellent location from which to explore the beautiful region of the Périgord.

Facilities

Three sanitary blocks, one has been totally refurbished, are kept clean and tidy. Facilities for babies and disabled visitors. Laundry. Shop with bread. Snack bar. Bar. Swimming and paddling pools. Minigolf. Play areas. TV room. Games room. Dance evenings. Karaoke. Sport tournaments. Bicycle hire. Canoe trips. Climbing. Free WiFi in reception and courtyard. Off site: Fishing 1 km. Riding 3 km. Golf 5 km. Canoeing.

Open: 1 April - 31 October.

Directions

From A20 exit 55 take D703 towards Sarlat and Beynac. Follow signs for D57 (Castelnaud la Chappelle). Site is well signed on edge of village. Caravans and large units over 5 m. are advised to continue on D57 for 2 km. then turn left. Site is signed here at the junction with D50. GPS: 44.80367, 1.15533

Charges guide

Per unit incl. 2 persons	€ 17.88 - € 25.28

For latest campsite news, availability and prices visit

alanrogers.com

Coux-et-Bigaroque

Camping les Valades

D703, F-24220 Coux-et-Bigaroque (Dordogne) T: 05 53 29 14 27. E: info@lesvalades.com
alanrogers.com/FR24420

Sometimes we come across small but beautifully kept campsites which seem to have been a well kept secret, and les Valades certainly fits the bill. Set on a hillside overlooking lovely countryside between the Dordogne and Vezère rivers, each pitch is surrounded by a variety of flowers, shrubs and trees. The 85 pitches are flat and grassy, mostly on terraces, all with 10A electricity and most with individual water and drainage as well. Ten very large pitches (over 300 sq. m) are available for weekly hire, each having a private sanitary unit, dishwashing, fridge and barbecue. At the bottom of the hill, away from the main area, is a swimming pool and a good sized lake for carp fishing, swimming and canoeing (free canoes). Rustic chalets for rent occupy 19 of the largest pitches, and mobile homes are on six. From the moment you arrive you can see that the owners, M. and Mme. Berger, take enormous pride in the appearance of their campsite and there is an abundance of well tended flowers and shrubs everywhere you look. A convivial and family atmosphere is very much in evidence and the site is therefore ideal for families with young children. Couples both young and mature will also enjoy this site.

Facilities

Two clean modern toilet blocks, one with family shower rooms. Facilities for disabled visitors. Washing machine. Shop, bar and restaurant (all July/Aug) and a terrace overlooking the valley. Heated swimming pool with sun terrace and paddling pool (July/Aug). Play area near the lake and pool. Fishing. Canoeing. WiFi (free). Off site: Small shop, bar, restaurant in Coux-et-Bigaroque 5 km. Supermarket at Le Bugue 10 km. Riding and bicycle hire 5 km. Golf 6 km.

Open: 1 April - 15 October.

Directions

Site is signed down a turning on west side of D703 Le Bugue - Siorac-en-Perigord road, about 3.5 km. north of village of Coux-et-Bigaroque. Turn off D703 and site is 1.5 km. along on right. GPS: 44.86056, 0.96385

Charges 2012

Per unit incl. 2 persons and electricity	€ 26.00
extra person	€ 6.30
child (under 7 yrs)	€ 4.40

No credit cards.

★★★ A quiet piece of nature in the Périgord Noir

Pitches and wooden chalets • Heated swimming pool • Fishing & Canoeing • Perfect for children
24220 - Coux et Bigaroque • www.lesvalades.com • +33 (0) 5.53.29.14.27

Daglan

Camping le Moulin de Paulhiac

F-24520 Daglan (Dordogne) T: 05 53 28 20 88. E: Francis.Armagnac@wanadoo.fr
alanrogers.com/FR24230

You will be guaranteed a friendly welcome from the Armagnac family, who are justifiably proud of their well-kept and attractive site built in the grounds surrounding an old mill. The facilities have been continually updated and improved over the years. The 150 shady pitches (93 for touring) are separated by hedges and shrubs, all fully serviced. Many pitches are next to a small river that runs through the site and joins the River Ceou along the far edge. A tent field slopes gently down to the river, which is quite shallow and used for swimming. This site will appeal especially to families with younger children.

Facilities

Two clean toilet blocks provide modern facilities, including those for disabled visitors. Good shop, restaurant, takeaway. Main pool, heated and covered by a sliding roof in low season, children's pool, a further small pool and a toboggan and slide. Boules. Bicycle hire. Small river with beach. Fishing. Canoe trips organised on the Dordogne. Organised evening activities. Children's club in high season. Off site: Riding 5 km. Golf 10 km.

Open: 15 May - 15 September.

Directions

Site is 17 km. south of Sarlat and is on the east side of the D57, about 5 km. north of the village of Daglan. GPS: 44.76762, 1.17635

Charges guide

Per unit incl. 2 persons and electricity	€ 17.95 - € 29.85
extra person	€ 5.00 - € 7.50
child (0-10 yrs)	€ 2.70 - € 5.20

For latest campsite news, availability and prices visit
alanrogers.com

Dax
Camping les Chênes

Bois de Boulogne, F-40100 Dax (Landes) T: 05 58 90 05 53. E: camping-chenes@wanadoo.fr
alanrogers.com/FR40020

Les Chênes is a well established site, popular with the French themselves and situated on the edge of town amongst parkland (also near the river) and close to the spa for the thermal treatments. The 176 touring pitches are of two types, some large and traditional with hedges, 109 with 5A electricity, water and drainage, and others more informal, set amongst tall pines with electricity if required. This is a reliable, well run site, with a little of something for everyone, but probably most popular for adults taking the treatments. Dax is not a place that springs at once to mind as a holiday town but, as well as being a spa, it promotes a comprehensive programme of events and shows during the summer season.

Facilities

Two toilet blocks, one new and modern with heating, washbasins in cubicles, facilities for disabled visitors, babies and young children. The older block has been refurbished. Laundry and dishwashing facilities. Shop also providing takeaway food (7/4-27/10). Swimming and paddling pools (5/5-15/9). Play area. Field for ball games. Boules. Bicycle hire. Miniclub for children (July/Aug). Occasional special evenings for adults. Charcoal barbecues are not permitted. WiFi (charged). Off site: Restaurant opposite. Riding, fishing and golf all within 200 m. Beaches 28 km.

Open: 24 March - 10 November.

Directions

Site is west of town on the south side of the river, signed after main river bridge and at many junctions in town – Bois de Boulogne (1.5 km). In very wet weather the access road to the site may be flooded (but not the site). GPS: 43.71182, -1.07329

Charges guide

Per unit incl. 2 persons	
and electricity	€ 14.90 - € 17.90
extra person	€ 6.00
child (2-10 yrs)	€ 4.00
dog	€ 1.50

Camping Les Chênes ★★★★

Hôtel de plein air
du Bois de Boulogne
4 0 1 0 0   D A X
Tel. 0033 558 90 05 53
Fax 0033 558 90 42 43

Devillac
Camping Fontaine du Roc

Dévillac, F-47210 Villeréal (Lot-et-Garonne) T: 05 53 36 08 16. E: fontaine.du.roc@wanadoo.fr
alanrogers.com/FR47070

Situated on the border between the lovely region of Périgord (Dordogne) and the Lot-et-Garonne, in the heart of the Pays des Bastides, is Camping Fontaine du Roc. It is a natural environment on a wooded hillside and quite isolated. The three hectare site has panoramic views of the nearby Château Biron. Each of the 70 pitches has access to electricity (5/10A Europlug); some are in the sun and others in the shade to suit your needs. A long-established site now run by Dutch owners, the site blends well with the natural surroundings. The narrow, single-track approach road may cause problems for large units.

Facilities

One centally located sanitary block is kept spotlessly clean and includes good facilities for babies, children and disabled visitors. Washing machine. Small shop with bread and milk daily. Bar and snack bar serving pizzas. Large swimming pool, children's pool, whirlpool. New wooden chalet with sauna, massage, whirlpool and bunkhouse. Two small play areas. Library with TV. Boules. Two purpose built stone barbecues (wood provided, no charcoal ones on pitches). Entertainment for children (high season). Free WiFi. Off site: Fishing 200 m. Riding 2 km. Monflanquin 9 km. Château Biron 10 km.

Open: 28 March - 1 October.

Directions

From Monflanquin, take D272 heading north towards Monpazier. Fontaine du Roc is 10 km. along the road on the left hand side. GPS: 44.61405, 0.81885

Charges 2012

Per unit incl. 2 persons	
and electricity	€ 18.50 - € 23.50
extra adult	€ 4.50 - € 5.50
child (under 6 yrs)	€ 3.00 - € 3.50
dog	€ 3.50

Less 10% outside 12/6-11/9. No credit cards.

For latest campsite news, availability and prices visit
alanrogers.com

Domme
Camping le Bosquet

La Riviere, F-24250 Domme (Dordogne) T: 05 53 28 37 39. E: info@lebosquet.com
alanrogers.com/FR24760

Located between Sarlat and Bergerac, this great little campsite is set in lovely countryside and is landscaped with flowers and shrubs, with trees offering some shade. The site is maintained to a good standard and is kept very clean. The natural environment gives a sense of tranquillity and calm – here you can relax. M. and Mme. Vrand will do everything they can to ensure you have a great holiday. There are 60 level pitches with 10A electricity, with 40 for touring units. The remainder are used for mobile homes to rent. The Dordogne river is 300 metres away and the canoeing here is good and convenient.

Facilities

The toilet block includes facilities for disabled visitors. Washing machine and iron. Restaurant. Takeaway. Small shop. Swimming pool. Library. Entertainment (July/Aug). Play area. Pétanque. TV. WiFi free in reception area. Charcoal barbecues allowed. Off site: Fishing 300m. Bicycle hire and canoeing 1 km. Golf and tennis 2 km. Riding 4 km.

Open: 1 April - 30 September.

Directions

Take D46 from Sarlat to Vitrac. Cross the river bridge in Vitrac and the site is on the right hand side 1 km. further on. Well signed. GPS: 44.82241, 1.225319

Charges 2012

Per unit incl. 2 persons and electricity	€ 13.40 - € 16.40
extra person	€ 3.40 - € 4.30

Duras
Le Cabri Holiday Village

Route de Savignac, F-47120 Duras (Lot-et-Garonne) T: 05 53 83 81 03. E: holidays@lecabri.eu.com
alanrogers.com/FR47110

This countryside site of 5.5 hectares is divided into three areas: camping, chalets and open fields. It is on the border of the Dordogne and the Lot-et-Garonne departments. Le Cabri Holiday Village is an English owned and run, small holiday complex. The owners, Peter and Eileen Marston who are keen caravanners themselves, have developed 24 new spacious pitches (generally 150 sq. m), all with electricity (4/16A) and water. The open, level pitches are all on hardstandings surrounded by grass and separated by young trees, so with limited shade. Access for large motorcaravans using the rear entrance is possible as this was considered when the site was planned. Open all year round, the site has a swimming pool, a small fishing pond and other leisure facilities. Wildlife watching is another pastime here with red deer and wild boar populating the area. Le Cabri also benefits from its own high quality restaurant which specialises in local cuisine. It draws clientele from the local area as well as those staying on the site. Although situated in a very rural and peaceful area, the historic village of Duras is only a ten minute walk, with its good selection of shops, restaurants, bars and the famous fortified château standing guard at the head of the village square.

Facilities

A recently refurbished sanitary block is centrally located, heated in low season and has three new private cabins. Separate cabin for disabled visitors. Washing machines, dryers and ironing board. Shop (all year) sells basics including bread. Restaurant (all year) with occasional entertainment, and Internet access. Swimming pool (June-Sept). Large play area. Boules. Fishing pond. WiFi (charged). Off site: Riding and tennis 1 km. Golf 10 km. Watersports 7 km. Canoeing 8 km.

Open: All year.

Directions

In Duras, look for the D203 and follow signs for site. It is less than 1 km. away. GPS: 44.68296, 0.18615

Charges guide

Per unit incl. 2 persons and 10A electricity	€ 18.00 - € 23.00
extra person	€ 4.00 - € 5.00
child (under 12 yrs)	€ 2.00 - € 3.00
dog	€ 2.00

Le Cabri Holiday Village
Route de Savignac - 47120 Duras
Tel-fax: 0033 (0) 553 838 103
Mobile: 0033 (0) 685 449 711
E-mail: holidays@lecabri.eu.com - www.lecabri.eu.com

For latest campsite news, availability and prices visit
alanrogers.com

Douville

Camping d'Orpheo Negro

Les trois Frères, (RN 21), F-24140 Douville (Dordogne) T: 05 53 82 96 58. E: camping@orpheonegro.com
alanrogers.com/FR24880

Camping d'Orpheo Negro can be found midway between Périgueux and Bergerac. Its 100 grassy pitches are in a park which extends over 16 hectares. They are large and generally well-shaded. Most have electrical connections (6A). A few chalets and mobile homes are available for rent. The site has been developed on the banks of a three-hectare lake, which is well stocked with carp, so this is a popular site with anglers. Rowing boats and pedaloes are provided free of charge too. Other leisure amenities include a swimming pool (with water slide), tennis, an open-air bowling alley and minigolf.

Facilities

The single toilet block was quite old when we visited but there are plans to renew it. Shop. Bar/snack bar. Swimming pool. Water slide. Fishing. Rowing boats and pedaloes. Tennis. Minigolf. Open-air bowling alley. Games room. Playground. Activity programme. WiFi (free). Off site: Cycle and walking tracks. Riding 1 km. Vergt 8 km. Périgueux and Bergerac 25 km.

Open: 1 April - 31 October.

Directions

Site is at Douville, north of Bergerac. From Bergerac, take northbound N21 towards Périgueux and follow signs to Douville (D36). Then, follow signs to site. GPS: 45.024654, 0.615967

Charges guide

Per unit incl. 2 persons and electricity	€ 16.20 - € 20.70
extra person (over 4 yrs)	€ 4.50 - € 5.50

Espelette

Camping Biper Gorri

Chemin de Lapitxague, F-64250 Espelette (Pyrénées-Atlantiques) T: 05 59 93 96 88.
E: info@camping-biper-gorri.com **alanrogers.com/FR64390**

Camping Biper Gorri has recently joined the Airotel group and can be found at the heart of Basque country, south of Cambo-les-Bains. This is a small site of 70 touring pitches, all of which are grassy and mostly shaded. There are a number of mobile homes and fully equipped bungalow-style tents available for rent. The site boasts an attractive pool complex with a large main pool and separate children's pool. The site is livelier in peak season with a children's club, regular entertainment and activities for all the family. A number of excursions are on offer, including accompanied rafting and canoe trips.

Facilities

One toilet block is partly heated and includes some washbasins in cabins and preset showers. Facilities for disabled visitors. Motorcaravan services. Basic shop (15/6-15/9). Bar, restaurant, snack bar and takeaway. Heated swimming pool. Spa. Play area. Entertainment and activity programme. Woodland walks. Tourist information. Mobile homes and tents for rent. WiFi over site (charged). Torches useful. Off site: Shops, bars and restaurants in Espelette. Mountain sports. Fishing.

Open: 1 April - 6 November.

Directions

Take the exit for Bayonne Sud from A64 motorway (Maignon) and take D932 to Ustaritz. Continue to Cambo-les-Bains and then take D10 to Espelette. The site is well signed in the village. GPS: 43.353374, -1.449635

Charges guide

Per unit incl. 2 persons and electricity	€ 17.60 - € 33.00
extra person	€ 3.00 - € 6.60

Groléjac-en-Perigord

Camping Caravaning les Granges

F-24250 Groléjac-en-Perigord (Dordogne) T: 05 53 28 11 15. E: contact@lesgranges-fr.com
alanrogers.com/FR24020

Situated only 500 metres from the village of Groléjac, les Granges is a lively and well maintained campsite set on sloping ground in woodland. There are 188 pitches, of which 100 are available for touring units. The pitches are marked and numbered on level terraces, some shaded by mature trees and shrubs whilst others are sunny. You can choose your preference when checking in at reception. All pitches have electricity (6A) and water either on the pitch or close by. The site has a good sized swimming pool and a large shallow pool for children. A bridge connects these to a fun pool with water slides. Around 88 pitches are used by tour operators.

Facilities

The toilet blocks are of a high standard with good facilities for disabled visitors. Bar/restaurant and snack bar with takeaway food (16/5-11/9). No shop, but bread and milk to order. Play area. Minigolf. Canoe and bicycle hire. New outdoor gym equipment. Paintball. Quad bikes. Climbing wall (2-12 yrs). Canoe trips. Entertainment, sporting tournaments and kids' club (high season). WiFi in the bar area (free). Off site: Shops in Groléjac 550 m.

Open: 21 April - 8 September.

Directions

In centre of village of Groléjac on main D704 road. Site signed through a gravel parking area on west side of road. Drive through this area and follow road around to T-junction. Turn right, under railway bridge, and immediately left (site signed). Site is just along this road on left. GPS: 44.81593, 1.29086

Charges 2012

Per unit incl. 2 persons and electricity	€ 18.20 - € 28.70

For latest campsite news, availability and prices visit

alanrogers.com

Labenne-Océan
Yelloh! Village le Sylvamar
Avenue de l'Océan, F-40530 Labenne-Océan (Landes) T: 05 59 45 75 16. E: camping@sylvamar.fr
alanrogers.com/FR40200

Less than a kilometre from a long sandy beach, this campsite has a good mix of tidy, well maintained chalets, mobile homes, a tree house and touring pitches. The 320 touring pitches (650 in total) are level, numbered and mostly separated by low hedges. A number of new, less shaded pitches have recently been added. Following development, all now have electricity (10A), water and drainage. They are set around a superb pool complex with pools of various sizes (one heated, one not) with a large one for paddling, a wild water river, toboggans and slides. In a sunny setting, all are surrounded by ample sunbathing terraces and overlooked by the excellent bar/restaurant. In the evenings, entertainment is organised for all ages. Every year new amenities are offered and new sporting facilities include a tennis court, multisports pitch and a 50x25 m. football pitch, all on all-weather surfaces. A member of Leading Campings group.

Facilities

Four modern toilet blocks have washbasins in cabins. Excellent facilities for babies and disabled visitors. Laundry. Fridge hire. Shop, bar/restaurant and takeaway (all season). Play area. Games room. Cinema, TV and video room. Fitness centre. Wellness amenities. Tennis. Football pitch. Bicycle hire. Library. Extensive entertainment programme for all ages. WiFi (Charged). No charcoal barbecues. Off site: Beach 900 m. Fishing and riding 1 km. Golf and boat launching 7 km.

Open: 31 March - 3 November.

Directions

Labenne is on the N10. In Labenne, head west on D126 signed Labenne-Océan and site is on right in 4 km. GPS: 43.59570, -1.45638

Charges guide

Per unit incl. 2 persons	
and electricity	€ 15.00 - € 44.00
extra person	€ 5.00 - € 8.00
child (3-7 yrs)	free - € 5.00
dog	€ 4.00

Between the forest, the dunes and the océan

CAMPING VILLAGE SYLVAMAR

Yelloh! village SYLVAMAR ***** - Avenue de l'Océan - 40530 Labenne Océan
Tél. : +33 (0)5 59 45 75 16 - Fax : +33 (0)5 59 45 46 39 - E mail : camping@sylvamar.fr - Site Web : www.sylvamar.fr

Lacanau-Océan
Yelloh! Village les Grands Pins
Plage Nord, F-33680 Lacanau-Océan (Gironde) T: 05 56 03 20 77. E: reception@lesgrandspins.com
alanrogers.com/FR33130

This Atlantic coast holiday site with direct access to a fine sandy beach, is on undulating terrain amongst tall pine trees. A large site with 576 pitches, there are 370 of varying sizes for touring units all with electricity (12A). One half of the site is a traffic free zone (except for arrival or departure day, caravans are placed on the pitch, with separate areas outside for parking). There are a good number of tent pitches, those in the centre of the site having some of the best views. This popular site has an excellent range of facilities available for the whole season.

Facilities

Four well equipped toilet blocks, one heated, including baby room and facilities for disabled visitors. Launderette. Motorcaravan services. Supermarket. Bar, restaurant and takeaway. Heated swimming pool complex (800 sq.m; lifeguard in July/Aug) with sunbathing surround and jacuzzi (all season). Fitness activities (charged) and fitness suite. Games room. Tennis. Two playgrounds. Adventure playground. Bicycle hire. Organised activities. WiFi in the bar (on payment). Only gas barbecues are permitted. Off site: Fishing, golf, riding and bicycle hire 5 km.

Open: 16 April - 24 September.

Directions

From Bordeaux take N125/D6 west to Lacanau-Océan. At second roundabout, take second exit: Plage Nord, follow signs to 'campings'. Les Grand Pins signed to right at the far end of road. GPS: 45.01107, -1.19337

Charges guide

Per unit incl. 2 persons	
and electricity	€ 15.00 - € 47.00
extra person	€ 5.00 - € 9.00
child (3-12 yrs)	free - € 5.00

For latest campsite news, availability and prices visit
alanrogers.com

We can book this site for you! Call 01580 214000

alan rogers travel

Hourtin-Plage

Airotel Camping de la Côte d'Argent

F-33990 Hourtin-Plage (Gironde) T: 05 56 09 10 25. E: info@cca33.com

alanrogers.com/FR33110

541

Côte d'Argent is a large, well equipped site for leisurely family holidays. It is an ideal base for walkers and cyclists with over 100 km. of cycle lanes in the area. Hourtin-Plage is a pleasant invigorating resort on the Atlantic coast and a popular location for watersports enthusiasts. The site's top attraction is its pool complex, where wooden bridges connect the pools and islands and there are sunbathing and play areas plus an indoor heated pool. The site has 588 touring pitches (all with 10A electricity), not always clearly defined, arranged under trees with some on sand. High quality entertainment takes place at the impressive bar/restaurant near the entrance. Spread over 20 hectares of undulating sand-based terrain and in the midst of a pine forest, the site is well organised and ideal for children.

Facilities	Directions
Very clean sanitary blocks include provision for disabled visitors. Washing machines. Motorcaravan service points. Large supermarket, restaurant, takeaway, pizzeria, bar (all open 1/6-15/9). Four outdoor pools with slides and flumes (1/6-19/9). Indoor pool (all season). Fitness room. Massage (Institut de Beauté). Tennis. Play areas. Miniclub, organised entertainment in season. Bicycle hire. WiFi (charged). ATM. Charcoal barbecues are not permitted. Hotel (12 rooms). Off site: Path to the beach 300 m. Fishing and riding. Golf 30 km.	Turn off D101 Hourtin-Soulac road 3 km. north of Hourtin. Then join D101E signed Hourtin-Plage. Site is 300 m. from the beach. GPS: 45.22297, -1.16465

Turn off D101 Hourtin-Soulac road 3 km. north of Hourtin. Then join D101E signed Hourtin-Plage. Site is 300 m. from the beach. GPS: 45.22297, -1.16465

Charges guide

Per unit incl. 2 persons and electricity	€ 26.00 - € 48.00
extra person	€ 4.00 - € 8.00
child (3-9 yrs)	€ 3.00 - € 7.00
dog	€ 2.00 - € 6.00

Camping Cheques accepted.

Open: 14 May - 18 September.

Lacanau-Lac

Camping le Tedey

Par le Moutchic, route de Longarisse, F-33680 Lacanau-Lac (Gironde) T: 05 56 03 00 15.
E: camping@le-tedey.com **alanrogers.com/FR33290**

With direct access to a large lake and beach, this site enjoys a beautiful tranquil position set in an area of 14 hectares amidst mature pine trees. There are 700 pitches of which 630 are for touring units, with just 38 mobile homes and chalets available for rent. The pitches are generally level and grassy although parts of the site are on a slope. The pitches are shady with dappled sunlight breaking through the trees. Electricity is available to all pitches and 223 also have water and waste water drainage. The bar is close to the lake with a large indoor and outdoor seating area. The owners and staff are friendly and helpful and English is spoken. There is an open-air cinema on Saturdays and Wednesdays as well as other entertainment in July and August. A children's club is also organised. The takeaway sells a variety of food and the shop next door is well stocked. This is an attractive, well maintained site where you get a feeling of space and calm. There are many places of interest nearby and it's a short drive from Bordeaux.

Facilities	Directions
Four modern sanitary blocks with facilities for disabled visitors and babies. Laundry facilities. Shop. Bar with terrace (1/6-15/9). Crêperie (16/6-11/9). Takeaway (25/6-3/9). Bicycle hire. Boating on the lake. Fishing. Pétanque. Playground. Gas barbecues only on pitches. Dogs are not accepted in July/Aug. WiFi (charged). Off site: Surfing. Riding. Golf. Cycling.	From Lacanau take the D6 to Lacanau-Océan. Take Route de Longarisse and the site is well signed. GPS: 44.98620, -1.13410

From Lacanau take the D6 to Lacanau-Océan. Take Route de Longarisse and the site is well signed. GPS: 44.98620, -1.13410

Charges guide

Per unit incl. 2 persons and electricity	€ 21.00 - € 26.00

Open: 28 April - 19 September.

Le Tedey
CAMPING CARAVANING ★★★

ROUTE DE LONGARISSE
33680 LACANAU
TEL: 0033(0) 5 56 03 00 15
FAX: 0033(0) 5 56 03 01 90

LACANAU - COTE ATLANTIQUE

E-MAIL: CAMPING@LE-TEDEY.COM - INTERNET: WWW.LE-TEDEY.COM

For latest campsite news, availability and prices visit
alanrogers.com

A 3500 m² aquatic complex with slides and jacuzzis, covered and heated swimming pool !

Club **Airotel** **Hourtin Plage**

★★★★★ Camping Caravaning

de la côte d'argent

Camping Special offer (except July and August) 14 = 11 and 7 = 6

WIFI - hotel - shops - restaurant - bar - food - sportive animations - tennis - archery - mini-club - games room - sailing (4 km) - surf (300m)

www.cca33.com

Campsite La Cote d'Argent is a very attractive 20 acre park, situated in the heart of the pine forest and on only 300m distance from the Atlantic Ocean Beach.

This characteristic park is protected for the ocean wind by the dunes and the forest. The Village Club Cote d'Argent is the perfect destination for your calm holiday in nature.

33990 Hourtin Plage
Tél : +33 (0)5.56.09.10.25   Fax : +33 (0)5.56.09.24.96
www.campingcotedargent.com   www.campingcoteouest.com
www.campingaquitaine.com

Laruns

Camping des Gaves

Quartier Pon, F-64440 Laruns (Pyrénées-Atlantiques) T: 05 59 05 32 37. E: campingdesgaves@wanadoo.fr

alanrogers.com/FR64040

Set in a secluded valley, Camping des Gaves is a clean, small and well managed site, open all year, with very friendly owners and staff. It is set high in Pyrenean walking country on one of the routes to Spain and is only 30 km. from the Spanish border. There are 99 pitches including 43 level grassed touring pitches of which 38 are fully serviced, numbered and separated (the remainder are used for seasonal units). Mature trees provide plenty of shade. The river runs alongside the site (well fenced) and fishing is possible. The busy little tourist town of Laruns is only a short walk.

Facilities	Directions
The clean toilet block can be heated in cool weather. Washbasins for ladies in curtained cubicles and one shower in ladies' suitable for children. Basic facilities for disabled visitors. Laundry room. Motorcaravan service point. No shop but baker calls daily (July/Aug). Small bar with TV, pool and video games (July/Aug). Larger bar with table tennis. Small play area. Boules. Volleyball. Fishing. Free WiFi. Accommodation to rent. Off site: Bicycle hire 500 m. Shops, restaurant and bars 1 km.	Take N134 from Pau towards Olorons and branch left on D934 at Gan. Follow to Laruns and just after town, turn left following signs to site. Note: the D918 to the east of Laruns is not recommended for large units. GPS: 42.98241, -0.41591

Open: All year.

Charges guide

Per unit incl. 2 persons and electricity	€ 16.90 - € 24.40
extra person	€ 3.20 - € 4.80

Le Buisson-de-Cadouin

Camping Domaine de Fromengal

F-24480 Le Buisson-de-Cadouin (Dordogne) T: 05 53 63 11 55. E: fromengal@domaine-fromengal.com

alanrogers.com/FR24810

Fromengal is a good quality site in the Périgord Noir. Set in over 22 acres, it was formerly an ancient farm and now offers a relaxed family atmosphere amid a calm, tranquil and natural setting. There is abundant vegetation. The pitches are of a good size, separated by shrubs and hedging with a mixture of sunshine and shade. There are 90 pitches, 34 for touring units with 6A electricity (ten also with water and drainage). The remaining pitches are used for chalets and mobile homes to rent. There is a good range of new amenities, notably a fine heated swimming pool and a restaurant built in the local style and serving food from the area. During the peak season there is an entertainment and activity programme.

Facilities	Directions
The single sanitary block includes facilities for disabled visitors. Washing machine and dryer. Bar, restaurant, takeaway and shop (July/Aug). Swimming pools and slides. Pétanque. BMX circuit. Play area. Entertainment programme. Library. Skate park. Bicycle hire. Tennis, archery and quad bikes (charged). WiFi (charged). Charcoal barbecues only. Off site: Hiking and cycle tracks.	Take the D703 Bergerac-Sarlat road turning off at Lalinde towards Le Buisson-de-Cadouin. Site is probably the best signed in the Dordogne. GPS: 44.82298, 0.8604

Open: 1 April - 31 October.

Charges guide

Per unit incl. 1 or 2 persons and electricity	€ 22.00 - € 38.00

Léon

Camping Lou Puntaou

Au bord du Lac, F-40550 Léon (Landes) T: 05 58 48 74 20. E: reception@loupuntaou.com

alanrogers.com/FR40280

Set between Lac de Léon and the nature reserve park of Huchet, this site offers plenty for young families. The level pitches are mainly grass, hedged and have electricity (15A). Trees offer reasonable shade. In July and August only, there may be some noise from the lake car park and activities. The lake is 200 metres away with watersports, fishing, restaurants and bars, plus plenty of cycle rides. In July and August a full range of activities is organised on the site with sports and clubs for children and activities and evening entertainment for adults. A number of tour operators use the site. The pool complex consists of a covered heated pool with a jacuzzi and another (unheated) with water slides and toboggan, plus a paddling pool. There is a pleasant bar/restaurant nearby.

Facilities	Directions
Three traditional style toilet blocks include facilities for disabled visitors and children. Laundry. Motorcaravan service point. Simple shop at site entrance. Bar, restaurant and takeaway. TV and games rooms. Tennis. ATM. Internet. Only electric barbecues are permitted (communal area available). Off site: Lake 200 m. Village 500 m. with shops, restaurants and bars. Bus to village (July/Aug).	From N10 take exit 12 towards Castets. Take D142 to Léon and at island take first exit 'Centre Ville'. At T-junction turn left on D652. After 300 m. turn left at sign for site and lake. After 500 m. site is on left. GPS: 43.88469, -1.31497

Open: 1 April - 30 September.

Charges guide

Per person	€ 3.00 - € 6.00
pitch incl. electricity	€ 9.00 - € 27.00

For latest campsite news, availability and prices visit

alanrogers.com

Léon
Yelloh! Village Punta Lago

Avenue du Lac, F-40550 Léon (Landes) T: 05 58 49 24 40. E: info@yellohvillage-punta-lago.com
alanrogers.com/FR40290

Five hundred metres from the charming village of Léon, this site offers above average size, level, grass pitches (some sandy). Most have electricity, water and drainage and they are separated by hedges. Shade is welcome from the tall oak trees. Whilst the pitches would be considered typical for the region, the buildings are a mix of old and new, the old being the sanitary block, in good order, clean and with all the usual facilities including a lovely new children's bathroom and facilities for disabled visitors. The new encompasses an impressive indoor heated pool, a recreation room serving as a gym and a TV room.

Facilities

The single toilet block is old, but kept clean and well maintained. Facilities for children and disabled visitors. Laundry facilities. Large shop. Restaurant and takeaway. Bar. Heated indoor and outdoor pools. Bicycle hire. Play area. Fridge hire. Pétanque. Beach volleyball. Sauna and jacuzzi. Miniclub (5-12 yrs). Entertainment and activities (July/Aug). Barbecues are not permitted. WiFi (charged). Off site: Lake 300 m. with sailing, windsurfing, kayak, swimming and fishing. Léon 800 m. with daily market (15/6-15/9). Riding 5 km. Beach 7 km. Golf 8 km.

Open: 8 April - 25 September.

Directions

From N10 take exit 12 towards Castets. Take D142 to Léon and at island take first exit to 'Centre Ville'. At T-junction turn left on D652 and after 300 m. turn left at sign for site and lake. After 500 m. site is on the left. GPS: 43.8842, -1.313

Charges guide

Per unit incl. 2 persons and electricity	€ 15.00 - € 41.00
extra person	€ 4.00 - € 6.00
child (3-7 yrs)	free - € 6.00
dog	€ 4.00

Les Eyzies-de-Tayac
Camping la Rivière

3 route du Sorcier, F-24620 Les Eyzies-de-Tayac (Dordogne) T: 05 53 06 97 14. E: la-riviere@wanadoo.fr
alanrogers.com/FR24680

This is a site with some Périgordine character situated beside the Vézère river. The buildings are in the traditional style of the area. It is owned and run by a French family who are friendly and helpful, and visitors to the site speak highly of them. They are proud of the site's ecological credentials. There are 120 pitches of which ten are used for chalets and mobile homes. All have 6/10A electricity connections, 75 also have water and a drain. The pitches are level, easily accessible and offer full shade. The site also provides a six-bedroom hotel. This attractive building also houses the bar, restaurant and shop. Outside, the attractive terrace overlooks the swimming pool. There are music evenings in July and August, together with shows for children. Access to the river provides opportunities for canoeing.

Facilities

Three sanitary blocks, two of them new. Facilities for disabled visitors and babies in the new, heated blocks. Washing machine and dryer. Motorcaravan service point. Small shop. Attractive bar/restaurant and outside eating area. Takeaway. Swimming pool and toddler's pool. Play area. Half tennis court. Canoeing. Fishing. Boules. Music evenings and children's shows. WiFi (free). Off site: Fishing 200 m. Bicycle hire and riding 1 km. Golf 20 km. The caves of Font de Gaume and Lascaux, listed by UNESCO, are nearby. Châteaux.

Open: 1 April - 1 November.

Directions

From Périgueux take D47 to Les Eyzies. After Manaurie and approaching Les Eyzies, turn right just before the bridge over the river. Then take the next left. Site is signed from D47. GPS: 44.93769, 1.00603

Charges guide

Per unit incl. 2 persons and electricity	€ 13.70 - € 22.00
extra person	€ 3.80 - € 6.25
child (3-12 yrs)	€ 2.80 - € 4.80

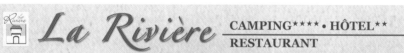

CAMPING★★★★ • HÔTEL★★
RESTAURANT

Come discover La Rivière in the Vérèze valley, at the heart of the Perigord Noir and the prehistory, with the famous "Old man of Cro-Magnon", at 10 minutes from the center of Eyzies.

3 route du Sorcier • 24620 Les Eyzies
Tèl : +33 (0)5 53 06 97 14 • Fax : +33 (0)5 53 35 20 85 • email : la-riviere@wanadoo.fr
Siret 448 442 582 00012 • APE 5530Z **WWW.LARIVIERELESEYZIES.COM**

Ecolabel

For latest campsite news, availability and prices visit
alanrogers.com

Les Eglisottes
Camping l'Eau Vive

6 bis Fond de Bournac, F-33230 Les Eglisottes (Gironde) T: 05 57 69 56 09. E: camping-leau-vive@sfr.fr
alanrogers.com/FR33830

This spacious, well maintained campsite with 100 larger than average level pitches is slightly out of the normal tourist areas, but ideal for a quiet break. It is run by a very friendly Dutch couple who speak excellent English. The campsite borders onto La Dronne river for fishing and is next to a swimming pool with diving board. All pitches have water and 16A electricity. One very clean toilet block has a separate suite for disabled campers. There is a small, very reasonable restaurant and shop on site, and the town of Les Eglisottes is a ten minute walk. Free WiFi.

Facilities

One clean and well equipped toilet block with facilities for babies and disabled visitors. Washing machine. Washing line. Dishwashing sinks. Motorcaravan services. Shop. Bar with TV. Restaurant and takeaway meals (July/Aug). Tourist information. 3 play areas. Children's club. Football. Basketball. Volleyball. Boules. Table tennis. WiFi. Communal barbecue. Mobile homes to rent. Off site: River fishing and swimming. Riverside walks. Large swimming pool with diving area (lifeguard July/Aug) 50 m.

Open: 1 May - 30 September.

Directions

Located 50 km. north east of Bordeaux. From La Roche-Chalais take D674 south for 7.5 km. to Les Eglisottes-et-Chalaures where the site is well signed. GPS: 45.097196, -0.04976

Charges guide

Per unit incl. 2 persons and electricity	€ 21.00
extra person	€ 3.40 - € 4.90
child (3-10 yrs)	€ 1.50 - € 2.50
dog	€ 1.50 - € 2.20

Limeuil
Camping la Ferme de Perdigat

F-24510 Limeuil (Dordogne) T: 05 53 63 31 54. E: accueil@perdigat.com
alanrogers.com/FR24750

The delightful French owners, Michel and Noelle Paille, make this a happy place to stay and everyone we spoke to praised it highly. The site nestles beautifully in a very natural environment at the base of tree-lined hills which provide a wonderful scenic background. Flowers, bushes and trees give a superb sense of well being and much care and attention is given to the environment. A superb lake is 100 m. from the site where visitors staying at the farm may fish without charge. The river is also the same distance away in a different direction. There are only 49 touring pitches (all with electricity 10A), and 15 mobile homes to rent.

Facilities

The completely refurbished shower block is bright and airy. Laundry facilities. Motorcaravan services. Shop (1/5-15/9). Bar (1/5-30/9) and restaurant with terrace (newly refurbished, 1/5-15/9). Swimming and paddling pools. Games room. WiFi in the bar area. Play area. Private fishing lake and the Vézère river. Canoes and kayaks. Max. 2 dogs. Off site: Riding 2 km. Supermarkets in Le Bugue 3 km. Golf 14 km.

Open: 1 March - 30 October.

Directions

From Le Bugue, take the D703 to La Borie and turn left to Limeuil. Campsite is well signed. GPS: 44.894765, 0.912509

Charges guide

Per unit incl. 2 persons and electricity	€ 12.00 - € 18.30
extra person	€ 3.00 - € 4.70
child (under 8 yrs)	€ 2.00 - € 3.10

Lit-et-Mixe
Village Center les Vignes

Route de la Plage du Cap de l'Homy, F-40170 Lit-et-Mixe (Landes) T: 05 58 42 85 60.
E: contact@village-center.com alanrogers.com/FR40160

Village Center les Vignes is a large holiday site close to the Atlantic coast with 475 pitches, all of which are occupied by a mix of mobile homes, bungalows and tents for rent. The site's amenities, including a supermarket, restaurant and bar, are located at the entrance to the site. The rather stylish swimming pool complex includes a six lane water slide. A wide range of activities is provided and during July and August a great variety of entertainment options for both adults and children, some of which take place in the new entertainment 'big top'.

Facilities

Four modern sanitary units. Facilities for babies and disabled visitors. Washing machines and dryers. Large supermarket, restaurant and bar. Takeaway (1/7-2/9). Swimming pool complex (all season), water complex (1/6-15/9). Tennis. Minigolf. Pétanque. Riding. Kids' club and playground. Bicycle hire. WiFi (charged). TV room. Play area. Barrier closed 23.00-07.00. Off site: Golf course, canoeing, kayaking, surfing, riding. Cycle tracks.

Open: 9 April - 2 October.

Directions

Lit-et-Mixe is on the D652 20 km. south of Mimizan. Turn west on D88 1 km. south of town towards Cap de l'Homy for 1.5 km. where site entrance is on left. GPS: 44.02292, -1.27978

Charges 2012

Contact the site for details.

For latest campsite news, availability and prices visit
alanrogers.com

Messages
Airotel le Vieux Port

We can book this site for you! Call 01580 214000   alan rogers ◉travel

541

Plage Sud, F-40660 Messanges (Landes) T: 01 76 76 70 00. E: contact@levieuxport.com

alanrogers.com/FR40180

A well established destination appealing particularly to families with teenage children, this lively site has 1,546 pitches of mixed sizes, most with electricity (6A). The camping area is well shaded by pines and pitches are generally of a good size, attractively grouped around the toilet blocks. There are many tour operators here and well over a third of the site is taken up with mobile homes and chalets. An enormous 7,000 sq. m. aquatic park is now open, and is the largest on any French campsite. This heated complex is exceptional, boasting five outdoor pools, three large water slides plus waves and a heated spa. There is also a heated indoor pool. The area to the north of Bayonne is heavily forested and a number of very large campsites are attractively located close to the superb Atlantic beaches. Le Vieux Port is probably the largest, and certainly one of the most impressive, of these. At the back of the site a path leads across the dunes to a good beach (400 m). Other recent innovations include an outdoor fitness area and a superb riding centre. All in all, this is a lively site with a great deal to offer an active family.

Facilities

Nine well appointed, recently renovated toilet blocks with facilities for disabled visitors. Motorcaravan services. Good supermarket and various smaller shops in high season. Several restaurants, takeaway and three bars (all open all season). Large pool complex (no Bermuda shorts; open all season) including new covered pool and Polynesian themed bar. Tennis. Multisports pitch. Minigolf. Outdoor fitness area. Fishing. Bicycle hire. Riding centre. Organised activities in high season including frequent discos and karaoke evenings. Only communal barbecues are allowed. WiFi (charged). Off site: Beach 400 m. Sailing 2 km. Golf 8 km.

Open: 31 March - 30 September.

Directions

Leave RN10 at Magescq exit heading for Soustons. Pass through Soustons following signs for Vieux-Boucau. Bypass this town and site is clearly signed to the left at second roundabout. GPS: 43.79778, -1.40111

Charges 2012

Per unit incl. 2 persons and electricity	€ 21.30 - € 61.00
extra person	€ 4.80 - € 9.00
child (under 13 yrs)	€ 3.80 - € 6.20
dog	€ 3.10 - € 5.80

Camping Cheques accepted.

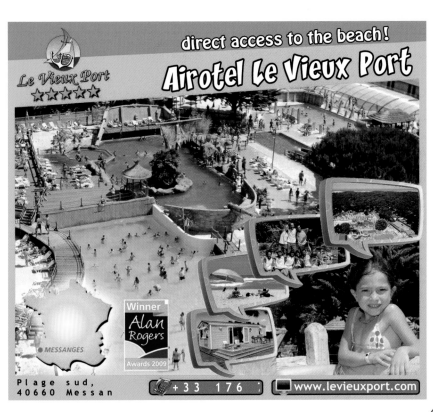

357

For latest campsite news, availability and prices visit
alanrogers.com

Messanges
Camping les Acacias

Quartier Delest, Route d'Azur (C3), F-40660 Messanges (Landes) T: 05 58 48 01 78.
E: lesacacias@lesacacias.com **alanrogers.com/FR40220**

Close to the Atlantic beaches of Les Landes, this small, well designed campsite is quiet and peaceful. Family run and well cared for, it is a site for couples looking for relaxation or families who want a safe environment for young children to play. There are 79 flat touring pitches, all with 6/10A electricity and separated by trees and shrubs. Mobile homes are arranged unobtrusively on two sides of the site. The pitches are easily accessed by tarmac roads, although units longer than 7 m. may have some difficulty. M. and Mme. Dourthe are constantly seeking to improve this charming campsite.

Facilities

One modern, clean and well designed toilet block with facilities for disabled campers. Laundry facilities. Motorcaravan services. Fridge hire. Shop (15/6-15/9). Takeaway (1/7-31/8). Games room. Play area. Children's entertainment. Small library. Boules. Football field. Bicycle hire. Tourist information. Security box hire. Communal barbecues only. WiFi. Off site: Bus 1 km. Riding 1.5 km. Beach and supermarket 2 km. Fishing 3 km. Golf 4 km.

Open: 25 March - 25 October.

Directions

Approaching Messanges from the north, continue through the centre of village on the D652 (site signed). At roundabout turn left onto C3 towards Azur and site is 1.5 km. on the left. GPS: 43.79836, -1.37550

Charges guide

Per unit incl. 2 persons and electricity	€ 13.60 - € 19.60
extra person	€ 3.30 - € 4.20

Messanges
Camping de Moisan

Route de la Plage, F-40660 Messanges (Landes) T: 05 58 48 92 06. E: camping.moisan@orange.fr
alanrogers.com/FR40470

This family site is located in the pine forests of the southern Landes, and close to the region's magnificent broad, sandy beach. There are 325 pitches here, dispersed beneath the pines. These are mostly equipped with 5 or 6A electricity. A wide range of mobile homes and chalets are available for rent. On-site amenities include a well stocked shop, a snack bar and cycle hire. There are miles of marked cycle tracks through the surrounding forest, including a track to the beach. A children's club is organised in peak season, and evening entertainment is also on offer.

Facilities

Two clean toilet blocks have equal numbers of Turkish and British style toilets, some washbasins in cabins, and preset showers. Facilities for disabled visitors. Washing machines and dryer. Shop (18/6-20/9). Bar/restaurant, snack bar and takeaway (11/6-20/9). Children's play area. Beach volleyball. Surf school (charged). Multisports court. Bicycle hire. Activity programme. Accommodation to rent. WiFi. Off site: Shops and restaurants in Messanges 800 m. Swimming pool. Archery. Tennis. Riding. Watersports.

Open: 14 May - 30 September.

Directions

Head south from Léon on 652 as far as Messanges. Turn right on Avenue de la Plage and the site is well signposted. GPS: 43.816121, -1.390319

Charges guide

Per unit incl. 2 persons and electricity	€ 11.50 - € 22.70
extra person	€ 2.50 - € 5.50
child (2-13 yrs)	free - € 3.30
dog	€ 1.50 - € 2.00

Mézos
Le Village Tropical Sen-Yan

Le Village Tropical, F-40170 Mézos (Landes) T: 05 58 42 60 05. E: reception@sen-yan.com
alanrogers.com/FR40110

This exotic family site is about 12 km. from the Atlantic coast in the Landes forest area, just outside the village. There are 100 touring pitches set around a similar number of mobile homes. Pitches are marked with hedges and have electricity (6A). The reception, bar and pool area is almost tropical with the luxuriant greenery of its banana trees, palm trees, tropical flowers and its straw sunshades. The covered, heated pool, new water slide, gym with sauna and jacuzzi all add to the attractiveness. A new covered animation area provides entertainment and discos during high season. A stunning new open swimming area (1/7-31/8) is surrounded by white sand.

Facilities

Three well maintained and clean toilet blocks with quality fittings and showers, washbasins in cabins and British style WCs. Facilities for babies and disabled campers. Shop (from 15/6). Bar, restaurant and snacks (1/7-31/8). Outdoor swimming pools (1/6-15/9). Heated indoor pool (1/5-15/9). Archery. Practice golf. Bicycle hire. No charcoal barbecues. WiFi (charged). Off site: Fishing 500 m. Riding 6 km. Beach 12 km.

Open: 1 May - 15 September.

Directions

From N10 take exit 14 (Onesse-Laharie), then D38 Bias/Mimizan road. After 13 km. turn south to Mézos from where site is signed. GPS: 44.07208, -1.15671

Charges guide

Per unit incl. 2 persons and electricity	€ 24.00 - € 34.50
extra person	€ 5.00 - € 6.00
child (under 7 yrs)	free - € 5.00

For latest campsite news, availability and prices visit
alanrogers.com

Mimizan-Plage
Airotel Club Marina-Landes

Rue Marina, F-40200 Mimizan (Landes) T: 05 58 09 12 66. E: contact@clubmarina.com

alanrogers.com/FR40080

Well maintained and clean, with helpful staff, Club Marina-Landes would be a very good choice for a family holiday. Activities include discos, play groups for children, specially trained staff to entertain teenagers and concerts for more mature campers. There are numerous sports opportunities and a superb sandy beach nearby. A nightly curfew ensures that all have a good night's sleep. A new leisure pool is planned for 2012. The site has 401 touring pitches (316 with 10A electricity) and 135 mobile homes and chalets for rent. The pitches are on firm grass, most with hedges and they are large (mostly 100 sq.m. or larger). If ever a campsite could be said to have two separate identities, then Club Marina-Landes is surely the one. In early and late season it is quiet, with the pace of life in low gear – come July and until 1st September, all the facilities are open and there is fun for all the family with the chance that family members will only meet together at meal times.

Facilities

Five toilet blocks (opened as required), well maintained with showers and many washbasins in cabins. Facilities for babies, children and disabled visitors. Laundry facilities. Motorcaravan services. Fridge hire. Shop (freshly baked bread) and bar (30/4-10/9). Restaurant, snack bar, pizzas and takeaway (1/5-10/9). Covered pool and outdoor pools (30/4-13/9). Minigolf. Tennis. Bicycle hire. Play area. Entertainment and activities (high season). Gas or electric barbecues only. WiFi (charged). Off site: Beach and fishing 500 m. Bus service and riding 1 km. Golf 8 km. Mimizan 8 km.

Open: 30 April - 13 September.

Directions

Heading west from Mimizan centre, take D626 passing Abbey Museum. Straight on at lights (crossing D87/D67). Next lights turn left. After 2 km. at T-junction turn left. Follow signs to site. GPS: 44.20447, -1.29099

Charges guide

Per unit incl. 3 persons	
and electricity	€ 18.00 - € 49.00
extra person	€ 4.00 - € 10.00
child (3-13 yrs)	€ 3.00 - € 8.00
dog	€ 2.00 - € 5.00

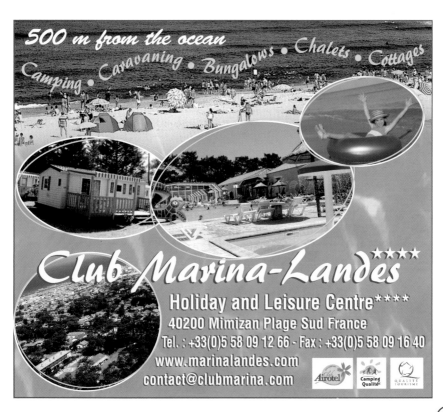

500 m from the ocean

Camping • Caravaning • Bungalows • Chalets • Cottages

Club Marina-Landes ★★★★

Holiday and Leisure Centre★★★★
40200 Mimizan Plage Sud France
Tel. : +33(0)5 58 09 12 66 - Fax : +33(0)5 58 09 16 40
www.marinalandes.com
contact@clubmarina.com

For latest campsite news, availability and prices visit
alanrogers.com

Mimizan-Plage

Camping de la Plage

Boulevard de l'Atlantique, F-40200 Mimizan-Plage (Landes) T: 05 58 09 00 32.
E: contact@mimizan-camping.com **alanrogers.com/FR40380**

This municipal site is located 800 m. from the Atlantic beach at Mimizan-Plage. This is a large site with 609 pitches of which 463 are available for touring units. The rest are occupied by mobile homes and chalets (available for rent; one adapted for campers with disabilities). Pitches are well shaded beneath pines and many are equipped with 6-10A electricity. A separate area (without electricity) is reserved for tents. Leisure amenities include a multisports terrain, beach volleyball courts and a climbing wall. An entertainment and activity programme is organised in peak season, including a programme for children.

Facilities

Seven toilet blocks. Facilities for babies and disabled visitors. Laundry facilites. Shop (bread available). Bar/snack bar, takeaway food. Fridge hire. No swimming pool, but beach nearby. Motorcaravan service point. Games room. Volleyball. Boules. Multisports terrain. Climbing wall. Play area. Bicycle hire. Picnic tables. Security barrier. Small train passes entrance in high season. WiFi (charged). Off site: Watersports adjacent. Nearest beach 800 m. Riding 3 km. Golf, covered swimming pool, adventure area, paintball, all 4 km.

Open: 7 April - 23 September.

Directions

Approaching from the north, leave N10 at Labouheyre and follow signs to Mimizan on D626. Drive though the town and follow signs for Mimizan-Plage. Site is clearly signed and is to the north of the river. GPS: 44.216482, -1.285653

Charges guide

Per unit incl. 2 persons and electricity	€ 17.00 - € 21.30
extra person	€ 7.00 - € 8.80

Moliets-Plage

Le Saint-Martin Camping

⌐ 542

Avenue de l'Océan, F-40660 Moliets-Plage (Landes) T: 05 58 48 52 30.
E: contact@camping-saint-martin.fr **alanrogers.com/FR40190**

A family site aimed mainly at couples and young families, le Saint-Martin is a welcome change from most of the sites in this area in that it has only a relatively small number of mobile homes (127) compared to the number of touring pitches (383). First impressions are of a neat, tidy, well cared for site and the direct access to a wonderful fine sandy beach is an added bonus. The pitches are mainly typically French in style with low hedges separating them, and with some shade. Electricity hook ups are 10/15A and a number of pitches also have water and drainage. Entertainment in high season is low key (with the emphasis on quiet nights) – daytime competitions and a miniclub, plus the occasional evening entertainment, well away from the pitches and with no discos or karaoke. With pleasant chalets and mobile homes to rent, a top-class pool complex and an 18-hole golf course 700 m. away (special rates negotiated), this would be an ideal destination for a golfing weekend or longer stay.

Facilities

Seven toilet blocks of a high standard and very well maintained, have washbasins in cabins, large showers, baby rooms and facilities for disabled visitors. Motorcaravan service point. Washing machines and dryers. Fridge rental. Supermarket. Bars, restaurants and takeaways. Indoor pool, jacuzzi and sauna (charged July/Aug). Outdoor pool area with jacuzzi and paddling pool (15/6-15/9). Multisports pitch. Play area. Bicycle hire. Beach access. Internet access. Electric barbecues only. Off site: Fishing and beach 300 m. Golf and tennis 700 m.

Open: Easter - 1 November.

Directions

From the N10 take D142 to Lèon, then D652 to Moliets-et-Mar. Follow signs to Moliets-Plage, site is well signed. GPS: 43.85242, -1.38732

Charges guide

Per unit incl. 2 persons and electricity	€ 22.70 - € 48.60
extra person	€ 6.00 - € 7.50
child (under 10 yrs)	€ 4.00 - € 5.30
dog	free - € 5.00

Prices are for reserved pitches.

Le Saint Martin
Camping & Caravan site ★★★★

2 swimming pools
1 heated indoor pool & Spa-Sauna
Chalets rental (2 to 6 persons)
Open from Easter to 1st November

DIRECT ACCESS TO THE BEACH

Tél. +33 (0)5 58 48 52 30 · MOLIETS PLAGE - Website: www.camping-saint-martin.fr

For latest campsite news, availability and prices visit
alanrogers.com

Monpazier

Camping le Moulin de David

Gaugeac, F-24540 Monpazier (Dordogne) T: 05 53 22 65 25. E: contact@moulindedavid.com

alanrogers.com/FR24080

Set in a 14 hectare wooded valley, it has 160 pitches split into two sections, 102 are available for touring units – 33 below the central reception complex in a shaded situation, and 69 above on partly terraced ground with varying degrees of shade. All pitches have electricity (3-16A). Spacing is good and there is no crowding. The site has been planted with a variety of shrubs and trees and combined with the small stream that runs through the centre they create a beautiful and tranquil setting. This pleasant and attractive site is one for those who enjoy peace, away from the hustle and bustle of the main Dordogne attractions, yet sufficiently close for them to be accessible.

Facilities

Three good toilet blocks, with facilities for disabled visitors and babies. Laundry room. Shop. Bar/restaurant with shaded patio, takeaway. Swimming pool and paddling pool, freshwater pool with waterslide. Play area. Boules. Half-court tennis. Trampoline. Library. Events, games and canoe trips. Barbecues for hire. Mobile homes for rent. WiFi in reception area (charged). Off site: Supermarket and cash point in Monpazier 2.5 km. Riding 3 km.

Open: 1 April - 30 September.

Directions

From Monpazier take the D2 Villeréal road. Take third turning left (after about 2 km), signed to Moulin de David and Gaugeac Mairie. Site is about 500 m. along this road on the left. GPS: 44.65949, 0.87898

Charges guide

Per unit incl. 2 persons and electricity	€ 18.00 - € 24.00
extra person	€ 3.00 - € 5.00

Montignac

Camping le Paradis

Saint Léon-sur-Vézère, F-24290 Montignac (Dordogne) T: 05 53 50 72 64.

E: le-paradis@perigord.com **alanrogers.com/FR24060**

Le Paradis is an excellent, very well maintained riverside site, halfway between Les Eyzies and Montignac. The site is landscaped with a variety of mature shrubs and trees. The gardens are beautiful, which gives a wonderful sense of tranquillity. It is very easy to relax on this ecologically friendly site. Systems of reed filters enhance the efficient natural drainage. This is a family run site and you are guaranteed a warm and friendly welcome. There are 200 good sized pitches, with 27 with mobile homes to rent. The pitches are level and with easy access, all with 10A electricity, water and drainage. There are some special pitches for motorcaravans. An excellent restaurant offers a good menu, reasonably priced and using fresh local produce where appropriate. The terraced area outside makes for a convivial family atmosphere. There are many sport and leisure activities. Direct access to the Vézère river for canoeing and swimming is possible at one end of the site. Organised games, competitions and evening events are aimed at maintaining a true French flavour. English is spoken. This is a site of real quality, which we thoroughly recommend.

Facilities

High quality, well equipped, heated toilet blocks are kept very clean. Well stocked shop (with gas). Good restaurant, takeaway. Good pool complex heated in low season, paddling pool. Play area. Tennis. BMX track. Multisports court. Canoe hire. Fishing. Bicycle hire. Quad bike and horse riding excursions. WiFi over site. Large units by arrangement. Mobile homes to rent, one for visitors with disabilities (no dogs permitted). Off site: Riding 3 km.

Open: 1 April - 19 October.

Directions

Site is 12 km. north of Les Eyzies and 3 km. south of St Léon-sur-Vézère, on the east side of the D706. GPS: 45.00207, 1.0711

Charges guide

Per unit incl. 2 persons and electricity	€ 22.10 - € 31.40
extra person	€ 5.60 - € 7.70
child (3-12 yrs)	€ 4.60 - € 6.70

Camping Cheques accepted.

Camping Le Paradis - 24290 St. Leon sur Vézère
tel.: 05 53 50 72 64 - fax: 05 53 50 75 90 - le-paradis@perigord.com - www.le-paradis.com

For latest campsite news, availability and prices visit

alanrogers.com

Navarrenx

Camping Beau Rivage

Allée des Marronniers, F-64190 Navarrenx (Pyrénées-Atlantiques) T: 05 59 66 10 00. E: beaucamping@free.fr
alanrogers.com/FR64120

This well cared for site lies just outside the walls of the bastide town of Navarrenx. It is owned and run by an English couple, Richard and Wendy Curtis, who take great pride in their site. Many bushes and trees have been planted and a total of 54 touring pitches are available either on hardstanding with full services or on grass, the latter having more shade. A traffic-free track leads to the town where all essential shops can be found. Richard trained as a pizzaiolo and offers fresh pizzas in the evenings. Within driving distance of the Atlantic Coast and the Pyrenees mountains, this is a good site for touring.

Facilities

Two very clean sanitary blocks with good separate facilities for ladies and men include facilities for babies and disabled visitors. Laundry facilities. Shop. Good quality local wines available in reception. Homemade pizzas. Small swimming pool (1/5-30/9). Playing field. Max. 2 dogs. Chalets for rent. Caravan storage. WiFi (charged). Off site: Municipal pool adjacent. Shop nearby. Town is five minutes walk for further shops, bars, restaurants, ATM and bicycle hire. Fishing 200 m. Riding 15 km. River sports.

Open: 25 March - 16 October.

Directions

From the north take D936 to Navarrenx. Turn left at first roundabout on D115 into Navarrenx. Turn left at T-junction, go over bridge and follow walls of town all the way around. At next island turn right on D947 and site is signed from here. GPS: 43.32001, -0.761

Charges guide

Per unit incl. 2 persons and electricity	€ 18.50 - € 24.50
extra person	€ 4.50 - € 5.50
child (0-7 yrs)	€ 2.00 - € 3.00

Parentis-en-Born

Camping l'Arbre d'Or

75 route du Lac, F-40160 Parentis-en-Born (Landes) T: 05 58 78 41 56. E: contact@arbre-dor.com
alanrogers.com/FR40350

L'Arbre d'Or is a friendly, family site on the outskirts of Parentis-en-Born. There are 200 pitches, most offering electrical connections (10A). Around 90 are occupied by mobile homes and chalets. L'Arbre d'Or lies 400 m. from the large Lac de Parentis where many watersports are available. The nearest coastal beach is at Biscarrosse-Plage, 19 km. distant. The site boasts two swimming pools, one of which is covered in inclement weather, as well as a convivial restaurant and an activity programme. Bicycle hire is available and there are hundreds of kilometres of cycle trails through the surrounding forest.

Facilities

Two well located toilet blocks are a good provision and are kept clean. Preset showers. Facilities for disabled visitors. Bar, restaurant and takeaway (15/5-15/9; weekends in low season). Two heated swimming pools. Play area. Bicycle hire. Entertainment and activities in peak season. Games room. Mobile homes and chalets for rent. WiFi (charged). Off site: Lac de Parentis, fishing and sailing 400 m. Shop 800 m. Golf and riding 9 km.

Open: 1 April - 31 October.

Directions

From Bordeaux head south on the A63 and then the N10 as far as Liposthey. Then head west on the D43 to Parentis-en-Born. The site is well signed from here on the Route du Lac. GPS: 44.34622, -1.0929

Charges guide

Per unit incl. 2 persons and electricity	€ 19.90 - € 24.10

Pauillac

Camping Municipal les Gabarreys

Route de la Rivière, F-33250 Pauillac (Gironde) T: 05 56 59 10 03. E: camping.les.gabarreys@wanadoo.fr
alanrogers.com/FR33150

An attractive, small site with well tended flower beds, les Gabarreys is surrounded by vineyards of the Médoc region. An excellent site, it has 59 pitches, most with hardstanding for motorcaravans (so pegging out awnings could be a problem), some grass pitches for tents and six mobile homes, most with electric hook-ups (5/10A, some may require long leads). The 'Maison du Tourisme et du Vin' should be your first port of call. The surrounding area is well supplied with wine caves, and being fairly level you could perhaps cycle to some of them.

Facilities

Two immaculate toilet blocks provide open and cubicle washbasins and excellent facilities for disabled visitors. Motorcaravan services. General room with satellite TV, fridge-freezer and a small library. New play area. Minigolf (free) and volleyball. New spa and sauna. WiFi (charged). Off site: Fishing 1 km.

Open: 2 April - 10 October.

Directions

Pauillac lies NNW of Bordeaux. From Bordeaux take D1 to St Laurent, then D206 to Pauillac. At roundabout turn right to Pauillac Guais, then straight ahead at next roundabout and turn right before the Maison du Tourisme. GPS: 45.1852, -0.742397

Charges guide

Per unit incl. 2 persons	€ 17.00 - € 20.20
extra person	€ 3.50 - € 4.50

For latest campsite news, availability and prices visit

alanrogers.com

Petit Palais-et-Cornemps
Flower Camping le Pressoir
29 Queyrai, F-33570 Petit Palais-et-Cornemps (Gironde) T: 05 57 69 73 25.
E: contact@campinglepressoir.com **alanrogers.com/FR33090**

Nestling in the famous wine producing countryside of the Lussac, Pomerol and St Emilion areas north of Bordeaux, Le Pressoir is surrounded by fields of vines. The 100 large pitches are arranged on either side of a gravel road leading up a slight hill. Most are shaded by attractive trees, but almost all are sloping. They are over 100 sq.m. and equipped with electricity (10A Europlug). The old barn has been converted into a stylish bar and a really charming, separate restaurant. A quiet, family site, le Pressoir provides a comfortable base for a holiday in this area famous for good food and wine.

Facilities

Fully equipped toilet block with excellent facilities for disabled visitors, and washing machine. Bar and pleasant restaurant with indoor and outdoor seating (open all year). Heated swimming pool (15/4-15/10, no Bermuda shorts). Sauna. Wellness (July/Aug). Playground. Bouncy castle. Trampoline. Kids' club. Pétanque. Mountain bike hire. Free WiFi. Mobile homes and bungalow tents to rent. Bicycle hire. No barbecues, but communal area provided. Off site: Tennis nearby. Fishing 1 km. Riding 5 km.

Open: All year.

Directions

From A89 Bordeaux - Périgueux take exit 11 to Saint Médard-de-Guizières where you turn south towards Lussac on the D21. From Castillon-la-Bataille on D936 Libourne-Bergerac road, south of site, take D17 north towards St Médard then D21 through Petit Palais. Site signed. GPS: 44.9971, -0.06326

Charges guide

Per unit incl. 2 persons	
and electricity	€ 16.50 - € 29.00
extra person	€ 4.00 - € 7.50

Pyla-sur-Mer
Village Center la Forêt
Route de Biscarrosse, F-33115 Pyla-sur-Mer (Gironde) T: 04 99 57 21 21. E: contact@village-center.com
alanrogers.com/FR33280

Village Center la Forêt is one of a number of sites in this area that is dominated by the massive Dune du Pyla. The dune has to be negotiated in order to get to the beach (either over it or around, which is about 3 km). And the virtual wall of bright sand is all you have by way of a view to the east. This is a very well kept site with good facilities, easy access for all types of unit, and plenty of attractions for adults and children. Set on a gentle slope, mixed pine and oak trees give shade on most pitches.

Facilities

Six unisex toilet blocks have good facilities. Bath with showers and mats for babies. Facilities for disabled visitors (key from reception). Washing machines and dryers. Motorcaravan service area. Shop. Bar, takeaway and restaurant (April-Oct). Swimming and paddling pools (May-Sept). Tennis court (charged July/Aug). Minigolf. Boules. Bicycle hire. Play area. Children's club (July/Aug). No charcoal barbecues. WiFi (charged). Off site: Bus (infrequent in low season) from outside site to Biscarrosse and to Bordeaux. Golf, riding and sailing all within 5 km.

Open: 8 April - 2 October.

Directions

From A63 (north or south) take A660 towards Arcachon. At La Teste turn off towards Dune du Pyla and at Dune car park roundabout take left turn towards Biscarrosse. Site is about 2 km. on the right. GPS: 44.5951, -1.1966

Charges guide

Per unit incl. 2 persons	€ 16.00 - € 32.00

Pyla-sur-Mer
Yelloh! Village Panorama du Pyla
Grande Dune du Pyla, route de Biscarrosse, F-33260 Pyla-sur-Mer (Gironde) T: 04 66 73 97 39.
E: info@yellohvillage-panorama.com **alanrogers.com/FR33310**

Many campsites set amongst pine trees have a rather untidy look, but Panorama is different. Here the entrance is inviting with well tended flower beds and a pleasant, airy reception. There is a steep climb up to the first of the touring pitches, passing the swimming pool and play area. Some are suitable for caravans and motorcaravans, and others for tents. The touring pitches are on terraces amongst the tall pines and most have electricity (3-10A). The sea views from almost all pitches are stunning. Access to the toilet blocks may involve a steep climb (the site is probably unsuitable for disabled visitors).

Facilities

Seven toilet blocks (two open in low season) are clean and well maintained with baby rooms and facilities for disabled visitors. Fridge hire. Laundry facilities. Motorcaravan services. Restaurant with panoramic sea view. Three heated swimming pools and jacuzzi. Adjacent play area. Tennis. Minigolf. Paragliding. Sub-aqua diving. Entertainment in high season for all ages. Library and Internet access in reception. Off site: Riding and golf 10 km.

Open: 18 April - 29 September.

Directions

From N250, just before La Teste, take D259 signed Biscarrosse and Dune du Pyla. At roundabout at end of road turn left (south) on D218 coast road signed Biscarrosse and Dune du Pyla. Site is 4 km. on right. GPS: 44.57265, -1.22053

Charges guide

Per unit incl. 2 persons	
and electricity	€ 17.00 - € 40.00
extra person	€ 4.00 - € 7.00

For latest campsite news, availability and prices visit
alanrogers.com

Rauzan
Camping du Vieux Château

D123, F-33420 Rauzan (Gironde) T: 05 57 84 15 38. E: contact@camping-levieuxchateau.com
alanrogers.com/FR33440

Camping du Vieux Château is located in the heart of the Bordeaux vineyards and adjacent to the fortress town of Rauzan. It was taken over by the present owners in 2010 and is an ideal starting point for walking and cycling along small tracks through the vineyards, and for day trips. The flat, grassy site has 78 well shaded pitches, many with views of the château. Fifty pitches are for touring (25 with 6/10A electricity); some are rather uneven and require long leads. Eight mobile homes are available to rent. Excellent German, Dutch and English are spoken at reception.

Facilities

The traditional sanitary block is clean and offers some washbasins, and preset showers in cubicles. Facilities for babies and disabled visitors. Washing machine. Shop. Bar, snack bar and takeaway. Outdoor swimming pool and children's pool (unheated). Play area and mini farm. TV. Small library. Boules. Bicycle hire. Electric barbecues to hire. Mobile homes and chalets to hire. WiFi (free). Off site: Shops and restaurants in Rauzan 200 m.

Open: 1 April - 31 October

Directions

From Libourne, join D670 in the direction of St Emilion and Castillon-la-Bataille. At St Laurent-des-Combes turn right towards Sauveterre-de-Guyenne. At sign for Rauzan turn right onto D231. Campsite is signed from the village. GPS: 44.782472, -0.127139

Charges guide

| Per unit incl. 2 persons and electricity | € 12.00 - € 19.00 |
| extra person | € 3.25 - € 5.00 |

Rouffignac-Saint Cernin
Camping BleuSoleil

Domaine Touvent, F-24580 Rouffignac-Saint Cernin (Dordogne) T: 05 53 05 48 30.
E: infos@camping-bleusoleil.com alanrogers.com/FR24380

Camping BleuSoleil is delightfully and quietly located in the countryside and has magnificent views from all areas of the site. It comprises 70 acres and, at present, has 110 pitches, 84 for touring units and 26 used for wooden chalets and 2 bungalow tents. Electricity (10A) is available on every pitch. Set in an open, woody, and hilly area, some of the pitches have partial shade from well sited trees and hedges. There is some terracing. The site's restaurant is bult in the style of the area. The site is divided by a very quiet minor road. The village of Rouffignac-St Cernin-de-Reilhac, is 1 km. away and is within walking distance. There you will find small bars, restaurants and other amenities. The wooden chalets on the site are available for rent from the owner. Noisy entertainment is actively discouraged and a peaceful and tranquil environment is promoted. A good sized supermarket is less than 2 km. The site is well placed for sightseeing and the famous caves of Lascaux, Font de Gaume, and the fossil depository are nearby. There is also the Troglodyte village at La Madeleine.

Facilities

Three modern unisex sanitary blocks are clean, well maintained and adequate for the number of pitches. En-suite toilet for disabled visitors. Baby room with bath. Enclosed laundry area with two washing machines and dryer. Small bar with TV (from 1/5). Restaurant (from 1/6). Large 200 sq.m. swimming pool and paddling pool (15/5-15/9). Multisports area. Boules. Small play area and a pen with donkeys and goats. WiFi (free). Off site: Supermarket 2 km. Riding 4 km. Golf 14 km. Fishing and bicycle hire 15 km.

Open: 1 April - 30 September.

Directions

From Périgueux take N89 east for 17 km. to Thenon, then D31 south signed Balou. Continue from Balou for 3 km. to the outskirts of Rouffignac-Saint Cernin-de-Reilhac and look for site sign on the left. Turn off main road to site (less than 1 km). GPS: 45.05497, 0.98691

Charges guide

Per unit incl. 2 persons and electricity (10A)	€ 14.50 - € 24.70
extra person	€ 3.00 - € 5.60
child (2-5 yrs)	€ 2.00 - € 3.80

www.camping-bleusoleil.com
Domaine Touvent
24580 Rouffignac St. Cernin de Reilhac
Phone n°: 33(0)5 53 05 48 30
Email: infos@camping-bleusoleil.com

For latest campsite news, availability and prices visit
alanrogers.com

Saint Amand-de-Coly
Yelloh! Village Lascaux Vacances
F-24290 Saint Amand-de-Coly (Dordogne) T: 04 66 73 97 39. E: info@yellohvillage-lascaux-vacances.com
alanrogers.com/FR24690

Situated on a wooded hillside in the heart of the Périgord Noir, this pleasant site has been totally redeveloped. It is owned by M. Cedric Rocher (also the owner of the very popular Panorama de Pyla) and managed by Phillipe and Jocelyne who are committed to ensuring that your stay is a memorable one. The pool complex is impressive and incorporates a spa bath and a terraced lounging area. The nearby village of St Armand-de-Coly is listed as one of the most beautiful in France and is a must to visit. There are 165 pitches, with 40 for touring units (20 can access electricity). The remainder are occupied by chalets, mobile homes and bungalow tents, some of which are for hire.

Facilities

The two main toilet blocks were very clean when we visited. Provision may be stretched in high season. One block has a baby room, the other has facilities for disabled visitors. Laundry area. Fridge hire. Shop. Bar. Restaurant. Takeaway. Swimming pools with spa bath. Play area. Bicycle hire. Riding. Small library. Activity and entertainment programme. WiFi in bar area (free). Electric barbecues are permitted. Off site: Lascaux caves 2 km.

Open: 16 April - 20 September.

Directions

Leave A89 (Bordeaux-Clermont-Ferrand) at exit 17 (Peyrignac) and head south on the D6089 to Le Lardin-Saint Lazare. Here, join southbound D62 to Coly, then signs to Saint Amand-de-Coly. Site is well signed from here. GPS: 45.05494, 1.24656

Charges guide

Per unit incl. 2 persons	€ 15.00 - € 30.00
extra person	€ 5.00 - € 6.00

Saint Antoine-de-Breuilh
Camping la Rivière Fleurie
180 rue Théophile Cart, F-24230 Saint Antoine-de-Breuilh (Dordogne) T: 05 53 24 82 80.
E: info@la-riviere-fleurie.com **alanrogers.com/FR24300**

This quiet, pleasant campsite is close to the vineyards of Pomerol and St Emilion, and not far from the extensive shopping of Saint Foy-la-Grande and Bergerac. The 66 pitches are all spacious, divided by shrubs and maturing trees, and are beginning to provide shade. All pitches have electricity (10A). There are no tour operators, but 19 pitches are used for mobile homes to rent and there are studio apartments to let throughout the year. The site has a tranquil and peaceful ambience, suitable for anyone looking for a relaxing holiday. You will receive a warm, friendly welcome and there is a convivial, family atmosphere.

Facilities

Sanitary facilities are plentiful and modern including an excellent new block. Bar and terrace restaurant. Heated swimming pool (100 sq.m) and toddlers' pool. TV room. Weekly soirées where the owners host an evening of French food and entertainment. Canoe trips arranged. Fishing. WiFi (free). Off site: Tennis court adjacent. Riding 4 km. Supermarket 5 km. Bicycle hire 8 km. Golf 10 km.

Open: 1 April - 30 September.

Directions

Site is in St Aulaye, 3 km. south of D936 Bordeaux - Bergerac road. 6 km. east of Lamothe-Montravel turn south on local roads and follow signs to site 150 m. from river. GPS: 44.82905, 0.12238

Charges guide

Per unit incl. 2 persons	€ 19.90 - € 25.90
extra person	€ 4.50 - € 5.90
Camping Cheques accepted.	

Saint Astier
Flower Camping le Pontet
Route D41, F-24110 Saint Astier (Dordogne) T: 05 53 54 14 22. E: camping.lepontet@flowercampings.com
alanrogers.com/FR24900

Le Pontet is a good choice for anglers, located on the banks of the small River Isle. Trout, carp, black bass and pike are all regularly caught here. The river is also popular for swimming and canoeing (canoe hire on site), but the site has its own small pool too. There are 131 level, grass pitches with 90 for touring, all with 6A electricity. On-site services include a bar/snack bar and a small shop. Pitches are grassy and of a good size. Most are equipped with electricity.(6A). Since the opening of the A89 motorway (Bordeaux - Clermont-Ferrand) access to this formerly remote region has become more straightforward, making the site a good base for exploring.

Facilities

Centrally located toilet blocks are open in style with washbasins and seatless WCs. Showers not controllable. En-suite room for disabled visitors. Bar/snack bar, small shop (15/6-15/9). Small swimming pool, paddling pool (July/Aug). Minigolf. TV/games room. Children's play area. Direct river access. Fishing. Canoe hire. WiFi by reception. Off site: Cycle and walking tracks in the local countryside. Supermarket. Périgueux. Riding 5 km. Golf 17 km.

Open: 1 April - 30 September.

Directions

Leave A89 autoroute, junction 14, southwest of Périgueux. Take D6089 west approx 1 km. At roundabout, turn north D43, site is on left in 1.3 km. GPS: 45.147353, 0.533121

Charges guide

Per unit incl. 2 persons and electricity	€ 13.90 - € 21.90
extra person	€ 2.50 - € 5.00

For latest campsite news, availability and prices visit
alanrogers.com

Saint-Avit-de-Vialard

Castel Camping Caravaning Saint-Avit Loisirs

Le Bugue, F-24260 Saint-Avit-de-Vialard (Dordogne) T: 05 53 02 64 00. E: contact@saint-avit-loisirs.com

alanrogers.com/FR24180

Although Saint-Avit Loisirs is set amidst rolling countryside, far from the hustle and bustle of the main tourist areas of the Dordogne, the facilities are first class, providing virtually everything you could possibly want without the need to leave the site. This makes it ideal for families with children of all ages. The site is in two sections. One part is dedicated to chalets and mobile homes which are available to rent, whilst the main section of the site contains 199 flat and mainly grassy, good sized pitches, 99 for touring, with electricity (6/10A). With a choice of sun or shade, they are arranged in cul-de-sacs off a main access road and are easily accessible. The café, shop and bar open onto a large terrace with pergola and hanging baskets, which overlooks the excellent pool complex. In high season a variety of activities and entertainments are organised – tournaments, aqua gym, bingo and weekly films in English.

Facilities

Three modern unisex toilet blocks provide high quality facilities. Shop, bar, good quality restaurant, caféteria. Outdoor swimming pool, children's pool, water slide, crazy river, heated indoor pool with jacuzzi. Fitness room. Soundproofed disco. Minigolf. Boules. BMX track. Tennis. Quad bikes. Play area. Bicycle hire. Canoeing and other sporting activities organised. Good cycle routes from site. Extra charge for some activities. Off site: Boulangerie, supermarket, Tuesday market, Birdland at Le Bugue 6 km.

Open: 2 April - 18 September.

Directions

Site is 6 km. north of Le Bugue. From D710 Le Bugue-Périgueux road, turn west on narrow and bumpy C201 towards St-Avit-de-Vialard. Follow road through St Avit, bearing right and site is 1.5 km. GPS: 44.95161, 0.85042

Charges guide

Per unit incl. 2 persons and electricity	€ 18.10 - € 44.00
extra person	€ 3.60 - € 10.20

Saint Crépin-Carlucet

Camping les Peneyrals

542

Le Poujol, F-24590 Saint Crépin-Carlucet (Dordogne) T: 05 53 28 85 71. E: infos@peneyrals.com

alanrogers.com/FR24320

Within easy reach of all the attractions of the Périgord region, M. and Mme. Havel have created an attractive and friendly family campsite at les Peneyrals. There are 250 pitches, 111 of which are for touring. The pitches at the bottom of the hill tend to be quieter as they are further from the main facilities, but are all level and grassy (some on terraces), with electricity (5/10A), and most have some shade. An attractive bar and restaurant with terrace overlook the excellent pool complex and at the bottom of the site is a small fishing lake. The site is set on a wooded hillside, with flowers in abundance (thanks to the dedication of Mme. Havel's mother). Activities are organised over a long season, including archery, various sports tournaments, aquagym, discos and a children's club. On-site entertainment is provided in and around the bar and terrace area every night except Saturdays.

Facilities

Two modern, unisex toilet blocks provide good quality facilities, including for babies and disabled visitors. Motorcaravan services. Shop, restaurant and takeaway (all season). Pool complex with two large pools (one heated), paddling pool and splash pool. Indoor heated pool. Bicycle hire. Minigolf. Tennis (charged). Badminton. Play area. Games room, WiFi (charged), TV room and small library. Fishing. Off site: Sarlat 11 km.

Open: 12 May - 15 September.

Directions

Site is 11 km. north of Sarlat. From D704 Sarlat - Montignac road turn east on D60 towards Salignac-Eyvigues. After 4 km. turn south on D56 towards St Crépin-Carlucet. Site is about 500 m. along this road on the right. GPS: 44.95776, 1.2729

Charges guide

Per unit incl. 2 persons and electricity	€ 19.40 - € 33.10
extra person	€ 4.90 - € 8.70

★ ★ ★ ★ ★ HEATED SWIMMING POOL AND PADDLING POOL, WATER SLIDES, HEATED SANITARY (LOW SEASON), RESTAURANT, BAR, SHOP, TENNIS, BASKET BALL, FISHING...

All facilities open from 12 May till 15 September

10 km from Sarlat, Dordogne-Périgord

Les Peneyrals

Tel: 0033 55 32 88 571
Fax: 0033 55 32 88 099

WWW.PENEYRALS.COM

Discount in May, June and September

For latest campsite news, availability and prices visit

alanrogers.com

5 stars + 5 red tents Michelin = 53 ha of fun ! Great aquatic resort with 4 swimming pools, including 1 inside exotic heated pool, Jacuzzi, aquatoon, crazy river, toboggan...

On site, multiple shops and activities (sport field, tennis, quad bikes, bungee jumping, driving range, putting green...). Relax in our various accommodations, just happiness! Seminaries, groups, contact us.

Saint Avit Loisirs le Bugue*** - 24260 Saint Avit de Vialard - France
Tél 05 53 02 64 00 - Fax 05 53 02 64 39
contact@saint-avit-loisirs.com - www.saint-avit-loisirs.com**

DOMAINE
cro **Magnon**
★ ★ ★ ★

On an estate covering 22 hectares dominating the Dordogne valley, 800 meters from the river and 20 km from Sarlat, the Domaine le Cro Magnon is the ideal location for visiting Perigord's 1001 treasures...

At the heart of a beautiful natural setting, at Cro Magnon you can choose from 160 demarcated pitches and a wide choice of accommodation: Chalets, Cottages

Domaine Le Cro Magnon** - 24220 Allas les Mines - France
Tél 05 53 29 13 70 - Fax 05 53 29 15 79
contact@domaine-cro-magnon.com - www.domaine-cro-magnon.com**

Saint Cybranet
Camping Bel Ombrage

F-24250 Saint Cybranet (Dordogne) T: 05 53 28 34 14. E: belombrage@wanadoo.fr

alanrogers.com/FR24140

Bel Ombrage is a quiet, well maintained site located in a pretty location by the little River Céou, with a pebble beach that is safe and clean for bathing. The site has a good pool complex, but otherwise there are few on-site facilities. The 180 well shaded, good sized and flat grass pitches are marked by trees and bushes and all have electricity. The quiet and tranquil setting makes the site particularly popular with couples. Bel Ombrage is very close to Domme and Castelnaud and would make an ideal and inexpensive base for visiting the southern Dordogne area. It is a short walk to the village of St Cybranet, with bar, restaurant and a small well stocked supermarket, and a short drive takes you to the beautifully restored village of Daglan.

Facilities

Two modern toilet blocks are kept spotlessly clean, with facilities for disabled visitors and babies. Laundry facilities. Bread van. Large swimming pool with sun terrace, children's pool. Paddling pool. Play area. Games room. Fishing. Excursions can be booked at reception. WiFi. Off site: Pizzeria next door. Tennis and canoeing nearby. Riding and bicycle hire 3 km. Golf 6 km. Shops at Cénac.

Open: 1 June - 5 September.

Directions

Site is about 14 km. south of Sarlat, on the east side of the D57 Castelnaud-la-Chapelle - St Cybranet road, about 1 km. north of the junction with the D50. GPS: 44.79128, 1.16214

Charges guide

Per unit incl. 2 persons and electricity	€ 21.80
extra person	€ 5.40
child (under 7 yrs)	€ 3.40

No credit cards.

Bel Ombrage camping-caravaning

24250 St. Cybranet • Tel: 0033 (0)553 28 34 14 • Fax: 0033 (0)553 59 64 64
E-mail: belombrage@wanadoo.fr • www.belombrage.com

Saint Emilion
Yelloh! Village Saint Emilion

Route de Montagne, D122, F-33330 Saint Emilion (Gironde) T: 05 57 24 75 80. E: barbanne@wanadoo.fr

alanrogers.com/FR33080

Yelloh! Village Saint Emilion (formerly La Barbanne) is a pleasant site in the heart of the Bordeaux wine region, only 2.5 km. from the famous town of Saint Emilion. It became part of the Yelloh! group in 2010. With 175 pitches, most for touring, the owners have created a carefully maintained, well equipped site. The large, level and grassy pitches have dividing hedges and electricity (long leads necessary). The original parts of the site bordering the lake have mature trees, good shade and pleasant surroundings, whilst in the newer area the trees have yet to provide full shade and it can be hot in summer. Twelve pitches for motorcaravans are on tarmac surrounded by grass.

Facilities

Two modern, fully equipped toilet blocks include facilities for children and for campers with disabilities. Motorcaravan services. Well stocked shop. Bar, terrace, takeaway, restaurant. Breakfast service. Two swimming pools, one heated with water slide. Enclosed play area with seats for parents. Children's club. Tennis. Boules. Volleyball. Fishing. Minigolf. Bicycle hire. Evening entertainment. WiFi (charged). Max. 1 dog. Off site: St Emilion and shops 2.5 km. Riding 8 km.

Open: 14 April - 22 September.

Directions

Site is 2.5 km. north of Saint Emilion. Caravans and motorcaravans are forbidden in the village of St Emilion, and must approach the site from Libourne on D243 or from Castillon – leave D936 and take D130/D243. GPS: 44.91679, -0.14148

Charges guide

Per unit incl. 2 persons	
and electricity	€ 17.00 - € 39.00
extra person	€ 6.00 - € 8.00
child (3-12 yrs)	free - € 6.00
dog	€ 4.00

For latest campsite news, availability and prices visit

alanrogers.com

Saint Geniès-en-Périgord
Camping Caravaning la Bouquerie

F-24590 Saint Geniès-en-Périgord (Dordogne) T: 05 53 28 98 22. E: labouquerie@wanadoo.fr

alanrogers.com/FR24310

La Bouquerie is situated within easy reach of the main road network in the Dordogne, but without any associated traffic noise. Recent new owners here are investing in new amenities. The main complex is based around some beautifully restored traditional Périgord buildings. There is a bar and restaurant that overlook the impressive pool complex, with a large outdoor terrace for fine weather. The excellent restaurant menu is varied and reasonably priced. Of the 185 pitches, 58 are used for touring units and these are of varying size (80-120 sq.m), flat and grassy, some with shade, and all with 10A electrical connections. The majority of the remainder are for mobile homes and chalets for rent. In high season the site offers a range of sporting activities (aqua-gym, archery, canoeing, walks etc), as well as a children's club each weekday morning. La Bouquerie is ideally situated for exploring the Périgord region, and has something to offer families with children of all ages. Reception has a very comprehensive supply of information leaflets and brochures so visitors can plan days out.

Facilities

Three toilet blocks with facilities for disabled visitors and baby rooms. Washing machines and covered drying lines. Shop (15/5-15/9). New bar and restaurant (12/5-15/9). Takeaway. Heated swimming pool complex including water slides, paddling pool and sunbathing areas with loungers (all season). Carp fishing in lake. Multisports area. Boules. Gym. Paintball. WiFi (charged). Off site: Shops, restaurants and Sunday market in the nearby village of St Geniès. The prehistoric caves at Lascaus. Museum and animal park at Le Thot. Golf 30 km.

Open: 7 April - 15 September.

Directions

Site is signed on east side D704 Sarlat - Montignac, about 500 m. north of junction with D64 St Geniès road. Turn off D704 at campsite sign and take first left turn signed La Bouquerie - site is straight ahead. GPS: 44.99865, 1.24549

Charges guide

Per unit incl. 2 persons	
and electricity	€ 19.00 - € 25.50
extra person	€ 4.60 - € 6.50
child (under 7 yrs)	€ 3.20 - € 4.50
dog	€ 2.50

VILLAGE VACANCES - CAMPING CLUB

La Bouquerie is situated within easy reach of the main road network in the Dordogne. The main complex is based around some beautifully restored traditional Périgordin buildings. Of the 185 pitches 55 are used for touring units and are flat and grassy, some with shade and all with electrical connections. The rest of the pitches are used for Mobil homes and Chalets.

It includes a shop, a bar and a restaurant overlooking the pool complex with a large outdoor terrace. Lots of entertainment during the day and in the evening.

CAMPING LA BOUQUERIE - F-24590 Saint Geniès en Périgord
Tel: +33 553 28 98 22 - Fax: +33 553 29 19 75
labouquerie@wanadoo.fr - www.labouquerie.com

For latest campsite news, availability and prices visit
alanrogers.com

Saint Jean-de-Luz
Camping Tamaris Plage

Quartier Acotz, 720 route des Plages, F-64500 Saint Jean-de-Luz (Pyrénées-Atlantiques) T: 05 59 26 55 90.
E: tamaris1@wanadoo.fr **alanrogers.com/FR64080**

This small, pleasant and popular site is well kept and open all year. It is situated outside the town and just across the road from a sandy beach. The 30 touring pitches, all with 7/10A electricity, are of a good size and separated by hedges, on slightly sloping ground with some shade. The site becomes full for July and August with families on long stays, so reservation then is essential. Mobile homes for rent occupy a further 40 pitches. A leisure centre and club provide a heated pool and various other free facilities for adults and children. A gym, Turkish bath, massage and other relaxing amenities are available at an extra charge. There is no shop, but bread is available daily across the road and some items can be bought in reception. Opposite the site, a popular surf school offers instruction to new and experienced surfers from the sandy Mayarco beach.

Facilities	Directions
The single heated toilet block of good quality and unusual design should be an ample provision. Facilities for disabled guests. Washing and drying machine. Wellness health club with free facilities: swimming pool, TV and play room and club for children (4-11 yrs), and some on payment: gym, Turkish bath and other spa facilities, sunbathing area, jacuzzi, TV lounge. WiFi. Off site: Beach, fishing, surfing (with instruction) 30 m. Ghéthary with supermarket 2 km. St Jean-de-Luz 4 km. Bicycle hire, boat launching and golf 5 km. Riding 7 km.	Proceed south on N10 and 1.5 km. after Ghéthary take first road on right (before access to the motorway and Carrefour centre commercial) and follow site signs. GPS: 43.41795, -1.623817

Open: All year.

Charges guide

Per unit incl. 2 persons	
and electricity	€ 18.00 - € 27.00
extra person (over 2 yrs)	€ 6.00 - € 8.00
dog	€ 6.00

TAMARIS PLAGE**** CAMPSITE HOLIDAY VILLAGE

TAMARIS Plage

ACOTZ 64500 ST. JEAN DE LUZ | TEL. 00 33 5 59 26 55 90 | FAX 0033 5 59 47 70 15
WWW.TAMARIS-PLAGE.COM | GPS: 43.413499. - 1.607297

Saint Jean-de-Luz
Camping International Erromardie

Avenue de la Source, F-64500 Saint Jean-de-Luz (Pyrénées-Atlantiques) T: 05 59 26 07 74.
E: camping-international@wanadoo.fr **alanrogers.com/FR64170**

There are not many sites right by the sea in this region. Erromardie, a new member of the Chadotel group, is a good one, with only a small access road to cross to reach a beach of coarse sand and fine shingle. The site is mainly flat and grassy, with several different parts separated by hedges, but not much shade. There are 215 pitches, mainly adjoining access roads and backing onto hedges, including 70 for tourers with electricity (10A), of which 20 also have water and waste water drainage. Some pitches have ocean views and others have views of the Pyrenees.

Facilities	Directions
The large sanitary buildings are of good quality, with individual cabins and free hot water. Baby changing area. Facilities for disabled visitors. Laundry room. Motorcaravan service point. Shop, bar, restaurant and takeaway (May-Sept). Basic outdoor heated swimming pool (15/5-10/9). Water play area. Playground. Games room. Boules. Fishing. Mobile homes for hire. WiFi throughout (charged). Off site: Beach 50 m. Golf 1 km. Boat ramp 2 km. Biarritz and Spain 15 km.	Take exit 3 from the A63 (E05, E70) St Jean-de-Luz Nord towards St Jean-de-Luz/Guéthary/Ascain onto Ave. de Lahanchipia, then left onto Ave. André Ithurralde (D810), first right Ave. Claude Farrère and follow site signs. GPS: 43.406247, -1.637286

Open: 3 April - 30 September.

Charges guide

Per unit incl. 2 persons	
and electricity	€ 17.60 - € 32.00
extra person	€ 5.80
child (2-13 yrs)	€ 3.80
dog	€ 3.20

For latest campsite news, availability and prices visit
alanrogers.com

Saint Jean-de-Luz
Camping Atlantica

Quartier Acotz, F-64500 Saint Jean-de-Luz (Pyrénées-Atlantiques) T: 05 59 47 72 44.
E: info@campingatlantica.com **alanrogers.com/FR64250**

This is a friendly, family run site with 200 shady and well kept grass pitches set amongst many shrubs, flowers and hedges. There are 99 pitches for touring, 69 have 6A electricity and 41 have water and drainage. The excellent swimming pool area is attractively landscaped with plenty of sunbeds. With a bar, restaurant and takeaway open June to September, the beach 500 m. and the cosmopolitan town of St Jean-de-Luz only 3 km. away, this site is suitable for families and couples of all ages. If excessively wet, motorcaravans are advised to call ahead to check availability. The three bright and very clean sanitary blocks are well maintained with large showers and piped music. A comprehensive fitness room includes a sauna and during July and August a trained attendant is available for advice.

Facilities

Three immaculate toilet blocks include facilities for babies and campers with disabilities. Excellent laundry. Motorcaravan services. Shop, bar, restaurant and takeaway (all 15/6-15/9). Swimming pool and fitness room (April-Sept). Games room. Multisports court. Modern, fenced children's play area. Family entertainment (July/Aug). WiFi (charged). Off site: Bus to major town 400 m. Large supermarket 1 km. Golf 4 km.

Open: 1 April - 30 September.

Directions

Leave A63, exit 3, taking N10 toward Bayonne. Take the second left turn signed 'Acotz Campings Plages'. At T-junction turn right and follow signs. Campsite is on the right. GPS: 43.41569, -1.61646

Charges guide

Per unit incl. 2 persons and electricity	€ 18.00 - € 34.90
extra person	€ 3.20 - € 7.00
child (under 7 yrs)	€ 2.20 - € 4.10
dog	free - € 2.50

CAMPING ATLANTICA ★★★★
Quartier Acotz - 64500 Saint-Jean-de-Luz
Tel: 0033 559 47 72 44 - Fax: 0033 559 54 72 27
info@campingatlantica.com - www.campingatlantica.com

On 500 m distance from the beach in a green and floral environment for a quiet and pleasant stay in a pleasant family ambiance. Heated water park, relaxing area with spa and sauna, mini golf, sports terrain. All facilities present for pleasant stay. Mobile homes for rent. Dogs not allowed in accommodation.
Campsite open from 1st April till 30th September.

Camping Holidays
Pyrénées Atlantiques (64)
Chadotel
International Erromardie ★★★★

Chadotel
Camping nternational Erromardie
F- 64500 Saint Jean de Luz
Tél. +33 (0)2 51 33 05 05 - info@chadotel.com - www.chadotel.com

Pitches for tents, caravans & motorhomes
Quality mobile homes
Swimming pool - Water games for children
Entertainment for adults & children

For latest campsite news, availability and prices visit
alanrogers.com

Saint Julien-en-Born

Yelloh! Village Lous Seurrots

606 avenue de l'Ocean, Contis Plage, F-40170 Saint Julien-en-Born (Landes) T: 05 58 42 85 82.
E: info@yellohvillage-lous-seurrots.com **alanrogers.com/FR40070**

Lous Seurrots is only a short 400 m. walk from the beach and parts of the site have views across the estuary. There are 602 pitches, mainly in pine woods on sandy undulating ground. They are numbered but many are only roughly marked out, most have good shade and all 277 touring pitches have 6/8A electricity (adaptors required). The site's pool complex (two are heated) is in a superb setting of palm trees and flower beds and the paved sunbathing areas have wonderful views out to the estuary and the sea. For all its size, Lous Seurrots is a family site with the emphasis on peace and tranquillity with some well-organised entertainment in peak season.

Facilities

Three well kept, modern toilet blocks, baby rooms and facilities for disabled visitors. Washing machines. Motorcaravan services. Large shop and bar (1/5-19/9). Restaurant (19/4-19/9) plus takeaway. Swimming pool complex (1/5-19/9) and a jacuzzi with keep fit classes (July/Aug). Tennis. Archery. Minigolf. Canoeing. Bicycle hire. Fishing. Miniclub. Evening entertainment twice weekly in high season in open-air auditorium. Electric barbecues are permitted. WiFi (charged). Off site: Beach 400 m. Riding 3 km.

Open: 31 March - 18 September.

Directions

Turn off D652 on D41 (15 km. south of Mimizan) to Contis-Plage and site is on left as you reach it. GPS: 44.08881, -1.31634

Charges guide

Per unit incl. 2 persons	
and electricity	€ 15.00 - € 41.00
extra person	€ 5.00 - € 7.00
child (3-7 yrs)	free - € 6.00
dog	€ 4.00

We can book this site for you! Call 01580 214000 alan rogers travel

Saint Martin-de-Seignanx

Camping Caravaning Lou P'tit Poun

542

110 avenue du Quartier Neuf, F-40390 Saint Martin-de-Seignanx (Landes) T: 05 59 56 55 79.
E: contact@louptitpoun.com **alanrogers.com/FR40140**

The manicured grounds surrounding Lou P'tit Poun give it a well kept appearance, a theme carried throughout this very pleasing site which celebrated its 20th anniversary in 2009. It is only after arriving at the car park that you feel confident it is not a private estate. Beyond this point an abundance of shrubs and trees is revealed. Behind a central sloping flower bed lies the open plan reception area. The avenues around the site are wide and the 168 pitches (142 for touring) are spacious. All have 10A electricity, many also have water and drainage and some are separated by low hedges. The jovial owners not only make their guests welcome, but extend their enthusiasm to organising weekly entertainment (at the café/restaurant) for young and old during high season. A Sites et Paysages member.

Facilities

Two unisex sanitary blocks, maintained to a high standard and kept clean, include washbasins in cabins, a baby bath and provision for disabled visitors. Laundry facilities with washing machine and dryer. Motorcaravan service point. Small shop (1/7-31/8). Café/restaurant (1/7-31/8). Swimming pool (1/6-15/9). Play area. Games room, TV. Half-court tennis. Off site: Bayonne 6 km. Fishing and riding 7 km. Golf 10 km. Sandy beaches of Basque coast ten minute drive. Trips to the pyrenees.

Open: 2 June - 12 September.

Directions

Leave A63 at exit 6 and join D817 in the direction of Pau. Site is signed at Leclerc supermarket. Continue for 3.5 km. and site is clearly signed on right. GPS: 43.52406, -1.41196

Charges guide

Per unit incl. 2 persons	
and electricity	€ 22.65 - € 33.80
extra person	€ 7.40 - € 7.80
child (under 7 yrs)	€ 5.55 - € 6.05
dog	€ 4.00 - € 5.00

Lou P'tit Poun ★★★

At 10 km from the ocean, a friendly welcome awaits you at this quality camp-site between Les Landes and the Basque country.

Rental of bungalows and mobil-homes

CAMPING LOU P'TIT POUN
40390 ST MARTIN DE SEIGNANX
Tél : 05 59 56 55 79 Fax : 05 59 56 53 71
E-mail : contact@louptitpoun.com
LANDES - AQUITAINE - FRANCE

For latest campsite news, availability and prices visit
alanrogers.com

Saint Pardoux-la-Riviere

Kawan Village Château le Verdoyer

Champs Romain, F-24470 Saint Pardoux-la-Riviere (Dordogne) T: 05 53 56 94 64. E: chateau@verdoyer.fr

alanrogers.com/FR24010

This 26-hectare estate has three lakes, two for fishing and one with a sandy beach and safe swimming area. There are 135 good sized touring pitches, level, terraced and hedged. With a choice of wooded area or open field, all have electricity (5/10A) and most share a water supply between four pitches. There is a swimming pool complex and high season activities are organised for children (5-13 yrs) but there is no disco. This site is well adapted for those with disabilities, with two fully adapted chalets, wheelchair access to all facilities and even a lift into the pool. Château le Verdoyer has been developed in the park of a restored château and is owned by a Dutch family. We particularly like this site for its beautiful buildings and lovely surroundings. It is situated in the lesser known area of the Dordogne sometimes referred to as the Périgord Vert, with its green forests and small lakes. The courtyard area between reception and the bar is home to evening activities, and provides a pleasant place to enjoy drinks and relax. The château itself has rooms to let and its excellent lakeside restaurant is also open to the public. There are Dutch tour operators on site with pre-erected tents for hire that occupy some touring pitches.

Facilities

Well appointed toilet blocks include facilities for disabled visitors and baby baths. Serviced launderette. Motorcaravan services. Shop (from 1/5). Bar, snacks, takeaway and restaurant (from 1/5). Bistro (July/Aug). Two pools, slide, paddling pool. Play areas. Tennis. Minigolf. Bicycle hire. Fishing. Small library. WiFi (charged). Internet access in reception. International newspapers daily. Off site: Riding 5 km. Golf 33 km. Vélo-rail at Bussière Galant. Market (Thu. and Sun) at Saint Pardoux 12 km.

Open: 28 April - 30 September.

Directions

Site is 2 km. from Limoges (N21) - Chalus (D6bis-D85) - Nontron road, 20 km. south of Chalus and is well signed from main road. Site on D96 about 4 km. north of Champs Romain. GPS: 45.55035, 0.7947

Charges guide

Per unit incl. 2 persons	
and electricity	€ 21.00 - € 38.50
extra person	€ 5.00 - € 6.50

Camping Cheques accepted.

We can book this site for you! **alan**rogers ● travel
Call 01580 214000

Dordogne
Périgord vert

Château · Le Verdoyer ★★★★ · Kawan Village Camping

www.verdoyer.fr

F 24470 Champs Romain
Tél. + 33 (0)5 53 56 94 64
Fax. + 33 (0)5 53 56 38 70
E mail : chateau@verdoyer.fr

Accomodations, restaurant, campsite ★★★★

Salignac-Eyvigues

Flower Camping le Temps de Vivre

Malmont, F-24590 Salignac-Eyvigues (Dordogne) T: 05 53 28 93 21. E: contact@temps-de-vivre.com

alanrogers.com/FR24460

Le Temps de Vivre is situated in the centre of the Périgord Noir, in the countryside and lies about 250 m. above sea level. The area of the campsite covers about 6.5 hectares in total, with 1.5 acres in use at present. It is a small, friendly, family run site with 50 pitches, 30 of which are for touring and 20 for mobile homes available for rent. The pitches are wide and terraces separate some of them. All have electricity connections available (10A) and you will find a variety of trees and bushes often as a natural separation. This is a delightful and peaceful rural site.

Facilities

One modern unisex sanitary block is very clean and well maintained. En-suite toilet for disabled visitors. Baby room with bath. Covered laundry area. Small shop in reception. Small bar (15/5-15/9), restaurant and takeaway (July/Aug). Two swimming pools (one for children). Boules. Play area. Pottery and painting for young children (July/Aug). Themed meals (weekly July/Aug). WiFi in reception (free). Electric barbecues are not permitted. Off site: Shops and restaurants within walking distance in Salignac-Eyvigues.

Open: 21 April - 23 September.

Directions

From Brive-La-Gaillarde heading south on the A20 continue for 30 km. to exit 55 signed Souillac. Take D62/D15 northwest for 12 km. until Salignac-Eyvigues. As you drive through the town centre look for blue sign for site. Follow the sign off the main road for about 2 km. GPS: 44.96374, 1.32813

Charges 2012

Per unit incl. 2 persons	
and electricity	€ 15.50 - € 26.90

For latest campsite news, availability and prices visit
alanrogers.com

Sanguinet

543

Camping les Grands Pins

1039 avenue de Losa, F-40460 Sanguinet (Landes) T: 05 58 78 61 74. E: info@campinglesgrandspins.com
alanrogers.com/FR40250

Approached by a road alongside the lake, this Airotel group site is surrounded by tall trees. Of the 345 pitches, the 80 sand/gravel pitches are of average size, mostly level with varying degrees of shade. Low hedges and young trees divide those available for tourers and most are set away from the mobile homes and chalets. An impressive central pool complex includes a covered heated indoor pool, an outdoor pool, water slide and flume, children's pool and jacuzzi. There are plenty of walks, cycle rides and the lake to enjoy. The poolside bar, restaurant and shops are open in July and August when the site becomes busier, offering watersports, minigolf, a children's club, boat trips and organised activities. Volleyball, tennis and boules are available all season. The charming small village of Sanguinet is 2 km. away with supermarket and shops, bank, bars, restaurants and an archaeological museum.

Facilities

Four toilet blocks include washbasins in cabins, showers and British style toilets (not all open in low seasons). Baby bath and provision for disabled visitors. Laundry facilities. Motorcaravan service point. Shop, bar, restaurant and takeaway (1/7-31/8). Indoor pool (all season). Outdoor pool complex with jacuzzi (1/4-15/9). Play area. Games room and TV in bar. Tennis, volleyball, boules. Sports equipment available to hire. Bicycle hire. Children's club (charged). Dogs are not accepted in July/Aug. Barbecues allowed in dedicated areas provided. Off site: Fishing 200 m. Boat launching 1 km. Golf and riding 15 km. Beach and windsurfing 18 km.

Open: 1 April - 30 September.

Directions

Enter Sanguinet from the north on the D46. At one way system turn right. Do not continue on one way system but go straight ahead toward lake (signed) on Rue de Lac. Site is 2 km. on left.
GPS: 44.48396, -1.089716

Charges guide

Per unit incl. 2 persons	
and electricity	€ 18.00 - € 41.00
extra person	€ 5.50 - € 9.00
child (3-7 yrs)	€ 4.50 - € 6.50
dog	€ 3.00

Salles

Camping des Bastides

Terre Rouge, F-47150 Salles (Lot-et-Garonne) T: 05 53 40 83 09. E: info@campingdesbastides.com
alanrogers.com/FR47130

Attractive and well maintained, this six and a half-hectare site is hilly and terraced with good views from the top of the site. The new French owners, Gaelle and Christian, are warm and welcoming. Although the terrain is hilly, most of the 90 medium sized touring pitches are fairly level and moderately shaded (all with 6A electricity). Tight turns with narrow gravel paths and overhanging trees may cause some difficulties for larger units. A range of different types of accommodation including Mongolian tents are available to rent. Reception keeps information on a variety of local walking and cycling routes.

Facilities

Two modern, clean and well maintained sanitary blocks can be heated. Facilities for disabled visitors. Excellent children's facilities with baby bath and child-size facilities. Private en-suite facilities for hire. Shop for essentials (with gas). Bar/reception and snack restaurant (including takeaway). Swimming pool complex with swimming pool, pool with slides, two paddling pools and a spa. Boules. Play area with bouncy castle. Small indoor play area with TV and small library. WiFi (charged). Entertainment (high season). Off site: Fishing 1 km. Fumel 8 km. Riding and bicycle hire 10 km. Golf 25 km.

Open: 1 May - 30 September.

Directions

From Fumel, take D710 north towards Cuzorn. Before reaching Cuzorn, turn northwest on D162 and site is 6 km. on the right hand side (well signed).
GPS: 44.5525, 0.8815

Charges guide

Per unit incl. 2 persons	
and electricity	€ 17.00 - € 28.50
extra person	€ 4.00 - € 5.00
child (2-12 yrs)	€ 2.25 - € 3.00
dog	free - € 2.00

For latest campsite news, availability and prices visit
alanrogers.com

Les Grands Pins

CAMPING CARAVANING ★★★★

Club Airotel

Sanguinet

Lac de Biscarrosse

Chalets and mobile homes for rent

Camping Caravaning les Grands Pins
Avenue de Losa (route du lac) 40460 SANGUINET
Tél : 00 33 (0)5 58 78 61 74 · Fax : 00 33 (0)5 58 78 69 15
info@campinglesgrandspins.com www.campingaquitaine.com

Situated
at the lakeside
Aquatic Parc
The best place to enjoy t
the Les Landes Sun!

www.campinglesgrandspins.com

Sanguinet

Campéole le Lac Sanguinet

526, rue de Pinton, F-40460 Sanguinet (Landes) T: 05 58 82 70 80. E: lac-sanguinet@campeole.com

alanrogers.com/FR40440

Le Lac Sanguinet is a member of the Campéole group, and is located just 100 m. from the large lake of the same name. There are 400 pitches here, of which 290 have electrical connections (10/16A). Around 70 pitches are occupied by mobile homes, chalets and fully equipped bungalow tents, all available for rent, including some models specially adapted for the disabled. An attractive swimming pool was added for the 2008 season and other amenities include volleyball and two children's playgrounds. A marquee is used for activities and entertainment during the peak season. The Lac de Sanguinet is one of Europe's largest lakes (6,800 hectares!) and is renowned for the clarity of its waters. It's understandably popular for fishing but also for watersports. A sailing and windsurfing centre is adjacent to the site. This is a region for superlatives – Europe's highest sand dune, the Dune de Pyla is close, and from the top, there are wonderful views of the Arcachon basin and surrounding forest.

Facilities

Four sanitary blocks have hot showers, washbasins in cabins and facilities for disabled visitors. Motorcaravan services. Laundry facilities. Snack bar and pizzas (July/Aug). Small shop. Heated swimming pool. Games room. Bicycle hire. Bouncy castle. Play areas. Activities and entertainment programme. Tourist information. Mobile homes, equipped tents and chalets for rent. Charcoal barbecues in a reserved area only. WiFi (charged). Off site: Lac de Sanguinet 100 m. Sailing centre. Walking and cycle tracks through the forest. Fishing. Dune du Pyla. Bordeaux 60 km.

Open: 1 May - 16 September.

Directions

Approaching from Bordeaux, head south on A63 and then join the A660 towards Arcachon. Leave this motorway at the first exit and follow signs to Sanguinet (D216). Upon arrival in Sanguinet follow signs to 'Le Lac' and from here the site is well indicated. GPS: 44.4816, -1.0938

Charges guide

Per unit incl. 2 persons	
and electricity	€ 17.90 - € 30.60
extra person	€ 4.60 - € 9.10
child (2-6 yrs)	€ 2.50 - € 3.50
dog	€ 2.50 - € 3.50

Campéole
CAMPSITES AND RENTALS

AQUITAINE

Le Lac Sanguinet★★

Magnificent site, new facilities, swimming pool, direct access to the lake, quality touring pitches and accommodations.

40460 Sanguinet - Tel.: +33-558-8270-80 - www.campeole.co.uk / lac-sanguinet@campeole.com

Sarlat-la-Canéda

Castel Camping le Moulin du Roch

Route des Eyzies-Le Roch (D47), F-24200 Sarlat-la-Canéda (Dordogne) T: 05 53 59 20 27.
E: moulin.du.roch@wanadoo.fr **alanrogers.com/FR24040**

The site has 195 large pitches, of which 124 are for touring units. They are mostly flat (some slope slightly) and grassy and all have electricity (6A). Pitches on the upper levels have plenty of shade, whilst those on the lower level near the amenities and the fishing lake are more open. Entertainment and activities are organised from June to September, with something for everyone, from quizzes and sports tournaments to canoeing and riding for the more adventurous. An excellent multilingual children's club runs in July/August. Walking and mountain biking routes lead from the site through the woodland.

Facilities

Well maintained, very clean toilet blocks. Washing machines, dryers. Good shop. Bar with WiFi and terrace. Takeaway. Superb restaurant. Attractive swimming pool, paddling pool, sun terrace, (all open all season). Fishing lake. Tennis. Boules. Playground. Evening entertainment throughout the high season. Pets are not accepted. Off site: Supermarkets, banks, etc. at Sarlat 10 km. Bicycle hire and riding 10 km. Golf 15 km.

Open: 9 May - 16 September.

Directions

Site is 10 km. west of Sarlat-la-Canéda, on south side of D47 Sarlat - Les Eyzies road. GPS: 44.90867, 1.1148

Charges guide

Per unit incl. 2 persons	€ 19.00 - € 35.00
incl. full services	€ 23.00 - € 39.00
extra person	€ 5.00 - € 9.50

Camping Cheques accepted.

For latest campsite news, availability and prices visit
alanrogers.com

Sarlat-la-Canéda
Domaine de Soleil Plage

Caudon par Montfort, Vitrac, F-24200 Sarlat-la-Canéda (Dordogne) T: 05 53 28 33 33. E: info@soleilplage.fr
alanrogers.com/FR24090

This site is in one of the most attractive sections of the Dordogne valley, with a riverside location. There are 199 pitches, in three sections, with 100 for touring units. Additionally there are 47 mobile homes and 27 chalets for rent. The site offers river swimming from a sizeable sandy bank or there is a very impressive heated pool complex. All pitches are bounded by hedges and are of adequate size with 16A electricity, water and a drain. Most pitches have some shade. If you like a holiday with lots going on, you will enjoy this site. Various activities are organised during high season including walks and sports tournaments, and daily canoe hire is available from the site. Once a week in July and August there is a 'soirée' (charged for) usually involving a barbecue or paella, with a band and lots of free wine – worth catching! The site is busy and reservation is advisable. English is spoken. The site is quite expensive in high season and you also pay more for a riverside pitch, but these have fine river views. There is some tour operator presence.

Facilities

Toilet facilities are in three modern unisex blocks. One has been completely renovated to a high standard with heating and family shower rooms. Washing machines and dryer. Motorcaravan service point. Well stocked shop, pleasant bar with TV and attractive, newly refurbished restaurant with local menus and a pleasant terrace (all from 1/5). Picnics available to order. Very impressive heated main pool, paddling pool, spa pool and two slides. Tennis. Minigolf. Three play areas. Fishing. Canoe and kayak hire. Bicycle hire. Currency exchange. Small library. WiFi throughout (charged). Activities and social events (high season). Off site: Golf 1 km. Riding 5 km. Many attractions of the Dordogne are within easy reach.

Open: Easter - 30 September.

Directions

Site is 6 km. south of Sarlat. From A20 take exit 55 (Souillac) towards Sarlat. Follow the D703 to Carsac and on to Montfort. At Montfort castle site is signed on left. Continue for 2 km. down to the river and site. GPS: 44.825, 1.25388

Charges guide

Per unit incl. 2 persons
electricity	€ 21.00 - € 35.50
incl. full services	€ 24.50 - € 50.50
extra person	€ 5.00 - € 7.50
child (2-8 yrs)	€ 3.00 - € 4.50
dog	€ 2.50 - € 3.50

Camping Cheques accepted.

Take advantage of our prices in low season to enjoy the heated pool & WIFI on all the campsite & New heated toilet block & the beautiful scenery from your chalet or your pitch along the river

Right on the Dordogne riverside (Sand beach, swimming, fishing, canoeing) An exceptional site, 6 km from Sarlat mediaeval town. In the heart of Périgord beautiful landscapes & castles

Many quality facilities for couples, families or groups: Mini-mart (fresh bread & croissants), restaurant périgourdin, pizzeria, take-away, bar. New heated toilet block Numerous activities: heated pool complex, tennis, mini-golf, multi-sport pitch, hiking, cycling, golf (1km), riding (5km), numerous visits (caves, castles, vines, farms...)

Domaine de Soleil Plage****
Caudon par Montfort, VITRAC, 24200 SARLAT
www.soleilplage.fr - info@soleilplage.fr
Tel: +33 5 53 28 33 33 - GPS: 44° 49' 30N - 1° 15' 14E

For latest campsite news, availability and prices visit
alanrogers.com

We can book this site for you! Call 01580 214000 alan rogers ◑ travel

Sarlat-la-Canéda
Camping les Grottes de Roffy

Sainte Nathalène, F-24200 Sarlat-la-Canéda (Dordogne) T: 05 53 59 15 61. E: contact@roffy.fr

alanrogers.com/FR24130

About 5 km. east of Sarlat, les Grottes de Roffy is a pleasantly laid out, family site. There are 162 clearly marked pitches, some very large, set on very well kept grass terraces. They have easy access and good views across an attractive valley. Some have plentiful shade, although others are more open, and all have 6A electricity. Those with very large units are advised to check availability in advance. The reception, bar, restaurant and shop are located within converted farm buildings surrounding a semi-courtyard. The site shop is well stocked with a variety of goods and a tempting épicerie. A good heated outdoor pool complex is open all season and is popular with visitors.

Facilities

Two toilet blocks with modern facilities. Well stocked shop. Bar and gastronomic restaurant. Takeaway. Good swimming pool complex comprising two deep pools (one heated), a paddling pool and heated jacuzzi. All amenities are available all season. Tennis. Games room. Room for teenagers. Play area. Bicycle hire. Entertainment for all ages. Internet access. Free WiFi in courtyard area. Off site: Fishing 2 km. Riding 10 km. Golf 15 km.

Open: 18 April - 21 September.

Directions

Take D47 east from Sarlat to Ste Nathalène. Just before Ste Nathalène the site is signed on the right hand side of the road. Turn here and the site is about 800 m. along the lane. GPS: 44.90404, 1.2821

Charges guide

Per pitch incl. 1-6 persons and electricity	€ 9.30 - € 21.40

Sarlat-la-Canéda
Camping les Tailladis

Marcillac-Saint Quentin, F-24200 Sarlat-la-Canéda (Dordogne) T: 05 53 59 10 95. E: tailladis@wanadoo.fr

alanrogers.com/FR24480

Les Tailladis is a well situated, mature campsite of some 17 hectares of woodland, owned by the same Dutch and French family for over 47 years. It is about 12 km. from Sarlat, Eyzies and Montignac-Lascaux, and 35 km. from Souillac. Four hectares provide 78 medium to large pitches which are grassy, terraced and partially shaded, with electricity (10A), and water points close by. There is also a small stream and pond. The access road and campsite roads/tracks are narrow and winding, which may cause difficulties for some larger units. The hosts are welcoming and enthusiastic and you will be greeted with a drink and warm, friendly service.

Facilities

One heated sanitary block. En-suite toilet for disabled visitors. Baby bath and changing area. Laundry. Shop (fresh bread and milk to order). Restaurant, bar. Swimming pool and paddling pool. Play area with trampoline. Library. Activities organised (high season). Internet access (charged). Fishing. Off site: Riding 3 km. Bicycle hire 12 km. Golf 25 km. Boat launching 25 km. Sarlat 12 km.

Open: 1 March - 30 November.

Directions

From Sarlat-la-Canéda, take D704 heading north. After 10 km. look for signs on the left for Marcillac-St Quentin. Take this road heading northwest, and site is less than 3 km. after Marcillac-St Quentin on the left hand side. GPS: 44.97450, 1.18832

Charges guide

Per unit incl. 2 persons	€ 14.60 - € 22.00

Sarlat-la-Canéda
Camping la Palombière

Sainte Nathalène, F-24200 Sarlat-la-Canéda (Dordogne) T: 05 53 59 42 34. E: la.palombiere@wanadoo.fr

alanrogers.com/FR24570

This site is set in a gorgeous, rural part of France amongst the beauty of the Périgord countryside with its rolling green hills and ancient buildings. The restored and preserved buildings at la Palombière add to the pleasure of this delightful site. It is evident that much investment has gone into making this holiday destination a place to remember. There are 200 pitches of which 68 are for touring caravans and tents. All have 10A electricity and some are fully serviced. Most are level and shaded from the sun, with some terracing because of the different levels. The remaining pitches are used for chalets and mobile home, of which 61 are for rent.

Facilities

Three modern sanitary blocks include facilities for babies and disabled visitors. Washing machines and dryers. Well stocked shop. Bar. Restaurant, snack bar and takeaway. Heated swimming pool complex with slide and toboggan. All amenities open all season. Gymnasium. Playgrounds. Library. Sports field. Tennis. Minigolf. Boules. Trampoline. Satellite TV. Games room. Bicycle hire. Internet facilities. WiFi (free). Off site: Riding and canoeing 3 km. Golf 10 km.

Open: 28 April - 15 September.

Directions

Take the D47 east from Sarlat to Sainte Nathalène. Site is signed from village and is reached by taking a left turn just beyond it. GPS: 44.90819, 1.29252

Charges guide

Per unit incl. 2 persons and electricity	€ 14.50 - € 29.70
extra person	€ 4.50 - € 7.80
child (1-7 yrs)	€ 4.50 - € 5.50

For latest campsite news, availability and prices visit
alanrogers.com

Sarlat-la-Canéda
Camping le Montant

Saint André-d'Allas, F-24200 Sarlat-la-Canéda (Dordogne) T: 05 53 59 18 50. E: lemontant@wanadoo.fr
alanrogers.com/FR24610

Camping le Montant is located on a hillside overlooking beautiful countryside only 2 km. from Sarlat. Run by a pleasant family, there is a friendly welcome. There are 131 pitches, of which 92 are large pitches for touring units, the remainder being used for a variety of high quality furnished accommodation for rent. The touring pitches, all with 6/10A electricity, are divided into two areas, each with its own sanitary block. One part of the site is shaded with hedges, the other area is more open with flat terraced pitches looking out over the wooded hills. Good amenities include an outdoor pool with slides, a heated indoor pool and large jacuzzi, and a bar/restaurant with terrace built in traditional style and surrounded by flowers. Recent additions and improvements include a large playground with modern activities and a large area for minigolf, boules and table tennis. In high season a daily supervised activity programme is arranged with pool activities, mountain bike outings, canoeing, a miniclub and sports tournaments. Many events and activities can be found in Sarlat and the surrounding area. Sarlat market takes place every Saturday.

Facilities

Both toilet blocks are very well equipped especially a newer one with its baby room and large laundry. Bar, restaurant and takeaway (all season). Swimming pool complex with outdoor pool (from 9/5), slides, heated indoor pool and large indoor jacuzzi. New playground. Tennis. Multisports area. Minigolf. Boules. Bicycle hire. Activities organised for children, teenagers and adults day and evening (July/Aug). WiFi (free). Off site: Historic Sarlat 2 km. Riding 3 km. Fishing and golf 5 km.

Open: 1 May - 20 September.

Directions

Site is 2 km. south of Sarlat off the D57 Sarlat -Baynac road. If approaching from Sarlat, site is signed to the right. Follow this road for about 1 km. GPS: 44.865344, 1.187704

Charges guide

Per unit incl. 2 persons	
and electricity	€ 19.60 - € 29.80
extra person	€ 4.80 - € 7.50
child (2-7 yrs)	€ 2.00 - € 5.20
dog	free - € 2.00

ONLY 4 KM FROM THE HISTORICAL VILLAGE OF SARLAT

LE MONTANT
★★★★
DOMAINE DE LOISIRS

YOUR HOLIDAY IN A LARGE FOREST DOMAIN
COVERED POOL & LARGE HEATED JACUZZI | RESTAURANT

Rte de Bergerac • 24200 Sarlat
Tél. 05 53 59 18 50 • Fax. 05 53 59 37 73
www.camping-sarlat.com
contact@camping-sarlat.com

• Camping / Camper service
• Gites / Chalets / Mobile homes
• Pitches
• Animation
• Free WiFi

Sarlat-la-Canéda
Camping les Terrasses du Périgord

Pech-d'Orance, F-24200 Sarlat-la-Canéda (Dordogne) T: 05 53 59 02 25.
E: terrasses-du-perigord@wanadoo.fr alanrogers.com/FR24670

Set on a hilltop on the edge of Sarlat, this site has panoramic views across the Périgord. There are 90 pitches, of which 75 are for touring units, with the remaining 15 for chalets and mobile homes for rent. The site is sloping on different levels but the pitches are generally level. All are shady, marked and separated by trees. Electricity is 6, 10 or 16A. For those with larger units, it is essential to phone in advance for pitches, as not all are suitable. A warm and friendly welcome is given by the French owners.

Facilities

One modern sanitary block divided into two provides all facilities including those for disabled visitors and babies. Washing machine and dryer. Motorcaravan services. Shop. Bar with snack bar and takeaway. Wine tastings. Swimming pool and toddler's pool. Play area with cable slide. Minigolf. Bicycle hire. Gas and electric barbecues only. Evening entertainment. Off site: Caves. Châteaux. Fishing and canoeing 2 km. Riding 8 km.

Open: 23 April - 18 September.

Directions

From Sarlat, take D47 to Proissans. Continue on D56 to Proissans and site is 500 m. on the left. In Sarlat, follow the signs for hospital as it is nearby. GPS: 44.9058, 1.23598

Charges guide

Per unit incl. 2 persons	
and electricity	€ 16.80 - € 22.00
extra person	€ 4.20 - € 5.40

No credit cards.

For latest campsite news, availability and prices visit
alanrogers.com

Sarlat-la-Canéda

Camping Domaine des Mathevies

Les Mathevies, Sainte Nathalène, F-24200 Sarlat-la-Canéda (Dordogne) T: 05 53 59 20 86.
E: mathevies@mac.com **alanrogers.com/FR24740**

This site is a rustic treasure, situated in the rural heart of the Périgord. Family run, the delightful owners, Patrick and Natalie McAlpine, will give you a warm and friendly welcome. The rural location gives a wonderful feeling of tranquillity. The 26 pitches are large and generous at 150-280 sq.m. and all have 10A electricity, five also have water and drainage. In addition, there are six wooden chalets, three mobile homes and a traditional stone gite to rent. A shaded terrace is next to the beautiful, original Périgordine building and the barn has been lovingly converted into the restaurant.

Facilities

Sanitary facilities include provision for disabled visitors. Washing machine and dryer. Bar. Restaurant. Swimming and paddling pools. Tennis court. Library. Selection of games. Satellite TV. Playground. Pétanque. Special interest groups catered for. Crèche (under 5 yrs). Badminton court. Basketball. Bicycle hire. WiFi over site (free). Off site: Riding 2 km. Fishing and canoeing 5 km.

Open: 13 April - 26 September.

Directions

From the A20 exit 55 for Souillac follow road to Roufillac and Carlux. Continue to Sainte Nathalène and site is signed from there.
GPS: 44.918056, 1.277778

Charges guide

Per unit incl. 2 persons and electricity	€ 14.00 - € 26.00
extra person	€ 4.50 - € 7.00

Sauveterre-la-Lemance

Flower Camping Moulin du Périé

F-47500 Sauveterre-la-Lemance (Lot-et-Garonne) T: 05 53 40 67 26. E: moulinduperie@wanadoo.fr
alanrogers.com/FR47010

Set in a quiet area and surrounded by woodlands, this peaceful little site is well away from much of the tourist bustle. It has 95 reasonably sized, grassy touring pitches, all with 6A electricity, divided by mixed trees and bushes with most having good shade. All are extremely well kept, as indeed is the entire site. The attractive front courtyard is complemented by an equally pleasant terrace at the rear. Two small, clean swimming pools overlook a shallow, spring water lake, ideal for inflatable boats and paddling, and bordering the lake, a large grass field is popular for games. The picturesque old mill buildings, adorned with flowers and creepers, now house the reception, bar and restaurant.

Facilities

Two clean and well maintained toilet blocks have facilities for disabled visitors. Motorcaravan services. Fridge, barbecue. Basic shop. Bar/reception, restaurant and takeaway. Two small swimming pools (no Bermuda-style shorts). Boules. Outdoor chess. Playground. Small indoor play area. Bicycle hire. Organised activities (high season). Internet access should be available using cable connection to your own equipment. Off site: Fishing 1 km. Riding 7 km. Small shop in village with larger stores in Fumel.

Open: 12 May - 18 September.

Directions

From D710, Fumel - Périgueux, turn southeast into Sauveterre-la-Lemance. Turn left (northeast) at far end on C201 signed Château Sauveterre and Loubejec (site also signed). Site is 3 km. on right.
GPS: 44.59016, 1.04761

Charges guide

Per unit incl. 2 persons and electricity	€ 18.15 - € 27.65
extra person	€ 4.50 - € 7.00

Camping Cheques accepted.

Sérignac-Péboudou

Camping la Vallée de Gardeleau

F-47410 Sérignac-Péboudou (Lot-et-Garonne) T: 05 53 36 96 96. E: valleegardeleau@wanadoo.fr
alanrogers.com/FR47120

Camping la Vallée is a delightful, well established family run site. It is well hidden, tranquil and private, some 9 km. from civilisation and deep in the countryside of Lot-et-Garonne, very close to the border of the Dordogne and 150 km. from the Atlantic coast. It has a total of 33 pitches, 26 for touring and seven mobile homes. The medium sized pitches are well laid out, all with hedges and shade, some with views. The owners, Virginie and Laurent Faivre, are very conscientious and work extremely hard to keep the site clean and well maintained.

Facilities

Two heated sanitary blocks are well sited and clean. Facilities for disabled visitors. Baby room. Washing machine. Shop with fresh bread daily. Bar with snack bar and TV. Restaurant (high season). Swimming pool. Large boules area (need to bring own boules). Small play area. Communal stone barbecue. Library in reception. Minigolf. Off site: Fishing and riding 2 km. Bicycle hire 9 km. Golf 20 km. Atlantic coast 150 km.

Open: 2 February - 31 October.

Directions

From Castillones on the N21 find the D254 to Sérignac-Péboudou and follow this. Some 10 km. along this road, look for signs to site, which is on the left-hand side. GPS: 44.61606, 0.51821

Charges guide

Per unit incl. 2 persons and electricity	€ 12.40 - € 17.50
extra person	€ 2.60 - € 4.00

For latest campsite news, availability and prices visit
alanrogers.com

Seignosse
Camping les Deux Etangs

1379 route de l'Etang Blanc, F-40510 Seignosse (Landes) T: 05 58 41 66 99. E: info@les2etangs.com
alanrogers.com/FR40750

Located in the Landes forest this site consists mainly of mobile homes and chalets of various designs with just a few touring pitches. The owner wishes to create a peaceful village for holidaymakers away from the hectic Atlantic coastal resorts whilst still being within thirty minutes drive of surfing and sailing attractions. The 12 touring pitches are on soft sand with shade provided by tall pines. Access is difficult for large units. The mobile homes are all new and furnished to a high standard. Evening entertainment is available for adults but there are no organised activities for children. The site is within walking distance of two lakes. Fishing is possible in the larger one and boats can also be used. At the smaller lake there is a designated nature reserve where just walking, cycling and nature observation is encouraged. Seignosse town is 2 km, where all essential amenities are available. Seignosse beach is a little further away, along with a large water and leisure park, play areas, a skate board park and plenty of restaurants and cafés. The beach can get crowded in peak season but it is very long and with a little effort quieter areas can be reached. If the beaches are a little too hot, a day out to visit the Grottes de Sare will help you cool down. There are many surf schools and good surfing beaches on the coast.

Facilities

One adequate toilet block. Laundry facilities. Basic shop, small bar, restaurant and takeaway (all 1/6-30/9). Basic swimming pool (July-Sept). Wellness centre (sauna, steam room, shower and therapy beds). Play area. Boules. Volleyball. Bicycle hire. Games room. Communal barbecues (individual barbecues not permitted). WiFi (charged). Off site: Basque Country. Fishing 250 m. Golf 3 km. Riding 5 km. Sea beach 5 km. Boat launching 8 km.

Open: All year.

Directions

Located 2 km. north of Seignosse town. From autoroute A63 take exit 8 on D112 signed Seignosse. Turn right signed Tosse and turn left onto Route de l'Etang. Site is on right within 4 km. GPS: 43.70047, -1.37273

Charges guide

Per unit incl. 2 persons and electricity	€ 18.00 - € 23.00
extra person	€ 4.00

LES DEUX ETANGS
CAMPING/VILLAGE VACANCES

LES DEUX ETANGS
CAMPING / VILLAGE VACANCES

Opened in May 2010, Les 2 Etangs defines a new generation of camping/holiday villages. With bold design and architecture it sets a new standard for environmentally friendly holidays with unrivalled comfort.

Camping les Deux Etangs | **1379 Route de l'Etang Blanc** | **40510 SEIGNOSSE**
Tel : 0033 (0)5 58 41 66 99 | **E-mail : info@les2etangs.com** | **Web : www.les2etangs.com**

Soulac-sur-Mer
Yelloh! Village Soulac-sur-Mer

8 allée Michel Montaigne, F-33780 Soulac-sur-Mer (Gironde) T: 05 56 09 77 63. E: contact@lelilhan.com
alanrogers.com/FR33330

This is a well established woodland site, popular with families. Now part of the Yelloh! Village group, it has benefited from an extensive programme of investment and development. There are around 50 large touring pitches (all with 10A electricity), the remainder used for mobile homes and chalets to rent. Most pitches are heavily shaded and on natural woodland floor terrain. A special area is kept for younger campers away from the quieter family areas. There is an attractive and well laid out pool complex, together with a small shop selling bread and basic provisions, a bar and a restaurant.

Facilities

Three unisex toilet blocks, with a family bathroom, facilities for babies, washbasins in cubicles, and a suite for disabled campers. Laundry facilities. Pool complex, new balnéo, sauna, jacuzzi (15/6-15/9). Shop, bar, restaurant and pizzeria, takeaway (15/6-15/9). Entertainment. Children's club (high season). Playground. Minigolf. Tennis. Archery. Riding. Bicycle hire. Internet access. WiFi. Gas and charcoal barbecues not permitted. Off site: Town 3 km.

Open: 1 April - 15 September.

Directions

Soulac-sur-Mer is on the Atlantic coast just south of the tip of the Gironde peninsula. Site is signed off the D101 – turn east on a minor road about 3 km. south of Soulac town, and site is on the left after a short distance. GPS: 45.48576, -1.1179

Charges guide

Per unit incl. 2 persons and electricity	€ 15.00 - € 39.00
No credit cards.	

For latest campsite news, availability and prices visit
alanrogers.com

Soulac-sur-Mer

Camping Club les Lacs

126 route des Lacs, F-33780 Soulac-sur-Mer (Gironde) T: 05 56 09 76 63. E: info@camping-les-lacs.com

alanrogers.com/FR33400

Given its proximity to the Gironde ferry terminal at Le Verdon, many campers head south through Soulac. It is, however, a smart resort with a fine sandy beach. Camping Club les Lacs is one of the best sites here and has 228 pitches on offer, of which 114 are available to touring units. All have electrical connnections (10A). Site amenities are impressive with a large, modern complex at the entrance with a large bar, restaurant, shop and stage for evening entertainment (high season). There is a large outdoor pool and covered pool adjacent (open for the full season). A member of Sites et Paysages.

Facilities

Good quality, modern toilet blocks. with showers and washbasins in cubicles. Facilities for disabled visitors. Washing machines and dryers. Shop. Bar, restaurant and takeaway (1/6-15/9). Swimming and paddling pools (1/6-15/9). Indoor pool all season. Water slide. Minigolf. Games room. Playground. Entertainment and children's club in peak season. WiFi. Communal barbecues only. Off site: Riding 200 m. Bicycle hire 2 km. Nearest beach 2.5 km. Fishing 4 km.

Open: 5 April - 8 November.

Directions

Site is 1 km. south of Soulac on the D101 (Routes des Lacs) and is well signed.
GPS: 45.48355, -1.11952

Charges guide

Per unit incl. 2 persons	
and electricity	€ 23.00 - € 33.00
extra person	€ 4.00 - € 5.00
child (3-10 yrs)	€ 2.00 - € 4.00
dog	€ 2.00

Soustons

Camping le Framissima Nature

63 avenue du Port d'Albret, F-40140 Soustons (Landes) T: 05 58 77 70 00. E: resa.soustons@fram.fr

alanrogers.com/FR40760

Framissima Nature is a new site (and a member of the Sunelia group) located in the heart of the vast Landes pine forest. It is close to Soustons and its huge lake, and around six kilometres from the Atlantic beaches. There are 250 well shaded pitches here. These are all occupied by chalet style mobile homes and other rentable accommodation. There are no touring pitches. The site does have an impressive pool complex with a wave pool, amongst other features. Unusually, in order to preserve a pleasant, tranquil aspect, cars are only allowed on site on arrival and departure. At other times, they must be left in a separate parking area. There is direct access to the large network of cycle tracks which run through the forest. The small town of Soustons is around two kilometres away and is a pleasant spot with a number of restaurants and cafés. There is a good golf course at Pinsolle, and the stylish resort of Biarritz is around 50 km. to the south, with the Spanish border and Pyrenees a little further.

Facilities

Bar. Restaurant. Takeaway food. Swimming pool complex (including covered pool). Children's playground. Football. Volleyball. Basketball. Tennis. Multisports terrain. Gym. Activity and entertainment programme. Mobile homes and chalets for hire. Please note that there are no touring pitches on this site. Off site: Supermarket 500 m. Shops and restaurants in Soustons. Cycle tracks through the forest. Golf 5 km. Beach 6 km. Watersports.

Open: 9 April - 16 October.

Directions

The site is located on the eastern side of the Etang de Soustons. Heading south on N10, leave at the Magesq exit and head for Soustons on D116. Before reaching Soustons follow signs to Azur on D60 and the site is clearly signed to the left.
GPS: 43.75579, -1.35384

Charges 2012

Contact the site for details.

FRAMISSIMA nature
Soustons - Landes - France

FRAMISSIMA NATURE *****
63 avenue de Port d'Albret - 40140 SOUSTONS
tél.: +33 (0)5 58 77 70 00 - fax: +33 (0)5 58 77 78 00
e-mail: resa.soustons@fram.fr

Situated in the heart of a pineforest of 14 ha, the first Framissima Nature offers you a new kind of holiday in an extraordinary environment.

For latest campsite news, availability and prices visit

alanrogers.com

Urrugne
Sunêlia Col d'Ibardin

F-64122 Urrugne (Pyrénées-Atlantiques) T: 05 59 54 31 21. E: info@col-ibardin.com
alanrogers.com/FR64110

This family owned site at the foot of the Basque Pyrenees is highly recommended and deserves praise. It is well run with emphasis on personal attention, the friendly family and their staff ensuring that all are made welcome, and is attractively set in the middle of an oak wood with a mountain stream cascading through it. Behind the forecourt, with its brightly coloured shrubs and modern reception area, various roadways lead to the 203 pitches. These are individual, spacious and enjoy the benefit of the shade (if preferred a more open aspect can be found). There are electricity hook-ups (6/10A) and adequate water points. A very attractive chalet 'village' has been added. From this site you can enjoy the mountain scenery, be on the beach in 7-10 km. or cross the border into Spain in about 14 km.

Facilities

Two toilet blocks, one rebuilt to a high specification, are kept very clean. WC for disabled campers. Dishwashing and laundry facilities. Motorcaravan service point. Shop for basics and bread orders (1/6-15/9). Restaurant, takeaway service and bar (1/6-15/9). Heated swimming pool and paddling pool (with water games). Playground and club (adult supervision). Tennis. Boules. Video games. Bicycle hire. Multisports area. WiFi (charged). Site is not suitable for American motorhomes. Off site: Supermarket and shopping centre 5 km. Fishing, boat launching, sailing and golf 7 km. Riding 20 km.

Open: 1 April - 30 September.

Directions

Leave A63 at St Jean-de-Luz sud, exit no. 2 and join RN10 in direction of Urrugne. Turn left at roundabout (Col d'Ibardin) on D4. Site on right after 5 km. Do not turn off to the Col itself, carry on towards Ascain. GPS: 43.33376, -1.68458

Charges guide

Per unit incl. 2 persons and electricity	€ 17.50 - € 38.50
extra person	€ 3.50 - € 6.50
child (2-7 yrs)	€ 2.50 - € 4.00
dog	€ 2.80

Le Col d'Ibardin***

Camping Sunelia
Le Col d'Ibardin***

Open 23th March – 11th November
Mobile-home, Chalet for rent from
23th March – 11th November
Pitches for rent from 1st April – 30th September
Facilities and amenities open all season:
reception 7 days, tennis, laundrette, hot water,
playground, little farm with animals for children
From 1st May – 30th September: Swimming pool
From June – September: Bar, restaurant, snacks, grocer's
July and August: animation for adults and children club

Tel: (0033) (0)559.54.31.21 – Fax: (0033) (0)559.54.62.28
Website: www.col-ibardin.com – E-mail: info@col-ibardin.com
220 Route d'Olhette – 64122 Urrugne – France

For latest campsite news, availability and prices visit
alanrogers.com

Urrugne
Camping Larrouleta

210 route de Socoa, F-64122 Urrugne (Pyrénées-Atlantiques) T: 05 59 47 37 84. E: info@larrouleta.com

alanrogers.com/FR64180

Camping Larrouleta is an all year site located at the heart of the Basque country. The site has been developed around a 7.5-hectare lake, which has a sandy beach and is ideal for fishing. On-site amenities include a swimming pool, which is covered in low season. There is also a bar/restaurant specialising in local cuisine, and where occasional Basque folk evenings are held in high season. Pitches are of a good size and are generally shaded by poplars. Most have electrical connections. A number of 'grand confort' pitches are available (large pitches with electricity, water and drainage – supplement charged).

Facilities

Toilet block (can be heated) with hot showers, washbasins in cabins and facilities for disabled visitors. Washing machine. Shop (July/Aug). Bar/restaurant. Swimming pool (covered in low season). Lake. Fishing. Tennis. Children's play area. Tourist information. Entertainment and activity programme. WiFi (charged). Off site: Nearest beach, sailing, golf and bicycle hire, all 3 km. Col d'Ibardin (Pyrenees) 7 km. Hendaye 8 km. Spanish border 10 km.

Open: All year.

Directions

Take exit 2 from A63 motorway (Saint Jean-de-Luz Sud) and follow signs to Port Fort, crossing N10. From here follow signs to the site. GPS: 43.37024, -1.686161

Charges guide

Per unit incl. 2 persons and electricity	€ 23.00
extra person	€ 7.00
child (under 7 yrs)	€ 3.00

Vielle-Saint-Girons

Campé●le

Campéole les Tourterelles

F-40560 Vielle-Saint-Girons (Landes) T: 05 58 47 93 12. E: tourterelles@campeole.com

alanrogers.com/FR40450

Les Tourterelles is a large site extending over 20 hectares of forest and is a member of the Campéole group. The site has direct access to the beach, using two footpaths, one of which is decked. The beach is vast and very popular with surfers. A life guard is in attendance during the high season. There are 822 pitches at les Tourterelles, of which around 300 are occupied by mobile homes, chalets and fully equipped bungalow tents, all available for rent, and including some units specially adapted for disabled visitors. Pitches are well shaded by pines and most have electrical connections. Leisure facilities here include a multisports terrain, cycle hire and several children's play areas. There are many appealing tracks through the surrounding forests and the site organises occasional accompanied walks (high season). Various other activities are on offer including beach volleyball and surfing lessons. A daily children's club is in operation as well as regular evening entertainment, including concerts and discos.

Facilities

Toilet blocks have hot showers, washbasins in cabins and facilities for disabled visitors. Motorcaravan service. Laundry facilities. Shop (1/5-30/9). Bar. Takeaway meals. Direct beach access. Volleyball. Beach volleyball. Bicycle hire. Bouncy castle. Play areas. Games room. Activity and entertainment programme. Tourist information. Mobile homes, chalets and equipped tents for rent. Only communal barbecues are permitted. WiFi (charged). Off site: St Girons Plage (attractive resort with all services) 200 m. Fishing. Walking and cycle tracks through the forest. Basque country.

Open: 1 May - 30 September.

Directions

Approaching from Bordeaux, take the A63 towards Bayonne. Leave at the Castets – Vielle-St-Girons exit and continue to Vielle-St-Girons. At the traffic lights follow signs to St Girons Plage (and the site). When you reach St Girons Plage turn right at roundabout and the site can be found after a further 50m. GPS: 43.9397, -1.3258

Charges guide

Per unit incl. 2 persons and electricity	€ 17.90 - € 31.70
extra person	€ 4.60 - € 9.50
child (2-6 yrs)	free - € 5.60

AQUITAINE

Campé●le
CAMPSITES AND RENTALS

Les Tourterelles ★★★
Three stars site with direct access to the Ocean, surfing spot, swimming pool, quality touring pitches, new accommodations.

40560 Vielle Saint Girons · Tel.: +33-558-4793-12 · www.campeole.co.uk / tourterelles@campeole.com

For latest campsite news, availability and prices visit

alanrogers.com

Veyrines-de-Domme

Camping les Pastourels

Le Brouillet - D 53, F-24250 Veyrines-de-Domme (Dordogne) T: 05 53 29 42 17. E: les.pastourels@orange.fr

alanrogers.com/FR24970

Les Pastourels enjoys an excellent location at the heart of the Périgord Noir, with views stretching across towards the Château de Milandes. The region's capital, Sarlat, can be reached in around 15 minutes. There are just 48 touring pitches (and 12 mobile homes) here, although the estate extends over 12 hectares. The pitches are vast (minimum 150 sq.m) and all have electrical connections. Much of the estate is covered by forest (with the characteristic walnut trees found in this area) and pasture. A number of footpaths converge at the site, including the long-distance GR64.

Facilities	Directions
Snack bar/pizzeria. Small shop (selling regional produce). Takeaway food. Outdoor swimming pool. Children's playground. Tourist information. Mobile homes for rent. Off site: Walking and cycling tracks. Shops and restaurants at Castelnaud and Beynac. Châteaux at Milandes, Beynac (4 km) and Castelnaud (3 km). La Roque Gageac 6 km.	From the north, leave A89 motorway at Terrasson exit and follow signs to Sarlat. After Sarlat, head for Bergerac on D67 and, at Castelnaud-la-Chapelle follow signs to Château de Milandes and the campsite. GPS: 44.815504, 1.10014

Open: 2 April - 24 October.

Charges 2012

Per unit incl. 2 persons   € 19.00 - € 23.00

We can book this site for you! Call 01580 214000   alan rogers travel

Vielle-Saint-Girons

Camping Club International Eurosol

Route de la Plage, F-40560 Vielle-Saint-Girons (Landes) T: 05 58 47 90 14. E: contact@camping-eurosol.com

alanrogers.com/FR40060

Eurosol is an attractive, friendly and well maintained site extending over 15 hectares of undulating ground amongst mature pine trees giving good shade. Of the 356 touring pitches, 209 have electricity (10A) with 120 fully serviced. A wide range of mobile homes and chalets are available for rent too. This is very much a family site with multilingual entertainers. Many games and tournaments are organised and a beach volleyball competition is held regularly in front of the bar. The adjacent boules terrain is also floodlit. An excellent sandy beach 700 metres from the site has supervised bathing in high season and is ideal for surfing. The landscaped swimming pool complex is impressive with three large pools, one of which is covered and heated, and a large children's paddling pool. There is a convivial restaurant and takeaway food service. A large supermarket is well stocked with fresh bread daily and international newspapers. A number of cycle trails lead from the site through the vast forests of Les Landes, and a riding centre is located just 100 m. from Eurosol. To the south, the Basque country and Biarritz are within easy access.

Facilities	Directions
Four main toilet blocks and two smaller blocks are comfortable and clean with facilities for babies and disabled visitors. Motorcaravan services. Fridge rental. Well stocked shop and bar (all season). Restaurant, takeaway (2/6-8/9). Stage for live shows (July/Aug). Outdoor swimming pool, paddling pool (all season) and heated covered pool (low season). Tennis. Multisports court. Bicycle hire. WiFi (charged). Charcoal barbecues are not permitted. Off site: Riding (July/Aug) 200 m. Surf school 500 m. Beach and fishing 700 m. Golf 18 km.	Turn off D652 at Saint-Girons on D42 towards Saint-Girons-Plage. Site is on left before coming to beach (4.5 km). GPS: 43.95166, -1.35212

Open: 19 May - 15 September.

Charges guide

Per unit incl. 2 persons and electricity	€ 18.00 - € 35.00
extra person (over 4 yrs)	€ 5.00
dog	€ 4.00

We can book this site for you! Call 01580 214000   alan rogers travel

EUROSOL **★★★★** Camping Club International

Route de la Plage • F-40560 Saint Girons Plage • Tel: 0033 558 479 014 • Fax: 0033 558 477 674
contact@camping-eurosol.com • www.camping-eurosol.com

Vielle-Saint-Girons

Sunêlia le Col-Vert

Lac de Léon, 1548, Route de L'Etang, F-40560 Vielle-Saint-Girons (Landes) T: 08 90 71 00 01.

E: contact@colvert.com **alanrogers.com/FR40050**

This large, well maintained campsite is well laid out on the shores of Lac de Léon and offers 185 mobile homes for rent and 380 touring pitches. The pitches range from simple ones to those with water and a drain, and there are eight with private, well designed, modern sanitary facilities. In low season it is a quiet site and those pitches beside the lake offer a wonderful backdrop to relaxing pastimes. During the main season it is a lively place for children of all ages. A pool complex offers a standard pool for swimming, a pool for children with a water canon and fountains, sunbeds and a heated indoor pool.

Facilities

Four toilet blocks, one heated. One has fun facilities for children based on Disney characters. Facilities for disabled campers. Laundry facilities. Motorcaravan services. Shops, bar/restaurant, takeaway (1/4-8/9). Swimming pool complex with three pools. Spa, fitness centre and sauna. Play area. Games room. Sports areas. Boules. Tennis. Bicycle hire. Minigolf. Fishing. Riding. Sailing school (15/6-15/9). Communal barbecues. WiFi (charged). Off site: Walking and cycle ways in the forest. Atlantic beaches 5 km. Golf 10 km.

Open: 1 April - 23 September.

Directions

Site is off D652 Mimizan - Léon road, 4 km. south of crossroads with D42 at St-Girons. The road to the lake and the site is signed at Vielle. GPS: 43.90285, -1.3125

Charges guide

Per unit incl. 2 persons and electricity	€ 16.90 - € 44.30
extra person	€ 2.00 - € 6.70
child (3-13 yrs)	€ 1.50 - € 5.70
dog	€ 1.10 - € 4.50

NEW digital iPad editions

alan rogers

Available on the **App Store**

NEW 2012

FREE Alan Rogers bookstore app - digital editions of all 2012 guides

alanrogers.com/digital

Vieux-Mareuil
Camping de l'Etang Bleu
F-24340 Vieux-Mareuil (Dordogne) T: 05 53 60 92 70. E: letangbleu@orange.fr
alanrogers.com/FR24330

The English owners at this site, Marc and Jo Finch, are warm and friendly and work hard to maintain high standards. Set in 42 acres, there are only 98 pitches, with three used for mobile homes for rent. All are generously sized and level, enjoying a mixture of sun and shade. Electricity is available (10A). The site's best features are the lake where anglers can fish for carp, the bistro which offers great food, reasonably priced, and the sparkling clean swimming pool. This site is spacious, tranquil and relaxing. A gym and a spa are planned. Entertainment is limited, but there are sporting facilities together with themed nights based around the bistro.

Facilities

Modern well maintained toilet block provides facilities for babies and disabled visitors. Laundry. Bar with terrace (all season). Bistro. Takeaway. Small shop. Swimming pool, sun terrace. Playground, paddling pool. Boules. Badminton. Entertainment, sporting activities, excursions in high season. WiFi (charged). Off site: Restaurant adjacent to campsite, small supermarket, post office etc. in Mareuil 7 km. Riding and bicycle hire 5 km. Golf 40 km.

Open: Easter/1 April - 21 October.

Directions

Site is between Angoulême and Périgueux. Leave D939 in Vieux Mareuil, take D93, and follow narrow road. Just after leaving village site signed on right, just past Auberge de L'Etang Bleu. Turn right, follow signs to site. GPS: 45.44614, 0.50859

Charges guide

Per unit incl. 2 persons	
and electricity	€ 17.25 - € 23.00
extra person	€ 3.75 - € 5.50

Villefranche-de-Queyran
Camping Moulin de Campech
F-47160 Villefranche-de-Queyran (Lot-et-Garonne) T: 05 53 88 72 43. E: camping@moulindecampech.co.uk
alanrogers.com/FR47050

This well shaded, pretty site is run by Sue and George Thomas along with Sue's parents, Dot and Bob Dunn. At the entrance to the site, a trout lake with graceful weeping willows feeds under the restored mill house, which is home to the owners, as well as housing the bar and restaurant. Children will need supervision around the lake and at the pool which is on an elevated area above the mill house. The 60 large-sized pitches are mostly divided by hedges, with electricity (6A, long leads may be necessary in places, but can be borrowed free of charge).

Facilities

The single, rather dated toilet block has modern fittings. Washing machine and dryer. Shop and bar (1/4-30/9). Restaurant (25/4-20/9). Terraced heated swimming pool (1/5-30/9). Open grassy games area. Board games and English library. Boules. Barbecue and quiz nights in high season. Fishing (discounted rate; no permit required). Torch useful. WiFi (charged). Off site: Watersports, bicycle hire, golf and riding 10 km.

Open: 1 April - 14 October.

Directions

Take A10 south to Bordeaux. Join A62 for Toulouse and take exit 6 for Damazan. Follow D8 to Mont de Marsan, at Cap du Bosc turn right onto D11 for Casteljaloux. Site is signed, 5 km. on right. GPS: 44.27179, 0.19093

Charges guide

Per unit incl. 2 persons	
and electricity	€ 20.00 - € 27.00

Villeréal
Camping le Château de Fonrives
Rives, F-47210 Villeréal (Lot-et-Garonne) T: 05 53 36 63 38. E: chateau.de.fonrives@wanadoo.fr
alanrogers.com/FR47030

Le Château de Fonrives is situated in Lot-et-Garonne. The site is set in pretty part-farmed, part-wooded countryside. It is a mixture of hazelnut woodland with a lake and château (mostly 16th century). An attractive tree-lined avenue leads to the barns adjacent to the château which have been converted to house the site's amenities. There are 251 pitches, 101 of which are for touring units, with electricity. They are of a generous size and are well defined by neatly trimmed hedges and small shrubs. Pitches near the woodland receive moderate shade, but elsewhere there is light shade from hedges and young trees.

Facilities

Three well positioned sanitary blocks with facilities for disabled visitors. Laundry facilities. Shop (20/5-15/9). Restaurant, snacks and takeaway (May-Sept). Bar with disco area and terrace (1/6-5/9). Covered swimming pool (April-Oct), outdoor pool, water slides, paddling pool. Jacuzzi. Gym. Sauna. Play area. Field for volleyball and football. Library. Minigolf, tennis, bicycle hire (all charged). Activities for children and adults in season. Hairdresser (July/Aug). WiFi in bar area (charged).

Open: 7 April - 30 September.

Directions

Site is about 2 km. northwest of Villeréal, on west side of the D14/D207 Bergerac - Villaréal road. Pass through Rives and site is signed on the left. GPS: 44.65723, 0.72847

Charges guide

Per unit incl. 2 persons	
and electricity	€ 15.00 - € 34.50
extra person	€ 4.00 - € 4.90
child (under 6 yrs)	€ 2.00 - € 2.80

For latest campsite news, availability and prices visit
alanrogers.com

Villeréal

Camping de Bergougne

D250, Rives, F-47210 Villeréal (Lot-et-Garonne) T: 05 53 36 01 30. E: info@camping-de-bergougne.com

alanrogers.com/FR47160

Camping de Bergougne is a small site located close to the 13th-century bastide of Villeréal in the Haut-Agenais. This restful site is a good choice for either relaxing at the poolside or exploring the surrounding country. There are 60 pitches, 48 for touring, with the remainder for mobile homes and tent-bungalows which are available for hire. The touring pitches are mainly in the shade and all have electricity. One toilet block is situated near the reception area and is converted from an original farm building – be careful, head room is limited!

Facilities

Two toilet blocks, one close to reception has limited head room. The second is newly built and of a high standard with facilities for babies and visitors with disabilities. Laundry and dishwashing area. Bar, restaurant, snack bar and takeaway (1/6-15/9). New swimming and paddling pools. Play area. Games room. Library. Pony riding. Fishing. WiFi in bar area (free). Tourist information. Off site: Shops and bicycle hire in Villaréal 2 km. Golf 15 km. Within 30 minutes of the Lot Valley and the Valley of the Dordogne.

Open: 1 May - 30 September.

Directions

Site is northwest of Villeréal. From Villeréal take the northbound D207 and at Rives, follow local signs to site. GPS: 44.652503, 0.723488

Charges guide

Per unit incl. 2 persons and electricity (6A)	€ 12.10 - € 18.60
extra person	€ 2.50 - € 3.80

Vitrac

Camping la Sagne

Lieu dit Lassagne, F-24200 Vitrac (Dordogne) T: 05 53 28 18 36. E: info@camping-la-sagne.com

alanrogers.com/FR24940

Camping la Sagne is a family run site and is being significantly rebuilt for the 2012 season. The rebuilding programme includes a new reception, bar and snack bar complex and a covered swimming pool and paddling pool with jacuzzi. There are 100 large, level pitches with 70 for touring, all with 16A electricity, but long leads are required. Those in the new area will be open and have no shade, but those in the older section are separated by hedges and mature trees providing good shade. The site is close to the Dordogne river and access is available via a track down through the trees. Fishing and bathing are possible in the river and canoe trips are organised from the site. There is a programme of entertainment in the high season and all the facilities are open all season.

Facilities

One old basic toilet block (refurbishment planned) with all necessary facilities including those for disabled visitors but no washing machine. Small shop. Bar with TV, snack bar and takeaway. Games room. Covered, heated swimming pool, paddling pool and jacuzzi. Playground. River fishing and bathing. WiFi near bar (free). Off site: Golf 800 m. Sarlat with range of shops, bars and restaurants 8 km. Riding 5 km. Bicycle hire 8 km. A good centre for touring the many old market towns with their châteaux and museums. Many marked walks and cycle routes.

Open: 1 May - 30 September.

Directions

Site is 6 km. south of Sarlat. Leave autoroute A20, exit 55 (Souillac) towards Sarlat. Take D703 to Montfort, turn left following site signs. Site entrance on right in 1 km. GPS: 44.825452, 1.242346

Charges guide

Per unit incl. 2 persons and electricity	€ 19.00 - € 30.00
extra person	€ 5.00 - € 7.00
child (2-13 yrs)	€ 3.00 - € 5.00
dog	€ 4.00 - € 5.00

CAMPING CARAVANING RENTAL

La Sagne
100% NATURE
PÉRIGORD
DORDOGNE

On the banks of the Dordogne

Camping LA SAGNE, 24200 VITRAC - FRANCE
Tél. +33 5 53 28 18 36 - www.camping-la-sagne.com - info@camping-la-sagne.com at 8km from Sarlat

For latest campsite news, availability and prices visit

alanrogers.com

Rolling fields of yellow sunflowers, the Armagnac vineyards and crumbling, ancient stone buildings amidst the sleepy villages make this colourful region popular with those who enjoy good food, good wine and a taste of the good life.

DÉPARTEMENTS: 09 ARIÈGE, 12 AVEYRON, 31 HAUTE-GARONNE, 32 GERS, 46 LOT, 65 HAUTES-PYRÉNÉES, 81 TARN, 82 TARN-ET GARONNE.

MAJOR CITY: TOULOUSE

Home of Armagnac, rugby and the Three Musketeers, the Midi-Pyrénées is the largest region of France, extending from the Dordogne in the north to the Spanish border.

It is blessed by radiant sunshine and a fascinating range of scenery. South of the cultivated fields and cliffside villages beside the Lot river, lie the stony lands of the Quercy Causse and the rocky gorges of the Aveyron and Tarn rivers. Centered around Millau, there are tortuous gorges and valleys, spectacular rivers, underground caves and grottoes, and forested mountains.

Further south, high chalk plateaux, majestic peaks, tiny hidden valleys and small fortified sleepy villages, which seem to have changed little since the Middle Ages, contrast with the high-tech, industrial and vibrant university city of Toulouse.

Lourdes is one of the most visited pilgrimage sites in the world. Toulouse-Lautrec, the artist, was born at Albi, the capital of the département of Tarn. In the east, the little town of Foix is a convenient centre from which to explore the prehistoric caves at Niaux and the Aladdin's Cave of duty-free gift shops in the independent state of Andorra.

Places of interest

Albi: birthplace and Museum of Toulouse-Lautrec, imposing Ste Cécile cathedral with 15th-century fresco of 'The Last Judgement'.

Auch: capital of ancient Gascony, boasts a fine statue of d'Artágnan.

Collonges-la-Rouge: picturesque village of Medieval- and Renaissance-style mansions and manors.

Conques: 11th-century Ste Foy Romanesque church.

Foix: 11th/12th-century towers on rocky peak above town; 14th-century cathedral.

Lourdes: famous pilgrimage site where Ste Bernadette is said to have spoken to the Virgin Mary in a grotto and known for the miracles said to have been performed there.

Cuisine of the region

Food is rich and strongly seasoned, making generous use of garlic and goose fat, and there are some excellent regional wines. Seafood such as oysters, salt-water fish, and piballes from the Adour river are popular.

Cassoulet: stew of duck, sausages and beans.

Confit de Canard (d'oie): preserved duck meat.

Grattons (Graisserons): a mélange of small pieces of rendered down duck, goose and pork fat.

Magret de canard: duck breast fillets

Ouillat (Ouliat): Pyrénées soup with onions, tomatoes, goose fat and garlic.

Tourtière Landaise: a sweet of Agen prunes, apples and Armagnac.

**www.tourisme-midi-pyrenees.com
information@crtmp.com
(0)5 61 13 55 48**

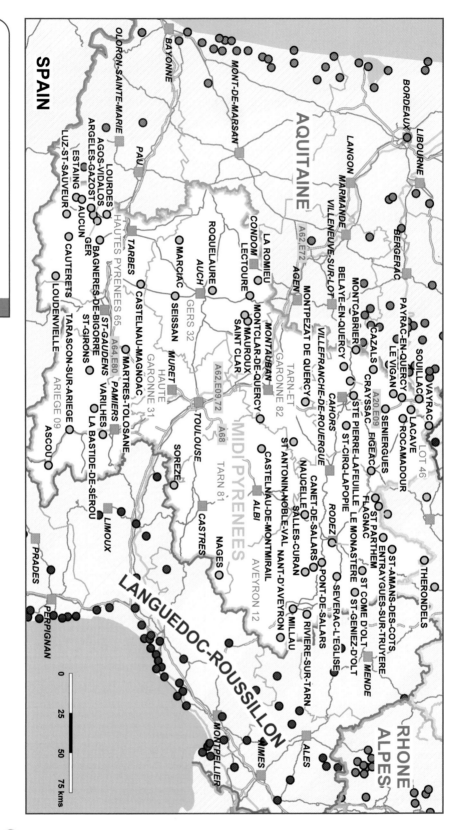

SPAIN

AQUITAINE

MIDI PYRÉNÉES

LANGUEDOC-ROUSSILLON

RHONE ALPES

BORDEAUX
LIBOURNE
BERGERAC
LANGON
MONT-DE-MARSAN
BAYONNE
OLORON-SAINTE-MARIE
PAU
LUZ-ST-SAUVEUR
ESTAING
ARGELES-GAZOST
AGOS-VIDALOS
LOURDES
AUCUN
GER
CAUTERETS
LOUDENVIELLE
TARBES
BAGNERES-DE-BIGORRE
ST-GIRONS
TARASCON-SUR-ARIEGE
ASCOU
ARIEGE 09
HAUTES PYRENEES 65
MARCIAC
SEISSAN
GERS 32
AUCH
ROQUELAURE
LECTOURE
CONDOM
LA ROMIEU
MARMANDE
VILLENEUVE-SUR-LOT
BELAYE-EN-QUERCY
MONTCABRIER
AGEN
A62.E72
MONTPEZAT DE QUERCY
VILLEFRANCHE-DE-ROUERGUE
SAINT CLAR
MAUROUX
MONTCLAR-DE-QUERCY
MONTAUBAN
TARN-ET-GARONNE 82
CASTELNAU-MAGNOAC
ST-GAUDENS
A64.E80
VARILHES
LA BASTIDE-DE-SÉROU
PAMIERS
MARTRES-TOLOSANE
HAUTE GARONNE 31
MURET
TOULOUSE
A62.E09.72
A68
LIMOUX
SOREZE
CASTRES
NAGES
TARN 81
PRADES
PERPIGNAN
MONTPELLIER
ALES
NIMES
MILLAU
AVEYRON 12
PONT-DE-SALARS
SALLES-CURAN
CANET-DE-SALARS
NAUCELLE
RIVIERE-SUR-TARN
NANT-D'AVEYRON
SEVERAC-L'EGLISE
ST-GENIEZ-D'OLT
ST COME D'OLT
RODEZ
CASTELNAU-DE-MONTMIRAIL
ST ANTONIN-NOBLE-VAL
ALBI
ST-CIRQ-LAPOPIE
LE MONASTERE
STE-PIERRE-LAFEUILLE
CAHORS
CRAYSSAC
CAZALS
LE VIGAN
PAYRAC-EN-QUERCY
SOUILLAC
VAYRAC
LACAVE
ROCAMADOUR
LOT 46
SENIERGUES
A20.E09
FIGEAC
FLAGNAC
ST PARTHEM
ENTRAYGUES-SUR-TRUYERE
ST-AMANS-DES-COTS
THERONDELS
MENDE
SEVERAC

For latest campsite news, availability and prices visit

alanrogers.com

Agos-Vidalos
Camping Soleil du Pibeste

16 avenue du Lavedan, F-65400 Agos-Vidalos (Hautes-Pyrénées) T: 05 62 97 53 23.
E: info@campingpibeste.com **alanrogers.com/FR65090**

The Dusserm family, the owners, are very proud of their regional culture and heritage and will ensure you are made welcome. The reception is friendly, with an area for local foods, maps and good tourist information. This site is special because of the range and type of activities that it offers. These include tai chi, qi gong, massage, archery, walking, climbing and canoeing. Choral and creative activities are offered. There are 38 touring pitches all with 3-15A electricity. Mobile homes and chalets are available to rent. The mountain view from the terrace is magnificent.

Facilities

Two heated toilet blocks. Baby room. Facilities for disabled visitors (key). Cleaning can be variable. Washing machine, dryer. Motorcaravan services. Bar, snack bar, restaurant and pizzeria (June-Sept). Shop for essentials. Bread can be ordered. Swimming pool (June-Sept). New play areas. Tennis. Multisports pitch. Volleyball. Badminton. Bowling. Basketball. Four free activities weekly, entertainment, children's activities and craft workshops (all July/Aug). Massage (charged). Library. WiFi (charged). Off site: Fishing 800 m. Rafting 2 km. Golf 10 km.

Open: 1 May - 30 September.

Directions

Agos Vidalos is on the N21, which becomes the D821, 5 km. south of Lourdes. Leave expressway at second exit, signed Agos Vidalos and continue on D921B to site, a short distance on the right. GPS: 43.03557, -0.07093

Charges guide

Per unit incl. 2 persons	
and electricity	€ 25.00 - € 34.00
extra person	€ 8.00
dog	€ 5.00

Argelès-Gazost
Sunêlia les Trois Vallées

Avenue des Pyrénées, F-65400 Argelès-Gazost (Hautes-Pyrénées) T: 05 62 90 35 47.
E: 3-vallees@wanadoo.fr **alanrogers.com/FR65020**

The attractive outdoor pools, jacuzzi, water chutes and heated indoor pool with opening roof are features of this large and lively site. It has 200 level grassy touring pitches, with some mountain views, and 283 mobile homes. All have electricity (3-6A). Reception staff are helpful and friendly. Visitors can gather in the new, imaginatively designed centre to eat, drink, chat, use the WiFi, watch events on the overhead TVs, and in season enjoy the daily programme of professional entertainers.

Facilities

The toilet blocks are a little dated and could be busy at peak times. Facilities for disabled visitors. Bar/disco. Café, takeaway, restaurant (15/6-15/9). Bread. Swimming pool complex (from 15/5), heated indoor pool (all year), paddling pool, spa bath, jacuzzi and water slides. TV room. Playground. Volleyball, football, boules, archery. Entertainment and activities (high season). Meeting, eating and greeting area. Large TV screens for events. WiFi (charged in high season). Off site: Supermarket across the road. Bicycle hire 50 m. Fishing 500 m. Riding 3 km.

Open: 1 April - 2 November.

Directions

Argelès-Gazost is 13 km. south of Lourdes. Take D821 towards Argelès-Gazost, then onto 'La Voie Rapide' and turn right at the first roundabout, after 300 m. right at the new roundabout and you are at the site. GPS: 43.01216, -0.09711

Charges guide

Per unit incl. 2 persons	
and electricity	€ 13.50 - € 34.00
extra person	€ 5.00 - € 10.00

Argelès-Gazost
Kawan Village du Lavedan

Lau-Balagnas, 44 Route des Vallees, F-65400 Argelès-Gazost (Hautes-Pyrénées) T: 05 62 97 18 84.
E: contact@lavedan.com **alanrogers.com/FR65080**

Camping du Lavedan is an old established, family owned site set in the Argelès-Gazost valley south of Lourdes, where a warm welcome and an impressive mountain view await you. There are 60 level touring pitches, all with electricity (2-10A) and most have shade from trees. They are set away from the 48 mobile homes, of which 12 are to rent. Landscaping has been carefully considered. The large, well designed restaurant and bar area is the scene of some lively evening entertainment in the summer. There is some noise from the road.

Facilities

Recent, well maintained toilet block. Baby room. Facilities for disabled visitors. Laundry facilities. Restaurant with terrace, pizzeria and snacks (1/5-15/9). Bar, TV (all year). No shop, bread delivery (1/5-15/9). Swimming pool (with cover), paddling pool. Play area. WiFi (charged). Boules, table tennis. Off site: Trout fishing, bicycle hire 1 km. Supermarket 2 km. Riding 5 km. Golf 15 km.

Open: All year.

Directions

From Lourdes take N21 (Voie rapide) south. This becomes N821/N821A. Take exit 3 (Argelès-Gazost). Take D921 then D921B (Lau-Balagnas). Site on right, southern edge of town. GPS: 42.98822, -0.089

Charges guide

Per unit incl. 2 persons	€ 15.00 - € 24.00
electricity (10A max)	€ 1.00

Camping Cheques accepted.

For latest campsite news, availability and prices visit
alanrogers.com

Ascou
Camping Ascou la Forge
F-09110 Ascou (Ariège) T: 05 61 64 60 03. E: info@ascou-la-forge.fr
alanrogers.com/FR09120

The Dutch owners of Ascou la Forge will give you a warm, friendly welcome at their oasis in the mountains of the Pyrenees, close to the borders of Andorra and Spain. The site is 3,500 feet above sea level but is easily accessible for motorcaravans and caravans. Lying alongside the Lauze river, there are 50 pitches. In low season, 44 mainly level, grass touring pitches with electricity are available, but this number reduces to 20 in July and August to allow more room for the large influx of campers with tents. There are also three chalets, two bungalows and one apartment available to rent. The site is quite open but a few trees scattered around provide some shade.

Facilities

Modern, bright, sanitary block is fully equipped including facilities for disabled visitors which double as a family shower room with a baby bath. Shop. Bar with large screen for major sports events and films about the local flora/fauna. Play area. Maps and walking routes are available from reception. Free WiFi. Off site: Restaurant next door to site (all year). Ax-les-Thermes 7 km.

Open: All year.

Directions

From Ax-Les-Thermes take D613 signed Quérigat, Quillan and Ascou-Pailhéres. After 3.6 km. turn right on D25 to site on right after 3.4 km.
GPS: 42.72444, 1.89274

Charges guide

Per unit incl. 2 persons and electricity	€ 15.00 - € 23.00
extra person	€ 3.50 - € 5.00

Aucun
Camping Azun Nature
1 route des Poueyes, F-65400 Aucun (Hautes-Pyrénées) T: 05 62 97 45 05. E: azun.nature@wanadoo.fr
alanrogers.com/FR65190

This site is attractively located on the edge of the National Park of the High Pyrenees with superb walking, mountain biking and paragliding opportunities. The 25 open and grassy touring pitches, most with electricity (3-6A), have fine views of the surrounding mountains. There are 12 rental chalets. The owner is friendly and enthusiastic. A small shop is provided and drinks can be served on the terrace in summer, though there is no bar. The site prides itself on its relative simplicity and its environmental ethos. The owners are delighted to recommend walking or cycling itineraries and to help organise excursions. There are also many kilometres of marked tracks.

Facilities

Good quality sanitary block with facilities for babies and visitors with disabilities. No restaurant/snack bar but drinks and coffee served on the terrace in high season. Bread delivery (1/7-31/8). Simple shop. Play area. Activities room. Simple shop. Maps and tourist information. Internet and WiFi. Large field area for sports and games. Off site: Walking. Mountain biking. Skiing. Paragliding schools. Shops and market at Arrens-Marsous 2 km.

Open: 15 May - 30 September.

Directions

From Argelès-Gazost take the 921B then the D918 following signs for Aucun. At sign for Aucun village turn left for 'Las Poueyes' and drive for 100 m. Azun Nature's entrance is on the right between the barns.
GPS: 42.97344, -0.18501

Charges guide

Per unit incl. electricity (6A)	€ 16.10
extra person	€ 4.20
child (under 7 yrs)	€ 2.50

Bélaye-en-Quercy
Camping la Tuque
F-46140 Bélaye (Lot) T: 05 65 21 34 34. E: camping@la-tuque.info
alanrogers.com/FR46130

The Quercy region of southwest France is renowned for its sunny climate and attractive terrain, ranging from the dry Causse landscape to the lusher Lot valley and vineyards of Cahors. La Tuque extends over 22 acres, close to the pretty village of Bélaye. The 90 pitches are large (some to 120 sq.m) and well shaded. Unusually, except for loading and unloading, cars are not allowed in the camping area, and large parking areas are provided at the entrance. This is a good centre for an active holiday – walking, mountain biking, canoeing and rock climbing are all possible.

Facilities

Small shop with daily delivery of fresh bread. Restaurant, bar and snack bar with freshly baked pizzas. Swimming pool with water slides and paddling pool. Tennis court. Minigolf. Library. Playground. Games room. Laundry carried out by site staff. Fridge hire. Mobile homes, Safari Lodge and tents for rent. WiFi in bar area (charged). Off site: Walking and cycle routes. Fishing 5 km. Prayssac with shops and cafés 10 km.

Open: 30 April - 10 September.

Directions

Leave the A20 at exit 57 (Cahors) and take the D811 (D911) towards Puy l'Evêque. In Prayssac, take the D67 (Bélaye/Boulvé). From Belaye the D6 to la Tuque. Site is well signed. GPS: 44.44407, 1.17244

Charges guide

Per unit incl. 2 persons	€ 19.50 - € 25.50
extra person	€ 5.00 - € 6.00
No credit cards.	

Bagnères-de-Bigorre
Camping le Monlôo

Chemin du Monlôo (RD8), F-65200 Bagnères-de-Bigorre (Hautes-Pyrénées) T: 05 62 95 19 65.
E: campingmonloo@yahoo.com **alanrogers.com/FR65160**

A relatively small site of 110 touring pitches, le Monlôo is set in a wide valley in the Pyrenees. The immediate surroundings of farmland, with crops growing and cows at pasture, give way to some magnificent views of the mountains towering away from the front of the site, whilst the back is right at the foot of some smaller foothills. This area is a paradise for walkers and cyclists and just travelling a short distance opens up new horizons with some large waterfalls not far away. The friendly family take their job seriously and will even show you a selection of available pitches from the comfort of their electric car. Shade is available on many pitches, with some tall dividing hedges. Electricity (10A) is available. Although lacking in modern day entertainments, the visitors we met were very content with having a good pitch, ample electricity and good facilities. There is a distinct air of friendliness here.

Facilities

Ample toilet facilities are provided in three blocks. Facilities for disabled visitors. Washing machines. Motorcaravan services. Bread to order. Open air heated pool with slide. Simple play area. Gas or electric barbecues are permitted. WiFi. Off site: Spa town of Bagnères-de-Bigorre 2 km.

Open: All year (except November).

Directions

From the A64 take exit 14 signed Bagnères-de-Bigorre. Enter town and take D8 road to the right for Ordizan. Site is just a few hundred metres along this road, well signed. GPS: 43.08180, 0.15139

Charges guide

Per unit incl. 3 persons	
and electricity	€ 19.00 - € 24.50
extra person	€ 3.50 - € 5.00
child (under 8 yrs)	€ 2.00 - € 3.50

Camping le Monlôo ****
Mail: campingmonloo@yahoo.com
Tel: 0033(0)5.62.95.19.65

65200 Bagnères de Bigorre
Hautes Pyrénées
France

Le Monlôo is situated in the touristique city of Bagnères de Bigorre at a hight of 550m. We offer you great service and the comfort of a 4 star campsite.

www.lemonloo.com

Castelnau-de-Montmirail
Camping du Chêne Vert

F-81140 Castelnau-de-Montmirail (Tarn) T: 05 63 33 16 10. E: campingduchenevert@wanadoo.fr
alanrogers.com/FR81170

Camping du Chêne Vert is surrounded by the vineyards of the Gaillac region and is located on the circuit of the 'bastides Albigeoises'. The site can be found just 3 km. from one of France's most beautiful villages, Castelnau de Montmiral. Some pitches are large and grassy. Most have 10A electrical connections. A number of chalets and fully equipped tents are available to rent. On site amenities include a well stocked shop, a bar and a swimming pool. During high season, pizzas and crepes are available, and a weekly themed meal is organised. A local wine producer visits the site on a regular basis with the opportunity to try and purchase his produce.

Facilities

Bar/restaurant. Takeaway food. Shop. Swimming pool. TV room. Games room. Volleyball. Play area. Activities and entertainment. Tourist information. WiFi. Chalets and equipped tents for rent. Off site: Hiking and cycle tracks. Riding. Golf. Albi 30 km.

Open: 1 June - 30 September.

Directions

Castelnau-de-Montmiral lies to the north of Gaillac. Leave the A68 motorway at exit 9 (Gaillac) and head north from Gaillac on D964 to Castelnau de Montmiral. The site is well signed. GPS: 43.97664, 1.79052

Charges guide

Per unit incl. 2 persons	
and electricity	€ 15.70 - € 19.00
extra person	€ 3.50 - € 4.70
child (4-7 yrs)	€ 2.50 - € 3.50

For latest campsite news, availability and prices visit
alanrogers.com

Canet-de-Salars

Castel Camping le Caussanel

Lac de Pareloup, F-12290 Canet-de-Salars (Aveyron) T: 05 65 46 85 19. E: info@lecaussanel.com

alanrogers.com/FR12170

This site has 228 large, fairly level, grassy pitches, 105 for touring. Most have 6A electricity but very long leads may be necessary, and 37 are fully serviced. The pitches are defined by a tree or boulder in each corner and offer little privacy but many have wonderful views over the lake. Most pitches have little shade, a few having good shade. The site has swimming pools with toboggan and slides and a large paddling pool for children with small slides. The adjacent lake offers a large area, 1 km. long, for swimming and all the usual watersports. This large, extremely spacious site on the banks of Lac de Pareloup is greatly improved. It is ideal, in low season, for those seeking a tranquil holiday in a beautiful region of France or in high season, for those seeking an active holiday.

Facilities

Modern toilet blocks have all the necessary facilities. Motorcaravan services. Shop. Bar. Restaurant, takeaway (5/6-4/9). Swimming pool complex (10/5-4/9). Large play area. Boules. Tennis. Football. Organised activities (July/Aug). Fishing. Bicycle hire (July/Aug). Motorboat launching. Water sports (July/Aug). Swimming in lake. Internet access. Max. 2 dogs. WiFi (charged).
Off site: Paths around lake (24 km). Other marked walks and cycle rides. Shops, banks, restaurants 8 km. Riding 10 km. Golf 30 km. Canoeing, rafting, paragliding caving, windsurfing.

Open: 23 May - 17 September.

Directions

From D911 Rodez - Millau road, just east of Pont de Salars, turn south on D993 signed Salles-Curan. In 6 km. at crossroads turn right on D538 signed le Caussanel. Very shortly turn left and continue to site. GPS: 44.21462, 2.76658

Charges guide

Per unit incl. 2 persons and electricity	€ 17.90 - € 44.20

Camping Cheques accepted.

 Le Caussanel ★★★ CASTELS *Hôtellerie de Plain Air*

Take the advantage of the fresh air in an unspoilt region with a wealth of natural treasures. Wide open spaces, great expanses of water and greenery... You are in the heart of Aveyron on the shores of Lac de Pareloup.

- Aquatic park, water slide, pentagliss, watergames (23-05 to 10-09), miniature farm and multisports area
- Chalets and Motorhomes for rent
- Services open from 01-06 to 10-09 (shop, bar, pizzeria-grill, entertainment...)

OPENING DATES: 23-05 TO 17-09-2011

Lac de Pareloup • 12290 Canet de Salars • Tél.: 0033 565 46 85 19 • Fax: 0033 565 46 89 85
Email: info@lecaussanel.com • www.lecaussanel.com

Cauterets

Camping Cabaliros

Pont de Secours, F-65110 Cauterets (Hautes-Pyrénées) T: 05 62 92 55 36. E: info@camping-cabaliros.com

alanrogers.com/FR65110

This is a delightful site, with friendly family owners who will give you a warm welcome to this magnificent mountain area. The open, grassy site has stupendous panoramic views. A separate field has 36 pitches for small tents and another 60 touring pitches with electricity (6A Europlug). These are large and grassy and some shade is provided by mature trees. A communal room is used by visitors to make music, play games, watch television, read the English books and enjoy themselves. The site is within walking distance of Cauterets, with its shops and restaurants, and Argelès-Gazost and the major pilgrimage town of Lourdes are suitable for day visits.

Facilities

Sanitary block near site entrance with WCs, hot showers and washbasins in cubicles. Facilities for disabled campers. Dishwashing and laundry sinks with cold water only. Washing machine and dryer. Motorcaravan service point. Large library (some English) and excellent meeting room with television. Play area for over 7s. Fishing.
Off site: Restaurant (July/Aug) 50 m. Supermarket 1 km. Shops, bars, restaurants, indoor and outdoor swimming pools 2 km. Walking. Route des Cascades (waterfalls) 4 km. Pont d'Espagne 9 km. Riding 10 km.

Open: 1 June - 30 September.

Directions

From Argelès-Gazost take D921B followed by the D920A to Cauterets. Site is on right 1 km. after 'SHOPI' supermarket just before Cauterets. GPS: 42.90347, -0.10714

Charges guide

Per unit incl. 2 persons and electricity (6A)	€ 15.80 - € 17.60
tent incl. 2 persons and car	€ 12.70 - € 14.10
extra person	€ 4.40 - € 4.90
child (under 7 yrs)	€ 2.30 - € 2.55

Cazals

Les Hameaux de Pomette

F-46250 Cazals (Lot) T: 05 55 84 34 48. E: infos@chalets-en-france.com

alanrogers.com/FR46570

Les Hameaux de Pomette is an attractive chalet park open all year round. Ideally situated in a lesser known region of France bordered by the departments of the Lot and the Dordogne, it lies in a wooded valley and is a good base for those seeking a quieter holiday in an area known for its culture, nature and gastronomy. The 42 modern chalets are spacious and well equipped with all necessary facilities and have solar panels on the roof to reduce the consumption of electricity. There are three chalets specially adapted for visitors with disabilities. A heated swimming pool can be covered in cooler weather. To the north lies the River Dordogne with its many perched castles and caves famous for their ancient wall paintings. To the south is the valley of the River Lot with its picturesque villages.

Facilities

Launderette. Small shop. Bar. Indoor heated swimming pool. Table tennis. Boules. Play area. TV/games room. Organised activities, excursions and children's club (high season). WiFi at bar and reception (free). Children's cot, iron and linen for hire. Electric barbecues for hire. Off site: Mountain biking. Riding. Tennis. Climbing. Fishing. Canoeing. Minigolf. Small shops, restaurants and Sunday market at Cazals 2 km. Supermarket in Gourdon 18 km.

Open: All year.

Directions

Leave A20 autoroute, exit 51, signed Souillac. Take N20 south, then D673 southwest through Gourdon to Cazals. Take D13 northwest to site (about 3 km). GPS: 44.64948, 1.21688

Charges 2012

Contact the site for details.

Crayssac

Campé●le

Campéole les Reflets du Quercy

Mas de Bastide, F-46150 Crayssac (Lot) T: 05 65 30 00 27. E: reflets-du-quercy@campeole.com

alanrogers.com/FR46170

Set in the west of the Lot department, this site is set on a wooded hill about 16 km. from the large town of Cahors. It is owned by the Campéole group and is classed as a holiday village. It is very lively here during July and August but otherwise very quiet. There are 150 uneven, stony pitches with shade, just 35 of which are for touring, most with 6A electricity (rock pegs are essential). At the rear of the site is a large area of independently owned mobile homes and residents here also have access to the campsite facilities. The site has a good 25 m. swimming pool overlooked by the terrace of the bar and snack bar. There are several play areas and sport facilities on site and in July and August there is an extensive programme of events for all the family, but probably more appealing to families with active teenagers. There are ancient market towns and villages to explore and the local produce is well worth sampling.

Facilities

One adequate toilet block with facilities for disabled visitors. Baby room with bath. Laundry facilities. Motorcaravan service point (charged). Shop, bar and snack bar (July/Aug). Swimming and paddling pools, TV and games room, bouncy castle (all July/Aug). Boules. Tennis. Multisports court. Play area. Entertainment (July/Aug). WiFi (charged). Off site: Shop, bar, restaurant at Mercuès 4 km. Canoeing and fishing on the River Lot. Riding 7 km. Bicycle hire 15 km. Water park (Souillac).

Open: 9 April - 25 September.

Directions

At Cahors leave RN20, take D811 northwest signed Fumel, through Mercuès. After a further 4.5 km. turn left D23, signed Crayssac. Just before Crayssac turn right, site signed, entrance in 1.5 km. GPS: 44.50993, 1.32269

Charges guide

Per unit incl. 2 persons and electricity	€ 15.10 - € 24.50
extra person	€ 4.00 - € 6.10
child (2-6 yrs)	free - € 4.00

Campé●le
CAMPSITES AND RENTALS

MIDI-PYRÉNÉES

Les reflets du Quercy★★★
At the heart of the vineyards, between the Lot and Dordogne Valley. Swimming pool, pitches and accommodations of good quality.

46150 Crayssac - Tel: +33-565-3000-27 - www.campeole.co.uk / reflets-du-quercy@campeole.com

For latest campsite news, availability and prices visit
alanrogers.com

Entraygues-sur-Truyère
Camping du Val de Saures

Village de Gîtes le Bastie, F-12140 Entraygues-sur-Truyère (Aveyron) T: 05 65 44 56 92.
E: info@camping-valdesaures.com **alanrogers.com/FR12260**

Camping du Val de Saures is a well presented, value for money site only five minutes across a river bridge from the interesting old town of Entraygues. Situated at the confluence of the rivers Lot and Truyère, it is a good base for relaxing and exploring this beautiful area of Aveyron. There are 110 good sized, level, grassy pitches (6A electricity) separated by small shrubs and trees with varying amounts of shade. Many overlook the river Lot. Although the site has no shop, bar or restaurant, these are all available in the town. In the area there are many wonderful medieval villages, with their narrow streets and Tudor houses with the famous grey Lauze tiles. Canoeing or rafting are possible and there are marked paths to explore on foot, on horseback or by bike.

Facilities	Directions
Three very clean and well appointed toilet blocks with all the necessary facilities including facilities for campers with disabilities. Motorcaravan service point. TV/games room. WiFi. Playground. River fishing but no bathing. Off site: Fortified town of Entraygues 400 m. (by footbridge) with a good range of shops, banks, bars and restaurants. Swimming pool (free), tennis courts and large playground close by. Watersports excursion 400 m. Riding 10 km. **Open:** 1 May - 30 September.	Entraygues-sur-Truyère is 42 km. southeast of Aurillac on the D920. At southern end of Entraygues on the D920 turn right (site signed), over river bridge onto the D904 and immediately right again. Just past the tennis courts fork right and follow lane down to site. GPS: 44.64243, 2.56414

Charges guide

Per unit incl. 2 persons	
and electricity	€ 13.50 - € 21.50
extra person	€ 2.50 - € 4.00
child (3-13 yrs)	free - € 3.00

Camping **le Val de Saures** ★★★

126 pitches • 11 chalets • at the riverside of the Lot • family campsite • 'municipal' swimming pool • games room with free WiFi • animation for children and adults • all shops on 300 meters distance • chalets for rent

Village de Gîtes du Bastié • 12140 Entraygues sur Truyère • Tel : 0033 565 44 56 92 • Fax : 0033 565 44 27 21
www.camping-valdesaures.com • info@camping-valdesaures.com

Estaing
Camping Pyrénées Natura

Route du Lac, F-65400 Estaing (Hautes-Pyrénées) T: 05 62 97 45 44. E: info@camping-pyrenees-natura.com
alanrogers.com/FR65060

Pyrénées Natura, at an altitude of 1,000 m, on the edge of the national park is the perfect site for lovers of nature. The 66 pitches (51 for tourers), all with electricity (3-10A), are in a landscaped area with 75 varieties of trees and shrubs – but they do not spoil the fantastic views. A traditional style building houses the reception, bar and indoor games/reading room. There is a small shop in the former water mill. Children will love the animals, including the unusual hens, the guinea pigs, goat and donkey. On the river there is a small beach belonging to the site for supervised water play. This site belongs to the prestigious Via Natura group of 11 campsites in France, committed to eco-tourism principles.

Facilities	Directions
First class toilet blocks. Facilities for disabled visitors and babies. Washing machine and airers (no lines allowed). Motorcaravan services. Bar, small shop and takeaway (1/5-15/9). Lounge, library, TV. Upstairs games/reading room. Bird watching with equipment available. Sauna, solarium and jacuzzi (free between 12.00-17.00). Music room. Play area for the very young. Small beach beside river. Boules. Weekly evening meal in May, June and Sept. Internet. Walks. Off site: Village with two restaurants. Bicycle hire and riding 4 km. Walking and hiking. **Open:** 1 May - 20 September.	At Argelès-Gazost, take D918 towards Aucun. After 8 km. turn left on D13 to Bun, cross the river, then right on D103 to site (5.5 km). Narrow road, few passing places. GPS: 42.94152, -0.17726

Charges guide

Per unit incl. 2 persons	
and electricity (3A)	€ 17.50 - € 42.00
extra person	€ 5.75
child (under 8 yrs)	€ 3.75
dog	€ 3.00
Less in low season.	

For latest campsite news, availability and prices visit
alanrogers.com

Figeac

Camping les Rives du Célé

Domaine du Surgié, F-46100 Figeac (Lot) T: 05 61 64 88 54. E: contact@marc-montmija.com
alanrogers.com/FR46320

Very conveniently placed, this rural site is only 2 km. from the centre of the interesting old town of Figeac. There are 163 pitches, of which 103 are for touring, the remaining 60 for mobile homes and gîtes, all of which are for rent. The grass pitches are level, with a mixture of shade and sun and all have 10A electricity. Access is easy for large outfits. The site is split into different areas with the aquatic centre next to the camping area. There are many organised activities on site and in the surrounding area making it an ideal choice for an active family including teenagers.

Facilities	Directions
Three modern toilet blocks include facilities for babies and disabled visitors. Laundry. Shop, bar, restaurant and takeaway. Swimming pool complex adjacent (15/5-15/9, open to the public). Sports competitions and party nights with themed dining. Children's clubs. Canoeing. Fishing. Minigolf. Boules. Bicycle hire. WiFi near reception (charged). Off site: Riding 2 km. Figeac with shops, bars, restaurants and museums 2 km.	From the west, enter Figeac on the D802 and then turn right across river, signed Base de Loisirs. Shortly turn left at small roundabout and then, at traffic lights, branch left uphill to site. Well signed from the centre of Figeac. GPS: 44.60989, 2.05015

Open: 1 April - 30 September.

Charges guide

Per unit incl. 2 persons and electricity	€ 14.00 - € 22.00
extra person	€ 4.00 - € 6.80

Flagnac

Flower Camping le Port de Lacombe

F-12300 Flagnac (Aveyron) T: 05 65 64 10 08. E: accueil@campingleportdelacombe.fr
alanrogers.com/FR12290

Le Port de Lacombe is well kept, situated on the banks of the Lot river, a location ideal for walking, cycling, fishing and canoeing. The 97 grass touring pitches (with 10A electricity) are level and range in size from 100-130 sq.m. A large natural swimming pool is fed by the river and provides a separate paddling area and a large slide. Using the D42, one can wind through the valley and climb to over 2,000 feet to the Plateau de la Viadene. The scenery is panoramic and picturesque. Running past the site, the Lot river provides a relaxing environment to laze away your holiday, should you wish to do so.

Facilities	Directions
Two separate sanitary blocks, each with the usual facilities including provision for disabled visitors. Washing machine. Shop and bar (all season) with restaurant and takeaway (both 15/6-15/9). TV in function room. Play area. Swimming pool fed from the river and paddling pool (15/6-15/9). Bicycle hire. Fishing in river. Entertainment (July/Aug). WiFi throughout (charged).	Driving south from Brive-la-Gaillarde, take N140 to Decazeville, turning north on D963 to Flagnac. Site is well signed on the left. From Rodez take N140 to Decazeville, then as above. GPS: 44.60915, 2.23597

Open: 1 April - 30 September.

Charges 2012

Per unit incl. 2 persons and electricity	€ 15.50 - € 26.90
extra person	€ 2.50 - € 5.50

Ger

Aire Naturelle de Camping l'Arrayade

Arrayade, 18 impasse de l'arremissant, F-65100 Ger (Hautes-Pyrénées) T: 05 62 94 17 73.
E: contact@arrayade.com **alanrogers.com/FR65170**

This unique little campsite, situated quite high up in the Pyrenees with some amazing views down the valley, could well be near perfect for anyone seeking a relaxing, informal and friendly atmosphere. On a very small site of just 16 large pitches, all with electricitry (6-10A), Mme. Piqué is a gracious host who will do her utmost to ensure your stay is as pleasant as possible. She has prepared plenty of information on the local area, the best walks to go on and the cycle pathway that runs past the site that takes you into Lourdes centre in just three kilometres. You can taste the freshness of the air up here and outdoor lovers will feel really at one with nature.

Facilities	Directions
One modern toilet block situated close to the reception area. Provision is adequate with good facilities for disabled visitors. Washing machine and dryer. Small bar where breakfast and evening meals are served. Peaceful lounge. Sauna, jacuzzi and small gym. Internet access and free WiFi throughout. Fishing. Bicycle hire. Off site: Walking, climbing, cycling and fishing all on the doorstep. Monsieur Pique, a qualified pilot, offers flights over the Pyrenees for the ultimate sightseeing experience. Golf and riding 5 km.	From Lourdes head south on the D921 signed Lugagnan. After 3 km. bear right on D13 for Ger. As you approach a few houses on your left the site entrance is on the right, set back a little in a layby. GPS: 43.05774, -0.04087

Open: 15 May - 15 September.

Charges guide

Per unit incl. 2 persons and electricity	€ 14.50 - € 17.00
extra person	€ 3.00
child (under 7 yrs)	€ 1.50

For latest campsite news, availability and prices visit
alanrogers.com

La Bastide-de-Sérou

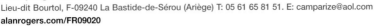

Camping l'Arize

Lieu-dit Bourtol, F-09240 La Bastide-de-Sérou (Ariège) T: 05 61 65 81 51. E: camparize@aol.com

alanrogers.com/FR09020

The site sits in a delightful, tranquil valley among the foothills of the Pyrenees and is just east of the interesting village of La Bastide-de-Sérou beside the River Arize (good trout fishing). The river is fenced for the safety of children on the site, but may be accessed just outside the gate. The 70 large pitches are neatly laid out on level grass within the spacious site. All have 3/6A electricity and are separated into bays by hedges and young trees. An extension to the site gives 24 large, fully serviced pitches (10A) and a small toilet block. You will receive a warm welcome from Dominique and Brigitte.

Facilities

Toilet block includes facilities for babies and disabled visitors. Laundry room. Motorcaravan services. New shop and restaurant planned. Small swimming pool and sunbathing area. Entertainment in high season. Weekly barbecues and welcome drinks on Sundays. Fishing, riding and bicycle hire. WiFi. Off site: Several restaurants and shops within a few minutes drive. A restaurant at the national stud for the famous Merens horses just 200 m. away will deliver takeaway meals to your pitch. Golf 5 km.

Open: 12 March - 10 November.

Directions

Site is southeast of the village La Bastide-de-Sérou. Take the D15 towards Nescus and site is on right after about 1 km. GPS: 43.00182, 1.44538

Charges guide

Per unit incl. 2 persons	
and electricity	€ 16.40 - € 28.30
extra person	€ 4.20 - € 5.80
child (2-12 yrs)	€ 2.80 - € 4.90
dog	€ 1.20 - € 2.20

Lacave

Camping la Rivière

Le Bougayrou, F-46200 Lacave (Lot) T: 05 65 37 02 04. E: camping.la.riviere@wanadoo.fr

alanrogers.com/FR46370

Camping la Rivière is situated on the banks of the Dordogne with direct access to the river and a sand and pebble beach. It is a natural rural site and in a pleasant location. The A20 motorway and the town of Souillac are just 15 km. away. The welcome from the owners is warm and friendly and they place much importance on customer service and a family atmosphere of conviviality. There are 110 pitches of which 15 are for mobile homes (all for rent). The remaining 95 pitches are for touring units. Of average size, all are level and on grass and divided by trees and shrubs which provide a good amount of shade. All have electricity (4/10A). There is a lagoon shaped swimming pool together with a paddling pool. Thoughtfully, there are two separate games areas, one for the toddlers and one for the rest. There is a children's club for 5-11 year olds and teen evenings for 11-15 year olds. The site has its own snack bar but within 4 km. there is a choice of numerous gastronomic restaurants. The closest one, which has an excellent reputation, is just 300 m. away. Many interesting places to visit are within a short distance.

Facilities

Three toilet blocks include facilities for disabled visitors and babies. Laundry. Shop. Bar. Snack bar. Takeaway. Two swimming pools including a children's pool. Two games areas. Minigolf. Barbecue and picnic areas. Organised excursions. Disco and karaoke evenings. Off site: The Caves of Padirac. Rocamadour. Sarlat and numerous theme parks. Museums. Off road cycling. Canoeing. Fishing. Kayaking. Climbing. Riding. Golf. Lacave 3 km. St Sozy 4 km.

Open: 7 April - 29 September.

Directions

From Souillac take the D43 and site is very well signed. GPS: 44.86171, 1.559372

Charges guide

Per unit incl. 2 persons	
and electricity	€ 16.00 - € 20.20
extra person	€ 4.20 - € 5.20
child (under 10 yrs)	€ 2.50 - € 3.10
dog	free - € 1.50

*Camping la Rivière****

Camping La Rivière is situated at the Dordogne with direct access to this river. 8 km from Rocamadour, centrally situated tot visit the nicest tourist attractions in the Lot and Dordogne region; Gouffre de Paridac, Sarlat, Grottes de Lascaux... Escape to these exceptional surroundings, in peace and quiet. Exceptional natur environment! We will offer you a warm welcome.

Open from 7 April till 29 September 2012

Camping La Rivière - F-46200 Lacave - France
Tel: +33 565 37 02 04 - Mobiel: +33 6 85 08 45 49
Fax: +33 565 37 03 06 - Tel low season: +33 565 41 47 22
camping.la.riviere@wanadoo.fr - **www.campinglariviere.com**

La Romieu
Kawan Village le Camp de Florence
Route Astaffort, F-32480 La Romieu (Gers) T: 05 62 28 15 58. E: info@lecampdeflorence.com

alanrogers.com/FR32010

We can book this site for you! Call 01580 214000 alanrogers ◉ travel

544

Camp de Florence is an attractive and very well equipped site on the edge of an historic village in pleasantly undulating Gers countryside. The 183 large, part terraced pitches (100 for tourers) all have electricity (10A), 20 with hardstanding and 16 fully serviced. They are arranged around a large field with rural views, giving a feeling of spaciousness. The 13th-century village of La Romieu is on the Santiago de Compostela pilgrim route. The Pyrénées are a two hour drive, the Atlantic coast a similar distance. The site has been developed by the friendly Mynsbergen family who are Dutch (although Susan is English). They have sympathetically converted the old farmhouse buildings to provide facilities for the site. The collegiate church, visible from the site, is well worth a visit (the views are magnificent from the top of the tower), as is the local arboretum, the biggest collection of trees in the Midi-Pyrénées.

Facilities

Three toilet blocks (one completely rebuilt for 2009), provide all the necessary facilities. Washing machines and dryers. Motorcaravan services. Restaurant (1/5-30/9, also open to the public). Takeaway. Bread. Swimming pool area with water slide. Jacuzzi, protected children's pool (open to public in afternoons). New playgrounds, games and animal park. Bouncy castle, trampoline. Outdoor fitness machines. Games room. Tennis. Pétanque. Bicycle hire. Discos, picnics, musical evenings. Excursions. WiFi (charged). Max. 2 dogs. Off site: Shop 500 m. in village. Fishing 5 km. Riding 10 km. Walking tours, excursions and wine tasting arranged.

Open: 1 April - 10 October.

Directions

Site signed from D931 Agen - Condom road. Small units turn left at Ligardes (signed), follow D36 for 1 km, turn right for La Romieu (signed). Otherwise continue until outskirts of Condom and take D41 left to La Romieu, through village to site. GPS: 43.98299, 0.50183

Charges guide

Per unit incl. 2 persons and electricity	€ 17.50 - € 34.90
extra person	€ 3.60 - € 7.40
child (4-9 yrs)	€ 3.50 - € 5.30
dog (max. 2)	€ 1.50 - € 2.30

Special prices for groups, rallies, etc.
Camping Cheques accepted.

Le Camp de Florence - 32480 La Romieu

Sun * Comfort * Nature * Water
The Gers - A region waiting to be discovered, an unspoilt landscape of rolling hills, sunflowers and historic fortified villages and castles. Peace, tranquillity, the home of Armagnac, Fois Gras and Magret de Canard. A 4* site with spacious pitches, panoramic views and luxury mobile homes for hire.

Tel: 0033 562 28 15 58 - Fax: 0033 562 28 20 04 — Camping Cheque
E-mail: info@lecampdeflorence.com - www.lecampdeflorence.com

For latest campsite news, availability and prices visit
alanrogers.com

Le Monastère

Campéole Domaine de Combelles

F-12000 Le Monastère (Aveyron) T: 05 65 78 29 53. E: combelles@campeole.com

alanrogers.com/FR12400

Campé•le

Domaine de Combelles is a well equipped 'parc résidentiel' which can be found at the heart of the Aveyron, quite close to the village of Le Monastère. Please note that there are no touring pitches here, but a range of attractive chalets and mobile homes are available for rent. This site is also unusual in that it incorporates an excellent riding centre, with opportunities for beginners as well as seasoned riders. Vehicle circulation is not allowed within the site – a large car park is available at the site entrance. This is a spacious site and most facilities are located some distance from the accommodation units, ensuring their tranquillity. On-site amenities include a bar and snack bar, and leisure facilities include a swimming pool and tennis court. Most leisure facilities (including tennis) are free of charge. Cycle hire and riding are available for a small charge. There are plenty of activities and a lively entertainment programme in the peak season, including a children's club as well as discos and karaoke. The surrounding country is ideal for walking and cycling and the site managers will be pleased to recommend possible routes.

Facilities

Bar/restaurant. Swimming pool. Riding centre. Bicycle hire. Volleyball. Bouncy castle. Play area. Activities and entertainment programme. Tourist information. Mobile homes and chalets and permanently erected tents for rent (there are no touring pitches). Off site: Le Monastère (attractive village with shops and restaurants). Walking and cycle tracks. Fishing. Rodez (cathedral city) 5 km. Tarn gorges.

Open: 1 May - 31 October.

Directions

From Albi head north on N88 towards Rodez via Luc la Primaube and Flavin. From here follow signs to the site which is well indicated. GPS: 44.3301, 2.5901

Charges 2012

Contact the site for details.

Campé•le

CAMPSITES AND RENTALS

Combelles

Beautiful traditional domain
in the Aveyron opposite Rodez.
Restaurant, swimming pool,
children's pool, equestrian centre...

MIDI-PYRÉNÉES

12000 Le Monastère - Tel.: +33-565-7829-53 - www.campeole.co.uk / domaine-de-combelles@campeole.com

Le Vigan

Camping le Rêve

F-46300 Le Vigan (Lot) T: 05 65 41 25 20. E: info@campinglereve.com

alanrogers.com/FR46050

Le Rêve is a peaceful site situated in the heart of rolling countryside where the Périgord runs into Quercy. You are assured of a warm reception from the van Iersels, a Dutch couple who have been providing a friendly and hospitable welcome to their clients since 1987. The 56 flat and grassy touring pitches are all of good size, with access to electricity (6A) and divided by shrubs and trees. A few of the pitches are situated at the edge of the forest and provide plenty of shade.

Facilities

The toilet block includes an enclosed area for cooler weather. Washbasins in cabins, special cubicles for disabled visitors and a baby room. New laundry facilities. Small shop for basics (bread, milk etc. 15/5-21/9), pleasant bar, restaurant and takeaway (all open all season). Heated swimming pool (all season) and large paddling pool with 'mushroom' fountain. Play area. Boules. Internet access and WiFi (charged). Charcoal barbecues not permitted. Off site: Fishing 5 km. Riding 8 km. Golf 20 km.

Open: 1 May - 21 September.

Directions

From D820 Souillac - Cahors road turn west onto D673 3 km. south of Payrac. After 2 km. site signed down lane on west side of road. Turn here, follow signs, site in 2.5 km. GPS: 44.77304, 1.44097

Charges 2012

Per unit incl. 2 persons and electricity	€ 22.20
extra person	€ 5.50
child (under 7 yrs)	€ 3.30
dog	€ 1.00

Less 20-30% outside July/Aug.
Credit cards accepted July and August only.

For latest campsite news, availability and prices visit

alanrogers.com

Lectoure
Yelloh! Village le Lac des Trois Vallées
F-32700 Lectoure (Gers) T: 04 66 73 97 39. E: contact@lacdes3vallees.fr
alanrogers.com/FR32060

This is a very large 140 hectare site with many facilities. It is a large holiday complex and good for families with young children or teenagers. The large lake provides the opportunity for canoeing, swimming, diving and there are four water slides. There is a large safe paddling area and a separate fishing lake. The impressive heated pool complex complete with gymnasium and jacuzzi also has paved areas for sunbathing and a large paddling pool. Of the 500 pitches, over 200 are well situated for touring on shaded or open ground, all with electricity (10A). A fireworks festival is held here in September.

Facilities

Eight modern sanitary blocks each with baby bathing facilities. Provision for disabled visitors. Laundry facilities. Motorcaravan services. Supermarket. Restaurants and bars. Lakeside snack bar and drinks kiosk. Heated swimming pool complex. Lake complex with water slides. Multisports pitch. BMX/skateboard area. Fishing. Tennis. Minigolf. Video. Disco. Cinema. Children's club. WiFi. Off site: Golf 10 km. Riding 20 km. Walking and mountain bike trails. Quad bikes. Hot air balloon rides.

Open: 1 June - 11 September (with all facilities).

Directions

Take N21 south from Lectoure for 2 km. Site is well signed and is a further 2 km. after turning left off the N21. GPS: 43.91250, 0.64852

Charges guide

Per unit incl. 2 persons	
and electricity	€ 19.00 - € 44.00
extra person	€ 5.00 - € 8.00
child (3-7 yrs)	free - € 8.00
dog	€ 4.00

Loudenvielle
Flower Camping Pène Blanche
9 chemin de la Mainette, F-65510 Loudenvielle (Hautes-Pyrénées) T: 05 62 99 68 85.
E: info@peneblanche.com **alanrogers.com/FR65140**

La Pène Blanche is spacious and well kept, in an idyllic location close to Lake Loudenvielle and surrounded by high mountains. There are 120 small, pitches which are not separated, 80 are for touring (40 with 5/10A electricity). The area is ideal for walking, hiking and biking in the mountains. An outdoor swimming pool is just 200 m. away and nearby is the Balnea centre with its spa waters. The resorts of Val Louron and Peyragudes are within easy reach for skiing. For the very brave there is paragliding and hang-gliding or you can relax in the park to watch them gracefully coming in to land.

Facilities

Two toilet blocks, one traditional, one modern and heated including facilities for disabled visitors. Laundry room. Play area. WiFi. Off site: Restaurant, snack bar, bar and local shops all within 100 m. Cinema 200 m. Motorcaravan services 300 m. Within walking distance is the Balnea Centre with its spa water baths and adjacent swimming pool with waterslide. Tennis. Minigolf. Hiking. Mountain biking. Paragliding. Hang-gliding. Skiing.

Open: 20 December - 31 October.

Directions

A64 Tarbes to Toulouse, exit junction 16, on D929 follow signs to Arreau, then D618 to D25 signed Loudenvielle. GPS: 42.796107, 0.406679

Charges guide

Per unit incl. 2 persons	
and electricity	€ 16.00 - € 23.50
extra person	€ 3.90 - € 5.50
child (2-7 yrs)	€ 2.90 - € 4.50

Lourdes
Camping le Moulin du Monge
Avenue Jean Moulin no 28, F-65100 Lourdes (Hautes-Pyrénées) T: 05 62 94 28 15.
E: camping.moulin.monge@wanadoo.fr **alanrogers.com/FR65100**

A well organised, family run site with a friendly welcome, Moulin du Monge is in an ideal location for visiting Lourdes, only 3 km. away. There will be some traffic noise from the nearby N21 and railway line. This attractive garden-like site has 57 pitches, all with electricity (2-6A) in three grassy areas, mostly shaded by trees and easy to access. The swimming pool is slightly apart from most of the pitches. There is a separate adjacent pool for children. There are ten mobile homes available to rent. The region is good for sightseeing, with the cities of Pau and Tarbes fairly near.

Facilities

The heated toilet blocks include laundry facilities. Facilities for disabled campers. Baby room. Motorcaravan services. Well stocked shop (15/6-20/9). Heated swimming pool, sliding cover (20/5-20/9), paddling pool. Sauna. Games/TV room. WiFi. Barbecue, terrace. Boules. Playground, trampolines. Off site: Good transport links to the city centre with its famous grotto. Bicycle hire 500 m. Fishing 3 km. Golf 4 km. Riding 15 km. Golf 16 km.

Open: 1 April - 10 October.

Directions

Site is just off the N21 on northern outskirts of Lourdes. From north, on N21 (2 km. south of Adé) be prepared to take slip lane in centre of road. Turn left into Ave. Jean Moulin. Site shortly on left. GPS: 43.115516, -0.031583

Charges guide

Per unit incl. 2 persons	
and electricity	€ 17.30 - € 19.30
extra person	€ 5.10

For latest campsite news, availability and prices visit
alanrogers.com

Luz-Saint-Sauveur
Camping Pyrenevasion

Route de Luz-Ardiden, Sazos, F-65120 Luz-Saint-Sauveur (Hautes-Pyrénées) T: 05 62 92 91 54.
E: camping-pyrenevasion@wanadoo.fr **alanrogers.com/FR65130**

In the heart of the Pyrenees, Camping Pyrenevasion has panoramic views of the mountains and the town of Luz-St-Sauveur in the valley below. This welcoming, family run site has 60 well laid out touring pitches, all with electricity (3-10A), on level, grassy hillside terraces partially shaded by young trees. There are 12 modern chalets for rent (all year), ideal for the nearby skiing, and in summer guided walks are arranged, with one free weekly walk. The heated outdoor pool has a separate paddling pool and jacuzzi. A member of Sites et Paysages.

Facilities

Heated sanitary block with showers, WCs, washbasins (cubicles and open area). Facilities for disabled visitors, steep access. Baby bath. Washing machine and dryer. Motorcaravan services. Bread can be ordered for next morning delivery. Bar. Takeaway (1/6-20/9). Heated swimming and paddling pools (15/5-1/10). Small play area. Sports area. WiFi (charged). Off site: Fishing 200 m. Shops, restaurant and bar 2 km. Riding and skiing 10 km. Col de Tourmalet and Pic du Midi observatory 22 km.

Open: All year excl. 21 October - 19 November.

Directions

From the north take the D921 to Luz-St-Sauveur. Follow signs from Luz-St-Sauveur to Luz-Ardiden (D12). Site is on right as you enter the village of Sazos. GPS: 42.88283, -0.02241

Charges guide

Per unit incl. 2 persons	
and electricity	€ 14.50 - € 33.50
extra person	€ 5.50
child (2-7 yrs)	€ 3.50
dog	€ 2.50

Marciac
Camping du Lac

F-32230 Marciac (Gers) T: 05 62 08 21 19. E: info@camping-mariac.com
alanrogers.com/FR32020

Summer wine and cheese tastings from local producers are a feature of this site, set in the beautiful Gers region, and close to the ancient fortified town of Marciac. Rob and Louise Robinson, the English owners since 2002, offer a quiet, relaxing stay. The well shaded site has 95 pitches, including 15 used for mobile homes and chalets for rent. There are 80 spacious touring pitches, 60 with electrical connections (6/10A, Europlug) and water. There are five with hardstanding for motorcaravans, and an attractive natural terrace has 20 pitches without electricity for tents.

Facilities

The centrally situated sanitary block uses solar energy to help to heat water. Washbasins in cubicles. Facilities for disabled visitors. Washing machine. Motorcaravan service point. Shop. Bar. Snacks. Bread to order (delivered daily). Swimming pool (15/4-30/9). Small library and communal room. Play area. WiFi (charged). Off site: Fishing, watersports, sailing and riding 300 m. Shops, restaurant and bars 1 km. Major international jazz festival in Marciac (first 2 weeks in August) 1 km. Golf 7 km.

Open: 20 March - 17 October.

Directions

The site is 800 m. from Marciac. From the town square take the D3 towards Plaisance. With the lake on your left, turn right and site is 300 m. on the left. GPS: 43.5323, 0.1667

Charges guide

Per unit incl. 2 persons	
and electricity (6A)	€ 13.00 - € 23.00
extra person	€ 2.50 - € 5.00
child (4-16 yrs)	€ 1.50 - € 3.50

Martres-Tolosane
Camping le Moulin

Lieu-dit le Moulin, F-31220 Martres-Tolosane (Haute-Garonne) T: 05 61 98 86 40.
E: info@campinglemoulin.com **alanrogers.com/FR31000**

With attractive shaded pitches and many activities, this family run campsite has 12 hectares of woods and fields beside the River Garonne. It is close to Martres-Tolosane, an interesting medieval village. Some of the 60 level and grassy pitches are supersize and all have electricity (6/10A). There are 24 chalets to rent. Summer brings opportunities for guided canoeing, archery and walking. A large sports field is available all season, with tennis, volleyball, basketball, boules and birdwatching on site. There may be some road noise. A member of Sites et Paysages.

Facilities

Large sanitary block with separate ladies' and gents WCs. Communal area with showers and washbasins in cubicles. Good facilities for disabled visitors. Baby bath. Laundry. Motorcaravan services. Outdoor bar with WiFi. Restaurant (1/7-20/8). Snack bar and takeaway (1/6-15/9). Heated swimming pool (1/6-15/9). Fishing. Tennis. Canoeing. Playground. Entertainment and children's club (high season). Massage (charged). Off site: Riding 4 km.

Open: 1 April - 30 September.

Directions

From the A64 motorway (Toulouse-Tarbes) take exit 21 (Boussens) or exit 22 (Martres-Tolosane) and follow signs to Martres-Tolosane. Site is well signed from village. GPS: 43.19048, 1.01788

Charges guide

Per unit incl. 2 persons	
and electricity	€ 18.50 - € 26.90
extra person	€ 4.50 - € 6.00
child (under 7 yrs)	€ 2.50 - € 3.00

For latest campsite news, availability and prices visit
alanrogers.com

Millau
Camping du Viaduc
121 avenue de Millau Plage, F-12100 Millau (Aveyron) T: 05 65 60 15 75. E: info@camping-du-viaduc.com
alanrogers.com/FR12280

Run by a French couple, this site is situated on the banks of the Tarn, across the river from Millau. Of medium size, the site has 237 pitches of which 199 are for touring units and the remainder for chalets. Being close to the town it has access to its services but there is also easy access for discovering the beauty and nature of the gorges. The pitches are flat, of average size, shaded under tall trees and have adequate water and electric points. The site is on the banks of the shallow Tarn, where a sandy beach has been created.

Facilities

One large, centrally situated sanitary block with the usual facilities. Bar with restaurant and takeaway. Swimming pool and children's pool. Shop (1/6-31/8). Laundry area. Entertainment in July/Aug. Free children's club in high season. Play area. Fishing and river bathing. Barbecues permitted. WiFi throughout (charged). Off site: Canoe hire 200 m. Bicycle hire 1 km. Hypermarket in Millau.

Open: 27 April - 30 September.

Directions

Follow signs for 'campings' from Millau centre across the Tarn to the east side. At roundabout take last exit signed Paulhe (D187) to second campsite on the left in a short distance. GPS: 44.10508, 3.08826

Charges 2012

Per unit incl. 2 persons and electricity	€ 19.00 - € 33.50
extra person	€ 3.00 - € 7.50

Millau
Camping Caravaning les Rivages
860 avenue de l'Aigoual, F-12100 Millau (Aveyron) T: 05 65 61 01 07. E: info@campinglesrivages.com
alanrogers.com/FR12020

Les Rivages is a large, well established site on the outskirts of the town. It is well situated, being close to the high limestone Causses and the dramatic gorges of the Tarn and Dourbie. Smaller pitches, used for small units, abut a pleasant riverside space suitable for sunbathing, fishing and picnics. Most of the 314 pitches are large, and well shaded. A newer part of the site has less shade but larger pitches. All pitches have electricity (6A), and 55 have water and drainage. The site offers a very wide range of sporting activities, close to 30 in all (see facilities).

Facilities

Four well kept modern toilet blocks. Special block for children. Small shop (1/6-15/9). Terrace, restaurant and bar overlooking swimming pool, children's pool (from 10/5). Play area. Entertainment, largely for children, child-minding, miniclub. Sports centre with tennis, squash and badminton. Boules. River activities. Fishing. WiFi by reception. Off site: Rafting and canoeing arranged. Bicycle hire 1 km. Riding 10 km. Abseiling, paragliding, caving and canyoning nearby. Hypermarket in Millau.

Open: 15 April - 30 September.

Directions

From Millau, cross the Tarn bridge and take D991 road east towards Nant. Site is about 400 m. from the roundabout on the right, on the banks of the Dourbie river. GPS: 44.10300, 3.095827

Charges guide

Per unit incl. 2 persons and electricity	€ 18.00 - € 30.00
extra person	€ 3.50 - € 6.50
child (2-7 yrs)	€ 2.00 - € 5.00

We can book this site for you! Call 01580 214000 alan rogers travel

Monclar-de-Quercy
Les Hameaux des Lacs
Base de Loisirs, F-82230 Monclar-de-Quercy (Tarn-et-Garonne) T: 05 55 84 34 48.
E: info@chalets-en-france.com alanrogers.com/FR82060

Les Hameaux des Lacs is a member of the Chalets en France group. This group comprises four chalet parks in southern France. Please note, however, that there are no touring pitches here. The site is open all year and can be found at the heart of the Tarn et Garonne department, south east of Montauban and forms part of a 'base de loisirs'. Leisure facilities on offer here include tennis, an equestrian centre, a swimming pool, and a multisports pitch. Sailing and windsurfing are popular on the lake, and fishing is also possible. Chalets here are attractively dispersed around the site and are all available for rent. During the summer months, the entertainment makes use of the lake and swimming pools. A comprehensive entertainment programme designed to suit ages 4-12 yrs is provided.

Facilities

Swimming pool (15/5-30/9). Play area. Children's club. Multisports pitch. Games room. Tourist information. Entertainment and activity programme. WiFi. Chalets for rent. Off site: Base de loisirs with swimming pool. Lake with beach. Sailing and windsurfing. Fishing. Riding centre. Cycle and walking trails.

Open: All year.

Directions

Take exit 61 from the A20 motorway (Montauban) and then head east on the D8 to Montclar de Quercy. The site is well signed at Base de Loisirs upon arrival in the town. GPS: 43.97000, 1.58855

Charges 2012

Contact the site for details.

For latest campsite news, availability and prices visit
alanrogers.com

Montcabrier
Camping Moulin de Laborde
F-46700 Montcabrier (Lot) T: 05 65 24 62 06. E: moulindelaborde@wanadoo.fr
alanrogers.com/FR46040

Based around a converted 17th-century watermill, Moulin de Laborde has been created by the van Bommel family to provide a tranquil and uncommercialised campsite for the whole family to enjoy. Bordered by woods, hills and a small river, there are 90 flat and grassy pitches, all of at least 100 sq.m. with electricity (6A). A variety of pretty shrubs and trees divide the pitches and provide a moderate amount of shade. A gate at the back of the site leads walkers onto a Grande Randonée footpath which passes through the village of Montcabrier, 1 km. away.

Facilities

Well designed, clean toilet block, unit for disabled visitors. Washing machine, dryer. Basic shop (all season). Small bar, restaurant, takeaway. Swimming pool, sunbathing area, paddling pool (all season). Play area. Small lake, free rafts and rowing boats. Fishing. Volleyball. Covered recreation area. Rock climbing. Archery. Dogs are not accepted. WiFi (free). Off site: Tennis nearby and canoeing on the Lot. Riding 15 km. The Château of Bonaquil 6 km. Cahors vineyards and golf 4 km. Fumel 12 km.

Open: 25 April - 8 September.

Directions

Site is on the north side of the D673 Fumel - Gourdon road about 1 km. northeast of the turn to village of Montcabrier. GPS: 44.5475, 1.08388

Charges guide

Per unit incl. 2 persons	
and electricity	€ 21.96 - € 26.70
extra person	€ 5.52 - € 6.90
child (under 7 yrs)	€ 3.36 - € 4.20

No credit cards.

Montpezat de Quercy
Camping le Faillal
F-82270 Montpezat de Quercy (Tarn-et-Garonne) T: 05 63 02 07 08. E: contact@revea-vacances.com
alanrogers.com/FR82050

Le Faillal is located at Montpézat de Quercy, around 35 km. north of Montauban. There are 69 pitches here, all of a good size and each has its own electricity (4/6A), water and light. The surrounding trees and hedges give shade and some privacy. The site forms a part of the Parc de Loisirs de Faillal and includes a swimming pool, tennis court and minigolf, all of which are free for campers. There is no bar, restaurant or snack provision. These amenities are available in the town, a short walk away. Le Faillal provides some activities for children in high season and some entertainment for families, including barbecues and karaoke evenings.

Facilities

One sanitary block with no facilities for disabled campers. Washing machines and irons. Municipal swimming pool, tennis court, basketball and minigolf (all open to public). Very small play area. Tourist information and limited WiFi in reception. Service for motorcaravans. Gîtes for rent. Communal barbecue area, no others allowed. Torch useful. Max. 1 dog. Off site: Village centre 800 m. Fishing 6 km. Riding 18 km. Golf 25 km.

Open: 4 April - 10 October.

Directions

Approaching from the north, leave A20 autoroute at exit 58 and head west on D19 and then south on D820 as far as La Baraque. Then head southwest on D20 to Montpezat de Quercy and follow signs to the site. GPS: 44.243139, 1.47764

Charges guide

Per unit incl. 2 persons	
and electricity	€ 16.50 - € 19.50
extra person	€ 3.20 - € 3.90
child (2-7 yrs)	free - € 2.00
dog	€ 1.50

Camping Cheques accepted.

Been to any good campsites lately?
We have

alan rogers

The UK's market leading independent guides to the best campsites
Also available on iPad alanrogers.com/digital

Nages
Village Center Rieu Montagné
Lac du Laouzas, F-81320 Nages (Tarn) T: 05 63 37 24 71. E: contact@village-center.com
alanrogers.com/FR81070

Rieu Montagné is a delightful site in the heart of the Haut Languedoc Regional park and at the corner of the départements of Tarn, Aveyron and Hérault. There are 123 touring pitches, mostly on broad terraces with reasonable shade, all with electrical connections (10A) and 56 fully serviced. A heated swimming pool overlooks the lake and is used for occasional aquagym. In high season there is a varied entertainment programme, and a number of guided walks. Most leisure facilities are available at the lakeside complex. The site is a member of the Village Center group.

Facilities

The two toilet blocks provide mostly British style toilets, washbasins in cubicles and facilities for disabled visitors and babies. Laundry. Shop with basic provisions, bar, restaurant and takeaway, swimming pool (all open all season). Entertainment programme (high season). Chalets, tents and mobile homes to let (53). Off site: Lakeside leisure complex.

Open: 13 June - 13 September.

Directions

Nages about 80 km. southeast of Albi. From Albi, D999 east towards St Affrique. 11 km. after Albon right, D607, to Lacaune. At T-junction left, D622, for 6.5 km. Right, D62, 2 km. South of town left over bridge, D162. First left uphill to site. GPS: 43.64795, 2.78147

Charges guide

Per unit incl. 2 persons and electricity	€ 14.00 - € 24.00
extra person	€ 3.00 - € 5.00

Camping Cheques accepted.

Nant-d'Aveyron
RCN Val de Cantobre
F-12230 Nant-d'Aveyron (Aveyron) T: 05 65 58 43 00. E: info@rcn-valdecantobre.fr
alanrogers.com/FR12010

Imaginatively and tastefully developed by the Dupond family over the past 30 years, this very pleasant terraced site is now owned by the RCN group. Most of the 200 touring pitches (all with electricity and water) are peaceful, generous in size and blessed with views of the valley. The terrace design provides some peace and privacy, especially on the upper levels. Rock pegs are advised. An activity programme is supervised by qualified instructors in July and August and a new pleasure pool has been added. The carved features in the bar create a delightful ambience, complemented by a recently built terrace.

Facilities

The fully equipped toilet blocks are well appointed. Fridge hire. Small shop including many regional specialities, attractive bar, restaurant, pizzeria and takeaway. There are some fairly steep up and down walking from furthest pitches to some facilities. Swimming pools. Minigolf. Play area. Activity programme. All-weather multisports pitch. Torch useful. Internet (charged). Off site: Fishing 4 km. Riding 15 km. Bicycle hire 25 km.

Open: 9 April - 1 October.

Directions

Site is 4 km. north of Nant, on D991 road to Millau. From Millau direction take D991 signed Gorge du Dourbie. Site is on left, just past turn to Cantobre. GPS: 44.04467, 3.30228

Charges guide

Per unit incl. 2 persons, electricity and water	€ 19.90 - € 43.90
extra person (4 yrs and over)	€ 2.50 - € 4.90

Camping Cheques accepted.

Naucelle
Flower Camping du Lac de Bonnefon
L'Etang de Bonnefon, F-12800 Naucelle (Aveyron) T: 05 65 69 33 20.
E: camping-du-lac-de-bonnefon@wanadoo.fr **alanrogers.com/FR12250**

This small, family run site, popular with French campers, lies in a picturesque region waiting to be discovered, with rolling hills, deep river valleys, lakes and many old fortified villages. There is more suitable for those seeking a quieter holiday with less in the way of entertainment. There are 112 good sized, grassy, slightly sloping pitches with 74 for touring (50 with 10A electricity). Some are separated by laurel hedging with others more open, and maturing trees give a little shade. The new, enthusiastic and friendly owners have recently extended the site and refurbished the facilities to a high standard.

Facilities

Two toilet blocks include some washbasins in cabins and good facilities for disabled visitors. No shop but bread to order. Bar with TV. Snack bar (July/Aug, other times on demand). Swimming and paddling pools (1/6-30/9). Playground. Archery. Lake fishing but no bathing. Activities for all in July/Aug. Off site: Riding 500 m. Small village of Naucelle with a few shops and heated pool complex 1 km.

Open: 1 April - 15 October.

Directions

Site is just off the N88 between Rodez and Albi. From Naucelle Gare take D997 towards Naucelle. In just over 1 km. turn left on D58 and follow signs to site in just under 1 km. GPS: 44.18805, 2.34827

Charges guide

Per unit incl. 2 persons and electricity	€ 15.50 - € 23.90
extra person	€ 3.50 - € 5.00

For latest campsite news, availability and prices visit
alanrogers.com

Payrac-en-Quercy
Flower Camping les Pins

F-46350 Payrac-en-Quercy (Lot) T: 05 65 37 96 32. E: info@les-pins-camping.com

alanrogers.com/FR46030

Set amongst 3.5 hectares of beautiful pine forest, Camping les Pins is well situated for exploring the historical and natural splendours of the Dordogne region, as well as being a convenient overnight stop when heading north or south. There are 125 clearly marked, level pitches (100 sq.m), of which 49 are for touring units. The pitches are well marked and separated by small shrubs or hedges. Many have shade from the abundant pine trees and all have 10A electricity connections. There is a bar and a good value restaurant with a terrace overlooking the pool area.

Facilities

Three toilet blocks (heated Apr/May), well maintained and include washbasins in cabins and good baby bath facilities. Laundry facilities (with plenty of drying lines). Motorcaravan service point. Shop with basics. Bar with TV. Restaurant and takeaway. Heated swimming pool, three slides and smaller paddling pool. Tennis. Small library. WiFi in bar area. Some entertainment in season, including weekly family discos. Walking routes. English and Dutch spoken. Off site: Fishing 7 km. Riding 10 km.

Open: 14 April - 16 September.

Directions

Site entrance is 16 km. from Souillac on western side of the N20 just south of the village of Payrac-en-Quercy. GPS: 44.78946, 1.47204

Charges guide

Per unit incl. 2 persons	
and electricity	€ 18.00 - € 33.40
extra person	€ 4.50 - € 6.90
child (under 7 yrs)	€ 2.00 - € 4.80
dog	€ 2.00 - € 3.00

Pont-de-Salars
Flower Camping les Terrasses du Lac

Route du Vibal, F-12290 Pont-de-Salars (Aveyron) T: 05 65 46 88 18. E: campinglesterrasses@orange.fr

alanrogers.com/FR12050

A terraced site, it provides 180 good sized, level pitches, 110 for touring, with or without shade, all with electricity. Some pitches have good views over the lake which has direct access from the site at two places – one for pedestrians and swimmers, the other for cars and trailers for launching small boats. This site is well placed for excursions into the Gorges du Tarn, Caves du Roquefort and nearby historic towns and villages. Although there are good facilities for disabled visitors, the terracing on the site may prove difficult. At an altitude of some 700 m. on the plateau of Le Lévézou, this outlying site enjoys attractive views over Lac de Pont-de-Salars.

Facilities

Four toilet blocks with adequate facilities. Fridge hire. Shop. Bar/restaurant with a lively French ambience serving full meals (high season), snacks (other times), takeaway (all 1/7-31/8). Heated swimming pool, children's pool (1/6-30/9). Solarium. Playground. Pétanque. Billiards. Games/TV rooms. Activities in high season. Fishing. Gas and charcoal barbecues permitted. WiFi. Off site: Tennis and bicycle hire 3 km. Riding 5 km. Golf 20 km.

Open: 1 April - 30 September.

Directions

Using D911 Millau - Rodez road, turn north at Pont-de-Salars towards lake on D523. Follow site signs. Ignore first site and continue, following lake until les Terraces du Lac on right (about 5 km). GPS: 44.30498, 2.73556

Charges 2012

Per unit incl. 2 persons	
and electricity	€ 16.50 - € 27.90
extra person	€ 3.50 - € 5.50
child (2-7 yrs)	€ 2.50 - € 4.00
dog	€ 1.50 - € 2.00

CAMPING - CARAVANING ★★★★

LES TERRASSES DU LAC

In overhanging of the lake, discover an exceptional place for your relaxation and your escape. Chalets and Mobile homes to rent. A 200 m^2 heated swimming pool. Free activities

Route de Vibal 12 290
PONT DE SALARS
Tel: 0033 565 46 88 18
Fax: 0033 565 46 85 38
www.campinglesterrasses.com
campinglesterrasses@orange.fr

For latest campsite news, availability and prices visit
alanrogers.com

Rivière-sur-Tarn

Kawan Village les Peupliers

Route des Gorges du Tarn, F-12640 Rivière-sur-Tarn (Aveyron) T: 05 65 59 85 17.
E: lespeupliers12640@orange.fr **alanrogers.com/FR12160**

Les Peupliers is a friendly, family site on the banks of the Tarn river. Most of the good sized pitches have shade, all have electricity, water and a waste water point and are divided by low hedges. It is possible to swim in the river and there is a landing place for canoes. The site has its own canoes (to rent). In a lovely, sunny situation on the site is a swimming pool with a paddling pool, sunbeds and a new slide, all protected by a beautifully clipped hedge and with a super view to the surrounding hills and the Château du Peyrelade perched above the village. A treat for us at dusk was to watch beavers playing and swimming on the far river bank. We were told this happens nearly every day. The site is near the village of Rivière-sur-Tarn and the mouth of the Gorges du Tarn. It is 10 km. from the town of Millau, now famous for its spectacular bridge designed by Norman Foster that carries the A75 over the Tarn valley. Some English is spoken.

Facilities

Large, light and airy toilet facilities, baby facilities with baths, showers and WCs, facilities for disabled visitors. Washing machines. Shop (1/6-30/9). Bar, TV. Internet. Snack bar, takeaway (1/5-30/9). Swimming pool (from 1/5). Games, competitions July/Aug. Fishing. Play area. Weekly dances July/Aug. Canoe hire. WiFi in bar area (free). Off site: Village with shops and restaurant 300 m. Riding 500 m. Bicycle hire 2 km. Golf 25 km. Rock climbing, canyoning, cycling and walking.

Open: 1 April - 30 September.

Directions

Heading south from Clermont-Ferrand to Millau on the A75 autoroute take exit 44-1 signed Aguessac/Gorges du Tarn. In Aguessac turn left and follow signs to Riviere-sur-Tarn (5 km). Site is clearly signed down a short road to the right. GPS: 44.18577, 3.13068

Charges guide

Per unit incl. 2 persons	
and electricity	€ 20.00 - € 32.00
extra person	€ 5.00 - € 7.00
child (2-7 yrs)	€ 2.00 - € 4.00
dog	€ 2.50

Camping Cheques accepted.

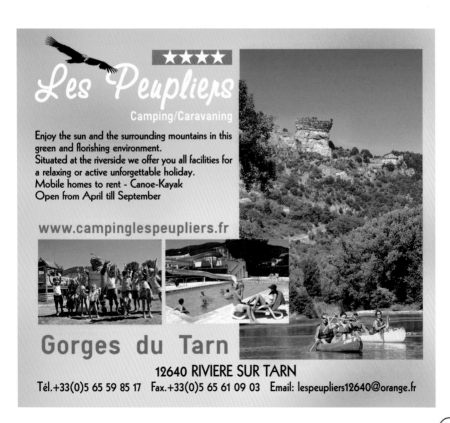

★★★★

Les Peupliers
Camping/Caravaning

Enjoy the sun and the surrounding mountains in this green and florishing environment.
Situated at the riverside we offer you all facilities for a relaxing or active unforgettable holiday.
Mobile homes to rent - Canoe-Kayak
Open from April till September

www.campinglespeupliers.fr

Gorges du Tarn

12640 RIVIERE SUR TARN
Tél.+33(0)5 65 59 85 17   Fax.+33(0)5 65 61 09 03   Email: lespeupliers12640@orange.fr

For latest campsite news, availability and prices visit
alanrogers.com

Rivière-sur-Tarn
Flower Camping Caravaning de Peyrelade

Route des Gorges du Tarn, F-12640 Rivière-sur-Tarn (Aveyron) T: 05 65 62 62 54.
E: campingpeyrelade@orange.fr **alanrogers.com/FR12000**

The 137 touring pitches (100-150 sq.m) are terraced, level and shady with 6A electricity hook-ups (long leads may be required for the riverside pitches). There are also 53 mobile homes for hire. The site is ideally placed for visiting the Tarn, Jonte and Dourbie gorges, and centres for rafting and canoeing are a short drive up the river. Other nearby attractions include the Caves of Aven Armand, the Chaos de Montpellier, Roquefort (of cheese fame) and the pleasant town of Millau.

Facilities

Two well equipped toilet blocks. Facilities for young children and disabled visitors. Laundry facilities. Bar, restaurant, pizzeria, takeaway (all from 1/6). A new aquapark with a 100 sq.m. children's pool, 120 sq.m. swimming pool and whirlpool (no shorts). Playground. Games room. Miniclub. Fishing. WiFi in bar area. Only charcoal barbecues allowed. Off site: Bicycle hire 100 m. Riding 3 km. Nearby leisure centre can be booked at reception. Millau with shops and night markets.

Open: 15 May - 15 September.

Directions

Take autoroute A75 to exit 44-1 Aguessac then onto D907 (follow Gorges du Tarn signs). Site is 2 km. past Rivière-sur-Tarn, on the right - the access road is quite steep. GPS: 44.19047, 3.15638

Charges 2012

Per unit incl. 2 persons	
and electricity	€ 19.00 - € 34.00
extra person	€ 3.50 - € 8.00
child (under 7 yrs)	€ 2.00 - € 5.00

Rocamadour
Camping Padimadour

La Châtaigneraie, F-46500 Rocamadour (Lot) T: 05 65 33 72 11. E: info@padimadour.fr
alanrogers.com/FR46410

Camping Padimadour is a small friendly, family run campsite in beautiful Quercy countryside, not far from the ancient town of Rocamadour in the Vallée de la Dordogne. There are 50 very large, grassy and slightly sloping pitches with 25 for touring, all with 10A electricity and most with water. There is some shade from maturing trees. The site is undergoing extensive refurbishment and has a superb new toilet block, small bar/snack bar and a games room. Many other improvements are planned. The site is aimed at couples and families with pre-teen children and there is low key family entertainment in July/August.

Facilities

Superb new toilet block with all necessary facilities including those for disabled visitors. Washing machine and dryer. Small shop for essentials. Snack bar, takeaway (July/Aug). Bar (Jun-Sept). Swimming pool (June-Sept). Children's play area. Trampolines. Activity and family entertainment programme (July/Aug). WiFi (charged). Off site: Cycling and walking tracks. Riding. Fishing. Rock climbing. Alvignac with shop and restaurant 2 km. Rocamadour 5 km. Padirac, Gouffre de Padirac 8 km.

Open: 9 April - 30 October.

Directions

From D840 (Figeac to Brive-la-Gaillarde road) turn east 7 km. north west of Gramat, site signed. Follow small lane to site in just under 2 km. GPS: 44.817742, 1.686267

Charges guide

Per unit incl. 2 persons	
and electricity	€ 16.80 - € 20.70
extra person	€ 4.20 - € 5.50
child (3-12 yrs)	€ 2.30 - € 3.50

Roquelaure
Yelloh! Village le Talouch

F-32810 Roquelaure (Gers) T: 05 62 65 52 43. E: info@camping-talouch.com
alanrogers.com/FR32080

Although enjoying a quiet and rural location, this neat and tidy site is only a short drive from the town of Auch with its famous legendary son, d'Artagnan. The entrance is fronted by a parking area with reception to the right and the bar and restaurant facing. Beyond this point lies the top half of the touring area with generous pitches of at least 120 sq.m. located between mature trees and divided by hedges, some with chalets. There are 100 pitches for touring, with electricity (4,6 or 10A). The rear half of the site has unshaded pitches in a more open aspect.

Facilities

Two toilet blocks with open style washbasins and controllable showers. Baby unit. One toilet for disabled visitors. Laundry facilities. Small shop (1/4-30/9). Bar, restaurant and takeaway. Two swimming pools, one heated and covered. Sauna and spa. Bicycle hire. GPS hire with pre-programmed walking routes. Activities for children. Play areas. Tennis. Hard surface sports area. Organised entertainment in high season. Small library. Internet and WiFi (charged) in reception. Charcoal barbecues only. Off site: Fishing and riding within 8 km.

Open: 6 April - 24 September.

Directions

Situated some 11 km. north of Auch on the D149, and 64 km. east of Toulouse the site is well signed. From the north approach via the A62 motorway, leaving at Layrac and heading towards Auch on the N21. GPS: 43.71283, 0.5645

Charges 2012

Per unit incl. 2 persons	
and electricity	€ 17.00 - € 38.00
extra person	€ 6.00 - € 8.00
child (3-7 yrs)	free - € 7.00

For latest campsite news, availability and prices visit
alanrogers.com

Saint Amans-des-Cots
Village Center les Tours

F-12460 Saint Amans-des-Cots (Aveyron) T: 04 99 57 21 21. E: contact@village-center.com
alanrogers.com/FR12040

This impressive campsite is set in beautiful countryside close to the Truyère Gorges, Upper Lot valley and the Aubrac Plateau. Efficiently run, it is situated on the shores of the Lac de la Selves. There are 275 average sized pitches (108 for touring) with 6A electricity, some bordering the lake, the rest terraced and hedged with views of the lake. About 100 pitches also have water points. The site has a spacious feel, enhanced by the thoughtfully planned terraced layout and it is well kept and very clean. There is some up and down walking to the facilities, especially from the upper terraces.

Facilities

Four very well equipped toilet blocks. Central complex housing the amenities. Shop. Restaurant, bar. Takeaway (high season). Swimming pools (May-Sept). Play area. Tennis. Daytime and evening activities, with miniclub and tree climbing (all supervised). Lake activities include fishing, canoeing, pedaloes, windsurfing, water skiing and provision for launching small boats. Internet. Max. 1 dog. Off site: Riding 6 km. Golf 9 km. Bicycle hire 12 km.

Open: 30 April - 5 September.

Directions

Take D34 from Entraygues-sur-Truyère to St Amans-des-Cots (14 km). In St Amans take D97 to Colombez and then D599 to Lac de la Selves (site signed, 5 km. from St Amans).
GPS: 44.66668, 2.68001

Charges guide

Per unit incl. 2 persons and electricity	€ 16.00 - € 34.00
extra person	€ 3.00 - € 5.00

Saint Antonin-Noble-Val
Flower Camping les Gorges de l'Aveyron

Marsac bas, F-82140 Saint Antonin-Noble-Val (Tarn-et-Garonne) T: 05 63 30 69 76.
E: info@camping-gorges-aveyron.com **alanrogers.com/FR82040**

This is a friendly, family site which is undergoing a process of renovation by its new owners, Stephane and Johanna Batlo. The site has an attractive wooded location, sloping down to the River Aveyron and facing the Roc d'Anglars. Reception and the two toilet blocks are housed in traditional, converted farm buildings. There are 80 pitches of which 50 are for touring units and these all have electrical connections (3-10A). The pitches are grassy and well shaded and may become very soft in times of poor weather. Some pitches are available close to the river but we would suggest that these are unsuitable for younger children as the river is unfenced. The current owners have built a swimming pool and a modern toilet block. This is a very quiet site in low season and some amenities, notably the snack bar and shop are only available in the peak season. The nearby artisan town of St Antonin-Noble-Val dates back to the eighth century, and is just 1.5 km. from the site. The town, with its medieval streets, is well worth a visit. The Gorges de l'Aveyron are well known for outdoor sports, canoeing, paragliding and potholing are all possible, with experienced guides. Fishing in the Aveyron is available directly from the campsite.

Facilities

Two toilet blocks with washing machines and dryers. Small shop, bar, snack bar and takeaway (June-Sept). Direct access to river. Fishing. Canoeing. Play area. Entertainment and activities in high season. WiFi. Mobile homes for rent. Off site: St Antonin-Noble-Val with a wide choice of shops, restaurants and bars 1.5 km. Bicycle hire 1.5 km. Riding 2 km. Cordes-sur-Ciel 35 km. Many walking paths and cycle trails.

Open: 7 April - 30 September.

Directions

From the north, take exit 59 from the A20 autoroute joining the D926 and follow signs to St Antonin. Site can be found on the D115, 1.5 km. east of the town.
GPS: 44.1519, 1.7715

Charges guide

Per unit incl. 2 persons and electricity	€ 14.40 - € 26.20
extra person	€ 3.20 - € 4.50

Camping Cheques accepted.

GORGES DE L'AVEYRON

LES GORGES DE L'AVEYRON
★★★
Open from 7/04 to 30/09 - 80 PITCHES
Pitches - Mobile homes and tents

flower
camping

friendly
camping
by nature.

JOHANNA AND STÉPHANE BATLO
Lieu dit Marsac Bas - 82140 St-Antonin-Noble-Val
Tel: 00 33 (0)3 25 04 13 20
E-mail: info@camping-gorges-aveyron.com
www.camping-gorges-aveyron.com

For latest campsite news, availability and prices visit
alanrogers.com

Saint Antonin-Noble-Val
Camping les Trois Cantons
F-82140 Saint Antonin-Noble-Val (Tarn-et-Garonne) T: 05 63 31 98 57. E: info@3cantons.fr
alanrogers.com/FR82010

Les Trois Cantons is a well established and very friendly family run site with 99 pitches (84 for tourers) set among mature trees that give dappled shade. The pitches are of average size, reasonably level and all have electricity connections. The main swimming pool is well separated from the children's pool, with activities organised there in July and August. There are also walks, archery and boules, a visiting hypnotist plus wine tastings and a weekly dance. When the trees are bare early in the season, there could be a little road noise when the wind is in a certain direction.

Facilities

The two sanitary blocks include British and Turkish style WCs, showers, washbasins (some in cubicles) and facilities for disabled visitors. Laundry facilities. Basic shop (1/6-30/9; bread daily). Bar serving snacks and takeaways. Restaurant. Swimming pool (1/5-15/9) and paddling pool. Climbing wall. Games area. Play area. Small farm enclosures. Tennis. Boules. English, Dutch and German spoken. WiFi. Torches useful. Off site: Riding 1 km. Caving and climbing 5 km. Fishing 7 km.

Open: 15 April - 30 September.

Directions

From A20 or N20 at Caussade, take D926 signed Caylus and Septfonds. Site is signed to right 5 km. after Septfonds. Do not take the D5 towards St Antonin-Noble-Val as it involves 5 km. of narrow roads. GPS: 44.19300, 1.69633

Charges guide

| Per unit incl. 2 persons and 10A electricity | € 21.00 - € 28.00 |
| extra person | € 3.70 - € 5.50 |

Saint Cirq-Lapopie
Camping de la Plage
F-46330 Saint Cirq-Lapopie (Lot) T: 05 65 30 29 51. E: camping-laplage@wanadoo.fr
alanrogers.com/FR46070

You are assured of a warm welcome at Camping la Plage from the English speaking owners. It is situated beside the River Lot and is within walking distance of the beautiful historic village of Saint Cirq-Lapopie. It provides a good base for those who want an active holiday with many organised activities available either on site or in the immediate area. There are 120 good sized, level stony/grass pitches, 98 of which are for touring. Most have electricity (6/10A), a few are fully serviced and some have hardstandings. They are separated by hedges and shrubs and a variety of mature trees give good shade.

Facilities

Two sanitary blocks are clean and well maintained. Facilities for disabled visitors. Laundry facilities. Motorcaravan service point (charged). Bar (1/4-30/9). Restaurant and takeaway (1/5-30/9). New swimming pool planned for 2012. Play area. Children's room. Canoeing, kayaking and swimming from beach (lifeguard July/Aug). Fishing. Bicycle hire. WiFi. Off site: Walking, rock climbing, caving, canyoning and shops all nearby. Riding 9 km.

Open: 1 April - 15 October.

Directions

From Cahors take D653 east to Vers, then D662 for 17 km. to Tour de Faure. Cross river and site entrance is on right by bar/restaurant. Do not approach via Saint Cirq-Lapopie - very steep, winding and narrow roads. GPS: 44.46926, 1.68135

Charges guide

| Per unit incl. 2 persons and electricity | € 20.00 - € 27.00 |

Saint Cirq-Lapopie
Camping la Truffière
F-46330 Saint Cirq-Lapopie (Lot) T: 05 65 30 20 22. E: contact@camping-truffiere.com
alanrogers.com/FR46150

This site is set in four hectares of mature oak woodland within the Parc Naturel Régional des Causses de Quercy with stunning natural scenery and only 2.5 km. from the cliff top village of St Cirq-Lapopie. La Truffière is well suited to those seeking a peaceful countryside holiday and it is a superb area for hiking. The 90 slightly sloping, terraced pitches are of varying sizes and on a mixture of grass and gravel. All have 6A electricity (long leads may be needed) and most have shade from mature trees. Access is good for large outfits but advanced booking is recommended.

Facilities

Two clean and modern toilet blocks (one heated) include facilities for disabled visitors. Motorcaravan services. Fridge hire. Small shop. Bar/restaurant (1/6-31/8). Takeaway (1/6-15/9). Swimming pool, paddling pool, sun terrace (1/5-15/9). Field for ball games. Adventure style play area. Boules. Trampolines. English spoken. Gas and electric barbecues only on pitches (3 communal areas). WiFi near bar. Off site: Small shop in village 4 km. Fishing and bathing (in the River Lot) and riding 3 km.

Open: 3 April - 15 September.

Directions

From D911 Cahors - Rodez road, at Concots, turn north on D26 (St Cirq-Lapopie). Shortly keep left, D42. Site about 6 km. on right. Coming from north on D42 via St Cirq-Lapopie not recommended (extremely tight turns). GPS: 44.44855, 1.67455

Charges guide

Per unit incl. 2 persons and electricity	€ 21.00
extra person	€ 5.50
Camping Cheques accepted.	

We can book this site for you! Call 01580 214000 alanrogers ❂ travel

For latest campsite news, availability and prices visit
alanrogers.com

Saint Côme-d'Olt
Camping Belle Rive

Rue du Terral, F-12500 Saint Côme-d'Olt (Aveyron) T: 05 65 44 05 85. E: bellerive12@voila.fr

alanrogers.com/FR12380

Small and simple, this family run campsite, beside the River Lot, is on the edge of a delightful medieval village. The region has many historic towns and villages with châteaux and ancient churches and is close to the Pilgrim route. The local produce, for example Roquefort cheese, is well worth sampling. The site is good for those seeking a tranquil spot with little in the way of on-site activities. There are 71 good sized, grassy pitches delineated by a variety of tall trees giving good shade on most pitches (6-10A electricity). Access to the site is not suitable for large outfits due to the many small twisting roads.

Facilities

Adequate but very clean old style central block with combined shower and washbasin cubicles. Washing machine. Facilities for disabled campers. Bar. Takeaway (all season). Play area. Some family activities (high season). River bathing and fishing. WiFi throughout (charged). Off site: Village with small shops, bank, bar/restaurants 400 m. Espalion with larger shops and market 4 km. Swimming pool 4 km. Riding 12 km. Beach 120 km. Canoeing. Ancient villages, châteaux, churches. Many walking and cycling routes.

Open: 1 April - 30 September.

Directions

Leave A75 at exit 42, signed Sévérac le Château. Take N88 west, then D28 to Espalion. Cross river on D987 to St Côme-d'Olt (4 km). On entering village bear left, following signs to site. Do not drive through the village. GPS: 44.51376, 2.81847

Charges 2012

Per unit incl. 2 persons and electricity	€ 14.00
extra person	€ 3.40
child (under 7 yrs)	€ 1.90

No credit cards.

Saint Geniez-d'Olt
Campéole la Boissière

Route de la Cascade, F-12130 Saint Geniez-d'Olt (Aveyron) T: 05 65 70 40 43. E: boissiere@campeole.com

alanrogers.com/FR12090

With trout in the river and carp in the lakes, la Boissière is a fisherman's paradise. The site is a member of the Campéole group and is situated on the banks of the River Lot, surrounded by wooded hills. Walking, swimming, canoeing or cycling are alternative pursuits here. Mature trees provide plenty of shade on the generous, partly hedged, grassy pitches, all of which have electricity connections (6A) and frequently placed water points. Reception is housed in an old, converted farmhouse. The nearby old town of St Geniez-d'Olt should satisfy all shopping needs day or longer fishing licences can be obtained there (the helpful site staff will advise). There is direct access through the site to the river, which is suitable for swimming and canoeing. La Boissière has 150 pitches, of which around 70 are used for mobile homes, chalets and fully equipped tents (available for rent) There is much of interest in the area and the Tarn gorges and Grandes Causses are both within easy reach.

Facilities

Two modern, clean toilet blocks with washbasins in cubicles and preset showers. Baby changing facilities in female area. Basic facilities for visitors with disabilities (no rails). Shop with basic provisions (milk and bread in high season only). Bar with terrace. Large, heated swimming pool and paddling pool. Multisports terrain. Bouncy castle and playground. Entertainment in July/Aug. Mobile homes, chalets and tents for rent. Internet (first 15 mins. free). Off site: St Géniez-d'Olt 500 m. Bicycle and canoe hire.

Open: 20 April - 30 September.

Directions

From Saint Geniez-d'Olt follow the D988 eastwards towards Banassac. After 500 m. follow signs on right to la Boissière campsite. GPS: 44.4686, 2.9825

Charges guide

Per unit incl. 2 persons and electricity	€ 15.10 - € 24.50
extra person	€ 4.00 - € 6.10
child (2-6 yrs)	€ 3.60 - € 4.00
dog	€ 2.00 - € 2.60

For latest campsite news, availability and prices visit
alanrogers.com

Saint Geniez-d'Olt

Kawan Village Marmotel

F-12130 Saint Geniez-d'Olt (Aveyron) T: 05 65 70 46 51. E: info@marmotel.com

alanrogers.com/FR12150

The road into Marmotel passes various industrial buildings and is a little off-putting – persevere, as they are soon left behind. The campsite itself is a mixture of old and new. The old part provides many pitches with lots of shade and separated by hedges. The new area is sunny until the trees grow. These pitches each have a private sanitary unit, with shower, WC, washbasin and dishwashing. New and very well designed, they are reasonably priced for such luxury. All the pitches have electricity (10A). A lovely restaurant has a wide terrace with views of the hills and overlooking the heated swimming and paddling pools. These have fountains, a toboggan and sun beds either on grass or the tiled surrounds. The Lot river runs alongside the site where you can fish or canoe.

Facilities

Good sanitary facilities include baby baths and facilities for disabled visitors. Washing machines. Bar/restaurant, takeaway. Swimming pools. Small play area. Multisports area. Entertainment (July/Aug) including disco below bar, cinema, karaoke, dances, miniclub for 4-12 yrs. Bicycle hire. Fishing. Canoeing. Off site: Large supermarket 500 m. Riding 10 km. Bicycle tours and canoe trips on the Lot and rafting on the Tarn are organised.

Open: 28 April - 22 September.

Directions

Heading south on autoroute 75 (free) take exit 41 and follow signs for St Geniez-d'Olt. Site is at western end of village. Site is signed onto D19 to Prades d'Aubrac, then 500 m. on left. GPS: 44.46165, 2.96318

Charges 2012

Per unit incl. 1 or 2 persons	
and electricity	€ 18.00 - € 31.00
with individual sanitary facility	€ 22.00 - € 38.00
extra person	€ 3.00 - € 8.00
child (under 5 yrs)	free - € 4.20

Camping Cheques accepted.

"VERY COMFORTABLE, VERY NATURAL"
5 ha in the Lot Valley, by the riverside. 190 pitches, of which 40 have an individual toilet. Chalets and Mobile homes for hire. 350 sqm swimming pools, waterslides, multi sports area, animations, kids club, bar, restaurant.

Open 28/04 – 22/09 2012

www.marmotel.com

Saint Girons

Parc d'Audinac les Bains

Montjoie-Audinac, F-09200 Saint Girons (Ariège) T: 05 61 66 44 50. E: accueil@audinac.com

alanrogers.com/FR09100

Remnants of an old thermal springs can be found on the site at Parc d'Audinac les Bains, a tranquil haven with wonderful views of the surrounding mountains. Owned by a charming French couple, Olivia and Jérôme Barbry, you are guaranteed a friendly welcome on this site which has 60 touring pitches and 40 chalets for rent. The terraced touring pitches are mostly level, although some do have a slight slope. They are on well drained grass and each has 10A electricity supplied (the older part of the site via French sockets). Water supplies are conveniently located for all pitches, as are the modern sanitary facilities.

Facilities

Two small bright and modern toilet blocks (one unisex) with hot and cold water to showers and washbasins. British and Turkish style WC's. Washing machines. Motorcaravan service point. Outdoor swimming pool and paddling pool with WCs, showers and changing facilities. Bar (11/4-30/9). Snacks (11/6-30/9). Small shop for drinks and ice creams (July/Aug). Tennis. Boules. Sports area. Bicycle hire. Children's club (July/Aug). Off site: Shops, bars, restaurants and supermarket at St Girons 3 km. Outdoor activities in the surrounding area.

Open: 1 April - 30 September.

Directions

From Saint Girons take D117 towards Foix. Turn left on D627 signed Saint Croix and Merigon. Site is on the right just after Audinac-les-Bains. GPS: 43.0074, 1.1826

Charges guide

Per unit incl. 2 persons	
and electricity	€ 15.00 - € 19.50
extra person	€ 4.00 - € 6.00
child (0-6 yrs)	€ 3.00 - € 5.00
dog	€ 1.00

For latest campsite news, availability and prices visit
alanrogers.com

Saint Parthem
Camping la Plaine
F-12300 Saint Parthem (Aveyron) T: 05 65 64 05 24. E: infos@camping-laplaine.fr
alanrogers.com/FR12360

Strung out along the bank of the Lot river, this small, spacious, delightful site is family run. The enthusiastic and very friendly Dutch owners are making many improvements here including the addition of a new swimming pool in 2008. There are 65 grassy, fairly level pitches with 61 for touring (6A electricity, long leads advised). The pitches are separated by maturing trees and some hedging with views over the river and the wooded gorge. Some pitches have little shade. Swimming and canoeing are possible from the small pebbly beach. The site makes a good base for exploring this beautiful region.

Facilities

Old style but very clean central block and small satellite block with all necessary facilities. Facilities for disabled visitors. Washing machine, ironing board. Small bar/restaurant with takeaway (all season). Bread to order. Swimming pool with patio. River fishing and bathing from pebble beach. Tennis. Boules. Off site: Small village with small shop 500 m. Riding 8 km. Canoeing 15 km. Medieval towns and villages, e.g. Conques 14 km.

Open: 5 April - 14 September.

Directions

Site is northeast of Decazeville. Leave Decazeville on the D963 signed Aurillac. After 6 km. cross river and turn east onto D42 to St Parthem (6 km). Site is well signed. GPS: 44.6292, 2.32059

Charges guide

Per unit incl. 2 persons	€ 12.50
extra person	€ 3.50
electricity (6A)	€ 3.00
No credit cards.	

Sainte Pierre-Lafeuille
Camping Quercy Vacances
Mas de la Combe, F-46090 Sainte Pierre-Lafeuille (Lot) T: 05 65 36 87 15. E: quercy-vacances@wanadoo.fr
alanrogers.com/FR46240

This clean and well run site is owned by a young, English speaking, French couple keen to improve the facilities and ambiance. It is only 4.5 km. from the A20 and is an ideal stopover site for holidaymakers travelling to and from Spain, but is also good for longer stays. It has 80 large, unmarked and slightly sloping grass pitches, some with shade from maturing trees. There are 52 pitches for touring units and most have 10A electricity. Access is good for larger outfits. The site facilities include a rustic bar and restaurant with hand painted murals on the walls.

Facilities

Clean, modern toilet block with all necessary facilities, including those for disabled visitors in a separate building. Small basic shop. Bar and takeaway. Restaurant serving specials like couscous and paella once a week (July/Aug). Large round swimming pool (20/6-15/9), children's pool. Live music, dancing (July/Aug). Small play area. WiFi near entrance. Off site: Riding 5 km. Bicycle hire, fishing 10 km. Cahors with many shops and bars etc. 10 km.

Open: 1 April - 30 September.

Directions

Leave A20 exit 57 (Cahors). Shortly turn left on N20 and then turn right on small un-named road (site signed) before reaching St Pierre-Lafeuille (about 4.5 km. from the A20). Site on right in about 600 m. GPS: 44.53136, 1.45926

Charges guide

Per unit incl. 2 persons and electricity	€ 18.70 - € 22.50
extra person	€ 3.80 - € 5.00

Salles-Curan
Kawan Village les Genêts
Lac de Pareloup, F-12410 Salles-Curan (Aveyron) T: 05 65 46 35 34. E: contact@camping-les-genets.fr
alanrogers.com/FR12080

This family run site is on the shores of Lac de Pareloup and offers both family holiday and watersports facilities. The 163 pitches include 80 grassy, mostly individual pitches for touring units. These are in two areas, one on each side of the entrance lane, and are divided by hedges, shrubs and trees. Most have electricity (6A) and many also have water and waste water drain. The site slopes gently down to the beach and lake with facilities for all watersports including water skiing. A full animation and activities programme is organised in high season, and there is much to see and do in this corner of Aveyron. Used by tour operators (25 pitches).

Facilities

Two sanitary units, one refurbished, with suite for disabled guests. Baby room. Laundry. Well stocked shop (from 1/6). Bar, restaurant, snacks (14/6-5/9). Swimming pool, spa pool (from 1/6; unsupervised). Playground. Minigolf. Boules. Bicycle hire. Pedaloes, windsurfers, kayaks. Fishing licences available. WiFi in bar.

Open: 21 May - 11 September.

Directions

From Salles-Curan take D577 for about 4 km. and turn right into a narrow lane immediately after a sharp right-hand bend. Site is signed at junction. GPS: 44.18933, 2.76693

Charges guide

Per unit incl. 2 persons and electricity	€ 18.00 - € 40.00
extra person	€ 4.00 - € 8.00
Camping Cheques accepted.	

For latest campsite news, availability and prices visit
alanrogers.com

Seissan

Domaine Lacs de Gascogne

Rue du Lac, F-32260 Seissan (Gers) T: 05 62 66 27 94. E: info@domainelacsdegascogne.eu

alanrogers.com/FR32180

This is a spacious site located at Seissan in the Pyrenean foothills. Its impressive drive sweeps around the largest of three lakes into the spacious and relaxing Domaine. The 50 large, grassy touring pitches mostly have shade and fine lake views. Electricity is 16A (some long leads required). Comfortable chalets and mobile homes (25) can be rented. The bar and restaurant are open all season and the food is very good. The lakes are perfect for fishing, kayaking, and evening beach campfires. Across the lakes is ideal for 'wilder' camping, this area also has five teepees to rent.

Facilities

Excellent sanitary facilities in a new block were clean, tidy and well maintained. There is a second older block across the lake. Baby changing mats and facilities for disabled visitors. Restaurant with lunch and à la carte menus. Breakfast service. Lounge. TV room. Swimming pool. Health pool. Sauna. Gym. Fishing (carp). Kayaks. Rope raft across lake. Play area. Play room. Tennis. Football. Basketball. Bicycle hire. Entertainment and activities including music and dancing. Mobile home, chalet, teepee and bed and breakfast accommodation. Off site: Riding 5 km. Golf 6 km. Supermarket 7 km. Auch 19 km.

Open: 1 April - 1 November.

Directions

Head south from Auch on N21 and, at Beaulieu, join the southbound D929. Continue on this road as far as Seissan and then follow signs to the site. GPS: 43.49535, 0.57826

Charges guide

Per unit incl. 2 persons	
and electricity	€ 12.50 - € 17.50
extra person	€ 6.00

Séniergues

Domaine de la Faurie

F-46240 Séniergues (Lot) T: 05 65 21 14 36. E: contact@camping-lafaurie.com

alanrogers.com/FR46190

A stunning array of tended shrubs and thoughtful flower plantings is spread throughout this very pretty 27-hectare site which is located on a hilltop with wide open views of the surrounding hills and valleys. Although hidden away, it is an excellent base for exploring the Lot and Dordogne regions. The site is separated into two distinct areas, an open, lightly shaded section and a much more densely shaded area with tall pine trees. The wooded section (total 42 touring), has small paths and tight turns which could cause difficulties for larger units. The pitches are large and most are at least 100 sq.m.

Facilities

The two sanitary blocks are clean and well maintained. Facilities for disabled visitors. Washing machine. Motorcaravan service point. Gift shop (bread available). Bar, restaurant and takeaway. Swimming pool and paddling pool. TV and games rooms. Boules. Bicycle hire. Play area. Small library. Weekly soirées in high season. Max. 1 dog. Off site: Fishing 3 km. Golf 8 km. Riding 15 km.

Open: 7 April - 30 September.

Directions

From the A20 exit on N56 and turn right towards St Germain du Bel Air. Continue for 5 km. and the site is on the right. GPS: 44.69197, 1.53461

Charges guide

Per unit incl. 2 persons	
and electricity	€ 19.50 - € 28.00
extra person	€ 4.50 - € 6.90
Camping Cheques accepted.	

Sévérac-l'Eglise

Flower Camping la Grange de Monteillac

F-12310 Sévérac-l'Eglise (Aveyron) T: 05 65 70 21 00. E: info@la-grange-de-monteillac.com

alanrogers.com/FR12070

La Grange de Monteillac is a modern, well equipped site in the beautiful, well preserved small village of Sévérac-l'Église. A spacious 4.5 hectare site, it provides 100 individual pitches, 70 for touring (eight extra large), on gently sloping grass, separated by flowering shrubs and trees offering some shade. All pitches have electricity (6A, long leads may be required), and 24 have water and waste water connections. There are 43 chalets, mobile homes and tents for rent in separate areas.

Facilities

Modern toilet block with facilities for babies and disabled visitors. Washing machine, dryer. Shop (1/7-31/8). Poolside restaurant/snack bar serving pizzas, grills etc, takeaway (15/5-15/9). Bar with music or groups (July/Aug). Two swimming pools (15/5-15/9). Playground. Bicycle hire. Archery. Boules. Organised activities. Children's and teen's clubs. Jacuzzi. WiFi. Off site: Fishing 1 km. Village 3 km. Riding 9 km. Golf 25 km. Canoeing, rafting, canyoning, rock climbing and hang-gliding.

Open: 27 April - 15 September.

Directions

Site is on the edge of Sévérac-l'Eglise village, just off N88 Rodez - Sévérac Le Château road. From A75 use exit 42. At Sévérac-l'Eglise turn south onto D28, site is signed. Site entrance is very shortly on left. GPS: 44.3652, 2.85142

Charges 2012

Per unit incl. 2 persons	
and electricity	€ 16.90 - € 34.90
extra person	€ 3.00 - € 6.50

For latest campsite news, availability and prices visit

alanrogers.com

Sorèze
Camping Saint Martin
F-81540 Sorèze (Tarn) T: 05 63 50 20 19. E: campings.occitanie@orange.fr
alanrogers.com/FR81110

There are 48 individual touring pitches with 10A electricity and six wooden chalets for rent at this site. The pitches are all on grass, some divided by newly planted hedging and there are some mature trees for shade. Six pitches are reserved for motorcaravans, although these are rather compact. A small swimming pool is well fenced and gated. Reception has a small bar and snack bar and can also provide basic supplies including drinks, sweets, speciality foods and snacks. However, you are only 100 metres from the town centre shops.

Facilities	Directions
Sanitary unit is well built. Facilities for disabled visitors. Laundry facilities. Small shop. Bar with TV. Snack bar. Swimming pool. WiFi (free). All amenities open 15/6-15/9. Boules. Communal barbecue. Small playground. Entertainment in high season. Off site: Municipal leisure and sports facilities including tennis courts adjacent.	Sorèze is on the D85 about 25 km. southwest of Castres, 5 km. east of Revel. The site is well signed within the town. GPS: 43.454517, 2.069583

Open: 15 June - 15 September.

Charges guide

Per unit incl. 2 persons	
and electricity	€ 15.05 - € 18.50
extra person	€ 3.40 - € 4.50

Souillac
Castel Camping le Domaine de la Paille Basse
F-46200 Souillac-sur-Dordogne (Lot) T: 05 65 37 85 48. E: info@lapaillebasse.com
alanrogers.com/FR46010

Set in a rural location some 8 km. from Souillac, this family owned site is easily accessible from the A20 and well placed to take advantage of excursions into the Dordogne. It is part of a large domain of 80 hectares, all available to campers for walks and recreation. The site is quite high up and there are excellent views over the surrounding countryside. The 262 pitches are in two main areas – one is level in cleared woodland with good shade, and the other on grass with limited shade. Numbered and marked, the pitches are a minimum 100 sq.m. and often considerably more. All have 10A electricity with 80 fully serviced. The site is well placed to take advantage of excursions into the Dordogne.

Facilities	Directions
Three main toilet blocks are and kept very clean. Laundry. Small shop with a large selection of wine. Restaurant, bar (open until 2 a.m. in high season), terrace, pizza takeaway. Crêperie. Main swimming pool, a smaller one, paddling pool (unheated), water slides. Sun terrace. Soundproofed disco (three times weekly in season). TV (with satellite). Cinema below the pool area. Tennis. Play area. Library. WiFi in office/bar area (charged). Mini-farm. Animation for all (July/Aug). Off site: Golf 4 km.	From Souillac take D15 and then D62 roads leading northwest (Salignac-Eyvignes) and after 6 km. turn right at site sign. Follow steep and narrow approach road for 2 km. GPS: 44.94728, 1.43924

Open: 15 May - 15 September.

Charges guide

Per person	€ 5.40 - € 7.50
pitch	€ 7.80 - € 10.80
incl. water and drainage	€ 9.80 - € 13.00

Camping Cheques accepted.

Souillac
Flower Camping les Ondines
Rue des Ondines, F-46200 Souillac (Lot) T: 05 65 37 86 44. E: info@camping-lesondines.com
alanrogers.com/FR46390

Souillac is a picturesque town lying between the Dordogne and Lot. It is just a five minute walk from les Ondines to the town's attractive pedestrianised centre where there are many cafés, restaurants and shops, as well as an abbey and, unusually, a robotic toy museum! There are 242 pitches here. These are grassy and well sized (mostly with electricity). A number of mobile homes and fully equipped tents are available for rent. In peak season, various activities are organised, including a children's club. The site lies on the banks of the Dordogne and canoe rental is available in the town.

Facilities	Directions
Two traditional toilet blocks with basic but clean facilities, including those for visitors with disabilities. Washing machine. Access to municipal swimming pool (free July/Aug). Pétanque. Volleyball. Play area. Tourist information. Activity and entertainment programme. Mobile homes and tents for rent. Off site: Swimming pool 300 m. Souillac (cafés, shops, restaurants and takeaway). Walking and cycle tracks. Riding. Canoeing. Supermarket.	Approaching from the north, leave the A20 motorway at exit 55 and head for Souilllac. Drive through the town and, around 500 m. beyond the traffic lights, turn right following signs to les Ondines and Quercyland. Continue to follow signs to the site. GPS: 44.888871, 1.474196

Open: 1 May - 30 September.

Charges guide

Per unit incl. 2 persons	
and electricity	€ 11.00 - € 16.00
extra person	€ 3.00 - € 4.90

For latest campsite news, availability and prices visit
alanrogers.com

Tarascon-sur-Ariege

Yelloh! Village le Pré Lombard

F-09400 Tarascon-sur-Ariege (Ariège) T: 05 61 05 61 94. E: leprelombard@wanadoo.fr
alanrogers.com/FR09060

This busy, good value site is located beside the attractive River Ariège and near the town. There are 180 level, grassy, pitches with shade provided by a variety of trees (electricity 10A). At the rear of the site are 70 site-owned chalets and mobile homes. A gate in the fence provides access to the riverbank for fishing. Open for a long season, it is an excellent choice for early or late breaks, or as a stopover en-route to the winter sun destinations in Spain. This region of Ariège is in the foothills of the Pyrenees and 85 km. from Andorra.

Facilities

Five toilet blocks of varying ages, facilities for disabled visitors. Laundry. Motorcaravan services. Bar and takeaway. Shop. Restaurant. Heated swimming pool (all 28/4-15/9). Playgrounds. Video games machines. Boules. Multisports court. Fishing. Internet and WiFi on payment. Satellite TV. Entertainment (high season). Activity programmes for small groups. Nightclub. Children's club. Sports tournaments. WiFi. No gas barbecues. Off site: Supermarket 300 m. Town 600 m. Archery, kayaking and fishing nearby. Riding 5 km. Skiing 20 km.

Open: 15 March - 15 October.

Directions

Site is 600 m. south of town, adjacent to the river. From north, turn off main N20 into the town, site well signed. From south (Andorra) site signed at roundabout on town approach.
GPS: 42.83985, 1.612

Charges 2012

Per unit incl. 2 persons	
and electricity	€ 17.00 - € 35.00
extra person	€ 6.00 - € 8.00
child (3-7 yrs)	free - € 7.00

Therondels

Flower Camping la Source

Presqu'île de Laussac, F-12600 Thérondels (Aveyron) T: 05 65 66 27 10. E: info@camping-la-source.com
alanrogers.com/FR12210

This extremely spacious, steeply terraced site borders the long and narrow Lac de Sarrans with its steep wooded sides. The site is run by a very friendly family and is better suited for the younger family wanting to 'get away from it all'. All the facilities are first class, although the layout of the site means that pitches may be some distance and a steep climb away. The owners prefer to provide tractor assistance for caravans. There are 101 medium to large, slightly sloping, grassy pitches with 62 for touring, all with 6/10A electricity, water and drainage.

Facilities

Two large, well appointed and clean toilet blocks with all the necessary facilities including those for babies and campers with disabilities. Bar with TV (all season). Shop, restaurant and takeaway (30/6-31/8). Heated swimming pool with toboggan and paddling pool. Play area. TV room. Activities in high season. Lake fishing. Barbecues permitted. WiFi (charged). Off site: Boat ramp 500 m. Golf 6 km. Riding and bicycle hire 15 km.

Open: 17 May - 9 September.

Directions

Leave the A75 at exit 28 or 29 (St Flour). Go through town and take D921 (Rodez). After 12 km. turn right on D990 (Pierrefort) and 3 km. after village turn left on D34 (Laussac). Follow narrow twisting lanes down to site (about 9 km). GPS: 44.853716, 2.77105

Charges 2012

Per unit incl. 2 persons	
and electricity	€ 17.00 - € 29.00
extra person	€ 3.00 - € 5.50

Vayrac

Camping les Granges

F-46110 Vayrac (Lot) T: 05 65 32 46 58. E: info@les-granges.com
alanrogers.com/FR46310

Situated just over 3 km. outside Vayrac in a very rural position, this site nestles quietly beside the river in a tranquil and peaceful area. Pitches along the river frontage are popular, but children will need to be supervised as the river is unfenced. There is access to the river at one end of the site, ideal for those wishing to discover the pleasures of the River Dordogne. There are 150 level grassy pitches, shaded by a variety of mature trees, with 116 for touring. Most have 10A electricity. In July and August there is some family entertainment, but only in French.

Facilities

Two modern toilet blocks include facilities for disabled visitors. Washing machine and ironing board. Small shop, bar, snack bar and takeaway (July/Aug). Swimming pool and paddling pool (May-Sept). Play area. Family entertainment (12/7-16/8). Fishing and river beach. Max. 1 dog. Electric barbecues not permitted. Off site: Bicycle hire 1 km. Shops, bars and restaurant in Vayrac 3 km. Golf and riding 10 km.

Open: 1 May - 18 September.

Directions

From Brive, take the D20 towards Figeac. In Vayrac turn right just before the church at sign for 'Campings' and 'Stade'. Site is signed from here in 3 km. GPS: 44.93462, 1.67981

Charges guide

Per unit incl. 2 persons	
and electricity	€ 16.72 - € 19.60
extra person	€ 4.08 - € 5.10

For latest campsite news, availability and prices visit
alanrogers.com

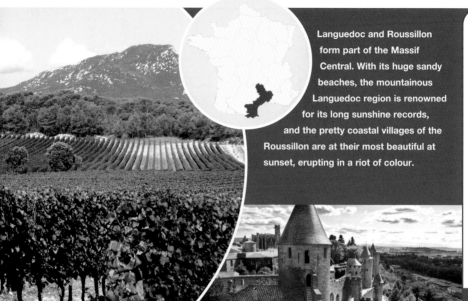

Languedoc and Roussillon form part of the Massif Central. With its huge sandy beaches, the mountainous Languedoc region is renowned for its long sunshine records, and the pretty coastal villages of the Roussillon are at their most beautiful at sunset, erupting in a riot of colour.

DÉPARTEMENTS: 11 AUDE, 30 GARD, 34 HÉRAULT, 48 LOZÈRE, 66 PYRÉNÉES-ORIENTALES

MAJOR CITIES: MONTPELLIER, PERPIGNAN, CARCASSONNE

Once an independent duchy, the ancient land of Languedoc combines two distinct regions: the vineyards of the Corbières and Minervois and the coastal plain stretching from the Rhône to the Spanish border. Much of the region is rugged and unspoilt, offering opportunities for walking and climbing.

There is ample evidence of the dramatic past. Ruins of the former Cathar castles can be seen throughout the region. The walled city of Carcassonne with its towers, dungeons, moats and drawbridges is one of the most impressive examples of medieval France.

Today, Languedoc and Roussillon are wine and agricultural regions. Languedoc, with considerable success, is now a producer of much of the nation's better value wines. But above all, vast hot sandy beaches and long hours of sunshine make this a paradise for beach enthusiasts. La Grande Motte, Cap d'Agde and Canet, are all being promoted as an alternative to the more famous Mediterranean stretches of the Côte d'Azur.

Places of interest

Aigues-Mortes: medieval city.

Béziers: wine capital of the region, St Nazaire cathedral, Canal du Midi.

Carcassonne: largest medieval walled city in Europe.

Limoux: medieval town, Notre Dame de Marseilla Basilica, St Martin church.

Montpellier: universities, Roman sites; Gothic cathedral.

Nîmes: Roman remains, Pont du Gard.

Perpignan: Kings Palace; Catalan characteristics, old fortress.

Villeneuve-lés-Avignon: Royal City and residence of popes in 14th century.

Cuisine of the region

Cooking is characterised by garlic and olive oil with sausages and smoked hams. Fish is popular along the coast. Wines include Corbières, Minervois, Banyuls and Muscat.

Aigo Bouido: garlic soup.

Boles de picoulat: small balls of diced beef and pork, garlic and eggs.

Bouillinade: a type of *bouillabaisse* with potatoes, oil, garlic and onions.

Boutifare: a sausage-shaped pudding of bacon and herbs.

Cargolade: snails, stewed in wine.

Ouillade: heavy soup of *boutifare* leeks, carrots, and potatoes..

Touron: a pastry of almonds, pistachio nuts and fruit.

www.sunfrance.com
contact.crtlr@sunfrance.com
(0) 4 67 20 02 20

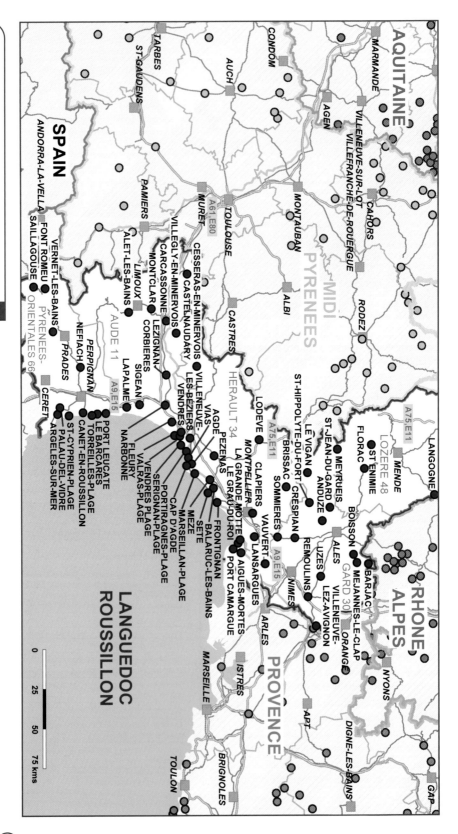

Agde
Camping le Neptune

46 boulevard du St Christ, F-34300 Agde (Hérault) T: 04 67 94 23 94. E: info@campingleneptune.com
alanrogers.com/FR34130

Camping le Neptune is a rare find in this area. This small, family run site with only 165 pitches makes a delightful change. The pitches are mostly separated by flowering bushes, with some shade, most with 6/10A electricity. There are also plenty of mobile homes to rent. The Fray family are welcoming, and even though this is a busy area, this site is an oasis of calm, suited to couples and young families. Situated alongside the splendid Hérault river, one can cycle or walk into the village of le Gau d'Agde or on into the historic centre of Agde itself. The site's swimming pool is in a sunny position, overlooked by the bar.

Facilities

Two toilet blocks provide roomy preset showers, washbasins in cabins, three cold showers for hot weather. Facilities for disabled visitors. Laundry. Small shop, bar (15/5-15/9). Snacks and takeaway (20/6-21/8). Heated swimming pool (15/4-30/9, bracelets required). Field for sports. WiFi (charged). Boat mooring facility on the River Hérault across the road. Barbecues not permitted. Max. 1 dog. Off site: Beach, riding, Canal du Midi and round lock 2 km. Golf 5 km.

Open: 1 April - 30 September.

Directions

From A9 exit 34 follow signs for Agde, Bessau, Vias, Cap d'Agde. Exit for Grau d'Agde. At roundabout (with statue) left following signs for Grau d'Agde, and again at second roundabout (left). Keep straight on to fifth roundabout where left and under bridge. Site is 600 m. on left. GPS: 43.29803, 3.45628

Charges guide

Per unit incl. 2 persons and electricity	€ 19.90 - € 29.60

Camping Cheques accepted.

Agde
Kawan Village les Champs Blancs

Route de Rochelongue, F-34300 Agde (Hérault) T: 04 67 94 23 42. E: champs.blancs@wanadoo.fr
alanrogers.com/FR34190

Les Champs Blancs is set amongst tall trees, 2 km. from Agde and 2 km. from the sea at Rochelongue in a shady environment. There are over 300 pitches, with 117 level, sandy pitches for touring units. Bordered with bushes and plenty of trees, all pitches have 10A electricity and unusually, 60 have private sanitary cabins. Mobile homes occupy separate areas. The area nearest the road is bordered by trees to deaden possible road noise. The pool area has been augmented by a super irregular pool, with toboggans, cascade, jacuzzi, bridges and palms but retaining the original pool and paddling pool. There are tennis courts and other leisure facilities. Games, shows and competitions are arranged in July and August. Champs Blancs is set in the centre of the three areas of Agde. There is the old town of Agde with a history going back to Greek and Roman times and known as the 'black pearl of the Mediterranean'. Its striking cathedral is made of black volcanic rock.

Facilities

Modern, fully equipped toilet blocks include 60 en-suite private cabins containing WC, shower and washbasin. Unit for disabled visitors. Washing machines and dryers. Motorcaravan services. Well stocked shop (high season, bread only in low season). Bar (from 1/6). Restaurant (20/6-15/9). Swimming complex (from 8/4 depending on weather; compulsory bracelet € 5). Good play area. Minigolf. Tennis. Multisports court. Off site: Riding 1 km. Beach, golf and bicycle hire 2 km.

Open: 8 April - 30 September.

Directions

From A9 exit 34, follow N312 for Agde, joins the N112 Béziers - Sète road. Cross bridge over river, take first turn signed Rochelongue, turn right at roundabout, next left, then next left (signed Agde). Site on left before another bridge back over N112. GPS: 43.29702, 3.47547

Charges guide

Per unit incl. 2 persons and electricity	€ 16.00 - € 45.00
extra person	€ 10.00

Camping Cheques accepted.

Camping les Champs Blancs ★★★★

Camping les Champs Blancs★★★★ - Route de Rochelongue - 34300 Agde
Tel: 0033 467 94 23 42 - Fax: 0033 467 94 87 81
champs.blancs@wanadoo.fr - www.champs-blancs.fr

For latest campsite news, availability and prices visit
alanrogers.com

Agde
Camping les Romarins

Route du Grau, F-34300 Agde (Hérault) T: 04 67 94 18 59. E: contact@romarins.com
alanrogers.com/FR34420

A small family campsite beside the River Hérault, les Romarins is only 1 km. from a wide sandy beach and 800 metres from the village. With 120 level pitches separated by shrubs, 80 are available for touring units, the rest are taken by mobile homes and chalets (40 to let). Electricity (6A) is available on all pitches, some of which have more shade than others. A pleasant walk beside the river and past the fish quay, takes you to the shops, restaurants and beach of Le Grau. You walk the other way for the town of Agde, famous for its Black Cathedral and Round Lock by which boats gain access to the Canal du Midi.

Facilities	Directions
Two modern toilet blocks are fully equipped. Good facilities for babies and disabled visitors. Motorcaravan services (charged). Bar with snacks. Bread can be ordered. Heated pool. Large playing field and play area at the back of the site (closed at night). Bicycle hire. Multisports court. Outdoor gym equipment. Sports activities and evening entertainment in season. WiFi (charged). Off site: Boat launching 50 m. Shops and restaurants 700 m. Beach 900 m. Riding and golf 2 km. Cap d'Agde and Aqualand 3 km.	From A9 exit 34, follow N112 towards Agde picking up N112. Cross river and take exit for Grau d'Agde and Rochelonge. Turn left at two roundabouts, then straight over next two roundabouts towards river. Left at roundabout beside river following sign for Berges de l'Hérault along riverside (one way). Site is third on left. GPS: 43.29446, 3.45005

Open: 2 April - 1 October.

Charges guide

Per unit incl. 2 persons and electricity	€ 18.00 - € 29.30
extra person	€ 4.40 - € 7.20

Agde
Village Center les 7 Fonts

Route de Sète, F-34300 Agde (Hérault) T: 04 99 57 21 21. E: contact@village-center.com
alanrogers.com/FR34590

If you are seeking a less hectic option, 7 Fonts has a rural feel to it, albeit that it is situated on the edge of the town of Agde, close to the Canal du Midi. A long time ago it was a vineyard but the traditional three storied house with its courtyard (now reception) is the only evidence remaining. The site is now owned by the Village Center Group. It is split into two parts separated by a small road. There are around 300 grass pitches, partially separated by shrubs and with good shade from tall trees. At least half are taken by mobile homes, some of which are for rent.

Facilities	Directions
Two traditional style toilet blocks. Facilities for disabled visitors. Small shop. Bar, simple restaurant and takeaway. Swimming pool complex with water slides and spa bath (1/5-15/9). Hairdressing and beauty salon (1/7-31/8). Bicycle hire. Entertainment programme (1/7-31/8). Mobile homes and equipped tents to rent. Free shuttle bus for beach (high season). WiFi around reception (charged). Off site: Riding, golf, beach and fishing all 4 km.	From autoroute take exit 34 towards Agde and Bessan. Follow N312 (Agde, Vias) then pick up N112 (Agde, Sète). Pass turnings for Agde until road divides. Take left for Agde and Centre Commercial. Site is signed some 250 m. up this road. Turn right after small garden centre. Carefully cross junction to site (narrow entrance). GPS: 43.31157, 3.49844

Open: 27 May - 18 September.

Charges guide

Per unit incl. 2 persons	€ 14.00 - € 34.00

Camping Cheques accepted.

Agde
Camping Le Rochelongue

Route de Rochelongue, F-34300 Aqde (Hérault) T: 04 67 21 25 51. E: le.rochelongue@wanadoo.fr
alanrogers.com/FR34610

Situated between le Grau d'Agde and Cap d'Agde, close to a long sandy beach, this small family site is worth consideration. A total of 106 pitches provide 48 for touring units (most with 10A electricity and water), 23 mobile homes to rent and 30 privately-owned mobile homes. Pitches are of a reasonable size on sandy soil with shade from tall trees. A large, fully equipped toilet block is centrally situated and the rest of the amenities are by the entrance. There is a pleasant pool area near the snack bar, and a shop and launderette beside reception, just outside the entrance.

Facilities	Directions
One fully equipped toilet block includes facilities for children. Washing machine. Shop (1/4-30/10). Bar, snack bar and takeaway (10/6-10/9). Heated pool (01/04-30/10). Children's entertainment (July/Aug). Aquagym and themed evenings in the bar for adults. WiFi. Gas or electric barbecues only. Off site: Beach and bicycle hire 500 m. Riding 1 km. Sailing 1.5 km. Golf and fishing 2 km.	From A9 at exit 3 follow N312 for Agde and follow as it joins N112 Béziers - Sète road. Cross bridge over Hérault river, turn right for Rochelonge. Turn left at next roundabout and right at next one. Site is on left. GPS: 43.279167, 3.481389

Open: 2 April - 30 October.

Charges guide

Per unit incl. 2 persons and electricity	€ 14.00 - € 43.00

For latest campsite news, availability and prices visit
alanrogers.com

Aigues-Mortes
Yelloh! Village la Petite Camargue

B.P. 21, D62, F-30220 Aigues-Mortes (Gard) T: 04 66 53 98 98. E: info@yellohvillage-petite-camargue.com
alanrogers.com/FR30020

This is a large, impressive site (553 pitches) with a huge swimming pool complex and other amenities to match, conveniently situated beside one of the main routes across the famous Camargue. The busy road is an advantage for access but could perhaps be a drawback in terms of traffic, although when we stayed overnight in season it was virtually silent. It offers a variety of good sized pitches on sandy grass, regularly laid out in shady avenues. There are 144 touring pitches (with 6/10A electricity) interspersed amongst more than 300 mobile homes and 145 tour operator pitches.

Facilities

Three toilet blocks provide combined showers and washbasins. Laundry facilities. Motorcaravan service point. Range of shops, bar/restaurant with pizzeria and takeaway. Hairdresser and beauty centre. Large L-shaped swimming pool with jacuzzi. Play area, and children's club. Mini animal park. Tennis. Bicycle hire. Quad bikes. Disco. Diving school. Free bus to the beach (July/Aug). Nightclub (over 16s). WiFi in reception. Off site: Riding adjacent. Fishing 3 km. Nearest beach 3.5 km.

Open: 22 April - 18 September (with all services).

Directions

From A9, exit 26 (Gallargues), towards Le Grau-du-Roi, site 18 km. Continue past Aigues-Mortes on D62, site is 2 km. on the right, just before large roundabout for La Grand-Motte and Le Grau-du-Roi junction. GPS: 43.56307, 4.15888

Charges guide

Per unit incl. 2 persons
and electricity € 19.00 - € 44.00
extra person € 4.00 - € 8.00

Alet-les-Bains
Camping Val d'Aleth

F-11580 Alet-les-Bains (Aude) T: 04 68 69 90 40. E: camping@valdaleth.com
alanrogers.com/FR11110

In the gateway to the upper Aude valley, open all year round, this popular small site is run by Christopher and Christine Cranmer, who offer a warm welcome. The mellow, medieval walls of Alet-les-Bains form one boundary of the site, while on the other and popular with anglers, is the River Aude (fenced for safety). Beyond this is the D118 and a railway which produces noise at times. The 37 mainly small, numbered pitches, around half of which are on hardstandings, all have electricity hook-ups (4-10A) and are separated by hedges and mature trees which give shade.

Facilities

Modern toilet blocks, fully equipped and heated in winter. Facilities for disabled visitors. Washing machine and dryer. Reception with small shop, drinks, wine, beer, use of freezer. Small play area. Mountain bike hire. Internet. Off site: White-water sports. Bus and train services to Carcassonne and Quillan. Shops and restaurants in town, full range at Limoux 10 km. Second weekend in June 'Fête de l'Eau' water festival (with jazz, food and wine).

Open: All year.

Directions

From Carcassonne take D118 south for 32 km. Ignore first sign to Alet (to avoid narrow stone bridge) and after crossing the river, turn into town. Site is 800 m. on the left (signed). GPS: 42.99482, 2.25605

Charges guide

Per unit incl. 2 persons
and electricity € 17.75 - € 20.00
extra person € 3.75 - € 3.95
child (under 10 yrs) € 2.30 - € 2.45

Anduze
Domaine de Gaujac

Boisset-et-Gaujac, F-30140 Anduze (Gard) T: 04 66 61 67 57. E: contact@domaine-de-gaujac.com
alanrogers.com/FR30000

The 293 level, well shaded pitches include 175 for touring, with electricity (4-10A), and 22 are fully serviced. Access to some areas can be difficult for larger units due to narrow winding access roads, trees and hedges. Larger units should ask for lower numbered pitches (1-148) where access is a little easier. In high season this region is dry and hot, thus grass quickly wears off many pitches leaving just a sandy base. There are 12 special hardstanding pitches for motorcaravans near the entrance. The site has a new covered entertainment area and courtyard terrace. Only gas and electric barbecues.

Facilities

Toilet blocks (one heated) include facilities for disabled visitors. Washing machines and dryer. Motorcaravan services. Shop (2/6-27/8). Newsagent. Bar, restaurant and takeaway/crêperie (5/5-15/9). New heated swimming, paddling pool (all season; lifeguard 5/7-15/8) and jacuzzi. Playground, sports field. Tennis. Minigolf. Communal barbecues (charcoal), only gas or electric on pitches. WiFi in bar/terrace area (free). Off site: Fishing 100 m. Riding, golf 8 km. Bicycle hire 10 km. River beach 70 km.

Open: 1 April - 20 September.

Directions

From Alès take N110 towards Montpellier. At St Christol-les-Alès fork right on D910 towards Anduze and in Bagard, at roundabout, turn left on D246 to Boisset et Gaujac. Follow signs to site in 5 km. GPS: 44.03580, 4.02425

Charges guide

Per unit incl. 2 persons
and electricity € 20.50 - € 31.50
Credit cards accepted in high season only.
Camping Cheques accepted.

For latest campsite news, availability and prices visit
alanrogers.com

Argelès-sur-Mer

Camping le Littoral

Route du Littoral, F-66700 Argelès-sur-Mer (Pyrénées-Orientales) T: 02 51 33 17 00.
E: infos@camping-le-littoral.fr **alanrogers.com/FR66060**

Sites with access to the beach are difficult to find and, even though le Littoral is not beside the beach, it is only 800 metres away by footpath. It offers much accommodation in mobile homes as well as 20 good sized, level touring pitches with shade and 6A electricity. An attractive pool area is open from May to September. Argelès is a very popular holiday resort with good sandy beaches. The border with Spain is only 30 km. The site is situated on the north side of Argelès, between the coast road and the beach, so access is good, although there could be some road noise in high season. The site has been taken over by a new group, Camp'Atlantic, and looks smart with a new reception and tarmac roadways. However, there are now fewer touring pitches and the emphasis is on mobile homes with over 127 to let and 105 privately owned. The site is well looked after and the pool area is particularly welcoming.

Facilities

Large modern toilet block, fully equipped and with some washbasins in cabins. Baby bath. Some facilities for disabled visitors. Washing machines. Shop. Bar, restaurant and takeaway (15/6-15/9). Heated swimming pool (May-Sept). Entertainment in high season. Play area. Bicycle hire. Internet. Path to beach. Communal barbecues only. Off site: Tourist train in high season. Aquatic park and adventure park within walking distance.

Open: 30 April - 24 September.

Directions

From A9 take exit 42 (Perpignan-Sud) and follow N114 for Argelès. At exit 10 follow directions for Taxo d'Avall then Plage Nord. Site is clearly signed off coast road in the St Cyprien direction. GPS: 42.580606, 3.032854

Charges guide

Per unit incl. 2 persons
and electricity   € 21.00 - € 44.00
Credit cards accepted.

Anduze

Camping Cévennes-Provence

Corbés-Thoiras, F-30140 Anduze (Gard) T: 04 66 61 73 10. E: marais@camping-cevennes-provence.com
alanrogers.com/FR30200

You are sure of a very warm welcome at this spacious, family owned site. New arrivals are taken on a tour so that they can select a good pitch. There are 250 pitches on the various levels, 200 with electricity (10A). Some are on the level land close to the river and others are scattered on high terraces having privacy and fine views across the Cévennes countryside. The river is very popular for swimming and in a separate section one can enjoy the rough and tumble of small 'rapids'. There are few on-site activities, however, the family is happy to advise visitors who wish to explore off site. There is a special area, away from the main site, where teenagers can safely 'let off steam'. This is easily accomplished in the 30 hectares of this natural and unusual site. The site lighting is turned off at 22.30, to encourage early nights. Young children can enjoy one of the best play areas we have seen. Cleanliness of the whole site, including the toilet blocks, is paramount (there are ten blocks so that no-one has to walk too far).

Facilities

Ten excellent, modern, clean toilet blocks (one heated). Good facilities for disabled visitors. Shop (1/4-1/10). Restaurant, takeaway, bar (1/5-15/9). Good play area. Minigolf. Volleyball. River bathing and fishing. Many off site activities arranged at reception. Internet point. Free WiFi near reception. Charcoal barbecues are not permitted. Communal barbecue. Bicycle hire. Off site: Riding 4 km. Golf 10 km. Adventure and discovery park.

Open: 20 March - 1 October.

Directions

Only viable access. From D907 Anduze, take the D284 alongside the river. Site signed on right about 3 km. from town. Take care on the approach – narrow lane for 100 m., then a narrow bridge, visibility good. GPS: 44.07763, 3.96484

Charges 2012

Per unit incl. 2 persons
and electricity   € 17.90 - € 27.90

Camping-Caravaning "CEVENNES PROVENCE"

At your service for 50 years...

Open from 20/03 to 01/10

Calm, shaded Places with open view Fishing, pedestrian path Swimming in river: direct access and private beach

Corbès - Thoiras F30140 Anduze Gard ✆: 00 334 66 61 73 10 www.camping-cevennes-provence.fr

Camp' Atlantique

Des campings à 2 pas de la plage...

LANGUEDOC-ROUSSILLON

Discover the southern ambiance and its typical villages at the Spanish border, and escape into the Catalan region.

Campsite le Littoral

At campsite le Littoral**** you will enjoy a wide view of the Pyrenees, at only 800m from the beach.

Route du Littoral - 66700 Argeles sur Mer

CAMP'ATLANTIQUE

Les Plantes de la Brunelle - 85560 LONGEVILLE sur MER
Tél: 0033 (0)2 51 33 17 00 - contact@camp-atlantique.com
www.camp-atlantique.com

Argelès-sur-Mer
Camping le Soleil

Route du Littoral, F-66702 Argelès-sur-Mer (Pyrénées-Orientales) T: 04 68 81 14 48.
E: camping.lesoleil@wanadoo.fr **alanrogers.com/FR66040**

Le Soleil is an attractive site with direct access to the sandy beach. It is a busy, popular, family owned site which over the years has developed into a small village. It has over 800 pitches of ample size, of which around 550 are used for touring units, on sandy/grassy ground and with a mixture of trees and shrubs providing plenty of shade, all with electricity (6A). Around 20 fully serviced pitches are to be added. Caravans sometimes need to take care on the narrow access roads. The site has a wide range of amenities, including an impressive pool complex with activities and entertainment for all the family. All facilities are open when the site is open. Spain and the Pyrénées are near enough for excursions.

Facilities

Seven toilet blocks of the type with external access to individual units. Some family cabins with washbasins, showers. Washing machines. Supermarket, general shop, press, tabac. Restaurant. Takeaway. Bar with disco (July/Aug), beach bar. Heated swimming pool complex and entertainment area. Adventure playground. TV room. Internet. WiFi. Tennis. Diving and riding in high season (charge). Dogs are not accepted.

Open: 14 May - 17 September.

Directions

Site is at north end of the beach, about 1 km. from Argelès-Plage village. GPS: 42.57552, 3.04232

Charges guide

Per unit incl. 2 persons and electricity	€ 25.97 - € 40.10
extra person (over 5 yrs)	€ 6.83 - € 10.50

Less 30% in May, June and August.

Argelès-sur-Mer
Camping le Dauphin

Route de Taxo à la Mer, F-66700 Argelès-sur-Mer (Pyrénées-Orientales) T: 04 68 81 17 54.
E: info@campingledauphin.com **alanrogers.com/FR66110**

Near Taxo in the quieter, northern part of Argelès (a somewhat frenzied resort in season), this family owned site on flat, grassy parkland with plenty of tall trees enjoys good views of the Pyrénées from the terrace area surrounding its excellent complex of swimming pools. There are 346 level, grassy, well shaded pitches, all with 10A electricity and some with individual sanitary units. Located some 1.5 km. from the town and beach, there is a regular connecting 'road train' service to and fro throughout the day and evening until midnight.

Facilities

Good central sanitary block with all modern facilities including washbasins en-suite and facilities for disabled visitors and children. A third of the pitches have individual sanitary units. Shops, bar/restaurant, pizzeria with takeaway (all 15/5-4/9). Two swimming pools and paddling pool. Two play areas. Tennis. Multisports courts. Minigolf. Games room. Entertainment programme in high season. Torches useful in some areas. WiFi in restaurant.

Open: 15 May - 17 September.

Directions

Site is on north side of Argelès. From autoroute take exit Perpignan-Nord for Argelès and follow directions for Plage-Nord and Taxo-d'Avall (similarly from the N114). GPS: 42.57229, 3.02167

Charges guide

Per unit incl. 2 persons and electricity	€ 18.00 - € 32.20
extra person	€ 4.00 - € 6.90

Argelès-sur-Mer
Castel Camping les Criques de Porteils

RD114, Corniche de Collioure, F-66701 Argelès-sur-Mer (Pyrénées-Orientales) T: 04 68 81 12 73.
E: contactcdp@lescriques.com **alanrogers.com/FR66150**

This is an amazing site situated on a clifftop with views across the sea to Argelès, against a backdrop of mountains and close to Collioure, the artists' paradise. What more could you ask for? A lot of work has been carried out to improve the facilities here and pitches have been redesigned for easier access. There are around 250 of varying sizes and shapes due to the nature of the terrain, level in places, up and down in others. All have 10A electricity available and either a sea view or views towards the mountains. There are eight small coves accessed by steep steps (gated). There is a new bar and restaurant and some unusual artistic workshops for children. Classical music sessions and guided walks are also available.

Facilities

Two renovated toilet blocks (one can be heated) are fully equipped with super children's room, and all small equipment. Laundry room with Internet point. Motorcaravan service point. Shop. New bar and terraced restaurant with takeaway. Swimming pool. TV/games room. Play area. Golf practice. Tennis. Fishing. Duck pond and small animal area. Only gas barbecues are allowed. WiFi over site. Off site: Collioure and sandy beach at Le Racou (both a 30 minute walk).

Open: 31 March - 20 October.

Directions

Exit A9 at Perpignan Sud or Le Boulou. Head for Argelès to pick up signs for 'Collioure par la Corniche'. Watch for site signs coming into a bend as you come down a hill by hotel. GPS: 42.53508, 3.06854

Charges guide

Per unit incl. 2 persons and electricity	€ 27.00 - € 48.00
extra person	€ 6.00 - € 11.00

For latest campsite news, availability and prices visit
alanrogers.com

Argelès-sur-Mer
Village Center le Neptune

Route du Tamariguer, F-66702 Argelès-sur-Mer (Pyrénées-Orientales) T: 04 99 57 21 21.
E: contact@village-center.com **alanrogers.com/FR66710**

Le Neptune belongs to the Village Centre Group which offers activities for children in the high season, good pool complexes and sports facilities. There is the additional bonus of the sea within 500 m. and a superb sandy beach. The site really comes to life in July and August, but the pool is heated earlier in the season. The accommodation available is mostly mobile homes and when visited there were only 14 touring pitches, and these are due to be used for mobile homes next year. A simple bar/snack bar operates in July and August, also the miniclub and teenagers' club with some entertainment provided.

Facilities

One small but adequate sanitary block. Laundry with washing machine and dryer. Bar, snack bar and fresh bread (July/Aug). Pool complex with slides and paddling pool (Apr-Sept). Football, volleyball and multisport court. Miniclub (4-12 yrs), teenagers' club (13-17 yrs). Sports and entertainment (July/Aug). Off site: Beach 500 m. Bicycle hire nearby.

Open: 3 April - 26 September.

Directions

Exit N114 Junction 10 signed Argelès-sur-Mer. At roundabout follow Argelès. At second roundabout follow direction Pujols. After 1.5 km. go left, signed Plage Centre/Sud. Site on left after 1 km.
GPS: 42.56549, 3.03647

Charges guide

Per unit incl. 2 persons
and electricity   € 18.00 - € 42.00

Balaruc-les-Bains
Camping le Mas du Padre

4 chemin du Mas du Padre, F-34540 Balaruc-les-Bains (Hérault) T: 04 67 48 53 41.
E: contact@mas-du-padre.com **alanrogers.com/FR34100**

Mas du Padre is a pleasant little site run by the Durand family and it makes a good base from which to explore the Sète area or 'take the waters' at Balaruc-les-Bains. Madame Durand speaks excellent English. On a hillside, just 2.5 km. from Balaruc-les-Bains and near the Etang de Thau (famous for oysters), this small site is unusually situated in a residential area that has obviously developed around it over the years. The secluded pitches are of varying sizes and are marked by hedges, mature trees and shrubs. Some are on a very gentle slope and hard ground. There are 112 touring pitches with 6/10A electricity and 18 mobile homes to let.

Facilities

Fully equipped toilet blocks include baby changing area, facilities for disabled campers, washing machines. Reception sells basics. Swimming pool (1/5-30/9), plus one for children. Half-court tennis, boules, mini adventure playground. Sports programme, tournaments, aquarobics, entertainment for children, weekly dance (all high season). WiFi. Torch useful. Off site: Bus service to historic city of Balaruc-les-Bains from outside site. Lake beach, sailing, bicycle hire and riding 2 km. Seaside beach 10 km.

Open: 2 April - 23 October.

Directions

From A9, exit Sète, follow N800 to Balaruc-le-Vieux, first roundabout (D2), second roundabout both following Balaruc-les-Bains/Sète. After 50 m. right for Balaruc-les-Bains, immediately left across road, double back down it (50 m). Immediately right, follow Chemin du Mas du Padre. GPS: 43.45219, 3.69241

Charges guide

Per unit incl. 2 persons
and electricity   € 15.25 - € 38.15

Boisson
Castel Camping le Château de Boisson

Boisson, F-30500 Allègre-les-Fumades (Gard) T: 04 66 24 85 61. E: reception@chateaudeboisson.com
alanrogers.com/FR30070

Château de Boisson is a quiet family site within easy reach of the Cévennes, Ardèche and Provence. The site is hilly and the 178 pitches, with 102 for touring are on two levels. They are separated by neat hedges and a variety of trees providing some shade. All have 6/10A electricity, 28 are fully serviced and seven have personal bathrooms. Rock pegs are essential. The large attractive swimming pools, one indoor (heated all season) with paddling pool and toboggan are near the château in a sunny location at the top of the site. Gas and electric barbecues only. Dogs are not accepted in July/Aug.

Facilities

Two very clean toilet blocks with all necessary facilities including those for disabled visitors. Shop (7/4-15/9). Good restaurant, bar, snacks. Play area. Pools: indoor (all season), outdoor (1/5-22/9). Bridge tournaments in low season. Painting classes. Tennis. Boules. WiFi over site (charged). Off site: Fishing 2 km. Riding 4 km. Allègre les Fumades (thermal baths and Casino) 5 km. Alès 16 km. Vallon Pont d'Arc and Ardèche gorges 30 km

Open: 7 April - 22 September.

Directions

From Alès take D16 northeast through Salindres and Auzon. After Auzon turn right across river, immediately left, signed Barjac and site. Shortly turn right to site entrance. Only route for trailers and motorcaravans. Do not drive through the village of Boissons. GPS: 44.20967, 4.25625

Charges guide

Per unit incl. 2 persons
and electricity   € 20.40 - € 56.00

We can book this site for you! alan rogers travel — Call 01580 214000

For latest campsite news, availability and prices visit
alanrogers.com

Argelès-sur-Mer
Camping la Sirène

Route de Taxo à la Mer, F-66702 Argelès-sur-Mer (Pyrénées-Orientales) T: 04 68 81 04 61.
E: contact@camping-lasirene.fr **alanrogers.com/FR66560**

From the moment you step into the hotel-like reception area you realise that this large site offers the holiday maker everything they could want in a well managed and convenient location close to Argelès-sur-Mer and the beaches. The 740 mobile homes and chalets vary in standard but all are less than five years old, very clean, comfortable and located on neat tidy pitches. There are also some touring pitches. In the summer there are 170 staff on duty to ensure your stay is as enjoyable as they can make it. All the shops and amenities are near reception making the accommodation areas peaceful and relaxing.

Facilities

Restaurant, bar and takeaway. Large shop (all season). Large aqua park, paddling pools, slides, jacuzzi. Games room. Multisports field, tennis, archery, minigolf, football. Theatre, evening entertainment, discos, show time spectacular. Riding. Bicycle hire. Off site: Resort of Argelès-sur-Mer with beaches, karting, 10-pin bowling, amusement park and the site's private Emeraude Beach Club, all 2 km. Interesting old town of Collioure close by.

Open: 17 April - 26 September.

Directions

Leave A9 motorway at exit 42, take D114, towards Argelès. Leave D114, exit 10, follow signs for Plage Nord. Site signed after first roundabout and on right 2 km. after last one. GPS: 42.57093, 3.02906

Charges guide

Per unit incl. 1-3 persons and electricity	€ 26.00 - € 43.00
extra person	€ 6.00 - € 9.00
child (under 5 yrs)	€ 4.00 - € 6.00

Argelès-sur-Mer
Camping l'Hippocampe

Route de Taxo à la Mer, F-66702 Argelès-sur-Mer (Pyrénées-Orientales) T: 04 68 81 04 61.
E: contact@camping-lasirene.fr **alanrogers.com/FR66570**

A sister site to la Sirène just opposite, this site has some touring pitches along with 170 mobile home and chalet pitches and is aimed at families with young children and adults looking for a quieter site. The mobile homes and chalets are all modern, well maintained and have space around them to provide privacy. The pool on site is dedicated to smaller children and is a great place for them to gain confidence in the water whilst still being able to play. Entertainment, shops, bars and the full range of activities offered by la Sirène, just across the road.

Facilities

Pool and laundry. Shop, small bar (all season). All other facilities are at la Sirène just across the road. Riding. Bicycle hire. Off site: Karting, 10-pin bowling, amusement park within 1 km. Beach at Argelès-sur-Mer within 2 km. Fishing 4 km. Golf 7 km.

Open: 17 April - 26 September.

Directions

Leave A9 junction 42. Take D114, Argelès road. Leave D114 junction 10, follow signs for Plage Nord. Site signed after the first roundabout, on left 2 km. after last roundabout. GPS: 42.5705, 3.03065

Charges guide

Per unit incl. 1-3 persons and electricity	€ 26.00 - € 43.00
extra person	€ 6.00 - € 9.00
child (under 5 yrs)	€ 4.00 - € 6.00
dog	free

Argelès-sur-Mer
Camping le Bois du Valmarie

F-66702 Argelès-sur-Mer (Pyrénées-Orientales) T: 04 68 81 09 92. E: contact@camping-lasirene.fr
alanrogers.com/FR66590

Pitches here are exclusively for mobile home and chalet accommodation. Le Bois du Valmarie is a member of the same group of sites as la Sirène (FR66560) and l'Hippocampe (FR66570). The site has 181 pitches, the majority of which are available for booking (none available for touring) and is located south of the port beside Racou beach. The site has a pleasant woodland location and a range of amenities including a large swimming pool complex with waterslides and a separate children's pool. The sea is just 50 m. from the site entrance with a sandy beach and within easy walking distance. The site has its own bar and a good restaurant but visitors are welcome at la Sirène to enjoy the entertainment and activities on offer. Popular with tour operators.

Facilities

Supermarket. Restaurant. Bar. Beach shop. Takeaway food. Swimming pool with waterslides and children's pool. Play area. Mobile homes for rent. Off site: Argelès town centre 3 km. Diving club. Blue Bear activity club. Emeraude Beach Club. Fishing 2 km. Riding 4 km. Golf 7 km.

Open: 7 April - 28 September.

Directions

Leave autoroute at Perpignan Sud exit and join the N114 southbound toward Argelès. Take exit 13 and follow signs to Le Racou. Site is well signed from here. GPS: 42.53784, 3.05445

Charges guide

Contact site.

For latest campsite news, availability and prices visit
alanrogers.com

CAMPINGS
CLUBS ★★★★
ARGELÈS/MER
MÉDITERRANÉE

LA SIRÈNE • LE BOIS DE VALMARIE • L'HIPPOCAMPE

Quick and easy, your reservation in just one click on:

route de Taxo
66702 Argelès-sur-Mer
Tél. : +33 (0)4 68 81 04 61
Fax : +33 (0)4 68 81 69 74
e-mail : contact@camping-lasirene.fr

www.camping-lasirene.fr

We can book this site for you! alan rogers travel

Call 01580 214000

Brissac
Domaine d'Anglas

F-34190 Brissac (Hérault) T: 04 67 73 70 18. E: contact@camping-anglas.com

alanrogers.com/FR34600

In the upper Hérault valley to the south of the Cévennes mountains, Camping d'Anglas is a delightful small site. The top part of the site is on quite stony ground with pitches divided by vines and mixed trees that provide a degree of shade. The lower part is more open, with some mature trees and pitches are not clearly divided but it makes a wonderful spot to camp. With 100 pitches in total, there are 78 for touring units. A stream runs through the site, dry when we visited, but it is quite possibly a torrent in winter time. Wooden bridges allow access to the toilet blocks on the other side.

Facilities

Two toilet blocks provide all necessary facilities. Baby bath. Facilities for disabled visitors but some up and down walking on site. Washing machine. Shop for bread and basics. Communal barbecue. Playing field. Wine evening. WiFi (free). Off site: Register at reception for canoeing, climbing, karting, mountain biking, walks and adventure tours through the woods. On Thursday (1/7-31/8) and Saturday (30/4-30/6) evenings tour the owner's vineyard, taste the wines and sample the 'assiettes du terroir'.

Open: 30 April - 5 September.

Directions

From Montpellier follow the D986 north towards Ganges. After about 40 km, just before entering the village of St Bauzille de Putois turn right signed Brissac. Cross the Hérault river over a narrow bridge and pick up site signs. GPS: 43.876056, 3.716083

Charges guide

Per unit incl. 2 persons and electricity	€ 12.00 - € 27.80
extra person	€ 3.50 - € 5.80

Canet-en-Roussillon
Kawan Village Caravaning Ma Prairie

1 avenue des Coteaux, F-66140 Canet-en-Roussillon (Pyrénées-Orientales) T: 04 68 73 26 17. E: ma.prairie@wanadoo.fr **alanrogers.com/FR66020**

Ma Prairie is an excellent site and its place in this guide goes back over 30 years. Then it was simply a field surrounded by vineyards. The trees planted then have now matured and more continue to be planted, along with colourful shrubs providing a comfortable, park-like setting with some 200 touring pitches, all with electricity and 15 with water and drainage. There are also 50 mobile homes available to rent and ten privately owned. It is a peaceful haven some 3 km. back from the sea but within walking distance of Canet village itself. The Gil family still provide a warm welcome and reception boasts an impressive international collection of hats, helmets and uniform caps. The restaurant and bar is across the road and overlooks a modern, attractive pool complex and wonderful old palm tree. Today there is Internet access, some mobile homes and modern housing has crept up but there are still vineyards close and the wine sold in reception is from the family vineyard.

Facilities

Fully equipped toilet blocks, baby bath. Washing machines and dryers. No shop but bread can be ordered. Covered snack bar and takeaway. Air-conditioned bar and restaurant. Large adult pool, splendid children's pool. Multisports court. TV. Amusement machines. Busy daily activity and entertainment programme in season for children aged 6-12. WiFi throughout (charged) and Internet access in reception. Charcoal barbecues not permitted. Communal barbecue. Off site: Supermarket 400 m. Riding 600 m. Sandy beach 3 km. Golf 6 km.

Open: 5 May - 25 September.

Directions

Leave autoroute A9 at Perpignan North towards Barcarès. Site access is from the D11 Perpignan road (exit 5), close to the junction with D617 in Canet-Village. Go under bridge, right at roundabout then left to site. GPS: 42.70135, 2.99968

Charges guide

Per unit incl. 2 persons and electricity	€ 21.50 - € 43.00
extra person	€ 4.00 - € 8.50
child (4-9 yrs)	free - € 6.00
Camping Cheques accepted.	

ma prairie ★★★★

Camping-Club Ma Prairie
1, avenue des Coteaux
66140 Canet-en-Roussillon

Tel. +33 (0)4 68 73 26 17 - ma.prairie@wanadoo.fr - www.maprairie.com

For latest campsite news, availability and prices visit

alanrogers.com

Canet-en-Roussillon
Yelloh! Village le Brasilia

544

B.P. 204, F-66141 Canet-en-Roussillon (Pyrénées-Orientales) T: 04 68 80 23 82. E: info@lebrasilia.fr
alanrogers.com/FR66070

Situated across the yacht harbour from the upmarket resort of Canet-Plage, le Brasilia is an impressive, well managed family site directly beside the beach. It is pretty, neat and well kept with an amazingly wide range of facilities – indeed, it is camping at its best. There are 428 neatly hedged touring pitches, all with electricity (6-10A) and 315 with water and drainage. They vary in size from 80 to 120 sq.m. and some of the longer pitches are suitable for two families together. With a range of shade from pines and flowering shrubs, less on pitches near the beach, there are neat access roads (sometimes narrow for large units). There are also 161 pitches with mobile homes and chalets to rent (the new ones have their own gardens). The sandy beach here is busy, with a beach club (you can hire windsurfing boards) and a naturist section is on the beach to the west of the site. A completely new pool complex is planned with pools catering for all ages and hydrotherapy facilities for adults and all overlooked by its own snack bar and restaurant. The village area of the site offers a range of shops, a busy restaurant and bar, entertainment (including a night club) and clubs for children of all ages. In fact you do not need to stir from the site which is almost a resort in itself. It does have a nice, lively atmosphere but is orderly and well run. If you would like to visit Canet-Plage, a free tourist train runs in summer and a small ferry crosses the harbour. A member of Yelloh! Village and Leading Campings group.

Facilities

Ten modern sanitary blocks are very well equipped and maintained, with British style WCs (some Turkish) and washbasins in cabins. Good facilities for children and for disabled visitors. Laundry room. Motorcaravan services. Range of shops. Gas supplies. Bars and restaurant. New pool complex (heated). Play areas. Sports field. Tennis. Sporting activities. Library, games and video room. Hairdresser. Internet café and WiFi. Daily entertainment programme. Bicycle hire. Fishing. ATM. Exchange facilities. Post office. Weather forecasts. Only gas or electric barbecues are allowed. Off site: Boat launchng and sailing 500 m. Riding 5 km. Golf 12 km.

Open: 21 April - 29 September.

Directions

From A9 exit 41 (Perpignan Centre, Rivesaltes) follow signs for Le Barcarès and Canet on D83 for 10 km. then for Canet (D81). At first Canet roundabout, turn fully back on yourself (Sainte-Marie) and watch for Brasilia sign almost immediately on right.
GPS: 42.70467, 3.03483

Charges guide

Per unit incl. 2 persons	
and electricity (6A)	€ 23.00 - € 55.00
extra person	€ 6.00 - € 9.00
child (3-6 yrs)	free - € 8.50
dog (max. 2)	€ 4.00

L E B R A S I L I A

CAMPING-VILLAGE
CANET-EN-ROUSSILLON - FRANCE
★ ★ ★ ★ ★
FONDÉ EN 1964

Your peninsula, your secret

Le Brasilia has chosen as its home port a beautiful, peaceful beach located at the far end of Canet-en-Roussillon. There, between the river and the port, in the hollow of a deep pine forest with its Mediterranean scents, Le Brasilia will reveal to you all the little secrets of well-being and the good life. The delightful Seychellois atmosphere of the 'Archipel' water park will immediately transport you to the Tropics. Our village is a garden of nature where you can get away from it all, and yet so much closer to your dream holidays.

Comfortable pitches, rental of cottages and bungalows, pool heated out of season, tropical water park, cardio-fitness training room, multi-sports pitches, entertainment, shops, disco, bar restaurant, cabaret, children's clubs, and so much more. All our shops and services are open throughout the whole time that the site is open.

2, avenue des Anneaux du Roussillon - 66140 Canet-en-Roussillon - France
Tél. : +33 (0)4 68 80 23 82 - Fax : +33 (0)4 68 73 32 97
info@lebrasilia.fr - www.brasilia.fr

yelloh! VILLAGE

The Leading Campings of Europe

429

For latest campsite news, availability and prices visit
alanrogers.com

Canet-en-Roussillon
Camping Mar Estang

Route de Saint-Cyprien, F-66140 Canet-en-Roussillon (Pyrénées-Orientales) T: 04 68 80 35 53.
E: contactme@marestang.com **alanrogers.com/FR66090**

Le Mar Estang is a large, impressive, 'all singing, all dancing' site with something for everyone. Situated on the edge of Canet, between the Etang (part of the Réserve Naturelle de Canet/Saint Nazaire) and the sea, there is access to the sandy beach from the site by two tunnels under the road. If you don't fancy the beach, the site has not one but two attractive pool complexes linked by a bridge. They are amazing, providing slides, togoggans, jacuzzi, paddling pool and a heated pool, all with lifeguards. You can swim seriously, learn to swim or scuba dive or just enjoy the fun pools. Who needs the beach! There are 600 pitches in total, some 300 for touring units, with 6A electricity, and some degree of shade, on sandy ground. The rest are used by tour operators and by site-owned mobile homes to rent. A very wide range of activities and entertainment is organised all season, with children's clubs in high season and a beach club for watersports. Children and teenagers would have a great time here and parents would enjoy Canet Plage with its esplanade, shops and restaurants. It is quite a smart resort watched over by Mount Canigou with its snowy peak.

Facilities

Nine well equipped sanitary blocks are well placed around the site. Facilities for babies. Laundry. Motorcaravan service point. Shops, bars, restaurant and takeaway all open when site is open. Swimming pools with lifeguards, jacuzzi and solarium. Fitness club. Children's clubs. Artistic workshops (pottery, crafts etc). Daily sports and entertainment programme. Day trips. Evening entertainment with cabaret. Disco. Communal barbecue. Sailing club. Beach club. Tennis. Bicycle hire. Play areas. WiFi. Direct access to beach. Off site: Riding nearby. Rafting, canoeing and quad bike treks by arrangement. Canet 500 m. with tourist train in high season. Perpignan 10 km. Collioure, Port Vendres and the Spanish border.

Open: 21 April - 15 September.

Directions

Take exit 41 from A9 autoroute and follow signs for Canet. On outskirts of town follow signs for St Cyprien/Plage Sud. Site is very clearly signed on southern edge of Canet Plage.
GPS: 42.6757, 3.03135

Charges guide

Per unit incl. 2 persons	
and electricity	€ 20.00 - € 44.00
extra person	€ 7.00 - € 13.00
child (0-5 yrs)	free - € 7.00
dog	free - € 4.00

Canet-en-Roussillon
Camping les Peupliers

Avenue des Anneaux du Roussillon, F-66141 Canet-en-Roussillon (Pyrénées-Orientales) T: 04 68 80 35 87.
E: contact@camping-les-peupliers.fr **alanrogers.com/FR66720**

Camping les Peupliers is situated in the harbour area 500 m. from a fine sandy beach. It is a neat, tidy and well organised site with shade from a mixture of tall trees and shrubs. There is an attractive pool complex here with several water slides, a spa bath and a shallower area for children. It is a lively site in peak season with music evenings and various games and competitions. There are 245 pitches in total, with 124 level, grass pitches for touring units. Most are supplied with 10A electricity. Mobile homes are available for rent. The bar/restaurant is the focal point of the site, and also hosts many of les Peupliers' social activities. Although the beach is the big draw here, Canet is just 45 km. from the Spanish border, and the foothills of the Pyrenees are also within easy reach. The snow capped summit of the Canigou can be seen for much of the year. 'Le train jaune' (named after the yellow and red Catalan flag) passes through Bolquère-Eyne, France's highest railway station.

Facilities

Excellent water park with water slides. Bar and snack bar. Shop. Games room. Play area. Tourist information. Activity and entertainment programme. WiFi. Communal barbecue. Mobile homes for rent. Off site: Nearest beach 500m. Fishing and boat launching 200 m. Golf 600 m. Riding 1 km. Spanish border 45 km.

Open: 21 May - 17 September.

Directions

From the A9 motorway take exit 41 and follow signs for Le Barcarès and Caneton D83 for 10 km. Then follow the D81 towards Canet-en-Roussillon. At the first Canet roundabout (Ch. de Gaulle) turn fully back on yourself to Barcarès-Ste Marie. Turn right towards 'ZA Las Bigues'. At the end of this road, turn right, then first left (following signs for Pole nautique) and the site is a further 800 m.
GPS: 42.706793, 3.030447

Charges guide

Per unit incl. 2 persons	
and electricity	€ 28.00 - € 44.50
extra person	€ 5.50 - € 6.50
child (1-4 yrs)	free - € 4.50
dog	€ 3.00 - € 5.50

For latest campsite news, availability and prices visit
alanrogers.com

Mar Estang

★★★★

Route de St Cyprien
66140 Canet Plage
www.marestang.com
contactme@marestang.com
TEL: +33(0)4 68 80 35 53
FAX: +33(0)4 68 73 32 94

LES CRIQUES DE PORTEILS

★★★★★

RD 114 - Corniche de Collioure
66701 Argelès-sur-Mer
www.lescriques.com
contactcdp@lescriques.com
TEL: +33(0)4 68 81 12 73
FAX: +33(0)4 68 95 85 76

LES CASTELS
★★★★
Hôtellerie de Plein Air

Cap d'Agde
Yelloh! Village Mer et Soleil

Chemin de Notre Dame à Saint Martin, Rochelongue, F-34300 Cap d'Agde (Hérault) T: 04 67 94 21 14.
E: contact@camping-mer-soleil.com **alanrogers.com/FR34290**

Close to Cap d'Agde, this is a popular, well equipped site with many facilities. The pool area is particularly attractive with large palm trees, a whirlpool and slides as well as a gym and wellness centre. An upstairs restaurant overlooks this area and the entertainment stage next to it. All ages are catered for and evening entertainment in July and August includes live shows. There are 477 pitches, around half taken by mobile homes and chalets (some to let, some privately owned). The touring pitches are hedged and have good shade from tall trees, all with 6A electricity. From the back of the site, a 1 km. long path leads to the white sandy beach at Rochelongue. A smart new reception has been built and a state-of-the-art balnéo can be found at the front of the site offering a wide range of treatments. It is open for public use with a 10% reduction offered to campers. The design inside is very impressive with a central grass area and fountain. The hydro pools are under a church-like roof and the massage rooms, sauna and Turkish bath are off to the sides providing a very calm and relaxed atmosphere.

Facilities

One large toilet block plus two smaller ones are fully equipped. Attractive units for children with small toilets, etc. Units for disabled visitors. Washing machine. Shop. Bar and restaurant. Heated swimming pools. Gym. State-of-the-art balnéo with hydro pools, massage rooms, sauna and Turkish bath. Hairdresser. Play area. Tennis. Archery. Sporting activities and evening entertainment. Miniclub. WiFi (charged). Off site: Sports and pool complex opposite site. Bus stop outside site. Beach and riding 1 km. Béziers airport within easy reach.

Open: 31 March - 6 October.

Directions

From A9 exit 34, follow N312 for Agde. It joins the N112 Béziers - Sète road. Cross bridge over Hérault river and turn right for Rochelongue. Take the second exit at next roundabout and site is a little further on the right. GPS: 43.286183, 3.478

Charges 2012

Per unit incl. 2 persons	
and electricity	€ 17.00 - € 41.00
extra person	€ 4.00 - € 8.00
child (3-7 yrs)	free - € 7.00

Carcassonne
Camping de la Cité

Route de Saint-Hilaire, F-11000 Carcassonne (Aude) T: 04 68 10 01 00. E: camping@carcassonne.fr
alanrogers.com/FR11100

A visit to the medieval cité of Carcassonne is a must and Campéole de la Cité is within walking distance along a shaded footpath beside a stream. The majority of pitches are very large, separated by bushes and with good shade. There are also some undefined places under trees for small tents. In total there are 200, with 143 for touring, 95 having 10A electricity and the rest used for mobile homes and chalets to hire. Because of its situation it is very popular and you need to arrive early in the high season. A swimming pool, snack bar and small shop make this a very comfortable and useful site.

Facilities

Three traditional, fully equipped toilet blocks, with (few) mainly Turkish toilets. Laundry. Motorcaravan service point. Fridge hire. Shop, bar and snack bar/takeaway meals (limited hours outside July/Aug). TV and games room. Multisport pitch. Swimming and paddling pools (15/6-15/9). Play area. Communal barbecue (only gas or electric permitted on pitches). Chalets and mobile homes to rent. WiFi (charged). Off site: Golf and bicycle hire 2 km. Riding 3 km. Lake with beaches 6 km.

Open: 2 April - 15 October.

Directions

From A61 autoroute take exit 24 onto N113 following signs for La Cité. Site is well signed (look carefully) from all roads into the city. Try not to arrive between 12.00 and 14.00 outside July/Aug. Reception will be closed with queues blocking the entrance! GPS: 43.200315, 2.353767

Charges guide

Per unit incl. 2 persons	
and electricity	€ 20.10 - € 29.00

For latest campsite news, availability and prices visit
alanrogers.com

Castelnaudary
Yelloh! Village le Bout du Monde

Ferme de Rhodes, Verdun-en-Lauragais, F-11400 Castelnaudary (Aude) T: 04 68 94 95 96.
E: info@yellohvillage-leboutdumonde.com **alanrogers.com/FR11230**

Le Bout du Monde is a really special place at the heart of the Montagne Noire, on the edge of the Haut Languedoc regional park. Here you can experience life as it used to be. Children help with the animals on the farm, roam the woods, swim in the natural pool and learn to make bread and pottery. Grown ups have a chance to unwind in wonderful natural surroundings. This small site is a member of the Yelloh! Village group and at present there are 26 large grass pitches with water and 8A electricity, most hedged. The toilet blocks are in keeping with the ethos; one is in a converted pigeon house, the other, under a turf roof, has a bees' nest behind glass – both however have modern fittings!

Facilities	Directions
Two fully equipped toilet bocks. Washing machine. Small shop, wine bar for simple food. Auberge (all year). Takeaway food. Swimming pool and natural swimming pool. Entertainment and activity programme. Archery. Sports field. Fishing lake. Children's farm. Electric barbecues only. Mobile homes for rent. WiFi. Off site: Riding 7 km. GR7 long-distance footpath. Haut Languedoc Regional Park. Sailing. Canoeing. **Open:** 6 April - 30 September.	From A61 take Castelnaudary exit and proceed to Castelnaudary. Here, take D103 towards Saissac. After passing through St Papoul, turn left to join the D803 to Verdun-en-Lauragais. Join the northbound D903 (narrow uphill road) and site is well signed with distinctive goat logo. GPS: 43.37671, 2.07463

Charges 2012

Per unit incl. 2 persons and electricity	€ 17.00 - € 33.00

Crespian
Kawan Village le Mas de Reilhe

Chemin du Mas de Reilhe, F-30260 Crespian (Gard) T: 04 66 77 82 12. E: info@camping-mas-de-reilhe.fr
alanrogers.com/FR30080

This is a pleasant family site in the heart of the Gard region with a favourable climate. There are 95 pitches, 70 for tourers, 57 have electricity (6/10A), 25 also have water and waste water and some of the upper ones may require long leads. The large lower pitches are separated by tall poplar trees and hedges, close to the main facilities but may experience some road noise. The large terraced pitches on the hillside are scattered under mature pine trees, some with good views, more suited to tents and trailer tents but with their own modern sanitary facilities. The heated swimming pool is in a sunny position and overlooked by the attractive bar/restaurant. There are no shops in the village, the nearest being in the medieval city of Sommières 10 km. away (and well worth a visit). From here you can explore the Cévennes gorges, enjoy the Mediterranean beaches, visit the Petite Camargue or Nîmes with its Roman remains, and other old Roman cities. The entertainment in July and August is mainly for children with just the occasional competition and musical evening for adults.

Facilities	Directions
Excellent, very clean toilet facilities with facilities for campers with disabilities. Dishwashing and laundry. Washing machine. Motorcaravan services. Limited shop (bread to order). Bar, takeaway, restaurant (1/5-16/9). Small play area on grass. Pétanque. Heated swimming pool (27/4-16/9). Internet access. WiFi over site (charged). Only gas or electric barbecues on pitches; communal barbecue. Bicycle hire. Off site: Tennis 500 m. Fishing 3 km. Riding 5 km. Golf 25 km. **Open:** 14 April - 16 September.	From the A9 take exit 25, Nimes-ouest signed Alès, then D999 towards Le Vigan (about 23 km). Turn north on the D6110, site shortly on right at southern edge of Crespian. GPS: 43.87931, 4.09637

Charges guide

Per unit incl. 2 persons and electricity	€ 20.00 - € 26.00
extra person	€ 5.00 - € 6.00
Camping Cheques accepted.	

LE MAS DE REILHE ★★★★
Camping Caravaning

"Situated between the Cevennes Mountains & the Mediterranean sea, a small charming & shaded camp site in the sun". Mobil-homes, chalets and bungalows A. Trigano to rent.

- Heated swimming-pool 140 m³ (27/4 - 16/9)
- Restaurant, pizzeria & takeaway (1/5 - 16/9)
- Animations for children (July - August)
- New heated sanitary blocks

Tel : 0033 466 77 82 12 - Fax : 0033 466 80 26 50
E-mail : info@camping-mas-de-reilhe.fr
Website : www.camping-mas-de-reilhe.fr

For latest campsite news, availability and prices visit
alanrogers.com

Clapiers
Camping le Plein Air des Chênes
Route de Castelnau, F-34830 Clapiers (Hérault) T: 04 67 02 02 53. E: pleinairdeschenes@free.fr
alanrogers.com/FR34230

Situated just outside the village of Clapiers, about 5 km. from the interesting city of Montpellier, yet merely 15 km. from the beach, this is one of few campsites which provides something for everyone, especially for those who prefer to spend their holidays without ever leaving the campsite. There are 130 touring pitches with 6A electricity (some large with individual toilet cabin), all in a shaded terraced setting. The site boasts an amazing landscaped swimming pool complex, with multi-lane toboggan, four pools and surrounding facilities such as bars and restaurants. It is also open to the public and obviously very popular and it could be noisy. There are chalets, bungalows and mobile homes to rent.

Facilities

Three well equipped modern toilet blocks provide washbasins in cabins and facilities for disabled visitors. Three washing machines. Restaurant open to the public (all year). Bar, pool side bar, café/takeaway (1/6-15/9). Swimming pools (1/6-15/9). Four tennis courts. Multisports court. Play area. Miniclub, evening entertainment in main season. Internet. Off site: Historic city of Montpellier 5 km.

Open: All year.

Directions

Site is north of Montpellier, 8 km. from A9. Exit 28 on N113 towards Montpellier passing Vendargues. Follow signs for Millau on D65, then Clapiers and follow site signs. GPS: 43.65135, 3.89607

Charges guide

Per unit incl. 2 persons and electricity	€ 23.00 - € 37.00

Camping Cheques accepted.

Florac
Camping le Pont du Tarn
Route de Pont de Montvert (RN106), F-48400 Florac (Lozère) T: 04 66 45 18 26.
E: contact@camping-florac.com **alanrogers.com/FR48100**

Le Pont du Tarn, just outside Florac and close to the River Tarn, is an excellent base for touring this beautiful Cévennes region of France. There are 181 pitches with 28 pitches occupied by mobile homes and chalets (available for rent). The pitches are large, level, grassy and well shaded. All have electricity (10A) and 36 are fully serviced. Access to this site and on-site is good for large outfits. Leisure amenities include a swimming pool, a paddling pool, minigolf and a sports area. A children's club is also operated in peak season. Only gas and electric barbecues allowed on site (communal one available).

Facilities

The clean toilet facilities are housed in older-style, heated buildings, with preset showers. Facilities for babies and disabled visitors. Dishwashing and laundry sinks. Shop. Bar/restaurant/takeaway (10/5-30/8). Swimming pool, paddling pool (8/5-30/9). Sports area. Minigolf. Play area. Motorcaravan services. River beach. Entertainment (high season). WiFi (free). Off site: Florac with bars, restaurants and shops 2.5 km. Bicycle hire 3 km. Riding 12 km.

Open: 1 April - 1 November.

Directions

Florac is 56 km northwest of Alès on N106. Bypass Florac and at roundabout turn right onto D998, signed Pont de Montvert, site shortly on left. GPS: 44.33569, 3.589729

Charges 2012

Per unit incl. 2 persons and electricity	€ 15.70 - € 22.20
extra person	€ 3.20 - € 4.00

Font-Romeu
Huttopia Font-Romeu

Route de Mont-Louis, F-66120 Font-Romeu (Pyrénées-Orientales) T: 04 68 30 09 32.
E: font-romeu@huttopia.com **alanrogers.com/FR66250**

This is a large, open site of some seven hectares, with 125 touring pitches (100 with 10A electricity), nestling on the side of the mountain at the entrance to Font-Romeu. This part of the Pyrenees offers some staggering views and the famous Mont Louis is close by. An ideal base for climbing, hiking and cycling, it would also provide a good stopover for a night or so whilst travelling between Spain and France, or to and from Andorra. The terraced pitches are easily accessed, with those dedicated to caravans and motorcaravans at the top of the site, whilst tents go on the lower slopes. Trees provide shade to many of the pitches from the sun, which can be quite hot at this altitude.

Facilities

Two toilet blocks are traditional in style, bright and clean with modern fittings. Toilet for children and good facilities for disabled visitors. Washing machines and dryers at each block. Shop (25/5-16/9). Bar, restaurant, takeaway (all July/Aug). Outdoor heated swimming pool (25/5-16/9). Large games hall. Only electric barbecues are permitted. Max. 1 dog. Off site: The small town of Font-Romeu is very near with shops and banking facilities. Beach 8 km.

Open: 25 May - 16 September.

Directions

Font-Romeu is on D118, some 12 km. after it branches off N116 heading west, just after Mont Louis. The site is just before the town, on the left and accessed off the car park. GPS: 42.51511, 2.05183

Charges guide

Per unit with 2 persons and electricity	€ 19.70 - € 29.70
extra person	€ 5.20 - € 6.60

We can book this site for you! Call 01580 214000 alanrogers travel

For latest campsite news, availability and prices visit
alanrogers.com

Frontignan
Camping les Tamaris
140 avenue d'Ingril, F-34110 Frontignan-Plage (Hérault) T: 04 67 43 44 77. E: les-tamaris@wanadoo.fr
alanrogers.com/FR34440

This is a super site, unusually situated on a strip of land that separates the sea from the étang, or inland lake, and therefore Fontignan Ville from Fontignan Plage. The design of the site is unusual which adds to its attractiveness. The pitches are laid out in hexagons divided by tall hedging and colourful shrubs. In total, there are 250 pitches with 100 taken by mobile homes which are let by the site. All are 'grand confort' with 10A electricity, water and waste water and on level sandy grass. Direct access to the sandy beach is possible via three gates.

Facilities	Directions
Three modern toilet blocks with some en-suite showers and washbasins. Excellent facilities for children. Unit for disabled visitors. Motorcaravan service point. Shop, bar, restaurant, takeaway, swimming pool (all season). Hairdresser. Gym. Play area. Miniclub. Archery. Bicycle hire. Internet access in reception and WiFi throughout (free). Entertainment for all ages. Off site: Riding 150 m. Sailing 1 km. Boat launching 2.5 km. Golf 15 km.	From the north on A9 take exit 32 and follow N112 towards Sète and Frontignan. After 16 km. ignore sign for Frontignan town and continue to Frontignan-Plage following site signs along the road between the sea and étang. GPS: 43.44970, 3.80603
Open: 3 April - 22 September.	**Charges 2012**

Per unit incl. 2 persons
and all services   € 25.00 - € 48.00
No credit cards.

Frontignan
Village Center l'Europe
Vic la Gardiole (CD114), F-34110 Frontignan (Hérault) T: 04 99 57 21 21. E: contact@village-center.com
alanrogers.com/FR34480

Situated between Montpellier and Sète and surrounded by vineyards which produce the Muscat wine, l'Europe could make an interesting holiday venue. There are 293 pitches, some for privately owned mobile homes but the majority featuring a range of chalets and mobile homes to rent. All the pitches are level and of reasonable size with good shade from flowering hedges. The focus is very much on families and the site boasts an excellent play area and a rather special pool for children. There could be some noise from the nearby railway.

Facilities	Directions
Fully equipped sanitary facilities. Laundry. Shop. Bar, restaurant and takeaway (June-Sept; hours may vary). Two swimming pools, one with toboggan and paddling pool (mid June-Sept). Large play area. Shuttle bus to beach (July/Aug). Miniclub. Sports activities. Evening entertainment. Bicycle hire. Internet access. Off site: Fishing 200 m. Riding 3 km. Beach 3.5 km. Boat launching 5 km.	From the A9 take exit 32 for Saint-Jean de Védas, then N112 (Séte). After Mireval, follow signs for Vic la Gardiole taking second left on CD114. This is a small road. Site is 800 m. on the right (park on the left). GPS: 43.49173, 3.77932
Open: 30 April - 7 September.	**Charges guide**

Contact the site for details.
No credit cards.

Langogne
Camping les Terrasses du Lac de Naussac
Lac de Naussac, F-48300 Langogne (Lozère) T: 04 66 69 29 62. E: info@naussac.com
alanrogers.com/FR48060

With friendly, family owners, this very spacious campsite and hotel complex is on the side of a steep hill at nearly 1,000 m. altitude (nights can be cold). There are 180 good sized, grassy, sloping pitches, often with part hardstanding (165 for touring). All have 6/10A electricity and many have panoramic views over the lake and surrounding hills. There are small trees on site offering a little shade. The lake offers a wide range of water based activities, notably sailing and fishing. The Lac de Naussac is the largest in the Lozère and this site has direct access to the lake.

Facilities	Directions
Three modern and well maintained, newly refurbished toilet blocks. Motorcaravan service point. Shop (1/5-30/9). Restaurant/takeaway in hotel. Swimming pool (1/6-30/9). Lively entertainment programme in peak season with children's club but no discos. Play area. Communal barbecue area. Gas and electric barbecues only. Internet point and WiFi. Off site: Disco 300 m. Watersports with equipment for hire on lake. Cycle route around 30 km. lake. Langogne (shops, restaurants, Stevenson trail etc) 2 km. 9-hole golf course, riding and bicycle hire 3 km.	Leave N88 (Le Puy - Mende) just southwest of Langogne. Turn north on D26 towards Lac de Naussac and follow signs to site (2.5 km). Park beside lake and just behind hotel. Reception inside hotel. GPS: 44.73472, 3.83527
	Charges guide

Per unit incl. 2 persons	€ 12.50 - € 13.50
extra person	€ 3.50
child (2-6 yrs)	€ 1.50
electricity	€ 2.50

Open: 15 April - 30 September.

For latest campsite news, availability and prices visit
alanrogers.com

La Grande Motte

Camping le Garden

44 place des Tamaris, F-34280 La Grande Motte (Hérault) T: 04 67 56 50 09. E: campinglegarden@orange.fr

alanrogers.com/FR34020

Le Garden is a well cared for and pretty site, situated amongst tall pines and flowering shrubs, some 400 m. back from a fine sandy beach. The pitches are of a good size (100 sq.m.) on sandy grass. There are 116 mobile homes to rent and 86 touring places, most with 10A electricity, water and waste water drain. An attractive pool is overlooked by the restaurant. The site also has a small 'centre commercial' with a range of shops and a bar which is next door and open to the public. Le Garden is a very comfortable and quiet site (possible road nose during the day) within pleasant walking distance of the town centre and port. La Grande Motte is a product of the sixties tourist boom when much building went on and, at the time the apartment blocks seemed very futuristic. It has now matured into a smart, upmarket seaside resort with plenty of green space. There is much to see in the area, being on the edge of the Petite Camargue and only a few kilometres from the old walled town of Aigues Mortes. A regular bus service (half hourly) runs from outside the site to Montpellier and other places.

Facilities

Three well situated toilet blocks, smartly refurbished in Mediterranean colours, include washbasins in cabins and baby bath. Laundry facilities. Unit for disabled visitors. Shops to one side of the site with groceries, cigarettes, newspapers, boutique and bar (1/3-31/10). Restaurant and takeaway on site (from 15/5). Swimming pool and paddling pool (15/5-30/9). Play area. TV room. Internet access and WiFi. Off site: Beach 400 m. Tennis, riding, bicycle hire and boat launching 500 m. Golf and fishing 2 km. Waterspoorts centre, casino and nightclub nearby.

Open: 1 April - 15 October.

Directions

Entering La Grande Motte from D62 dual-carriageway, keep right following signs for 'campings' and petite Motte. Turn right at traffic lights by the Office de Tourisme and right again by the Bar Le Garden and site almost immediately on right. GPS: 43.56322, 4.07278

Charges guide

Per unit incl. 1-3 persons	€ 29.50
incl. electricity, water and drainage	€ 39.50

Bracelet required for pool € 10.

CAMPING ★★★★
LE GARDEN
LA GRANDE MOTTE

Avenue de la Petite Motte
34280 La Grande Motte
France
Tél. : 00 33 (0)4 67 56 50 09
Fax : 00 33 (0)4 67 56 25 69
www.legarden.fr

Lansargues

Camping le Fou du Roi

Chemin des Codoniers, F-34130 Lansargues (Hérault) T: 04 67 86 78 08. E: campinglefouduroi@free.fr

alanrogers.com/FR34470

Beside the mellow stone village of Lansargues on the edge of the Camargue, le Fou du Roi was taken over by the Brunel family two years ago. They have done much to update it with a new reception/bar area complete with an attractive Tahitian style construction which can be left open or closed depending on the weather. Altogether this is a lovely little site. There are 82 pitches with 30 for touring units with 10A electricity, arranged in light shade amongst the vineyards. A small pool and play area for children make it a very comfortable site with a nice long season.

Facilities

Two toilet blocks, the first is modern and fully equipped with a baby bath, the second was not open when we visited. Facilities for disabled visitors. Washing machine and dryer. Motorcaravan service point. Small shop (July/Aug). Bar, simple snacks and takeaway (fully open July/Aug). Swimming pool (1/5-15/9). Play area. WiFi. Only gas barbecues are permitted (communal area provided). Off site: Village within easy walking distance with restaurants and shops. Nearest beach 20 km.

Open: 1 April - 15 October.

Directions

From A9 exit 27 follow signs for Lunel and from there pick up D24 going south. Lansargues is 7 km. Do not take 'village centre' sign but continue past and pick up site sign just past village on right. GPS: 43.65181, 4.06635

Charges guide

Per unit incl. 2 persons	€ 13.90 - € 20.80
extra person	€ 3.10 - € 6.20
electricity	€ 4.00

For latest campsite news, availability and prices visit
alanrogers.com

Le Barcarès
Yelloh! Village le Pré Catalan
Route de Saint-Laurent, F-66420 Le Barcarès (Pyrénées-Orientales) T: 04 68 86 12 60.
E: info@yellohvillage-pre-catalan.com **alanrogers.com/FR66300**

The green foliage from the mixed trees and the flowering shrubs makes this 4.5 hectare site very attractive and an avenue of palms is particularly spectacular. There has been a camping site on the spot since 1960 but the present owners, the Galidie family, took over in 1982 and the site is now run to a very high standard by their son Francois and his English wife Jenny. With 250 pitches in total, there are 140 taken by mobile homes and chalets either to let or privately owned and some are used by tour operators. These are mixed amongst the 80 touring pitches which are on level, sandy ground, clearly divided by hedging and all with 10A electricity. The newer part has been planted in the same way as the original areas. It has less shade but enjoys views across to the mountains. The facilities are opened all season but hours are adapted according to the number of visitors on site. An upstairs bar has a long terrace which overlooks the pool complex. A footpath of just less than 1 km. leads to the sandy beach. All in all, this a pleasant and comfortable place to stay.

Facilities

Good facilities include small showers for children. Laundry. Small shop. Bar, restaurant and takeaway (all season). Heated swimming pool complex including fun pools, whirlpool and paddling pool. Excellent play area. Tennis. Archery. Library. Activities for children with miniclub and evening entertainment (July/Aug). No charcoal barbecues. WiFi (free). Off site: Beach 900 m. River fishing 1 km. Riding 1.5 km. Boat launching 3 km.

Open: 27 April - 23 September.

Directions

From A9 exit 41 (Perpignan Nord), follow signs for Le Barcarès and Canet (D83). At exit 9 take D81 (Canet), then first left to Le Barcarès (D90). Site is on left after 500 m. next to Le California. Follow narrow lane to site entrance. GPS: 42.78106, 3.02282

Charges 2012

Per unit incl. 2 persons	
and electricity	€ 17.00 - € 40.00
child (3-7 yrs)	free - € 7.00

66420 Le Barcarès - Tel : 0033 468 86 12 60
Internet : www.precatalan.com - Email : info@precatalan.com

I heated pool of 200 m² and I heated pool of 300 m² with paddling pool. Bar, snack, restaurant, shop and animation for all ages. All our services are available from the opening date. Beach at 900 meter distance on foot. French/English owned.

Le Pré ★★★★ camping
Catalan

yelloh! VILLAGE

Le Barcarès
Camping Club le Floride et l'Embouchure
Route de Saint-Laurent, F-66423 Le Barcarès (Pyrénées-Orientales) T: 04 68 86 11 75.
E: campingfloride@aol.com **alanrogers.com/FR66290**

Essentially a family run enterprise, le Floride et l'Embouchure is really two sites in one – l'Embouchure is the smaller one with direct access to the beach, and le Floride is on the opposite side of the road into Le Barcarès village. There are a number of pitches with their own individual sanitary facility and in total the site offers 632 reasonably sized pitches, all with 10A electricity. A good range of chalets and mobile homes are available for rent. This is a very friendly family-centred site, very popular with Dutch visitors. It is relatively inexpensive, especially outside the July/August peak period. There is an excellent aquapark at le Floride with a number of water slides and a covered pool.

Facilities

Four fully equipped toilet blocks on le Floride and two on l'Embouchure where 50 pitches by the beach have individual facilities. Facilities for babies and disabled visitors. Motorcaravan service point. Shop, bar, restaurant and takeaway (all 15/6-5/9). Pool complex (indoor pool is heated outside July/Aug). Excellent play area. Multisports court. Gym. Tennis. Entertainment and sports programmes (mid June-mid Sept). Bicycle hire. Charcoal barbecues are not permitted. Max. 1 dog. Off site: Beach 100 m.

Open: 1 April - 30 September.

Directions

From A9 take exit 41 (Perpignan Nord) and follow signs for Canet and Le Barcarès via D83. At J9 follow D81 (Canet) then next left into Le Barcarès Village. Site is 1 km. on the left and right sides of the road. GPS: 42.77855, 3.0301

Charges guide

Per unit incl. 2 persons	
and electricity	€ 12.50 - € 34.00
incl. individual sanitary facility	€ 16.00 - € 42.00
extra person	€ 2.60 - € 6.20

For latest campsite news, availability and prices visit
alanrogers.com

Le Barcarès
Camping Club Village l'Europe

Route de Saint Laurent, F-66420 Le Barcarès (Pyrénées-Orientales) T: 04 68 86 15 36.
E: reception@europe-camping.com **alanrogers.com/FR66670**

Le Barcarès is a popular resort with a busy market and a fishing port. It has a good number of campsites but l'Europe is a little different in that it is open all year and each pitch has its own private sanitary facilities. There is a gate at the back of the site for the sandy beach which is a walk of some 600 m. However, the site has its own pool complex overlooked by the bar/restaurant and stage where nightly shows are performed in high season. In total, there are 339 pitches of a good size (100 for touring units) and with some shade from mixed trees and shrubs. The partly hedged pitches are level on sandy grass. The fact that the site is open all year round and that Perpignan airport is nearby has proved popular with visitors looking to buy their own mobile home. There are 75 mobile homes or chalets to rent and 145 privately owned. A new concept financed by the local authority has resulted in a tarmac path, the 'voie verte de l'Agly' which follows the Agly river running past the site. It is 15 km. long from Le Barcarès to Rivesaltes and is used for cycling, jogging, walking or roller skating (but no cars). It is popular with those who wish to keep fit.

Facilities

Individual sanitary facilities on every pitch including dishwashing sink. Laundry. Shop (15/4-30/9). Bar/restaurant and takeaway (high season, on demand at other times). Outdoor pool (15/4-30/9). Wellness. Play area. Tennis. Evening shows and children's club (high season). Only gas and electric barbecues allowed. WiFi at reception. Off site: Nearest beach 600 m. Supermarket. Fishing. Watersports. Le Barcarès resort with many shops, cafés, restaurants and market.

Open: All year.

Directions

From A9 take exit 41 (Perpignan Nord) and follow signs for Canet and Le Barcarès via the D83. At exit 9 follow the D81 (Canet), then next left for Le Barcarès. Site is almost immediately on the right. GPS: 42.774931, 3.021004

Charges guide

Per unit incl. 2 persons	
and electricity	€ 23.50 - € 49.00
extra person	€ 4.00 - € 8.00

www.europe-camping.com
66420 LE BARACARES
04 68 86 15 36

Le Grau-du-Roi
Camping Caravaning le Boucanet

B.P. 206, F-30240 Le Grau-du-Roi (Gard) T: 04 66 51 41 48. E: contact@campingboucanet.fr
alanrogers.com/FR30160

Le Boucanet has a superb situation beside the beach between La Grande Motte and Le Grau-du-Roi. Many trees have been planted and are growing, but as yet most are not tall enough to give much shade. As to be expected, the 458 pitches are sandy. They are on the small side, but are level and most have 6A electricity (long leads and adaptors useful). The 250 for touring are mixed amongst the mobile home and chalet pitches and are separated by small bushes. Plenty of flowers decorate the site and the pleasant restaurant (open lunchtimes and evenings) overlooks the pool area.

Facilities

The fully equipped toilet blocks include facilities for disabled visitors. Baby rooms. Laundry facilities. Fridge hire. Motorcaravan services. Range of shops. Restaurant, bar and snacks (16/5-15/9). Takeaway (1/7-31/8). Large swimming pool, smaller covered pool, toboggans and paddling pool. Play area on sand. Miniclub (July/Aug). Tennis. Bicycle hire. Windsurfing board hire (July/Aug). WiFi. Dogs are not accepted. Off site: Riding 1 km. Golf 2 km. Shops, restaurants and bars within 3 km.

Open: 11 April - 4 October.

Directions

Site is between La Grande Motte and Le Grau-du-Roi on the D255 coastal road, on the seaward side of the road. GPS: 43.5543, 4.10706

Charges guide

Per unit incl. 2 persons	
and electricity	€ 22.00 - € 39.00
pitch on first row of beach, plus	€ 5.00 - € 6.00
extra person	€ 6.00 - € 9.00

For latest campsite news, availability and prices visit
alanrogers.com

Le Grau-du-Roi
Yelloh! Village Secrets de Camargue
Route de l'Espiguette, F-30240 Le Grau-du-Roi (Gard) T: 04 66 80 08 00.
E: info@yellohvillage-secrets-de-camargue.com **alanrogers.com/FR30380**

Les Secrets de Camargue is a recent addition to the Yelloh! Village group, best described as 'stylish and elegant'. It has the unusual feature that it is reserved for over 18s and for families with children under three years old. In total there are 176 pitches with 28 for touring units (with 10A electricity) on level sandy grass. The majority of pitches are for mobile homes and chalets with the unusual feature of thatched roofs. The heart of the site is the Lodge Club which faces the pool and the surrounding sand dunes.

Facilities

Fully equipped sanitary block includes facilities for disabled visitors. Small shop (2/4-19/9). Restaurant, bar (all season). Swimming pool. Aquagym. Activities and entertainment. Mobile homes and chalets for rent. Off site: Free use of facilities at the nearby Camping les Petits Camarguais. Riding 0.8 km. Nearest beach 1.5 km. Village of Le Grau-du-Roi 3 km. Watersports 4 km. Fishing 5 km. Walled town of Aigues Mortes 12 km. Golf 16 km.

Open: 26 March - 3 October.

Directions

Leave the A9 at exit for Gallargues and head for Aigues Mortes on the D979. Continue to Le Grau-du-Roi and then follow signs to Port Camargue on the D62, continuing to join the D255. Site is well signed from this point. GPS: 43.48736, 4.14202

Charges guide

Per unit incl. 2 persons	€ 15.00 - € 44.00
extra person	€ 4.00 - € 8.00
pet	€ 4.00

Le Vigan
Camping le Val de l'Arre
Route du Pont de la Croix, F-30120 Le Vigan (Gard) T: 04 67 81 02 77. E: valdelarre@wanadoo.fr
alanrogers.com/FR30230

Camping Val de l'Arre is situated along the Arre river, a tributary of the Herault river and in the centre of the Cévennes National Park. The site is well managed by the very friendly Triaire family, who speak English, Dutch, Spanish and French. There are 180 grassy, level pitches, 145 for touring, many have some shade and most have electricity (10A). There is a pleasant swimming pool with an outdoor bar. A pebble beach at the river bank provides opportunities for play and fishing enthusiasts will also certainly appreciate the river. Only gas and electric barbecues are permitted on site. There are many possibilities for outdoor activities such as white water rafting, canoeing and mountain biking. Qualified guides may take you on mountain expeditions on foot or by bicycle. The nearby Les Grottes des Demoiselles are some of France's foremost caves. There is also the opportunity to taste the wines of the Hérault region.

Facilities

Three clean and well appointed toilet blocks are well spaced around the site with controllable showers. Facilities for babies and visitors with disabilities. Washing machines. Shop, open air bar with snacks and restaurant (all 1/6-31/8). Swimming and paddling pools (1/6-15/9). Boules. Play area. Motorcaravan services. Guided walks organised. Off site: Bicycle hire 2.5 km. Riding 8 km. Many opportunites for walkers, cyclists and mountain bikers.

Open: 1 April - 30 September.

Directions

Leave A75 at exit 48 and follow D7 and then the D999 east to Le Vigan (43 km). Drive through town, signed Nîmes, at roundabout turn right D110B, site signed. Cross river, turn left, site in 800 m. GPS: 43.992067, 3.6374

Charges guide

Per unit incl. 2 persons and electricity	€ 17.00 - € 21.50
extra person	€ 4.00 - € 5.00
child (2-6 yrs)	€ 3.00 - € 3.50

Camping le Val de l'Arre ★★★

Le Val de l'Arre - Route Du Pont de la Croix - Roudoulouse - 30120 Le Vigan

Cosy and shady family campsite in the south of the Cevennes region, situated at the Arre riverside. Many walking paths are close at hand for a day trip or excursion. We offer a swimming pool, modern sanitary facilities, a playground, WIFI, shop and a snack bar/restaurant with terrace. Mobile homes for rent. All ready to give you a relaxing and comfortable holiday.

Tel: 0033 467 810 277 - Fax: 0033 467 817 123 E-mail: valdelarre@wanadoo.fr - www.valdelarre.com

For latest campsite news, availability and prices visit
alanrogers.com

Lézignan-Corbières

Camping la Pinède

Rue des Rousillons, F-11200 Lézignan-Corbières (Aude) T: 04 68 27 05 08. E: reception@campinglapinede.fr
alanrogers.com/FR11030

Within walking distance of the town and only 28 km. from Narbonne Plage, la Pinède is set on terraces on a hillside, with good internal access on made-up roads. The 67 individual, level pitches vary in size and are divided up mainly by various trees and shrubs with 6A electricity (18 mobile homes). The guardian organises weekly local wine tasting and local walks to show visitors what is growing in the garden and how plants can be used as natural remedies. Outside the gates are a municipal swimming pool (free July/Aug), a disco, a restaurant and tennis courts.

Facilities

Three fully equipped sanitary blocks, one with facilities for babies. Not all blocks are opened outside high season. Washing machine. Motorcaravan service point. Gas. Pleasant bar providing decently priced hot food (July/Aug). Fresh vegetables can be sampled from the garden (small charge). Communal barbecue only. Torches necessary. Caravan storage. WiFi. Off site: Town centre 500 m. Bicycle hire 1 km. Riding 3 km. Fishing 4 km.

Open: 1 March - 30 October.

Directions

Access is directly off the main N113 on west side of Lézignan-Corbières. From A61 (to avoid low bridge) exit at Carcassonne or Narbonne onto N113 and follow to site. GPS: 43.2046, 2.7526

Charges guide

Per unit incl. 2 persons	
and electricity	€ 13.80 - € 17.20
extra person	€ 3.70 - € 4.70
child (under 10 yrs)	€ 2.20 - € 3.40

Lodève

Camping les Vailhés

Les Vailhés, Lac du Salagou, F-34700 Lodève (Hérault) T: 04 67 44 25 98. E: camping@lodevoisetlarzac.fr
alanrogers.com/FR34550

Les Vailhés is a popular municipal site with a wonderful situation on the shores of the Lac du Salagou which is a haven for watersports. Many pitches have views across the lake and the red volcanic rocks are most unusual. Of the 245 pitches, 55 are occupied by seasonal caravans and 190 are for touring, all with electricity; on ground sloping towards the lakeside beach. Most are hedged and there is plenty of shade from a variety of trees. The site is fenced off from the lake but the gates are open in the day.

Facilities

Two toilet blocks have good modern showers (unisex in low season), the rest are rather spartan, with unisex washbasins under cover but open to the fresh air, and old-fashioned sinks for dishwashing and laundry (with hot water). Washing machines. Very basic facilities for disabled visitors (no grab-rails). Small play area. Baker calls daily. Lake amenities (lifeguards July/Aug) and beach café. Windsurfing, sailing, canoes, rowing boats and pedalos. Off site: Riding 2 km. Ancient town of Lodève 9 km. Golf 25 km. Beaches one hour's drive.

Open: 1 April - 30 September.

Directions

Lac du Salagou is 50 km. west of Montpellier. From the A75 (Béziers/Clermont-Ferrand) take exit 54 or 55, and follow directions to Lac du Salagou. Then follow site signs to left. GPS: 43.67026, 3.35572

Charges guide

Per unit incl. 2 persons and electricity (16A)	€ 18.20
extra person	€ 3.95
child (under 13 yrs)	€ 2.15

Marseillan-Plage

Camping les Méditerranées

262 avenue des campings, F-34340 Marseillan-Plage (Hérault) T: 04 67 27 94 49.
E: info@nouvelle-floride.com alanrogers.com/FR34150

Marseillan-Plage is a small, busy resort east of Cap d'Adge and it enjoys a super position immediately beside a long, gently shelving sandy beach. Les Méditerranées is made up of two sites – Nouvelle Floride beside the beach and Charlemagne across the road, both with super pool complexes. Both are good quality sites set under tall trees with neat hedges separating around 500 pitches. There are about 200 for touring units on sandy soil, all with water and 6A electricity. The pitches nearer the sea have less shade. Amenities and facilities are generally of excellent quality and include a smart bar area overlooking the beach with a raised stage for entertainment.

Facilities

Very impressive toilet blocks include some en-suite showers and washbasins, facilities for disabled visitors, dog shower. Motorcaravan services. Shops. Bars, restaurants. Two swimming pool complexes, slides, jacuzzi, paddling pools. Play area. Fitness centre. Multisports court. Watersports. Weekly films. Organised entertainment. WiFi. Miniclub in school holidays. Bicycle hire. Off site: Riding and bicycle hire 500 m. Golf 5 km.

Open: 15 April - 1 October.

Directions

From A9 autoroute exit 34, follow N312 to Agde then take N112 towards Sète. Watch for signs to Marseillan-Plage from where site is well signed. GPS: 43.3087, 3.54168

Charges guide

Per unit incl. 2 persons	
and electricity	€ 15.00 - € 50.00
extra person	€ 6.00 - € 8.50

For latest campsite news, availability and prices visit
alanrogers.com

Marseillan-Plage

Camping la Créole

74 avenue des campings, F-34340 Marseillan-Plage (Hérault) T: 04 67 21 92 69.
E: campinglacreole@wanadoo.fr **alanrogers.com/FR34220**

This is a surprisingly tranquil, well cared for small campsite in the middle of this bustling resort that will appeal to those seeking a rather less frenetic ambience typical of many sites in this area. Essentially a family orientated site, it offers around 110 good sized, level, sandy pitches, all with 6A electricity and mostly with shade from trees and shrubs. There are also 15 mobile homes available to rent. It benefits from direct access to an extensive sandy beach (gated access) and the fact that there is no swimming pool or bar actually contributes to the tranquillity. It may even be seen as an advantage for families with younger children. The beach will be the main attraction here no doubt, and the town's extensive range of bars, restaurants and shops are all within a couple of minutes walk. It is well situated for visiting Sète, a miniature Venice, or Pézenas with an interesting history and lots of art and craft shops. Cap d'Agde, a modern resort with its large marina and super water park for children is popular. If you take a trip on the famous Canal du Midi you may get to see the oyster beds in the Etang de Thau, the inland saltwater lake. There are also many vineyards to visit and it is the home area of sweet Muscat wine.

Facilities

Toilet facilities are housed in a traditional building, modernised inside to provide perfectly adequate facilities including some washbasins in private cabins, a baby room and dog shower. Motorcaravan service point. Small play area. In high season beach games, dances, sangria evenings etc, are organised, all aimed particularly towards families. Communal barbecues only. WiFi. Off site: Local market day Tuesday. Bicycle hire outside site. Riding 1 km. Boat launching 1.5 km. Aqua park at Agde 5 km.

Open: 1 April - 15 October.

Directions

From A9 exit 34 take N312 towards Agde, then N112 towards Sète keeping a look-out for signs to Marseillan-Plage off this road. Site is well signed in Marseillan-Plage. GPS: 43.3206, 3.5501

Charges guide

Per unit incl. 2 persons and electricity	€ 16.30 - € 32.50
extra person (over 2 yrs)	€ 3.00 - € 6.00
dog	€ 2.00 - € 3.00

CAMPING ★★★
LA CREOLE

Direct access to the beach
Located in the Heart of Marseillan-Plage
Mobile home to rent
Low prices in low season

Open from 1/04 to 15/10

74 avenue des campings
34340 Marseillan-Plage
Tel : +33 (0)4 67 21 92 69
Fax : +33 (0)4 67 26 58 16

campinglacreole@wanadoo.fr
www.campinglacreole.com

Meyrueis

Camping Caravaning le Champ d'Ayres

Route de la Brèze, F-48150 Meyrueis (Lozère) T: 04 66 45 60 51. E: campinglechampdayres@wanadoo.fr
alanrogers.com/FR48000

You can be sure of a warm welcome at this traditional, family run site, set in the heart of the Cévennes and its magnificent gorges. Champ d'Ayres is neat, tidy and well kept and is run with young families in mind. The 85 slightly sloping grass pitches, 62 for touring, are mostly hedged with well trimmed bushes and many have some shade. All have electricity (6/10A) but some may require long leads. The area is surrounded by mountains and gorges and some of the narrow and winding roads are not for the faint-hearted or those with large and under-powered units.

Facilities

The toilet block is very clean and has all the necessary facilities. A new block is planned for 2012. Baby room. Facilities for disabled visitors. Laundry facilities. Shop, bar and takeaway (all 1/5-15/9). New heated swimming and paddling pools (8/5-15/9). Play area. Games room. Boules. Activities arranged (July/Aug). WiFi over site (free). Off site: Meyrueis (500 m) has many good shops and restaurants. Fishing 100 m. Riding and bicycle hire within 1 km. Maison du Vautours 18 km.

Open: 6 April - 22 September.

Directions

Leave A75 at exit 44-1, east on D29 through Aquessac, D907 to Le Rozier then D996 to Meyrueis. In Meyrueis (narrow roads) cross river and follow signs for Ayres. Site is 500 m. east of the town. GPS: 44.18077, 3.43507

Charges guide

Per unit incl. 2 persons and electricity	€ 13.00 - € 25.00
extra person	€ 3.50 - € 5.00

For latest campsite news, availability and prices visit
alanrogers.com

Meyrueis

Kawan Village de Capelan

Route de Millau, F-48150 Meyrueis (Lozère) T: 04 66 45 60 50. E: info@campingcapelan.com
alanrogers.com/FR48020

The Lozère is one of France's least populated regions but offers some truly spectacular, rugged scenery, wonderful flora and fauna and old towns and villages. Le Capelan, which is only 1 km. from the attractive market town of Meyrueis, has 116 level, grassy pitches strung out alongside the unfenced River Jonte. Of these, 72 are for touring, most with some shade and all with electrical connections (6/10A). There is direct river access from the site with a 3 km. stretch available for trout fishing. Although there are special facilities, the site is not ideal for disabled visitors. English and Dutch are spoken.

Facilities

Well maintained toilet blocks, facilities for disabled visitors. Three bathrooms for rent. Shop. Bar (both from 1/6). Takeaway (from 1/7). Swimming and paddling pools, sunbathing terrace (from 1/6), accessed via 60 steps. Multisports terrain. Satellite TV. Play area. Leisure activities. Fishing. Free WiFi. Communal barbecue area, only gas and electric barbecues. Off site: Town centre with many shops, bars and restaurants 1 km. Bicycle hire 1 km.

Open: 6 May - 15 September.

Directions

Exit A75 at 44-1, take D29 to Aguessac, D907 to Le Rozier, then D996 towards Meyrueis. The site is on the right 1 km. before town. It is well signed. GPS: 44.18583, 3.41988

Charges guide

Per unit incl. 2 persons	
and electricity	€ 18.00 - € 28.50
extra person	€ 3.70 - € 5.80

Camping Cheques accepted.

Méze

Kawan Village Beau Rivage

RD613, F-34140 Méze (Hérault) T: 04 67 43 81 48. E: reception@camping-beaurivage.fr
alanrogers.com/FR34260

Beau Rivage is situated on the inland shore of the 4.5 km. by 19.5 km. Etang du Thau. This inland salt lake, lying parallel to the Mediterranean and separated by a very narrow strip of land, is well known for its oyster beds. It is also popular for fishing, diving and watersports. The campsite, on the edge of the town, is within easy walking distance of the harbour and the shops. The site has 150 level, sandy grass pitches all with 6A electricity available for touring units and 134 mobile homes to rent. The main features of the site are a pleasant pool and paddling pool with a bar and snack restaurant for the high season.

Facilities

One fully equipped small toilet block is open all season and a larger block for the main season. Baby bath. Facilities for disabled visitors. Washing machine. Motorcaravan service point. Bar providing snacks and simple takeaway food (July/Aug). Swimming and paddling pools. Play area. Activities in July/Aug. Communal barbecues. Off site: Supermarket 200 m. Restaurant 300 m. Beach 500 m. Town within easy walking distance.

Open: 8 April - 17 September.

Directions

From A9 take exit 33 for Sète. Follow RN113 for Poussan, Bouzigues and Mèze. Continue for 5 km. to outskirts of Mèze and site is on left just after a petrol station. GPS: 43.43051, 3.61038

Charges guide

Per unit incl. 2 persons	
and electricity	€ 19.00 - € 38.00
extra person	€ 4.00 - € 7.00

Camping Cheques accepted.

Montclar

Yelloh! Village Domaine d'Arnauteille

F-11250 Montclar (Aude) T: 04 68 26 84 53. E: info@yellohvillage-domaine-arnauteille.com
alanrogers.com/FR11060

Enjoying some beautiful and varied views, this site is ideal for exploring the little known Aude département and for visiting the walled city of Carcassonne. The site is set in farmland on hilly ground with the original pitches on gently sloping, lightly wooded land. Newer ones are on open ground, of good size, with water, drainage and electricity (5/10A), semi-terraced and partly hedged. The most recent have views of Montclar village. Of the 198 pitches, 138 are for touring. The facilities are quite spread out with the swimming pool complex, in the style of a Roman amphitheatre, set in a hollow basin surrounded by fine views. Access, although much improved, could be difficult for large, twin-axle caravans.

Facilities

Three toilet blocks are fully equipped with some en-suite provision. Laundry, facilities for disabled visitors, children and babies. Motorcaravan services. Small shop, bar, restaurant and takeaway (all 15/5-15/9). Swimming pool (25 m; 1/5-30/9), two toboggans, paddling pool, river with water massage and sunbathing terrace. Multisports court. Boules. Play area. Riding (1/7-31/8). Day trips. Library, games room, TV. WiFi (charged). Gas barbecues only.

Open: 9 April - 25 September.

Directions

D118 from Carcassonne, pass Rouffiac d'Aude. Before the end of dual carriageway, turn right to Montclar up narrow road (passing places) for 2.5 km. Site signed very sharp left up hill before village. GPS: 43.12714, 2.25953

Charges guide

Per unit incl. 2 persons	
and electricity	€ 15.00 - € 44.00
extra person	€ 4.00 - € 8.00

For latest campsite news, availability and prices visit
alanrogers.com

Narbonne
Yelloh! Village les Mimosas

544

Chaussée de Mandirac, F-11100 Narbonne (Aude) T: 04 68 49 03 72. E: info@lesmimosas.com
alanrogers.com/FR11070

Six kilometres inland from the beaches of Narbonne and Gruissan, this site benefits from a less hectic situation than others by the sea. The site is lively with plenty to amuse and entertain the younger generation whilst offering facilities for the whole family. A free club card is available in July/August for use of the children's club, gym, sauna, tennis, minigolf, billiards etc. There are 250 pitches, 150 for touring, many in a circular layout of very good size, most with 6A electricity. There are a few 'grand confort', with reasonable shade, mostly from two metre high hedges. There are also a number of mobile homes and chalets to rent. This could be a very useful site offering many possibilities to meet a variety of needs, on-site entertainment (including an evening on Cathar history), and easy access to popular beaches. Nearby Gruissan is a fascinating village with its wooden houses on stilts, beaches, ruined castle, port and salt beds. Narbonne has Roman remains and inland Cathar castles are to be found perched on rugged hill tops.

Facilities

Sanitary buildings refurbished to a high standard include a baby room. Washing machines. Shop and 'Auberge' restaurant (open all season). Takeaway. Bar. Small lounge, amusements (July/Aug). Landscaped heated pool with slides and islands (open 1/5), plus the original pool and children's pool (high season). Play area. Minigolf. Mountain bike hire. Tennis. Sauna and new gym. Children's activities, sports, entertainment (high season). Bicycle hire. Multisports ground. WiFi. Off site: Lagoon with boating and fishing via footpath 200 m. Riding and windsurfing/sailing school 300 m. Gruissan's beach 10 minutes.

Open: 28 March - 1 November.

Directions

From A9 exit 38 (Narbonne Sud) take last exit on roundabout, back over the autoroute (site signed from here). Follow signs La Nautique and then Mandirac and site (6 km. from autoroute). Also signed from Narbonne centre.
GPS: 43.13662, 3.02562

Charges guide

Per unit incl. 2 persons	
and electricity	€ 17.50 - € 36.00
extra person	€ 4.10 - € 8.00
child (2-7 yrs)	free - € 6.00
dog	€ 1.50 - € 3.50

Discover the secret of successful holidays.

Nestling in the heart of lush greenery in the regional nature park, between the beaches of Gruissan and the Bages lagoon, Les Mimosas ensures a pleasant holiday experience.
The 2000 m² water complex with 3 swimming pools, 4 waterslides, Jacuzzi, sauna, mini-golf, fitness centre, 2 playgrounds, restaurant, bar, grocery shop and the proposed animation from April to September offering long hours of fun and relaxation for all ages. Without forgetting the large choice of rentals and shady places.

Les
Mimosas
village-camping
NARBONNE ★ ★ ★ ★ MÉDITERRANÉE

INFORMATIE-RESERVERING
Narbonne - France
Tel. +33 (0)4 68 49 03 72
www.lesmimosas.com

yelloh! VILLAGE

Un Air de Vacances.

For latest campsite news, availability and prices visit
alanrogers.com

We can book this site for you! alan rogers ⊗ travel Call 01580 214000

Narbonne

Camping la Nautique

La Nautique, F-11100 Narbonne (Aude) T: 04 68 90 48 19. E: info@campinglanautique.com

alanrogers.com/FR11080

Owned and run by a very welcoming Dutch family, this well established site has pitches each with an individual sanitary unit. It is an extremely spacious site situated on the Etang de Bages, where flat water combined with strong winds make it one of the best windsurfing areas in France. La Nautique has 390 huge, level pitches, 270 for touring, all with 10A electricity and water. Six or seven overnight pitches with electricity are in a separate area. A range of mobile homes are available to hire. The flowering shrubs and trees give a pleasant feel. Each pitch is separated by hedges making some quite private and providing shade. Entertainment is organised for adults and children from Easter to September (increasing in high season), plus windsurfing, sailing, rafting, walking, pedalos and canoeing (some activities are charged for). The unspoilt surrounding countryside is excellent for walking and cycling (reception has a booklet with routes), and locally there is horse riding and fishing. This site caters for families with children including teenagers and is fenced off from the water for the protection of children. Windsurfers can have a key for the gate (with deposit) that leads to launching points on the lake. English is spoken in reception by the welcoming Schutjes family.

Facilities

Each pitch has its own fully equipped sanitary unit. Specially equipped facilities for disabled visitors. Laundry. Shop. Bar/restaurant, terrace, TV. Takeaway (all 1/5-30/9). Snack bar (1/7-31/8). Swimming pool, water slide, paddling pool (1/5-30/9). Play areas. Tennis. Minigolf. Pétanque. Miniclub (high season). Games room. WiFi (charged). Only electric barbecues are permitted. Torch useful. Off site: Narbonne 4 km. Large sandy beaches at Gruissan (12 km) and Narbonne Plage (20 km). Kite surfing. Canoeing, sailing and windsurfing on the Etang.

Open: 15 February - 15 November.

Directions

From A9 take exit 38 (Narbonne Sud). Go round roundabout to last exit and follow signs for la Nautique and site, then further site signs to site on right in 2.5 km. GPS: 43.14696, 3.00439

Charges guide

Per unit incl. 2 persons, electricity, water and sanitary unit	€ 19.50 - € 42.00
extra person	€ 5.00 - € 8.00
child (2-7 yrs)	€ 3.00 - € 6.00
dog	€ 2.50 - € 4.00

LA NAUTIQUE
NARBONNE - FRANCE
★ ★ ★ ★
Créateur de belles vacances !

Individual Sanitary facilities

www.campinglanautique.com - +33 04 68 90 48 19

Néfiach

Flower Camping la Garenne

RD916, F-66170 Néfiach (Pyrénées-Orientales) T: 04 68 57 15 76. E: camping.lagarenne.nefiach@wanadoo.fr

alanrogers.com/FR66490

Situated beside the N116 which runs through the foothills of the Pyrenees from Perpignan to Andorra, this site is well situated for hiking, climbing, cycling and canoeing. The grass pitches are all level with very easy access and have a degree of privacy to them. There are several privately-owned mobile homes and some site-owned chalets available to rent. The bar/restaurant at the entrance is the focal point with the pool opposite. Great views of the surrounding hills and mountains are enjoyable from most areas of the site whilst at the back there are vineyards and orchards in abundance.

Facilities

Single toilet block in the centre of the site provides modern facilities. Baby area and facilities for disabled visitors. Washing machine. Bar and restaurant serving snacks (May-mid Oct). Weekly paella evening in summer. Small pool (April-Nov). Play area. Gas barbecues only. WiFi. Max. 1 dog. Off site: Shops in Ile-sur-Têt 3 km.

Open: All year.

Directions

From the N116 (Perpignan - Andorra), take exit for Néfiach and head up the old road to Ile-sur-Têt and the site is on the right. GPS: 42.69067, 2.65785

Charges guide

Per unit incl. 2 persons and 10A electricity	€ 16.90 - € 25.50
extra person	€ 4.00 - € 5.50

For latest campsite news, availability and prices visit

alanrogers.com

Palau-del-Vidre
Kawan Village le Haras

1 Ter avenue Joliot Curie, Domaine Sant Galdric, F-66690 Palau-del-Vidre (Pyrénées-Orientales)
T: 04 68 22 14 50. E: haras8@wanadoo.fr **alanrogers.com/FR66050**

Situated in the mature grounds of an old hunting lodge, later developed into an arboreum, le Haras is a rather special site. The 131 pitches are in bays of four arranged amidst an amazing variety of trees and shrubs that provide colour and shade for 97 touring units and some 34 mobile homes (18 to rent). All the touring pitches have 10A electricity, 29 are fully serviced. Some of the access roads are narrow. Under the same family management as Ma Prairie at Canet Village (FR66020), this is a comfortable site popular with British visitors. Rail noise is possible, although the line is screened by large trees.

Facilities

Fully equipped toilet blocks. Facilities for disabled visitors. Washing machines. Motorcaravan service point. Fridge hire. Bar, restaurant and takeaway (all 15/4-30/9). Swimming and paddling pools (1/5-15/9). Play area. Archery (10/7-25/8). Internet access (charged) and WiFi (free). Max. 1 dog. No charcoal barbecues. Off site: Three bakers in the village, two butchers and a general stores. Fishing 500 m. Riding 2 km. Bicycle hire 6 km. Golf 7 km.

Open: 1 April - 30 September.

Directions

From A9, exit 43 (Le Boulou) follow D618 towards Argelès for 13 km. From bypass at St André, turn left for Palau-del-Vidre (D11). Bear right through village, on D11 towards Elne. Site on right at end of village, before railway bridge. GPS: 42.57639, 2.96444

Charges guide

Per unit incl. two persons
and electricity (5A) € 19.00 - € 31.50
Camping Cheques accepted.

Pézenas
Domaine de Montrose

RN9, Tourbes, F-34120 Pézenas (Hérault) T: 04 67 98 52 10. E: reservation@camping-montrose.com
alanrogers.com/FR34900

Camping Montrose is set back from the hectic coastal resorts of Cap d'Agde, Vias and Sète, amongst 50 acres of vineyards on a three hundred-year-old wine 'domaine'. It is quiet, and very attractively laid out with large, level, hedged pitches (92 in total) which are well spaced. A selection of chalets blend into the environment, along with a few mobile homes. Approximately half are privately owned and half are to let, leaving 15 large grass pitches with water and 10A electricity for touring units. A mixture of trees and shrubs provide colour and light shade.

Facilities

Traditional, open-air toilet block but with modern fittings and fully equipped, works well. Washing machine and dryer. Basic necessities in bar including adapters. Bar and restaurant (main season and B.Hs). TV. Pool. Children's play area. Football field. Volleyball. 4 boulodromes. Wine tastings. WiFi (charged). Off site: Riding 200 m. Beach, Aqualand at Agde and Luna park at Vias 20 km.

Open: 1 May - 30 September.
(Chalets February - December).

Directions

Situated just off RN 119 between Pézenas and Béziers. Coming from the Béziers direction pass through Volros and watch for site sign, sharp left turn then right parallel to road. Site is set a good distance back from the road. The newly constructed A71 runs parallel to RN 119. GPS: 43.431779, 3.366121

Charges guide

Per unit incl. 2 persons
and electricity € 12.00 - € 26.00

Port Camargue
Camping Abri de Camargue

320 route du Phare de l'Espiguette, Port Camargue, F-30240 Le Grau-du-Roi (Gard) T: 04 66 51 54 83.
E: contact@abridecamargue.fr **alanrogers.com/FR30030**

Situated 1 km. from the Mediterranean and 1.5 km. from the town of Le Grau-du-Roi, this pleasant, family oriented site has an attractive pool area. Overlooked by the bar with its outdoor tables on a pleasant sheltered terrace, the larger outdoor pool has surrounds for sunbathing. The smaller indoor pool is heated. With 277 level pitches, there are 57 for touring units, mainly of 100 sq.m (there are also smaller ones). Electricity (6A) and water are available on most, and the pitches are well maintained and shaded, with trees and flowering shrubs, quite luxuriant in parts. Recent additions include an air-conditioned cinema and a new sports area.

Facilities

Well appointed toilet blocks and facilities for disabled visitors. Motorcaravan services. Shop. Bar with TV. Restaurant and takeaway. Heated indoor pool, outdoor pool and paddling pool. Outdoor fitness room. Cinema. High quality play area. Entertainment programme and children's club (high season). Pétanque. Music room for young people in high season. WiFi by restaurant (charged). Site access card (deposit € 15). Off site: Tennis 800 m. Nearest beach Port Camargue 900 m. Fishing 2 km.

Open: 1 April - 30 September.

Directions

Site is 45 km. southwest of Nîmes. From A9 exit 26, Gallargues to Le Grau-du-Roi. From bypass follow signs Port Camargue and Campings. Then Rive gauche signs towards Phare l'Espiguette. Site is on right opp. Toboggan Park. GPS: 43.5225, 4.1491

Charges guide

Per unit incl. 2 persons
and electricity € 27.00 - € 56.00

For latest campsite news, availability and prices visit
alanrogers.com

Port Leucate

Camping Rives des Corbières

Avenue du Languedoc, F-11370 Port Leucate (Aude) T: 04 68 40 90 31. E: rivescamping@wanadoo.fr
alanrogers.com/FR11050

Port Leucate is part of the major Languedoc development which took place during the sixties and seventies and it is now a thriving resort. The campsite is situated on the old coast road into Port Leucate between the Etang de Salas and the beach, 800 m. from the centre of the town and port and only 150 m. from the beach. A mixture of tall poplars and pine trees provide reasonable shade for the 305 pitches, on good sized sandy plots, all with 6A electricity connections. About 90 are used for mobile homes. With no tour operators this should be a good value site, now under new management.

Facilities

Four toilet blocks opened as required. Two have mainly Turkish toilets. Facilities for disabled visitors. Laundry room. Small supermarket, bar and takeaway (July/Aug). Swimming pools. Play area. Daytime and evening entertainment. WiFi. Off site: Beach 150 m. (lifeguards July/Aug). Watersports, tennis, riding and water park in Port Leucate 800 m. African wildlife reserve at Salses.

Open: 1 April - 30 September.

Directions

From A9 take exit 40, follow signs for Port Leucate on D627 (passing Leucate village) for 14 km. Exit the D627 which is like a bypass into Port Leucate village. Go right at roundabout into Avenue du Languedoc, site is on right after 800 m. GPS: 42.84932, 3.04083

Charges guide

Per unit incl. 2 persons and electricity	€ 14.00 - € 26.70

Portiragnes-Plage

Camping Caravaning les Mimosas

Port Cassafières, F-34420 Portiragnes-Plage (Hérault) T: 04 67 90 92 92.
E: les.mimosas.portiragnes@wanadoo.fr **alanrogers.com/FR34170**

Les Mimosas is quite a large site with 400 pitches – 200 for touring units, the remainder for mobile homes – in a rural situation. The level, grassy pitches are of average size, separated and numbered, all with 6A electricity (long leads may be required), some have good shade others have less. The pool area, a real feature of the site, includes a most impressive wave pool, various toboggans, the 'Space Hole' water slide, a large swimming pool and a super paddling pool (nine pools in all) with lots of free sun beds. This is a friendly, family run site with families in mind, and something new every year. Les Mimosas has a less hectic situation than sites closer to the beach. However, it is possible to walk to a lovely sandy beach (1.2 km). There is lots going on and many day trips and excursions are arranged all season, from canoeing to visiting castles. Portiragnes-Plage is about 2 km. away and it can be reached by cycle tracks. The Canal du Midi runs along the edge of the site (no access), providing another easy cycle route.

Facilities

Good, modern toilet blocks include baby rooms, children's toilets, facilities for disabled visitors (whole site wheelchair friendly). En-suite facilities on payment. Washing machines and dryers. Motorcaravan services. Fridge hire. Large well stocked shop, bar, restaurant, takeaway, swimming pool complex (all open as site), lifeguards all season. Good play area. Miniclub (4-8 yrs). Boules. Gym with instructor and sauna. Multisports court. Bicycle hire. Games/TV room. Variety of evening entertainment. Internet access and WiFi (charged). Communal barbecue (only gas and electric permitted on pitches). Off site: Fishing and riding 1 km. Portiragnes-Plage 2 km. Golf 10 km.

Open: 26 May - 5 September.

Directions

From A9 exit 35 (Béziers Est) take N112 south towards Serignan (1 km). Large roundabout follow signs for Cap d'Agde, watch carefully for D37. Portiragnes (1-2 km), follow signs for Portiragnes-Plage. Site well signed before Portiragnes-Plage (5 km). GPS: 43.29153, 3.37348

Charges 2012

Per unit incl. 2 persons and electricity	€ 20.00 - € 42.00
extra person	€ 5.00 - € 10.00
child (under 4 yrs)	free - € 4.00
private sanitary unit	€ 8.50 - € 10.00

les **M**imosas ★★★★
Camping Club
Mediterranean France

Camping - Mobile homes - Bengalis - Chalets
Port Cassafières - 34420 Portiragnes Plage
Tél : +33 (0)4 67 90 92 92
Fax : +33 (0)4 67 90 85 39
les.mimosas.portiragnes@wanadoo.fr

Leisure pool
Kamikazes
Jacuzzi
Rapid River
Space Hole

Portiragnes Plage   www.mimosas.com   www.camping-mediterranee.eu

For latest campsite news, availability and prices visit
alanrogers.com

Portiragnes-Plage
Camping les Sablons

Avenue des Muriers, F-34420 Portiragnes-Plage (Hérault) T: 04 67 90 90 55. E: contact@les-sablons.com
alanrogers.com/FR34400

Les Sablons is an impressive and popular site with lots going on, a village in itself. Most of the facilities are arranged around the entrance with shops, a restaurant, a bar and a large pool complex with no less than five slides and three heated pools. There is also direct access to a white sandy beach at the back of the site, close to a small lake. There is good shade on the majority of the site, although some of the newer touring pitches have less shade but are nearer the gate to the beach. On level sandy grass, all have 6A electricity. Of the 800 pitches, around half are taken by a range of mobile homes and chalets (many for hire, and a few for use by tour operators). A new entertainment office enables you to book a wide range of sporting, cultural and musical activities as well as excursions. Children's clubs and evening entertainment are organised. In fact, this is a real holiday venue aiming to keep all the family happy. Some visitors simply stay on the site for their entire holiday – it certainly has everything. The site is very convenient for Béziers airport.

Facilities

Well equipped, modernised toilet blocks include large showers, some with washbasins. Baby baths and facilities for disabled visitors. Supermarket, bakery and newsagent. Restaurant, bar and takeaway. Swimming pool complex. Entertainment and activity programme with sports, music and cultural activities. Children's club. Beach club. Tennis. Archery. Play areas. Electronic games. ATM. Internet access. WiFi throughout site. Off site: Village and bicycle hire 100 m. Beach and riding 200 m. Canal du Midi 1 km. Parc Adventure (high wire adventure park) 1.5 km.

Open: 1 April - 30 September.

Directions

From A9 exit 35 (Béziers Est) follow signs for Vias and Agde (N112). After large roundabout pass exit to Cers then take exit for Portiragnes (D37). Follow for about 5 km. and pass over Canal du Midi towards Portiragnes-Plage. Site is on left after roundabout. GPS: 43.28003, 3.36396

Charges guide

Per unit incl. 2 persons and electricity	€ 19.00 - € 48.00
extra person	€ 6.00 - € 10.00
child	free - € 8.00
dog	€ 4.00

For latest campsite news, availability and prices visit
alanrogers.com

Saint Cyprien-Plage
Camping Cala Gogo

Avenue Armand Lanoux, les Capellans, F-66750 Saint Cyprien-Plage (Pyrénées-Orientales)
T: 04 68 21 07 12. E: camping.calagogo@wanadoo.fr **alanrogers.com/FR66030**

This is an excellent, well organised site and it is agreeably situated by a superb sandy beach with a beach bar and boat launching. There are 654 pitches in total with 450 average sized, level, pitches for touring, electrical connections (6 or 10A) everywhere and some shade. Some fully serviced pitches have been added. The site has a most impressive pool complex carefully laid out with palm trees in ample sunbathing areas. The large bar complex becomes very busy in season and dancing or entertainment is arranged on some evenings on a large stage recently built alongside the bar. A feature of the site is the provision of special beach buggies for visitors with disabilities. The site is now part of the 'Les Pieds dans l'Eau' group (having direct access to water, either sea, river or lake). A large Aquapark, reputed to be amongst the best in southern France, is nearby. Used by tour operators (148 pitches). There are 57 chalets and mobile homes to rent.

Facilities

Fully equipped toilet blocks are of a high standard. Good supermarket and small shopping mall. Sophisticated restaurant with excellent cuisine. Self-service restaurant with simple menu. Takeaway. Bar. Small beach bar (high season). Fridge hire. Disco. TV. Three swimming pools (heated) plus one for children, water-jets, jacuzzi, waterfall. Play area. Tennis. Fishing. Diving club. Internet access and WiFi (free). Bicycle hire. Events, sports and entertainment organised in season. Torches useful. Only gas or electric barbecues allowed. Off site: Golf, riding and boat launching 3 km. Boat excursions and courses in skin-diving, windsurfing and sailing nearby.

Open: 28 April - 22 September.

Directions

Using D81 (southward) avoid St Cyprien-Plage and continue towards Argelès. Turn right at roundabout signed Le Port and Aquapark and pick up site signs. Site is just past Aquapark. GPS: 42.59939, 3.03761

Charges 2012

Per unit incl. 2 persons	
and electricity	€ 20.00 - € 42.40
extra person	€ 5.00 - € 10.80
child (under 5 yrs)	free
dog	€ 3.00 - € 4.00

Remoulins
Camping la Soubeyranne

1110 route de Beaucaire, F-30210 Remoulins (Gard) T: 04 66 37 03 21. E: soubeyranne@franceloc.fr
alanrogers.com/FR30140

Owned by the group FranceLoc, this site is well positioned for visiting the Pont du Gard, Nîmes and Uzès, famed for their Roman connections. The 200 pitches offer extremely generous amounts of shade and keeping the 6 hectares watered involves over 5 km. of hose pipe. The touring pitches, of which there are 79, are large, level, numbered and separated, and all have 6A electricity connections. An entertainment programme (July/August) is aimed mainly at young children (teenagers may find the site rather quiet).

Facilities

One unisex toilet block is basic but clean and has more than adequate facilities and include washbasins in cubicles. Motorcaravan service point. Fridges for hire. Small shop selling basics. Restaurant, bar and takeaway (all 4/4-27/9) – menu not extensive but adequate and moderately priced. Heated swimming pool complex (4/4-27/9) with 20x10 m. pool and smaller toddlers' pool (unsupervised). Play area including inflatable castle. Minigolf. Boules. Tennis. Bicycle hire. Off site: Fishing 1 km. Remoulins 1.5 km.

Open: 4 April - 27 September.

Directions

From Uzès take D981 to Remoulins, turn right at lights over river bridge, left at roundabout, then left (signed D986 Beaucaire). Site is 1.5 km. further on left. GPS: 43.942282, 4.559669

Charges guide

Per unit incl. 2 persons	
and electricity	€ 19.70 - € 31.20
extra person	€ 4.70 - € 7.00
child (under 7 yrs)	€ 2.60 - € 4.50
dog	€ 5.00

For latest campsite news, availability and prices visit
alanrogers.com

2 Campsites DIRECT ON THE BEACH !

Cala-Gogo

Avenue Armand Lanoux
F-66750 SAINT CYPRIEN
Tél. +33 4 68 21 07 12
Fax +33 4 68 21 02 19
www.campmed.com
e-mail : calagogo@campmed.com

Heated sanitary
Heated swimming pool

le Soleil
★★★★

Route du Littoral
F-66702 Argelès sur Mer
☎ +33 4 68 81 14 48 • Fax +33 4 68 81 44 34
www.campmed.com
e-mail : lesoleil@campmed.com

Saillagouse
PRL Le Vedrignans

545

Route de Vedrignans, F-66800 Saillagouse (Pyrénées-Orientales) T: 04 68 04 04 79.
E: contact@levedrignans.com **alanrogers.com/FR66700**

Le Vedrignans can be found deep in the Catalan Pyrenees Regional Park. It enjoys a spectacular natural setting, overlooked by towering mountains but with a very pleasant Mediterranean climate. This is a parc résidentiel de loisirs and there are no touring pitches here. Instead, accommodation is provided in a range of attractive wooden chalets. These range from the smaller 'Genets' model, which can sleep up to four, to the larger 'Edelweiss' chalets which can accommodate up to eight people. All chalets are fully equipped and are located on very large pitches of over 200 sq. m.

Facilities

Play area. Games room. Tourist information. Chalets to rent. Off site: Village centre 300 m. Le train jaune. Ski resorts. Walking and cycling tracks. Covered swimming pool. Tennis.

Open: All year.

Directions

Saillagouse lies around 90 km. west of Perpignan. From there head west on N116 to Prades and Mont Louis. Continue on this road to Saillagouse and the site is clearly indicated. GPS: 42.457712, 2.039638

Charges 2012

Contact the site for details.

Sainte Enimie
Camping Couderc

Route de Millau, F-48210 Sainte Enimie (Lozère) T: 04 66 48 50 53. E: contact@campingcouderc.fr
alanrogers.com/FR48080

A spacious rural site, Couderc is strung out along 1 km. of the clear shallow River Tarn, although access to the river is not easy. The beautiful Gorges du Tarn and the high plateaux are well worth exploring. Come in May and June to see the wonderful flowers and butterflies with vultures soaring overhead. There are 130 good sized, level, grassy/stony pitches here, separated by vines and mature trees. With 123 for touring units, most have welcome shade and 10A electricity (long leads may be needed). Rock pegs are advised. Although the local roads are winding and narrow, access on the site is good.

Facilities

Several toilet blocks with adequate facilities including those for children. Facilities for disabled visitors (the terrain is challenging for those with walking difficulties). Bar/TV room. Breakfast (all season). Basic shop, bread to order. Swimming and paddling pools (a steep climb from pitches). Play area. Canoe hire and trips run from site. Boules. River fishing. Electric barbecues only – communal barbecues provided. Off site: Ste Enimie 1.5 km. with shops, restaurants, bars, bank. Grottoes, canyoning, rock climbing, caving. Gorges of the Tarn, Jonte, high plateau with rare flowers and birds, interesting medieval villages.

Open: 19 April - 20 September.

Directions

Leave A75 at exit 40 for La Canourgue. Take the D998 to Ste Enimie (28 km) following signs for Millau, Gorges du Tarn. Take the D907 to site on left in 1.5 km. Approach from south not recommended for large outfits. GPS: 44.353606, 3.401347

Charges guide

Per unit incl. 2 persons	
and electricity	€ 15.00 - € 24.00
extra person	€ 3.00 - € 4.00
child (under 7 yrs)	€ 1.30 - € 1.60
dog	free

Saint Hippolyte-du-Fort
Camping de Graniers

Route de Monoblet, Graniers, F-30170 Saint Hippolyte-du-Fort (Gard) T: 04 66 25 19 24.
E: contact@camping-graniers.com **alanrogers.com/FR30430**

Les Graniers is a friendly site with new owners, located on the fringe of the magnificent Cevennes National Park. Pitches are well shaded by tall trees, and of a good size. Most have electrical connections. A number of mobile homes, chalets and fully equipped bungalow style tents are available for rent. Unusually, de Graniers also offers two Mongolian style yurts for rent. On-site leisure facilities include a swimming pool, volleyball and a snack bar. There are many footpaths and cycling routes close to the site, and the managers will be pleased to recommend routes. A day trip to the seaside is possible, around 1 hour's drive away at Le Grau-du-Roi.

Facilities

Fully equipped toilet block. Swimming pool (15/5-30/9). Bar/snack bar. Takeaway food. Games room. Children's play area. Volleyball. Fishing. Bicycle hire. Tourist information. Entertainment and activity programme. Accommodation for rent. Off site: Walking and cycling. St Hippolyte-du-Fort 3 km. Anduze 10 km. Riding 10 km. Beach 60 km.

Open: 13 March - 17 October.

Directions

Site is located to the north east of St Hippolyte-du-Fort. Approaching from Anduze, head south on D907 and D982 to St Hippolyte, follow signs in the village to de Graniers. GPS: 43.980104, 3.884885

Charges guide

Per unit incl. 2 persons and electricity	€ 23.50
extra person	€ 4.00
child (1-8 yrs)	€ 3.50

For latest campsite news, availability and prices visit
alanrogers.com

Saint Jean-du-Gard
Camping Mas de la Cam

Route de Saint-André de Valborgne, F-30270 Saint Jean-du-Gard (Gard) T: 04 66 85 12 02.
E: camping@masdelacam.fr **alanrogers.com/FR30180**

Camping Mas de la Cam is a superb, high quality family run touring site; you are assured of a warm welcome here (English and Dutch spoken). It is a very pleasant and spacious site with well trimmed grass and hedges and a profusion of flowers and shrubs. Lying alongside the small Gardon river, the banks have been left free of pitches giving neat grass for sunbathing and some trees for shade, whilst children can amuse themselves in the water (no good for canoes). The 200 medium to large pitches, all for touring, are on low level terraces, with varying amounts of shade, and electricity (6/10A). In the low season bridge drives, painting courses and boules are organised. In the high season there is some family entertainment and a musical evening once a week. Nearby one can walk in the footsteps of Robert Louis Stevenson (Travels with a Donkey), ride on a steam train, explore the deep underground caverns, and visit a giant bamboo forest. Entrance is via a narrow unfenced bridge, so not ideal for large outfits. Nine gîtes for rent in a beautiful old farmhouse. Only gas and electric barbecues are allowed on site.

Facilities

Three high quality, very clean toilet blocks with baby bath and facilities for visitors with disabilities. Washing machines. Bar/restaurant, terrace. Small shop. Attractive large swimming (heated) and paddling pools. Excellent play and sports areas, multisport court for football, volleyball and basketball. Boules, table tennis. Club, used in low season for bridge, in high season as games room. Fishing. WiFi. Off site: St Jean-du-Gard with shops and Tues. market 3 km. Riding 5 km. Bicycle hire 15 km. Many narrow lanes, old towns and villages to explore.

Open: 26 April - 20 September.

Directions

Site is 3 km. northwest of St Jean-du-Gard in direction of St André-de-Valborgne on D907, site signed, fork left, descend across a narrow unfenced bridge to site. Site entrance not accessible from north. GPS: 44.11235, 3.8541

Charges guide

Per unit incl. 2 persons	€ 15.00 - € 27.00
extra person	€ 3.60 - € 6.90
child (under 7 yrs)	€ 2.70 - € 4.50
electricity (6A)	€ 3.00 - € 5.50

camping mas de la cam ★★★
F-30270 St Jean du Gard
Cévennes
www.masdelacam.fr

Saint Jean-du-Gard
Camping les Sources

Route de Mialet, F-30270 Saint Jean-du-Gard (Gard) T: 04 66 85 38 03. E: camping-des-sources@orange.fr
alanrogers.com/FR30150

This is a small, family run site situated in the foothills of the beautiful Cévennes. There are 92 average to good sized, slightly sloping pitches on small terraces with 72 for touring units, all with electricity (6/10A). A number of attractive mobile homes and chalets are also available for rent. They are separated by a variety of flowering shrubs and trees offering good shade. Near the entrance is the attractive reception, bar, restaurant and terrace overlooking the swimming pools and children's play area. The emphasis here is on a quiet family holiday with little organised activity.

Facilities

Two toilet blocks with washbasins in cabins. Facilities for babies and visitors with disabilities. Washing machine. Motorcaravan service point. Bar/restaurant with takeaway, good menu and small shop (all season). Small swimming and paddling pools (from late May). Games/TV room. Play area. Gas and electric barbecues. Occasional children's activities and family evening meals. WiFi (free). Off site: St Jean-du-Gard 1.5 km. Daily bus service to Nîmes and Alès. Fishing and bathing 1.5 km. Riding 12 km.

Open: 1 April - 30 September.

Directions

From Alès take D910A to Anduze, then D907 to St Jean-du-Gard. Take ring road (autre directions) towards Florac. Turn right at traffic lights on D98. Right onto D50 (site signed). Very shortly, on sharp right-hand bend, fork right to site. Access impossible from the north. GPS: 44.11322, 3.89052

Charges 2012

Per unit incl. 2 persons and electricity	€ 17.50 - € 25.00
extra person	€ 3.50 - € 4.50

For latest campsite news, availability and prices visit
alanrogers.com

Sérignan-Plage

Yelloh! Village le Sérignan-Plage

Le Sérignan-Plage, F-34410 Sérignan-Plage (Hérault) T: 04 67 32 35 33. E: info@leserignanplage.com

alanrogers.com/FR34070

With direct access onto a superb 600 m. sandy beach (including a naturist section) and with three swimming pools, this is a must for a Mediterranean holiday. It is a busy, friendly, family orientated site with a very comprehensive range of amenities. Having recently acquired an adjacent site complete with a small lake, there are now over 1,100 pitches with 278 available for touring units. These vary in size and in terms of shade. They are mainly on sandy soil and all have 6A electricity. The collection of spa pools (balnéo) built in Romanesque style with colourful terracing and columns, overlooked by a very smart restaurant, Le Villa, is still the 'pièce de résistance' and available to use in the afternoons (used by the adjacent naturist site in the mornings). The enthusiastic owners, Jean-Guy and Catherine, continually surprise us with their unique style and new developments – this year a most dramatic play area featuring Hansel and Gretel style wooden play houses has been added. There are over 300 mobile homes and chalets to let, plus some 400 privately owned units. The heart of the site developed in the local Catalonian style is some distance from reception and is a busy and informal area with shops, another good restaurant, the Au Pas d'Oc, an indoor pool and a super roof-top bar. There is a range of sporting activities, children's clubs and evening entertainment, indeed something for all the family – a good holiday choice.

Facilities

Seven modern blocks of individual design with good facilities including showers with washbasin and WC. Facilities for disabled visitors. Baby bathroom. Launderette. Motorcaravan services. Supermarket, bakery and newsagent (all season). Other shops (21/4-2/10). ATM. Restaurants, bar and takeaway. Hairdresser. Balnéo spa (afternoons). Gym. Heated indoor pool. Outdoor pools (21/4-2/10). Tennis courts. Multisports courts. Play areas. Trampolines. Children's clubs. Evening entertainment. Sporting activities. Bicycle hire. Bus to Sérignan village July/Aug. Beach (lifeguards 15/6-15/9). WiFi (charged). Gas barbecues only. Off site: Riding 2 km. Golf 10 km. Sailing and windsurfing school on beach. Local markets.

Open: 26 April - 2 October.

Directions

From A9 exit 35 (Béziers Est) towards Sérignan, D64 (9 km). Before Sérignan, turn left, Sérignan-Plage (4 km). At small sign (blue) turn right. At T-junction turn left over small road bridge and after left hand bend. Site is 100 m. GPS: 43.26308, 3.31976

Charges guide

Per unit incl. 2 persons and electricity	€ 15.00 - € 52.00
extra person	€ 5.00 - € 8.50
child (3-7 yrs)	free - € 8.50
dog	€ 4.00

Sérignan-Plage

Yelloh! Village Aloha

F-34410 Sérignan-Plage (Hérault) T: 04 67 39 71 30. E: info@alohacamping.com

alanrogers.com/FR34390

An impressive and well run site beside the beach at Sérignan-Plage, Aloha offers a wide range of good quality facilities, all open when the site is open. There are 465 pitches with 170 mobile homes for hire in attractively landscaped settings. The 295 pitches for touring units are of a good size, regularly laid out on level, sandy grass. Easily accessed from tarmac roads, all have 10A electricity. Half are on one side of the small beach road with the swimming pools and other facilities, the other half are somewhat quieter with more grass but less shade across the road.

Facilities

Seven toilet blocks, including three large ones, offer all modern facilities and are well equipped for children. Laundry. Motorcaravan service point. Supermarket including fresh produce market. Bakery. Newsagent. Bazaar. Hairdresser. Bar, restaurant, snack bar, pizzeria and takeaway. Large heated pool and fun pools. Paddling pool. Playground. Tennis. Multisports facility. Bicycle hire. Miniclub. Activity programme and evening entertainment. Internet access and WiFi. ATM. Off site: Minigolf and trampolines 500 m. Riding 800 m. Boat launching 8 km. Golf 20 km.

Open: 25 April - 13 September.

Directions

From A9 exit 35 (Béziers Est) follow signs for Sérignan then Sérignan-Plage (D37, about 10 km). Once at Sérignan-Plage continue straight. Follow the sign for Aloha to right after the pink building. GPS: 43.273333, 3.348333

Charges guide

Per unit incl. 2 persons and electricity	€ 15.00 - € 46.00
extra person	€ 5.00 - € 8.00
child (3-7 yrs)	free - € 8.00
dog	€ 4.00

For latest campsite news, availability and prices visit
alanrogers.com

Imagine – hot sunshine, blue sea, vineyards, olive and eucalyptus trees, alongside a sandy beach – what a setting for a campsite – not just any campsite either! With three pool areas, one with four toboggans surrounded by sun bathing areas, an indoor pool for baby swimmers plus a magnificent landscaped, Romanesque spa-complex with half Olympic size pool and a superb range of hydromassage baths to let you unwind and re-charge after the stresses of work. And that's not all – two attractive restaurants, including the atmospheric "Villa" in its romantic Roman setting beside the spa, three bars, a mini-club and entertainment for all ages, all add up to a fantastic opportunity to enjoy a genuinely unique holiday experience.

Le Sérignan Plage

The Mediterranean
The place for your holidays

34410 Sérignan Tél : +33 (0)4 67 32 35 33 Fax : +33 (0)4 67 32 68 39
info@leserignanplage.com www.leserignanplage.com

yelloh! VILLAGE

Sérignan-Plage
Camping le Paradis

Route de Valras, F-34410 Sérignan (Hérault) T: 04 67 32 24 03. E: paradiscamping34@aol.com

alanrogers.com/FR34560

Family owned and run, le Paradis is a haven of tranquillity set some 3 km. back from the sea. With only 129 average sized, grassy pitches, of which 22 are taken by mobile homes to rent, it is comfortable and peaceful. Even the pool is hidden behind fencing so it does not intrude. A mix of trees and shrubs give shade and all the pitches are level with 6A electricity. There is a pleasant shaded area to one corner of the pool near the bar, where children can play table tennis. Entertainment is arranged on simple lines – music evenings two nights a week in July and August with darts or tennis tournaments for children.

Facilities

Fully equipped toilet facilities including those for disabled visitors. Baby bath. Washing machine and dryer. Small shop for essentials (15/5-30/9). Bar/restaurant (meals are pre-booked), takeaway (all 15/5-20/9). Reasonably sized pool. Play area. WiFi. Gas and electric barbecues only. Dogs are not accepted. Off site: Supermarket 200 m. Bicycle hire 1 km. Fishing and boat launching 2 km. Beach 2.5 km. Riding 3 km. Golf 15 km.

Open: 1 April - 30 September.

Directions

From A9 exit 35 (Béziers Est), follow signs for Valras Plage. At second roundabout beside McDonalds and Hyper U take left turn to site on right, clearly signed. GPS: 43.26926, 3.28727

Charges guide

Per unit incl. 2 persons and electricity	€ 16.00 - € 32.00
extra person	€ 3.00 - € 5.50

Sète
Village Center le Castellas

RN112, F-34200 Sète (Hérault) T: 04 99 57 21 21. E: contact@village-center.com

alanrogers.com/FR34240

One would expect a campsite beside a beachside main road and a railway to be noisy, whereas once within the confines of this site it is surprisingly peaceful offering everything one could want. It is situated across the road from 14 km. of superb sandy beach, with the Etang du Thau behind, yet within a short drive of Sète, Marseillan-Plage and Agde. It is a very large site with over 800 mobile homes and chalets to rent. There are also 200 sandy and hedged pitches for touring units, most with 6A electricity and some have been purpose-built for motorcaravans. Pitches are accessed by hard roads with a variety of shade – the sorts of shrubs that will grow by the sea.

Facilities

The toilet facilities include en-suite showers and basins. Laundry. Provision for disabled visitors. Fridge hire. Large supermarket, range of smaller shops and café open to public as well. Restaurant, bars, snack bars. Swimming pool with lifeguards (heated April-June). Toboggans. Games room. Multisport court. Sports field. Archery. Play area, bouncy castles. Outdoor fitness area. WiFi (charged). ATM. Wide range of entertainment. Miniclub and teenage club (July/Aug). Sea fishing. Watersports. Off site: Bus for Sète in July/Aug. Riding 3 km. Golf 10 km.

Open: 3 April - 26 September.

Directions

Site is beside the RN112 linking Marseillan-Plage and Sète (nearer Marseillian-Plage). This road can get very busy indeed in main season but it is being re-routed behind the site. GPS: 43.34192, 3.58449

Charges guide

Per unit incl. 2 persons and electricity (6A)	€ 18.00 - € 40.00
extra person (over 5 yrs)	€ 4.00 - € 8.00
dog	€ 3.00

Camping Cheques accepted.

Sigean
Village Center Ensoya

54 avenue de Perpignan, F-11130 Sigean (Aude) T: 08 25 00 20 30. E: contact@village-center.com

alanrogers.com/FR11350

Camping Ensoya is a new site, and a member of the Village Center group. It can be found in pleasant Garrigue countryside close to Sigean, a 14th century Languedoc border town, and now best known for its famous African animal reserve. There are 183 pitches, some of which are large (up to 150 sq.m). Most have electricity. A number of mobile homes, chalets and fully equipped tents are available to rent. This is a natural site with very few amenities (although some development is planned for the future). The nearest shops and restaurants can be found at Sigean.

Facilities

Motorcaravan services. Play area. Children's activity programme. Tourist information. Mobile homes, tents and chalets for rent. Off site: Nearest beaches 7 km. Shops and restaurants at Sigean. Walking and cycling tracks. Watersports on Etang de Bages.

Open: 2 April - 1 October.

Directions

Approaching from the north (Narbonne), leave A9 autoroute at exit 39 (Sigean) and head east to Sigean on D6139. The site is well signposted from here. GPS: 43.024785, 2.977123

Charges guide

Per unit incl. 2 persons and electricity	€ 18.00 - € 24.00

Camping Cheques accepted.

For latest campsite news, availability and prices visit
alanrogers.com

Sommières
Castel Camping Domaine de Massereau

Les Hauteurs de Sommières, route d'Aubais, F-30250 Sommières (Gard) T: 04 66 53 11 20.
E: info@massereau.fr **alanrogers.com/FR30290**

Two brothers, one a wine producer and one a hotelier, opened Domaine de Massereau in August 2006. It is set within a 50-hectare vineyard dating back to 1804, and the idea was to promote their wine, so tours are arranged and they now produce their own olive oil as well. There are 120 pitches, with 75 available for touring units (45 with 16A electricity, water and drainage). Pitch sizes range from 150-250 sq.m. but the positioning of trees on some of the pitches could limit the usable space. The area is lightly wooded and most pitches are now hedged with flowering shrubs. The other pitches are used for chalets and mobile homes to rent. Amenities include an attractive pool area with water slide and heated pool, a trim trail, mountain bike path and large grass play area including a trampoline. The camping area is accessed over a narrow bridge (3 m. wide) passing over a section of the 25 km. of cycle routes which enable the surrounding area to be explored safely. The pretty riverside town of Sommières is a 1.5 km. ride away with its historic centre, full of narrow streets lined with traditional shops.

Facilities

The modern toilet block has excellent facilities for children and disabled visitors. Laundry. Motorcaravan service point. Well stocked shop and newspapers. Restaurant. Bar. Pizzeria and outdoor grill. Takeaway (all 7/4-30/9). Heated swimming pool with slide. Paddling pool. Sauna, steam bath and jacuzzi. Play area. Trampoline. Minigolf. Bicycle hire. Fitness trail. Pétanque. Short tennis. TV room. Barbecue hire. Fridge hire. Tent hire (2 person). Gas. WiFi (charged). Charcoal barbecues are not allowed. Off site: Fishing and riding 3 km. Golf and sailing 30 km.

Open: 1 April - 15 November.

Directions

From south on A9 take exit 27 and D12 towards Sommières. Site is 5 km. on right. From the north, there is a width and weight restriction in Sommières. To avoid this remain on the N110, then take N2110 into Sommières, crossing river over a narrow bridge (traffic lights), and turn right onto the D12. Site is on left in 1 km. GPS: 43.765786, 4.097426

Charges 2012

Per unit incl. 2 persons	
and electricity	€ 21.40 - € 41.90
extra person	€ 3.50 - € 10.00

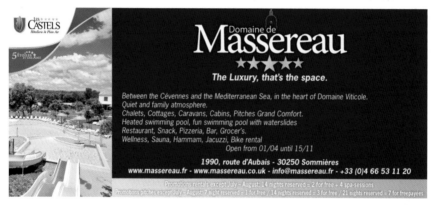

LES CASTELS
Hôtellerie de Plein Air

5 ÉTOILES

Domaine de Massereau
★★★★★
The Luxury, that's the space.

Between the Cévennes and the Mediterranean Sea, in the heart of Domaine Viticole.
Quiet and family atmosphere.
Chalets, Cottages, Caravans, Cabins, Pitches Grand Comfort.
Heated swimming pool, fun swimming pool with waterslides
Restaurant, Snack, Pizzeria, Bar, Grocer's.
Wellness, Sauna, Hammam, Jacuzzi, Bike rental
Open from 01/04 until 15/11

1990, route d'Aubais - 30250 Sommières
www.massereau.fr - www.massereau.co.uk - info@massereau.fr - +33 (0)4 66 53 11 20

Promotions rentals except July - August: 14 nights reserved = 2 for free + 4 spa-sessions
Promotions pitches except July - August: 7 night reserved = 1 for free / 14 nights reserved = 3 for free / 21 nights reserved = 7 for freepayees

Torreilles-Plage
Village Camping Spa Marisol

Boulevard de la Plage, F-66440 Torreilles-Plage (Pyrénées-Orientales) T: 04 68 28 04 07.
E: marisol@camping-marisol.com **alanrogers.com/FR66170**

Good quality sites with direct access to the beach are hard to find and Marisol is a useful option. It is a fairly large site, having 377 pitches with a significant number of mobile homes, but with 170 available for touring. These are sandy grass pitches of a good size with some shade. All have 10A electricity. There is a beauty centre where you can enjoy a sauna, Turkish or spa bath. This is essentially a holiday site with all the popular facilities and an extensive entertainment programme, gym and fitness courses and a children's club throughout the main season. The owners continue to make improvements and plan to add a heated children's pool.

Facilities

Three fully equipped toilet blocks, baby bath. Washing machine. Supermarket. Bar. TV. Restaurant. Takeaway. Heated swimming pool, water slide, children's pool. Beauty centre. Fitness room. Play area. Tennis. Archery. Children's club. Beach access through dunes. Watersports. Evening entertainment. WiFi. Max. 1 dog. Off site: Riding and minigolf 500 m. Microlights and karting 1.5 km.

Open: 9 April - 24 September.

Directions

From A9 take exit 41 (Perpignan Nord) towards Le Barcarès for 9 km. Then south on D81 towards Canet for 3 km. before turning to Torreilles-Plage. Site is signed. GPS: 42.78432, 3.0329

Charges guide

Per unit incl. 2 persons	
and electricity	€ 15.00 - € 54.00
extra person	€ 5.90 - € 9.90

For latest campsite news, availability and prices visit
alanrogers.com

Torreilles-Plage
Chadotel Camping le Trivoly

Route des Plages, F-66440 Torreilles-Plage (Pyrénées-Orientales) T: 04 68 28 20 28. E: info@chadotel.com

alanrogers.com/FR66240

The popularity of Torreilles derives mainly from its huge sandy beach and for some off-site nightlife, shopping, etc. but for smarter resorts one really needs to visit Le Barcarès or Canet a few kilometres distance in either direction. Le Trivoly (a member of the French Chadotel Group) is about 800 m. gentle stroll from the beach, in a fairly tranquil setting. In total there are 273 pitches, of which 60 are used for touring units. These are of a good size, well shaded and hedged with electricity (6A). The remainder are either used by tour operators or for site mobile homes to rent. It perhaps offers a rather more peaceful situation than do the other sites here.

Facilities

Four toilet blocks, although not new, provide modern facilities, including washbasins in (rather small) cabins, and were all clean and well cared for when we visited. Small shop (June-mid Sept). Snack restaurant and takeaway (June-mid Sept). Heated pool (1/5-15/9) with water slide and paddling pool. Terraced restaurant. Play area. Tennis. Minigolf. Bicycle hire. Entertainment programme in high season. WiFi (charged). Off site: Centre Commercial 500 m. Beach 800 m. Riding 1 km.

Open: 3 April - 25 September.

Directions

From A9 exit 42 (Perpignan-Nord) towards Le Barcarès for 9 km, then turn south on D81 towards Canet. After 3 km. turn left at roundabout, signed Torreilles-Plage. Site is on left, in about 500 m. GPS: 42.765808, 3.02681

Charges guide

Per unit incl. 2 persons	
and electricity	€ 19.60 - € 32.00
extra person	€ 5.80
child (2-13 yrs)	€ 3.80
dog	€ 3.20

Torreilles-Plage
Sunêlia les Tropiques

Boulevard de la plage, F-66440 Torreilles-Plage (Pyrénées-Orientales) T: 04 68 28 05 09.

E: contact@campinglestropiques.com **alanrogers.com/FR66190**

Les Tropiques makes a pleasant holiday destination, only 400 metres from a sandy beach and also boasting two pools. It will provide families with children of all ages with an ideal seaside holiday. There are 450 pitches with 200 given over to mobile homes and chalets. Pleasant pine and palm trees with other Mediterranean vegetation give shade and provide an attractive environment. Activities are provided for all including a large range of sports, activities, caberets and shows. An identity bracelet for entry to the site is obligatory in high season (a small payment is required).

Facilities

Modern, fully equipped sanitary facilities, provision for disabled visitors. Launderette. Shop (9/4-30/9). Bar (15/4-15/9). Restaurant (15/5-15/9). Takeaway and pizzeria (1/6-15/9). Heated pool (all season) and water slides. Paddling pool. Tennis (floodlit). Multisports area. Pétanque. Archery (1/7-31/8). TV, billiards room. Play area. Disco (every evening), miniclub for 6-12 ys in July/Aug. Bicycle hire (15/6-15/9). WiFi. Off site: Minigolf 300 m. Riding, windsurf board hire and sea fishing 400 m. Microlights, karting 1.5 km. Diving, waterskiing 4 km. Golf 15 km.

Open: 9 April - 1 October.

Directions

From A9 exit Perpignan-Nord, follow D83 towards Le Barcarès for 9 km. Take D81 south towards Canet for 3 km. turn left at roundabout for Torreilles-Plage. Site is the last but one on left. GPS: 42.7675, 3.02972

Charges guide

Per unit incl. 2 persons	
and electricity	€ 17.50 - € 44.00
extra person	€ 3.85 - € 8.75
child (0-13 yrs)	€ 2.55 - € 6.60
dog	€ 4.00

NEW digital
iPad editions

alan rogers

NEW 2012

Available on the App Store

FREE Alan Rogers bookstore app - digital editions of all 2012 guides

alanrogers.com/digital

For latest campsite news, availability and prices visit
alanrogers.com

Uzès
Camping du Mas de Rey

Arpaillargues, F-30700 Uzès (Gard) T: 04 66 22 18 27. E: info@campingmasderey.com

alanrogers.com/FR30110

A warm welcome from the English-speaking Maire family is guaranteed at this small, attractive, 70 pitch site. Most of the 60 large (150 sq.m) touring pitches are separated by bushes, many are shaded and all have 10A electricity. A good site for couples and families with young children. Due to the wonderful climate, grass can at times be hard to find. The reception, bar, restaurant and shop are in the same large airy building. The owners are always willing to give advice on the numerous things to see and do in the area. Gas and electric barbecues on site, communal charcoal barbecues.

Facilities

Two excellent, well maintained and very clean toilet blocks, with solar heating, facilities for disabled visitors, baby room and en-suite family cubicles. Laundry facilities. Shop (Jul/Aug), bread to order (all season). Takeaway meals (1/5-30/9) and restaurant (1/7-31/8). New heated swimming pool and paddling pool (1/5-15/10, closed lunchtimes). New chalets. WiFi over site (free). No charcoal barbecues. Off site: Golf 4 km. Canoeing 10 km.

Open: 1 April - 15 October.

Directions

Leave A9 autoroute, junction 23, signed Pont du Gard. Take N86 then D981 to Uzès (approx 18 km). Take D982 west, signed Arpaillargues, Moussac. Site signed on left, 3 km. GPS: 43.99843, 4.38424

Charges 2012

Per unit incl. 2 persons (3 in high season) and electricity	€ 20.80 - € 36.50
extra person	€ 5.60 - € 8.00

Credit cards accepted in July/August only.

Valras-Plage
Camping Blue Bayou

Vendres Plage Ouest, F-34350 Valras-Plage (Hérault) T: 04 67 37 41 97. E: infobluebayou@orange.fr

alanrogers.com/FR34370

A pleasant site, Blue Bayou is situated at the far end of Vendres Plage near Le Grau Vendres (the port of Vendres). It is therefore in a much quieter location than many other sites, away from the more hectic, built-up areas of Vendres and Valras-Plage. The beach is 300 m. across sand dunes and there are open views from the site creating a feeling of spaciousness. There are 256 pitches, all with 10A electricity, with 74 privately owned mobile homes and 92 to let, including some chalets. The touring pitches are large, some with their own sanitary arrangements. Light shade is provided by a mixture of trees. The restaurant and bar area is very attractive, overlooking two swimming pools, one with a toboggan, joined by a bridge where lifeguards station themselves. The owners and their family are very proud of their site and you are made to feel very welcome. The site would make a good choice for couples and families, perhaps best visited outside the height of the season when it becomes very busy. In July and August a tourist train runs to link Valras and Vendres.

Facilities

Individual toilet units for 66 touring pitches. Two separate blocks are fully equipped and were renovated for 2011. Baby bath and facilities for children. Facilities for disabled visitors. Laundry. Bar, restaurant and takeaway (open on demand in early season). Swimming pool (heated all season). Multisports court. Play area. Miniclub and entertainment in high season. WiFi throughout (charged). Bouncy castle (free) Tuesdays and Thursdays. Only electric barbecues permitted. Off site: Fishing, boat launching and riding 1 km. Bicycle hire 3 km. Golf 25 km.

Open: 7 April - 27 September.

Directions

From A9 exit 36 (Béziers Ouest) follow directions for Valras-Plage and Vendres Plage over four roundabouts. At fifth roundabout (Port Conchylicole) follow sign for Vendres Plage Ouest and site is 500 m. on the left past the Ranch and tourist office. The entrance is tight. GPS: 43.227408, 3.243536

Charges guide

Per unit incl. 2 persons and electricity	€ 21.00 - € 47.00
incl. private sanitary facility	€ 25.00 - € 55.00
extra person (over 4 yrs)	€ 5.00 - € 9.00

Blue Bayou ★★★★

300 meters from one of the most beautiful Mediterranean find-sand beaches, Blue Bayou welcomes you with its heated swimming pool area and with its various hosting arrangements in comfortable Mobile Homes, Chalets or its Camping area for tents and caravans.

We offer 40 pitches with private sanitary
New main sanitary block for the whole family!

Tennis, beach ball, biking, swimming for sportive holidays!
Entertainment, shows or thematic dinners for unforgettable holidays!

Open: 07/04/2012 - 27/09/2012

Vendres Plage Ouest - F-34350 Valras-Plage - France   infobluebayou@orange.fr
Tel: 0033 (0)4 67 37 41 97 - Fax: 0033 (0)4 67 37 53 00   www.bluebayou.fr

For latest campsite news, availability and prices visit
alanrogers.com

Valras-Plage

Camping Caravaning Domaine de la Yole

B.P. 23, F-34350 Valras-Plage (Hérault) T: 04 67 37 33 87. E: info@campinglayole.com

alanrogers.com/FR34090

A busy, happy holiday village with over 1,100 pitches could seem a little daunting. There are 590 pitches for touring with the remainder occupied by a range of mobile homes available to rent. Pitches are of a good size, all are level, hedged and have electricity (5A), water and waste water points and, very importantly for this area, they all have shade. The extensive pool area is impressive, more like an aqua park with its six pools and water slides. These are heated in low season and there are plenty of sunbathing areas. The central shopping and entertainment area form the heart of the site and provide everything you need. The beach, a long stretch of beautiful sand, is 500 m. away.

Facilities

Well maintained toilet blocks include baby rooms. Facilities for families and disabled visitors. Washing machines, dryers. Motorcaravan service points. Fridge hire. Shops. Restaurant, terrace, amphitheatre for entertainment (in season). Large pool complex. Tennis courts. Multisports court. Play areas. Bicycle hire. Boules. Miniclub. Youthclub. WiFi. Site-owned farm, vineyard and winery.

Open: 25 April - 19 September.

Directions

From A9 autoroute take Béziers Ouest exit for Valras-Plage (13-14 km) and follow Casino signs. Site is on left, just after sign for Vendres-Plage. GPS: 43.23708, 3.26234

Charges guide

Per unit incl. 2 persons	
and all services	€ 20.00 - € 57.40
extra person	€ 5.90 - € 8.50

Vauvert

Flower Camping Mas de Mourgues

Gallician, F-30600 Vauvert (Gard) T: 04 66 73 30 88. E: info@masdemourgues.com

alanrogers.com/FR30040

John and Lynn Foster are proud of their campsite on the edge of the Petite Camargue region, a unique area of France. It can be hot here, the Mistral can blow and you may have some road noise, but having said all that, the present owners, who moved from England over 10 years and live in the old Mas, have created quite a rural idyll and fit in well with the local community. There are 71 pitches with 46 for touring units (10A electricity), nine mobile homes to rent and four apartments. Originally a vineyard on stony ground (stong pegs needed), some of the vines are now used to mark the pitches, although many other varieties of trees and shrubs have been planted.

Facilities

Two small toilet blocks include facilities for disabled visitors. Washing machine. Motorcaravan service point. Takeaway food (high season). Reception sells essentials. Bread to order (day before). Play area. Weekly games (July/Aug). WiFi (charged). Communal barbecue but gas or electric ones are allowed. Accommodation to rent. Off site: Fishing 2 km. (licence not required). Riding 8 km. Bicycle hire 1 km. Golf 20 km. Beach 26 km.

Open: 1 April - 30 September.

Directions

Leave A9 autoroute at exit 26 (Gallargues) and follow signs for Vauvert. At Vauvert take N572 towards Arles and St Gilles. Site is on left after 4 km. at crossroads for Gallician. GPS: 43.6575, 4.2943

Charges guide

Per unit incl. 2 persons	
and electricity	€ 13.50 - € 20.40
extra person	€ 3.00 - € 4.40

Vendres

Camping Club les Vagues

F-34350 Valras-Plage (Hérault) T: 04 67 37 33 12. E: lesvagues34@free.fr

alanrogers.com/FR34120

Camping les Vagues is a member of the Sandaya group and can be found at the popular seaside resort of Valras-Plage, 500 m. from a fine sandy beach. Les Vagues has an excellent swimming pool complex extending over 2,000 sq.m. and an impressive range of amenities, including a buffet style restaurant (with carvery), a multisport pitch and a minigolf course. Pitches are well shaded and most have 6/10A electrical connections. A wide range of mobile homes and chalets are available for rent. This is a lively site in peak season with frequent evening entertainment and activities for all ages.

Facilities

Four modern toilet blocks with large showers, washbasins mainly in cabins, baby baths and provision for disabled visitors. Laundry facilities. Shop, bar, restaurant and snack bar. Swimming pool complex. Children's pool. Play area. Minigolf. Games room. Multisports court. Entertainment and miniclub (July/Aug). Tourist information. Gas or electric barbecues. Tourist train (July/Aug). WiFi (charged). Mobile homes and chalets for rent. Off site: Sandy beach, shops, bars and restaurants in Valras-Plage 500 m.

Open: 1 April - 30 September.

Directions

Approaching from A9 autoroute, leave at the Vendres exit and head south on the D64. Having passed Vendres and shortly before reaching Valras, watch for site signs at roundabout and turn right. GPS: 43.231023, 3.25356

Charges guide

Per unit incl. 2 persons	
and electricity	€ 20.00 - € 54.00
Camping Cheques accepted.	

For latest campsite news, availability and prices visit
alanrogers.com

Vendres Plage
Campéole les Mûriers

37E route départemental, F-34350 Vendres Plage (Hérault) T: 04 67 37 25 79. E: muriers@campeole.com
alanrogers.com/FR34620

Les Mûriers is a member of the Campéole group and is located among a group of sites situated on the route to le Grau de Vendres, the port of Vendre at the mouth of the River Aude. A marina has been developed there recently and there is also access to a lovely sandy beach, an 800 m. walk across the flat dunes. You need to look carefully for the Campéole reception as there is a large reception for a separate mobile home site under the same name. There are 105 bungalow tents available to rent, quite distinctive and fully equipped. They are arranged in a circular layout on grass pitches with hedging served by two toilet blocks. Please note that there are no pitches for tourers here.

Facilities	Directions
Two fully equipped toilet blocks. Washing machine. Bar/restaurant (28/06-30/08), takeaway, shop, heated swimming pool (all 15/06–15/09). Entertainment and miniclub (5-12 yrs; 28/06–28/08). Play area. Volleyball and basketball court. WiFi (charged). No barbecues allowed. Off site: Beach and sailing 800 m. Fishing 1 km.	From A9 take exit 36 (Béziers Ouest), towards Valras-Plage and Vendres-Plage. Continue over roundabouts. At 5th roundabout (Port Conchylicole) follow signs for Vendres Plage Ouest. Continue for 800 m, site is on right (Les Mûriers). GPS: 43.223433, 3.23945

Open: 12 June - 10 September.

Charges 2012

Contact the site for details.

Vernet-les-Bains
Hotel de Plein Air l'Eau Vive

Chemin de Saint-Saturnin, F-66820 Vernet-les-Bains (Pyrénées-Orientales) T: 04 68 05 54 14.
E: contact@leauvive-camping.com **alanrogers.com/FR66130**

Enjoying dramatic views of the Pic du Canigou (3,000 m), this rather special and peaceful, natural site is only 1.5 km. from the centre of Vernet-les-Bains in the Pyrenees. The 70 tourist pitches are on grass, with electricity (4/10A) and 45 fully serviced, are on a slight slope, part hedged and some terraced, with a separate tent field. Most pitches have some shade and there are 11 chalets and mobile homes to rent. The 'pièce de résistance' is the unique natural pool, 'le plan d'eau biologique'. It is fed from the nearby bubbling stream with a special filtration system. It is really quite impressive, and attractively landscaped in keeping with the site's green image – it's warm as well!

Facilities	Directions
Fully equipped toilet facilities and provision for babies and disabled visitors. Washing machine. Bread, main season. Bar/restaurant/takeaway with terrace (15/6-31/8). Natural swimming pool. New play area with trampoline, basketball and table tennis. WiFi (free) on the terrace. Off site: Fishing 200 m. Swimming pool, thermal centre 1 km. Organised rafting, canoeing, hydrospeed trips. Bicycle hire 2 km.	Following N116 towards Andorra. At Ville Franche, turn south, D116, for Vernet-les-Bains. After 5 km. keep right avoiding town. Turn right over bridge towards Sahorre. Immediately turn right (ave de Saturnin) for about 1 km. through a residential area (rather winding). GPS: 42.55506, 2.37779

Open: 15 May - 30 September.

Charges guide

Per unit incl. 2 persons	€ 19.50 - € 26.50

Credit cards accepted 1/6-31/8 only.

Vias
Yelloh! Village le Club Farret

F-34450 Vias-Plage (Hérault) T: 04 67 21 64 45. E: info@yellohvillage-club-farret.com
alanrogers.com/FR34110

An excellent site for families, well maintained and attractively landscaped with flowering shrubs, giving a truly Mediterranean feel. Staff are helpful and everywhere is neat and tidy. It is a large, busy site but well organised with a relaxed atmosphere. There are 785 good sized, level, grassy pitches, with 359 for touring (6A electricity) with some shade from many trees. The large heated pool has lots of sunbathing space and a special area with sand and a paddling pool has been created for youngsters and their parents. The safe beach is alongside the site, so some pitches have sea views.

Facilities	Directions
Very clean toilet blocks have good facilities for children. Baby rooms, facilities for disabled visitors. Washing machines. Well stocked supermarket. Hairdresser. Bars with pizzas, snacks, takeaway. Restaurant. Crêperie with minigolf. Heated swimming pool complex with lifeguard (all season). Wellness centre. Gym. Play areas. Miniclub. Teenagers' club. Tennis. Archery. Programme of games. Bicycle hire. WiFi (charged). Off site: Shops, bars and Luna Park within walking distance. Riding 1 km.	Site is south of Vias at Vias-Plage. From N112 (Béziers - Agde) take D137 signed Vias-Plage. Site is signed on the left. GPS: 43.29103, 3.41912

Open: 29 March - 29 September.

Charges guide

Per unit incl. 2 persons and electricity	€ 19.00 - € 50.00
extra person	€ 6.00 - € 8.00
extra tent	€ 3.00
dog	€ 4.00

---

(459)

For latest campsite news, availability and prices visit
alanrogers.com

Vias
Camping International le Napoléon
1171 avenue de la Méditerranée, F-34450 Vias-Plage (Hérault) T: 04 67 01 07 80
alanrogers.com/FR34030

Le Napoléon is a small, family run site situated in the village of Vias-Plage bordering the Mediterranean. The Graziani family celebrated their 40th anniversary at Napoléon in 2009. Vias-Plage is hectic to say the least in season, but once through the security barrier and entrance to le Napoléon, the contrast is marked – tranquillity, yet still only 150 m. from the beach and other attractions. It has a Californian-style pool, amphitheatre for entertainment and other new facilities, but thoughtful planning and design ensure that the camping area is quiet. With good shade from many tall trees, there are 239 fairly small, hedged and level pitches, 92 for touring units, all with 10A electricity. They are mixed in with a range of mobile homes for rent. The town of Vias itself is set further back from the sea, in the wine growing area of the Midi, an area which includes the Camargue, Béziers and popular modern resorts such as Cap d'Agde. The family own a range of shops, including a supermarket, a café, restaurant and gift shop, just outside the site on the main street. A good sandy beach is down the road.

Facilities
Fully equipped sanitary blocks are of a fair standard. Baby bath. Facilities for disabled visitors. Laundry. Motorcaravan services. Fridge hire. Supermarket and bakery. Bar. Restaurant/pizzeria. Swimming pool complex with lively piped music (heated in early and late season) includes a jacuzzi, hammam and solarium. Gym/fitness room with new equipment. Bicycle hire. Tennis, archery, boules. TV. Rooms for young campers. Children's club. Amphitheatre, with free entertainment until midnight. Disco outside site (Easter-Sept). WiFi (charged). Off site: Shops, restaurants, and laundry immediately adjacent. Beach 150 m.

Open: 6 April - 30 September.

Directions
From autoroute A9 take exit Agde-Pezenas, direction Béziers. Continue for 5 km. direction Vias – Vias-Plage. Site is on the right near the beach; watch carefully for turning between restaurant and shops. GPS: 43.29197, 3.41535

Charges guide
Per unit incl. 2 persons and electricity	€ 20.00 - € 45.00
extra person (over 4 yrs)	€ 6.00 - € 9.00
dog	€ 4.00

LE NAPOLÉON Camping Club ★★★★

Open from 2012/04/06 to 2012/09/30 - ☎ +33 (0)4 67 01 07 80

SEASIDE Rentals of CHALETS, MOBIL-HOMES, and APARTMENTS. FREE for children under 4 years

Booking (it's advisable to do it from January 3rd) and special offers : **www.camping-napoleon.fr**

SPA, HAMMAM, SAUNA, SOLARIUM, MASSAGES, KIDS CLUB - RELAXATION AND ENTERTAINMENT JULY AND AUGUST.

Vias
Camping le Méditerranée Plage
Côte Ouest, F-34450 Vias (Hérault) T: 04 67 90 99 07. E: contact@mediterranee-plage.com
alanrogers.com/FR34410

Set beside the beach in a quiet part of the coast, this site is somewhat different from the majority of beach sites. It has a most impressive entertainment complex situated to one side of the site with very comfortable outdoor seating facing a large stage for entertainment and a very smart bar and restaurant. The colourful furnishings and modern design reflect its Mediterranean setting. The site is very well cared for, with 410 pitches (some 185 used for touring units). Either grassy with a degree of shade or, as you get nearer the beach, more sandy with less shade, all have 6A electricity.

Facilities
Two large toilet blocks are modern, one very impressive with a special smart nursery unit. Two small ones are more traditional. Facilities for disabled visitors. Laundry. Motorcaravan service point. Supermarket. Restaurant and bar. Snack bar. Hairdressers. TV room. Play area. Games room. Multisports court. Tennis. Archery. Windsurfing from beach. Bicycle hire. Activity and entertainment. WiFi (charged). Off site: Riding and fishing 2 km. Golf 15 km.

Open: 31 March - 30 September.

Directions
From A9 exit 35 (Béziers Est) follow directions for Agde and Sète on N112. After 4.2 km. turn for Portiragnes. Pass village and continue for 2.5 km. over Canal du Midi then turn left and follow site signs. GPS: 43.28202, 3.37105

Charges guide
Per unit incl. 2 persons and electricity	€ 16.90 - € 40.50
extra person	€ 3.20 - € 7.20

For latest campsite news, availability and prices visit
alanrogers.com

Vias
Sunêlia Domaine de la Dragonnière

RD612, F-34450 Vias-sur-Mer (Hérault) T: 04 67 01 03 10. E: contact@dragonniere.com
alanrogers.com/FR34450

La Dragonnière makes up for being set back from the sea by offering an amazing selection of swimming pools and a wide range of sporting activities and entertainment. It is a busy holiday village, located between the popular resorts of Vias and Portiragnes, and very well organised. In total, there are 880 pitches split into two areas, most occupied by a range of smart mobile homes and chalets, but there are still around 50 grass touring pitches, with some shade. All have electrical connections (10A) as well as water and drainage. La Dragonnière lies 5 km. from the nearest beach and a free shuttle operates in peak season. This is a wonderful site for families with teenagers and young children.

Facilities

One fully equipped toilet block includes facilities for babies and disabled visitors. Laundry. Supermarket. Bar and restaurant complex (9/4-18/9) takeaway service (18/6-11/9). Two heated swimming pool complexes with children's pools. Play area. Sauna and gym (9/4-18/9). Multisports pitch. Entertainment and competitions (high season). Activity programme (low season). Bicycle hire. WiFi (charged). Mobile homes and chalets for rent. Off site: Nearest beach and boat launching 5 km.

Open: 9 April - 18 September.

Directions

Take the Béziers Est exit from the A9 autoroute. Follow directions to Villenevue, Serignan and Valras-Plage. After 800 m. at the large roundabout, follow signs to Vias aéroport on the N112. After a further 7 km, the campsite can be found on the right. GPS: 43.313, 3.36517

Charges guide

Per unit incl. 3 persons, water, drain and electricity	€ 20.00 - € 51.00
extra person	€ 7.00 - € 9.00

Vias
Camping les Salisses

Route de la Mer, F-34450 Vias-Plage (Hérault) T: 04 67 21 64 07. E: info@salisses.com
alanrogers.com/FR34520

A traditional style French campsite, les Salisses is well run and managed with an impressive range of swimming pools and other facilities. The 400 level pitches of average size are separated by flowering shrubs and trees that provide shade – all rather pretty. There are just over 100 places for tourers, with 8A electricity, the rest being taken by a range of mobile homes, some to let. Vias-Plage is a somewhat hectic resort and les Salisses has its own section of beach with a bar. However, the site's own pools are very welcoming, the covered one (heated in low season) is reserved for naturists in high season.

Facilities

Four fully equipped toilet blocks. Facilities for disabled visitors. Laundry. Shop (16/6-19/9). Bar and restaurant (16/6-19/9). Takeaway pizzeria (1/7-31/8). One indoor pool heated for low season, two other pool complexes. Play area. Sports field (rugby posts). Multisports court. Tennis. Minigolf. Bicycle hire. Wide range of entertainment and activities. WiFi (free). Off site: Watersports at beach 800 m. Riding 1 km. Golf 5 km. Bus stop for Vias town.

Open: 16 April - 19 September.

Directions

From the A9 take exit 34, then the N312 towards Vias and Agde. Join the N112 to avoid Vias town to pick up sign for Vias-Plage. Site is first on the right. GPS: 43.29657, 3.4164

Charges guide

Per unit incl. 2 persons and electricity	€ 26.00 - € 40.00

Camping Cheques accepted.

Villegly-en-Minervois
Camping le Moulin de Sainte Anne

Chemin de Sainte Anne, F-11600 Villegly-en-Minervois (Aude) T: 04 68 72 20 80.
E: campingstanne@wanadoo.fr **alanrogers.com/FR11210**

Just a few years ago le Moulin Sainte Anne was a vineyard but, with much hard work by Antoine and Magali Lacuve and the backing of the Mairie, there is now a flourishing campsite on the edge of the town. There are 45 level grass pitches of a good size and hedged. All have water and 10A electricity and are terraced where necessary and landscaped with growing trees and shrubs. The facilities are modern, well kept and in keeping with the area. They include a heated pool and a very attractive entertainment area. There is close co-operation with the village and villagers are welcome to the evening entertainment. A Sites et Paysages member.

Facilities

A modern toilet block is well equipped. Shared facilities for disabled visitors and babies. Washing machine. Motorcaravan service point. Bar, snack bar with takeaway (15/6-25/8). Heated swimming and paddling pools (1/5-30/9). Basket- and volleyball court. Games room. Play area. Communal barbecue (not allowed on pitches). Chalets to rent. WiFi over site. Off site: Multisports pitch.

Open: 1 April - 30 October.

Directions

Driving north from Carcassonne on D118 turn on D620 signed Villalier and Villegly for 7 km. Site is at entrance to village. Turn right over bridge just before the cemetery. GPS: 43.28308, 2.44152

Charges guide

Per unit incl. 2 persons and electricity	€ 15.00 - € 25.00
extra person	€ 3.00 - € 5.00

For latest campsite news, availability and prices visit
alanrogers.com

Villeneuve-lez-Avignon

Campé**o**le

Campéole Ile des Papes

1497 route départementale 780, F-30400 Villeneuve-lez-Avignon (Gard) T: 04 90 15 15 90.
E: ile-des-papes@campeole.com **alanrogers.com/FR30120**

Camping Ile des Papes is a large, open and very well equipped site. Avignon and its palace and museums are 8 km. away. The site has an extensive swimming pool area and a fishing lake with beautiful mature gardens. The railway is quite near but noise is not too intrusive. The 381 pitches, 176 for touring (all with 10A electricity), are of a good size on level grass, but with little shade. Games and competitions for all ages are organised in high season. This site is very popular with groups and is especially busy at weekends and in high season. In July and August a minibus is available for transport to Avignon, the airport and the railway station; the local bus can take you directly to Avignon. A good base to explore the famous Routes des Vins and the old villages and ancient towns of the Provençal region. There are many walks and cycle routes close by.

Facilities

Good quality toilet blocks (may be stretched when busy) include baby rooms and facilities for disabled campers. Washing machines. Motorcaravan services. Well stocked shop. Bar and restaurant (1/4-20/10 limited hours in low season). Large swimming pool complex and pool for children, all unheated, (15/4-31/10). Play area. Lake for fishing. Archery, tennis, minigolf and basketball (all free). Bicycle hire. Gas and electric barbecues only. Communal barbecue. Off site: Riding 3 km. Boat launching 5 km. Villeneuve-lez-Avignon with shops, bars, restaurants.

Open: 26 March - 5 November.

Directions

Leave the A9 at exit 22 (Roquemaure) and take D976 to Roquemaure, turn south D980 towards Villeneuve. Near railway bridge turn hard left, D780 (site signed). Cross river, immediately turn right to site. GPS: 43.97660, 4.79440

Charges guide

Per unit incl. 2 persons and electricity	€ 19.10 - € 29.00
extra person	€ 4.50 - € 4.90
child (under 7 years)	free - € 3.90

Campé**o**le
CAMPSITES AND RENTALS

Île des Papes ★★★★

Four stars site close to Avignon, famous for its architectural highlights and theatre festival. 2 swimming pools, touring pitches and quality accommodations for rent.

LANGUEDOC-ROUSSILLON

30400 Villeneuve-lez-Avignon - Tel.: +33-490-1515-90 - www.campeole.co.uk / ile-des-papes@campeole.com

Villeneuve-les-Béziers

Camping les Berges du Canal

Promenade les Vernets, F-34420 Villeneuve-les-Béziers (Hérault) T: 04 67 39 36 09.
E: contact@lesbergesducanal.com **alanrogers.com/FR34210**

There are surprisingly few campsites which provide an opportunity to enjoy the rather special ambience for which the Canal du Midi is renowned, but this pleasant little site is right alongside the canal at Villeneuve-les-Béziers. The campsite is in a peaceful and shady situation, separated from the canal by an unmade access road with a total of 75 level pitches on sandy grass. Some are large with 10A electricity, others are smaller and more suitable for tents. Of these, 20 are occupied by privately owned mobile homes and a further 25 are available to rent. There is a pleasant pool complex, one of the two pools being fitted with a jacuzzi-style facility.

Facilities

Fully equipped toilet block with some washbasins in cabins. Facilities for disabled visitors (with key) and children. Beauty therapist visits weekly. Laundry facilities. Motorcaravan service point. Bar/snack bar (serving breakfast too). Small restaurant attached to site. Two swimming pools. Multisport court. Play area. Fishing. Evening entertainment during high season. Only gas and electric barbecues allowed. Off site: Attractive old village centre of Villeneuve-les-Béziers. Beach at Portiragnes-Plage. Bicycle hire 100 m. Riding 5 km. Beach 7 km.

Open: 15 March - 15 October.

Directions

From A9 exit 35, follow signs for Agde, at first roundabout take N112 (Béziers). First left onto D37 (Villeneve-les-Béziers and Valras-Plage). Pass traffic lights, left at roundabout and follow site signs (take care at junction by bridge). GPS: 43.31673, 3.28433

Charges guide

Per unit incl. 2 persons and electricity	€ 17.00 - € 24.00
extra person (over 4 yrs)	€ 3.00 - € 5.00
dog	€ 3.00

This is a corner of France that evokes dreamy images of lazy afternoons amongst sleepy village squares, sunny vineyards and beautiful lavender fields basking under the dazzling blue of the sky.

DÉPARTEMENTS: 04 ALPES-DE-HAUTE-PROVENCE, 05 HAUTES-ALPES, 13 BOUCHES-DU-RHÔNE, 83 VAR, 84 VAUCLUSE

MAJOR CITY: MARSEILLES

Provence is a region of magical light, bleached landscapes, olive groves, herb-scented garrigue, vineyards and Roman and medieval antiquities. The river valleys provide natural routes through the mountain barrier. Roman monuments can be seen at Orange, and at Vaison-la-Romaine, where a 2,000-year-old bridge is still in use. Avignon was the site of the papal court and the Palais des Papes at Avignon is a spectacular construction.

The Hautes-Alpes will reward with stunning vistas, peace and quiet. Briançon is the highest town in Europe and many of the high passes are not for the faint-hearted. The Vaucluse, where in the late spring the southern slopes of the Montagne du Luberon are a mass of colour with wild flowers. The extinct volcanic cone of Mont Ventoux provides dramatic views. The scents, colours and an amazing intensity of light have encouraged artists and writers to settle amidst the sleepy villages, with narrow streets and ancient dwellings topped with sun-baked terracotta tiles, where the air is fragrant with the perfume of wild herbs and lavender.

Places of interest

Avignon: ramparts, old city, Papal Palace, old palace, Calvet museum.

Mont Ventoux: near Carpentras, one of the best known stages of the classic Tour de France annual cycle race.

Orange: Roman city, gateway to the Midi, Colline St Europe.

St Vaison la Romaine: Roman city, the French Pompeii.

Cuisine of the region

Influenced by the Savoie area to the north and the Côte d'Azur to the south, with emphasis on herbs and garlic, and fish. The wine region is mainly known for its dry, fruity rosé wines: Bandol, Bellet, Palette, Cassis. Red wines include Côtes du Rhône and Châteauneuf-du-Pape.

Aigo Bouido: garlic and sage soup with bread (or eggs and cheese).

Aïoli (ailloli): a mayonnaise sauce with garlic and olive oil.

Bouillabaisse: fish soup served with rouille sauce, saffron and aioli.

Bourride: a creamy fish soup (usually made with large white fish), thickened with aïoli and flavoured with crawfish.

Pissaladière: Provençal bread dough with onions, anchovies, olives.

Pollo pépitora: Provençal chicken fricassee thickened with lemon-flavoured mayonnaise.

Ratatouille: aubergines, courgettes, onions, garlic, red peppers and tomatoes in olive oil.

www.discover-southoffrance.com
information@cft-paca.fr
(0)4 91 56 47 00

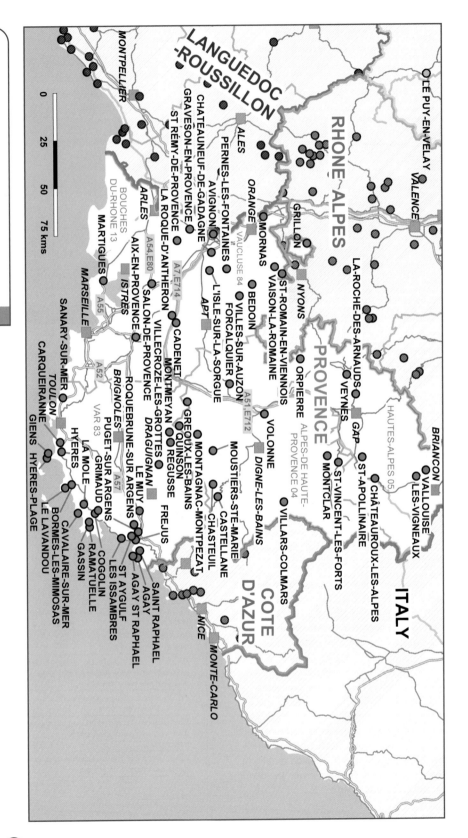

For latest campsite news, availability and prices visit

alanrogers.com

Agay
Camping Caravaning Esterel

Avenue des Golf, Agay, F-83530 Saint Raphaël (Var) T: 04 94 82 03 28. E: contact@esterel-caravaning.fr
alanrogers.com/FR83020

Esterel is a quality, award-winning caravan site east of St Raphaël, set among the hills beyond Agay. The site is 3.5 km. from the sandy beach at Agay where parking is perhaps a little easier than at most places on this coast, but a shuttle runs from the site to and from the beach several times daily in July and August (€1). It has 164 touring pitches for caravans but not tents; all have electricity (10A) and a water tap, 18 special ones have their own en-suite washroom adjoining whilst others also have a washing machine, dishwasher, jacuzzi, 16A electricity and free WiFi. Pitches are on shallow terraces, attractively landscaped with shade and a variety of flowers, giving a feeling of spaciousness.

Facilities

Excellent refurbished, heated toilet blocks. Individual toilet units on 18 pitches. Facilities for disabled visitors. Laundry room. Motorcaravan services. Shop. Gift shop. Takeaway. Bar/restaurant. Five circular swimming pools (two heated), one for adults, one for children (covered and heated), three arranged as a waterfall. Spa with sauna etc. Disco. Archery. Minigolf. Tennis. Pony rides. Pétanque. Squash. Playground. Nursery. Bicycle hire. Internet access. Organised events in season. No barbecues. WiFi throughout. Baby club (3 months to 3 years) all season. Off site: Golf nearby. Trekking by foot, bicycle or pony in L'Esterel forest park. Fishing and beach 3 km.

Open: 31 March - 29 September.

Directions

From A8, exit Fréjus, follow signs for Valescure, then for Agay, site is on left. The road from Agay is the easiest to follow but it is possible to approach from St Raphaël via Valescure. Look carefully for site sign, which is difficult to see. GPS: 43.453775, 6.832817

Charges guide

Per unit incl. 2 persons and electricity	€ 18.00 - € 83.00
extra person	€ 9.00 - € 11.00
child (acc. to age)	€ 5.00 - € 10.00
dog	€ 4.00

Agay-Saint Raphaël

Campé●le

Campéole du Dramont

986 bvd 36ème Division Texas, F-83530 Agay-Saint Raphaël (Var) T: 04 94 82 07 68.
E: dramont@campeole.com **alanrogers.com/FR83700**

Le Dramont stretches over a shady hillside, sloping gently down to a pebble beach (direct access), close to the attractive resort of Agay. This site is popular with scuba divers, and is an ideal base for exploring the turquoise waters. There is an international diving school on site and other amenities here include a beauty salon (July and August) and a sports field. Le Dramont has 400 pitches, of which 188 are occupied by mobile homes, chalets and fully equipped tents, for rent. Pitches are well shaded and generally of a good size. Some are near the main road so there may be some road noise. The site becomes lively in high season with a daily entertainment and activity programme.

Facilities

Three sanitary blocks include seatless toilets, modern preset showers and washbasins with hot and cold water. Good facilities for children. Wet room for disabled visitors. Rather dated laundry facilities. Shop. Snack bar. Beauty salon. Takeaway food. Games room. Playground. Diving school. Boat launching (charged). Multisports pitch. Activity and entertainment programme. Tourist information. Direct beach access. Mobile homes, chalets and tents for rent. WiFi (charged). Off site: Fishing. Golf. Rock climbing. Walking and mountain biking in the Esterel hills. St Raphaël and Fréjus.

Open: 20 March - 9 October.

Directions

From Saint Raphaël, take the RN98 towards Cannes. The site is 7 km beyond Saint Raphaël (between Boulouris and Agay). GPS: 43.417864, 6.848195

Charges guide

Per unit incl. 2 persons and electricity	€ 21.10 - € 43.00
extra person	€ 5.50 - € 9.30
child (2-6 yrs)	€ 3.20 - € 3.90
dog	€ 3.20 - € 3.90

For latest campsite news, availability and prices visit
alanrogers.com

Aix-en-Provence

Camping Chantecler

41 avenue du Val Saint André, F-13100 Aix-en-Provence (Bouches du Rhône) T: 04 42 26 12 98.
E: info@campingchantecler.com **alanrogers.com/FR13120**

Cézanne is amongst Aix's most famous former residents, but many just see the town as a stop on the journey south. This good, quiet campsite might change that image; on the southeast edge of the town, close to the motorway it is only minutes by the good bus service from the city centre. The site provides 240 pitches (160 for tourers) in mature woodland with good facilities. Under the new leadership of Serge Carcolse, the site is destined to change for the good whilst retaining the best that already exists. Cézanne's studio is amongst the numerous places to visit in Aix. The town has something to offer everyone, from modern pedestrian shopping to numerous museums and cultural sites and endless restaurants and bars. The Office du Tourisme also arranges a variety of excursions on a weekly basis to the surrounding area, ranging from bird sanctuaries in the Camargue to Marseille and the Luberon.

Facilities

Four sanitary blocks provide ample WCs, washbasins and hot showers around the site. Motorcaravan service point. Bar and restaurant (1/5-15/9). Swimming pool (1/5-15/9). Tennis. Boules. Internet access and WiFi. Barbecues are not permitted. Twin-axle units are not accepted. Mobile homes to rent. Off site: Bus service 200 m. Aix-en-Provence 2 km. Riding 2 km. Golf 5 km.

Open: All year.

Directions

Leave the A8 at exit 31 (Aix-Sud) and at roundabout turn right. At second set of lights turn left and within 300 m. at roundabout turn right to the site in 200 m. GPS: 43.51636, 5.47495

Charges guide

Per unit incl. 2 persons	
and electricity	€ 22.90 - € 24.20
extra person	€ 6.10 - € 6.50
child (under 7 yrs)	€ 3.60 - € 3.70
dog	€ 3.40 - € 3.50

Camping Chantecler****

Situated in a green quiet oasis and offering you all the sweetness of life, on only 5 minutes from Aix en Provence.
We warmly welcome you on this green 8 acres park, the favorite surroundings of Cézanne on only 30 minutes form Marseille and Cassis, and on only 45 minutes form Baux de Provence and Avignon.

Val St. André - 13100 Aix en Provence - Tel.: 0033 (0)4 42 26 12 98
info@campingchantecler.com - www.campingchantecler.com

Avignon

Camping du Pont d'Avignon

10 chemin de la Barthelasse, Ile de la Barthelasse, F-84000 Avignon (Vaucluse) T: 04 90 80 63 50.
E: info@camping-avignon.com **alanrogers.com/FR84090**

This is a city site, yet it is in a quiet location and only a short walk or free ferry ride from the town. The well shaded and neat layout of the pitches and the very good access will ensure a pleasant stay. There are 300 level pitches, some on grass and some with hardstanding, 120 with 10A electricity. A good play area, tennis courts and volleyball pitch are in the centre of the site separating the tent pitches on one side and the electric pitches on the other. Many pitches are separated by hedges. The restaurant, bar and terrace overlook the attractive pool. English is spoken at reception.

Facilities

Well maintained and clean toilet blocks, facilities for disabled visitors. Washing machines, dryer. Motorcaravan services. Well stocked (4/4-3/10). Bar/restaurant, takeaway (4/4-20/9). Swimming pool, paddling pool (2/5-20/9). Play area with climbing frame. Tennis (free). Bicycle hire (July/Aug). Internet access and WiFi (charged). Off site: Avignon with famous bridge and Pope's Palace. Ferry to town centre. Bicycle hire 2 km. Riding 3 km. Golf 10 km.

Open: 16 March - 1 November.

Directions

Site is on an island in River Rhône. Well signed from roads into Avignon, ring road has complex junctions. Accessed from Pont Daladier towards Villeneuve les Avignon. Just after crossing first section of river fork right, site signed, site about 1 km. GPS: 43.95153, 4.80193

Charges guide

Per unit incl. 2 persons	
and electricity	€ 16.82 - € 26.72
extra person	€ 3.41 - € 4.86
child (3-12 yrs)	free - € 4.30

For latest campsite news, availability and prices visit
alanrogers.com

Bormes-les-Mimosas
Camp du Domaine

B.P. 207 La Favière, F-83230 Bormes-les-Mimosas (Var) T: 04 94 71 03 12. E: mail@campdudomaine.com
alanrogers.com/FR83120

Camp du Domaine, 3 km. south of Le Lavandou, is a large, attractive beachside site with 1,200 pitches set in 45 hectares of pinewood, although surprisingly it does not give the impression of being so big. The pitches are large and most are reasonably level, 800 with 10A electricity. The most popular pitches are beside the beach, but the ones furthest away are generally larger and have more shade. Amongst the trees, many are more suitable for tents. The price for all the pitches is the same – smaller but near the beach or larger with shade. The beach is the attraction and everyone tries to get close. American motorhomes are not accepted. Despite its size, the site does not feel too busy, except perhaps around the supermarket. This is mainly because many pitches are hidden in the trees, the access roads are quite wide and it all covers quite a large area (some of the beach pitches are 600 m. from the entrance). Its popularity makes early reservation necessary over a long season (about mid June to mid Sept) as regular clients book from season to season. A good range of languages are spoken.

Facilities

Ten modern, well used but clean toilet blocks. Mostly Turkish WCs. Facilities for disabled visitors (but steep steps). Baby room. Washing machines. Fridge hire. Well stocked supermarket, bars, pizzeria (all open all season). No swimming pool. Excellent play area. Boats, pedaloes for hire. Wide range of watersports. Games, competitions (July/Aug). Children's club. Tennis. Multisports courts. Only gas and electric barbecues are allowed. Dogs are not accepted 10/7-21/8. WiFi throughout (charged). Off site: Bicycle hire 500 m. Riding and golf 15 km.

Open: 9 April - 5 November.

Directions

From Bormes-les-Mimosas, head east on D559 to Le Lavandou. At roundabout, turn off D559 towards the sea on road signed Favière. After 2 km. turn left at site signs. GPS: 43.11779, 6.35176

Charges guide

Per unit incl. 2 persons and electricity	€ 28.50 - € 43.00
extra person	€ 6.00 - € 9.50
child (under 7 yrs)	free - € 4.80
dog (not 10/7-21/8)	free

Camp du Domaine

★★★★

Var - Provence
Côte d'Azur

Bungalows
with sea view
Facing Iles d'Or
Animation
Shops

Campers
Caravans
Touring pitches
for tents
Mobile Homes

Direct access to one of
the most beautiful beaches
of the Côte d'Azur

BP 207 La Favière
83230 Bormes les Mimosas
Tél. +33 (0)4 94 71 03 12
Fax : +33 (0)4 94 15 18 67
e-mail : mail@campdudomaine.com
GPS :N 43°7'4" E 6°21'7"
Online booking
www.campdudomaine.com

For latest campsite news, availability and prices visit
alanrogers.com

Cadenet
Camping Val de Durance

F-84160 Cadenet (Vaucluse) T: 04 90 68 37 75. E: info@homair.com
alanrogers.com/FR84170

Val de Durance camping village is part of the Homair Vacances Group. It is an ideal holiday site for a family with young children yet will also suit a couple wishing to discover Provence or the Lubéron National Park. There are 232 pitches with just 36 for touring, all fully serviced with 10A electricity. Pitches are flat and most are shaded and have shrubs and hedges for privacy. This green, 27-acre campsite has its own ten-acre springwater lake and private sandy beach for sunbathing and paddling in the shallow roped area.

Facilities

Three well equipped toilet blocks, conveniently situated at various parts of the site. Children's WC and facilities for campers with disabilities. Small shop, bar/snack bar, takeaway (all season). Swimming and paddling pools (all season). Lake fishing, beach. WiFi. Off site: River fishing 500 m. Hiking trails. Canoeing at Cadenet 3 km. Lourmarin château 5 km. La Roque d'Atheron 7 km. Bicycle hire 12 km. Golf 25 km. Avignon and Orange.

Open: 1 April - 30 September.

Directions

A7 Autoroute, exit 26 (Senas), take N7 southeast towards Lambesc. At Pont Royal turn east onto D561. Beyond La Roque d'Antheron (14 km), turn north across river, onto D943 to Cadenet. GPS: 43.71971, 5.35499

Charges guide

| Per unit incl. 2 persons and electricity | € 15.00 - € 29.00 |
| extra person | € 3.00 - € 6.00 |

Carqueiranne
Camping le Beau Vezé

Route de la Moutonne, F-83320 Carqueiranne (Var) T: 04 94 57 65 30. E: info@camping-beauveze.com
alanrogers.com/FR83130

Le Beau Vezé is a quiet five-hectare site, inland from the busy resort of Hyères. The owner tries to keep it as a family site with its quiet position, although the superb beaches and hectic coastal areas are within easy reach. On a steep hillside it has terraced pitches and a plateau with more pitches on the top. The 120 pitches, all with electricity (10A Europlug) are well shaded and some will be rather difficult to manoeuvre onto due to overhanging trees and could be difficult for motorcaravans. There is some road noise on the lower pitches. The young staff here are friendly and helpful.

Facilities

Reasonable standard sanitary blocks, two heated, although maintenance may be variable. Some showers with washbasin. Baby room. Washing machines. Bar/restaurant, takeaway. Bread. Medium sized pool, paddling pool. Play area. Minigolf, boules and tennis. Jet-ski hire. Walking tours, visits to vineyard. Evening entertainment in restaurant. Off site: Golf 2 km. Fishing 3 km. Riding 5 km. The lovely old town of Hyères is only 8 km.

Open: 1 May - 15 September.

Directions

From A57 take exit for Toulon Est and follow D559 between Carqueiranne and Le Pradet. Take D76 northwards signed La Moutonne and site is signed on right of D76. GPS: 43.11413, 6.0564

Charges guide

Per unit incl. 2 persons and electricity	€ 20.00 - € 33.00
extra person	€ 4.50 - € 6.50
child (under 7 yrs)	€ 3.00 - € 4.50

No credit cards. Camping Cheques accepted.

Carqueiranne
Campéole les Arbousiers

Campé●le

Chemin des Arbousiers, Le Canebas, F-83320 Carqueiranne (Var) T: 04 94 58 56 56.
E: arbousiers@campeole.com **alanrogers.com/FR83670**

Les Arbousiers is a small site located on a hilltop overlooking the beautiful Gulf of Giens. There are 77 pitches occupied by mobile homes, chalets and fully equipped bungalow tents; a further 23 pitches are for small tents only. Access to pitches by car is authorised for arrivals and departures only, and vehicles are parked in a large car park close to reception. With all the activities taking place at the bar/restaurant area, this ensures a tranquil ambiance within the site. The pool area has plenty of relaxation space and will attract people looking for a peaceful vacation.

Facilities

Two modern, clean sanitary blocks. Laundry facilities. Bar/restaurant with takeaway (1/6-1/9). Swimming pool and children's pool with beach area (as site). Boules pitch. Volleyball. Play area. Activities and entertainment. Tourist information. Mobile homes, chalets and tents for rent. WiFi (charged). Off site: Beach 3 km. Riding and bicycle hire 5 km. Golf 6 km. Sailing 10 km. Hyères old town 10 km. Close to parc naturel.

Open: 1 April - 30 September.

Directions

From the A57 motorway (Aix en Provence - Toulon), take exit 2 and follow signs for Carqueiranne and Le Pradet. Upon reaching Carqueiranne, follow signs to Le Canebas and Fort de la Bayarde and the campsite. GPS: 43.093081, 6.058429

Charges guide

| Per unit incl. 2 persons and electricity | € 17.90 - € 27.60 |
| extra person | € 4.60 - € 7.90 |

Castellane
Castel Camping le Domaine du Verdon

545

Camp du Verdon, F-04120 Castellane (Alpes-de-Haute-Provence) T: 04 92 83 61 29.
E: contact@camp-du-verdon.com **alanrogers.com/FR04020**

Close to the Route des Alpes and the Gorges du Verdon. Two heated swimming pools and numerous on-site activities during high season help to keep non-canoeists here. Du Verdon is a large level site, part meadow, part wooded, with 500 partly shaded, rather stony pitches (390 for tourists). Numbered and separated by bushes, they vary in size, have 6A electricity, and 125 also have water and waste water. They are mostly separate from the mobile homes (60) and pitches used by tour operators. Some overlook the unfenced River Verdon, so watch the children. This is a very popular holiday area, the gorge, canoeing and rafting being the main attractions, ideal for active families. One can walk to Castellane without using the main road where there are numerous shops, cafés and restaurants. Dances and discos in July and August suit all age groups. The latest finishing time is around 23.00, after which time patrols make sure that the site is quiet. The site is popular and very busy in July and August.

Facilities

Refurbished toilet blocks include facilities for disabled visitors. Washing machines. Motorcaravan services. Babysitting service. Restaurant, terrace, log fire for cooler evenings. New supermarket. Pizzeria/crêperie. Takeaway. Heated swimming pools, paddling pool with 'mushroom' fountain (all open all season). Fitness equipment. Organised entertainment (July/Aug). Play areas. Minigolf. Archery. Organised walks. Bicycle hire. Riding. Small fishing lake. Room for games and TV. Internet access and WiFi (free). Off site: Bus stop outside main entrance (only one bus each day). Castellane and the Verdon Gorge 1 km. Riding 2 km. Boat launching 4.5 km. Golf 20 km. Watersports.

Open: 15 May - 15 September.

Directions

From Castellane take D952 westwards towards Gorges du Verdon and Moustiers. Site is 1 km. on left. GPS: 43.83921, 6.49396

Charges guide

Per unit (low season 2 or high season 3 persons) and electricity	€ 25.00 - € 42.00
extra person (over 4 yrs)	€ 8.00 - € 13.00
dog	€ 3.00

Domaine du VERDON
Camping Caravanning
★ ★ ★ ★

Close to the famous Gorges du Verdon on only 1,2 kilometres distance from the typical Provence village of Castellane you will love this lovely harmonius estate with many flowers and trees. Direct access to the river Verdon.

Animation in July and August - 500 pitches
14 acres - 220 mobile homes

Castel Camping Caravanning Domaine du Verdon
04120 Castellane - Tel.: +33 492 836 129 - Fax: +33 492 836 937
E-mail: contact@camp-du-verdon.com - www.camp-du-verdon.com

LES ★★★★
CASTELS
Hôtellerie de Plein Air

For latest campsite news, availability and prices visit
alanrogers.com

Castellane
RCN les Collines de Castellane

Route de Grasse, F-04120 Castellane (Alpes-de-Haute-Provence) T: 04 92 83 68 96. E: collines@rcn.fr
alanrogers.com/FR04040

RCN, a Dutch company, runs a chain of nine good campsites in the Netherlands. They also operate seven sites in France, all with Dutch managers who speak good French and English. Les Collines de Castellane is pleasantly situated in the mountainous landscape of the Alpes-de-Haute-Provence. There are 160 touring pitches spread over a series of flat terraces and most have shade provided by trees. Access roads are very steep and it is quite a long way down to the bottom of the site. At the top of the site, near the entrance, is a combined reception and small restaurant area.

Facilities

Tiled, modern toilet facilities include individual cabins and facilities for disabled visitors and babies. Washing machines, dryers and ironing area. Shop. Library. Small restaurant (including takeaway) with terrace. Heated swimming pool with slides and paddling pool. Tennis. Boules. Three play areas. Activities (May-Sept). WiFi room (charged). Off site: Castellane 6 km. with shops, bars and restaurants plus a market on Saturday mornings. Riding 6 km. Beach and golf 10 km.

Open: 14 April - 22 September.

Directions

Take the N85 (Route Napoléon) from Digné-les-Bains towards Castellane and Grasse. Site is 6 km. south of Castellane, on the right hand side of the road. GPS: 43.82412, 6.56962

Charges guide

Per unit incl. 2 persons,	
electricity and water	€ 18.90 - € 39.90
extra person	€ 2.50 - € 4.90

Camping Cheques accepted.

Castellane
Kawan Village International

Route Napoléon, F-04120 Castellane (Alpes-de-Haute-Provence) T: 04 92 83 66 67.
E: info@camping-international.fr **alanrogers.com/FR04100**

Camping International has very friendly, English speaking owners and is a reasonably priced, less commercialised site situated in some of the most dramatic scenery in France. The 274 pitches, 130 good sized ones for touring, are clearly marked, separated by trees and small hedges, some are on a slight slope and all have electricity and water. Access is good for larger units. The bar/restaurant overlooks the swimming pool with its sunbathing area set in a sunny location with fantastic views. In high season, English-speaking young people entertain children (3-8 years) and teenagers. Car hire can be arranged.

Facilities

Nine toilet blocks, some of the smaller blocks are of an older design. One newer block has modern facilities, including those for disabled visitors. Laundry facilities. Motorcaravan services. Shop. Restaurant/takeaway (May-Sept). Swimming pool (1/5-30/9). Play area. Club/TV room. Children's entertainment. Evening entertainment (July/Aug). Boules. Internet access. WiFi throughout (charged). Off site: Riding 800 m. Castellane 1.5 km. with river, canyon and rapids.

Open: 31 March - 1 October.

Directions

Site is 1 km. north of Castellane on the N85 'Route Napoléon'. GPS: 43.85866, 6.49803

Charges guide

Per unit incl. 2 persons	
and electricity	€ 18.00 - € 29.00
extra person	€ 3.00 - € 5.00
dog	€ 2.00

Camping Cheques accepted.

Cavalaire-sur-Mer
Camping Bonporteau

B.P. 18 (RD559), F-83240 Cavalaire-sur-Mer (Var) T: 04 94 64 03 24. E: contact@bonporteau.fr
alanrogers.com/FR83340

This terraced site is situated northeast of and above the pleasant and popular holiday resort of Cavalaire where there is a harbour, restaurants and shops. A long, sandy beach runs right round the bay and there are plenty of watersport activities nearby. The site is only 200 metres from the beach, accessed via a steep path, and only a short walk from a very good hypermarket. The 110 individual touring pitches are on sloping, sandy ground with terracing and good access roads, and all have electricity hook-ups (10A). The remaining 70 pitches are used for mobile homes and chalets.

Facilities

Three main toilet blocks are modern and include washbasins in cabins. Launderette. Small shop. Small restaurant (1/4-30/9). Bar. Takeaway. Entertainment with dance evenings. Swimming pool with terrace (15/3-30/9) and small paddling pool. Playground. Table tennis. TV and games room. Events including twice weekly concerts and aquagym sessions in high season. WiFi (charged). Off site: Beach 200 m. Bicycle hire 800 m. Riding 2 km.

Open: 15 March - 15 October.

Directions

Take D559 to Cavalaire-sur-Mer (not Cavalière, some 4 km. away). Site is signed by yellow signs from the main road before entering the town. GPS: 43.16681, 6.51953

Charges guide

Per unit incl. 2 persons	
and electricity	€ 24.00 - € 51.00
extra person	€ 5.00 - € 10.00

No credit cards.

For latest campsite news, availability and prices visit
alanrogers.com

Cavalaire-sur-Mer
Kawan Village Cros de Mouton

 546

B.P. 116, F-83240 Cavalaire-sur-Mer (Var) T: 04 94 64 10 87. E: campingcrosdemouton@wanadoo.fr

alanrogers.com/FR83220

Cros de Mouton is a reasonably priced campsite in a popular area. High on a steep hillside, about 2 km. from Cavalaire and its popular beaches, the site is a calm oasis away from the coast. There are stunning views of the bay but, due to the nature of the terrain, some of the site roads are very steep – the higher pitches with the best views are especially so. There are 199 large, terraced pitches (electricity 10A) under cork trees with 73 suitable only for tents with parking close by, and 80 for touring caravans. A range of languages is spoken by the welcoming and helpful owners. The terrace of the restaurant and the pool area share the wonderful view of Cavalaire and the bay. Olivier and Andre are happy to take your caravan up with their 4 x 4 Jeep if you are worried, and they will help you set up if necessary - all part of the service.

Facilities

Clean, well maintained toilet blocks have all the usual facilities including those for disabled customers (although site is perhaps a little steep in places for wheelchairs). Washing machine. Shop. Bar/restaurant with reasonably priced meals and takeaway. Swimming and paddling pools with many sun beds on the terrace and small bar for snacks and cold drinks. Small play area. Games room. Off site: Beach and bicycle hire 1.5 km. Riding 3 km. Golf 15 km.

Open: 15 March - 9 November.

Directions

Take the D559 to Cavalaire (not Cavalière 4 km. away). Site is about 1.5 km. north of Cavalière-sur-Mer, very well signed from the approach to the town. GPS: 43.18247, 6.5161

Charges guide

Per unit incl. 2 persons and electricity	€ 24.00 - € 29.10
extra person	€ 6.50 - € 8.20
child (under 7 yrs)	€ 4.10 - € 4.50
dog	free - € 2.00

Camping Cheques accepted.

★ ★ ★ ★
Le Cros de Mouton
Cavalaire - Côte d'Azur

Under the Mediterranean sun, 1.6 km from the beach and the town centre, appreciate the peace, comfort, quietness and the welcome of a family camping site in the heart of a shady forest. Heated swimming pool. Bungalows and mobile-homes for hire.

BP 116 – 83240 Cavalaire
Tel: 0033 494 64 10 87
Fax: 0033 494 64 63 12
campingcrosdemouton@wanadoo.fr
www.crosdemouton.com

Camping Cheque

For latest campsite news, availability and prices visit
alanrogers.com

Chasteuil/Castellane

Camping des Gorges du Verdon

Clos d'Arémus, F-04120 Chasteuil/Castellane (Alpes-de-Haute-Provence) T: 04 92 83 63 64.
E: aremus@camping-gorgesduverdon.com **alanrogers.com/FR04250**

Located at an altitude of 660 metres, between pinewoods and the River Verdon, Camping des Gorges du Verdon is a family site with large, shaded or semi-shaded pitches and a range of chalets and mobile homes. The site is bisected by the D952, has an inviting swimming pool, and offers direct access to the Verdon (with its own river beach). The main sight here is, of course, the stunning canyon of the Gorges du Verdon, a grandiose area of vertiginous cliffs towering above the emerald river below. There are some superb walks and this is also an ideal location for white-water rafting or canoeing.

Facilities

Two sanitary blocks with a mixture of French and English style toilets and controllable showers. Special toilets for children. Facilities for disabled visitors. Bar/restaurant. Shop. Swimming pool. River beach. Volleyball. Games room. Fishing. Play areas. Nursery rooms. Activities and entertainment. Mobile homes and chalets for rent. WiFi around most of site. Off site: Walking and cycling. Rafting and canoeing. Shops and restaurants in Castellane.

Open: 1 May - 15 September.

Directions

Site is west of Castellane. Leave the village on D952 headed towards the Gorges du Verdon and the site is around 9 km. GPS: 43.82343, 6.43095

Charges guide

Per unit incl. 2 persons	
and electricity	€ 19.90 - € 31.90
extra person	€ 4.50 - € 5.90
child (under 4 yrs)	€ 1.50 - € 2.50

Châteauroux-les-Alpes

Camping les Cariamas

Fontmolines, F-05380 Châteauroux-les-Alpes (Hautes-Alpes) T: 04 92 43 22 63. E: cariamas@hotmail.fr
alanrogers.com/FR05070

Set 1,000 metres up in the stunning scenery of the Alps, les Cariamas is at the gateway to the Ecrin National Park and within easy reach of the Serre-Ponçon lake and the Rabioux-Durance river. Of the 150 pitches, 120 are for touring and all have electrical connections (6-10A), are pleasantly shaded and many offer beautiful views of the surrounding countryside. These pitches are close to some of the mobile homes and chalets available for rent but they are large enough for this not to be a problem. Fully equipped tents are also available to rent. It would be an idea to check the availablity of the amenities prior to arrival, especially in low season. Part of the site is close to a main road so some noise may be experienced during peak times. The access barrier closes after 22.00 and cars should be parked in the car park beyond the site entrance. The site owner is very helpful and speaks good English. During high season many activities are arranged including guided walking tours of the area with picnics provided. There are five ski stations within the vicinity to cater for winter sports holidaymakers.

Facilities

Sanitary facilities include washbasins in cabins and hot showers. No facilities for disabled visitors. Laundry. Small shop and takeaway (from 1/5). Communal barbecue area. Swimming pool (1/5-30/9). Play area. Mountain bike hire. Fishing. WiFi (free). Off site: Bar and shop in the nearby village. Large supermarkets in Embrun approx 3 km. Bus service from village to Gap via several small villages. Riding 15 km. Canoeing, climbing, hiking, mountain biking and rafting. Tennis. Skiing.

Open: 1 April - 31 October (mobile homes all year).

Directions

From Gap follow signs to Embrun Briançon. Take turning for Châteauroux-les-Alpes at first roundabout after Embrun. Shortly (800 m.) before the village turn right and follow signs to site. Access to the site is via a 700 m. narrow lane with some passing places. GPS: 44.60293, 6.52180

Charges guide

Per unit incl. 2 persons and electricity	€ 20.75
extra person	€ 5.50
child (under 6 yrs)	€ 2.75
dog	€ 3.75

Camping, hôtel de plein air Les Cariamas

Les Cariamas

Fontmolines

05380 Châteauroux-les-Alpes

t. 00 33 (0)4 92 43 22 63

f. 00 33 (0)6 30 11 30 57

e. p.tim@free.fr

http://les.cariamas.free.fr

For latest campsite news, availability and prices visit
alanrogers.com

Châteauneuf-de-Gadagne

Camping Fontisson

1125 route d'Avignon, F-84470 Châteauneuf-de-Gadagne (Vaucluse) T: 04 90 22 59 77.
E: info@campingfontisson.com **alanrogers.com/FR84210**

Camping Fontisson is west of Avignon close to the pretty Provençal village of Châteauneuf-de-Gadagne. The site is well located for visiting the Lubéron and close to the fascinating city of Avignon and its Palais des Papes. There are 50 pitches here, 21 of which are occupied by mobile homes, chalets and equipped tents (available for rent). Pitches are large and generally well shaded and most have 10A electrical connections. On-site amenities include a swimming pool and a recently refurbished toilet block, as well as a tennis court and minigolf. During the high season there is regular activity and entertainment.

Facilities

Bar and snack bar (July/Aug). Bread and milk service. Swimming pool. Tennis. Multisports field. Boules. Children's play area. Entertainment and activities. WiFi (charged). Off site: Châteauneuf-de-Gadagne with shops, cafés and restaurants. Riding and fishing 2 km. Bicycle hire and golf 5 km. Grottes de Thouzon at Le Thor 8 km. L'Isle sur la Sorgue (antiques) 15 km. Avignon 15 km.

Open: 1 April - 15 October.

Directions

Leave A7 motorway at junction 23 (Avignon North). Head south on the D6 bypassing St Saturnin-lès-Avignon until you arrive at Châteauneuf-de-Gadagne. Site well signed from here. GPS: 43.92883, 4.93347

Charges guide

Per unit incl. 2 persons	
and electricity	€ 15.00 - € 25.60
extra person	€ 3.40 - € 6.40

Cogolin

Camping l'Argentière

Chemin de l'Argentiere (D48), F-83310 Cogolin (Var) T: 04 94 54 63 63. E: campinglargentiere@wanadoo.fr
alanrogers.com/FR83310

This little jewel of a site is in a pleasant setting and the intervening wooded area seems to give it sufficient screening to make the campsite itself quite peaceful. It is only 5 km. from the beach at Cogolin or St Tropez, so its position is handy for one of the showplaces of the Riviera, but away from the hustle and bustle of the beach resorts. There are 150 good sized touring pitches (out of 238 with the others used for mobile homes to rent). All have electricity although long leads may be necessary.

Facilities

Three toilet blocks are well kept and clean. Washbasins have warm water (some in cabins). Washing machines. Water has to be taken from the sanitary block. Fridge hire. Shop (15/6-30/9). Bar (15/4-30/9). Restaurant (15/6-15/9) and takeaway (15/6-15/9). Large swimming pool (15/5-30/9). Play equipment. Bicycle hire. Barbecues are only permitted on a communal area. WiFi around bar area (free). Off site: Shops nearby. Riding 2 km. Fishing 4 km. Beach 5 km. Golf 6 km.

Open: 1 April - 30 September.

Directions

From the A8 (Aix-en-Provence - Cannes) take exit 36 (Le Muy), then, D25 to Ste Maxime and the coast road N98 (St Tropez). After Grimaud follow signs for Cogolin. When near that village follow D48 (St Maur-en-Collobrière), then signs to site in suburb of L'Argentière. GPS: 43.256083, 6.5124

Charges guide

Per unit incl. 2 persons	
and electricity	€ 20.00 - € 41.00
extra person	€ 3.00 - € 6.00
No credit cards.	

Forcalquier

Camping le Moulin de Ventre

Niozelles, F-04300 Forcalquier (Alpes-de-Haute-Provence) T: 04 92 78 63 31. E: moulindeventre@aol.com
alanrogers.com/FR04030

This is a friendly, family run site in the heart of Haute-Provence, near Forcalquier, a bustling, small, French market town. Attractively located beside a small lake and 28 acres of wooded, hilly land, which is available for walking. Herbs of Provence can be found growing wild and flowers, birds and butterflies abound. The 124 level, grassy pitches for tourists are separated by a variety of trees and small shrubs, 114 of them having electricity (6A; long leads may be necessary). Some pitches are particularly attractive, bordering a small river which runs through the site. A Sites et Paysages member.

Facilities

Refurbished toilet block. Facilities for disabled visitors. Baby bath. Washing, drying machines. Fridge hire. Bread. Bar/restaurant, takeaway. Themed evenings (high season). Pizzeria. Swimming pools (15/5-30/9). New playground. Bouncy castle. Fishing, boules. Some activities organised in high season. No discos. Only electric or gas barbecues. Internet access and free WiFi. Off site: Shops, local market, doctor, tennis 2 km. Supermarket, chemist, riding, bicycle hire 5 km. Golf 20 km. Walking, cycling.

Open: 9 April - 30 September.

Directions

From A51 motorway take exit 19 (Brillanne). Turn right on N96 then turn left on N100 westwards (signed Forcalquier) for about 3 km. Site is signed on left, just after a bridge 3 km. southeast of Niozelles. GPS: 43.93364, 5.86815

Charges guide

Per unit incl. 2 persons	
and electricity	€ 20.00 - € 29.00
extra person (over 4 yrs)	€ 4.20 - € 6.00
No credit cards.	

For latest campsite news, availability and prices visit
alanrogers.com

Fréjus
Camping Resort la Baume – la Palmeraie

546

3775 rue des Combattants d'Afrique du Nord, F-83618 Fréjus (Var) T: 04 94 19 88 88.
E: reception@labaume-lapalmeraie.com **alanrogers.com/FR83060**

La Baume is a large, busy site about 5.5 km. from the long sandy beach of Fréjus-Plage, although with its fine and varied selection of swimming pools many people do not bother to make the trip. The pools with their palm trees are remarkable for their size and variety (water slides, etc) – the very large feature pool being a highlight. There is also an aquatic play area and two indoor pools with a slide and a spa area. The site has nearly 250 adequately sized, fully serviced pitches with some separators and most have shade. Although tents are accepted, the site concentrates mainly on caravanning. It becomes full in season. Adjoining la Baume is its sister site, la Palmeraie, providing self-catering accommodation, its own landscaped pool and some entertainment to supplement that at la Baume. There are 500 large pitches with mains sewerage for mobile homes. La Baume's convenient location has its downside as there is traffic noise on some pitches from the nearby autoroute – somewhat obtrusive at first but we soon failed to notice it. It is a popular site with tour operators.

Facilities

Five toilet blocks. Supermarket, several shops. Two bars, terrace overlooking pools, TV. Restaurant, takeaway. Six swimming pools (heated all season, two covered, plus steam room and jacuzzi). Fitness centre. Tennis. Archery (July/Aug). Skateboard park. Organised events, daytime and evening entertainment, some in English. Amphitheatre. Discos all season. Children's club (all season, 4-11 yrs). Two play areas renovated. Off site: Bus to Fréjus passes gate. Riding 2 km. Fishing 3 km. Golf and beach 5 km.

Open: 31 March - 29 September (with full services).

Directions

From west, A8, exit Fréjus, take N7 southwest (Fréjus). After 4 km, turn left on D4 and site is 3 km. From east, A8, exit 38 Fréjus and follow signs for Cais. Site is signed. GPS: 43.45998, 6.72048

Charges guide

Per unit incl. 2 persons, electricity, water and drainage	€ 19.00 - € 47.00
extra person	€ 5.00 - € 13.00
child (under 7 yrs)	free - € 7.00
dog	€ 5.00

Min. stay for motorcaravans 2 nights.
Large units should book.

We can book this site for you!
Call 01580 214000
alanrogers ● travel

Forcalquier
Camping Indigo Forcalquier

Route de Sigonce, F-04300 Forcalquier (Alpes-de-Haute-Provence) T: 04 92 75 27 94.
E: forcalquier@camping-indigo.com **alanrogers.com/FR04120**

Although Camping Indigo is an urban site, there are extensive views over the surrounding countryside where there are some excellent walks. The pitches are on grass and are of a good size, all with electricity, six fully serviced. The site is secure, with an electronic barrier (card deposit required) and there is no entry between 22.30 and 07.00. Local guides lead tours of the historic town and area. This is an excellent base for visiting Forcalquier, a 15th-century fortified hill town, and the Monday market (the best in Haute-Provence). Since Camping Indigo acquired this site, an extensive modernisation programme has been put into effect.

Facilities

Two refurbished toilet blocks with washbasins in cubicles and excellent facilities for disabled visitors. Bar (all season). Snack bar and takeaway (July and August). Play area. Heated swimming and paddling pools. Range of activities in high season, often involving local people, including astrology sessions, food tasting and storytelling. Free Internet access. Max. 1 dog. Off site: All shops, banks etc. in town centre 200 m. Riding 5 km. Fishing 15 km. Golf 20 km.

Open: 27 April - 7 October.

Directions

From town centre, follow D16 signed to Montlaux and Sigonce. Site is approx. 500 m. on the right. Well signed from town. GPS: 43.96206, 5.78743

Charges guide

Per unit incl. 2 persons and electricity	€ 19.70 - € 27.10
extra person	€ 4.90 - € 5.90
child (2-7 yrs)	€ 3.10 - € 4.10
dog	€ 4.00

Camping Cheques accepted.

For latest campsite news, availability and prices visit
alanrogers.com

La Baume ★★★★ *La Palmeraie* ★★

Camping Resort ★★★★   Résidence de Tourisme ★★

www.labaume-lapalmeraie.com

Fréjus Côte d'Azur

from April to September :
On going entertainment- Cabaret - Show
Disco - Children's club

Le Sud Grandeur Nature

Heated sanitary blocks,
marked-out pitches,
6 swimming pools including
2 covered and heated,
6 water-slides and jacuzzi.
5 kilometers from the sandy
beaches of Fréjus
and Saint Raphaël.

E.S.E COMMUNICATION - Draguignan Tel : 04 94 67 06 00

Bastidons for rent
1or 2 bedrooms - 4/6 persons
or 3 bedrooms - 6/8 persons
Mobil-homes 4/6 persons
Mobil-homes 6 persons
3 rooms - air conditioning
Appartment
6 or 10 persons

3775, Rue des Combattants d'Afrique du Nord   83618 FREJUS Cedex
Tel: +33(0)4 94 19 88 88   -   Fax:+33(0)4 94 19 83 50
E-mail : reception@labaume-lapalmeraie.com

Fréjus
Camping Caravaning les Pins Parasols

3360 rue des Combattants d'Afrique du Nord, F-83600 Fréjus (Var) T: 04 94 40 88 43.
E: lespinsparasols@wanadoo.fr **alanrogers.com/FR83010**

Les Pins Parasols with its 189 pitches is a comfortably sized site, which is quite easy to walk around. It is family owned and run. Although on very slightly undulating ground, virtually all the pitches (all have electricity 6A) are levelled or terraced and separated by hedges or bushes with pine trees for shade. There are 48 pitches equipped with their own fully enclosed, sanitary unit, with WC, washbasin, hot shower and dishwashing sink. These pitches naturally cost more but may well be of interest to those seeking a little bit of extra comfort. The nearest beach is Fréjus-Plage with its new marina, adjoining St Raphaël. The site is used by tour operators (10%).

Facilities

Good quality toilet blocks (one heated) providing facilities for disabled visitors. Small shop with reasonable stock, restaurant, takeaway (15/4-20/9). Heated swimming pool with attractive rock backdrop, separate long slide with landing pool and small paddling pool. Half-court tennis. General room, TV. Volleyball. Basketball court. Children's play area. Internet in reception and WiFi (charged). Off site: Bicycle hire and riding 2 km. Bus from the gate into Fréjus 5 km. Beach and fishing 6 km. Golf 10 km.

Open: 7 April - 29 September.

Directions

From A8 take exit 38 for Fréjus Est. Turn right immediately on leaving pay booths on a small road which leads across to D4, then right again and under 1 km. to site. GPS: 43.46290, 6.72570

Charges guide

Per unit incl. 2 persons	
and electricity	€ 18.40 - € 28.45
pitch with sanitary unit	€ 23.15 - € 35.48
extra person	€ 4.60 - € 6.58
child (under 7 yrs)	€ 3.05 - € 3.97
dog	€ 1.90 - € 2.85

LES PINS PARASOLS CAMPING CARAVANNING ★★★★

3360 Rue des Combattants d'Afrique du Nord
ROUTE DE BAGNOLS - F-83600 FRÉJUS
Tel.: 0033 494.40.88.43

HEATED SWIMMINGPOOL
Supermarket - Snackbar - Individual washing cabins and hot water in all sanitary facilities - Separated pitches (80-l00m²) all with electricity. Pitches with individual sanitary facilities (shower, washbasin, sink with hot water, WC) - Children's playground and solarium - Caravan pitches - Water points - Mini-tennis SUN AND SHADE near the beaches

Fax : 0033 494.40.81.99
Email : lespinsparasols@wanadoo.fr
Internet : www.lespinsparasols.com

Fréjus
Yelloh! Village Domaine du Colombier

Route de Bagnols-en-Forêt, 1052 rue des Combattants d'AFN, F-83600 Fréjus (Var) T: 04 66 73 97 39.
E: info@domaine-du-colombier.com **alanrogers.com/FR83230**

Domaine du Colombier is located between Cannes and St Tropez, alongside a main road 2 km. from the centre of Fréjus and 4 km. from the sandy beaches of Fréjus Saint-Raphaël. There are 52 touring pitches, ranging in size from 80-150 sq.m. and all with 16A electricity. Over recent years there has been much ongoing investment in high quality facilities. An attractive pool complex includes a heated pool (600 sq.m), a large paddling pool, water slides and jacuzzis and is surrounded by sunloungers, a fitness area and a grill restaurant. Plenty of activities and excursions are arranged all season and the site caters principally for families. A variety of accommodation to rent includes mobile homes and chalets.

Facilities

Three well maintained, fully equipped toilet blocks (two heated and with baby rooms). Facilities for disabled visitors. Laundry. Well stocked shop. Bar/restaurant, takeaway. Soundproofed nightclub. Large heated swimming pool with paddling pool, slides and jacuzzis (all season). Fitness facilities. Three play areas and four sports areas. Picnic area with communal barbecue. Internet access and WiFi over site. Fridge, safe and barbecue hire. Off site: Bus stop 50 m.

Open: 28 March - 12 October.

Directions

From A8 exit 37, follow signs for Fréjus, turning left at second lights (D4) and site is 1 km. on the right. From A8 exit 38 east (Nice) straight on at three roundabouts, then right at fourth and fifth. Site is 300 m. on right. From west (Aix) turn right at first roundabout, after 1 km. turn left and site is 1 km. on the left. GPS: 43.44583, 6.72727

Charges guide

Per unit incl. 2 persons	
and electricity	€ 15.00 - € 49.00
extra person	€ 5.00 - € 9.00

For latest campsite news, availability and prices visit
alanrogers.com

Fréjus
La Pierre Verte Camping Village
Rue des Combattants d'Afrique du Nord, F-83600 Fréjus (Var) T: 04 94 40 88 30.
E: info@campinglapierreverte.com **alanrogers.com/FR83360**

This attractive, terraced site, set on a hillside under umbrella pines, has been gradually and thoughtfully developed. The genuine, friendly welcome means many families return year upon year, bringing in turn new generations. The site is divided into terraces, each with its own toilet block. The 130 generously sized pitches for touring units enjoy good shade from trees and have either 6A or 10A electricity. There are 300 mobile homes in separate areas. For those seeking to 'get away from it all' in an area of outstanding natural beauty, there can be few more tranquil sites, but the many beaches, watersports and excursions the Gulf of St Tropez has to offer can also be enjoyed. Height restrictions could be an issue for larger units. For those staying on site, there are two large, (one heated) swimming pools with large sunbathing areas and exciting water slides. Not far away, some exhilarating hang-gliding and parascending can be enjoyed.

Facilities

Five toilet blocks with WCs and washbasins in cubicles are extremely clean and accessible from all levels. Baby bath. Laundry facilities. Supermarket. Bar with takeaway service. One heated (15x15 m) and one unheated swimming pool (25x15 m) and paddling pool. Play area. Boules. Games room. Bicycle hire. Activities and entertainment (high season). WiFi throughout (charged). Electric barbecues only. Off site: Riding 1 km. Shopping centre Fréjus 8 km. Fishing 8 km. Golf 12 km.

Open: 7 April - 30 September.

Directions

From the A8 (Aix-en-Provence - Nice) take exit 38 onto D4 towards Bagnols-en-Forêt. Site lies along this road past a military camp, clearly marked at the roundabout. GPS: 43.48389, 6.72058

Charges guide

Per unit incl. 2 persons	
and electricity	€ 20.00 - € 36.00
extra person	€ 7.00 - € 9.00
child (2-6 yrs)	€ 4.00 - € 6.00
dog	€ 3.00 - € 4.00

La Pierre Verte Camping Village ★★★★
8 km from the sandy beaches of Fréjus
www.campinglapierreverte.com
E-mail : info@campinglapierreverte.com
Rte de Bagnols en Forêt
83600 FREJUS
FRANCE
Tél : 00 33 4 94 40 88 30
Fax : 00 33 4 94 40 75 41

Gassin
Camping Parc Saint James-Gassin
Route de Bourrian, F-83580 Gassin (Var) T: 04 94 55 20 20. E: gassin@camping-parcsaintjames.com
alanrogers.com/FR83620

A member of the Parc Saint James Group, this attractive campsite was formerly known as Parc Montana and is very well positioned close to St Tropez. The majority of the pitches are occupied by individually owned mobile homes and chalets but there are also 30 touring pitches on the lower part of the site. The 30 hectare estate clings to the hillside with fragrant woodland providing good shade to the mainly terraced pitches. There is a good range of activities here, many concentrated around the large swimming pool complex. There are plans to include another heated fun pool area with flumes and jacuzzi.

Facilities

Five toilet blocks provide adequate facilities although rather dated. Facility for disabled visitors in one block. Laundry. Small supermarket. Swimming pools and separate children's pool. Bar and restaurant. Takeaway. Play area. Tennis. Multisports area. Games room. Children's club. Evening entertainment. Disco. Mobile homes and chalets for rent. WiFi. Off site: St Tropez, Port Grimaud and Cogolin. Nearest beaches 5 km. Riding. Fishing. Walking trails.

Open: 8 January - 19 November.

Directions

From A8 autoroute take Le Muy exit and follow signs to St Tropez and La Croix-Valmer. Pass Sainte Maxime and continue on the N98. At large roundabout take signs to Gassin. Cross first roundabout and turn left at next traffic lights. Site is also signed as Parc Montana in places. GPS: 43.24035, 6.57345

Charges guide

Per unit incl. 2 persons	
and electricity	€ 19.00 - € 40.00
extra person	€ 3.00 - € 6.00

For latest campsite news, availability and prices visit
alanrogers.com

Giens
Camping International (Giens)
1737 route de la Madrague, F-83400 Giens (Var) T: 04 94 58 90 16. E: thierry.coulomb@wanadoo.fr
alanrogers.com/FR83570

Camping International at Giens is a popular windsurfers' paradise. The site has its own school with the beach just across the quiet coast road. With approximately 200 pitches in total, there are 80 available for touring units, many of these just being used by tents. This site provides for those seeking an active holiday. As well as the opportunities for windsurfing, the beach is just 200 m. away and there are bicycles available to hire. The peninsula is a working area, as opposed to a bustling seaside resort like those to be found on the main coast nearby.

Facilities

Two sanitary blocks provide WCs, washbasins and showers. No facilities for disabled visitors. Washing machine. Bar, shop and restaurant. Swimming pool. Bicycle hire. Mobile homes to rent. WiFi (charged). Dogs are not accepted. Off site: Bus from outside the gate to Hyères (Saturday market). Les Iles des Hyères (Porquerolles and Port Cros). Toulon (naval base).

Open: 24 March - 3 November.

Directions

Site is on the peninsula some 6 km. south of Hyères. Turn right at third roundabout towards La Madrague and site is on the left. GPS: 43.041441, 6.128059

Charges guide

Per unit incl. 2 persons and electricity	€ 25.50 - € 28.50
extra person	€ 5.00

No credit cards.

Graveson-en-Provence
Camping les Micocouliers
445 route de Cassoulen, F-13690 Graveson-en-Provence (Bouches du Rhône) T: 04 90 95 81 49.
E: micocou@free.fr **alanrogers.com/FR13060**

M. et Mme. Riehl started work on les Micocouliers in 1997 and they have developed a comfortable site. On the outskirts of the town, the site is only some 10 km. from St Rémy and Avignon. Purpose built, terracotta houses in a raised position provide all the facilities at present. The 75 pitches radiate out from here with the pool and entrance to one side. The pitches are on level grass, separated by small bushes, and shade is developing well. Electricity connections are possible (4-13A). There are also a few mobile homes. The popular swimming pool is a welcome addition.

Facilities

Unisex facilities in one unit provide toilets and facilities for disabled visitors (by key), another showers and washbasins in cabins and another dishwashing and laundry facilities. Another block is planned. Reception and limited shop (July/Aug) are in another. Swimming pool (12x8 m; 5/5-15/9). Paddling pool (1/7-31/8). Play area. Gas and electric barbecues permitted. WiFi (charged). Off site: Riding next door. Bicycle hire 1 km. Golf and fishing 5 km. Beach 60 km. at Ste Marie-de-la-Mer.

Open: 15 March - 15 October.

Directions

Site is southeast of Graveson. From the N570 at new roundabout take D5 towards St Rémy and Maillane and site is 500 m. on the left. GPS: 43.84397, 4.78131

Charges guide

Per unit incl. 2 persons and electricity	€ 19.00 - € 25.00
extra person	€ 5.00 - € 7.00

Camping Cheques accepted.

Gréoux-les-Bains
Yelloh! Village Verdon Parc
Domaine de la Paludette, F-04800 Gréoux-les-Bains (Alpes-de-Haute-Provence) T: 04 66 73 97 39.
E: info@yellohvillage-verdon-parc.com **alanrogers.com/FR04110**

Friendly and family run, this very spacious site borders the River le Verdon and is close to the attractive spa town of Gréoux-les-Bains. The 280 medium to very large, stony or gravel pitches (150 for tourists) are in two sections. The main part of the campsite has large pitches laid out in rows separated by trees. Along the river bank the larger pitches are scattered amongst the trees and are of irregular shape and size with views. Electrical connections (10A) and water taps are reasonably close to most pitches.

Facilities

Several toilet blocks (one heated in low season) are clean and to a high standard and include facilities for disabled visitors. Laundry room. Motorcaravan service point. Shop. Bar and courtyard terrace. Restaurant and takeaway (April-Sept). TV. Internet point. Large play area. Miniclub for younger children (high season). Organised sports. Evening entertainment. Dogs are not accepted 30/6-25/8. Gas and electric barbecues only. Off site: Gréoux-les-Bains 1 km. Riding and bicycle hire 1 km. Small lakeside beach 8 km. Watersports on two lakes nearby.

Open: 21 March - 29 October.

Directions

Leave A51 autoroute at Manosque and take D907 southeast towards Gréoux-les-Bains. Turn right on D4, then left on D82 to Gréoux-les-Bains. Follow main road downhill through town to roundabout with fountain. Take second right, signed D8 St Pierre and descend for 1 km. Cross river and immediately turn left. Site shortly on the left. GPS: 43.75198, 5.89403

Charges guide

Per unit incl. 2 persons and electricity	€ 17.00 - € 34.00
extra person	€ 4.00 - € 6.00

For latest campsite news, availability and prices visit
alanrogers.com

Grillon
Camping le Garrigon
Chemin de Visan, F-84600 Grillon (Vaucluse) T: 04 90 28 72 94. E: contact@camping-garrigon.com
alanrogers.com/FR84200

Camping le Garrigon is a new site, first opened in 2010. It can be found in pleasant Provençal countryside at Grillon, one of the historical and cultural centres of the Vaucluse. There are 90 pitches here of varying sizes and surrounded by pine, mulberry and lime-blossom trees. All pitches have electricity and water. There are 24 air-conditioned chalet-style mobile homes available for rent with a minimum stay requirement of just two nights. There are superb views all around the site across the surrounding vineyards to Mont Ventoux and the Montagnes de la Lance.

Facilities
Central sanitary block is heated and has excellent, modern facilities, including those for children and disabled visitors. Small shop. Bar/snack bar (May-Sept). Takeaway food (July/Aug). Swimming pool. Waterslides. Paddling pool. Children's play area. TV room. Tourist information. Mobile homes and chalets for rent. WiFi. Off site: Shops and restaurants at Grillon 2 km. Walking and cycle tracks. Enclave des Papes itinerary. Historic town of Valréas with Wednesday market 5 km. Château and old town at Grignan 15 km.

Open: All year.

Directions
Approaching from the north (Lyon), leave the A7 autoroute at exit 18 (Montelimar Sud) and head south on N7, D133 and D641 to Grignan. By-pass this town and continue (on D641) to Grillon. The site is well signposted from here.
GPS: 44.382561, 4.93049

Charges guide
Per unit incl. 2 persons
and electricity € 19.00 - € 28.00
extra person € 4.80 - € 7.00
child (under 7 yrs) € 2.70 - € 4.50

Grimaud
Domaine des Naïades
546
Quartier Cros d'Entassi, Saint Pons-les-Mûres, F-83310 Grimaud (Var) T: 04 94 55 67 80.
E: info@lesnaiades.com **alanrogers.com/FR83640**

Les Naïades is a well equipped site with an enviable setting close to the modern resort of Port Grimaud and the Gulf of St Tropez. The 454 pitches (219 are mobile homes for rent) are of a good size and well shaded, most have electricity (10A). The site boasts an Olympic sized pool and two water slides, as well as a separate children's pool. The restaurant specialises in Mediterranean cuisine and local wines. Les Naïades becomes lively in high season with a full activity and entertainment programme, as well as a miniclub for children. Port Grimaud is a stylish resort, built in the 1960s in the marshy delta of the Giscle. It is modelled on Venice and is a car-free environment. Most property owners are able to moor their boats on the many canals which criss-cross the resort. Grimaud, in contrast, is a hilltop village dominated by its partially restored 11th century castle. St Tropez needs little introduction and, although very busy in the summer months, it resumes a rather more sedate character in the low season.

Facilities
Four basic but adequate toilet blocks. Facilities for disabled visitors, but access can be difficult. Laundry facilities. Covered dishwashing area. New supermarket for 2011. Bar. Restaurant. Swimming pool with water slides. Play area. Tourist information. Motorcaravan services. Mobile homes for rent. Off site: Port Grimaud. St Tropez. Fishing. Watersports. Walking and cycle routes in the Massif des Maures.

Open: 31 March - 21 October.

Directions
The site is located slightly to the north of Port Grimaud. From D98 head north to N98, Pons-les-Mûres and site is clearly signed.
GPS: 43.285278, 6.579722

Charges guide
Per unit incl. 3 persons
and electricity € 25.00 - € 52.00
extra person (over 7 yrs) € 5.00 - € 8.00
dog € 5.00

For latest campsite news, availability and prices visit
alanrogers.com

Grimaud
Club Holiday Marina

Le Ginestel, RN98/RD559, F-83310 Grimaud (Var) T: 04 94 56 08 43. E: info@holiday-marina.com
alanrogers.com/FR83400

Owned and operated by an English family this site is an established favourite with British families. It is located in the busy holiday area of the Gulf of St Tropez. Smaller than many sites in this area, there are 230 good sized pitches of which 49 are for touring units. Each of these has its own spacious bathroom and an outdoor sink. The Grand Luxe plus pitches have a small mobile home instead of the sanitary unit, with kitchen, bathroom, bedroom and terrace and are suitable for extra large motorhomes. On level, sandy ground, with variable shade, all have 16A electricity. Cars are parked separately to reduce noise.

Facilities

Private toilet blocks include washbasin, shower and WC, heated in low seasons. Laundry. Two restaurants with varied and full menu (15/6-31/8). Snacks and takeaway. Separate building houses a bar and games room. TV room. Heated swimming and paddling pools (1/4-31/9). Miniclub for children and evening entertainment in season. Fishing in adjacent canal. Mobile homes for hire. WiFi (charged). Off site: Beach and port within walking distance (busy road to cross) with shops and restaurants and some of the boats are available to hire. Golf 4 km. St Tropez.

Open: 1 March - 31 October.

Directions

From the A8 (Aix-en-Provence - Cannes) take exit 36 (Le Muy) and D25 to St Maxime. Follow N98 coast road towards St Tropez and site is 10 km. after busy roundabout at Grimaud. GPS: 43.26978, 6.57311

Charges guide

Per unit incl. 2 persons and electricity	€ 21.00 - € 79.00
family rate (2 adults, up to 3 children)	€ 21.00 - € 95.00
extra person	€ 5.00 - € 16.00

Hyères

Campé●le

Campéole Eurosurf

Plage de La Captel, F-83400 Hyères (Var) T: 04 94 58 00 20. E: eurosurf@campeole.com
alanrogers.com/FR83690

Facing towards the shimmering island of Porquerolles, Campéole Eurosurf has an enviable setting with direct access to a fine sandy beach. This is a large site with 402 pitches, of which just 13 are available for touring units. The remainder are occupied by mobile homes, chalets and fully equipped tents, available for rent. Pitches are mainly on sand, in the open and back onto the main road from which there is likely to be road noise. Some overhanging branches from trees are very low so care should be taken.

Facilities

The toilet blocks have showers and washbasins (some with cold water only). Facilities for disabled visitors. Baby room. Laundry facilities. Bar/restaurant. Snack bar. Shop. Takeaway. Games room. Playground. Diving school. Boat launching (charged). All terrain sports area. Activities and entertainment. Internet point and WiFi in reception area (charged). Direct beach access. Mobile homes, chalets and tents for rent. Off site: Sentier des Douaniers coastal walk. Fishing. Bird sanctuary. Windsurfing. Riding.

Open: 14 March - 4 November.

Directions

Take the A57 motorway as far as Hyères. Then follow signs to Giens/Les Iles. The site is on the left hand side of the road, 1 km. after the village of La Capte. GPS: 43.0561, 6.1475

Charges guide

Per unit incl. 2 persons and electricity	€ 21.10 - € 43.00
extra person	€ 5.50 - € 9.30
child (2-6 yrs)	€ 3.00 - € 4.70

Hyères-Plage
Camping la Presqu'île de Giens

153 route de la Madrague-Giens, F-83400 Hyères (Var) T: 04 94 58 22 86. E: info@camping-giens.com
alanrogers.com/FR83190

La Presqu'île de Giens is a well run, family campsite at the southern end of the Giens peninsula. The site is well maintained and extends over 17 acres of undulating terrain. Of the site's 460 pitches, 170 are reserved for touring. These are generally of a good size and well shaded – there is a separate area of smaller pitches reserved for tents. Electrical connections (16A) are available on all pitches. In high season this becomes a lively site with a well run children's club and an evening entertainment programme including discos, singers and dancers. Excursions are organised to the adjacent islands.

Facilities

Five toilet blocks, three very good new ones (heated in low season), and two refurbished. Facilities for disabled visitors. Laundry facilities. Shop. Bar, restaurant and takeaway. Play area. Children's club (small charge). Evening entertainment. Sports pitch. Diving classes. Sports tournaments. Electric barbecues only. WiFi. Off site: Bicycle hire 500 m. Beach 800 m. Fishing 1 km. Riding 5 km. Golf 20 km.

Open: 31 March - 7 October.

Directions

From west, leave A57 (Hyères). Continue to Hyères on the A570. At Hyères follow signs to Giens - Les Iles (D97). At end of this road, after 11 km. turn right (Madraque). Site on the left. GPS: 43.04071, 6.1435

Charges 2012

Per unit incl. 2 persons and electricity	€ 21.20 - € 31.00
extra person	€ 4.90 - € 7.90
Camping Cheques accepted.	

For latest campsite news, availability and prices visit
alanrogers.com

La Mole
Camping le Pachacaïd

Route du Canadel, F-83310 La Mole (Var) T: 04 94 55 70 80. E: pacha@pachacaid.com

alanrogers.com/FR83720

Pachacaïd is a very popular holiday village on the edge of the Massif des Maures. Please note that there are no touring pitches here. The site is located 17 km. from St Tropez and 8 km. from Rayol Canadel with its famous creeks and beaches. The heart of Pachacaïd is its amazing Niagara water park with seven massive water slides, a huge Californian style swimming pool and numerous jacuzzis and other water features. Other on-site amenities are of a very high standard, such as the Pacha Café restaurant and well stocked shop. The site extends over a 25 hectare pine forest, with a wide variety of mobile homes available for rent. Pachacaïd becomes lively in high season with a varied activity and entertainment programme including the Pacha Kids' club. For older guests, the Aqua Blue disco is open every night (in peak season) from 22.00. St Tropez and Port Grimaud are popular excursions but the villages of Bormes-les-Mimosas and Cogolin are also well worth exploration.

Facilities

Shop, bar, restaurant, café (all 30/4-18/9). Niagara water park (swimming pools and large water slides, 30/4-18/9). Water aerobics. Archery. Football. Volleyball. Play area. Tourist information. Entertainment and activity programme. Caravans for rent. Riding, bicycle and kayak activities organised. WiFi (charged). Off site: Nearest beach 8 km. St Tropez 15 km. Azur Park (Gassin) 15 km. Various watersports at Cavalaire.

Open: 8 April - 30 September.

Directions

Approaching from the A8, use the Le Luc exit and follow signs to St Tropez. Upon reaching Grimaud, take the westbound N98 (towards Toulon) and continue beyond Cogolin until you pass an aerodrome. At this point turn left following signs to the site (before reaching La Mole). GPS: 43.190181, 6.470887

Charges 2012

Contact the site for details.

CÔTE D'AZUR FRANCE

CAMP-HOTEL PACHACAÏD ★★★★
VILLAGE CLUB
WATER PARK

Rental of mobile-homes close to St-Tropez (17 km)
Not far from beautiful sandy beaches (8 km)
Huge water park with 7 slides, climbing wall over water. Californian swimming pool, Jacuzzi, paddling pool. Entertainment: kid's club, sports, themed evenings

OPEN : 8 April 30 September

83310 LA MOLE - Tel: 04 94 55 70 80 - e-mail: pacha@pachacaid.com
w w w . p a c h a c a i d . c o m

For latest campsite news, availability and prices visit
alanrogers.com

Isle-sur-la Sorgue
Camping Caravaning la Sorguette

Route d'Apt, F-84800 Isle-sur-la Sorgue (Vaucluse) T: 04 90 38 05 71. E: sorguette@wanadoo.fr
alanrogers.com/FR84050

This popular, well organised site is well placed, 1.5 km. from Isle-sur-la Sorgue. Arranged in groups of four, the 164 medium sized level pitches (124 for touring) all have electricity (6-10A). Each group is separated by tall hedges and most have a little shade during the day. In high season a few competitions are organised (boules or volleyball), plus some children's entertainment, but this is quite low key. Running alongside the site, the River Sorgue is only 6 km. from its source in the mountains. It is still very clear and used for canoeing, swimming and fishing.

Facilities

Well maintained toilet blocks. Washing machines. Units for disabled visitors. Baby room. Motorcaravan services. Fridge hire. Shop, bar, snacks (1/7-25/8). Entertainment in July/Aug. Play area, volleyball, half-court tennis, basketball. Canoe, bicycle hire. Internet point. Indian teepees and yurts. 40 mobile homes. WiFi throughout (charged). Off site: Indoor/outdoor swimming pools (preferential rates) 2 km. Fishing and riding 5 km. Walking and cycling circuits. Canoeing on River Sorgue.

Open: 15 March - 15 October.

Directions

Site is 1.5 km. east of Isle-sur-la Sorgue on the D901 towards Apt. It is well signed from the town. GPS: 43.91488, 5.07758

Charges 2012

Per unit incl. 2 persons	
and electricity	€ 21.50 - € 26.30
extra person	€ 6.05 - € 7.55
child (1-11 yrs)	€ 3.00 - € 3.80
dog	€ 2.50 - € 3.40

La Roche-des-Arnauds
Camping le Parc des Sérigons

F-05400 La Roche-des-Arnauds (Hautes-Alpes) T: 04 92 57 81 77. E: contact@camping-serigons.com
alanrogers.com/FR05160

Set in woodlands and surrounded by wooded mountain scenery this site gives the feeling of being with nature. The pitches are large and all numbered but are randomly situated amongst the trees with no obvious boundaries. Of the 94 touring pitches, 80 have electricity (5-10A). Mobile homes, chalets, bungalow tents and pre-erected furnished tents are available to rent. Located alongside the D994, just 15 km. from Gap and 1 km. from the small village of La Roche-des-Arnauds, the site is well placed to explore the various attractions the region has to offer.

Facilities

Three sanitary blocks include showers and some washbasins in cabins, one with facilities for disabled visitors. Washing machines. Motorhome service point. Outdoor swimming pool (unheated, 11/6-9/9). Shop (1/7-31/8). Bar, restaurant and takeaway (11/6-9/9). TV in bar. Tennis, volleyball, boules and table tennis. Children's play areas. WiFi around bar area. Torch useful. Off site: Village of La Roche-des-Arnauds 1 km. Veynes 10 km. Lake for watersports 12 km. Riding. Fishing.

Open: 1 April - 31 October.

Directions

From Gap follow D994 signed towards Orange, Valance and Veynes. Pass through small village of La Roche-des-Arnauds and site is signed on the right approx. 1 km. beyond village. GPS: 44.56416, 5.9175

Charges guide

Per unit incl. 2 persons	
and electricity	€ 11.80 - € 22.60
extra person	€ 2.40 - € 4.70

La Roque d'Anthéron
Village Center le Domaine des Iscles

B.P. 47, route du Plan d'Eau, F-13640 La Roque d'Anthéron (Bouches du Rhône) T: 04 99 57 21 21.
E: contact@village-center.com **alanrogers.com/FR13070**

Village Center le Domaine des Iscles is probably the best of the three sites in this area. There are over 400 pitches, including 234 mobile homes for rent. The remaining pitches for touring units are well laid out with shared electricity and water points. There is shade for some. An attractive feature is a lake with a pebble beach, used for swimming and with a high slide into the water. Fishing is also permitted here in the low seasons. There are 150 km. of footpaths around La Roque d'Anthéron and the Luberon hills are only 10 km. with good opportunities for excursions in this very pleasant landscape.

Facilities

Three basic toilet blocks (only one open in low season) have only two British WCs, the remainder are Turkish style. Small shower cubicles. One washing machine at each block. Shop and bar. Restaurant and snack bar. Circular swimming pool. Lake for swimming with slide. Some entertainment and activities for children (July/Aug). Bicycle hire. Off site: Fishing nearby. Riding 3 km.

Open: 8 April - 2 October.

Directions

From the A7 (Avignon - Marseille) take exit 26 (Senas) and N7 towards Pertuis. Turn left at Pont Royal on D561 towards Peyrolles. Pass town of La Roque d'Antheron and site is signed where the access road passes under the Canal de Marseille. GPS: 43.729683, 5.318283

Charges guide

Per unit incl. 2 persons	
and electricity	€ 16.00 - € 28.00

For latest campsite news, availability and prices visit
alanrogers.com

Le Lavandou
Camping Saint Pons

Avenue Maréchal Juin, F-83190 Le Lavandou (Var) T: 04 94 71 03 93. E: info@campingstpons.com
alanrogers.com/FR83680

Camping Saint Pons enjoys an attractive setting within walking distance of the delightful family resort of Le Lavandou. This is a park-like site extending over two hectares, with many flowering shrubs and bushes. There are 155 pitches here, well shaded and of a fair size. Most have electrical connections. A number of mobile homes are available for rent. There is no shop on site but there is a supermarket 500 m. away. The Littoral cycle track runs close to the site and provides an appealing way of exploring the coast and a number of pretty Provençal villages. Saint Pons is a relaxed site with little by way of on-site entertainment. There is a bar and restaurant next door. Le Lavandou is also one of the Riviera's more restrained resorts, named apparently after the river where local women came to do their washing because the water was so soft. The village boasts no fewer than 12 beaches, some wide and sandy, and others tiny, rocky coves. All can be reached by travelling on a small tourist train that runs along the coast. Boat trips are possible to the Ile du Levant, home to Heliopolis, Europe's first naturist resort, and also to the better known island of Porquerolles and as far afield as St Tropez. Visitors to the site can obtain a reduction in cost for these trips. Good English is spoken.

Facilities	Directions
Two clean sanitary blocks with controllable pushbutton showers. Wet room for disabled visitors. Laundry facilities. Children's playground. Boules. Tourist information. Mobile homes for rent. No pets (1/7-21/8). Off site: Le Lavandou 500 m. Nearest beach 800 m. Cycle tracks. Golf. Boat trips. Fishing.	From Hyères (A570) head east on D98 to Bormes-les-Mimosas and then south east on D559 to Le Lavandou, and then follow signs to the site. GPS: 43.136047, 6.354416

Open: 1 May - 1 October.

Charges guide

Per unit incl. 2 persons and electricity	€ 17.40 - € 28.20
extra person	€ 4.20 - € 6.00

Camping *** **SAINT-PONS**

Avenue Maréchal Juin - 83980 LE LAVANDOU
Tél : +33 (0)4 94 71 03 93 - Fax : +31 (0)4 94 71 09 46
info@campingstpons.com - www.campingstpons.com

Le Muy
RCN Domaine de la Noguière

1617 route de Fréjus, F-83490 Le Muy (Var) T: 04 94 45 13 78. E: noguiere@rcn.fr
alanrogers.com/FR83090

Domaine de la Noguière is located close to the town of Le Muy and is owned by RCN, a Dutch company with a chain of campsites in the Netherlands. Run by an enthusiastic young couple, this is a friendly and informal campsite. Set in 15 hectares, with delightful views of the beautiful Provençal scenery, it has 146 touring pitches, mainly level and with sizes to suit all units up to 120 sq. m. Reception has a small shop adjacent selling fresh bread daily, while the bar/restaurant serves local specialities. This site is ideally situated close to the Gorges du Verdon, yet only 16 km. from the Mediterranean beaches.

Facilities	Directions
Two modern sanitary buildings have been added with family showers and children's rooms. Toilets are fully tiled with individual cabins and access for disabled visitors. Laundry facilities. Shop. Bar/restaurant with terrace plus takeaway service, swimming pool complex with slides and snack bar (12/4-27/10). Small meeting room with library and large TV. Tennis. Boules. Games field. Play area. WiFi. Only gas and electric barbecues permitted. Off site: Riding 5 km. Bicycle hire, golf, beach and sailing 15 km.	From A8 autoroute exit 36 Le Muy, take DN7 Le Muy. At roundabout in town, take direction Route de Fréjus. Site is approx. 2 km. from centre of village. GPS: 43.46832, 6.59202

Open: 17 March - 27 October.

Charges guide

Per unit incl. 2 persons, electricity and water	€ 20.70 - € 45.65
incl. up to 4 persons	€ 25.90 - € 55.85

Camping Cheques accepted.

For latest campsite news, availability and prices visit
alanrogers.com

Le Muy

Parc Camping les Cigales

4 chemin du Jas de la Paro, F-83490 Le Muy (Var) T: 04 94 45 12 08. E: contact@camping-les-cigales-sud.fr

alanrogers.com/FR83160

Parc les Cigales is a pleasant site benefiting from the shady environment of cork umbrella pines, further enhanced by olives, palm trees and colourful shrubs. The terrain is typical of the area with rough, sloped and stony, dry ground but the pitches are of a good size, terraced where necessary and nestling amongst the trees. There are 356 pitches in total, 200 for tourers with 10A electricity and 119 mobile homes and chalets to rent. The site has undergone major rejuvenation. Convenient for the autoroute, this is a spacious family site away from the coast, to be enjoyed.

Facilities

Four sanitary blocks of varying size include facilities for disabled visitors. Laundry facilities. Shop, bar, restaurant and takeaway (1/4-30/9). Heated pool complex (19/3-15/10). An aqua park is planned. Adventure play area. Survival courses. Multisports area. Trampoline. Riding. Canoeing. Hang-gliding. Evening entertainment in season, disco twice weekly, daytime activities for children and senior citizens. WiFi around the restaurant area. No charcoal barbecues. Off site: Le Muy 2 km. Shopping mall at Les Arcs 5 km. Evening markets (high season) in Fréjus and Sainte-Maxime. Golf 10 km.

Open: 15 March - 15 October.

Directions

From A8, Le Muy exit, site is signed (west of Le Muy on N7, 2 km). After the toll booth, at the first roundabout turn left - site is well signed.
GPS: 43.46222, 6.54361

Charges guide

Per unit incl. 2 persons	
and electricity	€ 24.60 - € 40.35
extra person	€ 3.40 - € 10.20
child (under 7 yrs)	€ 2.25 - € 5.65
dog	free - € 2.50

Les Vigneaux

Campé●le

Campéole le Courounba

Le Pont du Rif, D994, F-05120 Les Vigneaux (Hautes-Alpes) T: 04 92 23 02 09. E: courounba@campeole.com

alanrogers.com/FR05140

Le Courounba is a member of the Campéole group, located at the entrance to the magnificent Parc National des Ecrins. Pitches are shady and spacious, dispersed around 12 hectares of woodland. Many of the 170 pitches have superb views of the surrounding mountain scenery. Ninety mobile homes are for rent (including specially adapted units for the disabled). There is also a good sized swimming pool with a water slide and other on-site amenities include two tennis courts and volleyball pitch. Most facilities are free of charge (including tennis). The site has a friendly bar/restaurant and also a small, basic shop (high season only). There is dramatic mountain scenery all around. The Mont Brison is the highest limestone rockface in France and the Mont Pelvoux, at 3943 metres has an all year snow cap. Le Courounba is on the banks of the River Gyronde, popular for fishing. A little further afield, Briançon is a superb town, fortified by Vauban and well worth a visit.

Facilities

Shop, bar/snack bar, swimming pool and water slide (all July-Aug). Volleyball. Tennis. Bouncy castle. Shop. Play area. Activity and entertainment programme. Tourist information. Mobile homes for rent. WiFi (charged). Multisports court. Off site: Fishing 100 m. Hiking and cycle tracks. Riding, bicycle hire 5 km. Briançon 17 km. White water sport. Rock climbing and bouldering.

Open: 22 May - 26 September.

Directions

The site is close to the village of Les Vigneaux, south of Briançon. From Briançon, head south on N94 as far as Prelles and then join the D4 to Les Vigneaux. The site is well indicated from here.
GPS: 44.82483, 6.52566

Charges guide

Per unit incl. 2 persons	
and electricity	€ 17.10 - € 24.70
dog	€ 2.30 - € 3.10

Campé●le

CAMPSITES AND RENTALS

RHÔNE-ALPES

Le Courounba*

In the middle of nature, at the foot of the mountains, beautiful site with swimming pool and restaurant. Pitches and accommodations of high quality.

05120 Les Vigneaux - Tel.: +33-492-2302-09 - www.campeole.co.uk / courounba@campeole.com

Les Issambres
Au Paradis des Campeurs
La Gaillarde-Plage, F-83380 Les Issambres (Var) T: 04 94 96 93 55
alanrogers.com/FR83080

Family owned and run, this popular site has 180 pitches, all with 6A electricity and 132 with water and drainage. The original pitches vary in size and shape but all are satisfactory and most have some shade. The newer pitches are all large and have rather less shade although trees and bushes are maturing nicely. There is no entertainment which gives peaceful nights. The gates are surveyed by CCTV (especially the beach gate) and a security man patrols all day. With direct access to a sandy beach (via an underpass) and being so well maintained, the site has become deservedly popular so it is essential to book for June, July and August.

Facilities

Excellent, refurbished, well maintained toilet blocks. Facilities for babies and children with shower at suitable height. En-suite for disabled visitors. Washing machines and dryer. Motorcaravan services. Shop, restaurant and takeaway service (all season). TV room. Internet and WiFi. Excellent play areas with top quality safety bases, catering for the under and over 5s. Boules. Car wash area. Mobile homes for rent. Off site: Bicycle hire 2.5 km. Riding 3 km. Golf 6 km.

Open: 1 April - 3 October.

Directions

Site is signed from N98 coast road at La Gaillarde, 2 km. south of St Aygulf. GPS: 43.36593, 6.71230

Charges guide

Per unit incl. 2 persons and electricity	€ 19.00 - € 29.00
incl. water and drainage	€ 21.00 - € 33.00
extra person	€ 6.00
child (under 5 yrs)	€ 3.00

Les Vigneaux

Campé●le

Campéole les Vaudois
Le Pont du Rif, F-05120 Les Vigneaux (Hautes-Alpes) T: 04 92 23 02 09. E: campeolelesvigneaux@orange.fr
alanrogers.com/FR05150

Les Vaudois is located at the edge of the Parc National des Ecrins. The site stands on the banks of the River Gyronde and at the foot of Mont Brison, France's highest limestone rock face. There are very few amenities on site but guests are able to use the facilities at the sister site, le Courounba, around 2 km. away. Amenities there include a swimming pool (with water slide) and a bar/restaurant. There are 141 touring pitches at les Vaudois, most equipped with electricity (6A). The site is ideal for groups and clubs seeking adventure sports and is well located for a wide range of activities, including white-water rafting, rock climbing and mountain biking. The Parc National des Ecrins is a vast area, one of only nine French national parks, established back in 1913 as the Parc National Bérarde. There are over 700 km. of marked footpaths in the park and a great wealth of wildlife.

Facilities

Play area. Tourist information. Off site: Swimming pool. Bar/restaurant. Cycle and walking tracks. Tennis. Canoeing. White-water sports on the Gyronde.

Open: 1 July - 28 August.

Directions

From Briançon, take N94 towards Prelles and St Martin de Queyrières, and then follow signs for l'Argentière. Take the D104A to La Batie des Vigneaux and then continue to Les Vigneaux and the campsite. GPS: 44.8213, 6.5355

Charges guide

Per unit incl. 2 persons and electricity	€ 15.10 - € 18.30

Campé●le
CAMPSITES AND RENTALS
Les Vaudois**
In the heart of nature, enjoy the pure mountain air of the Hautes Alpes, pitches and new mobile homes.
RHÔNE-ALPES
05120 Les Vigneaux - Tel.: +33-492-2302-09 - www.campeole.co.uk / vaudois@campeole.com

For latest campsite news, availability and prices visit
alanrogers.com

Martigues
Flower Camping Marius

Route de la Saulce, la Couronne, F-13500 Martigues (Bouches du Rhône) T: 04 42 80 70 29.
E: contact@camping-marius.com **alanrogers.com/FR13140**

East of the Camargue, past the oil tankers anchored in the Gulf de Fos and south of the Etang de Berre is Martigues. Camping Marius is 7 km. further south, tucked away beside a 'calanque' (or inlet) on this rocky coast. The site is a colourful oasis, regularly laid out with shade from shrubs and mixed trees. It provides 114 pitches, of which 53 are occupied by mobile homes for rent and 35 are seasonal pitches, leaving 25 for touring units. The pitches are rather small but each has its own sink and water supply.

Facilities

A good modern toilet block is well equipped and is supplemented by a smaller one. Baby bath. Facilities for disabled visitors. Very small shop. Bar and takeaway. Play area. Bicycle hire. Canoe hire. Activity and entertainment programme. Direct access via steep steps and some rough walking to beach 200 m. Mobile homes for rent. Only gas barbecues allowed. WiFi (free). Off site: Snack bar 200 m. Nearest village is La Couronne with shops, restaurants and railway station. Fishing village of Carro with daily fish market 3 km. Riding 5 km.

Open: 1 April - 31 October.

Directions

Approach Martigues from north on D5 and cross the Canal de Caronte. Contine south on D5, then D49 to La Couronne (7 km). At roundabout on outskirts of La Couronne, turn left (Sausset-les-Pins' and Saint Croix). Site signed. Using the A55 take left turn immediately on crossing bridge (Fos, exit 12). Follow road back under bridge until right sign for La Couronne. On A55 from Marseille take exit for Carry-le-Rouet. GPS: 43.335, 5.0673

Charges 2012

Per unit incl. 2 persons and electricity	€ 22.00 - € 31.00
extra person	€ 4.00 - € 7.00

Montagnac-Montpezat
Village Center Côteau de la Marine

Route de Baudinaud, F-04500 Montagnac-Montpezat (Alpes-de-Haute-Provence) T: 04 99 57 21 21.
E: contact@village-center.com **alanrogers.com/FR04200**

Located to the west of the Lac de Sainte Croix and the Gorges du Verdon, Côteau de la Marine is a well equipped site with a fine setting. The site is a member of the Village Center group and has direct access to the River Verdon and its own small harbour. There are 49 touring pitches (60-120 sq.m), mostly with electrical connections (10A). These are situated at the bottom end of the site overlooking the river but it is quite a steep climb up to the main site facilities. There is plenty of activity here in high season.

Facilities

Two toilet blocks include controllable pushbutton showers and washbasins with hot and cold water. Facilities for disabled visitors. Laundry. Restaurant/snack bar and takeaway. Bar. Small supermarket. Swimming and paddling pools. Play area. Sports field. Activities and entertainment. Direct river access. WiFi (charged). Mobile homes, chalets and tents for rent. Off site: Montagnac-Montpezat 5 km. Riez with shops, bars and restaurants 10 km. Gorges du Verdon. Lac de Sainte Croix.

Open: 8 April - 2 October.

Directions

From the north (Gap), leave the A51 at exit 19 (La Brillane). Follow signs to Oraison then head south on D4 and then D15 to Valensole. Then head southeast on D6 to Riez and follow signs to Montagnac-Montpezat. Site signed. GPS: 43.74768, 6.09845

Charges guide

Per unit incl. 2 persons and electricity	€ 16.00 - € 29.00
extra person	€ 3.00 - € 6.00
Camping Cheques accepted.	

Montclar
Yelloh! Village l'Etoile des Neiges

F-04140 Montclar (Alpes-de-Haute-Provence) T: 04 66 73 97 39. E: info@yellohvillage-etoile-des-neiges.com
alanrogers.com/FR04080

This attractive, family run site near the mountain village and ski resort of St Jean Montclar is open most of the year. Being at an altitude of 1,300 m. the nights can get quite cold in summer. The 130 shady terraced pitches, with 70 for touring, are separated by small shrubs and alpine trees. All pitches are close to electricity and water points. An attractive bar and restaurant overlooks the two outdoor swimming pools, with the shallow pool having a water slide ideal for children.

Facilities

Central toilet block (heated in winter) and facilities for disabled visitors. Washing machines. Motorcaravan services. Bar/restaurant. Two outdoor swimming pools and new indoor complex with heated pool, gym, jacuzzi, sauna and steam room (all 15/5-9/9). Tennis. Boules. Play areas. Multisports pitch. Rafting, walking (July/Aug). WiFi. Off site: Shops, bicycle hire and riding in village a few minutes walk. Fishing 1.5 km. Beach 7 km.

Open: All year excl. 26/3-29/4 and 16/9-19/12.

Directions

Site is 35 km. south of Gap via D900B. Beyond Serre Ponçon, turn right, D900 (Selonnet, St Jean Montclar). Entering St Jean Montclar turn left, pass chalets, shops, fork right down lane to site in 250 m. Steep roads (icy in winter). GPS: 44.40921, 6.34826

Charges guide

Per unit incl. 2 persons and electricity (6A)	€ 25.00 - € 33.00
extra person	€ 7.00

For latest campsite news, availability and prices visit
alanrogers.com

Montmeyan
Camping Château de l'Eouvière

Route de Tavernes, F-83670 Montmeyan (Var) T: 04 94 80 75 54. E: contact@leouviere.com
alanrogers.com/FR83260

This spacious site is in the grounds of an 18th-century château, close to the magnificent hill village of Montmeyan. Many of the terraced pitches, mostly behind the château, have magnificent views. The 80 large touring pitches are part grassy, part stony with varying amounts of shade from mature trees, all have electricity points and most have water nearby, although there may be reduced pressure on higher pitches. Access to the higher terraces of the site is very steep and may cause problems for some. The owner will assist with his 4x4 vehicle any visitor experiencing difficulty in siting their unit.

Facilities

Main refurbished toilet block (may be stretched in high season) includes facilities for disabled visitors. Washing machine, iron. Bar (15/5-30/9), restaurant (15/6-30/9), small shop (1/7-31/8). Swimming pool, sunbathing area. Small play area, paddling pool (some distance from the pool). Entertainment and children's activities in high season. Virtually soundproofed disco in the cellars of château. WiFi in bar area. Off site: Montmeyan 1 km. Beach at Lake Quinson 7 km. Other lakes with watersports. Gorges du Verdon. Regusse 5 km.

Open: 1 May - 30 September.

Directions

Leave A8 autoroute at St Maximin and take D560 to Barjols, then D71 to Montmeyan. At roundabout on entering village, take D13 southeast signed Cotignac and site entrance is very shortly on the right. GPS: 43.63709, 6.06102

Charges guide

| Per unit incl. 2 persons and electricity | € 22.00 - € 28.00 |
| extra person | € 6.00 - € 7.50 |

No credit cards.

Mornas
Camping Beauregard

Route d'Uchaux, F-84550 Mornas (Vaucluse) T: 04 90 37 02 08. E: beauregard@wanadoo.fr
alanrogers.com/FR84140

Just a kilometre off the N7 and near an A7 exit, this FranceLoc site may appeal to those needing a night stop when travelling to or from the Mediterranean coast. Although there are many mobile homes, there are 68 pitches available for tourers. The pitches are under large pine trees and are rather sandy and firm pegging might be difficult. They are of various shapes and sizes, mainly about 90 sq.m. The site is gradually being upgraded into a more modern and family oriented site.

Facilities

Two toilet blocks, one of which is heated when necessary, with washbasins in cabins. Facilities for disabled visitors (access by key). Laundry facilities. Shop (April-Sept). Bar, restaurant and takeaway (April-Sept). Swimming pools, one covered. Tennis. Play area. Boules. Quad bike hire. Fitness trail. Entertainment (high season). Barbecues are not permitted. WiFi. Off site: Fishing and riding 5 km. Golf 12 km.

Open: 25 March - 4 November.

Directions

From the A7 take exit for Bollene, then the N7 towards Orange. At north end of Mornas village, turn left on D74 signed Uchaux. Site is on left after 1.7 km. GPS: 44.21540, 4.74530

Charges guide

Per unit incl. 2 persons	€ 21.00 - € 24.00
extra person	€ 4.60 - € 7.00
child (under 7 yrs)	€ 2.50 - € 4.20
electricity	€ 4.70

Moustiers-Sainte-Marie
Camping Manaysse

Rue Fréderic Mistral, F-04360 Moustiers-Sainte-Marie (Alpes-de-Haute-Provence) T: 04 92 74 66 71.
E: manaysse@orange.fr **alanrogers.com/FR04190**

Manaysse is a little gem of a family campsite on the outskirts of the famous hillside village of Moustiers-Sainte-Marie (900 m) and is ideal for exploring the magnificent Gorges du Verdon region. There are 97 terraced pitches on grass and gravel, with 93 for touring (electricity 6/10A). Some of the pitches are on a slight slope, however those at the top of the site have a beautiful view of Moustiers-Sainte-Marie. There are both shady and sunny pitches available and the flowers, trees and shrubs make the site look very attractive. Large units should approach with care as there is a short, steep incline up to reception.

Facilities

Simple but clean toilet blocks. Facilities for disabled visitors. Washing machines. Bread is delivered. Small play area. Boules. Minigolf. No charcoal barbecues. Torches may be useful. WiFi (charged). Off site: Fishing 600 m. Moustiers 900 m. Bicycle hire 2 km. Lake, beach, water sports 4 km. Riding 12 km. Magnificent region waiting to be explored.

Open: 1 April - 2 November.

Directions

Moustiers is between Riez and Gorges du Verdon on the D952. From Riez turn north at first roundabout in Moustiers, site signed, entrance in 200 m. GPS: 43.84486, 6.21566

Charges guide

| Per unit incl. 2 persons and electricity (6/10A) | € 13.40 - € 14.40 |
| extra person | € 3.70 |

No credit cards.

For latest campsite news, availability and prices visit
alanrogers.com

Orpierre
Camping des Princes d'Orange

F-05700 Orpierre (Hautes-Alpes) T: 04 92 66 22 53. E: campingorpierre@wanadoo.fr

alanrogers.com/FR05000

This attractive, terraced site, set on a hillside above the village has been thoughtfully developed. Muriel, the owner, speaks excellent English and the genuine, friendly welcome means many families return year upon year, bringing in turn new generations. Divided into five terraces, each with its own toilet block, some of its 100 generously sized pitches (96 for touring) enjoy good shade from trees and have electricity connections (10A). In high season, one terrace is reserved as a one-star camping area for young people. Orpierre has an enchanting maze of medieval streets and houses, almost like a trip back through the centuries. Whether you choose to drive, climb, walk or cycle, there is plenty of wonderful scenery to discover in the immediate vicinity, whilst not far away, some exhilarating hang-gliding and parascending can be enjoyed. It is renowned as a world class rock climbing venue, with over 600 climbing routes in the surrounding mountains. For those seeking to 'get away from it all' in an area of outstanding natural beauty, there can be few more tranquil sites. There can be no doubt that you will be made most welcome and will enjoy the quiet splendours the region has to offer.

Facilities

Six well equipped toilet blocks. Baby bath. Laundry facilities. Bread. Bar (1/4-31/10). Heated swimming pool, paddling pool (15/6-15/9). Play area with inflatable climbing tower. Boules. Games room. Fridge hire. Only gas barbecues are permitted. Free WiFi around reception area. Off site: Orpierre with a few shops and bicycle hire 500 m. Fishing 7 km. Nearest shopping centre Laragne 12 km. Riding 19 km. Hang-gliding. Parascending. Rock climbing. Walking. Mountain biking. Gorges de Guil.

Open: 1 April - 31 October.

Directions

Turn off N75 road at Eyguians onto D30 – site is signed from left at crossroads in the centre of Orpierre village. GPS: 44.31121, 5.69677

Charges guide

Per unit incl. 2 persons and electricity	€ 21.10 - € 27.70
extra person	€ 5.50 - € 7.80
child (under 7 yrs)	€ 3.00 - € 3.70

No credit cards.

Camping des Princes d'Orange

05700 Orpierre
Tel: 0033 492 662 253
Fax: 0033 492 663 108
campingorpierre@wanadoo.fr
www.camping-orpierre.com

Pernes les Fontaines
Camping les Fontaines

125 chemin de la Chapelette, route de Sudre, F-84210 Pernes les Fontaines (Vaucluse) T: 04 90 46 82 55.
E: contact@campingfontaines.com alanrogers.com/FR84190

Camping les Fontaines is a small family run site set in two and a half hectares, with magnificent views of Mont Ventoux and the mountains of the Vaucluse. There are 90 pitches in total, with 60 for tourers. Good shade on most of the level pitches is provided by mature trees and shrubs, electricity (6A) and water are nearby. On-site amenities include a 200 sq.m. lagoon-style pool, an excellent restaurant and cocktail bar with a wide choice of smoothies. The whole site enjoys WiFi coverage at no extra charge. A warm welcome awaits the holidaymaker from the owners, Pierine and Pascal.

Facilities

Modern, clean sanitary block. Small nursery for babies and children and good facilities for disabled visitors. Laundry. Motorcaravan service point. Bar, restaurant with decked terrace overlooking the pool, takeaway food (all May-Sept). Lagoon-style pool with large 'beach' area. Small shop in reception selling basics and fresh bread daily. Children's play area. WiFi over site. Off site: Bicycle hire, riding 2 km. Golf, fishing 10 km.

Open: 1 April - 31 October.

Directions

From autoroute A7 take exit 23 Avignon Nord, direction Carpentras. Then D16 Entraigues. Follow signs for Pernes-les-Fontaines. Site is signed from roundabout in town. GPS: 44.006351, 5.038771

Charges guide

Per unit incl. 2 persons and electricity	€ 18.90 - € 29.50
extra person	€ 5.50 - € 7.50

Camping Cheques accepted.

For latest campsite news, availability and prices visit
alanrogers.com

Puget-sur-Argens

Camping Club la Bastiane

1056 chemin de Suvières, F-83480 Puget-sur-Argens (Var) T: 04 94 55 55 94. E: info@labastiane.com

alanrogers.com/FR83040

La Bastiane is an attractive, established site with good amenities, well located for exploring the Côte d'Azur and with easy access to nearby beaches. There are 180 pitches here of which 47 are reserved for touring. They are generally of a good size and are all supplied with electrical connections (6A). The terrain is somewhat undulating but most of the pitches are on level terraces. The site becomes lively in peak season with a range of activities and excursions to nearby places of interest such as Monaco and the Gorges du Verdon. The access road is limited, and therefore unsuitable for larger units.

Facilities

Three toilet blocks, clean and immaculately maintained. Facilities for disabled visitors. Washing machines, dryers. Shop, bar and takeaway (8/4-20/10). Restaurant (17/4-12/10). Heated swimming pool (8/4-20/10). Tennis. Multisports terrain. Children's club. Play area. Games/TV room. Bicycle hire. Evening entertainment in peak season. Excursions. Only electric barbecues. WiFi (charged). Max. 1 dog. Mobile homes and chalets for rent. Off site: Riding 500 m. Fishing 3 km. Beach 7 km. Lake beach 8 km.

Open: 7 April - 25 October.

Directions

Leave A8 at exit 37 (Puget), take right turn at first roundabout (signed Roquebrune), join N7. Turn right, first traffic lights (200 m), then left at roundabout. Site signed from here, on the right 2.5 km. from the motorway. GPS: 43.46966, 6.67845

Charges guide

Per unit incl. 2 persons and electricity	€ 19.90 - € 39.90

We can book this site for you! Call 01580 214000 alan rogers travel

---

Quinson

Village Center les Prés du Verdon

F-04500 Quinson (Alpes-de-Haute-Provence) T: 04 99 57 21 21. E: contact@village-center.com

alanrogers.com/FR04230

This family site is attractively located close to the River Verdon, and it is a good base for exploring the famous gorges. The site boasts a fine pool complex with a large main pool and separate paddling pool. There are 70 touring pitches here (from 70 to 110 sq. m), some well shaded and others rather sunnier. Most are equipped with electrical connections. A further 131 pitches are used for mobile homes and bungalow tents, most of which are available for rent. This is a great region for an active holiday.

Facilities

Two toilet blocks have controllable pushbutton showers and washbasins with hot and cold water. Wet room for disabled visitors. Baby room. Swimming pool with paddling pool. Play area. TV room. Children's club. Volleyball. Entertainment and activity programme. Off site: Tennis just beyond site entrance. Walking and cycling routes. River, lake, fishing and canoeing all 100 m. Supermarket 200 m. Climbing 500 m. Friday morning market in Quinson during summer.

Open: 6 April - 30 September.

Directions

Approaching on A51 motorway, head for Digne les Bains and leave at exit 17 (St Paul-les-Durance and Gréoux Les Bains). After Gréoux, follow signs to Quinson and Musée de la Préhistoire. The site is then clearly signed. GPS: 43.69713, 6.04162

Charges guide

Per unit incl. 2 persons and electricity	€ 14.00 - € 18.00

Camping Cheques accepted.

Ramatuelle

Yelloh! Village les Tournels

Route de Camarat, F-83350 Ramatuelle (Var) T: 04 94 55 90 90. E: info@yellohvillage-les-tournels.com

alanrogers.com/FR83210

Les Tournels is a large site set on a hillside and pitches have panoramic views of the Gulf of Saint Tropez and Pampelonne beach. The hillside is covered in parasol pines and old olive trees. The pitches are reasonably level, shady, of variable size, and most have electricity. The swimming pool, play area, shop and bar may be some distance away. The site has a superb new spa centre with gym, sauna and jacuzzi, with an excellent pool alongside, all reserved for adults (over 18 yrs), and a new restaurant with a large terrace. Competitions and shows are organised for adults and children in July and August.

Facilities

Well equipped toilet blocks, some heated, baby baths, children's WCs, facilities for disabled visitors. Laundry facilities. Fridge hire. Bar and restaurant (1/4-30/10). Takeaway. Bar and disco well away from most pitches. Large heated swimming pool (1/4-30/10). Fitness centre and pool. Good quality play area. Boules. Archery. Miniclub (over 5 yrs). Safety deposit boxes. Electric and gas barbecues permitted. Off site: Shopping centre with shuttle bus service 500 m. Beach 1.5 km. Golf 6 km.

Open: 1 April - 7 January.

Directions

From A8 exit 36 take D25 to Ste Maxime, then D98 towards St Tropez. Take D93 to Ramatuelle. Site is clearly marked after approx. 9 km. GPS: 43.20596, 6.65083

Charges guide

Per unit incl. 2 persons and electricity and water	€ 18.00 - € 52.00
extra person	€ 6.00 - € 7.00
child (3-6 yrs)	free - € 7.00

For latest campsite news, availability and prices visit

alanrogers.com

Ramatuelle

Campéole la Croix du Sud

Campé●le

Route des Plages, CD93, F-83350 Ramatuelle (Var) T: 04 94 55 51 23. E: croix-du-sud@campeole.com
alanrogers.com/FR83710

La Croix du Sud is perched on a little hill and pleasantly shaded by parasol pines and eucalyptus trees. The nearby fine sandy beach of Pampelonne is maybe the most celebrated in France, and famed for its association with St Tropez (although it is actually closer to Ramatuelle!). There are 120 pitches here, of which just 13 are available for touring units. Pitches are well shaded and mostly equipped with electricity. Other pitches are occupied by mobile homes, chalets and tents, available for rent.

Facilities

Sanitary facilities include a baby room but there is no provision for disabled visitors. Shop, restaurant, bar/snack bar (all 1/5-30/9). Takeaway pizza (all season). Swimming pool (1/5-30/9). Children's pool. Games room. Playground. Sports field. Activity and entertainment programme. Tourist information. WiFi (charged). Mobile homes, chalets and tents for rent. Off site: Nearest beach 1.6 km. Fishing. Golf. Walking and mountain biking. St Tropez. Ramatuelle.

Open: 1 April - 11 October.

Directions

From the A8 (La Provençale) motorway take the exit to Le Luc. Take the D558 (La Garde-Freinet and Saint Tropez), then D93 (Ramatuelle). In Ramatuelle, follow signs to Les Plages and Pampelonne, at second roundabout go straight on for 1.5 km and then turn left to the site. GPS: 43.21422, 6.64096

Charges guide

Per unit incl. 2 persons and electricity	€ 21.10 - € 43.00
extra person	€ 5.50 - € 9.30

Régusse

Camping les Lacs du Verdon

Domaine de Roquelande, F-83630 Régusse (Var) T: 04 94 70 17 95. E: info@lacs-verdon.com
alanrogers.com/FR83140

In beautiful countryside and within easy reach of the Grand Canyon du Verdon and its nearby lakes, this site is only 90 minutes from Cannes. It is now part of the Homair Vacances chain and is currently run by Christophe Laurent and his team who are proud of their site and the high standard they have achieved. The 30 acre wooded park is divided in two by a minor road. The 480 very stony but level pitches (rock pegs advised) are marked and separated by stones and trees. Of these, 107 are available for tourists, many an irregular shape, but all are of average size with 16A electricity (long leads may be necessary).

Facilities

Modernised toilet blocks have mainly British style WCs and some washbasins in cubicles. Laundry facilities. Small supermarket. Bar. Restaurant and pizzeria. Heated swimming pool/paddling pool complex. Tennis. Minigolf. Outdoor exercise equipment. Boules. Bicycle hire. Playground. TV and teenage games room. Entertainment. Discos, dances and theme nights. Electric barbecues only. WiFi (charged). Off site: Régusse 2.5 km. Aups 7 km. Riding 10 km. Fishing and beach at Saint Croix 15 km.

Open: 29 April - 23 September.

Directions

Leave A8 motorway at St Maximin and take the D560 northeast (Barjols). At Barjols turn left on the D71 (Montmeyan), turn right on D30 (Régusse) and follow site signs. GPS: 43.6602, 6.1511

Charges guide

Per unit incl. 1 or 2 persons and electricity	€ 15.00 - € 26.00
extra person	€ 3.00 - € 5.50

Roquebrune-sur-Argens

Camping Caravaning Moulin des Iscles

Chemin du Moulin des Iscles, F-83520 Roquebrune-sur-Argens (Var) T: 04 94 45 70 74.
E: moulin.iscles@wanadoo.fr alanrogers.com/FR83240

Moulin des Iscles is a small, pretty site beside the river Argens with access to the river in places for fishing, canoeing and swimming, with some sought after pitches overlooking the river. The 80 grassy, level pitches have water and electricity (6A). A mixture of deciduous trees provides natural shade. The old mill house is near the entrance, which has the security barrier closed at night. A quiet site with little on-site entertainment, but with a pleasant restaurant. Visitors with disabilities are made very welcome.

Facilities

Fully equipped toilet block, plus small block near entrance, ramped access for disabled visitors. Some Turkish style toilets. Washbasins have cold water. Baby bath and changing facilities. Washing machine. Restaurant. Shop. Library. TV, pool table, table tennis. Play area, minigolf, boules all outside the barrier. Internet terminal and WiFi. Canoeing possible. Off site: Excursions during the high season include rock climbing, visits to châteaux and olive oil mills. Roquebrune-sur-Argens is close by. Bicycle hire 1 km. Riding and golf 4 km. Beach 9 km.

Open: 1 April - 30 September.

Directions

From A8, exit Le Muy, follow N7 towards Fréjus for 13 km. Cross over A8 and turn right at roundabout through Roquebrune-sur-Argens towards St Aygulf for 1 km. Site signed on left. Follow private unmade road for 500 m. GPS: 43.44513, 6.65783

Charges guide

Per unit incl. 2 persons and electricity	€ 18.30 - € 24.20
extra person	€ 2.60 - € 3.30
Camping Cheques accepted.	

For latest campsite news, availability and prices visit
alanrogers.com

Roquebrune-sur-Argens
Camping Caravaning Leï Suves

Quartier du Blavet, F-83520 Roquebrune-sur-Argens (Var) T: 04 94 45 43 95.
E: camping.lei.suves@wanadoo.fr **alanrogers.com/FR83030**

This quiet, pretty site is a few kilometres inland from the coast, 2 km. north of the N7. Close to the unusual Roquebrune rock, it is within easy reach of Saint Tropez, Sainte Maxime, Saint Raphaël and Cannes. The site entrance is appealing – wide and spacious, with a large bank of well tended flowers. Mainly on a gently sloping hillside, the 310 pitches are terraced with shade provided by the many cork trees which give the site its name. All pitches have electricity and access to water. A pleasant pool area is beside the bar/restaurant and entertainment area. Please note that reception is closed on Sundays. It is possible to walk in the surrounding woods. There are 150 mobile homes available to rent.

Facilities

Modern, well kept toilet blocks include facilities for disabled visitors, washing machines and dryers. Shop. Good sized swimming pool, paddling pool. Bar, terrace, snack bar, takeaway (all 31/3-15/10). Outdoor stage near the bar for evening entertainment in high season. Excellent play area. Table tennis, tennis, sports area. WiFi over site. Only gas barbecues are permitted. Off site: Bus stop at site entrance. Riding 1 km. Fishing 3 km. Bicycle hire 5 km. Golf 7 km. Beach at St Aygulf 15 km.

Open: 2 April - 15 October.

Directions

Leave autoroute at Le Muy and take the N7 towards St Raphaël. Turn left at roundabout onto D7 heading north signed La Bouverie (site also signed). Site on right in 2 km. GPS: 43.47793, 6.63881

Charges 2012

Per unit incl. 2 persons	
and electricity	€ 26.50 - € 46.50
incl. 3 persons	€ 28.50 - € 49.70
extra person	€ 5.25 - € 9.90
child (under 7 yrs)	€ 3.25 - € 6.80
dog	€ 2.00 - € 3.50

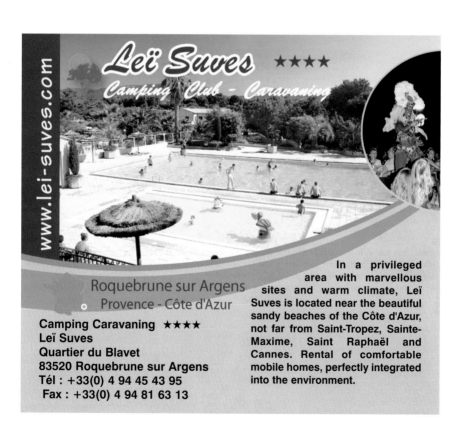

Leï Suves ★★★★
Camping Club - Caravaning

www.lei-suves.com

Roquebrune sur Argens
Provence - Côte d'Azur

**Camping Caravaning ★★★★
Leï Suves
Quartier du Blavet
83520 Roquebrune sur Argens
Tél : +33(0) 4 94 45 43 95
Fax : +33(0) 4 94 81 63 13**

In a privileged area with marvellous sites and warm climate, Leï Suves is located near the beautiful sandy beaches of the Côte d'Azur, not far from Saint-Tropez, Sainte-Maxime, Saint Raphaël and Cannes. Rental of comfortable mobile homes, perfectly integrated into the environment.

For latest campsite news, availability and prices visit
alanrogers.com

Roquebrune-sur-Argens
Camping Domaine de la Bergerie

Vallée du Fournel, route du Col-du-Bougnon, F-83520 Roquebrune-sur-Argens (Var) T: 04 98 11 45 45.
E: info@domainelabergerie.com **alanrogers.com/FR83170**

This excellent site near the Côte d'Azur will take you away from all the bustle of the Mediterranean to total relaxation amongst the cork, oak, pine and mimosa in its woodland setting. The 60 hectare site is quite spread out with semi-landscaped areas for mobile homes and 200 separated pitches for touring caravans and tents. All pitches average over 80 sq.m. and have electricity, with those in one area also having water and drainage. The restaurant/bar, a converted farm building, is surrounded by shady patios, whilst inside it oozes character with high beams and archways leading to intimate corners. Activities are organised daily and, in the evening, shows, cabarets, discos, cinema, karaoke and dancing at the amphitheatre prove popular (possibly until midnight). A superb new pool complex supplements the original pool, adding more outdoor pools with slides and a river feature, an indoor pool and a fitness centre with jacuzzi, sauna, turkish bath, massage, reflexology and gym.

Facilities

Four toilet blocks are kept clean and include washbasins in cubicles, facilities for disabled visitors and babies. Supermarket. Bar/restaurant. Takeaway. Pool complex (all season) with indoor pool and fitness centre (body building, sauna, gym, etc). Tennis courts. Archery. Roller skating. Minigolf. English speaking children's club. Mini farm for children. Fishing. Internet access and WiFi. Only gas barbecues are permitted. Off site: Riding and golf 2 km. Bicycle hire 7 km. Beach at St Aygulf and Ste Maxime 7 km. Water skiing and rock climbing nearby.

Open: 28 April - 30 September (mobile homes 1 March - 15 November).

Directions

Leave the A8 at Le Muy exit on the N7 towards Roquebrune. Proceed for 9 km. then right onto the D7 signed St Aygulf. Continue for 8 km. and then right at roundabout on D8; site is on the right. GPS: 43.4091, 6.6747

Charges 2012

Per unit incl. 2 persons and electricity	€ 19.00 - € 45.00
incl. water and drainage	€ 23.00 - € 50.50
extra person	€ 5.50 - € 10.00
child (under 7 yrs)	€ 3.90 - € 7.30
dog	free - € 5.20

Between Frejus and St. Tropez, in a natural wooded area of 60 ha., at only 10 min drive from the coast...

DOMAINE DE LA BERGERIE ★★★★

- Aquatic park with slides and Jacuzzi
- Steam bath • Fitness center • 5 tennis
- Shows • Animations • Kid's club

COTTAGES FOR RENT
1/03 to 15/11

Low season: Special price for two weeks or longer !

Camping : 23/04 to 30/09
Pool indoor : 09/04 to 30/10
Pool outdoor : 23/04 to 30/09

DOMAINE DE LA BERGERIE
Rte du Col du Bougnon
83520 Roquebrune sur Argens
04 98 11 45 45 • Fax 04 98 11 45 46
www.domainelabergerie.com

For latest campsite news, availability and prices visit

alanrogers.com

Roquebrune-sur-Argens
Camping les Pêcheurs

F-83520 Roquebrune-sur-Argens (Var) T: 04 94 45 71 25. E: info@camping-les-pecheurs.com

alanrogers.com/FR83200

Les Pêcheurs will appeal to families who appreciate natural surroundings together with many activities, cultural and sporting. Interspersed with mobile homes, the 123 good sized touring pitches (10A electricity) are separated by trees or flowering bushes. The Provençal style buildings are delightful, especially the bar, restaurant and games room, with its terrace down to the river and the site's own canoe station (locked gate). Across the road is a lake used exclusively for waterskiing with a sandy beach and restaurant. Enlarged spa facilities include a swimming pool, a large jacuzzi, massage, a steam pool and a sauna. Developed over three generations by the Simoncini family, this peaceful, friendly site is set in more than four hectares of mature, well shaded countryside at the foot of the Roquebrune Rock. Activities include climbing the Rock with a guide. We became more and more intrigued with stories about the Rock and the Holy Hole, the Three Crosses and the Hermit all call for further exploration which reception staff are happy to arrange, likewise trips to Monte Carlo, Ventimigua (Italy) and the Gorges du Verdon, etc. The medieval village of Roquebrune is within walking distance.

Facilities

Modern, refurbished, well designed toilet blocks, baby baths, facilities for disabled visitors. Washing machines. Shop. Bar and restaurant (all open all season). Heated outdoor swimming pool (all season), separate paddling pool (lifeguard in high season), ice cream bar. Games room. Spa facilities. Playing field. Fishing. Canoeing. Waterskiing. Rafting and diving schools. Minigolf. Activities for children and adults (high season), visits to local wine caves. Only electric barbecues allowed. WiFi in reception, bar/restaurant and pool area. Off site: Bicycle hire 1 km. Riding and golf 5 km. (reduced fees).

Open: 31 March - 30 September.

Directions

From A8 take Le Muy exit, follow N7 towards Fréjus for 13 km. bypassing Le Muy. After crossing A8, turn right at roundabout towards Roquebrune-sur-Argens. Site is on left after 1 km. just before bridge over river. GPS: 43.450783, 6.6335

Charges guide

Per unit incl. 2 persons	
and electricity	€ 23.00 - € 46.50
extra person	€ 4.00 - € 8.80
child (acc. to age)	free - € 6.75
dog (max. 1)	€ 3.20

We can book this site for you! alan rogers travel Call 01580 214000

★ *Les Pêcheurs*
★ *Village Camping*
★
★

10 km away from the beaches of Fréjus Saint Raphaël, calm and shady.

Un jardin en Provence

www.camping-les-pecheurs.com

10 km from the Fréjus Saint Raphaël beaches. Quiet and shady.
Wellness: spa, aqua sports trainer, sauna, restaurant, canoeing, family atmosphere. Mobile homes for rent. Cycle tracks to the beach

83520 Roquebrune sur Argens Tél : 00 33 (0)4 94 45 71 25
Provence - Côte d'Azur

For latest campsite news, availability and prices visit
alanrogers.com

Saint Aygulf
Caravaning l'Etoile d'Argens

F-83370 Saint Aygulf (Var) T: 04 94 81 01 41. E: info@etoiledargens.com

alanrogers.com/FR83070

First impressions of l'Etoile d'Argens are of space, cleanliness and calm. This is a site run with families in mind and many of the activities are free, making it an excellent choice for a good value holiday. There are 450 level, fully serviced grass pitches (all with 10/16A electricity). Separated by hedges, they range in size from 100-250 sq.m. and mainly have good shade. The pool and bar area is attractively landscaped with olive and palm trees on beautifully kept grass. There are two heated pools (one for adults, one for children), both of which are designed very much with families in mind. Reception staff are very friendly and English is spoken. The exceptionally large pitches could easily take two caravans and cars or one family could have a very spacious plot with a garden like atmosphere. The river runs alongside the site with a free boat service to the beach (15/6-15/9). This is an ideal family site for the summer, but also good in low season for a quiet stay in a great location with excellent pitches. There are 88 mobile homes to rent. For a large site, l'Etoile d'Argens is very calm and peaceful, even in July.

Facilities

Over 20, well kept, small toilet blocks. Supermarket and gas supplies. Bar, restaurant, pizzeria, takeaway. Two adult pools (heated 1/4-30/6), paddling pool, jacuzzi, solarium. Floodlit tennis with coaching. Minigolf. Aerobics. Archery (July/Aug). Football and swimming lessons. Boules. Good play area. Children's entertainment (July/Aug). Activity programme with games, dances and escorted walking trips to the surrounding hills within 3 km. Off site: Golf and riding 2 km. Beach 3.5 km.

Open: 1 April - 30 September (with all services).

Directions

From A8 exit 36, take the N7 towards Le Muy, Fréjus. After 8 km. at roundabout take D7 signed Roquebrune, St Aygulf. In 9.5 km. (after roundabout) turn left signed Fréjus. Site is signed. Ignore width and height limit signs as site is before the limit (500 m). GPS: 43.41581, 6.70545

Charges 2012

Per tent pitch (100 sq.m) incl. electricity and 2 persons	€ 14.00 - € 38.00
comfort pitch (130 sq.m) incl. water and drainage	€ 20.00 - € 63.00
luxury pitch (180 sq.m) incl. 4 persons	€ 36.00 - € 78.00
extra person	€ 6.00 - € 10.00
child (under 7 yrs)	€ 5.00 - € 8.00

Saint Aygulf
Camping Résidence du Campeur

B.P. 12, D7, F-83371 Saint Aygulf (Var) T: 04 94 81 01 59. E: info@residence-campeur.com

alanrogers.com/FR83050

This excellent site near the Côte d'Azur will take you away from all the bustle of the Mediterranean coast. Spread out over ten hectares, there are separate areas for mobile homes and touring caravans and tents, with pitches arranged along avenues. The 67 touring pitches average 100 sq.m. in size and all have electricity connections and private sanitary facilities (although washbasins double as dishwashing sinks). The bar/restaurant is surrounded by a shady terrace, whilst friendly staff provide an excellent service. A pleasant pool complex is available for those who wish to stay on site instead of going swimming in the nearby lake or from the Mediterranean beaches. Activities are organised daily during the summer season and the site has its own open-air cinema.

Facilities

Private toilet blocks are cleaned at regular intervals and include a washbasin, shower and WC. Laundry area with washing machines. Supermarket. Bar/restaurant. Takeaway (all open all season). New swimming pool complex with four water slides (high season). Two tennis courts. Minigolf. Boules. Fishing. Bicycle hire. Play area. Games/TV room. Only gas or electric barbecues are permitted. Off site: Riding 1.5 km. Golf 2 km. Beach and St Aygulf 2.5 km. Waterskiing nearby.

Open: 27 March - 30 September.

Directions

Leave A8 at Le Muy exit (no. 36) on N555 towards Draguignan then onto the N7 towards Fréjus. Turn right on D7 signed St Aygulf and site is on the right about 2.5 km. before the town. GPS: 43.40905, 6.70893

Charges guide

Per unit incl. 3 persons and electricity	€ 30.10 - € 50.15
extra person	€ 5.19 - € 8.65
child (under 7 yrs)	€ 3.54 - € 5.90
dog	€ 4.00

For latest campsite news, availability and prices visit
alanrogers.com

L'Etoile d'Argens

✦✦✦✦

2012

Camping-Caravaning

www.etoiledargens.com

E-mail : info@etoiledargens.com

83370 Saint Aygulf - Tel : +33 4 94 81 01 41

Saint Apollinaire

Campéole le Clos du Lac

Route des Lacs, F-05160 Saint Apollinaire (Hautes-Alpes) T: 04 92 44 27 43. E: clos-du-lac@campeole.com

alanrogers.com/FR05130

Le Clos du Lac is a member of the Campéole group and can be found close to the little mountain village of St Apollinaire on the southern fringe of the immense Ecrins National Park. The site is at an altitude of 1450 m. and has 68 pitches including 50 for tourers (most with electricity 7A), and 18 mobile homes for hire. Many of the pitches have fine views of the Lac de Serre Ponçon below and the mountain scenery all around. There is a smaller lake nearby, popular for its 'no kill' fly fishing, and also for swimming. This is also a great place to watch the night sky with a special astronomy week in August. The nearby Boscodon forest has been officially acknowledged as the least polluted place in France. On site amenities include a small shop and communal barbecue area. The Lac de Serre Ponçon is popular for many water sports and the site is well located for exploring this wonderful mountain landscape. The popular Montagne aux Marmottes animal park is close at hand, along with the Cathedral of Notre Dame du Réal at Embrun. Le Clos du Lac is a good base for walking and mountain biking and the site's friendly managers will be pleased to recommend possible itineraries.

Facilities

Shop. Play area. Tourist information. Mobile homes for rent. Off site: St Apollinaire (shops and restaurants). Canoe hire. Fishing. Mini golf. Water sports. Hiking and mountain biking. Bicycle hire. Les Ecrins National Park.

Open: 21 May - 24 September.

Directions

St Apollinaire is on the north side of Lac de Serre Ponçon. From Gap head west on N94 towards Embrun. At Chorges join the D9 to St Apollinaire from where the site is well indicated.
GPS: 44.5647, 6.3652

Charges guide

Per unit incl. 2 persons and electricity	€ 15.10 - € 18.30

Campéole
CAMPSITES AND RENTALS

Le Clos du Lac***

Beautifully located between lakes and mountains. Pitches and accommodations with views of the Lac de Serre-Ponçon.

05160 St Apollinaire - Tel.: +33-492-4427-43 - www.campeole.co.uk / clos-du-lac@campeole.com

RHÔNE-ALPES

Saint Aygulf

Camping de Saint Aygulf-Plage

270 avenue Salvarelli, F-83370 Saint Aygulf-Plage (Var) T: 04 94 17 62 49. E: info@campingdesaintaygulf.fr

alanrogers.com/FR83290

This is a large, well run and self-sufficient campsite with a range of good facilities and direct access to the beach. The pitches here are well marked, flat and arranged in long rows, many with good shade from the pine trees. There are 1,100 in total, with 700 for touring units and the remainder used for mobile homes and chalets. Electricity is available on 600 touring pitches. Although there is no swimming pool on the site, the direct access to the beach makes this a fine family holidaying campsite. The beach is part of a long sandy bay which shelves gradually into the sea, suitable for children of all ages.

Facilities

Four large toilet blocks provide good, clean facilities. No facilities for disabled visitors. Laundry facilities. Supermarket. Bakery. Two restaurants. Bar with patio and stage for discos and entertainment. Pizzeria and takeaways. Multisports court. Play areas. Boules. First aid. Caravan storage. Beach. No charcoal barbecues. Off site: Bicycle hire 100 m. Riding 1 km. Golf 6 km. Aquatica and Luna Park within 2 km. Fréjus and St. Raphael within 6 km.

Open: 7 April - 27 October.

Directions

From A8 take exits for Puget or Fréjus and RN7 to Fréjus town. Follow signs to seafront and join RN98. Saint Aygulf is 2 km. towards St Tropez. Site signed and is behind Hotel Van der Valk.
GPS: 43.39229, 6.72685

Charges guide

Per unit incl. 2 persons and electricity	€ 14.50 - € 32.50
extra person	€ 4.00 - € 9.50
child (0-7 yrs)	€ 2.00 - € 5.50
dog	€ 2.00 - € 4.00

For latest campsite news, availability and prices visit

alanrogers.com

Saint Raphaël

Castel Camping Douce Quiétude

3435 boulevard Jacques Baudino, F-83700 Saint Raphaël (Var) T: 04 94 44 30 00.
E: info@douce-quietude.com **alanrogers.com/FR83250**

Douce Quiétude is 5 km. from the beaches at Saint Raphaël and Agay but is quietly situated at the foot of the Estérel massif. There are 400 pitches, only 70 of these are for touring. Set in pleasant pine woodland or shaded, green areas, the pitches are of a comfortable size, separated by bushes and trees with electricity (10A), water, drainage and telephone/TV points provided. This mature site offers a wide range of services and facilities complete with a pool complex. It can be busy in the main season yet is relaxed and spacious. Security is good, with identity bracelets mandatory throughout your stay.

Facilities

Fully equipped modern toilet blocks, facilities for babies and disabled visitors. Launderette. Bar, restaurant, takeaway, pizzeria (3/4-3/9). Shop. Three swimming pools (two heated), water slide, jacuzzi. Play area. Children's club, activities for teenagers (all July/Aug). Sports area. Games room. Tennis. Minigolf. Archery. Fitness centre, sauna. Evening entertainment, shows, karaoke, discos (July/Aug). Mountain bike hire. Only gas barbecues. Off site: Bus route 1 km. Golf and riding 2 km. Windsurf hire and sea fishing 5 km.

Open: 3 April - 2 October.

Directions

From A8 exit 38 (Fréjus/St Raphaël) take D100, signed Valescure then Agay. Follow site signs. Access via N98 coast road turning north at Agay on D100. Pass Esterel Camping, then site signed. GPS: 43.44727, 6.80600

Charges guide

Per unit incl. 2 persons and electricity	€ 19.00 - € 52.50
extra person	€ 6.00 - € 10.00
child (3-13 yrs)	€ 5.00 - € 8.00

Camping Cheques accepted.

Saint Rémy-de-Provence

Camping Monplaisir

Chemin de Monplaisir, F-13210 Saint Rémy-de-Provence (Bouches du Rhône) T: 04 90 92 22 70.
E: reception@camping-monplaisir.fr **alanrogers.com/FR13040**

Only a kilometre from the centre of St Rémy, in the foothills of the Alpilles mountains, this is one of the most pleasant and well run sites we have come across. St Rémy is a very popular town and the site was full when we visited in mid June. Everything about it is of a high standard and quality. The good impression created by the reception and shop continues through the rest of the site. In all there are 130 level grass pitches with 9 taken by smart mobile homes, with 10A electricity everywhere. Flowering shrubs and greenery abounds, roads are tarmac and all is neat and tidy. There are six toilet blocks strategically placed for all areas. All are heated and one is larger, but all are unisex. The recreation area with a swimming pool (18x10 m), jacuzzi and paddling pool is overlooked by the bar. Open in July and August, it provides light meals and snacks and some entertainment.

Facilities

Six good quality, unisex toilet blocks are all heated in low season and have some washbasins in cabins. Family rooms and en-suite facilities for disabled visitors in two. Washing machines. Two motorcaravan service points. Shop with essentials (good cheese and cold meat counter). Bar with snacks (July/Aug). Swimming pool. Play area. Boules. Only gas and electric barbecues permitted. Mobile homes and chalets for hire. Off site: St Rémy 1 km. Bicycle hire 1 km. Fishing 2 km. Riding 5 km. Les Baux 5 km. Golf 10 km.

Open: 10 March - 20 October.

Directions

From St Rémy town centre follow signs for Arles and Nîmes. At roundabout on western side of town take D5 signed Maillane and immediately left by a supermarket. Site is signed and is 500 m. on left. GPS: 43.79695, 4.82372

Charges guide

Per unit incl. 2 persons and electricity (6A)	€ 18.90 - € 29.70
extra person	€ 5.00 - € 8.00
child (2-7 yrs)	€ 3.00 - € 6.00

CAMPING MONPLAISIR

- Overflowing swimming and paddling pool
- Snack bar in high season, Laundry

- 130 pitches, 2.8 ha of comfort, quietness and garden area
- Boules, children's games, table tennis, grocery

- Chalets & mobile homes to let

CHEMIN MONPLAISIR - F-13210 ST. RÉMY DE PROVENCE - FRANCE
TEL : +33 (0)4 90 92 22 70 - FAX : +33 (0)4 90 92 18 57
www.camping-monplaisir.fr
reception@camping-monplaisir.fr

For latest campsite news, availability and prices visit
alanrogers.com

Saint Rémy-de-Provence

Camping Mas de Nicolas

Avenue Plaisance du Touch, F-13210 Saint Rémy-de-Provence (Bouches du Rhône) T: 04 90 92 27 05.
E: camping-masdenicolas@nerim.fr **alanrogers.com/FR13050**

The site has a very spacious feel to it, due mainly to the central area of gently sloping grass, dotted with shrubs, that is kept clear of pitches and used for leisure and sunbathing. The 140 pitches are separated by hedges and flowering shrubs, 34 for mobile homes, the remainder for touring units. The pitches all have electricity, water and drainage, and access roads are wide. Some pitches are an irregular shape and some are sloping, but many have views and they are mostly organised into groups of two and four. There is a pool area with 'Balnéotherapie et Remise en form', or as we would call it a spa and gym.

Facilities

Good, modern toilet blocks including baby bathroom can be heated. Plans to refurbish one block. Dishwashing and laundry sinks, washing machines. Small bar (w/ends only until high season), occasional paella evenings. Swimming pool (15/5-15/9). Sauna, steam room, spa bath, gym. Play area. Bicycle hire. WiFi. Off site: Adjacent municipal gym, tennis, volleyball courts. Riding 1 km. Fishing 2 km. Golf 15 km. St Rémy has restaurants and a Wed. market.

Open: 15 March - 15 October.

Directions

St Rémy-de-Provence is located where the D571 from Avignon connects with the D99 Tarascon - Cavaillon road. Site is signed from the village centre on the north side. Leave the A7 at Cavaillon or Avignon-Sud. GPS: 43.79622, 4.83879

Charges guide

Per unit incl. 2 persons and electricity	€ 14.50 - € 21.50
extra person	€ 5.00 - € 7.00

Saint Romain-en-Viennois

Camping le Soleil de Provence

Route de Nyons, F-84110 Saint Romain-en-Viennois (Vaucluse) T: 04 90 46 46 00.
E: info@camping-soleil-de-provence.fr **alanrogers.com/FR84100**

The site has been developed to a high standard. The 162 average sized pitches, 150 for touring are separated by hedges and a variety of young trees offering only a little shade (10A electricity). The excellent pool, surrounded by a sunbathing terrace, and overlooked by the bar, is an unusual shape with an island in the centre. Although there is no paddling pool one end of the pool is very shallow. There is some organised entertainment in July and August but the emphasis is on a quiet and peaceful environment and is an ideal site for relaxing and unwinding.

Facilities

Modern well appointed, heated toilet blocks, facilities for disabled visitors, baby room. Washing machine, dryer. Motorcaravan services. Small shop for bread. Bar, snack bar. New aqua park with waterslides and paddling pool. Small play area. Volleyball. Boules. Off site: Tennis 1 km. Vaison-la-Romaine 4 km. Mountain biking 4 km. (Mont Ventoux is a challenge). Bicycle hire 5 km. Fishing 15 km.

Open: 15 March - 31 October.

Directions

Site is 4 km. north of Vaison-la-Romaine on the D938 road to Nyons. Turn right, signed St Romain-en-Viennois (site signed) and take first left to site. GPS: 44.26902, 5.10597

Charges guide

Per person	€ 3.50 - € 7.50
pitch	€ 3.00 - € 6.00
car	€ 3.00 - € 6.00
No credit cards.	

Salon-de-Provence

Camping le Nostradamus

Route d'Eyguières, F-13300 Salon-de-Provence (Bouches du Rhône) T: 04 90 56 08 36.
E: gilles.nostra@gmail.com **alanrogers.com/FR13030**

Only some 5 km. from Salon-de-Provence, near the village of Eyguières, this is a very pleasant campsite with grassy shaded pitches thanks to the many trees which have been preserved here as a result of the imaginative irrigation scheme developed by the owners in the 18th century. The campsite edging the canal was first opened 42 years ago as a farm site but has now been developed to offer 83 hedged pitches including 10 used for mobile homes. There are 20 with full services, the rest having electricity connections (4/6/10A). This is a family site, but having said that, the canal is unfenced.

Facilities

One large block with showers and toilets upstairs, and one small toilet block both provide all modern facilities including an en-suite unit for babies and children and another for disabled visitors (key). Washing machine (key). Motorcaravan service point. Shop (basic essentials) and bar. Takeaway/restaurant (15/5-30/9). Swimming and paddling pools (15/5-30/9). Play area outside entrance. Pétanque. Fishing. WiFi (charged). Off site: Regular bus service. Riding 5 km. Golf 12 km.

Open: 1 March - end October.

Directions

From A7 exit 26 (Senas) follow N538 south for 5 km. Take D175 west, pick up D17 going south to Salon. Site is at junction of D17 and CD72 with entrance off the CD72. From A54 exit 13 go north towards Eyguières and take first right on CD72 (site signed). GPS: 43.67772, 5.06476

Charges 2012

Per unit incl. 2 persons and electricity	€ 19.95 - € 26.65
Camping Cheques accepted.	

For latest campsite news, availability and prices visit
alanrogers.com

Saint Vincent-les-Forts

Campé⚫le

Campéole le Lac

Le Fein, F-04340 Saint Vincent-les-Forts (Alpes-de-Haute-Provence) T: 04 92 85 51 57.
E: lac@campeole.com **alanrogers.com/FR04210**

Le Lac is a member of the Campéole group and enjoys a fine location in the mountains of Haute-Provence. The site can be found at an altitude of 800 m. on the banks of the large Lac de Serre Ponçon and many of the site's 300 pitches (210 for tourers) have fine views of the lake and the surrounding mountains. All are of a good size with electricity hook ups and ample water points. The access road down to the site (3 km) is fairly steep and winding but it is certainly worth the effort. The waters of the lake have an alluring blue-green hue and shelve gradually from the site's beach. There is an ecological swimming pool, using natural water, consistent with this stunning natural setting. Other on-site amenities include a shop, restaurant and various sports facilities, notably volleyball and tennis. A number of pitches have lakeside locations and are particularly popular with fishermen. Water sports are popular and a hire service is offered, including canoes, electric boats and wakeboards. This is understandably a great area for hiking and mountain biking, with a number of excellent routes passing very close to the campsite. Reception staff have full details and will be pleased to make recommendations.

Facilities

Several toilet blocks have all the usual facilities. Wet room for disabled visitors. Laundry areas. Bar and restaurant (1/6-15/9). Shop and takeaway (1/7-31/8). Eco swimming pool (with lifeguard). Fishing. Volleyball. Tennis. Play area. Canoes and boat hire. Activity and entertainment programme. Tourist information. Mobile homes, chalets and equipped tents for rent. Free WiFi in reception area. Off site: Hiking and cycle. Montagne aux Marmottes (animal park). Riding 10 km. Serre Ponçon dam.

Open: 20 May - 25 September.

Directions

The site is close to the village of St Vincent-les-Forts. From Gap, head south on N85 and then join the D900b following signs to Barcelonnette. Continue on this road along the valley of the Durance passing the massive Barrage (dam) de Serre Ponçon and continue towards St Vincent-les-Forts. The site is well indicated from here. GPS: 44.45682, 6.36529

Charges guide

Per unit incl. 2 persons and electricity	€ 17.10 - € 26.60

Campé⚫le

CAMPSITES AND RENTALS

RHÔNE-ALPES

Le Lac ***

Direct access to the Lac de Serre Ponçon, natural swimming pool; amenities, pitches and accommodations of high quality.

04340 St Vincent Les Forts - Tel.: +33-492-8551-57 - www.campeole.co.uk / lac@campeole.com

Sanary-sur-Mer

Campasun Parc Mogador

167 chemin de Beaucours, F-83110 Sanary-sur-Mer (Var) T: 04 94 74 53 16. E: mogador@campasun.com
alanrogers.com/FR83320

This site in the Mediterranean countryside is very much geared for family holidays with children. Some 20 minutes on foot from the beach, the site has a very large and well kept pool area and a stage for entertainment. Somewhat smaller than other sites of this type, there are 180 good sized pitches (160 for touring units). The ground is mainly level, if rather stony and sandy. Variable shade is available and all pitches have 10A electricity. There are plans to enlarge some of the smaller, 80 sq.m. pitches. The attractive pool, is surrounded by ample paved sunbathing areas.

Facilities

Two large, deluxe toilet blocks, one with washbasins and showers in cabins. The high tech toilets are automatically cleaned and disinfected after every use. Laundry. Motorcaravan services. Restaurant (1/4-5/11), also snacks, pizzas and takeaway. Swimming pool and paddling pool, solarium. Boules. TV room also used for entertainment shows, cabarets, etc. Miniclub for children. Evening entertainment in season. Dogs are not accepted. Off site: Beach and fishing 800 m. Golf 6 km.

Open: 15 March - 5 November.

Directions

Take Bandol exit 12 from A50 and head for Six Fours on the N559. Arriving at Sanary-sur-Mer turn left towards Beaucours and site is on left after 100 m. GPS: 43.1488, 5.7732

Charges guide

Per unit incl. 2 persons and electricity (10A)	€ 18.00 - € 36.00
with individual sanitary facility	€ 22.00 - € 42.00
Camping Cheques accepted.	

499

We can book this site for you! alanrogers travel
Call 01580 214000

Vaison-la-Romaine
Camping de l'Ayguette
Faucon (CD86), F-84110 Vaison-la-Romaine (Vaucluse) T: 04 90 46 40 35. E: info@ayguette.com

alanrogers.com/FR84060

Set in four hectares of the beautiful region of north Provence, surrounded by vineyards and wooded hills, the 99 slightly sloping, stony pitches, 85 for touring, are widely spaced out on terraces amongst pine and oak trees giving plenty of dappled shade, only a few suitable for large units. All have 10A electricity (long leads necessary) but some are a considerable distance from the amenities, not ideal for those with walking difficulties. Rock pegs are essential. The reception building houses a bar, snack bar, small shop and terrace. Close by is an attractive swimming pool (heated all season) and sunbathing area.

Facilities

Two well equipped toilet blocks, one heated. Room for disabled campers or families with young children. Washing machines. Bar, snack bar, takeaway (July/Aug). Small shop, bread to order. Heated swimming pool, terrace. Volleyball. Badminton. Playground. Occasional entertainment, some activities for children. WiFi (free). Only gas and electric barbecues. Off site: Faucon with bar and restaurant 1 km. Roman town of Vaison la Romaine with shops, bar/restaurants, market and supermarkets 5 km.

Open: 7 April - 30 September.

Directions

From Nyons, follow signs for Vaison la Romaine. At the roundabout after Mirabel-aux-Baronnies, turn left through Puyméras-Faucon and then follow site signs. GPS: 44.26220, 5.129133

Charges guide

Per unit incl. 2 persons and electricity	€ 17.50 - € 27.00
extra person	€ 4.10 - € 5.90

Vallouise
Camping Indigo Vallouise
Petit Parcher, F-05290 Vallouise (Hautes-Alpes) T: 04 92 23 30 26

alanrogers.com/FR05440

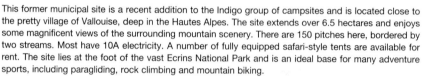

This former municipal site is a recent addition to the Indigo group of campsites and is located close to the pretty village of Vallouise, deep in the Hautes Alpes. The site extends over 6.5 hectares and enjoys some magnificent views of the surrounding mountain scenery. There are 150 pitches here, bordered by two streams. Most have 10A electricity. A number of fully equipped safari-style tents are available for rent. The site lies at the foot of the vast Ecrins National Park and is an ideal base for many adventure sports, including paragliding, rock climbing and mountain biking.

Facilities

Shop. Snack bar. Children's playground. Fishing. Tourist information. Fully equipped tents for rent. Off site: Shops and restaurants in Vallouise. Mountain sports. Hiking and mountain biking.

Open: 1 June - 31 August.

Directions

Vallouise can be found west of Briançon. From Grenoble, head south on N85 to Vizille, then the D1091 to Briançon, passing through Bourg d'Oisans. From Briançon, head south on N94 and then D4 and D994 to Vallouise. The site is well signposted. GPS: 44.835608, 6.507055

Charges guide

Per unit incl. 2 persons and electricity	€ 17.40 - € 18.00

Veynes
Camping Solaire
F-05400 Veynes (Hautes-Alpes) T: 04 92 58 12 34. E: info@camping-solaire.com

alanrogers.com/FR05080

An attractive, well kept site surrounded by mountains and scenes of pastural beauty, the owners have developed le Solaire to offer a wide range of facilities including a large jacuzzi heated to 30ºC. The swimming pools for adults and youngsters are supervised by a lifeguard, who also gives swimming lessons. The owners are particularly proud of their grasslands and of the 167 large pitches. There are 73 for touring in a separate area, many with good shade and all having 6A electricity with water close by. You can use the site's website to view and select your pitch. The site is well placed to explore the busy town of Gap and the surrounding countryside.

Facilities

New sanitary facilities with modern toilet and shower facilities including those for disabled visitors. Bar (1/6-30/9). Shop, snacks, takeaway. (1/7-30/9). Swimming pools (1/6-30/9). Jacuzzi (1/7-30/9). Large games room/TV. Football. Bicycle hire. WiFi over site (charged). Off site: Fishing 100 m. Lake, beach, swimming, boating 300 m. Veynes with range of shops and facilities 2 km.

Open: All year.

Directions

From Grenoble on N75, in town of Aspres-sur-Bu'ch, take D994a to join D994 travelling northeast towards Veynes. Site is signed on right 1 km. before village. After 300 m. take next right, entrance on right within 50 m. GPS: 44.52070, 5.80462

Charges guide

Per unit incl. 2 persons and electricity	€ 12.70 - € 22.20

For latest campsite news, availability and prices visit

alanrogers.com

Villars-Colmars

Camping Caravaning le Haut-Verdon

RD908, F-04370 Villars-Colmars (Alpes-de-Haute-Provence) T: 04 92 83 40 09.
E: campinglehautverdon@wanadoo.fr **alanrogers.com/FR04060**

For those seeking a quiet, family site set in most spectacular scenery, Camping le Haut-Verdon is ideal. It is on the banks of the Verdon, an excellent trout river, which flows through the spectacular gorge. The river can be fast flowing. Surrounded by the majestic peaks of the Alpes-de-Haute-Provence, it is on the doorstep of the Mercantour National Park. Set amongst the pines, the 109 pitches are mostly on the large size but are rather stony. With 73 for touring units, all have electricity (6/10A) but some require long leads. There is a small village nearby and the town of St André is 23 km. away.

Facilities

Refurbished, heated toilet block. Washing machines. Freezer for ice packs. Room for tenters for inclement weather. Motorcaravan services. Small shop. Bar and restaurant, takeaway. Heated swimming, paddling pools (from 1/6). Small play area. Giant chess. Boules. Skittle alley. Tennis. Trim trail in the woods. TV room. Organised games and competitions. Fishing. Barbecue areas (portable ones banned). Free WiFi in bar area. Off site: Pretty village of Colmars is nearby with a small supermarket, restaurants and bars. Riding adjacent. Bicycle hire 3 km.

Open: 1 May - 30 September.
Winter opening for mobile homes only.

Directions

Follow D955 north from St André-les-Alpes towards Colmar. After 11 km. road number changes to the D908. Site on right at southern edge of Villars-Colmars. Caravans not advised to use the D908 from Annot or Col d'Allos from Barcelonnette. GPS: 44.1601, 6.60625

Charges guide

Per unit incl. 2 persons and electricity (6A)	€ 16.00 - € 28.00
extra person	€ 3.00 - € 5.00
child (2-7 yrs)	€ 2.00 - € 3.00
dog	free - € 2.00

Villes-sur-Auzon

Camping les Verguettes

Route de Carpentras, F-84570 Villes-sur-Auzon (Vaucluse) T: 04 90 61 88 18.
E: info@provence-camping.com **alanrogers.com/FR84110**

Friendly and family run, this small campsite is surrounded by fields and vineyards and should appeal to those seeking a more relaxed holiday. It lies on the outskirts of the village of Villes sur Auzon and at the foot of Mont Ventoux and the Nesque Gorge (1 km). It is probably not the ideal site for active youngsters. The 89 compact pitches are attractively laid out and arranged in groups of six; 81 are for touring, separated by a variety of trees and shrubs, with electrical connections (5-10A) but long leads may be necessary. Close to the attractive swimming pool are the bar and small outside restaurant which offers a simple menu – a pleasant place to relax after a day sightseeing.

Facilities

Two toilet blocks, the buildings are old but have been refurbished to a high standard, one is heated in low season. Motorcaravan services. Bar (all season). Small outside restaurant (1/5-15/9) with simple menu and takeaway. Small swimming pool. Tennis. Minigolf. Boules. Table tennis, table football and small games/TV room. Internet point. Off site: Mont Ventoux, Nesque Gorge 1 km. Carpentras 10 km. Wine tasting, walking, cycling.

Open: 1 April - 15 October.

Directions

Leave A7 at exit 22 just south of Orange and take D950 to Carpentras. Take D942 east, signed Sault and Mazan. Site is about 10 km. on right just after a roundabout on entering village of Villes-sur-Auzon. GPS: 44.05685, 5.22820

Charges guide

Per unit incl. 2 persons and electricity	€ 19.30 - € 22.40
extra person	€ 4.70 - € 5.70
child (0-7 yrs)	€ 2.50 - € 3.00
dog	€ 2.20 - € 2.60

In Provence, between Luberon and Mont Ventoux
www.provence-camping.com
33 (0) 490 618 818
Les Verguettes ★★★★ Camping

For latest campsite news, availability and prices visit
alanrogers.com

Villecroze-les-Grottes

Camping Club le Ruou

Les Esparrus, 309, RD 560, F-83690 Villecroze-les-Grottes (Var) T: 04 94 70 67 70. E: info@leruou.com
alanrogers.com/FR83410

This is a family oriented site in the Provençal countryside, very much geared for family holidays with children. Some 45 minutes by car from the coast at Fréjus, the site has a large and well kept pool area and a mobile stage for entertainment. Smaller than some other sites of this type, there are 134 good sized pitches (50 for touring units). On mainly terraced, rather stony, ground with good shade, all have 6/10A electricity. Some of the pitches for caravans are along a steep path but there is a 4x4 available to assist. The attractive heated pool complex with three slides is surrounded by a sunbathing area and some shade. On the lower terraces there may be some road noise.

Facilities

One new deluxe toilet block with washbasins in cabins. Facilities for babies and disabled visitors. Laundry facilities. Snacks and takeaway (June-Sept). Main building houses a bar and entertainment room with TV. Area for shows, cabarets, etc. with mobile stage. Two swimming pools. Boules. Outdoor exercise equipment. Play area. Miniclub. Evening entertainment in season. Charcoal barbecues are not permitted. WiFi (charged). Off site: Fishing, riding and bicycle hire 5 km. Beach 35 km.

Open: 1 April - 30 October.

Directions

From the A8 (Toulon - Mandelieu-la-Napoule) take exit 13 onto the N7 towards Le Muy. At Les Arcs turn left on D555 (Draguignan), then onto D557 towards Villecroze. Approx. 4 km. before village turn onto D560. Site is on the left side of this road. GPS: 43.55345, 6.297983

Charges guide

Per unit incl. 2 persons
and electricity   € 18.20 - € 38.50
Camping Cheques accepted.

Volonne

Sunêlia Hippocampe

Route de Napoléon, F-04290 Volonne (Alpes-de-Haute-Provence) T: 04 92 33 50 00.
E: camping@l-hippocampe.com   **alanrogers.com/FR04010**

Hippocampe is a friendly family run, all action, lakeside site, with families in mind, situated in a beautiful area of France. The perfumes of thyme, lavender and wild herbs are everywhere and the higher hills of Haute-Provence are not too far away. There are 447 level, numbered pitches (177 for touring units), medium to very large (130 sq.m) in size. All have electricity (10A) and 140 have water and drainage, most are separated by bushes and cherry trees. Some of the best pitches border the lake. The restaurant, bar, takeaway and shop have all been completely renewed. Games, aerobics, competitions, entertainment and shows, plus a daily club for younger family members are organised in July/August. A soundproofed underground disco is set well away from the pitches and is very popular with teenage customers. Staff tour the site at night ensuring a good night's sleep. The site is much quieter in low season and, with its good discounts, is the time for those who do not want or need entertainment. English is spoken.

Facilities

Toilet blocks vary from old to modern, all with good clean facilities that include washbasins in cabins. Washing machines. Motorcaravan service point. Bread available (from 7/5). Shop, bar, restaurant and pizzeria (7/5-11/9). Large, heated pool complex (23/4-30/9) with five waterslides, (second pool 1/6-30/9). Tennis. Fishing. Canoeing. Boules. Bicycle hire. Several sports facilities (some with free instruction). Charcoal barbecues are not permitted. WiFi (charged). Off site: Volonne 600 m.

Open: 16 April - 30 September.

Directions

Approaching from the north turn off N85 across river bridge to Volonne, then right to site. From the south right on D4, 1 km. before Château Arnoux. GPS: 44.10462, 6.01688

Charges guide

Per unit incl. 2 persons
and electricity   € 16.00 - € 33.00
with full services   € 16.00 - € 43.00
Camping Cheques accepted.

★★★★
Camping L'Hippocampe

In the heart of the Alps of Haute Provence, near Verdon and Luberon, 12 km south of Sisteron. Relaxing holidays amidst olive and cherry orchards with a wide selection of activities.
(Reservation required)

Heated pool and water slides open from April 28

L'Hippocampe - Route Napoléon - 04290 VOLONNE - Tel: 00 33 492 33 50 00 - Fax: 00 33 492 33 50 49
http://www.l-hippocampe.com - e-mail: camping@l-hippocampe.com

Bathed in sunshine from early spring to late autumn, surrounded by stunning scenery, cosmopolitan towns and superb sandy beaches, no wonder this is one of France's most sought-after destinations.

DÉPARTEMENT: 06 ALPES-MARITIME

MAJOR CITIES: NICE, CANNES, MONTE CARLO (MONACO)

The glittering Côte d'Azur, perhaps better known as the French Riviera, is a beautiful stretch of coast studded with sophisticated towns such as the famous Monte Carlo, Nice, and Cannes, not forgetting the other famous and arguably the most glamorous resort of St Tropez. With its vast expanses of golden sandy beaches and long lazy hours of sunshine, this is a paradise for sun worshippers and beach enthusiasts.

It's a spectacular coast of rugged coves, sweeping beaches and warm seas. The quaint harbours and fishing villages have become chic destinations, now full of pleasure yachts, harbour-side cafés and crowded summertime beaches. Further up in the hills are quieter, tiny medieval villages with winding streets and white-walled houses with terracotta roofs, which have attracted artists for many years. In St Paul-de-Vence visitors browse through shops and galleries set on narrow winding cobblestone streets and inland Grasse is the perfume capital of the world, surrounded by the Provençal lavender fields and shady olive groves which pervade the air with a magical scent at certain times of the year.

Places of interest

Antibes: old city with 17th-century ramparts, 12th-century castle.

Cannes: popular for conventions and festivals, Cannes film festival, la Croisette, old city.

Grasse: capital of the perfume industry.

Menton: warmest of coastal cities, year round resort.

Nice: Promenade des Anglais, fine arts museum, Matisse museum.

Roquebrune: château, Ste Marguerite church.

Saint Paul-de-Vence: medieval village, Maeght Foundation.

Cuisine of the region

Aigo Bouido: garlic and sage soup.

Bouillabaisse: fish soup.

Rouille: an orange coloured sauce with peppers, garlic and saffron.

Bourride: a creamy fish soup.

Pissaladière: Provençal bread dough with onions, anchovies and olives.

Pistou (Soupe au): vegetable soup bound with *pommade*.

Pommade: a thick paste of garlic, basil, cheese and olive oil.

Ratatouille: aubergines, courgettes, onions, garlic, red peppers and tomatoes in olive oil.

www.guideriviera.com
info@guideriviera.com
(0)4 93 37 78 78

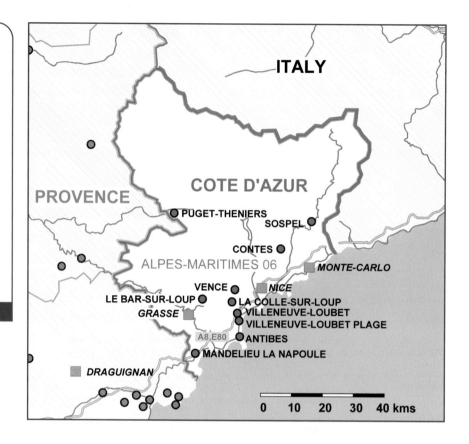

ITALY

COTE D'AZUR

PROVENCE

○ PUGET-THENIERS

SOSPEL ○

CONTES ○

ALPES-MARITIMES 06

■ MONTE-CARLO

VENCE ○ ■ NICE

LE BAR-SUR-LOUP ○ ○ LA COLLE-SUR-LOUP

GRASSE ■ ○ VILLENEUVE-LOUBET

VILLENEUVE-LOUBET PLAGE

A8,E80 ○ ANTIBES

○ MANDELIEU LA NAPOULE

■ DRAGUIGNAN

0   10   20   30   40 kms

Antibes
Camping Antipolis

Avenue du Pylône, La Brague, F-06600 Antibes (Alpes-Maritimes) T: 04 93 33 93 99.
E: contact@camping-antipolis.com **alanrogers.com/FR06200**

This quality site, set on four and a half hectares and just 800 m. from the beaches of the Côte d'Azur offers a truly unique style of camping – a Hollywood film set theme is presented throughout the site! The 180 pitches (60 for tourers) are level, with some shade. Each pitch has its own private washroom facilities with 10A electricity, and two of these have been adapted for campers with disabilities. There is an excellent pool complex with toboggan slides. The site's proximity to Marineland, one of Europe's largest sea animal parks, just a short walk away attracts most of its visitors. Good train and bus links are available nearby for those wishing to visit Nice, Cannes and the surrounding areas.

Facilities	Directions
Private washroom facilities. Laundry facilities. Restaurant/bar complex with takeaway. Supermarket. Pool complex with toboggan slides (heated out of season). Play area. Sports activities in high season. Aquagym. Tennis. Volleyball. Pétanque. Games room. Off site: Marineland 300 m. **Open:** 2 April - 25 September.	From autoroute A8, exit 46 Antibes, direction Biot - Marineland. At roundabout take first exit D/4 route de Biot. Turn left onto Avenue Mozart, turn right Avenue du Pylone and site is situtated on first left. GPS: 43.61097, 7.116968

Charges guide

Per unit incl. 2 persons
and electricity   € 21.00 - € 37.00
extra person   € 5.00 - € 9.00
Camping Cheques accepted.

For latest campsite news, availability and prices visit
alanrogers.com

Contes
La Ferme de Riola

5309 route des Clos, F-06390 Contes (Alpes-Maritimes) T: 04 93 79 03 02. E: la.riola@free.fr
alanrogers.com/FR06220

La Ferme de Riola is a very small site with just 35 pitches for touring and six gites, attractively dispersed amongst olive trees around the four-hectare terrain. Areas for tents are spread all around the site, mostly situated on the terraces amongst olive trees. Pitches are large and generally well shaded. All are equipped with electrical connections. Leisure facilities include a swimming pool, a volleyball court and a children's playground. This is a working farm and fresh produce including olives, olive oil and fresh eggs is available at the site's small shop.

Facilities

Two sanitary blocks have preset pushbutton showers and include a family shower room, baby room and facilities in one block for disabled visitors. Small shop. Swimming pool (April-Sept). Volleyball. Games room. Play area. WiFi around reception area. Off site: Sclos de Contes 1 km. Fishing 5 km. Contes 6 km. Riding 12 km. Nice 18 km.

Open: 1 April - 30 October.

Directions

Head north from Nice on the D2204 to La Pointe. Continue towards Sospel and then join the D1015. Pass La Vernea and join the D115 to Sclos de Contes. Site signed. GPS: 43.81612, 7.34324

Charges guide

Per unit incl. 2 persons and electricity	€ 21.00

No credit cards.

La Colle-sur-Loup
Camping les Pinèdes

Route du Pont de Pierre, F-06480 La Colle-sur-Loup (Alpes-Maritimes) T: 04 93 32 98 94.
E: info@lespinedes.com **alanrogers.com/FR06100**

Les Pinèdes is 7 km. inland from the busy coast, at the centre of all the attractions of the Côte d'Azur, yet far enough away to be a peaceful retreat at the end of a busy day. Run by the third generation of family owners, the site is terraced on a wooded hillside where olives and vines used to grow. All the level pitches have electricity (6-10A), most also with water and they are separated by low bushes. Twelve new pitches at the top of the site and also a small children's pool have recently been completed. In May the evenings are alive with fireflies. A Sites et Paysages member.

Facilities

Two excellent new toilet blocks. One block has facilities for disabled visitors. Baby room. Shop, bakery. Bar, restaurant, takeaway. Swimming pool. New children's play area. Field for volleyball, basketball, football, archery, boules. Fitness area. Riding. Entertainment (July/Aug). Weekly walks in the hills June-Sept. New mobile homes to rent. WiFi. Twin-axle caravans not accepted. Off site: River fishing 50 m. Village 1 km. (tennis, riding, leisure park, keep fit course, antiques quarter).

Open: 15 March - 30 September.

Directions

From A8 take D2 towards Vence. At Colle-sur-Loup roundabout take D6 signed Grasse, site on right in 3 km. at large sign after the restaurant entrance. GPS: 43.6817, 7.08335

Charges guide

Per unit incl. 2 persons and electricity	€ 23.80 - € 38.30
extra person	€ 4.30 - € 5.80
child (from 5 yrs)	€ 2.20 - € 3.50
dog	€ 2.40 - € 3.50

Le Bar-sur-Loup
Camping Caravaning les Gorges du Loup

965 chemin des Vergers, F-06620 Le Bar-sur-Loup (Alpes-Maritimes) T: 04 93 42 45 06.
E: info@lesgorgesduloup.com **alanrogers.com/FR06090**

Les Gorges du Loup is situated on a steep hillside above Grasse. The one kilometre lane which leads to the site is narrow with passing places. The 70 pitches are on level terraces, all with electricity and many have stupendous views. Some pitches are only suitable for tents and the site roads are quite steep. A quiet family site, there is no organised entertainment. Grasse (9 km) is surrounded by fields of lavender, mimosa and jasmine and has been famous for the manufacture of perfume since the 16th century. The friendly owners provide 4x4 assistance and there is a new parking area at the entrance.

Facilities

Clean toilet blocks with washbasins and hot showers, Laundry facilities. Reception, small shop, bread. Small bar/restaurant with terrace, takeaway (all 19/5-14/9). Swimming pool, small slide, diving board, but no pool for small children. Boules. Skittles. TV room, board games, library. WiFi (charged). Children's climbing frame, slide. Electric barbecues only. Fridge hire. Chalets, mobile homes for hire. Off site: Bar-sur-Loup with its few shops, restaurants is only a 500 m. walk. Fishing 1 km. Golf, riding and bicycle hire 5 km. Beach 15 km.

Open: 7 April - 29 September.

Directions

From Grasse, D2085 Nice road. D3 briefly to Châteauneuf Pré du Lac. D2210 to Pont-de-Loup, Vence. Site signed on right. Pass village of Bar-sur-Loup on left, after sharp right turn, follow narrow access road 750 m. (passing places). GPS: 43.7017, 6.9948

Charges 2012

Per unit incl. 2 persons and electricity	€ 18.70 - € 30.00
extra person	€ 5.00

No credit cards.

For latest campsite news, availability and prices visit
alanrogers.com

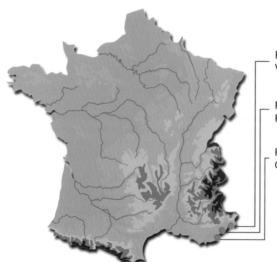

PARC SAINT-JAMES
VILLAGES CLUB

Parc Saint-James is a small group of 4* campsites, all located in the South of France on the Côte d'Azur.

These three 'village-club' style campsites offer a warm welcome, a decent range of facilities with a real family atmosphere and a great location for beach-based holidays.

Parc Saint-James 'Le Sourire'
Villeneuve Loubet

Parc Saint-James 'Oasis Village'
Puget sur Argens

Parc Saint-James 'Gassin'
Gassin

Parc Saint-James

In Their Own Words...

Come and discover the Côte d'Azur South of France

Enjoy the pleasure of spending your holidays outdoors in village-clubs where everything has been designed for your leisure and well being.

A superb environment, a warm welcome, a friendly setting where your family can get together in a privileged world and experience true moments of happiness.

Active holidays

Parc Saint-James offers the opportunity to enjoy many activities such as volleyball, tennis, badminton and fitness. Camping Parc Saint-James Le Sourire, is a hub of sports activities. Guests can also enjoy horse riding, windsurfing, rowing, diving and climbing.

...or relaxing holidays

Parc Saint-James campsites village club is for you! You'll find a swimming pool, sun deck and shady trees. Each campsite works hard to ensure you don't need to lift a finger – just relax and we'll take care of you. Enjoy our bars and TV lounges.

Your evening

Parc Saint-James ensures you are always close to some activity and entertainment. A short distance from Fréjus and Saint-Raphaël, our location in the Gulf of St. Tropez allows you to party through the night. And the Parc Saint-James campsites organise evenings exclusively for residents, with a different daily themed programme (musical groups and/or shows) and at Oasis, from 11pm, a disco party.

Children's kingdom

At Parc Saint-James campsites, children are heroes! Children from 4 to 10 years can enjoy our mini-club and a whole range of fun activities: treasure hunts, contests, make-up, crafts and sports. They will also enjoy our playground with slides and swings or go paddling safely under the eye of a lifeguard. Older children can do battle with friends in our arcades or play ping-pong, soccer and volleyball.

www.camping-parcsaintjames.com

We can book this site for you! Call 01580 214000 alan rogers 🌐 travel

Mandelieu-la-Napoule

Camping Caravaning les Cigales

505 avenue de la Mer, F-06210 Mandelieu-la-Napoule (Alpes-Maritimes) T: 04 93 49 23 53.
E: campingcigales@wanadoo.fr **alanrogers.com/FR06080**

It is hard to imagine that such a quiet, peaceful site could be in the middle of such a busy town and so near Cannes. The entrance (easily missed) has large electronic gates that ensure that the site is very secure. There are only 115 pitches (42 mobile homes) so this is quite a small, personal site. There are three pitch sizes, from small ones for tents to pitches for larger units and all have electricity (6A), some fully serviced. All are level with much needed shade in summer, although the sun will get through in winter when it is needed. The site is alongside the Canal de Siagne and for a fee, small boats can be launched at La Napoule, then moored outside the campsite's side gate. Les Cigales is open all year so it is useful for the Monte Carlo Rally, the Cannes Film Festival and the Mimosa Festival, all held out of the main season. English is spoken.

Facilities

Well appointed, clean, heated toilet blocks. Excellent facilities for babies and disabled visitors. Laundry area. Motorcaravan services. Restaurant and takeaway (May-Oct). Attractive swimming pool, heated according to the weather conditions and large sunbathing area (April-Oct). New play area. River fishing. WiFi (free). Only gas barbecues allowed. Max 1 dog per pitch. Off site: Beach 800 m. The town is an easy walk. Two golf courses within 1 km. Railway station 1 km. for trains to Cannes, Nice, Antibes, Monte Carlo. Hypermarket 2 km. Bus stop 30 m.

Open: All year.

Directions

From A8, exit 40, bear right. Remain in right-hand lane, continue right signed Plages-Ports, Creche-Campings. Casino supermarket on right. Continue under motorway to T-junction. Turn left, site is 60 m. on left opposite Chinese restaurant. Some other approaches have a 3.3 m. height restriction. GPS: 43.5391, 6.94275

Charges 2012

Per unit incl. 2 persons and electricity	€ 41.50 - € 55.00
extra person	€ 8.00
child (under 5 yrs)	€ 4.00

Camping Caravaning Mobil-homes Studios Solarium swimming-pool Private harbour

Les Cigales ★★★★ Baie de Cannes

New facilities to discover

www.lescigales.com

505, av. de la mer
06210 Mandelieu la Napoule
Tél. 00 33 493 49 23 53

Sospel

Camping Domaine Sainte Madeleine

Route de Moulinet, F-06380 Sospel (Alpes-Maritimes) T: 04 93 04 10 48.
E: camp@camping-sainte-madeleine.com **alanrogers.com/FR06010**

Domaine Sainte Madeleine is an attractive, peaceful site, with swimming pool, in spectacular mountain scenery. It is about 20 km. inland from Menton, and very near the Italian border. The approach to this site involves a 17 km. climb with hairpin bends and then a choice of going through the pass or an 800 m. long tunnel (3.5 m. high, 3 m. wide). Situated on a terraced hillside with mountain views towards Italy, manoeuvring within the site presents no problem as the pitches are on level, well drained grass. The lower ones have shade but those higher up on the hill have none. Electricity is available to 80 of the 90 pitches. There are few activities on site but the surrounding area is just waiting to be explored.

Facilities

Good quality toilet block with hot showers (token required). Laundry facilities. Motorcaravan services. Gas supplies. Bread can be ordered. Swimming pool (140 sq.m. and heated in spring and autumn). Bar and takeaway (July/Aug). WiFi (charged). Off site: Fishing 1 km. The attractive small town of Sospel is 4 km. with many restaurants, bars, cafés and shops and a Thursday market. Tennis, riding and a centre for mountain biking.

Open: 31 March - 3 October.

Directions

From A8 take Menton exit towards Sospel from where you turn onto the D2566 (route de Moulinet). Site is 4 km. north of Sospel on the left. GPS: 43.89702, 7.41685

Charges guide

| Per unit incl. 2 persons and electricity | € 22.90 |
| extra person | € 4.40 |

No credit cards.

For latest campsite news, availability and prices visit
alanrogers.com

Vence
Camping Caravaning Domaine de la Bergerie

1330 chemin de la Sine, F-06140 Vence (Alpes-Maritimes) T: 04 93 58 09 36.
E: info@camping-domainedelabergerie.com **alanrogers.com/FR06030**

La Bergerie is a quiet, family owned site that celebrates its 60th anniversary in 2012. It is situated in the hills 3 km. from Vence and 10 km. from the sea at Cagnes-sur-Mer. An extensive, natural, lightly wooded site, it is in a secluded position at about 300 m. above sea level. Most of the pitches are shaded and all are of a good size. There are 450 pitches, 245 with electricity (2/5A), including 65 also with water and drainage. Some areas are a little distance from the toilet blocks. With the aim of keeping this a quiet and tranquil place to stay, there are no organised activities and definitely no groups accepted.

Facilities

Refurbished toilet blocks are centrally positioned and include excellent provision for disabled visitors. Good shop. Small bar/restaurant, takeaway (all 1/5-30/9). Large swimming pool and smaller pool (1/5-30/9). Playground. Tennis. 12 boules pitches (lit at night) with competitions in season. No charcoal barbecues. Two mobile homes and new camping pods to rent. Off site: Beach at Cagnes-sur-Mer 10 km. Riding and fishing 10 km. Golf 18 km. Grasse, famous perfume centre 25 km.

Open: 25 March - 15 October.

Directions

From A8 exit 48 take Cagnes-sur-Mer road towards Vence (do not follow sat nav instructions to turn off this road before you reach Vence). At first roundabout in Vence follow signs for Centre Ville and site is well signed from here. GPS: 43.71174, 7.0905

Charges guide

Per unit incl. 2 persons and electricity (2A)	€ 20.00 - € 27.50
extra person	€ 5.00

Camping Cheques accepted.

Villeneuve-Loubet
Parc Saint James le Sourire

Route de Grasse, F-06270 Villeneuve-Loubet (Alpes-Maritimes) T: 04 93 20 96 11.
E: info@camping-parcsaintjames.com **alanrogers.com/FR06190**

Le Sourire is a member of the Parc Saint James group. There are 411 pitches here and many are occupied by mobile homes and chalets. There are however 241 touring pitches dispersed throughout the wooded terrain, some of which are on soft sandy soil. The site is close to the impressive La Vanade sports complex which has a massive range of activities including no fewer than 55 tennis courts, a riding centre and a 9-hole golf course. There is a good range of activities on site too. Some pitches are close to the main road so you may experience some road noise. Mobile homes and chalets for rent.

Facilities

Sanitary facilities (with key access) include preset pushbutton showers. Baby room planned. Laundry. Shop (June-Aug). Bar (July/Aug). Restaurant and takeaway (May-Aug). Swimming pool and separate children's pool (May-Aug). Play area. TV room. Gym. Games room. Sports competitions. Entertainment in high season. Off site: Cannes and Nice. Nearest beaches 4 km. Marineland water park. Leisure park at La Vanade.

Open: 7 April - 29 September.

Directions

Take the Villeneuve - Loubet exit from the A8 autoroute and follow signs to Grasse joining the D2085. The site can be found on the left, 2 km. from Villeneuve Loubet. GPS: 43.6603, 7.10429

Charges guide

Per unit incl. 2 persons and electricity	€ 17.00 - € 31.00
extra person	€ 3.00 - € 5.00

Villeneuve-Loubet-Plage
Camping la Vieille Ferme

296 boulevard des Groules, F-06270 Villeneuve-Loubet-Plage (Alpes-Maritimes) T: 04 93 33 41 44.
E: info@vieilleferme.com **alanrogers.com/FR06050**

In a popular resort area and open all year, la Vieille Ferme is a family owned site with good facilities. It has 113 leve,l gravel-based touring pitches, 95 fully serviced and the majority separated by hedges. Some are only small, simple pitches for little tents. There is also a fully serviced pitch on tarmac for motorcaravans. There are special winter rates for long stays with quite a few long stay units on site. The entrance to the site is very colourful with well tended flower beds. English is spoken at reception and the whole place has a very friendly feel to it.

Facilities

Modern, heated, well kept toilet blocks, children's toilets, baby room, facilities for disabled visitors. Motorcaravan services. Washing machines, dryer. Shop (Easter-Sept). Machine with drinks, sweets, ice in TV room. Gas, bread, milk to order. Swimming pool, children's pool, heated and covered for winter use (closed mid Nov-mid Dec). Jacuzzi. Internet. WiFi (charged). Boules. Games, competitions organised in July/Aug. Off site: Beach and fishing 1 km. Golf and bicycle hire 2 km. Riding 6 km.

Open: All year.

Directions

From west, A8, exit 44 Antibes, D35, 3.5 km. Left towards Nice, N7. After 3.5 km. turn left for site between Marineland and Parc de Vaugrenier. Site is 150 m. on right. Avoid N98 Route du Bord de Mer. GPS: 43.62002, 7.12586

Charges guide

Per unit incl. 2 persons and electricity (6A)	€ 25.50 - € 39.50
extra person	€ 5.00 - € 6.00

For latest campsite news, availability and prices visit
alanrogers.com

The island of Corsica is both dramatic and beautiful. The scenery is spectacular with bays of white sand lapped by the clear blue waters of the Mediterranean. At certain times of the year the entire island is ablaze with exotic flowers, aided by Corsica's excellent sunshine record.

DÉPARTEMENTS: 2A CORSE-SUD; 2B HAUTE-CORSE

MAJOR CITIES: AJACCIO AND BASTIA

Corsica is regarded by some as the jewel of the Mediterranean islands and is made up of two départements: Haute Corse (upper Corsica) and Corse du Sud (southern Corsica). The island has endured a bloody history, having been much disputed by the Greeks, Romans and Lombards. Five hundred years of Italian rule has influenced the look of the island with Italian-style hilltop hamlets and villages developed alongside mountain springs. Many of the villages feature rustic, unadorned churches and also a few Romanesque examples too.

The variety of scenery is spectacular. Across much of the island one can discover dramatic gorges, glacial lakes, gushing mountain torrents and magnificent pine and chestnut forests. You'll also experience the celebrated perfume of the Corsican maquis: a tangled undergrowth of fragrant herbs, flowers and bushes that fills the warm spring and summer air. The highest mountains lie to the west, while the gentler ranges, weathered to strange and often bizarre shapes, lie to the south and a continuous barrier forms the island's backbone.

Places of interest

Ajaccio: a dazzling white city full of Napoleonic memorabilia.

Bastia: historic citadel towering over the headland. The old town has preserved its streets in the form of steps connected by vaulted passages, converging on the Vieux port (the old port). The new port is the real commercial port of the island.

Cuisine of the region

Brocchui: sheeps' milk cheese is used much in cooking in both its soft form (savoury or sweet) or more mature and ripened.

Capone: local eels, cut up and grilled on a spit over a charcoal fire.

Dziminu: fish soup, like bouillabaise but much hotter. Made with peppers and pimentos.

Figatelli: a sausage made of dried and spiced pork with liver. A popular snack between meals.

Pibronata: a highly spiced local sauce.

Prizzutu: a peppered smoked ham; resembles the Italian prosciutto, but with chestnut flavour added.

www.visit-corsica.com
info@visit-corsica.com
(0)4 95 51 00 00

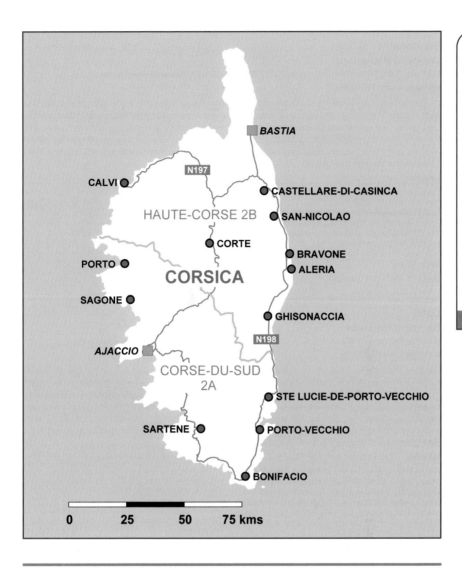

Bonifacio
Camping U-Farniente de Pertamina Village

RN198, F-20169 Bonifacio (Corse-du-Sud) T: 04 95 73 05 47. E: pertamina@wanadoo.fr

alanrogers.com/FR20000

This is a well run site with plenty to offer for a family holiday. The 120 pitches, many in delightful settings, have electricity (3A), are partially terraced and are hedged with trees and bushes, providing shade. They are fairly flat and vary in size, many being well over 100 sq.m. A central feature of the site is the large attractive swimming pool, surrounded by terraces. The bar, restaurant, pizzeria/grill and crêperie are on a series of terraces above the pool and patios. This site will suit campers who like a large pool complex and do not mind a drive to the beach. There is an entertainment programme for adults and children in high season.

Facilities

Two toilet blocks include washbasins in semi-private cubicles, British and Turkish style WCs, washing machines plus drying and ironing facilities. Motorcaravan service point at entrance (public usage). Shop. Takeaway. Bar, restaurant, pizzeria/grill serving set meals and à la carte menu at reasonable prices. Swimming pool. Tennis. Play area. TV room. Excellent gym. Off site: Excursions. Bonifacio 4 km.

Open: Easter - 15 October.

Directions

Site is on the RN198 road, 4 km. north of Bonifacio to the east. Well signed as Pertamina Village. GPS: 41.41790, 9.17990

Charges guide

Per unit incl. 2 persons
and electricity € 23.00 - € 36.00
extra person € 6.50 - € 10.00
child (0-10 yrs) free - € 6.00
Camping Cheques accepted.

For latest campsite news, availability and prices visit
alanrogers.com

Bonifacio
Camping Rondinara

Suartone, F-20169 Bonifacio (Corse-du-Sud) T: 04 95 70 43 15. E: reception@rondinara.fr
alanrogers.com/FR20240

The views from every pitch in this site are stunning, either coastal or the rolling hills and cliffs inland. 'The great outdoors' describes this campsite, which is away from any tourist over-development and is at one with nature. The natural and informal pitches sit on the hillside above a superb bay with sheltered water, fine silver sand and safe swimming. Most pitches have shade from foliage. Large boulders make natural divisions and some pitches need long leads for the 6A electricity. The beach is a 400 m. walk down a rough track through the maquis.

Facilities

Three excellent, modern toilet blocks are very clean and offer hot water throughout, hot showers and single sex British style toilets. Motorcaravan service point. Shop. Pizza restaurant. Bar. Swimming pool. Play area. Games room. Electronic games. Entertainment and family activities. Torches are essential here. Off site: Beach, boat launching and fishing 400 m. Golf, riding and sailing 15 km.

Open: 15 May - 30 September.

Directions

Site is midway between Bonifacio and Porto-Vecchio off the RN198. Take the D158 to Baie de la Rondinara for 7 km. (site is well signed). The road is rough and narrow but large units will have no trouble negotiating it. GPS: 41.47323, 9.26316

Charges guide

Per unit incl. 2 persons	
and electricity	€ 22.10 - € 27.00
extra person	€ 5.90 - € 7.70

Calvi
Camping Paduella

Route de Bastia, F-20260 Calvi (Haute-Corse) T: 04 95 65 06 16. E: campingpaduella@wanadoo.fr
alanrogers.com/FR20170

Camping Paduella is a beautifully maintained, simple site which has been run by the friendly Peretti family for 40 years. As it is a popular site, it is best to book ahead for high season. There is a wide choice of pleasant pitches (135 in total), some shaded under pines, others grassed and hedged with less shade. All are well maintained on level terraces with good access and 4/16A electricity. The surroundings are pleasant and the site is peaceful. The lovely white sand beach is 300 m. away and the picturesque town of Calvi is a delightful 30 minute walk. There is a fairly busy road and light railway to cross to get to the beach but most of the walk is through the shaded beach parkland.

Facilities

Two centrally located modern sanitary blocks (British style WCs). Well equipped showers. Baby bathroom. Laundry with washing machines, ironing board. Small shop with basic supplies and fresh bread. Pizzeria and bar. Internet access. WiFi (charged). Play area. Sports ground. Fridge hire can be arranged. Off site: Supermarket and ATM 200 m. Adventure activities 200 m. Riding and bicycle hire 700 m. Boat launching and marina 1 km. Scuba diving, rowing and sailing nearby.

Open: 10 May - 5 October.

Directions

From the north, site is just before the town of Calvi. It is directly off the RN197 on the left and is well signed. GPS: 42.5521, 8.7641

Charges guide

Per unit incl. 2 persons	
and electricity	€ 23.05 - € 27.65
extra person	€ 6.50 - € 8.00
child (under 7 yrs)	€ 3.25 - € 4.00

No credit cards. Cash only.

Calvi
Camping la Pinède

Route de la Pinède, F-20260 Calvi (Haute-Corse) T: 04 95 65 17 80. E: info@camping-calvi.com
alanrogers.com/FR20180

Camping la Pinède is a well ordered, family site of 185 touring pitches, all with 4-16A electricity. The pitches are marked and level (although the pine roots are a nuisance in places). There is access for large units in some areas. Water points are spread around the site and everything is kept tidy and clean. Under the mature pines it can be quite dark but there are plenty of alternatives in the light. The site is divided into areas of accommodation – pitches for tour operators, mobile homes and tourers. Unusually, all facilities are in separate buildings. English and Dutch are spoken at the efficient reception.

Facilities

Three well maintained and well placed sanitary buildings offer hot showers, facilities for disabled visitors and unisex toilets and showers. Washing machines. Motorcaravan service point. Shop (June-Sept). Bar. Restaurant (May-Sept). Swimming pool (no lifeguard). Play area. Tennis. Minigolf (charged). WiFi (charged). Overnight parking for late arrivals. Off site: Beach and fishing 200 m. Riding 500 m. Boat launching and bicycle hire 2 km. Golf 22 km.

Open: 1 April - 31 October.

Directions

Site is north of Calvi off the RN197, just south of the D251 road to the airport. Look for signs off the roundabout here and take care along a narrow road with leaning fir trees. GPS: 42.55320, 8.7686

Charges guide

Per unit incl. 2 persons	
and electricity	€ 21.50 - € 30.50
extra person	€ 6.50 - € 9.50

For latest campsite news, availability and prices visit
alanrogers.com

Castellare di Casinca

Village Center Domaine d'Anghione

F-20213 Castellare di Casinca (Corse-du-Sud) T: 04 99 57 21 21. E: contact@village-center.com

alanrogers.com/FR20270

Domaine d'Anghione is a sprawling and dated site built some forty years ago, which is being steadily upgraded. It is solely for bungalows and mobile homes which occupy a good deal of space here. The traditional pool and paddling pool are very welcome in the summer heat. A huge equestrian centre is on site and horses may be hired. The beachside self-service restaurant has excellent sea views as does the adjacent bar. The site has direct access to a wonderful long beach, which is of fine sand and shelves gently into the blue waters. Entertainment is provided in high season for both adults and children. Much of the site has a slightly tired look and needed watering and a general clean-up when seen. The very mature buildings on site added to this impression. Its main attractions are the beach and the amount of space available here.

Facilities	Directions
Self-service beach restaurant and bar. Pool bar. Swimming pool and paddling pool. Sauna. Tennis. Play area. Outdoor gym and sports area. Equestrian centre. Archery. Kids club. Minigolf. Squash. Entertainment in high season. WiFi (charged). Off site: Town of Folleli 7 km. Disco 7 km. Nature treks. Waterfall 15 km.	Site is on the eastern side of Corsica. From the RN198 at the 140 km. marker take the D106 towards the beach. The site is on the left as you approach the beach. GPS: 42.47599, 9.53242

Open: 1 April - 2 October.

Charges 2012

Contact the site for details.

Corte

Camping Restonica

Faubourg Saint Antoine, F-20250 Corte (Haute-Corse) T: 04 95 46 11 59. E: vero.camp@worldonline.fr

alanrogers.com/FR20110

Tucked away alongside the pretty Restonica river and near the Pont Neuf leading into the stunning mountainside old city of Corte, Camping Restonica is ideally placed for tourists wanting to visit Corte or travel on the popular inland mountain railway (the station is only a few hundred metres from the site). This is a small, simple site catering for those who want to enjoy the many delights of Corte. The entrance is steep but manageable, there are flat pitches for campers and caravans in the middle of the site, and many beautiful terraced pitches for tents dotted along the river bank under shady trees. The river is great for paddling or a shallow swim.

Facilities	Directions
Single, central toilet block is unisex and somewhat dated, although very clean. Toilet for disabled visitors but site not really suitable. Washing machine. Bread to order. Bar and snack bar. River fishing. WiFi throughout (charged). No barbecues. No pets. Off site: Sightseeing. Famous train journeys across Corsica. Museum. Only university in Corsica (politically significant).	Site is south of Corte town and the rivers Tavignnano and Restonica. Approaching the town, turn left at first roundabout onto Ave du 9 Septembre. Site is 300 m. on the right. It is signed from the roundabout and at the top of the steep, narrow access road. GPS: 42.3015, 9.152

Open: 15 April - 30 September.

Charges guide

Per unit incl. 2 persons and electricity	€ 19.40 - € 24.20
extra person	€ 7.60
child (0-7 yrs)	€ 3.80

For latest campsite news, availability and prices visit
alanrogers.com

Ghisonaccia
Camping Arinella Bianca
Route de la Mer, F-20240 Ghisonaccia (Haute-Corse) T: 04 95 56 04 78. E: arinella@arinellabianca.com
alanrogers.com/FR20010

Arinella is a lively, family oriented site on Corsica's east coast. The 381 level, grassy, good sized, irregularly-shaped pitches (141 for touring units with 10A electricity) have a variety of trees and shrubs providing ample shade. Some pitches overlook the attractive lakes which have fountains and are lit at night. The site has direct acess to a huge long beach of soft sand. The brilliantly designed resort style pools and paddling pool, overlooked by an attractive large restaurant, terraced bar and very professional entertainment area, form the hub of Arinella Bianca. The extremely active children's club with an information point, boutique and supermarket complete the facilities. When we visited the site was buzzing with activity at night and appeared to delight everyone by incorporating family entertainment. This excellent site includes a wellness centre and offers a vast range of services and plenty of sport and leisure facilities to choose from. This site is a tribute to its owner's design and development skills as it appears to be in entirely natural glades where, in fact, these have been created from former marshland.

Facilities

Four open plan sanitary blocks provide solar heated showers, washbasins in cabins, mainly British style WCs. Laundry. Motorcaravan services. Wellnes centre. Amphitheatre. Snack bar. Swimming pool (heated). Multisports centre. Windsurfing. Canoeing. Fishing. Tennis. Riding. Bicycle hire. Canyoning can be organised. Miniclub. Play area. Disco. Superb entertainment in the main season. Communal barbecue area. WiFi (charged). Only 1 dog per pitch. Off site: Sailing 300 m. Boat launching 2 km. Excursions. Subaqua diving.

Open: Mid April - 10 September.

Directions

Site is 4 km. east of Ghisonaccia. From N198 in Ghisonaccia look for sign 'La Plage, Li Mare'. Turn east on D144 at roundabout just south of town. Continue for 3.5 km. to further roundabout where site is signed to right. Site is 500 m. Speed bumps on approach road and on site. GPS: 41.9984, 9.442

Charges guide

Per unit incl. 2 persons and electricity	€ 29.00 - € 45.00

Camping Cheques accepted.

20240 Ghisonaccia – Corsica - tel: 0033 (0)4.95.56.04.78 - fax: 0033 (0)4.95.56.12.54

Welcome to Arinella Bianca, a Corsican campsite between sea and mountain, directly at the beach and with a family atmosphere. Animations, Mini Club, fishing, watersports, hiking and a beautiful spa.

web: www.arinellabianca.com - email: arinella@arinellabianca.com

Porto
Camping les Oliviers
F-20150 Porto (Corse-du-Sud) T: 04 95 26 14 49. E: lesoliviersporto@wanadoo.fr
alanrogers.com/FR20220

This attractive and modern, resort style campsite is by the Bay of Porto, set alongside a charming river suitable for fishing and swimming. It is located on the difficult to access and remote west coast of Corsica and reservations are essential. The site is on very steep slopes and has 190 pitches (120 with 10A electricity). The mainly small and terraced pitches reflect the rugged terrain, are unsuitable for motorcaravans and extremely challenging for larger units. The site is not suitable for disabled campers.

Facilities

Toilet facilities are unisex and in four blocks dotted around the site. Some washbasins in cubicles, British style WCs. No facilities for disabled visitors and unsuitable for those with mobility difficulty. Four washing machines. Fridge hire. Bread supplies. Restaurant. Pizzeria and bar (1/5-mid Sept). Swimming pool, gym, sauna, massage and Turkish bath. Play area. WiFi (charged). Fishing. Torches useful. Corsican trek agency. No dogs. Gas barbecues only. Off site: Supermarket in village 50 m. Bicycle hire 200 m. Garage 750 m. Fishing 1.5 km. Riding 30 km.

Open: 28 March - 7 November.

Directions

When approaching Porto from the North the road crosses a bridge over the river. Les Oliviers is on the left, well signed. Entrance is busy and gets quickly congested in high season. Allow extra time for transits on this coast road. Take care with larger units on mountain roads. GPS: 42.2619, 8.7103

Charges guide

Per unit incl. 2 persons and electricity	€ 25.60 - € 32.10
extra person	€ 7.30 - € 9.80

For latest campsite news, availability and prices visit
alanrogers.com

Porto-Vecchio

Camping la Vetta

Route de Bastia, la Trinité, F-20137 Porto-Vecchio (Corse-du-Sud) T: 04 95 70 09 86.
E: info@campinglavetta.com **alanrogers.com/FR20060**

The French/English owners Marieline and Nick Long have created a peaceful country park setting for their campsite to the north of La Trinité village. The 8.5 hectares of well maintained campsite are part sloping, part terraced, with an informal pitch allocation system. It seems to stretch endlessly. The abundance of tree varieties including many cork oaks give shade to 111 pitches which all have 10A electricity. The site has a pleasant lagoon-style pool with a bar, snacks and ice cream. Many of the delights of Corsica are only a short drive away and la Vetta is only 3 km. from Porto-Vecchio and its magnificent sandy beaches.

Facilities

Clean, traditional style toilet facilities have plenty of hot water. Laundry facilities. Bread and milk, lunchtime snacks and bar (all July/Aug). Swimming pool, paddling pool and water play area (all season). Snooker table. Play area. TV. Occasional Corsican evenings with food typical of the area (high season). WiFi. Off site: Public transport 800 m. Beach, fishing, watersports and boat launching 1.5 km. Good restaurant 1.5 km. Supermarket 2 km. Riding 4 km. Bicycle hire 5 km. Golf 7 km.

Open: 1 June - 1 October.

Directions

Site is in La Trinité village, off the RN198 (east side), north of Porto-Vecchio. GPS: 41.6316, 9.2929

Charges guide

Per unit incl. 2 persons	
and electricity	€ 22.00 - € 27.00
extra person	€ 6.50 - € 8.00
child (under 7 yrs)	€ 3.00 - € 4.00

Sagone

Camping le Sagone

Route de Vico, F-20118 Sagone (Corse-du-Sud) T: 04 95 28 04 15. E: sagone.camping@wanadoo.fr
alanrogers.com/FR20230

Situated outside the bustling seaside resort of Sagone, surrounded by protective hills, this campsite which used to be a fruit farm is in an ideal location for exploring Corsica's wild and rocky west coast or its mountainous interior. The large site borders a pleasant river and has 276 marked, shaded pitches, 250 with electricity (6A). The restaurant/bar overlooks the pool and they are the focal point of this well managed site. The site provides an amazing array of sports and specialises in 'à la carte' sports activities for groups in the low season.

Facilities

Clean, fully equipped toilet blocks with washbasins in cubicles. Facilities for disabled visitors. Baby baths. Washing machines, dryers. Motorcaravan services. Large supermarket (all year). Restaurant, pizzeria, bar. Swimming pools (June-Sept). Superb sports facilities. Fully equipped gymnasium. Tennis. Play area. Barbecues are not permitted. Satellite TV. WiFi in restaurant. Car wash. Putting and senior golf practice area. Off site: Riding 500 m. Diving, windsurfing, mountain biking, fishing, bicycle hire, climbing nearby. All manner of sports and activities can be arranged in the local area. Tours to local places of interest.

Open: 1 February - 1 December.

Directions

From Ajaccio take the RD81 in direction of Cergése and Calvilby (by coast road). In Sagone take RD70 in direction of Vico, Sagone can be found on left after 1.5 km. next to supermarket. GPS: 42.1304, 8.7055

Charges guide

Per unit incl. 2 persons	
and electricity	€ 22.00 - € 36.50
extra person	€ 5.00 - € 8.40
child (under 12 yrs)	€ 2.50 - € 5.25
dog	€ 2.20 - € 2.30
Camping Cheques accepted.	

For latest campsite news, availability and prices visit

alanrogers.com

Corsica

Sainte-Lucie-de-Porto-Vecchio
Camping Caravaning Santa Lucia
Lieu-dit Mulindinu, F-20144 Sainte Lucie-de-Porto-Vecchio (Corse-du-Sud) T: 04 95 71 45 28.
E: information@campingsantalucia.com **alanrogers.com/FR20070**

Camping Santa Lucia is a very small, friendly, family run site in a delightful southern Corsican setting. Behind the little reception hut is a simple restaurant and bar which have terraces overlooking the pool. It is very pleasant in the evenings when ornamental lamps light up the area. There are 160 informal pitches, 60 with 6A electrical connections. Some of the pitches are in enclosed bays created from huge boulders, making them very private and most have shade from mature trees. This site is only minutes by car from Porto-Vecchio and with very reasonable prices, will suit many.

Facilities

Two mature toilet blocks include British style toilets, some washbasins in cubicles and laundry facilities. Facilities for disabled visitors. Bread to order. Bar (15/6-15/9). Restaurant and takeaway (1/7-31/8). Swimming and paddling pools. Play area and high season miniclub. Minigolf. Communal barbecues. Satellite TV. WiFi (charged). Off site: Supermarket near site entrance and other shops and services in village. Beach, fishing and watersports 5 km. Riding 8 km. Golf 20 km. Canyoning, climbing and walking opportunities.

Open: 15 May - 10 October.

Directions

Site is at south end of Sainte-Lucie-de-Porto-Vecchio village, off N198 and well signed. GPS: 41.69660, 9.3434

Charges guide

Per unit incl. 2 persons	
and electricity	€ 16.10 - € 26.55
extra person	€ 5.50 - € 9.25
child (2-12 yrs)	free - € 6.20

San-Nicolao
Camping Merendella
Moriani-Plage, F-20230 San-Nicolao (Haute-Corse) T: 04 95 38 53 47. E: merendel@orange.fr
alanrogers.com/FR20030

This attractive site has the advantage of direct access to a very pleasant, 300 m. sandy beach. It is peacefully situated on level grass and sand with many trees and shrubs providing shade and colour. There are 196 pitches, all large and well spaced with electricity (10A, long leads may be required). The choice of placement is impressive with some hedged for privacy under the cool shade of mature trees. Many have direct beach access with brilliant sea views and the sound of the waves. An excellent bar, snack bar/pizzeria and restaurant are all available on the beach.

Facilities

Modern blocks, two smaller cabin units near the beach. Washbasins in private cubicles. Facilities for disabled visitors. Laundry facilities. Motorcaravan services. Shop. Bar/restaurant, pizzeria on the beach. Solar heated swimming pool with sliding cover (uncovered high season). TV room. Games room. Diving centre. Play area. WiFi (charged). Communal barbecue area. Night parking for late arrivals. Dogs are not accepted. Torches essential. Off site: Restaurant outside gate. All watersports 200 m. along beach from site. Village 800 m. Bicycle hire 800 m.

Open: 1 April - 10 October.

Directions

Site is to seaward side of the RN198, 800 m. south of Moriani Plage. GPS: 42.3656, 9.5296

Charges guide

Per unit incl. 2 persons	
and electricity	€ 30.10 - € 35.00
extra person	€ 7.45 - € 8.85
child (2-12 yrs)	€ 4.80 - € 5.55

Sartène
Campéole l'Avena
Tizzano, F-20100 Sartène (Corse-du-Sud) T: 04 95 77 02 18. E: avena@campeole.com
alanrogers.com/FR20290

Campéole l'Avena is a young site which is in the process of being improved. It sits in a valley with a beach 400 m. away along a sandy track. There are 211 flat pitches with 90 for tourers, all with 16A electricity. Some are closely placed and there are differing levels of shade. The small snack bar and shop provide an adequate service, but remember the closet village is 15 km. away. Reception is smart and air conditioned. A children's play area was supplemented with a bouncy castle when we visited.

Facilities

Single, dated unisex sanitary block, which was struggling when we visited. Hot showers. No provision for children or disabled visitors. Washing machines. Shop/bar/snack bar (high season). WiFi (charged). Communal barbecue. Off site: Beach, watersports and fishing 400 m. Riding 1 km. Archaeological sites. Walking. Diving.

Open: 28 May - 25 September.

Directions

Site is on the west coast of Corsica. From the RN196 take the D48 towards Tizzano, site is off to the left down a rough track and is well signed. GPS: 41.5343, 8.8633

Charges guide

Per unit incl. 2 persons	
and electricity	€ 17.90 - € 27.60
extra person	€ 4.60 - € 7.90

For latest campsite news, availability and prices visit
alanrogers.com

Naturism is something of a way of life, and today many more people than one might think enjoy the freedom and sense of equality found in naturist campsites. Being in harmony with nature, whether by the sea or in a woodland setting, can be a unique and liberating experience.

Some are dedicated naturists who practise their way of life wherever they may be, and who, in the UK, may well belong to clubs of like-minded people. For others, especially those who have enjoyed sunbathing on one of the many designated naturist areas on European beaches and feel comfortable with it, the logical next step is to try a holiday in a naturist village or campsite.

This growing number of 'holiday naturists' clearly enjoy the relaxed atmosphere prevailing on naturist sites. If they are not members of British Naturism, they can pick up a naturist card on the first site they visit. The rules are simple: respect for the environment and for other visitors. You are encouraged to strip off but, in reality, it is up to you, except in and around the swimming pool where there is always a 'no clothes' rule. Clothes do tend to label people and without them there is a relaxed informality and sense of equality often missing in today's 'designer society'.

We feature some 27 naturist campsites in this guide and have been impressed by the friendly welcome and cultural aspects of their entertainment and range of activities – classical music beside the pool, walking trails to discover local wildlife or book-binding classes, for example. Most campsites make an effort to provide good entertainment and to make your holiday memorable; on the naturist sites in particular, this is usually achieved quite elegantly without the frenzy that sometimes pervades more commercially-minded sites.

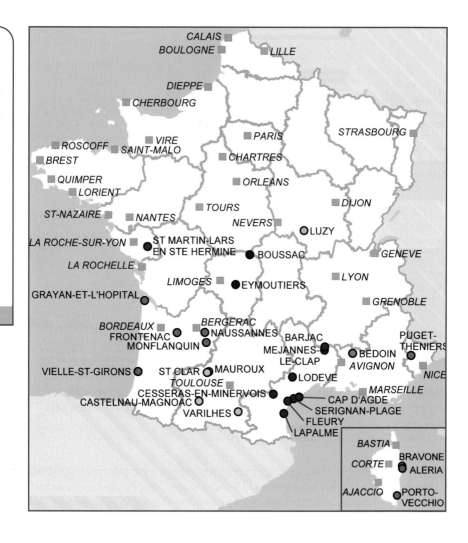

We can book this site for you! Call 01580 214000 alan rogers ◉ travel

Saint Martin-Lars en Sainte Hermine
Camping Naturiste le Colombier

Le Colombier, F-85210 Saint Martin-Lars en Sainte Hermine (Vendée) T: 02 51 27 83 84.
E: lecolombier.nat@wanadoo.fr **alanrogers.com/FR85140**

A countryside site for naturists near La Roche sur Yon, just right for those seeking a peaceful holiday. It provides around 160 pitches in seven very natural fields on different levels linked by informal tracks. There are level, terraced areas for caravans and a feeling of spaciousness with pitches around the edges of fields, unmarked and with electricity (6/10A, some may require long leads). The bar/restaurant is in a converted barn. The site's 125 acres provide many walks throughout the attractive, wooded valley and around the lake. Children are well catered for with some unusual activities.

Facilities

Fully equipped toilet blocks are good, providing some showers in cubicles. Laundry. Facilities for disabled visitors. Small shop. Bar/restaurant with à la carte and full menu (order before 12.00). Heated swimming pool (15/4-30/9). Sauna. Jacuzzi. Turkish steam bath. Masseuse visits. Fishing. Volleyball, boules and table tennis. Playground. Pony rides. One day a week children can make their own bread. Free WiFi. Off site: Charming towns such as Lucon, Bazoges and Fontenay-le-Comte. Puy du Fou 50 km.

Open: 1 April - 30 September.

Directions

From N148, La Roche-sur-Yon - Niort road, at St Hermine, turn onto D8 eastward for 4 km. Turn left on D10 to St Martin-Lars. Site is signed. GPS: 46.59795, -0.96936

Charges guide

Per unit incl. 2 persons	
and electricity	€ 21.50 - € 30.50
extra person	€ 4.00 - € 7.00
child (0-11 yrs)	free - € 4.50
dog	€ 3.00 - € 5.50

For latest campsite news, availability and prices visit
alanrogers.com

Luzy
Centre de Vacance Naturiste Domaine de la Gagère
F-58170 Luzy (Nièvre) T: 03 86 30 48 11. E: info@la-gagere.com
alanrogers.com/FR58060

At this secluded and attractive campsite, you will receive a really good welcome from the enthusiastic owners, Thom and Betty. The site is spacious and well equipped with 120 good sized, level, grassy pitches, some shaded, some open, of which 100 are available for tourers. Many are arranged in groups around three sides of rectangles, between hedges. Electricity (4-10A) is supplied to 84 pitches, six of which are fully serviced, but some require leads of up to 40 m. There are plenty of water points. In high season there are organised activities and entertainment and a children's club meets twice per week.

Facilities

Three modern unisex toilet blocks, one heated, have British style WCs, washbasins and preset showers. Facilities for disabled visitors. Laundry. Motorcaravan services. Shop (31/5-15/9). Bar. Restaurant with snack bar and takeaway (1/5-15/9). Satellite TV. Two heated swimming pools (one all season, the other 15/5-15/9). Sauna and health suite. Playgrounds. Bicycle hire. Gas and electric barbecues only (for hire). Off site: Luzy 10 km. Fishing 10 km. Riding 20 km. Golf 27 km.

Open: 1 April - 1 October.

Directions

Leave Autun on N81, southwest towards Bourbon-Lancy. In 27 km. turn left (signed Gagère) down a narrow lane. Site is 3 km. GPS: 46.81692, 4.05636

Charges guide

Per unit incl. 2 persons	€ 30.75 - € 34.00
extra person	€ 6.50
child (3-12 yrs)	€ 3.75
Admin fee for stays of 3 nights or less (€ 5).	

Boussac
Creuse Nature Naturisme
Route de Bétête (D15), F-23600 Boussac (Creuse) T: 05 55 65 18 01. E: creuse.nature@wanadoo.fr
alanrogers.com/FR23030

You are sure of a warm welcome by the Dutch owners of this very spacious, naturally laid out and well maintained naturist site. It is set in the beautiful but lesser known Limousin region in the centre of France. There are 100 large grassy/stony pitches, 80 of which are for touring with 10A electricity. Some are slightly sloping and there are varying degrees of shade. They are laid out in an open wooded parkland setting around the perimeter of the site or beside the small fishing lake. An attractive central feature is the swimming pool, sauna, bar and restaurant complex.

Facilities

Four modern, very clean toilet blocks with the usual facilities (open-plan, so little privacy). Facilities for disabled visitors. Small shop (baker calls). Indoor (heated) and outdoor pools. Paddling pool. Sauna. Bar and restaurant (all season). Archery (high season). Boules. Bicycle hire. Lake fishing. Internet access with free WiFi. Gas barbecues only. Accommodation for hire. Off site: Small, atttractive town of Boussac 3 km. Lake bathing 7 km. Riding 10 km. Golf 15 km.

Open: 1 April - 31 October.

Directions

Boussac lies 35 km. west of Montluçon between the A20 and A71 autoroutes. In Boussac site is well signed. Take D15 west for about 3 km. Site is on right. GPS: 46.34902, 2.18691

Charges guide

Per unit incl. 2 persons and electricity	€ 21,50 - € 29,50
extra person	€ 4,00 - € 7,00
child (3-12 yrs)	€ 2,50 - € 3,50

Eymoutiers
Camping Naturiste Domaine des Monts de Bussy
Bussy Varache, F-87120 Eymoutiers (Haute-Vienne) T: 05 55 69 68 20. E: montsdebussy@wanadoo.fr
alanrogers.com/FR87050

Domaine des Monts de Bussy is a naturist site in the Millevaches natural park in the Limousin. The site is located alongside a footpath leading to the River Vienne and extends over ten hectares, with some fine views over the surrounding country. Pitches are large, grassy and many are equipped with electricity. A number of fully equipped mobile homes are available for rent. On-site amenities include a swimming pool, a children's play area and a convivial bar. Canoe trips on the Vienne are popular and the site also has a rock climbing centre.

Facilities

Two toilet blocks with one controllable shower in a cubicle and two outdoor open showers. No facilities for children or disabled visitors. Washing machines (€ 3 incl. powder). Bar. Swimming pool (May-Oct). Playground. Rock climbing. Picnic areas. Naturist walks. Tourist information. Mobile homes for rent. Off site: Beach 300 m. Eymoutiers 3 km. Fishing, riding and bicycle hire 3 km. Golf 16 km.

Open: 16 April - 31 October.

Directions

Take exit 35 from the A20 and follow D979 in the direction of Eymoutiers (for 40 km). Just before Eymoutiers, turn left and take D129A towards Bussy. Follow D129A for 2 km, and drive through Bussy, then 300 m. beyond the take a small road to the right to the site. GPS: 45.750583, 1.692077

Charges guide

Per unit incl. 2 persons	€ 30.75 - € 34.00
Admin fee for stays of 3 nights or less (€ 5).	

For latest campsite news, availability and prices visit
alanrogers.com

We can book this site for you! Call 01580 214000 alan rogers ● travel

Frontenac

Domain Naturiste Château Guiton

F-33760 Frontenac (Gironde) T: 05 56 23 52 79. E: accueil@chateau-guiton.com

alanrogers.com/FR33450

A small naturist site situated in the park of an 18th-century castle, just 8 km. south of the Dordogne. The owners, Isabelle and Jean-Marc, offer a warm welcome and a family atmosphere. The site makes good use of the château's outbuildings, and wisteria hangs over the tiny reception area. There are 26 large pitches (electricity 6A) mainly on level grass, separated by mature hedges giving considerable privacy. The site is an excellent starting point for walking and cycling along small tracks through the vineyards.

Facilities

One small, unheated, unisex toilet block has washbasins (some in cubicles) and preset open showers. Baby bath and facilities for disabled visitors. Washing machine. Small swimming pool, but no children's pool. Small shop, fresh bread daily. Bar and snack bar. Entertainment (July/Aug). Play area. Boules. Badminton. Bicycle hire. Fitness room and sauna (charged). Bread oven. Communal barbecue area. WiFi. Off site: Frontenac with shops and restaurants. Fishing, golf 2 km. Riding 15 km.

Open: 15 May - 15 September.

Directions

From Libourne, join D670 (direction of St Emilion and Castillon-la-Bataille). At St Laurent-des-Combes turn right (Sauveterre-de-Guyenne). At sign for Rauzan turn right onto D231. Continue on this road and follow signs to Frontenac. Site is signed from outskirts of village. GPS: 44.725512, -0.150767

Charges guide

Per unit incl. 2 persons	€ 23.30 - € 27.00
extra person	€ 6.30 - € 7.00

Grayan et l'Hôpital

Espace Naturiste Euronat

F-33590 Grayan et l'Hôpital (Gironde) T: 05 56 09 33 33. E: info@euronat.fr

alanrogers.com/FR33160

Euronat is a well established naturist resort with extensive facilities, direct access to 1.5 km. of sandy beach and a thalassotherapy centre. With a total of 3,000 pitches, those for touring (around 1,200) are in two areas separated from the chalets and mobile homes. A variety of good sized, fairly flat and sandy pitches, include some suitable for large motorcaravans. All pitches have 5/10A electricity and some also have water and drainage. The recently enhanced 'town centre' is superb with supermarkets, butcher, fish shop, bakery, restaurants, brasserie, pizzeria/crêperie, and a takeaway.

Facilities

Sanitary blocks are well maintained with some heated. Facilities for disabled visitors. Launderette. Motorcaravan services. Shops, restaurants. Swimming pool, flumes, children's pool. Swimming lessons. Workshops, archery, pony club, riding, tennis, pétanque, fishing. Bicycle hire. Children's activities and day care. TV rooms, video/games centre. Library. Hall for dances, film nights, music evenings, sports activities. Supervised beach. No barbecues (communal areas provided). Torch may be useful. WiFi (charged). Off site: Cycle path passes site.

Open: 23 March - 3 November.

Directions

From Bordeaux ring road take exit 7, then D1215 to Lesparre and Vensac, then follow (large) signed route. GPS: 45.41627, -1.13178

Charges guide

Per unit incl. 2 persons and services	€ 17.00 - € 46.00
tent incl. 2 persons	€ 11.00 - € 32.00
incl. electricity (10A)	€ 17.00 - € 39.00
extra person	€ 4.00 - € 7.00
Camping Cheques accepted.	

Monflanquin

Camping Naturiste Domaine Laborde

Paulhiac, F-47150 Monflanquin (Lot-et-Garonne) T: 05 53 63 14 88. E: domainelaborde@wanadoo.fr

alanrogers.com/FR47140

Ideally situated on the border of Lot-et-Garonne and Dordogne, Domain Laborde is a naturist site of outstanding quality, with sweeping views from many of the higher pitches. This hilly and terraced site has 120 well maintained pitches, with 95 for touring; many are shaded, some partially shaded and all are surrounded by woodland. Electricity (3-15A) is available (long leads may be required). There are also 30 chalets for rent. This site is very popular even in low season. A Sites et Paysages member.

Facilities

The three sanitary blocks and a new wash block are well sited and clean. Washing machines and dryer. Shop with fresh bread and milk daily. Bar with TV. Snack bar serving pizzas. Restaurant (15/4-15/9). Swimming pool, whirlpool, sauna, children's pool and indoor heated pool. Massage. Trampoline. Play areas. Boules. Giant chess. Communal barbecue (no charcoal ones on pitches). Animation for children (high season). Internet access. WiFi (free). Off site: Riding 2 km. Golf 13 km. Castles and river trips.

Open: 1 April - 30 September.

Directions

From Monflanquin take D272 (Monpazier). About 10 km. along the road look for the signs to site. It is well signed at regular intervals and will read 'Domaine Laborde'. GPS: 44.613889, 0.835556

Charges guide

Per unit incl. 2 persons and electricity	€ 23.00 - € 31.50
extra person	€ 5.00 - € 6.50
child (under 6 yrs)	€ 4.00 - € 4.50

For latest campsite news, availability and prices visit

alanrogers.com

Vendays-Montalivet
Centre Naturiste Helio-Marin de Montalivet

46 avenue de l'Europe, F-33930 Vendays-Montalivet (Gironde) T: 05 56 73 73 73.
E: infos@chm-montalivet.com **alanrogers.com/FR33370**

This is a very large naturist village with everything that you could need during your holiday without leaving the site. It has direct access to the sea with its own beautiful, golden sandy beaches with coastguard surveillance in high season. Watersports are numerous with lessons if you require. The main emphasis here is to keep the family entertained. There is a total of 2,800 pitches, of which 622 are for touring. Pitches are level, on grass or sand, and mature trees provide shade in some areas. A circus school, dancing classes and skateboarding are just some of the activities organised here.

Facilities

Numerous sanitary blocks with facilities for children and disabled visitors. Launderette. Motorcaravan service point. Shops, restaurants and bars. Two swimming pool complexes with slides and toboggan. Children's clubs. Evening entertainment. Playgrounds. Sports grounds. TV rooms and cinema. Large library. Wellness centre including saunas and jacuzzis. Bicycle hire. Fishing. WiFi (charged). Off site: Riding 1 km. Sailing 6 km. Golf 40 km.

Open: All year.

Directions

From Royan, take the ferry to Verdon-sur-Mer and continue on N215 for 34 km. Turn right on D102 to Montalivet. Nearing the sea turn left for Hourtins and site is 1 km. on the right. GPS: 45.36348, -1.14575

Charges guide

Per unit incl. 2 persons and electricity	€ 16.90 - € 32.30
extra person	€ 3.60 - € 7.90

Naussannes
Centre Naturiste le Couderc

Le Couderc, F-24440 Naussannes (Dordogne) T: 05 53 22 40 40. E: info@lecouderc.com
alanrogers.com/FR24190

This is a very spacious site set in 28 hectares of open countryside with large pitches naturally laid out around sloping meadows. There is a feeling of calm and tranquillity and the family owners ensure that visitors enjoy their stay. There are 188 pitches of which 170 are for touring, all with 6A electricity. The site is on different levels with undulating slopes but the generous pitches are level and easily accessible. Generally open, but mature trees all around offer some shade. A varied programme of events, for all the family, are run throughout most of the season.

Facilities

Five very clean modern toilet blocks with facilities for children and disabled visitors. Outdoor showers. Washing machines and dryer. Restaurant and bar. Takeaway. Shop. Heated swimming pools. Jacuzzi. Sauna. Bicycle Hire. Two ponds, one for fishing the other with cable slide. Children's club (sculpture and circus lessons). Play area. Some entertainment. Walking tracks. Caravan storage. Off site: Caves. Châteaux. Riding 10 km. Golf 20 km.

Open: 1 April - 1 October.

Directions

From Bergerac take N21. Turn left on D25 to Issigeac. Continue towards Naussannes for 8 km. Turn left at signpost indicating Naussannes 2 km. Le Couderc is 350 m. on the right. GPS: 44.75602, 0.70212

Charges guide

Per unit incl. 2 persons and electricity	€ 22.15 - € 34.40
extra person	€ 4.50 - € 7.50

Vielle-Saint-Girons
Domaine Naturiste Arnaoutchot

5008 route du Pichelebe, F-40560 Vielle-Saint-Girons (Landes) T: 05 58 49 11 11. E: contact@arna.com
alanrogers.com/FR40120

Arnaoutchot is a large naturist site with extensive facilities and direct access to the beach. Even with 500 pitches, its layout in the form of a number of sections, each with its own character, make it quite relaxing and very natural. These sections amongst the trees and bushes of the Landes provide a variety of reasonably sized pitches, most with electricity (3/6A), although the hilly terrain means that only a limited number are flat enough for motorcaravans. We suggest that new visitors telephone before arrival as the site can require them to be proposed by a family who have stayed at the campsite for at least three years. A member of France 4 Naturisme.

Facilities

Heated sanitary facilities with communal hot showers and also a number of tiny blocks. Motorcaravan services. Supermarket. Shops. Bar/restaurant, pizzeria and tapita (fish) bar (all from 1/6). Heated indoor swimming pool with solarium, whirlpool and slide. Outdoor pool. New paddling pool. Spa, sauna, steam, whirlpool, massages. TV, games rooms. Cinema. Library. Internet point. Bicycle hire. Fishing. Torches useful. No charcoal barbecues. American motorhomes not accepted. Off site: Riding and golf 5 km.

Open: 1 April - 30 September.

Directions

Site is signed off the D652 road at Vielle-Saint-Girons. Follow D328 for 3-4 km. GPS: 43.9075, -1.361683

Charges guide

Per unit incl. 2 persons and electricity	€ 11.90 - € 37.95
extra person (over 3 yrs)	€ 2.00 - € 8.00
Deposit on arrival for accommodation € 50.	
Camping Cheques accepted.	

For latest campsite news, availability and prices visit
alanrogers.com

Castelnau-Magnoac
Domaine Naturiste l'Eglantière
Aries-Espenan, F-65230 Castelnau-Magnoac (Hautes-Pyrénées) T: 05 62 39 88 00. E: info@leglantiere.com
alanrogers.com/FR65010

A delightful site with an air of calm and repose, l'Eglantière is set within 50 hectares of organic farmland and woodland for walking. The fast-flowing River Gers runs through the site, bringing opportunities for watersports and fishing. Pitches are large and naturally shaped, most have electricity (16A, long leads). Many are separated by wild flowers, grasses and trees, ensuring shade and privacy. There is a separate wild area for tents. The clubhouse bar, restaurant and terrace overlook the attractive swimming pool area where nudity is compulsory. A member of France 4 Naturisme.

Facilities

Two toilet blocks provide undercover, open plan, facilities. Small block has individual cubicles. Shop (June-Aug). Clubhouse and bar. Takeaway food. Heated swimming pool. Soundproofed activities/disco area. Playroom. Play area. Children's entertainment (in season). Volleyball. Badminton. Archery. Pétanque. River activities. Canoe and mountain bike hire. Trekking. Cross-country cycling. Torches useful. WiFi. Chalets and mobile homes for rent. Off site: Restaurants in the nearby village.

Open: Easter - October.

Directions

From Auch take D929 south (Lannemezan). After Castelnau-Magnoac continue past aerodrome, turn onto D9 (Monleon-Magnoac). Take first left (Ariès-Espénan). Follow site signs. GPS: 43.26466, 0.52119

Charges guide

| Per unit incl. 2 persons and electricity | € 17.90 - € 40.40 |
| extra person | € 4.00 - € 7.20 |

Camping Cheques accepted.

Mauroux
Camping Naturiste les Roches
Le Néry, F-32380 Mauroux (Gers) T: 05 62 66 30 18. E: campinglesroches@wanadoo.fr
alanrogers.com/FR32190

A pleasant and friendly site in beautiful wooded countryside, where visitors can relax. The 36 large, shady pitches, some are 200 sq.m, have electricity (6A). The cool, traditional reception buildings include a bar, games room and seasonal restaurant. The site is calm with woodland walks and the swimming pool (20x8 m) is away from the pitches. Nudity is expected unless the weather prevents it. Activities are easy going: boules, lake fishing, archery and volleyball. The owners can arrange trips to local wine, garlic and foie gras producers. St Clar is a lovely village 4 km. away and well worth a visit.

Facilities

All necessary facilities, including those for disabled visitors. Laundry facilities. Restaurant (1/6-15/9) and bread in high season. Bar and takeaway. Swimming pool. Sauna (charged). Lake for fishing. Indoor games. Communal barbecue only. Playground. Saturday communal meal. Boules tournaments. Internet point. No motorcaravan services. Some lighting switched off after 23.00. Torches needed. Off site: Village of St Clar for most amenities 4 km. Bicycle hire and riding 15km. Golf 16 km.

Open: 1 May - 15 September.

Directions

From Lectoure take the D7 to St Clar. At St Clar turn left onto D13 then after 1 km. turn right onto D167 to Gaudonville. Site well signed and along a fairly narrow bumpy roadway. GPS: 43.898035, 0.811234

Charges guide

| Per unit incl. 2 persons and electricity (6A) | € 9.20 - € 13.00 |
| extra person | € 3.10 - € 4.75 |

No credit cards.

Saint Clar
Centre Naturiste Deveze
Gaudonville, F-32380 Saint Clar (Gers) T: 05 62 66 43 86. E: deveze@deveze-nat.com
alanrogers.com/FR32040

This is a well established and very pleasant, French owned naturist site in 50 acres of lovely Gers countryside. The 180 pitches, the majority with electricity and many terraced, are in several different areas. All are separated by mature hedges and trees, the amount of shade available varies from area to area and some pitches are flatter than others. This site would be an excellent introduction to naturist camping, being quite laid-back in terms of rules and regulations (although nudity is compulsory), but offering some activities for those who wish to join in without any pressure for those who don't!

Facilities

Sanitary facilities in three blocks include hot showers (communal) and washbasins (cold water only, but hot tap nearby), all very well maintained. Shop (1/7-31/8). Takeaway, pub and restaurant (1/4-1/11). Swimming pool and children's pool (1/5-30/9). Four acre lake for fishing or boating and woodland area. Adventure play area. Bicycle hire. Tennis, boules, archery, film shows and a small gym. TV rooms. Off site: Trips arranged to local attractions.

Open: All year (limited facilities Oct-May).

Directions

From Lectoure take the D7 to St Clar. At St Clar turn left onto D13 then after 1 km. turn right onto D167 to Gaudonville. After 4 km. turn left into narrow approach road to site. Site is a further 0.8 km. along narrow bumpy track. GPS: 43.891011, 0.828545

Charges guide

| Per unit incl. 2 persons and electricity | € 14.20 - € 23.30 |
| extra person | € 3.60 - € 7.10 |

For latest campsite news, availability and prices visit
alanrogers.com

Varilhes
Naturiste Camping Millefleurs

Le Tuilier Gudas, F-09120 Varilhes (Ariège) T: 05 61 60 77 56. E: simone.groot@orange.fr
alanrogers.com/FR09090

Millefleurs is a quiet site in a secluded location for naturists. It is peaceful with some 70 acres of woods and meadows providing guided naturist walks in total privacy. The site has 40 large, flat, mostly terraced pitches (34 with 6-10A electricity), long leads if pitching off the terraces. There are also very secluded pitches in wooded areas with shade, or you can pitch a tent in the meadows. There are few of the normal camping leisure facilities here and the site is definitely aimed at the more mature naturist camper.

Facilities	Directions
An excellent toilet block with facilities for disabled campers. Bread available to order in high season. Guests dine together in the 'salle de reunion' within the farmhouse two nights a week or just meet friends for a drink. Refrigerator with drinks. Pétanque. Guide book for walks and cycle rides. Torches essential. Pick ups from airports and stations arranged. Off site: The coast is 1.5 hours away.	From Varilhes, 8 km. south of Pamiers on D624 (parallel to N20). Take D13 for Dalou and Gudas cross railway and N20. The site is 2 km. past Gudas, on right. GPS: 42.9927, 1.6788

Charges guide

Per unit incl. 2 persons and electricity	€ 19.00 - € 19.50
extra person	€ 5.25
No credit cards.	

Open: 1 April - 1 November.

Barjac
Camping Naturiste de la Sablière

Domaine de la Sablière, Saint Privat-de-Champclos, F-30430 Barjac (Gard) T: 04 66 24 51 16.
E: contact@villagesabliere.com alanrogers.com/FR30100

Spectacularly situated in the Cèze Gorges, this well-equipped, spacious naturist site, tucked away within its wild and dramatic terrain offers a wide variety of facilities, all within a really peaceful, wooded setting. There are 497 pitches, 240 for touring. Many are large and most have electricity (6/10A). Long leads and rock pegs may possibly be needed. Nudity is only obligatory around the pool complex. There are long and steep walks between many pitches and the facilities. Cars can be used in low season and there is a shuttle service in July and August. Large outfits not advised.

Facilities	Directions
Six good open-plan unisex sanitary blocks. Naturist style baths and facilities for disabled visitors. Laundry. Good supermarket. Bar (1/4-22/9). Excellent open-air, covered restaurant and takeaway (1/4-22/9). Small café/crêperie. Swimming pool complex. Fitness room. TV room. Disco. Tennis. Minigolf. Children's play areas. River bathing. Fitness trail. Archery. Entertainment. Gas and electric barbecues only. Free WiFi at reception. Off site: Walking and cycling. Bicycle hire 8 km. Barjac with market 8 km. Riding 10 km. Golf 12 km. Vallon Pont d'Arc 20 km.	From Alès take D16 then D979 northeast towards Barjac. 5 km. beyond St Jean-de-Maruéjols turn right D266 signed St Privat and site. Site is 5 km, along winding lane. GPS: 44.26685, 4.35202

Charges guide

Per unit incl. 2 persons and electricity (10A)	€ 19.80 - € 35.30
extra person	€ 4.40 - € 8.00
child (0-10 yrs)	free - € 3.15
Camping Cheques accepted.	

Open: 2 April - 2 October.

Cesseras-en-Minervois
Camping Naturiste le Mas de Lignières

F-34210 Cesseras-en-Minervois (Hérault) T: 04 68 91 24 86. E: lemas1@wanadoo.fr
alanrogers.com/FR34050

A naturist site hidden in the hills of the Minervois, only 3 km. from the medieval town of Minerve. There are marvellous views to the Pyrenees, the Corbières and the coast at Narbonne. Jeanne continues to run the site and keep alive the memory of Gilles, offering a warm welcome to all. The site now has just 19 very large pitches (electricity 6/10A), two pitches for tents and five caravan holiday homes. Mainly on level grass, they are separated by mature hedges which give considerable privacy. There is natural shade and a variety of flora and fauna including four types of orchid.

Facilities	Directions
Clean toilet block has open washbasins and showers, facilities for disabled visitors. Washing machine. Bread (15/6-15/9). Bar (15/7-15/8). Swimming pool, sliding cover for use when cold. Paddling pool. Room for general use with TV, library, separate provision for young people. Playground. Tennis. Boules. Torch useful. WiFi (charged). Only gas barbecues are permitted. Off site: Sailing, riding and canoeing at nearby Lac de Jouarres. Canal du Midi.	From A61 take exit for Lézignan-Corbières, D611 to Homps, then D910 to Olonzac. Through village following signs to Minerve (D10). Continue. 4 km. Turn left to Cesseras (D168). At Cesseras follow signs Fauzan for 4 km. (site signed) on right, narrow, winding road. GPS: 43.34092, 2.70648

Charges guide

Per unit incl. 2 persons and electricity	€ 23.00 - € 26.00
extra person	€ 4.70

Open: 1 May - 30 September.

For latest campsite news, availability and prices visit
alanrogers.com

Fleury
Domaine Naturiste la Grande Cosse

Saint Pierre-la-Mer, F-11560 Fleury (Aude) T: 04 68 33 61 87. E: contact@grandecosse.com
alanrogers.com/FR11190

Any slight difficulty in finding this secluded naturist site is compensated for the moment you arrive. The abundance of flowers, shrubs and the generally peaceful ambience makes this a delightful place for a relaxing naturist holiday, and the extensive facilities mean you only need to leave the site for sightseeing rather than for necessities. In total there are 480 pitches, of which about 146 are for mobile homes, and the mainly large touring pitches, all with 8A electrical connections, are informally and very attractively arranged in a variety of different areas.

Facilities

Five sanitary blocks, one heated, are opened progressively as required. They include a choice of private or communal showers, and some washbasins in cabins. Laundry facilities. Motorcaravan service point. Gas. Well stocked shop, bar, restaurant and takeaway. Three heated swimming pools, two for adults and a smaller one for children. Play area. Tennis. Archery. Playing field. Bicycle hire. Internet and WiFi (charged). Communal barbecues. Off site: Riding 2 km. Sailing 3 km. Boat launching 5 km.

Open: 9 April - 9 October.

Directions

From the A9 take exit 36 to Vendres. Pass through town, on to Lespignan, then Fleury. At roundabout turn left (Cabanes-de-Fleury). Follow for 4 km. to pick up site sign to left. Continue for 2 km. and site signed to right. GPS: 43.20582, 3.21099

Charges guide

Per unit incl. 2 persons and electricity	€ 18.00 - € 41.00
extra person	€ 5.00 - € 7.00

Lapalme
Camping Naturiste le Clapotis

Lieu dit Pech-Redon, F-11480 Lapalme (Aude) T: 04 68 48 15 40. E: info@leclapotis.com
alanrogers.com/FR11090

Le Clapotis is a small and tranquil naturist site, situated between Narbonne and Perpignan in a secluded pine wood beside the Etang de Lapalme (a large sea lagoon). There is direct access to the lagoon which is popular with those in pursuit of the ideal conditions provided for windsurfing. In total there are 230 pitches with 173 for touring, all with electricity (4A). They are of a good size on stony or sandy ground. Pitches in the older part have excellent shade from the pine trees and in the newer area, shade is increasing as the hedges grow. There is a relaxed feeling of harmony and freedom about this site.

Facilities

Two large and three small sanitary blocks, a little basic but fully equipped. Showers are both open and in cabins. Facilities for babies and disabled campers. Washing machines. Shop (15/5-15/9). Bar, restaurant and takeaway (all 15/6-31/8). Swimming pool (15/5-15/9). Half tennis courts. Pétanque. Windsurfing. Fishing. Torches useful. WiFi (charged). Communal barbecue. Off site: Sandy beach 5 km. Bicycle hire 9 km. Golf and riding 10 km.

Open: 15 March - 15 October.

Directions

Exit N9 junction 40 (Port Leucate). At roundabout take N9 north for 3 km. to next roundabout. Turn right (Port-la-Nouvelle). Site sign in 500 m. on right. Follow narrow, rough road for 2 km. bearing left up hill to site. GPS: 42.958, 2.99586

Charges guide

Per unit incl. 2 persons and electricity	€ 23.50 - € 27.80
extra person	€ 4.30

Lodève
Domaine Naturiste de Lambeyran

Hameau De Lambeyran, F-34700 Lodève (Hérault) T: 04 67 44 13 99. E: lambeyran@wanadoo.fr
alanrogers.com/FR34540

A wooded valley covering 348 hectares allows Domaine de Lambeyran a place in the Guinness Book of Records for having the largest area available for naturists in the world. It is a wonderful natural area with amazing views across to Lodève and the spectacular surrounding countryside. Naturists can enjoy the marked trails around the valley or the large, heated pool whilst choosing from 160 huge pitches, 100 with electricity (4/6A) and many quite private. Some pitches have been levelled with local stone.

Facilities

Two large toilet blocks and a smaller one, include baby baths, but no facilities for disabled visitors. Washing machine. Small shop, bar and snack bar (all 7/6-31/8). Large, solar-heated swimming pool (from 20/5) with paddling pool. Some play equipment. Indoor area for older children. Dancing and films. Trips organised. Communal barbecue area. Dogs allowed in one area only. Off site: Tennis, fishing and riding 5 km. Lodève 5 km. Walking/hiking trails from 5-30 km. Watersports and beaches at Lac du Salagou 16 km. Golf 50 km.

Open: 10 May - 20 September.

Directions

Lodève is 50 km. west of Montpellier. From A75 (Béziers/Clermont-Ferrand) take exit for Lodève and follow signs for town centre. Cross town following signs for Lunas (D35). Ignore right turn for les Plans, take next right then up hill for 3 km. to site. Much of road is single file. GPS: 43.73648, 3.26483

Charges guide

Per unit incl. 2 persons and electricity	€ 21.10 - € 29.60
extra person	€ 4.60 - € 6.70

For latest campsite news, availability and prices visit
alanrogers.com

Méjannes-le-Clap
Camping Naturiste la Genèse

Route de la Genèse, F-30430 Méjannes-le-Clap (Gard) T: 04 66 24 51 82. E: info@lagenese.com
alanrogers.com/FR30400

La Genèse is a well equipped naturist site close to the banks of the River Cèze on the northern edge of the Cévennes national park. This is a large site with 480 well shaded pitches, 160 are for touring. These are divided into 'sauvage' (without electricity) and 'prairie' (with electricity 6A and closer to the main facilities). A wide variety of activities are on offer here, including art and craft workshops, bridge evenings and a cinema. Mobile homes and chalets available for rent. A good value site for lovers of nature.

Facilities

Five clean and well maintained toilet blocks, one refurbished. Facilities for campers with disabilities. Shop (1/5-31/8). Motorcaravan services. Bar, restaurant, takeaway. Swimming pool and children's pool. Sauna. Archery. Games room. Art and craft workshops. Cinema. Canoe hire. Play area. Activities and entertainment. Direct access to river, fishing. WiFi (charged). Electric or communal barbecues only. Off site: Bicycle hire and riding 7 km. Cycle and walking tracks. Méjannes-le-Clap.

Open: 2 April - 30 September.

Directions

From Pont St Esprit, take D901 west to Barjac, then D979 to Rochegude. Shortly beyond Rochegude, take D167 to Méjannes-le-Clap and follow signs to site (6 km). GPS: 44.26772, 4.37013

Charges guide

Per unit incl. 2 persons and electricity	€ 18.50 - € 25.50
extra person	€ 3.90 - € 5.90
child (4-17 yrs)	€ 2.95 - € 3.90

Sérignan-Plage
Camping le Sérignan-Plage Nature

Route de l'Orpellière, F-34410 Sérignan-Plage (Hérault) T: 04 67 32 09 61. E: info@leserignannature.com
alanrogers.com/FR34080

Sérignan-Plage Nature benefits from the same 600 m. of white, sandy beach as its sister site next door. Being a naturist site, it actually abuts the naturist section of the beach with direct access to it. It also has the use of the Sérignan-Plage balnéotherapy pool in the mornings, an excellent facility with spa and jacuzzi pools in a Romanesque style setting. The site has 286 good sized pitches on level sandy grass of which 99 are available for touring (6A electricity). There is plenty of shade except on the pitches beside the beach. Mobile homes and chalets are available to rent.

Facilities

Two well maintained toilet blocks (one refurbished) offer modern facilities with some washbasins in cabins. Washing machines. Supermarket, newsagent/souvenir shop and ice cream kiosk. Small bar/café. Evening entertainment. Play area, miniclub and disco for children. Facilities and pools at Sérignan-Plage. Gas barbecues only. WiFi throughout (charged). Off site: Bicycle hire 200 m. Fishing 500 m. Riding 800 km. Golf 2 km.

Open: 26 April - 6 October.

Directions

From A9 exit 35 (Béziers Est) towards Sérignan, D64 (9 km). Before Sérignan, take road to Sérignan-Plage. At small sign (blue) turn right for 500 m. At T-junction turn left over bridge, site is 75 m. immediately after left-hand bend (the second naturist site). GPS: 43.263409, 3.320148

Charges 2012

Per unit incl. 2 persons and electricity	€ 17.00 - € 53.00
extra person	€ 6.00 - € 10.00
Camping Cheques accepted.	

Cap d'Agde
Centre Hélio-Marin René Oltra

1 rue des Nérides, B.P. 884, F-34307 Cap d'Agde (Hérault) T: 04 67 01 06 36. E: infos@chm-reneoltra.fr
alanrogers.com/FR34270

A large, naturist site situated within the Cap d'Agde Village Naturiste and alongside a wonderful sandy beach. Regularly laid out in sheltered avenues covering 35 hectares, it is well organised with over 2,524 level sandy pitches and 1,000 privately-owned mobile homes. The remainder is divided between touring pitches (5A electricity) and site-owned mobile homes and chalets, some very smart and almost on the beach. A wide range of sports facilities are available including children's clubs. Bread, fresh fruit and vegetable stalls and several shops are at the Centre Naturiste and there is a smart new beach bar.

Facilities

Over 25 toilet blocks of varying sizes. Mainly open style showers. Laundry. Motorcaravan service point. Two bars, snack bar (1/5-30/9). Bread and fruit stalls (15/4-30/9). Children's clubs. Entertainment, cabarets, dancing. Open-air cinema. Beauty centre. Fiitness equipment. Multisports court. Football. Volleyball. Archery. Tennis. Play area. Communal barbecue. WiFi (charged). Off site: Centre Naturiste facilities (walking distance). Golf and riding 3 km.

Open: 15 March - 15 October.

Directions

Follow signs for Cap d'Agde Tourist office then pick up signs for 'Naturisme'. GPS: 43.29723, 3.52782

Charges guide

Per unit incl. 2 persons and electricity (5A)	€ 19.00 - € 34.00
extra person	€ 8.00 - € 14.00
child	free - € 6.00
dog	€ 3.20

For latest campsite news, availability and prices visit
alanrogers.com

Bédoin
Domaine Naturiste de Bélézy
F-84410 Bédoin (Vaucluse) T: 04 90 65 60 18. E: info@belezy.com

alanrogers.com/FR84020

At the foot of Mont Ventoux, surrounded by beautiful scenery, Bélézy is an excellent naturist site with many amenities and activities and the ambience is relaxed and comfortable. The 320 pitches, 248 for touring (12A electricity, long leads required) are set amongst many varieties of trees and shrubs giving space and privacy. The attractive bar/restaurant and terrace overlook the swimming pool area and have superb views over the large recreational area and hills beyond. The site has an ecological theme with a small farm, fish pond and a vegetable garden especially for the children. There is a good range of sports facilities and play areas. Only gas and electric barbecues are permitted. Pets are not accepted.

Facilities

Four toilet blocks with very good facilities for campers with disabilities – newer ones are excellent, some have hot showers in the open air. A superb children's section. Shop. Bar. Excellent restaurant/takeaway (all 31/3-30/9). Swimming pools. Sauna. Tennis. Adventure play area. Activities all season. Archery. Guided walks. Children's club. Hydrotherapy centre (31/3-30/9). Only gas barbecues are allowed. Off site: Bédoin with shops and restaurants 1.5 km. Discover the riches of Provence with its many interesting old market towns and villages. Superb area for walking and cycling with the challenge of Mont Ventoux.

Open: 31 March - 5 October.

Directions

From A7 autoroute (exit 22) or RN7, south of Orange, take D950 southeast to Carpentras, then D974 northeast to Bédoin. In Bédoin turn right at roundabout, site signed, site in 2 km. GPS: 44.13352, 5.18745

Charges 2012

Per unit incl. 2 persons and electricity	€ 15.00 - € 40.20
extra person	€ 6.00 - € 9.40
child (3-8 yrs)	free - € 9.30

Camping Cheques accepted.

Puget-Theniers
Domaine Naturiste Club Origan
F-06260 Puget-Theniers (Alpes-Maritimes) T: 04 93 05 06 00. E: origan@orange.fr

alanrogers.com/FR06070

Origan is a naturist site set in the mountains behind Nice at a height of 500 m. The access road is single track and winding with few passing places, so arrival is not recommended until late afternoon. The site's terrain is fairly wild and the roads stony, so it is unsuitable for caravans longer than six metres due to the steep slopes, although the site will assist with a 4x4 vehicle if requested. The 100 touring pitches, in three areas, are irregular sizes and shapes with good views. Electricity connection (6A) is possible on most pitches (by long cable). A variety of accommodation is also available to rent including Bengali tents and luxury chalets. Reservation is necessary in high season. A member of France 4 Naturisme.

Facilities

Sanitary facilities, are clean and of a standard and type associated with most good naturist sites – mostly open plan hot showers. Laundry facilities. Shop (1/6-30/8). Bar/restaurant. Takeaway. Heated swimming pools (1/6-30/8). Jacuzzi and sauna. Tennis. Fishing. Organised activities for all (high season). Only gas or electric barbecues are permitted. Torches advised. WiFi around reception. Off site: Puget-Theniers offers choice of bars, cafés, shops, etc. Steam train. Eco-museum of the Roudoule. Walled town of Entrevaux 6 km. with motorcycle museum.

Open: 15 April - 30 September.

Directions

Heading west on the N202, just past the town of Puget-Theniers, turn right at campsite sign at level crossing; site is 2 km. GPS: 43.957633, 6.860883

Charges guide

Per unit incl. 2 persons and electricity	€ 18.00 - € 34.00
extra person	€ 4.00 - € 9.00
child (3-8 yrs)	€ 3.00 - € 7.00
dog	€ 6.00

Camping Cheques accepted.

For latest campsite news, availability and prices visit

alanrogers.com

Aléria
Riva Bella Nature Resort & Spa

B.P. 21, F-20270 Aléria (Haute-Corse) T: 04 95 38 81 10. E: rivabella.corsica@gmail.com

alanrogers.com/FR20040

This is a relaxed, informal, spacious site alongside an extremely long and beautiful beach. Riva Bella is naturist from 16 May to 19 September only. It offers a variety of pitches situated in beautiful countryside and seaside. The site is divided into several areas with 200 pitches (133 for touring with 6A electricity), some of which are alongside the sandy beach with little shade. Others are in a shady wooded glade on the hillside. The huge fish-laden lakes are a fine feature of this site and a superb balnéotherapy centre offers the very latest beauty and relaxation treatments (men and women) based on marine techniques. The charming owner, Marie Claire Pasqual, is justifiably proud of the site and the fairly unobtrusive rules are designed to ensure that everyone is able to relax, whilst preserving the natural beauty of the environment. Cars are parked away from the pitches. The restaurant offers a sophisticated menu and the excellent beach restaurant/bar has superb sea views.

Facilities

High standard toilet facilities. Provision for disabled visitors, children and babies. Laundry. Large shop (15/5-15/10). Fridge hire. Two restaurants with sea and lake views with reasonable prices. Excellent beach restaurant/bar. Watersports, sailing school, pedaloes, fishing. Balnéotherapy centre. Sauna. Aerobics. Giant chess. Archery. Fishing. Riding. Mountain bike hire. Half-court tennis. Walking with llamas. Internet. WiFi (charged). Professional evening entertainment programme. Off site: Tours of the island. Walking. Riding 7 km. Scuba diving 10 km. Paragliding.

Open: All year (naturist 16/5-19/9).

Directions

Site is 12 km. north of Aleria on N198 (Bastia) road. Watch for large signs and unmade road to site and follow for 4 km. GPS: 42.16151, 9.55269

Charges guide

Per unit incl. 2 persons and electricity	€ 23.30 - € 40.30
extra person	€ 5.00 - € 9.00
child (3-8 yrs)	€ 2.00 - € 6.00
dog	€ 2.00 - € 3.50

Special offers and half-board arrangements available.

Camping Cheques accepted.

Domaine Naturiste Riva Bella
RIVA BELLA
THALASSO & SPA RESORT

For all: Village-Camping-Thalasso.

Yearly opening dates: NON NATURIST: from 20-09 untill 15-05. Closed from 20-12 untill 20-01

BP21 - 20270 Aleria
Corsica
Tel: +33 (0)495 38 81 10
riva-bella@orange.fr
www.rivabella-inf.com

Go camping and caravanning in the most relaxing way...

British Naturism
"Nothing's better"

There's a peace and tranquillity on naturist sites you don't find anywhere else. They also tend to be more natural and green. There's a great community spirit and friendly, welcoming people too. Stripping off your clothes helps to strip away the cares of daily life. Camping and caravanning is already a chilled out way to spend your leisure time, naturism takes that to the ultimate level. Come and join us – and get involved in a wide variety of other activities and benefits of membership.

Contact Us:

01604 620361 | headoffice@bn.org.uk
30-32 Wycliffe Road Northampton NN1 5JF   www.bn.org.uk

For latest campsite news, availability and prices visit
alanrogers.com

Bravone
Camping Bagheera Naturisme
Route 198, F-20230 Bravone (Haute-Corse) T: 04 95 38 80 30. E: bagheera@bagheera.fr
alanrogers.com/FR20080

An extremely long private road leads you to this naturist site which is alongside a 3 km. beach of fine sand and has been run by the same family for 30 years. There are 250 informal pitches which are separated from the bungalows. Well shaded under huge eucalyptus trees, all have 10A electricity (long leads may be necessary). Some beach-side pitches have sea views, the others are further back but all are within 200 m. of the sea. All pitches are on sandy grass and are kept clean and neat. The main restaurant and beach bar/restaurant have superb panoramic views of the sea and offer extensive menus with especially good seafood, served by enthusiastic staff. There is much to do here and many lovely walks in the area, or you may prefer to enjoy the relaxation of the beach and try the various massages and treatments offered. English is spoken in most areas. This is a popular site for families and has many activities available if you wish for a change from the safe beach and soft sand.

Facilities

Five very comfortable sanitary blocks can be heated and offer hot water throughout. Baby rooms. Washing machines. Excellent restaurant (Corsican menu, children's menu). Bar. Beach restaurant and bar. Pizzeria. Shop. All amenities 1/6-30/9. Play area. Fitness circuit. Gym. Massage. Sauna. Pedalos. Pétanque. Windsurfing. Subaqua diving. Beach umbrella rental. Refrigerated lockers for hire. Tennis. Bicycle hire. Fishing (lake or sea). Entertainment. TV. WiFi (charged). Off site: Commercial centre 6 km. Riding. Boat launching 15 km.

Open: All year.

Directions

Site is between Bastia and Aleria near Bravone, 7 km. north of Aleria on the RN198. It is well signed off the RN198. Follow site road 4 km. east to beach. GPS: 42.2206, 9.5380

Charges 2012

Per unit incl. 2 persons and electricity	€ 20.00 - € 32.50
extra person	€ 4.65 - € 9.90
child (acc. to age)	free - € 4.70
dog	€ 2.00 - € 4.10

A forest right behind the sea

A road invaded by the scents of rock-roses and wild flowers, leads to an almost unimaginable eucalyptus forest. A pond hidden under the reeds of the awaited blue between the sand and the infinite sea!
At Bagheera, it is so immense, that everything, including the welcoming structure, the accommodations, the catering, the supplying and the leisure activities, blends into the site, the dream of any naturist.
All this made in the hope of sharing, one day, a clean planet.

www.bagheera.fr - bagheera@bagheera.fr

Bagheera
Corsica, the sea and.. some guests.

Village de vacances et camping naturiste
20230 Bravone - Corse - France
Tél. +33 (04) 95 38 80 30
Fax +33 (04) 95 38 83 47

Porto-Vecchio
Village Naturiste la Chiappa
547

Route de Palombaggia, F-20137 Porto-Vecchio (Corse-du-Sud) T: 04 95 70 00 31.
E: chiappa@wanadoo.fr **alanrogers.com/FR20050**

This is a large naturist campsite on the Chiappa peninsula with 200 pitches, some with good sea views, for tourers and tents, plus 250 bungalows. The pitches are informally marked and are a variety of shapes and sizes, some with difficult slopes and access, especially for large units (75-125 sq.m). Cars are parked separately. Very long electricity leads are necessary here for most pitches (10A electricity). The beaches are between long rocky outcrops and it is generally safe to swim, or alternatively enjoy the swimming pool by the main beach.

Facilities

The sanitary facilities were clean when we visited. Washing machines. Well stocked shop. Two bars and restaurants with snacks. Bistro. Swimming pool. Play area for children. Riding. Tennis. Minigolf. Fishing. Diving, windsurfing and sailing schools. Keep fit, yoga, sauna (extra cost). Pottery. Riding. Satellite TV. WiFi. Torches essential. Off site: Excursions.

Open: 14 May - 8 October.

Directions

From Bastia, N198 heading south, take Porto-Vecchio bypass (signed Bonofaccio). At southern end, take first left signed Pont de la Chiappa, unclassified road. After 8 km. site signed. Turn left and follow rough track for 2 km. to site. GPS: 41.59387, 9.35713

Charges guide

| Per unit incl. 2 persons and electricity | € 27.00 - € 37.00 |
| per person | € 8.00 - € 10.00 |

For latest campsite news, availability and prices visit
alanrogers.com

Been to any good campsites lately?
We have

You'll find them here...

The UK's market leading independent
guides to the best campsites

Also available on iPad **alanrogers.com/digital**

GO THERE NOW!

Accommodation

Over recent years many of the campsites featured in this guide have added large numbers of high quality mobile homes and chalets. Many site owners believe that some former caravanners and motorcaravanners have been enticed by the extra comfort they can now provide, and that maybe this is the ideal solution to combine the freedom of camping with all the comforts of home.

Quality is consistently high and, although the exact size and inventory may vary from site to site, if you choose any of the sites detailed here, you can be sure that you're staying in some of the best quality and best value mobile homes available.

Home comforts are provided and typically these include a fridge with freezer compartment, gas hob, proper shower – often a microwave and radio/cassette hi-fi too, but do check for details. All mobile homes and chalets come fully equipped with a good range of kitchen utensils, pots and pans, crockery, cutlery and outdoor furniture. Some even have an attractive wooden sundeck or paved terrace – a perfect spot for outdoors eating or relaxing with a book and watching the world go by.

Regardless of model, colourful soft furnishings are the norm and a generally breezy décor helps to provide a real holiday feel.

Although some sites may have a large number of different accommodation types, we have restricted our choice to one or two of the most popular accommodation units (either mobile homes or chalets) for each of the sites listed.

The mobile homes here will be of modern design, and recent innovations, for example, often include pitched roofs which substantially improve their appearance.

Design will invariably include clever use of space and fittings/furniture to provide for comfortable holidays – usually light and airy, with big windows and patio-style doors, fully equipped kitchen areas, a shower room with shower, washbasin and WC, cleverly designed bedrooms and a comfortable lounge/dining area (often incorporating a sofa bed).

In general, modern campsite chalets incorporate all the best features of mobile homes in a more traditional structure, sometimes with the advantage of an upper mezzanine floor for an additional bedroom.

Our selected campsites offer a massive range of different types of mobile home and chalet, and it would be impractical to inspect every single accommodation unit. Our selection criteria, therefore, primarily takes account of the quality standards of the campsite itself.

However, there are a couple of important ground rules:

* Featured mobile homes must be no more than 5 years old

* chalets no more than 10 years old

* All listed accommodation must, of course, fully conform with all applicable local, national and European safety legislation.

For each campsite we have given details of the type, or types, of accommodation available to rent, but these details are necessarily quite brief. Sometimes internal layouts can differ quite substantially, particularly with regard to sleeping arrangements, where these include the flexible provision for 'extra persons' on sofa beds located in the living area. These arrangements may vary from accommodation to accommodation, and if you're planning a holiday which includes more people than are catered for by the main bedrooms you should check exactly how the extra sleeping arrangements are to be provided!

Charges

An indication of the tariff for each type of accommodation featured is also included, indicating the variance between the low and high season tariffs. However, given that many campsites have a large and often complex range of pricing options, incorporating special deals and various discounts, the charges we mention should be taken to be just an indication. We strongly recommend therefore that you confirm the actual cost when making a booking.

We also strongly recommend that you check with the campsite, when booking, what (if anything) will be provided by way of bed linen, blankets, pillows etc. Again, in our experience, this can vary widely from site to site.

On every campsite a fully refundable deposit (usually between 150 and 300 euros) is payable on arrival. There may also be an optional cleaning service for which a further charge is made. Other options may include sheet hire (typically 30 euros per unit) or baby pack hire (cot and high chair).

Low Cost Flights

An Inexpensive Way To Arrive At Your Campsite

Many campsites are conveniently served by a wide choice of low cost airlines. Cheap flights can be very easy to find and travellers increasingly find the regional airports often used to be smaller, quieter and generally a calmer, more pleasurable experience.

Low cost flights can make campsites in more distant regions a much more attractive option: quicker to reach, inexpensive flights, and simply more convenient.

Many campsites are seeing increased visitors using the low cost flights and are adapting their services to suit this clientele. An airport shuttle service is not uncommon, meaning you can take advantage of that cheap flight knowing you will be met at the other end and whisked to your campsite. No taxi queues or multiple drop-offs.

Obviously, these low cost flights are impractical when taking all your own camping gear but they do make a holiday in campsite owned accommodation much more straightforward. The low cost airline option makes mobile home holidays especially attractive: pack a suitcase and use bed linen and towels provided (which you will generally need to pre-book).

Pricing Tips

- Low cost airlines promote cheap flights but only a small percentage of seats are priced at the cheapest price. Book early for the best prices (and of course you also get a better choice of campsite or mobile home)
- Child seats are usually the same costs as adults
- Full payment is required at the time of booking
- Changes and amendments can be costly with low cost airlines
- Peak dates can be expensive compared to other carriers

Car Hire

For maximum flexibility you will probably hire a car from a car rental agency. Car hire provides convenience but also will allow you access to off-site shops, beaches and tourist sights.

FR35000 Camping le Vieux Chêne

see report page 35

Baguer-Pican, F-35120 Dol-de-Bretagne (Brittany)

AR1 – REVE CONFORT – Mobile home

Sleeping: 2 bedrooms, sleeps 5: 1 double, 2 singles, bunk bed, sofa bed, pillows and blankets provided

Living: living/kitchen area, heating, shower, separate WC

Eating: fitted kitchen with hob, oven, coffee maker, fridge, freezer

Outside: table & chairs

Pets: accepted (with supplement)

AR2 – COTTAGE DE BRETAGNE – Mobile Home

Sleeping: 2 bedrooms, sleeps 4: 2 singles, sofa bed, pillows and blankets provided

Living: living/kitchen area, heating, shower, separate WC

Eating: fitted kitchen with oven, fridge, freezer

Outside: table & chairs

Pets: accepted (with supplement)

Open: 1 April - 25 September

Weekly Charge	AR1	AR2
Low Season (from)	€ 325	€ 295
High Season (from)	€ 725	€ 695

FR29180 Camping les Embruns

see report page 53

2 rue du Philosophe Alain, Le Pouldu Plages, F-29360 Clohars-Carnoët (Brittany)

AR1 – ARMOR + VERANDA – Mobile home

Sleeping: 2 bedrooms, sleeps 4: 1 double, 2 singles

Living: living/kitchen area, heating, shower, WC

Eating: fitted kitchen with hob, oven, coffee maker, fridge

Outside: table & chairs

Pets: accepted (with supplement)

AR2 – ATLANTIQUE + VERANDA – Mobile home

Sleeping: 3 bedrooms, sleeps 6: 1 double, 2 singles, bunk bed

Living: living/kitchen area, heating, shower, WC

Eating: fitted kitchen with hob, oven, coffee maker, fridge

Outside: table & chairs

Pets: accepted (with supplement)

Other (AR1 and AR2): cot, highchair to hire

Open: 6 April - 22 September

Weekly Charge	AR1	AR2
Low Season (from)	€ 350	€ 400
High Season (from)	€ 690	€ 860

FR29010 Castel Camping le Ty-Nadan

see report page 54

Route d'Arzano, F-29310 Locunolé (Brittany)

AR1 – IRM – Mobile home

Sleeping: 2 bedrooms, sleeps 6: 1 double, 2 singles, sofa bed, pillows and blankets provided

Living: living/kitchen area, heating, shower, WC

Eating: fitted kitchen with hob, oven, fridge

Outside: table & chairs, parasol, 2 sun loungers

Pets: accepted

AR2 – CHALET – Chalet

Sleeping: 2 bedrooms, sleeps 6: 1 double, 2 singles, sofa bed, pillows and blankets provided

Living: living/kitchen area, heating, shower, WC

Eating: fitted kitchen with hob, oven, fridge

Outside: table & chairs, parasol, 2 sun loungers

Pets: accepted

Other (AR1 and AR2): bed linen, cot, highchair to hire

Open: 31 March - 2 September

Weekly Charge	AR1	AR2
Low Season (from)	€ 312	€ 426
High Season (from)	€ 952	€ 1211

FR29090 Camping le Raguénès-Plage

▶ see report page 56

19 rue des Iles, F-29920 Névez (Brittany)

AR1 – VARIANTE – Mobile home	AR2 – OHARA COTTAGE – Cottage
Sleeping: 2 bedrooms, sleeps 5: 1 double, 2 singles, sofa bed, pillows and blankets provided	Sleeping: 2 bedrooms, sleeps 4: 1 double, 2 singles, sofa bed, pillows and blankets provided
Living: living/kitchen area, heating, air conditioning, shower, separate WC	Living: living/kitchen area, heating, air conditioning, shower, separate WC
Eating: fitted kitchen with hob, oven, microwave, coffee maker, fridge, freezer	Eating: fitted kitchen with hob, microwave, coffee maker, fridge, freezer
Outside: table & chairs, parasol, 2 sun loungers, barbecue	Outside: table & chairs, parasol, 2 sun loungers, barbecue
Pets: accepted (with supplement)	Pets: accepted (with supplement)

Other (AR1 and AR2): bed linen to hire

Open: 1 April - 30 September

Weekly Charge	AR1	AR2
Low Season (from)	€ 320	€ 340
High Season (from)	€ 699	€ 745

FR29050 Castel Camping l'Orangerie de Lanniron

▶ see report page 64

Château de Lanniron, F-29336 Quimper (Brittany)

AR1 – ZEN – Mobile home	AR2 – CONFORT – Mobile home
Sleeping: 3 bedrooms, sleeps 6: 1 double, 3 singles, bunk bed, pillows and blankets provided	Sleeping: 2 bedrooms, sleeps 5: 1 double, 2 singles, sofa bed, pillows and blankets provided
Living: living/kitchen area, heating, air conditioning, shower, separate WC	Living: living/kitchen area, heating, shower, separate WC
Eating: fitted kitchen with hob, microwave, coffee maker, fridge, freezer	Eating: fitted kitchen with hob, microwave, coffee maker, fridge, freezer
Outside: table & chairs, parasol, 2 sun loungers, barbecue	Outside: table & chairs, parasol, 2 sun loungers, barbecue
Pets: not accepted	Pets: not accepted

Other (AR1 and AR2): bed linen, cot, highchair to hire

Open: 1 April - 31 October

Weekly Charge	AR1	AR2
Low Season (from)	€ 518	€ 420
High Season (from)	€ 1085	€ 966

FR29080 Camping le Panoramic

▶ see report page 72

Route de la Plage-Penker, F-29560 Telgruc-sur-Mer (Brittany)

AR1 – TRIGANO ELEGANTE 33 M2 – Mobile home	AR2 – TRIGANO ELEGANTE 25 M2 – Mobile home
Sleeping: 3 bedrooms, sleeps 6: 1 double, 4 singles, pillows and blankets provided	Sleeping: 2 bedrooms, sleeps 4: 1 double, 2 singles, sofa bed, pillows and blankets provided
Living: living/kitchen area, heating, shower, WC	Living: living/kitchen area, heating, shower, WC
Eating: fitted kitchen with hob, fridge, freezer	Eating: fitted kitchen with hob, fridge
Outside: table & chairs, parasol, 2 sun loungers, barbecue	Outside: table & chairs, parasol, 2 sun loungers, barbecue
Pets: accepted (with supplement)	Pets: accepted (with supplement)

Open: 1 May - 15 September

Weekly Charge	AR1	AR2
Low Season (from)	€ 320	€ 280
High Season (from)	€ 680	€ 590

`FR27070` Camping de l'Île des Trois Rois

▶ see report page 76

1 rue Gilles Nicolle, F-27700 Andelys (Normandy)

AR1 – MOBILE HOME 4 PERS – Mobile home	**AR2 – MOBILE HOME 6 PERS – Mobile home**
Sleeping: 2 bedrooms, sleeps 4: 1 double, 2 singles	Sleeping: 3 bedrooms, sleeps 6: 1 double, 4 singles
Living: living/kitchen area, heating, shower, WC	Living: living/kitchen area, heating, shower, WC, separate WC
Eating: fitted kitchen with hob, fridge	Eating: fitted kitchen with hob, fridge
Outside: table & chairs, barbecue	Outside: table & chairs, barbecue
Pets: not accepted	Pets: not accepted

Open: 13 March - 15 November		
Weekly Charge	AR1	AR2
Low Season (from)	€ 340	€ 400
High Season (from)	€ 540	€ 640

`FR80060` Camping le Val de Trie

▶ see report page 110

Rue des Sources, Bouillancourt-sous-Miannay, F-80870 Moyenneville (Picardy)

AR1 – MOREVA – Mobile home	**AR2 – GRAND CONFORT – Chalet**
Sleeping: 2 bedrooms, sleeps 6: 1 double, 2 singles, sofa bed, pillows and blankets provided	Sleeping: 3 bedrooms, sleeps 6: 1 double, 2 singles, bunk bed, pillows and blankets provided
Living: living/kitchen area, heating, shower, separate WC	Living: living/kitchen area, heating, shower, separate WC
Eating: fitted kitchen with hob, microwave, coffee maker, fridge, freezer	Eating: fitted kitchen with hob, microwave, dishwasher, coffee maker, fridge, freezer
Outside: table & chairs, parasol, barbecue	Outside: table & chairs, parasol, barbecue
Pets: not accepted	Pets: not accepted

Other (AR1 and AR2): bed linen, cot, highchair to hire

Open: 1 April - 15 October		
Weekly Charge	AR1	AR2
Low Season (from)	€ 343	€ 504
High Season (from)	€ 623	€ 854

`FR80070` Kawan Village la Ferme des Aulnes

▶ see report page 112

1 rue du Marais, Fresne-sur-Authie, F-80120 Nampont-Saint Martin (Picardy)

AR1 – CONFORT – Mobile home	**AR2 – PRIVILEGE – Mobile home**
Sleeping: 2 bedrooms, sleeps 5: 1 double, 2 singles, sofa bed, pillows and blankets provided	Sleeping: 3 bedrooms, sleeps 6: 1 double, 2 singles, bunk bed, pillows and blankets provided
Living: living/kitchen area, heating, TV, shower, separate WC	Living: living/kitchen area, heating, TV, shower, separate WC
Eating: fitted kitchen with hob, microwave, coffee maker, fridge, freezer	Eating: fitted kitchen with hob, microwave, coffee maker, fridge, freezer
Outside: table & chairs, parasol, barbecue	Outside: table & chairs, parasol, barbecue
Pets: accepted (with supplement)	Pets: accepted (with supplement)

Other (AR1 and AR2): bed linen, cot, highchair to hire

Open: 1 April - 1 November		
Weekly Charge	AR1	AR2
Low Season (from)	€ 490	€ 590
High Season (from)	€ 690	€ 790

FR80150 Camping Airotel Le Walric

▶ see report page 113

Route d'Eu, F-80230 Saint Valéry-sur-Somme (Picardy)

AR1 – COTTAGE 4 COUCHAGES – Mobile home	**AR2** – COTTAGE 6 COUCHAGES – Mobile home
Sleeping: 2 bedrooms, sleeps 4: 1 double, 2 singles, pillows and blankets provided	Sleeping: 3 bedrooms, sleeps 6: 1 double, 4 singles, pillows and blankets provided
Living: living/kitchen area, heating, TV, shower, WC	Living: living/kitchen area, heating, TV, shower, WC
Eating: fitted kitchen with hob, microwave, coffee maker, fridge, freezer	Eating: fitted kitchen with hob, microwave, coffee maker, fridge, freezer
Outside: table & chairs, parasol, barbecue	Outside: table & chairs, parasol, barbecue
Pets: accepted	Pets: accepted

Other (AR1 and AR2): cot, highchair to hire

Open: 1 April - 1 November

Weekly Charge	AR1	AR2
Low Season (from)	€ 300	€ 400
High Season (from)	€ 630	€ 725

FR57090 Parc Résidentiel de la Tensch

▶ see report page 135

F-57670 Francaltroff (Lorraine)

AR1 – CHALET – Chalet
Sleeping: 2 bedrooms, sleeps 5: 1 double, 2 singles, sofa bed, pillows and blankets provided
Living: living/kitchen area, heating, TV, shower, separate WC
Eating: fitted kitchen with hob, microwave, coffee maker, fridge, freezer
Outside: table & chairs, parasol
Pets: not accepted

Other (AR1 and AR2): bed linen, cot to hire

Open: 7 January - 15 December

Weekly Charge	AR1
Low Season (from)	€ 365
High Season (from)	€ 465

FR41070 Kawan Village la Grande Tortue

▶ see report page 154

3 route de Pontlevoy, F-41120 Candé-sur-Beuvron (Val de Loire)

AR1 – IRM SUPER MERCURE – Mobile home	**AR2** – LOUISIANE – Mobile home
Sleeping: 2 bedrooms, sleeps 5: 1 double, 2 singles, bunk bed, pillows and blankets provided	Sleeping: 3 bedrooms, sleeps 6: 1 double, 4 singles, pillows and blankets provided
Living: living/kitchen area, heating, shower, separate WC	Living: living/kitchen area, heating, shower, separate WC
Eating: fitted kitchen with hob, microwave, coffee maker, fridge	Eating: fitted kitchen with hob, microwave, coffee maker, fridge
Outside: table & chairs, 2 sun loungers	Outside: table & chairs, 2 sun loungers
Pets: accepted (with supplement)	Pets: accepted (with supplement)

Other (AR1 and AR2): bed linen, cot, highchair to hire

Open: 5 April - 20 September

Weekly Charge	AR1	AR2
Low Season (from)	€ 314	€ 441
High Season (from)	€ 700	€ 756

FR45050 Les Roulottes des Bords de Loire

see report page 161

Rue des Iris, F-45500 Poilly-lez-Gien (Val de Loire)

AR1 – LOUISIANA-O – Mobile home	AR2 – ROULOTTE – Gipsy wagon
Sleeping: 2 bedrooms, sleeps 6: 1 double, 2 singles, sofa bed, pillows and blankets provided	Sleeping: 1 bedroom, sleeps 3: 1 double, sofa bed, pillows and blankets provided
Living: living/kitchen area, heating, shower, separate WC	Living: living/kitchen area, heating, shower, separate WC
Eating: fitted kitchen with hob, microwave, coffee maker, fridge	Eating: fitted kitchen with hob, microwave, coffee maker, fridge
Outside: table & chairs, parasol, barbecue	Outside: table & chairs, parasol, barbecue
Pets: accepted (with supplement)	Pets: accepted (with supplement)

Other (AR1 and AR2): bed linen to hire

Open: 1 March - 8 November

Weekly Charge	AR1	AR2
Low Season (from)	€ 295	€ 425
High Season (from)	€ 545	€ 525

FR37060 Camping l'Arada Parc

see report page 164

Rue de la Baratière, F-37360 Sonzay (Val de Loire)

AR1 – SAMIBOIS – Chalet	AR2 – O HARA – Mobile home
Sleeping: 3 bedrooms, sleeps 6: 2 doubles, bunk bed, pillows and blankets provided	Sleeping: 2 bedrooms, sleeps 5: 1 double, 2 singles, sofa bed, pillows and blankets provided
Living: living/kitchen area, heating, shower, separate WC	Living: living/kitchen area, heating, shower, separate WC
Eating: fitted kitchen with hob, microwave, coffee maker, fridge, freezer	Eating: fitted kitchen with hob, microwave, coffee maker, fridge
Outside: table & chairs, barbecue	Outside: table & chairs, barbecue
Pets: accepted (with supplement)	Pets: accepted (with supplement)

Other (AR1 and AR2): bed linen, cot, highchair to hire

Open: 31 March - 18 October

Weekly Charge	AR1	AR2
Low Season (from)	€ 392	€ 343
High Season (from)	€ 714	€ 665

FR44220 Le Domaine de Léveno

see report page 172

Route de Sandun, F-44350 Guérande (Pays de la Loire)

AR1 – COTTAGE CONFORT – Mobile home	AR2 – COTTAGE CONFORT – Mobile home
Sleeping: 2 bedrooms, sleeps 6: 1 double, 2 singles, sofa bed, pillows and blankets provided	Sleeping: 3 bedrooms, sleeps 6: 1 double, 4 singles, pillows and blankets provided
Living: living/kitchen area, heating, shower, separate WC	Living: living/kitchen area, shower, separate WC
Eating: fitted kitchen with hob, fridge	Eating: fitted kitchen with hob, fridge
Outside: table & chairs, parasol	Outside: table & chairs, parasol
Pets: accepted (with supplement)	Pets: accepted (with supplement)

Other (AR1 and AR2): bed linen, cot, highchair to hire

Open: 7 April - 29 September

Weekly Charge	AR1	AR2
Low Season (from)	€ 315	€ 350
High Season (from)	€ 875	€ 903

FR44210 Camping de l'Océan

▶ see report page 177

15 route de la Maison Rouge, F-44490 Le Croisic (Pays de la Loire)

AR1 – COTTAGE OCEAN ESPACE – Mobile home	AR2 – OCEAN GRAND CONFORT FAMILLE – Mobile home
Sleeping: 2 bedrooms, sleeps 5: 1 double, 2 singles, sofa bed, pillows and blankets provided	Sleeping: 3 bedrooms, sleeps 6: 1 double, 4 singles, pillows and blankets provided
Living: living/kitchen area, heating, shower, WC	Living: living/kitchen area, shower, WC
Eating: fitted kitchen with hob, fridge	Eating: fitted kitchen with hob, fridge
Outside: table & chairs, parasol	Outside: table & chairs, parasol
Pets: accepted (with supplement)	Pets: accepted (with supplement)

Other (AR1 and AR2): bed linen, cot, highchair to hire

Open: 6 April - 30 September		
Weekly Charge	AR1	AR2
Low Season (from)	€ 511	€ 637
High Season (from)	€ 973	€ 1281

FR44090 Kawan Village du Deffay

▶ see report page 182

B.P. 18 Le Deffay, Sainte Reine-de-Bretagne, F-44160 Pontchâteau (Pays de la Loire)

AR1 – MOBILE HOME 5 – Mobile home	AR2 – CHALET 4/6 – Chalet
Sleeping: 2 bedrooms, sleeps 5: 1 double, 1 single, bunk bed, pillows and blankets provided	Sleeping: 2 bedrooms, sleeps 6: 1 double, bunk bed, sofa bed, pillows and blankets provided
Living: living/kitchen area, heating, shower, separate WC	Living: living/kitchen area, heating, shower, WC
Eating: fitted kitchen with hob, microwave, coffee maker, fridge, freezer	Eating: fitted kitchen with hob, microwave, grill, dishwasher, coffee maker, fridge, freezer
Outside: table & chairs, parasol, 2 sun loungers, barbecue	Outside: table & chairs, parasol, 2 sun loungers, barbecue
Pets: not accepted	Pets: not accepted

Other (AR1 and AR2): bed linen, cot, highchair to hire

Open: 1 April - 31 October		
Weekly Charge	AR1	AR2
Low Season (from)	€ 213	€ 250
High Season (from)	€ 671	€ 715

FR44180 Camping de la Boutinardière

▶ see report page 184

Rue de la Plage de la Boutinardière 23, F-44210 Pornic (Pays de la Loire)

AR1 – MOBILE HOME 5 PERS. – Mobile home	AR2 – MOBILE HOME 6 PERS. – Mobile home
Sleeping: 2 bedrooms, sleeps 5: 1 double, 2 singles, sofa bed, pillows and blankets provided	Sleeping: 3 bedrooms, sleeps 6: 1 double, 4 singles, pillows and blankets provided
Living: living/kitchen area, heating, shower, WC	Living: living/kitchen area, heating, shower, WC
Eating: fitted kitchen with hob, fridge	Eating: fitted kitchen with hob, fridge
Outside: table & chairs, parasol	Outside: table & chairs, parasol
Pets: accepted (with supplement)	Pets: accepted (with supplement)

Other (AR1 and AR2): bed linen, cot, highchair to hire

Open: 2 April - 1 October		
Weekly Charge	AR1	AR2
Low Season (from)	€ 260	€ 360
High Season (from)	€ 950	€ 1000

FR17280 Camping la Grainetière

▶ see report page 224

Route de Saint-Martin, F-17630 La Flotte-en-Ré (Poitou-Charentes)

AR1 – ROULOTTE – Mobile home	AR2 – LUXE – Mobile home
Sleeping: 2 bedrooms, sleeps 4: 1 double, 2 singles, pillows and blankets provided	Sleeping: 2 bedrooms, sleeps 5: 1 double, 2 singles, sofa bed, pillows and blankets provided
Living: living/kitchen area, TV, shower, separate WC	Living: living/kitchen area, TV, shower, separate WC
Eating: fitted kitchen with hob, oven, microwave, coffee maker, fridge, freezer	Eating: fitted kitchen with hob, oven, microwave, coffee maker, fridge, freezer
Outside: table & chairs, parasol	Outside: table & chairs, parasol
Pets: accepted (with supplement)	Pets: accepted (with supplement)

Other (AR1 and AR2): highchair to hire

Open: 1 April - 30 September

Weekly Charge	AR1	AR2
Low Season (from)	€ 275	€ 275
High Season (from)	€ 810	€ 810

FR17010 Camping Bois Soleil

▶ see report page 238

2 avenue de Suzac, F-17110 Saint Georges-de-Didonne (Poitou-Charentes)

AR1 – COTTAGE DE CHARME – Mobile home	AR2 – COTTAGE BOIS – Mobile home
Sleeping: 3 bedrooms, sleeps 6: 1 double, 4 singles, pillows and blankets provided	Sleeping: 2 bedrooms, sleeps 4: 1 double, 2 singles, pillows and blankets provided
Living: living/kitchen area, heating, TV, air conditioning, shower, WC	Living: living/kitchen area, heating, air conditioning, shower, WC
Eating: fitted kitchen with hob, microwave, fridge	Eating: fitted kitchen with hob, microwave, fridge
Outside: table & chairs, parasol	Outside: table & chairs, parasol
Pets: not accepted	Pets: not accepted

Open: 31 March - 7 October

Weekly Charge	AR1	AR2
Low Season (from)	€ 540	€ 300
High Season (from)	€ 1190	€ 980

FR71070 Kawan Village Château de l'Epervière

▶ see report page 248

Rue du Château, F-71240 Gigny-sur-Saône (Burgundy)

AR1 – LOUISIANE PACIFIQUE 3XL – Mobile home
Sleeping: 3 bedrooms, sleeps 6: 1 double, 4 singles, pillows and blankets provided
Living: living/kitchen area, heating, TV, shower, separate WC
Eating: fitted kitchen with hob, microwave, dishwasher, coffee maker, fridge, freezer
Outside: table & chairs, parasol, 2 sun loungers
Pets: not accepted

Other (AR1 and AR2): bed linen, cot, highchair to hire

Open: 1 April - 30 September

Weekly Charge	AR1
Low Season (from)	€ 399
High Season (from)	€ 849

FR26210 Camping les Bois du Chatelas

▶ see report page 291

Route de Dieulefit, F-26460 Bourdeaux (Rhône-Alpes)

AR1 – GOELAND – Bungalow	AR2 – TEXAS WATIPI – Bungalow
Sleeping: 2 bedrooms, sleeps 6: 2 doubles, 1 single, sofa bed, pillows and blankets provided	Sleeping: 3 bedrooms, sleeps 7: 1 double, 4 singles, sofa bed, pillows and blankets provided
Living: living/kitchen area, heating, shower, separate WC	Living: living/kitchen area, heating, shower, separate WC
Eating: fitted kitchen with hob, microwave, coffee maker, fridge, freezer	Eating: fitted kitchen with hob, microwave, coffee maker, fridge, freezer
Outside: table & chairs	Outside: table & chairs
Pets: accepted	Pets: accepted

Other (AR1 and AR2): bed linen, cot, highchair to hire

Open: 6 April - 16 September		
Weekly Charge	AR1	AR2
Low Season (from)	€ 392	€ 406
High Season (from)	€ 1050	€ 1036

FR07660 Castel Domaine de Sévenier

▶ see report page 303

F-07150 Lagorce (Rhône Alpes)

AR1 – CHENE BLANC – Chalet	AR2 – CHENE VERT – Chalet
Sleeping: 2 bedrooms, sleeps 4: 1 double, 2 singles, bunk bed, sofa bed, pillows and blankets provided	Sleeping: 3 bedrooms, sleeps 6: 1 double, 4 singles, sofa bed, pillows and blankets provided
Living: living/kitchen area, heating, air conditioning, shower, separate WC	Living: living/kitchen area, heating, air conditioning, shower, separate WC
Eating: fitted kitchen with hob, microwave, dishwasher, coffee maker, fridge, freezer	Eating: fitted kitchen with hob, microwave, dishwasher, coffee maker, fridge, freezer
Outside: table & chairs, 1 sun lounger	Outside: table & chairs, 1 sun lounger
Pets: accepted (with supplement)	Pets: accepted (with supplement)

Other (AR1 and AR2): bed linen, cot, highchair to hire

Open: 9 April - 2 November		
Weekly Charge	AR1	AR2
Low Season (from)	€ 448	€ 651
High Season (from)	€ 1232	€ 1673

FR38060 Domaine les Trois Lacs du Soleil

▶ see report page 325

La Plaine, F-38460 Trept (Rhône Alpes)

AR1 – CENTURY – Mobile home	AR2 – LOFT 83 LUX – Mobile home
Sleeping: 3 bedrooms, sleeps 6: 1 double, 2 singles, bunk bed, pillows and blankets provided	Sleeping: 3 bedrooms, sleeps 6: 1 double, 4 singles, pillows and blankets provided
Living: living/kitchen area, heating, air conditioning, shower, WC	Living: living/kitchen area, heating, air conditioning, shower, separate WC
Eating: fitted kitchen with hob, oven, microwave, coffee maker, fridge	Eating: fitted kitchen with hob, microwave, coffee maker, fridge
Outside: table & chairs, parasol, 2 sun loungers, barbecue	Outside: table & chairs, parasol, 2 sun loungers, barbecue
Pets: not accepted	Pets: not accepted

Other (AR1 and AR2): bed linen, cot, highchair to hire

Open: 28 April - 15 September		
Weekly Charge	AR1	AR2
Low Season (from)	€ 455	€ 490
High Season (from)	€ 773	€ 805

FR40100 Camping du Domaine de la Rive

see report page 340

Route de Bordeaux, F-40600 Biscarrosse (Aquitaine)

AR1 – SAVANNAH – Mobile home

Sleeping: 2 bedrooms, sleeps 6: 1 double, 2 singles, sofa bed, pillows and blankets provided

Living: living/kitchen area, heating, shower, WC

Eating: fitted kitchen with hob, microwave, fridge, freezer

Outside: table & chairs, parasol, 2 sun loungers

Pets: not accepted

AR2 – COTTAGE 3 – Mobile home

Sleeping: 3 bedrooms, sleeps 6: 1 double, 4 singles, pillows and blankets provided

Living: living/kitchen area, shower, WC

Eating: fitted kitchen with hob, microwave, fridge, freezer

Outside: table & chairs, parasol

Pets: not accepted

Other (AR1 and AR2): bed linen, cot, highchair to hire

Open: 6 April - 9 September		
Weekly Charge	AR1	AR2
Low Season (from)	€ 548	€ 555
High Season (from)	€ 1199	€ 1213

FR33110 Airotel Camping de la Côte d'Argent

see report page 352

F-33990 Hourtin-Plage (Aquitaine)

AR1 – SAVANNAH – Mobile home

Sleeping: 2 bedrooms, sleeps 5: 1 double, 2 singles, sofa bed, pillows and blankets provided

Living: living/kitchen area, shower, WC

Eating: fitted kitchen with hob, microwave, coffee maker, fridge, freezer

Outside: table & chairs, parasol

Pets: not accepted

AR2 – SUPER FAMILY – Mobile home

Sleeping: 3 bedrooms, sleeps 6: 1 double, 4 singles, pillows and blankets provided

Living: living/kitchen area, shower, WC

Eating: fitted kitchen with hob, microwave, coffee maker, fridge, freezer

Outside: table & chairs, parasol, 2 sun loungers

Pets: not accepted

Open: 17 May - 14 September		
Weekly Charge	AR1	AR2
Low Season (from)	€ 240	€ 272
High Season (from)	€ 1022	€ 1127

FR40180 Airotel le Vieux Port

see report page 357

Plage Sud, F-40660 Messanges (Aquitaine)

AR1 – MOBILE HOME SANS SANITAIRE – Mobile home

Sleeping: 2 bedrooms, sleeps 4: 1 double, 2 singles, pillows and blankets provided

Living: living/kitchen area, heating, shower, WC

Eating: fitted kitchen with hob, fridge

Outside: table & chairs, parasol

Pets: not accepted

AR2 – LODGE MEZZANINE – Mobile home

Sleeping: 3 bedrooms, sleeps 8: 1 double, 4 singles, pillows and blankets provided

Living: living/kitchen area, heating, TV, air conditioning, shower, WC, separate WC

Eating: fitted kitchen with hob, dishwasher, fridge, freezer

Outside: table & chairs, parasol, 2 sun loungers

Pets: not accepted

Other (AR1 and AR2): cot, highchair to hire

Open: 2 April - 25 September		
Weekly Charge	AR1	AR2
Low Season (from)	€ 199	€ 430
High Season (from)	€ 770	€ 1764

FR40190 Le Saint-Martin Camping

▶ see report page 360

Avenue de l'Océan, F-40660 Moliets-Plage (Aquitaine)

AR1 – DUO – Chalet	AR2 – ZEPHYR – Chalet
Sleeping: 1 bedroom, sleeps 3: 2 singles, pillows and blankets provided	Sleeping: 2 bedrooms, sleeps 5: 1 double, 2 singles, sofa bed, pillows and blankets provided
Living: living/kitchen area, heating, shower, separate WC	Living: living/kitchen area, heating, shower, separate WC
Eating: fitted kitchen with hob, microwave, coffee maker, fridge, freezer	Eating: fitted kitchen with hob, microwave, coffee maker, fridge, freezer
Outside: table & chairs	Outside: table & chairs
Pets: accepted (with supplement)	Pets: accepted (with supplement)

Other (AR1 and AR2): cot to hire

Open: 8 April - All Saints		
Weekly Charge	AR1	AR2
Low Season (from)	€ 220	€ 430
High Season (from)	€ 620	€ 1320

FR24320 Camping les Peneyrals

▶ see report page 366

Le Poujol, F-24590 Saint Crépin-Carlucet (Dordogne)

AR1 – MERCURE – Mobile home	AR2 – EQUINOXE – Chalet
Sleeping: 2 bedrooms, sleeps 5: 1 double, 2 singles, sofa bed, pillows and blankets provided	Sleeping: 3 bedrooms, sleeps 7: 1 double, 4 singles, sofa bed, pillows and blankets provided
Living: living/kitchen area, heating, shower, separate WC	Living: living/kitchen area, heating, TV, shower, separate WC
Eating: fitted kitchen with hob, microwave, coffee maker, fridge	Eating: fitted kitchen with hob, microwave, coffee maker, fridge
Outside: table & chairs, parasol, 2 sun loungers, barbecue	Outside: table & chairs, parasol, 2 sun loungers, barbecue
Pets: accepted (with supplement)	Pets: accepted (with supplement)

Other (AR1 and AR2): bed linen to hire

Open: 12 May - 14 September		
Weekly Charge	AR1	AR2
Low Season (from)	€ 310	€ 490
High Season (from)	€ 870	€ 1060

FR40140 Camping Caravaning Lou P'tit Poun

▶ see report page 372

110 avenue du Quartier Neuf, F-40390 Saint Martin-de-Seignanx (Aquitaine)

AR1 – FABRE REVE – Chalet
Sleeping: 2 bedrooms, sleeps 5: 1 double, 3 singles
Living: living/kitchen area, shower, WC
Eating: fitted kitchen with fridge
Outside: table & chairs, 2 sun loungers
Pets: not accepted

Open: 4 June - 10 September	
Weekly Charge	AR1
Low Season (from)	€ 465
High Season (from)	€ 790

FR40250 Camping les Grands Pins

▶ see report page 374

1039 avenue de Losa, F-40460 Sanguinet (Aquitaine)

AR1 – OHARA OCEANE – Mobile home

Sleeping: 3 bedrooms, sleeps 6: 1 double, 4 singles, pillows and blankets provided

Living: living/kitchen area, heating, shower, separate WC

Eating: fitted kitchen with hob, microwave, coffee maker, fridge, freezer

Outside: table & chairs, parasol, 1 sun lounger

Pets: not accepted

AR2 – GITOTEL FABRE – Chalet

Sleeping: 2 bedrooms, sleeps 4: 1 double, 2 singles, pillows and blankets provided

Living: living/kitchen area, heating, shower, WC

Eating: fitted kitchen with hob, microwave, fridge

Outside: table & chairs, parasol

Pets: not accepted

Open: 1 April - 30 September		
Weekly Charge	AR1	AR2
Low Season (from)	€ 623	€ 434
High Season (from)	€ 1057	€ 861

FR24090 Domaine de Soleil Plage

▶ see report page 377

Caudon par Montfort, Vitrac, F-24200 Sarlat-la-Canéda (Aquitaine)

AR1 – CHALET PRESTIGE – Chalet

Sleeping: 3 bedrooms, sleeps 7: 1 double, 4 singles, sofa bed, pillows and blankets provided

Living: living/kitchen area, heating, TV, shower, WC, separate WC

Eating: fitted kitchen with hob, microwave, grill, dishwasher, coffee maker, fridge, freezer

Outside: table & chairs, parasol, 2 sun loungers, barbecue

Pets: accepted (with supplement)

AR2 – MOBILE HOME 3 CHAMBRES – Mobile home

Sleeping: 3 bedrooms, sleeps 7: 1 double, 4 singles, sofa bed, pillows and blankets provided

Living: living/kitchen area, heating, shower, separate WC

Eating: fitted kitchen with hob, microwave, dishwasher, coffee maker, fridge

Outside: table & chairs, parasol, 2 sun loungers, barbecue

Pets: accepted (with supplement)

Other (AR1 and AR2): bed linen, cot, highchair to hire

Open: 6 April - 30 September		
Weekly Charge	AR1	AR2
Low Season (from)	€ 450	€ 390
High Season (from)	€ 1220	€ 1050

FR09020 Camping l'Arize

▶ see report page 398

Lieu-dit Bourtol, F-09240 La Bastide-de-Sérou (Midi-Pyrénées)

AR1 – LOUISIANE FLORES CONFORT PLUS – Mobile home

Sleeping: 2 bedrooms, sleeps 7: 1 double, 2 singles, bunk bed, sofa bed, pillows and blankets provided

Living: living/kitchen area, heating, shower, separate WC

Eating: fitted kitchen with hob, microwave, grill, fridge, freezer

Outside: table & chairs, parasol, barbecue

Pets: accepted (with supplement)

AR2 – CHALET 3 BEDROOMS – Chalet

Sleeping: 3 bedrooms, sleeps 8: 1 double, 3 singles, bunk bed, sofa bed, pillows and blankets provided

Living: living/kitchen area, heating, shower, separate WC

Eating: fitted kitchen with hob, microwave, grill, fridge, freezer

Outside: table & chairs, parasol, barbecue

Pets: accepted (with supplement)

Open: 30 January - 30 November		
Weekly Charge	AR1	AR2
Low Season (from)	€ 392	€ 455
High Season (from)	€ 749	€ 749

FR32010 Kawan Village le Camp de Florence

▶ see report page 399

Route Astaffort, F-32480 La Romieu (Midi-Pyrénées)

AR1 – LOUISIANE ZEN – Mobile home	AR2 – IRM DELUXE – Mobile home
Sleeping: 3 bedrooms, sleeps 6: 1 double, 2 singles, bunk bed, pillows and blankets provided	Sleeping: 2 bedrooms, sleeps 6: 1 double, 2 singles, sofa bed, pillows and blankets provided
Living: living/kitchen area, heating, shower, separate WC	Living: living/kitchen area, heating, shower, separate WC
Eating: fitted kitchen with microwave, fridge, freezer	Eating: fitted kitchen with microwave, fridge, freezer
Outside: table & chairs, 2 sun loungers	Outside: table & chairs, 2 sun loungers
Pets: accepted	Pets: accepted

Open: 1 April - 11 October

Weekly Charge	AR1	AR2
Low Season (from)	€ 406	€ 343
High Season (from)	€ 924	€ 854

FR66070 Yelloh! Village le Brasilia

▶ see report page 429

B.P. 204, F-66141 Canet-en-Roussillon (Languedoc-Roussillon)

AR1 – OKAVANGO – Mobile home	AR2 – PINÈDE – Bungalow
Sleeping: 2 bedrooms, sleeps 6: 1 double, 2 singles, bunk bed, pillows and blankets provided	Sleeping: 2 bedrooms, sleeps 4: 1 double, 2 singles, bunk bed, pillows and blankets provided
Living: living/kitchen area, heating, TV, shower, WC	Living: living/kitchen area, heating, TV, shower, WC
Eating: fitted kitchen with hob, microwave, grill, coffee maker, fridge, freezer	Eating: fitted kitchen with hob, microwave, grill, coffee maker, fridge, freezer
Outside: table & chairs, parasol, 2 sun loungers	Outside: table & chairs, 2 sun loungers
Pets: accepted (with supplement)	Pets: accepted (with supplement)

Other (AR1 and AR2): bed linen, cot, highchair to hire

Open: 21 April - 29 September

Weekly Charge	AR1	AR2
Low Season (from)	€ 301	€ 301
High Season (from)	€ 1155	€ 1155

FR11070 Yelloh! Village les Mimosas

▶ see report page 443

Chaussée de Mandirac, F-11100 Narbonne (Languedoc-Rousillon)

AR1 – MOBILE HOME PLANCHA – Mobile home	AR2 – FLORÈS – Mobile home
Sleeping: 2 bedrooms, sleeps 4: 1 double, 2 singles, pillows and blankets provided	Sleeping: 3 bedrooms, sleeps 6: 1 double, 4 singles, pillows and blankets provided
Living: living/kitchen area, shower, WC	Living: living/kitchen area, heating, air conditioning, shower, WC
Eating: fitted kitchen with hob, microwave, coffee maker, fridge, freezer	Eating: fitted kitchen with hob, microwave, coffee maker, fridge, freezer
Outside: table & chairs, 2 sun loungers, barbecue	Outside: table & chairs, 2 sun loungers
Pets: not accepted	Pets: not accepted

Other (AR1 and AR2): bed linen, cot, highchair to hire

Open: 27 March - 1 November

Weekly Charge	AR1	AR2
Low Season (from)	€ 301	€ 364
High Season (from)	€ 798	€ 1029

FR66700 PRL Le Vedrignans

▶ see report page 450

Route de Vedrignans, F-66800 Saillagouse (Languedoc-Roussillon)

AR1 – GENET – Chalet	**AR2 – EDELWEISS – Chalet**
Sleeping: 2 bedrooms, sleeps 4: 2 singles, bunk bed, pillows and blankets provided	Sleeping: 4 bedrooms, sleeps 8: 3 doubles, 2 singles, pillows and blankets provided
Living: living/kitchen area, heating, TV, shower, separate WC	Living: living/kitchen area, heating, TV, shower, separate WC
Eating: fitted kitchen with hob, microwave, grill, coffee maker, fridge, freezer	Eating: fitted kitchen with hob, oven, microwave, grill, dishwasher, coffee maker, fridge, freezer
Outside: table & chairs, parasol, 2 sun loungers, barbecue	Outside: table & chairs, parasol, 4 sun loungers, barbecue
Pets: accepted (with supplement)	Pets: accepted (with supplement)

Other (AR1 and AR2): bed linen, cot, highchair to hire

Open: All year		
Weekly Charge	AR1	AR2
Low Season (from)	€ 330	€ 630
High Season (from)	€ 480	€ 900

FR34070 Yelloh! Village le Sérignan-Plage

▶ see report page 452

Le Sérignan Plage, F-34410 Sérignan-Plage (Languedoc-Roussillon)

AR1 – CHALET ROBINSON – Chalet	**AR2 – COTTAGE CABANE – Mobile home**
Sleeping: 2 bedrooms, sleeps 5: 1 double, 2 singles, bunk bed, pillows and blankets provided	Sleeping: 3 bedrooms, sleeps 6: 1 double, 2 singles, bunk bed, pillows and blankets provided
Living: living/kitchen area, heating, air conditioning, shower, separate WC	Living: living/kitchen area, heating, TV, air conditioning, shower, separate WC
Eating: fitted kitchen with hob, microwave, dishwasher, coffee maker, fridge, freezer	Eating: fitted kitchen with hob, microwave, dishwasher, coffee maker, fridge, freezer
Outside: table & chairs, parasol, 2 sun loungers	Outside: table & chairs, 2 sun loungers
Pets: not accepted	Pets: not accepted

Other (AR1 and AR2): bed linen, cot, highchair to hire

Open: 21 April - 2 October		
Weekly Charge	AR1	AR2
Low Season (from)	€ 378	€ 455
High Season (from)	€ 1645	€ 2044

FR04020 Castel Camping le Domaine du Verdon

▶ see report page 469

Camp du Verdon, F-04120 Castellane (Provence)

AR1 – WATIPI – Mobile home	**AR2 – TITOM – Mobile home**
Sleeping: 2 bedrooms, sleeps 4: 1 double, 2 singles, pillows and blankets provided	Sleeping: 2 bedrooms, sleeps 4: 1 double, 2 singles, bunk bed, pillows and blankets provided
Living: living/kitchen area, shower, WC	Living: living/kitchen area, shower, WC
Eating: fitted kitchen with hob, fridge	Eating: fitted kitchen with hob, fridge
Outside: table & chairs, 2 sun loungers	Outside: table & chairs, 2 sun loungers
Pets: accepted	Pets: accepted

Other (AR1 and AR2): bed linen, cot, highchair to hire

Open: 15 May - 15 September		
Weekly Charge	AR1	AR2
Low Season (from)	€ 336	€ 378
High Season (from)	€ 742	€ 791

FR83220 Kawan Village Cros de Mouton

▶ see report page 471

B.P. 116, F-83240 Cavalaire-sur-Mer (Provence)

AR1 – PRESTIGE – Mobile home	AR2 – TEXAS – Mobile home
Sleeping: 2 bedrooms, sleeps 5: 1 double, 2 singles, sofa bed, pillows and blankets provided	Sleeping: 3 bedrooms, sleeps 6: 1 double, 4 singles, pillows and blankets provided
Living: living/kitchen area, heating, air conditioning, shower, separate WC	Living: living/kitchen area, heating, air conditioning, shower, separate WC
Eating: fitted kitchen with hob, microwave, coffee maker, fridge, freezer	Eating: fitted kitchen with hob, microwave, coffee maker, fridge, freezer
Outside: table & chairs, parasol, 2 sun loungers	Outside: table & chairs, parasol, 2 sun loungers
Pets: accepted	Pets: accepted

Other (AR1 and AR2): bed linen, cot, highchair to hire

Open: 15 March - 4 November		
Weekly Charge	AR1	AR2
Low Season (from)	€ 475	€ 555
High Season (from)	€ 872	€ 975

FR83060 Camping Resort la Baume – la Palmeraie

▶ see report page 474

3775 rue des Combattants d'Afrique du Nord, F-83618 Fréjus (Provence)

AR1 – BASTIDON – Bungalow	AR2 – CYCA – Mobile home
Sleeping: 3 bedrooms, sleeps 8: 1 double, 4 singles, sofa bed	Sleeping: 3 bedrooms, sleeps 6: 1 double, 4 singles, sofa bed
Living: living/kitchen area, TV, shower, WC	Living: living/kitchen area, TV, air conditioning, shower, WC
Eating: fitted kitchen with hob, microwave, fridge, freezer	Eating: fitted kitchen with hob, microwave, dishwasher, fridge, freezer
Outside: table & chairs, 4 sun loungers	Outside: table & chairs, 2 sun loungers
Pets: accepted	Pets: accepted

Other (AR1 and AR2): bed linen, cot, highchair to hire

Open: 9 April - 1 October		
Weekly Charge	AR1	AR2
Low Season (from)	€ 469	€ 525
High Season (from)	€ 1415	€ 1470

FR83640 Domaine des Naïades

▶ see report page 479

Quartier Cros d'Entassi, Saint Pons-les-Mûres, F-83310 Grimaud (Provence)

AR1 – MOBILE HOME CONFORT 4/5 PERSON – Mobile home	AR2 – MOBILE HOME PREMIUM – Mobile home
Sleeping: 2 bedrooms, sleeps 5: 1 double, 2 singles, sofa bed, pillows and blankets provided	Sleeping: 2 bedrooms, sleeps 5: 1 double, 2 singles, sofa bed, pillows and blankets provided
Living: living/kitchen area, heating, TV, air conditioning, shower, WC	Living: living/kitchen area, heating, TV, air conditioning, shower, separate WC
Eating: fitted kitchen with hob, microwave, coffee maker, fridge	Eating: fitted kitchen with hob, microwave, dishwasher, coffee maker, fridge, freezer
Outside: table & chairs, 2 sun loungers	Outside: table & chairs, parasol, 2 sun loungers
Pets: accepted (with supplement)	Pets: accepted (with supplement)

Other (AR1 and AR2): bed linen, cot, highchair to hire

Open: 31 March - 21 October		
Weekly Charge	AR1	AR2
Low Season (from)	€ 364	€ 490
High Season (from)	€ 966	€ 1225

FR83030 Camping Caravaning Leï Suves

⊙ see report page 491

Quartier du Blavet, F-83520 Roquebrune-sur-Argens (Provence)

AR1 – TYPE D – Mobile home	**AR2 – LUXE – Mobile home**
Sleeping: 2 bedrooms, sleeps 6: 1 double, 2 singles, sofa bed	Sleeping: 2 bedrooms, sleeps 5: 1 double, 2 singles, sofa bed
Living: living/kitchen area, shower, WC	Living: living/kitchen area, shower, WC
Eating: fitted kitchen with hob, oven, fridge	Eating: fitted kitchen with hob, oven, fridge
Outside: table & chairs	Outside: table & chairs, barbecue
Pets: not accepted	Pets: not accepted

Open: 2 April - 15 October

Weekly Charge	AR1	AR2
Low Season (from)	€ 470	€ 510
High Season (from)	€ 930	€ 970

FR20050 Village Naturiste la Chiappa

⊙ see report page 528

Route de Palombaggia, F-20137 Porto-Vecchio (Corsica)

AR1 – TYPE C – Bungalow	**AR2 – TYPE B – Bungalow**
Sleeping: 2 bedrooms, sleeps 4: 4 singles, pillows and blankets provided	Sleeping: 1 bedroom, sleeps 2: 2 singles
Living: living/kitchen area, shower, WC	Living: living/kitchen area, shower, WC
Eating: fitted kitchen with hob, fridge	Eating: fitted kitchen with hob, fridge
Outside: table & chairs	Outside: table & chairs
Pets: accepted	Pets: accepted

Other (AR1 and AR2): bed linen, cot, highchair to hire

Open: 15 May - 9 October

Weekly Charge	AR1	AR2
Low Season (from)	€ 660	€ 450
High Season (from)	€ 1050	€ 700

Been to any good campsites lately?
We have

alan rogers

The UK's market leading independent guides to the best campsites

Also available on iPad alanrogers.com/digital

Dogs

Since the introduction in 2000 of the Passports for Pets scheme many British campers and caravanners have been encouraged to take their pets with them on holiday. However, Pet Travel conditions are understandably strict, the procedure is quite lengthy and complicated so we would advise you to check the current situation before travelling. The Passports for Pets official website is: ww2.defra.gov.uk/wildlife-pets/pets/travel

For the benefit of those who want to take their dogs to France, we list here the sites which have indicated to us that they do not accept dogs or have certain restrictions. If you are planning to take your dog we do advise you to phone the site first to check – there may be limits on numbers, breeds, or times of the year when they are excluded.

Never – sites that do not accept dogs at any time:

Normandy		
FR14090	Brévedent	88

Alsace		
FR68080	Clair Vacances	146
FR67040	Ferme des Tuileries	146

Vendée		
FR85210	Ecureuils	194
FR85020	Jard	196

Poitou-Charentes		
FR16020	Gorges du Chambon	232

Aquitaine		
FR24040	Moulin du Roch	376
FR40040	Paillotte	337
FR64060	Pavillon Royal	338

Midi-Pyrénées		
FR46040	Moulin de Laborde	404

Languedoc-Roussillon		
FR30160	Boucanet	438
FR34560	Paradis	454
FR66040	Soleil	424

Provence		
FR83570	International (Giens)	478
FR83320	Mogador	499

Corsica		
FR20030	Merendella	516
FR20220	Oliviers	514
FR20110	Restonica	513

Sometimes – sites that accept dogs but with certain restrictions:

Brittany		
FR22210	Bellevue	45
FR29470	Deux Fontaines	56
FR29000	Mouettes	38

Normandy		
FR50060	Grand Large	85

Paris-Ile de France		
FR75020	Bois de Boulogne	119
FR78040	Rambouillet	120
FR91020	Roches	119
FR78060	Versailles	122

Champagne-Ardenne		
FR10020	Lac Forêt d'Orient	130

Val de Loire		
FR41040	Marais	158
FR37140	Rillé	162
FR28140	Senonches	163

Pays de la Loire		
FR72040	Molières	187

Vendée		
FR85870	Baie d'Aunis	197
FR85440	Brunelles	200
FR85480	Chaponnet	192
FR85770	Ferme du Latois	194
FR85930	Forges	190
FR85030	Loubine	203
FR85720	Noirmoutier	200
FR85270	Oceano d'Or	194
FR85000	Petit Rocher	199
FR85280	Places Dorées	206
FR85450	Roses	199
FR85310	Trévillière	192
FR85150	Yole	207

Poitou-Charentes		
FR17010	Bois Soleil	238
FR17580	Indigo Oléron	242
FR17470	Oléron	236
FR17290	Peupliers	226

Burgundy		
FR21000	Panthier	256

Limousin		
FR23010	Château Poinsouze	269

Auvergne		
FR15060	Pont du Rouffet	283
FR63070	Pré Bas	279
FR63050	Ribeyre	279
FR63120	Royat	282

Rhône Alpes		
FR07630	Aluna	316
FR07080	Bastide	323
FR38100	Belledonne	292
FR38120	Bontemps	328
FR74060	Colombière	311
FR07260	Cruses	302
FR26200	Ecluse	293
FR26030	Grand Lierne	294
FR01060	Ile de la Comtesse	311
FR07650	Indigo Moulin	322
FR69010	Lyon	296
FR07070	Ranchisses	304
FR26220	Soleil Fruité	295

Aquitaine

FR40250	Grands Pins	374
FR24350	Moulin de la Pique	337
FR24100	Moulinal	340
FR33080	Saint Emilion	368
FR33290	Tedey	352
FR33440	Vieux Château	364

Midi-Pyrénées

FR82050	Faillal	404
FR46190	Faurie	414
FR46310	Granges	416
FR12040	Tours	409
FR32060	Trois Vallées	401

Languedoc-Roussillon

FR30070	Boisson	425
FR48020	Capelan	442

FR66290	Floride l'Embouchure	437
FR66250	Font-Romeu	434
FR66490	Garenne	444
FR66050	Haras	445
FR34540	Lambeyran (Naturiste)	524
FR66170	Mar I Sol	455
FR30080	Mas de Reilhe	433
FR34130	Neptune	419

Provence

FR83040	Bastiane	489
FR83120	Domaine	467
FR04120	Forcalquier	474
FR13140	Marius	486
FR83680	Saint Pons	483
FR04110	Verdon Parc	478

Open All Year

The following sites are understood to accept caravanners and campers all year round. It is always wise to phone the site to check as the facilities available, for example, may be reduced.

Brittany

FR56150	Haras	73
FR56210	Merlin l'Enchanteur	55
FR56330	Saint Laurent	60

Normandy

FR76090	Etennemare (Mun)	93

Nord-Pas de Calais

FR62120	Eté Indien	104

Paris-Ile de France

FR91010	Beau Village de Paris	123
FR75020	Bois de Boulogne	119
FR77110	Parc de Paris	123
FR77140	Paris/Ile-de-France	118

Champagne-Ardenne

FR10060	Epine aux Moines	129

Lorraine

FR88050	Champé	134
FR88400	Gadémont Plage	135
FR88040	Lac de Bouzey	138
FR88090	Lac de la Moselotte	138

Alsace

FR68140	Bouleaux	145

Pays de la Loire

FR44430	Pindière	172
FR53020	Malidor	170

Vendée

FR85930	Forges	190

Poitou-Charentes

FR16130	Paradis	231
FR17070	Gros Joncs	237
FR17660	Hameaux des Marines	236
FR86120	Dienné	223
FR86040	Futuriste	240

Burgundy

FR21090	Arquebuse	246
FR58030	Bezolle	255

Limousin

FR19240	Cottages du Puy d'Agnoux	271
FR19200	Hameaux de Miel	268

FR19190	Hameaux du Perrier	271
FR19080	Vianon	271

Auvergne

FR63210	Haute Sioule	282

Rhône Alpes

FR26100	Sagittaire	330
FR74230	Giffre	322
FR69010	Lyon	296
FR73100	Reclus	324

Aquitaine

FR33410	Bordeaux Lac	345
FR33370	Montalivet (Naturiste)	521
FR33090	Pressoir	363
FR40750	Deux Etangs	381
FR47110	Cabri	349
FR64040	Gaves	354
FR64180	Larrouleta	384
FR64080	Tamaris Plage	370

Midi-Pyrénées

FR09120	Ascou la Forge	392
FR32040	Deveze (Naturiste)	522
FR65080	Lavedan	391
FR65160	Monlôo	393
FR46570	Hameaux de Pomette	395
FR82060	Hameaux des Lacs	403

Languedoc-Roussillon

FR11110	Val d'Aleth	421
FR34230	Chênes	434
FR66670	Europe	438
FR66490	Garenne	444
FR66700	PRL Le Vedrignans	450

Provence

FR13120	Chantecler	466
FR05080	Solaire	500
FR84200	Garrigon	479

Côte d'Azur

FR06080	Cigales	508
FR06050	Vieille Ferme	509

Corsica

FR20080	Bagheera (Naturiste)	528
FR20040	Riva Bella (Naturiste)	527

Travelling - in Europe

When taking your car (and caravan, tent or trailer tent) or motorcaravan to the continent you do need to plan in advance and to find out as much as possible about driving in the countries you plan to visit. Whilst European harmonisation has eliminated many of the differences between one country and another, it is well worth reading the short notes we provide in the introduction to each country in this guide in addition to this more general summary.

Of course, the main difference from driving in the UK is that in mainland Europe you will need to drive on the right. Without taking extra time and care, especially at busy junctions and conversely when roads are empty, it is easy to forget to drive on the right. Remember that traffic approaching from the right usually has priority unless otherwise indicated by road markings and signs. Harmonisation also means that most (but not all) common road signs are the same in all countries.

Your vehicle

Book your vehicle in for a good service well before your intended departure date. This will lessen the chance of an expensive breakdown. Make sure your brakes are working efficiently and that your tyres have plenty of tread (3 mm. is recommended, particularly if you are undertaking a long journey).

Also make sure that your caravan or trailer is roadworthy and that its tyres are in good order and correctly inflated. Plan your packing and be careful not to overload your vehicle, caravan or trailer – this is unsafe and may well invalidate your insurance cover (it must not be more fully loaded than the kerb weight of the insured vehicle).

CHECK ALL THE FOLLOWING:

- GB sticker. If you do not display a sticker, you may risk an on-the-spot fine as this identifier is compulsory in all countries. Euro-plates are an acceptable alternative within the EU (but not outside). Remember to attach another sticker (or Euro-plate) to caravans and trailers. Only GB stickers (not England, Scotland, Wales or N. Ireland) stickers are valid in the EU.

- Headlights. As you will be driving on the right you must adjust your headlights so that the dipped beam does not dazzle oncoming drivers. Converter kits are readily available for most vehicles, although if your car is fitted with high intensity headlights, you should check with your motor dealer. Check that any planned extra loading does not affect the beam height.

- Seatbelts. Rules for the fitting and wearing of seatbelts throughout Europe are similar to those in the UK, but it is worth checking before you go. Rules for carrying children in the front of vehicles vary from country to country. It is best to plan not to do this if possible.

- Door/wing mirrors. To help with driving on the right, if your vehicle is not fitted with a mirror on the left hand side, we recommend you have one fitted.

- Fuel. Leaded and Lead Replacement petrol is increasingly difficult to find in Northern Europe.

Compulsory additional equipment

The driving laws of the countries of Europe still vary in what you are required to carry in your vehicle, although the consequences of not carrying a required piece of equipment are almost always an on-the-spot fine.

To meet these requirements we suggest that you carry the following:

* FIRE EXTINGUISHER

* BASIC TOOL KIT

* FIRST AID KIT

* SPARE BULBS

* TWO WARNING TRIANGLES – two are required in some countries at all times, and are compulsory in most countries when towing.

* HIGH VISIBILITY VEST – now compulsory in France, Spain, Italy and Austria (and likely to become compulsory throughout the EU) in case you need to walk on a motorway.

Insurance and Motoring Documents

Vehicle insurance

Contact your insurer well before you depart to check that your car insurance policy covers driving outside the UK. Most do, but many policies only provide minimum cover (so if you have an accident your insurance may only cover the cost of damage to the other person's property, with no cover for fire and theft).

To maintain the same level of cover abroad as you enjoy at home you need to tell your vehicle insurer. Some will automatically cover you abroad with no extra cost and no extra paperwork. Some will say you need a Green Card (which is neither green nor on card) but won't charge for it. Some will charge extra for the Green Card. Ideally you should contact your vehicle insurer 3-4 weeks before you set off, and confirm your conversation with them in writing.

Breakdown insurance

Arrange breakdown cover for your trip in good time so that if your vehicle breaks down or is involved in an accident it (and your caravan or trailer) can be repaired or returned to this country. This cover can usually be arranged as part of your travel insurance policy (see below).

Documents you must take with you

You may be asked to show your documents at any time so make sure that they are in order, up-to-date and easily accessible while you travel.

These are what you need to take:

* Passports (you may also need a visa in some countries if you hold either a UK passport not issued in the UK or a passport that was issued outside the EU).

* Motor Insurance Certificate, including Green Card (or Continental Cover clause)

* DVLA Vehicle Registration Document plus, if not your own vehicle, the owner's written authority to drive.

* A full valid Driving Licence (not provisional). The new photo style licence is now mandatory in most European countries.

Personal Holiday insurance

Even though you are just travelling within Europe you must take out travel insurance. Few EU countries pay the full cost of medical treatment even under reciprocal health service arrangements. The first part of a holiday insurance policy covers people. It will include the cost of doctor, ambulance and hospital treatment if needed. If needed the better companies will even pay for English language speaking doctors and nurses and will bring a sick or injured holidaymaker home by air ambulance.

Personal Holiday insurance (continued)

An important part of the insurance, often ignored, is cancellation (and curtailment) cover. Few things are as heartbreaking as having to cancel a holiday because a member of the family falls ill. Cancellation insurance can't take away the disappointment, but it makes sure you don't suffer financially as well. For this reason you should arrange your holiday insurance at least eight weeks before you set off.

Whichever insurance you choose we would advise reading very carefully the policies sold by the High Street travel trade. Whilst they may be good, they may not cover the specific needs of campers, caravanners and motorcaravanners.

Telephone 01580 214000 for a quote for our Camping Travel Insurance with cover arranged through leading leisure insurance providers.
Alternatively visit our website at: alanrogers.com/insurance

European Health Insurance Card (EHIC)

Make sure you apply for your EHIC before travelling in Europe. Eligible travellers from the UK are entitled to receive free or reduced-cost medical care in many European countries on production of an EHIC. This free card is available by completing a form in the booklet 'Health Advice for Travellers' from local Post Offices. One should be completed for each family member. Alternatively visit www.ehic.org.uk and apply on-line. Please allow time to send your application off and have the EHIC returned to you.

The EHIC is valid in all European Community countries plus Iceland, Liechtenstein, Switzerland and Norway. If you or any of your dependants are suddenly taken ill or have an accident during a visit to any of these countries, free or reduced-cost emergency treatment is available – in most cases on production of a valid EHIC.

Only state-provided emergency treatment is covered, and you will receive treatment on the same terms as nationals of the country you are visiting. Private treatment is generally not covered, and state-provided treatment may not cover all of the things that you would expect to receive free of charge from the NHS.

Remember an EHIC does not cover you for all the medical costs that you can incur or for repatriation - it is not an alternative to travel insurance. You will still need appropriate insurance to ensure you are fully covered for all eventualities.

Travelling with children

Most countries in Europe are enforcing strict guidelines when you are travelling with children who are not your own. A minor (under the age of 18) must be accompanied by a parent or legal guardian or must carry a letter of authorisation from a parent or guardian. The letter should name the adult responsible for the minor during his or her stay. Similarly, a minor travelling with just one of his/her parents, must have a letter of authority to leave their home country from the parent staying behind. Full information is available at www.fco.gov.uk

Insurance Service

High quality, low cost insurance you can trust

Price Beater **GUARANTEE***

Caravan Insurance
SAVE UP TO 60%

We've been entrusted with readers' campsite-based holidays since 1968, and they have asked us for good value, good quality insurance.

We have teamed up with Shield Total Insurance – one of the leading names in outdoor leisure insurances – to bring you peace of mind and huge savings. Call or visit our website for a no obligation quote – there's no reason not to – and trust us to cover your valued possessions for you.

* Price Beater **GUARANTEE**
Motorhomes and Static Caravans
We guarantee to beat any genuine 'like for like' insurance renewal quote by at least £25. Subject to terms & conditions.

- Caravans - **Discounts up to 60%**
- Park Homes - **Fantastic low rates**
- Tents - **Prices from only £30**

Instant quote

Call **0844 824 6314**

alanrogers.com/insurance

Alan Rogers Insurance Services is a trading name of Mark Hammerton Travel Limited which is an Appointed Representative of ITC Compliance Ltd and is authorised and regulated by the Financial Services Authority. Insurance products featured in this advertisement are provided by Shield Total Insurance which is a trading name of Vantage Insurance Services Limited (VISL). VISL is a subsidiary of Vantage Holdings Ltd and is authorised and regulated by the Financial Services Authority. VISL is registered in England No. 3441136. Registered Office: 41 Eastcheap, London EC3M 1DT.

Been to any good campsites lately?
We have

You'll find them here...

The UK's market leading independent
guides to the best campsites

Also available on iPad **alanrogers.com/digital**

GO THERE NOW!

... also here...

101 great campsites, ideal for your specific
hobby, pastime or passion

Also available on iPad **alanrogers.com/digital**

GO THERE NOW!

Want independent campsite reviews at your fingertips?

You'll find them here...

Over 3,000 in-depth campsite reviews at
www.alanrogers.com

...and even here...

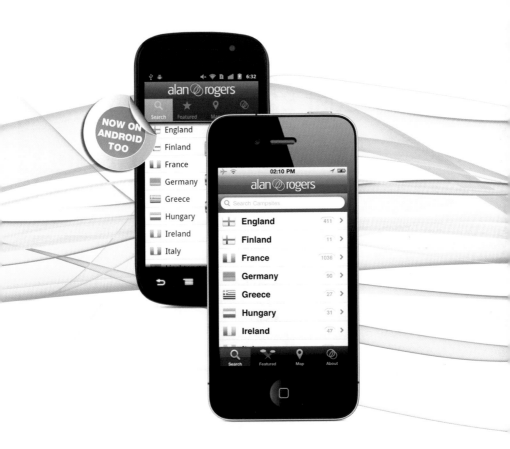

An exciting **FREE** app for both iPhone and Android

www.alanrogers.com/apps

Paying too much for your mobile home holiday?

EXTENDED MID-SEASON DATES AVAILABLE

Pay from Just £28 per night

Holiday Cheque gives you exclusive access to quality mobile homes and chalets on over 100 of Europe's finest campsites - in off peak periods and now closer to high season dates too. You'll find superb family facilities, including sensational pools, great value restaurants, friendly bars and real hospitality. And the kids can have the time of their lives!

HOLIDAY CHEQUE

- Over 100 top campsites
- From just £28 per night
- High quality mobile homes
- Luxury high specification chalets
- Fully equipped - down to the corkscrew!
- Plus unbeatable ferry prices

HUGE SAVINGS - BUT HURRY

HOLIDAY CHEQUES ARE PRICED AT A SPECIAL PROMOTIONAL RATE, SAVING UP TO 50% OFF CAMPSITE'S STANDARD PRICES. BUT IT'S FIRST COME, FIRST SERVED.

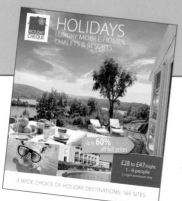

Call today for your FREE brochure

01580 214004

www.holidaycheque.co.uk

Some drive the long way round...
others sail with us

Why endure a long drive through northern France when you can sail direct to the finest holiday regions of France and Spain with us?

FRANCE
Just
£25
to reserve sailings now
SPAIN

Poole Portsmouth
Plymouth
Cherbourg Caen
Roscoff St Malo
Santander Bilbao

Visit **brittanyferries.com**
or call **0871 244 1448**

Brittany Ferries
where holidays begin

Calls costs 10p per minute plus network extras. Reserve your sailings for a deposit of £25 with balance payable 46 days before departure.

Use Camping Cheques on 17 top quality UK parks
all at £13.95 per night

Camping Cheque

£**13.95** /night
single tariff
2 people

Cambridgeshire	Parklands
Cornwall	Wooda Farm Park
	Carlyon Bay
Cumbria	The Quiet Site
Devon	Cofton Country Holidays
	River Dart Country Park
	Riverside Caravan Park
	Whitehill Country Park
Dorset	Newlands
Hampshire	Riverside
	Shamba
Ireland	Adare Caravan & Camping Park
	Cong Caravan & Camping Park
Isle of Wight	The Orchards
Scotland	Brighouse Bay
Suffolk	Westwood Caravan Park
Peak District	Rivendale

Camping Cheque
622 campsites 29 countries

alan rogers travel
Holiday Savings
Guide 2012
www.campingcheque.co.uk

www.campingcheque.co.uk
FREE Holiday Savings Guide
01580 214002

2012 warms up at ExCeL...

The ONLY SHOW in the spring where the leading caravan and motorhome manufacturers will be displaying their NEW 2012 SEASON MODELS.

The **MOTORHOME CARAVAN & CAMPING SHOW**

14-19 FEB 2012 · EXCEL LONDON

OFFICIAL PARTNER:

THE CARAVAN CLUB

SUPPORTER:
The Camping and Caravanning Club
The Friendly Club

WWW.MOTORHOMECARAVANANDCAMPING.CO.UK

The NATIONAL SHOW at the NEC where you'll see the NEW 2013 SEASON caravan and motorhome models from all the leading manufacturers.

The **MOTORHOME & CARAVAN SHOW**

16-21 OCT 2012 · NEC BIRMINGHAM

SUPPORTERS:

THE CARAVAN CLUB

The Camping and Caravanning Club
The Friendly Club

...and Autumn's looking hot too.

WWW.MOTORHOMEANDCARAVANSHOW.CO.UK

ORGANISED BY:

NCC events

NEW digital
iPad editions

Available on the
App Store

FREE Alan Rogers bookstore app
- digital editions of all 2012 guides

alanrogers.com/digital

GO THERE NOW!

Nord-Pas de Calais
page 98

Picardy
page 105

Normandy
page 74

Paris-Ile
de France
page 115

Brittany
page 32

Lorraine
page 132

Champagne-
Ardenne
page 124

Alsace
page 141

Pays de la Loire
page 166

Val de Loire
page 148

Burgundy
page 244

Franche-
Comté
page 257

Vendée
page 188

Poitou-
Charentes
page 215

Limousin
page 265

Auvergne
page 272

Rhône Alpes
page 286

Aquitaine
page 332

Midi-Pyrénées
page 389

Provence
page 463

Côte d'Azur
page 503

Languedoc-Roussillon
page 417

Corsica
page 510

Town & Village Index

Town & Village Index continued

Town & Village Index continued

Town & Village Index continued

Index by Campsite Region & Name

Images

© ATOUT FRANCE/Pierre Desheraud
© ATOUT FRANCE/Jean François Tripelon-Jarry
© ATOUT FRANCE/CRT Picardie/Sam Bellet
© ATOUT FRANCE/CRT Picardie/Didier Cry
© ATOUT FRANCE/CRT Bourgogne/Alain Doire
© ATOUT FRANCE/CRT Franche-Comté/J. Ambacher
© ATOUT FRANCE/CRT Franche-Comté/AC Tréboz
© ATOUT FRANCE/Jean Malburet
© ATOUT FRANCE/Michel Angot
© ATOUT FRANCE/Fabrice Milochau

© ATOUT FRANCE/Fabian Charaffi
© ATOUT FRANCE/R-Cast
© ATOUT FRANCE/Daniel Gallon – Dangal
© ATOUT FRANCE/Cédric Helsly
© ATOUT FRANCE/Fabrice Milochau
© ATOUT FRANCE/Michel Laurent/CRT Lorraine
© ATOUT FRANCE/CDT Calvados/CDT Calvados
© ATOUT FRANCE/Jean-François Tripelon-Jarry
© ATOUT FRANCE/Pierre Torset
© ATOUT FRANCE/Aquashot